S0-AJZ-027

THE MATHEMATICA® BOOK

STEPHEN WOLFRAM

THE MATHEMATICA® BOOK 5TH EDITION

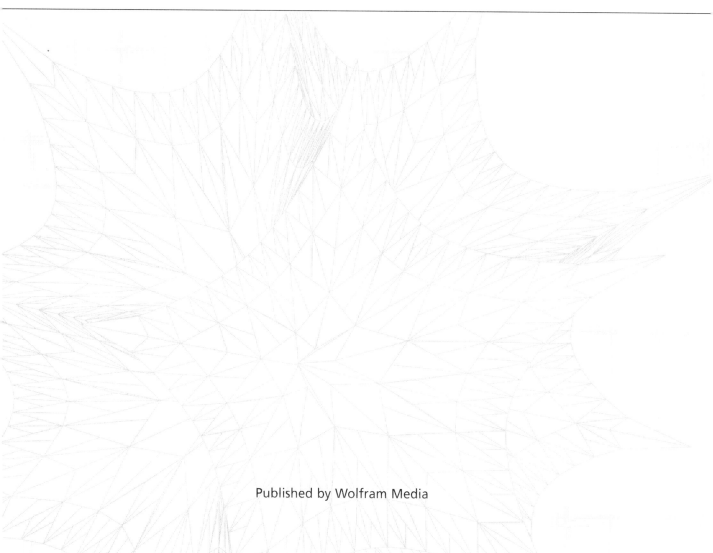

Published by Wolfram Media

Library of Congress Cataloging–in–Publication Data

Wolfram, Stephen, 1959 –
    Mathematica book / Stephen Wolfram. — 5th ed.
        p.   cm.
    Includes index.
    ISBN 1–57955–022–3 (hardbound).
    1. Mathematica (Computer file) 2. Mathematics—Data processing.
I. Title.
QA76.95.W65   2003
510'.285'5369—dc21

03–53794
CIP

Published by Wolfram Media, Inc.

Comments on this book will be welcomed at:
comments@wolfram.com

**In publications that refer to the *Mathematica*
system, please cite this book as:**
Stephen Wolfram, *The Mathematica Book*, 5th ed.
(Wolfram Media, 2003)

*First and second editions published by Addison–Wesley Publishing Company
under the title Mathematica: A System for Doing Mathematics by Computer.*

*Third and fourth editions co–published by Wolfram Media
and Cambridge University Press.*

Copyright © 1988, 1991, 1996, 1999, 2003 by Wolfram Research, Inc.

All rights reserved. No part of this book may be reproduced, stored in a retrieval system, or transmitted, in any form or by any means, electronic, mechanical, photocopying, recording or otherwise, without the prior written permission of the copyright holder.

Wolfram Research is the holder of the copyright to the *Mathematica* software system described in this book, including without limitation such aspects of the system as its code, structure, sequence, organization, "look and feel", programming language and compilation of command names. Use of the system unless pursuant to the terms of a license granted by Wolfram Research or as otherwise authorized by law is an infringement of the copyright.

The author, Wolfram Research, Inc. and Wolfram Media, Inc. make no representations, express or implied, with respect to this documentation or the software it describes, including without limitations, any implied warranties of merchantability, interoperability or fitness for a particular purpose, all of which are expressly disclaimed. Users should be aware that included in the terms and conditions under which Wolfram Research is willing to license *Mathematica* is a provision that the author, Wolfram Research, Wolfram Media, and their distribution licensees, distributors and dealers shall in no event be liable for any indirect, incidental or consequential damages, and that liability for direct damages shall be limited to the amount of the purchase price paid for *Mathematica*.

In addition to the foregoing, users should recognize that all complex software systems and their documentation contain errors and omissions. The author, Wolfram Research and Wolfram Media shall not be responsible under any circumstances for providing information on or corrections to errors and omissions discovered at any time in this book or the software it describes, whether or not they are aware of the errors or omissions. The author, Wolfram Research and Wolfram Media do not recommend the use of the software described in this book for applications in which errors or omissions could threaten life, injury or significant loss.

Mathematica, *MathLink* and *MathSource* are registered trademarks of Wolfram Research. *J/Link*, *MathLM*, *MathReader*, *.NET/Link*, Notebooks and web*Mathematica* are trademarks of Wolfram Research. All other trademarks used are the property of their respective owners. *Mathematica* is not associated with Mathematica Policy Research, Inc. or MathTech, Inc.

Printed in the United States of America. ⊗ Acid–free paper.   15   14   13   12   11   10   9   8   7   6   5   4   3   2   1

Author's website:
www.stephenwolfram.com

Author's address:
email: s.wolfram@wolfram.com
mail: c/o Wolfram Research, Inc.
        100 Trade Center Drive
        Champaign, IL 61820, USA

Other books by Stephen Wolfram:
• *Cellular Automata and Complexity: Collected Papers* (1993)
• *A New Kind of Science* (2002)

www.wolfram.com

About the Author

Stephen Wolfram is the creator of *Mathematica*, and a well-known scientist. He is widely regarded as the most important innovator in technical computing today, as well as one of the world's most original research scientists.

Born in London in 1959, he was educated at Eton, Oxford and Caltech. He published his first scientific paper at the age of fifteen, and had received his PhD in theoretical physics from Caltech by the age of twenty. Wolfram's early scientific work was mainly in high–energy physics, quantum field theory and cosmology, and included several now–classic results. Having started to use computers in 1973, Wolfram rapidly became a leader in the emerging field of scientific computing, and in 1979 he began the construction of SMP—the first modern computer algebra system—which he released commercially in 1981.

In recognition of his early work in physics and computing, Wolfram became in 1981 the youngest recipient of a Mac-Arthur Prize Fellowship. Late in 1981, Wolfram then set out on an ambitious new direction in science: to develop a general theory of complexity in nature. Wolfram's key idea was to use computer experiments to study the behavior of simple computer programs known as cellular automata. And in 1982 he made the first in a series of startling discoveries about the origins of complexity. The publication of Wolfram's papers on cellular automata led to a major shift in scientific thinking, and laid the groundwork for a new field of science that Wolfram named "complex systems research".

Through the mid–1980s, Wolfram continued his work on complexity, discovering a number of fundamental connections between computation and nature, and inventing such concepts as computational irreducibility. Wolfram's work led to a wide range of applications—and provided the main scientific foundations for the popular movements known as complexity theory and artificial life. Wolfram himself used his ideas to develop a new randomness generation system and a new approach to computational fluid dynamics—both of which are now in widespread use.

Following his scientific work on complex systems research, Wolfram in 1986 founded the first research center and first journal in the field. Then, after a highly successful career in academia—first at Caltech, then at the Institute for Advanced Study in Princeton, and finally as Professor of Physics, Mathematics and Computer Science at the University of Illinois—Wolfram launched Wolfram Research, Inc.

Wolfram began the development of *Mathematica* in late 1986. The first version of *Mathematica* was released on June 23, 1988, and was immediately hailed as a major advance in computing. In the years that followed, the popularity of *Mathematica* grew rapidly, and Wolfram Research became established as a world leader in the software industry, widely recognized for excellence in both technology and business. Wolfram has been president and CEO of Wolfram Research since its inception, and continues to be personally responsible for the overall design of its core technology.

Following the release of *Mathematica* Version 2 in 1991, Wolfram began to divide his time between *Mathematica* development and scientific research. Building on his work from the mid–1980s, and now with *Mathematica* as a tool, Wolfram made a rapid succession of major new discoveries. By the mid–1990s his discoveries led him to develop a fundamentally new conceptual framework, which he then spent the remainder of the 1990s applying not only to new kinds of questions, but also to many existing foundational problems in physics, biology, computer science, mathematics and several other fields.

After more than ten years of highly concentrated work, Wolfram finally described his achievements in his 1200–page book *A New Kind of Science*. Released on May 14, 2002, the book was widely acclaimed and immediately became a best-seller. Its publication has been seen as initiating a paradigm shift of historic importance in science.

In addition to leading Wolfram Research to break new ground with innovative technology, Wolfram is now developing a series of research and educational initiatives in the science he has created.

About *Mathematica*

Mathematica is the world's only fully integrated environment for technical computing. First released in 1988, it has had a profound effect on the way computers are used in many technical and other fields.

It is often said that the release of *Mathematica* marked the beginning of modern technical computing. Ever since the 1960s individual packages had existed for specific numerical, algebraic, graphical and other tasks. But the visionary concept of *Mathematica* was to create once and for all a single system that could handle all the various aspects of technical computing in a coherent and unified way. The key intellectual advance that made this possible was the invention of a new kind of symbolic computer language that could for the first time manipulate the very wide range of objects involved in technical computing using only a fairly small number of basic primitives.

When *Mathematica* Version 1 was released, the *New York Times* wrote that "the importance of the program cannot be overlooked", and *Business Week* later ranked *Mathematica* among the ten most important new products of the year. *Mathematica* was also hailed in the technical community as a major intellectual and practical revolution.

At first, *Mathematica*'s impact was felt mainly in the physical sciences, engineering and mathematics. But over the years, *Mathematica* has become important in a remarkably wide range of fields. *Mathematica* is used today throughout the sciences—physical, biological, social and other—and counts many of the world's foremost scientists among its enthusiastic supporters. It has played a crucial role in many important discoveries, and has been the basis for thousands of technical papers. In engineering, *Mathematica* has become a standard tool for both development and production, and by now many of the world's important new products rely at one stage or another in their design on *Mathematica*. In commerce, *Mathematica* has played a significant role in the growth of sophisticated financial modeling, as well as being widely used in many kinds of general planning and analysis. *Mathematica* has also emerged as an important tool in computer science and software development: its language component is widely used as a research, prototyping and interface environment.

The largest part of *Mathematica*'s user community consists of technical professionals. But *Mathematica* is also heavily used in education, and there are now many hundreds of courses—from high school to graduate school—based on it. In addition, with the availability of student versions, *Mathematica* has become an important tool for both technical and non-technical students around the world.

The diversity of *Mathematica*'s user base is striking. It spans all continents, ages from below ten up, and includes for example artists, composers, linguists and lawyers. There are also many hobbyists from all walks of life who use *Mathematica* to further their interests in science, mathematics and computing.

Ever since *Mathematica* was first released, its user base has grown steadily, and by now the total number of users is above a million. *Mathematica* has become a standard in a great many organizations, and it is used today in all of the Fortune 50 companies, all of the 15 major departments of the U.S. government, and all of the 50 largest universities in the world.

At a technical level, *Mathematica* is widely regarded as a major feat of software engineering. It is one of the largest single application programs ever developed, and it contains a vast array of novel algorithms and important technical innovations. Among its core innovations are its interconnected algorithm knowledge base, and its concepts of symbolic programming and of document-centered interfaces.

The development of *Mathematica* has been carried out at Wolfram Research by a world-class team led by Stephen Wolfram. The success of *Mathematica* has fueled the continuing growth of Wolfram Research, and has allowed a large community of independent *Mathematica*-related businesses to develop. There are today well over a hundred specialized commercial packages available for *Mathematica*, as well as more than three hundred books devoted to the system.

Features New in *Mathematica* Version 5

Mathematica Version 5 introduces important extensions to the *Mathematica* system, especially in scope and scalability of numeric and symbolic computation. Building on the core language and extensive algorithm knowledge base of *Mathematica*, Version 5 introduces a new generation of advanced algorithms for a wide range of numeric and symbolic operations.

Numerical Computation

- Major optimization of dense numerical linear algebra.
- New optimized sparse numerical linear algebra.
- Support for optimized arbitrary-precision linear algebra.
- Generalized eigenvalues and singular value decomposition.
- `LinearSolveFunction` for repeated linear-system solving.
- p norms for vectors and matrices.
- Built-in `MatrixRank` for exact and approximate matrices.
- Support for large-scale linear programming, with interior point methods.
- New methods and array variable support in `FindRoot` and `FindMinimum`.
- `FindFit` for full nonlinear curve fitting.
- Constrained global optimization with `NMinimize`.
- Support for n-dimensional PDEs in `NDSolve`.
- Support for differential-algebraic equations in `NDSolve`.
- Support for vector and array-valued functions in `NDSolve`.
- Highly extensive collection of automatically accessible algorithms in `NDSolve`.
- Finer precision and accuracy control for arbitrary-precision numbers.
- Higher-efficiency big number arithmetic, including processor-specific optimization.
- Enhanced algorithms for number-theoretical operations including `GCD` and `FactorInteger`.
- Direct support for high-performance basic statistics functions.

Symbolic Computation

- Solutions to mixed systems of equations and inequalities in `Reduce`.
- Complete solving of polynomial systems over real or complex numbers.
- Solving large classes of Diophantine equations.
- `ForAll` and `Exists` quantifiers and quantifier elimination.
- Representation of discrete and continuous algebraic and transcendental solution sets.
- `FindInstance` for finding instances of solutions over different domains.
- Exact constrained minimization over real and integer domains.
- Integrated support for assumptions using `Assuming` and `Refine`.
- `RSolve` for solving recurrence equations.
- Support for nonlinear, partial and q difference equations and systems.
- Full solutions to systems of rational ordinary differential equations.
- Support for differential-algebraic equations.
- `CoefficientArrays` for converting systems of equations to tensors.

Programming and Core System

- Integrated language support for sparse arrays.
- New list programming with `Sow` and `Reap`.
- `EvaluationMonitor` and `StepMonitor` for algorithm monitoring.
- Enhanced timing measurement, including `AbsoluteTiming`.
- Major performance enhancements for *MathLink*.
- Optimization for 64-bit operating systems and architectures.
- Support for computations in full 64-bit address spaces.

Interfaces

- Support for more than 50 import and export formats.

- High-efficiency import and export of tabular data.

- PNG, SVG and DICOM graphics and imaging formats.

- Import and export of sparse matrix formats.

- MPS linear programming format.

- Cascading style sheets and XHTML for notebook exporting.

- Preview version of *.NET/Link* for integration with .NET.

Notebook Interface

- Enhanced Help Browser design.

- Automatic copy/paste switching for Windows.

- Enhanced support for slide show presentation.

- *AuthorTools* support for notebook diffs.

Standard Add-on Packages

- Statistical plots and graphics.

- Algebraic number fields.

New in Versions 4.1 and 4.2

- Enhanced pattern matching of sequence objects.

- Enhanced optimizer for built-in *Mathematica* compiler.

- Enhanced continued fraction computation.

- Greatly enhanced `DSolve`.

- Additional `TraditionalForm` formats.

- Efficiency increases for multivariate polynomial operations.

- Support for import and export of DXF, STL, FITS and STDS data formats.

- Full support for CSV format import and export.

- Support for UTF character encodings.

- Extensive support for XML, including SymbolicXML subsystem and NotebookML.

- Native support for evaluation and formatting of `Nand` and `Nor`.

- High-efficiency `CellularAutomaton` function.

- *J/Link MathLink*-based Java capabilities.

- `MathMLForm` and extended MathML support.

- Extended simplification of `Floor`, `Erf`, `ProductLog` and related functions.

- Integration over regions defined by inequalities.

- Integration of piecewise functions.

- Standard package for visualization of regions defined by inequalities.

- ANOVA standard add-on package.

- Enhanced *Combinatorica* add-on package.

- *AuthorTools* notebook authoring environment.

The Role of This Book

The Scope of the Book

This book is intended to be a complete introduction to *Mathematica*. It describes essentially all the capabilities of *Mathematica*, and assumes no prior knowledge of the system.

In most uses of *Mathematica*, you will need to know only a small part of the system. This book is organized to make it easy for you to learn the part you need for a particular calculation. In many cases, for example, you may be able to set up your calculation simply by adapting some appropriate examples from the book.

You should understand, however, that the examples in this book are chosen primarily for their simplicity, rather than to correspond to realistic calculations in particular application areas.

There are many other publications that discuss *Mathematica* from the viewpoint of particular classes of applications. In some cases, you may find it better to read one of these publications first, and read this book only when you need a more general perspective on *Mathematica*.

Mathematica is a system built on a fairly small set of very powerful principles. This book describes those principles, but by no means spells out all of their implications. In particular, while the book describes the elements that go into *Mathematica* programs, it does not give detailed examples of complete programs. For those, you should look at other publications.

The Mathematica System Described in the Book

This book describes the standard *Mathematica* kernel, as it exists on all computers that run *Mathematica*. Most major supported features of the kernel in *Mathematica* Version 5 are covered in this book. Many of the important features of the front end are also discussed.

Mathematica is an open software system that can be customized in a wide variety of ways. It is important to realize that this book covers only the full basic *Mathematica* system. If your system is customized in some way, then it may behave differently from what is described in the book.

The most common form of customization is the addition of various *Mathematica* function definitions. These may come, for example, from loading a *Mathematica* package. Some-

times the definitions may actually modify the behavior of functions described in this book. In other cases, the definitions may simply add a collection of new functions that are not described in the book. In certain applications, it may be primarily these new functions that you use, rather than the standard ones described in the book.

This book describes what to do when you interact directly with the standard *Mathematica* kernel and notebook front end. Sometimes, however, you may not be using the standard *Mathematica* system directly. Instead, *Mathematica* may be an embedded component of another system that you are using. This system may for example call on *Mathematica* only for certain computations, and may hide the details of those computations from you. Most of what is in this book will only be useful if you can give explicit input to *Mathematica*. If all of your input is substantially modified by the system you are using, then you must rely on the documentation for that system.

Additional Mathematica Documentation

For all standard versions of *Mathematica*, the following is available in printed form, and can be ordered from Wolfram Research:

- *Getting Started with Mathematica*: a booklet describing installation, basic operation, and troubleshooting of *Mathematica* on specific computer systems.

Extensive online documentation is included with most versions of *Mathematica*. All such documentation can be accessed from the Help Browser in the *Mathematica* notebook front end.

In addition, the following sources of information are available on the web:

- www.wolfram.com: the main Wolfram Research website.
- documents.wolfram.com: full documentation for *Mathematica*.
- library.wolfram.com/infocenter: the *Mathematica Information Center*—a central web repository for information on *Mathematica* and its applications.

Suggestions about Learning *Mathematica*

Getting Started

As with any other computer system, there are a few points that you need to get straight before you can even start using *Mathematica*. For example, you absolutely must know how to type your input to *Mathematica*. To find out these kinds of basic points, you should read at least the first section of Part 1 in this book.

Once you know the basics, you can begin to get a feeling for *Mathematica* by typing in some examples from this book. Always be sure that you type in exactly what appears in the book—do not change any capitalization, bracketing, etc.

After you have tried a few examples from the book, you should start experimenting for yourself. Change the examples slightly, and see what happens. You should look at each piece of output carefully, and try to understand why it came out as it did.

After you have run through some simple examples, you should be ready to take the next step: learning to go through what is needed to solve a complete problem with *Mathematica*.

Solving a Complete Problem

You will probably find it best to start by picking a specific problem to work on. Pick a problem that you understand well—preferably one whose solution you could easily reproduce by hand. Then go through each step in solving the problem, learning what you need to know about *Mathematica* to do it. Always be ready to experiment with simple cases, and understand the results you get with these, before going back to your original problem.

In going through the steps to solve your problem, you will learn about various specific features of *Mathematica*, typically from sections of Part 1. After you have done a few problems with *Mathematica*, you should get a feeling for many of the basic features of the system.

When you have built up a reasonable knowledge of the features of *Mathematica*, you should go back and learn about the overall structure of the *Mathematica* system. You can do this by systematically reading Part 2 of this book. What you will discover is that many of the features that seemed unrelated actually fit together into a coherent overall structure. Knowing this structure will make it much easier for you to understand and remember the specific features you have already learned.

The Principles of Mathematica

You should not try to learn the overall structure of *Mathematica* too early. Unless you have had broad experience with advanced computer languages or pure mathematics, you will probably find Part 2 difficult to understand at first. You will find the structure and principles it describes difficult to remember, and you will always be wondering why particular aspects of them might be useful. However, if you first get some practical experience with *Mathematica*, you will find the overall structure much easier to grasp. You should realize that the principles on which *Mathematica* is built are very general, and it is usually difficult to understand such general principles before you have seen specific examples.

One of the most important aspects of *Mathematica* is that it applies a fairly small number of principles as widely as possible. This means that even though you have used a particular feature only in a specific situation, the principle on which that feature is based can probably be applied in many other situations. One reason it is so important to understand the underlying principles of *Mathematica* is that by doing so you can leverage your knowledge of specific features into a more general context. As an example, you may first learn about transformation rules in the context of algebraic expressions.

But the basic principle of transformation rules applies to any symbolic expression. Thus you can also use such rules to modify the structure of, say, an expression that represents a *Mathematica* graphics object.

Changing the Way You Work

Learning to use *Mathematica* well involves changing the way you solve problems. When you move from pencil and paper to *Mathematica* the balance of what aspects of problem solving are difficult changes. With pencil and paper, you can often get by with a fairly imprecise initial formulation of your problem. Then when you actually do calculations in solving the problem, you can usually fix up the formulation as you go along. However, the calculations you do have to be fairly simple, and you cannot afford to try out many different cases.

When you use *Mathematica*, on the other hand, the initial formulation of your problem has to be quite precise. However, once you have the formulation, you can easily do many different calculations with it. This means that you can effectively carry out many mathematical experiments on your problem. By looking at the results you get, you can then refine the original formulation of your problem.

There are typically many different ways to formulate a given problem in *Mathematica*. In almost all cases, however, the most direct and simple formulations will be best. The more you can formulate your problem in *Mathematica* from the beginning, the better. Often, in fact, you will find that formulating your problem directly in *Mathematica* is better than first trying to set up a traditional mathematical formulation, say an algebraic one. The main point is that *Mathematica* allows you to express not only traditional mathematical operations, but also algorithmic and structural ones. This greater range of possibilities gives you a better chance of being able to find a direct way to represent your original problem.

Writing Programs

For most of the more sophisticated problems that you want to solve with *Mathematica*, you will have to create *Mathematica* programs. *Mathematica* supports several types of programming, and you have to choose which one to use in each case. It turns out that no single type of programming suits all cases well. As a result, it is very important that you learn several different types of programming.

If you already know a traditional programming language such as BASIC, C, Fortran, Perl or Java, you will probably find it easiest to learn procedural programming in *Mathematica*, using Do, For and so on. But while almost any *Mathematica* program can, in principle, be written in a procedural way, this is rarely the best approach. In a symbolic system like *Mathematica*, functional and rule–based programming typically yields programs that are more efficient, and easier to understand.

If you find yourself using procedural programming a lot, you should make an active effort to convert at least some of your programs to other types. At first, you may find functional and rule–based programs difficult to understand. But after a while, you will find that their global structure is usually much easier to grasp than procedural programs. And as your experience with *Mathematica* grows over a period of months or years, you will probably find that you write more and more of your programs in non–procedural ways.

Learning the Whole System

As you proceed in using and learning *Mathematica*, it is important to remember that *Mathematica* is a large system. Although after a while you should know all of its basic principles, you may never learn the details of all its features. As a result, even after you have had a great deal of experience with *Mathematica*, you will undoubtedly still find it useful to look through this book. When you do so, you are quite likely to notice features that you never noticed before, but that with your experience, you can now see how to use.

How to Read This Book

If at all possible, you should read this book in conjunction with using an actual *Mathematica* system. When you see examples in the book, you should try them out on your computer.

You can get a basic feeling for what *Mathematica* does by looking at "A Tour of *Mathematica*" on page 3. You may also find it useful to try out examples from this Tour with your own copy of *Mathematica*.

Whatever your background, you should make sure to look at the first three or four sections in Part 1 before you start to use *Mathematica* on your own. These sections describe the basics that you need to know in order to use *Mathematica* at any level.

The remainder of Part 1 shows you how to do many different kinds of computations with *Mathematica*. If you are trying to do a specific calculation, you will often find it sufficient just to look at the sections of Part 1 that discuss the features of *Mathematica* you need to use. A good approach is to try and find examples in the book which are close to what you want to do.

The emphasis in Part 1 is on using the basic functions that are built into *Mathematica* to carry out various different kinds of computations.

Part 2, on the other hand, discusses the basic structure and principles that underlie all of *Mathematica*. Rather than describing a sequence of specific features, Part 2 takes a more global approach. If you want to learn how to create your own *Mathematica* functions, you should read Part 2.

Part 3 is intended for those with more sophisticated mathematical interests and knowledge. It covers the more advanced mathematical features of *Mathematica*, as well as describing some features already mentioned in Part 1 in greater mathematical detail.

Each part of the book is divided into sections and subsections. There are two special kinds of subsections, indicated by the following headings:

- **Advanced Topic:** Advanced material which can be omitted on a first reading.

- **Special Topic:** Material relevant only for certain users or certain computer systems.

The main parts in this book are intended to be pedagogical, and can meaningfully be read in a sequential fashion. The Appendix, however, is intended solely for reference purposes. Once you are familiar with *Mathematica*, you will probably find the list of functions in the Appendix the best place to look up details you need.

About the Examples in This Book

All the examples given in this book were generated by running an actual copy of *Mathematica* Version 5. If you have a copy of this version, you should be able to reproduce the examples on your computer as they appear in the book.

There are, however, a few points to watch:

- Until you are familiar with *Mathematica*, make sure to type the input *exactly* as it appears in the book. Do not change any of the capital letters or brackets. Later, you will learn what things you can change. When you start out, however, it is important that you do not make any changes; otherwise you may not get the same results as in the book.

- Never type the prompt `In[n]:=` that begins each input line. Type only the text that follows this prompt.

- You will see that the lines in each dialog are numbered in sequence. Most subsections in the book contain separate dialogs. To make sure you get exactly what the book says, you should start a new *Mathematica* session each time the book does.

- Some "Special Topic" subsections give examples that may be specific to particular computer systems.

- Any examples that involve random numbers will generally give different results than in the book, since the sequence of random numbers produced by *Mathematica* is different in every session.

- Some examples that use machine–precision arithmetic may come out differently on different computer systems. This is a result of differences in floating–point hardware. If you use arbitrary–precision *Mathematica* numbers, you should not see differences.

- Almost all of the examples show output as it would be generated in `StandardForm` with a notebook interface to *Mathematica*. Output with a text–based interface will look similar, but not identical.

- Almost all of the examples in this book assume that your computer or terminal uses a standard U.S. ASCII character set. If you cannot find some of the characters you need on your keyboard, or if *Mathematica* prints out different characters than you see in the book, you will need to look at your computer documentation to find the correspondence with the character set you are using. The most common problem is that the dollar sign character (SHIFT–4) may come out as your local currency character.

- If the version of *Mathematica* is more recent than the one used to produce this book, then it is possible that some results you get may be different.

- Most of the examples in "A Tour of *Mathematica*", as well as Parts 1 and 2, are chosen so as to be fairly quick to execute. Assuming you have a machine with a clock speed of over about 1 GHz (and most machines produced in 2003 or later do), then almost none of the examples should take anything more than a small fraction of a second to execute. If they do, there is probably something wrong. Section 1.3.12 describes how to stop the calculation.

Outline Table of Contents

Table of Contents

+■ a section new since Version 4
~■ a section substantially modified since Version 4

Part 2.   Principles of *Mathematica*

Part 3. Advanced Mathematics in *Mathematica*

Part A.   *Mathematica* Reference Guide

A Tour of *Mathematica*

The purpose of this Tour is to show examples of a few of the things that Mathematica can do. The Tour is in no way intended to be complete—it is just a sampling of a few of Mathematica's capabilities. It also concentrates only on general features, and does not address how these features can be applied in particular fields. Nevertheless, by reading through the Tour you should get at least some feeling for the basic Mathematica system.

Sometimes, you may be able to take examples from this Tour and immediately adapt them for your own purposes. But more often, you will have to look at some of Part 1, or at online Mathematica documentation, before you embark on serious work with Mathematica. If you do try repeating examples from the Tour, it is very important that you enter them exactly as they appear here. Do not change capitalization, types of brackets, etc.

On most versions of Mathematica, you will be able to find this Tour online as part of the Mathematica help system. Even if you do not have access to a running copy of Mathematica, you may still be able to try out the examples in this Tour by visiting ***www.wolfram.com/tour***.

A Tour of *Mathematica*

A Tour of *Mathematica*

Mathematica as a Calculator

You can use *Mathematica* just like a calculator: you type in questions, and *Mathematica* prints back the answers.

Note: *Most examples here use only ordinary keyboard input. Page 14 shows how to enter fully formatted input.*

Mathematica adds the In and Out labels; you do not type them. You end each line with [SHIFT]-[ENTER].

In[1]:= **3 + 5**

Out[1]= 8

This stands for "to the power of".

In[2]:= **57.1^100**

Out[2]= 4.60904×10^{175}

Ask Mathematica what 3 + 5 is; it prints back 8.

This asks Mathematica to work out the inverse of a 2 x 2 matrix.

Mathematica represents matrices as lists of lists.

In[3]:= **Inverse[{{1, 2}, {3, 4}}]**

Out[3]= $\left\{ \{-2, 1\}, \left\{ \frac{3}{2}, -\frac{1}{2} \right\} \right\}$

Mathematica can handle formulas as well as numbers.

This asks Mathematica to integrate a simple function.

In[1]:= **Integrate[Sqrt[x] Sqrt[1 + x], x]**

Out[1]= $\frac{1}{4} \left(\sqrt{x} \sqrt{1+x} \ (1 + 2x) - \text{ArcSinh}\left[\sqrt{x}\right] \right)$

This stands for mathematical equality.

This asks Mathematica to solve a quadratic equation.

In[2]:= **Solve[x^2 + x == a, x]**

Out[2]= $\left\{ \left\{ x \rightarrow \frac{1}{2} \left(-1 - \sqrt{1 + 4a} \right) \right\}, \left\{ x \rightarrow \frac{1}{2} \left(-1 + \sqrt{1 + 4a} \right) \right\} \right\}$

The result is a list of rules for x convenient for use in other calculations.

Mathematica can also create two- and three-dimensional graphics.

This creates a 2D plot of a simple function.

In[1]:= **Plot[Sin[x] + Sin[1.6 x], {x, 0, 40}]**

In[1]:= **Plot3D[Sin[x y], {x, 0, 4}, {y, 0, 4}]**

Here is a 3D plot.

Part of the Basic Calculations palette.

▶ **Arithmetic and Numbers**

▶ **Algebra**

▶ **Lists and Matrices**

▼ **Trigonometric and Exponential Functions**

　▼ **Trigonometric**

Sin[■]	ArcSin[■]
Cos[■]	ArcCos[■]
Tan[■]	ArcTan[■]

Manipulation of trigonometric expressions to alternate forms.

TrigExpand[■]
TrigFactor[■]

Mathematica comes with a collection of palettes that let you do many operations by clicking buttons rather than typing commands.

Power Computing with Mathematica

Even though you can use it as easily as a calculator, *Mathematica* gives you access to immense computational power.

This creates a 500 x 500 matrix of random numbers.

The semicolon tells *Mathematica* not to print the result.

On most computers it takes *Mathematica* only a few seconds to compute the eigenvalues of the matrix and plot them.

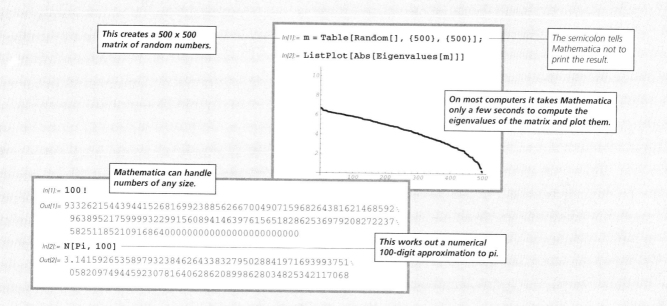

```
In[1]:= m = Table[Random[], {500}, {500}];

In[2]:= ListPlot[Abs[Eigenvalues[m]]]
```

Mathematica can handle numbers of any size.

This works out a numerical 100-digit approximation to pi.

```
In[1]:= 100!

Out[1]= 933262154439441526816992388562667004907159682643816214685929\
        638952175999932299156089414639761565182862536979208272237\
        5825118521091686400000000000000000000000000

In[2]:= N[Pi, 100]

Out[2]= 3.141592653589793238462643383279502884197169399375\
        105820974944592307816406286208998628034825342117068
```

Mathematica can work with formulas of any length—solving problems that would have taken years by hand.

This asks *Mathematica* to factor a polynomial.

```
In[1]:= Factor[x^99 + y^99]

Out[1]= (x + y) (x^2 - x y + y^2) (x^6 - x^3 y^3 + y^6) (x^10 - x^9 y + x^8 y^2 -
        x^7 y^3 + x^6 y^4 - x^5 y^5 + x^4 y^6 - x^3 y^7 + x^2 y^8 - x y^9 + y^10)
        (x^20 + x^19 y - x^17 y^3 - x^16 y^4 + x^14 y^6 + x^13 y^7 - x^11 y^9 - x^10 y^10 -
        x^9 y^11 + x^7 y^13 + x^6 y^14 - x^4 y^16 - x^3 y^17 + x y^19 + y^20)
        (x^60 + x^57 y^3 - x^51 y^9 - x^48 y^12 + x^42 y^18 + x^39 y^21 - x^33 y^27 - x^30 y^30 -
        x^27 y^33 + x^21 y^39 + x^18 y^42 - x^12 y^48 - x^9 y^51 + x^3 y^57 + y^60)

In[2]:= Simplify[%]

Out[2]= x^99 + y^99
```

Mathematica calls on sophisticated algorithms to simplify formulas.

This stands for the previous result.

Mathematica has achieved world records—for both size and speed—in many kinds of computations.

This tells *Mathematica* to show only a shortened version of the result.

```
In[1]:= PartitionsP[10^9] // Short

Out[1]= 16045350842809668832728039026391874671468439 <<35131>>
        856906686101897310304575268577797923685688339
```

Mathematica takes only a few seconds to work out how many ways a billion can be partitioned into sums—a frontier number theory calculation.

This indicates 35131 omitted digits.

Accessing Algorithms in Mathematica

Whenever you use *Mathematica* you are accessing the world's largest collection of computational algorithms.

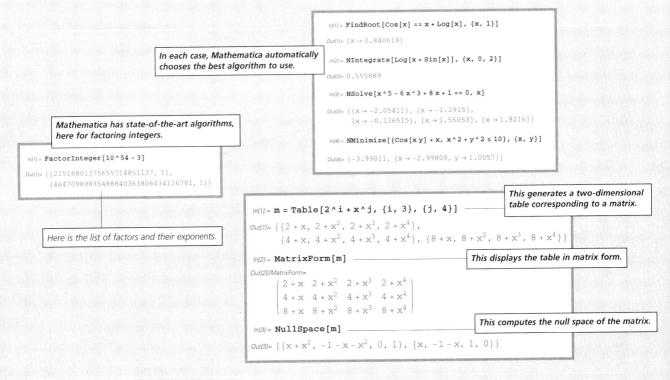

In each case, Mathematica automatically chooses the best algorithm to use.

```
In[1]:= FindRoot[Cos[x] == x + Log[x], {x, 1}]

Out[1]= {x → 0.840619}

In[2]:= NIntegrate[Log[x + Sin[x]], {x, 0, 2}]

Out[2]= 0.555889

In[3]:= NSolve[x^5 - 6 x^3 + 8 x + 1 == 0, x]

Out[3]= {{x → -2.05411}, {x → -1.2915},
         {x → -0.126515}, {x → 1.55053}, {x → 1.9216}}

In[4]:= NMinimize[{Cos[x y] + x, x^2 + y^2 ≤ 10}, {x, y}]

Out[4]= {-3.99011, {x → -2.99809, y → 1.0057}}
```

Mathematica has state-of-the-art algorithms, here for factoring integers.

```
In[1]:= FactorInteger[10^54 - 3]

Out[1]= {{215188013756557714851137, 1},
         {46470989835488840363806434126781, 1}}
```

Here is the list of factors and their exponents.

This generates a two-dimensional table corresponding to a matrix.

```
In[1]:= m = Table[2^i + x^j, {i, 3}, {j, 4}]

Out[1]= {{2 + x, 2 + x^2, 2 + x^3, 2 + x^4},
         {4 + x, 4 + x^2, 4 + x^3, 4 + x^4}, {8 + x, 8 + x^2, 8 + x^3, 8 + x^4}}

In[2]:= MatrixForm[m]

Out[2]//MatrixForm=
```
$$\begin{pmatrix} 2 + x & 2 + x^2 & 2 + x^3 & 2 + x^4 \\ 4 + x & 4 + x^2 & 4 + x^3 & 4 + x^4 \\ 8 + x & 8 + x^2 & 8 + x^3 & 8 + x^4 \end{pmatrix}$$

This displays the table in matrix form.

```
In[3]:= NullSpace[m]

Out[3]= {{x + x^2, -1 - x - x^2, 0, 1}, {x, -1 - x, 1, 0}}
```

This computes the null space of the matrix.

Mathematica can solve differential equations both symbolically and numerically.

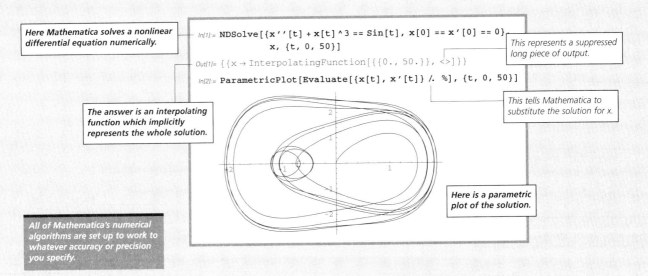

Here Mathematica solves a nonlinear differential equation numerically.

```
In[1]:= NDSolve[{x''[t] + x[t]^3 == Sin[t], x[0] == x'[0] == 0},
        x, {t, 0, 50}]

Out[1]= {{x → InterpolatingFunction[{{0., 50.}}, <>]}}

In[2]:= ParametricPlot[Evaluate[{x[t], x'[t]} /. %], {t, 0, 50}]
```

This represents a suppressed long piece of output.

This tells Mathematica to substitute the solution for x.

The answer is an interpolating function which implicitly represents the whole solution.

Here is a parametric plot of the solution.

All of Mathematica's numerical algorithms are set up to work to whatever accuracy or precision you specify.

Mathematical Knowledge in Mathematica

Mathematica incorporates the knowledge from the world's mathematical handbooks—and uses its own revolutionary algorithms to go much further.

Mathematica knows about all the hundreds of special functions in pure and applied mathematics.

```
In[1]:= LegendreQ[3, x]
```
$$Out[1]= \frac{2}{3} - \frac{5x^2}{2} - \frac{1}{4} x (3 - 5x^2) \log\left[\frac{1+x}{1-x}\right]$$

```
In[2]:= N[MathieuC[1 + i, 2 i, 3], 50]
```
$$Out[2]= 3.9251311374125198643497646168158379203627176844794 + \\ 1.8988239115433472411052747971439115776785813553761\,i$$

These both stand for $\sqrt{-1}$.

Mathematica can evaluate special functions with any parameters to any precision.

Mathematica is now able to do vastly more integrals than were ever before possible for either humans or computers.

```
In[1]:= Integrate[Sqrt[x] ArcTan[x], x]
```
$$Out[1]= \frac{1}{6}\left(-8\sqrt{x} - 2\sqrt{2}\,\text{ArcTan}\left[1 - \sqrt{2}\,\sqrt{x}\right] + 2\sqrt{2}\,\text{ArcTan}\left[1 + \sqrt{2}\,\sqrt{x}\right] + \right.$$
$$\left. 4x^{3/2}\,\text{ArcTan}[x] - \sqrt{2}\,\log\left[-1 + \sqrt{2}\,\sqrt{x} - x\right] + \sqrt{2}\,\log\left[1 + \sqrt{2}\,\sqrt{x} + x\right]\right)$$

Here is a definite integral.

```
In[1]:= Integrate[Log[x] Exp[-x^3], {x, 0, Infinity}]
```
$$Out[1]= \frac{1}{81}\,\text{Gamma}\left[-\frac{2}{3}\right](6\,\text{EulerGamma} + \sqrt{3}\,\pi + 9\,\log[3])$$

```
In[2]:= Integrate[x Sin[x^2] Exp[-x], {x, 0, Infinity}]
```
$$Out[2]= \frac{1}{8}\left(4\,\text{HypergeometricPFQ}\left[\{1\}, \left\{\frac{1}{4}, \frac{3}{4}\right\}, -\frac{1}{64}\right] + \sqrt{2\pi}\left(-\cos\left[\frac{1}{4}\right] + \sin\left[\frac{1}{4}\right]\right)\right)$$

Here is a symbolic sum.

```
In[1]:= Sum[1 / (k + 1)^6, {k, 0, n}]
```
$$Out[1]= \frac{\pi^6}{945} - \frac{1}{120}\,\text{PolyGamma}[5, 2 + n]$$

The results often require special functions.

Mathematica can solve a wide range of ordinary and partial differential equations.

```
In[1]:= DSolve[y''[x] + y'[x] + x y[x] == 0, y[x], x]
```
$$Out[1]= \left\{\left\{y[x] \to e^{-x/2}\,\text{AiryAi}\left[-(-1)^{1/3}\left(\frac{1}{4} - x\right)\right]C[1] + e^{-x/2}\,\text{AiryBi}\left[-(-1)^{1/3}\left(\frac{1}{4} - x\right)\right]C[2]\right\}\right\}$$

This finds the billionth prime number.

```
In[1]:= Prime[10^9]
```
$$Out[1]= 22801763489$$

Mathematica's algorithms can generate a huge range of mathematical results.

```
In[1]:= FullSimplify[Product[Gamma[2 n / 5], {n, 1, 5}]]
```
$$Out[1]= \frac{12\pi^2}{25\sqrt{5}}$$

```
In[1]:= Reduce[Exists[x, x^2 + a x + b == 0], {a, b}, Reals]
```
$$Out[1]= b \le \frac{a^2}{4}$$

```
In[1]:= Log[2] < Zeta[3] < Sqrt[2]
```
$$Out[1]= \text{True}$$

You can tell Mathematica assumptions about variables.

```
In[1]:= Simplify[Sin[x + 2 π n], n ∈ Integers]
```
$$Out[1]= \sin[x]$$

Building Up Computations

Being able to work with formulas lets you easily
integrate all the parts of a computation.

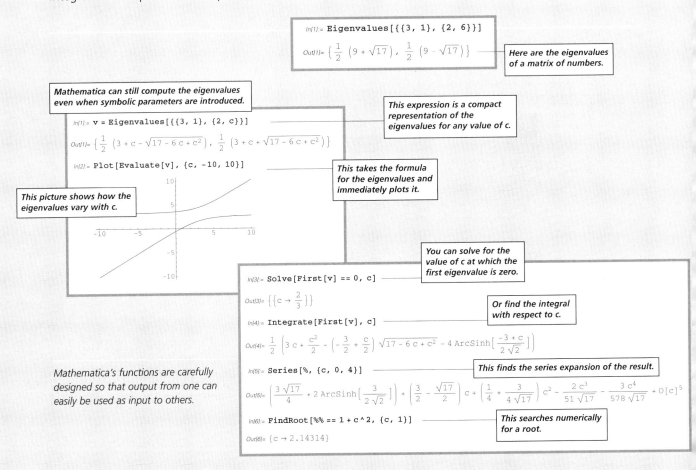

$In[1]:=$ **Eigenvalues[{{3, 1}, {2, 6}}]**

$Out[1]=$ $\left\{ \frac{1}{2} \left(9 + \sqrt{17}\right), \frac{1}{2} \left(9 - \sqrt{17}\right) \right\}$

Here are the eigenvalues of a matrix of numbers.

Mathematica can still compute the eigenvalues even when symbolic parameters are introduced.

$In[1]:=$ **v = Eigenvalues[{{3, 1}, {2, c}}]**

$Out[1]=$ $\left\{ \frac{1}{2} \left(3 + c - \sqrt{17 - 6\,c + c^2}\right), \frac{1}{2} \left(3 + c + \sqrt{17 - 6\,c + c^2}\right) \right\}$

$In[2]:=$ **Plot[Evaluate[v], {c, -10, 10}]**

This expression is a compact representation of the eigenvalues for any value of c.

This takes the formula for the eigenvalues and immediately plots it.

This picture shows how the eigenvalues vary with c.

You can solve for the value of c at which the first eigenvalue is zero.

$In[3]:=$ **Solve[First[v] == 0, c]**

$Out[3]=$ $\left\{ \left\{ c \rightarrow \frac{2}{3} \right\} \right\}$

Or find the integral with respect to c.

$In[4]:=$ **Integrate[First[v], c]**

$Out[4]=$ $\frac{1}{2} \left(3\,c + \frac{c^2}{2} - \left(-\frac{3}{2} + \frac{c}{2}\right) \sqrt{17 - 6\,c + c^2} - 4\,\text{ArcSinh}\left[\frac{-3 + c}{2\sqrt{2}}\right]\right)$

$In[5]:=$ **Series[%, {c, 0, 4}]**

This finds the series expansion of the result.

$Out[5]=$ $\left(\frac{3\sqrt{17}}{4} + 2\,\text{ArcSinh}\left[\frac{3}{2\sqrt{2}}\right]\right) + \left(\frac{3}{2} - \frac{\sqrt{17}}{2}\right) c + \left(\frac{1}{4} + \frac{3}{4\sqrt{17}}\right) c^2 - \frac{2\,c^3}{51\sqrt{17}} - \frac{3\,c^4}{578\sqrt{17}} + O[c]^5$

$In[6]:=$ **FindRoot[%% == 1 + c^2, {c, 1}]**

This searches numerically for a root.

$Out[6]=$ $\{c \rightarrow 2.14314\}$

Mathematica's functions are carefully designed so that output from one can easily be used as input to others.

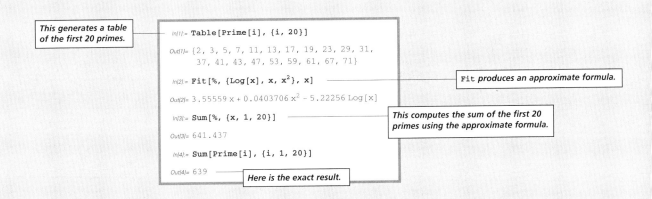

This generates a table of the first 20 primes.

$In[1]:=$ **Table[Prime[i], {i, 20}]**

$Out[1]=$ {2, 3, 5, 7, 11, 13, 17, 19, 23, 29, 31, 37, 41, 43, 47, 53, 59, 61, 67, 71}

$In[2]:=$ **Fit[%, {Log[x], x, x^2}, x]**

Fit *produces an approximate formula.*

$Out[2]=$ $3.55559\,x + 0.0403706\,x^2 - 5.22256\,\text{Log}[x]$

$In[3]:=$ **Sum[%, {x, 1, 20}]**

This computes the sum of the first 20 primes using the approximate formula.

$Out[3]=$ 641.437

$In[4]:=$ **Sum[Prime[i], {i, 1, 20}]**

$Out[4]=$ 639

Here is the exact result.

Handling Data

Mathematica lets you import data in any format, then manipulate it using powerful and flexible functions.

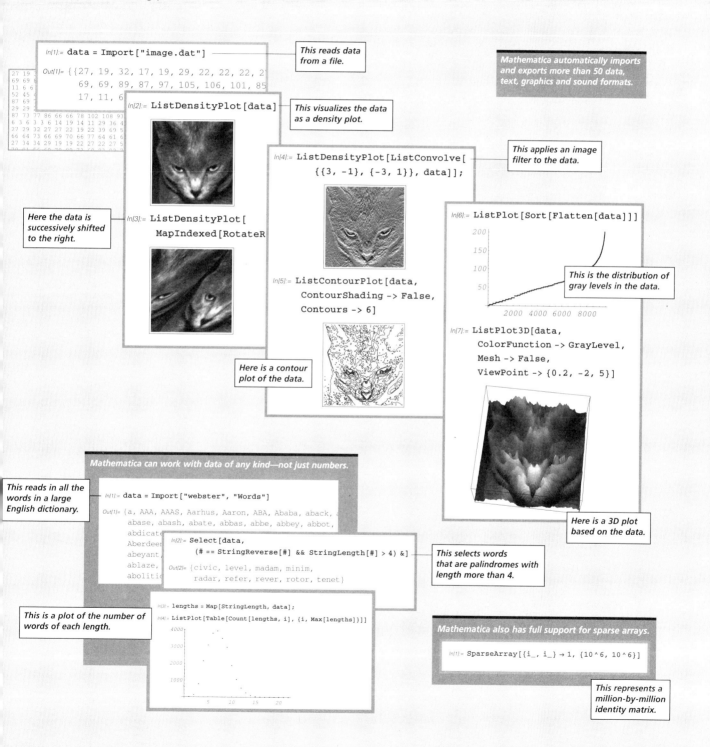

```
In[1]:= data = Import["image.dat"]
```
This reads data from a file.

```
Out[1]= {{27, 19, 32, 17, 19, 29, 22, 22, 22, 2
         69, 69, 89, 87, 97, 105, 106, 101, 85
         17, 11, 6
```

Mathematica automatically imports and exports more than 50 data, text, graphics and sound formats.

```
In[2]:= ListDensityPlot[data]
```
This visualizes the data as a density plot.

```
In[4]:= ListDensityPlot[ListConvolve[
          {{3, -1}, {-3, 1}}, data]];
```
This applies an image filter to the data.

Here the data is successively shifted to the right.

```
In[3]:= ListDensityPlot[
          MapIndexed[RotateR
```

```
In[6]:= ListPlot[Sort[Flatten[data]]]
```

This is the distribution of gray levels in the data.

```
In[5]:= ListContourPlot[data,
          ContourShading -> False,
          Contours -> 6]
```

Here is a contour plot of the data.

```
In[7]:= ListPlot3D[data,
          ColorFunction -> GrayLevel,
          Mesh -> False,
          ViewPoint -> {0.2, -2, 5}]
```

Mathematica can work with data of any kind—not just numbers.

This reads in all the words in a large English dictionary.

```
In[1]:= data = Import["webster", "Words"]
```

```
Out[1]= {a, AAA, AAAS, Aarhus, Aaron, ABA, Ababa, aback,
         abase, abash, abate, abbas, abbe, abbey, abbot,
         abdicate
         Aberdeen
         abeyant
         ablaze,
         abolitio
```

```
In[2]:= Select[data,
          (# == StringReverse[#] && StringLength[#] > 4) &]
```
This selects words that are palindromes with length more than 4.

```
Out[2]= {civic, level, madam, minim,
         radar, refer, rever, rotor, tenet}
```

Here is a 3D plot based on the data.

This is a plot of the number of words of each length.

```
In[3]:= lengths = Map[StringLength, data];
In[4]:= ListPlot[Table[Count[lengths, i], {i, Max[lengths]}]]
```

Mathematica also has full support for sparse arrays.

```
In[1]:= SparseArray[{i_, i_} -> 1, {10^6, 10^6}]
```

This represents a million-by-million identity matrix.

Visualization with Mathematica

Mathematica makes it easy to create stunning visual images.

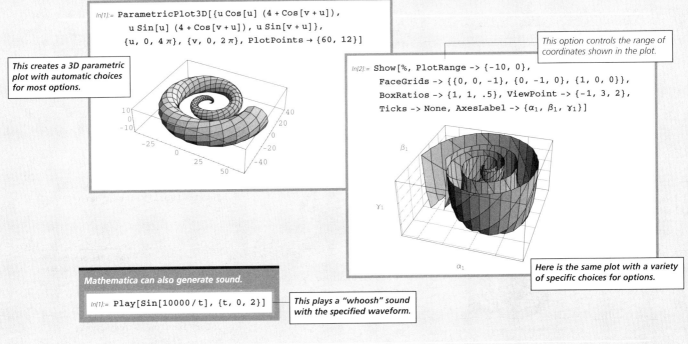

```
In[1]:= ParametricPlot3D[{u Cos[u] (4 + Cos[v + u]),
          u Sin[u] (4 + Cos[v + u]), u Sin[v + u]},
          {u, 0, 4 π}, {v, 0, 2 π}, PlotPoints → {60, 12}]
```

This creates a 3D parametric plot with automatic choices for most options.

This option controls the range of coordinates shown in the plot.

```
In[2]:= Show[%, PlotRange -> {-10, 0},
          FaceGrids -> {{0, 0, -1}, {0, -1, 0}, {1, 0, 0}},
          BoxRatios -> {1, 1, .5}, ViewPoint -> {-1, 3, 2},
          Ticks -> None, AxesLabel -> {α₁, β₁, γ₁}]
```

Here is the same plot with a variety of specific choices for options.

Mathematica can also generate sound.

```
In[1]:= Play[Sin[10000 / t], {t, 0, 2}]
```

This plays a "whoosh" sound with the specified waveform.

Mathematica includes primitives from which you can build up 2D and 3D graphics of any complexity.

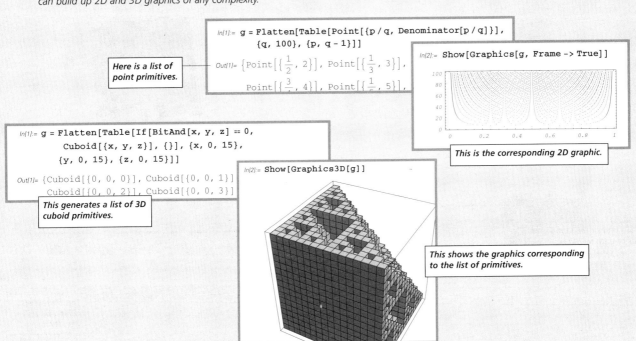

```
In[1]:= g = Flatten[Table[Point[{p / q, Denominator[p / q]}],
          {q, 100}, {p, q - 1}]]
```

$$Out[1]= \left\{ Point\left[\left\{\frac{1}{2}, 2\right\}\right], Point\left[\left\{\frac{1}{3}, 3\right\}\right], Point\left[\left\{\frac{3}{4}, 4\right\}\right], Point\left[\left\{\frac{1}{5}, 5\right\}\right], \right.$$

Here is a list of point primitives.

```
In[2]:= Show[Graphics[g, Frame -> True]]
```

This is the corresponding 2D graphic.

```
In[1]:= g = Flatten[Table[If[BitAnd[x, y, z] == 0,
          Cuboid[{x, y, z}], {}], {x, 0, 15},
          {y, 0, 15}, {z, 0, 15}]]

Out[1]= {Cuboid[{0, 0, 0}], Cuboid[{0, 0, 1}]
          Cuboid[{0, 0, 2}], Cuboid[{0, 0, 3}]
```

This generates a list of 3D cuboid primitives.

```
In[2]:= Show[Graphics3D[g]]
```

This shows the graphics corresponding to the list of primitives.

```
In[1]:= Table[Plot3D[Sin[2 x] Sin[2 y] Cos[t],
    {x, 0, Pi}, {y, 0, Pi}, PlotRange -> {-1, 1},
    BoxRatios -> {1, 1, 1}], {t, 0, Pi, Pi / 6}]
```

Mathematica lets you produce animated movies as well as static graphics.

Mathematica has made possible many new kinds of scientific, technical, and artistic images.

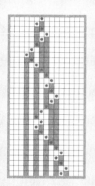

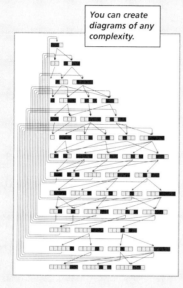

You can create diagrams of any complexity.

You can create representations of abstract mathematical objects.

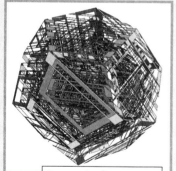

You can visualize structures of any kind.

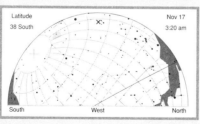

You can display data in any format.

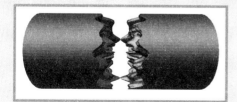

Mathematica Notebooks

Every *Mathematica* notebook is a complete interactive document which combines text, tables, graphics, calculations and other elements.

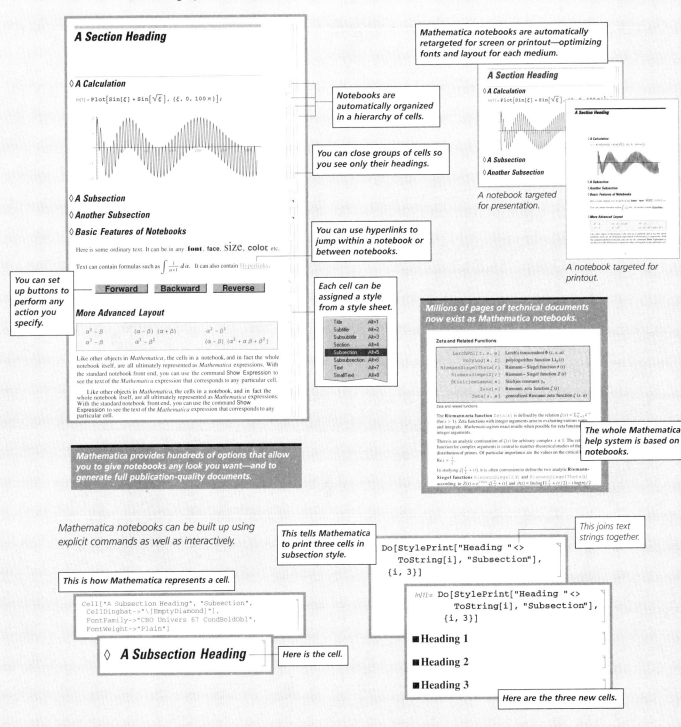

A Section Heading

◊ *A Calculation*

$In[1]:= \text{Plot}[\text{Sin}[\xi] + \text{Sin}[\sqrt{\xi}], \{\xi, 0, 100\,\pi\}];$

◊ *A Subsection*

◊ *Another Subsection*

◊ *Basic Features of Notebooks*

Here is some ordinary text. It can be in any **font**, face, size, color, etc.

Text can contain formulas such as $\int \frac{1}{\alpha+1}\,d\alpha$. It can also contain Hyperlinks.

| Forward | Backward | Reverse |

More Advanced Layout

| $\alpha^2 - \beta$ | $(\alpha - \beta)\ (\alpha + \beta)$ | $\alpha^2 - \beta^3$ |
| $\alpha^3 - \beta$ | $\alpha^2 - \beta^2$ | $(\alpha - \beta)\ (\alpha^2 + \alpha\,\beta + \beta^2)$ |

Like other objects in *Mathematica*, the cells in a notebook, and in fact the whole notebook itself, are all ultimately represented as *Mathematica* expressions. With the standard notebook front end, you can use the command Show Expression to see the text of the *Mathematica* expression that corresponds to any particular cell.

Like other objects in *Mathematica*, the cells in a notebook, and in fact the whole notebook itself, are all ultimately represented as *Mathematica* expressions. With the standard notebook front end, you can use the command Show Expression to see the text of the *Mathematica* expression that corresponds to any particular cell.

Mathematica notebooks are automatically retargeted for screen or printout—optimizing fonts and layout for each medium.

A notebook targeted for presentation.

A notebook targeted for printout.

Notebooks are automatically organized in a hierarchy of cells.

You can close groups of cells so you see only their headings.

You can use hyperlinks to jump within a notebook or between notebooks.

You can set up buttons to perform any action you specify.

Each cell can be assigned a style from a style sheet.

Title	Alt+1
Subtitle	Alt+2
Subsubtitle	Alt+3
Section	Alt+4
Subsection	Alt+5
Subsubsection	Alt+6
Text	Alt+7
SmallText	Alt+8

Millions of pages of technical documents now exist as Mathematica notebooks.

Zeta and Related Functions

LerchPhi[z, s, a]	Lerch's transcendent $\Phi(z, s, a)$
PolyLog[n, z]	polylogarithm function $\text{Li}_n(z)$
RiemannSiegelTheta[t]	Riemann–Siegel function $\vartheta(t)$
RiemannSiegelZ[t]	Riemann–Siegel function $Z(t)$
StieltjesGamma[n]	Stieltjes constants γ_n
Zeta[s]	Riemann zeta function $\zeta(s)$
Zeta[s, a]	generalized Riemann zeta function $\zeta(s, a)$

Zeta and related functions.

The **Riemann zeta function** Zeta[s] is defined by the relation $\zeta(s) = \sum_{k=1}^{\infty} k^{-s}$ (for $s > 1$). Zeta functions with integer arguments arise in evaluating various sums and integrals. *Mathematica* gives exact results when possible for zeta functions with integer arguments.

There is an analytic continuation of $\zeta(s)$ for arbitrary complex $s \neq 1$. The zeta function for complex arguments is central to number-theoretical studies of the distribution of primes. Of particular importance are the values on the critical line $\text{Re}\,s = \frac{1}{2}$.

In studying $\zeta(\frac{1}{2} + it)$, it is often convenient to define the two analytic **Riemann-Siegel functions** RiemannSiegelZ[t] and RiemannSiegelTheta[t] according to $Z(t) = e^{i\vartheta(t)} \zeta(\frac{1}{2} + it)$ and $\vartheta(t) = \text{Im}\log\Gamma(\frac{1}{4} + it/2) - t\log\pi/2$

The whole Mathematica help system is based on notebooks.

Mathematica provides hundreds of options that allow you to give notebooks any look you want—and to generate full publication-quality documents.

Mathematica notebooks can be built up using explicit commands as well as interactively.

This is how Mathematica represents a cell.

```
Cell["A Subsection Heading", "Subsection",
  CellDingbat->"\[EmptyDiamond]"],
  FontFamily->"CBO Univers 67 CondBoldObl",
  FontWeight->"Plain"]
```

◊ *A Subsection Heading*

Here is the cell.

This tells Mathematica to print three cells in subsection style.

This joins text strings together.

```
Do[StylePrint["Heading " <>
    ToString[i], "Subsection"],
  {i, 3}]
```

```
In[1]:= Do[StylePrint["Heading " <>
    ToString[i], "Subsection"],
  {i, 3}]
```

■ Heading 1

■ Heading 2

■ Heading 3

Here are the three new cells.

Palettes and Buttons

Palettes and buttons provide a simple but fully customizable point-and-click interface to *Mathematica*.

Mathematica comes with a collection of ready-to-use standard palettes.

Part of the standard Basic Calculations palette.

A standard palette for European characters.

The complete Basic Calculations palette is organized as a notebook with palettes inside it.

Palettes work like extensions to your keyboard.

Clicking the ε button pastes the ε character into your notebook.

The ■ indicates where the current selection should be inserted.

Clicking the button takes the highlighted selection and wraps a square root around it.

It is easy to create your own custom palettes.

Palettes can be part of a notebook or can stand alone.

A button waiting to be filled.

You can make custom palettes to execute any function or manipulate any expression.

Clicking the button immediately factors the part of the expression you have selected.

Polyhedron Explorer

Clicking a button performs a geometric operation on the current polyhedron.

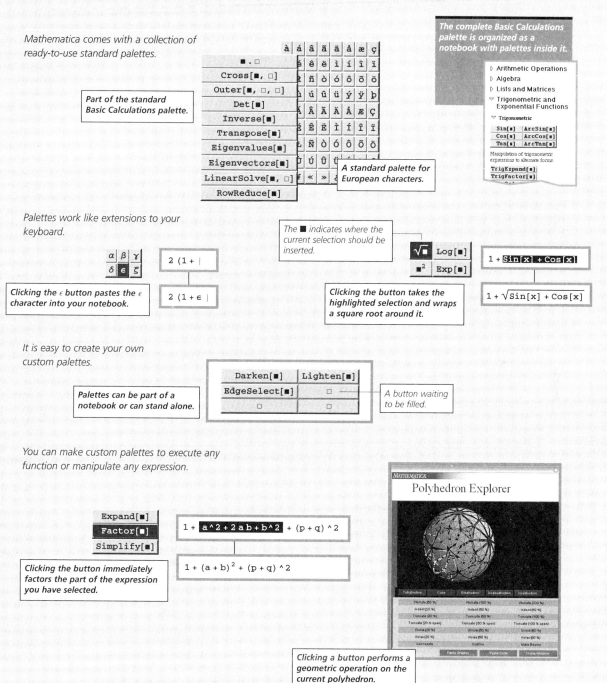

Mathematical Notation

Mathematica notebooks fully support standard mathematical notation—for both output and input.

Mathematica combines the compactness of mathematical notation with the precision of a computer language.

Here is an integral entered using only ordinary keyboard characters.

In[1]:= `Integrate[Log[1 + x] / Sqrt[x], x]`

Out[1]= $4 \, \text{ArcTan}\left[\sqrt{x}\right] + 2 \sqrt{x} \, (-2 + \text{Log}[1 + x])$

Here is the same integral entered in two-dimensional form with special characters.

You can enter this form using a palette or directly from the keyboard.

In[2]:= $\displaystyle\int \frac{\text{Log}[1 + \xi]}{\sqrt{\xi}} \, d\xi$

`⦂int⦂ Log[1 + ⦂x⦂] CTRL / CTRL 2 ⦂x⦂ CTRL␣ ⦂dd⦂ ⦂x⦂`

Out[2]= $4 \, \text{ArcTan}\left[\sqrt{\xi}\right] + 2 \sqrt{\xi} \, (-2 + \text{Log}[1 + \xi])$

This stands for the ESC key.

You can use any of the notation in this palette for input.

Mathematica always lets you edit output—and use it again as input.

Out[1]= $-4 \sqrt{\xi} + (4 \, \text{ArcTan}[\sqrt{\xi}] + 2 \pi) + 2 \sqrt{\xi} \, \text{Log}[1 + \xi]$

Mathematica can generate output in traditional textbook form.

In[2]:= `TraditionalForm[%]`

Out[2]//TraditionalForm=
$$4 \tan^{-1}\left(\sqrt{\xi}\right) + 2 \sqrt{\xi} \, (\log(\xi + 1) - 2)$$

Mathematica's StandardForm is precise and unambiguous. TraditionalForm requires heuristics for interpretation.

Mathematica supports over 700 special characters with new fonts optimized for both screen and printer.

Script
Double-struck
Gothic
Greek

All characters have consistent full names; some also have aliases and T$_E$X names.

Mathematica produces top-quality output for formulas of any size or complexity.

In[1]:= $\displaystyle\sum_{\mu=0}^{\infty} \frac{\varphi^{\mu} \, \text{Exp}\left[\frac{\pi \mu}{4}\right]}{\mu! \, 2 \, (\mu^2 + \kappa) \, (\mu^2 - \lambda)}$ `// TraditionalForm`

Out[1]//TraditionalForm=
$$\left(-\lambda \, _1F_2\left(-i\sqrt{\kappa}; 1, 1-i\sqrt{\kappa}; e^{\pi/4}\varphi\right) - \lambda \, _1F_2\left(i\sqrt{\kappa}; 1, i\sqrt{\kappa}+1; e^{\pi/4}\varphi\right) - \right.$$
$$\left. \kappa \, _1F_2\left(-\sqrt{\lambda}; 1, 1-\sqrt{\lambda}; e^{\pi/4}\varphi\right) - \kappa \, _1F_2\left(\sqrt{\lambda}; 1, \sqrt{\lambda}+1; e^{\pi/4}\varphi\right)\right) /$$
$$\left(2\kappa\left(\sqrt{\kappa}-i\sqrt{\lambda}\right)\left(\sqrt{\kappa}+i\sqrt{\lambda}\right)\lambda\right)$$

Mathematica makes it easy to work with abstract notation.

In[1]:= $\text{Table}\left[\mathcal{G} \circ \overline{\alpha_i \oplus \beta_i} \Rightarrow \underset{i}{\overset{3-i}{\partial}}, \{i, 3\}\right]$

Out[1]= $\left\{\mathcal{G} \circ \overline{\alpha_1 \oplus \beta_1} \Rightarrow \underset{1}{\overset{2}{\partial}}, \; \mathcal{G} \circ \overline{\alpha_2 \oplus \beta_2} \Rightarrow \underset{2}{\overset{1}{\partial}}, \; \mathcal{G} \circ \overline{\alpha_3 \oplus \beta_3} \Rightarrow \underset{3}{\overset{0}{\partial}}\right\}$

Mathematica includes full support for MathML.

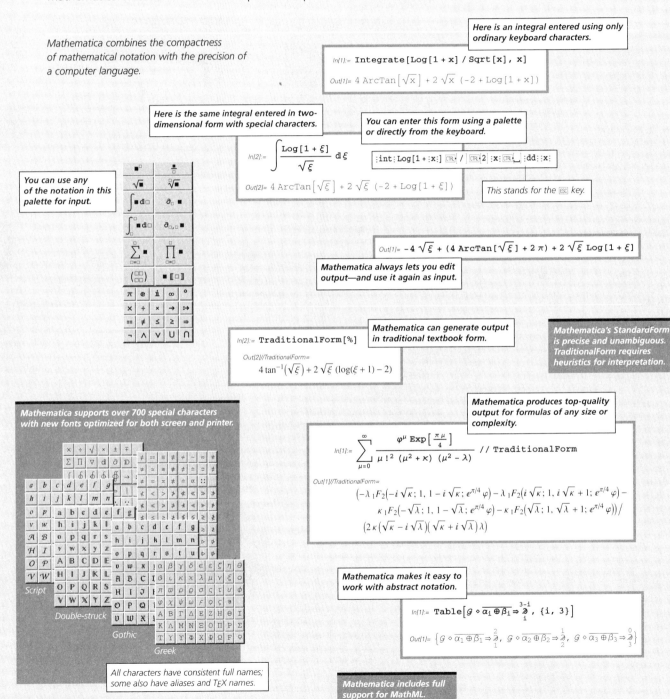

Mathematica and Your Computing Environment

Mathematica runs compatibly across all major computer systems, and lets you exchange data in many standard formats.

The standard Mathematica system consists of two parts:

The kernel—which actually does computations.

The front end—which handles user interaction and notebooks.

From within one notebook you can run several Mathematica kernels—on local or remote computers.

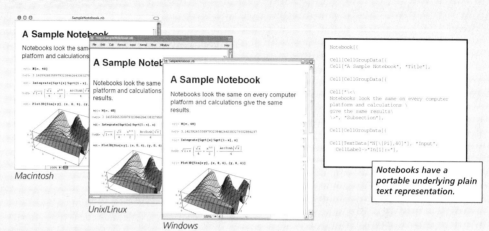

Macintosh

Unix/Linux

Windows

Notebooks have a portable underlying plain text representation.

This is what you get when you copy the integral into an external text application such as email.

$$\int \frac{\text{Log}[1 + \xi]}{\sqrt{\xi}}\, d\xi$$

```
\!\(\(\[Integral]\(Log[1 + \[Xi]]\)/\@\[Xi]\)\[DifferentialD]\[Xi]\)
```

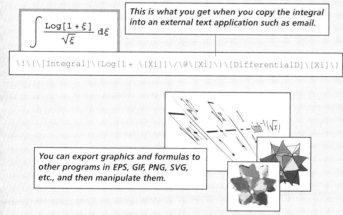

You can export graphics and formulas to other programs in EPS, GIF, PNG, SVG, etc., and then manipulate them.

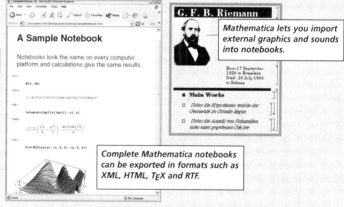

A Sample Notebook

Notebooks look the same on every computer platform and calculations give the same results.

Complete Mathematica notebooks can be exported in formats such as XML, HTML, T_EX and RTF.

Mathematica lets you import external graphics and sounds into notebooks.

Mathematica uses the Unicode standard to ensure portability of international character sets.

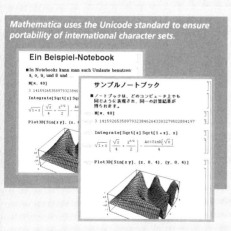

Mathematica provides system-independent functions for file manipulation.

```
In[1]:= all = FileNames["*",
            $HomeDirectory, Infinity];

In[2]:= sizes = Map[FileByteCount, all];

In[3]:= ListPlot[Sort[Log[10, 1 + sizes]]]
```

You can easily connect to external programs.

```
In[1]:= Install["sampler.exe"]

Out[1]= LinkObject[sampler.exe, 2, 2]

In[2]:= Table[getdata[i], {i, 3}]

Out[2]= {{x → 2.45, y → 5.78},
         {x → 1.16, y → 2.19},
         {x → 1.3, y → 4.35}}
```

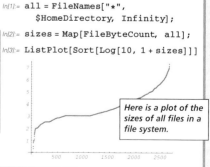

Here is a plot of the sizes of all files in a file system.

The Unifying Idea of Mathematica

Mathematica is built on the powerful unifying idea that everything can be represented as a symbolic expression.

All symbolic expressions are built up from combinations of the basic form: head[arg₁,arg₂,...].

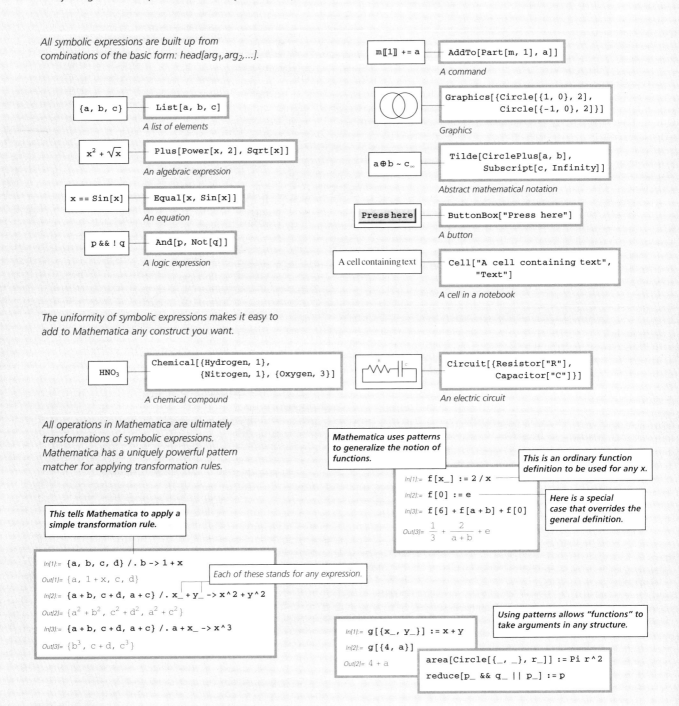

{a, b, c}	`List[a, b, c]`

A list of elements

$x^2 + \sqrt{x}$	`Plus[Power[x, 2], Sqrt[x]]`

An algebraic expression

x == Sin[x]	`Equal[x, Sin[x]]`

An equation

p && ! q	`And[p, Not[q]]`

A logic expression

m[[1]] += a	`AddTo[Part[m, 1], a]`

A command

	`Graphics[{Circle[{1, 0}, 2],` `          Circle[{-1, 0}, 2]}]`

Graphics

a⊕b ~ c∞	`Tilde[CirclePlus[a, b],` `      Subscript[c, Infinity]]`

Abstract mathematical notation

Press here	`ButtonBox["Press here"]`

A button

A cell containing text	`Cell["A cell containing text",` `     "Text"]`

A cell in a notebook

The uniformity of symbolic expressions makes it easy to add to Mathematica any construct you want.

HNO_3	`Chemical[{Hydrogen, 1},` `         {Nitrogen, 1}, {Oxygen, 3}]`

A chemical compound

	`Circuit[{Resistor["R"],` `        Capacitor["C"]}]`

An electric circuit

All operations in Mathematica are ultimately transformations of symbolic expressions. Mathematica has a uniquely powerful pattern matcher for applying transformation rules.

Mathematica uses patterns to generalize the notion of functions.

```
In[1]:= f[x_] := 2 / x
```

This is an ordinary function definition to be used for any x.

```
In[2]:= f[0] := e
```

```
In[3]:= f[6] + f[a + b] + f[0]
```

Here is a special case that overrides the general definition.

$$Out[3]= \frac{1}{3} + \frac{2}{a + b} + e$$

This tells Mathematica to apply a simple transformation rule.

```
In[1]:= {a, b, c, d} /. b -> 1 + x
```

```
Out[1]= {a, 1 + x, c, d}
```

Each of these stands for any expression.

```
In[2]:= {a + b, c + d, a + c} /. x_ + y_ -> x^2 + y^2
```

```
Out[2]= {a² + b², c² + d², a² + c²}
```

```
In[3]:= {a + b, c + d, a + c} /. a + x_ -> x^3
```

```
Out[3]= {b³, c + d, c³}
```

```
In[1]:= g[{x_, y_}] := x + y
```

```
In[2]:= g[{4, a}]
```

```
Out[2]= 4 + a
```

Using patterns allows "functions" to take arguments in any structure.

```
area[Circle[{_, _}, r_]] := Pi r^2
reduce[p_ && q_ || p_] := p
```

Mathematica as a Programming Language

Mathematica is an unprecedentedly flexible and productive programming language.

Mathematica incorporates a range of programming paradigms—so you can write every program in its most natural way.

> **Mathematica includes advanced programming methods from modern computer science—as well as adding a host of new ideas of its own.**

```
In[1]:= z = a;
        Do[Print[z *= z + i], {i, 3}]
        a (1 + a)
        a (1 + a) (2 + a (1 + a))
        a (1 + a) (2 + a (1 + a)) (3 + a (1 + a) (2 + a (1 + a)))
```

Procedural programming

```
In[1]:= 1 + {a, b, c} ^ 2
Out[1]= {1 + a², 1 + b², 1 + c²}
In[2]:= Table[i ^ j, {i, 4}, {j, i}]
Out[2]= {{1}, {2, 4}, {3, 9, 27}, {4, 16, 64, 256}}
In[3]:= Flatten[%]
Out[3]= {1, 2, 4, 3, 9, 27, 4, 16, 64, 256}
In[4]:= Partition[%, 2]
Out[4]= {{1, 2}, {4, 3}, {9, 27}, {4, 16}, {64, 256}}
```

Many operations are automatically threaded over lists.

This flattens out sublists.

This partitions into sublists of length 2.

List-based programming

```
In[1]:= NestList[f, x, 4]
Out[1]= {x, f[x], f[f[x]], f[f[f[x]]], f[f[f[f[x]]]]}
In[2]:= NestList[(1 + #) ^ 2 &, x, 3]
Out[2]= {x, (1 + x)², (1 + (1 + x)²)², (1 + (1 + (1 + x)²)²)²}
```

This is a pure function.

Functional programming

```
In[1]:= p[x_ + y_] := p[x] + p[y]
In[2]:= p[a + b + c]
Out[2]= p[a] + p[b] + p[c]
In[3]:= s[{x__, a_, y__}, a_] := {a, x, x, y, y}
In[4]:= s[{1, 2, 3, 4, 5, 6}, 4]
Out[4]= {4, 1, 2, 3, 1, 2, 3, 5, 6}
```

This stands for any sequence of expressions.

Rule-based programming

```
In[1]:= StringReplace["aababbaabaabababa",
          {"aa" -> "AAA", "ba" -> "V"}]
Out[1]= AAAVbVaVaVVV
```

String-based programming

```
h /: h[x_] + h[y_] := hplus[x, y]
h /: p[h[x_], x_] := hp[x]
h /: f_[h[x_]] := fh[f, x]
```

This associates the definition with the object h.

Here are three definitions to be associated with the object h.

Object-oriented programming

> **Mathematica gives you the flexibility to write programs in many different styles.**

```
f = Factorial
f[n_] := n!
f[n_] := Gamma[n + 1]
f[n_] := n f[n - 1] ; f[1] = 1
f[n_] := Product[i, {i, n}]
f[n_] := Module[{t = 1},
   Do[t = t * i, {i, n}]; t]
f[n_] := Module[{t = 1, i},
   For[i = 1, i <= n, i++, t *= i]; t]
f[n_] := Apply[Times, Range[n]]
f[n_] := Fold[Times, 1, Range[n]]
f[n_] := If[n == 1, 1, n f[n - 1]]
f = If[#1 == 1, 1, #1 #0[#1 - 1]] &
f[n_] := Fold[#2[#1] &, 1,
   Array[Function[t, # t] &, n]]
```

A dozen definitions of the factorial function

```
In[1]:= Position[{1, 2, 3, 4, 5} / 2, _Integer]
Out[1]= {{2}, {4}}
In[2]:= MapIndexed[Power, {a, b, c, d}]
Out[2]= {{a}, {b²}, {c³}, {d⁴}}
In[3]:= FixedPointList[If[EvenQ[#], # / 2, #] &, 10 ^ 5]
Out[3]= {100000, 50000, 25000, 12500, 6250, 3125, 3125}
In[4]:= ReplaceList[{a, b, c, d, e},
          {x__, y__} -> {{x}, {y}}]
Out[4]= {{{a}, {b, c, d, e}}, {{a, b}, {c, d, e}},
        {{a, b, c}, {d, e}}, {{a, b, c, d}, {e}}}
```

Many of Mathematica's most powerful functions mix different programming paradigms.

Mixed programming paradigms

Writing Programs in Mathematica

Mathematica's high-level programming constructs let you build sophisticated programs more quickly than ever before.

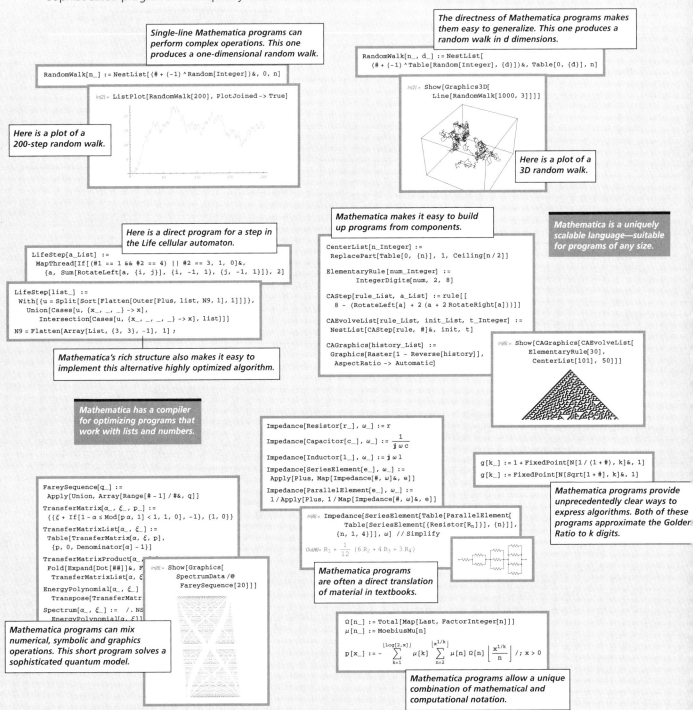

Single-line *Mathematica* programs can perform complex operations. This one produces a one-dimensional random walk.

```
RandomWalk[n_] := NestList[(# + (-1)^Random[Integer])&, 0, n]
```

```
In[2]:= ListPlot[RandomWalk[200], PlotJoined -> True]
```

Here is a plot of a 200-step random walk.

The directness of *Mathematica* programs makes them easy to generalize. This one produces a random walk in d dimensions.

```
RandomWalk[n_, d_] := NestList[
    (# + (-1)^Table[Random[Integer], {d}])&, Table[0, {d}], n]
```

```
In[2]:= Show[Graphics3D[
    Line[RandomWalk[1000, 3]]]]
```

Here is a plot of a 3D random walk.

Here is a direct program for a step in the Life cellular automaton.

```
LifeStep[a_List] :=
    MapThread[If[(#1 == 1 && #2 == 4) || #2 == 3, 1, 0]&,
    {a, Sum[RotateLeft[a, {i, j}], {i, -1, 1}, {j, -1, 1}]}, 2]
```

```
LifeStep[list_] :=
    With[{u = Split[Sort[Flatten[Outer[Plus, list, N9, 1], 1]]]},
    Union[Cases[u, {x_, _, _} -> x],
        Intersection[Cases[u, {x_, _, _, _} -> x], list]]]
N9 = Flatten[Array[List, {3, 3}, -1], 1] ;
```

Mathematica's rich structure also makes it easy to implement this alternative highly optimized algorithm.

Mathematica makes it easy to build up programs from components.

```
CenterList[n_Integer] :=
    ReplacePart[Table[0, {n}], 1, Ceiling[n/2]]
```

```
ElementaryRule[num_Integer] :=
    IntegerDigits[num, 2, 8]
```

```
CAStep[rule_List, a_List] := rule[[
    8 - (RotateLeft[a] + 2 (a + 2 RotateRight[a]))]]
```

```
CAEvolveList[rule_List, init_List, t_Integer] :=
    NestList[CAStep[rule, #]&, init, t]
```

```
CAGraphics[history_List] :=
    Graphics[Raster[1 - Reverse[history]],
    AspectRatio -> Automatic]
```

```
In[6]:= Show[CAGraphics[CAEvolveList[
    ElementaryRule[30],
    CenterList[101], 50]]]
```

Mathematica is a uniquely scalable language—suitable for programs of any size.

Mathematica has a compiler for optimizing programs that work with lists and numbers.

```
FareySequence[q_] :=
    Apply[Union, Array[Range[# - 1]/#&, q]]
```

```
TransferMatrix[α_, ξ_, p_] :=
    {{ξ + If[1 - α Mod[p α, 1] < 1, 1, 0], -1}, {1, 0}}
```

```
TransferMatrixList[α_, ξ_] :=
    Table[TransferMatrix[α, ξ, p],
    {p, 0, Denominator[α] -1}]
```

```
TransferMatrixProduct[α_,
    Fold[Expand[Dot[##]]&, F
    TransferMatrixList[α, ξ
```

```
EnergyPolynomial[α_, ξ_]
    Transpose[TransferMatr
```

```
Spectrum[α_, ξ_] := /. NS
    EnergyPolynomial[α, ξ]]
```

```
In[8]:= Show[Graphics[
    SpectrumData /@
    FareySequence[20]]]
```

Mathematica programs can mix numerical, symbolic and graphics operations. This short program solves a sophisticated quantum model.

```
Impedance[Resistor[r_], ω_] := r
```

$$\text{Impedance[Capacitor}[c\_], \omega\_] := \frac{1}{\mathbf{j}\, \omega\, c}$$

```
Impedance[Inductor[l_], ω_] := j ω l
```

```
Impedance[SeriesElement[e_], ω_] :=
    Apply[Plus, Map[Impedance[#, ω]&, e]]
```

```
Impedance[ParallelElement[e_], ω_] :=
    1/Apply[Plus, 1/Map[Impedance[#, ω]&, e]]
```

```
In[6]:= Impedance[SeriesElement[Table[ParallelElement[
    Table[SeriesElement[{Resistor[R_n]}], {n}]],
    {n, 1, 4}]], ω] // Simplify
```

$$Out[6]= R_1 + \frac{1}{12}\,(6 R_2 + 4 R_3 + 3 R_4)$$

Mathematica programs are often a direct translation of material in textbooks.

```
g[k_] := 1 + FixedPoint[N[1/(1 + #), k]&, 1]
g[k_] := FixedPoint[N[Sqrt[1 + #], k]&, 1]
```

Mathematica programs provide unprecedentedly clear ways to express algorithms. Both of these programs approximate the Golden Ratio to k digits.

```
Ω[n_] := Total[Map[Last, FactorInteger[n]]]
μ[n_] := MoebiusMu[n]
```

$$p[x\_] := -\sum_{k=1}^{\lfloor \text{Log}[2,x] \rfloor} \mu[k] \sum_{n=2}^{\lfloor x^{1/k} \rfloor} \mu[n]\,\Omega[n] \left\lfloor \frac{x^{1/k}}{n} \right\rfloor \; /; x > 0$$

Mathematica programs allow a unique combination of mathematical and computational notation.

Building Systems with Mathematica

Mathematica has everything you need to create complete systems for technical and non-technical applications.

```
In[1]:= << Miscellaneous`WorldPlot`

In[2]:= WorldPlot[World, WorldProjection ->
            N[{#2 (Abs[Sin[Degree / 60 #1]] + 1) / 2, #1} &],
            WorldBackground -> Hue[.5]];
```

This loads a Mathematica package called Combinatorica.

Combinatorica and WorldPlot are two examples of standard add-on packages that come with full versions of Mathematica.

```
In[1]:= << DiscreteMath`Combinatorica`

In[2]:= ShowGraph[LineGraph[LineGraph[
            CirculantGraph[5, Range[1, 3]]]]];
```

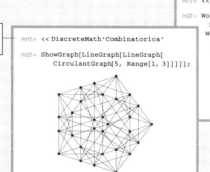

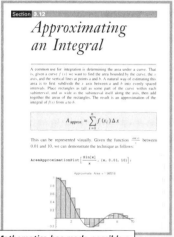

Approximating an Integral

$$A_{approx} = \sum_{i=1}^{n} f(x_i) \, \Delta x$$

```
AreaApproximationPlot[Sin[x]/x, {x, 0.01, 10}];
```

Mathematica has made possible a new generation of notebook-based interactive courseware.

Optica is a large Mathematica package for doing optical engineering.

```
In[1]:= << Optica`

In[2]:= DrawSystem[{
            ConeOfRays[10,NumberOfRays->10],
            Move[PlanoConvexLens[100,50,10],{100,0,0}],
            Move[PlanoConvexCylindricalLens[
                100, {50, 50},10], {130,0,0}],
            Move[BeamSplitter[{50,50},{50,50},10],{180,0,45}],
            Boundary[{-100,-100,-100},{250,100,200}]}];
```

Notebook documentation can automatically be integrated with the main Mathematica help system.

You can use palettes and buttons to build custom user interfaces.

Generate Stock Reports

Click the desired ticker symbol for a historical summary.

- Computer Hardware
- Computer Software

ADSK	Autodesk, Inc.
BORL	Borland International
INGR	Intergraph Corp.
INTU	Intuit
MSFT	Microsoft
NOVL	Novell, Inc.
ORCL	Oracle System Corp.
SY	Sybase

- Telecommunications

Clicking this button generates a report and puts it in a new notebook.

Historical Daily Data for Microsoft (MSFT)

This is the notebook produced by clicking the button.

You can create complete applications and user interfaces directly in Mathematica.

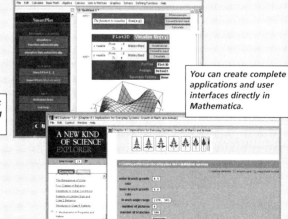
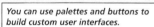

Mathematica as a Software Component

Mathematica's symbolic architecture and uniform linking mechanism make it uniquely powerful as a component in many kinds of software systems.

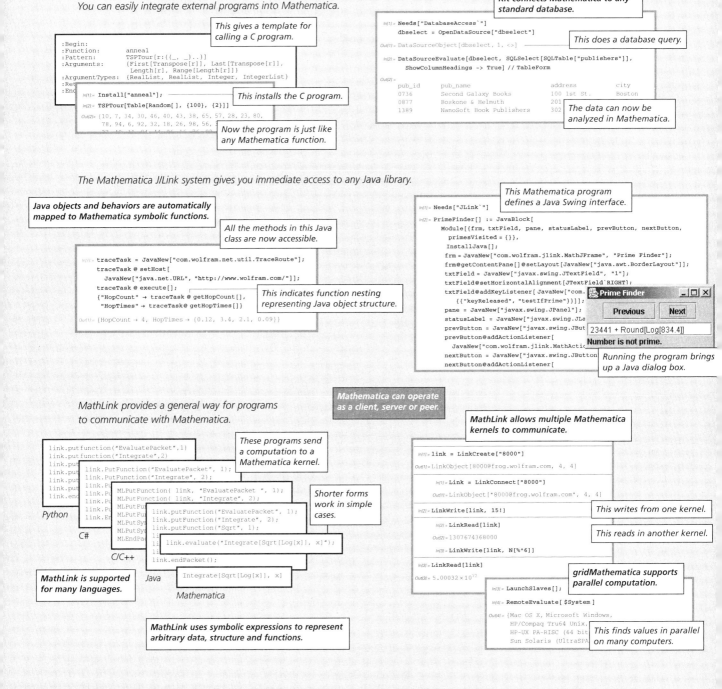

You can easily integrate external programs into Mathematica.

This gives a template for calling a C program.

```
:Begin:
:Function:      anneal
:Pattern:       TSPTour[r:{{_, _}..}]
:Arguments:     {First[Transpose[r]], Last[Transpose[r]],
                 Length[r], Range[Length[r]]}
:ArgumentTypes: {RealList, RealList, Integer, IntegerList}
:Ret
:End
```

In[1]:= `Install["anneal"];`

This installs the C program.

In[2]:= `TSPTour[Table[Random[], {100}, {2}]]`

Out[2]= {10, 7, 34, 30, 46, 40, 43, 38, 65, 57, 28, 23, 80,
          78, 94, 6, 92, 32, 18, 26, 98, 56,

Now the program is just like any Mathematica function.

The Mathematica Database Access Kit connects Mathematica to any standard database.

In[1]:= `Needs["DatabaseAccess`"]`
         `dbselect = OpenDataSource["dbselect"]`

Out[1]= `DataSourceObject[dbselect, 1, <>]`

This does a database query.

In[2]:= `DataSourceEvaluate[dbselect, SQLSelect[SQLTable["publishers"]],`
         `ShowColumnHeadings -> True] // TableForm`

Out[2]=

pub_id	pub_name	address	city
0736	Second Galaxy Books	100 1st St.	Boston
0877	Boskone & Helmuth	201	
1389	NanoSoft Book Publishers	302	

The data can now be analyzed in Mathematica.

The Mathematica J/Link system gives you immediate access to any Java library.

Java objects and behaviors are automatically mapped to Mathematica symbolic functions.

All the methods in this Java class are now accessible.

In[1]:= `traceTask = JavaNew["com.wolfram.net.util.TraceRoute"];`
         `traceTask @ setHost[`
         `   JavaNew["java.net.URL", "http://www.wolfram.com/"]];`
         `traceTask @ execute[];`
         `{HopCount → traceTask @ getHopCount[],`
         ` "HopTimes" → traceTask @ getHopTimes[]}`

This indicates function nesting representing Java object structure.

Out[1]= {HopCount → 4, HopTimes → {0.12, 3.4, 2.1, 0.09}}

This Mathematica program defines a Java Swing interface.

In[1]:= `Needs["JLink`"]`

In[2]:= `PrimeFinder[] := JavaBlock[`
         `  Module[{frm, txtField, pane, statusLabel, prevButton, nextButton,`
         `    primesVisited = {}},`
         `   InstallJava[];`
         `   frm = JavaNew["com.wolfram.jlink.MathJFrame", "Prime Finder"];`
         `   frm@getContentPane[]@setLayout[JavaNew["java.awt.BorderLayout"]];`
         `   txtField = JavaNew["javax.swing.JTextField", "1"];`
         `   txtField@setHorizontalAlignment[JTextField`RIGHT];`
         `   txtField@addKeyListener[ JavaNew["com.`
         `     {{"keyReleased", "testIfPrime"}}]];`
         `   pane = JavaNew["javax.swing.JPanel"];`
         `   statusLabel = JavaNew["javax.swing.JLa`
         `   prevButton = JavaNew["javax.swing.JBut`
         `   prevButton@addActionListener[`
         `     JavaNew["com.wolfram.jlink.MathActi`
         `   nextButton = JavaNew["javax.swing.JButton`
         `   nextButton@addActionListener[`

Prime Finder

| Previous | Next |

23441 + Round[Log[834.4]]

Number is not prime.

Running the program brings up a Java dialog box.

MathLink provides a general way for programs to communicate with Mathematica.

Mathematica can operate as a client, server or peer.

These programs send a computation to a Mathematica kernel.

```
link.putfunction("EvaluatePacket",1)
link.putfunction("Integrate",2)
link.put
link.put   link.PutFunction("EvaluatePacket", 1);
link.put   link.PutFunction("Integrate", 2);
link.put   link.Pu
link.put   link.Pu   MLPutFunction( link, "EvaluatePacket ", 1);
link.end   link.Pu   MLPutFunction( link, "Integrate", 2);
           link.Pu   MLPutFu
           link.Pu   MLPutFu   link.putFunction("EvaluatePacket", 1);
           link.Pu   MLPutSy   link.putFunction("Integrate", 2);
Python     link.En   MLPutSy   link.putFunction("Sqrt", 1);
                     MLPutSy   li
                     MLEndPa   li   link.evaluate("Integrate[Sqrt[Log[x]], x]");
                     li
           C#        li   Integrate[Sqrt[Log[x]], x]
                C/C++
                     link.endPacket();
```

Shorter forms work in simple cases.

MathLink is supported for many languages.

Java

Mathematica

MathLink uses symbolic expressions to represent arbitrary data, structure and functions.

MathLink allows multiple Mathematica kernels to communicate.

In[1]:= `link = LinkCreate["8000"]`

Out[1]= `LinkObject[8000@frog.wolfram.com, 4, 4]`

In[1]:= `Link = LinkConnect["8000"]`

Out[1]= `LinkObject["8000@frog.wolfram.com, 4, 4]`

In[2]:= `LinkWrite[link, 15!]`

This writes from one kernel.

In[2]:= `LinkRead[link]`

Out[2]= `1307674368000`

This reads in another kernel.

In[3]:= `LinkWrite[link, N[%^6]]`

In[3]:= `LinkRead[link]`

Out[3]= 5.00032×10^{72}

gridMathematica supports parallel computation.

In[3]:= `LaunchSlaves[];`

In[4]:= `RemoteEvaluate[ $System ]`

Out[4]= {Mac OS X, Microsoft Windows,
         HP/Compaq Tru64 Unix,
         HP-UX PA-RISC (64 bit
         Sun Solaris (UltraSPA

This finds values in parallel on many computers.

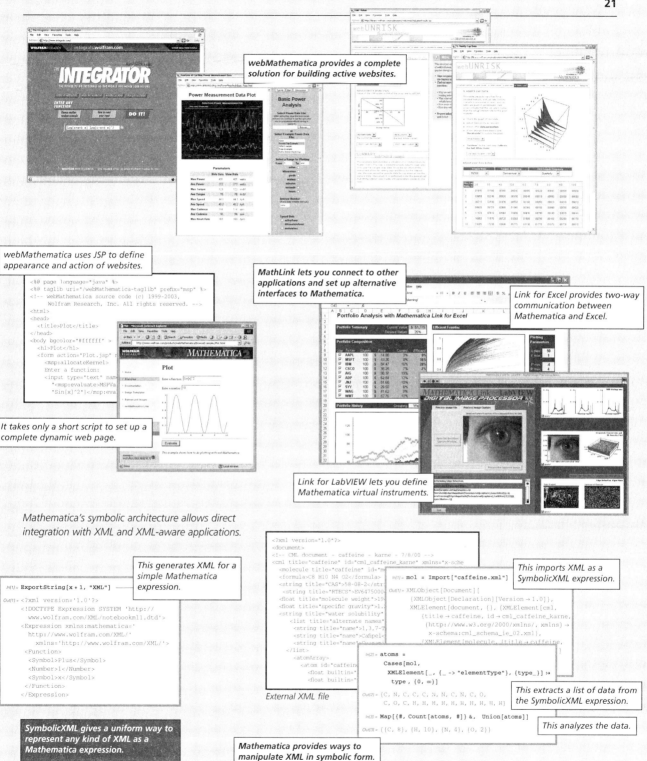

webMathematica provides a complete solution for building active websites.

webMathematica uses JSP to define appearance and action of websites.

```
<%@ page language="java" %>
<%@ taglib uri="/webMathematica-taglib" prefix="msp" %>
<!-- webMathematica source code (c) 1999-2003,
     Wolfram Research, Inc. All rights reserved. -->
<html>
<head>
  <title>Plot</title>
</head>
<body bgcolor="#ffffff" >
  <h1>Plot</h1>
  <form action="Plot.jsp" 
    <msp:allocateKernel>
      Enter a function:
      <input type="text" nam
        "<msp:evaluate>MSPVa
        "Sin[x]^2"]</msp:eva
```

MathLink lets you connect to other applications and set up alternative interfaces to Mathematica.

Link for Excel provides two-way communication between Mathematica and Excel.

It takes only a short script to set up a complete dynamic web page.

Link for LabVIEW lets you define Mathematica virtual instruments.

Mathematica's symbolic architecture allows direct integration with XML and XML-aware applications.

This generates XML for a simple Mathematica expression.

```
In[1]:= ExportString[x + 1, "XML"]

Out[1]= <?xml version='1.0'?>
        <!DOCTYPE Expression SYSTEM 'http://
          www.wolfram.com/XML/notebookml1.dtd'>
        <Expression xmlns:mathematica='
          http://www.wolfram.com/XML/'
          xmlns='http://www.wolfram.com/XML/'>
        <Function>
          <Symbol>Plus</Symbol>
          <Number>1</Number>
          <Symbol>x</Symbol>
        </Function>
        </Expression>
```

SymbolicXML gives a uniform way to represent any kind of XML as a Mathematica expression.

```
<?xml version="1.0"?>
<document>
<!-- CML document - caffeine - karne - 7/8/00 -->
<cml title="caffeine" id="cml_caffeine_karne" xmlns="x-sche
  <molecule title="caffeine" id="m
  <formula>C8 H10 N4 O2</formula>
  <string title="CAS">58-08-2</str
  <string title="RTECS">EV6475000
  <float title="molecule weight">194
  <float title="specific gravity">1.
  <string title="water solubility"
    <list title="alternate names"
      <string title="name">1,3,7-T
      <string title="name">Cafipel
      <string title="name">Cawaret
    </list>
    <atomArray>
      <atom id="caffeine
        <float builtin="
        <float builtin="
```

External XML file

This imports XML as a SymbolicXML expression.

```
In[1]:= mol = Import["caffeine.xml"]

Out[1]= XMLObject[Document][{
          {XMLObject[Declaration][Version → 1.0]},
          XMLElement[document, {}, {XMLElement[cml,
            {title → caffeine, id → cml_caffeine_karne,
            {http://www.w3.org/2000/xmlns/, xmlns} →
            x-schema:cml_schema_ie_02.xml},
            {XMLElement[molecule, {title → caffeine,
```

```
In[2]:= atoms =
        Cases[mol,
          XMLElement[_, {_ -> "elementType"}, {type_}] :>
          type , {0, ∞}]

Out[2]= {C, N, C, C, C, N, N, C, N, C, O,
        C, O, C, H, H, H, H, H, H, H, H, H, H}
```

This extracts a list of data from the SymbolicXML expression.

```
In[3]:= Map[{#, Count[atoms, #]} &,  Union[atoms]]

Out[3]= {{C, 8}, {H, 10}, {N, 4}, {O, 2}}
```

This analyzes the data.

Mathematica provides ways to manipulate XML in symbolic form.

Part 1

This part gives a self-contained introduction to Mathematica, concentrating on using Mathematica as an interactive problem-solving system.

When you have read this part, you should have sufficient knowledge of Mathematica to tackle many kinds of practical problems.

You should realize, however, that what is discussed in this part is in many respects just the surface of Mathematica. Underlying all the various features and capabilities that are discussed, there are powerful and general principles. These principles are discussed in Part 2. To get the most out of Mathematica, you will need to understand them.

This part does not assume that you have used a computer before. In addition, most of the material in it requires no knowledge of mathematics beyond high-school level. The more advanced mathematical aspects of Mathematica are discussed in Part 3 of this book.

Part 1

A Practical Introduction to *Mathematica*

1.0 Running *Mathematica*

To find out how to install and run *Mathematica* you should read the documentation that came with your copy of *Mathematica*. The details differ from one computer system to another, and are affected by various kinds of customization that can be done on *Mathematica*. Nevertheless, this section outlines two common cases.

Note that although the details of running *Mathematica* differ from one computer system to another, the structure of *Mathematica* calculations is the same in all cases. You enter input, then *Mathematica* processes it, and returns a result.

■ 1.0.1 Notebook Interfaces

use an icon or the Start menu	graphical ways to start *Mathematica*
mathematica	the shell command to start *Mathematica*
text ending with Shift-Enter	input for *Mathematica* (Shift-Return on some keyboards)
choose the Quit menu item	exiting *Mathematica*

Running *Mathematica* with a notebook interface.

In a "notebook" interface, you interact with *Mathematica* by creating interactive documents.

If you use your computer via a purely graphical interface, you will typically double-click the *Mathematica* icon to start *Mathematica*. If you use your computer via a textually based operating system, you will typically type the command `mathematica` to start *Mathematica*.

When *Mathematica* starts up, it usually gives you a blank notebook. You enter *Mathematica* input into the notebook, then type Shift-Enter to make *Mathematica* process your input. (To type Shift-Enter, hold down the Shift key, then press Enter.) You can use the standard editing features of your graphical interface to prepare your input, which may go on for several lines. Shift-Enter tells *Mathematica* that you have finished your input. If your keyboard has a numeric keypad, you can use its Enter key instead of Shift-Enter.

After you send *Mathematica* input from your notebook, *Mathematica* will label your input with `In[n]:=`. It labels the corresponding output `Out[n]=`.

You type 2 + 2, then end your input with SHIFT-ENTER. *Mathematica* processes the input, then adds the input label *In[1]:=*, and gives the output.

Throughout this book, "dialogs" with *Mathematica* are shown in the following way:

With a notebook interface, you just type in 2 + 2. *Mathematica* then adds the label *In[1]:=*, and prints the result.

In[1]:= **2 + 2**

Out[1]= 4

Page xv discusses some important details about reproducing the dialogs on your computer system. Section 1.3 gives more information about *Mathematica* notebooks.

You should realize that notebooks are part of the "front end" to *Mathematica*. The *Mathematica* kernel which actually performs computations may be run either on the same computer as the front end, or on another computer connected via some kind of network or line. In most cases, the kernel is not even started until you actually do a calculation with *Mathematica*.

To exit *Mathematica*, you typically choose the Quit menu item in the notebook interface.

■ 1.0.2 Text-Based Interfaces

	`math`	the operating system command to start *Mathematica*
	text ending with ENTER	input for *Mathematica*
	CONTROL-D or `Quit[ ]`	exiting *Mathematica*

Running *Mathematica* with a text-based interface.

With a text-based interface, you interact with your computer primarily by typing text on the keyboard.

To start *Mathematica* with a text-based interface, you typically type the command `math` at an operating system prompt. On some systems, you may also be able to start *Mathematica* with a text-based interface by double-clicking on a *Mathematica* Kernel icon.

When *Mathematica* has started, it will print the prompt *In[1]:=*, signifying that it is ready for your input. You can then type your input, ending with ENTER or RETURN.

Mathematica will then process the input, and generate a result. If it prints the result out, it will label it with *Out[1]=*.

Throughout this book, dialogs with *Mathematica* are shown in the following way:

The computer prints *In[1]:=*. You just type in 2 + 2. The line that starts with *Out[1]=* is the result from *Mathematica*.

```
In[1]:= 2 + 2
Out[1]= 4
```

Page xv discusses some important details about reproducing the dialogs on your computer system. Note that you do not explicitly type the *In[n]:=* prompt; only type the text that follows this prompt.

Note also that most of the actual dialogs given in the book show output in the form you get with a notebook interface to *Mathematica*; output with a text-based interface looks similar, but lacks such features as special characters and font size changes.

Section 1.3 gives more details on running *Mathematica* with a text-based interface. To exit *Mathematica*, either type CONTROL-D, CONTROL-Z or Quit[ ] at an input prompt.

1.1 Numerical Calculations

■ 1.1.1 Arithmetic

You can do arithmetic with *Mathematica* just as you would on an electronic calculator.

This is the sum of two numbers.	$In[1]:=$ **2.3 + 5.63** $Out[1]=$ 7.93
Here the / stands for division, and the ^ stands for power.	$In[2]:=$ **2.4 / 8.9 ^ 2** $Out[2]=$ 0.0302992
Spaces denote multiplication in *Mathematica*. You can use a * for multiplication if you want to.	$In[3]:=$ **2 3 4** $Out[3]=$ 24
You can type arithmetic expressions with parentheses.	$In[4]:=$ **(3 + 4) ^ 2 - 2 (3 + 1)** $Out[4]=$ 41
Spaces are not needed, though they often make your input easier to read.	$In[5]:=$ **(3+4)^2-2(3+1)** $Out[5]=$ 41

x^y	power
$-x$	minus
x/y	divide
$x\ y\ z$ or x*y*z	multiply
x+y+z	add

Arithmetic operations in *Mathematica*.

Arithmetic operations in *Mathematica* are grouped according to the standard mathematical conventions. As usual, 2 ^ 3 + 4, for example, means (2 ^ 3) + 4, and not 2 ^ (3 + 4). You can always control grouping by explicitly using parentheses.

This result is given in scientific notation.	$In[6]:=$ **2.4 ^ 45** $Out[6]=$ 1.28678×10^{17}
You can enter numbers in scientific notation like this.	$In[7]:=$ **2.3 10^70** $Out[7]=$ 2.3×10^{70}
Or like this.	$In[8]:=$ **2.3*^70** $Out[8]=$ 2.3×10^{70}

■ 1.1.2 Exact and Approximate Results

A standard electronic calculator does all your calculations to a particular accuracy, say ten decimal
digits. With *Mathematica*, however, you can often get *exact* results.

Mathematica gives an *exact* result for 2^{100}, even though it has 31 decimal digits.	*In[1]:=* **2 ^ 100** *Out[1]=* 1267650600228229401496703205376

You can tell *Mathematica* to give you an approximate numerical result, just as a calculator would,
by ending your input with //N. The N stands for "numerical". It must be a capital letter. Section 2.1.3
will explain what the // means.

This gives an approximate numerical result.	*In[2]:=* **2 ^ 100 //N** *Out[2]=* 1.26765×10^{30}
Mathematica can give results in terms of rational numbers.	*In[3]:=* **1/3 + 2/7** *Out[3]=* $\dfrac{13}{21}$
//N always gives the approximate numerical result.	*In[4]:=* **1/3 + 2/7 //N** *Out[4]=* 0.619048

---

expr //N	give an approximate numerical value for *expr*

Getting numerical approximations.

When you type in an integer like 7, *Mathematica* assumes that it is exact. If you type in a number
like 4.5, with an explicit decimal point, *Mathematica* assumes that it is accurate only to a fixed number
of decimal places.

This is taken to be an exact rational number, and reduced to its lowest terms.	*In[5]:=* **452/62** *Out[5]=* $\dfrac{226}{31}$
Whenever you give a number with an explicit decimal point, *Mathematica* produces an approximate numerical result.	*In[6]:=* **452.3/62** *Out[6]=* 7.29516
Here again, the presence of the decimal point makes *Mathematica* give you an approximate numerical result.	*In[7]:=* **452./62** *Out[7]=* 7.29032
When any number in an arithmetic expression is given with an explicit decimal point, you get an approximate numerical result for the whole expression.	*In[8]:=* **1. + 452/62** *Out[8]=* 8.29032

■ 1.1.3 Some Mathematical Functions

Mathematica includes a very large collection of mathematical functions. Section 3.2 gives the complete list. Here are a few of the common ones.

`Sqrt[x]`	square root ($\sqrt{x}$)
`Exp[x]`	exponential (e^x)
`Log[x]`	natural logarithm ($\log_e x$)
`Log[b, x]`	logarithm to base b ($\log_b x$)
`Sin[x]`, `Cos[x]`, `Tan[x]`	trigonometric functions (with arguments in radians)
`ArcSin[x]`, `ArcCos[x]`, `ArcTan[x]`	inverse trigonometric functions
$n!$	factorial (product of integers $1, 2, ..., n$)
`Abs[x]`	absolute value
`Round[x]`	closest integer to x
`Mod[n, m]`	n modulo m (remainder on division of n by m)
`Random[ ]`	pseudorandom number between 0 and 1
`Max[x, y, ... ]`, `Min[x, y, ... ]`	maximum, minimum of $x, y, ...$
`FactorInteger[n]`	prime factors of n (see page 750)

Some common mathematical functions.

- The arguments of all *Mathematica* functions are enclosed in *square brackets*.
- The names of built-in *Mathematica* functions begin with *capital letters*.

Two important points about functions in *Mathematica*.

It is important to remember that all function arguments in *Mathematica* are enclosed in *square brackets*, not parentheses. Parentheses in *Mathematica* are used only to indicate the grouping of terms, and never to give function arguments.

This gives $\log_e(8.4)$. Notice the capital letter for Log, and the *square brackets* for the argument.

```
In[1]:= Log[8.4]

Out[1]= 2.12823
```

Just as with arithmetic operations, *Mathematica* tries to give exact values for mathematical functions when you give it exact input.

This gives $\sqrt{16}$ as an exact integer.

```
In[2]:= Sqrt[16]
Out[2]= 4
```

This gives an approximate numerical result for $\sqrt{2}$.

```
In[3]:= Sqrt[2] //N
Out[3]= 1.41421
```

The presence of an explicit decimal point tells *Mathematica* to give an approximate numerical result.

```
In[4]:= Sqrt[2.]
Out[4]= 1.41421
```

Since you are not asking for an approximate numerical result, *Mathematica* leaves the number here in an exact symbolic form.

```
In[5]:= Sqrt[2]
Out[5]= √2
```

Here is the exact integer result for $30 \times 29 \times \ldots \times 1$. Computing factorials like this can give you very large numbers. You should be able to calculate up to at least 2000! in a short time.

```
In[6]:= 30!
Out[6]= 265252859812191058636308480000000
```

This gives the approximate numerical value of the factorial.

```
In[7]:= 30! //N
Out[7]= 2.65253 × 10^32
```

Pi	$\pi \simeq 3.14159$
E	$e \simeq 2.71828$ (normally output as e)
Degree	$\pi/180$: degrees-to-radians conversion factor (normally output as °)
I	$i = \sqrt{-1}$ (normally output as i)
Infinity	∞

Some common mathematical constants.

Notice that the names of these built-in constants all begin with capital letters.

This gives the numerical value of π^2.

```
In[8]:= Pi ^ 2 //N
Out[8]= 9.8696
```

This gives the exact result for $\sin(\pi/2)$. Notice that the arguments to trigonometric functions are always in radians.

```
In[9]:= Sin[Pi/2]
Out[9]= 1
```

This gives the numerical value of sin(20°). Multiplying by the constant Degree converts the argument to radians.

```
In[10]:= Sin[20 Degree] //N
Out[10]= 0.34202
```

Log[*x*] gives logarithms to base *e*.

```
In[11]:= Log[E ^ 5]
Out[11]= 5
```

You can get logarithms in any base *b* using Log[*b*, *x*]. As in standard mathematical notation, the *b* is optional.

```
In[12]:= Log[2, 256]
Out[12]= 8
```

■ 1.1.4 Arbitrary-Precision Calculations

When you use //N to get a numerical result, *Mathematica* does what a standard calculator would do: it gives you a result to a fixed number of significant figures. You can also tell *Mathematica* exactly how many significant figures to keep in a particular calculation. This allows you to get numerical results in *Mathematica* to any degree of precision.

expr//N or N[*expr*]	approximate numerical value of *expr*
N[*expr*, *n*]	numerical value of *expr* calculated with *n*-digit precision

Numerical evaluation functions.

This gives the numerical value of π to a fixed number of significant digits. Typing N[Pi] is exactly equivalent to Pi //N.

```
In[1]:= N[Pi]
Out[1]= 3.14159
```

This gives π to 40 digits.

```
In[2]:= N[Pi, 40]
Out[2]= 3.141592653589793238462643383279502884197
```

Here is $\sqrt{7}$ to 30 digits.

```
In[3]:= N[Sqrt[7], 30]
Out[3]= 2.64575131106459059050161575364
```

Doing any kind of numerical calculation can introduce small roundoff errors into your results. When you increase the numerical precision, these errors typically become correspondingly smaller. Making sure that you get the same answer when you increase numerical precision is often a good way to check your results.

The quantity $e^{\pi\sqrt{163}}$ turns out to be very close to an integer. To check that the result is not, in fact, an integer, you have to use sufficient numerical precision.

```
In[4]:= N[Exp[Pi Sqrt[163]], 40]
Out[4]= 2.625374126407687439999999999999992500725972 × 10^{17}
```

■ 1.1.5 Complex Numbers

You can enter complex numbers in *Mathematica* just by including the constant I, equal to $\sqrt{-1}$. Make sure that you type a capital I.

If you are using notebooks, you can also enter I as i by typing [ESC]ii[ESC] (see page 36). The form i is normally what is used in output. Note that an ordinary i means a variable named *i*, not $\sqrt{-1}$.

This gives the imaginary number result 2*i*.

```
In[1]:= Sqrt[-4]
Out[1]= 2 i
```

This gives the ratio of two complex numbers.

```
In[2]:= (4 + 3 I) / (2 - I)
Out[2]= 1 + 2 i
```

Here is the numerical value of a complex exponential.

```
In[3]:= Exp[2 + 9 I] //N
Out[3]= -6.73239 + 3.04517 i
```

x + I y	the complex number $x + i\,y$
Re[z]	real part
Im[z]	imaginary part
Conjugate[z]	complex conjugate z^* or $\bar{z}$
Abs[z]	absolute value $|z|$
Arg[z]	the argument φ in $|z|e^{i\varphi}$

Complex number operations.

■ 1.1.6 Getting Used to *Mathematica*

- Arguments of functions are given in *square brackets*.

- Names of built-in functions have their first letters capitalized.

- Multiplication can be represented by a space.

- Powers are denoted by ^.

- Numbers in scientific notation are entered, for example, as 2.5*^-4 or 2.5 10^-4.

Important points to remember in *Mathematica*.

This section has given you a first glimpse of *Mathematica*. If you have used other computer systems before, you will probably have noticed some similarities and some differences. Often you will find the differences the most difficult parts to remember. It may help you, however, to understand a little about *why Mathematica* is set up the way it is, and why such differences exist.

One important feature of *Mathematica* that differs from other computer languages, and from conventional mathematical notation, is that function arguments are enclosed in square brackets, not parentheses. Parentheses in *Mathematica* are reserved specifically for indicating the grouping of terms. There is obviously a conceptual distinction between giving arguments to a function and grouping terms together; the fact that the same notation has often been used for both is largely a consequence of typography and of early computer keyboards. In *Mathematica*, the concepts are distinguished by different notation.

This distinction has several advantages. In parenthesis notation, it is not clear whether $c(1 + x)$ means c[1 + x] or c*(1 + x). Using square brackets for function arguments removes this ambiguity. It also allows multiplication to be indicated without an explicit * or other character. As a result, *Mathematica* can handle expressions like 2x and a x or a (1 + x), treating them just as in standard mathematical notation.

You will have seen in this section that built-in *Mathematica* functions often have quite long names. You may wonder why, for example, the pseudorandom number function is called Random, rather than, say, Rand. The answer, which pervades much of the design of *Mathematica*, is consistency. There is a general convention in *Mathematica* that all function names are spelled out as full English words, unless there is a standard mathematical abbreviation for them. The great advantage of this scheme is that it is *predictable*. Once you know what a function does, you will usually be able to guess exactly what its name is. If the names were abbreviated, you would always have to remember which shortening of the standard English words was used.

Another feature of built-in *Mathematica* names is that they all start with capital letters. In later sections, you will see how to define variables and functions of your own. The capital letter convention makes it easy to distinguish built-in objects. If *Mathematica* used max instead of Max to represent the operation of finding a maximum, then you would never be able to use max as the name of one of your variables. In addition, when you read programs written in *Mathematica*, the capitalization of built-in names makes them easier to pick out.

■ 1.1.7 Mathematical Notation in Notebooks

If you use a text-based interface to *Mathematica*, then the input you give must consist only of characters that you can type directly on your computer keyboard. But if you use a notebook interface then other kinds of input become possible.

Usually there are palettes provided which operate like extensions of your keyboard, and which have buttons that you can click to enter particular forms. You can typically access standard palettes using the Palettes submenu of the File menu.

Clicking the π button in this palette
will enter a pi into your notebook.

Clicking the first button in this palette
will create an empty structure for
entering a power. You can use the
mouse to fill in the structure.

You can also give input by using special keys on your keyboard. Pressing one of these keys does
not lead to an ordinary character being entered, but instead typically causes some action to occur or
some structure to be created.

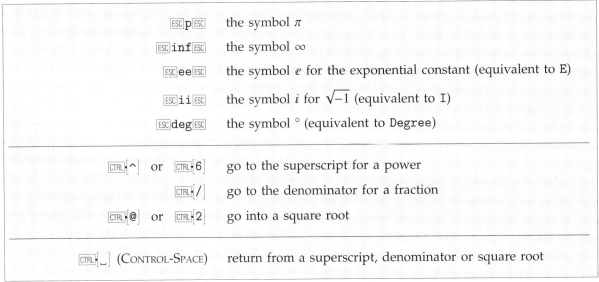

A few ways to enter special notations on a standard English-language keyboard.

Here is a computation entered using
ordinary characters on a keyboard.

$In[1]:=$ **N[Pi^2/6]**

$Out[1]=$ 1.64493

Here is the same computation entered
using a palette or special keys.

$In[2]:=$ **N$\left[\dfrac{\pi^2}{6}\right]$**

$Out[2]=$ 1.64493

Here is an actual sequence of keys that
can be used to enter the input.

$In[3]:=$ **N[ESC p ESC CTRL ^ 2 CTRL ⌴ CTRL / 6 CTRL ⌴]**

$Out[3]=$ 1.64493

In a traditional computer language such as C, Fortran, Java or Perl, the input you give must always consist of a string of ordinary characters that can be typed directly on a keyboard. But the *Mathematica* language also allows you to give input that contains special characters, superscripts, built-up fractions, and so on.

The language incorporates many features of traditional mathematical notation. But you should realize that the goal of the language is to provide a precise and consistent way to specify computations. And as a result, it does not follow all of the somewhat haphazard details of traditional mathematical notation.

Nevertheless, as discussed on page 193, it is always possible to get *Mathematica* to produce *output* that imitates every aspect of traditional mathematical notation. And as discussed on page 194, it is also possible for *Mathematica* to import text that uses such notation, and to some extent to translate it into its own more precise language.

1.2 Building Up Calculations

■ 1.2.1 Using Previous Results

In doing calculations, you will often need to use previous results that you have got. In *Mathematica*, % always stands for your last result.

%	the last result generated
%%	the next-to-last result
%% ... % (*k* times)	the *k*th previous result
%*n*	the result on output line Out[*n*] (to be used with care)

Ways to refer to your previous results.

Here is the first result.	In[1]:= **77 ^ 2** Out[1]= 5929
This adds 1 to the last result.	In[2]:= **% + 1** Out[2]= 5930
This uses both the last result, and the result before that.	In[3]:= **3 % + % ^ 2 + %%** Out[3]= 35188619

You will have noticed that all the input and output lines in *Mathematica* are numbered. You can use these numbers to refer to previous results.

This adds the results on lines 2 and 3 above.	In[4]:= **%2 + %3** Out[4]= 35194549

If you use a text-based interface to *Mathematica*, then successive input and output lines will always appear in order, as they do in the dialogs in this book. However, if you use a notebook interface to *Mathematica*, as discussed in Section 1.0.1, then successive input and output lines need not appear in order. You can for example "scroll back" and insert your next calculation wherever you want in the notebook. You should realize that % is always defined to be the last result that *Mathematica* generated. This may or may not be the result that appears immediately above your present position in the notebook. With a notebook interface, the only way to tell when a particular result was generated is to look at the Out[*n*] label that it has. Because you can insert and delete anywhere in a notebook, the textual ordering of results in a notebook need have no relation to the order in which the results were generated.

■ 1.2.2 Defining Variables

When you do long calculations, it is often convenient to give *names* to your intermediate results. Just as in standard mathematics, or in other computer languages, you can do this by introducing named *variables*.

This sets the value of the *variable* x to be 5.	`In[1]:= x = 5` `Out[1]= 5`
Whenever x appears, *Mathematica* now replaces it with the value 5.	`In[2]:= x ^ 2` `Out[2]= 25`
This assigns a new value to x.	`In[3]:= x = 7 + 4` `Out[3]= 11`
pi is set to be the numerical value of π to 40-digit accuracy.	`In[4]:= pi = N[Pi, 40]` `Out[4]= 3.141592653589793238462643383279502884197`
Here is the value you defined for pi.	`In[5]:= pi` `Out[5]= 3.141592653589793238462643383279502884197`
This gives the numerical value of π^2, to the same accuracy as pi.	`In[6]:= pi ^ 2` `Out[6]= 9.869604401089358618834490999987615113531`

$x = value$	assign a value to the variable x
$x = y = value$	assign a value to both x and y
$x =.$ or `Clear[x]`	remove any value assigned to x

Assigning values to variables.

It is very important to realize that values you assign to variables are *permanent*. Once you have assigned a value to a particular variable, the value will be kept until you explicitly remove it. The value will, of course, disappear if you start a whole new *Mathematica* session.

Forgetting about definitions you made earlier is the single most common cause of mistakes when using *Mathematica*. If you set x = 5, *Mathematica* assumes that you *always* want x to have the value 5, until or unless you explicitly tell it otherwise. To avoid mistakes, you should remove values you have defined as soon as you have finished using them.

> ■ Remove values you assign to variables as soon as you finish using them.

A useful principle in using *Mathematica*.

The variables you define can have almost any names. There is no limit on the length of their names. One constraint, however, is that variable names can never *start* with numbers. For example, x2 could be a variable, but 2x means 2*x.

Mathematica uses both upper- and lower-case letters. There is a convention that built-in *Mathematica* objects always have names starting with upper-case (capital) letters. To avoid confusion, you should always choose names for your own variables that start with lower-case letters.

aaaaa	a variable name containing only lower-case letters
Aaaaa	a built-in object whose name begins with a capital letter

Naming conventions.

You can type formulas involving variables in *Mathematica* almost exactly as you would in mathematics. There are a few important points to watch, however.

- x y means x times y.
- xy with no space is the variable with name xy.
- 5x means 5 times x.
- x^2y means (x^2) y, not x^(2y).

Some points to watch when using variables in *Mathematica*.

■ 1.2.3 Making Lists of Objects

In doing calculations, it is often convenient to collect together several objects, and treat them as a single entity. *Lists* give you a way to make collections of objects in *Mathematica*. As you will see later, lists are very important and general structures in *Mathematica*.

A list such as {3, 5, 1} is a collection of three objects. But in many ways, you can treat the whole list as a single object. You can, for example, do arithmetic on the whole list at once, or assign the whole list to be the value of a variable.

Here is a list of three numbers.	*In[1]:=* **{3, 5, 1}**
	Out[1]= {3, 5, 1}
This squares each number in the list, and adds 1 to it.	*In[2]:=* **{3, 5, 1}^2 + 1**
	Out[2]= {10, 26, 2}

This takes differences between corresponding elements in the two lists. The lists must be the same length.	*In[3]:=* **{6, 7, 8} - {3.5, 4, 2.5}**
	Out[3]= {2.5, 3, 5.5}
The value of % is the whole list.	*In[4]:=* **%**
	Out[4]= {2.5, 3, 5.5}
You can apply any of the mathematical functions in Section 1.1.3 to whole lists.	*In[5]:=* **Exp[%] // N**
	Out[5]= {12.1825, 20.0855, 244.692}

Just as you can set variables to be numbers, so also you can set them to be lists.

This assigns v to be a list.	*In[6]:=* **v = {2, 4, 3.1}**
	Out[6]= {2, 4, 3.1}
Wherever v appears, it is replaced by the list.	*In[7]:=* **v / (v - 1)**
	Out[7]= $\left\{2, \dfrac{4}{3}, 1.47619\right\}$

■ 1.2.4 Manipulating Elements of Lists

Many of the most powerful list manipulation operations in *Mathematica* treat whole lists as single objects. Sometimes, however, you need to pick out or set individual elements in a list.

You can refer to an element of a *Mathematica* list by giving its "index". The elements are numbered in order, starting at 1.

$\{a, b, c\}$	a list
Part[*list*, *i*] or *list*[[*i*]]	the ith element of *list* (the first element is *list*[[1]])
Part[*list*, $\{i, j, \dots\}$] or *list*[[$\{i, j, \dots\}$]]	
	a list of the ith, j^{th}, ... elements of *list*

Operations on list elements.

This extracts the second element of the list.	*In[1]:=* **{5, 8, 6, 9}[[2]]**
	Out[1]= 8
This extracts a list of elements.	*In[2]:=* **{5, 8, 6, 9}[[{3, 1, 3, 2, 4}]]**
	Out[2]= {6, 5, 6, 8, 9}
This assigns the value of v to be a list.	*In[3]:=* **v = {2, 4, 7}**
	Out[3]= {2, 4, 7}

You can extract elements of v.

$In[4]:= \mathbf{v[[2]]}$

$Out[4]= 4$

By assigning a variable to be a list, you can use *Mathematica* lists much like "arrays" in other computer languages. Thus, for example, you can reset an element of a list by assigning a value to $v[[i]]$.

Part[v, i] or $v[[i]]$	extract the ith element of a list
Part[v, i] = *value* or $v[[i]]$ = *value*	reset the ith element of a list

Array-like operations on lists.

Here is a list.

$In[5]:= \mathbf{v = \{4, -1, 8, 7\}}$

$Out[5]= \{4, -1, 8, 7\}$

This resets the third element of the list.

$In[6]:= \mathbf{v[[3]] = 0}$

$Out[6]= 0$

Now the list assigned to v has been modified.

$In[7]:= \mathbf{v}$

$Out[7]= \{4, -1, 0, 7\}$

■ 1.2.5 The Four Kinds of Bracketing in *Mathematica*

Over the course of the last few sections, we have introduced each of the four kinds of bracketing used in *Mathematica*. Each kind of bracketing has a very different meaning. It is important that you remember all of them.

(*term*)	parentheses for grouping
$f[x]$	square brackets for functions
$\{a, b, c\}$	curly braces for lists
$v[[i]]$	double brackets for indexing (Part[v, i])

The four kinds of bracketing in *Mathematica*.

When the expressions you type in are complicated, it is often a good idea to put extra space inside each set of brackets. This makes it somewhat easier for you to see matching pairs of brackets. $v[[\{a, b\}]]$ is, for example, easier to recognize than $v[[\{a, b\}]]$.

■ 1.2.6 Sequences of Operations

In doing a calculation with *Mathematica*, you usually go through a sequence of steps. If you want to, you can do each step on a separate line. Often, however, you will find it convenient to put several steps on the same line. You can do this simply by separating the pieces of input you want to give with semicolons.

$expr_1$; $expr_2$; $expr_3$	do several operations, and give the result of the last one
$expr_1$; $expr_2$;	do the operations, but print no output

Ways to do sequences of operations in *Mathematica*.

This does three operations on the same line. The result is the result from the last operation.

```
In[1]:= x = 4; y = 6; z = y + 6

Out[1]= 12
```

If you end your input with a semicolon, it is as if you are giving a sequence of operations, with an "empty" one at the end. This has the effect of making *Mathematica* perform the operations you specify, but display no output.

$expr$;	do an operation, but display no output

Inhibiting output.

Putting a semicolon at the end of the line tells *Mathematica* to show no output.

```
In[2]:= x = 67 - 5 ;
```

You can still use % to get the output that would have been shown.

```
In[3]:= %

Out[3]= 62
```

1.3 Using the *Mathematica* System

■ 1.3.1 The Structure of *Mathematica*

Mathematica kernel	the part that actually performs computations
Mathematica front end	the part that handles interaction with the user

The basic parts of the *Mathematica* system.

Mathematica is a modular software system in which the *kernel* which actually performs computations is separate from the *front end* which handles interaction with the user.

The most common type of front end for *Mathematica* is based on interactive documents known as *notebooks*. Notebooks mix *Mathematica* input and output with text, graphics, palettes and other material. You can use notebooks either for doing ongoing computations, or as means of presenting or publishing your results.

Notebook interface	interactive documents
Text-based interface	text from the keyboard
MathLink interface	communication with other programs

Common kinds of interfaces to *Mathematica*.

The notebook front end includes many menus and graphical tools for creating and reading notebook documents and for sending and receiving material from the *Mathematica* kernel.

A notebook mixing text, graphics and *Mathematica* input and output.

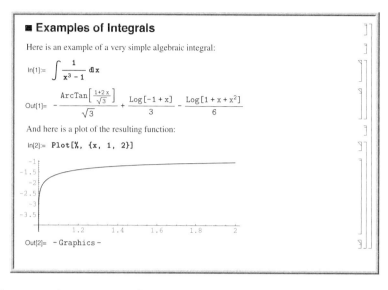

In some cases, you may not need to use the notebook front end, and you may want instead to interact more directly with the *Mathematica* kernel. You can do this by using a text-based interface, in which text you type on the keyboard goes straight to the kernel.

A dialog with *Mathematica* using a text-based interface.

```
In[1]:= 2^100

Out[1]= 1267650600228229401496703205376

In[2]:= Integrate[1/(x^3 - 1), x]

                        1 + 2 x
              ArcTan[-------]                                    2
                      Sqrt[3]      Log[-1 + x]   Log[1 + x + x ]
Out[2]= -(---------------) + ----------- - ----------------
                Sqrt[3]            3               6
```

An important aspect of *Mathematica* is that it can interact not only with human users but also with other programs. This is achieved primarily through *MathLink*, which is a standardized protocol for two-way communication between external programs and the *Mathematica* kernel.

A fragment of C code that communicates via *MathLink* with the *Mathematica* kernel.

```
MLPutFunction(stdlink,  "EvaluatePacket", 1);

  MLPutFunction(stdlink, "Gamma", 2);
    MLPutReal(stdlink, 2);
    MLPutInteger(stdlink, n);

MLEndPacket(stdlink);
MLCheckFunction(stdlink, "ReturnPacket", &n);

MLGetReal(stdlink, &result);
```

Among the many *MathLink*-compatible programs that are now available, some are set up to serve as complete front ends to *Mathematica*. Often such front ends provide their own special user interfaces, and treat the *Mathematica* kernel purely as an embedded computational engine. If you are using *Mathematica* in this way, then only some parts of the discussion in the remainder of this section will probably be relevant.

■ 1.3.2 Differences between Computer Systems

There are many detailed differences between different kinds of computer systems. But one of the important features of *Mathematica* is that it allows you to work and create material without being concerned about such differences.

In order to fit in as well as possible with particular computer systems, the user interface for *Mathematica* on different systems is inevitably at least slightly different. But the crucial point is that beyond superficial differences, *Mathematica* is set up to work in exactly the same way on every kind of computer system.

- ■ The language used by the *Mathematica* kernel
- ■ The structure of *Mathematica* notebooks
- ■ The *MathLink* communication protocol

Elements of *Mathematica* that are exactly the same on all computer systems.

The commands that you give to the *Mathematica* kernel, for example, are absolutely identical on every computer system. This means that when you write a program using these commands, you can immediately take the program and run it on any computer that supports *Mathematica*.

The structure of *Mathematica* notebooks is also the same on all computer systems. And as a result, if you create a notebook on one computer system, you can immediately take it and use it on any other system.

- The visual appearance of windows, fonts, etc.

- Mechanisms for importing and exporting material from notebooks

- Keyboard shortcuts for menu commands

Elements that can differ from one computer system to another.

Although the underlying structure of *Mathematica* notebooks is always the same, there are often superficial differences in the way notebooks look on different computer systems, and in some of the mechanisms provided for interacting with them.

The goal in each case is to make notebooks work in a way that is as familiar as possible to people who are used to a particular type of computer system.

And in addition, by adapting the details of notebooks to each specific computer system, it becomes easier to exchange material between notebooks and other programs running on that computer system.

The same *Mathematica* notebook on three different computer systems. The underlying structure is exactly the same, but some details of the presentation are different.

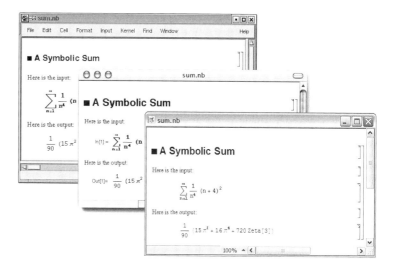

One consequence of the modular nature of the *Mathematica* system is that its parts can be run on different computers. Thus, for example, it is not uncommon to run the front end for *Mathematica* on one computer, while running the kernel on a quite separate computer.

Communications between the kernel and the front end are handled by *MathLink*, using whatever networking mechanisms are available.

■ 1.3.3 Special Topic: Using a Text-Based Interface

With a text-based interface, you interact with *Mathematica* just by typing successive lines of input, and getting back successive lines of output on your screen.

At each stage, *Mathematica* prints a prompt of the form In[n]:= to tell you that it is ready to receive input. When you have entered your input, *Mathematica* processes it, and then displays the result with a label of the form Out[n]=.

If your input is short, then you can give it on a single line, ending the line by pressing ENTER or RETURN. If your input is longer, you can give it on several lines. *Mathematica* will automatically continue reading successive lines until it has received a complete expression. Thus, for example, if you type an opening parenthesis on one line, *Mathematica* will go on reading successive lines of input until it sees the corresponding closing parenthesis. Note that if you enter a completely blank line, *Mathematica* will throw away the lines you have typed so far, and issue a new input prompt.

%n or Out[n]	the value of the nth output
InString[n]	the text of the nth input
In[n]	the nth input, for re-evaluation

Retrieving and re-evaluating previous input and output.

With a text-based interface, each line of *Mathematica* input and output appears sequentially. Often your computer system will allow you to scroll backwards to review previous work, and to cut-and-paste previous lines of input.

But whatever kind of computer system you have, you can always use *Mathematica* to retrieve or re-evaluate previous input and output. In general, re-evaluating a particular piece of input or output may give you a different result than when you evaluated it in the first place. The reason is that in between you may have reset the values of variables that are used in that piece of input or output. If you ask for Out[n], then *Mathematica* will give you the final form of your n^{th} output. On the other hand, if you ask for In[n], then *Mathematica* will take the nth input you gave, and re-evaluate it using whatever current assignments you have given for variables.

■ 1.3.4 Doing Computations in Notebooks

A typical *Mathematica* notebook containing text, graphics and *Mathematica* expressions. The brackets on the right indicate the extent of each cell.

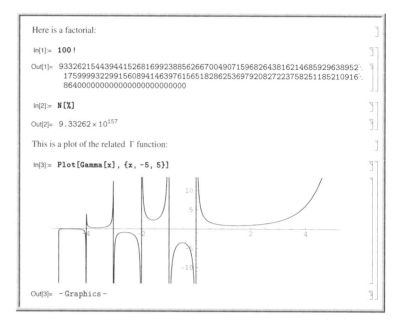

Mathematica notebooks are structured interactive documents that are organized into a sequence of *cells*. Each cell contains material of a definite type—usually text, graphics, sounds or *Mathematica* expressions. When a notebook is displayed on the screen, the extent of each cell is indicated by a bracket on the right.

The notebook front end for *Mathematica* provides many ways to enter and edit the material in a notebook. Some of these ways will be standard to whatever computer system or graphical interface you are using. Others are specific to *Mathematica*.

SHIFT-ENTER or SHIFT-RETURN	send a cell of input to the *Mathematica* kernel

Doing a computation in a *Mathematica* notebook.

Once you have prepared the material in a cell, you can send it as input to the *Mathematica* kernel simply by pressing SHIFT-ENTER or SHIFT-RETURN. The kernel will send back whatever output is generated, and the front end will create new cells in your notebook to display this output. Note that if you have a numeric keypad on your keyboard, then you can use its ENTER key as an alternative to SHIFT-ENTER.

Here is a cell ready to be sent as input to the *Mathematica* kernel.

> ```
> 3^100
> ```

The output from the computation is inserted in a new cell.

> ```
> In[1]:=  3^100
>
> Out[1]=  515377520732011331036461129765621272702107522001
> ```

Most kinds of output that you get in *Mathematica* notebooks can readily be edited, just like input. Usually *Mathematica* will make a copy of the output when you first start editing it, so you can keep track of the original output and its edited form.

Once you have done the editing you want, you can typically just press SHIFT-ENTER to send what you have created as input to the *Mathematica* kernel.

Here is a typical computation in a *Mathematica* notebook.

> ```
> In[1]:=  Integrate[Sqrt[x + 1] / Sqrt[x - 1], x]
> ```
> $$Out[1]= \sqrt{-1+x}\ \sqrt{1+x} + 2\,\mathrm{ArcSinh}\left[\frac{\sqrt{-1+x}}{\sqrt{2}}\right]$$

Mathematica will automatically make a copy if you start editing the output.

> ```
> In[1]:=  Integrate[Sqrt[x + 1] / Sqrt[x - 1], x]
> ```
> $$Out[1]= \sqrt{-1+x}\ \sqrt{1+x} + 2\,\mathrm{ArcSinh}\left[\frac{\sqrt{-1+x}}{\sqrt{2}}\right]$$
> $$\sqrt{-1+x}\ \sqrt{1+x} + D\left[2\,\mathrm{ArcSinh}\left[\frac{\sqrt{-1+x}}{\sqrt{2}}\right], x\right] \text{ // Simplify}$$

After you have edited the output, you can send it back as further input to the *Mathematica* kernel.

> ```
> In[1]:=  Integrate[Sqrt[x + 1] / Sqrt[x - 1], x]
> ```
> $$Out[1]= \sqrt{-1+x}\ \sqrt{1+x} + 2\,\mathrm{ArcSinh}\left[\frac{\sqrt{-1+x}}{\sqrt{2}}\right]$$
> $$In[2]:= \sqrt{-1+x}\ \sqrt{1+x} + D\left[2\,\mathrm{ArcSinh}\left[\frac{\sqrt{-1+x}}{\sqrt{2}}\right], x\right] \text{ // Simplify}$$
> $$Out[2]= \frac{x^2}{\sqrt{-1+x}\ \sqrt{1+x}}$$

When you do computations in a *Mathematica* notebook, each line of input is typically labeled with In[*n*]:=, while each line of output is labeled with the corresponding Out[*n*]=.

There is no reason, however, that successive lines of input and output should necessarily appear one after the other in your notebook. Often, for example, you will want to go back to an earlier part of your notebook, and re-evaluate some input you gave before.

It is important to realize that wherever a particular expression appears in your notebook, it is the line number given in In[*n*]:= or Out[*n*]= which determines when the expression was processed by the *Mathematica* kernel. Thus, for example, the fact that one expression may appear earlier than another in your notebook does not mean that it will have been evaluated first by the kernel. This will only be the case if it has a lower line number.

Each line of input and output is given a label when it is evaluated by the kernel. It is these labels, not the position of the expression in the notebook, that indicate the ordering of evaluation by the kernel.

```
Results:

In[2]:=  s^2 + 2

Out[2]=  146

In[4]:=  s^2 + 2

Out[4]=  10002

Settings for s:

In[1]:=  s = 12

Out[1]=  12

In[3]:=  s = 100

Out[3]=  100
```

If you make a mistake and try to enter input that the *Mathematica* kernel does not understand, then the front end will produce a beep. In general, you will get a beep whenever something goes wrong in the front end. You can find out the origin of the beep using the Why the Beep? item in the Help menu.

Animate graphics	double-click the first cell in the sequence of frames
Resize a graphic	click the graphic and move the handles that appear
Find coordinates in a graphic	move around in the graphic holding down the COMMAND or CONTROL key (or equivalent)
Play a sound	double-click the cell that contains it

Operations on graphics and sounds.

■ 1.3.5 Notebooks as Documents

Mathematica notebooks allow you to create documents that can be viewed interactively on screen or printed on paper.

Particularly in larger notebooks, it is common to have chapters, sections and so on, each represented by groups of cells. The extent of these groups is indicated by a bracket on the right.

The grouping of cells in a notebook is indicated by nested brackets on the right.

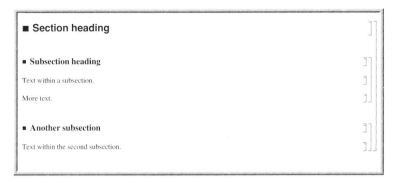

A group of cells can be either *open* or *closed*. When it is open, you can see all the cells in it explicitly. But when it is closed, you see only the first or *heading* cell in the group.

Large notebooks are often distributed with many closed groups of cells, so that when you first look at the notebook, you see just an outline of its contents. You can then open parts you are interested in by double-clicking the appropriate brackets.

Double-clicking the bracket that spans a group of cells closes the group, leaving only the first cell visible.

When a group is closed, the bracket for it has an arrow at the bottom. Double-clicking this arrow opens the group again.

Each cell within a notebook is assigned a particular *style* which indicates its role within the notebook. Thus, for example, material intended as input to be executed by the *Mathematica* kernel is typically in `Input` style, while text that is intended purely to be read is typically in `Text` style.

The *Mathematica* front end provides menus and keyboard shortcuts for creating cells with different styles, and for changing styles of existing cells.

This shows cells in various styles. The styles define not only the format of the cell contents, but also their placement and spacing.

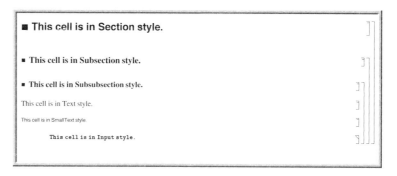

By putting a cell in a particular style, you specify a whole collection of properties for the cell, including for example how large and in what font text should be given.

The *Mathematica* front end allows you to modify such properties, either for complete cells, or for specific material within cells.

Even within a cell of a particular style, the *Mathematica* front end allows a wide range of properties to be modified separately.

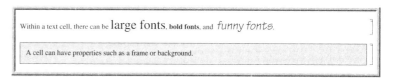

It is worth realizing that in doing different kinds of things with *Mathematica* notebooks, you are using different parts of the *Mathematica* system. Operations such as opening and closing groups of cells, doing animations and playing sounds use only a small part of the *Mathematica* front end, and these operations are supported by a widely available program known as *MathReader*.

To be able to create and edit notebooks, you need more of the *Mathematica* front end. And finally, to be able to actually do computations within a *Mathematica* notebook, you need a full *Mathematica* system, with both the front end and the kernel.

MathReader	reading *Mathematica* notebooks
Mathematica front end	creating and editing *Mathematica* notebooks
Mathematica kernel	doing computations in notebooks

Programs required for different kinds of operations with notebooks.

■ 1.3.6 Active Elements in Notebooks

One of the most powerful features of *Mathematica* notebooks is that their actions can be programmed. Thus, for example, you can set up a button in a *Mathematica* notebook which causes various operations to be performed whenever you click it.

Here is a notebook that contains a button.

Click the button to get the current date: Date[]

Clicking the button in this case causes the current date to be displayed.

Click the button to get the current date: Date[]

{1995, 9, 5, 10, 40, 53}

Later in this book, we will discuss how you can set up buttons and other similar objects in *Mathematica* notebooks. But here suffice it to say that whenever a cell is indicated as *active*, typically by the presence of a stylized "A" in its cell bracket, clicking on active elements within the cell will cause actions that have been programmed for these elements to be performed.

It is common to set up *palettes* which consist of arrays of buttons. Sometimes such palettes appear as cells within a notebook. But more often, a special kind of separate notebook window is used, which can conveniently be placed on the side of your computer screen and used in conjunction with any other notebook.

Palettes consisting of arrays of buttons are often placed in separate notebooks.

In the simplest cases, the buttons in palettes serve essentially like additional keys on your keyboard. Thus, when you press a button, the character or object shown in that button is inserted into your notebook just as if you had typed it.

Here is a palette of Greek letters with buttons that act like additional keys on your keyboard.

Often, however, a button may contain a placeholder indicated by ∎. This signifies that when you press the button, whatever is currently selected in your notebook will be inserted at the position of the placeholder.

The buttons here contain placeholders indicated by ∎.

Here is a notebook with an expression selected.

$$1 + \left(1 + \left(1 + \left(1 + x^2\right)^2\right)^2\right)^2$$

Pressing the top left button in the palette wraps the selected expression with a square root.

$$1 + \left(1 + \sqrt{\left(1 + \left(1 + x^2\right)^2\right)^2}\right)^2$$

Sometimes buttons that contain placeholders will be programmed simply to insert a certain expression in your notebook. But more often, they will be programmed to evaluate the result, sending it as input to the *Mathematica* kernel.

These buttons are set up to perform algebraic operations.

Here is a notebook with an expression selected.

$$\frac{2 + 2 \cos[2 x]}{4} + \frac{1}{32}\left(12 - 16 \cos[2 x] + 4 \cos[4 x]\right)$$

Pressing the top left button in the palette causes the selected expression to be simplified.

$$\frac{2 + 2 \cos[2 x]}{4} + \sin[x]^4$$

There are some situations in which it is convenient to have several placeholders in a single button. Your current selection is typically inserted at the position of the primary placeholder, indicated by ∎. Additional placeholders may however be indicated by □, and you can move to the positions of successive placeholders using TAB.

Here is a palette containing buttons with several placeholders.

Here is an expression in a notebook.

$$\frac{\text{Sin}[x]}{1+x}$$

Pressing the top left button in the palette inserts the expression in place of the ■.

$$\int \frac{\text{Sin}[x]}{1+x}\, d\Box$$

You can move to the other placeholders using TAB, and then edit them to insert whatever you want.

$$\int \frac{\text{Sin}[x]}{1+x}\, dx$$

■ 1.3.7 Special Topic: Hyperlinks and Active Text

The *Mathematica* front end provides a variety of ways to search for particular words or text in *Mathematica* notebooks. But particularly when large documents or collections of documents are involved, it is often convenient to insert hyperlinks which immediately take you to a specific point in a notebook, just as is often done on websites.

Hyperlinks are usually indicated by words or phrases that are underlined, and are often in a different color. Clicking on a hyperlink immediately takes you to wherever the hyperlink points.

Here is some text. The text can contain a <u>link</u>, which points elsewhere.

Hyperlinks in notebooks work very much like the buttons discussed in the previous section. And once again, all aspects of hyperlinks are programmable.

Indeed, it is possible to set up active text in notebooks that performs almost any kind of action.

■ 1.3.8 Getting Help in the Notebook Front End

In most versions of the *Mathematica* notebook front end, the Help menu gives you access to the *Help Browser*, which serves as an entry point into a large amount of online documentation for *Mathematica*.

Getting Started	a quick start to using *Mathematica*
Built-in Functions	information on all built-in functions
The Mathematica Book	the complete book online
Master Index	index of all online documentation material

Typical types of help available with the notebook front end.

An example of looking up basic information about a function in the Help Browser.

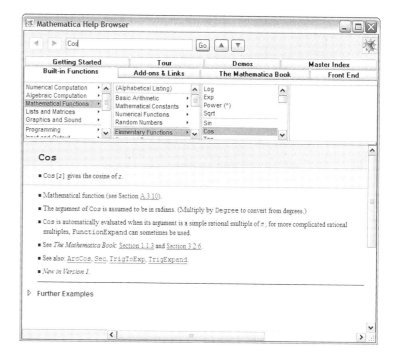

If you type the name of a function into a notebook, most versions of the front end allow you immediately to find information about the function by pressing an appropriate key (F1 under Windows).

When you first start *Mathematica*, you will typically be presented with a basic tutorial. You can visit the tutorial again with the Tutorial menu item in the Help menu.

■ 1.3.9 Getting Help with a Text-Based Interface

?Name	show information on *Name*
??Name	show extra information on *Name*
?Aaaa*	show information on all objects whose names begin with *Aaaa*

Ways to get information directly from the *Mathematica* kernel.

This gives information on the built-in function Log.

```
In[1]:= ?Log

Log[z] gives the natural logarithm of z (logarithm to base
    e). Log[b, z] gives the logarithm to base b.
```

You can ask for information about any object, whether it is built into *Mathematica*, has been read in from a *Mathematica* package, or has been introduced by you.

When you use ? to get information, you must make sure that the question mark appears as the first character in your input line. You need to do this so that *Mathematica* can tell when you are requesting information rather than giving ordinary input for evaluation.

You can get extra information by using ??. Attributes will be discussed in Section 2.6.3.

```
In[2]:= ??Log

Log[z] gives the natural logarithm of z (logarithm to base
    e). Log[b, z] gives the logarithm to base b.

Attributes[Log] = {Listable, NumericFunction, Protected}
```

This gives information on all *Mathematica* objects whose names begin with Lo. When there is more than one object, *Mathematica* just lists their names.

```
In[3]:= ?Lo*

Locked          LogGamma        LogIntegral    Loopback
Log             LogicalExpand   LongForm       LowerCaseQ
```

?Aaaa will give you information on the particular object whose name you specify. Using the "metacharacter" *, however, you can get information on collections of objects with similar names. The rule is that * is a "wild card" that can stand for any sequence of ordinary characters. So, for example, ?Lo* gets information on all objects whose names consist of the letters Lo, followed by any sequence of characters.

You can put * anywhere in the string you ask ? about. For example, ?*Expand would give you all objects whose names *end* with Expand. Similarly, ?x*0 would give you objects whose names start with x, end with 0, and have any sequence of characters in between. (You may notice that the way you use * to specify names in *Mathematica* is similar to the way you use * in Unix and other operating systems to specify file names.)

You can ask for information on most of the special input forms that *Mathematica* uses. This asks for information about the := operator.

```
In[4]:= ?:=

lhs := rhs assigns rhs to be the delayed value of lhs. rhs
    is maintained in an unevaluated form. When lhs appears,
    it is replaced by rhs, evaluated afresh each time.
```

■ 1.3.10 *Mathematica* Packages

One of the most important features of *Mathematica* is that it is an extensible system. There is a certain amount of mathematical and other functionality that is built into *Mathematica*. But by using the *Mathematica* language, it is always possible to add more functionality.

For many kinds of calculations, what is built into the standard version of *Mathematica* will be quite sufficient. However, if you work in a particular specialized area, you may find that you often need to use certain functions that are not built into *Mathematica*.

In such cases, you may well be able to find a *Mathematica* package that contains the functions you need. *Mathematica* packages are files written in the *Mathematica* language. They consist of collections of *Mathematica* definitions which "teach" *Mathematica* about particular application areas.

<<*package*	read in a *Mathematica* package

Reading in *Mathematica* packages.

If you want to use functions from a particular package, you must first read the package into *Mathematica*. The details of how to do this are discussed in Section 1.11. There are various conventions that govern the names you should use to refer to packages.

This command reads in a particular *Mathematica* package.

```
In[1]:= << DiscreteMath`CombinatorialFunctions`
```

The Subfactorial function is defined in the package.

```
In[2]:= Subfactorial[10]
Out[2]= 1334961
```

There are a number of subtleties associated with such issues as conflicts between names of functions in different packages. These are discussed in Section 2.7.9. One point to note, however, is that you must not refer to a function that you will read from a package before actually reading in the package. If you do this by mistake, you will have to execute the command Remove["*name*"] to get rid of the function before you read in the package which defines it. If you do not call Remove, *Mathematica* will use "your" version of the function, rather than the one from the package.

Remove["*name*"]	remove a function that has been introduced in error

Making sure that *Mathematica* uses correct definitions from packages.

The fact that *Mathematica* can be extended using packages means that the boundary of exactly what is "part of *Mathematica*" is quite blurred. As far as usage is concerned, there is actually no difference between functions defined in packages and functions that are fundamentally built into *Mathematica*.

In fact, a fair number of the functions described in this book are actually implemented as *Mathematica* packages. However, on most *Mathematica* systems, the necessary packages have been preloaded, so that the functions they define are always present.

To blur the boundary of what is part of *Mathematica* even further, Section 2.7.11 describes how you can tell *Mathematica* automatically to load a particular package if you ever try to use a certain function. If you never use that function, then it will not be present. But as soon as you try to use it, its definition will be read in from a *Mathematica* package.

As a practical matter, the functions that should be considered "part of *Mathematica*" are probably those that are present in all *Mathematica* systems. It is these functions that are primarily discussed in this book.

Nevertheless, most versions of *Mathematica* come with a standard set of *Mathematica* packages, which contain definitions for many more functions. Some of these functions are mentioned in this book. But to get them, you must usually read in the necessary packages explicitly.

You can use the Help Browser to get information on standard *Mathematica* add-on packages.

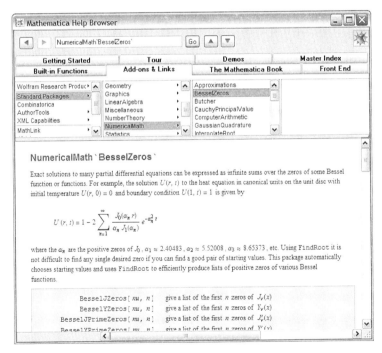

It is possible to set your *Mathematica* system up so that particular packages are pre-loaded, or are automatically loaded when needed. If you do this, then there may be many functions that appear as standard in your version of *Mathematica*, but which are not documented in this book.

One point that should be mentioned is the relationship between packages and notebooks. Both are stored as files on your computer system, and both can be read into *Mathematica*. However, a notebook is intended to be displayed, typically with a notebook interface, while a package is intended only to be used as *Mathematica* input. Many notebooks in fact contain sections that can be considered as packages, and which contain sequences of definitions intended for input to *Mathematica*. There are also capabilities that allow packages set up to correspond to notebooks to be maintained automatically.

■ 1.3.11 Warnings and Messages

Mathematica usually goes about its work silently, giving output only when it has finished doing the calculations you asked for.

However, if it looks as if *Mathematica* is doing something you definitely did not intend, *Mathematica* will usually print a message to warn you.

The square root function should have only one argument. *Mathematica* prints a message to warn you that you have given two arguments here.	*In[1]:=* **Sqrt[4, 5]** Sqrt::argx: Sqrt called with 2 arguments; 1 argument is expected. *Out[1]=* Sqrt[4, 5]
Each message has a name. You can switch off messages using Off.	*In[2]:=* **Off[Sqrt::argx]**
The message Sqrt::argx has now been switched off, and will no longer appear.	*In[3]:=* **Sqrt[4, 5]** *Out[3]=* Sqrt[4, 5]
This switches Sqrt::argx back on again.	*In[4]:=* **On[Sqrt::argx]**

Off[*Function*::*tag*]	switch off (suppress) a message
On[*Function*::*tag*]	switch on a message

Functions for controlling message output.

■ 1.3.12 Interrupting Calculations

There will probably be times when you want to stop *Mathematica* in the middle of a calculation. Perhaps you realize that you asked *Mathematica* to do the wrong thing. Or perhaps the calculation is just taking a long time, and you want to find out what is going on.

The way that you interrupt a *Mathematica* calculation depends on what kind of interface you are using.

ALT-COMMA or COMMAND-COMMA	notebook interfaces
CONTROL-C	text-based interfaces

Typical keys to interrupt calculations in *Mathematica*.

On some computer systems, it may take *Mathematica* some time to respond to your interrupt. When *Mathematica* does respond, it will typically give you a menu of possible things to do.

continue	continue the calculation
show	show what *Mathematica* is doing
inspect	inspect the current state of your calculation
abort	abort this particular calculation
exit	exit *Mathematica* completely

Some typical options available when you interrupt a calculation in *Mathematica*.

1.4 Algebraic Calculations

■ 1.4.1 Symbolic Computation

One of the important features of *Mathematica* is that it can do *symbolic*, as well as *numerical* calculations. This means that it can handle algebraic formulas as well as numbers.

Here is a typical numerical computation.

$In[1]:=$ **3 + 62 - 1**

$Out[1]=$ 64

This is a symbolic computation.

$In[2]:=$ **3x - x + 2**

$Out[2]=$ $2 + 2x$

Numerical computation	3 + 62 - 1	$\longrightarrow$ 64
Symbolic computation	3x - x + 2	$\longrightarrow$ 2 + 2 x

Numerical and symbolic computations.

You can type any algebraic expression into *Mathematica*.

$In[3]:=$ **-1 + 2x + x^3**

$Out[3]=$ $-1 + 2x + x^3$

Mathematica automatically carries out basic algebraic simplifications. Here it combines x^2 and $-4x^2$ to get $-3x^2$.

$In[4]:=$ **x^2 + x - 4 x^2**

$Out[4]=$ $x - 3x^2$

You can type in any algebraic expression, using the operators listed on page 29. You can use spaces to denote multiplication. Be careful not to forget the space in x y. If you type in xy with no space, *Mathematica* will interpret this as a single symbol, with the name xy, not as a product of the two symbols x and y.

Mathematica rearranges and combines terms using the standard rules of algebra.

$In[5]:=$ **x y + 2 x^2 y + y^2 x^2 - 2 y x**

$Out[5]=$ $-xy + 2x^2 y + x^2 y^2$

Here is another algebraic expression.

$In[6]:=$ **(x + 2y + 1)(x - 2)^2**

$Out[6]=$ $(-2 + x)^2 (1 + x + 2y)$

The function Expand multiplies out products and powers.

$In[7]:=$ **Expand[%]**

$Out[7]=$ $4 - 3x^2 + x^3 + 8y - 8xy + 2x^2 y$

Factor does essentially the inverse of Expand.

$In[8]:=$ **Factor[%]**

$Out[8]=$ $(-2 + x)^2 (1 + x + 2y)$

When you type in more complicated expressions, it is important that you put parentheses in the right places. Thus, for example, you have to give the expression x^{4y} in the form x^(4y). If you leave out the parentheses, you get x^4y instead. It never hurts to put in too many parentheses, but to find out exactly when you need to use parentheses, look at Section A.2.

Here is a more complicated formula, requiring several parentheses.

$In[9]:=$ **Sqrt[2]/9801 (4n)! (1103 + 26390 n) / (n!^4 396^(4n))**

$Out[9]=$ $\dfrac{2^{\frac{1}{2}-8n}\,99^{-2-4n}\,(1103+26390\,n)\,(4\,n)\,!}{(n\,!)^4}$

When you type in an expression, *Mathematica* automatically applies its large repertoire of rules for transforming expressions. These rules include the standard rules of algebra, such as $x - x = 0$, together with much more sophisticated rules involving higher mathematical functions.

Mathematica uses standard rules of algebra to replace $(\sqrt{1+x})^4$ by $(1+x)^2$.

$In[10]:=$ **Sqrt[1 + x]^4**

$Out[10]=$ $(1+x)^2$

Mathematica knows no rules for this expression, so it leaves the expression in the original form you gave.

$In[11]:=$ **Log[1 + Cos[x]]**

$Out[11]=$ $Log[1+Cos[x]]$

The notion of transformation rules is a very general one. In fact, you can think of the whole of *Mathematica* as simply a system for applying a collection of transformation rules to many different kinds of expressions.

The general principle that *Mathematica* follows is simple to state. It takes any expression you input, and gets results by applying a succession of transformation rules, stopping when it knows no more transformation rules that can be applied.

■ Take any expression, and apply transformation rules until the result no longer changes.

The fundamental principle of *Mathematica*.

■ 1.4.2 Values for Symbols

When *Mathematica* transforms an expression such as x + x into 2x, it is treating the variable x in a purely symbolic or formal fashion. In such cases, x is a symbol which can stand for any expression.

Often, however, you need to replace a symbol like x with a definite "value". Sometimes this value will be a number; often it will be another expression.

To take an expression such as 1 + 2x and replace the symbol x that appears in it with a definite value, you can create a *Mathematica* transformation rule, and then apply this rule to the expression. To replace x with the value 3, you would create the transformation rule x -> 3. You must type -> as a pair of characters, with no space in between. You can think of x -> 3 as being a rule in which "x goes to 3".

To apply a transformation rule to a particular *Mathematica* expression, you type *expr* /. *rule*. The "replacement operator" /. is typed as a pair of characters, with no space in between.

This uses the transformation rule x->3 in the expression 1 + 2x.	*In[1]:=* **1 + 2x /. x -> 3** *Out[1]=* 7
You can replace x with any expression. Here every occurrence of x is replaced by 2 - y.	*In[2]:=* **1 + x + x^2 /. x -> 2 - y** *Out[2]=* $3 + (2 - y)^2 - y$
Here is a transformation rule. *Mathematica* treats it like any other symbolic expression.	*In[3]:=* **x -> 3 + y** *Out[3]=* $x \rightarrow 3 + y$
This applies the transformation rule on the previous line to the expression x^2 - 9.	*In[4]:=* **x^2 - 9 /. %** *Out[4]=* $-9 + (3 + y)^2$

expr /. *x* -> *value*	replace *x* by *value* in the expression *expr*
expr /. {*x* -> *xval*, *y* -> *yval*}	perform several replacements

Replacing symbols by values in expressions.

You can apply rules together by putting the rules in a list.	*In[5]:=* **(x + y) (x - y)^2 /. {x -> 3, y -> 1 - a}** *Out[5]=* $(4 - a)(2 + a)^2$

The replacement operator /. allows you to apply transformation rules to a particular expression. Sometimes, however, you will want to define transformation rules that should *always* be applied. For example, you might want to replace x with 3 whenever x occurs.

As discussed in Section 1.2.2, you can do this by *assigning* the value 3 to x using x = 3. Once you have made the assignment x = 3, x will always be replaced by 3, whenever it appears.

This assigns the value 3 to x.	*In[6]:=* **x = 3** *Out[6]=* 3
Now x will automatically be replaced by 3 wherever it appears.	*In[7]:=* **x^2 - 1** *Out[7]=* 8
This assigns the expression 1 + a to be the value of x.	*In[8]:=* **x = 1 + a** *Out[8]=* $1 + a$
Now x is replaced by 1 + a.	*In[9]:=* **x^2 - 1** *Out[9]=* $-1 + (1 + a)^2$

You can define the value of a symbol to be any expression, not just a number. You should realize that once you have given such a definition, the definition will continue to be used whenever the symbol appears, until you explicitly change or remove the definition. For most people, forgetting to remove values you have assigned to symbols is the single most common source of mistakes in using *Mathematica*.

$x = value$	define a value for x which will always be used
$x =.$	remove any value defined for x

Assigning values to symbols.

The symbol x still has the value you assigned to it above.

```
In[10]:= x + 5 - 2x

Out[10]= 6 + a - 2 (1 + a)
```

This removes the value you assigned to x.

```
In[11]:= x =.
```

Now x has no value defined, so it can be used as a purely symbolic variable.

```
In[12]:= x + 5 - 2x

Out[12]= 5 - x
```

A symbol such as x can serve many different purposes in *Mathematica*, and in fact, much of the flexibility of *Mathematica* comes from being able to mix these purposes at will. However, you need to keep some of the different uses of x straight in order to avoid making mistakes. The most important distinction is between the use of x as a name for another expression, and as a symbolic variable that stands only for itself.

Traditional programming languages that do not support symbolic computation allow variables to be used only as names for objects, typically numbers, that have been assigned as values for them. In *Mathematica*, however, x can also be treated as a purely formal variable, to which various transformation rules can be applied. Of course, if you explicitly give a definition, such as x = 3, then x will always be replaced by 3, and can no longer serve as a formal variable.

You should understand that explicit definitions such as x = 3 have a global effect. On the other hand, a replacement such as *expr* /. x->3 affects only the specific expression *expr*. It is usually much easier to keep things straight if you avoid using explicit definitions except when absolutely necessary.

You can always mix replacements with assignments. With assignments, you can give names to expressions in which you want to do replacements, or to rules that you want to use to do the replacements.

This assigns a value to the symbol t.

```
In[13]:= t = 1 + x^2

Out[13]= 1 + x²
```

This finds the value of t, and then replaces x by 2 in it.

```
In[14]:= t /. x -> 2

Out[14]= 5
```

This finds the value of t for a different value of x.	$In[15]:=$ **t /. x -> 5a**
	$Out[15]=$ $1 + 25 a^2$
This finds the value of t when x is replaced by Pi, and then evaluates the result numerically.	$In[16]:=$ **t /. x -> Pi //N**
	$Out[16]=$ 10.8696

■ 1.4.3 Transforming Algebraic Expressions

There are often many different ways to write the same algebraic expression. As one example, the expression $(1 + x)^2$ can be written as $1 + 2x + x^2$. *Mathematica* provides a large collection of functions for converting between different forms of algebraic expressions.

Expand[*expr*]	multiply out products and powers, writing the result as a sum of terms
Factor[*expr*]	write *expr* as a product of minimal factors

Two common functions for transforming algebraic expressions.

Expand gives the "expanded form", with products and powers multiplied out.	$In[1]:=$ **Expand[(1 + x)^2]**
	$Out[1]=$ $1 + 2 x + x^2$
Factor recovers the original form.	$In[2]:=$ **Factor[%]**
	$Out[2]=$ $(1 + x)^2$
It is easy to generate complicated expressions with Expand.	$In[3]:=$ **Expand[(1 + x + 3 y)^4]**
	$Out[3]=$ $1 + 4 x + 6 x^2 + 4 x^3 + x^4 + 12 y + 36 x y + 36 x^2 y + 12 x^3 y +$ $54 y^2 + 108 x y^2 + 54 x^2 y^2 + 108 y^3 + 108 x y^3 + 81 y^4$
Factor often gives you simpler expressions.	$In[4]:=$ **Factor[%]**
	$Out[4]=$ $(1 + x + 3 y)^4$
There are some cases, though, where Factor can give you more complicated expressions.	$In[5]:=$ **Factor[x^10 - 1]**
	$Out[5]=$ $(-1 + x) (1 + x) (1 - x + x^2 - x^3 + x^4) (1 + x + x^2 + x^3 + x^4)$
In this case, Expand gives the "simpler" form.	$In[6]:=$ **Expand[%]**
	$Out[6]=$ $-1 + x^{10}$

■ 1.4.4 Simplifying Algebraic Expressions

There are many situations where you want to write a particular algebraic expression in the simplest possible form. Although it is difficult to know exactly what one means in all cases by the "simplest form", a worthwhile practical procedure is to look at many different forms of an expression, and pick out the one that involves the smallest number of parts.

Simplify[*expr*]	try to find the simplest form of *expr* by applying various standard algebraic transformations
FullSimplify[*expr*]	try to find the simplest form by applying a wide range of transformations

Simplifying algebraic expressions.

Simplify writes $x^2 + 2x + 1$ in factored form.

$In[1]:=$ **Simplify[x^2 + 2x + 1]**

$Out[1]=$ $(1 + x)^2$

Simplify leaves $x^{10} - 1$ in expanded form, since for this expression, the factored form is larger.

$In[2]:=$ **Simplify[x^10 - 1]**

$Out[2]=$ $-1 + x^{10}$

You can often use Simplify to "clean up" complicated expressions that you get as the results of computations.

Here is the integral of $1/(x^4 - 1)$. Integrals are discussed in more detail in Section 1.5.3.

$In[3]:=$ **Integrate[1/(x^4-1), x]**

$Out[3]=$ $\frac{1}{4} (-2\,\mathrm{ArcTan}[x] + \mathrm{Log}[-1 + x] - \mathrm{Log}[1 + x])$

Differentiating the result from Integrate should give back your original expression. In this case, as is common, you get a more complicated version of the expression.

$In[4]:=$ **D[%, x]**

$Out[4]=$ $\frac{1}{4} \left(\frac{1}{-1 + x} - \frac{1}{1 + x} - \frac{2}{1 + x^2} \right)$

Simplify succeeds in getting back the original, more simple, form of the expression.

$In[5]:=$ **Simplify[%]**

$Out[5]=$ $\frac{1}{-1 + x^4}$

Simplify is set up to try various standard algebraic transformations on the expressions you give. Sometimes, however, it can take more sophisticated transformations to make progress in finding the simplest form of an expression.

FullSimplify tries a much wider range of transformations, involving not only algebraic functions, but also many other kinds of functions.

Simplify does nothing to this expression.

$In[6]:=$ **Simplify[Gamma[x] Gamma[1 - x]]**

$Out[6]=$ $\mathrm{Gamma}[1 - x]\,\mathrm{Gamma}[x]$

FullSimplify, however, transforms it to a simpler form.

In[7]:= **FullSimplify[Gamma[x] Gamma[1 - x]]**

Out[7]= $\pi \, \text{Csc}[\pi x]$

For fairly small expressions, FullSimplify will often succeed in making some remarkable simplifications. But for larger expressions, it can become unmanageably slow.

The reason for this is that to do its job, FullSimplify effectively has to try combining every part of an expression with every other, and for large expressions the number of cases that it has to consider can be astronomically large.

Simplify also has a difficult task to do, but it is set up to avoid some of the most time-consuming transformations that are tried by FullSimplify. For simple algebraic calculations, therefore, you may often find it convenient to apply Simplify quite routinely to your results.

In more complicated calculations, however, even Simplify, let alone FullSimplify, may end up needing to try a very large number of different forms, and therefore taking a long time. In such cases, you typically need to do more controlled simplification, and use your knowledge of the form you want to get to guide the process.

■ 1.4.5 Advanced Topic: Putting Expressions into Different Forms

Complicated algebraic expressions can usually be written in many different ways. *Mathematica* provides a variety of functions for converting expressions from one form to another.

In many applications, the most common of these functions are Expand, Factor and Simplify. However, particularly when you have rational expressions that contain quotients, you may need to use other functions.

Expand[*expr*]	multiply out products and powers
ExpandAll[*expr*]	apply Expand everywhere
Factor[*expr*]	reduce to a product of factors
Together[*expr*]	put all terms over a common denominator
Apart[*expr*]	separate into terms with simple denominators
Cancel[*expr*]	cancel common factors between numerators and denominators
Simplify[*expr*]	try a sequence of algebraic transformations and give the smallest form of *expr* found

Functions for transforming algebraic expressions.

Here is a rational expression that can be written in many different forms.

$In[1]:=$ **e = (x - 1)^2 (2 + x) / ((1 + x) (x - 3)^2)**

$$Out[1]= \frac{(-1+x)^2 (2+x)}{(-3+x)^2 (1+x)}$$

Expand expands out the numerator, but leaves the denominator in factored form.

$In[2]:=$ **Expand[e]**

$$Out[2]= \frac{2}{(-3+x)^2 (1+x)} - \frac{3x}{(-3+x)^2 (1+x)} + \frac{x^3}{(-3+x)^2 (1+x)}$$

ExpandAll expands out everything, including the denominator.

$In[3]:=$ **ExpandAll[e]**

$$Out[3]= \frac{2}{9+3x-5x^2+x^3} - \frac{3x}{9+3x-5x^2+x^3} + \frac{x^3}{9+3x-5x^2+x^3}$$

Together collects all the terms together over a common denominator.

$In[4]:=$ **Together[%]**

$$Out[4]= \frac{2-3x+x^3}{(-3+x)^2 (1+x)}$$

Apart breaks the expression apart into terms with simple denominators.

$In[5]:=$ **Apart[%]**

$$Out[5]= 1 + \frac{5}{(-3+x)^2} + \frac{19}{4(-3+x)} + \frac{1}{4(1+x)}$$

Factor factors everything, in this case reproducing the original form.

$In[6]:=$ **Factor[%]**

$$Out[6]= \frac{(-1+x)^2 (2+x)}{(-3+x)^2 (1+x)}$$

According to Simplify, this is the simplest way to write the original expression.

$In[7]:=$ **Simplify[e]**

$$Out[7]= \frac{(-1+x)^2 (2+x)}{(-3+x)^2 (1+x)}$$

Getting expressions into the form you want is something of an art. In most cases, it is best simply to experiment, trying different transformations until you get what you want. Often you will be able to use palettes in the front end to do this.

When you have an expression with a single variable, you can choose to write it as a sum of terms, a product, and so on. If you have an expression with several variables, there is an even wider selection of possible forms. You can, for example, choose to group terms in the expression so that one or another of the variables is "dominant".

Collect[*expr*, *x*]	group together powers of *x*
FactorTerms[*expr*, *x*]	pull out factors that do not depend on *x*

Rearranging expressions in several variables.

Here is an algebraic expression in two variables.	*In[8]:=* **v = Expand[(3 + 2 x)^2 (x + 2 y)^2]**
	Out[8]= $9 x^2 + 12 x^3 + 4 x^4 + 36 x y +$ $48 x^2 y + 16 x^3 y + 36 y^2 + 48 x y^2 + 16 x^2 y^2$
This groups together terms in v that involve the same power of x.	*In[9]:=* **Collect[v, x]**
	Out[9]= $4 x^4 + 36 y^2 + x^3 (12 + 16 y) +$ $x^2 (9 + 48 y + 16 y^2) + x (36 y + 48 y^2)$
This groups together powers of y.	*In[10]:=* **Collect[v, y]**
	Out[10]= $9 x^2 + 12 x^3 + 4 x^4 +$ $(36 x + 48 x^2 + 16 x^3) y + (36 + 48 x + 16 x^2) y^2$
This factors out the piece that does not depend on y.	*In[11]:=* **FactorTerms[v, y]**
	Out[11]= $(9 + 12 x + 4 x^2) (x^2 + 4 x y + 4 y^2)$

As we have seen, even when you restrict yourself to polynomials and rational expressions, there are many different ways to write any particular expression. If you consider more complicated expressions, involving, for example, higher mathematical functions, the variety of possible forms becomes still greater. As a result, it is totally infeasible to have a specific function built into *Mathematica* to produce each possible form. Rather, *Mathematica* allows you to construct arbitrary sets of transformation rules for converting between different forms. Many *Mathematica* packages include such rules; the details of how to construct them for yourself are given in Section 2.5.

There are nevertheless a few additional built-in *Mathematica* functions for transforming expressions.

TrigExpand[*expr*]	expand out trigonometric expressions into a sum of terms
TrigFactor[*expr*]	factor trigonometric expressions into products of terms
TrigReduce[*expr*]	reduce trigonometric expressions using multiple angles
TrigToExp[*expr*]	convert trigonometric functions to exponentials
ExpToTrig[*expr*]	convert exponentials to trigonometric functions
FunctionExpand[*expr*]	expand out special and other functions
ComplexExpand[*expr*]	perform expansions assuming that all variables are real
PowerExpand[*expr*]	transform $(xy)^p$ into $x^p y^p$, etc.

Some other functions for transforming expressions.

This expands out the trigonometric expression, writing it so that all functions have argument x.	*In[12]:=* **TrigExpand[Tan[x] Cos[2x]]**
	Out[12]= $\frac{3}{2} \text{Cos}[x] \text{Sin}[x] - \frac{\text{Tan}[x]}{2} - \frac{1}{2} \text{Sin}[x]^2 \text{Tan}[x]$

This uses trigonometric identities to generate a factored form of the expression.	$In[13]:=$ **TrigFactor[%]** $Out[13]=$ $(Cos[x] - Sin[x])(Cos[x] + Sin[x])Tan[x]$

This reduces the expression by using multiple angles.	$In[14]:=$ **TrigReduce[%]** $Out[14]=$ $-\frac{1}{2} Sec[x](Sin[x] - Sin[3x])$

This expands the sine assuming that x and y are both real.	$In[15]:=$ **ComplexExpand[Sin[x + I y]]** $Out[15]=$ $Cosh[y] Sin[x] + i Cos[x] Sinh[y]$

This does the expansion allowing x and y to be complex.	$In[16]:=$ **ComplexExpand[Sin[x + I y], {x, y}]** $Out[16]=$ $-Cosh[Im[x] + Re[y]] Sin[Im[y] - Re[x]] +$ $i Cos[Im[y] - Re[x]] Sinh[Im[x] + Re[y]]$

The transformations on expressions done by functions like Expand and Factor are always correct, whatever values the symbolic variables in the expressions may have. Sometimes, however, it is useful to perform transformations that are only correct for some possible values of symbolic variables. One such transformation is performed by PowerExpand.

Mathematica does not automatically expand out non-integer powers of products.	$In[17]:=$ **Sqrt[x y]** $Out[17]=$ $\sqrt{xy}$

PowerExpand does the expansion.	$In[18]:=$ **PowerExpand[%]** $Out[18]=$ $\sqrt{x} \sqrt{y}$

■ 1.4.6 Advanced Topic: Simplifying with Assumptions

Simplify[*expr, assum*]	simplify *expr* with assumptions

Simplifying with assumptions.

Mathematica does not automatically simplify this, since it is only true for some values of x.	$In[1]:=$ **Simplify[Sqrt[x^2]]** $Out[1]=$ $\sqrt{x^2}$

$\sqrt{x^2}$ is equal to x for $x \geq 0$, but not otherwise.	$In[2]:=$ **{Sqrt[4^2], Sqrt[(-4)^2]}** $Out[2]=$ $\{4, 4\}$

This tells Simplify to make the assumption x > 0, so that simplification can proceed.	$In[3]:=$ **Simplify[Sqrt[x^2], x > 0]** $Out[3]=$ x

No automatic simplification can be done on this expression.	$In[4]:=$ **2 a + 2 Sqrt[a - Sqrt[-b]] Sqrt[a + Sqrt[-b]]** $Out[4]=$ $2a + 2\sqrt{a - \sqrt{-b}} \sqrt{a + \sqrt{-b}}$

If *a* and *b* are assumed to be positive, the expression can however be simplified.

In[5]:= **Simplify[%, a > 0 && b > 0]**

Out[5]= $2\left(a + \sqrt{a^2 + b}\right)$

Here is a simple example involving trigonometric functions.

In[6]:= **Simplify[ArcSin[Sin[x]], -Pi/2 < x < Pi/2]**

Out[6]= x

Element[*x*, *dom*]	state that *x* is an element of the domain *dom*
Element[{*x*$_1$, *x*$_2$, ... }, *dom*]	state that all the *x*$_i$ are elements of the domain *dom*
Reals	real numbers
Integers	integers
Primes	prime numbers

Some domains used in assumptions.

This simplifies $\sqrt{x^2}$ assuming that *x* is a real number.

In[7]:= **Simplify[Sqrt[x^2], Element[x, Reals]]**

Out[7]= Abs[x]

This simplifies the sine assuming that *n* is an integer.

In[8]:= **Simplify[Sin[x + 2 n Pi], Element[n, Integers]]**

Out[8]= Sin[x]

With the assumptions given, Fermat's Little Theorem can be used.

In[9]:= **Simplify[Mod[a^p, p], Element[a, Integers]**
&& **Element[p, Primes]]**

Out[9]= Mod[a, p]

This uses the fact that sin(*x*), but not arcsin(*x*), is real when *x* is real.

In[10]:= **Simplify[Re[{Sin[x], ArcSin[x]}], Element[x, Reals]]**

Out[10]= {Sin[x], Re[ArcSin[x]]}

■ 1.4.7 Picking Out Pieces of Algebraic Expressions

Coefficient[*expr*, *form*]	coefficient of *form* in *expr*
Exponent[*expr*, *form*]	maximum power of *form* in *expr*
Part[*expr*, *n*] or *expr*[[*n*]]	*n*th term of *expr*

Functions to pick out pieces of polynomials.

Here is an algebraic expression.

In[1]:= **e = Expand[(1 + 3x + 4y^2)^2]**

Out[1]= $1 + 6x + 9x^2 + 8y^2 + 24xy^2 + 16y^4$

This gives the coefficient of x in e.	*In[2]:=* **Coefficient[e, x]**
	Out[2]= $6 + 24 y^2$
Exponent[*expr*, *y*] gives the highest power of *y* that appears in *expr*.	*In[3]:=* **Exponent[e, y]**
	Out[3]= 4
This gives the fourth term in e.	*In[4]:=* **Part[e, 4]**
	Out[4]= $8 y^2$

You may notice that the function Part[*expr*, *n*] used to pick out the nth term in a sum is the same as the function described in Section 1.2.4 for picking out elements in lists. This is no coincidence. In fact, as discussed in Section 2.1.5, every *Mathematica* expression can be manipulated structurally much like a list. However, as discussed in Section 2.1.5, you must be careful, because *Mathematica* often shows algebraic expressions in a form that is different from the way it treats them internally.

Coefficient works even with polynomials that are not explicitly expanded out.	*In[5]:=* **Coefficient[(1 + 3x + 4y^2)^2, x]**
	Out[5]= $6 + 24 y^2$

Numerator[*expr*]	numerator of *expr*
Denominator[*expr*]	denominator of *expr*

Functions to pick out pieces of rational expressions.

Here is a rational expression.	*In[6]:=* **r = (1 + x)/(2 (2 - y))**
	Out[6]= $\dfrac{1 + x}{2 (2 - y)}$
Denominator picks out the denominator.	*In[7]:=* **Denominator[%]**
	Out[7]= $2 (2 - y)$
Denominator gives 1 for expressions that are not quotients.	*In[8]:=* **Denominator[1/x + 2/y]**
	Out[8]= 1

■ 1.4.8 Controlling the Display of Large Expressions

When you do symbolic calculations, it is quite easy to end up with extremely complicated expressions. Often, you will not even want to *see* the complete result of a computation.

If you end your input with a semicolon, *Mathematica* will do the computation you asked for, but will not display the result. You can nevertheless use % or Out[*n*] to refer to the result.

Even though you may not want to see the *whole* result from a computation, you often do need to see its basic form. You can use `Short` to display the *outline* of an expression, omitting some of the terms.

Ending your input with ; stops *Mathematica* from displaying the complicated result of the computation.	`In[1]:= Expand[(x + 5 y + 10)^8] ;`

You can still refer to the result as %. `//Short` displays a one-line outline of the result. The `<<n>>` stands for *n* terms that have been left out.

`In[2]:= % //Short`

`Out[2]//Short=` $100000000 + 80000000\,x + \ll 42 \gg + 390625\,y^8$

This shows a three-line version of the expression. More parts are now visible.

`In[3]:= Short[%, 3]`

`Out[3]//Short=` $100000000 + 80000000\,x + 28000000\,x^2 +$
$5600000\,x^3 + 700000\,x^4 + \ll 35 \gg + 8750000\,x\,y^6 +$
$437500\,x^2\,y^6 + 6250000\,y^7 + 625000\,x\,y^7 + 390625\,y^8$

This gives the total number of terms in the sum.

`In[4]:= Length[%]`

`Out[4]= 45`

---

command ;	execute *command*, but do not print the result
expr // `Short`	show a one-line outline form of *expr*
`Short[`*expr*, *n*`]`	show an *n*-line outline of *expr*

Some ways to shorten your output.

■ 1.4.9 The Limits of *Mathematica*

In just one *Mathematica* command, you can easily specify a calculation that is far too complicated for any computer to do. For example, you could ask for `Expand[(1+x)^(10^100)]`. The result of this calculation would have $10^{100} + 1$ terms—more than the total number of particles in the universe.

You should have no trouble working out `Expand[(1+x)^100]` on any computer that can run *Mathematica*. But as you increase the exponent of `(1+x)`, the results you get will eventually become too big for your computer's memory to hold. Exactly at what point this happens depends not only on the total amount of memory your computer has, but often also on such details as what other jobs happen to be running on your computer when you try to do your calculation.

If your computer does run out of memory in the middle of a calculation, most versions of *Mathematica* have no choice but to stop immediately. As a result, it is important to plan your calculations so that they never need more memory than your computer has.

Even if the result of an algebraic calculation is quite simple, the intermediate expressions that you generate in the course of the calculation can be very complicated. This means that even if the final result is small, the intermediate parts of a calculation can be too big for your computer to handle. If this happens, you can usually break your calculation into pieces, and succeed in doing each piece on its own. You should know that the internal scheme which *Mathematica* uses for memory management is such that once part of a calculation is finished, the memory used to store intermediate expressions that arose is immediately made available for new expressions.

Memory space is the most common limiting factor in *Mathematica* calculations. Time can also, however, be a limiting factor. You will usually be prepared to wait a second, or even a minute, for the result of a calculation. But you will less often be prepared to wait an hour or a day, and you will almost never be able to wait a year.

The internal code of *Mathematica* uses highly efficient and optimized algorithms. But there are some tasks for which the best known algorithms always eventually take a large amount of time. A typical issue is that the time required by the algorithm may increase almost exponentially with the size of the input. A classic case is integer factorization—where the best known algorithms require times that grow almost exponentially with the number of digits. In practice, you will find that FactorInteger[k] will give a result almost immediately when k has fewer than about 40 digits. But if k has 60 digits, FactorInteger[k] can start taking an unmanageably long time.

In some cases, there is progressive improvement in the algorithms that are known, so that successive versions of *Mathematica* can perform particular computations progressively faster. But ideas from the theory of computation strongly suggest that many computations will always in effect require an irreducible amount of computational work—so that no fast algorithm for them will ever be found.

Whether or not the only algorithms involve exponentially increasing amounts of time, there will always come a point where a computation is too large or time-consuming to do on your particular computer system. As you work with *Mathematica*, you should develop some feeling for the limits on the kinds of calculations you can do in your particular application area.

- Doing arithmetic with numbers containing a few hundred million digits.
- Generating a million digits of numbers like π and e.
- Expanding out a polynomial that gives a million terms.
- Factoring a polynomial in four variables with a hundred thousand terms.
- Reducing a system of quadratic inequalities to a few thousand independent components.
- Finding integer roots of a sparse polynomial with degree a million.
- Applying a recursive rule a million times.
- Calculating all the primes up to ten million.
- Finding the numerical inverse of a 1000×1000 dense matrix.
- Solving a million-variable sparse linear system with a hundred thousand non-zero coefficients.
- Finding the determinant of a 250×250 integer matrix.
- Finding the determinant of a 20×20 symbolic matrix.
- Finding numerical roots of a polynomial of degree 200.
- Solving a sparse linear programming problem with a few hundred thousand variables.
- Finding the Fourier transform of a list with a hundred million elements.
- Rendering a million graphics primitives.
- Sorting a list of ten million elements.
- Searching a string that is ten million characters long.
- Importing a few tens of megabytes of numerical data.
- Formatting a few hundred pages of `TraditionalForm` output.

Some operations that typically take a few seconds on a 2003 vintage PC.

■ 1.4.10 Using Symbols to Tag Objects

There are many ways to use symbols in *Mathematica*. So far, we have concentrated on using symbols to store values and to represent mathematical variables. This section describes another way to use symbols in *Mathematica*.

The idea is to use symbols as "tags" for different types of objects.

Working with physical units gives one simple example. When you specify the length of an object, you want to give not only a number, but also the units in which the length is measured. In standard notation, you might write a length as 12 meters.

You can imitate this notation almost directly in *Mathematica*. You can for example simply use a symbol `meters` to indicate the units of our measurement.

The symbol `meters` here acts as a tag, which indicates the units used.	*In[1]:=* **12 meters**
	Out[1]= 12 meters
You can add lengths like this.	*In[2]:=* **% + 5.3 meters**
	Out[2]= 17.3 meters
This gives a speed.	*In[3]:=* **% / (25 seconds)**
	Out[3]= $\dfrac{0.692\, \text{meters}}{\text{seconds}}$
This converts to a speed in feet per second.	*In[4]:=* **% /. meters -> 3.28084 feet**
	Out[4]= $\dfrac{2.27034\, \text{feet}}{\text{seconds}}$

There is in fact a standard *Mathematica* package that allows you to work with units. The package defines many symbols that represent standard types of units.

Load the *Mathematica* package for handling units.	*In[5]:=* **<<Miscellaneous`Units`**
The package uses standardized names for units.	*In[6]:=* **12 Meter/Second**
	Out[6]= $\dfrac{12\, \text{Meter}}{\text{Second}}$
The function `Convert[`*expr*, *units*`]` converts to the specified units.	*In[7]:=* **Convert[%, Mile/Hour]**
	Out[7]= $\dfrac{37500\, \text{Mile}}{1397\, \text{Hour}}$
Usually you have to give prefixes for units as separate words.	*In[8]:=* **Convert[3 Kilo Meter / Hour, Inch / Minute]**
	Out[8]= $\dfrac{250000\, \text{Inch}}{127\, \text{Minute}}$

1.5 Symbolic Mathematics

■ 1.5.1 Basic Operations

Mathematica's ability to deal with symbolic expressions, as well as numbers, allows you to use it for many kinds of mathematics.

Calculus is one example. With *Mathematica*, you can differentiate an expression *symbolically*, and get a formula for the result.

This finds the derivative of x^n.

```
In[1]:= D[ x^n, x ]
```

$$Out[1]= n\,x^{-1+n}$$

Here is a slightly more complicated example.

```
In[2]:= D[x^2 Log[x + a], x]
```

$$Out[2]= \frac{x^2}{a+x} + 2\,x\,Log[a+x]$$

D[f, x]	the (partial) derivative $\frac{\partial f}{\partial x}$
Integrate[f, x]	the indefinite integral $\int f\,dx$
Sum[f, {i, $imin$, $imax$}]	the sum $\sum_{i=imin}^{imax} f$
Solve[lhs==rhs, x]	solution to an equation for x
Series[f, {x, x_0, $order$}]	a power series expansion of f about the point $x = x_0$
Limit[f, x->x_0]	the limit $\lim_{x \to x_0} f$
Minimize[f, x]	minimization of f with respect to x

Some symbolic mathematical operations.

Getting formulas as the results of computations is usually desirable when it is possible. There are however many circumstances where it is mathematically impossible to get an explicit formula as the result of a computation. This happens, for example, when you try to solve an equation for which there is no "closed form" solution. In such cases, you must resort to numerical methods and approximations. These are discussed in Section 1.6.

■ 1.5.2 Differentiation

Here is the derivative of x^n with respect to x.

```
In[1]:= D[ x^n, x ]
```

$$Out[1]= n\,x^{-1+n}$$

Mathematica knows the derivatives of all the standard mathematical functions.

In[2]:= **D[ArcTan[x], x]**

$$Out[2]= \frac{1}{1+x^2}$$

This differentiates three times with respect to x.

In[3]:= **D[x^n, {x, 3}]**

$$Out[3]= (-2+n)\,(-1+n)\,n\,x^{-3+n}$$

The function D[x^n, x] really gives a *partial* derivative, in which n is assumed not to depend on x. *Mathematica* has another function, called Dt, which finds *total* derivatives, in which all variables are assumed to be related. In mathematical notation, D[*f*, *x*] is like $\frac{\partial f}{\partial x}$, while Dt[*f*, *x*] is like $\frac{df}{dx}$. You can think of Dt as standing for "derivative total".

Dt gives a *total derivative*, which assumes that n can depend on x. Dt[n, x] stands for $\frac{dn}{dx}$.

In[4]:= **Dt[x^n, x]**

$$Out[4]= x^n\left(\frac{n}{x}+Dt[n,\,x]\,Log[x]\right)$$

This gives the total differential $d(x^n)$. Dt[x] is the differential dx.

In[5]:= **Dt[x^n]**

$$Out[5]= x^n\left(\frac{n\,Dt[x]}{x}+Dt[n]\,Log[x]\right)$$

D[*f*, *x*]	partial derivative $\frac{\partial}{\partial x}f$	
D[*f*, x_1, x_2, ...]	multiple derivative $\frac{\partial}{\partial x_1}\frac{\partial}{\partial x_2}...f$	
D[*f*, {*x*, *n*}]	repeated derivative $\frac{\partial^n f}{\partial x^n}$	
Dt[*f*]	total differential df	
Dt[*f*, *x*]	total derivative $\frac{d}{dx}f$	

Some differentiation functions.

As well as treating variables like *x* symbolically, you can also treat functions in *Mathematica* symbolically. Thus, for example, you can find formulas for derivatives of f[x], without specifying any explicit form for the function f.

Mathematica does not know how to differentiate f, so it gives you back a symbolic result in terms of f'.

In[6]:= **D[f[x], x]**

Out[6]= f' [x]

Mathematica uses the chain rule to simplify derivatives.

In[7]:= **D[2 x f[x^2], x]**

$$Out[7]= 2\,f[x^2]+4\,x^2\,f'\,[x^2]$$

■ 1.5.3 Integration

Here is the integral $\int x^n \, dx$ in *Mathematica*.

In[1]:= **Integrate[x^n, x]**

Out[1]= $\dfrac{x^{1+n}}{1+n}$

Here is a slightly more complicated example.

In[2]:= **Integrate[1/(x^4 - a^4), x]**

Out[2]= $-\dfrac{2\,\mathrm{ArcTan}[\frac{x}{a}] - \mathrm{Log}[a - x] + \mathrm{Log}[a + x]}{4\,a^3}$

Mathematica knows how to do almost any integral that can be done in terms of standard mathematical functions. But you should realize that even though an integrand may contain only fairly simple functions, its integral may involve much more complicated functions—or may not be expressible at all in terms of standard mathematical functions.

Here is a fairly straightforward integral.

In[3]:= **Integrate[Log[1 - x^2], x]**

Out[3]= $-2\,x - \mathrm{Log}[-1 + x] + \mathrm{Log}[1 + x] + x\,\mathrm{Log}[1 - x^2]$

This integral can be done only in terms of a dilogarithm function.

In[4]:= **Integrate[Log[1 - x^2]/x, x]**

Out[4]= $-\dfrac{1}{2}\,\mathrm{PolyLog}[2, x^2]$

This integral involves **Erf**.

In[5]:= **Integrate[Exp[1 - x^2], x]**

Out[5]= $\dfrac{1}{2}\,e\,\sqrt{\pi}\,\mathrm{Erf}[x]$

And this one involves a Fresnel function.

In[6]:= **Integrate[Sin[x^2], x]**

Out[6]= $\sqrt{\dfrac{\pi}{2}}\,\mathrm{FresnelS}\!\left[\sqrt{\dfrac{2}{\pi}}\,x\right]$

Even this integral requires a hypergeometric function.

In[7]:= **Integrate[(1 - x^2)^n, x]**

Out[7]= $x\,\mathrm{Hypergeometric2F1}\!\left[\dfrac{1}{2},\, -n,\, \dfrac{3}{2},\, x^2\right]$

This integral simply cannot be done in terms of standard mathematical functions. As a result, *Mathematica* just leaves it undone.

In[8]:= **Integrate[x^x, x]**

Out[8]= $\displaystyle\int x^x \, dx$

Integrate[f, x]	the indefinite integral $\int f\ dx$
Integrate[f, x, y]	the multiple integral $\int dx\ dy\ f$
Integrate[f, {x, $xmin$, $xmax$}]	the definite integral $\int_{xmin}^{xmax} f\ dx$
Integrate[f, {x, $xmin$, $xmax$}, {y, $ymin$, $ymax$}]	
	the multiple integral $\int_{xmin}^{xmax} dx \int_{ymin}^{ymax} dy\ f$

Integration.

Here is the definite integral $\int_a^b \sin^2(x)\ dx$.

```
In[9]:= Integrate[Sin[x]^2, {x, a, b} ]
```

$$Out[9]= \frac{1}{2}\ (-a + b + Cos[a]\ Sin[a] - Cos[b]\ Sin[b])$$

Here is another definite integral.

```
In[10]:= Integrate[Exp[-x^2], {x, 0, Infinity}]
```

$$Out[10]= \frac{\sqrt{\pi}}{2}$$

Mathematica cannot give you a formula for this definite integral.

```
In[11]:= Integrate[ x^x, {x, 0, 1} ]
```

$$Out[11]= \int_0^1 x^x\ dx$$

You can still get a numerical result, though.

```
In[12]:= N[ % ]
Out[12]= 0.783431
```

This evaluates the multiple integral $\int_0^1 dx \int_0^x dy\ (x^2 + y^2)$. The range of the outermost integration variable appears first.

```
In[13]:= Integrate[ x^2 + y^2, {x, 0, 1}, {y, 0, x} ]
```

$$Out[13]= \frac{1}{3}$$

■ 1.5.4 Sums and Products

This constructs the sum $\sum_{i=1}^{7} \frac{x^i}{i}$.

```
In[1]:= Sum[x^i/i, {i, 1, 7}]
```

$$Out[1]= x + \frac{x^2}{2} + \frac{x^3}{3} + \frac{x^4}{4} + \frac{x^5}{5} + \frac{x^6}{6} + \frac{x^7}{7}$$

You can leave out the lower limit if it is equal to 1.

```
In[2]:= Sum[x^i/i, {i, 7}]
```

$$Out[2]= x + \frac{x^2}{2} + \frac{x^3}{3} + \frac{x^4}{4} + \frac{x^5}{5} + \frac{x^6}{6} + \frac{x^7}{7}$$

This makes *i* increase in steps of 2, so that only odd-numbered values are included.

```
In[3]:= Sum[x^i/i, {i, 1, 5, 2}]
```

$$Out[3]= x + \frac{x^3}{3} + \frac{x^5}{5}$$

Products work just like sums.

$In[4]:=$ **Product[x + i, {i, 1, 4}]**

$Out[4]=$ $(1 + x) (2 + x) (3 + x) (4 + x)$

Sum[f, {i, $imin$, $imax$}]	the sum $\sum_{i=imin}^{imax} f$
Sum[f, {i, $imin$, $imax$, di}]	the sum with i increasing in steps of di
Sum[f, {i, $imin$, $imax$}, {j, $jmin$, $jmax$}]	the nested sum $\sum_{i=imin}^{imax} \sum_{j=jmin}^{jmax} f$
Product[f, {i, $imin$, $imax$}]	the product $\prod_{i=imin}^{imax} f$

Sums and products.

This sum is computed symbolically as a function of n.

$In[5]:=$ **Sum[i^2, {i, 1, n}]**

$Out[5]=$ $\dfrac{1}{6} n (1 + n) (1 + 2 n)$

Mathematica can also give an exact result for this infinite sum.

$In[6]:=$ **Sum[1/i^4, {i, 1, Infinity}]**

$Out[6]=$ $\dfrac{\pi^4}{90}$

As with integrals, simple sums can lead to complicated results.

$In[7]:=$ **Sum[x^(i (i + 1)), {i, 1, Infinity}]**

$Out[7]=$ $\dfrac{-2 x^{1/4} + \text{EllipticTheta}[2, 0, x]}{2 x^{1/4}}$

This sum cannot be evaluated exactly using standard mathematical functions.

$In[8]:=$ **Sum[1/(i! + (2i)!), {i, 1, Infinity}]**

$Out[8]=$ $\displaystyle\sum_{i=1}^{\infty} \dfrac{1}{i! + (2 i)!}$

You can nevertheless find a numerical approximation to the result.

$In[9]:=$ **N[%]**

$Out[9]=$ 0.373197

Mathematica also has a notation for multiple sums and products.
Sum[f, {i, $imin$, $imax$}, {j, $jmin$, $jmax$}] represents a sum over i and j, which would be written in standard mathematical notation as $\sum_{i=imin}^{imax} \sum_{j=jmin}^{jmax} f$. Notice that in *Mathematica* notation, as in standard mathematical notation, the range of the *outermost* variable is given *first*.

This is the multiple sum $\sum_{i=1}^{3} \sum_{j=1}^{i} x^i y^j$. Notice that the outermost sum over i is given first, just as in the mathematical notation.

$In[10]:=$ **Sum[x^i y^j, {i, 1, 3}, {j, 1, i}]**

$Out[10]=$ $x y + x^2 y + x^3 y + x^2 y^2 + x^3 y^2 + x^3 y^3$

The way the ranges of variables are specified in Sum and Product is an example of the rather general *iterator notation* that *Mathematica* uses. You will see this notation again when we discuss generating tables and lists using Table (Section 1.8.2), and when we describe Do loops (Section 1.7.3).

{*imax*}	iterate *imax* times, without incrementing any variables
{*i, imax*}	*i* goes from 1 to *imax* in steps of 1
{*i, imin, imax*}	*i* goes from *imin* to *imax* in steps of 1
{*i, imin, imax, di*}	*i* goes from *imin* to *imax* in steps of *di*
{*i, imin, imax*}, {*j, jmin, jmax*}, ...	*i* goes from *imin* to *imax*, and for each such value, *j* goes from *jmin* to *jmax*, etc.

Mathematica iterator notation.

■ 1.5.5 Equations

Section 1.2.2 discussed *assignments* such as $x = y$ which *set* x equal to y. This section discusses *equations*, which *test* equality. The equation $x == y$ *tests* whether x is equal to y.

This *tests* whether 2 + 2 and 4 are
equal. The result is the symbol True.

```
In[1]:= 2 + 2 == 4
Out[1]= True
```

It is very important that you do not confuse $x = y$ with $x == y$. While $x = y$ is an *imperative* statement that actually causes an assignment to be done, $x == y$ merely *tests* whether x and y are equal, and causes no explicit action. If you have used the C programming language, you will recognize that the notation for assignment and testing in *Mathematica* is the same as in C.

$x = y$	assigns x to have value y
$x == y$	tests whether x and y are equal

Assignments and tests.

This *assigns* x to have value 4.

```
In[2]:= x = 4
Out[2]= 4
```

If you ask for x, you now get 4.

```
In[3]:= x
Out[3]= 4
```

This *tests* whether x is equal to 4. In
this case, it is.

```
In[4]:= x == 4
Out[4]= True
```

x is equal to 4, not 6.

```
In[5]:= x == 6
Out[5]= False
```

This removes the value assigned to x.

```
In[6]:= x =.
```

The tests we have used so far involve only numbers, and always give a definite answer, either `True` or `False`. You can also do tests on symbolic expressions.

Mathematica cannot get a definite result for this test unless you give x a specific numerical value.	`In[7]:= x == 5`
	`Out[7]= x == 5`

If you replace x by the specific numerical value 4, the test gives `False`.	`In[8]:= % /. x -> 4`
	`Out[8]= False`

Even when you do tests on symbolic expressions, there are some cases where you can get definite results. An important one is when you test the equality of two expressions that are *identical*. Whatever the numerical values of the variables in these expressions may be, *Mathematica* knows that the expressions must always be equal.

The two expressions are *identical*, so the result is `True`, whatever the value of x may be.	`In[9]:= 2 x + x^2 == 2 x + x^2`
	`Out[9]= True`

Mathematica does not try to tell whether these expressions are equal. In this case, using `Expand` would make them have the same form.	`In[10]:= 2 x + x^2 == x (2 + x)`
	`Out[10]= 2 x + x^2 == x (2 + x)`

Expressions like x == 4 represent *equations* in *Mathematica*. There are many functions in *Mathematica* for manipulating and solving equations.

This is an *equation* in *Mathematica*. Subsection 1.5.7 will discuss how to solve it for x.	`In[11]:= x^2 + 2 x - 7 == 0`
	`Out[11]= -7 + 2 x + x^2 == 0`

You can assign a name to the equation.	`In[12]:= eqn = %`
	`Out[12]= -7 + 2 x + x^2 == 0`

If you ask for eqn, you now get the equation.	`In[13]:= eqn`
	`Out[13]= -7 + 2 x + x^2 == 0`

■ 1.5.6 Relational and Logical Operators

$x == y$	equal (also input as $x == y$)
$x \mathrel{!}= y$	unequal (also input as $x \neq y$)
$x > y$	greater than
$x >= y$	greater than or equal to (also input as $x \geq y$)
$x < y$	less than
$x <= y$	less than or equal to (also input as $x \leq y$)
$x == y == z$	all equal
$x \mathrel{!}= y \mathrel{!}= z$	all unequal (distinct)
$x > y > z$, etc.	strictly decreasing, etc.

Relational operators.

This tests whether 10 is less than 7. The result is False.

```
In[1]:= 10 < 7
Out[1]= False
```

Not all of these numbers are unequal, so this gives False.

```
In[2]:= 3 != 2 != 3
Out[2]= False
```

You can mix < and <=.

```
In[3]:= 3 < 5 <= 6
Out[3]= True
```

Since both of the quantities involved are numeric, *Mathematica* can determine that this is true.

```
In[4]:= Pi^E < E^Pi
Out[4]= True
```

Mathematica does not know whether this is true or false.

```
In[5]:= x > y
Out[5]= x > y
```

!p	not (also input as ¬p)
p && q && ...	and (also input as $p \wedge q \wedge ...$)
p || q || ...	or (also input as $p \vee q \vee ...$)
Xor[p, q, ...]	exclusive or (also input as $p \veebar q \veebar ...$)
+ Nand[p, q, ...] and Nor[p, q, ...]	nand and nor (also input as $\bar{\wedge}$ and $\bar{\vee}$)
If[p, *then*, *else*]	give *then* if p is True, and *else* if p is False
LogicalExpand[*expr*]	expand out logical expressions

Logical operations.

Both tests give True, so the result is True.

```
In[6]:= 7 > 4 && 2 != 3
Out[6]= True
```

You should remember that the logical operations ==, && and || are all *double characters* in *Mathematica*. If you have used a programming language such as C, you will be familiar with this notation.

Mathematica does not know whether this is true or false.

```
In[7]:= p && q
Out[7]= p && q
```

Mathematica leaves this expression unchanged.

```
In[8]:= (p || q) && !(r || s)
Out[8]= (p || q) && ! (r || s)
```

You can use LogicalExpand to expand out the terms.

```
In[9]:= LogicalExpand[ % ]
Out[9]= p && ! r && ! s || q && ! r && ! s
```

■ 1.5.7 Solving Equations

An expression like x^2 + 2 x - 7 == 0 represents an *equation* in *Mathematica*. You will often need to *solve* equations like this, to find out for what values of x they are true.

This gives the two solutions to the quadratic equation $x^2 + 2x - 7 = 0$. The solutions are given as replacements for x.

```
In[1]:= Solve[x^2 + 2x - 7 == 0, x]
Out[1]= {{x → -1 - 2√2}, {x → -1 + 2√2}}
```

Here are the numerical values of the solutions.

```
In[2]:= N[ % ]
Out[2]= {{x → -3.82843}, {x → 1.82843}}
```

You can get a list of the actual solutions for x by applying the rules generated by Solve to x using the replacement operator.

In[3]:= **x /. %**

Out[3]= {-3.82843, 1.82843}

You can equally well apply the rules to any other expression involving x.

In[4]:= **x^2 + 3 x /. %%**

Out[4]= {3.17157, 8.82843}

Solve[*lhs* == *rhs*, *x*]	solve an equation, giving a list of rules for *x*
x /. *solution*	use the list of rules to get values for *x*
expr /. *solution*	use the list of rules to get values for an expression

Finding and using solutions to equations.

Solve always tries to give you explicit *formulas* for the solutions to equations. However, it is a basic mathematical result that, for sufficiently complicated equations, explicit algebraic formulas cannot be given. If you have an algebraic equation in one variable, and the highest power of the variable is at most four, then *Mathematica* can always give you formulas for the solutions. However, if the highest power is five or more, it may be mathematically impossible to give explicit algebraic formulas for all the solutions.

Mathematica can always solve algebraic equations in one variable when the highest power is less than five.

In[5]:= **Solve[x^4 - 5 x^2 - 3 == 0, x]**

$$Out[5]= \left\{\left\{x \to -\sqrt{\frac{5}{2} + \frac{\sqrt{37}}{2}}\right\}, \left\{x \to \sqrt{\frac{5}{2} + \frac{\sqrt{37}}{2}}\right\},\right.$$
$$\left.\left\{x \to -i\sqrt{\frac{1}{2}\left(-5 + \sqrt{37}\right)}\right\}, \left\{x \to i\sqrt{\frac{1}{2}\left(-5 + \sqrt{37}\right)}\right\}\right\}$$

It can solve some equations that involve higher powers.

In[6]:= **Solve[x^6 == 1, x]**

$$Out[6]= \left\{\{x \to -1\}, \{x \to 1\}, \left\{x \to -(-1)^{1/3}\right\},\right.$$
$$\left.\left\{x \to (-1)^{1/3}\right\}, \left\{x \to -(-1)^{2/3}\right\}, \left\{x \to (-1)^{2/3}\right\}\right\}$$

There are some equations, however, for which it is mathematically impossible to find explicit formulas for the solutions. *Mathematica* uses Root objects to represent the solutions in this case.

In[7]:= **Solve[2 - 4 x + x^5 == 0, x]**

$$Out[7]= \left\{\left\{x \to \text{Root}\left[2 - 4\,\#1 + \#1^5\,\&,\,1\right]\right\},\right.$$
$$\left\{x \to \text{Root}\left[2 - 4\,\#1 + \#1^5\,\&,\,2\right]\right\},$$
$$\left\{x \to \text{Root}\left[2 - 4\,\#1 + \#1^5\,\&,\,3\right]\right\},$$
$$\left\{x \to \text{Root}\left[2 - 4\,\#1 + \#1^5\,\&,\,4\right]\right\},$$
$$\left.\left\{x \to \text{Root}\left[2 - 4\,\#1 + \#1^5\,\&,\,5\right]\right\}\right\}$$

Even though you cannot get explicit formulas, you can still find the solutions numerically.

In[8]:= **N[%]**

$$Out[8]= \{\{x \to -1.51851\}, \{x \to 0.508499\},$$
$$\{x \to 1.2436\}, \{x \to -0.116792 - 1.43845\,i\},$$
$$\{x \to -0.116792 + 1.43845\,i\}\}$$

In addition to being able to solve purely algebraic equations, *Mathematica* can also solve some equations involving other functions.

After printing a warning, *Mathematica* returns one solution to this equation.

In[9]:= `Solve[ Sin[x] == a, x ]`

Solve::ifun:
    Inverse functions are being used by Solve, so some
      solutions may not be found; use Reduce for complete
      solution information.

Out[9]= `{{x → ArcSin[a]}}`

It is important to realize that an equation such as $\sin(x) = a$ actually has an infinite number of possible solutions, in this case differing by multiples of 2π. However, `Solve` by default returns just one solution, but prints a message telling you that other solutions may exist. You can use `Reduce` to get more information.

There is no explicit "closed form" solution for a transcendental equation like this.

In[10]:= `Solve[ Cos[x] == x, x ]`

Solve::tdep:
    The equations appear to involve the variables to be
      solved for in an essentially non-algebraic way.

Out[10]= `Solve[Cos[x] == x, x]`

You can find an approximate numerical solution using `FindRoot`, and giving a starting value for x.

In[11]:= `FindRoot[ Cos[x] == x, {x, 0} ]`

Out[11]= `{x → 0.739085}`

`Solve` can also handle equations involving symbolic functions. In such cases, it again prints a warning, then gives results in terms of formal inverse functions.

Mathematica returns a result in terms of the formal inverse function of f.

In[12]:= `Solve[ f[x^2] == a, x ]`

InverseFunction::ifun:
    Inverse functions are being used. Values may be lost
      for multivalued inverses.

Out[12]= $\left\{\left\{x \to -\sqrt{f^{(-1)}[a]}\right\}, \left\{x \to \sqrt{f^{(-1)}[a]}\right\}\right\}$

`Solve[{`*lhs*$_1$`==`*rhs*$_1$`, `*lhs*$_2$`==`*rhs*$_2$`, ... }, {`*x*`, `*y*`, ... }]`
           solve a set of simultaneous equations for *x*, *y*, ...

Solving sets of simultaneous equations.

You can also use *Mathematica* to solve sets of simultaneous equations. You simply give the list of equations, and specify the list of variables to solve for.

Here is a list of two simultaneous equations, to be solved for the variables *x* and *y*.

In[13]:= `Solve[{a x + y == 0, 2 x + (1-a) y == 1}, {x, y}]`

Out[13]= $\left\{\left\{x \to -\dfrac{1}{-2 + a - a^2}, y \to -\dfrac{a}{2 - a + a^2}\right\}\right\}$

Here are some more complicated simultaneous equations. The two solutions are given as two lists of replacements for x and y.

$In[14]:=$ `Solve[{x^2 + y^2 == 1, x + 3 y == 0}, {x, y}]`

$Out[14]= \left\{\left\{x \rightarrow -\dfrac{3}{\sqrt{10}}, y \rightarrow \dfrac{1}{\sqrt{10}}\right\}, \left\{x \rightarrow \dfrac{3}{\sqrt{10}}, y \rightarrow -\dfrac{1}{\sqrt{10}}\right\}\right\}$

This uses the solutions to evaluate the expression x + y.

$In[15]:=$ `x + y /. %`

$Out[15]= \left\{-\sqrt{\dfrac{2}{5}}, \sqrt{\dfrac{2}{5}}\right\}$

Mathematica can solve any set of simultaneous *linear* equations. It can also solve a large class of simultaneous polynomial equations. Even when it does not manage to solve the equations explicitly, *Mathematica* will still usually reduce them to a much simpler form.

When you are working with sets of equations in several variables, it is often convenient to reorganize the equations by eliminating some variables between them.

This eliminates y between the two equations, giving a single equation for x.

$In[16]:=$ `Eliminate[{a x + y == 0, 2 x + (1-a) y == 1}, y]`

$Out[16]= (2 - a + a^2) x == 1$

If you have several equations, there is no guarantee that there exists *any* consistent solution for a particular variable.

There is no consistent solution to these equations, so *Mathematica* returns {}, indicating that the set of solutions is empty.

$In[17]:=$ `Solve[{x==1, x==2}, x]`

$Out[17]= \{\}$

There is also no consistent solution to these equations for almost all values of a.

$In[18]:=$ `Solve[{x==1, x==a}, x]`

$Out[18]= \{\}$

The general question of whether a set of equations has any consistent solution is quite a subtle one. For example, for most values of a, the equations {x==1, x==a} are inconsistent, so there is no possible solution for x. However, if a is equal to 1, then the equations *do* have a solution. Solve is set up to give you *generic* solutions to equations. It discards any solutions that exist only when special constraints between parameters are satisfied.

If you use Reduce instead of Solve, *Mathematica* will however keep *all* the possible solutions to a set of equations, including those that require special conditions on parameters.

This shows that the equations have a solution only when a==1. The notation a==1 && x==1 represents the requirement that *both* a==1 *and* x==1 should be True.

$In[19]:=$ `Reduce[{x==a, x==1}, x]`

$Out[19]= a == 1 \&\& x == 1$

This gives the complete set of possible solutions to the equation. The answer is stated in terms of a combination of simpler equations. **&&** indicates equations that must simultaneously be true; **||** indicates alternatives.

In[20]:= **Reduce[a x - b == 0, x]**

Out[20]= $b == 0 \,\&\&\, a == 0 \,||\, a \neq 0 \,\&\&\, x == \dfrac{b}{a}$

This gives a more complicated combination of equations.

In[21]:= **Reduce[a x^2 - b == 0, x]**

Out[21]= $b == 0 \,\&\&\, a == 0 \,||\, a \neq 0 \,\&\&\, \left(x == -\dfrac{\sqrt{b}}{\sqrt{a}} \,||\, x == \dfrac{\sqrt{b}}{\sqrt{a}} \right)$

This gives a symbolic representation of all solutions.

In[22]:= **Reduce[Sin[x] == a, x]**

Out[22]= $C[1] \in \text{Integers} \,\&\&\, (x == \pi - \text{ArcSin}[a] + 2\pi C[1] \,||$
$x == \text{ArcSin}[a] + 2\pi C[1])$

`Solve[`*lhs==rhs*`, `*x*`]`	solve an equation for *x*
`Solve[{`*lhs₁==rhs₁*`, `*lhs₂==rhs₂*`, ... }, {`*x*`, `*y*`, ... }]`	
	solve a set of simultaneous equations for *x*, *y*, ...
`Eliminate[{`*lhs₁==rhs₁*`, `*lhs₂==rhs₂*`, ... }, {`*x*`, ... }]`	
	eliminate *x*, ... in a set of simultaneous equations
`Reduce[{`*lhs₁==rhs₁*`, `*lhs₂==rhs₂*`, ... }, {`*x*`, `*y*`, ... }]`	
	give a set of simplified equations, including all possible solutions

Functions for solving and manipulating equations.

Reduce also has powerful capabilities for handling equations specifically over real numbers or integers. Section 3.4.9 discusses this in more detail.

This reduces the equation assuming x and y are complex.

In[23]:= **Reduce[x^2 + y^2 == 1, y]**

Out[23]= $y == -\sqrt{1 - x^2} \,||\, y == \sqrt{1 - x^2}$

This includes the conditions for x and y to be real.

In[24]:= **Reduce[x^2 + y^2 == 1, y, Reals]**

Out[24]= $-1 \leq x \leq 1 \,\&\&\, \left(y == -\sqrt{1 - x^2} \,||\, y == \sqrt{1 - x^2} \right)$

This gives only the integer solutions.

In[25]:= **Reduce[x^2 + y^2 == 1, y, Integers]**

Out[25]= $x == -1 \,\&\&\, y == 0 \,||\, x == 0 \,\&\&\, y == -1 \,||$
$x == 0 \,\&\&\, y == 1 \,||\, x == 1 \,\&\&\, y == 0$

+■ 1.5.8 Inequalities

Reduce[*ineqs*, {*x*, *y*, ... }]	reduce a collection of inequalities
+ FindInstance[*ineqs*, {*x*, *y*, ... }]	find an instance that satisfies the *ineqs*

Handling inequalities.

This finds a reduced form for the inequalities.

In[1]:= **Reduce[x + y < 1 && y > x > 0, {x, y}]**

$Out[1]= \ 0 < x < \frac{1}{2} \ \&\& \ x < y < 1 - x$

These inequalities can never be satisfied.

In[2]:= **Reduce[x + y < 1 && y > x > 1, {x, y}]**

Out[2]= False

It is easy to end up with rather complicated results.

In[3]:= **Reduce[x + y < 1 && y^2 > x > 0, {x, y}]**

$Out[3]= \ 0 < x < \frac{1}{2} \left(3 - \sqrt{5}\right) \ \&\& \ \left(y < -\sqrt{x} \ || \ \sqrt{x} < y < 1 - x\right) \ ||$

$\qquad \frac{1}{2} \left(3 - \sqrt{5}\right) \le x < \frac{1}{2} \left(3 + \sqrt{5}\right) \ \&\& \ y < -\sqrt{x} \ ||$

$\qquad x \ge \frac{1}{2} \left(3 + \sqrt{5}\right) \ \&\& \ y < 1 - x$

Equations can often be solved to give definite values of variables. But inequalities typically just define regions that can only be specified by other inequalities. You can use FindInstance to find definite values of variables that satisfy a particular set of inequalities.

This finds a point in the region specified by the inequalities.

In[4]:= **FindInstance[x + y < 1 && y^2 > x > 0, {x, y}]**

$Out[4]= \ \left\{\left\{x \rightarrow \frac{7}{2}, \ y \rightarrow -3\right\}\right\}$

+ Minimize[{*expr*, *ineq*}, {*x*, *y*, ... }]	minimize *expr* while satisfying *ineqs*
+ Maximize[{*expr*, *ineq*}, {*x*, *y*, ... }]	maximize *expr* while satisfying *ineqs*

Constrained minimization and maximization.

This gives the maximum, together with where it occurs.

In[5]:= **Maximize[{x^2 + y, x^2 + y^2 <= 1}, {x, y}]**

$Out[5]= \ \left\{\frac{5}{4}, \ \left\{x \rightarrow -\frac{\sqrt{3}}{2}, \ y \rightarrow \frac{1}{2}\right\}\right\}$

▪ 1.5.9 Differential Equations

DSolve[*eqns*, y[x], x]	solve a differential equation for y[x], taking x as the independent variable
DSolve[*eqns*, y, x]	give a solution for y in pure function form

Solving an ordinary differential equation.

Here is the solution to the differential equation $y'(x) = ay(x) + 1$. C[1] is a coefficient which must be determined from boundary conditions.

In[1]:= **DSolve[y'[x] == a y[x] + 1, y[x], x]**

Out[1]= $\left\{\left\{y[x] \to -\frac{1}{a} + e^{ax} C[1]\right\}\right\}$

If you include an appropriate initial condition, there are no undetermined coefficients in the solution.

In[2]:= **DSolve[{y'[x] == a y[x] + 1, y[0] == 0}, y[x], x]**

Out[2]= $\left\{\left\{y[x] \to \frac{-1 + e^{ax}}{a}\right\}\right\}$

Whereas algebraic equations such as $x^2 + x = 1$ are equations for *variables*, differential equations such as $y''(x) + y'(x) = y(x)$ are equations for *functions*. In *Mathematica*, you must always give differential equations explicitly in terms of functions such as y[x], and you must specify the variables such as x on which the functions depend. As a result, you must write an equation such as $y''(x) + y'(x) = y(x)$ in the form y''[x] + y'[x] == y[x]. You cannot write it as y'' + y' == y.

Mathematica can solve both linear and nonlinear ordinary differential equations, as well as lists of simultaneous equations. If you do not specify enough initial or boundary conditions, *Mathematica* will give solutions that involve an appropriate number of undetermined coefficients. Each time you use DSolve, it names the undetermined coefficients C[1], C[2], etc.

Here is a pair of simultaneous differential equations, with no initial or boundary conditions. The solution you get involves two undetermined coefficients.

In[3]:= **DSolve[{x'[t] == y[t], y'[t] == x[t]},**
                         {x[t], y[t]}, t]

Out[3]= $\left\{\left\{x[t] \to \frac{1}{2} e^{-t} (1 + e^{2t}) C[1] + \frac{1}{2} e^{-t} (-1 + e^{2t}) C[2],\right.\right.$
            $\left.\left. y[t] \to \frac{1}{2} e^{-t} (-1 + e^{2t}) C[1] + \frac{1}{2} e^{-t} (1 + e^{2t}) C[2]\right\}\right\}$

When you ask DSolve to get you a solution for y[x], the rules it returns specify how to replace y[x] in any expression. However, these rules do not specify how to replace objects such as y'[x]. If you want to manipulate solutions that you get from DSolve, you will often find it better to ask for solutions for y, rather than for y[x].

This gives the solution for y as a "pure function".

In[4]:= **DSolve[y'[x] == x + y[x], y, x]**

Out[4]= {{y → Function[{x}, -1 - x + e^x C[1]]}}

You can now use the replacement operator to apply this solution to expressions involving y.

In[5]:= **y''[x] + y[x] /. %**

Out[5]= {-1 - x + 2 e^x C[1]}

Section 2.2.5 explains how the "pure function" indicated by & that appears in the result from DSolve works.

Note that DSolve can handle combinations of algebraic and differential equations. It can also handle partial differential equations, in which there is more than one independent variable.

■ 1.5.10 Power Series

The mathematical operations we have discussed so far are *exact*. Given precise input, their results are exact formulas.

In many situations, however, you do not need an exact result. It may be quite sufficient, for example, to find an *approximate* formula that is valid, say, when the quantity x is small.

This gives a power series approximation to $(1 + x)^n$ for x close to 0, up to terms of order x^3.

$In[1]:=$ **Series[(1 + x)^n, {x, 0, 3}]**

$Out[1]=$ $1 + n x + \frac{1}{2} (-1 + n) n x^2 + \frac{1}{6} (-2 + n) (-1 + n) n x^3 + O[x]^4$

Mathematica knows the power series expansions for many mathematical functions.

$In[2]:=$ **Series[Exp[-a t] (1 + Sin[2 t]), {t, 0, 4}]**

$Out[2]=$ $1 + (2 - a) t + \left(-2a + \frac{a^2}{2}\right) t^2 +$
$\left(-\frac{4}{3} + a^2 - \frac{a^3}{6}\right) t^3 + \left(\frac{4a}{3} - \frac{a^3}{3} + \frac{a^4}{24}\right) t^4 + O[t]^5$

If you give it a function that it does not know, Series writes out the power series in terms of derivatives.

$In[3]:=$ **Series[1 + f[t], {t, 0, 3}]**

$Out[3]=$ $1 + f[0] + f'[0] t + \frac{1}{2} f''[0] t^2 + \frac{1}{6} f^{(3)}[0] t^3 + O[t]^4$

Power series are approximate formulas that play much the same role with respect to algebraic expressions as approximate numbers play with respect to numerical expressions. *Mathematica* allows you to perform operations on power series, in all cases maintaining the appropriate order or "degree of precision" for the resulting power series.

Here is a simple power series, accurate to order x^5.

$In[4]:=$ **Series[Exp[x], {x, 0, 5}]**

$Out[4]=$ $1 + x + \frac{x^2}{2} + \frac{x^3}{6} + \frac{x^4}{24} + \frac{x^5}{120} + O[x]^6$

When you do operations on a power series, the result is computed only to the appropriate order in x.

$In[5]:=$ **%^2 (1 + %)**

$Out[5]=$ $2 + 5 x + \frac{13 x^2}{2} + \frac{35 x^3}{6} + \frac{97 x^4}{24} + \frac{55 x^5}{24} + O[x]^6$

This turns the power series back into an ordinary expression.

$In[6]:=$ **Normal[%]**

$Out[6]=$ $2 + 5 x + \frac{13 x^2}{2} + \frac{35 x^3}{6} + \frac{97 x^4}{24} + \frac{55 x^5}{24}$

Now the square is computed *exactly*.

$In[7]:=$ **%^2**

$Out[7]= \left(2 + 5x + \frac{13x^2}{2} + \frac{35x^3}{6} + \frac{97x^4}{24} + \frac{55x^5}{24}\right)^2$

Applying Expand gives a result with eleven terms.

$In[8]:=$ **Expand[%]**

$Out[8]= 4 + 20x + 51x^2 + \frac{265x^3}{3} + \frac{467x^4}{4} + \frac{1505x^5}{12} +$
$\frac{7883x^6}{72} + \frac{1385x^7}{18} + \frac{24809x^8}{576} + \frac{5335x^9}{288} + \frac{3025x^{10}}{576}$

`Series[`*expr*`, {`*x*`,` x_0`,` *n*`}]`	find the power series expansion of *expr* about the point $x = x_0$ to at most n^{th} order
`Normal[`*series*`]`	truncate a power series to give an ordinary expression

Power series operations.

■ 1.5.11 Limits

Here is the expression $\sin(x)/x$.

$In[1]:=$ **t = Sin[x]/x**

$Out[1]= \dfrac{Sin[x]}{x}$

If you replace x by 0, the expression becomes 0/0, and you get an indeterminate result.

$In[2]:=$ **t /. x->0**

```
                                 1
Power::infy: Infinite expression - encountered.
                                 0
Infinity::indet:
    Indeterminate expression 0 ComplexInfinity encountered.
```

$Out[2]=$ Indeterminate

If you find the numerical value of $\sin(x)/x$ for x close to 0, however, you get a result that is close to 1.

$In[3]:=$ **t /. x->0.01**

$Out[3]= 0.999983$

This finds the *limit* of $\sin(x)/x$ as x approaches 0. The result is indeed 1.

$In[4]:=$ **Limit[t, x->0]**

$Out[4]= 1$

`Limit[`*expr*`,` *x*`->`x_0`]`	the limit of *expr* as x approaches x_0

Limits.

■ 1.5.12 Integral Transforms

LaplaceTransform[*expr*, *t*, *s*]	find the Laplace transform of *expr*
InverseLaplaceTransform[*expr*, *s*, *t*]	
	find the inverse Laplace transform of *expr*

Laplace transforms.

This computes a Laplace transform.

In[1]:= **LaplaceTransform[t^3 Exp[a t], t, s]**

$$Out[1]= \frac{6}{(a-s)^4}$$

Here is the inverse transform.

In[2]:= **InverseLaplaceTransform[%, s, t]**

$$Out[2]= e^{a\,t}\,t^3$$

FourierTransform[*expr*, *t*, *w*]	find the symbolic Fourier transform of *expr*
InverseFourierTransform[*expr*, *w*, *t*]	
	find the inverse Fourier transform of *expr*

Fourier transforms.

This computes a Fourier transform.

In[3]:= **FourierTransform[t^4 Exp[-t^2], t, w]**

$$Out[3]= \frac{\frac{3}{4}\,e^{-\frac{w^2}{4}} - \frac{3}{4}\,e^{-\frac{w^2}{4}}\,w^2 + \frac{1}{16}\,e^{-\frac{w^2}{4}}\,w^4}{\sqrt{2}}$$

Here is the inverse transform.

In[4]:= **InverseFourierTransform[%, w, t]**

$$Out[4]= e^{-t^2}\,t^4$$

Note that in the scientific and technical literature many different conventions are used for defining Fourier transforms. Page 936 describes the setup in *Mathematica*.

■ 1.5.13 Recurrence Equations

RSolve[*eqns*, *a*[*n*], *n*]	solve the recurrence equations *eqns* for *a*[*n*]

Solving recurrence equations.

This solves a simple recurrence equation.

In[1]:= **RSolve[{a[n] == 3 a[n-1]+1, a[1]==1}, a[n], n]**

$$Out[1]= \left\{\left\{a[n] \to \frac{1}{2}\,(-1 + 3^n)\right\}\right\}$$

■ 1.5.14 Packages for Symbolic Mathematics

There are many *Mathematica* packages which implement symbolic mathematical operations. This section gives a few examples drawn from the standard set of packages distributed with *Mathematica*. As discussed in Section 1.3.10, some copies of *Mathematica* may be set up so that the functions described here are automatically loaded into *Mathematica* if they are ever needed.

Vector Analysis

`<<Calculus`VectorAnalysis``	load the vector analysis package
`SetCoordinates[`*system*`[`*names*`]]`	specify the coordinate system to be used (`Cartesian`, `Cylindrical`, `Spherical`, etc.), giving the names of the coordinates in that system
`Grad[`*f*`]`	evaluate the gradient ∇f of f in the coordinate system chosen
`Div[`*f*`]`	evaluate the divergence $\nabla \cdot f$ of the list f
`Curl[`*f*`]`	evaluate the curl $\nabla \times f$ of the list f
`Laplacian[`*f*`]`	evaluate the Laplacian $\nabla^2 f$ of f

Vector analysis.

This loads the vector analysis package. In some versions of *Mathematica*, you may not need to load the package explicitly.

```
In[1]:= <<Calculus`VectorAnalysis`
```

This specifies that a spherical coordinate system with coordinate names r, theta and phi should be used.

```
In[2]:= SetCoordinates[Spherical[r, theta, phi]]
Out[2]= Spherical[r, theta, phi]
```

This evaluates the gradient of $r^2 \sin(\theta)$ in the spherical coordinate system.

```
In[3]:= Grad[r^2 Sin[theta]]
Out[3]= {2 r Sin[theta], r Cos[theta], 0}
```

＋ Variational Methods

`<<Calculus`VariationalMethods``	load the variational methods package
`VariationalD[f, y[x], x]`	find the variational derivative of f

Variational methods.

This loads the variational methods package.

$In[1]:=$ `<<Calculus`VariationalMethods``

This finds the functional derivative of $y(x)\sqrt{y'(x)}$.

$In[2]:=$ `VariationalD[y[x] Sqrt[y'[x]], y[x], x]`

$$Out[2]= \frac{2\, y'\,[x]^2 + y[x]\, y''\,[x]}{4\, y'\,[x]^{3/2}}$$

＋ Quaternions

`<<Algebra`Quaternions``	load the quaternions package
`Quaternion[a, b, c, d]`	the quaternion $a + bi + cj + dk$

Quaternions.

This loads the quaternions package.

$In[1]:=$ `<<Algebra`Quaternions``

This finds the principal square root of a quaternion.

$In[2]:=$ `Sqrt[Quaternion[1, 1, 1, 0]]`

$$Out[2]= \text{Quaternion}\left[3^{1/4} \cos\left[\frac{\text{ArcTan}\left[\sqrt{2}\right]}{2}\right],\right.$$

$$\left.\frac{3^{1/4} \sin\left[\frac{\text{ArcTan}\left[\sqrt{2}\right]}{2}\right]}{\sqrt{2}}, \frac{3^{1/4} \sin\left[\frac{\text{ArcTan}\left[\sqrt{2}\right]}{2}\right]}{\sqrt{2}}, 0\right]$$

■ 1.5.15 Advanced Topic: Generic and Non-Generic Cases

This gives a result for the integral of x^n that is valid for almost all values of n.

$In[1]:=$ `Integrate[x^n, x]`

$$Out[1]= \frac{x^{1+n}}{1+n}$$

For the special case of x^{-1}, however, the correct result is different.

$In[2]:=$ `Integrate[x^-1, x]`

$Out[2]=$ `Log[x]`

The overall goal of symbolic computation is typically to get formulas that are valid for many possible values of the variables that appear in them. It is however often not practical to try to get formulas that are valid for absolutely every possible value of each variable.

Mathematica always replaces $0/x$ by 0.	`In[3]:= 0 / x`
	
	`Out[3]= 0`

If x is equal to 0, however, then the true result is not 0.	`In[4]:= 0 / 0`
	
	                                      1
	`Power::infy: Infinite expression - encountered.`
	                                      0
	
	`Infinity::indet:`
	    `Indeterminate expression 0 ComplexInfinity encountered.`
	
	`Out[4]= Indeterminate`

This construct treats both cases, but would be quite unwieldy to use.	`In[5]:= If[x != 0, 0, Indeterminate]`
	
	`Out[5]= If[x ≠ 0, 0, Indeterminate]`

If *Mathematica* did not automatically replace $0/x$ by 0, then few symbolic computations would get very far. But you should realize that the practical necessity of making such replacements can cause misleading results to be obtained when exceptional values of parameters are used.

The basic operations of *Mathematica* are nevertheless carefully set up so that whenever possible the results obtained will be valid for almost all values of each variable.

$\sqrt{x^2}$ is not automatically replaced by x.	`In[6]:= Sqrt[x^2]` `Out[6]=` $\sqrt{x^2}$

If it were, then the result here would be -2, which is incorrect.	`In[7]:= % /. x -> -2`
	
	`Out[7]= 2`

This makes the assumption that x is a positive real variable, and does the replacement.	`In[8]:= Simplify[Sqrt[x^2], x > 0]`
	
	`Out[8]= x`

■ **1.5.16 Mathematical Notation in Notebooks**

If you use the notebook front end for *Mathematica*, then you can enter some of the operations discussed in this section in special ways.

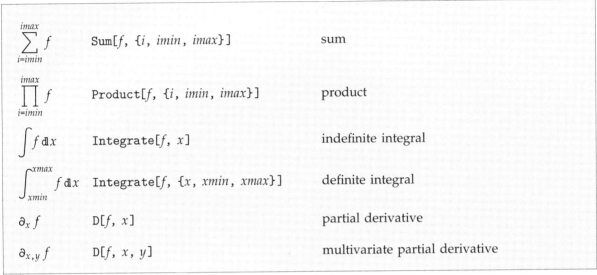

Special and ordinary ways to enter mathematical operations in notebooks.

This shows part of the standard palette for entering mathematical operations. When you press a button in the palette, the form shown in the button is inserted into your notebook, with the black square replaced by whatever you had selected in the notebook.

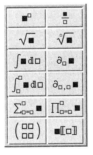

ESC sum ESC	summation sign $\sum$
ESC prod ESC	product sign $\prod$
ESC int ESC	integral sign $\int$
ESC dd ESC	special differential d for use in integrals
ESC pd ESC	partial derivative ∂

CTRL _ or CTRL -	move to the subscript position or lower limit of an integral
CTRL ^ or CTRL 6	move to the superscript position or upper limit of an integral
CTRL + or CTRL =	move to the underscript position or lower limit of a sum or product
CTRL & or CTRL 7	move to the overscript position or upper limit of a sum or product

CTRL % or CTRL 5	switch between upper and lower positions
CTRL ␣ (CONTROL-SPACE)	return from upper or lower positions

Ways to enter special notations on a standard English-language keyboard.

You can enter an integral like this. Be sure to use the special differential d entered as ESC dd ESC, not just an ordinary d.

$$In[1]:= \int x^n \, dx$$

$$Out[1]= \frac{x^{1+n}}{1+n}$$

Here is the actual key sequence you type to get the input.

$$In[2]:= \text{ESC int ESC } x \text{ CTRL ^ } n \text{ CTRL ␣ ESC dd ESC } x$$

$$Out[2]= \frac{x^{1+n}}{1+n}$$

1.6 Numerical Mathematics

◼ 1.6.1 Basic Operations

Exact symbolic results are usually very desirable when they can be found. In many calculations, however, it is not possible to get symbolic results. In such cases, you must resort to numerical methods.

N[*expr*]	numerical value of an expression (see Section 1.1)
NIntegrate[*f*, {*x*, *xmin*, *xmax*}]	numerical approximation to $\int_{xmin}^{xmax} f\, dx$
NSum[*f*, {*i*, *imin*, Infinity}]	numerical approximation to $\sum_{imin}^{\infty} f$
FindRoot[*lhs*==*rhs*, {*x*, x_0}]	search for a numerical solution to an equation, starting with $x = x_0$
NSolve[*lhs*==*rhs*, *x*]	numerical approximations to all solutions of an equation
FindMinimum[*f*, {*x*, x_0}]	search for a minimum of *f*, starting with $x = x_0$
NMinimize[*f*, *x*]	attempt to find the global minimum of *f*

Basic numerical operations.

Mathematica maintains this expression in an exact, symbolic, form.	In[1]:= **(3 + Sqrt[2])^3**
	Out[1]= $\left(3 + \sqrt{2}\right)^3$
You can even use standard symbolic operations on it.	In[2]:= **Expand[%]**
	Out[2]= $45 + 29\sqrt{2}$
N[*expr*] gives you a numerical approximation.	In[3]:= **N[%]**
	Out[3]= 86.0122

Functions such as Integrate always try to get exact results for computations. When they cannot get exact results, they typically return unevaluated. You can then find numerical approximations by explicitly applying N. Functions such as NIntegrate do the calculations numerically from the start, without first trying to get an exact result.

There is no exact formula for this integral, so *Mathematica* returns it unevaluated.

In[4]:= **Integrate[Sin[Sin[x]], {x, 1, 2}]**

$Out[4]= \int_1^2 Sin[Sin[x]] \, dx$

You can use N to get an approximate numerical result.

In[5]:= **N[%]**

Out[5]= 0.81645

NIntegrate does the integral numerically from the start.

In[6]:= **NIntegrate[Sin[Sin[x]], {x, 1, 2}]**

Out[6]= 0.81645

■ 1.6.2 Numerical Sums, Products and Integrals

NSum[*f*, {*i*, *imin*, Infinity}]	numerical approximation to $\sum_{imin}^{\infty} f$
NProduct[*f*, {*i*, *imin*, Infinity}]	numerical approximation to $\prod_{imin}^{\infty} f$
NIntegrate[*f*, {*x*, *xmin*, *xmax*}]	numerical approximation to $\int_{xmin}^{xmax} f \, dx$
NIntegrate[*f*, {*x*, *xmin*, *xmax*}, {*y*, *ymin*, *ymax*}]	the multiple integral $\int_{xmin}^{xmax} dx \int_{ymin}^{ymax} dy \, f$

Numerical sums, products and integrals.

Here is a numerical approximation to $\sum_{i=1}^{\infty} \frac{1}{i^3}$.

In[1]:= **NSum[1/i^3, {i, 1, Infinity}]**

Out[1]= 1.20206

NIntegrate can handle singularities at the end points of the integration region.

In[2]:= **NIntegrate[1/Sqrt[x (1-x)], {x, 0, 1}]**

$Out[2]= 3.14159 - 1.65678 \times 10^{-48} \, i$

You can do numerical integrals over infinite regions.

In[3]:= **NIntegrate[Exp[-x^2], {x, -Infinity, Infinity}]**

Out[3]= 1.77245

Here is a double integral over a triangular domain. Note the order in which the variables are given.

In[4]:= **NIntegrate[Sin[x y], {x, 0, 1}, {y, 0, x}]**

Out[4]= 0.119906

■ 1.6.3 Numerical Equation Solving

NSolve[*lhs*==*rhs*, *x*]	solve a polynomial equation numerically
NSolve[{*lhs*$_1$==*rhs*$_1$, *lhs*$_2$==*rhs*$_2$, ... }, {*x*, *y*, ... }]	
	solve a system of polynomial equations numerically
FindRoot[*lhs*==*rhs*, {*x*, *x*$_0$}]	search for a numerical solution to an equation, starting at $x = x_0$
FindRoot[{*lhs*$_1$==*rhs*$_1$, *lhs*$_2$==*rhs*$_2$, ... }, {{*x*, *x*$_0$}, {*y*, *y*$_0$}, ... }]	
	search for numerical solutions to simultaneous equations

Numerical root finding.

NSolve gives you numerical approximations to all the roots of a polynomial equation.

```
In[1]:= NSolve[ x^5 + x + 1 == 0, x ]
```
$Out[1]=$ {{x → -0.754878}, {x → -0.5 - 0.866025 i},
           {x → -0.5 + 0.866025 i}, {x → 0.877439 - 0.744862 i},
           {x → 0.877439 + 0.744862 i}}

You can also use NSolve to solve sets of simultaneous equations numerically.

```
In[2]:= NSolve[{x + y == 2, x - 3 y + z == 3, x - y + z == 0},
          {x, y, z}]
```
$Out[2]=$ {{x → 3.5, y → -1.5, z → -5.}}

If your equations involve only linear functions or polynomials, then you can use NSolve to get numerical approximations to all the solutions. However, when your equations involve more complicated functions, there is in general no systematic procedure for finding all solutions, even numerically. In such cases, you can use FindRoot to search for solutions. You have to give FindRoot a place to start its search.

This searches for a numerical solution, starting at $x = 1$.

```
In[3]:= FindRoot[ 3 Cos[x] == Log[x], {x, 1} ]
```
$Out[3]=$ {x → 1.44726}

The equation has several solutions. If you start at a different x, FindRoot may return a different solution.

```
In[4]:= FindRoot[ 3 Cos[x] == Log[x], {x, 10} ]
```
$Out[4]=$ {x → 13.1064}

You can search for solutions to sets of equations. Here the solution involves complex numbers.

```
In[5]:= FindRoot[{x==Log[y], y==Log[x]}, {{x, I}, {y, 2}}]
```
$Out[5]=$ {x → 0.318132 + 1.33724 i, y → 0.318132 + 1.33724 i}

■ 1.6.4 Numerical Differential Equations

> NDSolve[*eqns*, *y*, {*x*, *xmin*, *xmax*}]
>
> solve numerically for the function *y*, with the independent variable *x* in the range *xmin* to *xmax*
>
> NDSolve[*eqns*, {y_1, y_2, ... }, {*x*, *xmin*, *xmax*}]
>
> solve a system of equations for the y_i

Numerical solution of differential equations.

This generates a numerical solution to the equation $y'(x) = y(x)$ with $0 < x < 2$. The result is given in terms of an InterpolatingFunction.

```
In[1]:= NDSolve[{y'[x] == y[x], y[0] == 1}, y, {x, 0, 2}]
Out[1]= {{y → InterpolatingFunction[{{0., 2.}}, <>]}}
```

Here is the value of $y(1.5)$.

```
In[2]:= y[1.5] /. %
Out[2]= {4.48169}
```

With an algebraic equation such as $x^2 + 3x + 1 = 0$, each solution for *x* is simply a single number. For a differential equation, however, the solution is a *function*, rather than a single number. For example, in the equation $y'(x) = y(x)$, you want to get an approximation to the function $y(x)$ as the independent variable *x* varies over some range.

Mathematica represents numerical approximations to functions as InterpolatingFunction objects. These objects are functions which, when applied to a particular *x*, return the approximate value of $y(x)$ at that point. The InterpolatingFunction effectively stores a table of values for $y(x_i)$, then interpolates this table to find an approximation to $y(x)$ at the particular *x* you request.

> *y*[*x*] /. *solution*   use the list of rules for the function *y* to get values for *y*[*x*]
>
> InterpolatingFunction[*data*][*x*]
>
> evaluate an interpolated function at the point *x*
>
> Plot[Evaluate[*y*[*x*] /. *solution*], {*x*, *xmin*, *xmax*}]
>
> plot the solution to a differential equation

Using results from NDSolve.

This solves a system of two coupled differential equations.

```
In[3]:= NDSolve[ {y'[x] == z[x], z'[x] == -y[x], y[0] == 0,
                  z[0] == 1}, {y, z}, {x, 0, Pi} ]
Out[3]= {{y → InterpolatingFunction[{{0., 3.14159}}, <>],
          z → InterpolatingFunction[{{0., 3.14159}}, <>]}}
```

Here is the value of z[2] found from the solution.

```
In[4]:= z[2] /. %
Out[4]= {-0.416147}
```

Here is a plot of the solution for z[x] found on line 3. Plot is discussed in Section 1.9.1.

$In[5]:=$ **Plot[Evaluate[z[x] /. %3], {x, 0, Pi}]**

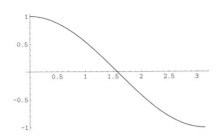

NDSolve[*eqn*, *u*, {*x*, *xmin*, *xmax*}, {*t*, *tmin*, *tmax*}, ...]
                    solve a partial differential equation

Numerical solution of partial differential equations.

■ 1.6.5 Numerical Optimization

+	NMinimize[*f*, {*x*, *y*, ... }]	minimize *f*
+	NMaximize[*f*, {*x*, *y*, ... }]	maximize *f*
+	NMinimize[{*f*, *ineqs*}, {*x*, *y*, ... }]	minimize *f* subject to the constraints *ineqs*
+	NMaximize[{*f*, *ineqs*}, {*x*, *y*, ... }]	maximize *f* subject to the constraints *ineqs*

Finding global minima and maxima.

This gives the maximum value, and where it occurs.

$In[1]:=$ **NMaximize[x/(1 + Exp[x]), x]**

$Out[1]=$ {0.278465, {x → 1.27846}}

This minimizes the function within the unit circle.

$In[2]:=$ **NMinimize[{Cos[x] - Exp[x y], x^2 + y^2 < 1}, {x, y}]**

$Out[2]=$ {-0.919441, {x → 0.795976, y → 0.605328}}

NMinimize and NMaximize can find the absolute minima and maxima of many functions. But in some cases it is not realistic to do this. You can search for local minima and maxima using FindMinimum and FindMaximum.

FindMinimum[f, {x, x_0}]   search for a local minimum of f, starting at $x = x_0$

FindMinimum[f, {{x, x_0}, {y, y_0}, ... }]
           search for a local minimum in several variables

+   FindMaximum[f, {x, x_0}]   search for a local maximum

Searching for local minima and maxima.

This searches for a local minimum of $x\cos(x)$, starting at $x = 2$.

```
In[3]:= FindMinimum[x Cos[x], {x, 2}]
Out[3]= {-3.28837, {x → 3.42562}}
```

With a different starting point, you may reach a different local minimum.

```
In[4]:= FindMinimum[x Cos[x], {x, 10}]
Out[4]= {-9.47729, {x → 9.52933}}
```

This finds a local minimum of $\sin(xy)$.

```
In[5]:= FindMinimum[Sin[x y], {{x, 2}, {y, 2}}]
Out[5]= {-1., {x → 2.1708, y → 2.1708}}
```

■ 1.6.6 Manipulating Numerical Data

When you have numerical data, it is often convenient to find a simple formula that approximates it. For example, you can try to "fit" a line or curve through the points in your data.

Fit[{y_1, y_2, ... }, {f_1, f_2, ... }, x]
           fit the values y_n to a linear combination of functions f_i

Fit[{{x_1, y_1}, {x_2, y_2}, ... }, {f_1, f_2, ... }, x]
           fit the points (x_n, y_n) to a linear combination of the f_i

Fitting curves to linear combinations of functions.

This generates a table of the numerical values of the exponential function. Table will be discussed in Section 1.8.2.

```
In[1]:= data = Table[ Exp[x/5.] , {x, 7}]
Out[1]= {1.2214, 1.49182, 1.82212,
          2.22554, 2.71828, 3.32012, 4.0552}
```

This finds a least-squares fit to data of the form $c_1 + c_2 x + c_3 x^2$. The elements of data are assumed to correspond to values 1, 2, ... of x.

```
In[2]:= Fit[data, {1, x, x^2}, x]
Out[2]= 1.09428 + 0.0986337 x + 0.0459482 x²
```

This finds a fit of the form $c_1 + c_2 x + c_3 x^3 + c_4 x^5$.

```
In[3]:= Fit[data, {1, x, x^3, x^5}, x]
Out[3]= 0.96806 + 0.246829 x + 0.00428281 x³ - 6.57948 × 10⁻⁶ x⁵
```

This gives a table of x, y pairs.

```
In[4]:= data = Table[ {x, Exp[Sin[x]]} , {x, 0., 1., 0.2}]

Out[4]= {{0., 1.}, {0.2, 1.21978}, {0.4, 1.47612},
          {0.6, 1.75882}, {0.8, 2.04901}, {1., 2.31978}}
```

This finds a fit to the new data, of the form $c_1 + c_2 \sin(x) + c_3 \sin(2x)$.

```
In[5]:= Fit[%, {1, Sin[x], Sin[2x]}, x]

Out[5]= 0.989559 + 2.04199 Sin[x] - 0.418176 Sin[2 x]
```

| + | FindFit[*data*, *form*, {p_1, p_2, ... }, x] | find a fit to *form* with parameters p_i |

Fitting data to general forms.

This finds the best parameters for a linear fit.

```
In[6]:= FindFit[data, a + b x + c x^2, {a, b, c}, x]

Out[6]= {a → 0.991251, b → 1.16421, c → 0.174256}
```

This does a nonlinear fit.

```
In[7]:= FindFit[data, a + b^(c + d x), {a, b, c, d}, x]

Out[7]= {a → -3.65199, b → 1.65713,
          c → 3.03947, d → 0.501815}
```

One common way of picking out "signals" in numerical data is to find the *Fourier transform*, or frequency spectrum, of the data.

| Fourier[*data*] | numerical Fourier transform |
| InverseFourier[*data*] | inverse Fourier transform |

Fourier transforms.

Here is a simple square pulse.

```
In[8]:= data = {1, 1, 1, 1, -1, -1, -1, -1}

Out[8]= {1, 1, 1, 1, -1, -1, -1, -1}
```

This takes the Fourier transform of the pulse.

```
In[9]:= Fourier[data]

Out[9]= {0. + 0. i, 0.707107 + 1.70711 i,
          0. + 0. i, 0.707107 + 0.292893 i, 0. + 0. i,
          0.707107 - 0.292893 i, 0. + 0. i, 0.707107 - 1.70711 i}
```

Note that the Fourier function in *Mathematica* is defined with the sign convention typically used in the physical sciences—opposite to the one often used in electrical engineering. Section 3.8.4 gives more details.

■ 1.6.7 Statistics

+	Mean[*data*]	mean (average value)
+	Median[*data*]	median (central value)
+	Variance[*data*]	variance
+	StandardDeviation[*data*]	standard deviation
+	Quantile[*data*, *q*]	q^{th} quantile
+	Total[*data*]	total of values

Basic descriptive statistics.

Here is some "data".

```
In[1]:= data = {4.3, 7.2, 8.4, 5.8, 9.2, 3.9}
Out[1]= {4.3, 7.2, 8.4, 5.8, 9.2, 3.9}
```

This gives the mean of your data.

```
In[2]:= Mean[data]
Out[2]= 6.46667
```

Here is the variance.

```
In[3]:= Variance[data]
Out[3]= 4.69467
```

The standard set of packages distributed with *Mathematica* includes several for doing more sophisticated statistical analyses of data.

Statistics`DescriptiveStatistics`	descriptive statistics functions
Statistics`MultivariateDescriptiveStatistics`	
	multivariate descriptive statistics functions
Statistics`ContinuousDistributions`	properties of continuous statistical distributions
Statistics`DiscreteDistributions`	properties of discrete statistical distributions
Statistics`HypothesisTests`	hypothesis tests based on the normal distribution
Statistics`ConfidenceIntervals`	confidence intervals derived from the normal distribution
Statistics`MultinormalDistribution`	properties of distributions based on the multivariate normal distribution
Statistics`LinearRegression`	linear regression analysis
Statistics`NonlinearFit`	nonlinear fitting of data
Statistics`DataSmoothing`	smoothing of data
Statistics`DataManipulation`	utilities for data manipulation

Some standard statistical analysis packages.

1.7 Functions and Programs

■ 1.7.1 Defining Functions

In this part of the book, we have seen many examples of functions that are built into *Mathematica*. In this section, we discuss how you can add your own simple functions to *Mathematica*. Part 2 will describe in much greater detail the mechanisms for adding functions to *Mathematica*.

As a first example, consider adding a function called f which squares its argument. The *Mathematica* command to define this function is f[x_] := x^2. The _ (referred to as "blank") on the left-hand side is very important; what it means will be discussed below. For now, just remember to put a _ on the left-hand side, but not on the right-hand side, of your definition.

This defines the function f. Notice the _ on the left-hand side.	*In[1]:=* **f[x_] := x^2**
f squares its argument.	*In[2]:=* **f[a+1]**
	Out[2]= $(1 + a)^2$
The argument can be a number.	*In[3]:=* **f[4]**
	Out[3]= 16
Or it can be a more complicated expression.	*In[4]:=* **f[3x + x^2]**
	Out[4]= $(3x + x^2)^2$
You can use f in a calculation.	*In[5]:=* **Expand[f[(x+1+y)]]**
	Out[5]= $1 + 2x + x^2 + 2y + 2xy + y^2$
This shows the definition you made for f.	*In[6]:=* **?f**
	Global`f
	f[x_] := x^2

f[x_] := x^2	define the function f
?f	show the definition of *f*
Clear[*f*]	clear all definitions for *f*

Defining a function in *Mathematica*.

The names like f that you use for functions in *Mathematica* are just symbols. Because of this, you should make sure to avoid using names that begin with capital letters, to prevent confusion with built-in *Mathematica* functions. You should also make sure that you have not used the names for anything else earlier in your session.

Mathematica functions can have any number of arguments.	*In[7]:=* **hump[x_, xmax_] := (x - xmax)^2 / xmax**
You can use the hump function just as you would any of the built-in functions.	*In[8]:=* **2 + hump[x, 3.5]** *Out[8]=* $2 + 0.285714 (-3.5 + x)^2$
This gives a new definition for hump, which overwrites the previous one.	*In[9]:=* **hump[x_, xmax_] := (x - xmax)^4**
The new definition is displayed.	*In[10]:=* **?hump** Global`hump hump[x_, xmax_] := (x - xmax)^4
This clears all definitions for hump.	*In[11]:=* **Clear[hump]**

When you have finished with a particular function, it is always a good idea to clear definitions you have made for it. If you do not do this, then you will run into trouble if you try to use the same function for a different purpose later in your *Mathematica* session. You can clear all definitions you have made for a function or symbol f by using Clear[f].

■ 1.7.2 Functions as Procedures

In many kinds of calculations, you may find yourself typing the same input to *Mathematica* over and over again. You can save yourself a lot of typing by defining a *function* that contains your input commands.

This constructs a product of three terms, and expands out the result.	*In[1]:=* **Expand[Product[x + i, {i, 3}]]** *Out[1]=* $6 + 11 x + 6 x^2 + x^3$
This does the same thing, but with four terms.	*In[2]:=* **Expand[Product[x + i, {i, 4}]]** *Out[2]=* $24 + 50 x + 35 x^2 + 10 x^3 + x^4$
This defines a function exprod which constructs a product of n terms, then expands it out.	*In[3]:=* **exprod[n_] := Expand[Product[x + i, {i, 1, n}]]**
Every time you use the function, it will execute the Product and Expand operations.	*In[4]:=* **exprod[5]** *Out[4]=* $120 + 274 x + 225 x^2 + 85 x^3 + 15 x^4 + x^5$

The functions you define in *Mathematica* are essentially procedures that execute the commands you give. You can have several steps in your procedures, separated by semicolons.

The result you get from the whole function is simply the last expression in the procedure. Notice that you have to put parentheses around the procedure when you define it like this.

```
In[5]:= cex[n_, i_] := ( t = exprod[n]; Coefficient[t, x^i] )
```

This "runs" the procedure.

```
In[6]:= cex[5, 3]
Out[6]= 85
```

$expr_1$; $expr_2$; ...	a sequence of expressions to evaluate
Module[{a, b, ... }, proc]	a procedure with local variables a, b, ...

Constructing procedures.

When you write procedures in *Mathematica*, it is usually a good idea to make variables you use inside the procedures *local*, so that they do not interfere with things outside the procedures. You can do this by setting up your procedures as *modules*, in which you give a list of variables to be treated as local.

The function cex defined above is not a module, so the value of t "escapes", and exists even after the function returns.

```
In[7]:= t
Out[7]= 120 + 274 x + 225 x^2 + 85 x^3 + 15 x^4 + x^5
```

This function is defined as a module with local variable u.

```
In[8]:= ncex[n_, i_] :=
              Module[{u}, u = exprod[n]; Coefficient[u, x^i]]
```

The function gives the same result as before.

```
In[9]:= ncex[5, 3]
Out[9]= 85
```

Now, however, the value of u does not escape from the function.

```
In[10]:= u
Out[10]= u
```

■ 1.7.3 Repetitive Operations

In using *Mathematica*, you sometimes need to repeat an operation many times. There are many ways to do this. Often the most natural is in fact to set up a structure such as a list with many elements, and then apply your operation to each of the elements.

Another approach is to use the *Mathematica* function Do, which works much like the iteration constructs in languages such as C and Fortran. Do uses the standard *Mathematica* iterator notation introduced for Sum and Product in Section 1.5.4.

Do[*expr*, {*i*, *imax*}]	evaluate *expr* with *i* running from 1 to *imax*
Do[*expr*, {*i*, *imin*, *imax*, *di*}]	evaluate *expr* with *i* running from *imin* to *imax* in steps of *di*
Print[*expr*]	print *expr*
Table[*expr*, {*i*, *imax*}]	make a list of the values of *expr* with *i* running from 1 to *imax*

Implementing repetitive operations.

This prints out the values of the first five factorials.

In[1]:= **Do[Print[i!], {i, 5}]**

```
1
2
6
24
120
```

It is often more useful to have a list of results, which you can then manipulate further.

In[2]:= **Table[i!, {i, 5}]**

Out[2]= {1, 2, 6, 24, 120}

If you do not give an iteration variable, *Mathematica* simply repeats the operation you have specified, without changing anything.

In[3]:= **r = 1; Do[r = 1/(1 + r), {100}]; r**

Out[3]= $\dfrac{573147844013817084101}{927372692193078999176}$

■ 1.7.4 Transformation Rules for Functions

Section 1.4.2 discussed how you can use transformation rules of the form x -> *value* to replace symbols by values. The notion of transformation rules in *Mathematica* is, however, quite general. You can set up transformation rules not only for symbols, but for any *Mathematica* expression.

Applying the transformation rule x -> 3 replaces x by 3.

In[1]:= **1 + f[x] + f[y] /. x -> 3**

Out[1]= 1 + f[3] + f[y]

You can also use a transformation rule for f[x]. This rule does not affect f[y].

In[2]:= **1 + f[x] + f[y] /. f[x] -> p**

Out[2]= 1 + p + f[y]

f[t_] is a *pattern* that stands for f with any argument.

In[3]:= **1 + f[x] + f[y] /. f[t_] -> t^2**

Out[3]= $1 + x^2 + y^2$

Probably the most powerful aspect of transformation rules in *Mathematica* is that they can involve not only literal expressions, but also *patterns*. A pattern is an expression such as f[t_] which contains a blank (underscore). The blank can stand for any expression. Thus, a transformation rule for f[t_] specifies how the function f with *any* argument should be transformed. Notice that, in contrast, a transformation rule for f[x] without a blank, specifies only how the literal expression f[x] should be transformed, and does not, for example, say anything about the transformation of f[y].

When you give a function definition such as `f[t_] := t^2`, all you are doing is telling *Mathematica* to automatically apply the transformation rule `f[t_] -> t^2` whenever possible.

You can set up transformation rules for expressions of any form.	`In[4]:= f[a b] + f[c d] /. f[x_ y_] -> f[x] + f[y]`
	`Out[4]= f[a] + f[b] + f[c] + f[d]`
This uses a transformation rule for `x^p_`.	`In[5]:= 1 + x^2 + x^4 /. x^p_ -> f[p]`
	`Out[5]= 1 + f[2] + f[4]`

Sections 2.3 and 2.5 will explain in detail how to set up patterns and transformation rules for any kind of expression. Suffice it to say here that in *Mathematica* all expressions have a definite symbolic structure; transformation rules allow you to transform parts of that structure.

1.8 Lists

■ 1.8.1 Collecting Objects Together

We first encountered lists in Section 1.2.3 as a way of collecting numbers together. In this section, we shall see many different ways to use lists. You will find that lists are some of the most flexible and powerful objects in *Mathematica*. You will see that lists in *Mathematica* represent generalizations of several standard concepts in mathematics and computer science.

At a basic level, what a *Mathematica* list essentially does is to provide a way for you to collect together several expressions of any kind.

Here is a list of numbers.	*In[1]:=* **{2, 3, 4}**
	Out[1]= {2, 3, 4}
This gives a list of symbolic expressions.	*In[2]:=* **x^% - 1**
	Out[2]= {$-1 + x^2$, $-1 + x^3$, $-1 + x^4$}
You can differentiate these expressions.	*In[3]:=* **D[%, x]**
	Out[3]= {$2x$, $3x^2$, $4x^3$}
And then you can find values when x is replaced with 3.	*In[4]:=* **% /. x -> 3**
	Out[4]= {6, 27, 108}

The mathematical functions that are built into *Mathematica* are mostly set up to be "listable" so that they act separately on each element of a list. This is, however, not true of all functions in *Mathematica*. Unless you set it up specially, a new function f that you introduce will treat lists just as single objects. Sections 2.2.4 and 2.2.10 will describe how you can use Map and Thread to apply a function like this separately to each element in a list.

■ 1.8.2 Making Tables of Values

You can use lists as tables of values. You can generate the tables, for example, by evaluating an expression for a sequence of different parameter values.

This gives a table of the values of i^2, with i running from 1 to 6.	*In[1]:=* **Table[i^2, {i, 6}]**
	Out[1]= {1, 4, 9, 16, 25, 36}
Here is a table of $\sin(n/5)$ for n from 0 to 4.	*In[2]:=* **Table[Sin[n/5], {n, 0, 4}]**
	Out[2]= $\left\{0, \sin\left[\frac{1}{5}\right], \sin\left[\frac{2}{5}\right], \sin\left[\frac{3}{5}\right], \sin\left[\frac{4}{5}\right]\right\}$

This gives the numerical values.	*In[3]:=* **N[%]**
	Out[3]= {0., 0.198669, 0.389418, 0.564642, 0.717356}
You can also make tables of formulas.	*In[4]:=* **Table[x^i + 2i, {i, 5}]**
	Out[4]= {2 + x, 4 + x², 6 + x³, 8 + x⁴, 10 + x⁵}

You can also make tables of formulas.

$In[4]:=$ **Table[x^i + 2i, {i, 5}]**

$Out[4]=$ $\{2 + x, 4 + x^2, 6 + x^3, 8 + x^4, 10 + x^5\}$

Table uses exactly the same iterator notation as the functions Sum and Product, which were discussed in Section 1.5.4.

$In[5]:=$ **Product[x^i + 2i, {i, 5}]**

$Out[5]=$ $(2 + x)(4 + x^2)(6 + x^3)(8 + x^4)(10 + x^5)$

This makes a table with values of x running from 0 to 1 in steps of 0.25.

$In[6]:=$ **Table[Sqrt[x], {x, 0, 1, 0.25}]**

$Out[6]=$ {0, 0.5, 0.707107, 0.866025, 1.}

You can perform other operations on the lists you get from Table.

$In[7]:=$ **%^2 + 3**

$Out[7]=$ {3, 3.25, 3.5, 3.75, 4.}

TableForm displays lists in a "tabular" format. Notice that both words in the name TableForm begin with capital letters.

$In[8]:=$ **% // TableForm**

$$
\begin{array}{l}
3 \\
3.25 \\
Out[8]//TableForm=\ 3.5 \\
3.75 \\
4.
\end{array}
$$

All the examples so far have been of tables obtained by varying a single parameter. You can also make tables that involve several parameters. These multidimensional tables are specified using the standard *Mathematica* iterator notation, discussed in Section 1.5.4.

This makes a table of $x^i + y^j$ with i running from 1 to 3 and j running from 1 to 2.

$In[9]:=$ **Table[x^i + y^j, {i, 3}, {j, 2}]**

$Out[9]=$ $\{\{x + y, x + y^2\}, \{x^2 + y, x^2 + y^2\}, \{x^3 + y, x^3 + y^2\}\}$

The table in this example is a *list of lists*. The elements of the outer list correspond to successive values of *i*. The elements of each inner list correspond to successive values of *j*, with *i* fixed.

Sometimes you may want to generate a table by evaluating a particular expression many times, without incrementing any variables.

This creates a list containing four copies of the symbol x.

$In[10]:=$ **Table[x, {4}]**

$Out[10]=$ {x, x, x, x}

This gives a list of four pseudorandom numbers. Table re-evaluates Random[ ] for each element in the list, so that you get a different pseudorandom number.

$In[11]:=$ **Table[Random[ ], {4}]**

$Out[11]=$ {0.0560708, 0.6303, 0.359894, 0.871377}

Table[f, {$imax$}]	give a list of *imax* values of f
Table[f, {i, $imax$}]	give a list of the values of f as i runs from 1 to *imax*
Table[f, {i, $imin$, $imax$}]	give a list of values with i running from *imin* to *imax*
Table[f, {i, $imin$, $imax$, di}]	use steps of *di*
Table[f, {i, $imin$, $imax$}, {j, $jmin$, $jmax$}, ...]	generate a multidimensional table
TableForm[$list$]	display a list in tabular form

Functions for generating tables.

You can use the operations discussed in Section 1.2.4 to extract elements of the table.

This creates a 2×2 table, and gives it the name m.	*In[12]:=* **m = Table[i - j, {i, 2}, {j, 2}]**
	Out[12]= {{0, -1}, {1, 0}}
This extracts the first sublist from the list of lists that makes up the table.	*In[13]:=* **m[[1]]**
	Out[13]= {0, -1}
This extracts the second element of that sublist.	*In[14]:=* **%[[2]]**
	Out[14]= -1
This does the two operations together.	*In[15]:=* **m[[1,2]]**
	Out[15]= -1
This displays m in a "tabular" form.	*In[16]:=* **TableForm[m]**
	Out[16]//TableForm= 0 -1 1 0

t[[i]] or Part[t, i]	give the ith sublist in t (also input as $t[\![i]\!]$)
t[[{i_1, i_2, ... }]] or Part[t, {i_1, i_2, ... }]	give a list of the $i_1{}^{\text{th}}$, $i_2{}^{\text{th}}$, ... parts of t
t[[i, j, ...]] or Part[t, i, j, ...]	give the part of t corresponding to t[[i]][[j]] ...

Ways to extract parts of tables.

As we mentioned in Section 1.2.4, you can think of lists in *Mathematica* as being analogous to "arrays". Lists of lists are then like two-dimensional arrays. When you lay them out in a tabular form, the two indices of each element are like its x and y coordinates.

You can use `Table` to generate arrays with any number of dimensions.

This generates a three-dimensional $2 \times 2 \times 2$ array. It is a list of lists of lists.	`In[17]:= Table[i j^2 k^3, {i, 2}, {j, 2}, {k, 2}]`
	
	`Out[17]= {{{1, 8}, {4, 32}}, {{2, 16}, {8, 64}}}`

■ 1.8.3 Vectors and Matrices

Vectors and matrices in *Mathematica* are simply represented by lists and by lists of lists, respectively.

$\{a, b, c\}$	vector (a, b, c)	
$\{\{a, b\}, \{c, d\}\}$	matrix $\begin{pmatrix} a & b \\ c & d \end{pmatrix}$	

The representation of vectors and matrices by lists.

This is a 2×2 matrix.	`In[1]:= m = {{a, b}, {c, d}}`
	
	`Out[1]= {{a, b}, {c, d}}`

Here is the first row.	`In[2]:= m[[1]]`
	
	`Out[2]= {a, b}`

Here is the element m_{12}.	`In[3]:= m[[1,2]]`
	
	`Out[3]= b`

This is a two-component vector.	`In[4]:= v = {x, y}`
	
	`Out[4]= {x, y}`

The objects p and q are treated as scalars.	`In[5]:= p v + q`
	
	`Out[5]= {q + p x, q + p y}`

Vectors are added component by component.	`In[6]:= v + {xp, yp} + {xpp, ypp}`
	
	`Out[6]= {x + xp + xpp, y + yp + ypp}`

This takes the dot ("scalar") product of two vectors.	`In[7]:= {x, y} . {xp, yp}`
	
	`Out[7]= x xp + y yp`

You can also multiply a matrix by a vector.	`In[8]:= m . v`
	
	`Out[8]= {a x + b y, c x + d y}`

Or a matrix by a matrix.	*In[9]:=* **m . m**
	Out[9]= $\{\{a^2 + bc, ab + bd\}, \{ac + cd, bc + d^2\}\}$
Or a vector by a matrix.	*In[10]:=* **v . m**
	Out[10]= $\{ax + cy, bx + dy\}$
This combination makes a scalar.	*In[11]:=* **v . m . v**
	Out[11]= $x(ax + cy) + y(bx + dy)$

Because of the way *Mathematica* uses lists to represent vectors and matrices, you never have to distinguish between "row" and "column" vectors.

Table[*f*, {*i*, *n*}]	build a length-*n* vector by evaluating *f* with *i* = 1, 2, ... , *n*
Array[*a*, *n*]	build a length-*n* vector of the form {*a*[1], *a*[2], ... }
Range[*n*]	create the list {1, 2, 3, ... , *n*}
Range[n_1, n_2]	create the list {n_1, n_1+1, ... , n_2}
Range[n_1, n_2, *dn*]	create the list {n_1, n_1+*dn*, ... , n_2}
list[[*i*]] or Part[*list*, *i*]	give the ith element in the vector *list*
Length[*list*]	give the number of elements in *list*
ColumnForm[*list*]	display the elements of *list* in a column
c v	multiply by a scalar
a . b	vector dot product
Cross[*a*, *b*]	vector cross product (also input as *a* × *b*)
Norm[*v*]	norm of a vector

Functions for vectors.

Table[f, {i, m}, {j, n}]	build an $m \times n$ matrix by evaluating f with i ranging from 1 to m and j ranging from 1 to n
Array[a, {m, n}]	build an $m \times n$ matrix with i,j^{th} element $a[i, j]$
IdentityMatrix[n]	generate an $n \times n$ identity matrix
DiagonalMatrix[$list$]	generate a square matrix with the elements in *list* on the diagonal
list[[i]] or Part[$list$, i]	give the ith row in the matrix *list*
list[[All, j]] or Part[$list$, All, j]	give the jth column in the matrix *list*
list[[i, j]] or Part[$list$, i, j]	give the i,j^{th} element in the matrix *list*
Dimensions[$list$]	give the dimensions of a matrix represented by *list*
MatrixForm[$list$]	display *list* in matrix form

Functions for matrices.

This builds a 3×3 matrix s with elements $s_{ij} = i + j$.

$In[12]:=$ **s = Table[i+j, {i, 3}, {j, 3}]**

$Out[12]=$ {{2, 3, 4}, {3, 4, 5}, {4, 5, 6}}

This displays s in standard two-dimensional matrix format.

$In[13]:=$ **MatrixForm[s]**

$Out[13]//MatrixForm=$ $\begin{pmatrix} 2 & 3 & 4 \\ 3 & 4 & 5 \\ 4 & 5 & 6 \end{pmatrix}$

This gives a vector with symbolic elements. You can use this in deriving general formulas that are valid with any choice of vector components.

$In[14]:=$ **Array[a, 4]**

$Out[14]=$ {a[1], a[2], a[3], a[4]}

This gives a 3×2 matrix with symbolic elements. Section 2.2.6 will discuss how you can produce other kinds of elements with Array.

$In[15]:=$ **Array[p, {3, 2}]**

$Out[15]=$ {{p[1, 1], p[1, 2]}, {p[2, 1], p[2, 2]}, {p[3, 1], p[3, 2]}}

Here are the dimensions of the matrix on the previous line.

$In[16]:=$ **Dimensions[%]**

$Out[16]=$ {3, 2}

This generates a 3×3 diagonal matrix.

$In[17]:=$ **DiagonalMatrix[{a, b, c}]**

$Out[17]=$ {{a, 0, 0}, {0, b, 0}, {0, 0, c}}

c m	multiply by a scalar
a . b	matrix product
Inverse[*m*]	matrix inverse
MatrixPower[*m*, *n*]	n^{th} power of a matrix
Det[*m*]	determinant
Tr[*m*]	trace
Transpose[*m*]	transpose
Eigenvalues[*m*]	eigenvalues
Eigenvectors[*m*]	eigenvectors

Some mathematical operations on matrices.

Here is the 2×2 matrix of symbolic variables that was defined above.

In[18]:= **m**

Out[18]= {{a, b}, {c, d}}

This gives its determinant.

In[19]:= **Det[m]**

Out[19]= -b c + a d

Here is the transpose of m.

In[20]:= **Transpose[m]**

Out[20]= {{a, c}, {b, d}}

This gives the inverse of m in symbolic form.

In[21]:= **Inverse[m]**

$$Out[21]= \left\{\left\{\frac{d}{-bc+ad}, -\frac{b}{-bc+ad}\right\}, \left\{-\frac{c}{-bc+ad}, \frac{a}{-bc+ad}\right\}\right\}$$

Here is a 3×3 rational matrix.

In[22]:= **h = Table[1/(i+j-1), {i, 3}, {j, 3}]**

$$Out[22]= \left\{\left\{1, \frac{1}{2}, \frac{1}{3}\right\}, \left\{\frac{1}{2}, \frac{1}{3}, \frac{1}{4}\right\}, \left\{\frac{1}{3}, \frac{1}{4}, \frac{1}{5}\right\}\right\}$$

This gives its inverse.

In[23]:= **Inverse[h]**

Out[23]= {{9, -36, 30}, {-36, 192, -180}, {30, -180, 180}}

Taking the dot product of the inverse with the original matrix gives the identity matrix.

In[24]:= **% . h**

Out[24]= {{1, 0, 0}, {0, 1, 0}, {0, 0, 1}}

Here is a 3×3 matrix.

In[25]:= **r = Table[i+j+1, {i, 3}, {j, 3}]**

Out[25]= {{3, 4, 5}, {4, 5, 6}, {5, 6, 7}}

Eigenvalues gives the eigenvalues of the matrix.

$In[26]:=$ **Eigenvalues[r]**

$Out[26]=$ $\left\{\frac{1}{2}\left(15+\sqrt{249}\right), \frac{1}{2}\left(15-\sqrt{249}\right), 0\right\}$

This gives a numerical approximation to the matrix.

$In[27]:=$ **rn = N[r]**

$Out[27]=$ {{3., 4., 5.}, {4., 5., 6.}, {5., 6., 7.}}

Here are numerical approximations to the eigenvalues.

$In[28]:=$ **Eigenvalues[rn]**

$Out[28]=$ $\left\{15.3899, -0.389867, -2.43881 \times 10^{-16}\right\}$

Section 3.7 discusses many other matrix operations that are built into *Mathematica*.

■ 1.8.4 Getting Pieces of Lists

First[*list*]	the first element in *list*
Last[*list*]	the last element
Part[*list*, *n*] or *list*[[*n*]]	the nth element
Part[*list*, -*n*] or *list*[[-*n*]]	the nth element from the end
Part[*list*, {n_1, n_2, ... }] or *list*[[{n_1, n_2, ... }]]	the list of elements at positions n_1, n_2, ...

Picking out elements of lists.

We will use this list for the examples.

$In[1]:=$ **t = {a,b,c,d,e,f,g}**

$Out[1]=$ {a, b, c, d, e, f, g}

Here is the last element of t.

$In[2]:=$ **Last[t]**

$Out[2]=$ g

This gives the third element.

$In[3]:=$ **t[[3]]**

$Out[3]=$ c

This gives a list of the first and fourth elements.

$In[4]:=$ **t[[{1, 4}]]**

$Out[4]=$ {a, d}

Take[*list*, *n*]	the first *n* elements in *list*
Take[*list*, -*n*]	the last *n* elements
Take[*list*, {*m*, *n*}]	elements *m* through *n* (inclusive)
Rest[*list*]	*list* with its first element dropped
Drop[*list*, *n*]	*list* with its first *n* elements dropped
Most[*list*]	*list* with its last element dropped
Drop[*list*, -*n*]	*list* with its last *n* elements dropped
Drop[*list*, {*m*, *n*}]	*list* with elements *m* through *n* dropped

Picking out sequences in lists.

This gives the first three elements of the list t defined above.	In[5]:= **Take[t, 3]** Out[5]= {a, b, c}
This gives the last three elements.	In[6]:= **Take[t, -3]** Out[6]= {e, f, g}
This gives elements 2 through 5 inclusive.	In[7]:= **Take[t, {2, 5}]** Out[7]= {b, c, d, e}
This gives elements 3 through 7 in steps of 2.	In[8]:= **Take[t, {3, 7, 2}]** Out[8]= {c, e, g}
This gives t with the first element dropped.	In[9]:= **Rest[t]** Out[9]= {b, c, d, e, f, g}
This gives t with its first three elements dropped.	In[10]:= **Drop[t, 3]** Out[10]= {d, e, f, g}
This gives t with only its third element dropped.	In[11]:= **Drop[t, {3, 3}]** Out[11]= {a, b, d, e, f, g}

Section 2.1.5 will show how all the functions in this section can be generalized to work not only on lists, but on any *Mathematica* expressions.

The functions in this section allow you to pick out pieces that occur at particular positions in lists. Section 2.3.2 will show how you can use functions like Select and Cases to pick out elements of lists based not on their positions, but instead on their properties.

■ 1.8.5 Testing and Searching List Elements

Position[*list*, *form*]	the positions at which *form* occurs in *list*
Count[*list*, *form*]	the number of times *form* appears as an element of *list*
MemberQ[*list*, *form*]	test whether *form* is an element of *list*
FreeQ[*list*, *form*]	test whether *form* occurs nowhere in *list*

Testing and searching for elements of lists.

The previous section discussed how to extract pieces of lists based on their positions or indices. *Mathematica* also has functions that search and test for elements of lists, based on the values of those elements.

This gives a list of the positions at which a appears in the list.

```
In[1]:= Position[{a, b, c, a, b}, a]
Out[1]= {{1}, {4}}
```

Count counts the number of occurrences of a.

```
In[2]:= Count[{a, b, c, a, b}, a]
Out[2]= 2
```

This shows that a is an element of {a, b, c}.

```
In[3]:= MemberQ[{a, b, c}, a]
Out[3]= True
```

On the other hand, d is not.

```
In[4]:= MemberQ[{a, b, c}, d]
Out[4]= False
```

This assigns m to be the 3×3 identity matrix.

```
In[5]:= m = IdentityMatrix[3]
Out[5]= {{1, 0, 0}, {0, 1, 0}, {0, 0, 1}}
```

This shows that 0 does occur *somewhere* in m.

```
In[6]:= FreeQ[m, 0]
Out[6]= False
```

This gives a list of the positions at which 0 occurs in m.

```
In[7]:= Position[m, 0]
Out[7]= {{1, 2}, {1, 3}, {2, 1}, {2, 3}, {3, 1}, {3, 2}}
```

As discussed in Section 2.3.2, the functions Count and Position, as well as MemberQ and FreeQ, can be used not only to search for *particular* list elements, but also to search for classes of elements which match specific "patterns".

■ 1.8.6 Adding, Removing and Modifying List Elements

Prepend[*list*, *element*]	add *element* at the beginning of *list*
Append[*list*, *element*]	add *element* at the end of *list*
Insert[*list*, *element*, *i*]	insert *element* at position *i* in *list*
Insert[*list*, *element*, -*i*]	insert at position *i* counting from the end of *list*
Delete[*list*, *i*]	delete the element at position *i* in *list*
ReplacePart[*list*, *new*, *i*]	replace the element at position *i* in *list* with *new*
ReplacePart[*list*, *new*, {*i*, *j*}]	replace *list*[[*i*, *j*]] with *new*

Functions for manipulating elements in explicit lists.

This gives a list with x prepended.	*In[1]:=* **Prepend[{a, b, c}, x]**
	Out[1]= {x, a, b, c}
This inserts x so that it becomes element number 2.	*In[2]:=* **Insert[{a, b, c}, x, 2]**
	Out[2]= {a, x, b, c}
This replaces the third element in the list with x.	*In[3]:=* **ReplacePart[{a, b, c, d}, x, 3]**
	Out[3]= {a, b, x, d}
This replaces the 1, 2 element in a 2 × 2 matrix.	*In[4]:=* **ReplacePart[{{a, b}, {c, d}}, x, {1, 2}]**
	Out[4]= {{a, x}, {c, d}}

Functions like ReplacePart take explicit lists and give you new lists. Sometimes, however, you may want to modify a list "in place", without explicitly generating a new list.

$v = \{e_1, e_2, \dots \}$	assign a variable to be a list
$v[[i]] = new$	assign a new value to the ith element

Resetting list elements.

This defines v to be a list.	*In[5]:=* **v = {a, b, c, d}**
	Out[5]= {a, b, c, d}
This sets the third element to be x.	*In[6]:=* **v[[3]] = x**
	Out[6]= x

Now v has been changed.

```
In[7]:= v
Out[7]= {a, b, x, d}
```

$m[[i, j]]$ = *new*	replace the $(i, j)^{th}$ element of a matrix
$m[[i]]$ = *new*	replace the ith row
$m[[\text{All}, i]]$ = *new*	replace the ith column

Resetting pieces of matrices.

This defines m to be a matrix.

```
In[8]:= m = {{a, b}, {c, d}}
Out[8]= {{a, b}, {c, d}}
```

This sets the first column of the matrix.

```
In[9]:= m[[All, 1]] = {x, y}; m
Out[9]= {{x, b}, {y, d}}
```

This sets every element in the first column to be 0.

```
In[10]:= m[[All, 1]] = 0; m
Out[10]= {{0, b}, {0, d}}
```

■ 1.8.7 Combining Lists

$\text{Join}[list_1, list_2, \ldots]$	concatenate lists together
$\text{Union}[list_1, list_2, \ldots]$	combine lists, removing repeated elements and sorting the result

Functions for combining lists.

Join concatenates any number of lists together.

```
In[1]:= Join[{a, b, c}, {x, y}, {t, u}]
Out[1]= {a, b, c, x, y, t, u}
```

Union combines lists, keeping only distinct elements.

```
In[2]:= Union[{a, b, c}, {c, a, d}, {a, d}]
Out[2]= {a, b, c, d}
```

■ 1.8.8 Advanced Topic: Lists as Sets

Mathematica usually keeps the elements of a list in exactly the order you originally entered them. If you want to treat a *Mathematica* list like a mathematical *set*, however, you may want to ignore the order of elements in the list.

Union[$list_1$, $list_2$, ...]	give a list of the distinct elements in the $list_i$
Intersection[$list_1$, $list_2$, ...]	give a list of the elements that are common to all the $list_i$
Complement[$universal$, $list_1$, ...]	give a list of the elements that are in $universal$, but not in any of the $list_i$

Set theoretical functions.

Union gives the elements that occur in *any* of the lists.	In[1]:= **Union[{c, a, b}, {d, a, c}, {a, e}]** Out[1]= {a, b, c, d, e}
Intersection gives only elements that occur in *all* the lists.	In[2]:= **Intersection[{a, c, b}, {b, a, d, a}]** Out[2]= {a, b}
Complement gives elements that occur in the first list, but not in any of the others.	In[3]:= **Complement[{a, b, c, d}, {a, d}]** Out[3]= {b, c}

■ 1.8.9 Rearranging Lists

Sort[$list$]	sort the elements of $list$ into a standard order
Union[$list$]	sort elements, removing any duplicates
Reverse[$list$]	reverse the order of elements in $list$
RotateLeft[$list$, n]	rotate the elements of $list$ n places to the left
RotateRight[$list$, n]	rotate n places to the right

Functions for rearranging lists.

This sorts the elements of a list into a standard order. In simple cases like this, the order is alphabetical or numerical.	In[1]:= **Sort[{b, a, c, a, b}]** Out[1]= {a, a, b, b, c}
This sorts the elements, removing any duplicates.	In[2]:= **Union[{b, a, c, a, b}]** Out[2]= {a, b, c}
This rotates ("shifts") the elements in the list two places to the left.	In[3]:= **RotateLeft[{a, b, c, d, e}, 2]** Out[3]= {c, d, e, a, b}

You can rotate to the right by giving a negative displacement, or by using RotateRight.

In[4]:= **RotateLeft[{a, b, c, d, e}, -2]**

Out[4]= {d, e, a, b, c}

PadLeft[*list*, *len*, *x*]	pad *list* on the left with *x* to make it length *len*
PadRight[*list*, *len*, *x*]	pad *list* on the right

Padding lists.

This pads a list with x's to make it length 10.

In[5]:= **PadLeft[{a, b, c}, 10, x]**

Out[5]= {x, x, x, x, x, x, x, a, b, c}

■ 1.8.10 Grouping Together Elements of Lists

Partition[*list*, *n*]	partition *list* into *n*-element pieces
Partition[*list*, *n*, *d*]	use offset *d* for successive pieces
Split[*list*]	split *list* into pieces consisting of runs of identical elements

Functions for grouping together elements of lists.

Here is a list.

In[1]:= **t = {a, b, c, d, e, f, g}**

Out[1]= {a, b, c, d, e, f, g}

This groups the elements of the list in pairs, throwing away the single element left at the end.

In[2]:= **Partition[t, 2]**

Out[2]= {{a, b}, {c, d}, {e, f}}

This groups elements in triples. There is no overlap between the triples.

In[3]:= **Partition[t, 3]**

Out[3]= {{a, b, c}, {d, e, f}}

This makes triples of elements, with each successive triple offset by just one element.

In[4]:= **Partition[t, 3, 1]**

Out[4]= {{a, b, c}, {b, c, d}, {c, d, e}, {d, e, f}, {e, f, g}}

This splits up the list into runs of identical elements.

In[5]:= **Split[{a, a, b, b, b, a, a, a, b}]**

Out[5]= {{a, a}, {b, b, b}, {a, a, a}, {b}}

◼ 1.8.11 Ordering in Lists

Sort[*list*]	sort the elements of *list* into order
Min[*list*]	the smallest element in *list*
Ordering[*list*, *n*]	the positions of the *n* smallest elements in *list*
Max[*list*]	the largest element in *list*
Ordering[*list*, -*n*]	the positions of the *n* largest elements in *list*
Ordering[*list*]	the ordering of all elements in *list*
Permutations[*list*]	all possible orderings of *list*

Ordering in lists.

Here is a list.

```
In[1]:= t = {17, 21, 14, 9, 18}
Out[1]= {17, 21, 14, 9, 18}
```

This gives the smallest element in the list.

```
In[2]:= Min[t]
Out[2]= 9
```

This gives in order the positions of the 3 smallest elements.

```
In[3]:= Ordering[t, 3]
Out[3]= {4, 3, 1}
```

Here are the actual elements.

```
In[4]:= t[[%]]
Out[4]= {9, 14, 17}
```

◼ 1.8.12 Advanced Topic: Rearranging Nested Lists

You will encounter nested lists if you use matrices or generate multidimensional arrays and tables. *Mathematica* provides many functions for handling such lists.

Flatten[*list*]	flatten out all levels in *list*
Flatten[*list*, *n*]	flatten out the top *n* levels in *list*
Partition[*list*, {n_1, n_2, ... }]	partition into blocks of size $n_1 \times n_2 \times ...$
Transpose[*list*]	interchange the top two levels of lists
RotateLeft[*list*, {n_1, n_2, ... }]	rotate successive levels by n_i places
PadLeft[*list*, {n_1, n_2, ... }]	pad successive levels to be length n_i

A few functions for rearranging nested lists.

This "flattens out" sublists. You can think of it as effectively just removing all inner braces.

In[1]:= **Flatten[{{a}, {b, {c}}, {d}}]**

Out[1]= {a, b, c, d}

This flattens out only one level of sublists.

In[2]:= **Flatten[{{a}, {b, {c}}, {d}}, 1]**

Out[2]= {a, b, {c}, d}

There are many other operations you can perform on nested lists. We will discuss more of them in Section 2.4.

1.9 Graphics and Sound

■ 1.9.1 Basic Plotting

Plot[*f*, {*x*, *xmin*, *xmax*}]	plot *f* as a function of *x* from *xmin* to *xmax*
Plot[{*f*₁, *f*₂, ... }, {*x*, *xmin*, *xmax*}]	plot several functions together

Basic plotting functions.

This plots a graph of sin(*x*) as a function of *x* from 0 to 2π.

In[1]:= **Plot[Sin[x], {x, 0, 2Pi}]**

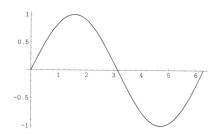

You can plot functions that have singularities. *Mathematica* will try to choose appropriate scales.

In[2]:= **Plot[Tan[x], {x, -3, 3}]**

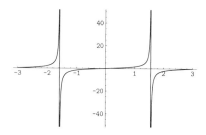

You can give a list of functions to plot.   *In[3]:=* `Plot[{Sin[x], Sin[2x], Sin[3x]}, {x, 0, 2Pi}]`

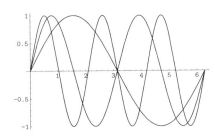

To get smooth curves, *Mathematica* has to evaluate functions you plot at a large number of points. As a result, it is important that you set things up so that each function evaluation is as quick as possible.

When you ask *Mathematica* to plot an object, say *f*, as a function of *x*, there are two possible approaches it can take. One approach is first to try and evaluate *f*, presumably getting a symbolic expression in terms of *x*, and then subsequently evaluate this expression numerically for the specific values of *x* needed in the plot. The second approach is first to work out what values of *x* are needed, and only subsequently to evaluate *f* with those values of *x*.

If you type Plot[*f*, {*x*, *xmin*, *xmax*}] it is the second of these approaches that is used. This has the advantage that *Mathematica* only tries to evaluate *f* for specific numerical values of *x*; it does not matter whether sensible values are defined for *f* when *x* is symbolic.

There are, however, some cases in which it is much better to have *Mathematica* evaluate *f* before it starts to make the plot. A typical case is when *f* is actually a command that generates a table of functions. You want to have *Mathematica* first produce the table, and then evaluate the functions, rather than trying to produce the table afresh for each value of *x*. You can do this by typing Plot[Evaluate[*f*], {*x*, *xmin*, *xmax*}].

This makes a plot of the Bessel functions $J_n(x)$ with *n* running from 1 to 4. The Evaluate tells *Mathematica* *first* to make the table of functions, and only *then* to evaluate them for particular values of x.

In[4]:= `Plot[Evaluate[Table[BesselJ[n, x], {n, 4}]],`
`{x, 0, 10}]`

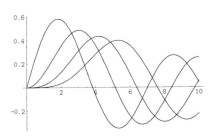

This finds the numerical solution to a differential equation, as discussed in Section 1.6.4.

In[5]:= `NDSolve[{y'[x] == Sin[y[x]], y[0] == 1}, y, {x, 0, 4}]`

Out[5]= `{{y → InterpolatingFunction[{{0., 4.}}, <>]}}`

Here is a plot of the solution. The Evaluate tells *Mathematica* to first set up an InterpolatingFunction object, then evaluate this at a sequence of x values.

In[6]:= `Plot[Evaluate[ y[x] /. % ], {x, 0, 4}]`

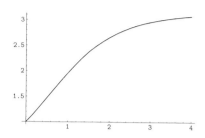

`Plot[f, {x, xmin, xmax}]`	*first* choose specific numerical values for x, then evaluate f for each value of x
`Plot[Evaluate[f], {x, xmin, xmax}]`	*first* evaluate f, then choose specific numerical values of x
`Plot[Evaluate[Table[f, ... ]], {x, xmin, xmax}]`	generate a list of functions, and then plot them
`Plot[Evaluate[y[x] /. solution], {x, xmin, xmax}]`	plot a numerical solution to a differential equation obtained from NDSolve

Methods for setting up objects to plot.

■ 1.9.2 Options

When *Mathematica* plots a graph for you, it has to make many choices. It has to work out what the scales should be, where the function should be sampled, how the axes should be drawn, and so on. Most of the time, *Mathematica* will probably make pretty good choices. However, if you want to get the very best possible pictures for your particular purposes, you may have to help *Mathematica* in making some of its choices.

There is a general mechanism for specifying "options" in *Mathematica* functions. Each option has a definite name. As the last arguments to a function like Plot, you can include a sequence of rules of the form *name->value*, to specify the values for various options. Any option for which you do not give an explicit rule is taken to have its "default" value.

| `Plot[f, {x, xmin, xmax}, option->value]` | make a plot, specifying a particular value for an option |

Choosing an option for a plot.

A function like `Plot` has many options that you can set. Usually you will need to use at most a few of them at a time. If you want to optimize a particular plot, you will probably do best to experiment, trying a sequence of different settings for various options.

Each time you produce a plot, you can specify options for it. Section 1.9.3 will also discuss how you can change some of the options, even after you have produced the plot.

option name	default value	
AspectRatio	1/GoldenRatio	the height-to-width ratio for the plot; Automatic sets it from the absolute x and y coordinates
Axes	Automatic	whether to include axes
AxesLabel	None	labels to be put on the axes; *ylabel* specifies a label for the y axis, {*xlabel*, *ylabel*} for both axes
AxesOrigin	Automatic	the point at which axes cross
TextStyle	$TextStyle	the default style to use for text in the plot
FormatType	StandardForm	the default format type to use for text in the plot
DisplayFunction	$DisplayFunction	how to display graphics; Identity causes no display
Frame	False	whether to draw a frame around the plot
FrameLabel	None	labels to be put around the frame; give a list in clockwise order starting with the lower x axis
FrameTicks	Automatic	what tick marks to draw if there is a frame; None gives no tick marks
GridLines	None	what grid lines to include; Automatic includes a grid line for every major tick mark
PlotLabel	None	an expression to be printed as a label for the plot
PlotRange	Automatic	the range of coordinates to include in the plot; All includes all points
Ticks	Automatic	what tick marks to draw if there are axes; None gives no tick marks

Some of the options for `Plot`. These can also be used in `Show`.

Here is a plot with all options having their default values.

In[7]:= `Plot[Sin[x^2], {x, 0, 3}]`

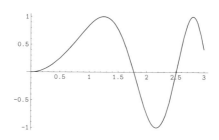

This draws axes on a frame around the plot.

In[8]:= `Plot[Sin[x^2], {x, 0, 3}, Frame->True]`

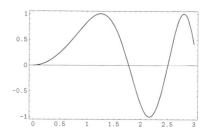

This specifies labels for the x and y axes. The expressions you give as labels are printed just as they would be if they appeared as *Mathematica* output. You can give any piece of text by putting it inside a pair of double quotes.

In[9]:= `Plot[Sin[x^2], {x, 0, 3},`
`            AxesLabel -> {"x value", "Sin[x^2]"} ]`

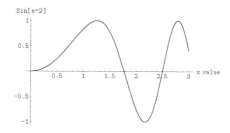

You can give several options at the
same time, in any order.

In[10]:= **Plot[Sin[x^2], {x, 0, 3}, Frame -> True,**
                      GridLines -> Automatic]

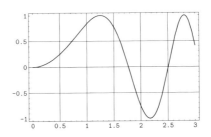

Setting the AspectRatio option
changes the whole shape of your plot.
AspectRatio gives the ratio of width
to height. Its default value is the
inverse of the Golden
Ratio—supposedly the most pleasing
shape for a rectangle.

In[11]:= **Plot[Sin[x^2], {x, 0, 3}, AspectRatio -> 1]**

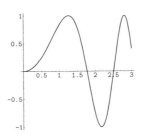

Automatic	use internal algorithms
None	do not include this
All	include everything
True	do this
False	do not do this

Some common settings for various options.

When *Mathematica* makes a plot, it tries to set the *x* and *y* scales to include only the "interesting" parts of the plot. If your function increases very rapidly, or has singularities, the parts where it gets too large will be cut off. By specifying the option PlotRange, you can control exactly what ranges of *x* and *y* coordinates are included in your plot.

Automatic	show at least a large fraction of the points, including the "interesting" region (the default setting)
All	show all points
{*ymin*, *ymax*}	show a specific range of *y* values
{*xrange*, *yrange*}	show the specified ranges of *x* and *y* values

Settings for the option `PlotRange`.

The setting for the option `PlotRange` gives explicit *y* limits for the graph. With the *y* limits specified here, the bottom of the curve is cut off.

In[12]:= `Plot[Sin[x^2], {x, 0, 3}, PlotRange -> {0, 1.2}]`

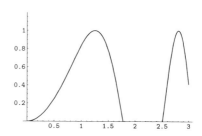

Mathematica always tries to plot functions as smooth curves. As a result, in places where your function wiggles a lot, *Mathematica* will use more points. In general, *Mathematica* tries to *adapt* its sampling of your function to the form of the function. There is, however, a limit, which you can set, to how finely *Mathematica* will ever sample a function.

The function $\sin(\frac{1}{x})$ wiggles infinitely often when $x \simeq 0$. *Mathematica* tries to sample more points in the region where the function wiggles a lot, but it can never sample the infinite number that you would need to reproduce the function exactly. As a result, there are slight glitches in the plot.

In[13]:= `Plot[Sin[1/x], {x, -1, 1}]`

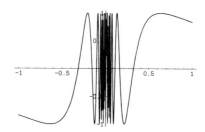

option name	default value	
PlotStyle	Automatic	a list of lists of graphics primitives to use for each curve (see Section 2.10.3)
PlotPoints	25	the minimum number of points at which to sample the function
MaxBend	10.	the maximum kink angle between successive segments of a curve
~ PlotDivision	30.	the maximum factor by which to subdivide in sampling the function
Compiled	True	whether to compile the function being plotted

More options for `Plot`. These cannot be used in `Show`.

It is important to realize that since *Mathematica* can only sample your function at a limited number of points, it can always miss features of the function. By increasing `PlotPoints`, you can make *Mathematica* sample your function at a larger number of points. Of course, the larger you set `PlotPoints` to be, the longer it will take *Mathematica* to plot *any* function, even a smooth one.

Since `Plot` needs to evaluate your function many times, it is important to make each evaluation as quick as possible. As a result, *Mathematica* usually *compiles* your function into a low-level pseudocode that can be executed very efficiently. One potential problem with this, however, is that the pseudocode allows only machine-precision numerical operations. If the function you are plotting requires higher-precision operations, you may have to switch off compilation in `Plot`. You can do this by setting the option `Compiled -> False`. Note that *Mathematica* can only compile "inline code"; it cannot for example compile functions that you have defined. As a result, you should, when possible, use `Evaluate` as described on page 132 to evaluate any such definitions and get a form that the *Mathematica* compiler can handle.

■ 1.9.3 **Redrawing and Combining Plots**

Mathematica saves information about every plot you produce, so that you can later redraw it. When you redraw plots, you can change some of the options you use.

Show[*plot*]	redraw a plot
Show[*plot*, *option->value*]	redraw with options changed
Show[*plot*₁, *plot*₂, ...]	combine several plots
Show[GraphicsArray[{{*plot*₁, *plot*₂, ... }, ... }]]	draw an array of plots
InputForm[*plot*]	show the information that is saved about a plot

Functions for manipulating plots.

Here is a simple plot. –Graphics– is usually printed on the output line to stand for the information that *Mathematica* saves about the plot.

In[1]:= **Plot[ChebyshevT[7, x], {x, -1, 1}]**

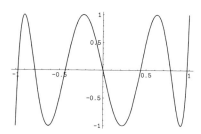

This redraws the plot from the previous line.

In[2]:= **Show[%]**

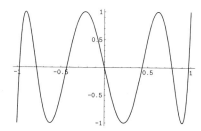

When you redraw the plot, you can change some of the options. This changes the choice of y scale.

In[3]:= **Show[%, PlotRange -> {-1, 2}]**

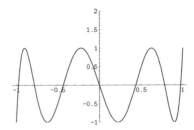

This takes the plot from the previous line, and changes another option in it.

In[4]:= **Show[%, PlotLabel -> "A Chebyshev Polynomial"]**

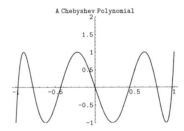

By using Show with a sequence of different options, you can look at the same plot in many different ways. You may want to do this, for example, if you are trying to find the best possible setting of options.

You can also use Show to combine plots. It does not matter whether the plots have the same scales: *Mathematica* will always choose new scales to include the points you want.

This sets gj0 to be a plot of $J_0(x)$ from $x = 0$ to 10.

In[5]:= **gj0 = Plot[BesselJ[0, x], {x, 0, 10}]**

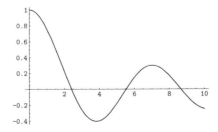

Here is a plot of $Y_1(x)$ from $x = 1$ to 10.

In[6]:= **gy1 = Plot[BesselY[1, x], {x, 1, 10}]**

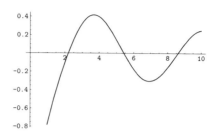

This shows the previous two plots combined into one. Notice that the scale is adjusted appropriately.

In[7]:= **gjy = Show[gj0, gy1]**

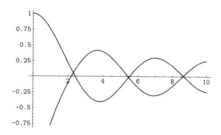

Using Show[*plot₁*, *plot₂*, ...] you can combine several plots into one. GraphicsArray allows you to draw several plots in an array.

Show[GraphicsArray[{*plot*₁, *plot*₂, ... }]]
                                      draw several plots side by side

Show[GraphicsArray[{{*plot*₁}, {*plot*₂}, ... }]]
                                      draw a column of plots

Show[GraphicsArray[{{*plot*₁₁, *plot*₁₂, ... }, ... }]]
                                      draw a rectangular array of plots

Show[GraphicsArray[*plots*, GraphicsSpacing -> {*h*, *v*}]]
                                      put the specified horizontal and vertical spacing between the plots

Drawing arrays of plots.

This shows the plots given above in an array.

In[8]:= **Show[GraphicsArray[{{gj0, gjy}, {gy1, gjy}}]]**

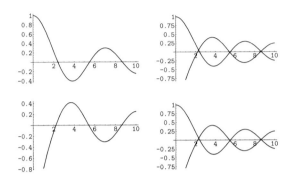

If you redisplay an array of plots using Show, any options you specify will be used for the whole array, rather than for individual plots.

In[9]:= **Show[%, Frame->True, FrameTicks->None]**

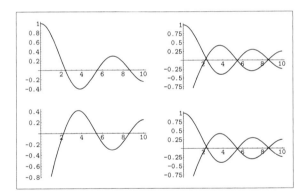

Here is a way to change options for all the plots in the array.

In[10]:= **Show[% /. (Ticks -> Automatic) -> (Ticks -> None)]**

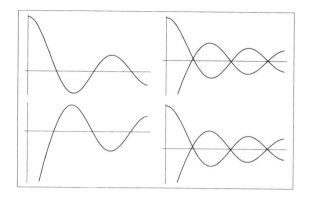

GraphicsArray by default puts a narrow border around each of the plots in the array it gives. You can change the size of this border by setting the option GraphicsSpacing -> {*h*, *v*}. The parameters *h* and *v* give the horizontal and vertical spacings to be used, as fractions of the width and height of the plots.

This increases the horizontal spacing, but decreases the vertical spacing between the plots in the array.

In[11]:= **Show[%, GraphicsSpacing -> {0.3, 0}]**

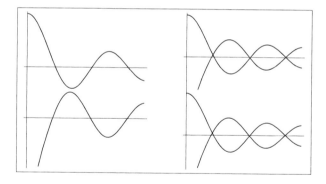

When you make a plot, *Mathematica* saves the list of points it used, together with some other information. Using what is saved, you can redraw plots in many different ways with Show. However, you should realize that no matter what options you specify, Show still has the same basic set of points to work with. So, for example, if you set the options so that *Mathematica* displays a small portion of your original plot magnified, you will probably be able to see the individual sample points that Plot used. Options like PlotPoints can only be set in the original Plot command itself. (*Mathematica* always plots the actual points it has; it avoids using smoothed or splined curves, which can give misleading results in mathematical graphics.)

Here is a simple plot.

In[12]:= **Plot[Cos[x], {x, -Pi, Pi}]**

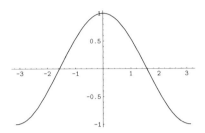

This shows a small region of the plot in a magnified form. At this resolution, you can see the individual line segments that were produced by the original **Plot** command.

In[13]:= **Show[%, PlotRange -> {{0, .3}, {.92, 1}}]**

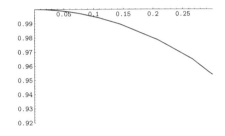

■ 1.9.4 Advanced Topic: Manipulating Options

There are a number of functions built into *Mathematica* which, like **Plot**, have various options you can set. *Mathematica* provides some general mechanisms for handling such options.

If you do not give a specific setting for an option to a function like **Plot**, then *Mathematica* will automatically use a default value for the option. The function **Options[***function***,** *option***]** allows you to find out the default value for a particular option. You can reset the default using **SetOptions[***function***,** *option->value***]**. Note that if you do this, the default value you have given will stay until you explicitly change it.

Options[*function***]**	give a list of the current default settings for all options
Options[*function***,** *option***]**	give the default setting for a particular option
SetOptions[*function***,** *option->value***, ...]**	reset defaults

Manipulating default settings for options.

Here is the default setting for the
PlotRange option of Plot.

In[1]:= **Options[Plot, PlotRange]**

Out[1]= {PlotRange → Automatic}

This resets the default for the
PlotRange option. The semicolon
stops *Mathematica* from printing out the
rather long list of options for Plot.

In[2]:= **SetOptions[Plot, PlotRange->All] ;**

Until you explicitly reset it, the default
for the PlotRange option will now be
All.

In[3]:= **Options[Plot, PlotRange]**

Out[3]= {PlotRange → All}

The graphics objects that you get from Plot or Show store information on the options they use.
You can get this information by applying the Options function to these graphics objects.

Options[*plot*]	show all the options used for a particular plot
Options[*plot*, *option*]	show the setting for a specific option
AbsoluteOptions[*plot*, *option*]	show the absolute form used for a specific option, even if the setting for the option is Automatic or All

Getting information on options used in plots.

Here is a plot, with default settings for
all options.

In[4]:= **g = Plot[SinIntegral[x], {x, 0, 20}]**

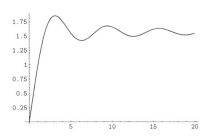

The setting used for the PlotRange
option was All.

In[5]:= **Options[g, PlotRange]**

Out[5]= {PlotRange → All}

AbsoluteOptions gives the *absolute*
automatically chosen values used for
PlotRange.

In[6]:= **AbsoluteOptions[g, PlotRange]**

Out[6]= {PlotRange →
          {{-0.499999, 20.5}, {-0.0462976, 1.89824}}}

■ 1.9.5 Contour and Density Plots

ContourPlot[f, {x, $xmin$, $xmax$}, {y, $ymin$, $ymax$}]
make a contour plot of f as a function of x and y

DensityPlot[f, {x, $xmin$, $xmax$}, {y, $ymin$, $ymax$}]
make a density plot of f

Contour and density plots.

This gives a contour plot of the function $\sin(x)\sin(y)$.

In[1]:= **ContourPlot[Sin[x] Sin[y], {x, -2, 2}, {y, -2, 2}]**

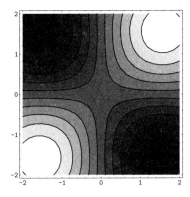

A contour plot gives you essentially a "topographic map" of a function. The contours join points on the surface that have the same height. The default is to have contours corresponding to a sequence of equally spaced z values. Contour plots produced by *Mathematica* are by default shaded, in such a way that regions with higher z values are lighter.

option name	default value	
ColorFunction	Automatic	what colors to use for shading; Hue uses a sequence of hues
Contours	10	the total number of contours, or the list of z values for contours
PlotRange	Automatic	the range of values to be included; you can specify {$zmin$, $zmax$}, All or Automatic
ContourShading	True	whether to use shading
PlotPoints	25	number of evaluation points in each direction
Compiled	True	whether to compile the function being plotted

Some options for ContourPlot. The first set can also be used in Show.

Particularly if you use a display or printer that does not handle gray levels well, you may find it better to switch off shading in contour plots.

In[2]:= **Show[%, ContourShading -> False]**

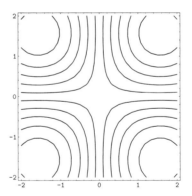

You should realize that if you do not evaluate your function on a fine enough grid, there may be inaccuracies in your contour plot. One point to notice is that whereas a curve generated by Plot may be inaccurate if your function varies too quickly in a particular region, the shape of contours can be inaccurate if your function varies too slowly. A rapidly varying function gives a regular pattern of contours, but a function that is almost flat can give irregular contours. You can typically overcome such problems by increasing the value of PlotPoints.

Density plots show the values of your function at a regular array of points. Lighter regions are higher.

In[3]:= **DensityPlot[Sin[x] Sin[y], {x, -2, 2}, {y, -2, 2}]**

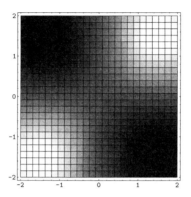

You can get rid of the mesh like this. But unless you have a very large number of regions, plots usually look better when you include the mesh.

In[4]:= **Show[%, Mesh -> False]**

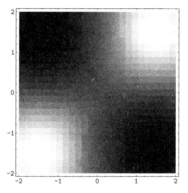

option name	default value	
ColorFunction	Automatic	what colors to use for shading; Hue uses a sequence of hues
Mesh	True	whether to draw a mesh
PlotPoints	25	number of evaluation points in each direction
Compiled	True	whether to compile the function being plotted

Some options for DensityPlot. The first set can also be used in Show.

■ 1.9.6 Three-Dimensional Surface Plots

Plot3D[*f*, {*x*, *xmin*, *xmax*}, {*y*, *ymin*, *ymax*}]
                   make a three-dimensional plot of *f* as a function of the
                   variables *x* and *y*

Basic 3D plotting function.

This makes a three-dimensional plot of   *In[1]:=* **Plot3D[Sin[x y], {x, 0, 3}, {y, 0, 3}]**
the function sin(*xy*).

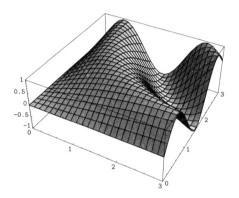

There are many options for three-dimensional plots in *Mathematica*. Some will be discussed in this section; others will be described in Section 2.10.

The first set of options for three-dimensional plots is largely analogous to those provided in the two-dimensional case.

option name	default value	
Axes	True	whether to include axes
AxesLabel	None	labels to be put on the axes: *zlabel* specifies a label for the z axis, {*xlabel*, *ylabel*, *zlabel*} for all axes
Boxed	True	whether to draw a three-dimensional box around the surface
ColorFunction	Automatic	what colors to use for shading; Hue uses a sequence of hues
TextStyle	$TextStyle	the default style to use for text in the plot
FormatType	StandardForm	the default format type to use for text in the plot
DisplayFunction	$DisplayFunction	how to display graphics; Identity causes no display
FaceGrids	None	how to draw grids on faces of the bounding box; All draws a grid on every face
HiddenSurface	True	whether to draw the surface as solid
Lighting	True	whether to color the surface using simulated lighting
Mesh	True	whether an *xy* mesh should be drawn on the surface
PlotRange	Automatic	the range of coordinates to include in the plot: you can specify All, {*zmin*, *zmax*} or {{*xmin*,*xmax*},{*ymin*,*ymax*},{*zmin*,*zmax*}}
Shading	True	whether the surface should be shaded or left white
ViewPoint	{1.3, -2.4, 2}	the point in space from which to look at the surface
PlotPoints	25	the number of points in each direction at which to sample the function; {n_x, n_y} specifies different numbers in the *x* and *y* directions
Compiled	True	whether to compile the function being plotted

Some options for Plot3D. The first set can also be used in Show.

This redraws the plot on the previous line, with options changed. With this setting for `PlotRange`, only the part of the surface in the range $-0.5 \leq z \leq 0.5$ is shown.

In[2]:= **Show[%, PlotRange -> {-0.5, 0.5}]**

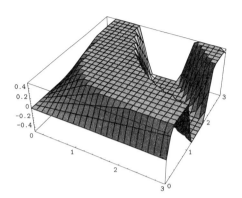

When you make the original plot, you can choose to sample more points. You will need to do this to get good pictures of functions that wiggle a lot.

In[3]:= **Plot3D[10 Sin[x + Sin[y]], {x, -10, 10}, {y, -10, 10}, PlotPoints -> 50]**

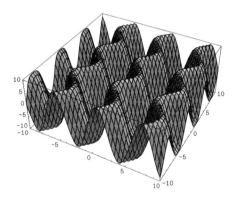

Here is the same plot, with labels for the axes, and grids added to each face.

In[4]:= **Show[%, AxesLabel -> {"Time", "Depth", "Value"},**
                                   FaceGrids -> All]

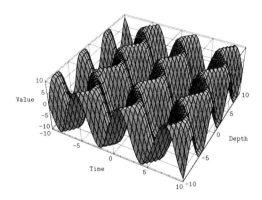

Probably the single most important issue in plotting a three-dimensional surface is specifying where you want to look at the surface from. The ViewPoint option for Plot3D and Show allows you to specify the point {x, y, z} in space from which you view a surface. The details of how the coordinates for this point are defined will be discussed in Section 2.10.10. In many versions of *Mathematica*, there are ways to choose three-dimensional view points interactively, then get the coordinates to give as settings for the ViewPoint option.

Here is a surface, viewed from the default view point {1.3, -2.4, 2}. This view point is chosen to be "generic", so that visually confusing coincidental alignments between different parts of your object are unlikely.

In[5]:= **Plot3D[Sin[x y], {x, 0, 3}, {y, 0, 3}]**

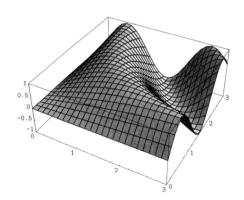

This redraws the picture, with the view point directly in front. Notice the perspective effect that makes the back of the box look much smaller than the front.

In[6]:= **Show[%, ViewPoint -> {0, -2, 0}]**

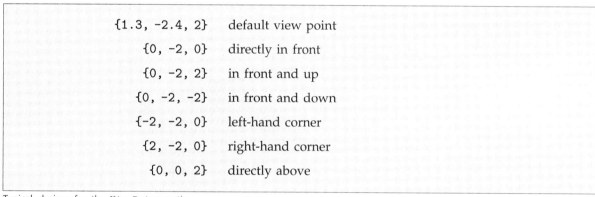

{1.3, -2.4, 2}	default view point
{0, -2, 0}	directly in front
{0, -2, 2}	in front and up
{0, -2, -2}	in front and down
{-2, -2, 0}	left-hand corner
{2, -2, 0}	right-hand corner
{0, 0, 2}	directly above

Typical choices for the **ViewPoint** option.

The human visual system is not particularly good at understanding complicated mathematical surfaces. As a result, you need to generate pictures that contain as many clues as possible about the form of the surface.

View points slightly above the surface usually work best. It is generally a good idea to keep the view point close enough to the surface that there is some perspective effect. Having a box explicitly drawn around the surface is helpful in recognizing the orientation of the surface.

Here is a plot with the default settings for surface rendering options.

In[7]:= **g = Plot3D[Exp[-(x^2+y^2)], {x, -2, 2}, {y, -2, 2}]**

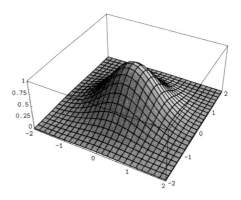

This shows the surface without the mesh drawn. It is usually much harder to see the form of the surface if the mesh is not there.

In[8]:= **Show[g, Mesh -> False]**

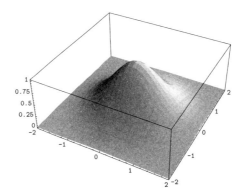

This shows the surface with no shading. Some display devices may not be able to show shading.

In[9]:= **Show[g, Shading -> False]**

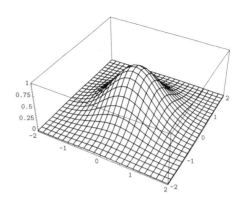

The inclusion of shading and a mesh are usually great assets in understanding the form of a surface. On some vector graphics output devices, however, you may not be able to get shading. You should also realize that when shading is included, it may take a long time to render the surface on your output device.

To add an extra element of realism to three-dimensional graphics, *Mathematica* by default colors three-dimensional surfaces using a simulated lighting model. In the default case, *Mathematica* assumes that there are three light sources shining on the object from the upper right of the picture. Section 2.10.12 describes how you can set up other light sources, and how you can specify the reflection properties of an object.

While in most cases, particularly with color output devices, simulated lighting is an asset, it can sometimes be confusing. If you set the option Lighting -> False, then *Mathematica* will not use simulated lighting, but will instead shade all surfaces with gray levels determined by their height.

Plot3D usually colors surfaces using a simulated lighting model.

In[10]:= **Plot3D[Sin[x y], {x, 0, 3}, {y, 0, 3}]**

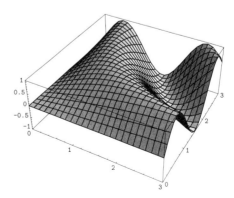

Lighting -> False switches off the
simulated lighting, and instead shades
surfaces with gray levels determined
by height.

In[11]:= **Show[%, Lighting -> False]**

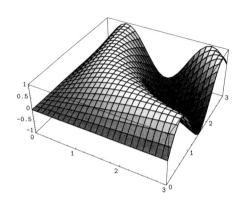

With Lighting -> False, *Mathematica* shades surfaces according to height. You can also tell *Mathematica* explicitly how to shade each element of a surface. This allows you effectively to use shading to display an extra coordinate at each point on your surface.

Plot3D[{*f*, GrayLevel[*s*]}, {*x*, *xmin*, *xmax*}, {*y*, *ymin*, *ymax*}]
                             plot a surface corresponding to *f*, shaded in gray according
                             to the function *s*

Plot3D[{*f*, Hue[*s*]}, {*x*, *xmin*, *xmax*}, {*y*, *ymin*, *ymax*}]
                             shade by varying color hue rather than gray level

---

Specifying shading functions for surfaces.

This shows a surface whose height is
determined by the function Sin[x y],
but whose shading is determined by
GrayLevel[x/3].

In[12]:= **Plot3D[{Sin[x y], GrayLevel[x/3]},**
                        {x, 0, 3}, {y, 0, 3}]

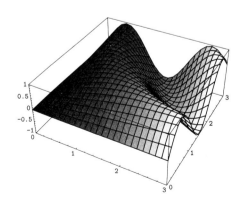

■ 1.9.7 Converting between Types of Graphics

Contour, density and surface plots are three different ways to display essentially the same information about a function. In all cases, you need the values of a function at a grid of points.

The *Mathematica* functions ContourPlot, DensityPlot and Plot3D all produce *Mathematica* graphics objects that include a list of the values of your function on a grid. As a result, having used any one of these functions, *Mathematica* can easily take its output and use it to produce another type of graphics.

Here is a surface plot.

In[1]:= **Plot3D[BesselJ[nu, 3x], {nu, 0, 3}, {x, 0, 3}]**

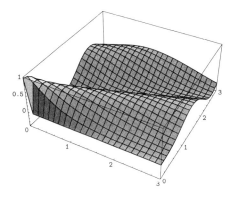

This converts the object produced by Plot3D into a contour plot.

In[2]:= **Show[ContourGraphics[%]]**

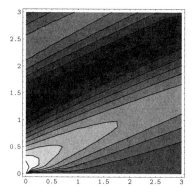

Show[ContourGraphics[*g*]]	convert to a contour plot
Show[DensityGraphics[*g*]]	convert to a density plot
Show[SurfaceGraphics[*g*]]	convert to a surface plot
Show[Graphics[*g*]]	convert to a two-dimensional image

Conversions between types of graphics.

You can use GraphicsArray to show different types of graphics together.

In[3]:= **Show[GraphicsArray[{%, %%}]]**

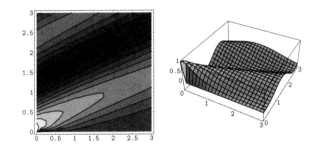

■ 1.9.8 Plotting Lists of Data

So far, we have discussed how you can use *Mathematica* to make plots of *functions*. You give *Mathematica* a function, and it builds up a curve or surface by evaluating the function at many different points.

This section describes how you can make plots from lists of data, instead of functions. (Section 1.11.3 discusses how to read data from external files and programs.) The *Mathematica* commands for plotting lists of data are direct analogs of the ones discussed above for plotting functions.

> ListPlot[{y_1, y_2, ... }]   plot y_1, y_2, ... at x values 1, 2, ...
>
> ListPlot[{{x_1, y_1}, {x_2, y_2}, ... }]
>   plot points (x_1, y_1), ...
>
> ListPlot[*list*, PlotJoined -> True]
>   join the points with lines
>
> ---
>
> ListPlot3D[{{z_{11}, z_{12}, ... }, {z_{21}, z_{22}, ... }, ... }]
>   make a three-dimensional plot of the array of heights z_{yx}
>
> ListContourPlot[*array*]   make a contour plot from an array of heights
>
> ListDensityPlot[*array*]   make a density plot

Functions for plotting lists of data.

Here is a list of values.	In[1]:= **t = Table[i^2, {i, 10}]**
	Out[1]= {1, 4, 9, 16, 25, 36, 49, 64, 81, 100}
This plots the values.	In[2]:= **ListPlot[t]**

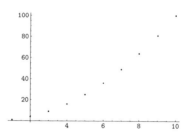

This joins the points with lines.	In[3]:= **ListPlot[t, PlotJoined -> True]**

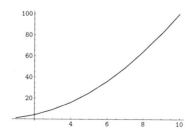

This gives a list of *x, y* pairs.	*In[4]:=* **Table[{i^2, 4 i^2 + i^3}, {i, 10}]**

Out[4]= {{1, 5}, {4, 24}, {9, 63}, {16, 128},
{25, 225}, {36, 360}, {49, 539},
{64, 768}, {81, 1053}, {100, 1400}}

This plots the points.

In[5]:= **ListPlot[%]**

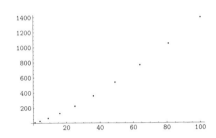

This gives a rectangular array of values. The array is quite large, so we end the input with a semicolon to stop the result from being printed out.

In[6]:= **t3 = Table[Mod[x, y], {y, 20}, {x, 30}] ;**

This makes a three-dimensional plot of the array of values.

In[7]:= **ListPlot3D[t3]**

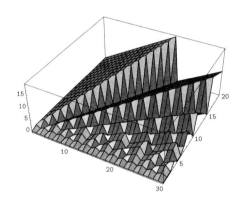

You can redraw the plot using Show, as usual.

In[8]:= **Show[%, ViewPoint -> {1.5, -0.5, 0}]**

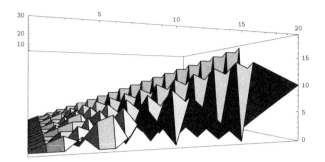

This gives a density plot of the array of values.

In[9]:= **ListDensityPlot[t3]**

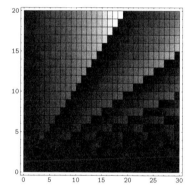

■ 1.9.9 Parametric Plots

Section 1.9.1 described how to plot curves in *Mathematica* in which you give the *y* coordinate of each point as a function of the *x* coordinate. You can also use *Mathematica* to make *parametric* plots. In a parametric plot, you give both the *x* and *y* coordinates of each point as a function of a third parameter, say *t*.

ParametricPlot[{f_x, f_y}, {t, $tmin$, $tmax$}]
                              make a parametric plot

ParametricPlot[{{f_x, f_y}, {g_x, g_y}, ... }, {t, $tmin$, $tmax$}]
                              plot several parametric curves together

ParametricPlot[{f_x, f_y}, {t, $tmin$, $tmax$}, AspectRatio -> Automatic]
                              attempt to preserve the shapes of curves

Functions for generating parametric plots.

Here is the curve made by taking the x coordinate of each point to be Sin[t] and the y coordinate to be Sin[2t].

In[1]:= **ParametricPlot[{Sin[t], Sin[2t]}, {t, 0, 2Pi}]**

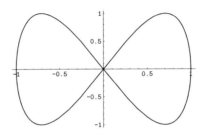

The "shape" of the curve produced depends on the ratio of height to width for the whole plot.

In[2]:= **ParametricPlot[{Sin[t], Cos[t]}, {t, 0, 2Pi}]**

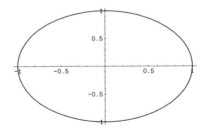

Setting the option AspectRatio to
Automatic makes *Mathematica* preserve
the "true shape" of the curve, as
defined by the actual coordinate values
it involves.

In[3]:= **Show[%, AspectRatio -> Automatic]**

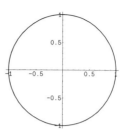

ParametricPlot3D[{f_x, f_y, f_z}, {t, *tmin*, *tmax*}]
        make a parametric plot of a three-dimensional curve

ParametricPlot3D[{f_x, f_y, f_z}, {t, *tmin*, *tmax*}, {u, *umin*, *umax*}]
        make a parametric plot of a three-dimensional surface

ParametricPlot3D[{f_x, f_y, f_z, s}, ...]
        shade the parts of the parametric plot according to the
        function *s*

ParametricPlot3D[{{f_x, f_y, f_z}, {g_x, g_y, g_z}, ... }, ...]
        plot several objects together

Three-dimensional parametric plots.

   ParametricPlot3D[{f_x, f_y, f_z}, {t, *tmin*, *tmax*}] is the direct analog in three dimensions of
ParametricPlot[{f_x, f_y}, {t, *tmin*, *tmax*}] in two dimensions. In both cases, *Mathematica* effectively
generates a sequence of points by varying the parameter *t*, then forms a curve by joining these
points. With ParametricPlot, the curve is in two dimensions; with ParametricPlot3D, it is in three
dimensions.

This makes a parametric plot of a helical curve. Varying t produces circular motion in the x, y plane, and linear motion in the z direction.

In[4]:= **ParametricPlot3D[{Sin[t], Cos[t], t/3}, {t, 0, 15}]**

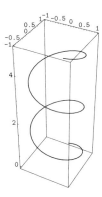

ParametricPlot3D[$\{f_x, f_y, f_z\}$, $\{t, tmin, tmax\}$, $\{u, umin, umax\}$] creates a surface, rather than a curve. The surface is formed from a collection of quadrilaterals. The corners of the quadrilaterals have coordinates corresponding to the values of the f_i when t and u take on values in a regular grid.

Here the x and y coordinates for the quadrilaterals are given simply by t and u. The result is a surface plot of the kind that can be produced by Plot3D.

In[5]:= **ParametricPlot3D[{t, u, Sin[t u]},**
{t, 0, 3}, {u, 0, 3}]

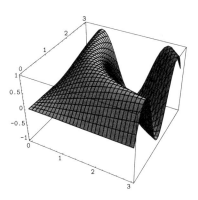

This shows the same surface as before, but with the *y* coordinates distorted by a quadratic transformation.

In[6]:= **ParametricPlot3D[{t, u^2, Sin[t u]},
{t, 0, 3}, {u, 0, 3}]**

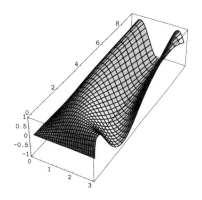

This produces a helicoid surface by taking the helical curve shown above, and at each section of the curve drawing a quadrilateral.

In[7]:= **ParametricPlot3D[{u Sin[t], u Cos[t], t/3},
{t, 0, 15}, {u, -1, 1}]**

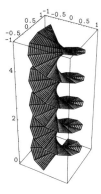

In general, it is possible to construct many complicated surfaces using `ParametricPlot3D`. In each case, you can think of the surfaces as being formed by "distorting" or "rolling up" the *t, u* coordinate grid in a certain way.

This produces a cylinder. Varying the t parameter yields a circle in the *x*, *y* plane, while varying u moves the circles in the *z* direction.

In[8]:= **ParametricPlot3D[{Sin[t], Cos[t], u},**
{t, 0, 2Pi}, {u, 0, 4}]

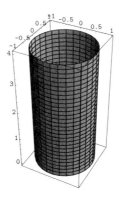

This produces a torus. Varying u yields a circle, while varying t rotates the circle around the *z* axis to form the torus.

In[9]:= **ParametricPlot3D[**
{Cos[t] (3 + Cos[u]), Sin[t] (3 + Cos[u]), Sin[u]},
{t, 0, 2Pi}, {u, 0, 2Pi}]

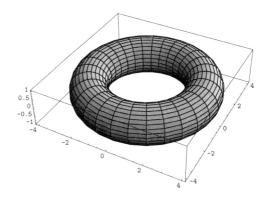

This produces a sphere.

```
In[10]:= ParametricPlot3D[
            {Cos[t] Cos[u], Sin[t] Cos[u], Sin[u]},
              {t, 0, 2Pi}, {u, -Pi/2, Pi/2}]
```

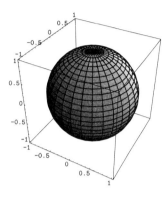

You should realize that when you draw surfaces with `ParametricPlot3D`, the exact choice of parametrization is often crucial. You should be careful, for example, to avoid parametrizations in which all or part of your surface is covered more than once. Such multiple coverings often lead to discontinuities in the mesh drawn on the surface, and may make `ParametricPlot3D` take much longer to render the surface.

■ 1.9.10 Some Special Plots

As discussed in Section 2.10, *Mathematica* includes a full graphics programming language. In this language, you can set up many different kinds of plots. A few of the common ones are included in standard *Mathematica* packages.

`<<Graphics``	load a package to set up additional graphics functions

`LogPlot[f, {x, xmin, xmax}]`	generate a log-linear plot
`LogLogPlot[f, {x, xmin, xmax}]`	generate a log-log plot
`LogListPlot[list]`	generate a log-linear plot from a list of data
`LogLogListPlot[list]`	generate a log-log plot from a list of data
`PolarPlot[r, {t, tmin, tmax}]`	generate a polar plot of the radius r as a function of angle t
`ErrorListPlot[{{x_1, y_1, dy_1}, ... }]`	generate a plot of data with error bars
`TextListPlot[{{x_1, y_1, "s_1"}, ... }]`	plot a list of data with each point given by the text string s_i
`BarChart[list]`	plot a list of data as a bar chart
`PieChart[list]`	plot a list of data as a pie chart
`PlotVectorField[{f_x, f_y}, {x, xmin, xmax}, {y, ymin, ymax}]`	plot the vector field corresponding to the vector function f
`ListPlotVectorField[list]`	plot the vector field corresponding to the two-dimensional array of vectors in *list*
`SphericalPlot3D[r, {theta, min, max}, {phi, min, max}]`	generate a three-dimensional spherical plot

Some special plotting functions defined in standard *Mathematica* packages.

This loads a standard *Mathematica* package to set up additional graphics functions.

`In[1]:= <<Graphics``

This generates a log-linear plot.

`In[2]:= LogPlot[ Exp[-x] + 4 Exp[-2x], {x, 0, 6} ]`

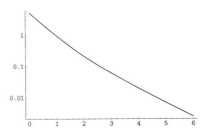

Here is a list of the first 10 primes.

In[3]:= **p = Table[Prime[n], {n, 10}]**

Out[3]= {2, 3, 5, 7, 11, 13, 17, 19, 23, 29}

This plots the primes using the integers 1, 2, 3, ... as plotting symbols.

In[4]:= **TextListPlot[p]**

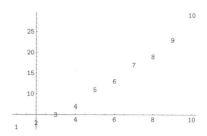

Here is a bar chart of the primes.

In[5]:= **BarChart[p]**

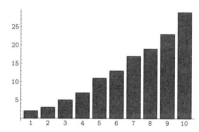

This gives a pie chart.

In[6]:= **PieChart[p]**

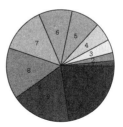

■ 1.9.11 Special Topic: Animated Graphics

On many computer systems, *Mathematica* can produce not only static images, but also animated graphics or "movies".

The basic idea in all cases is to generate a sequence of "frames" which can be displayed in rapid succession. You can use the standard *Mathematica* graphics functions described above to produce each frame. The mechanism for displaying the frames as a movie depends on the *Mathematica* interface you are using. With a notebook-based interface, you typically put the frames in a sequence of cells, then select the cells and choose a command to animate them. With text-based interfaces, there is often an external program provided for displaying animated graphics. The program can typically be accessed from inside *Mathematica* using the function `Animate`.

`<<Graphics`Animation``	load the animation package (if necessary)
`Animate[plot, {t, tmin, tmax}]`	execute the graphics command *plot* for a sequence of values of *t*, and animate the resulting sequence of frames
`ShowAnimation[{g`$_1$`, g`$_2$`, ... }]`	produce an animation from a sequence of graphics objects

Typical ways to produce animated graphics.

When you produce a sequence of frames for a movie, it is important that different frames be consistent. Thus, for example, you should typically give an explicit setting for the `PlotRange` option, rather than using the default `Automatic` setting, in order to ensure that the scales used in different frames are the same. If you have three-dimensional graphics with different view points, you should similarly set `SphericalRegion -> True` in order to ensure that the scaling of different plots is the same.

This generates a list of graphics objects. Setting `DisplayFunction -> Identity` stops `Plot3D` from rendering the graphics it produces. Explicitly setting `PlotRange` ensures that the scale is the same in each piece of graphics.

```
In[1]:= Table[ Plot3D[ BesselJ[0, Sqrt[x^2 + y^2] + t],
           {x, -10, 10}, {y, -10, 10}, Axes -> False,
           PlotRange -> {-0.5, 1.0},
           DisplayFunction -> Identity ],
        {t, 0, 8} ] // Short

Out[1]//Short= {-SurfaceGraphics-, <<7>>, -SurfaceGraphics-}
```

On an appropriate computer system, ShowAnimation[%] would animate the graphics. This partitions the graphics into three rows, and shows the resulting array of images.

In[2]:= **Show[GraphicsArray[Partition[%, 3]]]**

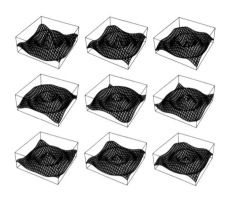

■ 1.9.12 Sound

On most computer systems, *Mathematica* can produce not only graphics but also sound. *Mathematica* treats graphics and sound in a closely analogous way.

For example, just as you can use Plot[*f*, {*x*, *xmin*, *xmax*}] to plot a function, so also you can use Play[*f*, {*t*, 0, *tmax*}] to "play" a function. Play takes the function to define the waveform for a sound: the values of the function give the amplitude of the sound as a function of time.

Play[*f*, {*t*, 0, *tmax*}]	play a sound with amplitude *f* as a function of time *t* in seconds

Playing a function.

On a suitable computer system, this plays a pure tone with a frequency of 440 hertz for one second.

In[1]:= **Play[Sin[2Pi 440 t], {t, 0, 1}]**

Out[1]= –Sound–

Sounds produced by Play can have any waveform. They do not, for example, have to consist of a collection of harmonic pieces. In general, the amplitude function you give to Play specifies the instantaneous signal associated with the sound. This signal is typically converted to a voltage, and ultimately to a displacement. Note that *amplitude* is sometimes defined to be the *peak* signal associated with a sound; in *Mathematica*, it is always the *instantaneous* signal as a function of time.

This plays a more complex sound.

In[2]:= **Play[Sin[700 t + 25 t Sin[350 t]], {t, 0, 4}]**

Out[2]= –Sound–

`Play` is set up so that the time variable that appears in it is always measured in absolute seconds. When a sound is actually played, its amplitude is sampled a certain number of times every second. You can specify the sample rate by setting the option `SampleRate`.

`Play[f, {t, 0, tmax}, SampleRate -> r]`
                    play a sound, sampling it r times a second

---

Specifying the sample rate for a sound.

In general, the higher the sample rate, the better high-frequency components in the sound will be rendered. A sample rate of r typically allows frequencies up to $r/2$ hertz. The human auditory system can typically perceive sounds in the frequency range 20 to 22000 hertz (depending somewhat on age and sex). The fundamental frequencies for the 88 notes on a piano range from 27.5 to 4096 hertz.

The standard sample rate used for compact disc players is 44100. The effective sample rate in a typical telephone system is around 8000. On most computer systems, the default sample rate used by *Mathematica* is around 8000.

You can use `Play[{f_1, f_2}, ... ]` to produce stereo sound. In general, *Mathematica* supports any number of sound channels.

`ListPlay[{a_1, a_2, ... }, SampleRate -> r]`
                    play a sound with a sequence of amplitude levels

---

Playing sampled sounds.

The function `ListPlay` allows you simply to give a list of values which are taken to be sound amplitudes sampled at a certain rate.

When sounds are actually rendered by *Mathematica*, only a certain range of amplitudes is allowed. The option `PlayRange` in `Play` and `ListPlay` specifies how the amplitudes you give should be scaled to fit in the allowed range. The settings for this option are analogous to those for the `PlotRange` graphics option discussed on page 137.

`PlayRange -> Automatic` (default)	use an internal procedure to scale amplitudes
`PlayRange -> All`	scale so that all amplitudes fit in the allowed range
`PlayRange -> {amin, amax}`	make amplitudes between *amin* and *amax* fit in the allowed range, and clip others

---

Specifying the scaling of sound amplitudes.

While it is often convenient to use the default setting PlayRange -> Automatic, you should realize that Play may run significantly faster if you give an explicit PlayRange specification, so it does not have to derive one.

Show[*sound*]   replay a sound object

Replaying a sound object.

Both Play and ListPlay return Sound objects which contain procedures for synthesizing sounds. You can replay a particular Sound object using the function Show that is also used for redisplaying graphics.

The internal structure of Sound objects is discussed in Section 2.10.18.

1.10 Input and Output in Notebooks

■ 1.10.1 Entering Greek Letters

click on α	use a button in a palette
\[Alpha]	use a full name
ESC a ESC or ESC alpha ESC	use a standard alias (shown below as ⦂a⦂)
ESC \alpha ESC	use a TeX alias
ESC &agr ESC	use an SGML alias

Ways to enter Greek letters in a notebook.

Here is a palette for entering common Greek letters.

You can use Greek letters just like the ordinary letters that you type on your keyboard.

$In[1]:=$ **Expand[(α + β)^3]**

$Out[1]=$ $\alpha^3 + 3\,\alpha^2\,\beta + 3\,\alpha\,\beta^2 + \beta^3$

There are several ways to enter Greek letters. This input uses full names.

$In[2]:=$ **Expand[(\[Alpha] + \[Beta])^3]**

$Out[2]=$ $\alpha^3 + 3\,\alpha^2\,\beta + 3\,\alpha\,\beta^2 + \beta^3$

	full name	aliases			full name	aliases
α	\[Alpha]	:a:, :alpha:		Γ	\[CapitalGamma]	:G:, :Gamma:
β	\[Beta]	:b:, :beta:		Δ	\[CapitalDelta]	:D:, :Delta:
γ	\[Gamma]	:g:, :gamma:		Θ	\[CapitalTheta]	:Q:, :Th:, :Theta:
δ	\[Delta]	:d:, :delta:		Λ	\[CapitalLambda]	:L:, :Lambda:
ϵ	\[Epsilon]	:e:, :epsilon:		Π	\[CapitalPi]	:P:, :Pi:
ζ	\[Zeta]	:z:, :zeta:		Σ	\[CapitalSigma]	:S:, :Sigma:
η	\[Eta]	:h:, :et:, :eta:		Υ	\[CapitalUpsilon]	:U:, :Upsilon:
θ	\[Theta]	:q:, :th:, :theta:		Φ	\[CapitalPhi]	:F:, :Ph:, :Phi:
κ	\[Kappa]	:k:, :kappa:		X	\[CapitalChi]	:C:, :Ch:, :Chi:
λ	\[Lambda]	:l:, :lambda:		Ψ	\[CapitalPsi]	:Y:, :Ps:, :Psi:
μ	\[Mu]	:m:, :mu:		Ω	\[CapitalOmega]	:O:, :W:, :Omega:
ν	\[Nu]	:n:, :nu:				
ξ	\[Xi]	:x:, :xi:				
π	\[Pi]	:p:, :pi:				
ρ	\[Rho]	:r:, :rho:				
σ	\[Sigma]	:s:, :sigma:				
τ	\[Tau]	:t:, :tau:				
ϕ	\[Phi]	:f:, :ph:, :phi:				
φ	\[CurlyPhi]	:j:, :cph:, :cphi:				
χ	\[Chi]	:c:, :ch:, :chi:				
ψ	\[Psi]	:y:, :ps:, :psi:				
ω	\[Omega]	:o:, :w:, :omega:				

Commonly used Greek letters. In aliases : stands for the key [ESC]. T_EX aliases are not listed explicitly.

Note that in *Mathematica* the letter π stands for Pi. None of the other Greek letters have special meanings.

π stands for Pi.	*In[3]:=* **N[π]**
	Out[3]= 3.14159
You can use Greek letters either on their own or with other letters.	*In[4]:=* **Expand[(Rαβ + Ξ)^4]**
	Out[4]= $R\alpha\beta^4 + 4\,R\alpha\beta^3\,\Xi + 6\,R\alpha\beta^2\,\Xi^2 + 4\,R\alpha\beta\,\Xi^3 + \Xi^4$
The symbol $\pi\alpha$ is not related to the symbol π.	*In[5]:=* **Factor[πα^4 - 1]**
	Out[5]= $(-1 + \pi\alpha)\,(1 + \pi\alpha)\,(1 + \pi\alpha^2)$

■ 1.10.2 Entering Two-Dimensional Input

When *Mathematica* reads the text x^y, it interprets it as x raised to the power y.

$In[1]:=$ **x^y**

$Out[1]=$ x^y

In a notebook, you can also give the two-dimensional input x^y directly. *Mathematica* again interprets this as a power.

$In[2]:=$ **x^y**

$Out[2]=$ x^y

One way to enter a two-dimensional form such as x^y into a *Mathematica* notebook is to copy this form from a palette by clicking the appropriate button in the palette.

Here is a palette for entering some common two-dimensional notations.

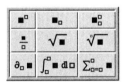

There are also several ways to enter two-dimensional forms directly from the keyboard.

x CTRL[^] y CTRL[␣]	use control keys that exist on most keyboards
x CTRL[6] y CTRL[␣]	use control keys that should exist on all keyboards
\!\(x\^y\) followed by Make 2D	use only ordinary printable characters

Ways to enter a superscript directly from the keyboard. CTRL[␣] stands for CONTROL-SPACE.

You type CTRL[^] by holding down the CONTROL key, then hitting the ^ key. As soon as you do this, your cursor will jump to a superscript position. You can then type anything you want and it will appear in that position.

When you have finished, press CTRL[␣] to move back down from the superscript position. CTRL[␣] stands for CONTROL-SPACE; you type it by holding down the CONTROL key, then pressing the space bar.

This sequence of keystrokes enters x^y.

$In[3]:=$ **x** CTRL[^] **y**

$Out[3]=$ x^y

Here the whole expression y+z is in the superscript.

$In[4]:=$ **x** CTRL[^] **y + z**

$Out[4]=$ x^{y+z}

Pressing CTRL[␣] (CONTROL-SPACE) takes you down from the superscript.

$In[5]:=$ **x** CTRL[^] **y** CTRL[␣] **+ z**

$Out[5]=$ $x^y + z$

You can remember the fact that CTRL[^] gives you a superscript by thinking of CTRL[^] as just a more immediate form of ^. When you type x^y, *Mathematica* will leave this one-dimensional form unchanged until you explicitly process it. But if you type x [CTRL][^] y then *Mathematica* will immediately give you a superscript.

On a standard English-language keyboard, the character ^ appears as the shifted version of 6. *Mathematica* therefore accepts [CTRL][6] as an alternative to [CTRL][^]. Note that if you are using something other than a standard English-language keyboard, *Mathematica* will almost always accept [CTRL][6] but may not accept [CTRL][^].

This is an alternative input form that avoids the use of control characters.	$In[6]:= \ !\ (\ x \ \backslash^\wedge \ y \ )$ $Out[6]= x^y$
With this input form, *Mathematica* automatically understands that the + z does not go in the superscript.	$In[7]:= \ !\ (\ x \ \backslash^\wedge \ y \ + \ z \ )$ $Out[7]= x^y + z$

Using control characters minimizes the number of keystrokes that you need to type in order to enter a superscript. But particularly if you want to save your input in a file, or send it to another program, it is often more convenient to use a form that does not involve control characters. You can do this using \! sequences.

If you copy a \! sequence into *Mathematica*, it will automatically jump into two-dimensional form. But if you enter the sequence directly from the keyboard, you explicitly need to choose the Make 2D menu item in order to get the two-dimensional form.

When entered from the keyboard \(... \) sequences are shown in literal form.	`\!\(x\^y + z\)`
Choosing the Make 2D item in the Edit menu converts these sequences into two-dimensional forms.	$x^y + z$

x [CTRL][_] y [CTRL][␣]	use control keys that exist on most keyboards
x [CTRL][-] y [CTRL][␣]	use control keys that should exist on all keyboards
\!\(x_y\) followed by Make 2D	use only ordinary printable characters

Ways to enter a subscript directly from the keyboard.

Subscripts in *Mathematica* work very much like superscripts. However, whereas *Mathematica* automatically interprets x^y as x raised to the power y, it has no similar interpretation for x_y. Instead, it just treats x_y as a purely symbolic object.

This enters y as a subscript.	$In[8]:= x$ [CTRL][_] y $Out[8]= x_y$

Here is another way to enter y as a subscript.

$In[9]:= \!\(x \_ y \)$

$Out[9]= x_y$

---

x ⌷CTRL⌷$/$ y ⌷CTRL⌷$␣$	use control keys
$\!\(x\/y\)$ followed by Make 2D	use only ordinary printable characters

Ways to enter a built-up fraction directly from the keyboard.

This enters the built-up fraction $\frac{x}{y}$.

$In[10]:= x$ ⌷CTRL⌷$/$ y

$Out[10]= \dfrac{x}{y}$

Here the whole y + z goes into the denominator.

$In[11]:= x$ ⌷CTRL⌷$/$ $y + z$

$Out[11]= \dfrac{x}{y+z}$

But pressing CONTROL-SPACE takes you out of the denominator, so the + z does not appear in the denominator.

$In[12]:= x$ ⌷CTRL⌷$/$ y ⌷CTRL⌷$␣$ $+ z$

$Out[12]= \dfrac{x}{y} + z$

Mathematica automatically interprets a built-up fraction as a division.

$In[13]:= \dfrac{8888}{2222}$

$Out[13]= 4$

Here is another way to enter a built-up fraction.

$In[14]:= \!\(8888 \/ 2222 \)$

$Out[14]= 4$

⌷CTRL⌷$@$ x ⌷CTRL⌷$␣$	use control keys that exist on most keyboards
⌷CTRL⌷2 x ⌷CTRL⌷$␣$	use control keys that should exist on all keyboards
$\!\(\@x\)$ followed by Make 2D	use only ordinary printable characters

Ways to enter a square root directly from the keyboard.

This enters a square root.

$In[15]:= $ ⌷CTRL⌷$@$ $x + y$

$Out[15]= \sqrt{x+y}$

CONTROL-SPACE takes you out of the square root.

$In[16]:= $ ⌷CTRL⌷$@$ x ⌷CTRL⌷$␣$ $+ y$

$Out[16]= \sqrt{x} + y$

Here is a form without control characters.

$In[17]:= \!\(\@ x + y \)$

$Out[17]= \sqrt{x} + y$

And here is the usual one-dimensional *Mathematica* input that gives the same output expression.

$In[18]:=$ **Sqrt[x] + y**

$Out[18]=$ $\sqrt{x} + y$

CTRL ^ or CTRL 6	go to the superscript position	
CTRL _ or CTRL -	go to the subscript position	
CTRL @ or CTRL 2	go into a square root	
CTRL % or CTRL 5	go from subscript to superscript or vice versa, or to the exponent position in a root	
CTRL /	go to the denominator for a fraction	
CTRL ␣	return from a special position (CONTROL-SPACE)	

Special input forms based on control characters. The second forms given should work on any keyboard.

This puts both a subscript and a superscript on x.

$In[19]:=$ **x** CTRL ^ **y** CTRL % **z**

$Out[19]=$ x_z^y

Here is another way to enter the same expression.

$In[20]:=$ **x** CTRL _ **z** CTRL % **y**

$Out[20]=$ x_z^y

\!\(... \)	all two-dimensional input and grouping within it
x \^ y	superscript x^y within \!\(... \)
x _ y	subscript x_y within \!\(... \)
x \^ y \% z	subscript and superscript x_z^y within \!\(... \)
\@ x	square root $\sqrt{x}$ within \!\(... \)
x \/ y	built-up fraction $\frac{x}{y}$ within \!\(... \)

Special input forms that generate two-dimensional input with the Make 2D menu item.

You must preface the outermost \(with \!.

$In[21]:=$ **\!\(a \/ b + \@ c \) + d**

$Out[21]=$ $\dfrac{a}{b} + \sqrt{c} + d$

You can use \(and \) to indicate the grouping of elements in an expression without introducing explicit parentheses.

$In[22]:= \verb|\!\(a \/ \(b + \@ c \) \) + d|$

$$Out[22]= \frac{a}{b + \sqrt{c}} + d$$

In addition to subscripts and superscripts, *Mathematica* also supports the notion of underscripts and overscripts—elements that go directly underneath or above. Among other things, you can use underscripts and overscripts to enter the limits of sums and products.

x [CTRL][+] y [CTRL][␣] or x [CTRL][=] y [CTRL][␣]	create an underscript $\underset{y}{x}$
\!\(x\+y\) followed by Make 2D	create an underscript $\underset{y}{x}$
x [CTRL][&] y [CTRL][␣] or x [CTRL][7] y [CTRL][␣]	create an overscript $\overset{y}{x}$
\!\(x\&y\) followed by Make 2D	create an overscript $\overset{y}{x}$

Creating underscripts and overscripts.

■ 1.10.3 Editing and Evaluating Two-Dimensional Expressions

When you see a two-dimensional expression on the screen, you can edit it much as you would edit text. You can for example place your cursor somewhere and start typing. Or you can select a part of the expression, then remove it using the DELETE key, or insert a new version by typing it in.

In addition to ordinary text editing features, there are some keys that you can use to move around in two-dimensional expressions.

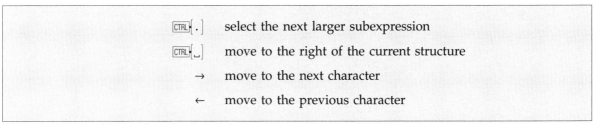

[CTRL][.]	select the next larger subexpression
[CTRL][␣]	move to the right of the current structure
→	move to the next character
←	move to the previous character

Ways to move around in two-dimensional expressions.

This shows the sequence of subexpressions selected by repeatedly typing [CTRL] . .

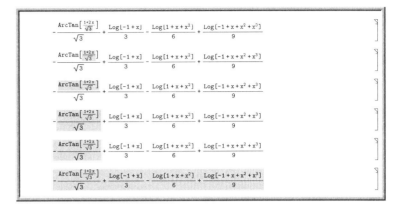

SHIFT-ENTER	evaluate the whole current cell
SHIFT-CONTROL-ENTER or COMMAND-RETURN	evaluate only the selected subexpression

Ways to evaluate two-dimensional expressions.

In most computations, you will want to go from one step to the next by taking the whole expression that you have generated, and then evaluating it. But if for example you are trying to manipulate a single formula to put it into a particular form, you may instead find it more convenient to perform a sequence of operations separately on different parts of the expression.

You do this by selecting each part you want to operate on, then inserting the operation you want to perform, then using SHIFT-CONTROL-ENTER or COMMAND-RETURN.

Here is an expression with one part selected.

{Factor[x⁴ - 1], **Factor[x⁵ - 1]**, Factor[x⁶ - 1], Factor[x⁷ - 1]}

Pressing SHIFT-CONTROL-ENTER evaluates the selected part.

{Factor[x⁴ - 1], (-1 + x) (1 + x + x² + x³ + x⁴), Factor[x⁶ - 1], Factor[x⁷ - 1]}

■ 1.10.4 Entering Formulas

character	short form	long form	symbol
π	⬚p⬚	\[Pi]	Pi
∞	⬚inf⬚	\[Infinity]	Infinity
$\circ$	⬚deg⬚	\[Degree]	Degree

Special forms for some common symbols. ⬚ stands for the key ESC.

This is equivalent to Sin[60 Degree].

$In[1]:=$ **Sin[60°]**

$Out[1]=$ $\dfrac{\sqrt{3}}{2}$

Here is the long form of the input.

$In[2]:=$ **Sin[60 \[Degree]]**

$Out[2]=$ $\dfrac{\sqrt{3}}{2}$

You can enter the same input like this.

$In[3]:=$ **Sin[60 ⬚deg⬚]**

$Out[3]=$ $\dfrac{\sqrt{3}}{2}$

Here the angle is in radians.

$In[4]:=$ **Sin$\left[\dfrac{\pi}{3}\right]$**

$Out[4]=$ $\dfrac{\sqrt{3}}{2}$

special characters	short form	long form	ordinary characters
$x \le y$	x ⬚<=⬚ y	x \[LessEqual] y	x <= y
$x \ge y$	x ⬚>=⬚ y	x \[GreaterEqual] y	x >= y
$x \ne y$	x ⬚!=⬚ y	x \[NotEqual] y	x != y
$x \in y$	x ⬚el⬚ y	x \[Element] y	Element[x, y]
$x \to y$	x ⬚->⬚ y	x \[Rule] y	x -> y

Special forms for a few operators. Pages 1024–1029 give a complete list.

Here the replacement rule is entered using two ordinary characters, as ->.

$In[5]:=$ **x/(x+1) /. x -> 3 + y**

$Out[5]=$ $\dfrac{3+y}{4+y}$

This means exactly the same.

$In[6]:=$ **x/(x+1) /. x \[Rule] 3 + y**

$Out[6]=$ $\dfrac{3+y}{4+y}$

As does this.

$In[7]:=$ **x/(x+1) /. x → 3 + y**

$Out[7]=$ $\dfrac{3+y}{4+y}$

Or this.

$In[8]:=$ **x/(x+1) /. x ⦂->⦂ 3 + y**

$Out[8]=$ $\dfrac{3+y}{4+y}$

The special arrow form → is by default also used for output.

$In[9]:=$ **Solve[x^2 == 1, x]**

$Out[9]=$ $\{\{x \to -1\}, \{x \to 1\}\}$

special characters	short form	long form	ordinary characters
$x \div y$	$x \,\text{⦂div⦂}\, y$	x \[Divide] y	$x\ /\ y$
$x \times y$	$x \,\text{⦂*⦂}\, y$	x \[Times] y	$x\ *\ y$
$x \times y$	$x \,\text{⦂cross⦂}\, y$	x \[Cross] y	Cross$[x,\ y]$
$x == y$	$x \,\text{⦂==⦂}\, y$	x \[Equal] y	$x == y$
$+\ x = y$	$x \,\text{⦂l=⦂}\, y$	x \[LongEqual] y	$x == y$
$x \wedge y$	$x \,\text{⦂\&\&⦂}\, y$	x \[And] y	x && y
$x \vee y$	$x \,\text{⦂||⦂}\, y$	x \[Or] y	x || y
$\neg\, x$	$\text{⦂!⦂}\, x$	\[Not] x	!x
$x \Rightarrow y$	$x \,\text{⦂=>⦂}\, y$	x \[Implies] y	Implies$[x,\ y]$
$x \cup y$	$x \,\text{⦂un⦂}\, y$	x \[Union] y	Union$[x,\ y]$
$x \cap y$	$x \,\text{⦂inter⦂}\, y$	x \[Intersection] y	Intersection$[x,\ y]$
xy	$x \,\text{⦂,⦂}\, y$	x \[InvisibleComma] y	x,y
fx	$f \,\text{⦂@⦂}\, x$	f \[InvisibleApplication] x	$f@x$ or $f[x]$

Some operators with special forms used for input but not output.

Mathematica understands ÷, but does
not use it by default for output.

$$In[10]:= \mathbf{x \div y}$$

$$Out[10]= \frac{x}{y}$$

The forms of input discussed so far in this section use special characters, but otherwise just consist of ordinary one-dimensional lines of text. *Mathematica* notebooks, however, also make it possible to use two-dimensional forms of input.

two-dimensional	one-dimensional	
x^y	x ^ y	power
$\dfrac{x}{y}$	x / y	division
$\sqrt{x}$	Sqrt[x]	square root
$\sqrt[n]{x}$	x ^ (1/n)	n^{th} root
$\displaystyle\sum_{i=imin}^{imax} f$	Sum[f, {i, imin, imax}]	sum
$\displaystyle\prod_{i=imin}^{imax} f$	Product[f, {i, imin, imax}]	product
$\displaystyle\int f\,dx$	Integrate[f, x]	indefinite integral
$\displaystyle\int_{xmin}^{xmax} f\,dx$	Integrate[f, {x, xmin, xmax}]	definite integral
$\partial_x f$	D[f, x]	partial derivative
$\partial_{x,y} f$	D[f, x, y]	multivariate partial derivative
$expr_{[i,j,...]}$	Part[expr, i, j, ...]	part extraction

Some two-dimensional forms that can be used in *Mathematica* notebooks.

You can enter two-dimensional forms using any of the mechanisms discussed on pages 176–180. Note that upper and lower limits for sums and products must be entered as overscripts and underscripts—not superscripts and subscripts.

This enters an indefinite integral. Note the use of ⁝dd⁝ to enter the "differential d".

$$In[11]:= \texttt{⁝int⁝ f[x] ⁝dd⁝ x}$$

$$Out[11]= \int f[x]\,dx$$

| Here is an indefinite integral that can be explicitly evaluated. | $In[12]:=$ $\int$ **Exp[-x^2] dx** |
| | $Out[12]=$ $\frac{1}{2}\sqrt{\pi}\,$ Erf[x] |

| Here is the usual *Mathematica* input for this integral. | $In[13]:=$ **Integrate[Exp[-x^2], x]** |
| | $Out[13]=$ $\frac{1}{2}\sqrt{\pi}\,$ Erf[x] |

| This enters exactly the same integral. | $In[14]:=$ **\!\(\[Integral] Exp[-x\^2] \[DifferentialD]x \)** |
| | $Out[14]=$ $\frac{1}{2}\sqrt{\pi}\,$ Erf[x] |

short form	long form	
⋮sum⋮	\[Sum]	summation sign $\sum$
⋮prod⋮	\[Product]	product sign $\prod$
⋮int⋮	\[Integral]	integral sign $\int$
⋮dd⋮	\[DifferentialD]	special d for use in integrals
⋮pd⋮	\[PartialD]	partial derivative operator ∂
⋮[[⋮, ⋮]]⋮	\[LeftDoubleBracket], \[RightDoubleBracket] part brackets	

Some special characters used in entering formulas. Section 3.10 gives a complete list.

You should realize that even though a summation sign can look almost identical to a capital sigma it is treated in a very different way by *Mathematica*. The point is that a sigma is just a letter; but a summation sign is an operator which tells *Mathematica* to perform a Sum operation.

| Capital sigma is just a letter. | $In[15]:=$ **a + \[CapitalSigma]^2** |
| | $Out[15]=$ $a + \Sigma^2$ |

| A summation sign, on the other hand, is an operator. | $In[16]:=$ ⎡ESC⎤**sum**⎡ESC⎤ ⎡CTRL⎤**+** **n=0** ⎡CTRL⎤**%** **m** ⎡CTRL⎤⎵ **1/f[n]** |
| | $Out[16]=$ $\displaystyle\sum_{n=0}^{m}\frac{1}{f[n]}$ |

| Here is another way to enter the same input. | $In[17]:=$ **\!\(\[Sum] \+ \(n = 0 \) \% m 1 \/ f[n] \)** |
| | $Out[17]=$ $\displaystyle\sum_{n=0}^{m}\frac{1}{f[n]}$ |

Much as *Mathematica* distinguishes between a summation sign and a capital sigma, it also distinguishes between an ordinary d and the special "differential d" $\mathbb{d}$ that is used in the standard notation for integrals. It is crucial that you use this differential $\mathbb{d}$—entered as ⎡ESC⎤dd⎡ESC⎤—when you type in an integral. If you try to use an ordinary d, *Mathematica* will just interpret this as a symbol called d—it will not understand that you are entering the second part of an integration operator.

This computes the derivative of x^n.	$In[18]:= \partial_x x^n$
	$Out[18]= n\, x^{-1+n}$

Here is the same derivative specified in ordinary one-dimensional form.	$In[19]:= D[x\char`\^n, x]$
	$Out[19]= n\, x^{-1+n}$

This computes the third derivative.	$In[20]:= \partial_{x,x,x} x^n$
	$Out[20]= (-2+n)\,(-1+n)\,n\,x^{-3+n}$

Here is the equivalent one-dimensional input form.	$In[21]:= D[x\char`\^n, x, x, x]$
	$Out[21]= (-2+n)\,(-1+n)\,n\,x^{-3+n}$

■ 1.10.5 Entering Tables and Matrices

The *Mathematica* front end typically provides a Create Table/Matrix/Palette menu item which allows you to create a blank array with any specified number of rows and columns. Once you have such an array, you can then edit it to fill in whatever elements you want.

Mathematica treats an array like this as a matrix represented by a list of lists.	$In[1]:= \begin{matrix} a & b & c \\ 1 & 2 & 3 \end{matrix}$
	$Out[1]= \{\{a, b, c\}, \{1, 2, 3\}\}$

Putting parentheses around the array makes it look more like a matrix, but does not affect its interpretation.	$In[2]:= \begin{pmatrix} a & b & c \\ 1 & 2 & 3 \end{pmatrix}$
	$Out[2]= \{\{a, b, c\}, \{1, 2, 3\}\}$

Using $\mathtt{MatrixForm}$ tells *Mathematica* to display the result of the $\mathtt{Transpose}$ as a matrix.	$In[3]:= \mathtt{MatrixForm}\left[\mathtt{Transpose}\left[\begin{pmatrix} a & b & c \\ 1 & 2 & 3 \end{pmatrix}\right]\right]$
	$Out[3]//MatrixForm= \begin{pmatrix} a & 1 \\ b & 2 \\ c & 3 \end{pmatrix}$

$\boxed{\text{CTRL}}\boxed{,}$	add a column
$\boxed{\text{CTRL}}\boxed{\leftarrow}$ (CONTROL-ENTER)	add a row
TAB	go to the next □ or ■ element
$\boxed{\text{CTRL}}\boxed{\ }$ (CONTROL-SPACE)	move out of the table or matrix

Entering tables and matrices.

Note that you can use $\boxed{\text{CTRL}}\boxed{,}$ and $\boxed{\text{CTRL}}\boxed{\leftarrow}$ to start building up an array, and particularly for small arrays this is often more convenient than using the Create Table/Matrix/Palette menu item.

Page 449 will describe how to adjust many aspects of the appearance of arrays you create in *Mathematica*. The Create Table/Matrix/Palette menu item typically allows you to make basic adjustments, such as drawing lines between rows or columns.

■ 1.10.6 Subscripts, Bars and Other Modifiers

Here is a typical palette of modifiers.

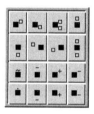

Mathematica allows you to use any expression as a subscript.

$In[1]:=$ **Expand$\left[(1 + x_{1+n})^4\right]$**

$Out[1]=$ $1 + 4\,x_{1+n} + 6\,x_{1+n}^2 + 4\,x_{1+n}^3 + x_{1+n}^4$

Unless you specifically tell it otherwise, *Mathematica* will interpret a superscript as a power.

$In[2]:=$ **Factor$[x_n^4 - 1]$**

$Out[2]=$ $(-1 + x_n)\,(1 + x_n)\,(1 + x_n^2)$

CTRL $\_$ or CTRL $-$	go to the position for a subscript
CTRL $+$ or CTRL $=$	go to the position underneath
CTRL $\wedge$ or CTRL 6	go to the position for a superscript
CTRL $\&$ or CTRL 7	go to the position on top
CTRL $\_$	return from a special position (CONTROL-SPACE)

Special input forms based on control characters. The second forms given should work on any keyboard.

This enters a subscript using control keys.

$In[3]:=$ **Expand[(1 + x** CTRL $\_$ **1+n** CTRL $\_$ **)^4]**

$Out[3]=$ $1 + 4\,x_{1+n} + 6\,x_{1+n}^2 + 4\,x_{1+n}^3 + x_{1+n}^4$

Just as CTRL $\wedge$ and CTRL $\_$ go to superscript and subscript positions, so also CTRL $\&$ and CTRL $=$ can be used to go to positions directly above and below. With the layout of a standard English-language keyboard CTRL $\&$ is directly to the right of CTRL $\wedge$ while CTRL $=$ is directly to the right of CTRL $\_$.

key sequence	displayed form	expression form
x CTRL $\&$ $\_$	$\bar{x}$	OverBar[x]
x CTRL $\&$: vec :	$\vec{x}$	OverVector[x]
x CTRL $\&$ $\sim$	$\tilde{x}$	OverTilde[x]
x CTRL $\&$ $\wedge$	$\hat{x}$	OverHat[x]
x CTRL $\&$.	$\dot{x}$	OverDot[x]
x CTRL $=$ $\_$	$\underline{x}$	UnderBar[x]

Ways to enter some common modifiers using control keys.

Here is $\bar{x}$.

$In[4]:=$ **x** CTRL $\&$ $\_$ CTRL $\_$

$Out[4]=$ $\bar{x}$

You can use $\bar{x}$ as a variable.

$In[5]:=$ **Solve[a^2 == %, a]**

$Out[5]=$ $\left\{ \left\{ a \to -\sqrt{\bar{x}} \right\}, \left\{ a \to \sqrt{\bar{x}} \right\} \right\}$

key sequence	displayed form	expression form
x _ y	x_y	Subscript[x, y]
x \\+ y	$\begin{smallmatrix}x\\y\end{smallmatrix}$	Underscript[x, y]
x \\^ y	x^y	Superscript[x, y] (interpreted as Power[x, y])
x \\& y	$\overset{y}{x}$	Overscript[x, y]
x \\&_	$\bar{x}$	OverBar[x]
x \\&\\[RightVector]	$\vec{x}$	OverVector[x]
x \\&~	$\tilde{x}$	OverTilde[x]
x \\&^	$\hat{x}$	OverHat[x]
x \\&.	$\dot{x}$	OverDot[x]
x \\+_	$\underline{x}$	UnderBar[x]

Ways to enter modifiers without control keys. All these forms can be used only inside \\!\\(... \\).

■ 1.10.7 Special Topic: Non-English Characters and Keyboards

If you enter text in languages other than English, you will typically need to use various additional accented and other characters. If your computer system is set up in an appropriate way, then you will often be able to enter such characters directly using standard keys on your keyboard. But however your system is set up, *Mathematica* always provides a uniform way to handle such characters.

	full name	*alias*		*full name*	*alias*
à	\[AGrave]	:a`:	ø	\[OSlash]	:o/:
å	\[ARing]	:ao:	ö	\[ODoubleDot]	:o":
ä	\[ADoubleDot]	:a":	ù	\[UGrave]	:u`:
ç	\[CCedilla]	:c,:	ü	\[UDoubleDot]	:u":
č	\[CHacek]	:cv:	ß	\[SZ]	:sz:, :ss:
é	\[EAcute]	:e':	Å	\[CapitalARing]	:Ao:
è	\[EGrave]	:e`:	Ä	\[CapitalADoubleDot]	:A":
í	\[IAcute]	:i':	Ö	\[CapitalODoubleDot]	:O":
ñ	\[NTilde]	:n~:	Ü	\[CapitalUDoubleDot]	:U":
ò	\[OGrave]	:o`:			

Some common European characters.

Here is a function whose name involves an accented character.	In[1]:= **Lam\[EAcute][x, y]** Out[1]= Lamé[x, y]
This is another way to enter the same input.	In[2]:= **Lam:e':[x, y]** Out[2]= Lamé[x, y]

You should realize that there is no uniform standard for computer keyboards around the world, and as a result it is inevitable that some details of what has been said in this chapter may not apply to your keyboard.

In particular, the identification for example of CTRL-6 with CTRL-^ is valid only for keyboards on which ^ appears as SHIFT-6. On other keyboards, *Mathematica* uses CTRL-6 to go to a superscript position, but not necessarily CTRL-^.

Regardless of how your keyboard is set up you can always use palettes or menu items to set up superscripts and other kinds of notation. And assuming you have some way to enter characters such as \, you can always give input using full names such as \[Infinity] and textual forms such as \(x\/y\).

■ 1.10.8 Other Mathematical Notation

Mathematica supports an extremely wide range of mathematical notation, although often it does not assign a pre-defined meaning to it. Thus, for example, you can enter an expression such as x ⊕ y, but *Mathematica* will not initially make any assumption about what you mean by ⊕.

Mathematica knows that ⊕ is an operator, but it does not initially assign any specific meaning to it.	In[1]:= **{17 ⊕ 5, 8 ⊕ 3}** Out[1]= {17⊕5, 8⊕3}

This gives *Mathematica* a definition for what the ⊕ operator does.

In[2]:= `x_ ⊕ y_ := Mod[x + y, 2]`

Now *Mathematica* can evaluate ⊕ operations.

In[3]:= `{17 ⊕ 5, 8 ⊕ 3}`

Out[3]= `{0, 1}`

	full name	alias			full name	alias
⊕	\[CirclePlus]	⦂c+⦂		⟶	\[LongRightArrow]	⦂-->⦂
⊗	\[CircleTimes]	⦂c*⦂		↔	\[LeftRightArrow]	⦂<->⦂
±	\[PlusMinus]	⦂+-⦂		↑	\[UpArrow]	
∧	\[Wedge]	⦂^⦂		⇌	\[Equilibrium]	⦂equi⦂
∨	\[Vee]	⦂v⦂		⊢	\[RightTee]	
≃	\[TildeEqual]	⦂~=⦂		⊃	\[Superset]	⦂sup⦂
≈	\[TildeTilde]	⦂~~⦂		⊓	\[SquareIntersection]	
∼	\[Tilde]	⦂~⦂		∈	\[Element]	⦂elem⦂
∝	\[Proportional]	⦂prop⦂		∉	\[NotElement]	⦂!elem⦂
≡	\[Congruent]	⦂===⦂		∘	\[SmallCircle]	⦂sc⦂
≳	\[GreaterTilde]	⦂>~⦂		∴	\[Therefore]	
≫	\[GreaterGreater]			|	\[VerticalSeparator]	⦂|⦂
≻	\[Succeeds]			❘	\[VerticalBar]	⦂ ⎵ |⦂
▷	\[RightTriangle]			\	\[Backslash]	⦂\\⦂

A few of the operators whose input is supported by *Mathematica*.

Mathematica assigns built-in meanings to ≥ and ≳, but not to ≧ or ≫.

In[4]:= `{3 ≥ 4, 3 ≳ 4, 3 ≧ 4, 3 ≫ 4}`

Out[4]= `{False, False, 3 ≧ 4, 3 ≫ 4}`

There are some forms which look like characters on a standard keyboard, but which are interpreted in a different way by *Mathematica*. Thus, for example, \[Backslash] or ⦂\⦂ displays as \ but is not interpreted in the same way as a \ typed directly on the keyboard.

The \ and ∧ characters used here are different from the \ and ^ you would type directly on a keyboard.

In[5]:= `{a ⦂\⦂ b, a ⦂^⦂ b}`

Out[5]= `{a \ b, a ∧ b}`

Most operators work like ⊕ and go in between their operands. But some operators can go in other places. Thus, for example, ⦂<⦂ and ⦂>⦂ or \[LeftAngleBracket] and \[RightAngleBracket] are effectively operators which go around their operand.

The elements of the angle bracket operator go around their operand.

In[6]:= `\[LeftAngleBracket] 1 + x \[RightAngleBracket]`

Out[6]= `⟨1 + x⟩`

	full name	alias		full name	alias
l	\[ScriptL]	:scl:	Å	\[Angstrom]	:Ang:
$\mathcal{E}$	\[ScriptCapitalE]	:scE:	$\hbar$	\[HBar]	:hb:
$\mathfrak{R}$	\[GothicCapitalR]	:goR:	£	\[Sterling]	
$\mathbb{Z}$	\[DoubleStruckCapitalZ]	:dsZ:	$\angle$	\[Angle]	
$\aleph$	\[Aleph]	:al:	•	\[Bullet]	:bu:
$\emptyset$	\[EmptySet]	:es:	†	\[Dagger]	:dg:
μ	\[Micro]	:mi:	$\natural$	\[Natural]	

Some additional letters and letter-like forms.

You can use letters and letter-like forms anywhere in symbol names.

```
In[7]:= {R∅, \[Angle]ABC}
Out[7]= {R∅, ∠ABC}
```

$\emptyset$ is assumed to be a symbol, and so is just multiplied by a and b.

```
In[8]:= a ∅ b
Out[8]= a b ∅
```

■ 1.10.9 Forms of Input and Output

Mathematica notebooks allow you to give input and get output in a variety of different forms. Typically the front end provides menu commands for converting cells from one form to another.

InputForm	a form that can be typed directly using characters on a standard keyboard
OutputForm	a form for output only that uses just characters on a standard keyboard
StandardForm	a form for input and output that makes use of special characters and positioning
TraditionalForm	a form primarily for output that imitates all aspects of traditional mathematical notation

Forms of input and output.

The input here works in both InputForm and StandardForm.

```
In[1]:= x^2 + y^2/z
```

$$Out[1]= x^2 + \frac{y^2}{z}$$

Here is a version of the input appropriate for StandardForm.

$In[2]:= \mathbf{x^2 + \dfrac{y^2}{z}}$

$Out[2]= x^2 + \dfrac{y^2}{z}$

InputForm is the most general form of input for *Mathematica*: it works whether you are using a notebook interface or a text-based interface.

With a notebook interface, output is by default produced in StandardForm.

$In[3]:= \mathbf{Sqrt[x] + 1/(2 + Sqrt[y])}$

$Out[3]= \sqrt{x} + \dfrac{1}{2 + \sqrt{y}}$

With a text-based interface, OutputForm is used instead.

$In[4]:= \mathbf{Sqrt[x] + 1/(2 + Sqrt[y]) \ // \ OutputForm}$

$Out[4]//OutputForm= \ Sqrt[x] + \dfrac{1}{2 + Sqrt[y]}$

With a notebook interface, the default form for both input and output is StandardForm.

The basic idea of StandardForm is to provide a precise but elegant representation of *Mathematica* expressions, making use of special characters, two-dimensional positioning, and so on.

Both input and output are given here in StandardForm.

$In[5]:= \displaystyle\int \dfrac{1}{(x^3 + 1)} \, \mathbf{d}x$

$Out[5]= \dfrac{ArcTan\left[\frac{-1+2x}{\sqrt{3}}\right]}{\sqrt{3}} + \dfrac{1}{3} Log[1 + x] - \dfrac{1}{6} Log[1 - x + x^2]$

An important feature of StandardForm is that any output you get in this form you can also directly use as input.

$In[6]:= \dfrac{ArcTan\left[\frac{-1+2x}{\sqrt{3}}\right]}{\sqrt{3}} + \dfrac{Log[1 + x]}{3} - \dfrac{Log[1 - x + x^2]}{6}$

$Out[6]= \dfrac{ArcTan\left[\frac{-1+2x}{\sqrt{3}}\right]}{\sqrt{3}} + \dfrac{1}{3} Log[1 + x] - \dfrac{1}{6} Log[1 - x + x^2]$

The precise nature of StandardForm prevents it from following all of the somewhat haphazard conventions of traditional mathematical notation. *Mathematica* however also supports TraditionalForm, which uses a large collection of rules to give a rather complete rendition of traditional mathematical notation.

TraditionalForm uses lower-case names for functions, and puts their arguments in parentheses rather than square brackets.

$In[7]:= \displaystyle\int \dfrac{1}{(x^3 + 1)} \, \mathbf{d}x \ // \ \mathbf{TraditionalForm}$

$Out[7]//TraditionalForm= \dfrac{\tan^{-1}\left(\frac{2x-1}{\sqrt{3}}\right)}{\sqrt{3}} + \dfrac{1}{3} \log(x + 1) - \dfrac{1}{6} \log(x^2 - x + 1)$

Here are a few transformations made by TraditionalForm.

$In[8]:= \mathbf{\{Abs[x], \ ArcTan[x], \ BesselJ[0, \ x], \ Binomial[i, \ j]\} \ //}$
$\mathbf{TraditionalForm}$

$Out[8]//TraditionalForm= \left\{|x|, \ \tan^{-1}(x), \ J_0(x), \ \binom{i}{j}\right\}$

`TraditionalForm` is often useful for generating output that can be inserted directly into documents which use traditional mathematical notation. But you should understand that `TraditionalForm` is intended primarily for output: it does not have the kind of precision that is needed to provide reliable input to *Mathematica*.

Thus, for example, in `TraditionalForm`, Ci(x) is the representation for both `Ci[x]` and `CosIntegral[x]`, so if this form appears on its own as input, *Mathematica* will have no idea which of the two interpretations is the correct one.

In StandardForm, these three expressions are all displayed in a unique and unambiguous way.	*In[9]:=* `{ Ci[1+x], CosIntegral[1+x], Ci(1+x) } // StandardForm` *Out[9]//StandardForm=* {Ci[1 + x], CosIntegral[1 + x], Ci (1 + x)}
In TraditionalForm, however, the first two are impossible to distinguish, and the third differs only in the presence of an extra space.	*In[10]:=* `{ Ci[1+x], CosIntegral[1+x], Ci(1+x) } // TraditionalForm` *Out[10]//TraditionalForm=* {Ci(x + 1), Ci(x + 1), Ci (x + 1)}

The ambiguities of `TraditionalForm` make it in general unsuitable for specifying input to the *Mathematica* kernel. But at least for sufficiently simple cases, *Mathematica* does include various heuristic rules for trying to interpret `TraditionalForm` expressions as *Mathematica* input.

Cells intended for input to the kernel are assumed by default to contain StandardForm expressions.	*In[1]:=* $c\left(\sqrt{x} + \frac{1}{x}\right) + \Gamma\ (x)$ *Out[1]=* $c\left(\frac{1}{x} + \sqrt{x}\right) + x\,\Gamma$

Here the front end was specifically told that input would be given in TraditionalForm. The cell bracket has a jagged line to indicate the difficulties involved.	*In[1]:=* $c\left(\sqrt{x} + \frac{1}{x}\right) + \Gamma(x)$ *Out[1]=* $c\left[\frac{1}{x} + \sqrt{x}\right] + \text{Gamma}\,[x]$

- ■ The input is a copy or simple edit of previous output.
- ■ The input has been converted from `StandardForm`, perhaps with simple edits.
- ■ The input contains explicit hidden information giving its interpretation.
- ■ The input contains only the simplest and most familiar notations.

Some situations in which `TraditionalForm` input can be expected to work.

Whenever *Mathematica* generates an expression in `TraditionalForm`, it automatically inserts various hidden tags so that the expression can later be interpreted unambiguously if it is given as input. And even if you edit the expression, the tags will often be left sufficiently undisturbed that unambiguous interpretation will still be possible.

This generates output in TraditionalForm.	*In[11]:=* **Exp[I Pi x] // TraditionalForm**
	Out[11]//TraditionalForm= $e^{i\pi x}$

Mathematica was told to expect TraditionalForm input here. The input was copied from the previous output line, and thus contains hidden tags that ensure the correct interpretation.	*In[12]:=* $e^{i\pi x}$ **// StandardForm**
	Out[12]//StandardForm= $\mathtext{e}^{i\pi x}$

Simple editing often does not disturb the hidden tags.	*In[13]:=* $e^{2i\pi x}$ **// StandardForm**
	Out[13]//StandardForm= $\mathe^{2i\pi x}$

If you enter a TraditionalForm expression from scratch, or import it from outside *Mathematica*, then *Mathematica* will still do its best to guess what the expression means. When there are ambiguities, what it typically does is to assume that you are using notation in whatever way is more common in elementary mathematical applications.

In TraditionalForm input, this is interpreted as a derivative.	*In[14]:=* $\dfrac{\partial y(x)}{\partial x}$ **// StandardForm**
	Out[14]//StandardForm= y'[x]

This is interpreted as an arc tangent.	*In[15]:=* $\tan^{-1}(x)$ **// StandardForm**
	Out[15]//StandardForm= ArcTan[x]

This is interpreted as the square of a tangent.	*In[16]:=* $\tan^{2}(x)$ **// StandardForm**
	Out[16]//StandardForm= Tan[x]^2

There is no particularly standard traditional interpretation for this; *Mathematica* assumes that it is 1/Tan[x]^2.	*In[17]:=* $\tan^{-2}(x)$ **// StandardForm**
	Out[17]//StandardForm= Cot[x]^2

You should realize that TraditionalForm does not provide any kind of precise or complete way of specifying *Mathematica* expressions. Nevertheless, for some elementary purposes it may be sufficient, particularly if you use a few additional tricks.

- Use $x(y)$ for functions; $x\ (y)$ for multiplication
- Use ⁝ee⁝ for the exponential constant E
- Use ⁝ii⁝ or ⁝jj⁝ for the imaginary unit I
- Use ⁝dd⁝ for differential operators in integrals and derivatives

A few tricks for `TraditionalForm` input.

With a space f (1 + x) is interpreted as multiplication. Without a space, g(1 + x) is interpreted as a function.

$In[18]:=$ $f(1+x)+g(1+x)$ // **StandardForm**

$Out[18]//StandardForm=$ f (1 + x) + g[1 + x]

The ordinary e is interpreted as a symbol e. The special "exponential e", entered as ⁝ee⁝, is interpreted as the exponential constant.

$In[19]:=$ $\{e^{3.7}, e^{3.7}\}$ // **StandardForm**

$Out[19]//StandardForm=$ {e$^{3.7}$, 40.4473}

■ 1.10.10 Mixing Text and Formulas

The simplest way to mix text and formulas in a *Mathematica* notebook is to put each kind of material in a separate cell. Sometimes, however, you may want to embed a formula within a cell of text, or vice versa.

CTRL-(or CTRL-9	begin entering a formula within text, or text within a formula	
CTRL-) or CTRL-0	end entering a formula within text, or text within a formula	

Entering a formula within text, or vice versa.

Here is a notebook with formulas embedded in a text cell.

This is a text cell, but it can contain formulas such as $\int \frac{1}{x^3-1} dx$ or $-\frac{\log(x^2+x+1)}{6} - \frac{\tan^{-1}\left(\frac{2x+1}{\sqrt{3}}\right)}{\sqrt{3}} + \frac{\log(x-1)}{3}$. The formulas flow with the text.

Mathematica notebooks often contain both formulas that are intended for actual evaluation by *Mathematica*, and ones that are intended just to be read in a more passive way.

When you insert a formula in text, you can use the Convert to StandardForm and Convert to TraditionalForm menu items within the formula to convert it to `StandardForm` or `TraditionalForm`. `StandardForm` is normally appropriate whenever the formula is thought of as a *Mathematica* program fragment.

In general, however, you can use exactly the same mechanisms for entering formulas, whether or not they will ultimately be given as *Mathematica* input.

You should realize, however, that to make the detailed typography of typical formulas look as good as possible, *Mathematica* automatically does things such as inserting spaces around certain operators. But these kinds of adjustments can potentially be inappropriate if you use notation in very different ways from the ones *Mathematica* is expecting.

In such cases, you may have to make detailed typographical adjustments by hand, using the mechanisms discussed on page 449.

■ 1.10.11 Displaying and Printing *Mathematica* Notebooks

Depending on the purpose for which you are using a *Mathematica* notebook, you may want to change its overall appearance. The front end allows you to specify independently the styles to be used for display on the screen and for printing. Typically you can do this by choosing appropriate items in the Format menu.

`ScreenStyleEnvironment`	styles to be used for screen display
`PrintingStyleEnvironment`	styles to be used for printed output
`Working`	standard style definitions for screen display
`Presentation`	style definitions for presentations
`Condensed`	style definitions for high display density
`Printout`	style definitions for printed output

Front end settings that define the global appearance of a notebook.

Here is a typical notebook as it appears in working form on the screen.

■ **A Symbolic Sum**

Here is the input:

$$\sum_{n=1}^{\infty} \frac{1}{n\,(n+4)^2}$$

Here is the output:

$$\left(615 + 1435\,\mathrm{m} + 1090\,\mathrm{m}^2 + 332\,\mathrm{m}^3 + 35\,\mathrm{m}^4 - 72\,\pi^2 - 150\,\mathrm{m}\,\pi^2 - 105\,\mathrm{m}^2\,\pi^2 - 30\,\mathrm{m}^3\,\pi^2 - 3\,\mathrm{m}^4\,\pi^2\right) / \left(72\,(1+\mathrm{m})\,(2+\mathrm{m})\,(3+\mathrm{m})\,(4+\mathrm{m})\right) + \frac{\mathrm{PolyGamma}[1,\,5+\mathrm{m}]}{4}$$

Here is the same notebook with condensed styles.

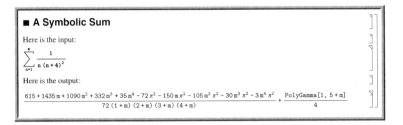

Here is a preview of how the notebook would appear when printed out.

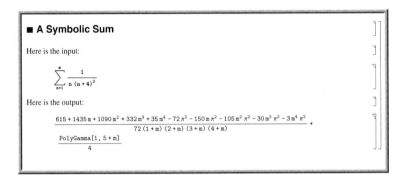

■ 1.10.12 Creating Your Own Palettes

The *Mathematica* notebook front end comes with a collection of standard palettes. But it also allows you to create your own palettes.

- Set up a blank palette using Create Table/Matrix/Palette under the Input menu

- Fill in the contents

- Make the palette active using Generate Palette from Selection under the File menu

The basic steps in creating a palette.

Create Table/Matrix/Palette will create a blank palette.

You can then insert whatever you want into each button.

The menu item Generate Palette from Selection makes a separate active palette.

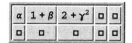

Clicking on a button in the palette now inserts its contents into your notebook.

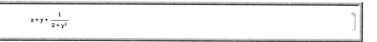

Create Table/Matrix/Palette	set up a blank palette
Generate Palette from Selection	make a separate active palette
Generate Notebook from Palette	convert a palette back into an editable notebook
Edit Button	edit the script associated with a palette or button

Menu items for setting up palettes.

When you are creating a palette, you can use the same mechanisms to add columns and rows as you can when you are creating any other kind of table, matrix or grid. Thus CTRL[,] will add a new column of buttons, and CTRL[↵] (CONTROL-ENTER) will add a new row.

button contents	action
X	replace current selection by X
text containing X■Y	replace current selection S by XSY

Contents of buttons.

In the simplest case, when you press a button in a palette what will happen is that the contents of the button will be inserted into your notebook, replacing whatever your current selection was.

Sometimes however you may not simply want to overwrite your current selection, but rather you may want to modify the selection in some way. As an example, you might want to wrap a function like Expand around your current selection.

You can do this by setting up a button with contents Expand[■]. The ■ can be entered as ⦂spl⦂ or \[SelectionPlaceholder]. In general, ■ serves as a placeholder for your current selection. When you press a button that contains ■, the ■ is first replaced by your current selection, and only then is the result inserted into your notebook.

Here is a cell in which the current selection is part of an expression.

$$1 + (1+x)^4 + (2+y)^3$$

Pressing a button containing Expand[■] wraps Expand around the current selection.

Mathematica allows you to associate any action you want with a button. You can set up some common actions by using the Edit Button menu, having selected either a single button or a whole palette.

Paste	paste the contents of the button (default)
Evaluate	paste then evaluate in place what has been pasted
EvaluateCell	paste then evaluate the whole cell
CopyEvaluate	copy the current selection into a new cell, then paste and evaluate in place
CopyEvaluateCell	copy the current selection into a new cell, then paste and evaluate the whole cell

Typical actions for buttons.

With the default Paste setting for a button action, pressing the button modifies the contents of a cell but does no evaluation. By choosing other button actions, however, you can tell *Mathematica* to perform an evaluation every time you press the button.

With the button action Evaluate the result of this evaluation is made to overwrite your current selection. This is useful if you want to set up a button which modifies parts of an expression in place, say by applying Expand[■] to them.

The button action Evaluate performs evaluation only on whatever was pasted into your current cell. The button action EvaluateCell, on the other hand, performs evaluation on the whole cell, generating a new cell to show the result.

Here is an expression with a part selected.

$$1 + (1+x)^4 + (2+y)^3$$

This shows the result of pressing a button containing Expand[■] with an EvaluateCell button action.

$$1 + (1+x)^4 + \text{Expand}[(2+y)^3]$$
$$9 + (1+x)^4 + 12y + 6y^2 + y^3$$

Sometimes it is useful to be able to extract the current selection from a cell, and then operate on it in a new cell. You can do this using the button actions CopyEvaluate and CopyEvaluateCell.

Here is an expression with a part selected.

$$1 + (1+x)^4 + (2+y)^3$$

A button with a `CopyEvaluateCell` button action copies the current selection into a new cell, then pastes the contents of the button, and then performs an evaluation, putting the result into a new cell.

$$1 + (1+x)^4 + (2+y)^3$$

$In[1]:=$ $\text{Expand}\left[(2+y)^3\right]$

$Out[1]=$ $8 + 12\,y + 6\,y^2 + y^3$

Create Table/Matrix/Palette	set up a blank palette
Create Button	set up a single button not in a palette
Generate Palette from Selection	make a separate window
Cell Active	activate buttons within a cell in a notebook

Ways to create active elements in the front end.

Mathematica allows you to set up a wide range of active elements in the notebook front end. In the most common case, you have a palette which consists of an array of buttons in a separate window. But you can also have arrays of buttons, or even single buttons, within the cells of an ordinary notebook.

In addition, you can make a button execute any action you want—performing computations in the *Mathematica* kernel, or changing the configuration of notebooks in the front end. Section 2.11.6 discusses how to do this.

■ 1.10.13 Setting Up Hyperlinks

Create Hyperlink	make the selected object a hyperlink

Menu item for setting up hyperlinks.

A hyperlink is a special kind of button which jumps to another part of a notebook when it is pressed. Typically hyperlinks are indicated in *Mathematica* by blue or underlined text.

To set up a hyperlink, just select the text or other object that you want to be a hyperlink. Then choose the menu item Create Hyperlink and fill in the specification of where you want the destination of the hyperlink to be.

■ 1.10.14 Automatic Numbering

- ■ Choose a cell style such as `NumberedEquation`
- ■ Use the Create Automatic Numbering Object menu, with a counter name such as `Section`

Two ways to set up automatic numbering in a *Mathematica* notebook.

The input for each cell here is exactly the same, but the cells contain an element that displays as a progressively larger number as one goes through the notebook.

> ■ **1. A Section**
>
> ■ **2. A Section**
>
> ■ **3. A Section**

These cells are in `NumberedEquation` style.

$$\int \frac{x}{x+1}\,dx \tag{1}$$

$$\int \frac{\mathrm{Sin}[x]}{x+1}\,dx \tag{2}$$

$$\int \frac{\mathrm{Log}[x]+\mathrm{Exp}[x]}{x+1}\,dx \tag{3}$$

■ 1.10.15 Exposition in *Mathematica* Notebooks

Mathematica notebooks provide the basic technology that you need to be able to create a very wide range of sophisticated interactive documents. But to get the best out of this technology you need to develop an appropriate style of exposition.

Many people at first tend to use *Mathematica* notebooks either as simple worksheets containing a sequence of input and output lines, or as on-screen versions of traditional books and other printed material. But the most effective and productive uses of *Mathematica* notebooks tend to lie at neither one of these extremes, and instead typically involve a fine-grained mixing of *Mathematica* input and output with explanatory text. In most cases the single most important factor in obtaining such fine-grained mixing is uniform use of the *Mathematica* language.

One might think that there would tend to be three kinds of material in a *Mathematica* notebook: plain text, mathematical formulas, and computer code. But one of the key ideas of *Mathematica* is to provide a single language that offers the best of both traditional mathematical formulas and computer code.

In `StandardForm`, *Mathematica* expressions have the same kind of compactness and elegance as traditional mathematical formulas. But unlike such formulas, *Mathematica* expressions are set up in a completely consistent and uniform way. As a result, if you use *Mathematica* expressions, then regardless of your subject matter, you never have to go back and reexplain your basic notation: it is always just the notation of the *Mathematica* language. In addition, if you set up your explanations in terms of *Mathematica* expressions, then a reader of your notebook can immediately take what you have given, and actually execute it as *Mathematica* input.

If one has spent many years working with traditional mathematical notation, then it takes a little time to get used to seeing mathematical facts presented as StandardForm *Mathematica* expressions. Indeed, at first one often has a tendency to try to use TraditionalForm whenever possible, perhaps with hidden tags to indicate its interpretation. But quite soon one tends to evolve to a mixture of StandardForm and TraditionalForm. And in the end it becomes clear that StandardForm alone is for most purposes the most effective form of presentation.

In traditional mathematical exposition, there are many tricks for replacing chunks of text by fragments of formulas. In StandardForm many of these same tricks can be used. But the fact that *Mathematica* expressions can represent not only mathematical objects but also procedures and algorithms increases greatly the extent to which chunks of text can be replaced by shorter and more precise material.

1.11 Files and External Operations

■ 1.11.1 Reading and Writing *Mathematica* Files

You can use files on your computer system to store definitions and results from *Mathematica*. The most general approach is to store everything as plain text that is appropriate for input to *Mathematica*. With this approach, a version of *Mathematica* running on one computer system produces files that can be read by a version running on any computer system. In addition, such files can be manipulated by other standard programs, such as text editors.

<< *name*	read in a *Mathematica* input file
expr >> *name*	output *expr* to a file as plain text
expr >>> *name*	append *expr* to a file
!! *name*	display the contents of a plain text file

Reading and writing files.

This expands $(x + y)^3$, and outputs the result to a file called tmp.	`In[1]:= Expand[ (x + y)^3 ] >> tmp`

Here are the contents of tmp. They can be used directly as input for *Mathematica*.	`In[2]:= !!tmp`
	
	`x^3 + 3*x^2*y + 3*x*y^2 + y^3`

This reads in tmp, evaluating the *Mathematica* input it contains.	`In[3]:= <<tmp` `Out[3]= ` $x^3 + 3 x^2 y + 3 x y^2 + y^3$

If you are familiar with Unix or MS-DOS operating systems, you will recognize the *Mathematica* redirection operators >>, >>> and << as being analogous to the shell operators >, >> and <.

The redirection operators >> and >>> are convenient for storing results you get from *Mathematica*. The function Save["*name*", *f*, *g*, ...] allows you to save definitions for variables and functions.

Save["*name*", *f*, *g*, ...]	save definitions for variables or functions in a file

Saving definitions in plain text files.

Here is a definition for a function f.	`In[4]:= f[x_] := x^2 + c`

This gives c the value 17.	`In[5]:= c = 17`
	
	`Out[5]= 17`

This saves the definition of f in the file ftmp.	*In[6]:=* **Save["ftmp", f]**
Mathematica automatically saves both the actual definition of f, and the definition of c on which it depends.	*In[7]:=* **!!ftmp** f[x_] := x^2 + c c = 17
This clears the definitions of f and c.	*In[8]:=* **Clear[f, c]**
You can reinstate the definitions you saved simply by reading in the file ftmp.	*In[9]:=* **<<ftmp** *Out[9]=* 17

file.m	*Mathematica* expression file in plain text format
file.nb	*Mathematica* notebook file
file.mx	*Mathematica* definitions in DumpSave format

Typical names of *Mathematica* files.

If you use a notebook interface to *Mathematica*, then the *Mathematica* front end allows you to save complete notebooks, including not only *Mathematica* input and output, but also text, graphics and other material.

It is conventional to give *Mathematica* notebook files names that end in .nb, and most versions of *Mathematica* enforce this convention.

When you open a notebook in the *Mathematica* front end, *Mathematica* will immediately display the contents of the notebook, but it will not normally send any of these contents to the kernel for evaluation until you explicitly request this to be done.

Within a *Mathematica* notebook, however, you can use the Cell menu in the front end to identify certain cells as *initialization cells*, and if you do this, then the contents of these cells will automatically be evaluated whenever you open the notebook.

The I in the cell bracket indicates that the second cell is an initialization cell that will be evaluated whenever the notebook is opened.	■ **Implementation** f[x_] := Log[x] + Log[1 - x]

It is sometimes convenient to maintain *Mathematica* material both in a notebook which contains explanatory text, and in a package which contains only raw *Mathematica* definitions. You can do this by putting the *Mathematica* definitions into initialization cells in the notebook. Every time you save the notebook, the front end will then allow you to save an associated .m file which contains only the raw *Mathematica* definitions.

■ 1.11.2 Advanced Topic: Finding and Manipulating Files

Although the details of how files are named and organized differ from one computer system to another, *Mathematica* provides some fairly general mechanisms for finding and handling files.

Mathematica assumes that files on your computer system are organized in a collection of *directories*. At any point, you have a *current working directory*. You can always refer to files in this directory just by giving their names.

Directory[ ]	give your current working directory
SetDirectory["*dir*"]	set your current working directory
FileNames[ ]	list the files in your current working directory
FileNames["*form*"]	list the files whose names match a certain form
<<*name*	read in a file with the specified name
<<*context*`	read in a file corresponding to the specified context
CopyFile["*file₁*", "*file₂*"]	copy *file₁* to *file₂*
DeleteFile["*file*"]	delete a file

Functions for finding and manipulating files.

This is the current working directory. The form it has differs from one computer system to another.	`In[1]:= Directory[ ]` `Out[1]= /users/sw`
This resets the current working directory.	`In[2]:= SetDirectory["Examples"]` `Out[2]= /users/sw/Examples`
This gives a list of all files in your current working directory whose names match the form Test*.m.	`In[3]:= FileNames["Test*.m"]` `Out[3]= {Test1.m, Test2.m, TestFinal.m}`

Although you usually want to create files only in your current working directory, you often need to read in files from other directories. As a result, when you ask *Mathematica* to read in a file with a particular name, *Mathematica* automatically searches a list of directories (specified by the value of the search path variable $Path) to try and find a file with that name.

One issue in handling files in *Mathematica* is that the form of file and directory names varies between computer systems. This means for example that names of files which contain standard *Mathematica* packages may be quite different on different systems. Through a sequence of conventions, it is however possible to read in a standard *Mathematica* package with the same command on all systems. The way this works is that each package defines a so-called *Mathematica* context, of the form *name`name`*. On each system, all files are named in correspondence with the contexts they define. Then when you use the command <<*name`name`* *Mathematica* automatically translates the context name into the file name appropriate for your particular computer system.

FindList["*file*", "*text*"]	give a list of all lines in a file that contain the specified text
FindList[FileNames[ ], "*text*"]	search in all files in your current directory

Searching for text in files.

This searches for all lines in the file BookIndex containing diagrams.

In[4]:= **FindList["BookIndex", "diagrams"]**

Out[4]= {Ferrers diagrams: DiscreteMath`Combinatorica`,
　　　　　Hasse diagrams: DiscreteMath`Combinatorica`}

■ 1.11.3 Importing and Exporting Data

Import["*file*", "Table"]	import a table of data from a file
Export["*file*", *list*, "Table"]	export *list* to a file as a table of data

Importing and exporting tabular data.

This exports an array of numbers to the file out.dat.

In[1]:= **Export["out.dat", {{5.7, 4.3}, {-1.2, 7.8}}]**

Out[1]= out.dat

Here are the contents of the file out.dat.

In[2]:= **!!out.dat**

5.7　　4.3

-1.2　　7.8

This imports the contents of out.dat as a table of data.

In[3]:= **Import["out.dat", "Table"]**

Out[3]= {{5.7, 4.3}, {-1.2, 7.8}}

Import["*file*", "Table"] will handle many kinds of tabular data, automatically deducing the details of the format whenever possible. Export["*file*", *list*, "Table"] writes out data separated by spaces, with numbers given in C or Fortran-like form, as in 2.3E5 and so on.

Import["*name.ext*"]	import data assuming a format deduced from the file name
Export["*name.ext*", *expr*]	export data in a format deduced from the file name

Importing and exporting general data.

~	table formats	"CSV", "TSV"
~	matrix formats	"MAT", "HDF", "MTX"
+	specialized data formats	"FITS", "SDTS"

Some common formats for tabular data.

Import and Export can handle not only tabular data, but also data corresponding to graphics, sounds, expressions and even whole documents. Import and Export can often deduce the appropriate format for data simply by looking at the extension of the file name for the file in which the data is being stored. Sections 2.10.19 and 2.12.7 discuss in more detail how Import and Export work. Note that you can also use Import and Export to manipulate raw files of binary data.

This imports a graphic in JPEG format.   *In[4]:=* **Import["turtle.jpg"]**

Out[4]= ▪Graphics▪

This displays the graphic.   *In[5]:=* **Show[%]**

$ImportFormats	import formats supported on your system
$ExportFormats	export formats supported on your system

Finding the complete list of supported import and export formats.

■ 1.11.4 Exporting Graphics and Sounds

Mathematica allows you to export graphics and sounds in a wide variety of formats. If you use the notebook front end for *Mathematica*, then you can typically just copy and paste graphics and sounds directly into other programs using the standard mechanism available on your computer system.

Export["*name.ext*", *graphics*]	export graphics to a file in a format deduced from the file name
Export["*file*", *graphics*, "*format*"]	export graphics in the specified format
Export["!*command*", *graphics*, "*format*"]	export graphics to an external command

Exporting *Mathematica* graphics and sounds.

| graphics formats | "EPS", "TIFF", "GIF", "JPEG", "PNG", "PDF", "SVG", etc. |
| sound formats | "SND", "WAV", "AIFF", "AU", etc. |

Some common formats for graphics and sounds. Page 568 gives a complete list.

This generates a plot.   *In[1]:=* **Plot[Sin[x] + Sin[Sqrt[2] x], {x, 0, 10}]**

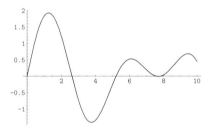

This exports the plot to a file in Encapsulated PostScript format.

In[2]:= **Export["sinplot.eps", %]**

```
Display::pserr:
   PostScript language error:
   Warning: substituting font Courier for WriCMTT9
```

Out[2]= sinplot.eps

■ 1.11.5 Exporting Formulas from Notebooks

Here is a cell containing a formula.

$$-\frac{\text{ArcTan}\left[\frac{1+2x}{\sqrt{3}}\right]}{\sqrt{3}} + \frac{\text{Log}[-1+x]}{3} - \frac{\text{Log}[1+x+x^2]}{6}$$

This is what you get if you copy the formula and paste it into an external text-based program.

```
\!\(-\(ArcTan[\(1 + 2 x\)\/\@3]\/\@3\) + Log[-1 + x]\/3
 - Log[1 + x + x\^2]\/6\)
```

Pasting the text back into a notebook immediately reproduces the original formula.

$$-\frac{\text{ArcTan}\left[\frac{1+2x}{\sqrt{3}}\right]}{\sqrt{3}} + \frac{\text{Log}[-1+x]}{3} - \frac{\text{Log}[1+x+x^2]}{6}$$

Mathematica allows you to export formulas both textually and visually. You can use Export to tell *Mathematica* to write a visual representation of a formula into a file.

Export["*file*.eps", ToBoxes[*expr*]]
        save the visual form of *expr* to a file in EPS format

Export["*file*", ToBoxes[*expr*], "*format*"]
        save the visual form of *expr* in the specified format

---

Exporting expressions in visual form.

■ 1.11.6 Generating T_EX

Mathematica notebooks provide a sophisticated environment for creating technical documents. But particularly if you want to merge your work with existing material in TEX, you may find it convenient to use TeXForm to convert expressions in *Mathematica* into a form suitable for input to TEX.

TeXForm[*expr*]   print *expr* in TEX input form

Mathematica output for TEX.

Here is an expression, printed in standard *Mathematica* form.

```
In[1]:= (x + y)^2 / Sqrt[x y]
```

$$Out[1]= \frac{(x+y)^2}{\sqrt{x\,y}}$$

Here is the expression in TEX input form.

```
In[2]:= TeXForm[%]
```

Out[2]//TeXForm= \frac{{\left(x + y \right) }^2}{{\sqrt{x\,y}}}

TeXSave["*file*.tex"]   save your complete current notebook in TEX input form

TeXSave["*file*.tex", "*source*.nb"]   save a TEX version of the notebook *source*.nb

---

Converting complete notebooks to TEX.

In addition to being able to convert individual expressions to T_EX, *Mathematica* also provides capabilities for translating complete notebooks. These capabilities can usually be accessed from the Save As Special menu in the notebook front end, where various options can be set.

■ 1.11.7 Exchanging Material with the Web

HTMLSave["*file*.html"]	save your complete current notebook in HTML form
HTMLSave["*file*.html", "*source*.nb"]	save an HTML version of the notebook *source*.nb

Converting notebooks to HTML.

HTMLSave has many options that allow you to specify how notebooks should be converted for web browsers with different capabilities. You can find details in the Additional Information section of the online Reference Guide entry for HTMLSave.

MathMLForm[*expr*]	print *expr* in MathML form
MathMLForm[StandardForm[*expr*]]	use StandardForm rather than traditional mathematical notation
ToExpression["*string*", MathMLForm]	interpret a string of MathML as *Mathematica* input

Converting to and from MathML.

Here is an expression printed in
MathML form.

```
In[1]:= MathMLForm[x^2/z]

Out[1]//MathMLForm= <math>
                      <mfrac>
                        <msup>
                          <mi>x</mi>
                          <mn>2</mn>
                        </msup>
                        <mi>z</mi>
                      </mfrac>
                    </math>
```

If you paste MathML into a *Mathematica* notebook, *Mathematica* will automatically try to convert it to *Mathematica* input. You can copy an expression from a notebook as MathML using the Copy As menu in the notebook front end.

+	Export["*file*.xml", *expr*]	export in XML format
+	Import["*file*.xml"]	import from XML
+	ImportString["*string*", "XML"]	import data from a string of XML

XML importing and exporting.

Somewhat like *Mathematica* expressions, XML is a general format for representing data. *Mathematica* automatically converts certain types of expressions to and from specific types of XML. MathML is one example. Other examples include NotebookML for notebook expressions, and SVG for graphics.

If you ask *Mathematica* to import a generic piece of XML, it will produce a *SymbolicXML* expression. Each XML element of the form <*elem attr='val'>data</elem*> is translated to a *Mathematica* SymbolicXML expression of the form XMLElement["*elem*", {"*attr*"->"*val*"}, {*data*}]. Once you have imported a piece of XML as SymbolicXML, you can use *Mathematica*'s powerful symbolic programming capabilities to manipulate the expression you get. You can then use Export to export the result in XML form.

This generates a SymbolicXML expression, with an XMLElement representing the a element in the XML string.	*In[2]:=* **ImportString["<a aa='va'>s</a>", "XML"]** *Out[2]=* XMLObject[Document] [{}, XMLElement[a, {aa → va}, {s}], {}]

There are now two nested levels in the SymbolicXML.	*In[3]:=* **ImportString[**
	          "<a><b bb='1'>ss</b><b bb='2'>ss</b></a>", "XML"]
	
	Out[3]= XMLObject[Document] [{},
	          XMLElement[a, {}, {XMLElement[b, {bb → 1}, {ss}],
	            XMLElement[b, {bb → 2}, {ss}]}], {}]

This does a simple transformation on the SymbolicXML.	*In[4]:=* **%/."ss" -> XMLElement["c",{},{"xx"}]**
	
	Out[4]= XMLObject[Document] [{},
	          XMLElement[a, {}, {XMLElement[b, {bb → 1},
	            {XMLElement[c, {}, {xx}]}], XMLElement[b,
	            {bb → 2}, {XMLElement[c, {}, {xx}]}]}], {}]

This shows the result as an XML string.	*In[5]:=* **ExportString[%, "XML"]** *Out[5]=* <a> <b bb='1'> <c>xx</c> </b> <b bb='2'> <c>xx</c> </b> </a>

■ 1.11.8 Generating C and Fortran Expressions

If you have special-purpose programs written in C or Fortran, you may want to take formulas you have generated in *Mathematica* and insert them into the source code of your programs. *Mathematica* allows you to convert mathematical expressions into C and Fortran expressions.

CForm[*expr*]	write out *expr* so it can be used in a C program
FortranForm[*expr*]	write out *expr* for Fortran

Mathematica output for programming languages.

Here is an expression, written out in standard *Mathematica* form.

$In[1]:=$ **Expand[(1 + x + y)^2]**

$Out[1]=$ $1 + 2x + x^2 + 2y + 2xy + y^2$

Here is the expression in Fortran form.

$In[2]:=$ **FortranForm[%]**

$Out[2]//FortranForm=$ 1 + 2*x + x**2 + 2*y + 2*x*y + y**2

Here is the same expression in C form. Macros for objects like Power are defined in the C header file mdefs.h that comes with most versions of *Mathematica*.

$In[3]:=$ **CForm[%]**

$Out[3]//CForm=$ 1 + 2*x + Power(x,2) + 2*y + 2*x*y + Power(y,2)

You should realize that there are many differences between *Mathematica* and C or Fortran. As a result, expressions you translate may not work exactly the same as they do in *Mathematica*. In addition, there are so many differences in programming constructs that no attempt is made to translate these automatically.

Compile[*x*, *expr*]	compile an expression into efficient internal code

A way to compile *Mathematica* expressions.

One of the common motivations for converting *Mathematica* expressions into C or Fortran is to try to make them faster to evaluate numerically. But the single most important reason that C and Fortran can potentially be more efficient than *Mathematica* is that in these languages one always specifies up front what type each variable one uses will be—integer, real number, array, and so on.

The *Mathematica* function Compile makes such assumptions within *Mathematica*, and generates highly efficient internal code. Usually this code runs not much if at all slower than custom C or Fortran.

■ 1.11.9 Splicing *Mathematica* Output into External Files

If you want to make use of *Mathematica* output in an external file such as a program or document, you will often find it useful to "splice" the output automatically into the file.

Splice["*file*.mx"]	splice *Mathematica* output into an external file named *file*.mx, putting the results in the file *file*.x
Splice["*infile*", "*outfile*"]	splice *Mathematica* output into *infile*, sending the output to *outfile*

Splicing *Mathematica* output into files.

The basic idea is to set up the definitions you need in a particular *Mathematica* session, then run Splice to use the definitions you have made to produce the appropriate output to insert into the external files.

```
#include "mdefs.h"

double f(x)
double x;
{
double y;

y = <* Integrate[Sin[x]^5, x] *> ;

return(2*y - 1) ;
}
```

A simple C program containing a *Mathematica* formula.

```
#include "mdefs.h"

double f(x)
double x;
{
double y;

y = -5*Cos(x)/8 + 5*Cos(3*x)/48 - Cos(5*x)/80 ;

return(2*y - 1) ;
}
```

The C program after processing with Splice.

■ 1.11.10 Running External Programs

Although *Mathematica* does many things well, there are some things that are inevitably better done by external programs. You can use *Mathematica* to control the external programs, or to analyze output they generate.

On almost all computer systems, it is possible to run external programs directly from within *Mathematica*. *Mathematica* communicates with the external programs through interprocess communication mechanisms such as pipes.

In the simplest cases, the only communication you need is to send and receive plain text. You can prepare input in *Mathematica*, then give it as the standard input for the external program. Or you can take the standard output of the external program, and use it as input to *Mathematica*.

In general, *Mathematica* allows you to treat streams of data exchanged with external programs just like files. In place of a file name, you give the external command to run, prefaced by an exclamation point.

<<*file*	read in a file
<<"!*command*"	run an external command, and read in the output it produces
expr >> "!*command*"	feed the textual form of *expr* to an external command
ReadList["!*command*", Number]	run an external command, and read in a list of the numbers it produces

Some ways to communicate with external programs.

This feeds the expression x^2 + y^2 as input to the external command lpr, which, on a typical Berkeley Unix system, sends output to a printer.

In[1]:= **x^2 + y^2 >> "!lpr"**

With a text-based interface, putting ! at the beginning of a line causes the remainder of the line to be executed as an external command. squares is an external program which prints numbers and their squares.

In[2]:= **!squares 4**

```
1   1
2   4
3   9
4   16
```

This runs the external command squares 4, then reads numbers from the output it produces.

In[3]:= **ReadList["!squares 4", Number, RecordLists->True]**

Out[3]= {{1, 1}, {2, 4}, {3, 9}, {4, 16}}

■ 1.11.11 *MathLink*

The previous section discussed how to exchange plain text with external programs. In many cases, however, you will find it convenient to communicate with external programs at a higher level, and to exchange more structured data with them.

On almost all computer systems, *Mathematica* supports the *MathLink* communication standard, which allows higher-level communication between *Mathematica* and external programs. In order to use *Math-Link*, an external program has to include some special source code, which is usually distributed with *Mathematica*.

MathLink allows external programs both to call *Mathematica*, and to be called by *Mathematica*. Section 2.13 discusses some of the details of *MathLink*. By using *MathLink*, you can, for example, treat *Mathematica* essentially like a subroutine embedded inside an external program. Or you can create a front end that implements your own user interface, and communicates with the *Mathematica* kernel via *MathLink*.

You can also use *MathLink* to let *Mathematica* call individual functions inside an external program. As described in Section 2.13, you can set up a *MathLink* template file to specify how particular functions in *Mathematica* should call functions inside your external program. From the *MathLink* template file, you can generate source code to include in your program. Then when you start your program, the appropriate *Mathematica* definitions are automatically made, and when you call a particular *Mathematica* function, code in your external program is executed.

Install["*command*"]	start an external program and install *Mathematica* definitions to call functions it contains
Uninstall[*link*]	terminate an external program and uninstall definitions for functions in it

Calling functions in external programs.

This starts the external program simul, and installs *Mathematica* definitions to call various functions in it.

```
In[1]:= Install["simul"]
Out[1]= LinkObject[simul, 5, 4]
```

Here is a usage message for a function that was installed in *Mathematica* to call a function in the external program.

```
In[2]:= ?srun
srun[{a, r, gamma}, x] performs a simulation with the
    specified parameters.
```

When you call this function, it executes code in the external program.

```
In[3]:= srun[{3, 0, 7}, 5]
Out[3]= 6.78124
```

This terminates the simul program.

```
In[4]:= Uninstall["simul"]
Out[4]= simul
```

You can use *MathLink* to communicate with many types of programs, including with *Mathematica* itself. There are versions of the *MathLink* library for a variety of common programming languages. The *J/Link* system provides a standard way to integrate *Mathematica* with Java, based on *MathLink*. With *J/Link* you can take any Java class, and immediately make its methods accessible as functions in *Mathematica*.

1.12 Special Topic: The Internals of *Mathematica*

■ 1.12.1 Why You Do Not Usually Need to Know about Internals

Most of this book is concerned with explaining *what Mathematica* does, not *how* it does it. But the purpose of this chapter is to say at least a little about how *Mathematica* does what it does. Appendix A.9 gives some more details.

You should realize at the outset that while knowing about the internals of *Mathematica* may be of intellectual interest, it is usually much less important in practice than one might at first suppose.

Indeed, one of the main points of *Mathematica* is that it provides an environment where you can perform mathematical and other operations without having to think in detail about how these operations are actually carried out inside your computer.

Thus, for example, if you want to factor the polynomial $x^{15} - 1$, you can do this just by giving *Mathematica* the command Factor[x^15 - 1]; you do not have to know the fairly complicated details of how such a factorization is actually carried out by the internal code of *Mathematica*.

Indeed, in almost all practical uses of *Mathematica*, issues about how *Mathematica* works inside turn out to be largely irrelevant. For most purposes it suffices to view *Mathematica* simply as an abstract system which performs certain specified mathematical and other operations.

You might think that knowing how *Mathematica* works inside would be necessary in determining what answers it will give. But this is only very rarely the case. For the vast majority of the computations that *Mathematica* does are completely specified by the definitions of mathematical or other operations.

Thus, for example, 3^40 will always be 12157665459056928801, regardless of how *Mathematica* internally computes this result.

There are some situations, however, where several different answers are all equally consistent with the formal mathematical definitions. Thus, for example, in computing symbolic integrals, there are often several different expressions which all yield the same derivative. Which of these expressions is actually generated by Integrate can then depend on how Integrate works inside.

Here is the answer generated by Integrate.

$$In[1]:= \textbf{Integrate[1/x + 1/x\^2, x]}$$

$$Out[1]= -\frac{1}{x} + \text{Log}[x]$$

This is an equivalent expression that might have been generated if Integrate worked differently inside.

$$In[2]:= \textbf{Together[\%]}$$

$$Out[2]= \frac{-1 + x \, \text{Log}[x]}{x}$$

In numerical computations, a similar phenomenon occurs. Thus, for example, `FindRoot` gives you a root of a function. But if there are several roots, which root is actually returned depends on the details of how `FindRoot` works inside.

This finds a particular root of $\cos(x) + \sin(x)$.	*In[3]:=* **FindRoot[Cos[x] + Sin[x], {x, 10.5}]** *Out[3]=* {x → 14.9226}
With a different starting point, a different root is found. Which root is found with each starting point depends in detail on the internal algorithm used.	*In[4]:=* **FindRoot[Cos[x] + Sin[x], {x, 10.8}]** *Out[4]=* {x → 11.781}

The dependence on the details of internal algorithms can be more significant if you push approximate numerical computations to the limits of their validity.

Thus, for example, if you give `NIntegrate` a pathological integrand, whether it yields a meaningful answer or not can depend on the details of the internal algorithm that it uses.

NIntegrate knows that this result is unreliable, and can depend on the details of the internal algorithm, so it prints warning messages.

```
In[5]:= NIntegrate[Sin[1/x], {x, 0, 1}]

NIntegrate::slwcon:
   Numerical integration converging too slowly; suspect
   one of the following: singularity, value of the
   integration being 0, oscillatory integrand, or
   insufficient WorkingPrecision. If your integrand is
   oscillatory try using the option Method->Oscillatory
   in NIntegrate.

NIntegrate::ncvb:
   NIntegrate failed to converge to prescribed accuracy
   after 7 recursive bisections in x near x = 0.0035126
   8.

Out[5]= 0.504894
```

Traditional numerical computation systems have tended to follow the idea that all computations should yield results that at least nominally have the same precision. A consequence of this idea is that it is not sufficient just to look at a result to know whether it is accurate; you typically also have to analyze the internal algorithm by which the result was found. This fact has tended to make people believe that it is always important to know internal algorithms for numerical computations.

But with the approach that *Mathematica* takes, this is rarely the case. For *Mathematica* can usually use its arbitrary-precision numerical computation capabilities to give results where every digit that is generated follows the exact mathematical specification of the operation being performed.

Even though this is an approximate numerical computation, every digit is determined by the mathematical definition for π.	*In[6]:=* **N[Pi, 30]** *Out[6]=* 3.14159265358979323846264338328
Once again, every digit here is determined by the mathematical definition for $\sin(x)$.	*In[7]:=* **N[Sin[10^50], 20]** *Out[7]=* -0.78967249342931008271

If you use machine-precision numbers, *Mathematica* cannot give a reliable result, and the answer depends on the details of the internal algorithm used.	`In[8]:= Sin[10.^50]` `Out[8]= 0.705222`

It is a general characteristic that whenever the results you get can be affected by the details of internal algorithms, you should not depend on these results. For if nothing else, different versions of *Mathematica* may exhibit differences in these results, either because the algorithms operate slightly differently on different computer systems, or because fundamentally different algorithms are used in versions released at different times.

This is the result for $\sin(10^{50})$ on one type of computer.	`In[1]:= Sin[10.^50]` `Out[1]= 0.705222`
Here is the same calculation on another type of computer.	`In[1]:= Sin[10.^50]` `Out[1]= -0.0528229`
And here is the result obtained in *Mathematica* Version 1.	`In[1]:= Sin[10.^50]` `Out[1]= 0.0937538`

Particularly in more advanced applications of *Mathematica*, it may sometimes seem worthwhile to try to analyze internal algorithms in order to predict which way of doing a given computation will be the most efficient. And there are indeed occasionally major improvements that you will be able to make in specific computations as a result of such analyses.

But most often the analyses will not be worthwhile. For the internals of *Mathematica* are quite complicated, and even given a basic description of the algorithm used for a particular purpose, it is usually extremely difficult to reach a reliable conclusion about how the detailed implementation of this algorithm will actually behave in particular circumstances.

A typical problem is that *Mathematica* has many internal optimizations, and the efficiency of a computation can be greatly affected by whether the details of the computation do or do not allow a given internal optimization to be used.

■ 1.12.2 Basic Internal Architecture

numbers	sequences of binary digits
strings	sequences of character code bytes or byte pairs
symbols	pointers to the central table of symbols
general expressions	sequences of pointers to the head and elements

Internal representations used by *Mathematica*.

When you type input into *Mathematica*, a data structure is created in the memory of your computer to represent the expression you have entered.

In general, different pieces of your expression will be stored at different places in memory. Thus, for example, for a list such as {2, x, y + z} the "backbone" of the list will be stored at one place, while each of the actual elements will be stored at a different place.

The backbone of the list then consists just of three "pointers" that specify the addresses in computer memory at which the actual expressions that form the elements of the list are to be found. These expressions then in turn contain pointers to their subexpressions. The chain of pointers ends when one reaches an object such as a number or a string, which is stored directly as a pattern of bits in computer memory.

Crucial to the operation of *Mathematica* is the notion of symbols such as x. Whenever x appears in an expression, *Mathematica* represents it by a pointer. But the pointer is always to the same place in computer memory—an entry in a central table of all symbols defined in your *Mathematica* session.

This table is a repository of all information about each symbol. It contains a pointer to a string giving the symbol's name, as well as pointers to expressions which give rules for evaluating the symbol.

■ Recycle memory as soon as the data in it is no longer referenced.

The basic principle of *Mathematica* memory management.

Every piece of memory used by *Mathematica* maintains a count of how many pointers currently point to it. When this count drops to zero, *Mathematica* knows that the piece of memory is no longer being referenced, and immediately makes the piece of memory available for something new.

This strategy essentially ensures that no memory is ever wasted, and that any piece of memory that *Mathematica* uses is actually storing data that you need to access in your *Mathematica* session.

■ Create an expression corresponding to the input you have given.

■ Process the expression using all rules known for the objects in it.

■ Generate output corresponding to the resulting expression.

The basic actions of *Mathematica*.

At the heart of *Mathematica* is a conceptually simple procedure known as the *evaluator* which takes every function that appears in an expression and evaluates that function.

When the function is one of the thousand or so that are built into *Mathematica*, what the evaluator does is to execute directly internal code in the *Mathematica* system. This code is set up to perform the operations corresponding to the function, and then to build a new expression representing the result.

■ The built-in functions of *Mathematica* support universal computation.

The basic feature that makes *Mathematica* a self-contained system.

A crucial feature of the built-in functions in *Mathematica* is that they support *universal computation*. What this means is that out of these functions you can construct programs that perform absolutely any kinds of operation that are possible for a computer.

As it turns out, small subsets of *Mathematica*'s built-in functions would be quite sufficient to support universal computation. But having the whole collection of functions makes it in practice easier to construct the programs one needs.

The underlying point, however, is that because *Mathematica* supports universal computation you never have to modify its built-in functions: all you have to do to perform a particular task is to combine these functions in an appropriate way.

Universal computation is the basis for all standard computer languages. But many of these languages rely on the idea of *compilation*. If you use C or Fortran, for example, you first write your program, then you compile it to generate machine code that can actually be executed on your computer.

Mathematica does not require you to go through the compilation step: once you have input an expression, the functions in the expression can immediately be executed.

Often *Mathematica* will preprocess expressions that you enter, arranging things so that subsequent execution will be as efficient as possible. But such preprocessing never affects the results that are generated, and can rarely be seen explicitly.

■ 1.12.3 The Algorithms of *Mathematica*

The built-in functions of *Mathematica* implement a very large number of algorithms from computer science and mathematics. Some of these algorithms are fairly old, but the vast majority had to be created or at least modified specifically for *Mathematica*. Most of the more mathematical algorithms in *Mathematica* ultimately carry out operations which at least at some time in the past were performed by hand. In almost all cases, however, the algorithms use methods very different from those common in hand calculation.

Symbolic integration provides an example. In hand calculation, symbolic integration is typically done by a large number of tricks involving changes of variables and the like.

But in *Mathematica* symbolic integration is performed by a fairly small number of very systematic procedures. For indefinite integration, the idea of these procedures is to find the most general form of the integral, then to differentiate this and try to match up undetermined coefficients.

Often this procedure produces at an intermediate stage immensely complicated algebraic expressions, and sometimes very sophisticated kinds of mathematical functions. But the great advantage of the procedure is that it is completely systematic, and its operation requires no special cleverness of the kind that only a human could be expected to provide.

In having *Mathematica* do integrals, therefore, one can be confident that it will systematically get results, but one cannot expect that the way these results are derived will have much at all to do with the way they would be derived by hand.

The same is true with most of the mathematical algorithms in *Mathematica*. One striking feature is that even for operations that are simple to describe, the systematic algorithms to perform these operations in *Mathematica* involve fairly advanced mathematical or computational ideas.

Thus, for example, factoring a polynomial in x is first done modulo a prime such as 17 by finding the null space of a matrix obtained by reducing high powers of x modulo the prime and the original polynomial. Then factorization over the integers is achieved by "lifting" modulo successive powers of the prime using a collection of intricate theorems in algebra and analysis.

The use of powerful systematic algorithms is important in making the built-in functions in *Mathematica* able to handle difficult and general cases. But for easy cases that may be fairly common in practice it is often possible to use simpler and more efficient algorithms.

As a result, built-in functions in *Mathematica* often have large numbers of extra pieces that handle various kinds of special cases. These extra pieces can contribute greatly to the complexity of the internal code, often taking what would otherwise be a five-page algorithm and making it hundreds of pages long.

Most of the algorithms in *Mathematica*, including all their special cases, were explicitly constructed by hand. But some algorithms were instead effectively created automatically by computer.

Many of the algorithms used for machine-precision numerical evaluation of mathematical functions are examples. The main parts of such algorithms are formulas which are as short as possible but which yield the best numerical approximations.

Most such formulas used in *Mathematica* were actually derived by *Mathematica* itself. Often many months of computation were required, but the result was a short formula that can be used to evaluate functions in an optimal way.

■ 1.12.4 The Software Engineering of *Mathematica*

Mathematica is one of the more complex software systems ever constructed. Its source code is written in a combination of C and *Mathematica*, and for Version 5, the code for the kernel consists of about 1.5 million lines of C and 150,000 lines of *Mathematica*. This corresponds to roughly 50 megabytes of data, or some 50,000 printed pages.

The C code in *Mathematica* is actually written in a custom extension of C which supports certain memory management and object-oriented features. The *Mathematica* code is optimized using `Share` and `DumpSave`.

In the *Mathematica* kernel the breakdown of different parts of the code is roughly as follows: language and system: 30%; numerical computation: 25%; algebraic computation: 25%; graphics and kernel output: 20%.

Most of this code is fairly dense and algorithmic: those parts that are in effect simple procedures or tables use minimal code since they tend to be written at a higher level—often directly in *Mathematica*.

The source code for the kernel, save a fraction of a percent, is identical for all computer systems on which *Mathematica* runs.

For the front end, however, a significant amount of specialized code is needed to support each different type of user interface environment. The front end contains about 650,000 lines of system-independent C source code, of which roughly 150,000 lines are concerned with expression formatting. Then there are between 50,000 and 100,000 lines of specific code customized for each user interface environment.

Mathematica uses a client-server model of computing. The front end and kernel are connected via *MathLink*—the same system as is used to communicate with other programs.

Within the C code portion of the *Mathematica* kernel, modularity and consistency are achieved by having different parts communicate primarily by exchanging complete *Mathematica* expressions.

But it should be noted that even though different parts of the system are quite independent at the level of source code, they have many algorithmic interdependencies. Thus, for example, it is common for numerical functions to make extensive use of algebraic algorithms, or for graphics code to use fairly advanced mathematical algorithms embodied in quite different *Mathematica* functions.

Since the beginning of its development in 1986, the effort spent directly on creating the source code for *Mathematica* is a substantial fraction of a thousand man-years. In addition, a comparable or somewhat larger effort has been spent on testing and verification.

The source code of *Mathematica* has changed greatly since Version 1 was released. The total number of lines of code in the kernel grew from 150,000 in Version 1 to 350,000 in Version 2, 600,000 in Version 3, 800,000 in Version 4 and about 1.5 million in Version 5. In addition, at every stage existing code has been revised—so that Version 5 has only a few percent of its code in common with Version 1.

Despite these changes in internal code, however, the user-level design of *Mathematica* has remained compatible from Version 1 on. Much functionality has been added, but programs created for *Mathematica* Version 1 will almost always run absolutely unchanged under Version 5.

■ 1.12.5 Testing and Verification

Every version of *Mathematica* is subjected to a large amount of testing before it is released. The vast majority of this testing is done by an automated system that is written in *Mathematica*.

The automated system feeds millions of pieces of input to *Mathematica*, and checks that the output obtained from them is correct. Often there is some subtlety in doing such checking: one must account for different behavior of randomized algorithms and for such issues as differences in machine-precision arithmetic on different computers.

The test inputs used by the automated system are obtained in several ways:

■ For every *Mathematica* function, inputs are devised that exercise both common and extreme cases.

■ Inputs are devised to exercise each feature of the internal code.

■ All the examples in this book and in other books about *Mathematica* are used.

■ Standard numerical tables are optically scanned for test inputs.

■ Formulas from all standard mathematical tables are entered.

■ Exercises from textbooks are entered.

■ For pairs of functions such as `Integrate` and `D` or `Factor` and `Expand`, random expressions are generated and tested.

When tests are run, the automated testing system checks not only the results, but also side effects such as messages, as well as memory usage and speed.

There is also a special instrumented version of *Mathematica* which is set up to perform internal consistency tests. This version of *Mathematica* runs at a small fraction of the speed of the real *Mathematica*, but at every step it checks internal memory consistency, interruptibility, and so on.

The instrumented version of *Mathematica* also records which pieces of *Mathematica* source code have been accessed, allowing one to confirm that all of the various internal functions in *Mathematica* have been exercised by the tests given.

All standard *Mathematica* tests are routinely run on each version of *Mathematica*, on each different computer system. Depending on the speed of the computer system, these tests take a few days to a few weeks of computer time.

In addition, huge numbers of tests based on random inputs are run for the equivalent of many years of computer time on a sampling of different computer systems.

Even with all this testing, however, it is inevitable in a system as complex as *Mathematica* that errors will remain.

The standards of correctness for *Mathematica* are certainly much higher than for typical mathematical proofs. But just as long proofs will inevitably contain errors that go undetected for many years, so also a complex software system such as *Mathematica* will contain errors that go undetected even after millions of people have used it.

Nevertheless, particularly after all the testing that has been done on it, the probability that you will actually discover an error in *Mathematica* in the course of your work is extremely low.

Doubtless there will be times when *Mathematica* does things you do not expect. But you should realize that the probabilities are such that it is vastly more likely that there is something wrong with your input to *Mathematica* or your understanding of what is happening than with the internal code of the *Mathematica* system itself.

If you do believe that you have found a genuine error in *Mathematica*, then you should contact Wolfram Research Technical Support, so that the error can be corrected in future versions.

Part 2

Part 1 introduced Mathematica by showing you how to use some of its more common features. This part looks at Mathematica in a different way. Instead of discussing individual features, it concentrates on the global structure of Mathematica, and describes the framework into which all the features fit.

When you first start doing calculations with Mathematica, you will probably find it sufficient just to read the relevant parts of Part 1. However, once you have some general familiarity with the Mathematica system, you should make a point of reading this part.

This part describes the basic structure of the Mathematica language, with which you can extend Mathematica, adding your own functions, objects or other constructs. This part shows how Mathematica uses a fairly small number of very powerful symbolic programming methods to allow you to build up many different kinds of programs.

Most of this part assumes no specific prior knowledge of computer science. Nevertheless, some of it ventures into some fairly complicated issues. You can probably ignore these issues unless they specifically affect programs you are writing.

If you are an expert on computer languages, you may be able to glean some understanding of Mathematica by looking at the Reference Guide at the end of this book. Nevertheless, to get a real appreciation for the principles of Mathematica, you will have to read this part.

Part 2

Principles of *Mathematica*

2.1 Expressions

■ 2.1.1 Everything Is an Expression

Mathematica handles many different kinds of things: mathematical formulas, lists and graphics, to name a few. Although they often look very different, *Mathematica* represents all of these things in one uniform way. They are all *expressions*.

A prototypical example of a *Mathematica* expression is f[x, y]. You might use f[x, y] to represent a mathematical function $f(x, y)$. The function is named f, and it has two arguments, x and y.

You do not always have to write expressions in the form $f[x, y, \ldots]$. For example, x + y is also an expression. When you type in x + y, *Mathematica* converts it to the standard form Plus[x, y]. Then, when it prints it out again, it gives it as x + y.

The same is true of other "operators", such as ^ (Power) and / (Divide).

In fact, everything you type into *Mathematica* is treated as an expression.

x + y + z	Plus[x, y, z]
x y z	Times[x, y, z]
x^n	Power[x, n]
{a, b, c}	List[a, b, c]
a -> b	Rule[a, b]
a = b	Set[a, b]

Some examples of *Mathematica* expressions.

You can see the full form of any expression by using FullForm[*expr*].

Here is an expression.

```
In[1]:= x + y + z
Out[1]= x + y + z
```

This is the full form of the expression.

```
In[2]:= FullForm[%]
Out[2]//FullForm= Plus[x, y, z]
```

Here is another expression.

```
In[3]:= 1 + x^2 + (y + z)^2
```

$$Out[3]= 1 + x^2 + (y + z)^2$$

Its full form has several nested pieces.

```
In[4]:= FullForm[%]
Out[4]//FullForm= Plus[1, Power[x, 2], Power[Plus[y, z], 2]]
```

The object *f* in an expression *f*[*x*, *y*, ...] is known as the *head* of the expression. You can extract it using Head[*expr*]. Particularly when you write programs in *Mathematica*, you will often want to test the head of an expression to find out what kind of thing the expression is.

Head gives the "function name" f.	*In[5]:=* **Head[f[x, y]]**
	Out[5]= f
Here Head gives the name of the "operator".	*In[6]:=* **Head[a + b + c]**
	Out[6]= Plus
Everything has a head.	*In[7]:=* **Head[{a, b, c}]**
	Out[7]= List
Numbers also have heads.	*In[8]:=* **Head[23432]**
	Out[8]= Integer
You can distinguish different kinds of numbers by their heads.	*In[9]:=* **Head[345.6]**
	Out[9]= Real

Head[*expr*]	give the head of an expression: the *f* in *f*[*x*, *y*]
FullForm[*expr*]	display an expression in the full form used by *Mathematica*

Functions for manipulating expressions.

■ 2.1.2 The Meaning of Expressions

The notion of expressions is a crucial unifying principle in *Mathematica*. It is the fact that every object in *Mathematica* has the same underlying structure that makes it possible for *Mathematica* to cover so many areas with a comparatively small number of basic operations.

Although all expressions have the same basic structure, there are many different ways that expressions can be used. Here are a few of the interpretations you can give to the parts of an expression.

meaning of f	*meaning of x, y, ...*	*examples*
Function	arguments or parameters	`Sin[x]`, `f[x, y]`
Command	arguments or parameters	`Expand[(x + 1)^2]`
Operator	operands	`x + y`, `a = b`
Head	elements	`{a, b, c}`
Object type	contents	`RGBColor[r, g, b]`

Some interpretations of parts of expressions.

Expressions in *Mathematica* are often used to specify operations. So, for example, typing in 2 + 3 causes 2 and 3 to be added together, while `Factor[x^6 - 1]` performs factorization.

Perhaps an even more important use of expressions in *Mathematica*, however, is to maintain a structure, which can then be acted on by other functions. An expression like `{a, b, c}` does not specify an operation. It merely maintains a list structure, which contains a collection of three elements. Other functions, such as `Reverse` or `Dot`, can act on this structure.

The full form of the expression `{a, b, c}` is `List[a, b, c]`. The head `List` performs no operations. Instead, its purpose is to serve as a "tag" to specify the "type" of the structure.

You can use expressions in *Mathematica* to create your own structures. For example, you might want to represent points in three-dimensional space, specified by three coordinates. You could give each point as `point[x, y, z]`. The "function" `point` again performs no operation. It serves merely to collect the three coordinates together, and to label the resulting object as a `point`.

You can think of expressions like `point[x, y, z]` as being "packets of data", tagged with a particular head. Even though all expressions have the same basic structure, you can distinguish different "types" of expressions by giving them different heads. You can then set up transformation rules and programs which treat different types of expressions in different ways.

■ 2.1.3 Special Ways to Input Expressions

Mathematica allows you to use special notation for many common operators. For example, although internally *Mathematica* represents a sum of two terms as `Plus[x, y]`, you can enter this expression in the much more convenient form *x + y*.

The *Mathematica* language has a definite grammar which specifies how your input should be converted to internal form. One aspect of the grammar is that it specifies how pieces of your input should be grouped. For example, if you enter an expression such as a + b ^ c, the *Mathematica* grammar specifies that this should be considered, following standard mathematical notation, as a + (b ^ c) rather than (a + b) ^ c. *Mathematica* chooses this grouping because it treats the operator ^ as having a higher *precedence* than +. In general, the arguments of operators with higher precedence are grouped before those of operators with lower precedence.

You should realize that absolutely every special input form in *Mathematica* is assigned a definite precedence. This includes not only the traditional mathematical operators, but also forms such as ->, := or the semicolons used to separate expressions in a *Mathematica* program.

The table on pages 1024–1029 gives all the operators of *Mathematica* in order of decreasing precedence. The precedence is arranged, where possible, to follow standard mathematical usage, and to minimize the number of parentheses that are usually needed.

You will find, for example, that relational operators such as < have lower precedence than arithmetic operators such as +. This means that you can write expressions such as x + y > 7 without using parentheses.

There are nevertheless many cases where you do have to use parentheses. For example, since ; has a lower precedence than =, you need to use parentheses to write x = (a ; b). *Mathematica* interprets the expression x = a ; b as (x = a) ; b. In general, it can never hurt to include extra parentheses, but it can cause a great deal of trouble if you leave parentheses out, and *Mathematica* interprets your input in a way you do not expect.

$f[x, y]$	standard form for $f[x, y]$
$f @ x$	prefix form for $f[x]$
$x // f$	postfix form for $f[x]$
$x \sim f \sim y$	infix form for $f[x, y]$

Four ways to write expressions in *Mathematica*.

There are several common types of operators in *Mathematica*. The + in $x + y$ is an "infix" operator. The − in $-p$ is a "prefix" operator. Even when you enter an expression such as $f[x, y, \ldots]$ *Mathematica* allows you to do it in ways that mimic infix, prefix and postfix forms.

This "postfix form" is exactly equivalent to f[x + y].

```
In[1]:= x + y //f
Out[1]= f[x + y]
```

You will often want to add functions like N as "afterthoughts", and give them in postfix form.

```
In[2]:= 3^(1/4) + 1  //N
Out[2]= 2.31607
```

It is sometimes easier to understand what a function is doing when you write it in infix form.

```
In[3]:= {a, b, c} ~Join~ {d, e}
Out[3]= {a, b, c, d, e}
```

You should notice that // has very low precedence. If you put //f at the end of any expression containing arithmetic or logical operators, the f is applied to the *whole expression.* So, for example, x+y //f means f[x+y], not x+f[y].

The prefix form @ has a much higher precedence. f @ x + y is equivalent to f[x] + y, not f[x + y]. You can write f[x + y] in prefix form as f @ (x + y).

■ 2.1.4 Parts of Expressions

Since lists are just a particular kind of expression, it will come as no surprise that you can refer to parts of any expression much as you refer to parts of a list.

This gets the second element in the list {a, b, c}.	*In[1]:=* **{a, b, c}[[2]]**
	Out[1]= b
You can use the same method to get the second element in the sum x + y + z.	*In[2]:=* **(x + y + z)[[2]]**
	Out[2]= y
This gives the last element in the sum.	*In[3]:=* **(x + y + z)[[-1]]**
	Out[3]= z
Part 0 is the head.	*In[4]:=* **(x + y + z)[[0]]**
	Out[4]= Plus

You can refer to parts of an expression such as *f[g[a], g[b]]* just as you refer to parts of nested lists.

This is part 1.	*In[5]:=* **f[g[a], g[b]] [[1]]**
	Out[5]= g[a]
This is part {1,1}.	*In[6]:=* **f[g[a], g[b]] [[1, 1]]**
	Out[6]= a
This extracts part {2,1} of the expression 1 + x^2.	*In[7]:=* **(1 + x^2) [[2, 1]]**
	Out[7]= x
To see what part is {2,1}, you can look at the full form of the expression.	*In[8]:=* **FullForm[1 + x^2]**
	Out[8]//FullForm= Plus[1, Power[x, 2]]

You should realize that the assignment of indices to parts of expressions is done on the basis of the internal *Mathematica* forms of the expression, as shown by FullForm. These forms do not always correspond directly with what you see printed out. This is particularly true for algebraic expressions, where *Mathematica* uses a standard internal form, but prints the expressions in special ways.

Here is the internal form of x / y.	*In[9]:=* **FullForm[x / y]**
	Out[9]//FullForm= Times[x, Power[y, -1]]

It is the internal form that is used in specifying parts.	$In[10]:=$ **(x / y)[[2]]**
	$Out[10]=$ $\dfrac{1}{y}$

You can manipulate parts of expressions just as you manipulate parts of lists.

This replaces the third part of a + b + c + d by x^2. Note that the sum is automatically rearranged when the replacement is done.	$In[11]:=$ **ReplacePart[a + b + c + d, x^2, 3]**
	$Out[11]=$ $a + b + d + x^2$

Here is an expression.	$In[12]:=$ **t = 1 + (3 + x)^2 / y**
	$Out[12]=$ $1 + \dfrac{(3 + x)^2}{y}$

This is the full form of t.	$In[13]:=$ **FullForm[t]**
	$Out[13]//FullForm=$ Plus[1, Times[Power[Plus[3, x], 2], Power[y, -1]]]

This resets a part of the expression t.	$In[14]:=$ **t[[2, 1, 1]] = x**
	$Out[14]=$ x

Now the form of t has been changed.	$In[15]:=$ **t**
	$Out[15]=$ $1 + \dfrac{x^2}{y}$

Part[*expr*, *n*] or *expr*[[*n*]]	the nth part of *expr*
Part[*expr*, {n_1, n_2, ... }] or *expr*[[{n_1, n_2, ... }]]	a combination of parts of an expression
ReplacePart[*expr*, *elem*, *n*]	replace the nth part of *expr* by *elem*

Functions for manipulating parts of expressions.

Section 1.2.4 discussed how you can use lists of indices to pick out several elements of a list at a time. You can use the same procedure to pick out several parts in an expression at a time.

This picks out elements 2 and 4 in the list, and gives a list of these elements.	$In[16]:=$ **{a, b, c, d, e}[[{2, 4}]]**
	$Out[16]=$ {b, d}

This picks out parts 2 and 4 of the sum, and gives a *sum* of these elements.	$In[17]:=$ **(a + b + c + d + e)[[{2, 4}]]**
	$Out[17]=$ b + d

Any part in an expression can be viewed as being an argument of some function. When you pick out several parts by giving a list of indices, the parts are combined using the same function as in the expression.

■ 2.1.5 Manipulating Expressions like Lists

You can use most of the list operations discussed in Section 1.8 on any kind of *Mathematica* expression. By using these operations, you can manipulate the structure of expressions in many ways.

Here is an expression that corresponds to a sum of terms.	*In[1]:=* **t = 1 + x + x^2 + y^2**
	Out[1]= $1 + x + x^2 + y^2$
Take[t, 2] takes the first two elements from t, just as if t were a list.	*In[2]:=* **Take[t, 2]**
	Out[2]= $1 + x$
Length gives the number of elements in t.	*In[3]:=* **Length[t]**
	Out[3]= 4
You can use FreeQ[*expr*, *form*] to test whether *form* appears nowhere in *expr*.	*In[4]:=* **FreeQ[t, x]**
	Out[4]= False
This gives a list of the positions at which x appears in t.	*In[5]:=* **Position[t, x]**
	Out[5]= {{2}, {3, 1}}

You should remember that all functions which manipulate the structure of expressions act on the internal forms of these expressions. You can see these forms using FullForm[*expr*]. They may not be what you would expect from the printed versions of the expressions.

Here is a function with four arguments.	*In[6]:=* **f[a, b, c, d]**
	Out[6]= f[a, b, c, d]
You can add an argument using Append.	*In[7]:=* **Append[%, e]**
	Out[7]= f[a, b, c, d, e]
This reverses the arguments.	*In[8]:=* **Reverse[%]**
	Out[8]= f[e, d, c, b, a]

There are a few extra functions that can be used with expressions, as discussed in Section 2.2.10.

■ 2.1.6 Expressions as Trees

Here is an expression in full form.	*In[1]:=* **FullForm[x^3 + (1 + x)^2]**
	Out[1]//FullForm= Plus[Power[x, 3], Power[Plus[1, x], 2]]
TreeForm prints out expressions to show their "tree" structure.	*In[2]:=* **TreeForm[x^3 + (1 + x)^2]**

$$Out[2]//TreeForm=\ Plus\left[\ \middle|\ ,\ \middle|\ \right]$$
$$Power[x, 3]\ \ \ \ \ Power\left[\ \middle|\ \ \ \ ,\ 2\right]$$
$$Plus[1, x]$$

You can think of any *Mathematica* expression as a tree. In the expression above, the top node in the tree consists of a Plus. From this node come two "branches", x^3 and (1 + x)^2. From the x^3 node, there are then two branches, x and 3, which can be viewed as "leaves" of the tree.

This matrix is a simple tree with just two levels.

In[3]:= **TreeForm[{{a, b}, {c, d}}]**

Out[3]//TreeForm= List[| , |]
                         List[a, b]   List[c, d]

Here is a more complicated expression.

In[4]:= **{{a b, c d^2}, {x^3 y^4}}**

Out[4]= {{a b, c d^2}, {x^3 y^4}}

The tree for this expression has several levels. The representation of the tree here was too long to fit on a single line, so it had to be broken onto two lines.

In[5]:= **TreeForm[%]**

Out[5]//TreeForm= List[| ,
                         List[| , |]
                             Times[a, b]   Times[c, |]
                                                   Power[d, 2]

                         |]
                         List[|]
                             Times[| , |]
                                  Power[x, 3]   Power[y, 4]

The indices that label each part of an expression have a simple interpretation in terms of trees. Descending from the top node of the tree, each index specifies which branch to take in order to reach the part you want.

■ 2.1.7 Levels in Expressions

The Part function allows you to access specific parts of *Mathematica* expressions. But particularly when your expressions have fairly uniform structure, it is often convenient to be able to refer to a whole collection of parts at the same time.

Levels provide a general way of specifying collections of parts in *Mathematica* expressions. Many *Mathematica* functions allow you to specify the levels in an expression on which they should act.

Here is a simple expression, displayed in tree form.

In[1]:= **(t = {x, {x, y}, y}) // TreeForm**

Out[1]//TreeForm= List[x, | , y]
                           List[x, y]

This searches for x in the expression t down to level 1. It finds only one occurrence.

In[2]:= **Position[t, x, 1]**

Out[2]= {{1}}

This searches down to level 2. Now it finds both occurrences of x.	*In[3]:=* **Position[t, x, 2]**
	Out[3]= {{1}, {2, 1}}
This searches only at level 2. It finds just one occurrence of x.	*In[4]:=* **Position[t, x, {2}]**
	Out[4]= {{2, 1}}

Position[*expr*, *form*, *n*]	give the positions at which *form* occurs in *expr* down to level *n*
Position[*expr*, *form*, {*n*}]	give the positions exactly at level *n*

Controlling Position using levels.

You can think of levels in expressions in terms of trees. The level of a particular part in an expression is simply the distance down the tree at which that part appears, with the top of the tree considered as level 0.

It is equivalent to say that the parts which appear at level *n* are those that can be specified by a sequence of exactly *n* indices.

n	levels 1 through *n*
Infinity	all levels (except 0)
{*n*}	level *n* only
{n_1, n_2}	levels n_1 through n_2
Heads -> True	include heads
Heads -> False	exclude heads

Level specifications.

Here is an expression, displayed in tree form.	*In[5]:=* **(u = f[f[g[a], a], a, h[a], f]) // TreeForm**
	Out[5]//TreeForm= f[| , a, | , f]
	f[| , a] h[a]
	g[a]
This searches for a at levels from 2 downwards.	*In[6]:=* **Position[u, a, {2, Infinity}]**
	Out[6]= {{1, 1, 1}, {1, 2}, {3, 1}}
This shows where f appears other than in the head of an expression.	*In[7]:=* **Position[u, f, Heads->False]**
	Out[7]= {{4}}

This includes occurrences of f in heads
of expressions.

In[8]:= **Position[u, f, Heads->True]**

Out[8]= {{0}, {1, 0}, {4}}

Level[*expr, lev*]	a list of the parts of *expr* at the levels specified by *lev*
Depth[*expr*]	the total number of levels in *expr*

Testing and extracting levels.

This gives a list of all parts of u that
occur down to level 2.

In[9]:= **Level[u, 2]**

Out[9]= {g[a], a, f[g[a], a], a, a, h[a], f}

Here are the parts specifically at
level 2.

In[10]:= **Level[u, {2}]**

Out[10]= {g[a], a, a}

When you have got the hang of ordinary levels, you can try thinking about *negative levels*. Negative
levels label parts of expressions starting at the *bottom* of the tree. Level −1 contains all the leaves of
the tree: objects like symbols and numbers.

This shows the parts of u at level −1.

In[11]:= **Level[u, {-1}]**

Out[11]= {a, a, a, a, f}

You can think of expressions as having a "depth", which is equal to the maximum number of levels
shown by **TreeForm**. In general, level −*n* in an expression is defined to consist of all subexpressions
whose depth is *n*.

The depth of g[a] is 2.

In[12]:= **Depth[g[a]]**

Out[12]= 2

The parts of u at level −2 are those
that have depth exactly 2.

In[13]:= **Level[u, {-2}]**

Out[13]= {g[a], h[a]}

2.2 Functional Operations

■ 2.2.1 Function Names as Expressions

In an expression like $f[x]$, the "function name" f is itself an expression, and you can treat it as you would any other expression.

You can replace names of functions using transformation rules.

$In[1]:=$ **f[x] + f[1 - x] /. f -> g**

$Out[1]=$ g[1 - x] + g[x]

Any assignments you have made are used on function names.

$In[2]:=$ **p1 = p2; p1[x, y]**

$Out[2]=$ p2[x, y]

This defines a function which takes a function name as an argument.

$In[3]:=$ **pf[f_, x_] := f[x] + f[1 - x]**

This gives Log as the function name to use.

$In[4]:=$ **pf[Log, q]**

$Out[4]=$ Log[1 - q] + Log[q]

The ability to treat the names of functions just like other kinds of expressions is an important consequence of the symbolic nature of the *Mathematica* language. It makes possible the whole range of *functional operations* discussed in the sections that follow.

Ordinary *Mathematica* functions such as Log or Integrate typically operate on data such as numbers and algebraic expressions. *Mathematica* functions that represent functional operations, however, can operate not only on ordinary data, but also on functions themselves. Thus, for example, the functional operation InverseFunction takes a *Mathematica* function name as an argument, and represents the inverse of that function.

InverseFunction is a functional operation: it takes a *Mathematica* function as an argument, and returns another function which represents its inverse.

$In[5]:=$ **InverseFunction[ArcSin]**

$Out[5]=$ Sin

The result obtained from InverseFunction is a function which you can apply to data.

$In[6]:=$ **%[x]**

$Out[6]=$ Sin[x]

You can also use InverseFunction in a purely symbolic way.

$In[7]:=$ **InverseFunction[f] [x]**

$Out[7]=$ $f^{(-1)}[x]$

There are many kinds of functional operations in *Mathematica*. Some represent mathematical operations; others represent various kinds of procedures and algorithms.

Unless you are familiar with advanced symbolic languages, you will probably not recognize most of the functional operations discussed in the sections that follow. At first, the operations may seem difficult to understand. But it is worth persisting. Functional operations provide one of the most conceptually and practically efficient ways to use *Mathematica*.

■ 2.2.2 Applying Functions Repeatedly

Many programs you write will involve operations that need to be iterated several times. Nest and NestList are powerful constructs for doing this.

Nest[*f*, *x*, *n*]	apply the function *f* nested *n* times to *x*
NestList[*f*, *x*, *n*]	generate the list {*x*, *f*[*x*], *f*[*f*[*x*]], ... }, where *f* is nested up to *n* deep

Applying functions of one argument repeatedly.

Nest[*f*, *x*, *n*] takes the "name" *f* of a function, and applies the function *n* times to *x*.

```
In[1]:= Nest[f, x, 4]
Out[1]= f[f[f[f[x]]]]
```

This makes a list of each successive nesting.

```
In[2]:= NestList[f, x, 4]
Out[2]= {x, f[x], f[f[x]], f[f[f[x]]], f[f[f[f[x]]]]}
```

Here is a simple function.

```
In[3]:= recip[x_] := 1/(1 + x)
```

You can iterate the function using Nest.

```
In[4]:= Nest[recip, x, 3]
```

$$Out[4]= \cfrac{1}{1 + \cfrac{1}{1 + \cfrac{1}{1+x}}}$$

Nest and NestList allow you to apply functions a fixed number of times. Often you may want to apply functions until the result no longer changes. You can do this using FixedPoint and FixedPointList.

FixedPoint[*f*, *x*]	apply the function *f* repeatedly until the result no longer changes
FixedPointList[*f*, *x*]	generate the list {*x*, *f*[*x*], *f*[*f*[*x*]], ... }, stopping when the elements no longer change

Applying functions until the result no longer changes.

Here is a function that takes one step in Newton's approximation to $\sqrt{3}$.

```
In[5]:= newton3[x_] := N[ 1/2 ( x + 3/x ) ]
```

Here are five successive iterates of the function, starting at *x* = 1.

```
In[6]:= NestList[newton3, 1.0, 5]
Out[6]= {1., 2., 1.75, 1.73214, 1.73205, 1.73205}
```

Using the function FixedPoint, you can automatically continue applying newton3 until the result no longer changes.

```
In[7]:= FixedPoint[newton3, 1.0]
Out[7]= 1.73205
```

Here is the sequence of results.

```
In[8]:= FixedPointList[newton3, 1.0]
Out[8]= {1., 2., 1.75, 1.73214, 1.73205, 1.73205, 1.73205}
```

NestWhile[*f*, *x*, *test*]	apply the function *f* repeatedly until applying *test* to the result no longer yields True
NestWhileList[*f*, *x*, *test*]	generate the list {*x*, *f*[*x*], *f*[*f*[*x*]], ... }, stopping when applying *test* to the result no longer yields True
NestWhile[*f*, *x*, *test*, *m*], NestWhileList[*f*, *x*, *test*, *m*]	supply the *m* most recent results as arguments for *test* at each step
NestWhile[*f*, *x*, *test*, All], NestWhileList[*f*, *x*, *test*, All]	supply all results so far as arguments for *test*

Applying functions repeatedly until a test fails.

Here is a function which divides a number by 2.

```
In[9]:= divide2[n_] := n/2
```

This repeatedly applies divide2 until the result is no longer an even number.

```
In[10]:= NestWhileList[divide2, 123456, EvenQ]
Out[10]= {123456, 61728, 30864, 15432, 7716, 3858, 1929}
```

This repeatedly applies newton3, stopping when two successive results are no longer considered unequal, just as in FixedPointList.

```
In[11]:= NestWhileList[newton3, 1.0, Unequal, 2]
Out[11]= {1., 2., 1.75, 1.73214, 1.73205, 1.73205, 1.73205}
```

This goes on until the first time a result that has been seen before reappears.

```
In[12]:= NestWhileList[Mod[5 #, 7]&, 1, Unequal, All]
Out[12]= {1, 5, 4, 6, 2, 3, 1}
```

Operations such as Nest take a function *f* of one argument, and apply it repeatedly. At each step, they use the result of the previous step as the new argument of *f*.

It is important to generalize this notion to functions of two arguments. You can again apply the function repeatedly, but now each result you get supplies only one of the new arguments you need. A convenient approach is to get the other argument at each step from the successive elements of a list.

FoldList[*f*, *x*, {*a*, *b*, ... }]	create the list {*x*, *f*[*x*, *a*], *f*[*f*[*x*, *a*], *b*], ... }
Fold[*f*, *x*, {*a*, *b*, ... }]	give the last element of the list produced by FoldList[*f*, *x*, {*a*, *b*, ... }]

Ways to repeatedly apply functions of two arguments.

Here is an example of what FoldList does.	*In[13]:=* **FoldList[f, x, {a, b, c}]** *Out[13]=* {x, f[x, a], f[f[x, a], b], f[f[f[x, a], b], c]}
Fold gives the last element of the list produced by FoldList.	*In[14]:=* **Fold[f, x, {a, b, c}]** *Out[14]=* f[f[f[x, a], b], c]
This gives a list of cumulative sums.	*In[15]:=* **FoldList[Plus, 0, {a, b, c}]** *Out[15]=* {0, a, a + b, a + b + c}

Using Fold and FoldList you can write many elegant and efficient programs in *Mathematica*. In some cases, you may find it helpful to think of Fold and FoldList as producing a simple nesting of a family of functions indexed by their second argument.

This defines a function nextdigit.	*In[16]:=* **nextdigit[a_, b_] := 10 a + b**
This is now like the built-in function FromDigits.	*In[17]:=* **fromdigits[digits_] := Fold[nextdigit, 0, digits]**
Here is an example of the function in action.	*In[18]:=* **fromdigits[{1, 3, 7, 2, 9, 1}]** *Out[18]=* 137291

■ 2.2.3 Applying Functions to Lists and Other Expressions

In an expression like f[{a, b, c}] you are giving a list as the argument to a function. Often you need instead to apply a function directly to the elements of a list, rather than to the list as a whole. You can do this in *Mathematica* using Apply.

This makes each element of the list an argument of the function f.	*In[1]:=* **Apply[f, {a, b, c}]** *Out[1]=* f[a, b, c]
This gives Plus[a, b, c] which yields the sum of the elements in the list.	*In[2]:=* **Apply[Plus, {a, b, c}]** *Out[2]=* a + b + c
Here is the definition of the statistical mean, written using Apply.	*In[3]:=* **mean[list_] := Apply[Plus, list] / Length[list]**

Apply[*f*, {*a*, *b*, ... }]	apply *f* to a list, giving *f*[*a*, *b*, ...]
Apply[*f*, *expr*] or *f* @@ *expr*	apply *f* to the top level of an expression
Apply[*f*, *expr*, {1}] or *f* @@@ *expr*	apply *f* at the first level in an expression
Apply[*f*, *expr*, *lev*]	apply *f* at the specified levels in an expression

Applying functions to lists and other expressions.

What Apply does in general is to replace the head of an expression with the function you specify. Here it replaces Plus by List.

```
In[4]:= Apply[List, a + b + c]

Out[4]= {a, b, c}
```

Here is a matrix.

```
In[5]:= m = {{a, b, c}, {b, c, d}}

Out[5]= {{a, b, c}, {b, c, d}}
```

Using Apply without an explicit level specification replaces the top-level list with f.

```
In[6]:= Apply[f, m]

Out[6]= f[{a, b, c}, {b, c, d}]
```

This applies f only to parts of m at level 1.

```
In[7]:= Apply[f, m, {1}]

Out[7]= {f[a, b, c], f[b, c, d]}
```

This applies f at levels 0 through 1.

```
In[8]:= Apply[f, m, {0, 1}]

Out[8]= f[f[a, b, c], f[b, c, d]]
```

■ 2.2.4 Applying Functions to Parts of Expressions

If you have a list of elements, it is often important to be able to apply a function separately to each of the elements. You can do this in *Mathematica* using Map.

This applies f separately to each element in a list.

```
In[1]:= Map[f, {a, b, c}]

Out[1]= {f[a], f[b], f[c]}
```

This defines a function which takes the first two elements from a list.

```
In[2]:= take2[list_] := Take[list, 2]
```

You can use Map to apply take2 to each element of a list.

```
In[3]:= Map[take2, {{1, 3, 4}, {5, 6, 7}, {2, 1, 6, 6}}]

Out[3]= {{1, 3}, {5, 6}, {2, 1}}
```

Map[*f*, {*a*, *b*, ... }]	apply *f* to each element in a list, giving {*f*[*a*], *f*[*b*], ... }

Applying a function to each element in a list.

What Map[*f*, *expr*] effectively does is to "wrap" the function *f* around each element of the expression *expr*. You can use Map on any expression, not just a list.

This applies f to each element in the sum.	*In[4]:=* **Map[f, a + b + c]**
	Out[4]= f[a] + f[b] + f[c]

This applies Sqrt to each argument of g.	*In[5]:=* **Map[Sqrt, g[x^2, x^3]]**
	Out[5]= g$\left[\sqrt{x^2}, \sqrt{x^3}\right]$

Map[*f*, *expr*] applies *f* to the first level of parts in *expr*. You can use MapAll[*f*, *expr*] to apply *f* to *all* the parts of *expr*.

This defines a 2 × 2 matrix m.	*In[6]:=* **m = {{a, b}, {c, d}}**
	Out[6]= {{a, b}, {c, d}}

Map applies f to the first level of m, in this case the rows of the matrix.	*In[7]:=* **Map[f, m]**
	Out[7]= {f[{a, b}], f[{c, d}]}

MapAll applies f at *all* levels in m. If you look carefully at this expression, you will see an f wrapped around every part.	*In[8]:=* **MapAll[f, m]**
	Out[8]= f[{f[{f[a], f[b]}], f[{f[c], f[d]}]}]

In general, you can use level specifications as described on page 238 to tell Map to which parts of an expression to apply your function.

This applies f only to the parts of m at level 2.	*In[9]:=* **Map[f, m, {2}]**
	Out[9]= {{f[a], f[b]}, {f[c], f[d]}}

Setting the option Heads->True wraps f around the head of each part, as well as its elements.	*In[10]:=* **Map[f, m, Heads->True]**
	Out[10]= f[List][f[{a, b}], f[{c, d}]]

Map[*f*, *expr*] or *f* /@ *expr*	apply *f* to the first-level parts of *expr*
MapAll[*f*, *expr*] or *f* //@ *expr*	apply *f* to all parts of *expr*
Map[*f*, *expr*, *lev*]	apply *f* to each part of *expr* at levels specified by *lev*

Ways to apply a function to different parts of expressions.

Level specifications allow you to tell Map to which levels of parts in an expression you want a function applied. With MapAt, however, you can instead give an explicit list of parts where you want a function applied. You specify each part by giving its indices, as discussed in Section 2.1.4.

Here is a 2 × 3 matrix.	*In[11]:=* **mm = {{a, b, c}, {b, c, d}}**
	Out[11]= {{a, b, c}, {b, c, d}}

This applies f to parts {1, 2} and {2, 3}.	In[12]:= **MapAt[f, mm, {{1, 2}, {2, 3}}]**
	Out[12]= {{a, f[b], c}, {b, c, f[d]}}
This gives a list of the positions at which b occurs in mm.	In[13]:= **Position[mm, b]**
	Out[13]= {{1, 2}, {2, 1}}
You can feed the list of positions you get from Position directly into MapAt.	In[14]:= **MapAt[f, mm, %]**
	Out[14]= {{a, f[b], c}, {f[b], c, d}}
To avoid ambiguity, you must put each part specification in a list, even when it involves only one index.	In[15]:= **MapAt[f, {a, b, c, d}, {{2}, {3}}]**
	Out[15]= {a, f[b], f[c], d}

MapAt[*f*, *expr*, {*part₁*, *part₂*, ... }]	apply *f* to specified parts of *expr*

Applying a function to specific parts of an expression.

Here is an expression.	In[16]:= **t = 1 + (3 + x)^2 / x**
	Out[16]= $1 + \dfrac{(3+x)^2}{x}$
This is the full form of t.	In[17]:= **FullForm[t]**
	Out[17]//FullForm= Plus[1, Times[Power[x, -1], Power[Plus[3, x], 2]]]
You can use MapAt on any expression. Remember that parts are numbered on the basis of the full forms of expressions.	In[18]:= **MapAt[f, t, {{2, 1, 1}, {2, 2}}]**
	Out[18]= $1 + \dfrac{f\left[(3+x)^2\right]}{f[x]}$

MapIndexed[*f*, *expr*]	apply *f* to the elements of an expression, giving the part specification of each element as a second argument to *f*
MapIndexed[*f*, *expr*, *lev*]	apply *f* to parts at specified levels, giving the list of indices for each part as a second argument to *f*

Applying a function to parts and their indices.

This applies f to each element in a list, giving the index of the element as a second argument to f.	In[19]:= **MapIndexed[f, {a, b, c}]**
	Out[19]= {f[a, {1}], f[b, {2}], f[c, {3}]}
This applies f to both levels in a matrix.	In[20]:= **MapIndexed[f, {{a, b}, {c, d}}, 2]**
	Out[20]= {f[{f[a, {1, 1}], f[b, {1, 2}]}, {1}], f[{f[c, {2, 1}], f[d, {2, 2}]}, {2}]}

Map allows you to apply a function of one argument to parts of an expression. Sometimes, however, you may instead want to apply a function of several arguments to corresponding parts of several different expressions. You can do this using MapThread.

MapThread[*f*, {*expr*$_1$, *expr*$_2$, ... }]	apply *f* to corresponding elements in each of the *expr*$_i$
MapThread[*f*, {*expr*$_1$, *expr*$_2$, ... }, *lev*]	apply *f* to parts of the *expr*$_i$ at the specified level

Applying a function to several expressions at once.

This applies f to corresponding pairs of list elements.

```
In[21]:= MapThread[f, {{a, b, c}, {ap, bp, cp}}]
Out[21]= {f[a, ap], f[b, bp], f[c, cp]}
```

MapThread works with any number of expressions, so long as they have the same structure.

```
In[22]:= MapThread[f, {{a, b}, {ap, bp}, {app, bpp}}]
Out[22]= {f[a, ap, app], f[b, bp, bpp]}
```

Functions like Map allow you to create expressions with parts modified. Sometimes you simply want to go through an expression, and apply a particular function to some parts of it, without building a new expression. A typical case is when the function you apply has certain "side effects", such as making assignments, or generating output.

Scan[*f*, *expr*]	evaluate *f* applied to each element of *expr* in turn
Scan[*f*, *expr*, *lev*]	evaluate *f* applied to parts of *expr* on levels specified by *lev*

Evaluating functions on parts of expressions.

Map constructs a new list in which f has been applied to each element of the list.

```
In[23]:= Map[f, {a, b, c}]
Out[23]= {f[a], f[b], f[c]}
```

Scan evaluates the result of applying a function to each element, but does not construct a new expression.

```
In[24]:= Scan[Print, {a, b, c}]
a
b
c
```

Scan visits the parts of an expression in a depth-first walk, with the leaves visited first.

```
In[25]:= Scan[Print, 1 + x^2, Infinity]
1
x
2
 2
x
```

■ 2.2.5 Pure Functions

Function[x, *body*]	a pure function in which x is replaced by any argument you provide
Function[{x_1, x_2, ... }, *body*]	a pure function that takes several arguments
body &	a pure function in which arguments are specified as # or #1, #2, #3, etc.

Pure functions.

When you use functional operations such as Nest and Map, you always have to specify a function to apply. In all the examples above, we have used the "name" of a function to specify the function. Pure functions allow you to give functions which can be applied to arguments, without having to define explicit names for the functions.

This defines a function h.

In[1]:= **h[x_] := f[x] + g[x]**

Having defined h, you can now use its name in Map.

In[2]:= **Map[h, {a, b, c}]**

Out[2]= {f[a] + g[a], f[b] + g[b], f[c] + g[c]}

Here is a way to get the same result using a pure function.

In[3]:= **Map[f[#] + g[#] &, {a, b, c}]**

Out[3]= {f[a] + g[a], f[b] + g[b], f[c] + g[c]}

There are several equivalent ways to write pure functions in *Mathematica*. The idea in all cases is to construct an object which, when supplied with appropriate arguments, computes a particular function. Thus, for example, if *fun* is a pure function, then *fun*[a] evaluates the function with argument a.

Here is a pure function which represents the operation of squaring.

In[4]:= **Function[x, x^2]**

Out[4]= Function[x, x^2]

Supplying the argument n to the pure function yields the square of n.

In[5]:= **%[n]**

Out[5]= n^2

You can use a pure function wherever you would usually give the name of a function.

You can use a pure function in Map.

In[6]:= **Map[Function[x, x^2], a + b + c]**

Out[6]= $a^2 + b^2 + c^2$

Or in Nest.

In[7]:= **Nest[Function[q, 1/(1+q)], x, 3]**

Out[7]= $\dfrac{1}{1 + \dfrac{1}{1+\frac{1}{1+x}}}$

This sets up a pure function with two arguments and then applies the function to the arguments a and b.

In[8]:= **Function[{x, y}, x^2 + y^3] [a, b]**

Out[8]= $a^2 + b^3$

If you are going to use a particular function repeatedly, then you can define the function using *f*[*x_*] := *body*, and refer to the function by its name *f*. On the other hand, if you only intend to use a function once, you will probably find it better to give the function in pure function form, without ever naming it.

If you are familiar with formal logic or the LISP programming language, you will recognize *Mathematica* pure functions as being like λ expressions or anonymous functions. Pure functions are also close to the pure mathematical notion of operators.

#	the first variable in a pure function
#*n*	the nth variable in a pure function
##	the sequence of all variables in a pure function
##*n*	the sequence of variables starting with the nth one

Short forms for pure functions.

Just as the name of a function is irrelevant if you do not intend to refer to the function again, so also the names of arguments in a pure function are irrelevant. *Mathematica* allows you to avoid using explicit names for the arguments of pure functions, and instead to specify the arguments by giving "slot numbers" **#***n*. In a *Mathematica* pure function, **#***n* stands for the nth argument you supply. **#** stands for the first argument.

#^2 & is a short form for a pure function that squares its argument.	*In[9]:=* **Map[#^2 &, a + b + c]** *Out[9]=* $a^2 + b^2 + c^2$
This applies a function that takes the first two elements from each list. By using a pure function, you avoid having to define the function separately.	*In[10]:=* **Map[Take[#, 2]&, {{2, 1, 7}, {4, 1, 5}, {3, 1, 2}}]** *Out[10]=* {{2, 1}, {4, 1}, {3, 1}}
Using short forms for pure functions, you can simplify the definition of **fromdigits** given on page 243.	*In[11]:=* **fromdigits[digits_] := Fold[(10 #1 + #2)&, 0, digits]**

When you use short forms for pure functions, it is very important that you do not forget the ampersand. If you leave the ampersand out, *Mathematica* will not know that the expression you give is to be used as a pure function.

When you use the ampersand notation for pure functions, you must be careful about the grouping of pieces in your input. As shown on page 1029 the ampersand notation has fairly low precedence, which means that you can type expressions like **#1 + #2 &** without parentheses. On the other hand, if you want, for example, to set an option to be a pure function, you need to use parentheses, as in *option* -> (*fun* &).

Pure functions in *Mathematica* can take any number of arguments. You can use ## to stand for all the arguments that are given, and ##*n* to stand for the *n*th and subsequent arguments.

## stands for all arguments.	*In[12]:=* **f[##, ##]& [x, y]**
	Out[12]= f[x, y, x, y]
##2 stands for all arguments except the first one.	*In[13]:=* **Apply[f[##2, #1]&, {{a, b, c}, {ap, bp}}, {1}]**
	Out[13]= {f[b, c, a], f[bp, ap]}

■ 2.2.6 Building Lists from Functions

Array[*f*, *n*]	generate a length *n* list of the form {*f*[1], *f*[2], ... }
Array[*f*, {*n*$_1$, *n*$_2$, ... }]	generate an *n*$_1$ × *n*$_2$ × ... nested list, each of whose entries consists of *f* applied to its indices
NestList[*f*, *x*, *n*]	generate a list of the form {*x*, *f*[*x*], *f*[*f*[*x*]], ... }, where *f* is nested up to *n* deep
FoldList[*f*, *x*, {*a*, *b*, ... }]	generate a list of the form {*x*, *f*[*x*, *a*], *f*[*f*[*x*, *a*], *b*], ... }
ComposeList[{*f*$_1$, *f*$_2$, ... }, *x*]	generate a list of the form {*x*, *f*$_1$[*x*], *f*$_2$[*f*$_1$[*x*]], ... }

Making lists from functions.

This makes a list of 5 elements, each of the form p[*i*].	*In[1]:=* **Array[p, 5]**
	Out[1]= {p[1], p[2], p[3], p[4], p[5]}
Here is another way to produce the same list.	*In[2]:=* **Table[p[i], {i, 5}]**
	Out[2]= {p[1], p[2], p[3], p[4], p[5]}
This produces a list whose elements are $i + i^2$.	*In[3]:=* **Array[# + #^2 &, 5]**
	Out[3]= {2, 6, 12, 20, 30}
This generates a 2 × 3 matrix whose entries are m[*i*, *j*].	*In[4]:=* **Array[m, {2, 3}]**
	Out[4]= {{m[1, 1], m[1, 2], m[1, 3]}, {m[2, 1], m[2, 2], m[2, 3]}}
This generates a 3 × 3 matrix whose elements are the squares of the sums of their indices.	*In[5]:=* **Array[Plus[##]^2 &, {3, 3}]**
	Out[5]= {{4, 9, 16}, {9, 16, 25}, {16, 25, 36}}

NestList and FoldList were discussed in Section 2.2.2. Particularly by using them with pure functions, you can construct some very elegant and efficient *Mathematica* programs.

This gives a list of results obtained by successively differentiating x^n with respect to *x*.	*In[6]:=* **NestList[D[#, x]&, x^n, 3]**
	Out[6]= {x^n, n x^{-1+n}, (-1+n) n x^{-2+n}, (-2+n) (-1+n) n x^{-3+n}}

■ 2.2.7 Selecting Parts of Expressions with Functions

Section 1.2.4 showed how you can pick out elements of lists based on their *positions*. Often, however, you will need to select elements based not on *where* they are, but rather on *what* they are.

`Select[`*list*`, `*f*`]` selects elements of *list* using the function *f* as a criterion. `Select` applies *f* to each element of *list* in turn, and keeps only those for which the result is `True`.

This selects the elements of the list for which the pure function yields True, i.e., those numerically greater than 4.	$In[1]:=$ `Select[{2, 15, 1, a, 16, 17}, # > 4 &]` $Out[1]=$ `{15, 16, 17}`

You can use `Select` to pick out pieces of any expression, not just elements of a list.

This gives a sum of terms involving x, y and z.	$In[2]:=$ `t = Expand[(x + y + z)^2]` $Out[2]=$ $x^2 + 2xy + y^2 + 2xz + 2yz + z^2$
You can use Select to pick out only those terms in the sum that do not involve the symbol x.	$In[3]:=$ `Select[t, FreeQ[#, x]&]` $Out[3]=$ $y^2 + 2yz + z^2$

`Select[`*expr*`, `*f*`]`	select the elements in *expr* for which the function *f* gives `True`
`Select[`*expr*`, `*f*`, `*n*`]`	select the first *n* elements in *expr* for which the function *f* gives `True`

Selecting pieces of expressions.

Section 2.3.5 discusses some "predicates" that are often used as criteria in `Select`.

This gives the first element which satisfies the criterion you specify.	$In[4]:=$ `Select[{-1, 3, 10, 12, 14}, # > 3 &, 1]` $Out[4]=$ `{10}`

■ 2.2.8 Expressions with Heads That Are Not Symbols

In most cases, you want the head *f* of a *Mathematica* expression like *f*[*x*] to be a single symbol. There are, however, some important applications of heads that are not symbols.

This expression has f[3] as a head. You can use heads like this to represent "indexed functions".	$In[1]:=$ `f[3][x, y]` $Out[1]=$ `f[3][x, y]`
You can use any expression as a head. Remember to put in the necessary parentheses.	$In[2]:=$ `(a + b)[x]` $Out[2]=$ `(a + b)[x]`

One case where we have already encountered the use of complicated expressions as heads is in working with pure functions in Section 2.2.5. By giving Function[*vars*, *body*] as the head of an expression, you specify a function of the arguments to be evaluated.

With the head Function[x, x^2], the value of the expression is the square of the argument.

In[3]:= **Function[x, x^2] [a + b]**

Out[3]= $(a + b)^2$

There are several constructs in *Mathematica* which work much like pure functions, but which represent specific kinds of functions, typically numerical ones. In all cases, the basic mechanism involves giving a head which contains complete information about the function you want to use.

Function[*vars*, *body*][*args*]	pure function
InterpolatingFunction[*data*][*args*]	approximate numerical function (generated by Interpolation and NDSolve)
CompiledFunction[*data*][*args*]	compiled numerical function (generated by Compile)
+ LinearSolveFunction[*data*][*vec*]	matrix solution function (generated by LinearSolve)

Some expressions which have heads that are not symbols.

NDSolve returns a list of rules that give y as an InterpolatingFunction object.

In[4]:= **NDSolve[{y''[x] == y[x], y[0]==y'[0]==1}, y, {x, 0, 5}]**

Out[4]= {{y → InterpolatingFunction[{{0., 5.}}, <>]}}

Here is the InterpolatingFunction object.

In[5]:= **y /. First[%]**

Out[5]= InterpolatingFunction[{{0., 5.}}, <>]

You can use the InterpolatingFunction object as a head to get numerical approximations to values of the function y.

In[6]:= **% [3.8]**

Out[6]= 44.7012

Another important use of more complicated expressions as heads is in implementing *functionals* and *functional operators* in mathematics.

As one example, consider the operation of differentiation. As will be discussed in Section 3.5.4, an expression like f' represents a *derivative function*, obtained from f by applying a functional operator to it. In *Mathematica*, f' is represented as Derivative[1][f]: the "functional operator" Derivative[1] is applied to f to give another function, represented as f'.

This expression has a head which represents the application of the "functional operator" Derivative[1] to the "function" f.

In[7]:= **f'[x] // FullForm**

Out[7]//FullForm= Derivative[1][f][x]

You can replace the head `f'` with another head, such as `fp`. This effectively takes `fp` to be a "derivative function" obtained from `f`.

```
In[8]:= % /. f' -> fp

Out[8]= fp[x]
```

■ 2.2.9 Advanced Topic: Working with Operators

You can think of an expression like $f[x]$ as being formed by applying an *operator f* to the expression x. You can think of an expression like $f[g[x]]$ as the result of *composing* the operators f and g, and applying the result to x.

`Composition[`f`, `g`, ... ]`	the composition of functions f, g, ...
`InverseFunction[`f`]`	the inverse of a function f
`Identity`	the identity function

Some functional operations.

This represents the composition of the functions f, g and h.

```
In[1]:= Composition[f, g, h]

Out[1]= Composition[f, g, h]
```

You can manipulate compositions of functions symbolically.

```
In[2]:= InverseFunction[Composition[%, q]]

Out[2]= Composition[q^(-1), h^(-1), g^(-1), f^(-1)]
```

The composition is evaluated explicitly when you supply a specific argument.

```
In[3]:= %[x]

Out[3]= q^(-1)[h^(-1)[g^(-1)[f^(-1)[x]]]]
```

You can get the sum of two expressions in *Mathematica* just by typing $x + y$. Sometimes it is also worthwhile to consider performing operations like addition on *operators*.

You can think of this as containing a sum of two operators f and g.

```
In[4]:= (f + g)[x]

Out[4]= (f + g)[x]
```

Using `Through`, you can convert the expression to a more explicit form.

```
In[5]:= Through[%, Plus]

Out[5]= f[x] + g[x]
```

This corresponds to the mathematical operator $1 + \frac{\partial}{\partial x}$.

```
In[6]:= Identity + (D[#, x]&)

Out[6]= Identity + (∂_x #1 &)
```

Mathematica does not automatically apply the separate pieces of the operator to an expression.

```
In[7]:= % [x^2]

Out[7]= (Identity + (∂_x #1 &))[x^2]
```

You can use `Through` to apply the operator.

```
In[8]:= Through[%, Plus]

Out[8]= 2 x + x^2
```

Identity[*expr*]	the identity function
Through[$p[f_1, f_2][x]$, q]	give $p[f_1[x], f_2[x]]$ if p is the same as q
Operate[p, $f[x]$]	give $p[f][x]$
Operate[p, $f[x]$, n]	apply p at level n in f
MapAll[p, *expr*, Heads->True]	apply p to all parts of *expr*, including heads

Operations for working with operators.

This has a complicated expression as a head.

```
In[9]:= t = ((1 + a)(1 + b))[x]
Out[9]= ((1 + a) (1 + b)) [x]
```

Functions like Expand do not automatically go inside heads of expressions.

```
In[10]:= Expand[%]
Out[10]= ((1 + a) (1 + b)) [x]
```

With the Heads option set to True, MapAll goes inside heads.

```
In[11]:= MapAll[Expand, t, Heads->True]
Out[11]= (1 + a + b + a b) [x]
```

The replacement operator /. does go inside heads of expressions.

```
In[12]:= t /. a->1
Out[12]= (2 (1 + b)) [x]
```

You can use Operate to apply a function specifically to the head of an expression.

```
In[13]:= Operate[p, t]
Out[13]= p[(1 + a) (1 + b)] [x]
```

■ 2.2.10 Structural Operations

Mathematica contains some powerful primitives for making structural changes to expressions. You can use these primitives both to implement mathematical properties such as associativity and distributivity, and to provide the basis for some succinct and efficient programs.

This section describes various operations that you can explicitly perform on expressions. Section 2.6.3 will describe how some of these operations can be performed automatically on all expressions with a particular head by assigning appropriate attributes to that head.

You can use the *Mathematica* function Sort[*expr*] to sort elements not only of lists, but of expressions with any head. In this way, you can implement the mathematical properties of commutativity or symmetry for arbitrary functions.

You can use Sort to put the arguments of any function into a standard order.

```
In[1]:= Sort[ f[c, a, b] ]
Out[1]= f[a, b, c]
```

Sort[*expr*]	sort the elements of a list or other expression into a standard order
Sort[*expr*, *pred*]	sort using the function *pred* to determine whether pairs are in order
Ordering[*expr*]	give the ordering of elements when sorted
Ordering[*expr*, *n*]	give the ordering of the first *n* elements when sorted
Ordering[*expr*, *n*, *pred*]	use the function *pred* to determine whether pairs are in order
OrderedQ[*expr*]	give True if the elements of *expr* are in standard order, and False otherwise
Order[*expr*$_1$, *expr*$_2$]	give 1 if *expr*$_1$ comes before *expr*$_2$ in standard order, and −1 if it comes after

Sorting into order.

The second argument to Sort is a function used to determine whether pairs are in order. This sorts numbers into descending order.

```
In[2]:= Sort[ {5, 1, 8, 2}, (#2 < #1)& ]
Out[2]= {8, 5, 2, 1}
```

This sorting criterion puts elements that do not depend on x before those that do.

```
In[3]:= Sort[ {x^2, y, x+y, y-2}, FreeQ[#1, x]& ]
Out[3]= {y, -2 + y, x + y, x²}
```

Flatten[*expr*]	flatten out all nested functions with the same head as *expr*
Flatten[*expr*, *n*]	flatten at most *n* levels of nesting
Flatten[*expr*, *n*, *h*]	flatten functions with head *h*
FlattenAt[*expr*, *i*]	flatten only the *i*th element of *expr*

Flattening out expressions.

Flatten removes nested occurrences of a function.

```
In[4]:= Flatten[ f[a, f[b, c], f[f[d]]] ]
Out[4]= f[a, b, c, d]
```

You can use Flatten to "splice" sequences of elements into lists or other expressions.

```
In[5]:= Flatten[ {a, f[b, c], f[a, b, d]}, 1, f ]
Out[5]= {a, b, c, a, b, d}
```

You can use Flatten to implement the mathematical property of associativity. The function Distribute allows you to implement properties such as distributivity and linearity.

Distribute[$f[a + b + ... , ...]$]	distribute f over sums to give $f[a, ...] + f[b, ...] + ...$
Distribute[$f[args], g$]	distribute f over any arguments which have head g
Distribute[$expr, g, f$]	distribute only when the head is f
Distribute[$expr, g, f, gp, fp$]	distribute f over g, replacing them with fp and gp, respectively

Applying distributive laws.

This "distributes" f over a + b.

```
In[6]:= Distribute[ f[a + b] ]
Out[6]= f[a] + f[b]
```

Here is a more complicated example.

```
In[7]:= Distribute[ f[a + b, c + d] ]
Out[7]= f[a, c] + f[a, d] + f[b, c] + f[b, d]
```

In general, if f is distributive over Plus, then an expression like $f[a + b]$ can be "expanded" to give $f[a] + f[b]$. The function Expand does this kind of expansion for standard algebraic operators such as Times. Distribute allows you to perform the same kind of expansion for arbitrary operators.

Expand uses the distributivity of Times over Plus to perform algebraic expansions.

```
In[8]:= Expand[ (a + b) (c + d) ]
Out[8]= a c + b c + a d + b d
```

This applies distributivity over lists, rather than sums. The result contains all possible pairs of arguments.

```
In[9]:= Distribute[ f[{a, b}, {c, d}], List ]
Out[9]= {f[a, c], f[a, d], f[b, c], f[b, d]}
```

This distributes over lists, but does so only if the head of the whole expression is f.

```
In[10]:= Distribute[ f[{a, b}, {c, d}], List, f ]
Out[10]= {f[a, c], f[a, d], f[b, c], f[b, d]}
```

This distributes over lists, making sure that the head of the whole expression is f. In the result, it uses gp in place of List, and fp in place of f.

```
In[11]:= Distribute[ f[{a, b}, {c, d}], List, f, gp, fp ]
Out[11]= gp[fp[a, c], fp[a, d], fp[b, c], fp[b, d]]
```

Related to Distribute is the function Thread. What Thread effectively does is to apply a function in parallel to all the elements of a list or other expression.

Thread[$f[\{a_1, a_2\}, \{b_1, b_2\}]$]	thread f over lists to give $\{f[a_1, b_1], f[a_2, b_2]\}$
Thread[$f[args], g$]	thread f over objects with head g in *args*

Functions for threading expressions.

Here is a function whose arguments are lists.	*In[12]:=* **f[{a1, a2}, {b1, b2}]**
	Out[12]= f[{a1, a2}, {b1, b2}]
Thread applies the function "in parallel" to each element of the lists.	*In[13]:=* **Thread[%]**
	Out[13]= {f[a1, b1], f[a2, b2]}
Arguments that are not lists get repeated.	*In[14]:=* **Thread[f[{a1, a2}, {b1, b2}, c, d]]**
	Out[14]= {f[a1, b1, c, d], f[a2, b2, c, d]}

As mentioned in Section 1.8.1, and discussed in more detail in Section 2.6.3, many built-in *Mathematica* functions have the property of being "listable", so that they are automatically threaded over any lists that appear as arguments.

Built-in mathematical functions such as Log are listable, so that they are automatically threaded over lists.	*In[15]:=* **Log[{a, b, c}]**
	Out[15]= {Log[a], Log[b], Log[c]}
Log is, however, not automatically threaded over equations.	*In[16]:=* **Log[x == y]**
	Out[16]= Log[x == y]
You can use Thread to get functions applied to both sides of an equation.	*In[17]:=* **Thread[%, Equal]**
	Out[17]= Log[x] == Log[y]

Outer[*f*, *list*$_1$, *list*$_2$]	generalized outer product
Inner[*f*, *list*$_1$, *list*$_2$, *g*]	generalized inner product

Generalized outer and inner products.

Outer[*f*, *list*$_1$, *list*$_2$] takes all possible combinations of elements from *list*$_1$ and *list*$_2$, and combines them with *f*. Outer can be viewed as a generalization of a Cartesian product for tensors, as discussed in Section 3.7.11.

Outer forms all possible combinations of elements, and applies f to them.	*In[18]:=* **Outer[f, {a, b}, {1, 2, 3}]**
	Out[18]= {{f[a, 1], f[a, 2], f[a, 3]},
	{f[b, 1], f[b, 2], f[b, 3]}}
Here Outer produces a lower-triangular Boolean matrix.	*In[19]:=* **Outer[Greater, {1, 2, 3}, {1, 2, 3}]**
	Out[19]= {{False, False, False},
	{True, False, False}, {True, True, False}}
You can use Outer on any sequence of expressions with the same head.	*In[20]:=* **Outer[g, f[a, b], f[c, d]]**
	Out[20]= f[f[g[a, c], g[a, d]], f[g[b, c], g[b, d]]]

Outer, like Distribute, constructs all possible combinations of elements. On the other hand, Inner, like Thread, constructs only combinations of elements that have corresponding positions in the expressions it acts on.

Here is a structure built by Inner.

In[21]:= **Inner[f, {a, b}, {c, d}, g]**

Out[21]= g[f[a, c], f[b, d]]

Inner is a generalization of Dot.

In[22]:= **Inner[Times, {a, b}, {c, d}, Plus]**

Out[22]= a c + b d

■ 2.2.11 Sequences

The function Flatten allows you to explicitly flatten out all sublists.

In[1]:= **Flatten[{a, {b, c}, {d, e}}]**

Out[1]= {a, b, c, d, e}

FlattenAt lets you specify at what positions you want sublists flattened.

In[2]:= **FlattenAt[{a, {b, c}, {d, e}}, 2]**

Out[2]= {a, b, c, {d, e}}

Sequence objects automatically get spliced in, and do not require any explicit flattening.

In[3]:= **{a, Sequence[b, c], Sequence[d, e]}**

Out[3]= {a, b, c, d, e}

Sequence[e_1, e_2, ...]	a sequence of arguments that will automatically be spliced into any function

Representing sequences of arguments in functions.

Sequence works in any function.

In[4]:= **f[Sequence[a, b], c]**

Out[4]= f[a, b, c]

This includes functions with special input forms.

In[5]:= **a == Sequence[b, c]**

Out[5]= a == b == c

Here is a common way that Sequence is used.

In[6]:= **{a, b, f[x, y], g[w], f[z, y]} /. f->Sequence**

Out[6]= {a, b, x, y, g[w], z, y}

2.3 Patterns

■ 2.3.1 Introduction

Patterns are used throughout *Mathematica* to represent classes of expressions. A simple example of a pattern is the expression f[x_]. This pattern represents the class of expressions with the form f[*anything*].

The main power of patterns comes from the fact that many operations in *Mathematica* can be done not only with single expressions, but also with patterns that represent whole classes of expressions.

You can use patterns in transformation rules to specify how classes of expressions should be transformed.	*In[1]:=* **f[a] + f[b] /. f[x_] -> x^2** *Out[1]=* $a^2 + b^2$
You can use patterns to find the positions of all expressions in a particular class.	*In[2]:=* **Position[{f[a], g[b], f[c]}, f[x_]]** *Out[2]=* {{1}, {3}}

The basic object that appears in almost all *Mathematica* patterns is _ (traditionally called "blank" by *Mathematica* programmers). The fundamental rule is simply that _ *stands for any expression*. On most keyboards the _ underscore character appears as the shifted version of the – dash character.

Thus, for example, the pattern f[_] stands for any expression of the form f[*anything*]. The pattern f[x_] also stands for any expression of the form f[*anything*], but gives the name x to the expression *anything*, allowing you to refer to it on the right-hand side of a transformation rule.

You can put blanks anywhere in an expression. What you get is a pattern which matches all expressions that can be made by "filling in the blanks" in any way.

f[n_]	f with any argument, named n
f[n_, m_]	f with two arguments, named n and m
x^n_	x to any power, with the power named n
x_^n_	any expression to any power
a_ + b_	a sum of two expressions
{a1_, a2_}	a list of two expressions
f[n_, n_]	f with two *identical* arguments

Some examples of patterns.

You can construct patterns for expressions with any structure.

In[3]:= **f[{a, b}] + f[c] /. f[{x_, y_}] -> p[x + y]**

Out[3]= f[c] + p[a + b]

One of the most common uses of patterns is for "destructuring" function arguments. If you make a definition for f[list_], then you need to use functions like Part explicitly in order to pick out elements of the list. But if you know for example that the list will always have two elements, then it is usually much more convenient instead to give a definition instead for f[{x_, y_}]. Then you can refer to the elements of the list directly as x and y. In addition, *Mathematica* will not use the definition you have given unless the argument of f really is of the required form of a list of two expressions.

Here is one way to define a function which takes a list of two elements, and evaluates the first element raised to the power of the second element.

In[4]:= **g[list_] := Part[list, 1] ^ Part[list, 2]**

Here is a much more elegant way to make the definition, using a pattern.

In[5]:= **h[{x_, y_}] := x ^ y**

A crucial point to understand is that *Mathematica* patterns represent classes of expressions with a given *structure*. One pattern will match a particular expression if the structure of the pattern is the same as the structure of the expression, in the sense that by filling in blanks in the pattern you can get the expression. Even though two expressions may be *mathematically equal*, they cannot be represented by the same *Mathematica* pattern unless they have the same structure.

Thus, for example, the pattern (1 + x_)^2 can stand for expressions like (1 + a)^2 or (1 + b^3)^2 that have the same *structure*. However, it cannot stand for the expression 1 + 2 a + a^2. Although this expression is *mathematically equal* to (1 + a)^2, it does not have the same *structure* as the pattern (1 + x_)^2.

The fact that patterns in *Mathematica* specify the *structure* of expressions is crucial in making it possible to set up transformation rules which change the *structure* of expressions, while leaving them mathematically equal.

It is worth realizing that in general it would be quite impossible for *Mathematica* to match patterns by mathematical, rather than structural, equivalence. In the case of expressions like (1 + a)^2 and 1 + 2 a + a^2, you can determine equivalence just by using functions like Expand and Factor. But, as discussed on page 327 there is no general way to find out whether an arbitrary pair of mathematical expressions are equal.

As another example, the pattern x^_ will match the expression x^2. It will not, however, match the expression 1, even though this could be considered as x^0. Section 2.3.9 will discuss how to construct a pattern for which this particular case will match. But you should understand that in all cases pattern matching in *Mathematica* is fundamentally structural.

The x^n_ matches only x^2 and x^3. 1 and x can mathematically be written as x^n, but do not have the same structure.

In[6]:= **{1, x, x^2, x^3} /. x^n_ -> r[n]**

Out[6]= {1, x, r[2], r[3]}

Another point to realize is that the structure *Mathematica* uses in pattern matching is the full form of expressions printed by `FullForm`. Thus, for example, an object such as 1/x, whose full form is `Power[x, -1]` will be matched by the pattern `x_^n_`, but not by the pattern `x_/y_`, whose full form is `Times[x_, Power[y_, -1]]`. Again, Section 2.3.9 will discuss how you can construct patterns which can match all these cases.

The expressions in the list contain explicit powers of b, so the transformation rule can be applied.	`In[7]:= {a/b, 1/b^2, 2/b^2} /. b^n_ -> d[n]`
	
	`Out[7]= {a d[-1], d[-2], 2 d[-2]}`

Here is the full form of the list.	`In[8]:= FullForm[{a/b, 1/b^2, 2/b^2}]`
	
	`Out[8]//FullForm= List[Times[a, Power[b, -1]],`
	`Power[b, -2], Times[2, Power[b, -2]]]`

Although *Mathematica* does not use mathematical equivalences such as $x^1 = x$ when matching patterns, it does use certain structural equivalences. Thus, for example, *Mathematica* takes account of properties such as commutativity and associativity in pattern matching.

To apply this transformation rule, *Mathematica* makes use of the commutativity and associativity of addition.	`In[9]:= f[a + b] + f[a + c] + f[b + d] /.`
	`f[a + x_] + f[c + y_] -> p[x, y]`
	
	`Out[9]= f[b + d] + p[b, a]`

The discussion so far has considered only pattern objects such as `x_` which can stand for any single expression. In later subsections, we discuss the constructs that *Mathematica* uses to extend and restrict the classes of expressions represented by patterns.

■ 2.3.2 Finding Expressions That Match a Pattern

`Cases[`*list*`, `*form*`]`	give the elements of *list* that match *form*
`Count[`*list*`, `*form*`]`	give the number of elements in *list* that match *form*
`Position[`*list*`, `*form*`, {1}]`	give the positions of elements in *list* that match *form*
`Select[`*list*`, `*test*`]`	give the elements of *list* on which *test* gives True

Picking out elements that match a pattern.

This gives the elements of the list which match the pattern x^_.	`In[1]:= Cases[ {3, 4, x, x^2, x^3}, x^_ ]`
	
	`Out[1]= {x^2, x^3}`

Here is the total number of elements which match the pattern.	`In[2]:= Count[ {3, 4, x, x^2, x^3}, x^_ ]`
	
	`Out[2]= 2`

You can apply functions like `Cases` not only to lists, but to expressions of any kind. In addition, you can specify the level of parts at which you want to look.

Cases[*expr*, *lhs*->*rhs*]	find elements of *expr* that match *lhs,* and give a list of the results of applying the transformation rule to them
Cases[*expr*, *lhs*->*rhs*, *lev*]	test parts of *expr* at levels specified by *lev*
Count[*expr*, *form*, *lev*]	give the total number of parts that match *form* at levels specified by *lev*
Position[*expr*, *form*, *lev*]	give the positions of parts that match *form* at levels specified by *lev*

Searching for parts of expressions that match a pattern.

This returns a list of the exponents n.

```
In[3]:= Cases[ {3, 4, x, x^2, x^3}, x^n_ -> n]
Out[3]= {2, 3}
```

The pattern _Integer matches any integer. This gives a list of integers appearing at any level.

```
In[4]:= Cases[ {3, 4, x, x^2, x^3}, _Integer, Infinity]
Out[4]= {3, 4, 2, 3}
```

Cases[*expr*, *form*, *lev*, *n*]	find only the first *n* parts that match *form*
Position[*expr*, *form*, *lev*, *n*]	give the positions of the first *n* parts that match *form*

Limiting the number of parts to search for.

This gives the positions of the first two powers of x appearing at any level.

```
In[5]:= Position[ {4, 4 + x^a, x^b, 6 + x^5}, x^_, Infinity, 2]
Out[5]= {{2, 2}, {3}}
```

The positions are specified in exactly the form used by functions such as Extract and ReplacePart discussed in Section 1.8.

```
In[6]:= ReplacePart[ {4, 4 + x^a, x^b, 6 + x^5}, zzz, % ]
Out[6]= {4, 4 + zzz, zzz, 6 + x^5}
```

DeleteCases[*expr*, *form*]	delete elements of *expr* that match *form*
DeleteCases[*expr*, *form*, *lev*]	delete parts of *expr* that match *form* at levels specified by *lev*

Deleting parts of expressions that match a pattern.

This deletes the elements which match x^n_.

```
In[7]:= DeleteCases[ {3, 4, x, x^2, x^3}, x^n_ ]
Out[7]= {3, 4, x}
```

This deletes all integers appearing at any level.

```
In[8]:= DeleteCases[ {3, 4, x, 2+x, 3+x}, _Integer, Infinity ]
Out[8]= {x, x, x}
```

`ReplaceList[`*expr*`, `*lhs*` -> `*rhs*`]`	find all ways that *expr* can match *lhs*

Finding arrangements of an expression that match a pattern.

This finds all ways that the sum can be written in two parts.

In[9]:= `ReplaceList[a + b + c, x_ + y_ -> g[x, y]]`

Out[9]= {g[a, b+c], g[b, a+c], g[c, a+b],
  g[a+b, c], g[a+c, b], g[b+c, a]}

This finds all pairs of identical elements. The pattern `___` stands for any sequence of elements.

In[10]:= `ReplaceList[{a, b, b, b, c, c, a},`
  `{___, x_, x_, ___} -> x]`

Out[10]= {b, b, c}

■ 2.3.3 Naming Pieces of Patterns

Particularly when you use transformation rules, you often need to name pieces of patterns. An object like *x_* stands for any expression, but gives the expression the name *x*. You can then, for example, use this name on the right-hand side of a transformation rule.

An important point is that when you use *x_*, *Mathematica* requires that all occurrences of blanks with the same name *x* in a particular expression must stand for the same expression.

Thus `f[x_, x_]` can only stand for expressions in which the two arguments of `f` are exactly the same. `f[_, _]`, on the other hand, can stand for any expression of the form f[*x*, *y*], where *x* and *y* need not be the same.

The transformation rule applies only to cases where the two arguments of `f` are identical.

In[1]:= `{f[a, a], f[a, b]} /. f[x_, x_] -> p[x]`

Out[1]= {p[a], f[a, b]}

Mathematica allows you to give names not just to single blanks, but to any piece of a pattern. The object *x*:*pattern* in general represents a pattern which is assigned the name *x*. In transformation rules, you can use this mechanism to name exactly those pieces of a pattern that you need to refer to on the right-hand side of the rule.

`_`	any expression
*x_*	any expression, to be named *x*
x:*pattern*	an expression to be named *x*, matching *pattern*

Patterns with names.

This gives a name to the complete form _^_ so you can refer to it as a whole on the right-hand side of the transformation rule.	*In[2]:=* **f[a^b] /. f[x:_^_] -> p[x]** *Out[2]=* p[a^b]
Here the exponent is named n, while the whole object is x.	*In[3]:=* **f[a^b] /. f[x:_^n_] -> p[x, n]** *Out[3]=* p[a^b, b]

When you give the same name to two pieces of a pattern, you constrain the pattern to match only those expressions in which the corresponding pieces are identical.

Here the pattern matches both cases.	*In[4]:=* **{f[h[4], h[4]], f[h[4], h[5]]} /. f[h[_], h[_]] -> q** *Out[4]=* {q, q}
Now both arguments of f are constrained to be the same, and only the first case matches.	*In[5]:=* **{f[h[4], h[4]], f[h[4], h[5]]} /. f[x:h[_], x_] -> r[x]** *Out[5]=* {r[h[4]], f[h[4], h[5]]}

■ 2.3.4 Specifying Types of Expression in Patterns

You can tell a lot about what "type" of expression something is by looking at its head. Thus, for example, an integer has head Integer, while a list has head List.

In a pattern, _h and x_h represent expressions that are constrained to have head h. Thus, for example, _Integer represents any integer, while _List represents any list.

x_h	an expression with head *h*
*x_*Integer	an integer
*x_*Real	an approximate real number
*x_*Complex	a complex number
*x_*List	a list
*x_*Symbol	a symbol

Patterns for objects with specified heads.

This replaces just those elements that are integers.	*In[1]:=* **{a, 4, 5, b} /. x_Integer -> p[x]** *Out[1]=* {a, p[4], p[5], b}

You can think of making an assignment for f[x_Integer] as like defining a function f that must take an argument of "type" Integer.

This defines a value for the function gamma when its argument is an integer.	*In[2]:=* **gamma[n_Integer] := (n - 1)!**

The definition applies only when the argument of gamma is an integer.	*In[3]:=* **gamma[4] + gamma[x]**
	Uut[3]– 6 + gamma[x]
The object 4. has head Real, so the definition does not apply.	*In[4]:=* **gamma[4.]**
	Out[4]= gamma[4.]
This defines values for expressions with integer exponents.	*In[5]:=* **d[x_^n_Integer] := n x^(n-1)**
The definition is used only when the exponent is an integer.	*In[6]:=* **d[x^4] + d[(a+b)^3] + d[x^(1/2)]**
	Out[6]= $3 (a+b)^2 + 4 x^3 + d\left[\sqrt{x}\right]$

■ 2.3.5 Putting Constraints on Patterns

Mathematica provides a general mechanism for specifying constraints on patterns. All you need do is to put /; *condition* at the end of a pattern to signify that it applies only when the specified condition is True. You can read the operator /; as "slash-semi", "whenever" or "provided that".

pattern /; *condition*	a pattern that matches only when a condition is satisfied
lhs :> *rhs* /; *condition*	a rule that applies only when a condition is satisfied
lhs := *rhs* /; *condition*	a definition that applies only when a condition is satisfied

Putting conditions on patterns and transformation rules.

This gives a definition for fac that applies only when its argument n is positive.	*In[1]:=* **fac[n_ /; n > 0] := n!**
The definition for fac is used only when the argument is positive.	*In[2]:=* **fac[6] + fac[-4]**
	Out[2]= 720 + fac[-4]
This gives the negative elements in the list.	*In[3]:=* **Cases[{3, -4, 5, -2}, x_ /; x < 0]**
	Out[3]= {-4, -2}

You can use /; on whole definitions and transformation rules, as well as on individual patterns. In general, you can put /; *condition* at the end of any := definition or :> rule to tell *Mathematica* that the definition or rule applies only when the specified condition holds. Note that /; conditions should not usually be put at the end of = definitions or -> rules, since they will then be evaluated immediately, as discussed in Section 2.5.8.

Here is another way to give a definition which applies only when its argument n is positive.	*In[4]:=* **fac2[n_] := n! /; n > 0**

Once again, the factorial functions evaluate only when their arguments are positive.

In[5]:= **fac2[6] + fac2[-4]**

Out[5]= 720 + fac2[-4]

You can use the /; operator to implement arbitrary mathematical constraints on the applicability of rules. In typical cases, you give patterns which *structurally* match a wide range of expressions, but then use *mathematical* constraints to reduce the range of expressions to a much smaller set.

This rule applies only to expressions that have the structure v[x_, 1 - x_].

In[6]:= **v[x_, 1 - x_] := p[x]**

This expression has the appropriate structure, so the rule applies.

In[7]:= **v[a^2, 1 - a^2]**

Out[7]= p[a^2]

This expression, while mathematically of the correct form, does not have the appropriate structure, so the rule does not apply.

In[8]:= **v[4, -3]**

Out[8]= v[4, -3]

This rule applies to any expression of the form w[x_, y_], with the added restriction that y == 1 - x.

In[9]:= **w[x_, y_] := p[x] /; y == 1 - x**

The new rule does apply to this expression.

In[10]:= **w[4, -3]**

Out[10]= p[4]

In setting up patterns and transformation rules, there is often a choice of where to put /; conditions. For example, you can put a /; condition on the right-hand side of a rule in the form *lhs* :> *rhs* /; *condition*, or you can put it on the left-hand side in the form *lhs* /; *condition* -> *rhs*. You may also be able to insert the condition inside the expression *lhs*. The only constraint is that all the names of patterns that you use in a particular condition must appear in the pattern to which the condition is attached. If this is not the case, then some of the names needed to evaluate the condition may not yet have been "bound" in the pattern-matching process. If this happens, then *Mathematica* uses the global values for the corresponding variables, rather than the values determined by pattern matching.

Thus, for example, the condition in f[x_, y_] /; (x + y < 2) will use values for x and y that are found by matching f[x_, y_], but the condition in f[x_ /; x + y < 2, y_] will use the global value for y, rather than the one found by matching the pattern.

As long as you make sure that the appropriate names are defined, it is usually most efficient to put /; conditions on the smallest possible parts of patterns. The reason for this is that *Mathematica* matches pieces of patterns sequentially, and the sooner it finds a /; condition which fails, the sooner it can reject a match.

Putting the /; condition around the x_ is slightly more efficient than putting it around the whole pattern.

In[11]:= **Cases[{z[1, 1], z[-1, 1], z[-2, 2]}, z[x_ /; x < 0, y_]]**

Out[11]= {z[-1, 1], z[-2, 2]}

You need to put parentheses around
the /; piece in a case like this.

In[12]:= **{1 + a, 2 + a, -3 + a} /. (x_ /; x < 0) + a -> p[x]**

Out[12]= {1 + a, 2 + a, p[-3]}

It is common to use /; to set up patterns and transformation rules that apply only to expressions with certain properties. There is a collection of functions built into *Mathematica* for testing the properties of expressions. It is a convention that functions of this kind have names that end with the letter Q, indicating that they "ask a question".

IntegerQ[*expr*]	integer
EvenQ[*expr*]	even number
OddQ[*expr*]	odd number
PrimeQ[*expr*]	prime number
NumberQ[*expr*]	explicit number of any kind
NumericQ[*expr*]	numeric quantity
PolynomialQ[*expr*, {x_1, x_2, ... }]	polynomial in x_1, x_2, ...
VectorQ[*expr*]	a list representing a vector
MatrixQ[*expr*]	a list of lists representing a matrix
VectorQ[*expr*, NumericQ], MatrixQ[*expr*, NumericQ]	vectors and matrices where all elements are numeric
VectorQ[*expr*, *test*], MatrixQ[*expr*, *test*]	vectors and matrices for which the function *test* yields True on every element
ArrayQ[*expr*, *d*]	full array with depth matching *d*

Some functions for testing mathematical properties of expressions.

The rule applies to all elements of the list that are numbers.

In[13]:= **{2.3, 4, 7/8, a, b} /. (x_ /; NumberQ[x]) -> x^2**

Out[13]= $\left\{5.29, 16, \dfrac{49}{64}, a, b\right\}$

This definition applies only to vectors of integers.

In[14]:= **mi[list_] := list^2 /; VectorQ[list, IntegerQ]**

The definition is now used only in the first case.

In[15]:= **{mi[{2, 3}], mi[{2.1, 2.2}], mi[{a, b}]}**

Out[15]= {{4, 9}, mi[{2.1, 2.2}], mi[{a, b}]}

An important feature of all the *Mathematica* property-testing functions whose names end in Q is that they always return False if they cannot determine whether the expression you give has a particular property.

4561 is an integer, so this returns True.	*In[16]:=* **IntegerQ[4561]**
	Out[16]= True
This returns False, since x is not known to be an integer.	*In[17]:=* **IntegerQ[x]**
	Out[17]= False

In some cases, you can explicitly specify the results that property-testing functions should give. Thus, with a definition such as x /: IntegerQ[x] = True, as discussed in Section 2.5.10, *Mathematica* will assume that x is an integer. This means that if you explicitly ask for IntegerQ[x], you will now get True, rather than False. However, *Mathematica* does not automatically propagate assertions, so it cannot determine for example that IntegerQ[x^2] is True. You must load an appropriate *Mathematica* package to make this possible.

SameQ[x, y] or x === y	x and y are identical
UnsameQ[x, y] or x =!= y	x and y are not identical
OrderedQ[{a, b, ... }]	a, b, ... are in standard order
MemberQ[*expr*, *form*]	*form* matches an element of *expr*
FreeQ[*expr*, *form*]	*form* matches nothing in *expr*
MatchQ[*expr*, *form*]	*expr* matches the pattern *form*
ValueQ[*expr*]	a value has been defined for *expr*
AtomQ[*expr*]	*expr* has no subexpressions

Some functions for testing structural properties of expressions.

With ==, the equation remains in symbolic form; === yields False unless the expressions are manifestly equal.	*In[18]:=* **{x == y, x === y}**
	Out[18]= {x == y, False}
The expression n is not a *member* of the list {x, x^n}.	*In[19]:=* **MemberQ[{x, x^n}, n]**
	Out[19]= False
However, {x, x^n} is not completely free of n.	*In[20]:=* **FreeQ[{x, x^n}, n]**
	Out[20]= False
You can use FreeQ to define a "linearity" rule for h.	*In[21]:=* **h[a_ b_, x_] := a h[b, x] /; FreeQ[a, x]**

| Terms free of x are pulled out of each h. | In[22]:= **h[a b x, x] + h[2 (1+x) x^2, x]** |
| | Out[22]= $a\,b\,h[x, x] + 2\,h[x^2\,(1+x), x]$ |

| *pattern* ? *test* | a pattern which matches an expression only if *test* yields True when applied to the expression |

Another way to constrain patterns.

The construction *pattern* /; *condition* allows you to evaluate a condition involving pattern names to determine whether there is a match. The construction *pattern* ? *test* instead applies a function *test* to the whole expression matched by *pattern* to determine whether there is a match. Using ? instead of /; sometimes leads to more succinct definitions.

| With this definition matches for x_ are tested with the function NumberQ. | In[23]:= **p[x_?NumberQ] := x^2** |

| The definition applies only when p has a numerical argument. | In[24]:= **p[4.5] + p[3/2] + p[u]** |
| | Out[24]= $22.5 + p[u]$ |

| Here is a more complicated definition. Do not forget the parentheses around the pure function. | In[25]:= **q[{x_Integer, y_Integer} ?**
           (Function[v, v.v > 4])] := qp[x + y] |

| The definition applies only in certain cases. | In[26]:= **{q[{3, 4}], q[{1, 1}], q[{-5, -7}]}** |
| | Out[26]= {qp[7], q[{1, 1}], qp[-12]} |

■ 2.3.6 Patterns Involving Alternatives

| *patt*$_1$ | *patt*$_2$ | ... | a pattern that can have one of several forms |

Specifying patterns that involve alternatives.

| This defines h to give p when its argument is either a or b. | In[1]:= **h[a | b] := p** |

| The first two cases give p. | In[2]:= **{h[a], h[b], h[c], h[d]}** |
| | Out[2]= {p, p, h[c], h[d]} |

| You can also use alternatives in transformation rules. | In[3]:= **{a, b, c, d} /. (a | b) -> p** |
| | Out[3]= {p, p, c, d} |

| Here is another example, in which one of the alternatives is itself a pattern. | In[4]:= **{1, x, x^2, x^3, y^2} /. (x | x^_) -> q** |
| | Out[4]= {1, q, q, q, y^2} |

When you use alternatives in patterns, you should make sure that the same set of names appear in each alternative. When a pattern like (a[x_] | b[x_]) matches an expression, there will always be a definite expression that corresponds to the object x. On the other hand, if you try to match a pattern like (a[x_] | b[y_]), then there will be a definite expression corresponding either to x, or to y, but not to both. As a result, you cannot use x and y to refer to definite expressions, for example on the right-hand side of a transformation rule.

Here f is used to name the head, which can be either a or b.	*In[5]:=* {a[2], b[3], c[4], a[5]} /. (f:(a|b))[x_] -> r[f, x] *Out[5]=* {r[a, 2], r[b, 3], c[4], r[a, 5]}

■ 2.3.7 Flat and Orderless Functions

Although *Mathematica* matches patterns in a purely structural fashion, its notion of structural equivalence is quite sophisticated. In particular, it takes account of properties such as commutativity and associativity in functions like Plus and Times.

This means, for example, that *Mathematica* considers the expressions $x + y$ and $y + x$ equivalent for the purposes of pattern matching. As a result, a pattern like g[x_ + y_, x_] can match not only g[a + b, a], but also g[a + b, b].

This expression has exactly the same form as the pattern.	*In[1]:=* g[a + b, a] /. g[x_ + y_, x_] -> p[x, y] *Out[1]=* p[a, b]
In this case, the expression has to be put in the form g[b + a, b] in order to have the same structure as the pattern.	*In[2]:=* g[a + b, b] /. g[x_ + y_, x_] -> p[x, y] *Out[2]=* p[b, a]

Whenever *Mathematica* encounters an *orderless* or *commutative* function such as Plus or Times in a pattern, it effectively tests all the possible orders of arguments to try and find a match. Sometimes, there may be several orderings that lead to matches. In such cases, *Mathematica* just uses the first ordering it finds. For example, h[x_ + y_, x_ + z_] could match h[a + b, a + b] with x→a, y→b, z→b or with x→b, y→a, z→a. *Mathematica* tries the case x→a, y→b, z→b first, and so uses this match.

This can match either with x → a or with x → b. *Mathematica* tries x → a first, and so uses this match.	*In[3]:=* h[a + b, a + b] /. h[x_ + y_, x_ + z_] -> p[x, y, z] *Out[3]=* p[a, b, b]
ReplaceList shows both possible matches.	*In[4]:=* ReplaceList[h[a + b, a + b], h[x_ + y_, x_ + z_] -> p[x, y, z]] *Out[4]=* {p[a, b, b], p[b, a, a]}

As discussed in Section 2.6.3, *Mathematica* allows you to assign certain attributes to functions, which specify how those functions should be treated in evaluation and pattern matching. Functions can for example be assigned the attribute Orderless, which specifies that they should be treated as commutative or symmetric, and allows their arguments to be rearranged in trying to match patterns.

Orderless	commutative function: $f[b, c, a]$, etc., are equivalent to $f[a, b, c]$
Flat	associative function: $f[f[a], b]$, etc., are equivalent to $f[a, b]$
OneIdentity	$f[f[a]]$, etc., are equivalent to a
Attributes[f]	give the attributes assigned to f
SetAttributes[f, *attr*]	add *attr* to the attributes of f
ClearAttributes[f, *attr*]	remove *attr* from the attributes of f

Some attributes that can be assigned to functions.

Plus has attributes Orderless and Flat, as well as others.	*In[5]:=* **Attributes[Plus]** *Out[5]=* {Flat, Listable, NumericFunction, OneIdentity, Orderless, Protected}
This defines q to be an orderless or commutative function.	*In[6]:=* **SetAttributes[q, Orderless]**
The arguments of q are automatically sorted into order.	*In[7]:=* **q[b, a, c]** *Out[7]=* q[a, b, c]
Mathematica rearranges the arguments of q functions to find a match.	*In[8]:=* **f[q[a, b], q[b, c]] /.** **f[q[x_, y_], q[x_, z_]] -> p[x, y, z]** *Out[8]=* p[b, a, c]

In addition to being orderless, functions like Plus and Times also have the property of being *flat* or *associative*. This means that you can effectively "parenthesize" their arguments in any way, so that, for example, x + (y + z) is equivalent to x + y + z, and so on.

Mathematica takes account of flatness in matching patterns. As a result, a pattern like g[x_ + y_] can match g[a + b + c], with x → a and y → (b + c).

The argument of g is written as a + (b + c) so as to match the pattern.	*In[9]:=* **g[a + b + c] /. g[x_ + y_] -> p[x, y]** *Out[9]=* p[a, b+c]
If there are no other constraints, *Mathematica* will match x_ to the first element of the sum.	*In[10]:=* **g[a + b + c + d] /. g[x_ + y_] -> p[x, y]** *Out[10]=* p[a, b+c+d]
This shows all the possible matches.	*In[11]:=* **ReplaceList[g[a + b + c], g[x_ + y_] -> p[x, y]]** *Out[11]=* {p[a, b+c], p[b, a+c], p[c, a+b], p[a+b, c], p[a+c, b], p[b+c, a]}

Here x_ is forced to match b + d.
$$In[12]:= \textbf{g[a + b + c + d, b + d] /. g[x\_ + y\_, x\_] -> p[x, y]}$$
$$Out[12]= \text{p[b+d, a+c]}$$

Mathematica can usually apply a transformation rule to a function only if the pattern in the rule covers all the arguments in the function. However, if you have a flat function, it is sometimes possible to apply transformation rules even though not all the arguments are covered.

This rule applies even though it does not cover all the terms in the sum.
$$In[13]:= \textbf{a + b + c /. a + c -> p}$$
$$Out[13]= \text{b+p}$$

This combines two of the terms in the sum.
$$In[14]:= \textbf{u[a] + u[b] + v[c] + v[d] /. u[x\_] + u[y\_] -> u[x + y]}$$
$$Out[14]= \text{u[a+b] + v[c] + v[d]}$$

Functions like Plus and Times are both flat and orderless. There are, however, some functions, such as Dot, which are flat, but not orderless.

Both x_ and y_ can match any sequence of terms in the dot product.
$$In[15]:= \textbf{a . b . c . d . a . b /. x\_ . y\_ . x\_ -> p[x, y]}$$
$$Out[15]= \text{p[a.b, c.d]}$$

This assigns the attribute Flat to the function r.
$$In[16]:= \textbf{SetAttributes[r, Flat]}$$

Mathematica writes the expression in the form r[r[a, b], r[a, b]] to match the pattern.
$$In[17]:= \textbf{r[a, b, a, b] /. r[x\_, x\_] -> rp[x]}$$
$$Out[17]= \text{rp[r[a, b]]}$$

Mathematica writes this expression in the form r[a, r[r[b], r[b]], c] to match the pattern.
$$In[18]:= \textbf{r[a, b, b, c] /. r[x\_, x\_] -> rp[x]}$$
$$Out[18]= \text{r[a, rp[r[b]], c]}$$

In an ordinary function that is not flat, a pattern such as x_ matches an individual argument of the function. But in a function $f[a, b, c, \ldots]$ that is flat, x_ can match objects such as $f[b, c]$ which effectively correspond to a sequence of arguments. However, in the case where x_ matches a single argument in a flat function, the question comes up as to whether the object it matches is really just the argument *a* itself, or $f[a]$. *Mathematica* chooses the first of these cases if the function carries the attribute OneIdentity, and chooses the second case otherwise.

This adds the attribute OneIdentity to the function r.
$$In[19]:= \textbf{SetAttributes[r, OneIdentity]}$$

Now x_ matches individual arguments, without r wrapped around them.
$$In[20]:= \textbf{r[a, b, b, c] /. r[x\_, x\_] -> rp[x]}$$
$$Out[20]= \text{r[a, rp[b], c]}$$

The functions Plus, Times and Dot all have the attribute OneIdentity, reflecting the fact that Plus[x] is equivalent to x, and so on. However, in representing mathematical objects, it is often convenient to deal with flat functions that do not have the attribute OneIdentity.

■ 2.3.8 Functions with Variable Numbers of Arguments

Unless *f* is a flat function, a pattern like *f*[*x_*, *y_*] stands only for instances of the function with exactly two arguments. Sometimes you need to set up patterns that can allow any number of arguments.

You can do this using *multiple blanks*. While a single blank such as x_ stands for a single *Mathematica* expression, a double blank such as x__ stands for a sequence of one or more expressions.

Here x__ stands for the sequence of expressions (a, b, c).	*In[1]:=* **f[a, b, c] /. f[x__] -> p[x, x, x]**
	Out[1]= p[a, b, c, a, b, c, a, b, c]
Here is a more complicated definition, which picks out pairs of duplicated elements in h.	*In[2]:=* **h[a___, x_, b___, x_, c___] := hh[x] h[a, b, c]**
The definition is applied twice, picking out the two paired elements.	*In[3]:=* **h[2, 3, 2, 4, 5, 3]**
	Out[3]= h[4, 5] hh[2] hh[3]

"Double blanks" __ stand for sequences of one or more expressions. "Triple blanks" ___ stand for sequences of zero or more expressions. You should be very careful whenever you use triple blank patterns. It is easy to make a mistake that can lead to an infinite loop. For example, if you define p[x_, y___] := p[x] q[y], then typing in p[a] will lead to an infinite loop, with y repeatedly matching a sequence with zero elements. Unless you are sure you want to include the case of zero elements, you should always use double blanks rather than triple blanks.

_	any single expression
*x_*	any single expression, to be named *x*
__	any sequence of one or more expressions
x__	sequence named *x*
x__h	sequence of expressions, all of whose heads are *h*
___	any sequence of zero or more expressions
x___	sequence of zero or more expressions named *x*
x___h	sequence of zero or more expressions, all of whose heads are *h*

More kinds of pattern objects.

Notice that with flat functions such as Plus and Times, *Mathematica* automatically handles variable numbers of arguments, so you do not explicitly need to use double or triple blanks, as discussed in Section 2.3.7.

When you use multiple blanks, there are often several matches that are possible for a particular expression. In general, *Mathematica* tries first those matches that assign the shortest sequences of arguments to the first multiple blanks that appear in the pattern.

This gives a list of all the matches that *Mathematica* tries.	`In[4]:= ReplaceList[f[a, b, c, d], f[x__, y__] -> g[{x}, {y}]]`
	`Out[4]= {g[{a}, {b, c, d}],`
	`          g[{a, b}, {c, d}], g[{a, b, c}, {d}]}`

Many kinds of enumeration can be done by using `ReplaceList` with various kinds of patterns.	`In[5]:= ReplaceList[f[a, b, c, d], f[___, x__] -> g[x]]` `Out[5]= {g[a, b, c, d], g[b, c, d], g[c, d], g[d]}`

This effectively enumerates all sublists with at least one element.	`In[6]:= ReplaceList[f[a, b, c, d], f[___, x__, ___] -> g[x]]`
	`Out[6]= {g[a], g[a, b], g[b], g[a, b, c], g[b, c],`
	`          g[c], g[a, b, c, d], g[b, c, d], g[c, d], g[d]}`

■ 2.3.9 Optional and Default Arguments

Sometimes you may want to set up functions where certain arguments, if omitted, are given "default values". The pattern $x\_:v$ stands for an object that can be omitted, and if so, will be replaced by the default value v.

This defines a function j with a required argument x, and optional arguments y and z, with default values 1 and 2, respectively.	`In[1]:= j[x_, y_:1, z_:2] := jp[x, y, z]`
The default value of z is used here.	`In[2]:= j[a, b]` `Out[2]= jp[a, b, 2]`
Now the default values of both y and z are used.	`In[3]:= j[a]` `Out[3]= jp[a, 1, 2]`

$x\_:v$	an expression which, if omitted, is taken to have default value v
$x\_h:v$	an expression with head h and default value v
$x\_.$	an expression with a built-in default value

Pattern objects with default values.

Some common *Mathematica* functions have built-in default values for their arguments. In such cases, you need not explicitly give the default value in $x\_:v$, but instead you can use the more convenient notation $x\_.$ in which a built-in default value is assumed.

x_ + y_.	default for y is 0
x_ y_.	default for y is 1
x_^y_.	default for y is 1

Some patterns with optional pieces.

Here a matches the pattern x_ + y_.
with y taken to have the default
value 0.

```
In[4]:= {f[a], f[a + b]} /. f[x_ + y_.] -> p[x, y]
Out[4]= {p[a, 0], p[b, a]}
```

Because Plus is a flat function, a pattern such as x_ + y_ can match a sum with any number of terms. This pattern cannot, however, match a single term such as a. However, the pattern x_ + y_. contains an optional piece, and can match either an explicit sum of terms in which both x_ and y_ appear, or a single term x_, with y taken to be 0.

Using constructs such as $x_.$, you can easily construct single patterns that match expressions with several different structures. This is particularly useful when you want to match several mathematically equal forms that do not have the same structure.

The pattern matches g[a^2], but not
g[a + b].

```
In[5]:= {g[a^2], g[a + b]} /. g[x_^n_] -> p[x, n]
Out[5]= {p[a, 2], g[a + b]}
```

By giving a pattern in which the
exponent is optional, you can match
both cases.

```
In[6]:= {g[a^2], g[a + b]} /. g[x_^n_.] -> p[x, n]
Out[6]= {p[a, 2], p[a + b, 1]}
```

The pattern a_. + b_. x_ matches any
linear function of x_.

```
In[7]:= lin[a_. + b_. x_, x_] := p[a, b]
```

In this case, b → 1.

```
In[8]:= lin[1 + x, x]
Out[8]= p[1, 1]
```

Here b → 1 and a → 0.

```
In[9]:= lin[y, y]
Out[9]= p[0, 1]
```

Standard *Mathematica* functions such as Plus and Times have built-in default values for their arguments. You can also set up defaults for your own functions, as described in Section A.5.1.

■ 2.3.10 Setting Up Functions with Optional Arguments

When you define a complicated function, you will often want to let some of the arguments of the function be "optional". If you do not give those arguments explicitly, you want them to take on certain "default" values.

Built-in *Mathematica* functions use two basic methods for dealing with optional arguments. You can choose between the same two methods when you define your own functions in *Mathematica*.

The first method is to have the meaning of each argument determined by its position, and then to allow one to drop arguments, replacing them by default values. Almost all built-in *Mathematica* functions that use this method drop arguments from the end. For example, the built-in function Flatten[*list*, *n*] allows you to drop the second argument, which is taken to have a default value of Infinity.

You can implement this kind of "positional" argument using _: patterns.

> *f*[*x_*, *k_:kdef*] := *value*   a typical definition for a function whose second argument is optional, with default value *kdef*

Defining a function with positional arguments.

This defines a function with an optional second argument. When the second argument is omitted, it is taken to have the default value Infinity.	`In[1]:= f[list_, n_:Infinity] := f0[list, n]`
Here is a function with two optional arguments.	`In[2]:= fx[list_, n1_:1, n2_:2] := fx0[list, n1, n2]`

Mathematica assumes that arguments are dropped from the end. As a result m here gives the value of n1, while n2 has its default value of 2.	`In[3]:= fx[k, m]`
	
	`Out[3]= fx0[k, m, 2]`

The second method that built-in *Mathematica* functions use for dealing with optional arguments is to give explicit names to the optional arguments, and then to allow their values to be given using transformation rules. This method is particularly convenient for functions like Plot which have a very large number of optional parameters, only a few of which usually need to be set in any particular instance.

The typical arrangement is that values for "named" optional arguments can be specified by including the appropriate transformation rules at the end of the arguments to a particular function. Thus, for example, the rule PlotJoined->True, which specifies the setting for the named optional argument PlotJoined, could appear as ListPlot[*list*, PlotJoined->True].

When you set up named optional arguments for a function *f*, it is conventional to store the default values of these arguments as a list of transformation rules assigned to Options[*f*].

$f[x\_, opts\_\_\_] := value$	a typical definition for a function with zero or more named optional arguments
$name$ /. {$opts$} /. Options[f]	replacements used to get the value of a named optional argument in the body of the function

Named arguments.

This sets up default values for two named optional arguments opt1 and opt2 in the function fn.

In[4]:= **Options[fn] = { opt1 -> 1, opt2 -> 2 }**

Out[4]= {opt1 → 1, opt2 → 2}

This gives the default value for opt1.

In[5]:= **opt1 /. Options[fn]**

Out[5]= 1

The rule opt1->3 is applied first, so the default rule for opt1 in Options[fn] is not used.

In[6]:= **opt1 /. opt1->3 /. Options[fn]**

Out[6]= 3

Here is the definition for a function fn which allows zero or more named optional arguments to be specified.

In[7]:= **fn[x_, opts___] := k[x, opt2/.{opts}/.Options[fn]]**

With no optional arguments specified, the default rule for opt2 is used.

In[8]:= **fn[4]**

Out[8]= k[4, 2]

If you explicitly give a rule for opt2, it will be used before the default rules stored in Options[fn] are tried.

In[9]:= **fn[4, opt2->7]**

Out[9]= k[4, 7]

■ 2.3.11 Repeated Patterns

expr..	a pattern or other expression repeated one or more times
expr...	a pattern or other expression repeated zero or more times

Repeated patterns.

Multiple blanks such as $x\_\_$ allow you to give patterns in which sequences of arbitrary expressions can occur. The *Mathematica pattern repetition operators* .. and ... allow you to construct patterns in which particular forms can be repeated any number of times. Thus, for example, f[a..] represents any expression of the form f[a], f[a, a], f[a, a, a] and so on.

The pattern f[a..] allows the argument a to be repeated any number of times.

In[1]:= **Cases[{ f[a], f[a, b, a], f[a, a, a] }, f[a..]]**

Out[1]= {f[a], f[a, a, a]}

This pattern allows any number of a arguments, followed by any number of b arguments.

```
In[2]:= Cases[{ f[a], f[a, a, b], f[a, b, a], f[a, b, b] },
                                        f[a.., b..]]
Out[2]= {f[a, a, b], f[a, b, b]}
```

Here each argument can be either a or b.

```
In[3]:= Cases[{ f[a], f[a, b, a], f[a, c, a] }, f[(a | b)..]]
Out[3]= {f[a], f[a, b, a]}
```

You can use .. and ... to represent repetitions of any pattern. If the pattern contains named parts, then each instance of these parts must be identical.

This defines a function whose argument must consist of a list of pairs.

```
In[4]:= v[x:{{_, _}..}] := Transpose[x]
```

The definition applies in this case.

```
In[5]:= v[{{a1, b1}, {a2, b2}, {a3, b3}}]
Out[5]= {{a1, a2, a3}, {b1, b2, b3}}
```

With this definition, the second elements of all the pairs must be the same.

```
In[6]:= vn[x:{{_, n_}..}] := Transpose[x]
```

The definition applies in this case.

```
In[7]:= vn[{{a, 2}, {b, 2}, {c, 2}}]
Out[7]= {{a, b, c}, {2, 2, 2}}
```

■ 2.3.12 Verbatim Patterns

Verbatim[*expr*]	an expression that must be matched verbatim

Verbatim patterns.

Here the x_ in the rule matches any expression.

```
In[1]:= {f[2], f[a], f[x_], f[y_]} /. f[x_] -> x^2
Out[1]= {4, a², x_², y_²}
```

The Verbatim tells *Mathematica* that only the exact expression x_ should be matched.

```
In[2]:= {f[2], f[a], f[x_], f[y_]} /. f[Verbatim[x_]] -> x^2
Out[2]= {f[2], f[a], x_², f[y_]}
```

■ 2.3.13 Patterns for Some Common Types of Expression

Using the objects described above, you can set up patterns for many kinds of expressions. In all cases, you must remember that the patterns must represent the structure of the expressions in *Mathematica* internal form, as shown by FullForm.

Especially for some common kinds of expressions, the standard output format used by *Mathematica* is not particularly close to the full internal form. But it is the internal form that you must use in setting up patterns.

n_Integer	an integer n
x_Real	an approximate real number x
z_Complex	a complex number z
Complex[x_, y_]	a complex number $x + iy$
Complex[x_Integer, y_Integer]	a complex number where both real and imaginary parts are integers
(r_Rational | r_Integer)	rational number or integer r
Rational[n_, d_]	a rational number $\frac{n}{d}$
(x_ /; NumberQ[x] && Im[x]==0)	a real number of any kind
(x_ /; NumberQ[x])	a number of any kind

Some typical patterns for numbers.

Here are the full forms of some numbers.

```
In[1]:= {2, 2.5, 2.5 + I, 2/7} // FullForm
Out[1]//FullForm= List[2, 2.5`, Complex[2.5`, 1], Rational[2, 7]]
```

The rule picks out each piece of the complex numbers.

```
In[2]:= {2.5 - I, 3 + I} /. Complex[x_, y_] -> p[x, y]
Out[2]= {p[2.5, -1], p[3, 1]}
```

The fact that these expressions have different full forms means that you cannot use $x\_ + I\ y\_$ to match a complex number.

```
In[3]:= {2.5 - I, x + I y} // FullForm
Out[3]//FullForm= List[Complex[2.5`, -1],
                    Plus[x, Times[Complex[0, 1], y]]]
```

The pattern here matches both ordinary integers, and complex numbers where both the real and imaginary parts are integers.

```
In[4]:= Cases[ {2.5 - I, 2, 3 + I, 2 - 0.5 I, 2 + 2 I},
              _Integer | Complex[_Integer, _Integer] ]
Out[4]= {2, 3 + i, 2 + 2 i}
```

As discussed in Section 1.4.1, *Mathematica* puts all algebraic expressions into a standard form, in which they are written essentially as a sum of products of powers. In addition, ratios are converted into products of powers, with denominator terms having negative exponents, and differences are converted into sums with negated terms. To construct patterns for algebraic expressions, you must use this standard form. This form often differs from the way *Mathematica* prints out the algebraic expressions. But in all cases, you can find the full internal form using FullForm[*expr*].

Here is a typical algebraic expression.

$In[5]:=$ **-1/z^2 - z/y + 2 (x z)^2 y**

$Out[5]=$ $-\dfrac{1}{z^2} - \dfrac{z}{y} + 2\,x^2\,y\,z^2$

This is the full internal form of the expression.

$In[6]:=$ **FullForm[%]**

$Out[6]//FullForm=$ Plus[Times[-1, Power[z, -2]],
                    Times[-1, Power[y, -1], z],
                    Times[2, Power[x, 2], y, Power[z, 2]]]

This is what you get by applying a transformation rule to all powers in the expression.

$In[7]:=$ **% /. x_^n_ -> e[x, n]**

$Out[7]=$ $-z\,e[y, -1] - e[z, -2] + 2\,y\,e[x, 2]\,e[z, 2]$

$x\_ + y\_$	a sum of two or more terms
$x\_ + y\_.$	a single term or a sum of terms
$n\_$Integer $x\_$	an expression with an explicit integer multiplier
$a\_. + b\_.\ x\_$	a linear expression $a + bx$
$x\_ \wedge n\_$	x^n with $n \neq 0, 1$
$x\_ \wedge n\_.$	x^n with $n \neq 0$
$a\_. + b\_.\ x\_ + c\_.\ x\_^2$	a quadratic expression with non-zero linear term

Some typical patterns for algebraic expressions.

This pattern picks out linear functions of x.

$In[8]:=$ **{1, a, x, 2 x, 1 + 2 x} /. a_. + b_. x -> p[a, b]**

$Out[8]=$ {1, a, p[0, 1], p[0, 2], p[1, 2]}

$x\_$List or x:{___}	a list
$x\_$List /; VectorQ[x]	a vector containing no sublists
$x\_$List /; VectorQ[x, NumberQ]	a vector of numbers
x:{___List} or x:{{___}...}	a list of lists
$x\_$List /; MatrixQ[x]	a matrix containing no sublists
$x\_$List /; MatrixQ[x, NumberQ]	a matrix of numbers
x:{{_, _}...}	a list of pairs

Some typical patterns for lists.

This defines a function whose argument must be a list containing lists with either one or two elements.

In[9]:= **h[x:{ ({_} | {_, _})... }] := q**

The definition applies in the second and third cases.

In[10]:= **{h[{a, b}], h[{{a}, {b}}], h[{{a}, {b, c}}]}**

Out[10]= {h[{a, b}], q, q}

■ 2.3.14 An Example: Defining Your Own Integration Function

Now that we have introduced the basic features of patterns in *Mathematica*, we can use them to give a more or less complete example. We will show how you could define your own simple integration function in *Mathematica*.

From a mathematical point of view, the integration function is defined by a sequence of mathematical relations. By setting up transformation rules for patterns, you can implement these mathematical relations quite directly in *Mathematica*.

mathematical form	*Mathematica definition*
$\int (y + z)\, dx = \int y\, dx + \int z\, dx$	`integrate[y_ + z_, x_] :=` `integrate[y, x] + integrate[z, x]`
$\int c\, y\, dx = c \int y\, dx$ (*c* independent of *x*)	`integrate[c_ y_, x_] :=` `c integrate[y, x] /; FreeQ[c, x]`
$\int c\, dx = c\, x$	`integrate[c_, x_] := c x /; FreeQ[c, x]`
$\int x^n\, dx = \frac{x^{(n+1)}}{n+1}, \; n \neq -1$	`integrate[x_^n_., x_] := x^(n+1)/(n+1) /;` `FreeQ[n, x] && n != -1`
$\int \frac{1}{ax+b}\, dx = \frac{\log(ax+b)}{a}$	`integrate[1/(a_. x_ + b_.), x_] :=` `Log[a x + b]/a /; FreeQ[{a,b}, x]`
$\int e^{ax+b}\, dx = \frac{1}{a}\, e^{ax+b}$	`integrate[Exp[a_. x_ + b_.], x_] :=` `Exp[a x + b]/a /; FreeQ[{a,b}, x]`

Definitions for an integration function.

This implements the linearity relation for integrals:
$\int (y + z)\, dx = \int y\, dx + \int z\, dx$.

In[1]:= **integrate[y_ + z_, x_] :=**
              integrate[y, x] + integrate[z, x]

The associativity of Plus makes the linearity relation work with any number of terms in the sum.

```
In[2]:= integrate[a x + b x^2 + 3, x]
```

```
Out[2]= integrate[3, x] +
            integrate[a x, x] + integrate[b x², x]
```

This makes `integrate` pull out factors that are independent of the integration variable x.

```
In[3]:= integrate[c_ y_, x_] := c integrate[y, x] /; FreeQ[c, x]
```

Mathematica tests each term in each product to see whether it satisfies the FreeQ condition, and so can be pulled out.

```
In[4]:= integrate[a x + b x^2 + 3, x]
```

```
Out[4]= integrate[3, x] +
            a integrate[x, x] + b integrate[x², x]
```

This gives the integral $\int c\,dx = c\,x$ of a constant.

```
In[5]:= integrate[c_, x_] := c x /; FreeQ[c, x]
```

Now the constant term in the sum can be integrated.

```
In[6]:= integrate[a x + b x^2 + 3, x]
```

```
Out[6]= 3 x + a integrate[x, x] + b integrate[x², x]
```

This gives the standard formula for the integral of x^n. By using the pattern x_^n_., rather than x_^n_, we include the case of $x^1 = x$.

```
In[7]:= integrate[x_^n_., x_] :=
                    x^(n+1)/(n+1) /; FreeQ[n, x] && n != -1
```

Now this integral can be done completely.

```
In[8]:= integrate[a x + b x^2 + 3, x]
```

$$Out[8]= 3 x + \frac{a\,x^2}{2} + \frac{b\,x^3}{3}$$

Of course, the built-in integration function Integrate (with a capital I) could have done the integral anyway.

```
In[9]:= Integrate[a x + b x^2 + 3, x]
```

$$Out[9]= 3 x + \frac{a\,x^2}{2} + \frac{b\,x^3}{3}$$

Here is the rule for integrating the reciprocal of a linear function. The pattern a_. x_ + b_. stands for any linear function of x.

```
In[10]:= integrate[1/(a_. x_ + b_.), x_] :=
                    Log[a x + b]/a /; FreeQ[{a,b}, x]
```

Here both a and b take on their default values.

```
In[11]:= integrate[1/x, x]
```

```
Out[11]= Log[x]
```

Here is a more complicated case. The symbol a now matches 2 p.

```
In[12]:= integrate[1/(2 p x - 1), x]
```

$$Out[12]= \frac{Log[-1 + 2\,p\,x]}{2\,p}$$

You can go on and add many more rules for integration. Here is a rule for integrating exponentials.

```
In[13]:= integrate[Exp[a_. x_ + b_.], x_] :=
                    Exp[a x + b]/a /; FreeQ[{a,b}, x]
```

2.4 Manipulating Lists

■ 2.4.1 Constructing Lists

Lists are widely used in *Mathematica,* and there are many ways to construct them.

Range[n]	the list {1, 2, 3, ... , n}
Table[$expr$, {i, n}]	the values of *expr* with i from 1 to n
Array[f, n]	the list {f[1], f[2], ... , f[n]}
NestList[f, x, n]	{x, f[x], f[f[x]], ... } with up to n nestings
Normal[SparseArray[{i_1->v_1, ... }, n]]	a length n list with element i_k being v_k
Apply[List, f[e_1, e_2, ...]]	the list {e_1, e_2, ... }

Some explicit ways to construct lists.

This gives a table of the first five powers of two.

```
In[1]:= Table[2^i, {i, 5}]
Out[1]= {2, 4, 8, 16, 32}
```

Here is another way to get the same result.

```
In[2]:= Array[2^# &, 5]
Out[2]= {2, 4, 8, 16, 32}
```

This gives a similar list.

```
In[3]:= NestList[2 #&, 1, 5]
Out[3]= {1, 2, 4, 8, 16, 32}
```

SparseArray lets you specify values at particular positions.

```
In[4]:= Normal[SparseArray[{3->x, 4->y}, 5]]
Out[4]= {0, 0, x, y, 0}
```

You can also use patterns to specify values.

```
In[5]:= Normal[SparseArray[{i_ -> 2^i}, 5]]
Out[5]= {2, 4, 8, 16, 32}
```

Often you will know in advance how long a list is supposed to be, and how each of its elements should be generated. And often you may get one list from another.

Map[*f*, *list*]	apply *f* to each element of *list*
MapIndexed[*f*, *list*]	give *f*[*elem*, {*i*}] for the ith element
Cases[*list*, *form*]	give elements of *list* that match *form*
Select[*list*, *test*]	select elements for which *test*[*elem*] is True
list[[{i_1, i_2, ... }]] or Part[*list*, {i_1, i_2, ... }]	
	give a list of the specified parts of *list*

Constructing lists from other lists.

This selects elements larger than 5.

```
In[6]:= Select[{1, 3, 6, 8, 10}, # > 5&]
Out[6]= {6, 8, 10}
```

This explicitly picks out numbered parts.

```
In[7]:= {a, b, c, d}[[{2, 1, 4}]]
Out[7]= {b, a, d}
```

Sometimes you may want to accumulate a list of results during the execution of a program. You can do this using Sow and Reap.

+	Sow[*val*]	sow the value *val* for the nearest enclosing Reap
+	Reap[*expr*]	evaluate *expr*, returning also a list of values sown by Sow

Using Sow and Reap.

This program iteratively squares a number.

```
In[8]:= Nest[#^2&, 2, 5]
Out[8]= 4294967296
```

This does the same computation, but accumulating a list of intermediate results above 1000.

```
In[9]:= Reap[Nest[(If[# > 1000, Sow[#]]; #^2) &, 2, 6]]
Out[9]= {18446744073709551616, {{65536, 4294967296}}}
```

An alternative but less efficient approach involves introducing a temporary variable, then starting with *t* = {}, and successively using AppendTo[*t*, *elem*].

■ 2.4.2 Manipulating Lists by Their Indices

Part[*list*, *spec*] or *list*[[*spec*]]	part or parts of a list
Part[*list*, *spec*$_1$, *spec*$_2$, ...] or *list*[[*spec*$_1$, *spec*$_2$, ...]]	part or parts of a nested list

n	the nth part from the beginning
$-n$	the nth part from the end
$\{i_1, i_2, ... \}$	a list of parts
All	all parts

Getting parts of lists.

This gives a list of parts 1 and 3.	*In[1]:=* **{a, b, c, d}[[{1, 3}]]**
	Out[1]= {a, c}
Here is a nested list.	*In[2]:=* **m = {{a, b, c}, {d, e}, {f, g, h}};**
This gives a list of its first and third parts.	*In[3]:=* **m[[{1, 3}]]**
	Out[3]= {{a, b, c}, {f, g, h}}
This gives a list of the first part of each of these.	*In[4]:=* **m[[{1, 3}, 1]]**
	Out[4]= {a, f}
And this gives a list of the first two parts.	*In[5]:=* **m[[{1, 3}, {1, 2}]]**
	Out[5]= {{a, b}, {f, g}}
This gives the second part of all sublists.	*In[6]:=* **m[[All, 2]]**
	Out[6]= {b, e, g}

You can always reset one or more pieces of a list by doing an assignment like *m*[[...]] = *value*.

This resets part 1,2 of m.	*In[7]:=* **m[[1, 2]] = x**
	Out[7]= x
This is now the form of m.	*In[8]:=* **m**
	Out[8]= {{a, x, c}, {d, e}, {f, g, h}}
This resets part 1 to x and part 3 to y.	*In[9]:=* **m[[{1, 3}]] = {x, y}; m**
	Out[9]= {x, {d, e}, y}
This resets parts 1 and 3 both to p.	*In[10]:=* **m[[{1, 3}]] = p; m**
	Out[10]= {p, {d, e}, p}

This restores the original form of m.	$In[11]:=$ **m = {{a, b, c}, {d, e}, {f, g, h}};**
This now resets all parts specified by m[[{1, 3}, {1, 2}]].	$In[12]:=$ **m[[{1, 3}, {1, 2}]] = x; m**
	$Out[12]=$ {{x, x, c}, {d, e}, {x, x, h}}
You can use Range to indicate all indices in a given range.	$In[13]:=$ **m[[Range[1, 3], 2]] = y; m**
	$Out[13]=$ {{x, y, c}, {d, y}, {x, y, h}}

It is sometimes useful to think of a nested list as being laid out in space, with each element being at a coordinate position given by its indices. There is then a direct geometrical interpretation for $list[[spec_1, spec_2, \dots]]$. If a given $spec_k$ is a single integer, then it represents extracting a single slice in the kth dimension, while if it is a list, it represents extracting a list of parallel slices. The final result for $list[[spec_1, spec_2, \dots]]$ is then the collection of elements obtained by slicing in each successive dimension.

Here is a nested list laid out as a two-dimensional array.	$In[14]:=$ **(m = {{a, b, c}, {d, e, f}, {g, h, i}}) // TableForm**
	$Out[14]//TableForm=$

$$\begin{matrix} a & b & c \\ d & e & f \\ g & h & i \end{matrix}$$

This picks out rows 1 and 3, then columns 1 and 2.	$In[15]:=$ **m[[{1, 3}, {1, 2}]] // TableForm**
	$Out[15]//TableForm=$

$$\begin{matrix} a & b \\ g & h \end{matrix}$$

Part is set up to make it easy to pick out structured slices of nested lists. Sometimes, however, you may want to pick out arbitrary collections of individual parts. You can do this conveniently with Extract.

Part[*list*, {i_1, i_2, … }]	the list {$list[[i_1]]$, $list[[i_2]]$, … }
Extract[*list*, {i_1, i_2, … }]	the element $list[[i_1, i_2, \dots]]$

Part[*list*, $spec_1$, $spec_2$, …]	parts specified by successive slicing
Extract[*list*, {{i_1, i_2, … }, {j_1, j_2, … }, … }]	the list of individual parts {$list[[i_1, i_2, \dots]]$, $list[[j_1, j_2, \dots]]$, … }

Getting slices versus lists of individual parts.

This extracts the individual parts 1,3 and 1,2.	$In[16]:=$ **Extract[m, {{1, 3}, {1, 2}}]**
	$Out[16]=$ {c, b}

An important feature of Extract is that it takes lists of part positions in the same form as they are returned by functions like Position.

This sets up a nested list.	*In[17]:=* **m = {{a[1], a[2], b[1]}, {b[2], c[1]}, {{b[3]}}};**
This gives a list of positions in m.	*In[18]:=* **Position[m, b[_]]**
	Out[18]= {{1, 3}, {2, 1}, {3, 1, 1}}
This extracts the elements at those positions.	*In[19]:=* **Extract[m, %]**
	Out[19]= {b[1], b[2], b[3]}

Take[*list*, *spec*]	take the specified parts of a list
Drop[*list*, *spec*]	drop the specified parts of a list
Take[*list*, *spec*₁, *spec*₂, ...], Drop[*list*, *spec*₁, *spec*₂, ...]	
	take or drop specified parts at each level in nested lists
n	the first *n* elements
−*n*	the last *n* elements
{*n*}	element *n* only
{*m*, *n*}	elements *m* through *n* (inclusive)
{*m*, *n*, *s*}	elements *m* through *n* in steps of *s*
All	all parts
None	no parts

Taking and dropping sequences of elements in lists.

This takes every second element starting at position 2.	*In[20]:=* **Take[{a, b, c, d, e, f, g}, {2, -1, 2}]**
	Out[20]= {b, d, f}
This drops every second element.	*In[21]:=* **Drop[{a, b, c, d, e, f, g}, {2, -1, 2}]**
	Out[21]= {a, c, e, g}

Much like Part, Take and Drop can be viewed as picking out sequences of slices at successive levels in a nested list. You can use Take and Drop to work with blocks of elements in arrays.

Here is a 3×3 array.	*In[22]:=* **(m = {{a, b, c}, {d, e, f}, {g, h, i}}) // TableForm**

```
                 a      b      c
Out[22]//TableForm= d      e      f
                 g      h      i
```

Here is the first 2×2 subarray.	*In[23]:=* **Take[m, 2, 2] // TableForm**

```
                 a      b
Out[23]//TableForm= d      e
```

This takes all elements in the first two columns.

```
In[24]:= Take[m, All, 2] // TableForm
                      a       b
Out[24]//TableForm=   d       e
                      g       h
```

This leaves no elements from the first two columns.

```
In[25]:= Drop[m, None, 2] // TableForm
                      c
Out[25]//TableForm=   f
                      i
```

Prepend[*list*, *elem*]	add *element* at the beginning of *list*
Append[*list*, *elem*]	add *element* at the end of *list*
Insert[*list*, *elem*, *i*]	insert *element* at position *i*
Insert[*list*, *elem*, {*i*, *j*, ... }]	insert at position *i*, *j*, ...
Delete[*list*, *i*]	delete the element at position *i*
Delete[*list*, {*i*, *j*, ... }]	delete at position *i*, *j*, ...

Adding and deleting elements in lists.

This makes the 2,1 element of the list be x.

```
In[26]:= Insert[{{a, b, c}, {d, e}}, x, {2, 1}]
Out[26]= {{a, b, c}, {x, d, e}}
```

This deletes the element again.

```
In[27]:= Delete[%, {2, 1}]
Out[27]= {{a, b, c}, {d, e}}
```

ReplacePart[*list*, *new*, *i*]	replace the element at position *i* in *list* with *new*
ReplacePart[*list*, *new*, {*i*, *j*, ... }]	replace *list*[[*i*, *j*, ...]] with *new*
ReplacePart[*list*, *new*, {{i_1, j_1, ... }, {i_2, ... }, ... }]	replace all parts *list*[[i_k, j_k, ...]] with *new*
ReplacePart[*list*, *new*, {{i_1, ... }, ... }, {n_1, ... }]	replace part *list*[[i_k, ...]] with *new*[[n_k]]

Replacing parts of lists.

This replaces the third element in the list with x.

```
In[28]:= ReplacePart[{a, b, c, d}, x, 3]
Out[28]= {a, b, x, d}
```

This replaces the first and fourth parts of the list. Notice the need for double lists in specifying multiple parts to replace.

In[29]:= **ReplacePart[{a, b, c, d}, x, {{1}, {4}}]**

Out[29]= {x, b, c, x}

Here is a 3×3 identity matrix.

In[30]:= **IdentityMatrix[3]**

Out[30]= {{1, 0, 0}, {0, 1, 0}, {0, 0, 1}}

This replaces the 2,2 component of the matrix by x.

In[31]:= **ReplacePart[%, x, {2, 2}]**

Out[31]= {{1, 0, 0}, {0, x, 0}, {0, 0, 1}}

■ 2.4.3 Nested Lists

{$list_1$, $list_2$, ... }	list of lists
Table[*expr*, {i, m}, {j, n}, ...]	$m \times n \times \dots$ table of values of *expr*
Array[f, {m, n, ... }]	$m \times n \times \dots$ array of values $f[i, j, \dots]$
Normal[SparseArray[{{i_1, j_1,... } -> v_1, ... }, {m, n, ... }]]	
	$m \times n \times \dots$ array with element {i_s, j_s,... } being v_s
Outer[f, $list_1$, $list_2$, ...]	generalized outer product with elements combined using f

Ways to construct nested lists.

This generates a table corresponding to a 2×3 nested list.

In[1]:= **Table[x^i + j, {i, 2}, {j, 3}]**

Out[1]= {{1 + x, 2 + x, 3 + x}, {1 + x^2, 2 + x^2, 3 + x^2}}

This generates an array corresponding to the same nested list.

In[2]:= **Array[x^#1 + #2 &, {2, 3}]**

Out[2]= {{1 + x, 2 + x, 3 + x}, {1 + x^2, 2 + x^2, 3 + x^2}}

Elements not explicitly specified in the sparse array are taken to be 0.

In[3]:= **Normal[SparseArray[{{1, 3} -> 3 + x}, {2, 3}]]**

Out[3]= {{0, 0, 3 + x}, {0, 0, 0}}

Each element in the final list contains one element from each input list.

In[4]:= **Outer[f, {a, b}, {c, d}]**

Out[4]= {{f[a, c], f[a, d]}, {f[b, c], f[b, d]}}

Functions like **Array**, **SparseArray** and **Outer** always generate *full arrays*, in which all sublists at a particular level are the same length.

Dimensions[*list*]	the dimensions of a full array
+ ArrayQ[*list*]	test whether all sublists at a given level are the same length
+ ArrayDepth[*list*]	the depth to which all sublists are the same length

Functions for full arrays.

Mathematica can handle arbitrary nested lists. There is no need for the lists to form a full array. You can easily generate ragged arrays using Table.

This generates a triangular array.

In[5]:= **Table[x^i + j, {i, 3}, {j, i}]**

Out[5]= $\{\{1 + x\}, \{1 + x^2, 2 + x^2\}, \{1 + x^3, 2 + x^3, 3 + x^3\}\}$

Flatten[*list*]	flatten out all levels of *list*
Flatten[*list*, *n*]	flatten out the top *n* levels

Flattening out sublists.

This generates a 2 × 3 array.

In[6]:= **Array[a, {2, 3}]**

Out[6]= {{a[1, 1], a[1, 2], a[1, 3]},
        {a[2, 1], a[2, 2], a[2, 3]}}

Flatten in effect puts elements in lexicographic order of their indices.

In[7]:= **Flatten[%]**

Out[7]= {a[1, 1], a[1, 2], a[1, 3], a[2, 1], a[2, 2], a[2, 3]}

Transpose[*list*]	transpose the top two levels of *list*
Transpose[*list*, {n_1, n_2, ... }]	put the kth level in *list* at level n_k

Transposing levels in nested lists.

This generates a 2 × 2 × 2 array.

In[8]:= **Array[a, {2, 2, 2}]**

Out[8]= {{{a[1, 1, 1], a[1, 1, 2]}, {a[1, 2, 1], a[1, 2, 2]}},
        {{a[2, 1, 1], a[2, 1, 2]}, {a[2, 2, 1], a[2, 2, 2]}}}

This permutes levels so that level 3 appears at level 1.

In[9]:= **Transpose[%, {3, 1, 2}]**

Out[9]= {{{a[1, 1, 1], a[2, 1, 1]}, {a[1, 1, 2], a[2, 1, 2]}},
        {{a[1, 2, 1], a[2, 2, 1]}, {a[1, 2, 2], a[2, 2, 2]}}}

This restores the original array.

In[10]:= **Transpose[%, {2, 3, 1}]**

Out[10]= {{{a[1, 1, 1], a[1, 1, 2]}, {a[1, 2, 1], a[1, 2, 2]}},
         {{a[2, 1, 1], a[2, 1, 2]}, {a[2, 2, 1], a[2, 2, 2]}}}

Map[*f*, *list*, {*n*}]	map *f* across elements at level *n*
Apply[*f*, *list*, {*n*}]	apply *f* to the elements at level *n*
MapIndexed[*f*, *list*, {*n*}]	map *f* onto parts at level *n* and their indices

Applying functions in nested lists.

Here is a nested list.

In[11]:= **m = {{{a, b}, {c, d}}, {{e, f}, {g, h}, {i}}};**

This maps a function f at level 2.

In[12]:= **Map[f, m, {2}]**

Out[12]= {{f[{a, b}], f[{c, d}]},
　　　　　{f[{e, f}], f[{g, h}], f[{i}]}}

This applies the function at level 2.

In[13]:= **Apply[f, m, {2}]**

Out[13]= {{f[a, b], f[c, d]}, {f[e, f], f[g, h], f[i]}}

This applies f to both parts and their indices.

In[14]:= **MapIndexed[f, m, {2}]**

Out[14]= {{f[{a, b}, {1, 1}], f[{c, d}, {1, 2}]},
　　　　　{f[{e, f}, {2, 1}],
　　　　　f[{g, h}, {2, 2}], f[{i}, {2, 3}]}}

Partition[*list*, {n_1, n_2, ... }]	partition into $n_1 \times n_2 \times ...$ blocks
PadLeft[*list*, {n_1, n_2, ... }]	pad on the left to make an $n_1 \times n_2 \times ...$ array
PadRight[*list*, {n_1, n_2, ... }]	pad on the right to make an $n_1 \times n_2 \times ...$ array
RotateLeft[*list*, {n_1, n_2, ... }]	rotate n_k places to the left at level *k*
RotateRight[*list*, {n_1, n_2, ... }]	rotate n_k places to the right at level *k*

Operations on nested lists.

Here is a nested list.

In[15]:= **m = {{{a, b, c}, {d, e}}, {{f, g}, {h}, {i}}};**

This rotates different amounts at each level.

In[16]:= **RotateLeft[m, {0, 1, -1}]**

Out[16]= {{{e, d}, {c, a, b}}, {{h}, {i}, {g, f}}}

This pads with zeros to make a 2 × 3 × 3 array.

In[17]:= **PadRight[%, {2, 3, 3}]**

Out[17]= {{{e, d, 0}, {c, a, b}, {0, 0, 0}},
　　　　　{{h, 0, 0}, {i, 0, 0}, {g, f, 0}}}

＋■ 2.4.4 Partitioning and Padding Lists

Partition[*list*, *n*]	partition *list* into sublists of length *n*
Partition[*list*, *n*, *d*]	partition into sublists with offset *d*
Split[*list*]	split *list* into runs of identical elements
Split[*list*, *test*]	split into runs with adjacent elements satisfying *test*

Partitioning elements in a list.

This partitions in blocks of 3.

In[1]:= **Partition[{a, b, c, d, e, f}, 3]**

Out[1]= {{a, b, c}, {d, e, f}}

This partitions in blocks of 3 with offset 1.

In[2]:= **Partition[{a, b, c, d, e, f}, 3, 1]**

Out[2]= {{a, b, c}, {b, c, d}, {c, d, e}, {d, e, f}}

The offset can be larger than the block size.

In[3]:= **Partition[{a, b, c, d, e, f}, 2, 3]**

Out[3]= {{a, b}, {d, e}}

This splits into runs of identical elements.

In[4]:= **Split[{1, 4, 1, 1, 1, 2, 2, 3, 3}]**

Out[4]= {{1}, {4}, {1, 1, 1}, {2, 2}, {3, 3}}

This splits into runs where adjacent elements are unequal.

In[5]:= **Split[{1, 4, 1, 1, 1, 2, 2, 3, 3}, Unequal]**

Out[5]= {{1, 4, 1}, {1}, {1, 2}, {2, 3}, {3}}

Partition in effect goes through a list, grouping successive elements into sublists. By default it does not include any sublists that would "overhang" the original list.

This stops before any overhang occurs.

In[6]:= **Partition[{a, b, c, d, e}, 2]**

Out[6]= {{a, b}, {c, d}}

The same is true here.

In[7]:= **Partition[{a, b, c, d, e}, 3, 1]**

Out[7]= {{a, b, c}, {b, c, d}, {c, d, e}}

You can tell **Partition** to include sublists that overhang the ends of the original list. By default, it fills in additional elements by treating the original list as cyclic. It can also treat it as being padded with elements that you specify.

This includes additional sublists, treating the original list as cyclic.

In[8]:= **Partition[{a, b, c, d, e}, 3, 1, {1, 1}]**

Out[8]= {{a, b, c}, {b, c, d}, {c, d, e}, {d, e, a}, {e, a, b}}

Now the original list is treated as being padded with the element x.

In[9]:= **Partition[{a, b, c, d, e}, 3, 1, {1, 1}, x]**

Out[9]= {{a, b, c}, {b, c, d}, {c, d, e}, {d, e, x}, {e, x, x}}

This pads cyclically with elements x and y.	In[10]:= **Partition[{a, b, c, d, e}, 3, 1, {1, 1}, {x, y}]** Out[10]= {{a, b, c}, {b, c, d}, {c, d, e}, {d, e, y}, {e, y, x}}
This introduces no padding, yielding sublists of differing lengths.	In[11]:= **Partition[{a, b, c, d, e}, 3, 1, {1, 1}, {}]** Out[11]= {{a, b, c}, {b, c, d}, {c, d, e}, {d, e}, {e}}

You can think of **Partition** as extracting sublists by sliding a template along and picking out elements from the original list. You can tell **Partition** where to start and stop this process.

This gives all sublists that overlap the original list.	In[12]:= **Partition[{a, b, c, d}, 3, 1, {-1, 1}, x]** Out[12]= {{x, x, a}, {x, a, b}, {a, b, c}, {b, c, d}, {c, d, x}, {d, x, x}}
This allows overlaps only at the beginning.	In[13]:= **Partition[{a, b, c, d}, 3, 1, {-1, -1}, x]** Out[13]= {{x, x, a}, {x, a, b}, {a, b, c}, {b, c, d}}

Partition[*list*, *n*, *d*] or Partition[*list*, *n*, *d*, {1, -1}]	keep only sublists with no overhangs
Partition[*list*, *n*, *d*, {1, 1}]	allow an overhang at the end
Partition[*list*, *n*, *d*, {-1, -1}]	allow an overhang at the beginning
Partition[*list*, *n*, *d*, {-1, 1}]	allow overhangs at both the beginning and end
Partition[*list*, *n*, *d*, {k_L, k_R}]	specify alignments of first and last sublists
Partition[*list*, *n*, *d*, *spec*]	pad by cyclically repeating elements in *list*
Partition[*list*, *n*, *d*, *spec*, *x*]	pad by repeating the element *x*
Partition[*list*, *n*, *d*, *spec*, {x_1, x_2, ... }]	pad by cyclically repeating the x_i
Partition[*list*, *n*, *d*, *spec*, {}]	use no padding

Specifying alignment and padding.

An alignment specification $\{k_L, k_R\}$ tells **Partition** to give the sequence of sublists in which the first element of the original list appears at position k_L in the first sublist, and the last element of the original list appears at position k_R in the last sublist.

This makes a appear at position 1 in the first sublist.	In[14]:= **Partition[{a, b, c, d}, 3, 1, {1, 1}, x]** Out[14]= {{a, b, c}, {b, c, d}, {c, d, x}, {d, x, x}}

This makes a appear at position 2 in the first sublist.	*In[15]:=* **Partition[{a, b, c, d}, 3, 1, {2, 1}, x]**
	Out[15]= {{x, a, b}, {a, b, c}, {b, c, d}, {c, d, x}, {d, x, x}}
Here a is in effect made to appear first at position 4.	*In[16]:=* **Partition[{a, b, c, d}, 3, 1, {4, 1}, x]**
	Out[16]= {{x, x, x}, {x, x, a}, {x, a, b}, {a, b, c}, {b, c, d}, {c, d, x}, {d, x, x}}
This fills in padding cyclically from the list given.	*In[17]:=* **Partition[{a, b, c, d}, 3, 1, {4, 1}, {x, y}]**
	Out[17]= {{y, x, y}, {x, y, a}, {y, a, b}, {a, b, c}, {b, c, d}, {c, d, x}, {d, x, y}}

Functions like ListConvolve use the same alignment and padding specifications as Partition.

In some cases it may be convenient to insert explicit padding into a list. You can do this using PadLeft and PadRight.

PadLeft[*list*, *n*]	pad to length *n* by inserting zeros on the left
PadLeft[*list*, *n*, *x*]	pad by repeating the element *x*
PadLeft[*list*, *n*, {x_1, x_2, ... }]	pad by cyclically repeating the x_i
PadLeft[*list*, *n*, *list*]	pad by cyclically repeating *list*
PadLeft[*list*, *n*, *padding*, *m*]	leave a margin of *m* elements on the right
PadRight[*list*, *n*]	pad by inserting zeros on the right

Padding a list.

This pads the list to make it length 6.	*In[18]:=* **PadLeft[{a, b, c}, 6]**
	Out[18]= {0, 0, 0, a, b, c}
This cyclically inserts {x, y} as the padding.	*In[19]:=* **PadLeft[{a, b, c}, 6, {x, y}]**
	Out[19]= {x, y, x, a, b, c}
This also leaves a margin of 3 on the right.	*In[20]:=* **PadLeft[{a, b, c}, 10, {x, y}, 3]**
	Out[20]= {y, x, y, x, a, b, c, x, y, x}

PadLeft, PadRight and Partition can all be used on nested lists.

This creates a 3 × 3 array.	*In[21]:=* **PadLeft[{{a, b}, {e}, {f}}, {3, 3}, x]**
	Out[21]= {{x, a, b}, {x, x, e}, {x, x, f}}
This partitions the array into 2 × 2 blocks with offset 1.	*In[22]:=* **Partition[%, {2, 2}, {1, 1}]**
	Out[22]= {{{{x, a}, {x, x}}, {{a, b}, {x, e}}}, {{{x, x}, {x, x}}, {{x, e}, {x, f}}}}

If you give a nested list as a padding specification, its elements are picked up cyclically at each level.

This cyclically fills in copies of the padding list.

In[23]:= **PadLeft[{{a, b}, {e}, {f}}, {4, 4}, {{x, y}, {z, w}}]**

Out[23]= {{x, y, x, y}, {z, w, a, b}, {x, y, x, e}, {z, w, z, f}}

Here is a list containing only padding.

In[24]:= **PadLeft[{{}}, {4, 4}, {{x, y}, {z, w}}]**

Out[24]= {{x, y, x, y}, {z, w, z, w}, {x, y, x, y}, {z, w, z, w}}

■ 2.4.5 Sparse Arrays

Lists are normally specified in *Mathematica* just by giving explicit lists of their elements. But particularly in working with large arrays, it is often useful instead to be able to say what the values of elements are only at certain positions, with all other elements taken to have a default value, usually zero. You can do this in *Mathematica* using `SparseArray` objects.

$\{e_1, e_2, \dots \}, \{\{e_{11}, e_{12}, \dots \}, \dots \}, \dots$ ordinary lists

+ **SparseArray[**$\{pos_1$ -> val_1, pos_2 -> $val_2, \dots \}$**]**   sparse arrays

Ordinary lists and sparse arrays.

This specifies a sparse array.

In[1]:= **SparseArray[{2->a, 5->b}]**

Out[1]= SparseArray[<2>, {5}]

Here it is as an ordinary list.

In[2]:= **Normal[%]**

Out[2]= {0, a, 0, 0, b}

This specifies a two-dimensional sparse array.

In[3]:= **SparseArray[{{1,2}->a, {3,2}->b, {3,3}->c}]**

Out[3]= SparseArray[<3>, {3, 3}]

Here it is an ordinary list of lists.

In[4]:= **Normal[%]**

Out[4]= {{0, a, 0}, {0, 0, 0}, {0, b, c}}

+	SparseArray[*list*]	sparse array version of *list*
+	SparseArray[{pos_1->val_1, pos_2->val_2, ... }]	
		sparse array with values val_i at positions pos_i
+	SparseArray[{pos_1, pos_2, ... }->{val_1, val_2, ... }]	
		the same sparse array
+	SparseArray[*data*, {d_1, d_2, ... }]	$d_1 \times d_2 \times$ ... sparse array
+	SparseArray[*data*, *dims*, *val*]	sparse array with default value *val*
+	Normal[*array*]	ordinary list version of *array*
+	ArrayRules[*array*]	position-value rules for *array*

Creating and converting sparse arrays.

This generates a sparse array version of a list.

$In[5]:=$ **SparseArray[{a, b, c, d}]**

$Out[5]=$ SparseArray[<4>, {4}]

This converts back to an ordinary list.

$In[6]:=$ **Normal[%]**

$Out[6]=$ {a, b, c, d}

This makes a length 7 sparse array with default value x.

$In[7]:=$ **SparseArray[{3->a, 5->b}, 7, x]**

$Out[7]=$ SparseArray[<2>, {7}, x]

Here is the corresponding ordinary list.

$In[8]:=$ **Normal[%]**

$Out[8]=$ {x, x, a, x, b, x, x}

This shows the rules used in the sparse array.

$In[9]:=$ **ArrayRules[%%]**

$Out[9]=$ {{3} → a, {5} → b, {_} → x}

An important feature of SparseArray is that the positions you specify can be patterns.

This specifies a 4×4 sparse array with 1 at every position matching {i_, i_}.

$In[10]:=$ **SparseArray[{i_, i_} -> 1, {4, 4}]**

$Out[10]=$ SparseArray[<4>, {4, 4}]

The result is a 4×4 identity matrix.

$In[11]:=$ **Normal[%]**

$Out[11]=$ {{1, 0, 0, 0}, {0, 1, 0, 0}, {0, 0, 1, 0}, {0, 0, 0, 1}}

Here is an identity matrix with an extra element.

$In[12]:=$ **Normal[SparseArray[{{1, 3}->a, {i_, i_}->1}, {4, 4}]]**

$Out[12]=$ {{1, 0, a, 0}, {0, 1, 0, 0}, {0, 0, 1, 0}, {0, 0, 0, 1}}

This makes the whole third column be a.

$In[13]:=$ **Normal[SparseArray[{{_, 3}->a, {i_, i_}->1}, {4, 4}]]**

$Out[13]=$ {{1, 0, a, 0}, {0, 1, a, 0}, {0, 0, a, 0}, {0, 0, a, 1}}

You can think of `SparseArray[`*rules*`]` as taking all possible position specifications, then applying *rules* to determine values in each case. As usual, rules given earlier in the list will be tried first.

This generates a random diagonal matrix.

`In[14]:= Normal[SparseArray[{{i_, i_} :> Random[]}, {3, 3}]]`

`Out[14]= {{0.0560708, 0, 0}, {0, 0.6303, 0}, {0, 0, 0.359894}}`

You can have rules where values depend on indices.

`In[15]:= Normal[SparseArray[i_ -> i^2, 10]]`

`Out[15]= {1, 4, 9, 16, 25, 36, 49, 64, 81, 100}`

This fills in even-numbered positions with p.

`In[16]:= Normal[SparseArray[{_?EvenQ->p, i_->i^2}, 10]]`

`Out[16]= {1, p, 9, p, 25, p, 49, p, 81, p}`

You can use patterns involving alternatives.

`In[17]:= Normal[SparseArray[{1|3, 2|4}->a, {4, 4}]]`

`Out[17]= {{0, a, 0, a}, {0, 0, 0, 0}, {0, a, 0, a}, {0, 0, 0, 0}}`

You can also give conditions on patterns.

`In[18]:= Normal[SparseArray[i_/;3<i<7 -> p, 10]]`

`Out[18]= {0, 0, 0, p, p, p, 0, 0, 0, 0}`

This makes a band-diagonal matrix.

`In[19]:= Normal[SparseArray[{{i_, j_} /;`
`            Abs[i - j] < 2 -> i + j}, {5, 5}]]`

`Out[19]= {{2, 3, 0, 0, 0}, {3, 4, 5, 0, 0},`
`            {0, 5, 6, 7, 0}, {0, 0, 7, 8, 9}, {0, 0, 0, 9, 10}}`

For many purposes, *Mathematica* treats `SparseArray` objects just like the ordinary lists to which they correspond. Thus, for example, if you ask for parts of a sparse array object, *Mathematica* will operate as if you had asked for parts in the corresponding ordinary list.

This generates a sparse array object.

`In[20]:= s = SparseArray[{2->a, 4->b, 5->c}, 10]`

`Out[20]= SparseArray[<3>, {10}]`

Here is the corresponding ordinary list.

`In[21]:= Normal[s]`

`Out[21]= {0, a, 0, b, c, 0, 0, 0, 0, 0}`

Parts of the sparse array are just like parts of the corresponding ordinary list.

`In[22]:= s[[2]]`

`Out[22]= a`

This part has the default value 0.

`In[23]:= s[[3]]`

`Out[23]= 0`

Many operations treat `SparseArray` objects just like ordinary lists. When possible, they give sparse arrays as results.

This gives a sparse array.

`In[24]:= 3 s + x`

`Out[24]= SparseArray[<3>, {10}, x]`

Here is the corresponding ordinary list.

`In[25]:= Normal[%]`

`Out[25]= {x, 3a+x, x, 3b+x, 3c+x, x, x, x, x, x}`

| Dot works directly with sparse array objects. | $In[26]:=$ **s . s** |
| | $Out[26]=$ $a^2 + b^2 + c^2$ |

| You can mix sparse arrays and ordinary lists. | $In[27]:=$ **s . Range[10]** |
| | $Out[27]=$ $2\,a + 4\,b + 5\,c$ |

Mathematica represents sparse arrays as expressions with head SparseArray. Whenever a sparse array is evaluated, it is automatically converted to an optimized standard form with structure SparseArray[Automatic, *dims*, *val*, ...].

This structure is, however, rarely evident, since even operations like Length are set up to give results for the corresponding ordinary list, not for the raw SparseArray expression structure.

| This generates a sparse array. | $In[28]:=$ **t = SparseArray[{1->a, 5->b}, 10]** |
| | $Out[28]=$ SparseArray[<2>, {10}] |

Here is the underlying optimized expression structure.	$In[29]:=$ **InputForm[%]**
	$Out[29]//InputForm=$ SparseArray[Automatic, {10}, 0,
	{1, {{0, 1, 1, 1, 1, 2, 2, 2, 2, 2, 2}, {}}, {a, b}}]

| Length gives the length of the corresponding ordinary list. | $In[30]:=$ **Length[t]** |
| | $Out[30]=$ 10 |

Map also operates on individual values.	$In[31]:=$ **Normal[Map[f, t]]**
	$Out[31]=$ {f[a], f[0], f[0], f[0],
	f[b], f[0], f[0], f[0], f[0], f[0]}

2.5 Transformation Rules and Definitions

■ 2.5.1 Applying Transformation Rules

expr /. *lhs* -> *rhs*	apply a transformation rule to *expr*
expr /. {*lhs*$_1$ -> *rhs*$_1$, *lhs*$_2$ -> *rhs*$_2$, ... }	try a sequence of rules on each part of *expr*

Applying transformation rules.

The replacement operator /.
(pronounced "slash-dot") applies rules
to expressions.

```
In[1]:= x + y /. x -> 3
Out[1]= 3 + y
```

You can give a list of rules to apply.
Each rule will be tried once on each
part of the expression.

```
In[2]:= x + y /. {x -> a, y -> b}
Out[2]= a + b
```

expr /. {*rules*$_1$, *rules*$_2$, ... }	give a list of the results from applying each of the *rules*$_i$ to *expr*

Applying lists of transformation rules.

If you give a list of lists of rules, you
get a list of results.

```
In[3]:= x + y /. {{x -> 1, y -> 2}, {x -> 4, y -> 2}}
Out[3]= {3, 6}
```

Functions such as Solve and NSolve
return lists whose elements are lists of
rules, each representing a solution.

```
In[4]:= Solve[x^3 - 5x^2 +2x + 8 == 0, x]
Out[4]= {{x → -1}, {x → 2}, {x → 4}}
```

When you apply these rules, you get a
list of results, one corresponding to
each solution.

```
In[5]:= x^2 + 6 /. %
Out[5]= {7, 10, 22}
```

When you use *expr* /. *rules*, each rule is tried in turn on each part of *expr*. As soon as a rule applies,
the appropriate transformation is made, and the resulting part is returned.

The rule for x^3 is tried first; if it does
not apply, the rule for x^n_ is used.

```
In[6]:= {x^2, x^3, x^4} /. {x^3 -> u, x^n_ -> p[n]}
Out[6]= {p[2], u, p[4]}
```

A result is returned as soon as the rule
has been applied, so the inner instance
of h is not replaced.

```
In[7]:= h[x + h[y]] /. h[u_] -> u^2
Out[7]= (x + h[y])^2
```

The replacement *expr* /. *rules* tries each rule just once on each part of *expr*.

Since each rule is tried just once, this serves to swap x and y.

```
In[8]:= {x^2, y^3} /. {x -> y, y -> x}

Out[8]= {y^2, x^3}
```

You can use this notation to apply one set of rules, followed by another.

```
In[9]:= x^2 /. x -> (1 + y) /. y -> b

Out[9]= (1 + b)^2
```

Sometimes you may need to go on applying rules over and over again, until the expression you are working on no longer changes. You can do this using the repeated replacement operation *expr* //. *rules* (or ReplaceRepeated[*expr*, *rules*]).

expr /. *rules*	try rules once on each part of *expr*
expr //. *rules*	try rules repeatedly until the result no longer changes

Single and repeated rule application.

With the single replacement operator /. each rule is tried only once on each part of the expression.

```
In[10]:= x^2 + y^6 /. {x -> 2 + a, a -> 3}

Out[10]= (2 + a)^2 + y^6
```

With the repeated replacement operator //. the rules are tried repeatedly until the expression no longer changes.

```
In[11]:= x^2 + y^6 //. {x -> 2 + a, a -> 3}

Out[11]= 25 + y^6
```

Here the rule is applied only once.

```
In[12]:= log[a b c d] /. log[x_ y_] -> log[x] + log[y]

Out[12]= log[a] + log[b c d]
```

With the repeated replacement operator, the rule is applied repeatedly, until the result no longer changes.

```
In[13]:= log[a b c d] //. log[x_ y_] -> log[x] + log[y]

Out[13]= log[a] + log[b] + log[c] + log[d]
```

When you use //. (pronounced "slash-slash-dot"), *Mathematica* repeatedly passes through your expression, trying each of the rules given. It goes on doing this until it gets the same result on two successive passes.

If you give a set of rules that is circular, then //. can keep on getting different results forever. In practice, the maximum number of passes that //. makes on a particular expression is determined by the setting for the option MaxIterations. If you want to keep going for as long as possible, you can use ReplaceRepeated[*expr*, *rules*, MaxIterations -> Infinity]. You can always stop by explicitly interrupting *Mathematica*.

By setting the option MaxIterations, you can explicitly tell ReplaceRepeated how many times to try the rules you give.

```
In[14]:= ReplaceRepeated[x, x -> x + 1, MaxIterations -> 1000]

ReplaceRepeated::rrlim:
   Exiting after x scanned 1000 times.

Out[14]= 1000 + x
```

The replacement operators /. and //. share the feature that they try each rule on every subpart of your expression. On the other hand, Replace[*expr*, *rules*] tries the rules only on the whole of *expr*, and not on any of its subparts.

You can use Replace, together with functions like Map and MapAt, to control exactly which parts of an expression a replacement is applied to. Remember that you can use the function ReplacePart[*expr*, *new*, *pos*] to replace part of an expression with a specific object.

The operator /. applies rules to all subparts of an expression.	*In[15]:=* **x^2 /. x -> a**
	Out[15]= a^2
Without a level specification, Replace applies rules only to the whole expression.	*In[16]:=* **Replace[x^2, x^2 -> b]**
	Out[16]= b
No replacement is done here.	*In[17]:=* **Replace[x^2, x -> a]**
	Out[17]= x^2
This applies rules down to level 2, and so replaces x.	*In[18]:=* **Replace[x^2, x -> a, 2]**
	Out[18]= a^2

expr /. *rules*	apply rules to all subparts of *expr*
Replace[*expr*, *rules*]	apply rules to the whole of *expr* only
Replace[*expr*, *rules*, *levspec*]	apply rules to parts of *expr* on levels specified by *levspec*

Applying rules to whole expressions.

Replace returns the result from using the first rule that applies.	*In[19]:=* **Replace[f[u], {f[x_] -> x^2, f[x_] -> x^3}]**
	Out[19]= u^2
ReplaceList gives a list of the results from every rule that applies.	*In[20]:=* **ReplaceList[f[u], {f[x_] -> x^2, f[x_] -> x^3}]**
	Out[20]= $\{u^2, u^3\}$
If a single rule can be applied in several ways, ReplaceList gives a list of all the results.	*In[21]:=* **ReplaceList[a + b + c, x_ + y_ -> g[x, y]]**
	Out[21]= {g[a, b + c], g[b, a + c], g[c, a + b],
	g[a + b, c], g[a + c, b], g[b + c, a]}
This gives a list of ways of breaking the original list in two.	*In[22]:=* **ReplaceList[{a, b, c, d}, {x__, y__} -> g[{x}, {y}]]**
	Out[22]= {g[{a}, {b, c, d}],
	g[{a, b}, {c, d}], g[{a, b, c}, {d}]}
This finds all sublists that are flanked by the same element.	*In[23]:=* **ReplaceList[{a, b, c, a, d, b, d},**
	{___, x_, y__, x_, ___} -> g[x, {y}]]
	Out[23]= {g[a, {b, c}], g[b, {c, a, d}], g[d, {b}]}

| Replace[*expr*, *rules*] | apply *rules* in one way only |
| ReplaceList[*expr*, *rules*] | apply *rules* in all possible ways |

Applying rules in one way or all possible ways.

■ 2.5.2 Manipulating Sets of Transformation Rules

You can manipulate lists of transformation rules in *Mathematica* just like other symbolic expressions. It is common to assign a name to a rule or set of rules.

| This assigns the "name" sinexp to the trigonometric expansion rule. | *In[1]:=* **sinexp = Sin[2 x_] -> 2 Sin[x] Cos[x]** |
| | *Out[1]=* $Sin[2 x_] \to 2 Cos[x] Sin[x]$ |

| You can now request the rule "by name". | *In[2]:=* **Sin[2 (1 + x)^2] /. sinexp** |
| | *Out[2]=* $2 Cos\left[(1+x)^2\right] Sin\left[(1+x)^2\right]$ |

You can use lists of rules to represent mathematical and other relations. Typically you will find it convenient to give names to the lists, so that you can easily specify the list you want in a particular case.

In most situations, it is only one rule from any given list that actually applies to a particular expression. Nevertheless, the /. operator tests each of the rules in the list in turn. If the list is very long, this process can take a long time.

Mathematica allows you to preprocess lists of rules so that /. can operate more quickly on them. You can take any list of rules and apply the function Dispatch to them. The result is a representation of the original list of rules, but including dispatch tables which allow /. to "dispatch" to potentially applicable rules immediately, rather than testing all the rules in turn.

| Here is a list of rules for the first five factorials. | *In[3]:=* **facs = Table[f[i] -> i!, {i, 5}]** |
| | *Out[3]=* $\{f[1] \to 1, f[2] \to 2, f[3] \to 6, f[4] \to 24, f[5] \to 120\}$ |

This sets up dispatch tables that make the rules faster to use.	*In[4]:=* **dfacs = Dispatch[facs]**
	Out[4]= $Dispatch[\{f[1] \to 1, f[2] \to 2, f[3] \to 6,$
	$f[4] \to 24, f[5] \to 120\}, -DispatchTables -]$

| You can apply the rules using the /. operator. | *In[5]:=* **f[4] /. dfacs** |
| | *Out[5]=* 24 |

Dispatch[*rules*]	create a representation of a list of rules that includes dispatch tables
expr /. drules	apply rules that include dispatch tables

Creating and using dispatch tables.

For long lists of rules, you will find that setting up dispatch tables makes replacement operations much faster. This is particularly true when your rules are for individual symbols or other expressions that do not involve pattern objects. Once you have built dispatch tables in such cases, you will find that the /. operator takes a time that is more or less independent of the number of rules you have. Without dispatch tables, however, /. will take a time directly proportional to the total number of rules.

■ 2.5.3 Making Definitions

The replacement operator /. allows you to apply transformation rules to a specific expression. Often, however, you want to have transformation rules automatically applied whenever possible.

You can do this by assigning explicit values to *Mathematica* expressions and patterns. Each assignment specifies a transformation rule to be applied whenever an expression of the appropriate form occurs.

expr /. lhs -> rhs	apply a transformation rule to a specific expression
lhs = rhs	assign a value which defines a transformation rule to be used whenever possible

Manual and automatic application of transformation rules.

This applies a transformation rule for x to a specific expression.	`In[1]:= (1 + x)^6 /. x -> 3 - a` $Out[1]= (4-a)^6$
By assigning a value to x, you tell *Mathematica* to apply a transformation rule for x whenever possible.	`In[2]:= x = 3 - a` $Out[2]= 3-a$
Now x is transformed automatically.	`In[3]:= (1 + x)^7` $Out[3]= (4-a)^7$

You should realize that except inside constructs like Module and Block, all assignments you make in a *Mathematica* session are *permanent*. They continue to be used for the duration of the session, unless you explicitly clear or overwrite them.

The fact that assignments are permanent means that they must be made with care. Probably the single most common mistake in using *Mathematica* is to make an assignment for a variable like x at one point in your session, and then later to use x having forgotten about the assignment you made.

There are several ways to avoid this kind of mistake. First, you should avoid using assignments whenever possible, and instead use more controlled constructs such as the /. replacement operator. Second, you should explicitly use the deassignment operator =. or the function Clear to remove values you have assigned when you have finished with them.

Another important way to avoid mistakes is to think particularly carefully before assigning values to variables with common or simple names. You will often want to use a variable such as x as a symbolic parameter. But if you make an assignment such as x = 3, then x will be replaced by 3 whenever it occurs, and you can no longer use x as a symbolic parameter.

In general, you should be sure not to assign permanent values to any variables that you might want to use for more than one purpose. If at one point in your session you wanted the variable c to stand for the speed of light, you might assign it a value such as 3.*10^8. But then you cannot use c later in your session to stand, say, for an undetermined coefficient. One way to avoid this kind of problem is to make assignments only for variables with more explicit names, such as SpeedOfLight.

x =.	remove the value assigned to the object x
Clear[x, y, ...]	clear all the values of x, y, ...

Removing assignments.

This does not give what you might expect, because x still has the value you assigned it above.	*In[4]:=* **Factor[x^2 - 1]**
	Out[4]= $(-4+a)(-2+a)$
This removes any value assigned to x.	*In[5]:=* **Clear[x]**
Now this gives the result you expect.	*In[6]:=* **Factor[x^2 - 1]**
	Out[6]= $(-1+x)(1+x)$

■ 2.5.4 Special Forms of Assignment

Particularly when you write procedural programs in *Mathematica*, you will often need to modify the value of a particular variable repeatedly. You can always do this by constructing the new value and explicitly performing an assignment such as x = *value*. *Mathematica*, however, provides special notations for incrementing the values of variables, and for some other common cases.

i++	increment the value of i by 1
i--	decrement i
++i	pre-increment i
--i	pre-decrement i
i += di	add di to the value of i
i -= di	subtract di from i
x *= c	multiply x by c
x /= c	divide x by c

Modifying values of variables.

This assigns the value 7x to the variable t.	`In[1]:= t = 7x` `Out[1]= 7 x`
This increments the value of t by 18x.	`In[2]:= t += 18x` `Out[2]= 25 x`
The value of t has been modified.	`In[3]:= t` `Out[3]= 25 x`
This sets t to 8, multiplies its value by 7, then gives the final value of t.	`In[4]:= t = 8; t *= 7; t` `Out[4]= 56`

The value of i++ is the value of i *before* the increment is done.	`In[5]:= i=5; Print[i++]; Print[i]`
	`5`
	`6`

The value of ++i is the value of i *after* the increment.	`In[6]:= i=5; Print[++i]; Print[i]`
	`6`
	`6`

$x = y = value$	assign the same value to both x and y
$\{x, y\} = \{value_1, value_2\}$	assign different values to x and y
$\{x, y\} = \{y, x\}$	interchange the values of x and y

Assigning values to several variables at a time.

This assigns the value 5 to x and 8 to y.	`In[7]:= {x, y} = {5, 8}` `Out[7]= {5, 8}`

| This interchanges the values of x and y. | *In[8]:=* **{x, y} = {y, x}** |
| | *Out[8]=* {8, 5} |

| Now x has value 8. | *In[9]:=* **x** |
| | *Out[9]=* 8 |

| And y has value 5. | *In[10]:=* **y** |
| | *Out[10]=* 5 |

| You can use assignments to lists to permute values of variables in any way. | *In[11]:=* **{a, b, c} = {1, 2, 3}; {b, a, c} = {a, c, b}; {a, b, c}** |
| | *Out[11]=* {3, 1, 2} |

When you write programs in *Mathematica*, you will sometimes find it convenient to take a list, and successively add elements to it. You can do this using the functions PrependTo and AppendTo.

PrependTo[v, *elem*]	prepend *elem* to the value of v
AppendTo[v, *elem*]	append *elem*
v = {v, *elem*}	make a nested list containing *elem*

Assignments for modifying lists.

| This assigns the value of v to be the list {5, 7, 9}. | *In[12]:=* **v = {5, 7, 9}** |
| | *Out[12]=* {5, 7, 9} |

| This appends the element 11 to the value of v. | *In[13]:=* **AppendTo[v, 11]** |
| | *Out[13]=* {5, 7, 9, 11} |

| Now the value of v has been modified. | *In[14]:=* **v** |
| | *Out[14]=* {5, 7, 9, 11} |

Although AppendTo[v, *elem*] is always equivalent to v = Append[v, *elem*], it is often a convenient notation. However, you should realize that because of the way *Mathematica* stores lists, it is usually less efficient to add a sequence of elements to a particular list than to create a nested structure that consists, for example, of lists of length 2 at each level. When you have built up such a structure, you can always reduce it to a single list using Flatten.

| This sets up a nested list structure for w. | *In[15]:=* **w = {1}; Do[w = {w, k^2}, {k, 1, 4}]; w** |
| | *Out[15]=* {{{{{1}, 1}, 4}, 9}, 16} |

| You can use Flatten to unravel the structure. | *In[16]:=* **Flatten[w]** |
| | *Out[16]=* {1, 1, 4, 9, 16} |

■ 2.5.5 Making Definitions for Indexed Objects

In many kinds of calculations, you need to set up "arrays" which contain sequences of expressions, each specified by a certain index. One way to implement arrays in *Mathematica* is by using lists. You can define a list, say $a = \{x, y, z, \ldots\}$, then access its elements using $a[[i]]$, or modify them using $a[[i]] = value$. This approach has a drawback, however, in that it requires you to fill in all the elements when you first create the list.

Often, it is more convenient to set up arrays in which you can fill in only those elements that you need at a particular time. You can do this by making definitions for expressions such as $a[i]$.

This defines a value for a[1].	`In[1]:= ` **a[1] = 9** `Out[1]= 9`
This defines a value for a[2].	`In[2]:= ` **a[2] = 7** `Out[2]= 7`
This shows all the values you have defined for expressions associated with a so far.	`In[3]:= ` **?a** `Global`a`  `a[1] = 9`  `a[2] = 7`
You can define a value for a[5], even though you have not yet given values to a[3] and a[4].	`In[4]:= ` **a[5] = 0** `Out[4]= 0`
This generates a list of the values of the a[i].	`In[5]:= ` **Table[a[i], {i, 5}]** `Out[5]= {9, 7, a[3], a[4], 0}`

You can think of the expression $a[i]$ as being like an "indexed" or "subscripted" variable.

$a[i] = value$	add or overwrite a value
$a[i]$	access a value
$a[i] =.$	remove a value
$?a$	show all defined values
$Clear[a]$	clear all defined values
Table[a[i], {i, 1, n}] or Array[a, n]	convert to an explicit List

Manipulating indexed variables.

When you have an expression of the form $a[i]$, there is no requirement that the "index" i be a number. In fact, *Mathematica* allows the index to be any expression whatsoever. By using indices that are symbols, you can for example build up simple databases in *Mathematica*.

This defines the "object" area with "index" square to have value 1.	*In[6]:=* **area[square] = 1**
	Out[6]= 1
This adds another result to the area "database".	*In[7]:=* **area[triangle] = 1/2**
	Out[7]= $\dfrac{1}{2}$
Here are the entries in the area database so far.	*In[8]:=* **?area**
	Global`area
	area[square] = 1
	area[triangle] = 1/2
You can use these definitions wherever you want. You have not yet assigned a value for `area[pentagon]`.	*In[9]:=* **4 area[square] + area[pentagon]**
	Out[9]= 4 + area[pentagon]

■ 2.5.6 Making Definitions for Functions

Section 1.7.1 discussed how you can define functions in *Mathematica*. In a typical case, you would type in f[x_] = x^2 to define a function f. (Actually, the definitions in Section 1.7.1 used the := operator, rather than the = one. Section 2.5.8 will explain exactly when to use each of the := and = operators.)

The definition f[x_] = x^2 specifies that whenever *Mathematica* encounters an expression which matches the pattern f[x_], it should replace the expression by x^2. Since the pattern f[x_] matches all expressions of the form f[*anything*], the definition applies to functions f with any "argument".

Function definitions like f[x_] = x^2 can be compared with definitions like f[a] = b for indexed variables discussed in the previous subsection. The definition f[a] = b specifies that whenever the *particular* expression f[a] occurs, it is to be replaced by b. But the definition says nothing about expressions such as f[y], where f appears with another "index".

To define a "function", you need to specify values for expressions of the form f[x], where the argument x can be anything. You can do this by giving a definition for the pattern f[x_], where the pattern object x_ stands for any expression.

f[x] = *value*	definition for a *specific expression* x
f[x_] = *value*	definition for *any expression*, referred to as x

The difference between defining an indexed variable and a function.

Making definitions for f[2] or f[a] can be thought of as being like giving values to various elements of an "array" named f. Making a definition for f[x_] is like giving a value for a set of "array elements" with arbitrary "indices". In fact, you can actually think of any function as being like an array with an arbitrarily variable index.

In mathematical terms, you can think of f as a *mapping*. When you define values for, say, f[1] and f[2], you specify the image of this mapping for various discrete points in its domain. Defining a value for f[x_] specifies the image of f on a continuum of points.

This defines a transformation rule for the *specific expression* f[x].	*In[1]:=* **f[x] = u** *Out[1]=* u
When the specific expression f[x] appears, it is replaced by u. Other expressions of the form f[*argument*] are, however, not modified.	*In[2]:=* **f[x] + f[y]** *Out[2]=* u + f[y]
This defines a value for f with *any expression* as an "argument".	*In[3]:=* **f[x_] = x^2** *Out[3]=* x^2
The old definition for the *specific expression* f[x] is still used, but the new general definition for f[x_] is now used to find a value for f[y].	*In[4]:=* **f[x] + f[y]** *Out[4]=* u + y^2
This removes all definitions for f.	*In[5]:=* **Clear[f]**

Mathematica allows you to define transformation rules for any expression or pattern. You can mix definitions for specific expressions such as f[1] or f[a] with definitions for patterns such as f[x_].

Many kinds of mathematical functions can be set up by mixing specific and general definitions in *Mathematica*. As an example, consider the factorial function. This particular function is in fact built into *Mathematica* (it is written *n*!). But you can use *Mathematica* definitions to set up the function for yourself.

The standard mathematical definition for the factorial function can be entered almost directly into *Mathematica*, in the form: f[n_] := n f[n-1]; f[1] = 1. This definition specifies that for any *n*, f[*n*] should be replaced by *n* f[*n*-1], except that when *n* is 1, f[1] should simply be replaced by 1.

Here is the value of the factorial function with argument 1.	*In[6]:=* **f[1] = 1** *Out[6]=* 1
Here is the general recursion relation for the factorial function.	*In[7]:=* **f[n_] := n f[n-1]**
Now you can use these definitions to find values for the factorial function.	*In[8]:=* **f[10]** *Out[8]=* 3628800
The results are the same as you get from the built-in version of factorial.	*In[9]:=* **10!** *Out[9]=* 3628800

■ 2.5.7 The Ordering of Definitions

When you make a sequence of definitions in *Mathematica*, some may be more general than others. *Mathematica* follows the principle of trying to put more general definitions after more specific ones. This means that special cases of rules are typically tried before more general cases.

This behavior is crucial to the factorial function example given in the previous section. Regardless of the order in which you entered them, *Mathematica* will always put the rule for the special case f[1] ahead of the rule for the general case f[n_]. This means that when *Mathematica* looks for the value of an expression of the form f[*n*], it tries the special case f[1] first, and only if this does not apply, it tries the general case f[n_]. As a result, when you ask for f[5], *Mathematica* will keep on using the general rule until the "end condition" rule for f[1] applies.

■ *Mathematica* tries to put specific definitions before more general definitions.

Treatment of definitions in *Mathematica*.

If *Mathematica* did not follow the principle of putting special rules before more general ones, then the special rules would always be "shadowed" by more general ones. In the factorial example, if the rule for f[n_] was ahead of the rule for f[1], then even when *Mathematica* tried to evaluate f[1], it would use the general f[n_] rule, and it would never find the special f[1] rule.

Here is a general definition for f[n_].	*In[1]:=* **f[n_] := n f[n-1]**
Here is a definition for the special case f[1].	*In[2]:=* **f[1] = 1**
	Out[2]= 1
Mathematica puts the special case before the general one.	*In[3]:=* **?f**
	Global`f
	f[1] = 1
	f[n_] := n*f[n - 1]

In the factorial function example used above, it is clear which rule is more general. Often, however, there is no definite ordering in generality of the rules you give. In such cases, *Mathematica* simply tries the rules in the order you give them.

These rules have no definite ordering in generality.	*In[4]:=* **log[x_ y_] := log[x] + log[y] ; log[x_^n_] := n log[x]**
Mathematica stores the rules in the order you gave them.	*In[5]:=* **?log**
	Global`log
	log[(x_)*(y_)] := log[x] + log[y]
	log[(x_)^(n_)] := n*log[x]
This rule is a special case of the rule for log[x_ y_].	*In[6]:=* **log[2 x_] := log[x] + log2**

Mathematica puts the special rule before the more general one.	*In[7]:=* **?log**

```
Global`log

log[2*(x_)] := log[x] + log2

log[(x_)*(y_)] := log[x] + log[y]

log[(x_)^(n_)] := n*log[x]
```

Although in many practical cases, *Mathematica* can recognize when one rule is more general than another, you should realize that this is not always possible. For example, if two rules both contain complicated /; conditions, it may not be possible to work out which is more general, and, in fact, there may not be a definite ordering. Whenever the appropriate ordering is not clear, *Mathematica* stores rules in the order you give them.

■ 2.5.8 Immediate and Delayed Definitions

You may have noticed that there are two different ways to make assignments in *Mathematica*: *lhs = rhs* and *lhs := rhs*. The basic difference between these forms is *when* the expression *rhs* is evaluated. *lhs = rhs* is an *immediate assignment*, in which *rhs* is evaluated at the time when the assignment is made. *lhs := rhs*, on the other hand, is a *delayed assignment*, in which *rhs* is not evaluated when the assignment is made, but is instead evaluated each time the value of *lhs* is requested.

lhs = *rhs* (immediate assignment)	*rhs* is evaluated when the assignment is made
lhs := *rhs* (delayed assignment)	*rhs* is evaluated each time the value of *lhs* is requested

The two types of assignments in *Mathematica*.

This uses the := operator to define the function ex.	*In[1]:=* **ex[x_] := Expand[(1 + x)^2]**
Because := was used, the definition is maintained in an unevaluated form.	*In[2]:=* **?ex**

```
Global`ex

ex[x_] := Expand[(1 + x)^2]
```

When you make an assignment with the = operator, the right-hand side is evaluated immediately.	*In[3]:=* **iex[x_] = Expand[(1 + x)^2]** *Out[3]=* $1 + 2x + x^2$
The definition now stored is the result of the Expand command.	*In[4]:=* **?iex**

```
Global`iex

iex[x_] = 1 + 2*x + x^2
```

When you execute ex, the Expand is performed.	*In[5]:=* **ex[y + 2]** *Out[5]=* $9 + 6y + y^2$

iex simply substitutes its argument
into the already expanded form, giving
a different answer.

$In[6]:= $ **iex[y + 2]**

$Out[6]= 1 + 2 (2 + y) + (2 + y)^2$

As you can see from the example above, both = and := can be useful in defining functions, but they have different meanings, and you must be careful about which one to use in a particular case.

One rule of thumb is the following. If you think of an assignment as giving the final "value" of an expression, use the = operator. If instead you think of the assignment as specifying a "command" for finding the value, use the := operator. If in doubt, it is usually better to use the := operator than the = one.

lhs = *rhs*	*rhs* is intended to be the "final value" of *lhs* (e.g., f[x_] = 1 - x^2)
lhs := *rhs*	*rhs* gives a "command" or "program" to be executed whenever you ask for the value of *lhs* (e.g., f[x_] := Expand[1 - x^2])

Interpretations of assignments with the = and := operators.

Although := is probably used more often than = in defining functions, there is one important case in which you must use = to define a function. If you do a calculation, and get an answer in terms of a symbolic parameter x, you often want to go on and find results for various specific values of x. One way to do this is to use the /. operator to apply appropriate rules for x in each case. It is usually more convenient however, to use = to define a function whose argument is x.

Here is an expression involving x.

$In[7]:= $ **D[Log[Sin[x]]^2, x]**

$Out[7]= 2 Cot[x] Log[Sin[x]]$

This defines a function whose
argument is the value to be taken
for x.

$In[8]:= $ **dlog[x_] = %**

$Out[8]= 2 Cot[x] Log[Sin[x]]$

Here is the result when x is taken to
be 1 + a.

$In[9]:= $ **dlog[1 + a]**

$Out[9]= 2 Cot[1 + a] Log[Sin[1 + a]]$

An important point to notice in the example above is that there is nothing special about the name x that appears in the x_ pattern. It is just a symbol, indistinguishable from an x that appears in any other expression.

f[*x_*] = *expr*	define a function which gives the value *expr* for any particular value of *x*

Defining functions for evaluating expressions.

You can use = and := not only to define functions, but also to assign values to variables. If you type *x* = *value*, then *value* is immediately evaluated, and the result is assigned to *x*. On the other hand, if you type *x* := *value*, then *value* is not immediately evaluated. Instead, it is maintained in an unevaluated form, and is evaluated afresh each time *x* is used.

This evaluates Random[ ] to find a pseudorandom number, then assigns this number to r1.	*In[10]:=* **r1 = Random[ ]** *Out[10]=* 0.0560708
Here Random[ ] is maintained in an unevaluated form, to be evaluated afresh each time r2 is used.	*In[11]:=* **r2 := Random[ ]**
Here are values for r1 and r2.	*In[12]:=* **{r1, r2}** *Out[12]=* {0.0560708, 0.6303}
The value of r1 never changes. Every time r2 is used, however, a new pseudorandom number is generated.	*In[13]:=* **{r1, r2}** *Out[13]=* {0.0560708, 0.359894}

The distinction between immediate and delayed assignments is particularly important when you set up chains of assignments.

This defines a to be 1.	*In[14]:=* **a = 1** *Out[14]=* 1
Here a + 2 is evaluated to give 3, and the result is assigned to be the value of ri.	*In[15]:=* **ri = a + 2** *Out[15]=* 3
Here a + 2 is maintained in an unevaluated form, to be evaluated every time the value of rd is requested.	*In[16]:=* **rd := a + 2**
In this case, ri and rd give the same values.	*In[17]:=* **{ri, rd}** *Out[17]=* {3, 3}
Now the value of a is changed.	*In[18]:=* **a = 2** *Out[18]=* 2
Now rd uses the new value for a, while ri keeps its original value.	*In[19]:=* **{ri, rd}** *Out[19]=* {3, 4}

You can use delayed assignments such as *t* := *rhs* to set up variables whose values you can find in a variety of different "environments". Every time you ask for *t*, the expression *rhs* is evaluated using the current values of the objects on which it depends.

The right-hand side of the delayed assignment is maintained in an unevaluated form.	*In[20]:=* **t := {a, Factor[x^a - 1]}**

This sets a to 4, then finds the value
of t.

$In[21]:=$ **a = 4; t**

$Out[21]=$ $\{4, (-1+x)(1+x)(1+x^2)\}$

Here a is 6.

$In[22]:=$ **a = 6; t**

$Out[22]=$ $\{6, (-1+x)(1+x)(1-x+x^2)(1+x+x^2)\}$

In the example above, the symbol a acts as a "global variable", whose value affects the value of t. When you have a large number of parameters, many of which change only occasionally, you may find this kind of setup convenient. However, you should realize that implicit or hidden dependence of one variable on others can often become quite confusing. When possible, you should make all dependencies explicit, by defining functions which take all necessary parameters as arguments.

lhs -> *rhs*	*rhs* is evaluated when the rule is given
lhs :> *rhs*	*rhs* is evaluated when the rule is used

Two types of transformation rules in *Mathematica*.

Just as you can make immediate and delayed assignments in *Mathematica*, so you can also set up immediate and delayed transformation rules.

The right-hand side of this rule is
evaluated when you give the rule.

$In[23]:=$ **f[x_] -> Expand[(1 + x)^2]**

$Out[23]=$ $f[x\_] \to 1 + 2x + x^2$

A rule like this is probably not
particularly useful.

$In[24]:=$ **f[x_] -> Expand[x]**

$Out[24]=$ $f[x\_] \to x$

Here the right-hand side of the rule is
maintained in an unevaluated form, to
be evaluated every time the rule is
used.

$In[25]:=$ **f[x_] :> Expand[x]**

$Out[25]=$ $f[x\_] :\to Expand[x]$

Applying the rule causes the expansion
to be done.

$In[26]:=$ **f[(1 + p)^2] /. f[x_] :> Expand[x]**

$Out[26]=$ $1 + 2p + p^2$

In analogy with assignments, you should typically use -> when you want to replace an expression with a definite value, and you should use :> when you want to give a command for finding the value.

■ 2.5.9 Functions That Remember Values They Have Found

When you make a function definition using :=, the value of the function is recomputed every time you ask for it. In some kinds of calculations, you may end up asking for the same function value many times. You can save time in these cases by having *Mathematica* remember all the function values it finds. Here is an "idiom" for defining a function that does this.

---

f[x_] := f[x] = rhs	define a function which remembers values that it finds

Defining a function that remembers values it finds.

This defines a function f which stores all values that it finds.

In[1]:= **f[x_] := f[x] = f[x - 1] + f[x - 2]**

Here are the end conditions for the recursive function f.

In[2]:= **f[0] = f[1] = 1**

Out[2]= 1

Here is the original definition of f.

In[3]:= **?f**

Global`f

f[1] = 1

f[0] = 1

f[x_] := f[x] = f[x - 1] + f[x - 2]

This computes f[5]. The computation involves finding the sequence of values f[5], f[4], ... f[2].

In[4]:= **f[5]**

Out[4]= 8

All the values of f found so far are explicitly stored.

In[5]:= **?f**

Global`f

f[1] = 1

f[0] = 1

f[2] = 2

f[3] = 3

f[4] = 5

f[5] = 8

f[x_] := f[x] = f[x - 1] + f[x - 2]

If you ask for f[5] again, *Mathematica* can just look up the value immediately; it does not have to recompute it.

In[6]:= **f[5]**

Out[6]= 8

You can see how a definition like f[x_] := f[x] = f[x-1] + f[x-2] works. The function f[x_] is defined to be the "program" f[x] = f[x-1] + f[x-2]. When you ask for a value of the function f, the "program" is executed. The program first calculates the value of f[x-1] + f[x-2], then saves the result as f[x].

It is often a good idea to use functions that remember values when you implement mathematical *recursion relations* in *Mathematica*. In a typical case, a recursion relation gives the value of a function f with an integer argument x in terms of values of the same function with arguments $x - 1$, $x - 2$, etc. The Fibonacci function definition $f(x) = f(x - 1) + f(x - 2)$ used above is an example of this kind of recursion relation. The point is that if you calculate say $f(10)$ by just applying the recursion relation over and over again, you end up having to recalculate quantities like $f(5)$ many times. In a case like this, it is therefore better just to *remember* the value of $f(5)$, and look it up when you need it, rather than having to recalculate it.

There is of course a trade-off involved in remembering values. It is faster to find a particular value, but it takes more memory space to store all of them. You should usually define functions to remember values only if the total number of different values that will be produced is comparatively small, or the expense of recomputing them is very great.

■ 2.5.10 Associating Definitions with Different Symbols

When you make a definition in the form $f[args]$ = *rhs* or $f[args]$:= *rhs*, *Mathematica* associates your definition with the object f. This means, for example, that such definitions are displayed when you type ?f. In general, definitions for expressions in which the symbol f appears as the head are termed *downvalues* of f.

Mathematica however also supports *upvalues*, which allow definitions to be associated with symbols that do not appear directly as their head.

Consider for example a definition like Exp[g[x_]] := *rhs*. One possibility is that this definition could be associated with the symbol Exp, and considered as a downvalue of Exp. This is however probably not the best thing either from the point of view of organization or efficiency.

Better is to consider Exp[g[x_]] := *rhs* to be associated with g, and to correspond to an upvalue of g.

$f[args]$:= *rhs*	define a downvalue for f
$f[g[args],\ ...\ ]$ ^:= *rhs*	define an upvalue for g

Associating definitions with different symbols.

This is taken to define a downvalue for f.	*In[1]:=* **f[g[x_]] := fg[x]**
You can see the definition when you ask about f.	*In[2]:=* **?f**
	Global`f
	f[g[x_]] := fg[x]
This defines an upvalue for g.	*In[3]:=* **Exp[g[x_]] ^:= expg[x]**
The definition is associated with g.	*In[4]:=* **?g**
	Global`g
	Exp[g[x_]] ^:= expg[x]

It is not associated with Exp.	*In[5]:=* **??Exp**
	Exp[z] is the exponential function.
	Attributes[Exp] = {Listable, NumericFunction, Protected,
	ReadProtected}
The definition is used to evaluate this expression.	*In[6]:=* **Exp[g[5]]**
	Out[6]= expg[5]

In simple cases, you will get the same answers to calculations whether you give a definition for $f[g[x]]$ as a downvalue for f or an upvalue for g. However, one of the two choices is usually much more natural and efficient than the other.

A good rule of thumb is that a definition for $f[g[x]]$ should be given as an upvalue for g in cases where the function f is more common than g. Thus, for example, in the case of Exp[$g[x]$], Exp is a built-in *Mathematica* function, while g is presumably a function you have added. In such a case, you will typically think of definitions for Exp[$g[x]$] as giving relations satisfied by g. As a result, it is more natural to treat the definitions as upvalues for g than as downvalues for Exp.

This gives the definition as an upvalue for g.	*In[7]:=* **g/: g[x_] + g[y_] := gplus[x, y]**
Here are the definitions for g so far.	*In[8]:=* **?g**
	Global`g
	Exp[g[x_]] ^:= expg[x]
	g[x_] + g[y_] ^:= gplus[x, y]
The definition for a sum of g's is used whenever possible.	*In[9]:=* **g[5] + g[7]**
	Out[9]= gplus[5, 7]

Since the full form of the pattern g[x_] + g[y_] is Plus[g[x_], g[y_]], a definition for this pattern could be given as a downvalue for Plus. It is almost always better, however, to give the definition as an upvalue for g.

In general, whenever *Mathematica* encounters a particular function, it tries all the definitions you have given for that function. If you had made the definition for g[x_] + g[y_] a downvalue for Plus, then *Mathematica* would have tried this definition whenever Plus occurs. The definition would thus be tested every time *Mathematica* added expressions together, making this very common operation slower in all cases.

However, by giving a definition for g[x_] + g[y_] as an upvalue for g, you associate the definition with g. In this case, *Mathematica* only tries the definition when it finds a g inside a function such as Plus. Since g presumably occurs much less frequently than Plus, this is a much more efficient procedure.

$f[g]$ ^= *value*   or $f[g[args]]$ ^= *value*
>   make assignments to be associated with g, rather than f

$f[g]$ ^:= *value*   or $f[g[args]]$ ^:= *value*
>   make delayed assignments associated with g

> $f[arg_1, arg_2, \ldots]$ ^= *value*   make assignments associated with the heads of *all* the arg_i

---

Shorter ways to define upvalues.

A typical use of upvalues is in setting up a "database" of properties of a particular object. With upvalues, you can associate each definition you make with the object that it concerns, rather than with the property you are specifying.

This defines an upvalue for square which gives its area.	`In[10]:= area[square] ^= 1`
	
	`Out[10]= 1`

This adds a definition for the perimeter.	`In[11]:= perimeter[square] ^= 4`
	
	`Out[11]= 4`

Both definitions are now associated with the object square.	`In[12]:= ?square` `Global`square`  `area[square] ^= 1`  `perimeter[square] ^= 4`

In general, you can associate definitions for an expression with any symbol that occurs at a sufficiently high level in the expression. With an expression of the form $f[args]$, you can define an upvalue for a symbol g so long as either g itself, or an object with head g, occurs in *args*. If g occurs at a lower level in an expression, however, you cannot associate definitions with it.

g occurs as the head of an argument, so you can associate a definition with it.	`In[13]:= g/: h[w[x_], g[y_]] := hwg[x, y]`

Here g appears too deep in the left-hand side for you to associate a definition with it.	`In[14]:= g/: h[w[g[x_]], y_] := hw[x, y]`
	
	`TagSetDelayed::tagpos:`
	`    Tag g in h[w[g[x_]], y_]`
	`        is too deep for an assigned rule to be found.`
	
	`Out[14]= $Failed`

$f[\ \dots\ ] := rhs$	downvalue for f
$f/: f[g[\ \dots\ ]][\ \dots\ ] := rhs$	downvalue for f
$g/: f[\ \dots\ , g, \ \dots\ ] := rhs$	upvalue for g
$g/: f[\ \dots\ , g[\ \dots\ ], \ \dots\ ] := rhs$	upvalue for g

Possible positions for symbols in definitions.

As discussed in Section 2.1.2, you can use *Mathematica* symbols as "tags", to indicate the "type" of an expression. For example, complex numbers in *Mathematica* are represented internally in the form Complex[x, y], where the symbol Complex serves as a tag to indicate that the object is a complex number.

Upvalues provide a convenient mechanism for specifying how operations act on objects that are tagged to have a certain type. For example, you might want to introduce a class of abstract mathematical objects of type quat. You can represent each object of this type by a *Mathematica* expression of the form quat[*data*].

In a typical case, you might want quat objects to have special properties with respect to arithmetic operations such as addition and multiplication. You can set up such properties by defining upvalues for quat with respect to Plus and Times.

This defines an upvalue for quat with respect to Plus.	*In[15]:=* **quat[x_] + quat[y_] ^:= quat[x + y]**
The upvalue you have defined is used to simplify this expression.	*In[16]:=* **quat[a] + quat[b] + quat[c]**
	Out[16]= quat[a + b + c]

When you define an upvalue for quat with respect to an operation like Plus, what you are effectively doing is to extend the domain of the Plus operation to include quat objects. You are telling *Mathematica* to use special rules for addition in the case where the things to be added together are quat objects.

In defining addition for quat objects, you could always have a special addition operation, say quatPlus, to which you assign an appropriate downvalue. It is usually much more convenient, however, to use the standard *Mathematica* Plus operation to represent addition, but then to "overload" this operation by specifying special behavior when quat objects are encountered.

You can think of upvalues as a way to implement certain aspects of object-oriented programming. A symbol like quat represents a particular type of object. Then the various upvalues for quat specify "methods" that define how quat objects should behave under certain operations, or on receipt of certain "messages".

■ 2.5.11 Defining Numerical Values

If you make a definition such as f[x_] := *value*, *Mathematica* will use the value you give for any f function it encounters. In some cases, however, you may want to define a value that is to be used specifically when you ask for numerical values.

expr = *value*	define a value to be used whenever possible
N[*expr*] = *value*	define a value to be used for numerical approximation

Defining ordinary and numerical values.

This defines a numerical value for the function f.	*In[1]:=* **N[f[x_]] := Sum[x^-i/i^2, {i, 20}]**
Defining the numerical value does not tell *Mathematica* anything about the ordinary value of f.	*In[2]:=* **f[2] + f[5]** *Out[2]=* f[2] + f[5]
If you ask for a numerical approximation, however, *Mathematica* uses the numerical values you have defined.	*In[3]:=* **N[%]** *Out[3]=* 0.793244

You can define numerical values for both functions and symbols. The numerical values are used by all numerical *Mathematica* functions, including NIntegrate, FindRoot and so on.

N[*expr*] = *value*	define a numerical value to be used when default numerical precision is requested
+ N[*expr*, {*n*, Infinity}] = *value*	define a numerical value to be used when *n*-digit precision and any accuracy is requested

Defining numerical values that depend on numerical precision.

This defines a numerical value for the symbol const, using 4n + 5 terms in the product for n-digit precision.	*In[4]:=* **N[const, {n_, Infinity}] := Product[1 - 2^-i, {i, 2, 4n + 5}]**
Here is the value of const, computed to 30-digit precision using the value you specified.	*In[5]:=* **N[const, 30]** *Out[5]=* 0.577576190173204842557799443858

Mathematica treats numerical values essentially like upvalues. When you define a numerical value for f, *Mathematica* effectively enters your definition as an upvalue for f with respect to the numerical evaluation operation N.

■ 2.5.12 Modifying Built-in Functions

Mathematica allows you to define transformation rules for any expression. You can define such rules not only for functions that you add to *Mathematica*, but also for intrinsic functions that are already built into *Mathematica*. As a result, you can enhance, or modify, the features of built-in *Mathematica* functions.

This capability is powerful, but potentially dangerous. *Mathematica* will always follow the rules you give it. This means that if the rules you give are incorrect, then *Mathematica* will give you incorrect answers.

To avoid the possibility of changing built-in functions by mistake, *Mathematica* "protects" all built-in functions from redefinition. If you want to give a definition for a built-in function, you have to remove the protection first. After you give the definition, you should usually restore the protection, to prevent future mistakes.

Unprotect[*f*]	remove protection
Protect[*f*]	add protection

Protection for functions.

Built-in functions are usually "protected", so you cannot redefine them.

```
In[1]:= Log[7] = 2
Set::write: Tag Log in Log[7] is Protected.
Out[1]= 2
```

This removes protection for Log.

```
In[2]:= Unprotect[Log]
Out[2]= {Log}
```

Now you can give your own definitions for Log. This particular definition is not mathematically correct, but *Mathematica* will still allow you to give it.

```
In[3]:= Log[7] = 2
Out[3]= 2
```

Mathematica will use your definitions whenever it can, whether they are mathematically correct or not.

```
In[4]:= Log[7] + Log[3]
Out[4]= 2 + Log[3]
```

This removes the incorrect definition for Log.

```
In[5]:= Log[7] =.
```

This restores the protection for Log.

```
In[6]:= Protect[Log]
Out[6]= {Log}
```

Definitions you give can override built-in features of *Mathematica*. In general, *Mathematica* tries to use your definitions before it uses built-in definitions.

The rules that are built into *Mathematica* are intended to be appropriate for the broadest range of calculations. In specific cases, however, you may not like what the built-in rules do. In such cases, you can give your own rules to override the ones that are built in.

There is a built-in rule for simplifying Exp[Log[*expr*]].	`In[7]:= Exp[Log[y]]`
	
	`Out[7]= y`

You can give your own rule for Exp[Log[*expr*]], overriding the built-in rule.	`In[8]:= (`
	
	`        Unprotect[Exp] ;`
	`        Exp[Log[expr_]] := explog[expr] ;`
	`        Protect[Exp] ;`
	`        )`

Now your rule is used, rather than the built-in one.	`In[9]:= Exp[Log[y]]`
	
	`Out[9]= explog[y]`

■ 2.5.13 Advanced Topic: Manipulating Value Lists

DownValues[*f*]	give the list of downvalues of *f*
UpValues[*f*]	give the list of upvalues of *f*
DownValues[*f*] = *rules*	set the downvalues of *f*
UpValues[*f*] = *rules*	set the upvalues of *f*

Finding and setting values of symbols.

Mathematica effectively stores all definitions you give as lists of transformation rules. When a particular symbol is encountered, the lists of rules associated with it are tried.

Under most circumstances, you do not need direct access to the actual transformation rules associated with definitions you have given. Instead, you can simply use *lhs* = *rhs* and *lhs* =. to add and remove rules. In some cases, however, you may find it useful to have direct access to the actual rules.

Here is a definition for f.	`In[1]:= f[x_] := x^2`

This gives the explicit rule corresponding to the definition you made for f.	`In[2]:= DownValues[f]`
	
	`Out[2]= {HoldPattern[f[x_]] :> x^2}`

Notice that the rules returned by `DownValues` and `UpValues` are set up so that neither their left- nor right-hand sides get evaluated. The left-hand sides are wrapped in `HoldPattern`, and the rules are delayed, so that the right-hand sides are not immediately evaluated.

As discussed in Section 2.5.6, *Mathematica* tries to order definitions so that more specific ones appear before more general ones. In general, however, there is no unique way to make this ordering, and you may want to choose a different ordering from the one that *Mathematica* chooses by default. You can do this by reordering the list of rules obtained from DownValues or UpValues.

Here are some definitions for the object g.	*In[3]:=* **g[x_ + y_] := gp[x, y] ; g[x_ y_] := gm[x, y]**

This shows the default ordering used for the definitions.	*In[4]:=* **DownValues[g]**
	Out[4]= {HoldPattern[g[x_ + y_]] :→ gp[x, y], HoldPattern[g[x_ y_]] :→ gm[x, y]}

This reverses the order of the definitions for g.	*In[5]:=* **DownValues[g] = Reverse[DownValues[g]]**
	Out[5]= {HoldPattern[g[x_ y_]] :→ gm[x, y], HoldPattern[g[x_ + y_]] :→ gp[x, y]}

2.6 Evaluation of Expressions

■ 2.6.1 Principles of Evaluation

The fundamental operation that *Mathematica* performs is *evaluation*. Whenever you enter an expression, *Mathematica* evaluates the expression, then returns the result.

Evaluation in *Mathematica* works by applying a sequence of definitions. The definitions can either be ones you explicitly entered, or ones that are built into *Mathematica*.

Thus, for example, *Mathematica* evaluates the expression 6 + 7 using a built-in procedure for adding integers. Similarly, *Mathematica* evaluates the algebraic expression x − 3x + 1 using a built-in simplification procedure. If you had made the definition x = 5, then *Mathematica* would use this definition to reduce x − 3x + 1 to −9.

The two most central concepts in *Mathematica* are probably *expressions* and *evaluation*. Section 2.1 discussed how all the different kinds of objects that *Mathematica* handles are represented in a uniform way using expressions. This section describes how all the operations that *Mathematica* can perform can also be viewed in a uniform way as examples of evaluation.

Computation	5 + 6	$\longrightarrow$ 11
Simplification	x − 3x + 1	$\longrightarrow$ 1 − 2x
Execution	x = 5	$\longrightarrow$ 5

Some interpretations of evaluation.

Mathematica is an *infinite evaluation* system. When you enter an expression, *Mathematica* will keep on using definitions it knows until it gets a result to which no definitions apply.

This defines x1 in terms of x2, and then defines x2.	*In[1]:=* **x1 = x2 + 2 ; x2 = 7** *Out[1]=* 7
If you ask for x1, *Mathematica* uses all the definitions it knows to give you a result.	*In[2]:=* **x1** *Out[2]=* 9
Here is a recursive definition in which the factorial function is defined in terms of itself.	*In[3]:=* **fac[1] = 1 ; fac[n_] := n fac[n-1]**
If you ask for fac[10], *Mathematica* will keep on applying the definitions you have given until the result it gets no longer changes.	*In[4]:=* **fac[10]** *Out[4]=* 3628800

When *Mathematica* has used all the definitions it knows, it gives whatever expression it has obtained as the result. Sometimes the result may be an object such as a number. But usually the result is an expression in which some objects are represented in a symbolic form.

Mathematica uses its built-in definitions for simplifying sums, but knows no definitions for f[3], so leaves this in symbolic form.

In[5]:= **f[3] + 4f[3] + 1**

Out[5]= $1 + 5 \, f[3]$

Mathematica follows the principle of applying definitions until the result it gets no longer changes. This means that if you take the final result that *Mathematica* gives, and enter it as *Mathematica* input, you will get back the same result again. (There are some subtle cases discussed in Section 2.6.13 in which this does not occur.)

If you type in a result from *Mathematica*, you get back the same expression again.

In[6]:= **1 + 5 f[3]**

Out[6]= $1 + 5 \, f[3]$

At any given time, *Mathematica* can only use those definitions that it knows at that time. If you add more definitions later, however, *Mathematica* will be able to use these. The results you get from *Mathematica* may change in this case.

Here is a new definition for the function f.

In[7]:= **f[x_] = x^2**

Out[7]= x^2

With the new definition, the results you get can change.

In[8]:= **1 + 5 f[3]**

Out[8]= 46

The simplest examples of evaluation involve using definitions such as f[x_] = x^2 which transform one expression directly into another. But evaluation is also the process used to execute programs written in *Mathematica*. Thus, for example, if you have a procedure consisting of a sequence of *Mathematica* expressions, some perhaps representing conditionals and loops, the execution of this procedure corresponds to the evaluation of these expressions. Sometimes the evaluation process may involve evaluating a particular expression several times, as in a loop.

The expression Print[zzzz] is evaluated three times during the evaluation of the Do expression.

In[9]:= **Do[Print[zzzz], {3}]**

zzzz
zzzz
zzzz

■ 2.6.2 Reducing Expressions to Their Standard Form

The built-in functions in *Mathematica* operate in a wide variety of ways. But many of the mathematical functions share an important approach: they are set up so as to reduce classes of mathematical expressions to standard forms.

The built-in definitions for the Plus function, for example, are set up to write any sum of terms in a standard unparenthesized form. The associativity of addition means that expressions like (a + b) + c, a + (b + c) and a + b + c are all equivalent. But for many purposes it is convenient for all these forms to be reduced to the single standard form a + b + c. The built-in definitions for Plus are set up to do this.

Through the built-in definitions for Plus, this expression is reduced to a standard unparenthesized form.

```
In[1]:= (a + b) + c
Out[1]= a + b + c
```

Whenever *Mathematica* knows that a function is associative, it tries to remove parentheses (or nested invocations of the function) to get the function into a standard "flattened" form.

A function like addition is not only associative, but also commutative, which means that expressions like a + c + b and a + b + c with terms in different orders are equal. Once again, *Mathematica* tries to put all such expressions into a "standard" form. The standard form it chooses is the one in which all the terms are in a definite order, corresponding roughly to alphabetical order.

Mathematica sorts the terms in this sum into a standard order.

```
In[2]:= c + a + b
Out[2]= a + b + c
```

flat (associative)	$f[f[a, b], c]$ is equivalent to $f[a, b, c]$, etc.
orderless (commutative)	$f[b, a]$ is equivalent to $f[a, b]$, etc.

Two important properties that *Mathematica* uses in reducing certain functions to standard form.

There are several reasons to try to put expressions into standard forms. The most important is that if two expressions are really in standard form, it is obvious whether or not they are equal.

When the two sums are put into standard order, they are immediately seen to be equal, so that two f's cancel, leaving the result 0.

```
In[3]:= f[a + c + b] - f[c + a + b]
Out[3]= 0
```

You could imagine finding out whether a + c + b was equal to c + a + b by testing all possible orderings of each sum. It is clear that simply reducing both sums to standard form is a much more efficient procedure.

One might think that *Mathematica* should somehow automatically reduce *all* mathematical expressions to a single standard canonical form. With all but the simplest kinds of expressions, however, it is quite easy to see that you do not want the *same* standard form for all purposes.

For polynomials, for example, there are two obvious standard forms, which are good for different purposes. The first standard form for a polynomial is a simple sum of terms, as would be generated in *Mathematica* by applying the function Expand. This standard form is most appropriate if you need to add and subtract polynomials.

There is, however, another possible standard form that you can use for polynomials. By applying Factor, you can write any polynomial as a product of irreducible factors. This canonical form is useful if you want to do operations like division.

Expanded and factored forms are in a sense both equally good standard forms for polynomials. Which one you decide to use simply depends on what you want to use it for. As a result, *Mathematica* does not automatically put polynomials into one of these two forms. Instead, it gives you functions like Expand and Factor that allow you explicitly to put polynomials in whatever form you want.

Here is a list of two polynomials that are mathematically equal.	*In[4]:=* **t = {x^2 - 1, (x + 1)(x - 1)}**
	Out[4]= $\{-1 + x^2, (-1 + x)(1 + x)\}$
You can write both of them in expanded form just by applying Expand. In this form, the equality of the polynomials is obvious.	*In[5]:=* **Expand[t]**
	Out[5]= $\{-1 + x^2, -1 + x^2\}$
You can also see that the polynomials are equal by writing them both in factored form.	*In[6]:=* **Factor[t]**
	Out[6]= $\{(-1 + x)(1 + x), (-1 + x)(1 + x)\}$

Although it is clear that you do not always want expressions reduced to the *same* standard form, you may wonder whether it is at least *possible* to reduce all expressions to *some* standard form.

There is a basic result in the mathematical theory of computation which shows that this is, in fact, not always possible. You cannot guarantee that any finite sequence of transformations will take any two arbitrarily chosen expressions to a standard form.

In a sense, this is not particularly surprising. If you could in fact reduce all mathematical expressions to a standard form, then it would be quite easy to tell whether any two expressions were equal. The fact that so many of the difficult problems of mathematics can be stated as questions about the equality of expressions suggests that this can in fact be difficult.

■ 2.6.3 Attributes

Definitions such as f[x_] = x^2 specify *values* for functions. Sometimes, however, you need to specify general properties of functions, without necessarily giving explicit values.

Mathematica provides a selection of *attributes* that you can use to specify various properties of functions. For example, you can use the attribute Flat to specify that a particular function is "flat", so that nested invocations are automatically flattened, and it behaves as if it were associative.

This assigns the attribute Flat to the function f.

In[1]:= **SetAttributes[f, Flat]**

Now f behaves as a flat, or associative, function, so that nested invocations are automatically flattened.

In[2]:= **f[f[a, b], c]**

Out[2]= f[a, b, c]

Attributes like **Flat** can affect not only evaluation, but also operations such as pattern matching. If you give definitions or transformation rules for a function, you must be sure to have specified the attributes of the function first.

Here is a definition for the flat function f.

In[3]:= **f[x_, x_] := f[x]**

Because f is flat, the definition is automatically applied to every subsequence of arguments.

In[4]:= **f[a, a, a, b, b, b, c, c]**

Out[4]= f[a, b, c]

Attributes[*f*]	give the attributes of *f*
Attributes[*f*] = {*attr₁*, *attr₂*, ... }	set the attributes of *f*
Attributes[*f*] = {}	set *f* to have no attributes
SetAttributes[*f*, *attr*]	add *attr* to the attributes of *f*
ClearAttributes[*f*, *attr*]	remove *attr* from the attributes of *f*

Manipulating attributes of symbols.

This shows the attributes assigned to f.

In[5]:= **Attributes[f]**

Out[5]= {Flat}

This removes the attributes assigned to f.

In[6]:= **Attributes[f] = { }**

Out[6]= {}

Orderless	orderless, commutative function (arguments are sorted into standard order)
Flat	flat, associative function (arguments are "flattened out")
OneIdentity	$f[f[a]]$, etc. are equivalent to a for pattern matching
Listable	f is automatically "threaded" over lists that appear as arguments (e.g., $f[\{a,b\}]$ becomes $\{f[a],\ f[b]\}$)
Constant	all derivatives of f are zero
NumericFunction	f is assumed to have a numerical value when its arguments are numeric quantities
Protected	values of f cannot be changed
Locked	attributes of f cannot be changed
ReadProtected	values of f cannot be read
HoldFirst	the first argument of f is not evaluated
HoldRest	all but the first argument of f is not evaluated
HoldAll	none of the arguments of f are evaluated
HoldAllComplete	the arguments of f are treated as completely inert
NHoldFirst	the first argument of f is not affected by N
NHoldRest	all but the first argument of f is not affected by N
NHoldAll	none of the arguments of f are affected by N
SequenceHold	Sequence objects appearing in the arguments of f are not flattened out
Temporary	f is a local variable, removed when no longer used
Stub	Needs is automatically called if f is ever explicitly input

The complete list of attributes for symbols in *Mathematica*.

Here are the attributes for the built-in function Plus.

```
In[7]:= Attributes[Plus]

Out[7]= {Flat, Listable, NumericFunction,
         OneIdentity, Orderless, Protected}
```

An important attribute assigned to built-in mathematical functions in *Mathematica* is the attribute Listable. This attribute specifies that a function should automatically be distributed or "threaded" over lists that appear as its arguments. This means that the function effectively gets applied separately to each element in any lists that appear as its arguments.

The built-in Log function is Listable.	*In[8]:=* **Log[{5, 8, 11}]**
	Out[8]= {Log[5], Log[8], Log[11]}
This defines the function p to be listable.	*In[9]:=* **SetAttributes[p, Listable]**
Now p is automatically threaded over lists that appear as its arguments.	*In[10]:=* **p[{a, b, c}, d]**
	Out[10]= {p[a, d], p[b, d], p[c, d]}

Many of the attributes you can assign to functions in *Mathematica* directly affect the evaluation of those functions. Some attributes, however, affect only other aspects of the treatment of functions. For example, the attribute OneIdentity affects only pattern matching, as discussed in Section 2.3.7. Similarly, the attribute Constant is only relevant in differentiation, and operations that rely on differentiation.

The Protected attribute affects assignments. *Mathematica* does not allow you to make any definition associated with a symbol that carries this attribute. The functions Protect and Unprotect discussed in Section 2.5.12 can be used as alternatives to SetAttributes and ClearAttributes to set and clear this attribute. As discussed in Section 2.5.12 most built-in *Mathematica* objects are initially protected so that you do not make definitions for them by mistake.

Here is a definition for the function g.	*In[11]:=* **g[x_] = x + 1**
	Out[11]= 1 + x
This sets the Protected attribute for g.	*In[12]:=* **Protect[g]**
	Out[12]= {g}
Now you cannot modify the definition of g.	*In[13]:=* **g[x_] = x**
	Set::write: Tag g in g[x_] is Protected.
	Out[13]= x

You can usually see the definitions you have made for a particular symbol by typing ?*f*, or by using a variety of built-in *Mathematica* functions. However, if you set the attribute ReadProtected, *Mathematica* will not allow you to look at the definition of a particular symbol. It will nevertheless continue to use the definitions in performing evaluation.

Although you cannot modify it, you can still look at the definition of g.	*In[14]:=* **?g**
	Global`g
	Attributes[g] = {Protected}
	g[x_] = 1 + x
This sets the ReadProtected attribute for g.	*In[15]:=* **SetAttributes[g, ReadProtected]**
Now you can no longer read the definition of g.	*In[16]:=* **?g**
	Global`g
	Attributes[g] = {Protected, ReadProtected}

Functions like `SetAttributes` and `ClearAttributes` usually allow you to modify the attributes of a symbol in any way. However, if you once set the `Locked` attribute on a symbol, then *Mathematica* will not allow you to modify the attributes of that symbol for the remainder of your *Mathematica* session. Using the `Locked` attribute in addition to `Protected` or `ReadProtected`, you can arrange for it to be impossible for users to modify or read definitions.

`Clear[f]`	remove values for *f*, but not attributes
`ClearAll[f]`	remove both values and attributes of *f*

Clearing values and attributes.

This clears values and attributes of p which was given attribute `Listable` above.	*In[17]:=* `ClearAll[p]`
Now p is no longer listable.	*In[18]:=* `p[{a, b, c}, d]`
	Out[18]= p[{a, b, c}, d]

By defining attributes for a function you specify properties that *Mathematica* should assume whenever that function appears. Often, however, you want to assume the properties only in a particular instance. In such cases, you will be better off not to use attributes, but instead to call a particular function to implement the transformation associated with the attributes.

By explicitly calling `Thread`, you can implement the transformation that would be done automatically if p were listable.	*In[19]:=* `Thread[p[{a, b, c}, d]]`
	Out[19]= {p[a, d], p[b, d], p[c, d]}

`Orderless`	`Sort[`*f*`[`*args*`]]`
`Flat`	`Flatten[`*f*`[`*args*`]]`
`Listable`	`Thread[`*f*`[`*args*`]]`
`Constant`	`Dt[`*expr*`, Constants->`*f*`]`

Functions that perform transformations associated with some attributes.

Attributes in *Mathematica* can only be permanently defined for single symbols. However, *Mathematica* also allows you to set up pure functions which behave as if they carry attributes.

> `Function[`*vars*`,` *body*`, {`*attr₁*`, ... }]`   a pure function with attributes *attr₁*, ...

Pure functions with attributes.

| This pure function applies p to the whole list. | `In[20]:= Function[{x}, p[x]] [{a, b, c}]` |
| | `Out[20]= p[{a, b, c}]` |

| By adding the attribute Listable, the function gets distributed over the elements of the list before applying p. | `In[21]:= Function[{x}, p[x], {Listable}] [{a, b, c}]` |
| | `Out[21]= {p[a], p[b], p[c]}` |

■ 2.6.4 The Standard Evaluation Procedure

This section describes the standard procedure used by *Mathematica* to evaluate expressions. This procedure is the one followed for most kinds of expressions. There are however some kinds of expressions, such as those used to represent *Mathematica* programs and control structures, which are evaluated in a non-standard way. The treatment of such expressions is discussed in the sections that follow this one.

In the standard evaluation procedure, *Mathematica* first evaluates the head of an expression, and then evaluates each element of the expressions. These elements are in general themselves expressions, to which the same evaluation procedure is recursively applied.

The three Print functions are evaluated in turn, each printing its argument, then returning the value Null.	`In[1]:= {Print[1], Print[2], Print[3]}`
	1
	2
	3
	`Out[1]= {Null, Null, Null}`

| This assigns the symbol ps to be Plus. | `In[2]:= ps = Plus` |
| | `Out[2]= Plus` |

| The head ps is evaluated first, so this expression behaves just like a sum of terms. | `In[3]:= ps[ps[a, b], c]` |
| | `Out[3]= a + b + c` |

As soon as *Mathematica* has evaluated the head of an expression, it sees whether the head is a symbol that has attributes. If the symbol has the attributes `Orderless`, `Flat` or `Listable`, then immediately after evaluating the elements of the expression *Mathematica* performs the transformations associated with these attributes.

The next step in the standard evaluation procedure is to use definitions that *Mathematica* knows for the expression it is evaluating. *Mathematica* first tries to use definitions that you have made, and if there are none that apply, it tries built-in definitions.

If *Mathematica* finds a definition that applies, it performs the corresponding transformation on the expression. The result is another expression, which must then in turn be evaluated according to the standard evaluation procedure.

- Evaluate the head of the expression.

- Evaluate each element in turn.

- Apply transformations associated with the attributes Orderless, Listable and Flat.

- Apply any definitions that you have given.

- Apply any built-in definitions.

- Evaluate the result.

The standard evaluation procedure.

As discussed in Section 2.6.1, *Mathematica* follows the principle that each expression is evaluated until no further definitions apply. This means that *Mathematica* must continue re-evaluating results until it gets an expression which remains unchanged through the evaluation procedure.

Here is an example that shows how the standard evaluation procedure works on a simple expression. We assume that a = 7.

2 a x + a^2 + 1	here is the original expression
Plus[Times[2, a, x], Power[a, 2], 1]	this is the internal form
Times[2, a, x]	this is evaluated first
Times[2, 7, x]	a is evaluated to give 7
Times[14, x]	built-in definitions for Times give this result
Power[a, 2]	this is evaluated next
Power[7, 2]	here is the result after evaluating a
49	built-in definitions for Power give this result
Plus[Times[14, x], 49, 1]	here is the result after the arguments of Plus have been evaluated
Plus[50, Times[14, x]]	built-in definitions for Plus give this result
50 + 14 x	the result is printed like this

A simple example of evaluation in *Mathematica*.

Mathematica provides various ways to "trace" the evaluation process, as discussed in Section 2.6.11. The function Trace[*expr*] gives a nested list showing each subexpression generated during evaluation. (Note that the standard evaluation traverses the expression tree in a depth-first way, so that the smallest subparts of the expression appear first in the results of Trace.)

First set a to 7.	*In[4]:=* **a = 7**
	Out[4]= 7

This gives a nested list of all the subexpressions generated during the evaluation of the expression.	*In[5]:=* **Trace[2 a x + a^2 + 1]**
	Out[5]= {{{a, 7}, 27 x, 14 x},
	{{a, 7}, 7^2, 49}, 14 x + 49 + 1, 50 + 14 x}

The order in which *Mathematica* applies different kinds of definitions is important. The fact that *Mathematica* applies definitions you have given before it applies built-in definitions means that you can give definitions which override the built-in ones, as discussed in Section 2.5.12.

This expression is evaluated using the built-in definition for ArcSin.	*In[6]:=* **ArcSin[1]**
	Out[6]= $\dfrac{\pi}{2}$

You can give your own definitions for ArcSin. You need to remove the protection attribute first.	*In[7]:=* **Unprotect[ArcSin]; ArcSin[1] = 5Pi/2;**

Your definition is used before the one that is built in.	*In[8]:=* **ArcSin[1]**
	Out[8]= $\dfrac{5\pi}{2}$

As discussed in Section 2.5.10, you can associate definitions with symbols either as upvalues or downvalues. *Mathematica* always tries upvalue definitions before downvalue ones.

If you have an expression like *f*[*g*[*x*]], there are in general two sets of definitions that could apply: downvalues associated with *f*, and upvalues associated with *g*. *Mathematica* tries the definitions associated with *g* before those associated with *f*.

This ordering follows the general strategy of trying specific definitions before more general ones. By applying upvalues associated with arguments before applying downvalues associated with a function, *Mathematica* allows you to make definitions for special arguments which override the general definitions for the function with any arguments.

This defines a rule for f[g[x_]], to be associated with f.	*In[9]:=* **f/: f[g[x_]] := frule[x]**

This defines a rule for f[g[x_]], to be associated with g.	*In[10]:=* **g/: f[g[x_]] := grule[x]**

The rule associated with g is tried before the rule associated with f.	*In[11]:=* **f[g[2]]**
	Out[11]= grule[2]

If you remove rules associated with g, the rule associated with f is used.	*In[12]:=* **Clear[g] ; f[g[1]]**
	Out[12]= frule[1]

> ■ Definitions associated with g are applied before definitions associated with f in the expression $f[g[x]]$.

The order in which definitions are applied.

Most functions such as Plus that are built into *Mathematica* have downvalues. There are, however, some objects in *Mathematica* which have built-in upvalues. For example, SeriesData objects, which represent power series, have built-in upvalues with respect to various mathematical operations.

For an expression like $f[g[x]]$, the complete sequence of definitions that are tried in the standard evaluation procedure is:

■ Definitions you have given associated with g;

■ Built-in definitions associated with g;

■ Definitions you have given associated with f;

■ Built-in definitions associated with f.

The fact that upvalues are used before downvalues is important in many situations. In a typical case, you might want to define an operation such as composition. If you give upvalues for various objects with respect to composition, these upvalues will be used whenever such objects appear. However, you can also give a general procedure for composition, to be used if no special objects are present. You can give this procedure as a downvalue for composition. Since downvalues are tried after upvalues, the general procedure will be used only if no objects with upvalues are present.

Here is a definition associated with q for composition of "q objects".	*In[13]:=* **q/: comp[q[x_], q[y_]] := qcomp[x, y]**
Here is a general rule for composition, associated with comp.	*In[14]:=* **comp[f_[x_], f_[y_]] := gencomp[f, x, y]**
If you compose two q objects, the rule associated with q is used.	*In[15]:=* **comp[q[1], q[2]]**
	Out[15]= qcomp[1, 2]
If you compose r objects, the general rule associated with comp is used.	*In[16]:=* **comp[r[1], r[2]]**
	Out[16]= gencomp[r, 1, 2]

In general, there can be several objects that have upvalues in a particular expression. *Mathematica* first looks at the head of the expression, and tries any upvalues associated with it. Then it successively looks at each element of the expression, trying any upvalues that exist. *Mathematica* performs this procedure first for upvalues that you have explicitly defined, and then for upvalues that are built in.

The procedure means that in a sequence of elements, upvalues associated with earlier elements take precedence over those associated with later elements.

This defines an upvalue for p with respect to c.	*In[17]:=* **p/: c[l___, p[x_], r___] := cp[x, {l, r}]**
This defines an upvalue for q.	*In[18]:=* **q/: c[l___, q[x_], r___] := cq[x, {l, r}]**
Which upvalue is used depends on which occurs first in the sequence of arguments to c.	*In[19]:=* **{c[p[1], q[2]], c[q[1], p[2]]}** *Out[19]=* **{cp[1, {q[2]}], cq[1, {p[2]}]}**

■ 2.6.5 Non-Standard Evaluation

While most built-in *Mathematica* functions follow the standard evaluation procedure, some important ones do not. For example, most of the *Mathematica* functions associated with the construction and execution of programs use non-standard evaluation procedures. In typical cases, the functions either never evaluate some of their arguments, or do so in a special way under their own control.

$x = y$	do not evaluate the left-hand side
If[p, a, b]	evaluate a if p is True, and b if it is False
Do[*expr*, {n}]	evaluate *expr* n times
Plot[f, {x, … }]	evaluate f with a sequence of numerical values for x
Function[{x}, *body*]	do not evaluate until the function is applied

Some functions that use non-standard evaluation procedures.

When you give a definition such as a = 1, *Mathematica* does not evaluate the a that appears on the left-hand side. You can see that there would be trouble if the a was evaluated. The reason is that if you had previously set a = 7, then evaluating a in the definition a = 1 would put the definition into the nonsensical form 7 = 1.

In the standard evaluation procedure, each argument of a function is evaluated in turn. This is prevented by setting the attributes HoldFirst, HoldRest and HoldAll. These attributes make *Mathematica* "hold" particular arguments in an unevaluated form.

HoldFirst	do not evaluate the first argument
HoldRest	evaluate only the first argument
HoldAll	evaluate none of the arguments

Attributes for holding function arguments in unevaluated form.

With the standard evaluation procedure, all arguments to a function are evaluated.

```
In[1]:= f[1 + 1, 2 + 4]
Out[1]= f[2, 6]
```

This assigns the attribute HoldFirst to h.

```
In[2]:= SetAttributes[h, HoldFirst]
```

The first argument to h is now held in an unevaluated form.

```
In[3]:= h[1 + 1, 2 + 4]
Out[3]= h[1 + 1, 6]
```

When you use the first argument to h like this, it will get evaluated.

```
In[4]:= h[1 + 1, 2 + 4] /. h[x_, y_] -> x^y
Out[4]= 64
```

Built-in functions like Set carry attributes such as HoldFirst.

```
In[5]:= Attributes[Set]
Out[5]= {HoldFirst, Protected, SequenceHold}
```

Even though a function may have attributes which specify that it should hold certain arguments unevaluated, you can always explicitly tell *Mathematica* to evaluate those arguments by giving the arguments in the form Evaluate[*arg*].

Evaluate effectively overrides the HoldFirst attribute, and causes the first argument to be evaluated.

```
In[6]:= h[Evaluate[1 + 1], 2 + 4]
Out[6]= h[2, 6]
```

| *f*[Evaluate[*arg*]] | evaluate *arg* immediately, even though attributes of *f* may specify that it should be held |

Forcing the evaluation of function arguments.

By holding its arguments, a function can control when those arguments are evaluated. By using Evaluate, you can force the arguments to be evaluated immediately, rather than being evaluated under the control of the function. This capability is useful in a number of circumstances.

One example discussed on page 132 occurs when plotting graphs of expressions. The *Mathematica* Plot function holds unevaluated the expression you are going to plot, then evaluates it at a sequence of numerical positions. In some cases, you may instead want to evaluate the expression immediately, and have Plot work with the evaluated form. For example, if you want to plot a list of functions generated by `Table`, then you will want the `Table` operation done immediately, rather than being done every time a point is to be plotted.

Evaluate causes the list of functions to be constructed immediately, rather than being constructed at each value of x chosen by Plot.

```
In[7]:= Plot[
            Evaluate[Table[Sin[n x], {n, 1, 3}]],
                                {x, 0, 2Pi} ]
```

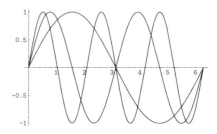

There are a number of built-in *Mathematica* functions which, like `Plot`, are set up to hold some of their arguments. You can always override this behavior using `Evaluate`.

The *Mathematica* `Set` function holds its first argument, so the symbol a is not evaluated in this case.

```
In[8]:= a = b
Out[8]= b
```

You can make `Set` evaluate its first argument using `Evaluate`. In this case, the result is the object which is the *value* of a, namely b is set to 6.

```
In[9]:= Evaluate[a] = 6
Out[9]= 6
```

b has now been set to 6.

```
In[10]:= b
Out[10]= 6
```

In most cases, you want all expressions you give to *Mathematica* to be evaluated. Sometimes, however, you may want to prevent the evaluation of certain expressions. For example, if you want to manipulate pieces of a *Mathematica* program symbolically, then you must prevent those pieces from being evaluated while you are manipulating them.

You can use the functions `Hold` and `HoldForm` to keep expressions unevaluated. These functions work simply by carrying the attribute `HoldAll`, which prevents their arguments from being evaluated. The functions provide "wrappers" inside which expressions remain unevaluated.

The difference between `Hold[`*expr*`]` and `HoldForm[`*expr*`]` is that in standard *Mathematica* output format, `Hold` is printed explicitly, while `HoldForm` is not. If you look at the full internal *Mathematica* form, you can however see both functions.

Hold maintains expressions in an unevaluated form.

```
In[11]:= Hold[1 + 1]
Out[11]= Hold[1 + 1]
```

HoldForm also keeps expressions unevaluated, but is invisible in standard *Mathematica* output format.

In[12]:= **HoldForm[1 + 1]**

Out[12]= 1 + 1

HoldForm is still present internally.

In[13]:= **FullForm[%]**

Out[13]//FullForm= HoldForm[Plus[1, 1]]

The function ReleaseHold removes Hold and HoldForm, so the expressions they contain get evaluated.

In[14]:= **ReleaseHold[%]**

Out[14]= 2

Hold[*expr*]	keep *expr* unevaluated
HoldComplete[*expr*]	keep *expr* unevaluated and prevent upvalues associated with *expr* from being used
HoldForm[*expr*]	keep *expr* unevaluated, and print without HoldForm
ReleaseHold[*expr*]	remove Hold and HoldForm in *expr*
Extract[*expr*, *index*, Hold]	get a part of *expr*, wrapping it with Hold to prevent evaluation
ReplacePart[*expr*, Hold[*value*], *index*, 1]	
	replace part of *expr*, extracting *value* without evaluating it

Functions for handling unevaluated expressions.

Parts of expressions are usually evaluated as soon as you extract them.

In[15]:= **Extract[Hold[1 + 1, 2 + 3], 2]**

Out[15]= 5

This extracts a part and immediately wraps it with Hold, so it does not get evaluated.

In[16]:= **Extract[Hold[1 + 1, 2 + 3], 2, Hold]**

Out[16]= Hold[2 + 3]

The last argument of 1 tells ReplacePart to extract the first part of Hold[7 + 8] before inserting it.

In[17]:= **ReplacePart[Hold[1 + 1, 2 + 3], Hold[7 + 8], 2, 1]**

Out[17]= Hold[1 + 1, 7 + 8]

f[... , Unevaluated[*expr*], ...]	give *expr* unevaluated as an argument to *f*

Temporary prevention of argument evaluation.

1 + 1 evaluates to 2, and Length[2] gives 0.

In[18]:= **Length[1 + 1]**

Out[18]= 0

This gives the unevaluated form 1 + 1
as the argument of Length.

In[19]:= **Length[Unevaluated[1 + 1]]**

Out[19]= 2

Unevaluated[*expr*] effectively works by temporarily giving a function an attribute like HoldFirst, and then supplying *expr* as an argument to the function.

SequenceHold	do not flatten out Sequence objects that appear as arguments
HoldAllComplete	treat all arguments as completely inert

Attributes for preventing other aspects of evaluation.

By setting the attribute HoldAll, you can prevent *Mathematica* from evaluating the arguments of a function. But even with this attribute set, *Mathematica* will still do some transformations on the arguments. By setting SequenceHold you can prevent it from flattening out Sequence objects that appear in the arguments. And by setting HoldAllComplete you can also inhibit the stripping of Unevaluated, and prevent *Mathematica* from using any upvalues it finds associated with the arguments.

■ 2.6.6 Evaluation in Patterns, Rules and Definitions

There are a number of important interactions in *Mathematica* between evaluation and pattern matching. The first observation is that pattern matching is usually done on expressions that have already been at least partly evaluated. As a result, it is usually appropriate that the patterns to which these expressions are matched should themselves be evaluated.

The fact that the pattern is evaluated means that it matches the expression given.

In[1]:= **f[k^2] /. f[x_^(1 + 1)] -> p[x]**

Out[1]= p[k]

The right-hand side of the /; condition is not evaluated until it is used during pattern matching.

In[2]:= **f[{a, b}] /. f[list_ /; Length[list] > 1] -> list^2**

Out[2]= {a^2, b^2}

There are some cases, however, where you may want to keep all or part of a pattern unevaluated. You can do this by wrapping the parts you do not want to evaluate with HoldPattern. In general, whenever HoldPattern[*patt*] appears within a pattern, this form is taken to be equivalent to *patt* for the purpose of pattern matching, but the expression *patt* is maintained unevaluated.

HoldPattern[*patt*]	equivalent to *patt* for pattern matching, with *patt* kept unevaluated

Preventing evaluation in patterns.

One application for `HoldPattern` is in specifying patterns which can apply to unevaluated expressions, or expressions held in an unevaluated form.

`HoldPattern` keeps the 1 + 1 from being evaluated, and allows it to match the 1 + 1 on the left-hand side of the /. operator.	`In[3]:= Hold[u[1 + 1]] /. HoldPattern[1 + 1] -> x`
	
	`Out[3]= Hold[u[x]]`

Notice that while functions like `Hold` prevent evaluation of expressions, they do not affect the manipulation of parts of those expressions with /. and other operators.

This defines values for r whenever its argument is not an atomic object.	`In[4]:= r[x_] := x^2 /; !AtomQ[x]`

According to the definition, expressions like r[3] are left unchanged.	`In[5]:= r[3]`
	
	`Out[5]= r[3]`

However, the pattern r[x_] is transformed according to the definition for r.	`In[6]:= r[x_]` `Out[6]= x_`^{2}

You need to wrap `HoldPattern` around r[x_] to prevent it from being evaluated.	`In[7]:= {r[3], r[5]} /. HoldPattern[r[x_]] -> x`
	
	`Out[7]= {3, 5}`

As illustrated above, the left-hand sides of transformation rules such as *lhs -> rhs* are usually evaluated immediately, since the rules are usually applied to expressions which have already been evaluated. The right-hand side of *lhs -> rhs* is also evaluated immediately. With the delayed rule *lhs :> rhs*, however, the expression *rhs* is not evaluated.

The right-hand side is evaluated immediately in -> but not :> rules.	`In[8]:= {{x -> 1 + 1}, {x :> 1 + 1}}`
	
	`Out[8]= {{x → 2}, {x :→ 1 + 1}}`

Here are the results of applying the rules. The right-hand side of the :> rule gets inserted inside the `Hold` without evaluation.	`In[9]:= {x^2, Hold[x]} /. %`
	
	`Out[9]= {{4, Hold[2]}, {4, Hold[1 + 1]}}`

lhs -> rhs	evaluate both *lhs* and *rhs*
lhs :> rhs	evaluate *lhs* but not *rhs*

Evaluation in transformation rules.

While the left-hand sides of transformation rules are usually evaluated, the left-hand sides of definitions are usually not. The reason for the difference is as follows. Transformation rules are typically applied using /. to expressions that have already been evaluated. Definitions, however, are used during the evaluation of expressions, and are applied to expressions that have not yet been completely evaluated. To work on such expressions, the left-hand sides of definitions must be maintained in a form that is at least partially unevaluated.

Definitions for symbols are the simplest case. As discussed in the previous section, a symbol on the left-hand side of a definition such as $x = value$ is not evaluated. If x had previously been assigned a value y, then if the left-hand side of $x = value$ were evaluated, it would turn into the quite unrelated definition $y = value$.

Here is a definition. The symbol on the left-hand side is not evaluated.	*In[10]:=* **k = w[3]**
	Out[10]= w[3]
This redefines the symbol.	*In[11]:=* **k = w[4]**
	Out[11]= w[4]
If you evaluate the left-hand side, then you define not the symbol k, but the *value* w[4] of the symbol k.	*In[12]:=* **Evaluate[k] = w[5]**
	Out[12]= w[5]
Now w[4] has value w[5].	*In[13]:=* **w[4]**
	Out[13]= w[5]

Although individual symbols that appear on the left-hand sides of definitions are not evaluated, more complicated expressions are partially evaluated. In an expression such as $f[args]$ on the left-hand side of a definition, the *args* are evaluated.

The 1 + 1 is evaluated, so that a value is defined for g[2].	*In[14]:=* **g[1 + 1] = 5**
	Out[14]= 5
This shows the value defined for g.	*In[15]:=* **?g**
	Global`g
	g[2] = 5

You can see why the arguments of a function that appears on the left-hand side of a definition must be evaluated by considering how the definition is used during the evaluation of an expression. As discussed in Section 2.6.1, when *Mathematica* evaluates a function, it first evaluates each of the arguments, then tries to find definitions for the function. As a result, by the time *Mathematica* applies any definition you have given for a function, the arguments of the function must already have been evaluated. An exception to this occurs when the function in question has attributes which specify that it should hold some of its arguments unevaluated.

symbol = *value*	*symbol* is not evaluated; *value* is evaluated
symbol := *value*	neither *symbol* nor *value* is evaluated
f[*args*] = *value*	*args* are evaluated; left-hand side as a whole is not
f[HoldPattern[*arg*]] = *value*	*f*[*arg*] is assigned, without evaluating *arg*
Evaluate[*lhs*] = *value*	left-hand side is evaluated completely

Evaluation in definitions.

While in most cases it is appropriate for the arguments of a function that appears on the left-hand side of a definition to be evaluated, there are some situations in which you do not want this to happen. In such cases, you can wrap HoldPattern around the parts that you do not want to be evaluated.

■ 2.6.7 Evaluation in Iteration Functions

The built-in *Mathematica* iteration functions such as Table and Sum, as well as Plot and Plot3D, evaluate their arguments in a slightly special way.

When evaluating an expression like Table[*f*, {*i*, *imax*}], the first step, as discussed on page 390, is to make the value of *i* local. Next, the limit *imax* in the iterator specification is evaluated. The expression *f* is maintained in an unevaluated form, but is repeatedly evaluated as a succession of values are assigned to *i*. When this is finished, the global value of *i* is restored.

The function Random[ ] is evaluated four separate times here, so four different pseudorandom numbers are generated.	*In[1]:=* **Table[Random[ ], {4}]** *Out[1]=* {0.0560708, 0.6303, 0.359894, 0.871377}
This evaluates Random[ ] before feeding it to Table. The result is a list of four identical numbers.	*In[2]:=* **Table[Evaluate[Random[ ]], {4}]** *Out[2]=* {0.858645, 0.858645, 0.858645, 0.858645}

In most cases, it is convenient for the function *f* in an expression like Table[*f*, {*i*, *imax*}] to be maintained in an unevaluated form until specific values have been assigned to *i*. This is true in particular if a complete symbolic form for *f* valid for any *i* cannot be found.

This defines fac to give the factorial when it has an integer argument, and to give NaN (standing for "Not a Number") otherwise.	*In[3]:=* **fac[n_Integer] := n! ; fac[x_] := NaN**
In this form, fac[i] is not evaluated until an explicit integer value has been assigned to i.	*In[4]:=* **Table[fac[i], {i, 5}]** *Out[4]=* {1, 2, 6, 24, 120}

Using Evaluate forces fac[i] to be evaluated with i left as a symbolic object.

In[5]:= **Table[Evaluate[fac[i]], {i, 5}]**

Out[5]= {NaN, NaN, NaN, NaN, NaN}

In cases where a complete symbolic form for *f* with arbitrary *i* in expressions such as Table[*f*, {*i*, *imax*}] *can* be found, it is often more efficient to compute this form first, and then feed it to Table. You can do this using Table[Evaluate[*f*], {*i*, *imax*}].

The Sum in this case is evaluated separately for each value of i.

In[6]:= **Table[Sum[i^k, {k, 4}], {i, 8}]**

Out[6]= {4, 30, 120, 340, 780, 1554, 2800, 4680}

It is however possible to get a symbolic formula for the sum, valid for any value of i.

In[7]:= **Sum[i^k, {k, 4}]**

Out[7]= $i + i^2 + i^3 + i^4$

By inserting Evaluate, you tell *Mathematica* first to evaluate the sum symbolically, then to iterate over i.

In[8]:= **Table[Evaluate[Sum[i^k, {k, 4}]], {i, 8}]**

Out[8]= {4, 30, 120, 340, 780, 1554, 2800, 4680}

Table[*f*, {*i*, *imax*}]	keep *f* unevaluated until specific values are assigned to *i*
Table[Evaluate[*f*], {*i*, *imax*}]	evaluate *f* first with *i* left symbolic

Evaluation in iteration functions.

As discussed on page 132, it is convenient to use Evaluate when you plot a graph of a function or a list of functions. This causes the symbolic form of the function or list to be found first, before the iteration begins.

■ 2.6.8 Conditionals

Mathematica provides various ways to set up *conditionals*, which specify that particular expressions should be evaluated only if certain conditions hold.

lhs := *rhs* /; *test*	use the definition only if *test* evaluates to True
If[*test*, *then*, *else*]	evaluate *then* if *test* is True, and *else* if it is False
Which[*test*$_1$, *value*$_1$, *test*$_2$, ...]	evaluate the *test*$_i$ in turn, giving the value associated with the first one that is True
Switch[*expr*, *form*$_1$, *value*$_1$, *form*$_2$, ...]	compare *expr* with each of the *form*$_i$, giving the value associated with the first form it matches
Switch[*expr*, *form*$_1$, *value*$_1$, *form*$_2$, ... , _, *def*]	use *def* as a default value

Conditional constructs.

The test gives False, so the *"else"* expression y is returned.	In[1]:= If[7 > 8, x, y] Out[1]= y
Only the *"else"* expression is evaluated in this case.	In[2]:= If[7 > 8, Print[x], Print[y]] y

When you write programs in *Mathematica*, you will often have a choice between making a single definition whose right-hand side involves several branches controlled by If functions, or making several definitions, each controlled by an appropriate /; condition. By using several definitions, you can often produce programs that are both clearer, and easier to modify.

This defines a step function, with value 1 for x > 0, and –1 otherwise.	In[3]:= f[x_] := If[x > 0, 1, -1]
This defines the positive part of the step function using a /; condition.	In[4]:= g[x_] := 1 /; x > 0
Here is the negative part of the step function.	In[5]:= g[x_] := -1 /; x <= 0
This shows the complete definition using /; conditions.	In[6]:= ?g Global`g g[x_] := 1 /; x > 0 g[x_] := -1 /; x <= 0

The function If provides a way to choose between two alternatives. Often, however, there will be more than two alternatives. One way to handle this is to use a nested set of If functions. Usually, however, it is instead better to use functions like Which and Switch.

This defines a function with three regions. Using `True` as the third test makes this the default case.	`In[7]:= h[x_] := Which[x < 0, x^2, x > 5, x^3, True, 0]`
This uses the first case in the `Which`.	`In[8]:= h[-5]` `Out[8]= 25`
This uses the third case.	`In[9]:= h[2]` `Out[9]= 0`
This defines a function that depends on the values of its argument modulo 3.	`In[10]:= r[x_] := Switch[Mod[x, 3], 0, a, 1, b, 2, c]`
`Mod[7, 3]` is 1, so this uses the second case in the `Switch`.	`In[11]:= r[7]` `Out[11]= b`
17 matches neither 0 nor 1, but does match `_`.	`In[12]:= Switch[17, 0, a, 1, b, _, q]` `Out[12]= q`

An important point about symbolic systems such as *Mathematica* is that the conditions you give may yield neither `True` nor `False`. Thus, for example, the condition `x == y` does not yield `True` or `False` unless `x` and `y` have specific values, such as numerical ones.

In this case, the test gives neither `True` nor `False`, so both branches in the `If` remain unevaluated.	`In[13]:= If[x == y, a, b]` `Out[13]= If[x == y, a, b]`
You can add a special fourth argument to `If`, which is used if the test does not yield `True` or `False`.	`In[14]:= If[x == y, a, b, c]` `Out[14]= c`

`If[`*test*, *then*, *else*, *unknown*`]`	a form of `If` which includes the expression to use if *test* is neither `True` nor `False`
`TrueQ[`*expr*`]`	give `True` if *expr* is `True`, and `False` otherwise
lhs `===` *rhs* or `SameQ[`*lhs*, *rhs*`]`	give `True` if *lhs* and *rhs* are identical, and `False` otherwise
lhs `=!=` *rhs* or `UnsameQ[`*lhs*, *rhs*`]`	give `True` if *lhs* and *rhs* are not identical, and `False` otherwise
`MatchQ[`*expr*, *form*`]`	give `True` if the pattern *form* matches *expr*, and give `False` otherwise

Functions for dealing with symbolic conditions.

Mathematica leaves this as a symbolic equation.	`In[15]:= x == y` `Out[15]= x == y`

Unless *expr* is manifestly True, TrueQ[*expr*] effectively assumes that *expr* is False.

In[16]:= **TrueQ[x == y]**

Out[16]= False

Unlike ==, === tests whether two expressions are manifestly identical. In this case, they are not.

In[17]:= **x === y**

Out[17]= False

The main difference between *lhs* === *rhs* and *lhs* == *rhs* is that === always returns True or False, whereas == can leave its input in symbolic form, representing a symbolic equation, as discussed in Section 1.5.5. You should typically use === when you want to test the *structure* of an expression, and == if you want to test mathematical equality. The *Mathematica* pattern matcher effectively uses === to determine when one literal expression matches another.

You can use === to test the structure of expressions.

In[18]:= **Head[a + b + c] === Times**

Out[18]= False

The == operator gives a less useful result.

In[19]:= **Head[a + b + c] == Times**

Out[19]= Plus == Times

In setting up conditionals, you will often need to use combinations of tests, such as *test*$_1$ && *test*$_2$ && ... . An important point is that the result from this combination of tests will be False if *any* of the *test*$_i$ yield False. *Mathematica* always evaluates the *test*$_i$ in turn, stopping if any of the *test*$_i$ yield False.

expr$_1$ && *expr*$_2$ && *expr*$_3$	evaluate until one of the *expr*$_i$ is found to be False
expr$_1$ || *expr*$_2$ || *expr*$_3$	evaluate until one of the *expr*$_i$ is found to be True

Evaluation of logical expressions.

This function involves a combination of two tests.

In[20]:= **t[x_] := (x != 0 && 1/x < 3)**

Here both tests are evaluated.

In[21]:= **t[2]**

Out[21]= True

Here the first test yields False, so the second test is not tried. The second test would involve 1/0, and would generate an error.

In[22]:= **t[0]**

Out[22]= False

The way that *Mathematica* evaluates logical expressions allows you to combine sequences of tests where later tests may make sense only if the earlier ones are satisfied. The behavior, which is analogous to that found in languages such as C, is convenient in constructing many kinds of *Mathematica* programs.

■ 2.6.9 Loops and Control Structures

The execution of a *Mathematica* program involves the evaluation of a sequence of *Mathematica* expressions. In simple programs, the expressions to be evaluated may be separated by semicolons, and evaluated one after another. Often, however, you need to evaluate expressions several times, in some kind of "loop".

Do[*expr*, {*i*, *imax*}]	evaluate *expr* repetitively, with *i* varying from 1 to *imax* in steps of 1
Do[*expr*, {*i*, *imin*, *imax*, *di*}]	evaluate *expr* with *i* varying from *imin* to *imax* in steps of *di*
Do[*expr*, {*n*}]	evaluate *expr* n times

Simple looping constructs.

This evaluates Print[i^2], with i running from 1 to 4.

In[1]:= Do[Print[i^2], {i, 4}]

```
1
4
9
16
```

This executes an assignment for t in a loop with k running from 2 to 6 in steps of 2.

In[2]:= t = x; Do[t = 1/(1 + k t), {k, 2, 6, 2}]; t

$$Out[2]= \cfrac{1}{1 + \cfrac{6}{1 + \cfrac{4}{1 + 2x}}}$$

The way iteration is specified in Do is exactly the same as in functions like Table and Sum. Just as in those functions, you can set up several nested loops by giving a sequence of iteration specifications to Do.

This loops over values of i from 1 to 4, and for each value of i, loops over j from 1 to i-1.

In[3]:= Do[Print[{i,j}], {i, 4}, {j, i-1}]

```
{2, 1}
{3, 1}
{3, 2}
{4, 1}
{4, 2}
{4, 3}
```

Sometimes you may want to repeat a particular operation a certain number of times, without changing the value of an iteration variable. You can specify this kind of repetition in Do just as you can in Table and other iteration functions.

This repeats the assignment t = 1/(1+t) three times.

In[4]:= t = x; Do[t = 1/(1+t), {3}]; t

$$Out[4]= \cfrac{1}{1 + \cfrac{1}{1 + \cfrac{1}{1+x}}}$$

You can put a procedure inside Do.

In[5]:= t = 67; Do[Print[t]; t = Floor[t/2], {3}]

```
67
33
16
```

Nest[*f*, *expr*, *n*]	apply *f* to *expr* *n* times
FixedPoint[*f*, *expr*]	start with *expr*, and apply *f* repeatedly until the result no longer changes
NestWhile[*f*, *expr*, *test*]	start with *expr*, and apply *f* repeatedly until applying *test* to the result no longer yields True

Applying functions repetitively.

Do allows you to repeat operations by evaluating a particular expression many times with different values for iteration variables. Often, however, you can make more elegant and efficient programs using the functional programming constructs discussed in Section 2.2.2. Nest[*f*, *x*, *n*], for example, allows you to apply a function repeatedly to an expression.

This nests f three times.

In[6]:= **Nest[f, x, 3]**

Out[6]= f[f[f[x]]]

By nesting a pure function, you can get the same result as in the example with Do above.

In[7]:= **Nest[Function[t, 1/(1+t)], x, 3]**

$$Out[7]= \cfrac{1}{1 + \cfrac{1}{1 + \cfrac{1}{1+x}}}$$

Nest allows you to apply a function a specified number of times. Sometimes, however, you may simply want to go on applying a function until the results you get no longer change. You can do this using FixedPoint[*f*, *x*].

FixedPoint goes on applying a function until the result no longer changes.

In[8]:= **FixedPoint[Function[t, Print[t]; Floor[t/2]], 67]**

```
67
33
16
8
4
2
1
0
```

Out[8]= 0

You can use FixedPoint to imitate the evaluation process in *Mathematica*, or the operation of functions such as *expr //. rules*. FixedPoint goes on until two successive results it gets are the same. NestWhile allows you to go on until an arbitrary function no longer yields True.

Catch[*expr*]	evaluate *expr* until Throw[*value*] is encountered, then return *value*
Catch[*expr*, *form*]	evaluate *expr* until Throw[*value*, *tag*] is encountered, where *form* matches *tag*
Catch[*expr*, *form*, *f*]	return *f*[*value*, *tag*] instead of *value*

Non-local control of evaluation.

When the Throw is encountered, evaluation stops, and the current value of i is returned as the value of the enclosing Catch.

```
In[9]:= Catch[Do[Print[i]; If[i > 3, Throw[i]], {i, 10}]]
1
2
3
4

Out[9]= 4
```

Throw and Catch provide a flexible way to control the process of evaluation in *Mathematica*. The basic idea is that whenever a Throw is encountered, the evaluation that is then being done is stopped, and *Mathematica* immediately returns to the nearest appropriate enclosing Catch.

Scan applies the function Print to each successive element in the list, and in the end just returns Null.

```
In[10]:= Scan[Print, {7, 6, 5, 4}]
7
6
5
4
```

The evaluation of Scan stops as soon as Throw is encountered, and the enclosing Catch returns as its value the argument of Throw.

```
In[11]:= Catch[Scan[(Print[#];
                 If[# < 6, Throw[#]])&, {7, 6, 5, 4}]]
7
6
5

Out[11]= 5
```

The same result is obtained with Map, even though Map would have returned a list if its evaluation had not been stopped by encountering a Throw.

```
In[12]:= Catch[Map[(Print[#];
                 If[# < 6, Throw[#]])&, {7, 6, 5, 4}]]
7
6
5

Out[12]= 5
```

You can use Throw and Catch to divert the operation of functional programming constructs, allowing for example the evaluation of such constructs to continue only until some condition has been met. Note that if you stop evaluation using Throw, then the structure of the result you get may be quite different from what you would have got if you had allowed the evaluation to complete.

Here is a list generated by repeated application of a function.

```
In[13]:= NestList[1/(# + 1)&, -2.5, 6]
Out[13]= {-2.5, -0.666667, 3., 0.25, 0.8, 0.555556, 0.642857}
```

Since there is no `Throw` encountered, the result here is just as before.

In[14]:= **Catch[NestList[1/(# + 1)&, -2.5, 6]]**

Out[14]= {-2.5, -0.666667, 3., 0.25, 0.8, 0.555556, 0.642857}

Now the evaluation of the `NestList` is diverted, and the single number given as the argument of `Throw` is returned.

In[15]:= **Catch[NestList**
[If[# > 1, Throw[#], 1/(# + 1)]&, -2.5, 6]]

Out[15]= 3.

`Throw` and `Catch` operate in a completely global way: it does not matter how or where a `Throw` is generated—it will always stop evaluation and return to the enclosing `Catch`.

The `Throw` stops the evaluation of `f`, and causes the `Catch` to return just `a`, with no trace of `f` left.

In[16]:= **Catch[f[Throw[a]]]**

Out[16]= a

This defines a function which generates a `Throw` when its argument is larger than 10.

In[17]:= **g[x_] := If[x > 10, Throw[overflow], x!]**

No `Throw` is generated here.

In[18]:= **Catch[g[4]]**

Out[18]= 24

But here the `Throw` generated inside the evaluation of `g` returns to the enclosing `Catch`.

In[19]:= **Catch[g[40]]**

Out[19]= overflow

In small programs, it is often adequate to use `Throw`[*value*] and `Catch`[*expr*] in their simplest form. But particularly if you write larger programs that contain many separate pieces, it is usually much better to use `Throw`[*value*, *tag*] and `Catch`[*expr*, *form*]. By keeping the expressions *tag* and *form* local to a particular piece of your program, you can then ensure that your `Throw` and `Catch` will also operate only within that piece.

Here the `Throw` is caught by the inner `Catch`.

In[20]:= **Catch[f [Catch[Throw[x, a], a]], b]**

Out[20]= f [x]

But here it is caught only by the outer `Catch`.

In[21]:= **Catch[f [Catch[Throw[x, b], a]], b]**

Out[21]= x

You can use patterns in specifying the tags which a particular `Catch` should catch.

In[22]:= **Catch[Throw[x, a], a | b]**

Out[22]= x

This keeps the tag a completely local.

In[23]:= **Module[{a}, Catch[Throw[x, a], a]]**

Out[23]= x

You should realize that there is no need for the tag that appears in `Throw` to be a constant; in general it can be any expression.

Here the inner `Catch` catches all throws with tags less than 4, and continues the `Do`. But as soon as the tag reaches 4, the outer `Catch` is needed.

In[24]:= **Catch[Do[Catch[Throw[i^2, i], n_ /; n < 4],**
{i, 10}], _]

Out[24]= 16

When you use Catch[*expr*, *form*] with Throw[*value*, *tag*], the value returned by Catch is simply the expression *value* given in the Throw. If you use Catch[*expr*, *form*, *f*], however, then the value returned by Catch is instead *f*[*value*, *tag*].

Here f is applied to the value and tag in the Throw.

In[25]:= **Catch[Throw[x, a], a, f]**

Out[25]= f[x, a]

If there is no Throw, f is never used.

In[26]:= **Catch[x, a, f]**

Out[26]= x

| While[*test*, *body*] | evaluate *body* repetitively, so long as *test* is True |
| For[*start*, *test*, *incr*, *body*] | evaluate *start*, then repetitively evaluate *body* and *incr*, until *test* fails |

General loop constructs.

Functions like Do, Nest and FixedPoint provide structured ways to make loops in *Mathematica* programs, while Throw and Catch provide opportunities for modifying this structure. Sometimes, however, you may want to create loops that even from the outset have less structure. And in such cases, you may find it convenient to use the functions While and For, which perform operations repeatedly, stopping when a specified condition fails to be true.

The While loop continues until the condition fails.

In[27]:= **n = 17; While[(n = Floor[n/2]) != 0, Print[n]]**

```
8
4
2
1
```

The functions While and For in *Mathematica* are similar to the control structures while and for in languages such as C. Notice, however, that there are a number of important differences. For example, the roles of comma and semicolon are reversed in *Mathematica* For loops relative to C language ones.

This is a very common form for a For loop. i++ increments the value of i.

In[28]:= **For[i=1, i < 4, i++, Print[i]]**

```
1
2
3
```

Here is a more complicated For loop. Notice that the loop terminates as soon as the test i^2 < 10 fails.

In[29]:= **For[i=1; t=x, i^2 < 10, i++, t = t^2 + i;**
                        Print[t]]

$$1 + x^2$$
$$2 + (1 + x^2)^2$$
$$3 + (2 + (1 + x^2)^2)^2$$

In *Mathematica*, both While and For always evaluate the loop test before evaluating the body of the loop. As soon as the loop test fails to be True, While and For terminate. The body of the loop is thus only evaluated in situations where the loop test is True.

The loop test fails immediately, so the body of the loop is never evaluated.

In[30]:= **While[False, Print[x]]**

In a While or For loop, or in general in any *Mathematica* procedure, the *Mathematica* expressions you give are evaluated in a definite sequence. You can think of this sequence as defining the "flow of control" in the execution of a *Mathematica* program.

In most cases, you should try to keep the flow of control in your *Mathematica* programs as simple as possible. The more the flow of control depends for example on specific values generated during the execution of the program, the more difficult you will typically find it to understand the structure and operation of the program.

Functional programming constructs typically involve very simple flow of control. While and For loops are always more complicated, since they are set up to make the flow of control depend on the values of the expressions given as tests. Nevertheless, even in such loops, the flow of control does not usually depend on the values of expressions given in the body of the loop.

In some cases, however, you may need to construct *Mathematica* programs in which the flow of control is affected by values generated during the execution of a procedure or of the body of a loop. One way to do this, which fits in with functional programming ideas, is to use Throw and Catch. But *Mathematica* also provides various functions for modifying the flow of control which work like in languages such as C.

Break[ ]	exit the nearest enclosing loop
Continue[ ]	go to the next step in the current loop
Return[*expr*]	return the value *expr*, exiting all procedures and loops in a function
Goto[*name*]	go to the element Label[*name*] in the current procedure
Throw[*value*]	return *value* as the value of the nearest enclosing Catch (non-local return)

Control flow functions.

The Break[ ] causes the loop to terminate as soon as t exceeds 19.

In[31]:= **t = 1; Do[t *= k; Print[t];**
            If[t > 19, Break[]], {k, 10}]

```
1
2
6
24
```

When k < 3, the Continue[ ] causes the loop to be continued, without executing t += 2.

```
In[32]:= t = 1; Do[t *= k; Print[t];
            If[k < 3, Continue[]]; t += 2, {k, 10}]
```
```
1
2
6
32
170
1032
7238
57920
521298
5213000
```

Return[*expr*] allows you to exit a particular function, returning a value. You can think of Throw as a kind of non-local return which allows you to exit a whole sequence of nested functions. Such behavior can be convenient for handling certain error conditions.

Here is an example of the use of Return. This particular procedure could equally well have been written without using Return.

```
In[33]:= f[x_] :=
            (If[x > 5, Return[big]]; t = x^3; Return[t - 7])
```

When the argument is greater than 5, the first Return in the procedure is used.

```
In[34]:= f[10]
Out[34]= big
```

This function "throws" error if its argument is negative.

```
In[35]:= h[x_] := If[x < 0, Throw[error], Sqrt[x]]
```

No Throw is generated here.

```
In[36]:= Catch[ h[6] + 2 ]
Out[36]= 2 + √6
```

But in this case a Throw is generated, and the whole Catch returns the value error.

```
In[37]:= Catch[ h[-6] + 2 ]
Out[37]= error
```

Functions like Continue[ ] and Break[ ] allow you to "transfer control" to the beginning or end of a loop in a *Mathematica* program. Sometimes you may instead need to transfer control to a particular element in a *Mathematica* procedure. If you give a Label as an element in a procedure, you can use Goto to transfer control to this element.

This goes on looping until q exceeds 6.

```
In[38]:= (q = 2; Label[begin]; Print[q]; q += 3;
            If[q < 6, Goto[begin]])
```
```
2
5
```

Note that you can use Goto in a particular *Mathematica* procedure only when the Label it specifies occurs as an element of the same *Mathematica* procedure. In general, use of Goto reduces the degree of structure that can readily be perceived in a program, and therefore makes the operation of the program more difficult to understand.

■ 2.6.10 Collecting Expressions During Evaluation

In many computations one is concerned only with the final result of evaluating the expression given as input. But sometimes one also wants to collect expressions that were generated in the course of the evaluation. You can do this using Sow and Reap.

+ Sow[*val*]	sow the value *val* for the nearest enclosing Reap
+ Reap[*expr*]	evaluate *expr*, returning also a list of values sown by Sow

Using Sow and Reap.

Here the output contains only the final result.

```
In[1]:= a = 3; a += a^2 + 1; a = Sqrt[a + a^2]

Out[1]= √182
```

Here two intermediate results are also given.

```
In[2]:= Reap[Sow[a = 3]; a += Sow[a^2 + 1]; a = Sqrt[a + a^2]]

Out[2]= {√182, {{3, 10}}}
```

This computes a sum, collecting all terms that are even.

```
In[3]:= Reap[Sum[If[EvenQ[#], Sow[#], #]& [i^2 + 1], {i, 10}]]

Out[3]= {395, {{2, 10, 26, 50, 82}}}
```

Like Throw and Catch, Sow and Reap can be used anywhere in a computation.

This defines a function that can do a Sow.

```
In[4]:= f[x_] := (If[x < 1/2, Sow[x]]; 3.5 x (1 - x))
```

This nests the function, reaping all cases below 1/2.

```
In[5]:= Reap[Nest[f, 0.8, 10]]

Out[5]= {0.868312,
          {{0.415332, 0.446472, 0.408785, 0.456285}}}
```

+ Sow[*val*, *tag*]	sow *val* with a tag to indicate when to reap
+ Sow[*val*, {*tag*₁, *tag*₂, ... }]	sow *val* for each of the *tag*ᵢ
+ Reap[*expr*, *form*]	reap all values whose tags match *form*
+ Reap[*expr*, {*form*₁, *form*₂, ... }]	make separate lists for each of the *form*ᵢ
+ Reap[*expr*, {*form*₁, ... }, *f*]	apply *f* to each distinct tag and list of values

Sowing and reaping with tags.

This reaps only values sown with tag x.

```
In[6]:= Reap[Sow[1, x]; Sow[2, y]; Sow[3, x], x]

Out[6]= {3, {{1, 3}}}
```

Here 1 is sown twice with tag x.

$In[7]:=$ `Reap[Sow[1, {x, x}]; Sow[2, y]; Sow[3, x], x]`

$Out[7]=$ {3, {{1, 1, 3}}}

Values sown with different tags always appear in different sublists.

$In[8]:=$ `Reap[Sow[1, {x, x}]; Sow[2, y]; Sow[3, x]]`

$Out[8]=$ {3, {{1, 1, 3}, {2}}}

The makes a sublist for each form of tag being reaped.

$In[9]:=$ `Reap[Sow[1, {x, x}]; Sow[2, y]; Sow[3, x], {x, x, y}]`

$Out[9]=$ {3, {{{1, 1, 3}}, {{1, 1, 3}}, {{2}}}}

This applies f to each distinct tag and list of values.

$In[10]:=$ `Reap[Sow[1, {x, x}]; Sow[2, y]; Sow[3, x], _, f]`

$Out[10]=$ {3, {f[x, {1, 1, 3}], f[y, {2}]}}

The tags can be part of the computation.

$In[11]:=$ `Reap[Do[Sow[i/j, GCD[i, j]], {i, 4}, {j, i}]]`

$Out[11]=$ $\left\{\text{Null}, \left\{\left\{1, 2, 3, \frac{3}{2}, 4, \frac{4}{3}\right\}, \{1, 2\}, \{1\}, \{1\}\right\}\right\}$

■ 2.6.11 Advanced Topic: Tracing Evaluation

The standard way in which *Mathematica* works is to take any expression you give as input, evaluate the expression completely, and then return the result. When you are trying to understand what *Mathematica* is doing, however, it is often worthwhile to look not just at the final result of evaluation, but also at intermediate steps in the evaluation process.

Trace[*expr*]	generate a list of all expressions used in the evaluation of *expr*
Trace[*expr*, *form*]	include only expressions which match the pattern *form*

Tracing the evaluation of expressions.

The expression 1 + 1 is evaluated immediately to 2.

$In[1]:=$ `Trace[1 + 1]`

$Out[1]=$ {1 + 1, 2}

The 2^3 is evaluated before the addition is done.

$In[2]:=$ `Trace[2^3 + 4]`

$Out[2]=$ {{2^3, 8}, 8 + 4, 12}

The evaluation of each subexpression is shown in a separate sublist.

$In[3]:=$ `Trace[2^3 + 4^2 + 1]`

$Out[3]=$ {{2^3, 8}, {4^2, 16}, 8 + 16 + 1, 25}

Trace[*expr*] gives a list which includes *all* the intermediate expressions involved in the evaluation of *expr*. Except in rather simple cases, however, the number of intermediate expressions generated in this way is typically very large, and the list returned by Trace is difficult to understand.

Trace[*expr*, *form*] allows you to "filter" the expressions that Trace records, keeping only those which match the pattern *form*.

Here is a recursive definition of a factorial function.	*In[4]:=* **fac[n_] := n fac[n-1]; fac[1] = 1** *Out[4]=* 1
This gives *all* the intermediate expressions generated in the evaluation of fac[3]. The result is quite complicated.	*In[5]:=* **Trace[fac[3]]** *Out[5]=* {fac[3], 3 fac[3-1], {{3-1, 2}, fac[2], 2 fac[2-1], {{2-1, 1}, fac[1], 1}, 21, 2}, 32, 6}
This shows only intermediate expressions of the form fac[n_].	*In[6]:=* **Trace[fac[3], fac[n_]]** *Out[6]=* {fac[3], {fac[2], {fac[1]}}}
You can specify any pattern in Trace.	*In[7]:=* **Trace[fac[10], fac[n_/;n > 5]]** *Out[7]=* {fac[10], {fac[9], {fac[8], {fac[7], {fac[6]}}}}}

Trace[*expr*, *form*] effectively works by intercepting every expression that is about to be evaluated during the evaluation of *expr*, and picking out those that match the pattern *form*.

If you want to trace "calls" to a function like fac, you can do so simply by telling Trace to pick out expressions of the form fac[n_]. You can also use patterns like f[n_, 2] to pick out calls with particular argument structure.

A typical *Mathematica* program, however, consists not only of "function calls" like fac[n], but also of other elements, such as assignments to variables, control structures, and so on. All of these elements are represented as expressions. As a result, you can use patterns in Trace to pick out any kind of *Mathematica* program element. Thus, for example, you can use a pattern like k = _ to pick out all assignments to the symbol k.

This shows the sequence of assignments made for k.	*In[8]:=* **Trace[(k=2; For[i=1, i<4, i++, k = i/k]; k), k=_]** *Out[8]=* $\left\{\{k = 2\}, \left\{\left\{k = \frac{1}{2}\right\}, \{k = 4\}, \left\{k = \frac{3}{4}\right\}\right\}\right\}$

Trace[*expr*, *form*] can pick out expressions that occur at any time in the evaluation of *expr*. The expressions need not, for example, appear directly in the form of *expr* that you give. They may instead occur, say, during the evaluation of functions that are called as part of the evaluation of *expr*.

Here is a function definition.	*In[9]:=* **h[n_] := (k=n/2; Do[k = i/k, {i, n}]; k)**
You can look for expressions generated during the evaluation of h.	*In[10]:=* **Trace[h[3], k=_]** *Out[10]=* $\left\{\left\{k = \frac{3}{2}\right\}, \left\{\left\{k = \frac{2}{3}\right\}, \{k = 3\}, \{k = 1\}\right\}\right\}$

Trace allows you to monitor intermediate steps in the evaluation not only of functions that you define, but also of some functions that are built into *Mathematica*. You should realize, however, that the specific sequence of intermediate steps followed by built-in *Mathematica* functions depends in detail on their implementation and optimization in a particular version of *Mathematica*.

Trace[*expr*, *f*[___]]	show all calls to the function *f*
Trace[*expr*, *i* = _]	show assignments to *i*
Trace[*expr*, _ = _]	show all assignments
Trace[*expr*, Message[___]]	show messages generated

Some ways to use Trace.

The function Trace returns a list that represents the "history" of a *Mathematica* computation. The expressions in the list are given in the order that they were generated during the computation. In most cases, the list returned by Trace has a nested structure, which represents the "structure" of the computation.

The basic idea is that each sublist in the list returned by Trace represents the "evaluation chain" for a particular *Mathematica* expression. The elements of this chain correspond to different forms of the same expression. Usually, however, the evaluation of one expression requires the evaluation of a number of other expressions, often subexpressions. Each subsidiary evaluation is represented by a sublist in the structure returned by Trace.

Here is a sequence of assignments.

In[11]:= **a[1] = a[2]; a[2] = a[3]; a[3] = a[4]**

Out[11]= a[4]

This yields an evaluation chain reflecting the sequence of transformations for a[*i*] used.

In[12]:= **Trace[a[1]]**

Out[12]= {a[1], a[2], a[3], a[4]}

The successive forms generated in the simplification of y + x + y show up as successive elements in its evaluation chain.

In[13]:= **Trace[y + x + y]**

Out[13]= {y + x + y, x + y + y, x + 2 y}

Each argument of the function f has a separate evaluation chain, given in a sublist.

In[14]:= **Trace[f[1 + 1, 2 + 3, 4 + 5]]**

Out[14]= {{1 + 1, 2}, {2 + 3, 5}, {4 + 5, 9}, f[2, 5, 9]}

The evaluation chain for each subexpression is given in a separate sublist.

In[15]:= **Trace[x x + y y]**

Out[15]= {{x x, x^2}, {y y, y^2}, $x^2 + y^2$}

Tracing the evaluation of a nested expression yields a nested list.

In[16]:= **Trace[f[f[f[1 + 1]]]]**

Out[16]= {{{{1 + 1, 2}, f[2]}, f[f[2]]}, f[f[f[2]]]}

There are two basic ways that subsidiary evaluations can be required during the evaluation of a *Mathematica* expression. The first way is that the expression may contain subexpressions, each of which has to be evaluated. The second way is that there may be rules for the evaluation of the expression that involve other expressions which themselves must be evaluated. Both kinds of subsidiary evaluations are represented by sublists in the structure returned by Trace.

The subsidiary evaluations here come from evaluation of the arguments of f and g.	*In[17]:=* **Trace[f[g[1 + 1], 2 + 3]]** *Out[17]=* {{{1 + 1, 2}, g[2]}, {2 + 3, 5}, f[g[2], 5]}
Here is a function with a condition attached.	*In[18]:=* **fe[n_] := n + 1 /; EvenQ[n]**
The evaluation of fe[6] involves a subsidiary evaluation associated with the condition.	*In[19]:=* **Trace[fe[6]]** *Out[19]=* {fe[6], {{EvenQ[6], True}, RuleCondition[$ConditionHold[$ConditionHold[6 + 1]], True], $ConditionHold[$ConditionHold[6 + 1]]}, 6 + 1, 7}

You often get nested lists when you trace the evaluation of functions that are defined "recursively" in terms of other instances of themselves. The reason is typically that each new instance of the function appears as a subexpression in the expressions obtained by evaluating previous instances of the function.

Thus, for example, with the definition fac[n_] := n fac[n-1], the evaluation of fac[6] yields the expression 6 fac[5], which contains fac[5] as a subexpression.

The successive instances of fac generated appear in successively nested sublists.	*In[20]:=* **Trace[fac[6], fac[_]]** *Out[20]=* {fac[6], {fac[5], {fac[4], {fac[3], {fac[2], {fac[1]}}}}}}
With this definition, fp[*n*-1] is obtained directly as the value of fp[*n*].	*In[21]:=* **fp[n_] := fp[n - 1] /; n > 1**
fp[*n*] never appears in a subexpression, so no sublists are generated.	*In[22]:=* **Trace[fp[6], fp[_]]** *Out[22]=* {fp[6], fp[6 - 1], fp[5], fp[5 - 1], fp[4], fp[4 - 1], fp[3], fp[3 - 1], fp[2], fp[2 - 1], fp[1]}
Here is the recursive definition of the Fibonacci numbers.	*In[23]:=* **fib[n_] := fib[n - 1] + fib[n - 2]**
Here are the end conditions for the recursion.	*In[24]:=* **fib[0] = fib[1] = 1** *Out[24]=* 1
This shows all the steps in the recursive evaluation of fib[5].	*In[25]:=* **Trace[fib[5], fib[_]]** *Out[25]=* {fib[5], {fib[4], {fib[3], {fib[2], {fib[1]}, {fib[0]}}, {fib[1]}}, {fib[2], {fib[1]}, {fib[0]}}}, {fib[3], {fib[2], {fib[1]}, {fib[0]}}, {fib[1]}}}

Each step in the evaluation of any *Mathematica* expression can be thought of as the result of applying a particular transformation rule. As discussed in Section 2.5.10, all the rules that *Mathematica* knows are associated with specific symbols or "tags". You can use Trace[*expr*, *f*] to see all the steps in the evaluation of *expr* that are performed using transformation rules associated with the symbol *f*. In this case, Trace gives not only the expressions to which each rule is applied, but also the results of applying the rules.

In general, Trace[*expr*, *form*] picks out all the steps in the evaluation of *expr* where *form* matches *either* the expression about to be evaluated, *or* the tag associated with the rule used.

Trace[*expr*, *f*]	show all evaluations which use transformation rules associated with the symbol *f*
Trace[*expr*, *f* | *g*]	show all evaluations associated with either *f* or *g*

Tracing evaluations associated with particular tags.

This shows only intermediate expressions that match fac[_].

```
In[26]:= Trace[fac[3], fac[_]]
Out[26]= {fac[3], {fac[2], {fac[1]}}}
```

This shows all evaluations that use transformation rules associated with the symbol fac.

```
In[27]:= Trace[fac[3], fac]
Out[27]= {fac[3], 3 fac[3 - 1],
            {fac[2], 2 fac[2 - 1], {fac[1], 1}}}
```

Here is a rule for the log function.

```
In[28]:= log[x_ y_] := log[x] + log[y]
```

This traces the evaluation of log[a b c d], showing all transformations associated with log.

```
In[29]:= Trace[log[a b c d], log]
Out[29]= {log[a b c d], log[a] + log[b c d], {log[b c d],
            log[b] + log[c d], {log[c d], log[c] + log[d]}}}
```

Trace[*expr*, *form*, TraceOn -> *oform*]	switch on tracing only within forms matching *oform*
Trace[*expr*, *form*, TraceOff -> *oform*]	switch off tracing within any form matching *oform*

Switching off tracing inside certain forms.

Trace[*expr*, *form*] allows you to trace expressions matching *form* generated at any point in the evaluation of *expr*. Sometimes, you may want to trace only expressions generated during certain parts of the evaluation of *expr*.

By setting the option TraceOn -> *oform*, you can specify that tracing should be done only during the evaluation of forms which match *oform*. Similarly, by setting TraceOff -> *oform*, you can specify that tracing should be switched off during the evaluation of forms which match *oform*.

This shows all steps in the evaluation.

```
In[30]:= Trace[log[fac[2] x]]
Out[30]= {{{fac[2], 2 fac[2 - 1], {{2 - 1, 1}, fac[1], 1},
            2 1, 2}, 2 x}, log[2 x], log[2] + log[x]}
```

This shows only those steps that occur during the evaluation of fac.

In[31]:= **Trace[log[fac[2] x], TraceOn -> fac]**

Out[31]= {{{fac[2], 2 fac[2 - 1],
{{2 - 1, 1}, fac[1], 1}, 2 1, 2}}}

This shows only those steps that do not occur during the evaluation of fac.

In[32]:= **Trace[log[fac[2] x], TraceOff -> fac]**

Out[32]= {{{fac[2], 2}, 2 x}, log[2 x], log[2] + log[x]}

Trace[*expr*, *lhs* -> *rhs*]	find all expressions matching *lhs* that arise during the evaluation of *expr*, and replace them with *rhs*

Applying rules to expressions encountered during evaluation.

This tells Trace to return only the arguments of fib used in the evaluation of fib[5].

In[33]:= **Trace[fib[5], fib[n_] -> n]**

Out[33]= {5, {4, {3, {2, {1}, {0}}, {1}}, {2, {1}, {0}}},
{3, {2, {1}, {0}}, {1}}}

A powerful aspect of the *Mathematica* Trace function is that the object it returns is basically a standard *Mathematica* expression which you can manipulate using other *Mathematica* functions. One important point to realize, however, is that Trace wraps all expressions that appear in the list it produces with HoldForm to prevent them from being evaluated. The HoldForm is not displayed in standard *Mathematica* output format, but it is still present in the internal structure of the expression.

This shows the expressions generated at intermediate stages in the evaluation process.

In[34]:= **Trace[1 + 3^2]**

Out[34]= {{3^2, 9}, 1 + 9, 10}

The expressions are wrapped with HoldForm to prevent them from evaluating.

In[35]:= **Trace[1 + 3^2] // InputForm**

Out[35]//InputForm= {{HoldForm[3^2], HoldForm[9]}, HoldForm[1 + 9],
HoldForm[10]}

In standard *Mathematica* output format, it is sometimes difficult to tell which lists are associated with the structure returned by Trace, and which are expressions being evaluated.

In[36]:= **Trace[{1 + 1, 2 + 3}]**

Out[36]= {{1 + 1, 2}, {2 + 3, 5}, {2, 5}}

Looking at the input form resolves any ambiguities.

In[37]:= **InputForm[%]**

Out[37]//InputForm= {{HoldForm[1 + 1], HoldForm[2]},
{HoldForm[2 + 3], HoldForm[5]}, HoldForm[{2, 5}]}

When you use a transformation rule in Trace, the result is evaluated before being wrapped with HoldForm.

In[38]:= **Trace[fac[4], fac[n_] -> n + 1]**

Out[38]= {5, {4, {3, {2}}}}

For sophisticated computations, the list structures returned by Trace can be quite complicated. When you use Trace[*expr*, *form*], Trace will include as elements in the lists only those expressions which match the pattern *form*. But whatever pattern you give, the nesting structure of the lists remains the same.

<table>
<tr><td>This shows all occurrences of fib[_]
in the evaluation of fib[3].</td><td><code>In[39]:= Trace[fib[3], fib[_]]</code>
<code>Out[39]= {fib[3], {fib[2], {fib[1]}, {fib[0]}}, {fib[1]}}</code></td></tr>
<tr><td>This shows only occurrences of fib[1],
but the nesting of the lists is the same
as for fib[_].</td><td><code>In[40]:= Trace[fib[3], fib[1]]</code>
<code>Out[40]= {{{fib[1]}}, {fib[1]}}</code></td></tr>
</table>

You can set the option TraceDepth -> *n* to tell Trace to include only lists nested at most *n* levels deep. In this way, you can often pick out the "big steps" in a computation, without seeing the details. Note that by setting TraceDepth or TraceOff you can avoid looking at many of the steps in a computation, and thereby significantly speed up the operation of Trace for that computation.

<table>
<tr><td>This shows only steps that appear in
lists nested at most two levels deep.</td><td><code>In[41]:= Trace[fib[3], fib[_], TraceDepth->2]</code>
<code>Out[41]= {fib[3], {fib[1]}}</code></td></tr>
</table>

Trace[*expr*, *form*, TraceDepth -> *n*]	trace the evaluation of *expr*, ignoring steps that lead to lists nested more than *n* levels deep

Restricting the depth of tracing.

When you use Trace[*expr*, *form*], you get a list of all the expressions which match *form* produced during the evaluation of *expr*. Sometimes it is useful to see not only these expressions, but also the results that were obtained by evaluating them. You can do this by setting the option TraceForward -> True in Trace.

<table>
<tr><td>This shows not only expressions which
match fac[_], but also the results of
evaluating those expressions.</td><td><code>In[42]:= Trace[fac[4], fac[_], TraceForward->True]</code>
<code>Out[42]= {fac[4], {fac[3], {fac[2], {fac[1], 1}, 2}, 6}, 24}</code></td></tr>
</table>

Expressions picked out using Trace[*expr*, *form*] typically lie in the middle of an evaluation chain. By setting TraceForward -> True, you tell Trace to include also the expression obtained at the end of the evaluation chain. If you set TraceForward -> All, Trace will include *all* the expressions that occur after the expression matching *form* on the evaluation chain.

<table>
<tr><td>With TraceForward->All, all elements
on the evaluation chain after the one
that matches fac[_] are included.</td><td><code>In[43]:= Trace[fac[4], fac[_], TraceForward->All]</code>
<code>Out[43]= {fac[4], 4 fac[4 - 1],</code>
<code>　　　{fac[3], 3 fac[3 - 1], {fac[2], 2 fac[2 - 1],</code>
<code>　　　　{fac[1], 1}, 2 1, 2}, 3 2, 6}, 4 6, 24}</code></td></tr>
</table>

By setting the option TraceForward, you can effectively see what happens to a particular form of expression during an evaluation. Sometimes, however, you want to find out not what happens to a particular expression, but instead how that expression was generated. You can do this by setting the option `TraceBackward`. What `TraceBackward` does is to show you what *preceded* a particular form of expression on an evaluation chain.

This shows that the number 120 came from the evaluation of `fac[5]` during the evaluation of `fac[10]`.

`In[44]:= Trace[fac[10], 120, TraceBackward->True]`

`Out[44]= {{{{{{fac[5], 120}}}}}}`

Here is the whole evaluation chain associated with the generation of the number 120.

`In[45]:= Trace[fac[10], 120, TraceBackward->All]`

`Out[45]= {{{{{{fac[5], 5 fac[5 - 1], 5 24, 120}}}}}}`

`TraceForward` and `TraceBackward` allow you to look forward and backward in a particular evaluation chain. Sometimes, you may also want to look at the evaluation chains within which the particular evaluation chain occurs. You can do this using `TraceAbove`. If you set the option `TraceAbove -> True`, then `Trace` will include the initial and final expressions in all the relevant evaluation chains. With `TraceAbove -> All`, `Trace` includes all the expressions in all these evaluation chains.

This includes the initial and final expressions in all evaluation chains which contain the chain that contains 120.

`In[46]:= Trace[fac[7], 120, TraceAbove->True]`

`Out[46]= {fac[7], {fac[6], {fac[5], 120}, 720}, 5040}`

This shows all the ways that `fib[2]` is generated during the evaluation of `fib[5]`.

`In[47]:= Trace[fib[5], fib[2], TraceAbove->True]`

```
Out[47]= {fib[5],
          {fib[4], {fib[3], {fib[2], 2}, 3}, {fib[2], 2}, 5},
          {fib[3], {fib[2], 2}, 3}, 8}
```

`Trace[`*expr*`, `*form*`, `*opts*`]`	trace the evaluation of *expr* using the specified options
`TraceForward -> True`	include the final expression in the evaluation chain containing *form*
`TraceForward -> All`	include all expressions following *form* in the evaluation chain
`TraceBackward -> True`	include the first expression in the evaluation chain containing *form*
`TraceBackward -> All`	include all expressions preceding *form* in the evaluation chain
`TraceAbove -> True`	include the first and last expressions in all evaluation chains which contain the chain containing *form*
`TraceAbove -> All`	include all expressions in all evaluation chains which contain the chain containing *form*

Option settings for including extra steps in trace lists.

The basic way that Trace[*expr*, ...] works is to intercept each expression encountered during the evaluation of *expr*, and then to use various criteria to determine whether this expression should be recorded. Normally, however, Trace intercepts expressions only *after* function arguments have been evaluated. By setting TraceOriginal -> True, you can get Trace also to look at expressions *before* function arguments have been evaluated.

This includes expressions which match fac[_] both before and after argument evaluation.	*In[48]:=* **Trace[fac[3], fac[_], TraceOriginal -> True]** *Out[48]=* {fac[3], {fac[3 - 1], fac[2], {fac[2 - 1], fac[1]}}}

The list structure produced by Trace normally includes only expressions that constitute steps in non-trivial evaluation chains. Thus, for example, individual symbols that evaluate to themselves are not normally included. Nevertheless, if you set TraceOriginal -> True, then Trace looks at absolutely every expression involved in the evaluation process, including those that have trivial evaluation chains.

In this case, Trace includes absolutely all expressions, even those with trivial evaluation chains.	*In[49]:=* **Trace[fac[1], TraceOriginal -> True]** *Out[49]=* {fac[1], {fac}, {1}, fac[1], 1}

option name	default value	
TraceForward	False	whether to show expressions following *form* in the evaluation chain
TraceBackward	False	whether to show expressions preceding *form* in the evaluation chain
TraceAbove	False	whether to show evaluation chains leading to the evaluation chain containing *form*
TraceOriginal	False	whether to look at expressions before their heads and arguments are evaluated

Additional options for Trace.

When you use Trace to study the execution of a program, there is an issue about how local variables in the program should be treated. As discussed in Section 2.7.3, *Mathematica* scoping constructs such as Module create symbols with new names to represent local variables. Thus, even if you called a variable x in the original code for your program, the variable may effectively be renamed x$*nnn* when the program is executed.

Trace[*expr*, *form*] is set up so that by default a symbol *x* that appears in *form* will match all symbols with names of the form x$*nnn* that arise in the execution of *expr*. As a result, you can for example use Trace[*expr*, x = _] to trace assignment to all variables, local and global, that were named x in your original program.

> Trace[*expr*, *form*, MatchLocalNames -> False]
> > include all steps in the execution of *expr* that match *form*,
> > with no replacements for local variable names allowed

Preventing the matching of local variables.

In some cases, you may want to trace only the global variable x, and not any local variables that were originally named x. You can do this by setting the option MatchLocalNames -> False.

This traces assignments to all variables with names of the form x$*nnn*.	*In[50]:=* **Trace[Module[{x}, x = 5], x = _]** *Out[50]=* {{x$1 = 5}}
This traces assignments only to the specific global variable x.	*In[51]:=* **Trace[Module[{x}, x = 5], x = _,** **MatchLocalNames -> False]** *Out[51]=* {}

The function Trace performs a complete computation, then returns a structure which represents the history of the computation. Particularly in very long computations, it is however sometimes useful to see traces of the computation as it proceeds. The function TracePrint works essentially like Trace, except that it prints expressions when it encounters them, rather than saving up all of the expressions to create a list structure.

This prints expressions encountered in the evaluation of fib[3].

```
In[52]:= TracePrint[fib[3], fib[_]]
   fib[3]
     fib[3 - 1]
     fib[2]
       fib[2 - 1]
       fib[1]
       fib[2 - 2]
       fib[0]
     fib[3 - 2]
     fib[1]
Out[52]= 3
```

The sequence of expressions printed by TracePrint corresponds to the sequence of expressions given in the list structure returned by Trace. Indentation in the output from TracePrint corresponds to nesting in the list structure from Trace. You can use the Trace options TraceOn, TraceOff and TraceForward in TracePrint. However, since TracePrint produces output as it goes, it cannot support the option TraceBackward. In addition, TracePrint is set up so that TraceOriginal is effectively always set to True.

Trace[*expr*, ...]	trace the evaluation of *expr*, returning a list structure containing the expressions encountered
TracePrint[*expr*, ...]	trace the evaluation of *expr*, printing the expressions encountered
TraceDialog[*expr*, ...]	trace the evaluation of *expr*, initiating a dialog when each specified expression is encountered
TraceScan[*f*, *expr*, ...]	trace the evaluation of *expr*, applying *f* to HoldForm of each expression encountered

Functions for tracing evaluation.

This enters a dialog when fac[5] is encountered during the evaluation of fac[10].

```
In[53]:= TraceDialog[fac[10], fac[5]]

TraceDialog::dgbgn: Entering Dialog; use Return[] to exit.

Out[54]= fac[5]
```

Inside the dialog you can for example find out where you are by looking at the "stack".

```
In[55]:= Stack[ ]

Out[55]= {TraceDialog, Times,
            Times, Times, Times, Times, fac}
```

This returns from the dialog, and gives the final result from the evaluation of fac[10].

```
In[56]:= Return[ ]

TraceDialog::dgend: Exiting Dialog.

Out[53]= 3628800
```

The function TraceDialog effectively allows you to stop in the middle of a computation, and interact with the *Mathematica* environment that exists at that time. You can for example find values of intermediate variables in the computation, and even reset those values. There are however a number of subtleties, mostly associated with pattern and module variables.

What TraceDialog does is to call the function Dialog on a sequence of expressions. The Dialog function is discussed in detail in Section 2.14.2. When you call Dialog, you are effectively starting a subsidiary *Mathematica* session with its own sequence of input and output lines.

In general, you may need to apply arbitrary functions to the expressions you get while tracing an evaluation. TraceScan[*f*, *expr*, ...] applies *f* to each expression that arises. The expression is wrapped with HoldForm to prevent it from evaluating.

In TraceScan[*f*, *expr*, ...], the function *f* is applied to expressions before they are evaluated. TraceScan[*f*, *expr*, *patt*, *fp*] applies *f* before evaluation, and *fp* after evaluation.

■ 2.6.12 Advanced Topic: The Evaluation Stack

Throughout any computation, *Mathematica* maintains an *evaluation stack* containing the expressions it is currently evaluating. You can use the function Stack to look at the stack. This means, for example, that if you interrupt *Mathematica* in the middle of a computation, you can use Stack to find out what *Mathematica* is doing.

The expression that *Mathematica* most recently started to evaluate always appears as the last element of the evaluation stack. The previous elements of the stack are the other expressions whose evaluation is currently in progress.

Thus at the point when x is being evaluated, the stack associated with the evaluation of an expression like $f[g[x]]$ will have the form $\{f[g[x]], g[x], x\}$.

Stack[_] gives the expressions that are being evaluated at the time when it is called, in this case including the Print function.	*In[1]:=* **f[g[Print[Stack[_]]]] ;** {f[g[Print[Stack[_]]]]; , f[g[Print[Stack[_]]]], g[Print[Stack[_]]], Print[Stack[_]]}
Stack[ ] gives the tags associated with the evaluations that are being done when it is called.	*In[2]:=* **f[g[Print[Stack[ ]]]] ;** {CompoundExpression, f, g, Print}

In general, you can think of the evaluation stack as showing what functions called what other functions to get to the point *Mathematica* is at in your computation. The sequence of expressions corresponds to the first elements in the successively nested lists returned by Trace with the option TraceAbove set to True.

Stack[ ]	give a list of the tags associated with evaluations that are currently being done
Stack[_]	give a list of all expressions currently being evaluated
Stack[*form*]	include only expressions which match *form*

Looking at the evaluation stack.

It is rather rare to call Stack directly in your main *Mathematica* session. More often, you will want to call Stack in the middle of a computation. Typically, you can do this from within a dialog, or subsidiary session, as discussed in Section 2.14.2.

Here is the standard recursive definition of the factorial function.	*In[3]:=* **fac[1] = 1; fac[n_] := n fac[n-1]**
This evaluates fac[10], starting a dialog when it encounters fac[4].	*In[4]:=* **TraceDialog[fac[10], fac[4]]** TraceDialog::dgbgn: Entering Dialog; use Return[] to exit. *Out[5]=* fac[4]

This shows what objects were being evaluated when the dialog was started.	*In[6]:=* **Stack[ ]** *Out[6]=* {TraceDialog, Times, Times, 　　　　　　Times, Times, Times, Times, fac}
This ends the dialog.	*In[7]:=* **Return[ ]** TraceDialog::dgend: Exiting Dialog. *Out[4]=* 3628800

In the simplest cases, the *Mathematica* evaluation stack is set up to record *all* expressions currently being evaluated. Under some circumstances, however, this may be inconvenient. For example, executing Print[Stack[ ]] will always show a stack with Print as the last function.

The function StackInhibit allows you to avoid this kind of problem. StackInhibit[*expr*] evaluates *expr* without modifying the stack.

StackInhibit prevents Print from being included on the stack.	*In[5]:=* **f[g[StackInhibit[Print[Stack[ ]]]]] ;** *Out[5]=* {CompoundExpression, f, g}

Functions like TraceDialog automatically call StackInhibit each time they start a dialog. This means that Stack does not show functions that are called within the dialog, only those outside.

StackInhibit[*expr*]	evaluate *expr* without modifying the stack
StackBegin[*expr*]	evaluate *expr* with a fresh stack
StackComplete[*expr*]	evaluate *expr* with intermediate expressions in evaluation chains included on the stack

Controlling the evaluation stack.

By using StackInhibit and StackBegin, you can control which parts of the evaluation process are recorded on the stack. StackBegin[*expr*] evaluates *expr*, starting a fresh stack. This means that during the evaluation of *expr*, the stack does not include anything outside the StackBegin. Functions like TraceDialog[*expr*, ...] call StackBegin before they begin evaluating *expr*, so that the stack shows how *expr* is evaluated, but not how TraceDialog was called.

StackBegin[*expr*] uses a fresh stack in the evaluation of *expr*.	*In[6]:=* **f[StackBegin[g[h[StackInhibit[Print[Stack[ ]]]]]]]** {g, h} *Out[6]=* f[g[h[Null]]]

Stack normally shows you only those expressions that are currently being evaluated. As a result, it includes only the latest form of each expression. Sometimes, however, you may find it useful also to see earlier forms of the expressions. You can do this using StackComplete.

What StackComplete[*expr*] effectively does is to keep on the stack the complete evaluation chain for each expression that is currently being evaluated. In this case, the stack corresponds to the sequence of expressions obtained from Trace with the option TraceBackward -> All as well as TraceAbove -> True.

■ 2.6.13 Advanced Topic: Controlling Infinite Evaluation

The general principle that *Mathematica* follows in evaluating expressions is to go on applying transformation rules until the expressions no longer change. This means, for example, that if you make an assignment like x = x + 1, *Mathematica* should go into an infinite loop. In fact, *Mathematica* stops after a definite number of steps, determined by the value of the global variable $RecursionLimit. You can always stop *Mathematica* earlier by explicitly interrupting it.

This assignment could cause an infinite loop. *Mathematica* stops after a number of steps determined by $RecursionLimit.	*In[1]:=* **x = x + 1** $RecursionLimit::reclim: Recursion depth of 256 exceeded. *Out[1]=* $255 + \text{Hold}[1 + x]$
When *Mathematica* stops without finishing evaluation, it returns a held result. You can continue the evaluation by explicitly calling ReleaseHold.	*In[2]:=* **ReleaseHold[%]** $RecursionLimit::reclim: Recursion depth of 256 exceeded. *Out[2]=* $510 + \text{Hold}[1 + x]$

$RecursionLimit	maximum depth of the evaluation stack
$IterationLimit	maximum length of an evaluation chain

Global variables that limit infinite evaluation.

Here is a circular definition, whose evaluation is stopped by $IterationLimit.	*In[3]:=* **{a, b} = {b, a}** $IterationLimit::itlim: Iteration limit of 4096 exceeded. $IterationLimit::itlim: Iteration limit of 4096 exceeded. *Out[3]=* {Hold[b], Hold[a]}

The variables $RecursionLimit and $IterationLimit control the two basic ways that an evaluation can become infinite in *Mathematica*. $RecursionLimit limits the maximum depth of the evaluation stack, or equivalently, the maximum nesting depth that would occur in the list structure produced by Trace. $IterationLimit limits the maximum length of any particular evaluation chain, or the maximum length of any single list in the structure produced by Trace.

$RecursionLimit and $IterationLimit are by default set to values that are appropriate for most computations, and most computer systems. You can, however, reset these variables to any integer (above a lower limit), or to Infinity. Note that on most computer systems, you should never set $RecursionLimit = Infinity, as discussed on page 715.

This resets $RecursionLimit and $IterationLimit to 20.	*In[4]:=* **$RecursionLimit = $IterationLimit = 20** *Out[4]=* 20
Now infinite definitions like this are stopped after just 20 steps.	*In[5]:=* **t = {t}** $RecursionLimit::reclim: Recursion depth of 20 exceeded. *Out[5]=* {{{{{{{{{{{{{{{{{{Hold[{t}]}}}}}}}}}}}}}}}}}}

Without an end condition, this recursive definition leads to infinite computations.

```
In[6]:= fn[n_] := {fn[n-1], n}
```

A fairly large structure is built up before the computation is stopped.

```
In[7]:= fn[10]
```

$RecursionLimit::reclim: Recursion depth of 20 exceeded.

```
Out[7]= {{{{{{{{{{{{{{{{{{Hold[fn[-8 - 1]], -8}, -7}, -6},
                             -5}, -4}, -3}, -2}, -1}, 0}, 1}, 2},
                   3}, 4}, 5}, 6}, 7}, 8}, 9}, 10}
```

Here is another recursive definition.

```
In[8]:= fm[n_] := fm[n - 1]
```

In this case, no complicated structure is built up, and the computation is stopped by $IterationLimit.

```
In[9]:= fm[0]
```

$IterationLimit::itlim: Iteration limit of 20 exceeded.

```
Out[9]= Hold[fm[-19 - 1]]
```

It is important to realize that infinite loops can take up not only time but also computer memory. Computations limited by $IterationLimit do not normally build up large intermediate structures. But those limited by $RecursionLimit often do. In many cases, the size of the structures produced is a linear function of the value of $RecursionLimit. But in some cases, the size can grow exponentially, or worse, with $RecursionLimit.

An assignment like x = x + 1 is obviously circular. When you set up more complicated recursive definitions, however, it can be much more difficult to be sure that the recursion terminates, and that you will not end up in an infinite loop. The main thing to check is that the right-hand sides of your transformation rules will always be different from the left-hand sides. This ensures that evaluation will always "make progress", and *Mathematica* will not simply end up applying the same transformation rule to the same expression over and over again.

Some of the trickiest cases occur when you have rules that depend on complicated /; conditions (see Section 2.3.5). One particularly awkward case is when the condition involves a "global variable". *Mathematica* may think that the evaluation is finished because the expression did not change. However, a side effect of some other operation could change the value of the global variable, and so should lead to a new result in the evaluation. The best way to avoid this kind of difficulty is not to use global variables in /; conditions. If all else fails, you can type Update[s] to tell *Mathematica* to update all expressions involving s. Update[ ] tells *Mathematica* to update absolutely all expressions.

■ 2.6.14 Advanced Topic: Interrupts and Aborts

Section 1.3.12 described how you can interrupt a *Mathematica* computation by pressing appropriate keys on your keyboard.

In some cases, you may want to simulate such interrupts from within a *Mathematica* program. In general, executing Interrupt[ ] has the same effect as pressing interrupt keys. On a typical system, a menu of options is displayed, as discussed in Section 1.3.12.

Interrupt[ ]	interrupt a computation
Abort[ ]	abort a computation
CheckAbort[*expr*, *failexpr*]	evaluate *expr* and return the result, or *failexpr* if an abort occurs
AbortProtect[*expr*]	evaluate *expr*, masking the effect of aborts until the evaluation is complete

Interrupts and aborts.

The function Abort[ ] has the same effect as interrupting a computation, and selecting the abort option in the interrupt menu.

You can use Abort[ ] to implement an "emergency stop" in a program. In almost all cases, however, you should try to use functions like Return and Throw, which lead to more controlled behavior.

Abort terminates the computation, so only the first Print is executed.

```
In[1]:= Print[a]; Abort[ ]; Print[b]

a

Out[1]= $Aborted
```

If you abort at any point during the evaluation of a *Mathematica* expression, *Mathematica* normally abandons the evaluation of the whole expression, and returns the value $Aborted.

You can, however, "catch" aborts using the function CheckAbort. If an abort occurs during the evaluation of *expr* in CheckAbort[*expr*, *failexpr*], then CheckAbort returns *failexpr*, but the abort propagates no further. Functions like Dialog use CheckAbort in this way to contain the effect of aborts.

CheckAbort catches the abort, prints c and returns the value aborted.

```
In[2]:= CheckAbort[Print[a]; Abort[ ]; Print[b], Print[c]; aborted]

a
c

Out[2]= aborted
```

The effect of the Abort is contained by CheckAbort, so b is printed.

```
In[3]:= CheckAbort[Print[a]; Abort[ ], Print[c]; aborted]; Print[b]

a
c
b
```

When you construct sophisticated programs in *Mathematica*, you may sometimes want to guarantee that a particular section of code in a program cannot be aborted, either interactively or by calling Abort. The function AbortProtect allows you to evaluate an expression, saving up any aborts until after the evaluation of the expression is complete.

The `Abort` is saved up until `AbortProtect` is finished.

In[4]:= **AbortProtect[Abort[ ]; Print[a]]; Print[b]**

a

Out[4]= $Aborted

The `CheckAbort` sees the abort, but does not propagate it further.

In[5]:= **AbortProtect[Abort[ ]; CheckAbort[Print[a], x]]; Print[b]**

b

Even inside `AbortProtect`, `CheckAbort` will see any aborts that occur, and will return the appropriate *failexpr*. Unless this *failexpr* itself contains `Abort[ ]`, the aborts will be "absorbed" by the `CheckAbort`.

■ 2.6.15 Compiling *Mathematica* Expressions

If you make a definition like `f[x_] := x Sin[x]`, *Mathematica* will store the expression `x Sin[x]` in a form that can be evaluated for any `x`. Then when you give a particular value for `x`, *Mathematica* substitutes this value into `x Sin[x]`, and evaluates the result. The internal code that *Mathematica* uses to perform this evaluation is set up to work equally well whether the value you give for `x` is a number, a list, an algebraic object, or any other kind of expression.

Having to take account of all these possibilities inevitably makes the evaluation process slower. However, if *Mathematica* could *assume* that `x` will be a machine number, then it could avoid many steps, and potentially evaluate an expression like `x Sin[x]` much more quickly.

Using `Compile`, you can construct *compiled functions* in *Mathematica*, which evaluate *Mathematica* expressions assuming that all the parameters which appear are numbers (or logical variables). `Compile[{`x_1, x_2, ... `}`, *expr*] takes an expression *expr* and returns a "compiled function" which evaluates this expression when given arguments x_1, x_2, ...

In general, `Compile` creates a `CompiledFunction` object which contains a sequence of simple instructions for evaluating the compiled function. The instructions are chosen to be close to those found in the machine code of a typical computer, and can thus be executed quickly.

`Compile[{`x_1, x_2, ... `}`, *expr*]	create a compiled function which evaluates *expr* for numerical values of the x_i

Creating compiled functions.

This defines `f` to be a pure function which evaluates `x Sin[x]` for any `x`.

In[1]:= **f = Function[{x}, x Sin[x]]**

Out[1]= Function[{x}, x Sin[x]]

This creates a compiled function for evaluating `x Sin[x]`.

In[2]:= **fc = Compile[{x}, x Sin[x]]**

Out[2]= CompiledFunction[{x}, x Sin[x], -CompiledCode-]

f and fc yield the same results, but fc runs faster when the argument you give is a number.

In[3]:= **{f[2.5], fc[2.5]}**

Out[3]= {1.49618, 1.49618}

Compile is useful in situations where you have to evaluate a particular numerical or logical expression many times. By taking the time to call Compile, you can get a compiled function which can be executed more quickly than an ordinary *Mathematica* function.

For simple expressions such as x Sin[x], there is usually little difference between the execution speed for ordinary and compiled functions. However, as the size of the expressions involved increases, the advantage of compilation also increases. For large expressions, compilation can speed up execution by a factor as large as 20.

Compilation makes the biggest difference for expressions containing a large number of simple, say arithmetic, functions. For more complicated functions, such as BesselK or Eigenvalues, most of the computation time is spent executing internal *Mathematica* algorithms, on which compilation has no effect.

This creates a compiled function for finding values of the tenth Legendre polynomial. The Evaluate tells *Mathematica* to construct the polynomial explicitly before doing compilation.

In[4]:= **pc = Compile[{x}, Evaluate[LegendreP[10, x]]]**

$$Out[4]= \text{CompiledFunction}\Big[\{x\},$$
$$-\frac{63}{256} + \frac{3465\,x^2}{256} - \frac{15015\,x^4}{128} + \frac{45045\,x^6}{128} -$$
$$\frac{109395\,x^8}{256} + \frac{46189\,x^{10}}{256}, \text{-CompiledCode-}\Big]$$

This finds the value of the tenth Legendre polynomial with argument 0.4.

In[5]:= **pc[0.4]**

Out[5]= 0.0968391

This uses built-in numerical code.

In[6]:= **LegendreP[10, 0.4]**

Out[6]= 0.0968391

Even though you can use compilation to speed up numerical functions that you write, you should still try to use built-in *Mathematica* functions whenever possible. Built-in functions will usually run faster than any compiled *Mathematica* programs you can create. In addition, they typically use more extensive algorithms, with more complete control over numerical precision and so on.

You should realize that built-in *Mathematica* functions quite often themselves use Compile. Thus, for example, NIntegrate by default automatically uses Compile on the expression you tell it to integrate. Similarly, functions like Plot and Plot3D use Compile on the expressions you ask them to plot. Built-in functions that use Compile typically have the option Compiled. Setting Compiled -> False tells the functions not to use Compile.

Compile[{{x_1, t_1}, {x_2, t_2}, ... }, *expr*]

compile *expr* assuming that x_i is of type t_i

Compile[{{x_1, t_1, n_1}, {x_2, t_2, n_2}, ... }, *expr*]

compile *expr* assuming that x_i is a rank n_i array of objects each of type t_i

Compile[*vars*, *expr*, {{p_1, pt_1}, ... }]

compile *expr*, assuming that subexpressions which match p_i are of type pt_i

_Integer	machine-size integer
_Real	machine-precision approximate real number
_Complex	machine-precision approximate complex number
True | False	logical variable

Specifying types for compilation.

Compile works by making assumptions about the types of objects that occur in evaluating the expression you give. The default assumption is that all variables in the expression are approximate real numbers.

Compile nevertheless also allows integers, complex numbers and logical variables (True or False), as well as arrays of numbers. You can specify the type of a particular variable by giving a pattern which matches only values that have that type. Thus, for example, you can use the pattern _Integer to specify the integer type. Similarly, you can use True | False to specify a logical variable that must be either True or False.

This compiles the expression 5 i + j with the assumption that i and j are integers.	*In[7]:=* **Compile[{{i, _Integer}, {j, _Integer}}, 5 i + j]** *Out[7]=* CompiledFunction[{i, j}, 5 i + j, -CompiledCode-]
This yields an integer result.	*In[8]:=* **%[8, 7]** *Out[8]=* 47
This compiles an expression that performs an operation on a matrix of integers.	*In[9]:=* **Compile[{{m, _Integer, 2}}, Apply[Plus, Flatten[m]]]** *Out[9]=* CompiledFunction[{m}, Plus @@ Flatten[m], -CompiledCode-]
The list operations are now carried out in a compiled way, and the result is an integer.	*In[10]:=* **%[{{1, 2, 3}, {7, 8, 9}}]** *Out[10]=* 30

The types that `Compile` handles correspond essentially to the types that computers typically handle at a machine-code level. Thus, for example, `Compile` can handle approximate real numbers that have machine precision, but it cannot handle arbitrary-precision numbers. In addition, if you specify that a particular variable is an integer, `Compile` generates code only for the case when the integer is of "machine size", typically between $\pm 2^{31}$.

When the expression you ask to compile involves only standard arithmetic and logical operations, `Compile` can deduce the types of objects generated at every step simply from the types of the input variables. However, if you call other functions, `Compile` will typically not know what type of value they return. If you do not specify otherwise, `Compile` assumes that any other function yields an approximate real number value. You can, however, also give an explicit list of patterns, specifying what type to assume for an expression that matches a particular pattern.

This defines a function which yields an integer result when given an integer argument.	`In[11]:= com[i_] := Binomial[2i, i]`

This compiles x^com[i] using the assumption that com[_] is always an integer.	`In[12]:= Compile[{x, {i, _Integer}}, x^com[i],`
	`                    {{com[_], _Integer}}]`
	
	`Out[12]= CompiledFunction[{x, i}, x`$^{\text{com[i]}}$`, -CompiledCode-]`

This evaluates the compiled function.	`In[13]:= %[5.6, 1]`
	
	`Out[13]= 31.36`

The idea of `Compile` is to create a function which is optimized for certain types of arguments. `Compile` is nevertheless set up so that the functions it creates work with whatever types of arguments they are given. When the optimization cannot be used, a standard *Mathematica* expression is evaluated to find the value of the function.

Here is a compiled function for taking the square root of a variable.	`In[14]:= sq = Compile[{x}, Sqrt[x]]` `Out[14]= CompiledFunction`$\left[\{x\}, \sqrt{x}, \text{-CompiledCode-}\right]$

If you give a real number argument, optimized code is used.	`In[15]:= sq[4.5]`
	
	`Out[15]= 2.12132`

The compiled code cannot be used, so *Mathematica* prints a warning, then just evaluates the original symbolic expression.	`In[16]:= sq[1 + u]`
	
	`CompiledFunction::cfsa:`
	`    Argument 1 + u at position 1 should be a`
	`    machine-size real number.`
	
	`Out[16]=` $\sqrt{1+u}$

The compiled code generated by `Compile` must make assumptions not only about the types of arguments you will supply, but also about the types of all objects that arise during the execution of the code. Sometimes these types depend on the actual *values* of the arguments you specify. Thus, for example, `Sqrt[x]` yields a real number result for real x if x is not negative, but yields a complex number if x is negative.

Compile always makes a definite assumption about the type returned by a particular function. If this assumption turns out to be invalid in a particular case when the code generated by Compile is executed, then *Mathematica* simply abandons the compiled code in this case, and evaluates an ordinary *Mathematica* expression to get the result.

The compiled code does not expect a complex number, so *Mathematica* has to revert to explicitly evaluating the original symbolic expression.	*In[17]:=* **sq[-4.5]**
	
	CompiledFunction::cfn:
	    Numerical error encountered at instruction 2;
	        proceeding with uncompiled evaluation.
	
	Out[17]= 0. + 2.12132 i

An important feature of Compile is that it can handle not only mathematical expressions, but also various simple *Mathematica* programs. Thus, for example, Compile can handle conditionals and control flow structures.

In all cases, Compile[*vars*, *expr*] holds its arguments unevaluated. This means that you can explicitly give a "program" as the expression to compile.

This creates a compiled version of a *Mathematica* program which implements Newton's approximation to square roots.	*In[18]:=* **newt = Compile[{x, {n, _Integer}},**
	            Module[{t}, t = x; Do[t = (t + x/t)/2, {n}]; t]
	        ]
	
	Out[18]= CompiledFunction$\Big[$\{x, n\},
	
	Module$\Big[$\{t\}, t = x; Do$\Big[$t = $\frac{1}{2}\Big(t + \frac{x}{t}\Big)$, \{n\}$\Big]$; t$\Big]$,
	
	-CompiledCode-$\Big]$

This executes the compiled code.	*In[19]:=* **newt[2.4, 6]** *Out[19]=* 1.54919

■ 2.6.16 Advanced Topic: Manipulating Compiled Code

If you use compiled code created by Compile only within *Mathematica* itself, then you should never need to know the details of its internal form. Nevertheless, the compiled code can be represented by an ordinary *Mathematica* expression, and it is sometimes useful to manipulate it.

For example, you can take compiled code generated by Compile, and feed it to external programs or devices. You can also create CompiledFunction objects yourself, then execute them in *Mathematica*.

In all of these cases, you need to know the internal form of CompiledFunction objects. The first element of a CompiledFunction object is always a list of patterns which specifies the types of arguments accepted by the object. The fifth element of a CompiledFunction object is a *Mathematica* pure function that is used if the compiled code instruction stream fails for any reason to give a result.

CompiledFunction[{*arg*$_1$, *arg*$_2$, ... }, {*reg*$_1$, *reg*$_2$, ... }, {n_l, n_i, n_r, n_c, n_t}, *instr*, *func*]
compiled code taking arguments of type *arg*$_i$ and executing
the instruction stream *instr* using n_k registers of type k

The structure of a compiled code object.

This shows the explicit form of the
compiled code generated by Compile.

```
In[1]:= Compile[{x}, x^2] // InputForm

Out[1]//InputForm= CompiledFunction[{_Real}, {{3, 0, 0}, {3, 0, 1}},
                   {0, 0, 2, 0, 0}, {{1, 5}, {29, 0, 0, 1}, {2}},
                   Function[{x}, x^2], Evaluate]
```

The instruction stream in a CompiledFunction object consists of a list of instructions for a simple idealized computer. The computer is assumed to have numbered "registers", on which operations can be performed. There are five basic types of registers: logical, integer, real, complex and tensor. For each of these basic types it is then possible to have either a single scalar register or an array of registers of any rank. A list of the total number of registers of each type required to evaluate a particular CompiledFunction object is given as the second element of the object.

The actual instructions in the compiled code object are given as lists. The first element is an integer "opcode" which specifies what operation should be performed. Subsequent elements are either the numbers of registers of particular types, or literal constants. Typically the last element of the list is the number of a "destination register", into which the result of the operation should be put.

2.7 Modularity and the Naming of Things

■ 2.7.1 Modules and Local Variables

Mathematica normally assumes that all your variables are *global*. This means that every time you use a name like x, *Mathematica* normally assumes that you are referring to the *same* object.

Particularly when you write programs, however, you may not want all your variables to be global. You may, for example, want to use the name x to refer to two quite different variables in two different programs. In this case, you need the x in each program to be treated as a *local* variable.

You can set up local variables in *Mathematica* using *modules*. Within each module, you can give a list of variables which are to be treated as local to the module.

Module[{x, y, ... }, *body*]	a module with local variables x, y, ...

Creating modules in *Mathematica*.

This defines the global variable t to have value 17.	*In[1]:=* t = 17
	Out[1]= 17
The t inside the module is local, so it can be treated independently of the global t.	*In[2]:=* Module[{t}, t=8; Print[t]]
	8
The global t still has value 17.	*In[3]:=* t
	Out[3]= 17

The most common way that modules are used is to set up temporary or intermediate variables inside functions you define. It is important to make sure that such variables are kept local. If they are not, then you will run into trouble whenever their names happen to coincide with the names of other variables.

The intermediate variable t is specified to be local to the module.	*In[4]:=* f[v_] := Module[{t}, t = (1 + v)^2; t = Expand[t]]
This runs the function f.	*In[5]:=* f[a + b]
	Out[5]= $1 + 2\,a + a^2 + 2\,b + 2\,a\,b + b^2$
The global t still has value 17.	*In[6]:=* t
	Out[6]= 17

You can treat local variables in modules just like other symbols. Thus, for example, you can use them as names for local functions, you can assign attributes to them, and so on.

This sets up a module which defines a local function f.	`In[7]:= gfac10[k_] :=` `Module[{f, n}, f[1] = 1; f[n_] := k + n f[n-1]; f[10]]`
In this case, the local function f is just an ordinary factorial.	`In[8]:= gfac10[0]` `Out[8]= 3628800`
In this case, f is set up as a generalized factorial.	`In[9]:= gfac10[2]` `Out[9]= 8841802`

When you set up a local variable in a module, *Mathematica* initially assigns no value to the variable. This means that you can use the variable in a purely symbolic way, even if there was a global value defined for the variable outside the module.

This uses the global value of t defined above, and so yields a number.	`In[10]:= Expand[(1 + t)^3]` `Out[10]= 5832`
Here Length simply receives a number as its argument.	`In[11]:= Length[Expand[(1 + t)^3]]` `Out[11]= 0`
The local variable t has no value, so it acts as a symbol, and Expand produces the anticipated algebraic result.	`In[12]:= Module[{t}, Length[Expand[(1 + t)^3]]]` `Out[12]= 4`

`Module[{`$x = x_0$`, `$y = y_0$`, ... }, `*body*`]`   a module with initial values for local variables

---

Assigning initial values to local variables.

This specifies t to be a local variable, with initial value u.	`In[13]:= g[u_] := Module[{ t = u }, t += t/(1 + u)]`
This uses the definition of g.	`In[14]:= g[a]` `Out[14]= `$a + \dfrac{a}{1+a}$

You can define initial values for any of the local variables in a module. The initial values are always evaluated before the module is executed. As a result, even if a variable x is defined as local to the module, the global x will be used if it appears in an expression for an initial value.

The initial value of u is taken to be the global value of t.	`In[15]:= Module[{t = 6, u = t}, u^2]` `Out[15]= 289`

---

lhs `:= Module[`*vars*`, `*rhs* `/; `*cond*`]`   share local variables between *rhs* and *cond*

Using local variables in definitions with conditions.

When you set up /; conditions for definitions, you often need to introduce temporary variables. In many cases, you may want to share these temporary variables with the body of the right-hand side of the definition. *Mathematica* allows you to enclose the whole right-hand side of your definition in a module, including the condition.

This defines a function with a condition attached.	`In[16]:= h[x_] := Module[{t}, t^2 - 1 /; (t = x - 4) > 1]`

Mathematica shares the value of the local variable t between the condition and the body of the right-hand side.	`In[17]:= h[10]`
	
	`Out[17]= 35`

■ 2.7.2 Local Constants

`With[{x = `x_0`, y = `y_0`, ... }, `*body*`]`	define local constants *x*, *y*, ...

Defining local constants.

Module allows you to set up local *variables*, to which you can assign any sequence of values. Often, however, all you really need are local *constants*, to which you assign a value only once. The *Mathematica* With construct allows you to set up such local constants.

This defines a global value for t.	`In[1]:= t = 17`
	
	`Out[1]= 17`

This defines a function using t as a local constant.	`In[2]:= w[x_] := With[{t = x + 1}, t + t^3]`

This uses the definition of w.	`In[3]:= w[a]` `Out[3]= `$1 + a + (1 + a)^3$

t still has its global value.	`In[4]:= t`
	
	`Out[4]= 17`

Just as in Module, the initial values you define in With are evaluated before the With is executed.

The expression t + 1 which gives the value of the local constant t is evaluated using the global t.	`In[5]:= With[{t = t + 1}, t^2]`
	
	`Out[5]= 324`

The way `With[{x = `x_0`, ... }, `*body*`]` works is to take *body*, and replace every occurrence of *x*, etc. in it by x_0, etc. You can think of With as a generalization of the /. operator, suitable for application to *Mathematica* code instead of other expressions.

This replaces x with a.	`In[6]:= With[{x = a}, x = 5]`
	
	`Out[6]= 5`

| After the replacement, the body of the With is a = 5, so a gets the global value 5. | *In[7]:=* **a** |
| | *Out[7]=* 5 |

| This clears the value of a. | *In[8]:=* **Clear[a]** |

In some respects, `With` is like a special case of `Module`, in which each local variable is assigned a value exactly once.

One of the main reasons for using `With` rather than `Module` is that it typically makes the *Mathematica* programs you write easier to understand. In a module, if you see a local variable x at a particular point, you potentially have to trace through all of the code in the module to work out the value of x at that point. In a `With` construct, however, you can always find out the value of a local constant simply by looking at the initial list of values, without having to trace through specific code.

If you have several `With` constructs, it is always the innermost one for a particular variable that is in effect. You can mix `Module` and `With`. The general rule is that the innermost one for a particular variable is the one that is in effect.

| With nested With constructs, the innermost one is always the one in effect. | *In[9]:=* **With[{t = 8}, With[{t = 9}, t^2]]** |
| | *Out[9]=* 81 |

| You can mix Module and With constructs. | *In[10]:=* **Module[{t = 8}, With[{t = 9}, t^2]]** |
| | *Out[10]=* 81 |

| Local variables in inner constructs do not mask ones outside unless the names conflict. | *In[11]:=* **With[{t = a}, With[{u = b}, t + u]]** |
| | *Out[11]=* a + b |

Except for the question of when x and *body* are evaluated, `With[{`$x = x_0$`},` *body*`]` works essentially like *body* `/.` x `->` x_0. However, `With` behaves in a special way when the expression *body* itself contains `With` or `Module` constructs. The main issue is to prevent the local constants in the various `With` constructs from conflicting with each other, or with global objects. The details of how this is done are discussed in Section 2.7.3.

| The y in the inner With is renamed to prevent it from conflicting with the global y. | *In[12]:=* **With[{x = 2 + y}, Hold[With[{y = 4}, x + y]]]** |
| | *Out[12]=* Hold[With[{y$ = 4}, (2 + y) + y$]] |

■ 2.7.3 How Modules Work

The way modules work in *Mathematica* is basically very simple. Every time any module is used, a new symbol is created to represent each of its local variables. The new symbol is given a unique name which cannot conflict with any other names. The name is formed by taking the name you specify for the local variable, followed by $, with a unique "serial number" appended.

The serial number is found from the value of the global variable `$ModuleNumber`. This variable counts the total number of times any `Module` of any form has been used.

> ■ `Module` generates symbols with names of the form *x$nnn* to represent each local variable.

The basic principle of modules in *Mathematica*.

This shows the symbol generated for t within the module.

In[1]:= `Module[{t}, Print[t]]`

t$1

The symbols are different every time any module is used.

In[2]:= `Module[{t, u}, Print[t]; Print[u]]`

t$2
u$2

For most purposes, you will never have to deal directly with the actual symbols generated inside modules. However, if for example you start up a dialog while a module is being executed, then you will see these symbols. The same is true whenever you use functions like `Trace` to watch the evaluation of modules.

You see the symbols that are generated inside modules when you use `Trace`.

In[3]:= `Trace[ Module[{t}, t = 3] ]`

Out[3]= {Module[{t}, t = 3], {t$3 = 3, 3}, 3}

This starts a dialog inside a module.

In[4]:= `Module[{t}, t = 6; Dialog[ ]]`

Inside the dialog, you see the symbols generated for local variables such as t.

In[5]:= `Stack[_]`

Out[5]= {Module[{t}, t = 6; Dialog[]],
         t$4 = 6; Dialog[], Dialog[]}

You can work with these symbols as you would with any other symbols.

In[6]:= `t$4 + 1`

Out[6]= 7

This returns from the dialog.

In[7]:= `Return[t$4 ^ 2]`

Out[4]= 36

Under some circumstances, it is convenient explicitly to return symbols that are generated inside modules.

You can explicitly return symbols that are generated inside modules.

In[5]:= `Module[{t}, t]`

Out[5]= t$6

You can treat these symbols as you would any others.

In[6]:= `%^2 + 1`

Out[6]= $1 + t\$6^2$

`Unique[x]`	generate a new symbol with a unique name of the form *x$nnn*
`Unique[{x, y, ... }]`	generate a list of new symbols

Generating new symbols with unique names.

The function `Unique` allows you to generate new symbols in the same way as `Module` does. Each time you call `Unique`, `$ModuleNumber` is incremented, so that the names of new symbols are guaranteed to be unique.

| This generates a unique new symbol whose name starts with x. | *In[7]:=* **Unique[x]** |
| | *Out[7]=* x$7 |

| Each time you call `Unique` you get a symbol with a larger serial number. | *In[8]:=* **{Unique[x], Unique[x], Unique[x]}** |
| | *Out[8]=* {x$8, x$9, x$10} |

| If you call `Unique` with a list of names, you get the same serial number for each of the symbols. | *In[9]:=* **Unique[{x, xa, xb}]** |
| | *Out[9]=* {x$11, xa$11, xb$11} |

You can use the standard *Mathematica* ?*name* mechanism to get information on symbols that were generated inside modules or by the function `Unique`.

| Executing this module generates the symbol q$*nnn*. | *In[10]:=* **Module[{q}, q^2 + 1]** |
| | *Out[10]=* $1 + q\$12^2$ |

| You can see the generated symbol here. | *In[11]:=* **?q*** |
| | q   q$12 |

Symbols generated by `Module` behave in exactly the same way as other symbols for the purposes of evaluation. However, these symbols carry the attribute `Temporary`, which specifies that they should be removed completely from the system when they are no longer used. Thus most symbols that are generated inside modules are removed when the execution of those modules is finished. The symbols survive only if they are explicitly returned.

| This shows a new q variable generated inside a module. | *In[12]:=* **Module[{q}, Print[q]]** |
| | q$13 |

| The new variable is removed when the execution of the module is finished, so it does not show up here. | *In[13]:=* **?q*** |
| | q   q$12 |

You should realize that the use of names such as *x*$*nnn* for generated symbols is purely a convention. You can in principle give any symbol a name of this form. But if you do, the symbol may collide with one that is produced by `Module`.

An important point to note is that symbols generated by `Module` are in general unique only within a particular *Mathematica* session. The variable `$ModuleNumber` which determines the serial numbers for these symbols is always reset at the beginning of each session.

This means in particular that if you save expressions containing generated symbols in a file, and then read them into another session, there is no guarantee that conflicts will not occur.

One way to avoid such conflicts is explicitly to set `$ModuleNumber` differently at the beginning of each session. In particular, if you set `$ModuleNumber = 10^10 $SessionID`, you should avoid any conflicts. The global variable `$SessionID` should give a unique number which characterizes a particular *Mathematica* session on a particular computer. The value of this variable is determined from such quantities as the absolute date and time, the ID of your computer, and, if appropriate, the ID of the particular *Mathematica* process.

`$ModuleNumber`	the serial number for symbols generated by `Module` and `Unique`
`$SessionID`	a number that should be different for every *Mathematica* session

Variables to be used in determining serial numbers for generated symbols.

Having generated appropriate symbols to represent the local variables you have specified, `Module[`*vars*`, `*body*`]` then has to evaluate *body* using these symbols. The first step is to take the actual expression *body* as it appears inside the module, and effectively to use `With` to replace all occurrences of each local variable name with the appropriate generated symbol. After this is done, `Module` actually performs the evaluation of the resulting expression.

An important point to note is that `Module[`*vars*`, `*body*`]` inserts generated symbols only into the actual expression *body*. It does not, for example, insert such symbols into code that is called from *body*, but does not explicitly appear in *body*.

Section 2.7.6 will discuss how you can use `Block` to set up "local values" which work in a different way.

Since x does not appear explicitly in the body of the module, the local value is not used.

```
In[14]:= tmp = x^2 + 1; Module[{x = 4}, tmp]
```

$Out[14]= 1 + x^2$

Most of the time, you will probably set up modules by giving explicit *Mathematica* input of the form `Module[`*vars*`, `*body*`]`. Since the function `Module` has the attribute `HoldAll`, the form of *body* will usually be kept unevaluated until the module is executed.

It is, however, possible to build modules dynamically in *Mathematica*. The generation of new symbols, and their insertion into *body* are always done only when a module is actually executed, not when the module is first given as *Mathematica* input.

This evaluates the body of the module immediately, making x appear explicitly.

```
In[15]:= tmp = x^2 + 1; Module[{x = 4}, Evaluate[tmp]]
```

$Out[15]= 17$

■ 2.7.4 Advanced Topic: Variables in Pure Functions and Rules

`Module` and `With` allow you to give a specific list of symbols whose names you want to treat as local. In some situations, however, you want to automatically treat certain symbol names as local.

For example, if you use a pure function such as `Function[{x}, x + a]`, you want `x` to be treated as a "formal parameter", whose specific name is local. The same is true of the `x` that appears in a rule like `f[x_] -> x^2`, or a definition like `f[x_] := x^2`.

Mathematica uses a uniform scheme to make sure that the names of formal parameters which appear in constructs like pure functions and rules are kept local, and are never confused with global names. The basic idea is to replace formal parameters when necessary by symbols with names of the form $x\$$. By convention, $x\$$ is never used as a global name.

Here is a nested pure function.	*In[1]:=* `Function[{x}, Function[{y}, x + y]]`
	Out[1]= $\text{Function}[\{x\}, \text{Function}[\{y\}, x + y]]$
Mathematica renames the formal parameter y in the inner function to avoid conflict with the global object y.	*In[2]:=* `%[2y]`
	Out[2]= $\text{Function}[\{y\$\}, 2y + y\$]$
The resulting pure function behaves as it should.	*In[3]:=* `%[a]`
	Out[3]= $a + 2y$

In general, *Mathematica* renames the formal parameters in an object like `Function[`*vars*`, `*body*`]` whenever *body* is modified in any way by the action of another pure function.

The formal parameter y is renamed because the body of the inner pure function was changed.	*In[4]:=* `Function[{x}, Function[{y}, x + y]] [a]`
	Out[4]= $\text{Function}[\{y\$\}, a + y\$]$
Since the body of the inner function does not change, the formal parameter is not renamed.	*In[5]:=* `Function[{x}, x + Function[{y}, y^2]] [a]`
	Out[5]= $a + \text{Function}[\{y\}, y^2]$

Mathematica renames formal parameters in pure functions more liberally than is strictly necessary. In principle, renaming could be avoided if the names of the formal parameters in a particular function do not actually conflict with parts of expressions substituted into the body of the pure function. For uniformity, however, *Mathematica* still renames formal parameters even in such cases.

In this case, the formal parameter x in the inner function shields the body of the function, so no renaming is needed.	*In[6]:=* `Function[{x}, Function[{x}, x + y]] [a]`
	Out[6]= $\text{Function}[\{x\}, x + y]$
Here are three nested functions.	*In[7]:=* `Function[{x}, Function[{y}, Function[{z}, x + y + z]]]`
	Out[7]= $\text{Function}[\{x\},$
	$\text{Function}[\{y\}, \text{Function}[\{z\}, x + y + z]]]$
Both inner functions are renamed in this case.	*In[8]:=* `%[a]`
	Out[8]= $\text{Function}[\{y\$\}, \text{Function}[\{z\$\}, a + y\$ + z\$]]$

As mentioned on page 249, pure functions in *Mathematica* are like λ expressions in formal logic. The renaming of formal parameters allows *Mathematica* pure functions to reproduce all the semantics of standard λ expressions faithfully.

`Function[{`x`, ... }, `*body*`]`	local parameters
lhs `-> ` *rhs* and *lhs* `:> ` *rhs*	local pattern names
lhs `= ` *rhs* and *lhs* `:= ` *rhs*	local pattern names
`With[{`$x = x_0$`, ... }, `*body*`]`	local constants
`Module[{`x`, ... }, `*body*`]`	local variables

Scoping constructs in *Mathematica*.

Mathematica has several "scoping constructs" in which certain names are treated as local. When you mix these constructs in any way, *Mathematica* does appropriate renamings to avoid conflicts.

Mathematica renames the formal parameter of the pure function to avoid a conflict.

In[9]:= `With[{x = a}, Function[{a}, a + x]]`

Out[9]= `Function[{a$}, a$ + a]`

Here the local constant in the inner With is renamed to avoid a conflict.

In[10]:= `With[{x = y}, Hold[With[{y = 4}, x + y]]]`

Out[10]= `Hold[With[{y$ = 4}, y + y$]]`

There is no conflict between names in this case, so no renaming is done.

In[11]:= `With[{x = y}, Hold[With[{z = x + 2}, z + 2]]]`

Out[11]= `Hold[With[{z = y + 2}, z + 2]]`

The local variable y in the module is renamed to avoid a conflict.

In[12]:= `With[{x = y}, Hold[Module[{y}, x + y]]]`

Out[12]= `Hold[Module[{y$}, y + y$]]`

If you execute the module, however, the local variable is renamed again to make its name unique.

In[13]:= `ReleaseHold[%]`

Out[13]= `y + y$1`

Mathematica treats transformation rules as scoping constructs, in which the names you give to patterns are local. You can set up named patterns either using $x\_$, $x\_\_$ and so on, or using x`:`*patt*.

The x in the h goes with the x_, and is considered local to the rule.

In[14]:= `With[{x = 5}, g[x_, x] -> h[x]]`

Out[14]= `g[x_, 5] → h[x]`

In a rule like `f[x_] -> x + y`, the x which appears on the right-hand side goes with the name of the x_ pattern. As a result, this x is treated as a variable local to the rule, and cannot be modified by other scoping constructs.

The y, on the other hand, is not local to the rule, and *can* be modified by other scoping constructs. When this happens, *Mathematica* renames the patterns in the rule to prevent the possibility of a conflict.

| *Mathematica* renames the x in the rule to prevent a conflict. | *In[15]:=* **With[{w = x}, f[x_] -> w + x]** |
| | *Out[15]=* f[x$_] → x + x$ |

When you use **With** on a scoping construct, *Mathematica* automatically performs appropriate renamings. In some cases, however, you may want to make substitutions inside scoping constructs, without any renaming. You can do this using the **/.** operator.

| When you substitute for y using **With**, the x in the pure function is renamed to prevent a conflict. | *In[16]:=* **With[{y = x + a}, Function[{x}, x + y]]** |
| | *Out[16]=* Function[{x$}, x$ + (a + x)] |

| If you use **/.** rather than **With**, no such renaming is done. | *In[17]:=* **Function[{x}, x + y] /. y -> a + x** |
| | *Out[17]=* Function[{x}, x + (a + x)] |

When you apply a rule such as $f[x\_] \to rhs$, or use a definition such as $f[x\_] := rhs$, *Mathematica* implicitly has to substitute for x everywhere in the expression *rhs*. It effectively does this using the **/.** operator. As a result, such substitution does not respect scoping constructs. However, when the insides of a scoping construct are modified by the substitution, the other variables in the scoping construct are renamed.

| This defines a function for creating pure functions. | *In[18]:=* **mkfun[var_, body_] := Function[{var}, body]** |

| The x and x^2 are explicitly inserted into the pure function, effectively by using the **/.** operator. | *In[19]:=* **mkfun[x, x^2]** |
| | *Out[19]=* Function[{x}, x^2] |

| This defines a function that creates a pair of nested pure functions. | *In[20]:=* **mkfun2[var_, body_] := Function[{x},** |
| | **Function[{var}, body + x]]** |

| The x in the outer pure function is renamed in this case. | *In[21]:=* **mkfun2[x, x^2]** |
| | *Out[21]=* Function[{x$}, Function[{x}, $x^2 + x\$$]] |

■ 2.7.5 Dummy Variables in Mathematics

When you set up mathematical formulas, you often have to introduce various kinds of local objects or "dummy variables". You can treat such dummy variables using modules and other *Mathematica* scoping constructs.

Integration variables are a common example of dummy variables in mathematics. When you write down a formal integral, conventional notation requires you to introduce an integration variable with a definite name. This variable is essentially "local" to the integral, and its name, while arbitrary, must not conflict with any other names in your mathematical expression.

| Here is a function for evaluating an integral. | *In[1]:=* **p[n_] := Integrate[f[s] s^n, {s, 0, 1}]** |

The s here conflicts with the integration variable.

$In[2]:=$ **p[s + 1]**

$Out[2]=$ $\displaystyle\int_0^1 s^{1+s}\, f[s]\, \mathrm{d}s$

Here is a definition with the integration variable specified as local to a module.

$In[3]:=$ **pm[n_] := Module[{s}, Integrate[f[s] s^n, {s, 0, 1}]]**

Since you have used a module, *Mathematica* automatically renames the integration variable to avoid a conflict.

$In[4]:=$ **pm[s + 1]**

$Out[4]=$ $\displaystyle\int_0^1 s\$242^{1+s}\, f[s\$242]\, \mathrm{d}s\$242$

In many cases, the most important issue is that dummy variables should be kept local, and should not interfere with other variables in your mathematical expression. In some cases, however, what is instead important is that different uses of the *same* dummy variable should not conflict.

Repeated dummy variables often appear in products of vectors and tensors. With the "summation convention", any vector or tensor index that appears exactly twice is summed over all its possible values. The actual name of the repeated index never matters, but if there are two separate repeated indices, it is essential that their names do not conflict.

This sets up the repeated index j as a dummy variable.

$In[5]:=$ **q[i_] := Module[{j}, a[i, j] b[j]]**

The module gives different instances of the dummy variable different names.

$In[6]:=$ **q[i1] q[i2]**

$Out[6]=$ a[i1, j\$387] a[i2, j\$388] b[j\$387] b[j\$388]

There are many situations in mathematics where you need to have variables with unique names. One example is in representing solutions to equations. With an equation like $\sin(x) = 0$, there are an infinite number of solutions, each of the form $x = n\pi$, where n is a dummy variable that can be equal to any integer. If you generate solutions to the equation on two separate occasions, there is no guarantee that the value of n should be the same in both cases. As a result, you must set up the solution so that the object n is different every time.

This defines a value for sinsol, with n as a dummy variable.

$In[7]:=$ **sinsol := Module[{n}, n Pi]**

Different occurrences of the dummy variable are distinguished.

$In[8]:=$ **sinsol - sinsol**

$Out[8]=$ n\$389 π - n\$390 π

Another place where unique objects are needed is in representing "constants of integration". When you do an integral, you are effectively solving an equation for a derivative. In general, there are many possible solutions to the equation, differing by additive "constants of integration". The standard *Mathematica* Integrate function always returns a solution with no constant of integration. But if you were to introduce constants of integration, you would need to use modules to make sure that they are always unique.

■ 2.7.6 Blocks and Local Values

Modules in *Mathematica* allow you to treat the *names* of variables as local. Sometimes, however, you want the names to be global, but *values* to be local. You can do this in *Mathematica* using `Block`.

`Block[{x, y, ... }, body]`	evaluate *body* using local values for *x, y, ...*
`Block[{x = `x_0`, y = `y_0`, ... }, body]`	assign initial values to *x, y, ...*

Setting up local values.

Here is an expression involving x.

$In[1]:=$ **x^2 + 3**

$Out[1]= 3 + x^2$

This evaluates the previous expression, using a local value for x.

$In[2]:=$ **Block[{x = a + 1}, %]**

$Out[2]= 3 + (1 + a)^2$

There is no global value for x.

$In[3]:=$ **x**

$Out[3]= x$

As described in the sections above, the variable *x* in a module such as `Module[{x}, `*body*`]` is always set up to refer to a unique symbol, different each time the module is used, and distinct from the global symbol *x*. The *x* in a block such as `Block[{x}, `*body*`]` is, however, taken to be the global symbol *x*. What the block does is to make the *value* of *x* local. The value *x* had when you entered the block is always restored when you exit the block. And during the execution of the block, *x* can take on any value.

This sets the symbol t to have value 17.

$In[4]:=$ **t = 17**

$Out[4]= 17$

Variables in modules have unique local names.

$In[5]:=$ **Module[{t}, Print[t]]**

t$1

In blocks, variables retain their global names, but can have local values.

$In[6]:=$ **Block[{t}, Print[t]]**

t

t is given a local value inside the block.

$In[7]:=$ **Block[{t}, t = 6; t^4 + 1]**

$Out[7]= 1297$

When the execution of the block is over, the previous value of t is restored.

$In[8]:=$ **t**

$Out[8]= 17$

Blocks in *Mathematica* effectively allow you to set up "environments" in which you can temporarily change the values of variables. Expressions you evaluate at any point during the execution of a block will use the values currently defined for variables in the block. This is true whether the expressions appear directly as part of the body of the block, or are produced at any point in its evaluation.

This defines a delayed value for the symbol u.	*In[9]:=* **u := x^2 + t^2**
If you evaluate u outside a block, the global value for t is used.	*In[10]:=* **u** *Out[10]=* $289 + x^2$
You can specify a temporary value for t to use inside the block.	*In[11]:=* **Block[{t = 5}, u + 7]** *Out[11]=* $32 + x^2$

An important implicit use of Block in *Mathematica* is for iteration constructs such as Do, Sum and Table. *Mathematica* effectively uses Block to set up local values for the iteration variables in all of these constructs.

Sum automatically makes the value of the iterator t local.	*In[12]:=* **Sum[t^2, {t, 10}]** *Out[12]=* 385
The local values in iteration constructs are slightly more general than in Block. They handle variables such as a[1], as well as pure symbols.	*In[13]:=* **Sum[a[1]^2, {a[1], 10}]** *Out[13]=* 385

When you set up functions in *Mathematica*, it is sometimes convenient to have "global variables" which can affect the functions without being given explicitly as arguments. Thus, for example, *Mathematica* itself has a global variable \$RecursionLimit which affects the evaluation of all functions, but is never explicitly given as an argument.

Mathematica will usually keep any value you define for a global variable until you explicitly change it. Often, however, you want to set up values which last only for the duration of a particular computation, or part of a computation. You can do this by making the values local to a *Mathematica* block.

This defines a function which depends on the "global variable" t.	*In[14]:=* **f[x_] := x^2 + t**
In this case, the global value of t is used.	*In[15]:=* **f[a]** *Out[15]=* $17 + a^2$
Inside a block, you can set up a local value for t.	*In[16]:=* **Block[{t = 2}, f[b]]** *Out[16]=* $2 + b^2$

You can use global variables not only to set parameters in functions, but also to accumulate results from functions. By setting up such variables to be local to a block, you can arrange to accumulate results only from functions called during the execution of the block.

This function increments the global variable t, and returns its current value.	*In[17]:=* **h[x_] := (t += x^2)**

If you do not use a block, evaluating h[a] changes the global value of t.

In[18]:= **h[a]**

Out[18]= $17 + a^2$

With a block, only the local value of t is affected.

In[19]:= **Block[{t = 0}, h[c]]**

Out[19]= c^2

The global value of t remains unchanged.

In[20]:= **t**

Out[20]= $17 + a^2$

When you enter a block such as Block[{*x*}, *body*], any value for *x* is removed. This means that you can in principle treat *x* as a "symbolic variable" inside the block. However, if you explicitly return *x* from the block, it will be replaced by its value outside the block as soon as it is evaluated.

The value of t is removed when you enter the block.

In[21]:= **Block[{t}, Print[Expand[(t + 1)^2]]]**

$1 + 2 t + t^2$

If you return an expression involving t, however, it is evaluated using the global value for t.

In[22]:= **Block[{t}, t^2 - 3]**

Out[22]= $-3 + (17 + a^2)^2$

■ 2.7.7 Blocks Compared with Modules

When you write a program in *Mathematica*, you should always try to set it up so that its parts are as independent as possible. In this way, the program will be easier for you to understand, maintain and add to.

One of the main ways to ensure that different parts of a program do not interfere is to give their variables only a certain "scope". *Mathematica* provides two basic mechanisms for limiting the scope of variables: modules and blocks.

In writing actual programs, modules are far more common than blocks. When scoping is needed in interactive calculations, however, blocks are often convenient.

Module[*vars*, *body*]	lexical scoping
Block[*vars*, *body*]	dynamic scoping

Mathematica variable scoping mechanisms.

Most traditional computer languages use a so-called "lexical scoping" mechanism for variables, which is analogous to the module mechanism in *Mathematica*. Some symbolic computer languages such as LISP also allow "dynamic scoping", analogous to *Mathematica* blocks.

When lexical scoping is used, variables are treated as local to a particular section of the *code* in a program. In dynamic scoping, the values of variables are local to a part of the *execution history* of the program.

In compiled languages like C and Java, there is a very clear distinction between "code" and "execution history". The symbolic nature of *Mathematica* makes this distinction slightly less clear, since "code" can in principle be built up dynamically during the execution of a program.

What `Module[vars, body]` does is to treat the form of the expression *body* at the time when the module is executed as the "code" of a *Mathematica* program. Then when any of the *vars* explicitly appears in this "code", it is considered to be local.

`Block[vars, body]` does not look at the *form* of the expression *body*. Instead, throughout the evaluation of *body*, the block uses local values for the *vars*.

This defines m in terms of i.	$In[1]:=$ **m = i^2**
	$Out[1]=$ i^2
The local value for i in the block is used throughout the evaluation of i + m.	$In[2]:=$ **Block[{i = a}, i + m]**
	$Out[2]=$ $a + a^2$
Here only the i that appears explicitly in i + m is treated as a local variable.	$In[3]:=$ **Module[{i = a}, i + m]**
	$Out[3]=$ $a + i^2$

■ 2.7.8 Contexts

It is always a good idea to give variables and functions names that are as explicit as possible. Sometimes, however, such names may get inconveniently long.

In *Mathematica*, you can use the notion of "contexts" to organize the names of symbols. Contexts are particularly important in *Mathematica* packages which introduce symbols whose names must not conflict with those of any other symbols. If you write *Mathematica* packages, or make sophisticated use of packages that others have written, then you will need to know about contexts.

The basic idea is that the *full name* of any symbol is broken into two parts: a *context* and a *short name*. The full name is written as *context`short*, where the ` is the backquote or grave accent character (ASCII decimal code 96), called a "context mark" in *Mathematica*.

Here is a symbol with short name x, and context aaaa.	$In[1]:=$ **aaaa`x**
	$Out[1]=$ aaaa`x
You can use this symbol just like any other symbol.	$In[2]:=$ **%^2 - %**
	$Out[2]=$ $-aaaa`x + aaaa`x^2$
You can for example define a value for the symbol.	$In[3]:=$ **aaaa`x = 78**
	$Out[3]=$ 78

Mathematica treats a`x and b`x as completely different symbols.	`In[4]:= a`x == b`x` `Out[4]= a`x == b`x`

It is typical to have all the symbols that relate a particular topic in a particular context. Thus, for example, symbols that represent physical units might have a context `PhysicalUnits``. Such symbols might have full names like `PhysicalUnits`Joule` or `PhysicalUnits`Mole`.

Although you can always refer to a symbol by its full name, it is often convenient to use a shorter name.

At any given point in a *Mathematica* session, there is always a *current context* `$Context`. You can refer to symbols that are in this context simply by giving their short names.

The default context for *Mathematica* sessions is Global`.	`In[5]:= $Context` `Out[5]= Global``
Short names are sufficient for symbols that are in the current context.	`In[6]:= {x, Global`x}` `Out[6]= {x, x}`

Contexts in *Mathematica* work somewhat like file directories in many operating systems. You can always specify a particular file by giving its complete name, including its directory. But at any given point, there is usually a current working directory, analogous to the current *Mathematica* context. Files that are in this directory can then be specified just by giving their short names.

Like directories in many operating systems, contexts in *Mathematica* can be hierarchical. Thus, for example, the full name of a symbol can involve a sequence of context names, as in c_1`$c_2$`c_3`*name*.

context`*name*  or  $c_1$`c_2` ... `*name*	a symbol in an explicitly specified context
`*name*	a symbol in the current context
`*context*`*name* or `$c_1$`c_2` ... `*name*	a symbol in a specific context relative to the current context
name	a symbol in the current context, or found on the context search path

Specifying symbols in various contexts.

Here is a symbol in the context a`b`.	`In[7]:= a`b`x` `Out[7]= a`b`x`

When you start a *Mathematica* session, the default current context is `Global``. Symbols that you introduce will usually be in this context. However, built-in symbols such as `Pi` are in the context `System``.

In order to let you easily access not only symbols in the context Global`, but also in contexts such as System`, *Mathematica* supports the notion of a *context search path*. At any point in a *Mathematica* session, there is both a current context $Context, and also a current context search path $ContextPath. The idea of the search path is to allow you to type in the short name of a symbol, then have *Mathematica* search in a sequence of contexts to find a symbol with that short name.

The context search path for symbols in *Mathematica* is analogous to the "search path" for program files provided in operating systems such as Unix and MS-DOS.

The default context path includes the
contexts for system-defined symbols.

In[8]:= **$ContextPath**

Out[8]= {Global`, System`}

When you type in Pi, *Mathematica*
interprets it as the symbol with full
name System`Pi.

In[9]:= **Context[Pi]**

Out[9]= System`

Context[*s*]	the context of a symbol
$Context	the current context in a *Mathematica* session
$ContextPath	the current context search path
Contexts[ ]	a list of all contexts

Finding contexts and context search paths.

When you use contexts in *Mathematica*, there is no reason that two symbols which are in different contexts cannot have the same short name. Thus, for example, you can have symbols with the short name Mole both in the context PhysicalUnits` and in the context BiologicalOrganisms`.

There is, however, then the question of which symbol you actually get when you type in only the short name Mole. The answer to this question is determined by which of the contexts comes first in the sequence of contexts listed in the context search path.

This introduces two symbols, both with
short name Mole.

In[10]:= **{PhysicalUnits`Mole, BiologicalOrganisms`Mole}**

Out[10]= {PhysicalUnits`Mole, BiologicalOrganisms`Mole}

This adds two additional contexts to
$ContextPath.

In[11]:= **$ContextPath =**
        Join[$ContextPath,
           {"PhysicalUnits`", "BiologicalOrganisms`"}]

Out[11]= {Global`, System`,
       PhysicalUnits`, BiologicalOrganisms`}

Now if you type in Mole, you get the
symbol in the context PhysicalUnits`.

In[12]:= **Context[Mole]**

Out[12]= PhysicalUnits`

In general, when you type in a short name for a symbol, *Mathematica* assumes that you want the symbol with that name whose context appears earliest in the context search path. As a result, symbols with the same short name whose contexts appear later in the context search path are effectively "shadowed". To refer to these symbols, you need to use their full names.

Mathematica always warns you when you introduce new symbols that "shadow" existing symbols with your current choice for $ContextPath. If you use a notebook front end, *Mathematica* will typically let you select in such cases which symbol you want to keep.

This introduces a symbol with short name Mole in the context Global`. *Mathematica* warns you that the new symbol shadows existing symbols with short name Mole.	`In[13]:= Global`Mole`  `Mole::shdw:` ` Symbol Mole appears in multiple contexts` ` {Global`, P<<11>>s`, BiologicalOrganisms`}` ` ; definitions in context Global`` `    may shadow or be shadowed by other definitions.` `Out[13]= Mole`
Now when you type in Mole, you get the symbol in context Global`.	`In[14]:= Context[Mole]` `Out[14]= Global``

If you once introduce a symbol which shadows existing symbols, it will continue to do so until you either rearrange $ContextPath, or explicitly remove the symbol. You should realize that it is not sufficient to clear the *value* of the symbol; you need to actually remove the symbol completely from *Mathematica*. You can do this using the function Remove[*s*].

Clear[*s*]	clear the values of a symbol
Remove[*s*]	remove a symbol completely from the system

Clearing and removing symbols in *Mathematica*.

This removes the symbol Global`Mole.	`In[15]:= Remove[Mole]`
Now if you type in Mole, you get the symbol PhysicalUnits`Mole.	`In[16]:= Context[Mole]` `Out[16]= PhysicalUnits``

When *Mathematica* prints out the name of a symbol, it has to choose whether to give the full name, or just the short name. What it does is to give whatever version of the name you would have to type in to get the particular symbol, given your current settings for $Context and $ContextPath.

The short name is printed for the first symbol, so this would give that symbol if you typed it in.	`In[17]:= {PhysicalUnits`Mole, BiologicalOrganisms`Mole}` `Out[17]= {Mole, BiologicalOrganisms`Mole}`

If you type in a short name for which there is no symbol either in the current context, or in any context on the context search path, then *Mathematica* has to *create* a new symbol with this name. It always puts new symbols of this kind in the current context, as specified by $Context.

This introduces the new symbol with short name tree.	`In[18]:= tree` `Out[18]= tree`

Mathematica puts tree in the current context Global`.	`In[19]:=` **Context[tree]** `Out[19]=` Global`

■ 2.7.9 Contexts and Packages

A typical package written in *Mathematica* introduces several new symbols intended for use outside the package. These symbols may correspond for example to new functions or new objects defined in the package.

There is a general convention that all new symbols introduced in a particular package are put into a context whose name is related to the name of the package. When you read in the package, it adds this context at the beginning of your context search path $ContextPath.

This reads in a package for finding Padé approximants.	`In[1]:=` **<<Calculus`Pade`**
The package prepends its context to $ContextPath.	`In[2]:=` **$ContextPath** `Out[2]=` {Calculus`Pade`, Global`, System`}
The symbol Pade is in the context set up by the package.	`In[3]:=` **Context[Pade]** `Out[3]=` Calculus`Pade`
You can refer to the symbol using its short name.	`In[4]:=` **Pade[Exp[x], {x, 0, 2, 4}]** `Out[4]=` $\dfrac{1 + \frac{x}{3} + \frac{x^2}{30}}{1 - \frac{2x}{3} + \frac{x^2}{5} - \frac{x^3}{30} + \frac{x^4}{360}}$

The full names of symbols defined in packages are often quite long. In most cases, however, you will only need to use their short names. The reason for this is that after you have read in a package, its context is added to $ContextPath, so the context is automatically searched whenever you type in a short name.

There is a complication, however, when two symbols with the same short name appear in two different packages. In such a case, *Mathematica* will warn you when you read in the second package. It will tell you which symbols will be "shadowed" by the new symbols that are being introduced.

The symbol Pade in the context Calculus`Pade` is shadowed by the symbol with the same short name in the new package.	`In[5]:=` **<<NewPade`**  Pade::shdw: 　Symbol Pade appears in multiple contexts 　　{NewPade`, Calculus`Pade`}; definitions in context 　　NewPade` may shadow or be shadowed by other 　　definitions.
You can access the shadowed symbol by giving its full name.	`In[6]:=` **Calculus`Pade`Pade[Exp[x], {x, 0, 2, 4}]** `Out[6]=` $\dfrac{1 + \frac{x}{3} + \frac{x^2}{30}}{1 - \frac{2x}{3} + \frac{x^2}{5} - \frac{x^3}{30} + \frac{x^4}{360}}$

Conflicts can occur not only between symbols in different packages, but also between symbols in packages and symbols that you introduce directly in your *Mathematica* session. If you define a symbol in your current context, then this symbol will shadow any other symbol with the same short name in packages that you read in. The reason for this is that *Mathematica* always searches for symbols in the current context before looking in contexts on the context search path.

This defines a function in the current context.	$In[7]:=$ **Div[f_] = 1/f**
	$Out[7]=$ $\dfrac{1}{f}$

Any other functions with short name Div will be shadowed by the one in your current context.	$In[8]:=$ **<<Calculus`VectorAnalysis`** Div::shdw: Symbol Div appears in multiple contexts {Calculus`VectorAnalysis`, Global`}      ; definitions in context Calculus`VectorAnalysis` may shadow or be shadowed by other definitions.

This sets up the coordinate system for vector analysis.	$In[9]:=$ **SetCoordinates[Cartesian[x, y, z]]** $Out[9]=$ Cartesian[x, y, z]

This removes Div completely from the current context.	$In[10]:=$ **Clear[Div]; Remove[Div]**

Now the Div from the package is used.	$In[11]:=$ **Div[{x, y^2, x}]** $Out[11]=$ $1 + 2y$

If you get into the situation where unwanted symbols are shadowing the symbols you want, the best thing to do is usually to get rid of the unwanted symbols using Remove[s]. An alternative that is sometimes appropriate is to rearrange the entries in $ContextPath and to reset the value of $Context so as to make the contexts that contain the symbols you want be the ones that are searched first.

$Packages	a list of the contexts corresponding to all packages loaded into your *Mathematica* session

Getting a list of packages.

■ 2.7.10 Setting Up *Mathematica* Packages

In a typical *Mathematica* package, there are generally two kinds of new symbols that are introduced. The first kind are ones that you want to "export" for use outside the package. The second kind are ones that you want to use only internally within the package. You can distinguish these two kinds of symbols by putting them in different contexts.

The usual convention is to put symbols intended for export in a context with a name *Package`* that corresponds to the name of the package. Whenever the package is read in, it adds this context to the context search path, so that the symbols in this context can be referred to by their short names.

Symbols that are not intended for export, but are instead intended only for internal use within the package, are conventionally put into a context with the name *Package*`Private`. This context is *not* added to the context search path. As a result, the symbols in this context cannot be accessed except by giving their full names.

Package`	symbols for export
Package`Private`	symbols for internal use only
System`	built-in *Mathematica* symbols
Needed$_1$`, *Needed*$_2$`, ...	other contexts needed in the package

Contexts conventionally used in *Mathematica* packages.

There is a standard sequence of *Mathematica* commands that is typically used to set up the contexts in a package. These commands set the values of $Context and $ContextPath so that the new symbols which are introduced are created in the appropriate contexts.

BeginPackage["*Package*`"]	set *Package*` to be the current context, and put only System` on the context search path
f::usage = "*text*", ...	introduce the objects intended for export (and no others)
Begin["`Private`"]	set the current context to *Package*`Private`
f[*args*] = *value*, ...	give the main body of definitions in the package
End[ ]	revert to the previous context (here *Package*`)
EndPackage[ ]	end the package, prepending the *Package*` to the context search path

The standard sequence of context control commands in a package.

```
BeginPackage["Collatz`"]

Collatz::usage =
        "Collatz[n] gives a list of the iterates in the 3n+1 problem,
        starting from n. The conjecture is that this sequence always
        terminates."

Begin["`Private`"]

Collatz[1] := {1}

Collatz[n_Integer]  := Prepend[Collatz[3 n + 1], n] /; OddQ[n] && n > 0

Collatz[n_Integer] := Prepend[Collatz[n/2], n] /; EvenQ[n] && n > 0

End[ ]

EndPackage[ ]
```

The sample package `Collatz.m`.

Defining usage messages at the beginning of a package is the standard way of making sure that symbols you want to export are created in the appropriate context. The way this works is that in defining these messages, the only symbols you mention are exactly the ones you want to export. These symbols are then created in the context *Package*`, which is then current.

In the actual definitions of the functions in a package, there are typically many new symbols, introduced as parameters, temporary variables, and so on. The convention is to put all these symbols in the context *Package*`Private`, which is not put on the context search path when the package is read in.

This reads in the sample package given above.	*In[1]:=* `<<Collatz.m`
The EndPackage command in the package adds the context associated with the package to the context search path.	*In[2]:=* `$ContextPath` *Out[2]=* {Collatz`, Global`, System`}
The Collatz function was created in the context Collatz`.	*In[3]:=* `Context[Collatz]` *Out[3]=* Collatz`
The parameter n is put in the private context Collatz`Private`.	*In[4]:=* `?Collatz`Private`*` Collatz`Private`n

In the `Collatz` package, the functions that are defined depend only on built-in *Mathematica* functions. Often, however, the functions defined in one package may depend on functions defined in another package.

Two things are needed to make this work. First, the other package must be read in, so that the functions needed are defined. And second, the context search path must include the context that these functions are in.

You can explicitly tell *Mathematica* to read in a package at any point using the command <<*context*`. (Section 2.12.5 discusses the tricky issue of translation from system-independent context names to system-dependent file names.) Often, however, you want to set it up so that a particular package is read in only if it is needed. The command Needs["*context*`"] tells *Mathematica* to read in a package if the context associated with that package is not already in the list $Packages.

Get["*context*`"]   or   <<*context*`	read in the package corresponding to the specified context
Needs["*context*`"]	read in the package if the specified context is not already in $Packages
BeginPackage["*Package*`", {"*Needed*₁`", ... }]	begin a package, specifying that certain contexts in addition to System` are needed

Functions for specifying interdependence of packages.

If you use BeginPackage["*Package*`"] with a single argument, *Mathematica* puts on the context search path only the *Package*` context and the contexts for built-in *Mathematica* symbols. If the definitions you give in your package involve functions from other packages, you must make sure that the contexts for these packages are also included in your context search path. You can do this by giving a list of the additional contexts as a second argument to BeginPackage. BeginPackage automatically calls Needs on these contexts, reading in the corresponding packages if necessary, and then making sure that the contexts are on the context search path.

Begin["*context*`"]	switch to a new current context
End[ ]	revert to the previous context

Context manipulation functions.

Executing a function like Begin which manipulates contexts changes the way that *Mathematica* interprets names you type in. However, you should realize that the change is effective only in subsequent expressions that you type in. The point is that *Mathematica* always reads in a complete input expression, and interprets the names in it, before it executes any part of the expression. As a result, by the time Begin is executed in a particular expression, the names in the expression have already been interpreted, and it is too late for Begin to have an effect.

The fact that context manipulation functions do not have an effect until the *next* complete expression is read in means that you must be sure to give those functions as separate expressions, typically on separate lines, when you write *Mathematica* packages.

The name x is interpreted before this expression is executed, so the Begin has no effect.	*In[5]:=* `Begin["a`"]; Print[Context[x]]; End[ ]`  `Global`  *Out[5]=* `a``

Context manipulation functions are used primarily as part of packages intended to be read into *Mathematica*. Sometimes, however, you may find it convenient to use such functions interactively.

This can happen, for example, if you go into a dialog, say using `TraceDialog`, while executing a function defined in a package. The parameters and temporary variables in the function are typically in a private context associated with the package. Since this context is not on your context search path, *Mathematica* will print out the full names of the symbols, and will require you to type in these full names in order to refer to the symbols. You can however use `Begin["Package`Private`"]` to make the private context of the package your current context. This will make *Mathematica* print out short names for the symbols, and allow you to refer to the symbols by their short names.

■ 2.7.11 Automatic Loading of Packages

Previous sections have discussed explicit loading of *Mathematica* packages using <<*package* and `Needs[`*package*`]`. Sometimes, however, you may want to set *Mathematica* up so that it automatically loads a particular package when the package is needed.

You can use `DeclarePackage` to give the names of symbols which are defined in a particular package. Then, when one of these symbols is actually used, *Mathematica* will automatically load the package where the symbol is defined.

`DeclarePackage["`*context*`\`", {"`*name*₁`", "`*name*₂`", ... }]`   declare that a package should automatically be loaded if a symbol with any of the names *name*ᵢ is used

Arranging for automatic loading of packages.

This specifies that the symbols Div, Grad and Curl are defined in Calculus`VectorAnalysis`.	*In[1]:=* `DeclarePackage["Calculus`VectorAnalysis`",` `{"Div", "Grad", "Curl"}]` *Out[1]=* `Calculus`VectorAnalysis``
When you first use Grad, *Mathematica* automatically loads the package that defines it.	*In[2]:=* `Grad[x^2 + y^2, Cartesian[x, y, z]]` *Out[2]=* `{2 x, 2 y, 0}`

When you set up a large collection of *Mathematica* packages, it is often a good idea to create an additional "names file" which contains a sequence of `DeclarePackage` commands, specifying packages to load when particular names are used. Within a particular *Mathematica* session, you then need to load explicitly only the names file. When you have done this, all the other packages will automatically be loaded if and when they are needed.

`DeclarePackage` works by immediately creating symbols with the names you specify, but giving each of these symbols the special attribute `Stub`. Whenever *Mathematica* finds a symbol with the `Stub` attribute, it automatically loads the package corresponding to the context of the symbol, in an attempt to find the definition of the symbol.

■ 2.7.12 Manipulating Symbols and Contexts by Name

Symbol["*name*"]	construct a symbol with a given name
SymbolName[*symb*]	find the name of a symbol

Converting between symbols and their names.

Here is the symbol x.

```
In[1]:= x // InputForm
Out[1]//InputForm= x
```

Its name is a string.

```
In[2]:= SymbolName[x] // InputForm
Out[2]//InputForm= "x"
```

This gives the symbol x again.

```
In[3]:= Symbol["x"] // InputForm
Out[3]//InputForm= x
```

Once you have made an assignment such as x = 2, then whenever x is evaluated, it is replaced by 2. Sometimes, however, you may want to continue to refer to x itself, without immediately getting the value of x.

You can do this by referring to x by name. The name of the symbol x is the string "x", and even though x itself may be replaced by a value, the string "x" will always stay the same.

The names of the symbols x and xp are the strings "x" and "xp".

```
In[4]:= t = {SymbolName[x], SymbolName[xp]} // InputForm
Out[4]//InputForm= {"x", "xp"}
```

This assigns a value to x.

```
In[5]:= x = 2
Out[5]= 2
```

Whenever you enter x it is now replaced by 2.

```
In[6]:= {x, xp} // InputForm
Out[6]//InputForm= {2, xp}
```

The name "x" is not affected, however.

In[7]:= **t // InputForm**

Out[7]//InputForm= InputForm[{"x", "xp"}]

NameQ["*form*"]	test whether any symbol has a name which matches *form*
Names["*form*"]	give a list of all symbol names which match *form*
Contexts["*form`*"]	give a list of all context names which match *form*

Referring to symbols and contexts by name.

x and xp are symbols that have been created in this *Mathematica* session; xpp is not.

In[8]:= **{NameQ["x"], NameQ["xp"], NameQ["xpp"]}**

Out[8]= {True, True, False}

You can specify the form of symbol names using *string patterns* of the kind discussed on page 411. "x*" stands, for example, for all names that start with x.

This gives a list of all symbol names in this *Mathematica* session that begin with x.

In[9]:= **Names["x*"] // InputForm**

Out[9]//InputForm= {"x", "xp", "x$"}

These names correspond to built-in functions in *Mathematica*.

In[10]:= **Names["Qu*"] // InputForm**

Out[10]//InputForm= {"Quantile", "Quartics", "QuasiMonteCarlo", "QuasiNewton", "Quit", "Quotient"}

This asks for names "close" to WeierstrssP.

In[11]:= **Names["WeierstrssP", SpellingCorrection->True]**

Out[11]= {WeierstrassP}

Clear["*form*"]	clear the values of all symbols whose names match *form*
Clear["*context`*"]	clear the values of all symbols in the specified context
Remove["*form*"]	remove completely all symbols whose names match *form*
Remove["*context`*"]	remove completely all symbols in the specified context

Getting rid of symbols by name.

This clears the values of all symbols whose names start with x.

In[12]:= **Clear["x*"]**

The name "x" is still known, however.

In[13]:= **Names["x*"]**

Out[13]= {x, xp, x$}

But the value of x has been cleared.

In[14]:= **{x, xp}**

Out[14]= {x, xp}

This removes completely all symbols whose names start with x.

In[15]:= **Remove["x*"]**

Now not even the name "x" is known.

In[16]:= **Names["x*"]**

Out[16]= {}

Remove["Global`*"]      remove completely all symbols in the Global` context

Removing all symbols you have introduced.

If you do not set up any additional contexts, then all the symbols that you introduce in a *Mathematica* session will be placed in the Global` context. You can remove these symbols completely using Remove["Global`*"]. Built-in *Mathematica* objects are in the System` context, and are thus unaffected by this.

■ 2.7.13 Advanced Topic: Intercepting the Creation of New Symbols

Mathematica creates a new symbol when you first enter a particular name. Sometimes it is useful to "intercept" the process of creating a new symbol. *Mathematica* provides several ways to do this.

On[General::newsym]   print a message whenever a new symbol is created

Off[General::newsym]   switch off the message printed when new symbols are created

---

Printing a message when new symbols are created.

This tells *Mathematica* to print a message whenever a new symbol is created.

In[1]:= **On[General::newsym]**

Mathematica now prints a message about each new symbol that it creates.

In[2]:= **sin[k]**

General::newsym: Symbol sin is new.

General::newsym: Symbol k is new.

Out[2]= sin[k]

This switches off the message.

In[3]:= **Off[General::newsym]**

Generating a message when *Mathematica* creates a new symbol is often a good way to catch typing mistakes. *Mathematica* itself cannot tell the difference between an intentionally new name, and a misspelling of a name it already knows. But by reporting all new names it encounters, *Mathematica* allows you to see whether any of them are mistakes.

$NewSymbol	a function to be applied to the name and context of new symbols which are created

Performing operations when new symbols are created.

When *Mathematica* creates a new symbol, you may want it not just to print a message, but instead to perform some other action. Any function you specify as the value of the global variable $NewSymbol will automatically be applied to strings giving the name and context of each new symbol that *Mathematica* creates.

This defines a function to be applied to each new symbol which is created.

```
In[4]:= $NewSymbol = Print["Name: ", #1, " Context: ", #2]&

Out[4]= Print[Name: , #1,  Context: , #2] &
```

The function is applied once to v and once to w.

```
In[5]:= v + w

Name: v  Context: Global`
Name: w  Context: Global`

Out[5]= v + w
```

2.8 Strings and Characters

■ 2.8.1 Properties of Strings

Much of what *Mathematica* does revolves around manipulating structured expressions. But you can also use *Mathematica* as a system for handling unstructured strings of text.

"*text*"　　a string containing arbitrary text

Text strings.

When you input a string of text to *Mathematica* you must always enclose it in quotes. However, when *Mathematica* outputs the string it usually does not explicitly show the quotes.

You can see the quotes by asking for the input form of the string. In addition, in a *Mathematica* notebook, quotes will typically appear automatically as soon as you start to edit a string.

When *Mathematica* outputs a string, it usually does not explicitly show the quotes.

```
In[1]:= "This is a string."
Out[1]= This is a string.
```

You can see the quotes, however, by asking for the input form of the string.

```
In[2]:= InputForm[%]
Out[2]//InputForm= "This is a string."
```

The fact that *Mathematica* does not usually show explicit quotes around strings makes it possible for you to use strings to specify quite directly the textual output you want.

The strings are printed out here without explicit quotes.

```
In[3]:= Print["The value is ", 567, "."]
The value is 567.
```

You should understand, however, that even though the string "x" often appears as x in output, it is still a quite different object from the symbol x.

The string "x" is not the same as the symbol x.

```
In[4]:= "x" === x
Out[4]= False
```

You can test whether any particular expression is a string by looking at its head. The head of any string is always String.

All strings have head String.

```
In[5]:= Head["x"]
Out[5]= String
```

The pattern _String matches any string.

```
In[6]:= Cases[{"ab", x, "a", y}, _String]
Out[6]= {ab, a}
```

You can use strings just like other expressions as elements of patterns and transformations. Note, however, that you cannot assign values directly to strings.

This gives a definition for an expression that involves a string.	*In[7]:=* z["gold"] = 79
	Out[7]= 79
This replaces each occurrence of the string "aa" by the symbol x.	*In[8]:=* {"aaa", "aa", "bb", "aa"} /. "aa" -> x
	Out[8]= {aaa, x, bb, x}

■ 2.8.2 Operations on Strings

Mathematica provides a variety of functions for manipulating strings. Most of these functions are based on viewing strings as a sequence of characters, and many of the functions are analogous to ones for manipulating lists.

s_1 <> s_2 <> ... or StringJoin[{s_1, s_2, ... }]	
	join several strings together
StringLength[s]	give the number of characters in a string
StringReverse[s]	reverse the characters in a string

Operations on complete strings.

You can join together any number of strings using <>.	*In[1]:=* "aaaaaaa" <> "bbb" <> "cccccccccc"
	Out[1]= aaaaaaabbbcccccccccc
StringLength gives the number of characters in a string.	*In[2]:=* StringLength[%]
	Out[2]= 20
StringReverse reverses the characters in a string.	*In[3]:=* StringReverse["A string."]
	Out[3]= .gnirts A

StringTake[s, n]	make a string by taking the first n characters from s
StringTake[s, {n}]	take the nth character from s
StringTake[s, {n_1, n_2}]	take characters n_1 through n_2
StringDrop[s, n]	make a string by dropping the first n characters in s
StringDrop[s, {n_1, n_2}]	drop characters n_1 through n_2

Taking and dropping substrings.

StringTake and StringDrop are the analogs for strings of Take and Drop for lists. Like Take and Drop, they use standard *Mathematica* sequence specifications, so that, for example, negative numbers count character positions from the end of a string. Note that the first character of a string is taken to have position 1.

Here is a sample string.

```
In[4]:= alpha = "ABCDEFGHIJKLMNOPQRSTUVWXYZ"
Out[4]= ABCDEFGHIJKLMNOPQRSTUVWXYZ
```

This takes the first five characters from alpha.

```
In[5]:= StringTake[alpha, 5]
Out[5]= ABCDE
```

Here is the fifth character in alpha.

```
In[6]:= StringTake[alpha, {5}]
Out[6]= E
```

This drops the characters 10 through 2, counting from the end of the string.

```
In[7]:= StringDrop[alpha, {-10, -2}]
Out[7]= ABCDEFGHIJKLMNOPZ
```

StringInsert[s, *snew*, n]	insert the string *snew* at position n in s
StringInsert[s, *snew*, $\{n_1, n_2, \ldots\}$]	insert several copies of *snew* into s

Inserting into a string.

StringInsert[s, *snew*, n] is set up to produce a string whose n^{th} character is the first character of *snew*.

This produces a new string whose fourth character is the first character of the string "XX".

```
In[8]:= StringInsert["abcdefgh", "XX", 4]
Out[8]= abcXXdefgh
```

Negative positions are counted from the end of the string.

```
In[9]:= StringInsert["abcdefgh", "XXX", -1]
Out[9]= abcdefghXXX
```

Each copy of "XXX" is inserted at the specified position in the original string.

```
In[10]:= StringInsert["abcdefgh", "XXX", {2, 4, -1}]
Out[10]= aXXXbcXXXdefghXXX
```

> StringReplacePart[*s*, *snew*, {*m*, *n*}]
>
> replace the characters at positions *m* through *n* in *s* by the string *snew*
>
> StringReplacePart[*s*, *snew*, {{*m₁*, *n₁*}, {*m₂*, *n₂*}, ... }]
>
> replace several substrings in *s* by *snew*
>
> StringReplacePart[*s*, {*snew₁*, *snew₂*, ... }, {{*m₁*, *n₁*}, {*m₂*, *n₂*}, ... }]
>
> replace substrings in *s* by the corresponding *snewᵢ*

Replacing parts of a string.

This replaces characters 2 through 6 by the string "XXX".	*In[11]:=* **StringReplacePart["abcdefgh", "XXX", {2, 6}]** *Out[11]=* aXXXgh
This replaces two runs of characters by the string "XXX".	*In[12]:=* **StringReplacePart["abcdefgh", "XXX", {{2, 3}, {5, -1}}]** *Out[12]=* aXXXdXXX
Now the two runs of characters are replaced by different strings.	*In[13]:=* **StringReplacePart["abcdefgh", {"XXX", "YYYY"}, {{2, 3}, {5, -1}}]** *Out[13]=* aXXXdYYYY

> StringPosition[*s*, *sub*]   give a list of the starting and ending positions at which *sub* appears as a substring of *s*
>
> StringPosition[*s*, *sub*, *k*]   include only the first *k* occurrences of *sub* in *s*
>
> StringPosition[*s*, {*sub₁*, *sub₂*, ... }]
>
> include occurrences of any of the *subᵢ*

Finding positions of substrings.

You can use StringPosition to find where a particular substring appears within a given string. StringPosition returns a list, each of whose elements corresponds to an occurrence of the substring. The elements consist of lists giving the starting and ending character positions for the substring. These lists are in the form used as sequence specifications in StringTake, StringDrop and StringReplacePart.

This gives a list of the positions of the substring "abc".	*In[14]:=* **StringPosition["abcdabcdaabcabcd", "abc"]** *Out[14]=* {{1, 3}, {5, 7}, {10, 12}, {13, 15}}
This gives only the first occurrence of "abc".	*In[15]:=* **StringPosition["abcdabcdaabcabcd", "abc", 1]** *Out[15]=* {{1, 3}}

This shows where both "abc" and "cd" appear. Overlaps between these strings are taken into account.

In[16]:= **StringPosition["abcdabcdaabcabcd", {"abc", "cd"}]**

Out[16]= {{1, 3}, {3, 4}, {5, 7},
          {7, 8}, {10, 12}, {13, 15}, {15, 16}}

StringReplace[s, {s_1 -> sp_1, s_2 -> sp_2, ... }]
replace the s_i by the corresponding sp_i whenever they appear as substrings of s

Replacing substrings according to rules.

StringReplace allows you to perform replacements for substrings within a string. **StringReplace** sequentially goes through a string, testing substrings that start at each successive character position. To each substring, it tries in turn each of the transformation rules you have specified. If any of the rules apply, it replaces the substring, then continues to go through the string, starting at the character position after the end of the substring.

This replaces all occurrences of the character a by the string XX.

In[17]:= **StringReplace["abcdabcdaabcabcd", "a" -> "XX"]**

Out[17]= XXbcdXXbcdXXXXbcXXbcd

This replaces abc by Y, and d by XXX.

In[18]:= **StringReplace["abcdabcdaabcabcd",
                        {"abc" -> "Y", "d" -> "XXX"}]**

Out[18]= YXXXYXXXaYYXXX

The first occurrence of cde is not replaced because it overlaps with abc.

In[19]:= **StringReplace["abcde abacde",
                        {"abc" -> "X", "cde" -> "Y"}]**

Out[19]= Xde abaY

StringPosition[s, sub, IgnoreCase -> True]
find where sub occurs in s, treating lower- and upper-case letters as equivalent

StringReplace[s, {s_1 -> sp_1, ... }, IgnoreCase -> True]
replace s_i by sp_i in s, treating lower- and upper-case letters as equivalent

Case-independent operations.

This replaces all occurrences of "the", independent of case.

In[20]:= **StringReplace["The cat in the hat.", "the" -> "a",
                        IgnoreCase -> True]**

Out[20]= a cat in a hat.

Sort[{s_1, s_2, s_3, ... }]	sort a list of strings

Sorting strings.

Sort sorts strings into standard dictionary order.

In[21]:= **Sort[{"cat", "fish", "catfish", "Cat"}]**

Out[21]= {cat, Cat, catfish, fish}

■ 2.8.3 String Patterns

You can use the standard *Mathematica* equality test $s_1 == s_2$ to test whether two strings are identical. Sometimes, however, you may want to find out whether a particular string matches a certain *string pattern*.

Mathematica allows you to define *string patterns* which consist of ordinary strings in which certain characters are interpreted as special "metacharacters". You can then use the function StringMatchQ to find out whether a particular string matches a string pattern you have defined. You should realize however that string patterns have nothing to do with the ordinary *Mathematica* patterns for expressions that were discussed in Section 2.3.

"*string*$_1$" == "*string*$_2$"	test whether two strings are identical
StringMatchQ["*string*", "*pattern*"]	test whether a string matches a particular string pattern

Matching strings.

The character ∗ can be used in a string pattern as a metacharacter to stand for any sequence of alphanumeric characters. Thus, for example, the string pattern "a∗b" would match any string which begins with an a, ends with a b, and has any number of alphanumeric characters in between. Similarly, "a∗b∗" would match any string that starts with a, and has any number of other characters, including at least one b.

The string matches the string pattern you have given.

In[1]:= **StringMatchQ["aaaaabbbbcccbbb", "a∗b∗"]**

Out[1]= True

The way ∗ is used in *Mathematica* string patterns is analogous to the way it is used for file-name patterns in many operating systems. *Mathematica* however provides some other string pattern metacharacters that are tailored to matching different classes of *Mathematica* symbol names.

*	zero or more characters
@	one or more characters which are not upper-case letters
* etc.	literal * etc.

Metacharacters used in string patterns.

In *Mathematica* there is a general convention that only built-in names should contain upper-case characters. Assuming that you follow this convention, you can use @ as a metacharacter to set up string patterns which match names you have defined, but avoid matching built-in names.

StringMatchQ["*string*", "*pattern*", SpellingCorrection -> True]	
	test whether *pattern* matches *string*, allowing a small fraction of characters to differ
StringMatchQ["*string*", "*pattern*", IgnoreCase -> True]	
	test whether *pattern* matches *string*, treating lower- and upper-case letters as equivalent

Options for matching strings.

These strings do not match.

```
In[2]:= StringMatchQ["platypus", "paltypus"]
Out[2]= False
```

Allowing for spelling correction, these strings are considered to match.

```
In[3]:= StringMatchQ["platypus", "paltypus",
                    SpellingCorrection -> True]
Out[3]= True
```

These strings match when lower- and upper-case letters are treated as equivalent.

```
In[4]:= StringMatchQ["AAaaBBbb", "a*b*", IgnoreCase -> True]
Out[4]= True
```

■ 2.8.4 Characters in Strings

Characters["*string*"]	convert a string to a list of characters
StringJoin[{"c_1", "c_2", ... }]	convert a list of characters to a string

Converting between strings and lists of characters.

This gives a list of the characters in the string.

```
In[1]:= Characters["A string."]
Out[1]= {A, , s, t, r, i, n, g, .}
```

You can apply standard list manipulation operations to this list.

```
In[2]:= RotateLeft[%, 3]
Out[2]= {t, r, i, n, g, ., A, , s}
```

StringJoin converts the list of characters back to a single string.

```
In[3]:= StringJoin[%]
Out[3]= tring.A s
```

DigitQ[*string*]	test whether all characters in a string are digits
LetterQ[*string*]	test whether all characters in a string are letters
UpperCaseQ[*string*]	test whether all characters in a string are upper-case letters
LowerCaseQ[*string*]	test whether all characters in a string are lower-case letters

Testing characters in a string.

All characters in the string given are letters.

```
In[4]:= LetterQ["Mixed"]
Out[4]= True
```

Not all the letters are upper case, so the result is False.

```
In[5]:= UpperCaseQ["Mixed"]
Out[5]= False
```

ToUpperCase[*string*]	generate a string in which all letters are upper case
ToLowerCase[*string*]	generate a string in which all letters are lower case

Converting between upper and lower case.

This converts all letters to upper case.

```
In[6]:= ToUpperCase["Mixed Form"]
Out[6]= MIXED FORM
```

CharacterRange["c_1", "c_2"]	generate a list of all characters from c_1 and c_2

Generating ranges of characters.

This generates a list of lower-case letters in alphabetical order.

```
In[7]:= CharacterRange["a", "h"]
Out[7]= {a, b, c, d, e, f, g, h}
```

Here is a list of upper-case letters.

```
In[8]:= CharacterRange["T", "Z"]
Out[8]= {T, U, V, W, X, Y, Z}
```

Here are some digits.

```
In[9]:= CharacterRange["0", "7"]
Out[9]= {0, 1, 2, 3, 4, 5, 6, 7}
```

`CharacterRange` will usually give meaningful results for any range of characters that have a natural ordering. The way `CharacterRange` works is by using the character codes that *Mathematica* internally assigns to every character.

This shows the ordering defined by the internal character codes used by *Mathematica*.	*In[10]:=* **CharacterRange["T", "e"]** *Out[10]=* {T, U, V, W, X, Y, Z, [, \,], ^, _, `, a, b, c, d, e}

■ 2.8.5 Special Characters

In addition to the ordinary characters that appear on a standard keyboard, you can include in *Mathematica* strings any of the special characters that are supported by *Mathematica*.

Here is a string containing special characters.	*In[1]:=* **"α⊕βⴱ..."** *Out[1]=* α⊕βⴱ...
You can manipulate this string just as you would any other.	*In[2]:=* **StringReplace[%, "⊕" -> " ⊙⊙ "]** *Out[2]=* α ⊙⊙ β ⊙⊙ ...
Here is the list of the characters in the string.	*In[3]:=* **Characters[%]** *Out[3]=* {α, , ⊙, ⊙, , β, , ⊙, ⊙, , ...}

In a *Mathematica* notebook, a special character such as α can always be displayed directly. But if you use a text-based interface, then typically the only characters that can readily be displayed are the ones that appear on your keyboard.

As a result, what *Mathematica* does in such situations is to try to approximate special characters by similar-looking sequences of ordinary characters. And when this is not practical, *Mathematica* just gives the full name of the special character.

In a *Mathematica* notebook using `StandardForm`, special characters can be displayed directly.	*In[4]:=* **"Lamé → αβ+"** *Out[4]=* Lamé → αβ+
In `OutputForm`, however, the special characters are approximated when possible by sequences of ordinary ones.	*In[5]:=* **% // OutputForm** *Out[5]//OutputForm=* Lame' —> \[Alpha]\[Beta]+

Mathematica always uses full names for special characters in `InputForm`. This means that when special characters are written out to files or external programs, they are by default represented purely as sequences of ordinary characters.

This uniform representation is crucial in allowing special characters in *Mathematica* to be used in a way that does not depend on the details of particular computer systems.

In `InputForm` the full names of all special characters are always written out explicitly.	*In[6]:=* **"Lamé → αβ+" // InputForm** *Out[6]//InputForm=* "Lamé \[LongRightArrow] \[Alpha]\[Beta]+"

a	a literal character
\[*Name*]	a character specified using its full name
\"	a " to be included in a string
\\	a \ to be included in a string

Ways to enter characters in a string.

You have to use \ to "escape" any " or \ characters in strings that you enter.

```
In[7]:= "Strings can contain \"quotes\" and \\ characters."
Out[7]= Strings can contain "quotes" and \ characters.
```

\\ produces a literal \ rather than forming part of the specification of α.

```
In[8]:= "\\[Alpha] is \[Alpha]."
Out[8]= \[Alpha] is α.
```

This breaks the string into a list of individual characters.

```
In[9]:= Characters[%]
Out[9]= {\, [, A, l, p, h, a, ], , i, s, , α, .}
```

This creates a list of the characters in the full name of α.

```
In[10]:= Characters[ ToString[InputForm["α"]] ]
Out[10]= {", \, [, A, l, p, h, a, ], "}
```

And this produces a string consisting of an actual α from its full name.

```
In[11]:= ToExpression[ "\"\\[" <> "Alpha" <> "]\"" ]
Out[11]= α
```

■ 2.8.6 Advanced Topic: Newlines and Tabs in Strings

\n	a newline (line feed) to be included in a string
\t	a tab to be included in a string

Explicit representations of newlines and tabs in strings.

This prints on two lines.

```
In[1]:= "First line.\nSecond line."
Out[1]= First line.
        Second line.
```

In InputForm there is an explicit \n to represent the newline.

```
In[2]:= InputForm[%]
Out[2]//InputForm= "First line.\nSecond line."
```

When you enter a long string in *Mathematica*, it is often convenient to break your input across several lines. *Mathematica* will by default ignore such breaks, so that if you subsequently output the string, it can then be broken in whatever way is appropriate.

Mathematica ignores the line break and any tabs that follow it.	*In[3]:=* **"A string on** **two lines."** *Out[3]=* A string on two lines.
There is no newline in the string.	*In[4]:=* **InputForm[%]** *Out[4]//InputForm=* "A string on two lines."

"text"	line breaks in *text* are ignored
"\<text\>"	line breaks in *text* are stored explicitly as \n

Input forms for strings.

Now *Mathematica* keeps the newline.	*In[5]:=* **"\<A string on**
	    two lines.\>"
	
	Out[5]= A string on
	    two lines.

In InputForm, the newline is shown as an explicit \n.	*In[6]:=* **InputForm[%]** *Out[6]//InputForm=* "A string on\ntwo lines."

You should realize that even though it is possible to achieve some formatting of *Mathematica* output by creating strings which contain raw tabs and newlines, this is rarely a good idea. Typically a much better approach is to use the higher-level *Mathematica* formatting primitives to be discussed in the next two sections. These primitives will always yield consistent output, independent of such issues as the positions of tab settings on a particular device.

In strings with newlines, text is always aligned on the left.	*In[7]:=* **{"Here is\na string\non several lines.",**
	    "Here is\nanother"}
	
	Out[7]= {Here is
	    a string
	    on several lines., Here is
	    another}

The ColumnForm formatting primitive gives more control. Here text is aligned on the right.	*In[8]:=* **ColumnForm[{"First line", "Second", "Third"}, Right]**
	
	Out[8]= First line
	    Second
	      Third

And here the text is centered.	*In[9]:=* **ColumnForm[{"First line", "Second", "Third"}, Center]**
	
	Out[9]= First line
	    Second
	     Third

Within *Mathematica* you can use formatting primitives to avoid raw tabs and newlines. But if you intend to send your output in textual form to external programs, then these programs will often expect to get raw tabs and newlines.

Note that you must either use WriteString or give your output in OutputForm in order for the raw tabs and newlines to show up. In InputForm, they will just be given as \t and \n.

This outputs a string to a file.	*In[10]:=* **"First line.\nSecond line." >> test**
Here are the contents of the file. By default, >> generates output in InputForm.	*In[11]:=* **!!test** "First line.\nSecond line."
This explicitly tells *Mathematica* to use OutputForm for the output.	*In[12]:=* **OutputForm["First line.\nSecond line."] >> test**
Now there is a raw newline in the file.	*In[13]:=* **!!test** First line. Second line.

■ 2.8.7 Advanced Topic: Character Codes

ToCharacterCode["*string*"]	give a list of the character codes for the characters in a string
FromCharacterCode[*n*]	construct a character from its character code
FromCharacterCode[{n_1, n_2, ... }]	construct a string of characters from a list of character codes

Converting to and from character codes.

Mathematica assigns every character that can appear in a string a unique *character code*. This code is used internally as a way to represent the character.

This gives the character codes for the characters in the string.	*In[1]:=* **ToCharacterCode["ABCD abcd"]** *Out[1]=* {65, 66, 67, 68, 32, 97, 98, 99, 100}
FromCharacterCode reconstructs the original string.	*In[2]:=* **FromCharacterCode[%]** *Out[2]=* ABCD abcd
Special characters also have character codes.	*In[3]:=* **ToCharacterCode["α⊕Γϴ∅"]** *Out[3]=* {945, 8853, 915, 8854, 8709}

CharacterRange["c_1", "c_2"]	generate a list of characters with successive character codes

Generating sequences of characters.

This gives part of the English alphabet.

In[4]:= **CharacterRange["a", "k"]**

Out[4]= {a, b, c, d, e, f, g, h, i, j, k}

Here is the Greek alphabet.

In[5]:= **CharacterRange["α", "ω"]**

Out[5]= {α, β, γ, δ, ε, ζ, η, θ, ι, κ, λ,
μ, ν, ξ, ο, π, ρ, ς, σ, τ, υ, φ, χ, ψ, ω}

Mathematica assigns names such as \[Alpha] to a large number of special characters. This means that you can always refer to such characters just by giving their names, without ever having to know their character codes.

This generates a string of special characters from their character codes.

In[6]:= **FromCharacterCode[{8706, 8709, 8711, 8712}]**

Out[6]= ∂∅∇∈

You can always refer to these characters by their names, without knowing their character codes.

In[7]:= **InputForm[%]**

Out[7]//InputForm= "\[PartialD]\[EmptySet]\[Del]\[Element]"

Mathematica has names for all the common characters that are used in mathematical notation and in standard European languages. But for a language such as Japanese, there are more than 3,000 additional characters, and *Mathematica* does not assign an explicit name to each of them. Instead, it refers to such characters by standardized character codes.

Here is a string containing Japanese characters.

In[8]:= **"数学"**

Out[8]= 数学

In InputForm, these characters are referred to by standardized character codes. The character codes are given in hexadecimal.

In[9]:= **InputForm[%]**

Out[9]//InputForm= "\:6570\:5b66"

The notebook front end for *Mathematica* is typically set up so that when you enter a character in a particular font, *Mathematica* will automatically work out the character code for that character.

Sometimes, however, you may find it convenient to be able to enter characters directly using character codes.

\0	null byte (code 0)
nnn	a character with octal code *nnn*
\.*nn*	a character with hexadecimal code *nn*
\:*nnnn*	a character with hexadecimal code *nnnn*

Ways to enter characters directly in terms of character codes.

For characters with character codes below 256, you can use *nnn* or \.*nn*. For characters with character codes above 256, you must use \:*nnnn*. Note that in all cases you must give a fixed number of octal or hexadecimal digits, padding with leading 0s if necessary.

This gives character codes in hexadecimal for a few characters.	*In[10]:=* **BaseForm[ToCharacterCode["Aàαℵ"], 16]**
	Out[10]//BaseForm= $\{41_{16}, e0_{16}, 3b1_{16}, 2135_{16}\}$
This enters the characters using their character codes. Note the leading 0 inserted in the character code for α.	*In[11]:=* **"\.41\.e0\:03b1\:2135"**
	Out[11]= Aàαℵ

In assigning codes to characters, *Mathematica* follows three compatible standards: ASCII, ISO Latin-1, and Unicode. ASCII covers the characters on a normal American English keyboard. ISO Latin-1 covers characters in many European languages. Unicode is a more general standard which defines character codes for several tens of thousands of characters used in languages and notations around the world.

0 – 127 (\000 – \177)	ASCII characters
1 – 31 (\001 – \037)	ASCII control characters
32 – 126 (\040 – \176)	printable ASCII characters
97 – 122 (\141 – \172)	lower-case English letters
129 – 255 (\201 – \377)	ISO Latin-1 characters
192 – 255 (\240 – \377)	letters in European languages
0 – 59391 (\:0000 – \:e7ff)	Unicode standard public characters
913 – 1009 (\:0391 – \:03f1)	Greek letters
12288 – 35839 (\:3000 – \:8bff)	Chinese, Japanese and Korean characters
8450 – 8504 (\:2102 – \:2138)	modified letters used in mathematical notation
8592 – 8677 (\:2190 – \:21e5)	arrows
8704 – 8945 (\:2200 – \:22f1)	mathematical symbols and operators
64256 – 64300 (\:fb00 – \:fb2c)	Unicode private characters defined specially by *Mathematica*

A few ranges of character codes used by *Mathematica*.

Here are all the printable ASCII characters.

In[12]:= **FromCharacterCode[Range[32, 126]]**

Out[12]= !"#$%&'()*+,-./0123456789:;<=>
?@ABCDEFGHIJKLMNOPQRSTUVWXYZ[\]^
_`abcdefghijklmnopqrstuvwxyz{|}~

Here are some ISO Latin-1 letters.

In[13]:= **FromCharacterCode[Range[192, 255]]**

Out[13]= ÀÁÂÃÄÅÆÇÈÉÊËÌÍÎÏÐÑÒÓÔÕÖ×
ØÙÚÛÜÝÞßàáâãäåæçèéêëìíîïðñòóôõö÷øùúûüýþÿ

Here are some special characters used in mathematical notation. The black blobs correspond to characters not available in the current font.

In[14]:= **FromCharacterCode[Range[8704, 8750]]**

Out[14]= ∀■∂∃∄∅■∇∈∉■∋∌∍■∏∐∑■∓■/\■∘■√■■∝
∞ᒻᒻ∢∣∤∥∦∧∨■■∫■■■∮

Here are a few Japanese characters.

In[15]:= **FromCharacterCode[Range[30000, 30030]]**

Out[15]= 田由甲申■■■男■町画甼■■■■甾■甿■畀畁畂界畄■

■ 2.8.8 Advanced Topic: Raw Character Encodings

Mathematica always allows you to refer to special characters by using names such as \[Alpha] or explicit hexadecimal codes such as \:03b1. And when *Mathematica* writes out files, it by default uses these names or hexadecimal codes.

But sometimes you may find it convenient to use raw encodings for at least some special characters. What this means is that rather than representing special characters by names or explicit hexadecimal codes, you instead represent them by raw bit patterns appropriate for a particular computer system or particular font.

`$CharacterEncoding = None`	use printable ASCII names for all special characters
`$CharacterEncoding = "name"`	use the raw character encoding specified by *name*
`$SystemCharacterEncoding`	the default raw character encoding for your particular computer system

Setting up raw character encodings.

When you press a key or combination of keys on your keyboard, the operating system of your computer sends a certain bit pattern to *Mathematica*. How this bit pattern is interpreted as a character within *Mathematica* will depend on the character encoding that has been set up.

The notebook front end for *Mathematica* typically takes care of setting up the appropriate character encoding automatically for whatever font you are using. But if you use *Mathematica* with a text-based interface or via files or pipes, then you may need to set $CharacterEncoding explicitly.

By specifying an appropriate value for $CharacterEncoding you will typically be able to get *Mathematica* to handle raw text generated by whatever language-specific text editor or operating system you use.

You should realize, however, that while the standard representation of special characters used in *Mathematica* is completely portable across different computer systems, any representation that involves raw character encodings will inevitably not be.

"PrintableASCII"	printable ASCII characters only (default)
"ASCII"	all ASCII including control characters
"ISOLatin1"	characters for common western European languages
"ISOLatin2"	characters for central and eastern European languages
"ISOLatin3"	characters for additional European languages (e.g. Catalan, Turkish)
"ISOLatin4"	characters for other additional European languages (e.g. Estonian, Lappish)
"ISOLatinCyrillic"	English and Cyrillic characters
"AdobeStandard"	Adobe standard PostScript font encoding
"MacintoshRoman"	Macintosh roman font encoding
"WindowsANSI"	Windows standard font encoding
"Symbol"	symbol font encoding
"ZapfDingbats"	Zapf dingbats font encoding
"ShiftJIS"	shift-JIS for Japanese (mixture of 8- and 16-bit)
"EUC"	extended Unix code for Japanese (mixture of 8- and 16-bit)
"UTF8"	Unicode transformation format encoding
"Unicode"	raw 16-bit Unicode bit patterns

Some raw character encodings supported by *Mathematica*.

Mathematica knows about various raw character encodings, appropriate for different computer systems and different languages.

Any character that is included in a particular raw encoding will be written out in raw form by *Mathematica* if you specify that encoding. But characters which are not included in the encoding will still be written out using standard *Mathematica* full names or hexadecimal codes.

In addition, any character included in a particular encoding can be given in raw form as input to *Mathematica* if you specify that encoding. *Mathematica* will automatically translate the character to its own standard internal form.

This writes a string to the file `tmp`.	`In[1]:= "a b c \[EAcute] \[Alpha] \[Pi] \:2766" >> tmp`

Special characters are by default written out using full names or explicit hexadecimal codes.	`In[2]:= !!tmp`
	
	`"a b c \[EAcute] \[Alpha] \[Pi] \:2766"`

This tells *Mathematica* to use a raw character encoding appropriate for Macintosh roman fonts.	`In[3]:= $CharacterEncoding = "MacintoshRoman"` `Out[3]= MacintoshRoman`
Now those special characters that can will be written out in raw form.	`In[4]:= "a b c \[EAcute] \[Alpha] \[Pi] \:2766" >> tmp`

You can only read the raw characters if you have a system that uses the Macintosh roman encoding.	`In[5]:= !!tmp`
	
	`"a b c \[EAcute] \[Alpha] \[Pi] \:2766"`

This tells *Mathematica* to use no raw encoding by default.	`In[6]:= $CharacterEncoding = None` `Out[6]= None`
You can still explicitly request raw encodings to be used in certain functions.	`In[7]:= Get["tmp", CharacterEncoding->"MacintoshRoman"]` `Out[7]= a b c é α π ∎`

Mathematica supports both 8- and 16-bit raw character encodings. In an encoding such as `"ISOLatin1"`, all characters are represented by bit patterns containing 8 bits. But in an encoding such as `"ShiftJIS"` some characters instead involve bit patterns containing 16 bits.

Most of the raw character encodings supported by *Mathematica* include basic ASCII as a subset. This means that even when you are using such encodings, you can still give ordinary *Mathematica* input in the usual way, and you can specify special characters using \[and \: sequences.

Some raw character encodings, however, do not include basic ASCII as a subset. An example is the `"Symbol"` encoding, in which the character codes normally used for a and b are instead used for α and β.

This gives the usual ASCII character codes for a few English letters.	`In[8]:= ToCharacterCode["abcdefgh"]` `Out[8]= {97, 98, 99, 100, 101, 102, 103, 104}`
In the `"Symbol"` encoding, these character codes are used for Greek letters.	`In[9]:= FromCharacterCode[%, "Symbol"]` `Out[9]= αβχδεφγη`

ToCharacterCode["*string*"]	generate codes for characters using the standard *Mathematica* encoding
ToCharacterCode["*string*", "*encoding*"]	generate codes for characters using the specified encoding
FromCharacterCode[{n_1, n_2, ... }]	generate characters from codes using the standard *Mathematica* encoding
FromCharacterCode[{n_1, n_2, ... }, "*encoding*"]	generate characters from codes using the specified encoding

Handling character codes with different encodings.

This gives the codes assigned to various characters by *Mathematica*.

```
In[10]:= ToCharacterCode["abc\[EAcute]\[Pi]"]
Out[10]= {97, 98, 99, 233, 960}
```

Here are the codes assigned to the same characters in the Macintosh roman encoding.

```
In[11]:= ToCharacterCode["abc\[EAcute]\[Pi]", "MacintoshRoman"]
Out[11]= {97, 98, 99, 142, 185}
```

Here are the codes in the Windows standard encoding. There is no code for \[Pi] in that encoding.

```
In[12]:= ToCharacterCode["abc\[EAcute]\[Pi]", "WindowsANSI"]
Out[12]= {97, 98, 99, 233, None}
```

The character codes used internally by *Mathematica* are based on Unicode. But externally *Mathematica* by default always uses plain ASCII sequences such as \[*Name*] or \:*xxxx* to refer to special characters. By telling it to use the raw "Unicode" character encoding, however, you can get *Mathematica* to read and write characters in raw 16-bit Unicode form.

2.9 Textual Input and Output

■ 2.9.1 Forms of Input and Output

Here is one way to enter a particular expression.

$In[1]:=$ **x^2 + Sqrt[y]**

$Out[1]=$ $x^2 + \sqrt{y}$

Here is another way to enter the same expression.

$In[2]:=$ **Plus[Power[x, 2], Sqrt[y]]**

$Out[2]=$ $x^2 + \sqrt{y}$

With a notebook front end, you can also enter the expression directly in this way.

$In[3]:=$ **$x^2 + \sqrt{y}$**

$Out[3]=$ $x^2 + \sqrt{y}$

Mathematica allows you to output expressions in many different ways.

In *Mathematica* notebooks, expressions are by default output in StandardForm.

$In[4]:=$ **x^2 + Sqrt[y]**

$Out[4]=$ $x^2 + \sqrt{y}$

OutputForm uses only ordinary keyboard characters and is the default for text-based interfaces to *Mathematica*.

$In[5]:=$ **OutputForm[x^2 + Sqrt[y]]**

$Out[5]//OutputForm=$ x^2 + Sqrt[y]

InputForm yields a form that can be typed directly on a keyboard.

$In[6]:=$ **InputForm[x^2 + Sqrt[y]]**

$Out[6]//InputForm=$ x^2 + Sqrt[y]

FullForm shows the internal form of an expression in explicit functional notation.

$In[7]:=$ **FullForm[x^2 + Sqrt[y]]**

$Out[7]//FullForm=$ Plus[Power[x, 2], Power[y, Rational[1, 2]]]

FullForm[*expr*]	the internal form of an expression
InputForm[*expr*]	a form suitable for direct keyboard input
OutputForm[*expr*]	a two-dimensional form using only keyboard characters
StandardForm[*expr*]	the default form used in *Mathematica* notebooks

Some output forms for expressions.

Output forms provide textual representations of *Mathematica* expressions. In some cases these textual representations are also suitable for input to *Mathematica*. But in other cases they are intended just to be looked at, or to be exported to other programs, rather than to be used as input to *Mathematica*.

TraditionalForm uses a large collection of ad hoc rules to produce an approximation to traditional mathematical notation.

In[8]:= **TraditionalForm[x^2 + Sqrt[y] + Gamma[z] EllipticK[z]]**

Out[8]//TraditionalForm= $x^2 + K(z)\,\Gamma(z) + \sqrt{y}$

TeXForm yields output suitable for export to TEX.

In[9]:= **TeXForm[x^2 + Sqrt[y]]**

Out[9]//TeXForm= x^2 + {\sqrt{y}}

CForm yields output that can be included in a C program. Macros for objects like Power are included in the header file mdefs.h.

In[10]:= **CForm[x^2 + Sqrt[y]]**

Out[10]//CForm= Power(x,2) + Sqrt(y)

FortranForm yields output suitable for export to Fortran.

In[11]:= **FortranForm[x^2 + Sqrt[y]]**

Out[11]//FortranForm= x**2 + Sqrt(y)

TraditionalForm[*expr*]	traditional mathematical notation
TeXForm[*expr*]	output suitable for export to TEX
MathMLForm[*expr*]	output suitable for use with MathML on the web
CForm[*expr*]	output suitable for export to C
FortranForm[*expr*]	output suitable for export to Fortran

Output forms not normally used for *Mathematica* input.

Section 2.9.17 will discuss how you can create your own output forms. You should realize however that in communicating with external programs it is often better to use *MathLink* to send expressions directly than to generate a textual representation for these expressions.

- Exchange textual representations of expressions.
- Exchange expressions directly via *MathLink*.

Two ways to communicate between *Mathematica* and other programs.

■ 2.9.2 How Input and Output Work

Input	convert from a textual form to an expression
Processing	do computations on the expression
Output	convert the resulting expression to textual form

Steps in the operation of *Mathematica*.

When you type something like x^2 what *Mathematica* at first sees is just the string of characters x, ^, 2. But with the usual way that *Mathematica* is set up, it immediately knows to convert this string of characters into the expression Power[x, 2].

Then, after whatever processing is possible has been done, *Mathematica* takes the expression Power[x, 2] and converts it into some kind of textual representation for output.

Mathematica reads the string of characters x, ^, 2 and converts it to the expression Power[x, 2].	$In[1]:=$ **x ^ 2** $Out[1]=$ x^2
This shows the expression in Fortran form.	$In[2]:=$ **FortranForm[%]** $Out[2]//FortranForm=$ x**2
FortranForm is just a "wrapper": the value of Out[2] is still the expression Power[x, 2].	$In[3]:=$ **%** $Out[3]=$ x^2

It is important to understand that in a typical *Mathematica* session In[n] and Out[n] record only the underlying expressions that are processed, not the textual representations that happen to be used for their input or output.

If you explicitly request a particular kind of output, say by using TraditionalForm[*expr*], then what you get will be labeled with Out[n]//TraditionalForm. This indicates that what you are seeing is *expr*//TraditionalForm, even though the value of Out[n] itself is just *expr*.

Mathematica also allows you to specify globally that you want output to be displayed in a particular form. And if you do this, then the form will no longer be indicated explicitly in the label for each line. But it is still the case that In[n] and Out[n] will record only underlying expressions, not the textual representations used for their input and output.

This sets t to be an expression with FortranForm explicitly wrapped around it.	$In[4]:=$ **t = FortranForm[x^2 + y^2]** $Out[4]//FortranForm=$ x**2 + y**2
The result on the previous line is just the expression.	$In[5]:=$ **%** $Out[5]=$ $x^2 + y^2$

But t contains the `FortranForm` wrapper, and so is displayed in `FortranForm`.

In[6]:= **t**

Out[6]//FortranForm= x**2 + y**2

Wherever t appears, it is formatted in `FortranForm`.

In[7]:= **{t^2, 1/t}**

Out[7]= $\left\{ x ** 2 + y ** 2^2, \dfrac{1}{x ** 2 + y ** 2} \right\}$

■ 2.9.3 The Representation of Textual Forms

Like everything else in *Mathematica* the textual forms of expressions can themselves be represented as expressions. Textual forms that consist of one-dimensional sequences of characters can be represented directly as ordinary *Mathematica* strings. Textual forms that involve subscripts, superscripts and other two-dimensional constructs, however, can be represented by nested collections of two-dimensional boxes.

| One-dimensional strings | `InputForm`, `FullForm`, etc. |
| Two-dimensional boxes | `StandardForm`, `TraditionalForm`, etc. |

Typical representations of textual forms.

This generates the string corresponding to the textual representation of the expression in `InputForm`.

In[1]:= **ToString[x^2 + y^3, InputForm]**

Out[1]= x^2 + y^3

`FullForm` shows the string explicitly.

In[2]:= **FullForm[%]**

Out[2]//FullForm= "x^2 + y^3"

Here are the individual characters in the string.

In[3]:= **Characters[%]**

Out[3]= {x, ^, 2, , +, , y, ^, 3}

Here is the box structure corresponding to the expression in `StandardForm`.

In[4]:= **ToBoxes[x^2 + y^3, StandardForm]**

Out[4]= RowBox[
{SuperscriptBox[x, 2], +, SuperscriptBox[y, 3]}]

Here is the `InputForm` of the box structure. In this form the structure is effectively represented by an ordinary string.

In[5]:= **ToBoxes[x^2 + y^3, StandardForm] // InputForm**

Out[5]//InputForm= \(x\^2 + y\^3\)

If you use the notebook front end for *Mathematica*, then you can see the expression that corresponds to the textual form of each cell by using the Show Expression menu item.

Here is a cell containing an expression in `StandardForm`.

$$\dfrac{1}{2\,(1+x^2)} + \text{Log}[x] - \dfrac{\text{Log}[1+x^2]}{2}$$

Here is the underlying representation
of that expression in terms of boxes,
displayed using the Show Expression
menu item.

```
Cell[BoxData[
  RowBox[{
    FractionBox["1",
      RowBox[{"2", " ",
        RowBox[{"(",
          RowBox[{"1", "+",
            SuperscriptBox["x", "2"]}], ")"}]}]], "+",
    RowBox[{"Log", "[", "x", "]"}], "-",
    FractionBox[
      RowBox[{"Log", "[",
        RowBox[{"1", "+",
          SuperscriptBox["x", "2"]}], "]"}], "2"]}]], "Output"]
```

ToString[*expr*, *form*]	create a string representing the specified textual form of *expr*
ToBoxes[*expr*, *form*]	create a box structure representing the specified textual form of *expr*

Creating strings and boxes from expressions.

■ 2.9.4 The Interpretation of Textual Forms

ToExpression[*input*]	create an expression by interpreting strings or boxes

Converting from strings or boxes to expressions.

This takes a string and interprets it as
an expression.

In[1]:= **ToExpression["2 + 3 + x/y"]**

$Out[1]= 5 + \dfrac{x}{y}$

Here is the box structure corresponding
to the textual form of an expression in
StandardForm.

In[2]:= **ToBoxes[2 + x^2, StandardForm]**

Out[2]= RowBox[{2, +, SuperscriptBox[x, 2]}]

ToExpression interprets this box
structure and yields the original
expression again.

In[3]:= **ToExpression[%]**

$Out[3]= 2 + x^2$

In any *Mathematica* session, *Mathematica* is always effectively using ToExpression to interpret the textual form of your input as an actual expression to evaluate.

If you use the notebook front end for *Mathematica*, then the interpretation only takes place when the contents of a cell are sent to the kernel, say for evaluation. This means that within a notebook there is no need for the textual forms you set up to correspond to meaningful *Mathematica* expressions; this is only necessary if you want to send these forms to the kernel.

FullForm	explicit functional notation
InputForm	one-dimensional notation
StandardForm	two-dimensional notation

The hierarchy of forms for standard *Mathematica* input.

Here is an expression entered in FullForm.	*In[4]:=* **Plus[1, Power[x, 2]]**
	Out[4]= $1 + x^2$
Here is the same expression entered in InputForm.	*In[5]:=* **1 + x^2**
	Out[5]= $1 + x^2$
And here is the expression entered in StandardForm.	*In[6]:=* **1 + x²**
	Out[6]= $1 + x^2$

Built into *Mathematica* is a collection of standard rules for use by ToExpression in converting textual forms to expressions.

These rules define the *grammar* of *Mathematica*. They state, for example, that $x + y$ should be interpreted as Plus[x, y], and that x^y should be interpreted as Power[x, y]. If the input you give is in FullForm, then the rules for interpretation are very straightforward: every expression consists just of a head followed by a sequence of elements enclosed in brackets. The rules for InputForm are slightly more sophisticated: they allow operators such as +, =, and ->, and understand the meaning of expressions where these operators appear between operands. StandardForm involves still more sophisticated rules, which allow operators and operands to be arranged not just in a one-dimensional sequence, but in a full two-dimensional structure.

Mathematica is set up so that FullForm, InputForm and StandardForm form a strict hierarchy: anything you can enter in FullForm will also work in InputForm, and anything you can enter in InputForm will also work in StandardForm.

If you use a notebook front end for *Mathematica*, then you will typically want to use all the features of StandardForm. If you use a text-based interface, however, then you will typically be able to use only features of InputForm.

| x^2 | ordinary InputForm |
| \!\(x\^2\) | one-dimensional representation of StandardForm |

Two versions of InputForm.

When you use StandardForm in a *Mathematica* notebook, you can enter directly two-dimensional forms such as x^2. But InputForm allows only one-dimensional forms. Nevertheless, even though the actual text you give in InputForm must be one-dimensional, it is still possible to make it represent a two-dimensional form. Thus, for example, \!\(x\^2\) represents the two-dimensional form x^2, and is interpreted by *Mathematica* as Power[x, 2].

Here is ordinary one-dimensional input.	*In[7]:=* **x^2 + 1/y**
	Out[7]= $x^2 + \dfrac{1}{y}$
Here is input that represents a two-dimensional form.	*In[8]:=* **\!\(x\^2 + 1\/y \)**
	Out[8]= $x^2 + \dfrac{1}{y}$
Even though the input is given differently, the expressions obtained on the last two lines are exactly the same.	*In[9]:=* **% == %%**
	Out[9]= True

If you copy a two-dimensional form out of *Mathematica*, it is normally given in \!\(... \) form. When you paste this one-dimensional form back into a *Mathematica* notebook, it will automatically "snap" into two-dimensional form. If you simply type a \!\(... \) form into a notebook, you can get it to snap into two-dimensional form using the Make 2D menu item.

ToExpression[*input*, *form*]	attempt to create an expression assuming that *input* is given in the specified textual form

Importing from other textual forms.

StandardForm and its subsets FullForm and InputForm provide precise ways to represent any *Mathematica* expression in textual form. And given such a textual form, it is always possible to convert it unambiguously to the expression it represents.

TraditionalForm is an example of a textual form intended primarily for output. It is possible to take any *Mathematica* expression and display it in TraditionalForm. But TraditionalForm does not have the precision of StandardForm, and as a result there is in general no unambiguous way to go back from a TraditionalForm representation and get the expression it represents.

Nevertheless, ToExpression[*input*, TraditionalForm] takes text in TraditionalForm and attempts to interpret it as an expression.

This takes a string and interprets it as TraditionalForm input.	*In[10]:=* **ToExpression["f(6)", TraditionalForm]**
	Out[10]= f[6]
In StandardForm the same string would mean a product of terms.	*In[11]:=* **ToExpression["f(6)", StandardForm]**
	Out[11]= 6 f

When `TraditionalForm` output is generated as the result of a computation, the actual collection of boxes that represent the output typically contains special `InterpretationBox` and `TagBox` objects which specify how an expression can be reconstructed from the `TraditionalForm` output.

The same is true of `TraditionalForm` that is obtained by explicit conversion from `StandardForm`. But if you edit `TraditionalForm` extensively, or enter it from scratch, then *Mathematica* will have to try to interpret it without the benefit of any additional embedded information.

■ 2.9.5 Short and Shallow Output

When you generate a very large output expression in *Mathematica*, you often do not want to see the whole expression at once. Rather, you would first like to get an idea of the general structure of the expression, and then, perhaps, go in and look at particular parts in more detail.

The functions `Short` and `Shallow` allow you to see "outlines" of large *Mathematica* expressions.

`Short[`*expr*`]`	show a one-line outline of *expr*
`Short[`*expr, n*`]`	show an *n*-line outline of *expr*
`Shallow[`*expr*`]`	show the "top parts" of *expr*
`Shallow[`*expr, {depth, length}*`]`	show the parts of *expr* to the specified depth and length

Showing outlines of expressions.

This generates a long expression. If the whole expression were printed out here, it would go on for 23 lines.

$In[1]:= $ `t = Expand[(1 + x + y)^12] ;`

This gives a one-line "outline" of t. The <<87>> indicates that 87 terms are omitted.

$In[2]:= $ `Short[t]`

$Out[2]//Short= $ $1 + 12 x + \ll 87 \gg + 12 x y^{11} + y^{12}$

When *Mathematica* generates output, it first effectively writes the output in one long row. Then it looks at the width of text you have asked for, and it chops the row of output into a sequence of separate "lines". Each of the "lines" may of course contain superscripts and built-up fractions, and so may take up more than one actual line on your output device. When you specify a particular number of lines in `Short`, *Mathematica* takes this to be the number of "logical lines" that you want, not the number of actual physical lines on your particular output device.

Here is a four-line version of t. More terms are shown in this case.

$In[3]:= $ `Short[t, 4]`

$Out[3]//Short= $ $1 + 12 x + 66 x^2 + 220 x^3 + 495 x^4 + 792 x^5 + 924 x^6 +$
$792 x^7 + 495 x^8 + 220 x^9 + 66 x^{10} + 12 x^{11} + \ll 68 \gg +$
$495 x^4 y^8 + 220 y^9 + 660 x y^9 + 660 x^2 y^9 + 220 x^3 y^9 +$
$66 y^{10} + 132 x y^{10} + 66 x^2 y^{10} + 12 y^{11} + 12 x y^{11} + y^{12}$

You can use Short with other output forms, such as InputForm.

```
In[4]:= Short[InputForm[t]]
Out[4]//Short= 1 + 12*x + 66*x^2 + 220*x^3 + <<85>> + 12*x*y^11 + y^12
```

Short works by removing a sequence of parts from an expression until the output form of the result fits on the number of lines you specify. Sometimes, however, you may find it better to specify not how many final output lines you want, but which parts of the expression to drop. Shallow[*expr*, {*depth*, *length*}] includes only *length* arguments to any function, and drops all subexpressions that are below the specified depth.

Shallow shows a different outline of t.

```
In[5]:= Shallow[t]
Out[5]//Shallow= 1 + 12 x + 66 Power[<<2>>] + 220 Power[<<2>>] +
                  495 Power[<<2>>] + 792 Power[<<2>>] +
                  924 Power[<<2>>] + 792 Power[<<2>>] +
                  495 Power[<<2>>] + 220 Power[<<2>>] + <<81>>
```

This includes only 10 arguments to each function, but allows any depth.

```
In[6]:= Shallow[t, {Infinity, 10}]
Out[6]//Shallow= 1 + 12 x + 66 x^2 + 220 x^3 + 495 x^4 + 792 x^5 +
                  924 x^6 + 792 x^7 + 495 x^8 + 220 x^9 + <<81>>
```

Shallow is particularly useful when you want to drop parts in a uniform way throughout a highly nested expression, such as a large list structure returned by Trace.

Here is the recursive definition of the Fibonacci function.

```
In[7]:= fib[n_] := fib[n-1] + fib[n-2] ; fib[0] = fib[1] = 1
Out[7]= 1
```

This generates a large list structure.

```
In[8]:= tr = Trace[fib[8]] ;
```

You can use Shallow to see an outline of the structure.

```
In[9]:= Shallow[tr]
Out[9]//Shallow= {fib[<<1>>], Plus[<<2>>], {{<<2>>}, <<1>>,
                  <<1>>, {<<7>>}, {<<7>>}, <<1>>, <<1>>},
                  {{<<2>>}, <<1>>, <<1>>, {<<7>>}, {<<7>>},
                  <<1>>, <<1>>}, Plus[<<2>>], 34}
```

Short gives you a less uniform outline, which can be more difficult to understand.

```
In[10]:= Short[tr, 4]
Out[10]//Short= {fib[8], fib[8 - 1] + fib[8 - 2],
                  {{8 - 1, 7}, fib[7], <<3>>, 13 + 8, 21},
                  {<<1>>}, 21 + 13, 34}
```

■ 2.9.6 String-Oriented Output Formats

"*text*"	a string containing arbitrary text

Text strings.

The quotes are not included in standard *Mathematica* output form.

```
In[1]:= "This is a string."
Out[1]= This is a string.
```

In input form, the quotes are included.   *In[2]:=* **InputForm[%]**

Out[2]//InputForm= "This is a string."

You can put any kind of text into a *Mathematica* string. This includes non-English characters, as well as newlines and other control information. Section 2.8 discusses in more detail how strings work.

StringForm["*cccc*``*cccc*", x_1, x_2, ...]
  output a string in which successive `` are replaced by successive x_i

StringForm["*cccc*`*i*`*cccc*", x_1, x_2, ...]
  output a string in which each `*i*` is replaced by the corresponding x_i

---

Using format strings.

In many situations, you may want to generate output using a string as a "template", but "splicing" in various *Mathematica* expressions. You can do this using StringForm.

This generates output with each successive `` replaced by an expression.

In[3]:= **StringForm["x = ``, y = ``", 3, (1 + u)^2]**

Out[3]= x = 3, y = $(1+u)^2$

You can use numbers to pick out expressions in any order.

In[4]:= **StringForm["{`1`, `2`, `1`}", a, b]**

Out[4]= {a, b, a}

The string in StringForm acts somewhat like a "format directive" in the formatted output statements of languages such as C and Fortran. You can determine how the expressions in StringForm will be formatted by wrapping them with standard output format functions.

You can specify how the expressions in StringForm are formatted using standard output format functions.

In[5]:= **StringForm["The `` of `` is ``.", TeXForm, a/b, TeXForm[a/b]]**

Out[5]= The TeXForm of $\frac{a}{b}$ is \ frac {a} {b}.

You should realize that StringForm is only an output format. It does not evaluate in any way. You can use the function ToString to create an ordinary string from a StringForm object.

StringForm generates formatted output in standard *Mathematica* output form.

In[6]:= **StringForm["Q: `` -> ``", a, b]**

Out[6]= Q: a -> b

In input form, you can see the actual StringForm object.

In[7]:= **InputForm[%]**

Out[7]//InputForm= StringForm["Q: `` -> ``", a, b]

This creates an ordinary string from the StringForm object.

In[8]:= **InputForm[ToString[%]]**

Out[8]//InputForm= "Q: a -> b"

StringForm allows you to specify a "template string", then fill in various expressions. Sometimes all you want to do is to concatenate together the output forms for a sequence of expressions. You can do this using SequenceForm.

SequenceForm[*expr*₁, *expr*₂, ...]	give the output forms of the *expr*ᵢ concatenated together

Output of sequences of expressions.

SequenceForm prints as a sequence of expressions concatenated together.	*In[9]:=* **SequenceForm["[x = ", 56, "]"]** *Out[9]=* [x = 56]

ColumnForm[{*expr*₁, *expr*₂, ... }]	a left-aligned column of objects
ColumnForm[*list*, *h*, *v*]	a column with horizontal alignment *h* (Left, Center or Right), and vertical alignment *v* (Below, Center or Above)

Output of columns of expressions.

This arranges the two expressions in a column.	*In[10]:=* **ColumnForm[{a + b, x^2}]** *Out[10]=* a + b x²

HoldForm[*expr*]	give the output form of *expr*, with *expr* maintained unevaluated

Output of unevaluated expressions.

Using text strings and functions like StringForm, you can generate pieces of output that do not necessarily correspond to valid *Mathematica* expressions. Sometimes, however, you want to generate output that corresponds to a valid *Mathematica* expression, but only so long as the expression is not evaluated. The function HoldForm maintains its argument unevaluated, but allows it to be formatted in the standard *Mathematica* output form.

HoldForm maintains 1 + 1 unevaluated.	*In[11]:=* **HoldForm[1 + 1]** *Out[11]=* 1 + 1

The HoldForm prevents the actual assignment from being done.	*In[12]:=* **HoldForm[x = 3]** *Out[12]=* x = 3

If it was not for the HoldForm, the power would be evaluated.	*In[13]:=* **HoldForm[34^78]** *Out[13]=* 34^{78}

■ 2.9.7 Output Formats for Numbers

ScientificForm[*expr*]	print all numbers in scientific notation
EngineeringForm[*expr*]	print all numbers in engineering notation (exponents divisible by 3)
AccountingForm[*expr*]	print all numbers in standard accounting format

Output formats for numbers.

These numbers are given in the default output format. Large numbers are given in scientific notation.	*In[1]:=* **{6.7^-4, 6.7^6, 6.7^8}** *Out[1]=* $\left\{0.00049625,\ 90458.4,\ 4.06068 \times 10^{6}\right\}$
This gives all numbers in scientific notation.	*In[2]:=* **ScientificForm[%]** *Out[2]//ScientificForm=* $\left\{4.9625 \times 10^{-4},\ 9.04584 \times 10^{4},\ 4.06068 \times 10^{6}\right\}$
This gives the numbers in engineering notation, with exponents arranged to be multiples of three.	*In[3]:=* **EngineeringForm[%]** *Out[3]//EngineeringForm=* $\left\{496.25 \times 10^{-6},\ 90.4584 \times 10^{3},\ 4.06068 \times 10^{6}\right\}$
In accounting form, negative numbers are given in parentheses, and scientific notation is never used.	*In[4]:=* **AccountingForm[{5.6, -6.7, 10.^7}]** *Out[4]//AccountingForm=* {5.6, (6.7), 10000000.}

NumberForm[*expr*, *tot*]	print at most *tot* digits of all approximate real numbers in *expr*
ScientificForm[*expr*, *tot*]	use scientific notation with at most *tot* digits
EngineeringForm[*expr*, *tot*]	use engineering notation with at most *tot* digits

Controlling the printed precision of real numbers.

Here is π^{9} to 30 decimal places.	*In[5]:=* **N[Pi^9, 30]** *Out[5]=* 29809.0993334462116665094024012
This prints just 10 digits of π^{9}.	*In[6]:=* **NumberForm[%, 10]** *Out[6]//NumberForm=* 29809.09933

This gives 12 digits, in engineering notation.

In[7]:= **EngineeringForm[%, 12]**

Out[7]//EngineeringForm= $29.8090993334 \times 10^3$

option name	default value	
DigitBlock	Infinity	maximum length of blocks of digits between breaks
NumberSeparator	{",", " "}	strings to insert at breaks between blocks of digits to the left and right of a decimal point
NumberPoint	"."	string to use for a decimal point
NumberMultiplier	"\[Times]"	string to use for the multiplication sign in scientific notation
NumberSigns	{"-", ""}	strings to use for signs of negative and positive numbers
NumberPadding	{"", ""}	strings to use for padding on the left and right
SignPadding	False	whether to insert padding after the sign
NumberFormat	Automatic	function to generate final format of number
ExponentFunction	Automatic	function to determine the exponent to use

Options for number formatting.

All the options in the table except the last one apply to both integers and approximate real numbers.

All the options can be used in any of the functions NumberForm, ScientificForm, EngineeringForm and AccountingForm. In fact, you can in principle reproduce the behavior of any one of these functions simply by giving appropriate option settings in one of the others. The default option settings listed in the table are those for NumberForm.

Setting DigitBlock->n breaks digits into blocks of length n.

In[8]:= **NumberForm[30!, DigitBlock->3]**

Out[8]//NumberForm= 265,252,859,812,191,058,636,308,480,000,000

You can specify any string to use as a separator between blocks of digits.

In[9]:= **NumberForm[30!, DigitBlock->5, NumberSeparator->" "]**

Out[9]//NumberForm= 265 25285 98121 91058 63630 84800 00000

This gives an explicit plus sign for positive numbers, and uses | in place of a decimal point.

In[10]:= **NumberForm[{4.5, -6.8}, NumberSigns->{"-", "+"},**
              NumberPoint->"|"]

Out[10]//NumberForm= {+4|5, -6|8}

When *Mathematica* prints an approximate real number, it has to choose whether scientific notation should be used, and if so, how many digits should appear to the left of the decimal point. What *Mathematica* does is first to find out what the exponent would be if scientific notation were used, and one digit were given to the left of the decimal point. Then it takes this exponent, and applies any function given as the setting for the option `ExponentFunction`. This function should return the actual exponent to be used, or `Null` if scientific notation should not be used.

The default is to use scientific notation for all numbers with exponents outside the range −5 to 5.	*In[11]:=* `{8.^5, 11.^7, 13.^9}`
	Out[11]= $\left\{32768., 1.94872 \times 10^7, 1.06045 \times 10^{10}\right\}$
This uses scientific notation only for numbers with exponents of 10 or more.	*In[12]:=* `NumberForm[%,` `      ExponentFunction -> (If[-10 < # < 10, Null, #]&)]`
	Out[12]//NumberForm= $\left\{32768., 19487171., 1.06045 \times 10^{10}\right\}$
This forces all exponents to be multiples of 3.	*In[13]:=* `NumberForm[%, ExponentFunction -> (3 Quotient[#, 3]&)]`
	Out[13]//NumberForm= $\left\{32.768 \times 10^3, 19.4872 \times 10^6, 10.6045 \times 10^9\right\}$

Having determined what the mantissa and exponent for a number should be, the final step is to assemble these into the object to print. The option `NumberFormat` allows you to give an arbitrary function which specifies the print form for the number. The function takes as arguments three strings: the mantissa, the base, and the exponent for the number. If there is no exponent, it is given as `""`.

This gives the exponents in Fortran-like "e" format.	*In[14]:=* `NumberForm[{5.6^10, 7.8^20},` `            NumberFormat -> (SequenceForm[#1, "e", #3]&) ]`
	Out[14]//NumberForm= `{3.03305e7, 6.94852e17}`
You can use `FortranForm` to print individual numbers in Fortran format.	*In[15]:=* `FortranForm[7.8^20]`
	Out[15]//FortranForm= `6.948515870862152e17`

`PaddedForm[`*expr*`, `*tot*`]`	print with all numbers having room for *tot* digits, padding with leading spaces if necessary
`PaddedForm[`*expr*`, {`*tot*`, `*frac*`}]`	print with all numbers having room for *tot* digits, with exactly *frac* digits to the right of the decimal point
`NumberForm[`*expr*`, {`*tot*`, `*frac*`}]`	print with all numbers having at most *tot* digits, exactly *frac* of them to the right of the decimal point
`ColumnForm[{`*expr*$_1$`, `*expr*$_2$`, ... }]`	print with the *expr*$_i$ left aligned in a column

Controlling the alignment of numbers in output.

Whenever you print a collection of numbers in a column or some other definite arrangement, you typically need to be able to align the numbers in a definite way. Usually you want all the numbers to be set up so that the digit corresponding to a particular power of 10 always appears at the same position within the region used to print a number.

You can change the positions of digits in the printed form of a number by "padding" it in various ways. You can pad on the right, typically adding zeros somewhere after the decimal. Or you can pad on the left, typically inserting spaces in place of leading zeros.

This pads with spaces to make room for up to 7 digits in each integer.	`In[16]:= PaddedForm[{456, 12345, 12}, 7]`
	
	`Out[16]//PaddedForm= {   456,   12345,      12}`

This creates a column of integers.

```
In[17]:= PaddedForm[ColumnForm[{456, 12345, 12}], 7]
Out[17]//PaddedForm=      456
                        12345
                           12
```

This prints each number with room for a total of 7 digits, and with 4 digits to the right of the decimal point.

```
In[18]:= PaddedForm[{-6.7, 6.888, 6.99999}, {7, 4}]
Out[18]//PaddedForm= { -6.7000,   6.8880,   7.0000}
```

In NumberForm, the 7 specifies the maximum precision, but does not make *Mathematica* pad with spaces.

```
In[19]:= NumberForm[{-6.7, 6.888, 6.99999}, {7, 4}]
Out[19]//NumberForm= {-6.7, 6.888, 7.}
```

If you set the option SignPadding-> True, *Mathematica* will insert leading spaces *after* the sign.

```
In[20]:= PaddedForm[{-6.7, 6.888, 6.99999}, {7, 4},
                                    SignPadding->True]
Out[20]//PaddedForm= {-  6.7000,   6.8880,   7.0000}
```

Only the mantissa portion is aligned when scientific notation is used.

```
In[21]:= PaddedForm[
            ColumnForm[{6.7 10^8, 48.7, -2.3 10^-16}], {4, 2}]
```

$$Out[21]//PaddedForm=   6.70 \times 10^{8}$$
$$48.70$$
$$-2.30 \times 10^{-16}$$

With the default setting for the option NumberPadding, both NumberForm and PaddedForm insert trailing zeros when they pad a number on the right. You can use spaces for padding on both the left and the right by setting NumberPadding -> {" ", " "}.

This uses spaces instead of zeros for padding on the right.

```
In[22]:= PaddedForm[{-6.7, 6.888, 6.99999}, {7, 4},
                        NumberPadding -> {" ", " "}]
Out[22]//PaddedForm= { -6.7  ,   6.888 ,   7.   }
```

BaseForm[*expr*, *b*]	print with all numbers given in base *b*

Printing numbers in other bases.

This prints a number in base 2.

$In[23]:=$ **BaseForm[2342424, 2]**

$Out[23]//BaseForm=$ 1000111011111000011000_2

In bases higher than 10, letters are used for the extra digits.

$In[24]:=$ **BaseForm[242345341, 16]**

$Out[24]//BaseForm=$ $e71e57d_{16}$

BaseForm also works with approximate real numbers.

$In[25]:=$ **BaseForm[2.3, 2]**

$Out[25]//BaseForm=$ 10.010011001100110011_2

You can even use BaseForm for numbers printed in scientific notation.

$In[26]:=$ **BaseForm[2.3 10^8, 2]**

$Out[26]//BaseForm=$ $1.1011011010110000101_2 \times 2^{27}$

Section 3.1.3 discusses how to enter numbers in arbitrary bases, and also how to get lists of the digits in a number.

■ 2.9.8 Tables and Matrices

TableForm[*list*]	print in tabular form
MatrixForm[*list*]	print in matrix form

Formatting lists as tables and matrices.

Here is a list.

$In[1]:=$ **Table[(i + 45)^j, {i, 3}, {j, 3}]**

$Out[1]=$ {{46, 2116, 97336}, {47, 2209, 103823}, {48, 2304, 110592}}

TableForm displays the list in a tabular format.

$In[2]:=$ **TableForm[%]**

$$Out[2]//TableForm= \begin{array}{ccc} 46 & 2116 & 97336 \\ 47 & 2209 & 103823 \\ 48 & 2304 & 110592 \end{array}$$

MatrixForm displays the list as a matrix.

$In[3]:=$ **MatrixForm[%]**

$$Out[3]//MatrixForm= \begin{pmatrix} 46 & 2116 & 97336 \\ 47 & 2209 & 103823 \\ 48 & 2304 & 110592 \end{pmatrix}$$

This displays an array of algebraic expressions as a matrix.

$In[4]:=$ **MatrixForm[Table[x^i - y^j, {i, 3}, {j, 3}]]**

$$Out[4]//MatrixForm= \begin{pmatrix} x - y & x - y^2 & x - y^3 \\ x^2 - y & x^2 - y^2 & x^2 - y^3 \\ x^3 - y & x^3 - y^2 & x^3 - y^3 \end{pmatrix}$$

PaddedForm[TableForm[*list*], *tot*]	print a table with all numbers padded to have room for *tot* digits
PaddedForm[TableForm[*list*], {*tot*, *frac*}]	put *frac* digits to the right of the decimal point in all approximate real numbers

Printing tables of numbers.

Here is a list of numbers.

$In[5]:=$ **fac = {10!, 15!, 20!}**

$Out[5]=$ {3628800, 1307674368000, 2432902008176640000}

TableForm displays the list in a column.

$In[6]:=$ **TableForm[fac]**

$Out[6]//TableForm=$
$$\begin{array}{l} 3628800 \\ 1307674368000 \\ 2432902008176640000 \end{array}$$

This aligns the numbers by padding each one to leave room for up to 20 digits.

$In[7]:=$ **PaddedForm[TableForm[fac], 20]**

$Out[7]//PaddedForm=$
$$\begin{array}{r} 3628800 \\ 1307674368000 \\ 2432902008176640000 \end{array}$$

In this particular case, you could also align the numbers using the TableAlignments option.

$In[8]:=$ **TableForm[fac, TableAlignments -> {Right}]**

$Out[8]//TableForm=$
$$\begin{array}{r} 3628800 \\ 1307674368000 \\ 2432902008176640000 \end{array}$$

This lines up the numbers, padding each one to have room for 8 digits, with 5 digits to the right of the decimal point.

$In[9]:=$ **PaddedForm[TableForm[{6.7, 6.888, 6.99999}], {8, 5}]**

$Out[9]//PaddedForm=$
$$\begin{array}{l} 6.70000 \\ 6.88800 \\ 6.99999 \end{array}$$

You can use TableForm and MatrixForm to format lists that are nested to any depth, corresponding to arrays with any number of dimensions.

Here is the format for a 2 × 2 array of elements a[*i*, *j*].

$In[10]:=$ **TableForm[Array[a, {2, 2}]]**

$Out[10]//TableForm=$
$$\begin{array}{ll} a[1, 1] & a[1, 2] \\ a[2, 1] & a[2, 2] \end{array}$$

Here is a 2 × 2 × 2 array.

```
In[11]:= TableForm[ { Array[a, {2, 2}], Array[b, {2, 2}] } ]
```

```
Out[11]//TableForm=   a[1, 1]    a[2, 1]
                      a[1, 2]    a[2, 2]
                      b[1, 1]    b[2, 1]
                      b[1, 2]    b[2, 2]
```

And here is a 2 × 2 × 2 × 2 array.

```
In[12]:= TableForm[ { {Array[a, {2, 2}], Array[b, {2, 2}]},
                      {Array[c, {2, 2}], Array[d, {2, 2}]} } ]
```

```
Out[12]//TableForm=   a[1, 1]  a[1, 2]    b[1, 1]  b[1, 2]
                      a[2, 1]  a[2, 2]    b[2, 1]  b[2, 2]
                      c[1, 1]  c[1, 2]    d[1, 1]  d[1, 2]
                      c[2, 1]  c[2, 2]    d[2, 1]  d[2, 2]
```

In general, when you print an *n*-dimensional table, successive dimensions are alternately given as columns and rows. By setting the option TableDirections -> {*dir*$_1$, *dir*$_2$, ... }, where the *dir*$_i$ are Column or Row, you can specify explicitly which way each dimension should be given. By default, the option is effectively set to {Column, Row, Column, Row, ... }.

The option TableDirections allows you to specify explicitly how each dimension in a multidimensional table should be given.

```
In[13]:= TableForm[ { Array[a, {2, 2}], Array[b, {2, 2}] },
                      TableDirections -> {Row, Row, Column} ]
```

```
Out[13]//TableForm=   a[1, 1]      a[2, 1]  b[1, 1]      b[2, 1]
                      a[1, 2]      a[2, 2]  b[1, 2]      b[2, 2]
```

Whenever you make a table from a nested list such as {*list*$_1$, *list*$_2$, ... }, there is a question of whether it should be the *list*$_i$ or their elements which appear as the basic entries in the table. The default behavior is slightly different for MatrixForm and TableForm.

MatrixForm handles only arrays that are "rectangular". Thus, for example, to consider an array as two-dimensional, all the rows must have the same length. If they do not, MatrixForm treats the array as one-dimensional, with elements that are lists.

MatrixForm treats this as a one-dimensional array, since the rows are of differing lengths.

```
In[14]:= MatrixForm[{{a, a, a}, {b, b}}]
```

$$Out[14]//MatrixForm= \begin{pmatrix} \{a, a, a\} \\ \{b, b\} \end{pmatrix}$$

While MatrixForm can handle only "rectangular arrays", TableForm can handle arbitrary "ragged" arrays. It leaves blanks wherever there are no elements supplied.

TableForm can handle "ragged" arrays.

```
In[15]:= TableForm[{{a, a, a}, {b, b}}]
```

```
Out[15]//TableForm=   a        a        a
                      b        b
```

You can include objects that behave as "subtables".

```
In[16]:= TableForm[{{a, {{p, q}, {r, s}}, a, a},
                     {{x, y}, b, b}}]
```

```
Out[16]//TableForm=            p  q
                      a        r  s     a        a
                      x
                      y        b        b
```

You can control the number of levels in a nested list to which both `TableForm` and `MatrixForm` go by setting the option `TableDepth`.

This tells `TableForm` only to go down to depth 2. As a result {x, y} is treated as a single table entry.

In[17]:= `TableForm[{{a, {x, y}}, {c, d}}, TableDepth -> 2]`

Out[17]//TableForm=
```
a    {x, y}
c    d
```

option name	default value	
TableDepth	Infinity	maximum number of levels to include in the table
TableDirections	{Column, Row, Column, ... }	whether to arrange dimensions as rows or columns
TableAlignments	{Left, Bottom, Left, ... }	how to align the entries in each dimension
TableSpacing	{1, 3, 0, 1, 0, ... }	how many spaces to put between entries in each dimension
TableHeadings	{None, None, ... }	how to label the entries in each dimension

Options for `TableForm`.

With the option `TableAlignments`, you can specify how each entry in the table should be aligned with its row or column. For columns, you can specify `Left`, `Center` or `Right`. For rows, you can specify `Bottom`, `Center` or `Top`. If you set `TableAlignments -> Center`, all entries will be centered both horizontally and vertically. `TableAlignments -> Automatic` uses the default choice of alignments.

Entries in columns are by default aligned on the left.

In[18]:= `TableForm[{a, bbbb, ccccccccc}]`

Out[18]//TableForm=
```
a
bbbb
ccccccccc
```

This centers all entries.

In[19]:= `TableForm[{a, bbbb, ccccccccc},`
`                TableAlignments -> Center]`

Out[19]//TableForm=
```
    a
  bbbb
ccccccccc
```

You can use the option `TableSpacing` to specify how much horizontal space there should be between successive columns, or how much vertical space there should be between successive rows. A setting of 0 specifies that successive objects should abut.

This leaves 6 spaces between the entries in each row, and no space between successive rows.

```
In[20]:= TableForm[{{a, b}, {ccc, d}}, TableSpacing -> {0, 6}]

Out[20]//TableForm=  a              b
                     ccc            d
```

None	no labels in any dimension
Automatic	successive integer labels in each dimension
$\{\{lab_{11}, \ lab_{12}, \ \dots \ \}, \ \dots \ \}$	explicit labels

Settings for the option `TableHeadings`.

This puts integer labels in a $2 \times 2 \times 2$ array.

```
In[21]:= TableForm[Array[a, {2, 2, 2}],
                     TableHeadings -> Automatic]

Out[21]//TableForm=        1              2

                    1   a[1, 1, 1]    a[1, 2, 1]
                  1 2   a[1, 1, 2]    a[1, 2, 2]

                    1   a[2, 1, 1]    a[2, 2, 1]
                  2 2   a[2, 1, 2]    a[2, 2, 2]
```

This gives a table in which the rows are labeled by integers, and the columns by a list of strings.

```
In[22]:= TableForm[{{a, b, c}, {ap, bp, cp}},
                     TableHeadings ->
                       {Automatic, {"first", "middle", "last"}}]

                          first      middle      last
Out[22]//TableForm=  1      a          b          c
                     2      ap         bp         cp
```

This labels the rows but not the columns. TableForm automatically inserts a blank row to go with the third label.

```
In[23]:= TableForm[{{2, 3, 4}, {5, 6, 1}},
                     TableHeadings ->
                       {{"row a", "row b", "row c"}, None}]

                     row a    2     3     4
Out[23]//TableForm=  row b    5     6     1
                     row c
```

■ 2.9.9 Styles and Fonts in Output

| StyleForm[*expr*, *options*] | print with the specified style options |
| StyleForm[*expr*, *"style"*] | print with the specified cell style |

Specifying output styles.

The second x^2 is here shown in boldface.

```
In[1]:= {x^2, StyleForm[x^2, FontWeight->"Bold"]}

Out[1]= {x^2 , x^2}
```

This shows the word text in font sizes from 10 to 20 points.

$In[2]:=$ **Table[StyleForm["text", FontSize->s], {s, 10, 20}]**

$Out[2]=$ {text, text, text, text, text, text, text, text, text, text, text}

This shows the text in the Tekton font.

$In[3]:=$ **StyleForm["some text", FontFamily->"Tekton"]**

$Out[3]//StyleForm=$ some text

option	typical setting(s)	
FontSize	12	size of characters in printer's points
FontWeight	"Plain" or "Bold"	weight of characters
FontSlant	"Plain" or "Italic"	slant of characters
FontFamily	"Courier", "Times", "Helvetica"	font family
FontColor	GrayLevel[0]	color of characters
Background	GrayLevel[1]	background color for characters

A few options that can be used in StyleForm.

If you use the notebook front end for *Mathematica*, then each piece of output that is generated will by default be in the style of the cell in which the output appears. By using StyleForm[*expr*, "*style*"], however, you can tell *Mathematica* to output a particular expression in a different style.

Here is an expression output in the style normally used for section headings.

$In[4]:=$ **StyleForm[x^2 + y^2, "Section"]**

$Out[4]//StyleForm=$ $\mathbf{x^2 + y^2}$

Page 572 describes in more detail how cell styles work. By using StyleForm[*expr*, "*style*", *options*] you can generate output that is in a particular style, but with certain options modified.

■ 2.9.10 Representing Textual Forms by Boxes

All textual forms in *Mathematica* are ultimately represented in terms of nested collections of *boxes*. Typically the elements of these boxes correspond to objects that are to be placed at definite relative positions in two dimensions.

Here are the boxes corresponding to the expression a + b.

$In[1]:=$ **ToBoxes[a + b]**

$Out[1]=$ RowBox[{a, +, b}]

DisplayForm shows how these boxes would be displayed.

In[2]:= **DisplayForm[%]**

Out[2]//DisplayForm= a + b

DisplayForm[*boxes*]	show *boxes* as they would be displayed

Showing the displayed form of boxes.

This displays three strings in a row.

In[3]:= **RowBox[{"a", "+", "b"}] // DisplayForm**

Out[3]//DisplayForm= a + b

This displays one string as a subscript of another.

In[4]:= **SubscriptBox["a", "i"] // DisplayForm**

Out[4]//DisplayForm= a_i

This puts two subscript boxes in a row.

In[5]:= **RowBox[{SubscriptBox["a", "1"], SubscriptBox["b", "2"]}] // DisplayForm**

Out[5]//DisplayForm= a_1 b_2

"*text*"	literal text
RowBox[{*a*, *b*, ... }]	a row of boxes or strings a b ...
GridBox[{{*a*₁, *b*₁, ... }, {*a*₂, *b*₂, ... }, ... }]	a grid of boxes $\begin{matrix} a_1 & b_1 & ... \\ a_2 & b_2 & ... \\ \vdots & \vdots \end{matrix}$
SubscriptBox[*a*, *b*]	subscript a_b
SuperscriptBox[*a*, *b*]	superscript a^b
SubsuperscriptBox[*a*, *b*, *c*]	subscript and superscript a_b^c
UnderscriptBox[*a*, *b*]	underscript $\underset{b}{a}$
OverscriptBox[*a*, *b*]	overscript $\overset{b}{a}$
UnderoverscriptBox[*a*, *b*, *c*]	underscript and overscript $\underset{b}{\overset{c}{a}}$
FractionBox[*a*, *b*]	fraction $\dfrac{a}{b}$
SqrtBox[*a*]	square root $\sqrt{a}$
RadicalBox[*a*, *b*]	b^{th} root $\sqrt[b]{a}$

Some basic box types.

This nests a fraction inside a radical.

In[6]:= **RadicalBox[FractionBox[x, y], n] // DisplayForm**

$Out[6]//DisplayForm=$ $\sqrt[n]{\dfrac{x}{y}}$

This puts a superscript on a subscripted object.

In[7]:= **SuperscriptBox[SubscriptBox[a, b], c] // DisplayForm**

$Out[7]//DisplayForm=$ $a_b{}^c$

This puts both a subscript and a superscript on the same object.

In[8]:= **SubsuperscriptBox[a, b, c] // DisplayForm**

$Out[8]//DisplayForm=$ a_b^c

FrameBox[*box*]	render *box* with a frame drawn around it
GridBox[*list*, RowLines->True]	put lines between rows in a GridBox
GridBox[*list*, ColumnLines->True]	put lines between columns in a GridBox
GridBox[*list*, RowLines->{True, False}]	
	put a line below the first row, but not subsequent ones

Inserting frames and grid lines.

This shows a fraction with a frame drawn around it.

In[9]:= **FrameBox[FractionBox["x", "y"]] // DisplayForm**

$Out[9]//DisplayForm=$ $\boxed{\dfrac{x}{y}}$

This puts lines between rows and columns of an array.

In[10]:= **GridBox[Table[i+j, {i, 3}, {j, 3}], RowLines->True,**
            ColumnLines->True] // DisplayForm

$Out[10]//DisplayForm=$
$$\begin{array}{c|c|c} 2 & 3 & 4 \\ \hline 3 & 4 & 5 \\ \hline 4 & 5 & 6 \end{array}$$

And this also puts a frame around the outside.

In[11]:= **FrameBox[%] // DisplayForm**

$Out[11]//DisplayForm=$
$$\boxed{\begin{array}{c|c|c} 2 & 3 & 4 \\ \hline 3 & 4 & 5 \\ \hline 4 & 5 & 6 \end{array}}$$

StyleBox[*boxes*, *options*]	render *boxes* with the specified option settings
StyleBox[*boxes*, *"style"*]	render *boxes* in the specified style

Modifying the appearance of boxes.

StyleBox takes the same options as StyleForm. The difference is that StyleForm acts as a "wrapper" for any expression, while StyleBox represents underlying box structure.

This shows the string "name" in italics.	*In[12]:=* **StyleBox["name", FontSlant->"Italic"] // DisplayForm**
	Out[12]//DisplayForm= *name*
This shows "name" in the style used for section headings in your current notebook.	*In[13]:=* **StyleBox["name", "Section"] // DisplayForm**
	Out[13]//DisplayForm= **name**
This uses section heading style, but with characters shown in gray.	*In[14]:=* **StyleBox["name", "Section", FontColor->GrayLevel[0.5]] // DisplayForm**
	Out[14]//DisplayForm= name

If you use a notebook front end for *Mathematica*, then you will be able to change the style and appearance of what you see on the screen directly by using menu items. Internally, however, these changes will still be recorded by the insertion of appropriate StyleBox objects.

FormBox[*boxes*, *form*]	interpret *boxes* using rules associated with the specified form
InterpretationBox[*boxes*, *expr*]	interpret *boxes* as representing the expression *expr*
TagBox[*boxes*, *tag*]	use *tag* to guide the interpretation of *boxes*
ErrorBox[*boxes*]	indicate an error and do not attempt further interpretation of *boxes*

Controlling the interpretation of boxes.

This prints as x with a superscript.	*In[15]:=* **SuperscriptBox["x", "2"] // DisplayForm**
	Out[15]//DisplayForm= x^2
It is normally interpreted as a power.	*In[16]:=* **ToExpression[%] // InputForm**
	Out[16]//InputForm= x^2
This again prints as x with a superscript.	*In[17]:=* **InterpretationBox[SuperscriptBox["x", "2"], vec[x, 2]] // DisplayForm**
	Out[17]//DisplayForm= x^2
But now it is interpreted as vec[x, 2], following the specification given in the InterpretationBox.	*In[18]:=* **ToExpression[%] // InputForm**
	Out[18]//InputForm= vec[x, 2]

If you edit the boxes given in an InterpretationBox, then there is no guarantee that the interpretation specified by the interpretation box will still be correct. As a result, *Mathematica* provides various options that allow you to control the selection and editing of InterpretationBox objects.

option	default value	
Editable	False	whether to allow the contents to be edited
Selectable	True	whether to allow the contents to be selected
Deletable	True	whether to allow the box to be deleted
DeletionWarning	False	whether to issue a warning if the box is deleted
BoxAutoDelete	False	whether to strip the box if its contents are modified
StripWrapperBoxes	False	whether to remove StyleBox etc. from within *boxes* in TagBox[*boxes*, ...]

Options for `InterpretationBox` and related boxes.

`TagBox` objects are used to store information that will not be displayed but which can nevertheless be used by the rules that interpret boxes. Typically the *tag* in `TagBox[`*boxes*`,` *tag*`]` is a symbol which gives the head of the expression corresponding to *boxes*. If you edit only the arguments of this expression then there is a good chance that the interpretation specified by the `TagBox` will still be appropriate. As a result, `Editable->True` is the default setting for a `TagBox`.

The rules that *Mathematica* uses for interpreting boxes are in general set up to ignore details of formatting, such as those defined by `StyleBox` objects. Thus, unless `StripWrapperBoxes->False`, a red x, for example, will normally not be distinguished from an ordinary black x.

A red x is usually treated as identical to an ordinary one.

```
In[19]:= ToExpression[
              StyleBox[x, FontColor->RGBColor[1,0,0]]] == x

Out[19]= True
```

ButtonBox[*boxes*]	display like *boxes* but perform an action whenever *boxes* are clicked on

Setting up active elements.

In a *Mathematica* notebook it is possible to set up elements which perform an action whenever you click on them. These elements are represented internally by `ButtonBox` objects. When you create an expression containing a `ButtonBox`, you will be able to edit the contents of the `ButtonBox` directly so long as the `Active` option is `False` for the cell containing the expression. As soon as you set `Active->True`, the `ButtonBox` will perform its action whenever you click on it.

Section 2.11.6 discusses how to set up actions for `ButtonBox` objects.

■ 2.9.11 Adjusting Details of Formatting

Mathematica provides a large number of options for adjusting the details of how expressions are formatted. In most cases, the default settings for these options will be quite adequate. But sometimes special features in the expressions you are dealing with may require you to change the options.

option	default value	
ColumnAlignments	Center	how to align columns
RowAlignments	Baseline	how to align rows
ColumnSpacings	0.8	spacings between columns in ems
RowSpacings	1.0	spacings between rows in x-heights
ColumnsEqual	False	whether to make all columns equal width
RowsEqual	False	whether to make all rows equal total height
ColumnWidths	Automatic	the actual width of each column in ems
RowMinHeight	1	the minimum total height in units of font size assigned to each row
GridBaseline	Axis	with what part of the whole grid the baselines of boxes around it should be aligned
ColumnLines	False	whether to draw lines between columns
RowLines	False	whether to draw lines between rows
GridDefaultElement	"□"	what to insert when a new element is interactively created

Options to GridBox.

This sets up an array of numbers.

In[1]:= **t = Table[{i, (2i)!, (3i)!}, {i, 4}] ;**

Here is how the array is displayed with the default settings for all GridBox options.

In[2]:= **GridBox[t] // DisplayForm**

```
           1    2       6
           2    24      720
Out[2]//DisplayForm=
           3    720     362880
           4    40320   479001600
```

This right justifies all the columns.

`In[3]:= GridBox[t, ColumnAlignments->Right] // DisplayForm`

Out[3]//DisplayForm=
```
1      2          6
2     24        720
3    720     362880
4  40320  479001600
```

This left justifies the first two columns and right justifies the last one.

`In[4]:= GridBox[t,`
`       ColumnAlignments->{Left, Left, Right}] // DisplayForm`

Out[4]//DisplayForm=
```
1  2           6
2  24        720
3  720    362880
4  40320  479001600
```

This sets the gutters between columns.

`In[5]:= GridBox[t, ColumnSpacings->{5, 10}] // DisplayForm`

Out[5]//DisplayForm=
```
1        2              6
2       24            720
3      720         362880
4    40320      479001600
```

This forces all columns to be the same width.

`In[6]:= GridBox[t, ColumnsEqual->True] // DisplayForm`

Out[6]//DisplayForm=
```
1      2       6
2     24     720
3    720  362880
4  40320  479001600
```

Usually a `GridBox` leaves room for any character in the current font to appear in each row. But with `RowMinHeight->0` it packs rows in more tightly.

`In[7]:= {GridBox[{{x, x}, {x, x}}],`
`        GridBox[{{x, x}, {x, x}}, RowMinHeight->0]} // DisplayForm`

Out[7]//DisplayForm= $\left\{ \begin{matrix} x & x \\ x & x \end{matrix}, \begin{matrix} x & x \\ x & x \end{matrix} \right\}$

Center	centered (default)
Left	left justified (aligned on left edge)
Right	right justified (aligned on right edge)
"."	aligned at decimal points
"c"	aligned at the first occurrence of the specified character
{pos_1, pos_2, ... }	separate specifications for each column in the grid

Settings for the `ColumnAlignments` option.

In formatting complicated tables, it is often important to be able to control in detail the alignment of table entries. By setting `ColumnAlignments->"c"` you tell *Mathematica* to arrange the elements in each column so that the first occurrence of the character "*c*" in each entry is aligned.

Choosing `ColumnAlignments->"."` will therefore align numbers according to the positions of their decimal points. *Mathematica* also provides a special `\[AlignmentMarker]` character, which can be entered as ⦂am⦂. This character does not display explicitly, but can be inserted in entries in a table to mark which point in these entries should be lined up.

Center	centered
Top	tops aligned
Bottom	bottoms aligned
Baseline	baselines aligned (default)
Axis	axes aligned
{pos_1, pos_2, ... }	separate specifications for each row in the grid

Settings for the `RowAlignments` option.

This is the default alignment of elements in a row of a GridBox.	`In[8]:= GridBox[{{SuperscriptBox[x, 2], FractionBox[y, z]}}] // DisplayForm` `Out[8]//DisplayForm=` $x^2 \ \frac{y}{z}$
Here is what happens if the bottom of each element is aligned.	`In[9]:= GridBox[{{SuperscriptBox[x, 2], FractionBox[y, z]}}, RowAlignments->Bottom] // DisplayForm` `Out[9]//DisplayForm=` $x^2 \ \frac{y}{z}$

In a piece of ordinary text, successive characters are normally positioned so that their baselines are aligned. For many characters, such as m and x, the baseline coincides with the bottom of the character. But in general the baseline is the bottom of the main part of the character, and for example, in most fonts g and y have "descenders" that extend below the baseline.

This shows the alignment of characters with the default setting `RowAlignments->Baseline`.	`In[10]:= GridBox[{{"x", "m", "g", "y"}}] // DisplayForm` `Out[10]//DisplayForm=` x m g y
This is what happens if instead the bottom of each character is aligned.	`In[11]:= GridBox[{{"x", "m", "g", "y"}}, RowAlignments->Bottom] // DisplayForm` `Out[11]//DisplayForm=` x m g y

Like characters in ordinary text, *Mathematica* will normally position sequences of boxes so that their baselines are aligned. For many kinds of boxes the baseline is simply taken to be the baseline of the main element of the box. Thus, for example, the baseline of a SuperScript box x^y is taken to be the baseline of x.

For a FractionBox $\dfrac{x}{y}$, the fraction bar defines the *axis* of the box. In text in a particular font, one can also define an axis—a line going through the centers of symmetrical characters such as + and (. The baseline for a FractionBox is then taken to be the same distance below its axis as the baseline for text in the current font is below its axis.

For a GridBox, you can use the option GridBaseline to specify where the baseline should be taken to lie. The possible settings are the same as the ones for RowAlignments. The default is Axis, which makes the center of the GridBox be aligned with the axis of text around it.

The GridBaseline option specifies where the baseline of the GridBox should be assumed to be.

```
In[12]:= {GridBox[{{x,x},{x,x}}, GridBaseline->Top],
            GridBox[{{x,x},{x,x}}, GridBaseline->Bottom]} //
          DisplayForm
```

$$
Out[12]//DisplayForm= \left\{ \begin{matrix} x & x \\ x & x \end{matrix} , \begin{matrix} x & x \\ x & x \end{matrix} \right\}
$$

option	default value	
Background	GrayLevel[0.8]	button background color
ButtonFrame	"Palette"	the type of frame for the button
ButtonExpandable	True	whether a button should expand to fill a position in a GridBox
ButtonMargins	3	the margin in printer's points around the contents of a button
ButtonMinHeight	1	the minimum total height of a button in units of font size
ButtonStyle	"Paste"	the style from which properties of the button not explicitly specified should be inherited

Formatting options for ButtonBox objects.

This makes a button that looks like an element of a dialog box.

```
In[13]:= ButtonBox["abcd",
             ButtonFrame->"DialogBox"] // DisplayForm
```

$$
Out[13]//DisplayForm= \boxed{abcd}
$$

Palettes are typically constructed using grids of ButtonBox objects with zero row and column spacing.

```
In[14]:= GridBox[{{ButtonBox["abc"], ButtonBox["xyz"]}},
              ColumnSpacings->0] // DisplayForm
```

Out[14]//DisplayForm= abc | xyz

Buttons usually expand to be aligned in a GridBox.

```
In[15]:= GridBox[{{ButtonBox["abcd"]},
                 {ButtonBox["x"]}}] // DisplayForm
```

Out[15]//DisplayForm=
  abcd
  x

Here the lower button is made not to expand.

```
In[16]:= GridBox[{{ButtonBox["abcd"]}, {ButtonBox["x",
              ButtonExpandable->False]}}] // DisplayForm
```

Out[16]//DisplayForm=
  abcd
  x

Section 2.11.6 will discuss how to set up actions for ButtonBox objects.

printer's point	approximately 1/72 inch (or sometimes the size of a pixel on a display)
pica	12 printer's points, or 1/6 inch
font point size	the maximum distance in printer's points between the top and bottom of any character in a particular font
em	a width equal to the point font size—approximately the width of an "M"
en	half an em
x-height	the height of an "x" character in the current font

Units of distance.

full name	alias	
\[InvisibleSpace]	⋮is⋮	zero-width space
\[VeryThinSpace]	⋮␣⋮	1/18 em (x x)
\[ThinSpace]	⋮␣␣⋮	3/18 em (x x)
\[MediumSpace]	⋮␣␣␣⋮	4/18 em (x x)
\[ThickSpace]	⋮␣␣␣␣⋮	5/18 em (x x)
\[NegativeVeryThinSpace]	⋮-␣⋮	−1/18 em (xx)
\[NegativeThinSpace]	⋮-␣␣⋮	−3/18 em (xx)
\[NegativeMediumSpace]	⋮-␣␣␣⋮	−4/18 em (x)
\[NegativeThickSpace]	⋮-␣␣␣␣⋮	−5/18 em (x)
\[RawSpace]	␣	keyboard space character
\[SpaceIndicator]	⋮space⋮	the ␣ character indicating a space

Spacing characters of various widths. ␣ indicates the space key on your keyboard.

When you enter input such as x+y, *Mathematica* will automatically convert this to RowBox[{"x","+","y"}]. When the RowBox is output, *Mathematica* will then try to insert appropriate space between each element. Typically, it will put more space around characters such as + that are usually used as operators, and less space around characters such as x that are not. You can however always modify spacing by inserting explicit spacing characters. Positive spacing characters will move successive elements further apart, while negative ones will bring them closer together.

Mathematica by default leaves more space around characters such as + and − that are usually used as operators.

```
In[17]:= RowBox[{"a", "b", "+", "c", "-", "+"}] // DisplayForm
Out[17]//DisplayForm= a b + c − +
```

You can explicitly insert positive and negative spacing characters to change spacing.

```
In[18]:= RowBox[{"a", "\[ThickSpace]", "b", "+",
            "\[NegativeMediumSpace]", "c", "-", "+"}]  // DisplayForm
Out[18]//DisplayForm= a b +c − +
```

> StyleBox[*boxes*, AutoSpacing->False]
>
>   leave the same space around every character in *boxes*

Inhibiting automatic spacing in *Mathematica*.

This makes *Mathematica* leave the same space between successive characters.

```
In[19]:= StyleBox[RowBox[{"a", "b", "+", "c", "-", "+"}],
            AutoSpacing->False] // DisplayForm

Out[19]//DisplayForm= a b+c-+
```

When you have an expression displayed on the screen, the notebook front end allows you interactively to make detailed adjustments to the positions of elements. Typically CTRL←, CTRL→, CTRL↑, CTRL↓ "nudge" whatever you have selected by one pixel at your current screen magnification. Such adjustments are represented within *Mathematica* using AdjustmentBox objects.

AdjustmentBox[*box*, BoxMargins->{{*left*, *right*}, {*bottom*, *top*}}]
  draw margins of the specified widths around *box*

AdjustmentBox[*box*, BoxBaselineShift->*up*]
  shift the height at which baselines of boxes around *box* should be aligned

---

Adjusting the position of a box.

This adds space to the left of the B and removes space to its right.

```
In[20]:= RowBox[{"A", AdjustmentBox["B", BoxMargins->
            {{1, -0.3}, {0, 0}}], "C", "D"}] // DisplayForm

Out[20]//DisplayForm= A  B CD
```

By careful adjustment, you can set things up to put two characters on top of each other.

```
In[21]:= RowBox[{"C", AdjustmentBox["/",
            BoxMargins->{{-.8, .8}, {0, 0}}]}] // DisplayForm

Out[21]//DisplayForm= ₵
```

The left and right margins in an AdjustmentBox are given in ems; the bottom and top ones in x-heights. By giving positive values for margins you can force there to be space around a box. By giving negative values you can effectively trim space away, and force other boxes to be closer. Note that in a RowBox, vertical alignment is determined by the position of the baseline; in a FractionBox or an OverscriptBox, for example, it is instead determined by top and bottom margins.

StyleBox[*boxes*, ShowContents->False]
  leave space for *boxes* but do not display them

Leaving space for boxes without displaying them.

If you are trying to line up different elements of your output, you can use ShowContents->False in StyleBox to leave space for boxes without actually displaying them.

This leaves space for the Y, but does not display it.

```
In[22]:= RowBox[{"X", StyleBox["Y", ShowContents->False], "Z"}] //
            DisplayForm

Out[22]//DisplayForm= X Z
```

The sizes of most characters are determined solely by what font they are in, as specified for example by the `FontSize` option in `StyleBox`. But there are some special expandable characters whose size can change even within a particular font. Examples are parentheses, which by default are taken to expand so as to span any expression they contain.

Parentheses by default expand to span whatever expressions they contain.

```
In[23]:= {RowBox[{"(", "X", ")"}],
          RowBox[{"(", FractionBox["X", "Y"], ")"}]} // DisplayForm
```

$$Out[23]//DisplayForm= \left\{(X), \left(\frac{X}{Y}\right)\right\}$$

option	default value	
SpanMinSize	Automatic	minimum size of expandable characters in units of font size
SpanMaxSize	Automatic	maximum size of expandable characters in units of font size
SpanSymmetric	True	whether vertically expandable characters should be symmetric about the axis of the box they are in
SpanLineThickness	Automatic	thickness in printer's points of fraction lines etc.

`StyleBox` options for controlling expandable characters.

Parentheses within a single `RowBox` by default grow to span whatever other objects appear in the `RowBox`.

```
In[24]:= RowBox[{"(", "(", GridBox[{{X},{Y},{Z}}]}] // DisplayForm
```

$$Out[24]//DisplayForm= \left(\left(\begin{matrix}X\\Y\\Z\end{matrix}\right.\right.$$

Some expandable characters, however, grow by default only to a limited extent.

```
In[25]:= RowBox[{"{", "[", "(",
          GridBox[{{X},{Y},{Z}}]}] // DisplayForm
```

$$Out[25]//DisplayForm= \left\{\left[\left(\begin{matrix}X\\Y\\Z\end{matrix}\right.\right.\right.$$

This specifies that all characters inside the `StyleBox` should be allowed to grow as large as they need.

```
In[26]:= StyleBox[%, SpanMaxSize->Infinity] // DisplayForm
```

$$Out[26]//DisplayForm= \left\{\left[\left(\begin{matrix}X\\Y\\Z\end{matrix}\right.\right.\right.$$

By default, expandable characters grow symmetrically.

```
In[27]:= RowBox[{"(", GridBox[{{X},{Y}},
                    GridBaseline->Bottom], ")"}] // DisplayForm
```

$$Out[27]//DisplayForm= \begin{pmatrix} X \\ Y \end{pmatrix}$$

Setting SpanSymmetric->False allows expandable characters to grow asymmetrically.

```
In[28]:= {X, StyleBox[%, SpanSymmetric->False]} // DisplayForm
```

$$Out[28]//DisplayForm= \left\{ X, \binom{X}{Y} \right\}$$

The notebook front end typically provides a Spanning Characters menu which allows you to change the spanning characteristics of all characters within your current selection.

parentheses, arrows, bracketing bars	grow without bound
brackets, braces, slash	grow to limited size

Default characteristics of expandable characters.

The top bracket by default grows to span the OverscriptBox.

```
In[29]:= OverscriptBox["xxxxxx", "\[OverBracket]"] // DisplayForm
```

$$Out[29]//DisplayForm= \overline{xxxxxx}$$

The right arrow by default grows horizontally to span the column it is in.

```
In[30]:= GridBox[{{"a", "xxxxxxx", "b"},
                  {"a", "\[RightArrow]", "b"}}] // DisplayForm
```

$$Out[30]//DisplayForm= \begin{matrix} a & xxxxxxx & b \\ a & \longrightarrow & b \end{matrix}$$

The up arrow similarly grows vertically to span the row it is in.

```
In[31]:= GridBox[{{FractionBox[X, Y],
                  "\[UpArrow]"}}] // DisplayForm
```

$$Out[31]//DisplayForm= \frac{X}{Y} \uparrow$$

option	default value	
ScriptSizeMultipliers	0.71	how much smaller to make each level of subscripts, etc.
ScriptMinSize	4	the minimum point size to use for subscripts, etc.
ScriptBaselineShifts	{Automatic, Automatic}	the distance in x-heights to shift subscripts and superscripts

StyleBox options for controlling the size and positioning of subscripts, etc.

This sets up a collection of nested SuperscriptBox objects.

$In[32]:=$ **b = ToBoxes[X^X^X^X^X]**

$Out[32]=$ SuperscriptBox[X, SuperscriptBox[X,
               SuperscriptBox[X, SuperscriptBox[X, X]]]]

By default, successive superscripts get progressively smaller.

$In[33]:=$ **b // DisplayForm**

$Out[33]//DisplayForm=$ $X^{X^{X^{X^X}}}$

This tells *Mathematica* to make all levels of superscripts the same size.

$In[34]:=$ **StyleBox[b, ScriptSizeMultipliers->1] // DisplayForm**

$Out[34]//DisplayForm=$ $X^{X^{X^{X^X}}}$

Here successive levels of superscripts are smaller, but only down to 5-point size.

$In[35]:=$ **StyleBox[b, ScriptMinSize->5] // DisplayForm**

$Out[35]//DisplayForm=$ $X^{X^{X^{X^X}}}$

Mathematica will usually optimize the position of subscripts and superscripts in a way that depends on their environment. If you want to line up several different subscripts or superscripts you therefore typically have to use the option ScriptBaselineShifts to specify an explicit distance to shift each one.

The second subscript is by default shifted down slightly more than the first.

$In[36]:=$ **RowBox[{SubscriptBox["x", "0"], "+",**
             SubsuperscriptBox["x", "0", "2"]}] // DisplayForm

$Out[36]//DisplayForm=$ $x_0 + x_0^2$

This tells *Mathematica* to apply exactly the same shift to both subscripts.

$In[37]:=$ **StyleBox[%, ScriptBaselineShifts->{1, Automatic}] //**
                                    DisplayForm

$Out[37]//DisplayForm=$ $x_0 + x_0^2$

option	default value	
LimitsPositioning	Automatic	whether to change positioning in the way conventional for limits

An option to UnderoverscriptBox and related boxes.

The limits of a sum are usually displayed as underscripts and overscripts.

$In[38]:=$ **Sum[f[i], {i, 0, n}]**

$Out[38]=$ $\displaystyle\sum_{i=0}^{n} f[i]$

When the sum is shown smaller, however, it is conventional for the limits to be displayed as subscripts and superscripts.

$In[39]:=$ **1/%**

$Out[39]=$ $\dfrac{1}{\sum_{i=0}^{n} f[i]}$

Here low and high still display directly above and below XX.

$In[40]:=$ **UnderoverscriptBox["XX", "low", "high",**
                                    LimitsPositioning->True] // DisplayForm

$Out[40]//DisplayForm=$ $\underset{\text{low}}{\overset{\text{high}}{\text{XX}}}$

But now low and high are moved to subscript and superscript positions.

$In[41]:=$ **FractionBox["a", %] // DisplayForm**

$Out[41]//DisplayForm=$ $\dfrac{a}{XX_{\text{low}}^{\text{high}}}$

LimitsPositioning->Automatic will act as if LimitsPositioning->True when the first argument of the box is an object such as \[Sum] or \[Product]. You can specify the list of such characters by setting the option LimitsPositioningTokens.

option	default value	
MultilineFunction	Automatic	what to do when a box breaks across several lines

Line breaking option for boxes.

When you are dealing with long expressions it is inevitable that they will continue beyond the length of a single line. Many kinds of boxes change their display characteristics when they break across several lines.

This displays as a built-up fraction on a single line.

$In[42]:=$ **Expand[(1 + x)^5]/Expand[(1 + y)^5]**

$Out[42]=$ $\dfrac{1 + 5 x + 10 x^2 + 10 x^3 + 5 x^4 + x^5}{1 + 5 y + 10 y^2 + 10 y^3 + 5 y^4 + y^5}$

This breaks across several lines.

$In[43]:=$ **Expand[(1 + x)^10]/Expand[(1 + y)^5]**

$Out[43]=$ $(1 + 10 x + 45 x^2 + 120 x^3 + 210 x^4 +$
            $252 x^5 + 210 x^6 + 120 x^7 + 45 x^8 + 10 x^9 + x^{10}) /$
            $(1 + 5 y + 10 y^2 + 10 y^3 + 5 y^4 + y^5)$

You can use the option MultilineFunction to specify how a particular box should be displayed if it breaks across several lines. The setting MultilineFunction->None prevents the box from breaking at all.

You can to some extent control where expressions break across lines by inserting \[NoBreak] and \[NonBreakingSpace] characters. *Mathematica* will try to avoid ever breaking an expression at the position of such characters.

You can force *Mathematica* to break a line by explicitly inserting a \[NewLine] character, obtained in the standard notebook front end simply by typing RETURN. With default settings for options, *Mathematica* will automatically indent the next line after you type a RETURN. However, the level of indenting used will be fixed as soon as the line is started, and will not change when you edit around it. By inserting an \[IndentingNewLine] character, you can tell *Mathematica* always to maintain the correct level of indenting based on the actual environment in which a line occurs.

full name	alias	
\[NoBreak]	⁚nb⁚	inhibit a line break
\[NonBreakingSpace]	⁚nbs⁚	insert a space, inhibiting a line break on either side of it
\[NewLine]	↵	insert a line break, setting the indenting level at the time the new line is started
\[IndentingNewLine]	⁚nl⁚	insert a line break, always maintaining the correct indenting level

Characters for controlling line breaking.

When *Mathematica* breaks an expression across several lines, it indents intermediate lines by an amount proportional to the nesting level in the expression at which the break occurred.

The line breaks here occur only at level 1.

```
In[44]:= Range[30]

Out[44]= {1, 2, 3, 4, 5, 6, 7, 8, 9, 10, 11, 12, 13, 14, 15, 16, 17, 18,
          19, 20, 21, 22, 23, 24, 25, 26, 27, 28, 29, 30}
```

But here the break is at a much deeper level.

```
In[45]:= Nest[List, x+y, 30]

Out[45]= {{{{{{{{{{{{{{{{{{{{{{{{{{{{{{x +
                                     y}}}}}}}}}}}}}}}}}}}}}}}}}}}}}}
```

■ 2.9.12 String Representation of Boxes

Mathematica provides a compact way of representing boxes in terms of strings. This is particularly convenient when you want to import or export specifications of boxes as ordinary text.

This generates an InputForm string that represents the SuperscriptBox.

```
In[1]:= ToString[SuperscriptBox["x", "2"], InputForm]

Out[1]= \(x\^2\)
```

This creates the SuperscriptBox.

```
In[2]:= \( x \^ 2 \)

Out[2]= SuperscriptBox[x, 2]
```

ToExpression interprets the SuperscriptBox as a power.

```
In[3]:= ToExpression[%] // FullForm

Out[3]//FullForm= Power[x, 2]
```

It is important to distinguish between forms that represent just raw boxes, and forms that represent the *meaning* of the boxes.

This corresponds to a raw SuperscriptBox.	`In[4]:= \( x \^ 2 \)`
	`Out[4]= SuperscriptBox[x, 2]`
This corresponds to the power that the SuperscriptBox represents.	`In[5]:= \!\( x \^ 2 \)`
	`Out[5]= `x^2
The expression generated here is a power.	`In[6]:= FullForm[ \!\( x \^ 2 \) ]`
	`Out[6]//FullForm= Power[x, 2]`

\(*input*\)	raw boxes
\!\(*input*\)	the meaning of the boxes

Distinguishing raw boxes from the expressions they represent.

If you copy the contents of a **StandardForm** cell into another program, such as a text editor, *Mathematica* will automatically generate a \!\(... \) form. This is done so that if you subsequently paste the form back into *Mathematica*, the original contents of the **StandardForm** cell will automatically be re-created. Without the \!, only the raw boxes corresponding to these contents would be obtained.

With default settings for options, \!\(... \) forms pasted into *Mathematica* notebooks are automatically displayed in two-dimensional form. \!\(... \) forms entered directly from the keyboard can be displayed in two-dimensional form using the Make 2D item in the Edit menu.

"\(*input*\)"	a raw character string
"\!\(*input*\)"	a string containing boxes

Embedding two-dimensional box structures in strings.

Mathematica will usually treat a \(... \) form that appears within a string just like any other sequence of characters. But by inserting a \! you can tell *Mathematica* instead to treat this form like the boxes it represents. In this way you can therefore embed box structures within ordinary character strings.

Mathematica treats this as an ordinary character string.	`In[7]:= "\( x \^ 2 \)"`
	`Out[7]= \( x \^ 2 \)`
The \! tells *Mathematica* that this string contains boxes.	`In[8]:= "\!\( x \^ 2 \)"`
	`Out[8]= `x^2
You can mix boxes with ordinary text.	`In[9]:= "box 1: \!\(x\^2\); box 2: \!\(y\^3\)"`
	`Out[9]= box 1: `x^2`; box 2: `y^3

$\backslash(box_1, box_2, \ldots \backslash)$	RowBox[box_1, box_2, ...]
$box_1 \backslash\hat{} \; box_2$	SuperscriptBox[box_1, box_2]
$box_1 \backslash\_ \; box_2$	SubscriptBox[box_1, box_2]
$box_1 \backslash\_ \; box_2 \backslash\% \; box_3$	SubsuperscriptBox[box_1, box_2, box_3]
$box_1 \backslash\& \; box_2$	OverscriptBox[box_1, box_2]
$box_1 \backslash+ \; box_2$	UnderscriptBox[box_1, box_2]
$box_1 \backslash+ \; box_2 \backslash\% \; box_3$	UnderoverscriptBox[box_1, box_2, box_3]
$box_1 \backslash/ \; box_2$	FractionBox[box_1, box_2]
$\backslash@ \; box$	SqrtBox[box]
$\backslash@ \; box_1 \backslash\% \; box_2$	RadicalBox[box_1, box_2]
$form \backslash\grave{} \; box$	FormBox[box, $form$]
$\backslash* \; input$	construct boxes from *input*

Input forms for boxes.

Mathematica requires that any input forms you give for boxes be enclosed within \(and \). But within these outermost \(and \) you can use additional \(and \) to specify grouping.

Here ordinary parentheses are used to indicate grouping.

In[10]:= \(x \/ (y + z) \) // **DisplayForm**

Out[10]//DisplayForm= $\dfrac{x}{(y+z)}$

Without the parentheses, the grouping would be different.

In[11]:= \(x \/ y + z \) // **DisplayForm**

Out[11]//DisplayForm= $\dfrac{x}{y} + z$

\(and \) specify grouping, but are not displayed as explicit parentheses.

In[12]:= \(x \/ \(y + z\) \) // **DisplayForm**

Out[12]//DisplayForm= $\dfrac{x}{y+z}$

The inner \(and \) lead to the construction of a RowBox.

In[13]:= \(x \/ \(y + z\) \)

Out[13]= FractionBox[x, RowBox[{y, +, z}]]

When you type aa+bb as input to *Mathematica*, the first thing that happens is that aa, + and bb are recognized as being separate "tokens". The same separation into tokens is done when boxes are constructed from input enclosed in \(... \). However, inside the boxes each token is given as a string, rather than in its raw form.

The RowBox has aa, + and bb broken into separate strings.

In[14]:= \(aa+bb \) // **FullForm**

Out[14]//FullForm= RowBox[List["aa", "+", "bb"]]

The spaces around the + are by default discarded.

In[15]:= \(aa + bb \) // FullForm

Out[15]//FullForm= RowBox[List["aa", "+", "bb"]]

Backslash-space inserts a literal space.

In[16]:= \(aa \ + \ bb \) // FullForm

Out[16]//FullForm= RowBox[List["aa", " ", "+", " ", "bb"]]

Here two nested RowBox objects are formed.

In[17]:= \(aa+bb/cc \) // FullForm

Out[17]//FullForm= RowBox[
List["aa", "+", RowBox[List["bb", "/", "cc"]]]]

The same box structure is formed even when the string given does not correspond to a complete *Mathematica* expression.

In[18]:= \(aa+bb/ \) // FullForm

Out[18]//FullForm= RowBox[List["aa", "+", RowBox[List["bb", "/"]]]]

Within \(... \) sequences, you can set up certain kinds of boxes by using backslash notations such as \^ and \@. But for other kinds of boxes, you need to give ordinary *Mathematica* input, prefaced by *.

This constructs a GridBox.

In[19]:= \(*GridBox[{{"a", "b"}, {"c", "d"}}] \) // DisplayForm

Out[19]//DisplayForm=
a b
c d

This constructs a StyleBox.

In[20]:= \(*StyleBox["text", FontWeight->"Bold"] \) // DisplayForm

Out[20]//DisplayForm= **text**

* in effect acts like an escape: it allows you to enter ordinary *Mathematica* syntax even within a \(... \) sequence. Note that the input you give after a * can itself in turn contain \(... \) sequences.

You can alternate nested * and \(... \). Explicit quotes are needed outside of \(... \).

In[21]:= \(x + *GridBox[{{"a", "b"}, {\(c \^ 2\), \(d \/
*GridBox[{{"x","y"},{"x","y"}}] \)}}] \) // DisplayForm

Out[21]//DisplayForm= $x + c^2 \begin{matrix} a & b \\ \frac{d}{x \ y} \\ x \ y \end{matrix}$

In the notebook front end, you can typically use CTRL-* or CTRL-8 to get a dialog box in which you can enter raw boxes—just as you do after *.

\!\(*input*\)	interpret input in the current form
\!\(*form* \` *input*\)	interpret input using the specified form

Controlling the way input is interpreted.

In a StandardForm cell, this will be interpreted in StandardForm, yielding a product.	*In[22]:=* \!\(c(1+x) \) *Out[22]=* c (1 + x)
The backslash backquote sequence tells *Mathematica* to interpret this in TraditionalForm.	*In[23]:=* \!\(TraditionalForm\` c(1+x) \) *Out[23]=* c [1 + x]

When you copy the contents of a cell from a notebook into a program such as a text editor, no explicit backslash backquote sequence is usually included. But if you expect to paste what you get back into a cell of a different type from the one it came from, then you will typically need to include a backslash backquote sequence in order to ensure that everything is interpreted correctly.

■ 2.9.13 Converting between Strings, Boxes and Expressions

ToString[*expr*, *form*]	create a string representing the specified textual form of *expr*
ToBoxes[*expr*, *form*]	create boxes representing the specified textual form of *expr*
ToExpression[*input*, *form*]	create an expression by interpreting a string or boxes as input in the specified textual form
ToString[*expr*]	create a string using OutputForm
ToBoxes[*expr*]	create boxes using StandardForm
ToExpression[*input*]	create an expression using StandardForm

Converting between strings, boxes and expressions.

Here is a simple expression.	*In[1]:=* x^2 + y^2 *Out[1]=* $x^2 + y^2$
This gives the InputForm of the expression as a string.	*In[2]:=* ToString[x^2 + y^2, InputForm] *Out[2]=* x^2 + y^2
In FullForm explicit quotes are shown around the string.	*In[3]:=* FullForm[%] *Out[3]//FullForm=* "x^2 + y^2"
This gives a string representation for the StandardForm boxes that correspond to the expression.	*In[4]:=* ToString[x^2 + y^2, StandardForm] // FullForm *Out[4]//FullForm=* "\!\(x\^2 + y\^2\)"
ToBoxes yields the boxes themselves.	*In[5]:=* ToBoxes[x^2 + y^2, StandardForm] *Out[5]=* RowBox[{SuperscriptBox[x, 2], +, SuperscriptBox[y, 2]}]

In generating data for files and external programs, it is sometimes necessary to produce two-dimensional forms which use only ordinary keyboard characters. You can do this using OutputForm.

This produces a string which gives a two-dimensional rendering of the expression, using only ordinary keyboard characters.

```
In[6]:= ToString[x^2 + y^2, OutputForm]

Out[6]=  2    2
        x  + y
```

The string consists of two lines, separated by an explicit \n newline.

```
In[7]:= FullForm[%]

Out[7]//FullForm= "  2     2\nx  + y"
```

The string looks right only in a monospaced font.

```
In[8]:= StyleBox[%, FontFamily->"Times"] // DisplayForm

Out[8]//DisplayForm=  2 2
                     x + y
```

If you operate only with one-dimensional structures, you can effectively use ToString to do string manipulation with formatting functions.

This generates a string corresponding to the OutputForm of StringForm.

```
In[9]:= ToString[StringForm["``^10 = ``", 4, 4^10]] // InputForm

Out[9]//InputForm= "4^10 = 1048576"
```

InputForm	strings corresponding to keyboard input
StandardForm	strings or boxes corresponding to standard two-dimensional input (default)
TraditionalForm	strings or boxes mimicking traditional mathematical notation

Some forms handled by ToExpression.

This creates an expression from an InputForm string.

```
In[10]:= ToExpression["x^2 + y^2"]

Out[10]= x^2 + y^2
```

This creates the same expression from StandardForm boxes.

```
In[11]:= ToExpression[RowBox[{SuperscriptBox["x", "2"], "+",
                SuperscriptBox["y", "2"]}]]

Out[11]= x^2 + y^2
```

Here the boxes are represented in InputForm.

```
In[12]:= ToExpression[\(x\^2 + y\^2\)]

Out[12]= x^2 + y^2
```

This returns raw boxes.

```
In[13]:= ToExpression["\(x\^2 + y\^2\)"]

Out[13]= RowBox[
            {SuperscriptBox[x, 2], +, SuperscriptBox[y, 2]}]
```

This interprets the boxes.

```
In[14]:= ToExpression["\!\(x\^2 + y\^2\)"]

Out[14]= x^2 + y^2
```

In TraditionalForm these are interpreted as functions.

In[15]:= **ToExpression["c(1 + x) + log(x)", TraditionalForm]**

Out[15]= c[1 + x] + Log[x]

ToExpression[*input*, *form*, *h*]	create an expression, then wrap it with head *h*

Creating expressions wrapped with special heads.

This creates an expression, then immediately evaluates it.

In[16]:= **ToExpression["1 + 1"]**

Out[16]= 2

This creates an expression using StandardForm rules, then wraps it in Hold.

In[17]:= **ToExpression["1 + 1", StandardForm, Hold]**

Out[17]= Hold[1 + 1]

You can get rid of the Hold using ReleaseHold.

In[18]:= **ReleaseHold[%]**

Out[18]= 2

SyntaxQ["*string*"]	determine whether a string represents syntactically correct *Mathematica* input
SyntaxLength["*string*"]	find out how long a sequence of characters starting at the beginning of a string is syntactically correct

Testing correctness of strings as input.

ToExpression will attempt to interpret any string as *Mathematica* input. But if you give it a string that does not correspond to syntactically correct input, then it will print a message, and return $Failed.

This is not syntactically correct input, so ToExpression does not convert it to an expression.

In[19]:= **ToExpression["1 +/+ 2"]**

ToExpression::sntx: Syntax error in or before "1 +/+ 2".
                                                      ^

Out[19]= $Failed

ToExpression requires that the string correspond to a *complete Mathematica* expression.

In[20]:= **ToExpression["1 + 2 + "]**

ToExpression::sntxi:
     Incomplete expression; more input is needed.

Out[20]= $Failed

You can use the function SyntaxQ to test whether a particular string corresponds to syntactically correct *Mathematica* input. If SyntaxQ returns False, you can find out where the error occurred using SyntaxLength. SyntaxLength returns the number of characters which were successfully processed before a syntax error was detected.

SyntaxQ shows that this string does not correspond to syntactically correct *Mathematica* input.

In[21]:= **SyntaxQ["1 +/+ 2"]**

Out[21]= False

SyntaxLength reveals that an error was detected after the third character in the string.

In[22]:= **SyntaxLength["1 +/+ 2"]**

Out[22]= 3

Here SyntaxLength returns a value greater than the length of the string, indicating that the input was correct so far as it went, but needs to be continued.

In[23]:= **SyntaxLength["1 + 2 + "]**

Out[23]= 10

■ 2.9.14 The Syntax of the *Mathematica* Language

Mathematica uses various syntactic rules to interpret input that you give, and to convert strings and boxes into expressions. The version of these rules that is used for StandardForm and InputForm in effect defines the basic *Mathematica* language. The rules used for other forms, such as TraditionalForm, follow the same overall principles, but differ in many details.

a, xyz, $\alpha\beta\gamma$	symbols
"some text", "$\alpha + \beta$"	strings
123.456, 3*^45	numbers
+, ->, ≠	operators
(* comment *)	input to be ignored

Types of tokens in the *Mathematica* language.

When you give text as input to *Mathematica*, the first thing that *Mathematica* does is to break the text into a sequence of *tokens*, with each token representing a separate syntactic unit.

Thus, for example, if you give the input xx+yy-zzzz, *Mathematica* will break this into the sequence of tokens xx, +, yy, - and zzzz. Here xx, yy and zzzz are tokens that correspond to symbols, while + and - are operators.

Operators are ultimately what determine the structure of the expression formed from a particular piece of input. The *Mathematica* language involves several general classes of operators, distinguished by the different positions in which they appear with respect to their operands.

prefix	!x	Not[x]
postfix	x!	Factorial[x]
infix	$x + y + z$	Plus[x, y, z]
matchfix	{x, y, z}	List[x, y, z]
compound	x /: y = z	TagSet[x, y, z]
overfix	$\hat{x}$	OverHat[x]

Examples of classes of operators in the *Mathematica* language.

Operators typically work by picking up operands from definite positions around them. But when a string contains more than one operator, the result can in general depend on which operator picks up its operands first.

Thus, for example, a*b+c could potentially be interpreted either as (a*b)+c or as a*(b+c) depending on whether * or + picks up its operands first.

To avoid such ambiguities, *Mathematica* assigns a *precedence* to each operator that can appear. Operators with higher precedence are then taken to pick up their operands first.

Thus, for example, the multiplication operator * is assigned higher precedence than +, so that it picks up its operands first, and a*b+c is interpreted as (a*b)+c rather than a*(b+c).

The * operator has higher precedence than +, so in both cases Times is the innermost function.

```
In[1]:= {FullForm[a * b + c], FullForm[a + b * c]}
Out[1]= {Plus[Times[a, b], c], Plus[a, Times[b, c]]}
```

The // operator has rather low precedence.

```
In[2]:= a * b + c // f
Out[2]= f[a b + c]
```

The @ operator has high precedence.

```
In[3]:= f @ a * b + c
Out[3]= c + b f[a]
```

Whatever the precedence of the operators you are using, you can always specify the structure of the expressions you want to form by explicitly inserting appropriate parentheses.

Inserting parentheses makes Plus rather than Times the innermost function.

```
In[4]:= FullForm[a * (b + c)]
Out[4]//FullForm= Times[a, Plus[b, c]]
```

Extensions of symbol names	$x\_$, #2, e::s, etc.
Function application variants	$e[e]$, e @@ e, etc.
Power-related operators	$\sqrt{e}$, $e^{\wedge}e$, etc.
Multiplication-related operators	∇e, e/e, $e \otimes e$, $e\,e$, etc.
Addition-related operators	$e \oplus e$, $e + e$, $e \cup e$, etc.
Relational operators	$e == e$, $e \sim e$, $e \lessdot e$, $e \lhd e$, $e \in e$, etc.
Arrow and vector operators	$e \to e$, $e \nearrow e$, $e \rightleftharpoons e$, $e \twoheadleftarrow e$, etc.
Logic operators	$\forall_e\, e$, e && e, $e \lor e$, $e \vdash e$, etc.
Pattern and rule operators	$e..$, $e \mid e$, e -> e, $e\,/.\,e$, etc.
Pure function operator	e &
Assignment operators	$e = e$, $e := e$, etc.
Compound expression	$e; e$

Outline of operators in order of decreasing precedence.

The table on pages 1024–1029 gives the complete ordering by precedence of all operators in *Mathematica*. Much of this ordering, as in the case of * and +, is determined directly by standard mathematical usage. But in general the ordering is simply set up to make it less likely for explicit parentheses to have to be inserted in typical pieces of input.

Operator precedences are such that this requires no parentheses.

```
In[5]:= ∀ₓ ∃ᵧ x⊗y > y ⋀ m ≠ 0 ⇒ n ⊮ m

Out[5]= Implies[∀ₓ (∃ᵧ x⊗y > y) && m ≠ 0, n ⊮ m]
```

FullForm shows the structure of the expression that was constructed.

```
In[6]:= FullForm[%]

Out[6]//FullForm= Implies[And[ForAll[x,
                    Exists[y, Succeeds[CircleTimes[x, y], y]]],
                    Unequal[m, 0]], NotRightTriangleBar[n, m]]
```

Note that the first and second forms here are identical; the third requires explicit parentheses.

```
In[7]:= {x -> #^2 &, (x -> #^2)&, x -> (#^2 &)}

Out[7]= {x → #1² &, x → #1² &, x → (#1² &)}
```

flat	$x + y + z$		$x + y + z$
left grouping	$x / y / z$		$(x / y) / z$
right grouping	$x \wedge y \wedge z$		$x \wedge (y \wedge z)$

Types of grouping for infix operators.

Plus is a Flat function, so no grouping is necessary here.

```
In[8]:= FullForm[a + b + c + d]
Out[8]//FullForm= Plus[a, b, c, d]
```

Power is not Flat, so the operands have to be grouped in pairs.

```
In[9]:= FullForm[a ^ b ^ c ^ d]
Out[9]//FullForm= Power[a, Power[b, Power[c, d]]]
```

The syntax of the *Mathematica* language is defined not only for characters that you can type on a typical keyboard, but also for all the various special characters that *Mathematica* supports.

Letters such as γ, $\mathcal{L}$ and $\aleph$ from any alphabet are treated just like ordinary English letters, and can for example appear in the names of symbols. The same is true of letter-like forms such as ∞, $\hbar$ and L.

But many other special characters are treated as operators. Thus, for example, $\oplus$ and $\uplus$ are infix operators, while $\neg$ is a prefix operator, and $\langle$ and $\rangle$ are matchfix operators.

$\oplus$ is an infix operator.

```
In[10]:= a ⊕ b ⊕ c // FullForm
Out[10]//FullForm= CirclePlus[a, b, c]
```

$\times$ is an infix operator which means the same as *.

```
In[11]:= a × a × a × b × b × c
Out[11]= a^3 b^2 c
```

Some special characters form elements of fairly complicated compound operators. Thus, for example, $\int f \, dx$ contains the compound operator with elements $\int$ and d.

The $\int$ and d form parts of a compound operator.

```
In[12]:= ∫ k[x] dx // FullForm
Out[12]//FullForm= Integrate[k[x], x]
```

No parentheses are needed here: the "inner precedence" of $\int \ldots d$ is lower than Times.

```
In[13]:= ∫ a[x] b[x] dx + c[x]
Out[13]= c[x] + ∫ a[x] b[x] dx
```

Parentheses are needed here, however.

```
In[14]:= ∫ (a[x] + b[x]) dx + c[x]
Out[14]= c[x] + ∫ (a[x] + b[x]) dx
```

Input to *Mathematica* can be given not only in the form of one-dimensional strings, but also in the form of two-dimensional boxes. The syntax of the *Mathematica* language covers not only one-dimensional constructs but also two-dimensional ones.

This superscript is interpreted as a power.

```
In[15]:= x^{a+b}
Out[15]= x^{a+b}
```

$\partial_x f$ is a two-dimensional compound operator.

```
In[16]:= ∂_x x^n
Out[16]= n x^{-1+n}
```

$\sum$ is part of a more complicated two-dimensional compound operator.

$In[17]:= \sum\limits_{n=1}^{\infty} \dfrac{1}{n^\circ}$

$Out[17]= \text{Zeta}[s]$

The $\sum$ operator has higher precedence than +.

$In[18]:= \sum\limits_{n=1}^{\infty} \dfrac{1}{n^s} + n$

$Out[18]= n + \text{Zeta}[s]$

■ 2.9.15 Operators without Built-in Meanings

When you enter a piece of input such as 2 + 2, *Mathematica* first recognizes the + as an operator and constructs the expression Plus[2, 2], then uses the built-in rules for Plus to evaluate the expression and get the result 4.

But not all operators recognized by *Mathematica* are associated with functions that have built-in meanings. *Mathematica* also supports several hundred additional operators that can be used in constructing expressions, but for which no evaluation rules are initially defined.

You can use these operators as a way to build up your own notation within the *Mathematica* language.

The ⊕ is recognized as an infix operator, but has no predefined value.

$In[1]:= \textbf{2} \oplus \textbf{3} \,\textbf{// FullForm}$

$Out[1]//FullForm= \text{CirclePlus}[2, 3]$

In StandardForm, ⊕ prints as an infix operator.

$In[2]:= \textbf{2} \oplus \textbf{3}$

$Out[2]= 2 \oplus 3$

You can define a value for ⊕.

$In[3]:= \textbf{x\_} \oplus \textbf{y\_} \,\textbf{:= Mod[x + y, 2]}$

Now ⊕ is not only recognized as an operator, but can also be evaluated.

$In[4]:= \textbf{2} \oplus \textbf{3}$

$Out[4]= 1$

$x \oplus y$	CirclePlus[x, y]
$x \approx y$	TildeTilde[x, y]
$x \therefore y$	Therefore[x, y]
$x \leftrightarrow y$	LeftRightArrow[x, y]
∇x	Del[x]
$\square x$	Square[x]
$\langle x, y, \ldots \rangle$	AngleBracket[x, y, ...]

A few *Mathematica* operators corresponding to functions without predefined values.

Mathematica follows the general convention that the function associated with a particular operator should have the same name as the special character that represents that operator.

\[Congruent] is displayed as ≡.	*In[5]:=* **x \[Congruent] y**
	Out[5]= x ≡ y
It corresponds to the function Congruent.	*In[6]:=* **FullForm[%]**
	Out[6]//FullForm= Congruent[x, y]

$$x \text{ \[}name\text{]} y \qquad name[x, y]$$

$$\text{\[}name\text{]} x \qquad name[x]$$

$$\text{\[Left}name\text{]} x, y, ... \text{\[Right}name\text{]} \qquad name[x, y, ...]$$

The conventional correspondence in *Mathematica* between operator names and function names.

You should realize that even though the functions CirclePlus and CircleTimes do not have built-in evaluation rules, the operators ⊕ and ⊗ do have built-in precedences. Pages 1024–1029 list all the operators recognized by *Mathematica*, in order of their precedence.

The operators ⊗ and ⊕ have definite precedences—with ⊗ higher than ⊕.	*In[7]:=* **x ⊗ y ⊕ z // FullForm**
	Out[7]//FullForm= Mod[Plus[z, CircleTimes[x, y]], 2]

x_y	Subscript[x, y]		$\overset{y}{x}$	Overscript[x, y]
x_+	SubPlus[x]		$\underset{y}{x}$	Underscript[x, y]
x_-	SubMinus[x]		$\bar{x}$	OverBar[x]
x_*	SubStar[x]		$\vec{x}$	OverVector[x]
x^+	SuperPlus[x]		$\tilde{x}$	OverTilde[x]
x^-	SuperMinus[x]		$\hat{x}$	OverHat[x]
x^*	SuperStar[x]		$\dot{x}$	OverDot[x]
$x^\dagger$	SuperDagger[x]		$\underline{x}$	UnderBar[x]

Some two-dimensional forms without built-in meanings.

Subscripts have no built-in meaning in *Mathematica*.	*In[8]:=* **x_2 + y_2 // InputForm**
	Out[8]//InputForm= Subscript[x, 2] + Subscript[y, 2]
Most superscripts are however interpreted as powers by default.	*In[9]:=* **x^2 + y^2 // InputForm**
	Out[9]//InputForm= x^2 + y^2

A few special superscripts are not interpreted as powers.

$In[10]:=$ **$x^\dagger + y^+$ // InputForm**

$Out[10]//InputForm=$ SuperDagger[x] + SuperPlus[y]

Bar and hat are interpreted as `OverBar` and `OverHat`.

$In[11]:=$ **$\bar{x} + \hat{y}$ // InputForm**

$Out[11]//InputForm=$ OverBar[x] + OverHat[y]

■ 2.9.16 Defining Output Formats

Just as *Mathematica* allows you to define how expressions should be evaluated, so also it allows you to define how expressions should be formatted for output. The basic idea is that whenever *Mathematica* is given an expression to format for output, it first calls `Format[`*expr*`]` to find out whether any special rules for formatting the expression have been defined. By assigning a value to `Format[`*expr*`]` you can therefore tell *Mathematica* that you want a particular kind of expression to be output in a special way.

This tells *Mathematica* to format bin objects in a special way.

$In[1]:=$ **Format[bin[x_, y_]] := MatrixForm[{{x}, {y}}]**

Now `bin` objects are output to look like binomial coefficients.

$In[2]:=$ **bin[i + j, k]**

$Out[2]=$ $\begin{pmatrix} i+j \\ k \end{pmatrix}$

Internally, however, bin objects are still exactly the same.

$In[3]:=$ **FullForm[%]**

$Out[3]//FullForm=$ bin[Plus[i, j], k]

`Format[`*expr*$_1$`] := `*expr*$_2$	define *expr*$_1$ to be formatted like *expr*$_2$
`Format[`*expr*$_1$`, `*form*`] := `*expr*$_2$	give a definition only for a particular output form

Defining your own rules for formatting.

By making definitions for `Format`, you can tell *Mathematica* to format a particular expression so as to look like another expression. You can also tell *Mathematica* to run a program to determine how a particular expression should be formatted.

This specifies that *Mathematica* should run a simple program to determine how xrep objects should be formatted.

$In[4]:=$ **Format[xrep[n_]] := StringJoin[Table["x", {n}]]**

The strings are created when each xrep is formatted.

$In[5]:=$ **xrep[1] + xrep[4] + xrep[9]**

$Out[5]=$ x + xxxx + xxxxxxxxx

Internally however the expression still contains xrep objects.

$In[6]:=$ **% /. xrep[n_] -> x^n**

$Out[6]=$ $x + x^4 + x^9$

Prefix[$f[x]$, h]	prefix form $h\ x$
Postfix[$f[x]$, h]	postfix form $x\ h$
Infix[$f[x,\ y,\ \dots\ ]$, h]	infix form $x\ h\ y\ h\ \dots$
Prefix[$f[x]$]	standard prefix form $f\ @\ x$
Postfix[$f[x]$]	standard postfix form $x\ //\ f$
Infix[$f[x,\ y,\ \dots\ ]$]	standard infix form $x \sim f \sim y \sim f \sim \dots$
PrecedenceForm[$expr$, n]	an object to be parenthesized with a precedence level n

Output forms for operators.

This prints with f represented by the "prefix operator" <>.

In[7]:= **Prefix[f[x], "<>"]**

Out[7]= <> x

Here is output with the "infix operator" <>.

In[8]:= **s = Infix[{a, b, c}, "<>"]**

Out[8]= a <> b <> c

By default, the "infix operator" <> is assumed to have "higher precedence" than ^, so no parentheses are inserted.

In[9]:= **s^2**

Out[9]= $(a <> b <> c)^2$

When you have an output form involving operators, the question arises of whether the arguments of some of them should be parenthesized. As discussed in Section 2.1.3, this depends on the "precedence" of the operators. When you set up output forms involving operators, you can use PrecedenceForm to specify the precedence to assign to each operator. *Mathematica* uses integers from 1 to 1000 to represent "precedence levels". The higher the precedence level for an operator, the less it needs to be parenthesized.

Here <> is treated as an operator with precedence 100. This precedence turns out to be low enough that parentheses are inserted.

In[10]:= **PrecedenceForm[s, 100]^2**

Out[10]= $(a <> b <> c)^2$

When you make an assignment for Format[*expr*], you are defining the output format for *expr* in all standard types of *Mathematica* output. By making definitions for Format[*expr*, *form*], you can specify formats to be used in specific output forms.

This specifies the TeXForm for the symbol x.

In[11]:= **Format[x, TeXForm] := "{\\bf x}"**

The output format for x that you specified is now used whenever the TEX form is needed.

In[12]:= **TeXForm[1 + x^2]**

Out[12]//TeXForm= 1 + {{\bf x}}^2

■ 2.9.17 Advanced Topic: Low-Level Input and Output Rules

MakeBoxes[*expr*, *form*]	construct boxes to represent *expr* in the specified form
MakeExpression[*boxes*, *form*]	construct an expression corresponding to *boxes*

Low-level functions for converting between expressions and boxes.

MakeBoxes generates boxes without evaluating its input.

```
In[1]:= MakeBoxes[2 + 2, StandardForm]

Out[1]= RowBox[{2, +, 2}]
```

MakeExpression interprets boxes but uses HoldComplete to prevent the resulting expression from being evaluated.

```
In[2]:= MakeExpression[%, StandardForm]

Out[2]= HoldComplete[2 + 2]
```

Built into *Mathematica* are a large number of rules for generating output and interpreting input. Particularly in StandardForm, these rules are carefully set up to be consistent, and to allow input and output to be used interchangeably.

It is fairly rare that you will need to modify these rules. The main reason is that *Mathematica* already has built-in rules for the input and output of many operators to which it does not itself assign specific meanings.

Thus, if you want to add, for example, a generalized form of addition, you can usually just use an operator like ⊕ for which *Mathematica* already has built-in input and output rules.

This outputs using the ⊕ operator.

```
In[3]:= CirclePlus[u, v, w]

Out[3]= u ⊕ v ⊕ w
```

Mathematica understands ⊕ on input.

```
In[4]:= u ⊕ v ⊕ w // FullForm

Out[4]//FullForm= CirclePlus[u, v, w]
```

In dealing with output, you can make definitions for Format[*expr*] to change the way that a particular expression will be formatted. You should realize, however, that as soon as you do this, there is no guarantee that the output form of your expression will be interpreted correctly if it is given as *Mathematica* input.

If you want to, *Mathematica* allows you to redefine the basic rules that it uses for the input and output of all expressions. You can do this by making definitions for MakeBoxes and MakeExpression. You should realize, however, that unless you make such definitions with great care, you are likely to end up with inconsistent results.

This defines how gplus objects should be output in StandardForm.

```
In[5]:= gplus /: MakeBoxes[gplus[x_, y_, n_], StandardForm] :=
          RowBox[ {MakeBoxes[x, StandardForm],
            SubscriptBox["\[CirclePlus]", MakeBoxes[n, StandardForm]],
              MakeBoxes[y, StandardForm]} ]
```

gplus is now output using a subscripted ⊕.	*In[6]:=* **gplus[a, b, m+n]** *Out[6]=* a ⊕ₘ₊ₙ b

Mathematica cannot however interpret this as input.

In[7]:= **a ⊕ₘ₊ₙ b**

Syntax::sntxi:
   Incomplete expression; more input is needed.

This tells *Mathematica* to interpret a subscripted ⊕ as a specific piece of FullForm input.

In[7]:= **MakeExpression[RowBox[{x_, SubscriptBox[**
        "\[CirclePlus]", n_], y_}], StandardForm] :=
     MakeExpression[RowBox[
       {"gplus", "[", x, ",", y, ",", n, "]"}], StandardForm]

Now the subscripted ⊕ is interpreted as a gplus.

In[8]:= **a ⊕ₘ₊ₙ b // FullForm**

Out[8]//FullForm= gplus[a, b, Plus[m, n]]

When you give definitions for MakeBoxes, you can think of this as essentially a lower-level version of giving definitions for Format. An important difference is that MakeBoxes does not evaluate its argument, so you can define rules for formatting expressions without being concerned about how these expressions would evaluate.

In addition, while Format is automatically called again on any results obtained by applying it, the same is not true of MakeBoxes. This means that in giving definitions for MakeBoxes you explicitly have to call MakeBoxes again on any subexpressions that still need to be formatted.

- Break input into tokens.

- Strip spacing characters.

- Construct boxes using built-in operator precedences.

- Strip StyleBox and other boxes not intended for interpretation.

- Apply rules defined for MakeExpression.

Operations done on *Mathematica* input.

■ 2.9.18 Generating Unstructured Output

The functions described so far in this section determine *how* expressions should be formatted when they are printed, but they do not actually cause anything to be printed.

In the most common way of using *Mathematica* you never in fact explicitly have to issue a command to generate output. Usually, *Mathematica* automatically prints out the final result that it gets from processing input you gave. Sometimes, however, you may want to get *Mathematica* to print out expressions at intermediate stages in its operation. You can do this using the function Print.

Print[$expr_1$, $expr_2$, ...]	print the $expr_i$, with no spaces in between, but with a newline (line feed) at the end

Printing expressions.

Print prints its arguments, with no spaces in between, but with a newline (line feed) at the end.

```
In[1]:= Print[a, b]; Print[c]
ab
c
```

This prints a table of the first five integers and their squares.

```
In[2]:= Do[Print[i, "  ", i^2], {i, 5}]
1   1
2   4
3   9
4   16
5   25
```

Print simply takes the arguments you give, and prints them out one after the other, with no spaces in between. In many cases, you will need to print output in a more complicated format. You can do this by giving an output form as an argument to Print.

This prints the matrix in the form of a table.

```
In[3]:= Print[TableForm[{{1, 2}, {3, 4}}]]
1   2

3   4
```

Here the output format is specified using StringForm.

```
In[4]:= Print[StringForm["x = ``, y = ``", a^2, b^2]]
     2      2
x = a , y = b
```

The output generated by Print is usually given in the standard *Mathematica* output format. You can however explicitly specify that some other output format should be used.

This prints output in *Mathematica* input form.

```
In[5]:= Print[InputForm[a^2 + b^2]]
a^2 + b^2
```

You should realize that Print is only one of several mechanisms available in *Mathematica* for generating output. Another is the function Message described in Section 2.9.21, used for generating named messages. There are also a variety of lower-level functions described in Section 2.12.3 which allow you to produce output in various formats both as part of an interactive session, and for files and external programs.

■ 2.9.19 Generating Styled Output in Notebooks

StylePrint[$expr$, "*style*"]	create a new cell containing *expr* in the specified style
StylePrint[$expr$]	use the default style for the notebook

Generating styled output in notebooks.

This generates a cell in section heading style.

In[1]:= `StylePrint["The heading", "Section"];`

■ **The heading**

This generates a cell in input style.

In[2]:= `StylePrint[x^2 + y^2, "Input"]`

■ **The heading**

$x^2 + y^2$

Mathematica provides many capabilities for manipulating the contents of notebooks, as discussed in Section 2.11. `StylePrint` handles the simple case when all you want to do is to add a cell of a particular style.

■ 2.9.20 Requesting Input

Mathematica usually works by taking whatever input you give, and then processing it. Sometimes, however, you may want to have a program you write explicitly request more input. You can do this using `Input` and `InputString`.

Input[ ]	read an expression as input
InputString[ ]	read a string as input
Input["*prompt*"]	issue a prompt, then read an expression
InputString["*prompt*"]	issue a prompt then read a string

Interactive input.

Exactly how `Input` and `InputString` work depends on the computer system and *Mathematica* interface you are using. With a text-based interface, they typically just wait for standard input, terminated with a newline. With a notebook interface, however, they typically get the front end to put up a "dialog box", in which the user can enter input.

In general, `Input` is intended for reading complete *Mathematica* expressions. `InputString`, on the other hand, is for reading arbitrary strings.

■ 2.9.21 Messages

Mathematica has a general mechanism for handling messages generated during computations. Many built-in *Mathematica* functions use this mechanism to produce error and warning messages. You can also use the mechanism for messages associated with functions you write.

The basic idea is that every message has a definite name, of the form *symbol::tag*. You can use this name to refer to the message. (The object *symbol::tag* has head `MessageName`.)

`Off[`*s::tag*`]`	switch off a message, so it is not printed
`On[`*s::tag*`]`	switch on a message

Controlling the printing of messages.

As discussed in Section 1.3.11, you can use `On` and `Off` to control the printing of particular messages. Most messages associated with built-in functions are switched on by default. You can use `Off` to switch them off if you do not want to see them.

This prints a warning message.	*In[1]:=* **`Log[a, b, c]`**
	`Log::argt: Log called with 3 arguments; 1 or 2` `    arguments are expected.`
	Out[1]= `Log[a, b, c]`
You can switch off the message like this.	*In[2]:=* **`Off[Log::argt]`**
Now no warning message is produced.	*In[3]:=* **`Log[a, b, c]`**
	Out[3]= `Log[a, b, c]`

Although most messages associated with built-in functions are switched on by default, there are some which are switched off by default, and which you will see only if you explicitly switch them on. An example is the message `General::newsym`, discussed in Section 2.7.13, which tells you every time a new symbol is created.

s::tag	give the text of a message
s::tag = *string*	set the text of a message
`Messages[`*s*`]`	show all messages associated with *s*

Manipulating messages.

The text of a message with the name *s::tag* is stored simply as the value of *s::tag*, associated with the symbol *s*. You can therefore see the text of a message simply by asking for *s::tag*. You can set the text by assigning a value to *s::tag*.

If you give LinearSolve a singular matrix, it prints a warning message.

```
In[4]:= LinearSolve[{{1, 1}, {2, 2}}, {3, 5}]

LinearSolve::nosol:
   Linear equation encountered which has no solution.

Out[4]= LinearSolve[{{1, 1}, {2, 2}}, {3, 5}]
```

Here is the text of the message.

```
In[5]:= LinearSolve::nosol

Out[5]= Linear equation encountered which has no solution.
```

This redefines the message.

```
In[6]:= LinearSolve::nosol = "Matrix encountered is not invertible."

Out[6]= Matrix encountered is not invertible.
```

Now the new form will be used.

```
In[7]:= LinearSolve[{{1, 1}, {2, 2}}, {3, 5}]

LinearSolve::nosol: Matrix encountered is not invertible.

Out[7]= LinearSolve[{{1, 1}, {2, 2}}, {3, 5}]
```

Messages are always stored as strings suitable for use with StringForm. When the message is printed, the appropriate expressions are "spliced" into it. The expressions are wrapped with HoldForm to prevent evaluation. In addition, any function that is assigned as the value of the global variable $MessagePrePrint is applied to the resulting expressions before they are given to StringForm. The default for $MessagePrePrint is Short.

Most messages are associated directly with the functions that generate them. There are, however, some "general" messages, which can be produced by a variety of functions.

If you give the wrong number of arguments to a function *F*, *Mathematica* will warn you by printing a message such as *F*::argx. If *Mathematica* cannot find a message named *F*::argx, it will use the text of the "general" message General::argx instead. You can use Off[*F*::argx] to switch off the argument count message specifically for the function *F*. You can also use Off[General::argx] to switch off all messages that use the text of the general message.

Mathematica prints a message if you give the wrong number of arguments to a built-in function.

```
In[8]:= Sqrt[a, b]

Sqrt::argx:
   Sqrt called with 2 arguments; 1 argument is expected.

Out[8]= Sqrt[a, b]
```

This argument count message is a general one, used by many different functions.

```
In[9]:= General::argx

Out[9]= `1` called with `2`
              arguments; 1 argument is expected.
```

If something goes very wrong with a calculation you are doing, it is common to find that the same warning message is generated over and over again. This is usually more confusing than useful. As a result, *Mathematica* keeps track of all messages that are produced during a particular calculation, and stops printing a particular message if it comes up more than three times. Whenever this happens, *Mathematica* prints the message General::stop to let you know. If you really want to see all the messages that *Mathematica* tries to print, you can do this by switching off General::stop.

| $MessageList | a list of the messages produced during a particular computation |
| MessageList[n] | a list of the messages produced during the processing of the nth input line in a *Mathematica* session |

Finding out what messages were produced during a computation.

In every computation you do, *Mathematica* maintains a list $MessageList of all the messages that are produced. In a standard *Mathematica* session, this list is cleared after each line of output is generated. However, during a computation, you can access the list. In addition, when the nth output line in a session is generated, the value of $MessageList is assigned to MessageList[n].

This returns $MessageList, which gives a list of the messages produced.

```
In[10]:= Sqrt[a, b, c]; Exp[a, b]; $MessageList
```
Sqrt::argx:
    Sqrt called with 3 arguments; 1 argument is expected.

Exp::argx: Exp called with 2
        arguments; 1 argument is expected.

```
Out[10]= {Sqrt::argx, Exp::argx}
```

The message names are wrapped in HoldForm to stop them from evaluating.

```
In[11]:= InputForm[%]
```
```
Out[11]//InputForm= {HoldForm[Sqrt::argx], HoldForm[Exp::argx]}
```

In writing programs, it is often important to be able to check automatically whether any messages were generated during a particular calculation. If messages were generated, say as a consequence of producing indeterminate numerical results, then the result of the calculation may be meaningless.

| Check[*expr*, *failexpr*] | if no messages are generated during the evaluation of *expr*, then return *expr*, otherwise return *failexpr* |
| Check[*expr*, *failexpr*, s_1::t_1, s_2::t_2, ...] | check only for the messages s_i::t_i |

Checking for warning messages.

Evaluating 1^0 produces no messages, so the result of the evaluation is returned.

```
In[12]:= Check[1^0, err]
```
```
Out[12]= 1
```

Evaluating 0^0 produces a message, so the second argument of Check is returned.

```
In[13]:= Check[0^0, err]
```
Power::indet: Indeterminate expression 0^0 encountered.

```
Out[13]= err
```

Check[*expr*, *failexpr*] tests for all messages that are actually printed out. It does not test for messages whose output has been suppressed using Off.

In some cases you may want to test only for a specific set of messages, say ones associated with numerical overflow. You can do this by explicitly telling Check the names of the messages you want to look for.

The message generated by Sin[1, 2] is ignored by Check, since it is not the one specified.	*In[14]:=* **Check[Sin[1, 2], err, General::ind]** Sin::argx: Sin called with 2 arguments; 1 argument is expected. *Out[14]=* Sin[1, 2]

Message[*s*::*tag*]	print a message
Message[*s*::*tag*, *expr*₁, ...]	print a message, with the *expr*ᵢ spliced into its string form

Generating messages.

By using the function Message, you can mimic all aspects of the way in which built-in *Mathematica* functions generate messages. You can for example switch on and off messages using On and Off, and Message will automatically look for General::*tag* if it does not find the specific message *s*::*tag*.

This defines the text of a message associated with f.	*In[15]:=* **f::overflow = "Factorial argument \`1\` too large."** *Out[15]=* Factorial argument \`1\` too large.

Here is the function f.	*In[16]:=* **f[x_] :=**
	          If[x > 10,
	             (Message[f::overflow, x]; Infinity), x!]

When the argument of f is greater than 10, the message is generated.	*In[17]:=* **f[20]** f::overflow: Factorial argument 20 too large. *Out[17]=* ∞
This switches off the message.	*In[18]:=* **Off[f::overflow]**
Now the message is no longer generated.	*In[19]:=* **f[20]** *Out[19]=* ∞

When you call Message, it first tries to find a message with the explicit name you have specified. If this fails, it tries to find a message with the appropriate tag associated with the symbol General. If this too fails, then *Mathematica* takes any function you have defined as the value of the global variable $NewMessage, and applies this function to the symbol and tag of the message you have requested.

By setting up the value of $NewMessage appropriately, you can, for example, get *Mathematica* to read in the text of a message from a file when that message is first needed.

■ 2.9.22 International Messages

The standard set of messages for built-in *Mathematica* functions are written in American English. In some versions of *Mathematica*, messages are also available in other languages. In addition, if you set up messages yourself, you can give ones in other languages.

Languages in *Mathematica* are conventionally specified by strings. The languages are given in English, in order to avoid the possibility of needing special characters. Thus, for example, the French language is specified in *Mathematica* as "French".

\$Language = "*lang*"	set the language to use
\$Language = {"*lang*$_1$", "*lang*$_2$", ... }	set a sequence of languages to try

Setting the language to use for messages.

This tells *Mathematica* to use French-language versions of messages.	`In[1]:= `**`$Language = "French"`**
	`Out[1]= French`

This tells *Mathematica* to use French-language versions of messages.

```
In[1]:= $Language = "French"
Out[1]= French
```

If your version of *Mathematica* has French-language messages, the message generated here will be in French.

```
In[2]:= Sqrt[a, b, c]
Sqrt::argx:
    Sqrt  est appelée avec 3 arguments; il faut y avoir 1.

Out[2]= Sqrt[a, b, c]
```

symbol::*tag*	the default form of a message
symbol::*tag*::*Language*	a message in a particular language

Messages in different languages.

When built-in *Mathematica* functions generate messages, they look first for messages of the form *s*::*t*::*Language*, in the language specified by \$Language. If they fail to find any such messages, then they use instead the form *s*::*t* without an explicit language specification.

The procedure used by built-in functions will also be followed by functions you define if you call `Message` with message names of the form *s*::*t*. If you give explicit languages in message names, however, only those languages will be used.

■ 2.9.23 Documentation Constructs

When you write programs in *Mathematica*, there are various ways to document your code. As always, by far the best thing is to write clear code, and to name the objects you define as explicitly as possible.

Sometimes, however, you may want to add some "commentary text" to your code, to make it easier to understand. You can add such text at any point in your code simply by enclosing it in matching (* and *). Notice that in *Mathematica*, "comments" enclosed in (* and *) can be nested in any way.

You can use comments anywhere in the *Mathematica* code you write.

```
In[1]:= If[a > b, (* then *) p, (* else *) q]

Out[1]= If[a > b, p, q]
```

(* *text* *)	a comment that can be inserted anywhere in *Mathematica* code

Comments in *Mathematica*.

There is a convention in *Mathematica* that all functions intended for later use should be given a definite "usage message", which documents their basic usage. This message is defined as the value of f::usage, and is retrieved when you type ?f.

f::usage = "*text*"	define the usage message for a function
?f	get information about a function
??f	get more information about a function

Usage messages for functions.

Here is the definition of a function f.

```
In[2]:= f[x_] := x^2
```

Here is a "usage message" for f.

```
In[3]:= f::usage = "f[x] gives the square of x."

Out[3]= f[x] gives the square of x.
```

This gives the usage message for f.

```
In[4]:= ?f

f[x] gives the square of x.
```

??f gives all the information *Mathematica* has about f, including the actual definition.

```
In[5]:= ??f

f[x] gives the square of x.

f[x_] := x^2
```

When you define a function f, you can usually display its value using ?f. However, if you give a usage message for f, then ?f just gives the usage message. Only when you type ??f do you get all the details about f, including its actual definition.

If you ask for information using ? about just one function, *Mathematica* will print out the complete usage messages for the function. If you ask for information on several functions at the same time, however, *Mathematica* will just give you the name of each function.

f::usage	main usage message
f::notes	notes about the function
f::usage::*Language*, etc.	messages in a particular language

Some typical documentation messages.

In addition to the usage message, there are some messages such as notes and qv that are often defined to document functions.

If you use *Mathematica* with a text-based interface, then messages and comments are the primary mechanisms for documenting your definitions. However, if you use *Mathematica* with a notebook interface, then you will be able to give much more extensive documentation in text cells in the notebook.

2.10 The Structure of Graphics and Sound

■ 2.10.1 The Structure of Graphics

Section 1.9 discussed how to use functions like `Plot` and `ListPlot` to plot graphs of functions and data. In this section, we discuss how *Mathematica* represents such graphics, and how you can program *Mathematica* to create more complicated images.

The basic idea is that *Mathematica* represents all graphics in terms of a collection of *graphics primitives*. The primitives are objects like `Point`, `Line` and `Polygon`, that represent elements of a graphical image, as well as directives such as `RGBColor`, `Thickness` and `SurfaceColor`.

This generates a plot of a list of points.   *In[1]:=* **ListPlot[Table[Prime[n], {n, 20}]]**

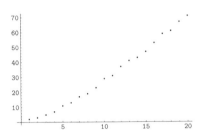

InputForm shows how *Mathematica* represents the graphics. Each point is represented as a `Point` graphics primitive. All the various graphics options used in this case are also given.

```
In[2]:= InputForm[%]

Out[2]//InputForm= Graphics[{Point[{1, 2}], Point[{2, 3}],
          Point[{3, 5}], Point[{4, 7}], Point[{5, 11}],
          Point[{6, 13}], Point[{7, 17}], Point[{8, 19}],
          Point[{9, 23}], Point[{10, 29}], Point[{11, 31}],
          Point[{12, 37}], Point[{13, 41}], Point[{14, 43}],
          Point[{15, 47}], Point[{16, 53}], Point[{17, 59}],
          Point[{18, 61}], Point[{19, 67}], Point[{20, 71}]},
       {PlotRange -> Automatic,
        AspectRatio -> GoldenRatio^(-1),
        DisplayFunction :> $DisplayFunction,
        ColorOutput -> Automatic, Axes -> Automatic,
        AxesOrigin -> Automatic, PlotLabel -> None,
        AxesLabel -> None, Ticks -> Automatic,
        GridLines -> None, Prolog -> {}, Epilog -> {},
        AxesStyle -> Automatic, Background -> Automatic,
        DefaultColor -> Automatic,
        DefaultFont :> $DefaultFont, RotateLabel -> True,
        Frame -> False, FrameStyle -> Automatic,
        FrameTicks -> Automatic, FrameLabel -> None,
        PlotRegion -> Automatic, ImageSize -> Automatic,
        TextStyle :> $TextStyle, FormatType :> $FormatType}]
```

Each complete piece of graphics in *Mathematica* is represented as a *graphics object*. There are several different kinds of graphics object, corresponding to different types of graphics. Each kind of graphics object has a definite head which identifies its type.

Graphics[*list*]	general two-dimensional graphics
DensityGraphics[*list*]	density plot
ContourGraphics[*list*]	contour plot
SurfaceGraphics[*list*]	three-dimensional surface
Graphics3D[*list*]	general three-dimensional graphics
GraphicsArray[*list*]	array of other graphics objects

Graphics objects in *Mathematica*.

The functions like Plot and ListPlot discussed in Section 1.9 all work by building up *Mathematica* graphics objects, and then displaying them.

Graphics	Plot, ListPlot, ParametricPlot
DensityGraphics	DensityPlot, ListDensityPlot
ContourGraphics	ContourPlot, ListContourPlot
SurfaceGraphics	Plot3D, ListPlot3D
Graphics3D	ParametricPlot3D

Generating graphics objects by plotting functions and data.

You can create other kinds of graphical images in *Mathematica* by building up your own graphics objects. Since graphics objects in *Mathematica* are just symbolic expressions, you can use all the standard *Mathematica* functions to manipulate them.

Once you have created a graphics object, you must then display it. The function Show allows you to display any *Mathematica* graphics object.

Show[g]	display a graphics object
Show[g_1, g_2, ...]	display several graphics objects combined
Show[GraphicsArray[{{g_{11}, g_{12}, ... }, ... }]]	
	display an array of graphics objects

Displaying graphics objects.

This uses `Table` to generate a polygon graphics primitive.

```
In[3]:= poly = Polygon[
          Table[N[{Cos[n Pi/5], Sin[n Pi/5]}], {n, 0, 5}] ]
Out[3]= Polygon[{{1., 0.}, {0.809017, 0.587785},
          {0.309017, 0.951057}, {-0.309017, 0.951057},
          {-0.809017, 0.587785}, {-1., 0.}}]
```

This creates a two-dimensional graphics object that contains the polygon graphics primitive. In standard output format, the graphics object is given simply as -Graphics-.

```
In[4]:= Graphics[ poly ]
Out[4]= -Graphics-
```

`InputForm` shows the complete graphics object.

```
In[5]:= InputForm[%]
Out[5]//InputForm=
          Graphics[Polygon[{{1., 0.},
            {0.8090169943749475, 0.5877852522924731},
            {0.30901699437494745, 0.9510565162951535},
            {-0.30901699437494745, 0.9510565162951535},
            {-0.8090169943749475, 0.5877852522924731}, {-1., 0.}}]]
```

This displays the graphics object you have created.

```
In[6]:= Show[%]
```

Graphics directives	Examples: RGBColor, Thickness, SurfaceColor
Graphics options	Examples: PlotRange, Ticks, AspectRatio, ViewPoint

Local and global ways to modify graphics.

Given a particular list of graphics primitives, *Mathematica* provides two basic mechanisms for modifying the final form of graphics you get. First, you can insert into the list of graphics primitives certain *graphics directives*, such as RGBColor, which modify the subsequent graphical elements in the list. In this way, you can specify how a particular set of graphical elements should be rendered.

This takes the list of graphics primitives created above, and adds the graphics directive GrayLevel[0.3].

```
In[7]:= Graphics[ {GrayLevel[0.3], poly} ]
Out[7]= -Graphics-
```

Now the polygon is rendered in gray.   *In[8]:=* **Show[%]**

By inserting graphics directives, you can specify how particular graphical elements should be rendered. Often, however, you want to make global modifications to the way a whole graphics object is rendered. You can do this using *graphics options*.

By adding the graphics option Frame   *In[9]:=* **Show[%, Frame -> True]**
you can modify the overall appearance
of the graphics.

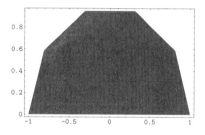

Show returns a graphics object with the   *In[10]:=* **InputForm[%]**
options in it.

Out[10]//InputForm=
        Graphics[{GrayLevel[0.3],
            Polygon[{{1., 0.}, {0.8090169943749475,
                0.5877852522924731},
              {0.30901699437494745, 0.9510565162951535},
              {-0.30901699437494745, 0.9510565162951535},
              {-0.8090169943749475, 0.5877852522924731}, {-1., 0.}}
          ]}, {Frame -> True}]

You can specify graphics options in Show. As a result, it is straightforward to take a single graphics object, and show it with many different choices of graphics options.

Notice however that Show always returns the graphics objects it has displayed. If you specify graphics options in Show, then these options are automatically inserted into the graphics objects that Show returns. As a result, if you call Show again on the same objects, the same graphics options will be used, unless you explicitly specify other ones. Note that in all cases new options you specify will overwrite ones already there.

Options[*g*]	give a list of all graphics options for a graphics object
Options[*g*, *opt*]	give the setting for a particular option
AbsoluteOptions[*g*, *opt*]	give the absolute value used for a particular option, even if the setting is Automatic

Finding the options for a graphics object.

Some graphics options work by requiring you to specify a particular value for a parameter related to a piece of graphics. Other options allow you to give the setting Automatic, which makes *Mathematica* use internal algorithms to choose appropriate values for parameters. In such cases, you can find out the values that *Mathematica* actually used by applying the function AbsoluteOptions.

Here is a plot.

In[11]:= **zplot = Plot[Abs[Zeta[1/2 + I x]], {x, 0, 10}]**

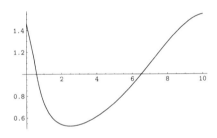

The option PlotRange is set to its default value of Automatic, specifying that *Mathematica* should use internal algorithms to determine the actual plot range.

In[12]:= **Options[zplot, PlotRange]**

Out[12]= {PlotRange → Automatic}

AbsoluteOptions gives the actual plot range determined by *Mathematica* in this case.

In[13]:= **AbsoluteOptions[zplot, PlotRange]**

Out[13]= {PlotRange → {{-0.25, 10.25}, {0.500681, 1.57477}}}

FullGraphics[*g*]	translate objects specified by graphics options into lists of explicit graphics primitives

Finding the complete form of a piece of graphics.

When you use a graphics option such as Axes, *Mathematica* effectively has to construct a list of graphics elements to represent the objects such as axes that you have requested. Usually *Mathematica* does not explicitly return the list it constructs in this way. Sometimes, however, you may find it useful to get this list. The function `FullGraphics` gives the complete list of graphics primitives needed to generate a particular plot, without any options being used.

This plots a list of values. `In[14]:= ListPlot[ Table[EulerPhi[n], {n, 10}] ]`

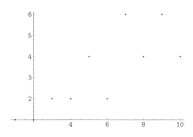

FullGraphics yields a graphics object that includes graphics primitives representing axes and so on.

`In[15]:= Short[ InputForm[ FullGraphics[%] ], 6]`

`Out[15]//Short= Graphics[{{Point[{1, 1}], Point[{2, 1}],`
`                Point[{3, 2}], Point[{4, 2}],`
`                Point[{5, 4}], Point[{6, 2}],`
`                Point[{7, 6}], Point[{8, 4}],`
`                Point[{9, 6}], Point[{10, 4}],`
`                <<1>>}]`

With their default option settings, functions like `Plot` and `Show` actually cause *Mathematica* to generate graphical output. In general, the actual generation of graphical output is controlled by the graphics option `DisplayFunction`. The default setting for this option is the value of the global variable `$DisplayFunction`.

In most cases, `$DisplayFunction` and the `DisplayFunction` option are set to use the lower-level rendering function `Display` to produce output, perhaps after some preprocessing. Sometimes, however, you may want to get a function like `Plot` to produce a graphics object, but you may not immediately want that graphics object actually rendered as output. You can tell *Mathematica* to generate the object, but not render it, by setting the option `DisplayFunction -> Identity`. Section 2.10.14 will explain exactly how this works.

`Plot[f, ... , DisplayFunction -> Identity]`, etc.
  generate a graphics object for a plot, but do not actually display it

`Show[g, DisplayFunction -> $DisplayFunction]`
  show a graphics object using the default display function

Generating and displaying graphics objects.

This generates a graphics object, but does not actually display it.

```
In[16]:= Plot[BesselJ[0, x], {x, 0, 10},
                          DisplayFunction -> Identity]
Out[16]= -Graphics-
```

This modifies the graphics object, but still does not actually display it.

```
In[17]:= Show[%, Frame -> True]
Out[17]= -Graphics-
```

To display the graphic, you explicitly have to tell *Mathematica* to use the default display function.

```
In[18]:= Show[%, DisplayFunction -> $DisplayFunction]
```

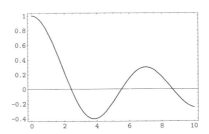

■ 2.10.2 Two-Dimensional Graphics Elements

Point[{x, y}]	point at position x, y
Line[{{x_1, y_1}, {x_2, y_2}, ... }]	line through the points {x_1, y_1}, {x_2, y_2}, ...
Rectangle[{$xmin$, $ymin$}, {$xmax$, $ymax$}]	filled rectangle
Polygon[{{x_1, y_1}, {x_2, y_2}, ... }]	filled polygon with the specified list of corners
Circle[{x, y}, r]	circle with radius r centered at x, y
Disk[{x, y}, r]	filled disk with radius r centered at x, y
Raster[{{a_{11}, a_{12}, ... }, {a_{21}, ... }, ... }]	rectangular array of gray levels between 0 and 1
Text[$expr$, {x, y}]	the text of *expr*, centered at x, y (see Section 2.10.16)

Basic two-dimensional graphics elements.

Here is a line primitive.

```
In[1]:= sawline = Line[Table[{n, (-1)^n}, {n, 6}]]
Out[1]= Line[
            {{1, -1}, {2, 1}, {3, -1}, {4, 1}, {5, -1}, {6, 1}}]
```

This shows the line as a
two dimensional graphics object.

In[2]:= **sawgraph = Show[Graphics[sawline]]**

This redisplays the line, with axes
added.

In[3]:= **Show[%, Axes -> True]**

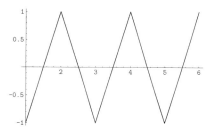

You can combine graphics objects that you have created explicitly from graphics primitives with ones
that are produced by functions like Plot.

This produces an ordinary *Mathematica*
plot.

In[4]:= **Plot[Sin[Pi x], {x, 0, 6}]**

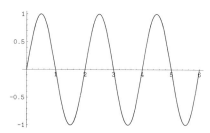

This combines the plot with the sawtooth picture made above.

$In[5]:=$ **Show[%, sawgraph]**

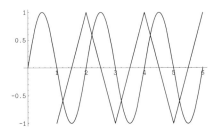

You can combine different graphical elements simply by giving them in a list. In two-dimensional graphics, *Mathematica* will render the elements in exactly the order you give them. Later elements are therefore effectively drawn on top of earlier ones.

Here is a list of two Rectangle graphics elements.

$In[6]:=$ **{Rectangle[{1, -1}, {2, -0.6}],**
Rectangle[{4, .3}, {5, .8}]}

$Out[6]=$ {Rectangle[{1, -1}, {2, -0.6}],
Rectangle[{4, 0.3}, {5, 0.8}]}

This draws the rectangles on top of the line that was defined above.

$In[7]:=$ **Show[Graphics[{sawline, %}]]**

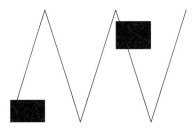

The Polygon graphics primitive takes a list of x, y coordinates, corresponding to the corners of a polygon. *Mathematica* joins the last corner with the first one, and then fills the resulting area.

Here are the coordinates of the corners of a regular pentagon.

$In[8]:=$ **pentagon = Table[{Sin[2 Pi n/5], Cos[2 Pi n/5]}, {n, 5}]**

$Out[8]=$ $\left\{\left\{\frac{1}{2}\sqrt{\frac{1}{2}\left(5+\sqrt{5}\right)}, \frac{1}{4}\left(-1+\sqrt{5}\right)\right\},\right.$

$\left\{\frac{1}{2}\sqrt{\frac{1}{2}\left(5-\sqrt{5}\right)}, -\frac{1}{4}\left(1+\sqrt{5}\right)\right\},$

$\left\{-\frac{1}{2}\sqrt{\frac{1}{2}\left(5-\sqrt{5}\right)}, -\frac{1}{4}\left(1+\sqrt{5}\right)\right\},$

$\left.\left\{-\frac{1}{2}\sqrt{\frac{1}{2}\left(5+\sqrt{5}\right)}, \frac{1}{4}\left(-1+\sqrt{5}\right)\right\}, \{0, 1\}\right\}$

This displays the pentagon. With the default choice of aspect ratio, the pentagon looks somewhat squashed.

In[9]:= **Show[Graphics[Polygon[pentagon]]]**

This chooses the aspect ratio so that the shape of the pentagon is preserved.

In[10]:= **Show[%, AspectRatio -> Automatic]**

Mathematica can handle polygons which fold over themselves.

In[11]:= **Show[Graphics[**
               Polygon[{{-1, -1}, {1, 1}, {1, -1}, {-1, 1}}]]]

Circle[{x, y}, r]	a circle with radius r centered at the point {x, y}
Circle[{x, y}, {r_x, r_y}]	an ellipse with semi-axes r_x and r_y
Circle[{x, y}, r, {$theta_1$, $theta_2$}]	a circular arc
Circle[{x, y}, {r_x, r_y}, {$theta_1$, $theta_2$}]	an elliptical arc
Disk[{x, y}, r], etc.	filled disks

Circles and disks.

This shows two circles with radius 2. Setting the option AspectRatio -> Automatic makes the circles come out with their natural aspect ratio.

```
In[12]:= Show[ Graphics[
            {Circle[{0, 0}, 2], Circle[{1, 1}, 2]} ],
                    AspectRatio -> Automatic ]
```

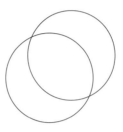

This shows a sequence of disks with progressively larger semi-axes in the x direction, and progressively smaller ones in the y direction.

```
In[13]:= Show[ Graphics[
            Table[Disk[{3n, 0}, {n/4, 2-n/4}], {n, 4}] ],
                    AspectRatio -> Automatic ]
```

Mathematica allows you to generate arcs of circles, and segments of ellipses. In both cases, the objects are specified by starting and finishing angles. The angles are measured counterclockwise in radians with zero corresponding to the positive x direction.

This draws a 140° wedge centered at the origin.

In[14]:= **Show[Graphics[Disk[{0, 0}, 1, {0, 140 Degree}]],
AspectRatio -> Automatic]**

Raster[{{a_{11}, a_{12}, ... }, {a_{21}, ... }, ... }]
array of gray levels between 0 and 1

Raster[*array*, {{*xmin*, *ymin*}, {*xmax*, *ymax*}}, {*zmin*, *zmax*}]
array of gray levels between *zmin* and *zmax* drawn in the rectangle defined by {*xmin*, *ymin*} and {*xmax*, *ymax*}

RasterArray[{{g_{11}, g_{12}, ... }, {g_{21}, ... }, ... }]
rectangular array of cells colored according to the graphics directives g_{ij}

Raster-based graphics elements.

Here is a 4 × 4 array of values between 0 and 1.

In[15]:= **modtab = Table[Mod[i, j]/3, {i, 4}, {j, 4}] // N**

Out[15]= {{0., 0.333333, 0.333333, 0.333333},
{0., 0., 0.666667, 0.666667},
{0., 0.333333, 0., 1.}, {0., 0., 0.333333, 0.}}

This uses the array of values as gray levels in a raster.

In[16]:= **Show[Graphics[Raster[%]]]**

This shows two overlapping copies of the raster.

In[17]:= **Show[Graphics[{Raster[modtab, {{0, 0}, {2, 2}}],**
                               Raster[modtab, {{1.5, 1.5}, {3, 2}}]}]]

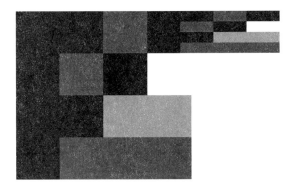

In the default case, `Raster` always generates an array of gray cells. As described on page 517, you can use the option `ColorFunction` to apply a "coloring function" to all the cells.

You can also use the graphics primitive `RasterArray`. While `Raster` takes an array of *values*, `RasterArray` takes an array of *Mathematica graphics directives*. The directives associated with each cell are taken to determine the color of that cell. Typically the directives are chosen from the set `GrayLevel`, `RGBColor` or `Hue`. By using `RGBColor` and `Hue` directives, you can create color rasters using `RasterArray`.

■ 2.10.3 Graphics Directives and Options

When you set up a graphics object in *Mathematica*, you typically give a list of graphical elements. You can include in that list *graphics directives* which specify how subsequent elements in the list should be rendered.

In general, the graphical elements in a particular graphics object can be given in a collection of nested lists. When you insert graphics directives in this kind of structure, the rule is that a particular graphics directive affects all subsequent elements of the list it is in, together with all elements of sublists that may occur. The graphics directive does not, however, have any effect outside the list it is in.

The first sublist contains the graphics directive GrayLevel.

```
In[1]:= {{GrayLevel[0.5], Rectangle[{0, 0}, {1, 1}]},
         Rectangle[{1, 1}, {2, 2}]}

Out[1]= {{GrayLevel[0.5], Rectangle[{0, 0}, {1, 1}]},
         Rectangle[{1, 1}, {2, 2}]}
```

Only the rectangle in the first sublist is affected by the GrayLevel directive.

```
In[2]:= Show[Graphics[ % ]]
```

Mathematica provides various kinds of graphics directives. One important set is those for specifying the colors of graphical elements. Even if you have a black-and-white display device, you can still give color graphics directives. The colors you specify will be converted to gray levels at the last step in the graphics rendering process. Note that you can get gray-level display even on a color device by setting the option ColorOutput -> GrayLevel.

GrayLevel[i]	gray level between 0 (black) and 1 (white)
RGBColor[r, g, b]	color with specified red, green and blue components, each between 0 and 1
Hue[h]	color with hue h between 0 and 1
Hue[h, s, b]	color with specified hue, saturation and brightness, each between 0 and 1

Basic *Mathematica* color specifications.

On a color display, the two curves are shown in color. In black and white they are shown in gray.

```
In[3]:= Plot[{BesselI[1, x], BesselI[2, x]}, {x, 0, 5},
          PlotStyle ->
            {{RGBColor[1, 0, 0]}, {RGBColor[0, 1, 0]}}]
```

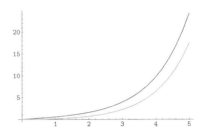

The function Hue[*h*] provides a convenient way to specify a range of colors using just one parameter. As *h* varies from 0 to 1, Hue[*h*] runs through red, yellow, green, cyan, blue, magenta, and back to red again. Hue[*h*, *s*, *b*] allows you to specify not only the "hue", but also the "saturation" and "brightness" of a color. Taking the saturation to be equal to one gives the deepest colors; decreasing the saturation toward zero leads to progressively more "washed out" colors.

For most purposes, you will be able to specify the colors you need simply by giving appropriate RGBColor or Hue directives. However, if you need very precise or repeatable colors, particularly for color printing, there are a number of subtleties which arise, as discussed in Section 2.10.17.

When you give a graphics directive such as RGBColor, it affects *all* subsequent graphical elements that appear in a particular list. *Mathematica* also supports various graphics directives which affect only specific types of graphical elements.

The graphics directive PointSize[*d*] specifies that all Point elements which appear in a graphics object should be drawn as circles with diameter *d*. In PointSize, the diameter *d* is measured as a fraction of the width of your whole plot.

Mathematica also provides the graphics directive AbsolutePointSize[*d*], which allows you to specify the "absolute" diameter of points, measured in fixed units. The units are $\frac{1}{72}$ of an inch, approximately printer's points.

PointSize[*d*]	give all points a diameter *d* as a fraction of the width of the whole plot
AbsolutePointSize[*d*]	give all points a diameter *d* measured in absolute units

Graphics directives for points.

Here is a list of points.

```
In[4]:= Table[Point[{n, Prime[n]}], {n, 6}]

Out[4]= {Point[{1, 2}], Point[{2, 3}], Point[{3, 5}],
          Point[{4, 7}], Point[{5, 11}], Point[{6, 13}]}
```

This makes each point have a diameter equal to one-tenth of the width of the plot.

In[5]:= **Show[Graphics[{PointSize[0.1], %}], PlotRange -> All]**

Here each point has size 3 in absolute units.

In[6]:= **ListPlot[Table[Prime[n], {n, 20}],**
**   Prolog -> AbsolutePointSize[3]]**

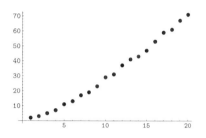

Thickness[w]	give all lines a thickness w as a fraction of the width of the whole plot
AbsoluteThickness[w]	give all lines a thickness w measured in absolute units
Dashing[{w_1, w_2, ... }]	show all lines as a sequence of dashed segments, with lengths w_1, w_2, ...
AbsoluteDashing[{w_1, w_2, ... }]	use absolute units to measure dashed segments

Graphics directives for lines.

This generates a list of lines with different absolute thicknesses.

```
In[7]:= Table[
           {AbsoluteThickness[n], Line[{{0, 0}, {n, 1}}]}, {n, 4}]
```

```
Out[7]= {{AbsoluteThickness[1], Line[{{0, 0}, {1, 1}}]},
          {AbsoluteThickness[2], Line[{{0, 0}, {2, 1}}]},
          {AbsoluteThickness[3], Line[{{0, 0}, {3, 1}}]},
          {AbsoluteThickness[4], Line[{{0, 0}, {4, 1}}]}}
```

Here is a picture of the lines.

```
In[8]:= Show[Graphics[%]]
```

The Dashing graphics directive allows you to create lines with various kinds of dashing. The basic idea is to break lines into segments which are alternately drawn and omitted. By changing the lengths of the segments, you can get different line styles. Dashing allows you to specify a sequence of segment lengths. This sequence is repeated as many times as necessary in drawing the whole line.

This gives a dashed line with a succession of equal-length segments.

```
In[9]:= Show[Graphics[ {Dashing[{0.05, 0.05}],
                         Line[{{-1, -1}, {1, 1}}]} ]]
```

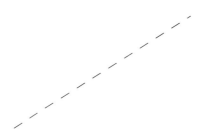

This gives a dot-dashed line.

In[10]:= **Show[Graphics[{Dashing[{0.01, 0.05, 0.05, 0.05}],**
Line[{{-1, -1}, {1, 1}}]}]]

One way to use *Mathematica* graphics directives is to insert them directly into the lists of graphics primitives used by graphics objects. Sometimes, however, you want the graphics directives to be applied more globally, and for example to determine the overall "style" with which a particular type of graphical element should be rendered. There are typically graphics options which can be set to specify such styles in terms of lists of graphics directives.

PlotStyle -> *style*	specify a style to be used for all curves in Plot
PlotStyle -> {{*style₁*}, {*style₂*}, ... }	specify styles to be used (cyclically) for a sequence of curves in Plot
MeshStyle -> *style*	specify a style to be used for a mesh in density and surface graphics
BoxStyle -> *style*	specify a style to be used for the bounding box in three-dimensional graphics

Some graphics options for specifying styles.

This generates a plot in which the curve is given in a style specified by graphics directives.

In[11]:= **Plot[BesselJ[2, x], {x, 0, 10},**
PlotStyle -> {{Thickness[0.02], GrayLevel[0.5]}}]

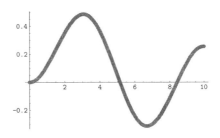

GrayLevel[0.5]	gray
RGBColor[1, 0, 0], etc.	red, etc.
Thickness[0.05]	thick
Dashing[{0.05, 0.05}]	dashed
Dashing[{0.01, 0.05, 0.05, 0.05}]	dot-dashed

Some typical styles.

The various "style options" allow you to specify how particular graphical elements in a plot should be rendered. *Mathematica* also provides options that affect the rendering of the whole plot.

Background -> *color*	specify the background color for a plot
DefaultColor -> *color*	specify the default color for a plot
Prolog -> *g*	give graphics to render before a plot is started
Epilog -> *g*	give graphics to render after a plot is finished

Graphics options that affect whole plots.

This draws the whole plot on a gray background.

In[12]:= **Plot[Sin[Sin[x]], {x, 0, 10},**
              Background -> GrayLevel[0.6]]

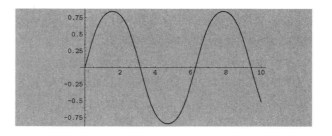

This makes the default color white.   *In[13]:=* **Show[%, DefaultColor -> GrayLevel[1]]**

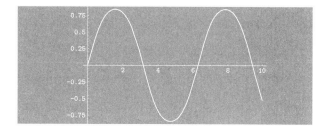

■ 2.10.4 Coordinate Systems for Two-Dimensional Graphics

When you set up a graphics object in *Mathematica*, you give coordinates for the various graphical elements that appear. When *Mathematica* renders the graphics object, it has to translate the original coordinates you gave into "display coordinates" which specify where each element should be placed in the final display area.

Sometimes, you may find it convenient to specify the display coordinates for a graphical element directly. You can do this by using "scaled coordinates" Scaled[{sx, sy}] rather than {x, y}. The scaled coordinates are defined to run from 0 to 1 in x and y, with the origin taken to be at the lower-left corner of the display area.

{x, y}	original coordinates
Scaled[{sx, sy}]	scaled coordinates

Coordinate systems for two-dimensional graphics.

The rectangle is drawn at a fixed position relative to the display area, independent of the original coordinates used for the plot.

In[1]:= **Plot[Tan[x], {x, 0, 2Pi},**
        Prolog ->
            Rectangle[Scaled[{0.7, 0.7}], Scaled[{1, 1}]]]

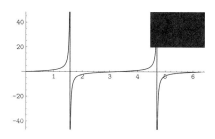

When you use {*x*, *y*} or `Scaled[{`*sx*, *sy*`}]`, you are specifying position either completely in original coordinates, or completely in scaled coordinates. Sometimes, however, you may need to use a combination of these coordinate systems. For example, if you want to draw a line at a particular point whose length is a definite fraction of the width of the plot, you will have to use original coordinates to specify the basic position of the line, and scaled coordinates to specify its length.

You can use `Scaled[{`*dsx*, *dsy*`}`, {*x*, *y*`}]` to specify a position using a mixture of original and scaled coordinates. In this case, {*x*, *y*} gives a position in original coordinates, and {*dsx*, *dsy*} gives the offset from the position in scaled coordinates.

Note that you can use `Scaled` with either one or two arguments to specify radii in `Disk` and `Circle` graphics elements.

`Scaled[{`*sdx*, *sdy*`}`, {*x*, *y*`}]`	scaled offset from original coordinates
`Offset[{`*adx*, *ady*`}`, {*x*, *y*`}]`	absolute offset from original coordinates
`Offset[{`*adx*, *ady*`}`, `Scaled[{`*sx*, *sy*`}]]`	absolute offset from scaled coordinates

Positions specified as offsets.

Each line drawn here has an absolute length of 6 printer's points.

```
In[2]:= Show[Graphics[Table[
            Line[{{x, x^2}, Offset[{0, 6}, {x, x^2}]}],
            {x, 10}], Frame->True]]
```

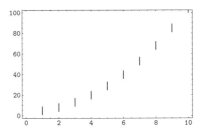

You can also use `Offset` inside `Circle` with just one argument to create a circle with a certain absolute radius.

In[3]:= `Show[Graphics[Table[`
       `Circle[{x, x^2}, Offset[{2, 2}]],`
       `{x, 10}], Frame->True]]`

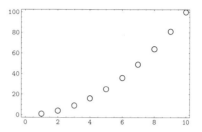

In most kinds of graphics, you typically want the relative positions of different objects to adjust automatically when you change the coordinates or the overall size of your plot. But sometimes you may instead want the offset from one object to another to be constrained to remain fixed. This can be the case, for example, when you are making a collection of plots in which you want certain features to remain consistent, even though the different plots have different forms.

`Offset[{`*adx*`, `*ady*`}, `*position*`]` allows you to specify the position of an object by giving an absolute offset from a position that is specified in original or scaled coordinates. The units for the offset are printer's points, equal to $\frac{1}{72}$ of an inch.

When you give text in a plot, the size of the font that is used is also specified in printer's points. A 10-point font, for example, therefore has letters whose basic height is 10 printer's points. You can use `Offset` to move text around in a plot, and to create plotting symbols or icons which match the size of text.

`PlotRange -> {{`*xmin*`, `*xmax*`}, {`*ymin*`, `*ymax*`}}`
 the range of original coordinates to include in the plot

`PlotRegion -> {{`*sxmin*`, `*sxmax*`}, {`*symin*`, `*symax*`}}`
 the region of the display specified in scaled coordinates which the plot fills

---

Options which determine translation from original to display coordinates.

When *Mathematica* renders a graphics object, one of the first things it has to do is to work out what range of original x and y coordinates it should actually display. Any graphical elements that are outside this range will be "clipped", and not shown.

The option `PlotRange` specifies the range of original coordinates to include. As discussed on page 136, the default setting is `PlotRange -> Automatic`, which makes *Mathematica* try to choose a range which includes all "interesting" parts of a plot, while dropping "outliers". By setting

PlotRange -> All, you can tell *Mathematica* to include everything. You can also give explicit ranges of coordinates to include.

This sets up a polygonal object whose corners have coordinates between roughly ±1.

```
In[4]:= obj = Polygon[
             Table[{Sin[n Pi/10], Cos[n Pi/10]} + 0.05 (-1)^n,
                                    {n, 20}]] ;
```

In this case, the polygonal object fills almost the whole display area.

```
In[5]:= Show[Graphics[obj]]
```

With the default PlotRange -> Automatic, the outlying point is not included, but does affect the range of coordinates chosen.

```
In[6]:= Show[ Graphics[{obj, Point[{20, 20}]}] ]
```

With PlotRange -> All, the outlying point is included, and the coordinate system is correspondingly modified.

```
In[7]:= Show[%, PlotRange -> All]
```

The option PlotRange allows you to specify a rectangular region in the original coordinate system, and to drop any graphical elements that lie outside this region. In order to render the remaining elements, however, *Mathematica* then has to determine how to position this rectangular region with respect to the final display area.

The option `PlotRegion` allows you to specify where the corners of the rectangular region lie within the final display area. The positions of the corners are specified in scaled coordinates, which are defined to run from 0 to 1 across the display area. The default is `PlotRegion -> {{0, 1}, {0, 1}}`, which specifies that the rectangular region should fill the whole display area.

By specifying `PlotRegion`, you can effectively add "margins" around your plot.

```
In[8]:= Plot[ArcTan[x], {x, 0, 10},
              PlotRegion -> {{0.2, 0.8}, {0.3, 0.7}}]
```

AspectRatio -> r	make the ratio of height to width for the display area equal to r
AspectRatio -> Automatic	determine the shape of the display area from the original coordinate system

Specifying the shape of the display area.

What we have discussed so far is how *Mathematica* translates the original coordinates you specify into positions in the final display area. What remains to discuss, however, is what the final display area is like.

On most computer systems, there is a certain fixed region of screen or paper into which the *Mathematica* display area must fit. How it fits into this region is determined by its "shape" or aspect ratio. In general, the option `AspectRatio` specifies the ratio of height to width for the final display area.

It is important to note that the setting of `AspectRatio` does not affect the meaning of the scaled or display coordinates. These coordinates always run from 0 to 1 across the display area. What `AspectRatio` does is to change the shape of this display area.

This generates a graphic object corresponding to a hexagon.

```
In[9]:= hex = Graphics[Polygon[
              Table[{Sin[n Pi/3], Cos[n Pi/3]}, {n, 6}] ]] ;
```

This renders the hexagon in a display area whose height is three times its width.

In[10]:= **Show[hex, AspectRatio -> 3]**

For two-dimensional graphics, AspectRatio is set by default to the fixed value of 1/GoldenRatio. Sometimes, however, you may want to determine the aspect ratio for a plot from the original coordinate system used in the plot. Typically what you want is for one unit in the x direction in the original coordinate system to correspond to the same distance in the final display as one unit in the y direction. In this way, objects that you define in the original coordinate system are displayed with their "natural shape". You can make this happen by setting the option AspectRatio -> Automatic.

With AspectRatio -> Automatic, the aspect ratio of the final display area is determined from the original coordinate system, and the hexagon is shown with its "natural shape".

In[11]:= **Show[hex, AspectRatio -> Automatic]**

Using scaled coordinates, you can specify the sizes of graphical elements as fractions of the size of the display area. You cannot, however, tell *Mathematica* the actual physical size at which a particular graphical element should be rendered. Of course, this size ultimately depends on the details of your graphics output device, and cannot be determined for certain within *Mathematica*. Nevertheless, graphics directives such as AbsoluteThickness discussed on page 501 do allow you to indicate "absolute sizes" to use for particular graphical elements. The sizes you request in this way will be respected by most, but not all, output devices. (For example, if you optically project an image, it is neither possible nor desirable to maintain the same absolute size for a graphical element within it.)

■ 2.10.5 Labeling Two-Dimensional Graphics

Axes -> True	give a pair of axes
GridLines -> Automatic	draw grid lines on the plot
Frame -> True	put axes on a frame around the plot
PlotLabel -> "*text*"	give an overall label for the plot

Ways to label two-dimensional plots.

Here is a plot, using the default
Axes -> True.

In[1]:= **bp = Plot[BesselJ[2, x], {x, 0, 10}]**

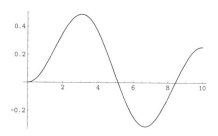

Setting Frame -> True generates a
frame with axes, and removes tick
marks from the ordinary axes.

In[2]:= **Show[bp, Frame -> True]**

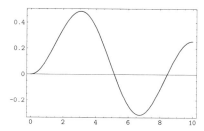

This includes grid lines, which are
shown in light blue on color displays.

In[3]:= **Show[%, GridLines -> Automatic]**

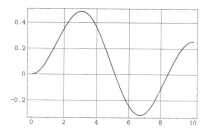

`Axes -> False`	draw no axes
`Axes -> True`	draw both x and y axes
`Axes -> {False, True}`	draw a y axis but no x axis
`AxesOrigin -> Automatic`	choose the crossing point for the axes automatically
`AxesOrigin -> {x, y}`	specify the crossing point
`AxesStyle -> style`	specify the style for axes
`AxesStyle -> {{xstyle}, {ystyle}}`	specify individual styles for axes
`AxesLabel -> None`	give no axis labels
`AxesLabel -> ylabel`	put a label on the y axis
`AxesLabel -> {xlabel, ylabel}`	put labels on both x and y axes

Options for axes.

This makes the axes cross at the point {5, 0}, and puts a label on each axis.

`In[4]:= Show[bp, AxesOrigin->{5, 0}, AxesLabel->{"x", "y"}]`

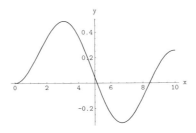

`Ticks -> None`	draw no tick marks
`Ticks -> Automatic`	place tick marks automatically
`Ticks -> {xticks, yticks}`	tick mark specifications for each axis

Settings for the `Ticks` option.

With the default setting `Ticks -> Automatic`, *Mathematica* creates a certain number of major and minor tick marks, and places them on axes at positions which yield the minimum number of decimal digits in the tick labels. In some cases, however, you may want to specify the positions and properties of tick marks explicitly. You will need to do this, for example, if you want to have tick marks at multiples of π, or if you want to put a nonlinear scale on an axis.

None	draw no tick marks
Automatic	place tick marks automatically
$\{x_1, x_2, \ldots \}$	draw tick marks at the specified positions
$\{\{x_1, label_1\}, \{x_2, label_2\}, \ldots \}$	draw tick marks with the specified labels
$\{\{x_1, label_1, len_1\}, \ldots \}$	draw tick marks with the specified scaled lengths
$\{\{x_1, label_1, \{plen_1, mlen_1\}\}, \ldots \}$	draw tick marks with the specified lengths in the positive and negative directions
$\{\{x_1, label_1, len_1, style_1\}, \ldots \}$	draw tick marks with the specified styles
func	a function to be applied to *xmin, xmax* to get the tick mark option

Tick mark options for each axis.

This gives tick marks at specified positions on the *x* axis, and chooses the tick marks automatically on the *y* axis.

In[5]:= **Show[bp, Ticks -> {{0, Pi, 2Pi, 3Pi}, Automatic}]**

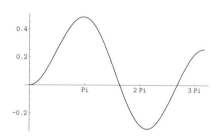

This adds tick marks with no labels at multiples of $\pi/2$.

In[6]:= **Show[bp,
    Ticks -> {{0, {Pi/2, ""}, Pi, {3Pi/2, ""},
        2Pi, {5Pi/2, ""}, 3Pi}, Automatic}]**

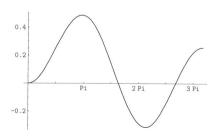

Particularly when you want to create complicated tick mark specifications, it is often convenient to define a "tick mark function" which creates the appropriate tick mark specification given the minimum and maximum values on a particular axis.

This defines a function which gives a list of tick mark positions with a spacing of 1.	`In[7]:= units[xmin_, xmax_] :=` `                    Range[Floor[xmin], Floor[xmax], 1]`
This uses the `units` function to specify tick marks for the *x* axis.	`In[8]:= Show[bp, Ticks -> {units, Automatic}]`

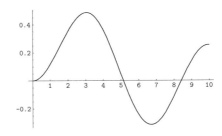

Sometimes you may want to generate tick marks which differ only slightly from those produced automatically with the setting `Ticks -> Automatic`. You can get the complete specification for tick marks that were generated automatically in a particular plot by using `AbsoluteOptions[g, Ticks]`, as discussed on page 490.

`Frame -> False`	draw no frame
`Frame -> True`	draw a frame around the plot
`FrameStyle -> style`	specify a style for the frame
`FrameStyle -> {{xmstyle}, {ymstyle}, ... }`	specify styles for each edge of the frame
`FrameLabel -> None`	give no frame labels
`FrameLabel -> {xmlabel, ymlabel, ... }`	put labels on edges of the frame
`RotateLabel -> False`	do not rotate text in labels
`FrameTicks -> None`	draw no tick marks on frame edges
`FrameTicks -> Automatic`	position tick marks automatically
`FrameTicks -> {{xmticks, ymticks, ... }}`	specify tick marks for frame edges

Options for frame axes.

The `Axes` option allows you to draw a single pair of axes in a plot. Sometimes, however, you may instead want to show the scales for a plot on a frame, typically drawn around the whole plot. The option `Frame` allows you effectively to draw four axes, corresponding to the four edges of the frame around a plot. These four axes are ordered clockwise, starting from the one at the bottom.

<table>
<tr><td>This draws frame axes, and labels each of them.</td><td>In[9]:= Show[bp, Frame -> True,
        FrameLabel -> {"label 1", "label 2",
                  "label 3", "label 4"}]</td></tr>
</table>

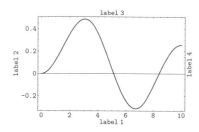

`GridLines -> None`	draw no grid lines
`GridLines -> Automatic`	position grid lines automatically
`GridLines -> {xgrid, ygrid}`	specify grid lines in analogy with tick marks

Options for grid lines.

Grid lines in *Mathematica* work very much like tick marks. As with tick marks, you can specify explicit positions for grid lines. There is no label or length to specify for grid lines. However, you can specify a style.

This generates *x* but not *y* grid lines.   *In[10]:=* **Show[bp, GridLines -> {Automatic, None}]**

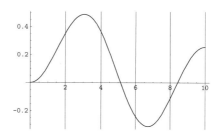

■ 2.10.6 Making Plots within Plots

Section 1.9.3 described how you can make regular arrays of plots using GraphicsArray. Using the Rectangle graphics primitive, however, you can combine and superimpose plots in any way.

Rectangle[{*xmin*, *ymin*}, {*xmax*, *ymax*}, *graphics*]
                    render a graphics object within the specified rectangle

Creating a subplot.

Here is a three-dimensional plot.   *In[1]:=* **p3 = Plot3D[Sin[x] Exp[y], {x, -5, 5}, {y, -2, 2}]**

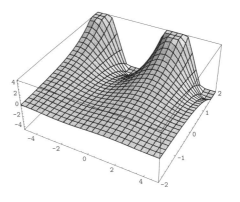

This creates a two-dimensional   *In[2]:=* **Show[Graphics[{Rectangle[{0, 0}, {1, 1}, p3],**
graphics object which contains two   **Rectangle[{0.8, 0.8}, {1.2, 1.4}, p3]}]]**
copies of the three-dimensional plot.

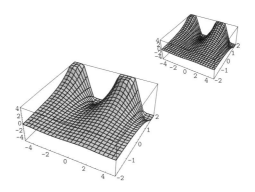

Mathematica can render any graphics object within a `Rectangle`. In all cases, what it puts in the rectangle is a scaled down version of what would be obtained if you displayed the graphics object on its own. Notice that in general the display area for the graphics object will be sized so as to touch at least one pair of edges of the rectangle.

■ 2.10.7 Density and Contour Plots

`DensityGraphics[`*array*`]`	density plot
`ContourGraphics[`*array*`]`	contour plot

Graphics objects that represent density and contour plots.

The functions `DensityPlot` and `ContourPlot` discussed in Section 1.9.5 work by creating `ContourGraphics` and `DensityGraphics` objects containing arrays of values.

Most of the options for density and contour plots are the same as those for ordinary two-dimensional plots. There are, however, a few additional options.

option name	default value	
`ColorFunction`	`Automatic`	how to assign colors to each cell
`ColorFunctionScaling`	`True`	whether to scale values before applying a color function
`Mesh`	`True`	whether to draw a mesh
`MeshStyle`	`Automatic`	a style for the mesh

Additional options for density plots.

In a density plot, the color of each cell represents its value. By default, each cell is assigned a gray level, running from black to white as the value of the cell increases. In general, however, you can specify other "color maps" for the relation between the value of a cell and its color. The option `ColorFunction` allows you to specify a function which is applied to each cell value to find the color of the cell. With `ColorFunctionScaling->True` the cell values are scaled so as to run between 0 and 1 in a particular density plot; with `ColorFunctionScaling->False` no such scaling is performed. The function you give as the setting for `ColorFunction` may return any *Mathematica* color directive, such as `GrayLevel`, `Hue` or `RGBColor`. A common setting to use is `ColorFunction -> Hue`.

Here is a density plot with the default ColorFunction.

In[1]:= **DensityPlot[Sin[x y], {x, -1, 1}, {y, -1, 1}]**

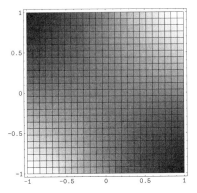

This gives a density plot with a different "color map".

In[2]:= **Show[%, ColorFunction -> (GrayLevel[#^3]&)]**

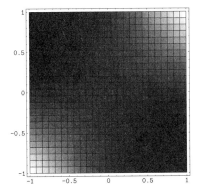

option name	default value	
Contours	10	what contours to use
ContourLines	True	whether to draw contour lines
ContourStyle	Automatic	style to use for contour lines
ContourShading	True	whether to shade regions in the plot
ColorFunction	Automatic	how to assign colors to contour levels
ColorFunctionScaling	True	whether to scale values before applying a color function

Options for contour plots.

In constructing a contour plot, the first issue is what contours to use. With the default setting Contours -> 10, *Mathematica* uses a sequence of 10 contour levels equally spaced between the minimum and maximum values defined by the PlotRange option.

Contours -> n	use a sequence of n equally spaced contours
Contours -> $\{z_1, z_2, \ldots\}$	use contours with values $z_1, z_2, \ldots$

Specifying contours.

This creates a contour plot with two contours.

$In[3]:=$ **ContourPlot[Sin[x y], {x, -1, 1}, {y, -1, 1}, Contours -> {-.5, .5}]**

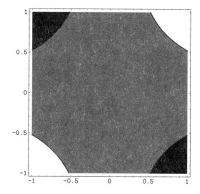

There are some slight subtleties associated with labeling density and contour plots. Both the Axes and Frame options from ordinary two-dimensional graphics can be used. But setting AxesOrigin -> Automatic keeps the axes outside the plot in both cases.

■ 2.10.8 Three-Dimensional Graphics Primitives

One of the most powerful aspects of graphics in *Mathematica* is the availability of three-dimensional as well as two-dimensional graphics primitives. By combining three-dimensional graphics primitives, you can represent and render three-dimensional objects in *Mathematica*.

Point[{x, y, z}]	point with coordinates x, y, z
Line[{{x_1, y_1, z_1}, {x_2, y_2, z_2}, ... }]	line through the points {x_1, y_1, z_1}, {x_2, y_2, z_2}, ...
Polygon[{{x_1, y_1, z_1}, {x_2, y_2, z_2}, ... }]	filled polygon with the specified list of corners
Cuboid[{$xmin$, $ymin$, $zmin$}, {$xmax$, $ymax$, $zmax$}]	cuboid
Text[$expr$, {x, y, z}]	text at position {x, y, z} (see Section 2.10.16)

Three-dimensional graphics elements.

Every time you evaluate rcoord, it generates a random coordinate in three dimensions.

```
In[1]:= rcoord := {Random[ ], Random[ ], Random[ ]}
```

This generates a list of 20 random points in three-dimensional space.

```
In[2]:= pts = Table[Point[rcoord], {20}] ;
```

Here is a plot of the points.

In[3]:= **Show[Graphics3D[pts]]**

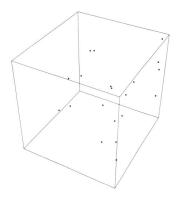

This gives a plot showing a line through 10 random points in three dimensions.

In[4]:= **Show[Graphics3D[Line[Table[rcoord, {10}]]]]**

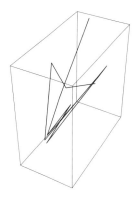

If you give a list of graphics elements in two dimensions, *Mathematica* simply draws each element in turn, with later elements obscuring earlier ones. In three dimensions, however, *Mathematica* collects together all the graphics elements you specify, then displays them as three-dimensional objects, with the ones in front in three-dimensional space obscuring those behind.

Every time you evaluate rantri, it generates a random triangle in three-dimensional space.

In[5]:= **rantri := Polygon[Table[rcoord, {3}]]**

This draws a single random triangle.   *In[6]:=* **Show[Graphics3D[rantri]]**

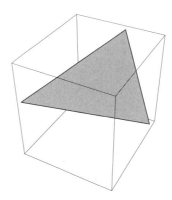

This draws a collection of 5 random triangles. The triangles in front obscure those behind.

In[7]:= **Show[Graphics3D[Table[rantri, {5}]]]**

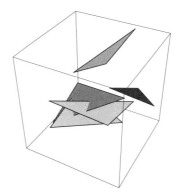

By creating an appropriate list of polygons, you can build up any three-dimensional object in *Mathematica*. Thus, for example, all the surfaces produced by `ParametricPlot3D` are represented simply as lists of polygons.

The package `Graphics`Polyhedra`` contains examples of lists of polygons which correspond to polyhedra in three dimensions.

This loads a package which defines various polyhedra.   *In[8]:=* **<<Graphics`Polyhedra`**

Here is the list of polygons corresponding to a tetrahedron centered at the origin.

```
In[9]:= Tetrahedron[ ]

Out[9]= {Polygon[
            {{0., 0., 1.73205}, {0., 1.63299, -0.57735},
            {-1.41421, -0.816497, -0.57735}}],
         Polygon[{{0., 0., 1.73205}, {-1.41421, -0.816497,
            -0.57735}, {1.41421, -0.816497, -0.57735}}],
         Polygon[{{0., 0., 1.73205}, {1.41421, -0.816497,
            -0.57735}, {0., 1.63299, -0.57735}}],
         Polygon[{{0., 1.63299, -0.57735},
            {1.41421, -0.816497, -0.57735},
            {-1.41421, -0.816497, -0.57735}}]]}
```

This displays the tetrahedron as a three-dimensional object.

```
In[10]:= Show[ Graphics3D[ % ] ]
```

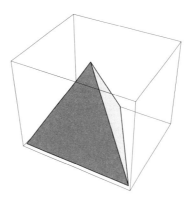

Dodecahedron[ ] is another three-dimensional object defined in the polyhedra package.

```
In[11]:= Show[ Graphics3D[ Dodecahedron[ ] ] ]
```

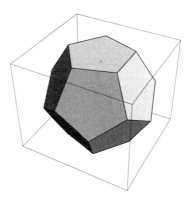

This shows four intersecting dodecahedra.

In[12]:= **Show[Graphics3D[**
                Table[Dodecahedron[0.8 {k, k, k}], {k, 0, 3}]]]

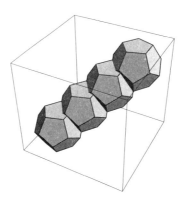

Mathematica allows polygons in three dimensions to have any number of vertices. However, these vertices should lie in a plane, and should form a convex figure. If they do not, then *Mathematica* will break the polygon into triangles, which are planar by definition, before rendering it.

Cuboid[{*x*, *y*, *z*}]	a unit cube with opposite corners having coordinates {*x*, *y*, *z*} and {*x*+1, *y*+1, *z*+1}
Cuboid[{*xmin*, *ymin*, *zmin*}, {*xmax*, *ymax*, *zmax*}]	
	a cuboid (rectangular parallelepiped) with opposite corners having the specified coordinates

Cuboid graphics elements.

This draws 20 random unit cubes in three-dimensional space.

In[13]:= **Show[Graphics3D[Table[Cuboid[10 rcoord], {20}]]]**

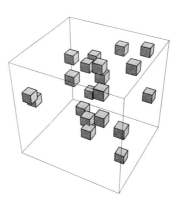

■ 2.10.9 Three-Dimensional Graphics Directives

In three dimensions, just as in two dimensions, you can give various graphics directives to specify how the different elements in a graphics object should be rendered.

All the graphics directives for two dimensions also work in three dimensions. There are however some additional directives in three dimensions.

Just as in two dimensions, you can use the directives PointSize, Thickness and Dashing to tell *Mathematica* how to render Point and Line elements. Note that in three dimensions, the lengths that appear in these directives are measured as fractions of the total width of the display area for your plot.

This generates a list of 20 random points in three dimensions.	`In[1]:= pts = Table[Point[Table[Random[ ], {3}]], {20}];`
This displays the points, with each one being a circle whose diameter is 5% of the display area width.	`In[2]:= Show[Graphics3D[ { PointSize[0.05], pts } ]]`

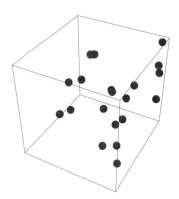

As in two dimensions, you can use AbsolutePointSize, AbsoluteThickness and AbsoluteDashing if you want to measure length in absolute units.

This generates a line through 10 random points in three dimensions.	`In[3]:= line = Line[Table[Random[ ], {10}, {3}]] ;`

This shows the line dashed, with a thickness of 2 printer's points.

In[4]:= **Show[Graphics3D[{ AbsoluteThickness[2],**
                  AbsoluteDashing[{5, 5}], line }]]

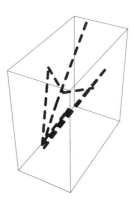

For `Point` and `Line` objects, the color specification directives also work the same in three dimensions as in two dimensions. For `Polygon` objects, however, they can work differently.

In two dimensions, polygons are always assumed to have an intrinsic color, specified directly by graphics directives such as `RGBColor`. In three dimensions, however, *Mathematica* also provides the option of generating colors for polygons using a more physical approach based on simulated illumination. With the default option setting `Lighting -> True` for `Graphics3D` objects, *Mathematica* ignores explicit colors specified for polygons, and instead determines all polygon colors using the simulated illumination model. Even in this case, however, explicit colors are used for points and lines.

`Lighting -> False`	intrinsic colors
`Lighting -> True`	colors based on simulated illumination (default)

The two schemes for coloring polygons in three dimensions.

This loads a package which defines various polyhedra.

In[5]:= **<<Graphics`Polyhedra`**

This draws an icosahedron, using the same gray level for all faces.

In[6]:= **Show[Graphics3D[{GrayLevel[0.7], Icosahedron[ ]}],**
Lighting -> False]

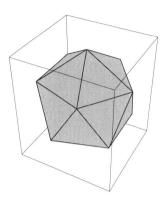

With the default setting
Lighting -> True, the colors of
polygons are determined by the
simulated illumination model, and
explicit color specifications are ignored.

In[7]:= **Show[%, Lighting -> True]**

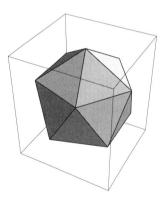

Explicit color directives are, however, always followed for points and lines.

```
In[8]:= Show[{%, Graphics3D[{GrayLevel[0.5], Thickness[0.05],
              Line[{{0, 0, -2}, {0, 0, 2}}]}]}]
```

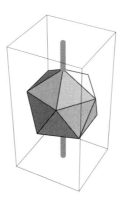

EdgeForm[ ]	draw no lines at the edges of polygons
EdgeForm[*g*]	use the graphics directives *g* to determine how to draw lines at the edges of polygons

Giving graphics directives for all the edges of polygons.

When you render a three-dimensional graphics object in *Mathematica*, there are two kinds of lines that can appear. The first kind are lines from explicit Line primitives that you included in the graphics object. The second kind are lines that were generated as the edges of polygons.

You can tell *Mathematica* how to render all lines of the second kind by giving a list of graphics directives inside EdgeForm.

This renders a dodecahedron with its edges shown as thick gray lines.

```
In[9]:= Show[Graphics3D[
              {EdgeForm[{GrayLevel[0.5], Thickness[0.02]}],
               Dodecahedron[ ]}]]
```

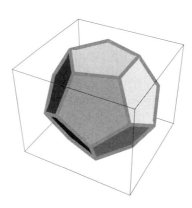

FaceForm[*gfront*, *gback*]	use *gfront* graphics directives for the front face of each polygon, and *gback* for the back

Rendering the fronts and backs of polygons differently.

An important aspect of polygons in three dimensions is that they have both front and back faces. *Mathematica* uses the following convention to define the "front face" of a polygon: if you look at a polygon from the front, then the corners of the polygon will appear counterclockwise, when taken in the order that you specified them.

This defines a dodecahedron with one face removed.

In[10]:= **d = Drop[Dodecahedron[ ], {6}] ;**

You can now see inside the dodecahedron.

In[11]:= **Show[Graphics3D[d]]**

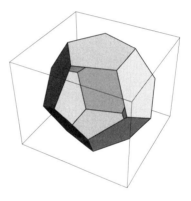

This makes the front (outside) face of each polygon light gray, and the back (inside) face dark gray.

In[12]:= **Show[Graphics3D[**
{FaceForm[GrayLevel[0.8], GrayLevel[0.3]], d}],
Lighting -> False]

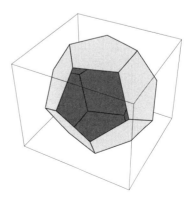

■ 2.10.10 Coordinate Systems for Three-Dimensional Graphics

Whenever *Mathematica* draws a three-dimensional object, it always effectively puts a cuboidal box around the object. With the default option setting Boxed -> True, *Mathematica* in fact draws the edges of this box explicitly. But in general, *Mathematica* automatically "clips" any parts of your object that extend outside of the cuboidal box.

The option PlotRange specifies the range of *x*, *y* and *z* coordinates that *Mathematica* should include in the box. As in two dimensions the default setting is PlotRange -> Automatic, which makes *Mathematica* use an internal algorithm to try and include the "interesting parts" of a plot, but drop outlying parts. With PlotRange -> All, *Mathematica* will include all parts.

This loads a package defining various polyhedra.	In[1]:= **<<Graphics`Polyhedra`**
This creates a stellated icosahedron.	In[2]:= **stel = Stellate[Icosahedron[ ]] ;**
Here is the stellated icosahedron, drawn in a box.	In[3]:= **Show[Graphics3D[stel], Axes -> True]**

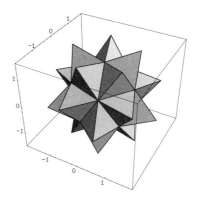

With this setting for PlotRange, many parts of the stellated icosahedron lie outside the box, and are clipped.	In[4]:= **Show[%, PlotRange -> {-1, 1}]**

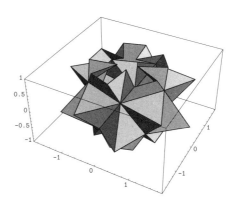

Much as in two dimensions, you can use either "original" or "scaled" coordinates to specify the positions of elements in three-dimensional objects. Scaled coordinates, specified as Scaled[{sx, sy, sz}] are taken to run from 0 to 1 in each dimension. The coordinates are set up to define a right-handed coordinate system on the box.

{x, y, z}	original coordinates
Scaled[{sx, sy, sz}]	scaled coordinates, running from 0 to 1 in each dimension

Coordinate systems for three-dimensional objects.

This puts a cuboid in one corner of the box.

```
In[5]:= Show[Graphics3D[{stel,
            Cuboid[Scaled[{0, 0, 0}],
                Scaled[{0.2, 0.2, 0.2}]]}]]
```

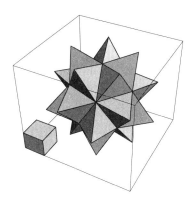

Once you have specified where various graphical elements go inside a three-dimensional box, you must then tell *Mathematica* how to draw the box. The first step is to specify what shape the box should be. This is analogous to specifying the aspect ratio of a two-dimensional plot. In three dimensions, you can use the option BoxRatios to specify the ratio of side lengths for the box. For Graphics3D objects, the default is BoxRatios -> Automatic, specifying that the shape of the box should be determined from the ranges of actual coordinates for its contents.

BoxRatios -> {xr, yr, zr}	specify the ratio of side lengths for the box
BoxRatios -> Automatic	determine the ratio of side lengths from the range of actual coordinates (default for Graphics3D)
BoxRatios -> {1, 1, 0.4}	specify a fixed shape of box (default for SurfaceGraphics)

Specifying the shape of the bounding box for three-dimensional objects.

This displays the stellated icosahedron in a tall box.

In[6]:= **Show[Graphics3D[stel], BoxRatios -> {1, 1, 5}]**

To produce an image of a three-dimensional object, you have to tell *Mathematica* from what view point you want to look at the object. You can do this using the option `ViewPoint`.

Some common settings for this option were given on page 153. In general, however, you can tell *Mathematica* to use any view point, so long as it lies outside the box.

View points are specified in the form `ViewPoint -> {sx, sy, sz}`. The values *si* are given in a special coordinate system, in which the center of the box is {0, 0, 0}. The special coordinates are scaled so that the longest side of the box corresponds to one unit. The lengths of the other sides of the box in this coordinate system are determined by the setting for the `BoxRatios` option. For a cubical box, therefore, each of the special coordinates runs from −1/2 to 1/2 across the box. Note that the view point must always lie outside the box.

This generates a picture using the default view point {1.3, -2.4, 2}.

In[7]:= **surf = Plot3D[(2 + Sin[x]) Cos[2 y],**
        {x, -2, 2}, {y, -3, 3},
            AxesLabel -> {"x", "y", "z"}]

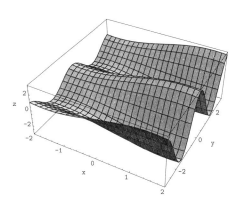

This is what you get with a view point close to one of the corners of the box.

In[8]:= **Show[surf, ViewPoint -> {1.2, 1.2, 1.2}]**

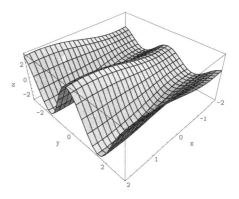

As you move away from the box, the perspective effect gets smaller.

In[9]:= **Show[surf, ViewPoint -> {5, 5, 5}]**

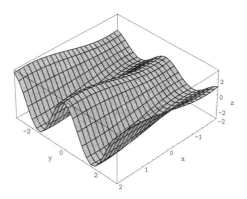

option name	*default value*	
ViewPoint	{1.3, -2.4, 2}	the point in a special scaled coordinate system from which to view the object
ViewCenter	Automatic	the point in the scaled coordinate system which appears at the center of the final image
ViewVertical	{0, 0, 1}	the direction in the scaled coordinate system which appears as vertical in the final image

Specifying the position and orientation of three-dimensional objects.

In making a picture of a three-dimensional object you have to specify more than just *where* you want to look at the object from. You also have to specify how you want to "frame" the object in your final image. You can do this using the additional options `ViewCenter` and `ViewVertical`.

`ViewCenter` allows you to tell *Mathematica* what point in the object should appear at the center of your final image. The point is specified by giving its scaled coordinates, running from 0 to 1 in each direction across the box. With the setting `ViewCenter -> {1/2, 1/2, 1/2}`, the center of the box will therefore appear at the center of your final image. With many choices of view point, however, the box will not appear symmetrical, so this setting for `ViewCenter` will not center the whole box in the final image area. You can do this by setting `ViewCenter -> Automatic`.

`ViewVertical` specifies which way up the object should appear in your final image. The setting for `ViewVertical` gives the direction in scaled coordinates which ends up vertical in the final image. With the default setting `ViewVertical -> {0, 0, 1}`, the *z* direction in your original coordinate system always ends up vertical in the final image.

With this setting for `ViewCenter`, a corner of the box appears in the center of your image.

In[10]:= **Show[surf, ViewCenter -> {1, 1, 1}]**

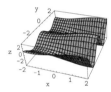

This setting for `ViewVertical` makes the *x* axis of the box appear vertical in your image.

In[11]:= **Show[surf, ViewVertical -> {1, 0, 0}]**

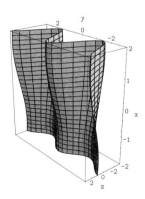

When you set the options `ViewPoint`, `ViewCenter` and `ViewVertical`, you can think about it as specifying how you would look at a physical object. `ViewPoint` specifies where your head is relative to the object. `ViewCenter` specifies where you are looking (the center of your gaze). And `ViewVertical` specifies which way up your head is.

In terms of coordinate systems, settings for `ViewPoint`, `ViewCenter` and `ViewVertical` specify how coordinates in the three-dimensional box should be transformed into coordinates for your image in the final display area.

For some purposes, it is useful to think of the coordinates in the final display area as three dimensional. The x and y axes run horizontally and vertically, respectively, while the z axis points out of the page. Positions specified in this "display coordinate system" remain fixed when you change `ViewPoint` and so on. The positions of light sources discussed in the next section are defined in this display coordinate system.

Box coordinate system	measured relative to the box around your object
Display coordinate system	measured relative to your final display area

Coordinate systems for three-dimensional graphics.

Once you have obtained a two-dimensional image of a three-dimensional object, there are still some issues about how this image should be rendered. The issues however are identical to those that occur for two-dimensional graphics. Thus, for example, you can modify the final shape of your image by changing the `AspectRatio` option. And you specify what region of your whole display area your image should take up by setting the `PlotRegion` option.

This modifies the aspect ratio of the final image.

`In[12]:= ` **`Show[surf, Axes -> False, AspectRatio -> 0.3]`**

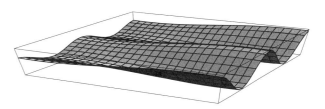

Mathematica usually scales the images of three-dimensional objects to be as large as possible, given the display area you specify. Although in most cases this scaling is what you want, it does have the consequence that the size at which a particular three-dimensional object is drawn may vary with the orientation of the object. You can set the option `SphericalRegion -> True` to avoid such variation. With this option setting, *Mathematica* effectively puts a sphere around the three-dimensional bounding box, and scales the final image so that the whole of this sphere fits inside the display area you specify. The sphere has its center at the center of the bounding box, and is drawn so that the bounding box just fits inside it.

This draws a rather elongated version of the plot.

`In[13]:= Show[surf, BoxRatios -> {1, 5, 1}]`

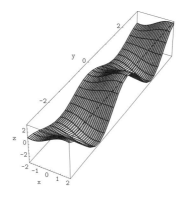

With `SphericalRegion -> True`, the final image is scaled so that a sphere placed around the bounding box would fit in the display area.

`In[14]:= Show[%, SphericalRegion -> True]`

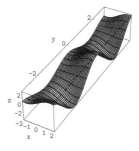

By setting `SphericalRegion -> True`, you can make the scaling of an object consistent for all orientations of the object. This is useful if you create animated sequences which show a particular object in several different orientations.

| SphericalRegion -> False | scale three-dimensional images to be as large as possible |
| SphericalRegion -> True | scale images so that a sphere drawn around the three-dimensional bounding box would fit in the final display area |

Changing the magnification of three-dimensional images.

■ 2.10.11 Plotting Three-Dimensional Surfaces

By giving an appropriate list of graphics primitives, you can represent essentially any three-dimensional object in *Mathematica* with `Graphics3D`. You can represent three-dimensional surfaces with `Graphics3D` by giving explicit lists of polygons with adjacent edges.

If you need to represent arbitrary surfaces which can fold over and perhaps intersect themselves, there is no choice but to use explicit lists of polygons with `Graphics3D`, as `ParametricPlot3D` does.

However, there are many cases in which you get simpler surfaces. For example, `Plot3D` and `ListPlot3D` yield surfaces which never fold over, and have a definite height at every x, y point. You can represent simple surfaces like these in *Mathematica* without giving an explicit list of polygons. Instead, all you need do is to give an array which specifies the z height at every point in an x, y grid. The graphics object `SurfaceGraphics[`*array*`]` represents a surface constructed in this way.

| Graphics3D[*primitives*] | arbitrary three-dimensional objects, including folded surfaces |
| SurfaceGraphics[*array*] | simple three-dimensional surfaces |

Three-dimensional graphics objects.

| Here is a 4×4 array of values. | *In[1]:=* **moda = Table[Mod[i, j], {i, 4}, {j, 4}]** |
| | *Out[1]=* {{0, 1, 1, 1}, {0, 0, 2, 2}, {0, 1, 0, 3}, {0, 0, 1, 0}} |

This uses the array to give the height of each point on the surface.

In[2]:= **Show[SurfaceGraphics[moda]]**

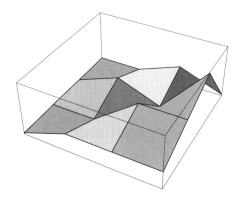

Both `Plot3D` and `ListPlot3D` work by creating `SurfaceGraphics` objects.

Graphics3D[*surface*]   convert SurfaceGraphics to Graphics3D

Converting between representations of surfaces.

If you apply `Graphics3D` to a `SurfaceGraphics` object, *Mathematica* will generate a `Graphics3D` object containing an explicit list of polygons representing the surface in the `SurfaceGraphics` object. Whenever you ask *Mathematica* to combine two `SurfaceGraphics` objects together, it automatically converts them both to `Graphics3D` objects.

Here is a surface represented by a `SurfaceGraphics` object.

In[3]:= **Plot3D[(1 - Sin[x]) (2 - Cos[2 y]),
                    {x, -2, 2}, {y, -2, 2}]**

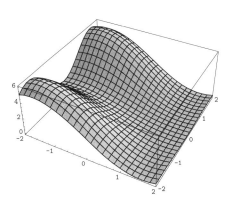

Here is another surface.

In[4]:= `Plot3D[(2 + Sin[x]) (1 + Cos[2 y]),`
`                {x, -2, 2}, {y, -2, 2}]`

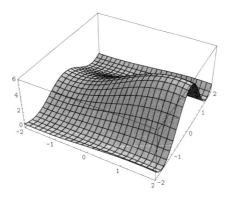

Mathematica shows the two surfaces together by converting each of them to a `Graphics3D` object containing an explicit list of polygons.

In[5]:= `Show[%, %%]`

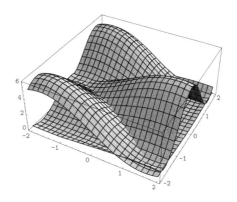

option name	default value	
Mesh	True	whether to draw a mesh on the surface
MeshStyle	Automatic	graphics directives specifying how to render the mesh
MeshRange	Automatic	the original range of coordinates corresponding to the mesh

Mesh options in `SurfaceGraphics`.

When you create a surface using `SurfaceGraphics`, the default is to draw a rectangular mesh on the surface. As discussed on page 154, including this mesh typically makes it easier for one to see the shape of the surface. You can nevertheless get rid of the mesh by setting the option `Mesh -> False`. You can also set the option `MeshStyle` to a list of graphics directives which specify thickness, color or other properties of the mesh lines.

A `SurfaceGraphics` object contains an array of values which specify the height of a surface at points in an x, y grid. By setting the option `MeshRange`, you can give the range of original x and y coordinates that correspond to the points in this grid. When you use `Plot3D[f, {x, xmin, xmax}, {y, ymin, ymax}]` to generate a `SurfaceGraphics` object, the setting `MeshRange -> {{xmin, xmax}, {ymin, ymax}}` is automatically generated. The setting for `MeshRange` is used in labeling the x and y axes in surface plots, and in working out polygon coordinates if you convert a `SurfaceGraphics` object to an explicit list of polygons in a `Graphics3D` object.

None	leave out clipped parts of the surface, so that you can see through
Automatic	show the clipped part of the surface with the same shading as an actual surface in the same position would have (default setting)
`GrayLevel[i]`, `RGBColor[r, g, b]`, etc.	show the clipped part of the surface with a particular gray level, color, etc.
{bottom, top}	give different specifications for parts that are clipped at the bottom and top

Settings for the `ClipFill` option.

The option `PlotRange` works for `SurfaceGraphics` as it does for other *Mathematica* graphics objects. Any parts of a surface that lie outside the range of coordinates defined by `PlotRange` will be "clipped". The option `ClipFill` allows you to specify what should happen to the parts of a surface that are clipped.

Here is a three-dimensional plot in which the top and bottom of the surface are clipped. With the default setting for ClipFill, the clipped parts are shown as they would be if they were part of the actual surface.

In[6]:= **Plot3D[Sin[x y], {x, 0, 3}, {y, 0, 3},
            PlotRange -> {-.5, .5}]**

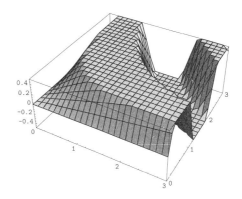

With ClipFill->None, parts of the surface which are clipped are left out, so that you can "see through" the surface there. *Mathematica* always leaves out parts of the surface that correspond to places where the value of the function you are plotting is not a real number.

In[7]:= **Show[%, ClipFill -> None]**

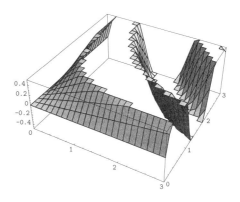

This makes the bottom clipped face white (gray level 1), and the top one black.

In[8]:= **Show[%, ClipFill -> {GrayLevel[1], GrayLevel[0]}]**

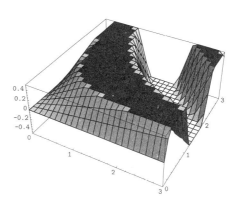

Whenever *Mathematica* draws a surface, it has to know not only the height, but also the color of the surface at each point. With the default setting `Lighting -> True`, *Mathematica* colors the surface using a simulated lighted model. However, with `Lighting -> False`, *Mathematica* uses a "color function" to determine how to color the surface.

The default color function takes the height of the surface, normalized to run from 0 to 1, and colors each part of the surface with a gray level corresponding to this height. There are two ways to change the default.

First, if you set the option `ColorFunction -> c`, then *Mathematica* will apply the function *c* to each height value to determine the color to use at that point. With `ColorFunction -> Hue`, *Mathematica* will for example color the surface with a range of hues.

`Plot3D[f, ... , ColorFunction -> c]`
> apply *c* to the normalized values of *f* to determine the color of each point on a surface

`ListPlot3D[array, ColorFunction -> c]`
> apply *c* to the elements of *array* to determine color

`SurfaceGraphics[array, ColorFunction -> c]`
> apply *c* to the elements of *array* to determine color

Specifying functions for coloring surfaces.

With `Lighting -> False`, the default is to color surfaces with gray scales determined by height.

`In[9]:= exp = Plot3D[Exp[-Sqrt[x^2 + y^2]],`
`        {x, -2, 2}, {y, -2, 2}, Lighting -> False]`

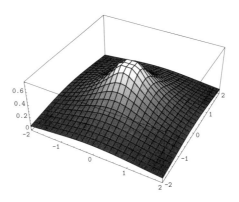

This defines a function which maps alternating ranges of values into black and white.

`In[10]:= stripes[f_] :=`
`        If[Mod[f, 1] > 0.5, GrayLevel[1], GrayLevel[0]]`

This shows the surface colored with black and white stripes.

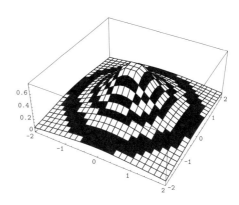

The second way to change the default coloring of surfaces is to supply an explicit second array along with the array of heights. ColorFunction is then applied to the elements of this second array, rather than the array of heights, to find the color directives to use. In the second array, you can effectively specify the value of another coordinate for each point on the surface. This coordinate will be plotted using color, rather than position.

You can generate an array of color values automatically using Plot3D[{*f*, *s*}, ...]. If you give the array explicitly in ListPlot3D or SurfaceGraphics, you should realize that with an $n \times n$ array of heights, you need an $(n-1) \times (n-1)$ array to specify colors. The reason is that the heights are specified for *points* on a grid, whereas the colors are specified for *squares* on the grid.

When you supply a second function or array to Plot3D, ListPlot3D, and so on, the default setting for the ColorFunction option is Automatic. This means that the function or array should contain explicit *Mathematica* color directives, such as GrayLevel or RGBColor. However, if you give another setting, such as ColorFunction -> Hue, then the function or array can yield pure numbers or other data which are converted to color directives when the function specified by ColorFunction is applied.

Plot3D[{*f*, *s*}, {*x*, *xmin*, *xmax*}, {*y*, *ymin*, *ymax*}]	
	plot a surface whose height is determined by *f* and whose color is determined by *s*
ListPlot3D[*height*, *color*]	generate a colored surface plot from an array of heights and colors
SurfaceGraphics[*height*, *color*]	a graphics object representing a surface with a specified array of heights and colors

Specifying arrays of colors for surfaces.

This plots a surface with gray level determined by the *y* coordinate.

```
In[12]:= Plot3D[{Sin[x] Sin[y]^2, GrayLevel[y/3]},
                {x, 0, 3}, {y, 0, 3}]
```

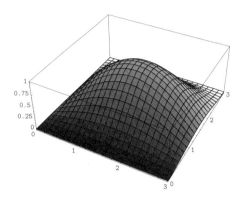

This puts a random gray level in each grid square. Notice that the array of grid squares is 9 × 9, whereas the array of grid points is 10 × 10.

```
In[13]:= ListPlot3D[ Table[i/j, {i, 10}, {j, 10}],
               Table[GrayLevel[Random[ ]], {i, 9}, {j, 9}] ]
```

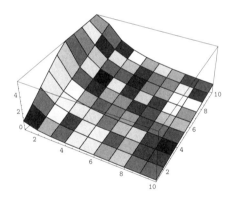

■ 2.10.12 Lighting and Surface Properties

With the default option setting Lighting -> True, *Mathematica* uses a simulated lighting model to determine how to color polygons in three-dimensional graphics.

Mathematica allows you to specify two components to the illumination of an object. The first is "ambient lighting", which produces uniform shading all over the object. The second is light from a collection of point sources, each with a particular position and color. *Mathematica* adds together the light from all of these sources in determining the total illumination of a particular polygon.

AmbientLight -> *color*   diffuse isotropic lighting

LightSources -> {{*pos*$_1$, *col*$_1$}, {*pos*$_2$, *col*$_2$}, ... }
                        point light sources with specified positions and colors

Options for simulated illumination.

The default lighting used by *Mathematica* involves three point light sources, and no ambient component. The light sources are colored respectively red, green and blue, and are placed at 45° angles on the right-hand side of the object.

Here is a surface, shaded using simulated lighting using the default set of lights.

In[1]:= **Plot3D[Sin[x + Sin[y]], {x, -3, 3}, {y, -3, 3},
                        Lighting -> True]**

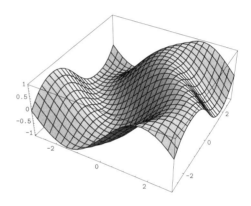

This shows the result of adding ambient light, and removing all point light sources.

In[2]:= **Show[%, AmbientLight -> GrayLevel[0.5],
                        LightSources -> {}]**

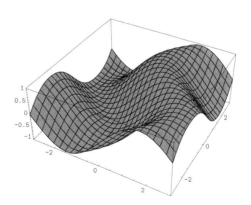

This adds a single point light source at the left-hand side of the image.

In[3]:= **Show[%,**
        LightSources -> {{{-1, 0, 0.5}, GrayLevel[0.5]}}]

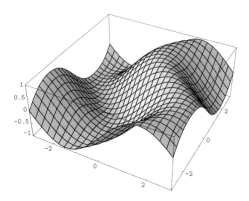

The positions of light sources in *Mathematica* are specified in the *display* coordinate system. The *x* and *y* coordinates are in the plane of the final display, and the *z* coordinate comes out of the plane. Using this coordinate system ensures that the light sources remain fixed with respect to the viewer, even when the relative positions of the viewer and object change.

Even though the view point is changed, the light source is kept fixed on the left-hand side of the image.

In[4]:= **Show[%, ViewPoint -> {2, 2, 6}]**

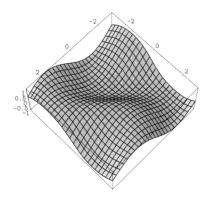

The perceived color of a polygon depends not only on the light which falls on the polygon, but also on how the polygon reflects that light. You can use the graphics directive **SurfaceColor** to specify the way that polygons reflect light.

If you do not explicitly use **SurfaceColor** directives, *Mathematica* effectively assumes that all polygons have matte white surfaces. Thus the polygons reflect light of any color incident on them, and do so equally in all directions. This is an appropriate model for materials such as uncoated white paper.

Using `SurfaceColor`, however, you can specify more complicated models. The basic idea is to distinguish two kinds of reflection: *diffuse* and *specular*.

In diffuse reflection, light incident on a surface is scattered equally in all directions. When this kind of reflection occurs, a surface has a "dull" or "matte" appearance. Diffuse reflectors obey Lambert's Law of light reflection, which states that the intensity of reflected light is $\cos(\alpha)$ times the intensity of the incident light, where α is the angle between the incident light direction and the surface normal vector. Note that when $\alpha > 90°$, there is no reflected light.

In specular reflection, a surface reflects light in a mirror-like way. As a result, the surface has a "shiny" or "gloss" appearance. With a perfect mirror, light incident at a particular angle is reflected at exactly the same angle. Most materials, however, scatter light to some extent, and so lead to reflected light that is distributed over a range of angles. *Mathematica* allows you to specify how broad the distribution is by giving a *specular exponent*, defined according to the Phong lighting model. With specular exponent n, the intensity of light at an angle θ away from the mirror reflection direction is assumed to vary like $\cos(\theta)^n$. As $n \to \infty$, therefore, the surface behaves like a perfect mirror. As n decreases, however, the surface becomes less "shiny", and for $n = 0$, the surface is a completely diffuse reflector. Typical values of n for actual materials range from about 1 to several hundred.

Most actual materials show a mixture of diffuse and specular reflection. In addition, they typically behave as if they have a certain intrinsic color. When the incident light is white, the reflected light has the color of the material. When the incident light is not white, each color component in the reflected light is a product of the corresponding component in the incident light and in the intrinsic color of the material.

In *Mathematica*, you can specify reflection properties by giving an intrinsic color associated with diffuse reflection, and another one associated with specular reflection. To get no reflection of a particular kind, you must give the corresponding intrinsic color as black, or `GrayLevel[0]`. For materials that are effectively "white", you can specify intrinsic colors of the form `GrayLevel[a]`, where a is the reflectance or albedo of the surface.

`SurfaceColor[GrayLevel[a]]`	matte surface with albedo a
`SurfaceColor[RGBColor[r, g, b]]`	matte surface with intrinsic color
`SurfaceColor[`*diff*`, `*spec*`]`	surface with diffuse intrinsic color *diff* and specular intrinsic color *spec*
`SurfaceColor[`*diff*`, `*spec*`, `*n*`]`	surface with specular exponent n

Specifying surface properties of lighted polygons.

This loads a package containing various graphics objects.

In[5]:= `<<Graphics`Shapes``

Sphere creates a graphics object which represents a sphere.

In[6]:= **s = Sphere[ ] ;**

This shows the sphere with the default matte white surface.

In[7]:= **Show[Graphics3D[s]]**

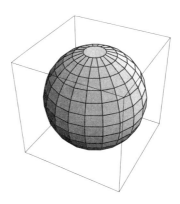

This makes the sphere have low diffuse reflectance, but high specular reflectance. As a result, the sphere has a "specular highlight" near the light sources, and is quite dark elsewhere.

In[8]:= **Show[Graphics3D[{**
            SurfaceColor[GrayLevel[0.2],
                GrayLevel[0.8], 5], s}]]

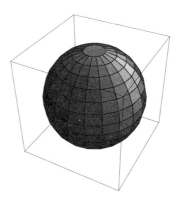

When you set up light sources and surface colors, it is important to make sure that the total intensity of light reflected from a particular polygon is never larger than 1. You will get strange effects if the intensity is larger than 1.

■ 2.10.13 Labeling Three-Dimensional Graphics

Mathematica provides various options for labeling three-dimensional graphics. Some of these options are directly analogous to those for two-dimensional graphics, discussed in Section 2.10.5. Others are different.

Boxed -> True	draw a cuboidal bounding box around the graphics (default)
Axes -> True	draw *x*, *y* and *z* axes on the edges of the box (default for SurfaceGraphics)
Axes -> {False, False, True}	draw the *z* axis only
FaceGrids -> All	draw grid lines on the faces of the box
PlotLabel -> *text*	give an overall label for the plot

Some options for labeling three-dimensional graphics.

This loads a package containing various polyhedra.

In[1]:= <<Graphics`Polyhedra`

The default for Graphics3D is to include a box, but no other forms of labeling.

In[2]:= Show[Graphics3D[Dodecahedron[ ]]]

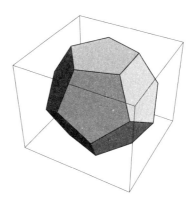

Setting Axes -> True adds *x*, *y* and *z* axes.

In[3]:= Show[%, Axes -> True]

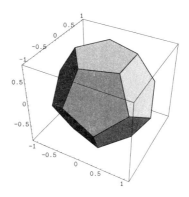

This adds grid lines to each face of the box.

In[4]:= **Show[%, FaceGrids -> All]**

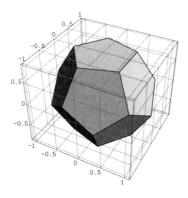

BoxStyle -> *style*	specify the style for the box
AxesStyle -> *style*	specify the style for axes
AxesStyle -> {{*xstyle*}, {*ystyle*}, {*zstyle*}}	
	specify separate styles for each axis

Style options.

This makes the box dashed, and draws axes which are thicker than normal.

In[5]:= **Show[Graphics3D[Dodecahedron[ ]],**
BoxStyle -> Dashing[{0.02, 0.02}],
Axes -> True, AxesStyle -> Thickness[0.01]]

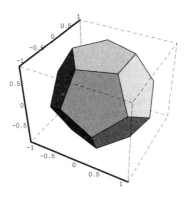

By setting the option Axes -> True, you tell *Mathematica* to draw axes on the edges of the three-dimensional box. However, for each axis, there are in principle four possible edges on which it can be drawn. The option AxesEdge allows you to specify on which edge to draw each of the axes.

AxesEdge -> Automatic	use an internal algorithm to choose where to draw all axes
AxesEdge -> {*xspec*, *yspec*, *zspec*}	
	give separate specifications for each of the *x*, *y* and *z* axes
None	do not draw this axis
Automatic	decide automatically where to draw this axis
{*dir_i*, *dir_j*}	specify on which of the four possible edges to draw this axis

Specifying where to draw three-dimensional axes.

This draws the *x* on the edge with larger *y* and *z* coordinates, draws no *y* axis, and chooses automatically where to draw the *z* axis.

In[6]:= **Show[Graphics3D[Dodecahedron[ ]], Axes -> True,**
         AxesEdge -> {{1, 1}, None, Automatic}]

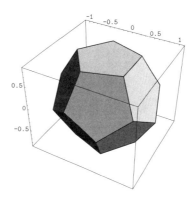

When you draw the *x* axis on a three-dimensional box, there are four possible edges on which the axis can be drawn. These edges are distinguished by having larger or smaller *y* and *z* coordinates. When you use the specification {*dir_y*, *dir_z*} for where to draw the *x* axis, you can set the *dir_i* to be +1 or −1 to represent larger or smaller values for the *y* and *z* coordinates.

AxesLabel -> None	give no axis labels
AxesLabel -> *zlabel*	put a label on the *z* axis
AxesLabel -> {*xlabel*, *ylabel*, *zlabel*}	put labels on all three axes

Axis labels in three-dimensional graphics.

You can use AxesLabel to label edges of the box, without necessarily drawing scales on them.

In[7]:= **Show[Graphics3D[Dodecahedron[ ]], Axes -> True,**
      AxesLabel -> {"x", "y", "z"}, Ticks -> None]

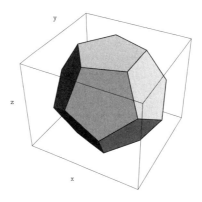

Ticks -> None	draw no tick marks
Ticks -> Automatic	place tick marks automatically
Ticks -> {*xticks*, *yticks*, *zticks*}	tick mark specifications for each axis

Settings for the Ticks option.

You can give the same kind of tick mark specifications in three dimensions as were described for two-dimensional graphics in Section 2.10.5.

FaceGrids -> None	draw no grid lines on faces
FaceGrids -> All	draw grid lines on all faces
FaceGrids -> {$face_1$, $face_2$, ... }	draw grid lines on the faces specified by the $face_i$
FaceGrids -> {{$face_1$, {$xgrid_1$, $ygrid_1$}}, ... }	use $xgrid_i$, $ygrid_i$ to determine where and how to draw grid lines on each face

Drawing grid lines in three dimensions.

Mathematica allows you to draw grid lines on the faces of the box that surrounds a three-dimensional object. If you set FaceGrids -> All, grid lines are drawn in gray on every face. By setting FaceGrids -> {$face_1$, $face_2$, ... } you can tell *Mathematica* to draw grid lines only on specific faces. Each face is specified by a list {dir_x, dir_y, dir_z}, where two of the dir_i must be 0, and the third one is +1 or −1. For each face, you can also explicitly tell *Mathematica* where and how to draw the grid lines, using the same kind of specifications as you give for the GridLines option in two-dimensional graphics.

This draws grid lines only on the top and bottom faces of the box.

In[8]:= **Show[Graphics3D[Dodecahedron[ ]],**
              FaceGrids -> {{0, 0, 1}, {0, 0, -1}}]

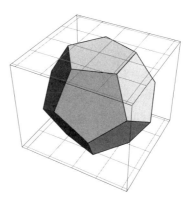

■ 2.10.14 Advanced Topic: Low-Level Graphics Rendering

All *Mathematica* graphics functions such as Show and Plot have an option DisplayFunction, which specifies how the *Mathematica* graphics objects they produce should actually be displayed. The way this works is that the setting you give for DisplayFunction is automatically applied to each graphics object that is produced.

DisplayFunction -> $DisplayFunction	default setting
DisplayFunction -> Identity	generate no display
DisplayFunction -> *f*	apply *f* to graphics objects to produce display

Settings for the `DisplayFunction` option.

Within the *Mathematica* kernel, graphics are always represented by graphics objects involving graphics primitives. When you actually render graphics, however, they must be converted to a lower-level form which can be processed by a *Mathematica* front end, such as a notebook interface, or by other external programs.

The standard low-level form that *Mathematica* uses for graphics is *PostScript*. The *Mathematica* function `Display` takes any *Mathematica* graphics object, and converts it into a block of PostScript code. It can then send this code to a file, an external program, or in general any output stream.

Display["*file*", *graphics*]	store the PostScript for a piece of *Mathematica* graphics in a file
Display["!*program*", *graphics*]	send the PostScript to an external program
Display[*stream*, *graphics*]	send the PostScript to an arbitrary stream
DisplayString[*graphics*]	generate a string of PostScript

Converting *Mathematica* graphics to PostScript.

The default value of the global variable $DisplayFunction is Function[Display[$Display, #]]. With this default, graphics objects produced by functions like Show and Plot are automatically converted to PostScript, and sent to whatever stream is specified by the value of the global variable $Display. The variable $Display is typically set during the initialization of a particular *Mathematica* session.

PostScript["*string*$_1$", "*string*$_2$", ...]	a two-dimensional graphics primitive giving PostScript code to include verbatim

Inserting verbatim PostScript code.

With the standard two-dimensional graphics primitives in *Mathematica* you can produce most of the effects that can be obtained with PostScript. Sometimes, however, you may find it necessary to give PostScript code directly. You can do this using the special two-dimensional graphics primitive PostScript.

The strings you specify in the PostScript primitive will be inserted verbatim into the final PostScript code generated by Display. You should use the PostScript primitive with care. For example, it is crucial that the code you give restores the PostScript stack to exactly its original state when it is finished. In addition, to specify positions of objects, you will have to understand the coordinate scaling that *Mathematica* does in its PostScript output. Finally, any PostScript primitives that you insert can only work if they are supported in the final PostScript interpreter that you use to display your graphics.

The PostScript primitive gives raw PostScript code which draws a Bézier curve.

```
In[1]:= Show[Graphics[ {
            PostScript[".008 setlinewidth"],
            PostScript[".1 .1 moveto"],
            PostScript["1.1 .6 -.1 .6 .9 .1 curveto stroke"] },
                Frame -> True]]
```

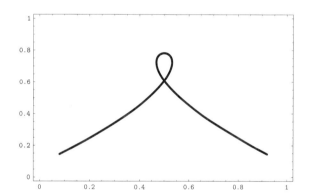

In most cases, a particular *Mathematica* graphics object always generates PostScript of a particular form. For Graphics3D objects, the option RenderAll allows you to choose between two different forms.

The main issue is how the polygons which make up three-dimensional objects should be rendered. With the default setting RenderAll -> True, all polygons you specify are drawn in full, but those behind are drawn first. When all the polygons are drawn, only those in front are visible. However, while an object is being drawn on a display, you can typically see the polygons inside it.

The problem with this approach is that for an object with many layers, you may generate a large amount of spurious PostScript code associated with polygons that are not visible in the final image. You can potentially avoid this by setting RenderAll -> False. In this case, *Mathematica* works out exactly which polygons or parts of polygons will actually be visible in your final image, and renders only these. So long as there are fairly few intersections between polygons, this approach will typically yield less PostScript code, though it may be much slower.

RenderAll -> True	draw all polygons, starting from the back (default)
RenderAll -> False	draw only those polygons or parts of polygons that are visible in the final image

An option for rendering three-dimensional pictures.

When you generate a PostScript representation of a three-dimensional object, you lose all information about the depths of the parts of the object. Sometimes, you may want to send to external programs a representation which includes depth information. Often, the original Graphics3D object in *Mathematica* form is then the appropriate representation. But some external programs cannot handle intersecting polygons. To deal with this, Graphics3D includes the option PolygonIntersections. If you set PolygonIntersections -> False, then Show will return not your original Graphics3D object, but rather one in which intersecting polygons have been broken into disjoint pieces, at least with the setting for ViewPoint and so on that you have given.

■ 2.10.15 Formats for Text in Graphics

$TextStyle = *value*	set the default text style for all graphics
$FormatType = *value*	set the default text format type for all graphics
TextStyle -> *value*	an option for the text style in a particular graphic
FormatType -> *value*	an option for the text format type in a particular graphic

Specifying formats for text in graphics.

Here is a plot with default settings for all formats.

In[1]:= **Plot[Sin[x]^2, {x, 0, 2 Pi}, PlotLabel->Sin[x]^2]**

Here is the same plot, but now using a 7-point italic font.

In[2]:= **Plot[Sin[x]^2, {x, 0, 2 Pi}, PlotLabel->Sin[x]^2, TextStyle->{FontSlant->"Italic", FontSize->7}]**

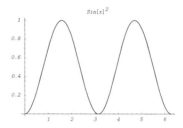

This uses `TraditionalForm` rather than `StandardForm`.

In[3]:= **Plot[Sin[x]^2, {x, 0, 2 Pi}, PlotLabel->Sin[x]^2, FormatType -> TraditionalForm]**

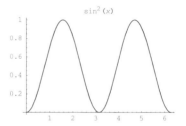

This tells *Mathematica* what default text style to use for all subsequent plots.

In[4]:= **$TextStyle = {FontFamily -> "Times", FontSize -> 7}**

Out[4]= {FontFamily → Times, FontSize → 7}

Now all the text is in 7-point Times font.

In[5]:= **Plot[Sin[x]^2, {x, 0, 2 Pi}, PlotLabel->Sin[x]^2]**

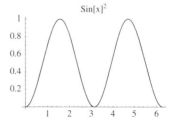

"*style*"	a cell style in your current notebook
FontSize -> *n*	the size of font to use in printer's points
FontSlant -> "Italic"	use an italic font
FontWeight -> "Bold"	use a bold font
FontFamily -> "*name*"	specify the name of the font family to use (e.g. "Times", "Courier", "Helvetica")

Typical elements used in the setting for TextStyle or $TextStyle.

If you use the standard notebook front end for *Mathematica*, then you can set $TextStyle or TextStyle to be the name of a cell style in your current notebook. This tells *Mathematica* to use that cell style as the default for formatting any text that appears in graphics.

You can also explicitly specify how text should be formatted by using options such as FontSize and FontFamily. Note that FontSize gives the absolute size of the font to use, measured in units of printer's points, with one point being $\frac{1}{72}$ inches. If you resize a plot, the text in it will not by default change size: to get text of a different size you must explicitly specify a new value for the FontSize option.

StyleForm[*expr*, "*style*"]	output *expr* in the specified cell style
StyleForm[*expr*, *options*]	output *expr* using the specified font and style options
TraditionalForm[*expr*]	output *expr* in TraditionalForm

Changing the formats of individual pieces of output.

This outputs the plot label using the section heading style in your current notebook.

```
In[6]:= Plot[Sin[x]^2, {x, 0, 2 Pi},
            PlotLabel->StyleForm[Sin[x]^2, "Section"]]
```

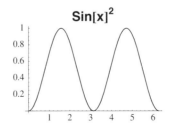

This uses the section heading style, but modified to be in italics.

```
In[7]:= Plot[Sin[x]^2, {x, 0, 2 Pi},
          PlotLabel->StyleForm[Sin[x]^2, "Section",
                    FontSlant->"Italic"]]
```

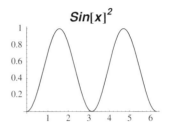

This produces TraditionalForm output, with a 12-point font.

```
In[8]:= Plot[Sin[x]^2, {x, 0, 2 Pi},
          PlotLabel->StyleForm[TraditionalForm[Sin[x]^2],
                    FontSize->12]]
```

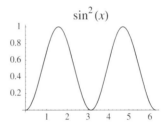

You should realize that the ability to refer to cell styles such as "Section" depends on using the standard *Mathematica* notebook front end. Even if you are just using a text-based interface to *Mathematica*, however, you can still specify formatting of text in graphics using options such as FontSize. The complete collection of options that you can use is given on page 612.

■ 2.10.16 Graphics Primitives for Text

With the Text graphics primitive, you can insert text at any position in two- or three-dimensional *Mathematica* graphics. Unless you explicitly specify a style or font using StyleForm, the text will be given in your current default style.

Text[*expr*, {*x*, *y*}]	text centered at the point {*x*, *y*}
Text[*expr*, {*x*, *y*}, {-1, 0}]	text with its left-hand end at {*x*, *y*}
Text[*expr*, {*x*, *y*}, {1, 0}]	right-hand end at {*x*, *y*}
Text[*expr*, {*x*, *y*}, {0, -1}]	centered above {*x*, *y*}
Text[*expr*, {*x*, *y*}, {0, 1}]	centered below {*x*, *y*}
Text[*expr*, {*x*, *y*}, {*dx*, *dy*}]	text positioned so that {*x*, *y*} is at relative coordinates {*dx*, *dy*} within the box that bounds the text
Text[*expr*, {*x*, *y*}, {*dx*, *dy*}, {0, 1}]	text oriented vertically to read from bottom to top
Text[*expr*, {*x*, *y*}, {*dx*, *dy*}, {0, -1}]	text that reads from top to bottom
Text[*expr*, {*x*, *y*}, {*dx*, *dy*}, {-1, 0}]	text that is upside-down

Two-dimensional text.

This generates five pieces of text, and displays them in a plot.

```
In[1]:= Show[Graphics[
            Table[ Text[Expand[(1 + x)^n], {n, n}], {n, 5} ] ],
               PlotRange -> All]
```

$$1 + 5x + 10x^2 + 10x^3 + 5x^4 + x^5$$

$$1 + 4x + 6x^2 + 4x^3 + x^4$$

$$1 + 3x + 3x^2 + x^3$$

$$1 + 2x + x^2$$

$$1 + x$$

Here is some vertically oriented text with its left hand side at the point {2, 2}.

```
In[2]:= Show[Graphics[Text[
            StyleForm["Some text", FontSize->14, FontWeight->"Bold"],
            {2, 2}, {-1, 0}, {0, 1}]], Frame -> True]
```

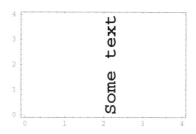

When you specify an offset for text, the relative coordinates that are used are taken to run from -1 to 1 in each direction across the box that bounds the text. The point {0, 0} in this coordinate system is defined to be center of the text. Note that the offsets you specify need not lie in the range -1 to 1.

Note that you can specify the color of a piece of text by preceding the Text graphics primitive with an appropriate RGBColor or other graphics directive.

Text[*expr*, {*x*, *y*, *z*}]	text centered at the point {*x*, *y*, *z*}
Text[*expr*, {*x*, *y*, *z*}, {*sdx*, *sdy*}]	text with a two-dimensional offset

Three-dimensional text.

This loads a package containing definitions of polyhedra.

```
In[3]:= <<Graphics`Polyhedra`
```

This puts text at the specified position in three dimensions.

```
In[4]:= Show[Graphics3D[{Dodecahedron[ ],
                Text["a point", {2, 2, 2}, {1, 1}]}]]
```

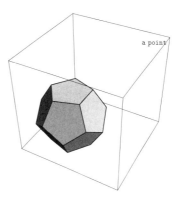

Note that when you use text in three-dimensional graphics, *Mathematica* assumes that the text is never hidden by any polygons or other objects.

option name	default value	
Background	None	background color
TextStyle	{}	style or font specification
FormatType	StandardForm	format type

Options for Text.

By default the text is just put straight on top of whatever graphics have already been drawn.

```
In[5]:= Show[Graphics[{{GrayLevel[0.5],
            Rectangle[{0, 0}, {1, 1}]},
          Text["Some text", {0.5, 0.5}]}]]
```

Now there is a rectangle with the background color of the whole plot enclosing the text.

```
In[6]:= Show[Graphics[{{GrayLevel[0.5],
          Rectangle[{0, 0}, {1, 1}]},
         Text["Some text", {0.5, 0.5},
              Background->Automatic]}]]
```

■ 2.10.17 Advanced Topic: Color Output

Monochrome displays	gray levels
Color displays	red, green and blue mixtures
Color printing	cyan, magenta, yellow and black mixtures

Specifications of color for different kinds of output devices.

When you generate graphics output in *Mathematica*, there are different specifications of color which are natural for different kinds of output devices. Sometimes output devices may automatically convert from one form of color specification to another. But *Mathematica* provides graphics directives which allow you directly to produce color specifications appropriate for particular devices.

GrayLevel[*i*]	gray level (setgray in PostScript)
RGBColor[*r*, *g*, *b*]	red, green and blue components for a display (setrgbcolor)
Hue[*h*, *s*, *b*]	hue, saturation and brightness components for a display (setrgbcolor)
CMYKColor[*c*, *m*, *y*, *k*]	cyan, magenta, yellow and black components for four-color process printing (setcmykcolor)

Color directives in *Mathematica*.

Each color directive in *Mathematica* yields a definite color directive in the PostScript code that *Mathematica* sends to your output device. Thus, for example, the RGBColor directive in *Mathematica* yields setrgbcolor in PostScript. The final treatment of the PostScript color directives is determined by your output device, and the PostScript interpreter that is used.

Nevertheless, in most cases, the parameters specified in the *Mathematica* color directives will be used fairly directly to set the intensities or densities of the components of the color output.

When this is done, it is important to realize that a given set of parameters in a *Mathematica* color directive may yield different perceived colors on different output devices. For example, the actual intensities of red, green and blue components will often differ between different color displays even when the settings for these components are the same. Such differences also occur when the brightness or contrast of a particular color display is changed.

In addition, you should realize that the complete "gamut" of colors that you can produce by varying parameters on a particular output device is smaller, often substantially so, than the gamut of colors which can be perceived by the human visual system. Even though the space of colors that we can perceive can be described with three parameters, it is not possible to reach all parts of this space with mixtures of a fixed number of "primary colors".

Different choices of primary colors are typically made for different types of output devices. Color displays, which work with emitted or transmitted light, typically use red, green and blue primary colors. However, color printing, which works with reflected light, typically uses cyan, magenta, yellow and black as primary colors. When a color image is printed, four separate passes are typically made, each time laying down one of these primary colors.

Thus, while RGBColor and Hue are natural color specifications for color displays, CMYKColor is the natural specification for color printing.

By default, *Mathematica* takes whatever color specifications you give, and uses them directly. The option ColorOutput, however, allows you to make *Mathematica* always convert the color specifications you give to ones appropriate for a particular kind of output device.

ColorOutput -> Automatic	use color specifications as given (default)
ColorOutput -> None	convert to monochrome
ColorOutput -> GrayLevel	convert all color specifications to gray levels
ColorOutput -> RGBColor	convert to RGBColor form
ColorOutput -> CMYKColor	convert to CMYKColor form
ColorOutput -> *f*	apply *f* to each color directive

Color output conversions.

One of the most complicated issues in color output is performing the "color separation" necessary to take a color specified using red, green and blue primaries, and render the color using cyan, magenta, yellow and black printing inks. *Mathematica* has a built-in algorithm for doing this conversion. The algorithm is based on an approximation to typical monitor colors and the standard set of four-color process printing inks. Note that the colors of these printing inks are not even close to complementary to typical monitor colors, and the actual transformation is quite nonlinear.

While *Mathematica* has built-in capabilities for various color conversions, you can also specify your own color conversions using ColorOutput -> *f*. With this option setting, the function *f* is automatically applied to each color directive generated by *Mathematica*.

Note that while any of the color directives given above can be used in setting up graphics objects, simulated lighting calculations in *Mathematica* are always done using RGBColor, and so all color directives are automatically converted to this form when simulated lighting is used.

This defines a transformation on RGBColor objects, which extracts the red component, and squares it.	*In[1]:=* **red[RGBColor[r_, g_, b_]] = GrayLevel[r^2]** *Out[1]=* GrayLevel[r^2]
This specifies that red should simply square any GrayLevel specification.	*In[2]:=* **red[GrayLevel[g_]] = GrayLevel[g^2]** *Out[2]=* GrayLevel[g^2]

This plots the squared red component, rather than using the usual transformation from color to black and white.

In[3]:= `Plot3D[Sin[x + y], {x, -3, 3}, {y, -3, 3},`
`ColorOutput -> red]`

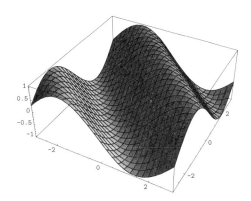

Note that if you give your own `ColorOutput` transformation, you must specify how the transformation acts on every color directive that arises in the image you are producing. For three-dimensional plots shaded with simulated lighting, you must typically specify the transformation at least for `RGBColor` and `GrayLevel`.

■ 2.10.18 The Representation of Sound

Section 1.9.12 described how you can take functions and lists of data and produce sounds from them. This subsection discusses how sounds are represented in *Mathematica*.

Mathematica treats sounds much like graphics. In fact, *Mathematica* allows you to combine graphics with sound to create pictures with "sound tracks".

In analogy with graphics, sounds in *Mathematica* are represented by symbolic sound objects. The sound objects have head `Sound`, and contain a list of sound primitives, which represent sounds to be played in sequence.

`Sound[{`s_1`, `s_2`, ... }]`   a sound object containing a list of sound primitives

---

The structure of a sound object.

The functions `Play` and `ListPlay` discussed in Section 1.9.12 return Sound objects.

Play returns a Sound object. On appropriate computer systems, it also produces sound.

In[1]:= `Play[Sin[300 t + 2 Sin[400 t]], {t, 0, 2}]`

Out[1]= `-Sound-`

The Sound object contains a
SampledSoundFunction primitive
which uses a compiled function to
generate amplitude samples for the
sound.

```
In[2]:= Short[ InputForm[%] ]

Out[2]//Short= Sound[SampledSoundFunction[<<3>>]]
```

SampledSoundList[{a_1, a_2, ... }, r]	a sound with a sequence of amplitude levels, sampled at rate r
SampledSoundFunction[f, n, r]	a sound whose amplitude levels sampled at rate r are found by applying the function f to n successive integers

Mathematica sound primitives.

At the lowest level, all sounds in *Mathematica* are represented as a sequence of amplitude samples. In SampledSoundList, these amplitude samples are given explicitly in a list. In SampledSoundFunction, however, they are generated when the sound is output, by applying the specified function to a sequence of integer arguments. In both cases, all amplitude values obtained must be between -1 and 1.

ListPlay generates SampledSoundList primitives, while Play generates SampledSoundFunction primitives. With the default option setting Compiled -> True, Play will produce a SampledSoundFunction object containing a CompiledFunction.

Once you have generated a Sound object containing various sound primitives, you must then output it as a sound. Much as with graphics, the basic scheme is to take the *Mathematica* representation of the sound, and convert it to a lower-level form that can be handled by an external program, such as a *Mathematica* front end.

The low-level representation of sound used by *Mathematica* consists of a sequence of hexadecimal numbers specifying amplitude levels. Within *Mathematica*, amplitude levels are given as approximate real numbers between -1 and 1. In producing the low-level form, the amplitude levels are "quantized". You can use the option SampleDepth to specify how many bits should be used for each sample. The default is SampleDepth -> 8, which yields 256 possible amplitude levels, sufficient for most purposes.

You can use the option SampleDepth in any of the functions Play, ListPlay and PlaySound. In sound primitives, you can specify the sample depth by replacing the sample rate argument by the list {*rate*, *depth*}.

Since graphics and sound can be combined in *Mathematica*, their low-level representations must not conflict. As discussed in Section 2.10.14, all graphics in *Mathematica* are generated in the PostScript language. Sounds are also generated as a special PostScript function, which can be ignored by PostScript interpreters on devices which do not support sound output.

Display[*stream*, *sound*]	output sound to a stream
Display[*stream*, {*graphics*, *sound*}]	output graphics and sound to a stream

Sending sound to a stream.

Mathematica uses the same function Display to output sound, graphics, and combinations of the two.

In Play, ListPlay and Sound, the option DisplayFunction specifies how the sound should ultimately be output. The default for this option is the global variable $SoundDisplayFunction. Typically, this is set to an appropriate call to Display.

■ 2.10.19 Exporting Graphics and Sounds

Export["*name.ext*", *graphics*]	export graphics in a format deduced from the file name
Export["*file*", *graphics*, "*format*"]	export graphics in the specified format
Export["*file*", {g_1, g_2, ... }, ...]	export a sequence of graphics for an animation
ExportString[*graphics*, "*format*"]	generate a string representation of exported graphics

Exporting graphics and sounds.

`"EPS"`	Encapsulated PostScript (`.eps`)
`"PDF"`	Adobe Acrobat portable document format (`.pdf`)
`"SVG"`	Scalable Vector Graphics (`.svg`)
`"PICT"`	Macintosh PICT
`"WMF"`	Windows metafile format (`.wmf`)
`"TIFF"`	TIFF (`.tif`, `.tiff`)
`"GIF"`	GIF and animated GIF (`.gif`)
`"JPEG"`	JPEG (`.jpg`, `.jpeg`)
`"PNG"`	PNG format (`.png`)
`"BMP"`	Microsoft bitmap format (`.bmp`)
`"EPSI"`	Encapsulated PostScript with device-independent preview (`.epsi`)
`"EPSTIFF"`	Encapsulated PostScript with TIFF preview
`"XBitmap"`	X window system bitmap (`.xbm`)
`"PBM"`	portable bitmap format (`.pbm`)
`"PPM"`	portable pixmap format (`.ppm`)
`"PGM"`	portable graymap format (`.pgm`)
`"PNM"`	portable anymap format (`.pnm`)
`"DICOM"`	DICOM medical imaging format (`.dcm`, `.dic`)

Typical graphics formats supported by *Mathematica*. The first group are resolution independent.

When you export a graphic outside of *Mathematica*, you usually have to specify the absolute size at which the graphic should be rendered. You can do this using the `ImageSize` option to `Export`.

`ImageSize->`x makes the width of the graphic be x printer's points; `ImageSize->72` xi thus makes the width xi inches. The default is to produce an image that is four inches wide. `ImageSize->{`x, y`}` scales the graphic so that it fits in an $x \times y$ region.

ImageSize	Automatic	absolute image size in printer's points
ImageRotated	False	whether to rotate the image (landscape mode)
ImageResolution	Automatic	resolution in dpi for the image

Options for `Export`.

Within *Mathematica*, graphics are manipulated in a way that is completely independent of the resolution of the computer screen or other output device on which the graphics will eventually be rendered.

Many programs and devices accept graphics in resolution-independent formats such as Encapsulated PostScript (EPS). But some require that the graphics be converted to rasters or bitmaps with a specific resolution. The `ImageResolution` option for `Export` allows you to determine what resolution in dots per inch (dpi) should be used. The lower you set this resolution, the lower the quality of the image you will get, but also the less memory the image will take to store. For screen display, typical resolutions are 72 dpi and above; for printers, 300 dpi and above.

| "DXF" | AutoCAD drawing interchange format (`.dxf`) |
| "STL" | STL stereolithography format (`.stl`) |

Typical 3D geometry formats supported by *Mathematica*.

"WAV"	Microsoft wave format (`.wav`)
"AU"	μ law encoding (`.au`)
"SND"	sound file format (`.snd`)
"AIFF"	AIFF format (`.aif`, `.aiff`)

Typical sound formats supported by *Mathematica*.

■ 2.10.20 Importing Graphics and Sounds

Mathematica allows you not only to export graphics and sounds, but also to import them. With `Import` you can read graphics and sounds in a wide variety of formats, and bring them into *Mathematica* as *Mathematica* expressions.

Import["*name.ext*"]	import graphics from the file *name.ext* in a format deduced from the file name
Import["*file*", "*format*"]	import graphics in the specified format
ImportString["*string*", "*format*"]	import graphics from a string

Importing graphics and sounds.

This imports an image stored in JPEG format.

In[1]:= **g = Import["ocelot.jpg"]**

Out[1]= ▪ Graphics ▪

Here is the image.

In[2]:= **Show[g]**

This shows an array of four copies of the image.

In[3]:= **Show[GraphicsArray[{{g, g}, {g, g}}]]**

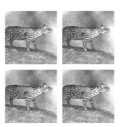

Import yields expressions with different structures depending on the type of data it reads. Typically you will need to know the structure if you want to manipulate the data that is returned.

Graphics[*primitives*, *opts*]	resolution-independent graphics
Graphics[Raster[*data*], *opts*]	resolution-dependent bitmap images
{*graphics*$_1$, *graphics*$_2$, ... }	animated graphics
Sound[SampledSoundList[*data*, *r*]]	sounds

Structures of expressions returned by Import.

This shows the overall structure of the graphics object imported above.

```
In[4]:= Shallow[InputForm[g]]

Out[4]//Shallow= Graphics[Raster[<<4>>], Rule[<<2>>]]
```

This extracts the array of pixel values used.

```
In[5]:= d = g[[1, 1]] ;
```

Here are the dimensions of the array.

```
In[6]:= Dimensions[d]

Out[6]= {200, 200}
```

This shows the distribution of pixel values.

```
In[7]:= ListPlot[Sort[Flatten[d]]]
```

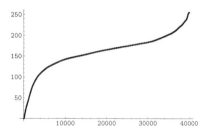

This shows a transformed version of the image.

```
In[8]:= Show[Graphics[Raster[d^2 / Max[d^2]]],
              AspectRatio->Automatic]
```

2.11 Manipulating Notebooks

■ 2.11.1 Cells as *Mathematica* Expressions

Like other objects in *Mathematica*, the cells in a notebook, and in fact the whole notebook itself, are all ultimately represented as *Mathematica* expressions. With the standard notebook front end, you can use the command Show Expression to see the text of the *Mathematica* expression that corresponds to any particular cell.

Show Expression menu item	toggle between displayed form and underlying *Mathematica* expression
[CTRL] * or [CTRL] 8 (between existing cells)	put up a dialog box to allow input of a cell in *Mathematica* expression form

Handling Cell expressions in the notebook front end.

Here is a cell displayed in its usual way in the front end.

This is a text cell.

Here is the underlying *Mathematica* expression that corresponds to the cell.

Cell["This is a text cell.", "Text"]

Cell[*contents*, "*style*"]	a cell with a specific style
Cell[*contents*, "*style*", *options*]	a cell with additional options specified

Mathematica expressions corresponding to cells in notebooks.

Within a given notebook, there is always a collection of *styles* that can be used to determine the appearance and behavior of cells. Typically the styles are named so as to reflect what role cells which have them will play in the notebook.

"Title"	the title of the notebook
"Section"	a section heading
"Subsection"	a subsection heading
"Text"	ordinary text
"Input"	*Mathematica* input
"Output"	*Mathematica* output

Some typical cell styles defined in notebooks.

Here are several cells in different styles.

■ **This is in Section style.**

This is in Text style.

     This is in Input style.

Here are the expressions that correspond to these cells.

```
Cell["This is in Section style.", "Section"]
Cell["This is in Text style.", "Text"]
Cell["This is in Input style.", "Input"]
```

A particular style such as "Section" or "Text" defines various settings for the options associated with a cell. You can override these settings by explicitly setting options within a specific cell.

Here is the expression for a cell in which options are set to use a gray background and to put a frame around the cell.

```
Cell["This is some text.", "Text", CellFrame->True,
  Background->GrayLevel[.8]]
```

This is how the cell looks in a notebook.

This is some text.

option	default value	
CellFrame	False	whether to draw a frame around the cell
Background	GrayLevel[1]	what color to draw the background for the cell
Editable	True	whether to allow the contents of the cell to be edited
TextAlignment	Left	how to align text in the cell
FontSize	12	the point size of the font for text
CellTags	{ }	tags to be associated with the cell

A few of the large number of possible options for cells.

The standard notebook front end for *Mathematica* provides several ways to change the options of a cell. In simple cases, such as changing the size or color of text, there will often be a specific menu item for the purpose. But in general you can use the *option inspector* that is built into the front end. This is typically accessed using the Option Inspector menu item in the Format menu.

- Change settings for specific options with menus.

- Look at and modify all options with the option inspector.

- Edit the textual form of the expression corresponding to the cell.

- Change the settings for all cells with a particular style.

Ways to manipulate cells in the front end.

Sometimes you will want just to change the options associated with a specific cell. But often you may want to change the options associated with all cells in your notebook that have a particular style. You can do this by using the Edit Style Sheet command in the front end to open up the style sheet associated with your notebook, and then modifying the options for the cells in this style sheet that represent the style you want to change.

<table>
<tr><td>CellPrint[Cell[...]]</td><td>insert a cell into your currently selected notebook</td></tr>
<tr><td>CellPrint[{Cell[...], Cell[...], ... }]</td><td></td></tr>
<tr><td></td><td>insert a sequence of cells into your currently selected notebook</td></tr>
</table>

Inserting cells into a notebook.

This inserts a section cell into the current notebook.

In[1]:= CellPrint[Cell["The heading", "Section"]]

This inserts a text cell with a frame around it.

In[2]:= CellPrint[Cell["Some text", "Text", CellFrame->True]]

CellPrint allows you to take a raw Cell expression and insert it into your current notebook. Sometimes, however, you may find it more convenient to give an ordinary *Mathematica* expression, and then have *Mathematica* convert it into a Cell of a certain style, and insert this cell into a notebook. You can do this using the function StylePrint.

<table>
<tr><td>StylePrint[*expr*, "*style*"]</td><td>create a new cell of the specified style, and write *expr* into it</td></tr>
<tr><td>StylePrint[*contents*, "*style*", *options*]</td><td></td></tr>
<tr><td></td><td>use the specified options for the new cell</td></tr>
</table>

Writing expressions into cells with specified styles.

This inserts a cell in section style into your current notebook.

In[3]:= StylePrint["The heading", "Section"]

This creates several cells in output style.

In[4]:= `Do[StylePrint[Factor[x^i - 1], "Output"], {i, 7, 10}]`

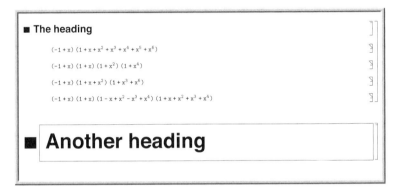

You can use any cell options in `StylePrint`.

In[5]:= `StylePrint["Another heading", "Section", CellFrame->True, FontSize->28]`

`CellPrint` and `StylePrint` provide simple ways to modify open notebooks in the front end from within the kernel. Later in this section we will discuss more sophisticated and flexible ways to do this.

■ 2.11.2 Notebooks as *Mathematica* Expressions

`Notebook[{cell`$_1$`, cell`$_2$`, ... }]`	a notebook containing a sequence of cells
`Notebook[cells, options]`	a notebook with options specified

Expressions corresponding to notebooks.

Here is a simple *Mathematica* notebook.

■ **Section heading**

Some text.

More text.

Here is the expression that corresponds
to this notebook.

```
Notebook[{
    Cell["Section heading", "Section"],
    Cell["Some text.", "Text"],
    Cell["More text.", "Text"]}]
```

Just like individual cells, notebooks in *Mathematica* can also have options. You can look at and
modify these options using the options inspector in the standard notebook front end.

option	default value	
WindowSize	{*nx*, *ny*}	the size in pixels of the window used to display the notebook
WindowFloating	False	whether the window should float on top of others
WindowToolbars	{ }	what toolbars to include at the top of the window
ShowPageBreaks	False	whether to show where page breaks would occur if the notebook were printed
CellGrouping	Automatic	how to group cells in the notebook
Evaluator	"Local"	what kernel should be used to do evaluations in the notebook

A few of the large number of possible options for notebooks.

In addition to notebook options, you can also set any cell option at the notebook level. Doing this
tells *Mathematica* to use that option setting as the default for all the cells in the notebook. You can
override the default by explicitly setting the options within a particular cell.

Here is the expression corresponding to
a notebook with a ruler displayed in
the toolbar at the top of the window.

```
Notebook[{
    Cell["Section heading", "Section"],
    Cell["Some text.", "Text"]},
      WindowToolbars->{"RulerBar"}]
```

This is what the notebook looks like in
the front end.

This sets the default background color
for all cells in the notebook.

```
Notebook[{
    Cell["Section heading", "Section"],
    Cell["Some text.", "Text"]},
        Background->GrayLevel[.7]]
```

Now each cell has a gray background.

If you go outside of *Mathematica* and look at the raw text of the file that corresponds to a *Mathematica* notebook, you will find that what is in the file is just the textual form of the expression that represents the notebook. One way to create a *Mathematica* notebook is therefore to construct an appropriate expression and put it in a file.

In notebook files that are written out by *Mathematica*, some additional information is typically included to make it faster for *Mathematica* to read the file in again. The information is enclosed in *Mathematica* comments indicated by (∗ ... ∗) so that it does not affect the actual expression stored in the file.

`NotebookOpen["file.nb"]`	open a notebook file in the front end
`NotebookPut[expr]`	create a notebook corresponding to *expr* in the front end
`NotebookGet[obj]`	get the expression corresponding to an open notebook in the front end

Setting up notebooks in the front end from the kernel.

This writes a notebook expression out
to the file `sample.nb`.

In[1]:= **Notebook[{Cell["Section heading", "Section"],
            Cell["Some text.", "Text"]}] >> "sample.nb"**

This reads the notebook expression
back from the file.

In[2]:= **<<sample.nb**

Out[2]= Notebook[{Cell[Section heading, Section],
            Cell[Some text., Text]}]

This opens `sample.nb` as a notebook in
the front end.

In[3]:= **NotebookOpen["sample.nb"]**

■ **Section heading**

Some text.

Once you have set up a notebook in the front end using `NotebookOpen`, you can then manipulate the notebook interactively just as you would any other notebook. But in order to use `NotebookOpen`, you have to explicitly have a notebook expression in a file. With `NotebookPut`, however, you can take a notebook expression that you have created in the kernel, and immediately display it as a notebook in the front end.

Here is a notebook expression in the kernel.

```
In[4]:= Notebook[{Cell["Section heading", "Section"],
            Cell["Some text.", "Text"]}]
```

```
Out[4]= Notebook[{Cell[Section heading, Section],
            Cell[Some text., Text]}]
```

This uses the expression to set up a notebook in the front end.

```
In[5]:= NotebookPut[%]
```

■ **Section heading**

Some text.

```
Out[5]= -NotebookObject-
```

You can use `NotebookGet` to get the notebook corresponding to a particular `NotebookObject` back into the kernel.

```
In[6]:= NotebookGet[%]
```

```
Out[6]= Notebook[{Cell[CellGroupData[
            {Cell[TextData[Section heading], Section],
            Cell[TextData[Some text.], Text]}, Open]]}]
```

■ 2.11.3 Manipulating Notebooks from the Kernel

If you want to do simple operations on *Mathematica* notebooks, then you will usually find it convenient just to use the interactive capabilities of the standard *Mathematica* front end. But if you want to do more complicated and systematic operations, then you will often find it better to use the kernel.

`Notebooks[ ]`	a list of all your open notebooks
`Notebooks["`*name*`"]`	a list of all open notebooks with the specified name
`SelectedNotebook[ ]`	the notebook that is currently selected
`InputNotebook[ ]`	the notebook into which typed input will go
`EvaluationNotebook[ ]`	the notebook in which this function is being evaluated
`ButtonNotebook[ ]`	the notebook containing the button (if any) which initiated this evaluation

Functions that give the notebook objects corresponding to particular notebooks.

Within the *Mathematica* kernel, notebooks that you have open in the front end are referred to by *notebook objects* of the form NotebookObject[*fe*, *id*]. The first argument of NotebookObject specifies the FrontEndObject for the front end in which the notebook resides, while the second argument gives a unique serial number for the notebook.

Here is a notebook named Example.nb.

■ **First Heading**

■ **Second Heading**

This finds the corresponding notebook object in the front end.

```
In[1]:= Notebooks["Example.nb"]
```
```
Out[1]= {NotebookObject[<<Example.nb>>]}
```

This gets the expression corresponding to the notebook into the kernel.

```
In[2]:= NotebookGet[First[%]]
```
```
Out[2]= Notebook[{Cell[First Heading, Section],
           Cell[Second Heading, Section]}]
```

This replaces every occurrence of the string "Section" by "Text".

```
In[3]:= % /. "Section" -> "Text"
```
```
Out[3]= Notebook[{Cell[First Heading, Text],
           Cell[Second Heading, Text]}]
```

This creates a new modified notebook in the front end.

```
In[4]:= NotebookPut[%]
```

First Heading

Second Heading

```
Out[4]= {NotebookObject[<<Untitled-1.nb>>]}
```

NotebookGet[*obj*]	get the notebook expression corresponding to the notebook object *obj*
NotebookPut[*expr*, *obj*]	make *expr* the expression corresponding to the notebook object *obj*
NotebookPut[*expr*]	make *expr* the expression corresponding to the currently selected notebook

Exchanging whole notebook expressions between the kernel and front end.

If you want to do extensive manipulations on a particular notebook you will usually find it convenient to use NotebookGet to get the whole notebook into the kernel as a single expression. But if instead you want to do a sequence of small operations on a notebook, then it is often better to leave the notebook in the front end, and then to send specific commands from the kernel to the front end to tell it what operations to do.

Mathematica is set up so that anything you can do interactively to a notebook in the front end you can also do by sending appropriate commands to the front end from the kernel.

Options[*obj*]	give a list of all options set for the notebook corresponding to notebook object *obj*
Options[*obj*, *option*]	give the value of a specific option
AbsoluteOptions[*obj*, *option*]	give absolute option values even when the actual setting is Automatic
SetOptions[*obj*, *option*->*value*]	set the value of an option

Finding and setting options for notebooks.

This gives the setting of the WindowSize option for your currently selected notebook.

In[5]:= **Options[SelectedNotebook[ ], WindowSize]**

Out[5]= {WindowSize → {550., 600.}}

This changes the size of the currently selected notebook on the screen.

In[6]:= **SetOptions[SelectedNotebook[ ], WindowSize -> {250, 100}]**

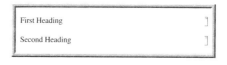

Out[6]= {WindowSize → {250., 100.}}

Within any open notebook, the front end always maintains a *current selection*. The selection can consist for example of a region of text within a cell or of a complete cell. Usually the selection is indicated on the screen by some form of highlighting. The selection can also be between two characters of text, or between two cells, in which case it is usually indicated on the screen by a vertical or horizontal insertion bar.

You can modify the current selection in an open notebook by issuing commands from the kernel.

SelectionMove[*obj*, Next, *unit*]	move the current selection to make it be the next unit of the specified type
SelectionMove[*obj*, Previous, *unit*]	move to the previous unit
SelectionMove[*obj*, After, *unit*]	move to just after the end of the present unit of the specified type
SelectionMove[*obj*, Before, *unit*]	move to just before the beginning of the present unit
SelectionMove[*obj*, All, *unit*]	extend the current selection to cover the whole unit of the specified type

Moving the current selection in a notebook.

Character	individual character
Word	word or other token
Expression	complete subexpression
TextLine	line of text
TextParagraph	paragraph of text
CellContents	the contents of the cell
Cell	complete cell
CellGroup	cell group
EvaluationCell	cell associated with the current evaluation
ButtonCell	cell associated with any button that initiated the evaluation
GeneratedCell	cell generated by the current evaluation
Notebook	complete notebook

Units used in specifying selections.

Here is a simple notebook.

- Here is a **first** cell.

- Here is a second one.

This sets nb to be the notebook object corresponding to the currently selected notebook.

In[7]:= **nb = SelectedNotebook[ ];**

This moves the current selection within the notebook to be the next word.

In[8]:= **SelectionMove[nb, Next, Word]**

- Here is a first **cell**.

- Here is a second one.

This extends the selection to the complete first cell.

In[9]:= **SelectionMove[nb, All, Cell]**

- Here is a first cell.

- Here is a second one.

This puts the selection at the end of the whole notebook.

In[10]:= **SelectionMove[nb, After, Notebook]**

- Here is a first cell.

- Here is a second one.

`NotebookFind[`*obj*, *data*`]`	move the current selection to the next occurrence of the specified data in a notebook
`NotebookFind[`*obj*, *data*, `Previous]`	move to the previous occurrence
`NotebookFind[`*obj*, *data*, `All]`	make the current selection cover all occurrences
`NotebookFind[`*obj*, *data*, *dir*, *elems*`]`	search in the specified elements of each cell, going in direction *dir*
`NotebookFind[`*obj*, `"`*text*`", IgnoreCase->True]`	do not distinguish upper- and lower-case letters in text

Searching the contents of a notebook.

This moves the current selection to the position of the previous occurrence of the word `cell`.

In[11]:= `NotebookFind[nb, "cell", Previous]`

> ■ **Here is a first cell.**
>
> ■ **Here is a second one.**

Out[11]= `$Failed`

The letter α does not appear in the current notebook, so `$Failed` is returned, and the selection is not moved.

In[12]:= `NotebookFind[nb, "\[Alpha]", Next]`

> ■ **Here is a first cell.**
>
> ■ **Here is a second one.**

Out[12]= `$Failed`

`CellContents`	contents of each cell
`CellStyle`	the name of the style for each cell
`CellLabel`	the label for each cell
`CellTags`	tags associated with each cell
`{`*elem*$_1$, *elem*$_2$, ... `}`	several kinds of elements

Possible elements of cells to be searched by `NotebookFind`.

In setting up large notebooks, it is often convenient to insert tags which are not usually displayed, but which mark particular cells in such a way that they can be found using `NotebookFind`. You can set up tags for cells either interactively in the front end, or by explicitly setting the `CellTags` option for a cell.

`NotebookLocate["`*tag*`"]`	locate and select cells with the specified tag in the current notebook
`NotebookLocate[{"`*file*`", "`*tag*`"}]`	open another notebook if necessary

Globally locating cells in notebooks.

`NotebookLocate` is the underlying function that *Mathematica* calls when you follow a hyperlink in a notebook. The menu item Create Hyperlink sets up the appropriate `NotebookLocate` as part of the script for a particular hyperlink button.

`NotebookWrite[`*obj*`, `*data*`]`	write *data* into a notebook at the current selection
`NotebookApply[`*obj*`, `*data*`]`	write *data* into a notebook, inserting the current selection in place of the first ■ that appears in *data*
`NotebookDelete[`*obj*`]`	delete whatever is currently selected in a notebook
`NotebookRead[`*obj*`]`	get the expression that corresponds to the current selection in a notebook

Writing and reading in notebooks.

`NotebookWrite[`*obj*`, `*data*`]` is similar to a Paste operation in the front end: it replaces the current selection in your notebook by *data*. If the current selection is a cell `NotebookWrite[`*obj*`, `*data*`]` will replace the cell with *data*. If the current selection lies between two cells, however, then NotebookWrite[*obj*, *data*] will create an appropriate new cell or cells.

Here is a notebook with a word of text selected.	■ **Here is a first cell.** ■ **Here is a second one.**

This replaces the selected word by new text.	*In[13]:=* NotebookWrite[nb, "<<inserted text>>"]

■ **Here is a first <<inserted text>>.**

■ **Here is a second one.**

This moves the current selection to just after the first cell in the notebook.	*In[14]:=* SelectionMove[nb, After, Cell]

■ **Here is a first <<inserted text>>.**

■ **Here is a second one.**

This now inserts a text cell after the first cell in the notebook.	*In[15]:=* NotebookWrite[nb, Cell["This cell contains text.", "Text"]]

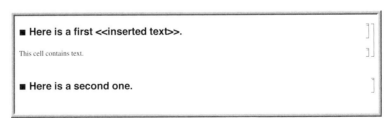

■ **Here is a first <<inserted text>>.**

This cell contains text.

■ **Here is a second one.**

This makes the current selection be the next cell in the notebook.

In[16]:= **SelectionMove[nb, Next, Cell]**

■ **Here is a first <<inserted text>>.**

This cell contains text.

■ **Here is a second one.**

This reads the current selection, returning it as an expression in the kernel.

In[17]:= **NotebookRead[nb]**

■ **Here is a first <<inserted text>>.**

This cell contains text.

■ **Here is a second one.**

Out[17]= Cell[Here is a second one., Section]

NotebookWrite[*obj*, *data*] just discards the current selection and replaces it with *data*. But particularly if you are setting up palettes, it is often convenient first to modify *data* by inserting the current selection somewhere inside it. You can do this using *selection placeholders* and NotebookApply. The first time the character ■ , entered as \[SelectionPlaceholder] or ⎋spl⎋, appears anywhere in *data*, NotebookApply will replace this character by the current selection.

Here is a simple notebook with the current selection being the contents of a cell.

In[18]:= **nb = SelectedNotebook[ ] ;**

Expand$[(1 + x)^4]$

This replaces the current selection by a string that contains a copy of its previous form.

In[19]:= **NotebookApply[nb, "x + 1/■"]**

$x + 1/\text{Expand}[(1 + x)^4]$

SelectionEvaluate[*obj*]	evaluate the current selection in place
SelectionCreateCell[*obj*]	create a new cell containing just the current selection
SelectionEvaluateCreateCell[*obj*]	evaluate the current selection and create a new cell for the result
SelectionAnimate[*obj*]	animate graphics in the current selection
SelectionAnimate[*obj*, *t*]	animate graphics for *t* seconds

Operations on the current selection.

This makes the current selection be the whole contents of the cell.

In[20]:= **SelectionMove[nb, All, CellContents]**

$x + 1 / \text{Expand}\left[(1+x)^4\right]$

This evaluates the current selection in place.

In[21]:= **SelectionEvaluate[nb]**

$x + \dfrac{1}{1 + 4\,x + 6\,x^2 + 4\,x^3 + x^4}$

SelectionEvaluate allows you to take material from a notebook and send it through the kernel for evaluation. On its own, however, SelectionEvaluate always overwrites the material you took. But by using functions like SelectionCreateCell you can maintain a record of the sequence of forms that are generated—just like in a standard *Mathematica* session.

This makes the current selection be the whole cell.

In[22]:= **SelectionMove[nb, All, Cell]**

$x + \dfrac{1}{1 + 4\,x + 6\,x^2 + 4\,x^3 + x^4}$

This creates a new cell, and copies the current selection into it.

In[23]:= **SelectionCreateCell[nb]**

$x + \dfrac{1}{1 + 4\,x + 6\,x^2 + 4\,x^3 + x^4}$

$x + \dfrac{1}{1 + 4\,x + 6\,x^2 + 4\,x^3 + x^4}$

This wraps Factor around the contents of the current cell.

In[24]:= **NotebookApply[nb, "Factor[■]"]**

$$x + \frac{1}{1 + 4 x + 6 x^2 + 4 x^3 + x^4}$$

$$\text{Factor}\left[x + \frac{1}{1 + 4 x + 6 x^2 + 4 x^3 + x^4}\right]$$

This evaluates the contents of the current cell, and creates a new cell to give the result.

In[25]:= **SelectionEvaluateCreateCell[nb]**

$$x + \frac{1}{1 + 4 x + 6 x^2 + 4 x^3 + x^4}$$

$$\text{Factor}\left[x + \frac{1}{1 + 4 x + 6 x^2 + 4 x^3 + x^4}\right]$$

$$\frac{1 + x + 4 x^2 + 6 x^3 + 4 x^4 + x^5}{(1 + x)^4}$$

Functions like NotebookWrite and SelectionEvaluate by default leave the current selection just after whatever material they insert into your notebook. You can then always move the selection by explicitly using SelectionMove. But functions like NotebookWrite and SelectionEvaluate can also take an additional argument which specifies where the current selection should be left after they do their work.

NotebookWrite[*obj*, *data*, *sel*]	write *data* into a notebook, leaving the current selection as specified by *sel*
NotebookApply[*obj*, *data*, *sel*]	write *data* replacing ■ by the previous current selection, then leaving the current selection as specified by *sel*
SelectionEvaluate[*obj*, *sel*]	evaluate the current selection, making the new current selection be as specified by *sel*
SelectionCreateCell[*obj*, *sel*]	create a new cell containing just the current selection, and make the new current selection be as specified by *sel*
SelectionEvaluateCreateCell[*obj*, *sel*]	evaluate the current selection, make a new cell for the result, and make the new current selection be as specified by *sel*

Performing operations and specifying what the new current selection should be.

After	immediately after whatever material is inserted (default)
Before	immediately before whatever material is inserted
All	the inserted material itself
Placeholder	the first ■ in the inserted material
None	leave the current selection unchanged

Specifications for the new current selection.

Here is a blank notebook.

$In[26]:=$ **nb = SelectedNotebook[ ] ;**

This writes 10! into the notebook, making the current selection be what was written.

$In[27]:=$ **NotebookWrite[nb, "10!", All]**

> 10!

This evaluates the current selection, creating a new cell for the result, and making the current selection be the whole of the result.

$In[28]:=$ **SelectionEvaluateCreateCell[nb, All]**

> 10!
>
> 3628800

This wraps FactorInteger around the current selection.

$In[29]:=$ **NotebookApply[nb, "FactorInteger[■]", All]**

> 10!
>
> FactorInteger[3628800]

This evaluates the current selection, leaving the selection just before the result.

$In[30]:=$ **SelectionEvaluate[nb, Before]**

> 10!
>
> I {{2, 8}, {3, 4}, {5, 2}, {7, 1}}

This now inserts additional text at the position of the current selection.

$In[31]:=$ **NotebookWrite[nb, "a = "]**

> 10!
>
> a = {{2, 8}, {3, 4}, {5, 2}, {7, 1}}

Options[*obj*, *option*]   find the value of an option for a complete notebook

Options[NotebookSelection[*obj*], *option*]
find the value for the current selection

SetOptions[*obj*, *option->value*]   set the value of an option for a complete notebook

SetOptions[NotebookSelection[*obj*], *option->value*]
set the value for the current selection

Finding and setting options for whole notebooks and for the current selection.

Make the current selection be a complete cell.

In[32]:= **SelectionMove[nb, All, Cell]**

> 10!
>
> a = {{2, 8}, {3, 4}, {5, 2}, {7, 1}}

Put a frame around the cell that is the current selection.

In[33]:= **SetOptions[NotebookSelection[nb], CellFrame->True]**

> 10!
>
> a = {{2, 8}, {3, 4}, {5, 2}, {7, 1}}

NotebookCreate[ ]	create a new notebook
NotebookCreate[*options*]	create a notebook with specified options
NotebookOpen["*name*"]	open an existing notebook
NotebookOpen["*name*", *options*]	open a notebook with specified options
SetSelectedNotebook[*obj*]	make the specified notebook the selected one
NotebookPrint[*obj*]	send a notebook to your printer
NotebookPrint[*obj*, "*file*"]	send a PostScript version of a notebook to a file
NotebookPrint[*obj*, "!*command*"]	send a PostScript version of a notebook to an external command
NotebookSave[*obj*]	save the current version of a notebook in a file
NotebookSave[*obj*, "*file*"]	save the notebook in a file with the specified name
NotebookClose[*obj*]	close a notebook

Operations on whole notebooks.

If you call NotebookCreate[ ] a new empty notebook will appear on your screen.

By executing commands like SetSelectedNotebook and NotebookOpen, you tell the *Mathematica* front end to change the windows you see. Sometimes you may want to manipulate a notebook without ever having it displayed on the screen. You can do this by using the option setting Visible->False in NotebookOpen or NotebookCreate.

■ 2.11.4 Manipulating the Front End from the Kernel

$FrontEnd	the front end currently in use
Options[$FrontEnd, *option*]	the setting for a global option in the front end
AbsoluteOptions[$FrontEnd, *option*]	
	the absolute setting for an option
SetOptions[$FrontEnd, *option*->value*]	
	reset an option in the front end

Manipulating global options in the front end.

Just like cells and notebooks, the complete *Mathematica* front end has various options, which you can look at and manipulate from the kernel.

This gives the object corresponding to the front end currently in use.

In[1]:= **$FrontEnd**

Out[1]= -FrontEndObject-

This gives the current directory used by the front end for notebook files.

In[2]:= **Options[$FrontEnd, NotebookDirectory]**

Out[2]= {NotebookDirectory:→$InstallationDirectory}

option	default value	
NotebookDirectory	"~$"	the current directory for notebook files
NotebookPath	(system dependent)	the path to search when trying to open notebooks
Language	"English"	default language for text
MessageOptions	(list of settings)	how to handle various help and warning messages

A few global options for the *Mathematica* front end.

By using `NotebookWrite` you can effectively input to the front end any ordinary text that you can enter on the keyboard. `FrontEndTokenExecute` allows you to send from the kernel any command that the front end can execute. These commands include both menu items and control sequences.

`FrontEndTokenExecute["`*name*`"]`	execute a named command in the front end

Executing a named command in the front end.

`"Indent"`	indent all selected lines by one tab
`"NotebookStatisticsDialog"`	display statistics about the current notebook
`"OpenCloseGroup"`	toggle a cell group between open and closed
`"CellSplit"`	split a cell in two at the current insertion point
`"DuplicatePreviousInput"`	create a new cell which is a duplicate of the nearest input cell above
`"FindDialog"`	bring up the find dialog
`"ColorSelectorDialog"`	bring up the color selector dialog
`"GraphicsAlign"`	align selected graphics
`"CompleteSelection"`	complete the command name that is the current selection

A few named commands that can be given to the front end. These commands usually correspond to menu items.

■ 2.11.5 Advanced Topic: Executing Notebook Commands Directly in the Front End

When you execute a command like `NotebookWrite[`*obj, data*`]` the actual operation of inserting data into your notebook is performed in the front end. Normally, however, the kernel is needed in order to evaluate the original command, and to construct the appropriate request to send to the front end. But it turns out that the front end is set up to execute a limited collection of commands directly, without ever involving the kernel.

> NotebookWrite[*obj*, *data*]   version of NotebookWrite to be executed in the kernel
>
> FrontEnd`NotebookWrite[*obj*, *data*]
>   version of NotebookWrite to be executed directly in the
>   front end

Distinguishing kernel and front end versions of commands.

The basic way that *Mathematica* distinguishes between commands to be executed in the kernel and to be executed directly in the front end is by using contexts. The kernel commands are in the usual System` context, but the front end commands are in the FrontEnd` context.

> FrontEndExecute[*expr*]   send *expr* to be executed in the front end

Sending an expression to be executed in the front end.

Here is a blank notebook.

This uses kernel commands to write data into the notebook.

```
In[1]:= NotebookWrite[SelectedNotebook[ ], "x + y + z"]
```

x + y + z

In the kernel, these commands do absolutely nothing.

```
In[2]:= FrontEnd`NotebookWrite[FrontEnd`SelectedNotebook[ ],
            "a + b + c + d"]
```

x + y + z

```
Out[2]= FrontEnd`NotebookWrite[
            FrontEnd`SelectedNotebook[], a + b + c + d]
```

If they are sent to the front end, however, they cause data to be written into the notebook.

```
In[3]:= FrontEndExecute[%]
```

x + y + z

a + b + c + d

If you write sophisticated programs for manipulating notebooks, then you will have no choice but to execute these programs primarily in the kernel. But for the kinds of operations typically performed by simple buttons, you may find that it is possible to execute all the commands you need directly in the front end—without the kernel even needing to be running.

■ 2.11.6 Button Boxes and Active Elements in Notebooks

Within any cell in a notebook it is possible to set up `ButtonBox` objects that perform actions whenever you click on them. `ButtonBox` objects are the way that palette buttons, hyperlinks and other active elements are implemented in *Mathematica* notebooks.

When you first enter a `ButtonBox` object in a cell, it will behave just like any other expression, and by clicking on it you can select it, edit it, and so on. But if you set the `Active` option for the cell, say by choosing the Cell Active item in the Cell Properties menu, then the `ButtonBox` will become active, and when you click on it, it will perform whatever action you have specified for it.

Here is a button.	`In[1]:= ButtonBox["Expand[■]"] // DisplayForm`
	`Out[1]//DisplayForm=` `Expand[■]`

When the button appears in an active cell, it will paste its contents whenever you click on it.

> `Expand[■]`

Here is a typical palette.

> `abc` `xy`

In the expression corresponding to the palette each button corresponds to a ButtonBox object.

```
Cell[BoxData[GridBox[{
    {
      ButtonBox["abc"],
      ButtonBox["xy"]}
    },
    ColumnSpacings->0]], "Input", Active->True]
```

`ButtonBox[`*boxes*`]`	a button that will paste its contents when it appears in an active cell
`ButtonBox[`*boxes*`, Active->True]`	a button that will always be active
`ButtonBox[`*boxes*`, ButtonStyle->"`*style*`"]`	a button whose properties are taken from the specified style

Basic `ButtonBox` objects.

By setting the `ButtonStyle` you can specify defaults both for how a button will be displayed, and what its action will be. The notebook front end provides a number of standard `ButtonStyle` settings, which you can access from the Create Button and Edit Button menu items.

"Paste"	paste the contents of the button (default)
"Evaluate"	paste then evaluate in place what has been pasted
"EvaluateCell"	paste then evaluate the whole cell
"CopyEvaluate"	copy the current selection into a new cell, then paste and evaluate in place
"CopyEvaluateCell"	copy the current selection into a new cell, then paste and evaluate the whole cell
"Hyperlink"	jump to a different location in the notebook

Standard settings for the `ButtonStyle` option.

Here is the expression corresponding to a CopyEvaluateCell button.

```
Cell[BoxData[
  ButtonBox[
    RowBox[{"Expand", "[", "\[SelectionPlaceholder]", "]"}],
    ButtonStyle->"CopyEvaluateCell"]], "Input",
  Active->True]
```

This is what the button looks like.

Expand[■]

Here is a notebook with a selection made.

$(1+x)^6$

This is what happens when one then clicks on the button.

$(1+x)^6$

$In[1]:=$ Expand$\left[(1+x)^6\right]$

$Out[1]=$ $1 + 6x + 15x^2 + 20x^3 + 15x^4 + 6x^5 + x^6$

option	default value	
ButtonFunction	(pasting function)	the function to apply when the button is clicked
ButtonSource	Automatic	where to get the first argument of the button function from
ButtonData	Automatic	the second argument to supply to the button function
ButtonEvaluator	None	where to send the button function for evaluation
ButtonNote	None	what to display in the window status line when the cursor is over the button

Options that affect the action of buttons.

A particular `ButtonStyle` setting will specify defaults for all other button options. Some of these options will affect the display of the button, as discussed on page 452. Others affect the action it performs.

What ultimately determines the action of a button is the setting for the `ButtonFunction` option. This setting gives the *Mathematica* function which is to be executed whenever the button is clicked. Typically this function will be a combination of various notebook manipulation commands.

Thus, for example, in its most basic form, a `Paste` button will have a `ButtonFunction` given effectively by `NotebookApply[SelectedNotebook[ ], #]&`, while a `Hyperlink` button will have a `ButtonFunction` given effectively by `NotebookLocate[#2]&`.

When a button is clicked, two arguments are supplied to its `ButtonFunction`. The first is specified by `ButtonSource`, and the second by `ButtonData`.

Typically `ButtonData` is set to be a fixed expression, defined when the button was first created. `ButtonSource`, on the other hand, usually changes with the contents of the button, or the environment in which the button appears.

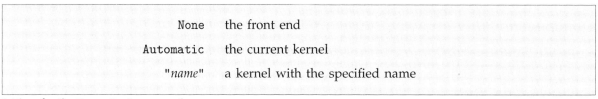

Automatic	`ButtonData` if it is set, otherwise `ButtonContents`
ButtonContents	the expression displayed on the button
ButtonData	the setting for the `ButtonData` option
CellContents	the contents of the cell in which the button appears
Cell	the whole cell in which the button appears
Notebook	the whole notebook in which the button appears
n	the expression n levels up from the button in the notebook

Possible settings for the `ButtonSource` option.

For a simple `Paste` button, the setting for `ButtonSource` is typically `ButtonContents`. This means that whatever is displayed in the button will be what is passed as the first argument of the button function. The button function can then take this argument and feed it to `NotebookApply`, thereby actually pasting it into the notebook.

By using settings other than `ButtonContents` for `ButtonSource`, you can create buttons which effectively pull in various aspects of their environment for processing. Thus, for example, with the setting `ButtonSource->Cell`, the first argument to the button function will be the expression that represents the whole cell in which the button appears. By having the button function manipulate this expression you can then make the button have a global effect on the whole cell, say by restructuring it in some specified way.

None	the front end
Automatic	the current kernel
"name"	a kernel with the specified name

Settings for the `ButtonEvaluator` option.

Once the arguments to a `ButtonFunction` have been found, and an expression has been constructed, there is then the question of where that expression should be sent for evaluation. The `ButtonEvaluator` option for a `ButtonBox` allows you to specify this.

In general, if the expression involves a range of *Mathematica* functions, then there will be no choice but to evaluate it in an actual *Mathematica* kernel. But if the expression involves only simple notebook manipulation commands, then it may be possible to execute the expression directly in the front end, without ever involving the kernel. You can specify that this should be done by setting the option `ButtonEvaluator->None`.

FrontEndExecute[*expr*]	execute an expression in the front end
FrontEnd`NotebookApply[...], etc.	front end versions of notebook commands

Expressions to be executed directly in the front end.

As discussed in the previous section, the standard notebook front end can handle only a limited set of commands, all identified as being in the FrontEnd` context. But these commands are sufficient to be able to implement all of the actions associated with standard button styles such as Paste, EvaluateCell and Hyperlink.

Note that even if an expression is sent to the front end, it will be executed only if it is wrapped in a FrontEndExecute.

■ 2.11.7 Advanced Topic: The Structure of Cells

Cell[*contents*, "*style*"]	a cell in a particular style
Cell[*contents*, "*style*", *options*]	a cell with additional options set

Expressions corresponding to cells.

Here is a notebook containing a text cell and a *Mathematica* input cell.

```
Here is some ordinary text.

   x^α / y
```

Here are the expressions corresponding to these cells.

```
Cell["Here is some ordinary text.", "Text"]

Cell[BoxData[
  RowBox[{
    SuperscriptBox["x", "α"], "/", "y"}]], "Input"]
```

Here is a notebook containing a text cell with *Mathematica* input inside.

```
Text with the formula xyz^α inside.
```

This is the expression corresponding to the cell. The *Mathematica* input is in a cell embedded inside the text.

```
Cell[TextData[{
  "Text with the formula ",
  Cell[BoxData[
    FormBox[
      SuperscriptBox["xyz", "\[Alpha]"], TraditionalForm]]],
  " inside."
}], "Text"]
```

"text"	plain text
TextData[{*text₁*, *text₂*, ... }]	text potentially in different styles, or containing cells
BoxData[*boxes*]	formatted *Mathematica* expressions
GraphicsData["*type*", *data*]	graphics or sounds
OutputFormData["*itext*", "*otext*"]	
	text as generated by InputForm and OutputForm
RawData["*data*"]	unformatted expressions as obtained using Show Expression
CellGroupData[{*cell₁*, *cell₂*, ... }, Open]	
	an open group of cells
CellGroupData[{*cell₁*, *cell₂*, ... }, Closed]	
	a closed group of cells
StyleData["*style*"]	a style definition cell

Expressions representing possible forms of cell contents.

■ 2.11.8 Styles and the Inheritance of Option Settings

Global	the complete front end and all open notebooks
Notebook	the current notebook
Style	the style of the current cell
Cell	the specific current cell
Selection	a selection within a cell

The hierarchy of levels at which options can be set.

Here is a notebook containing three cells.

This is what happens when the setting `CellFrame->True` is made specifically for the third cell.

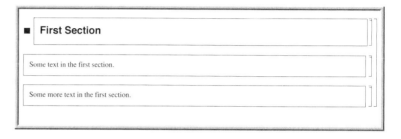

This is what happens when the setting `CellFrame->True` is made globally for the whole notebook.

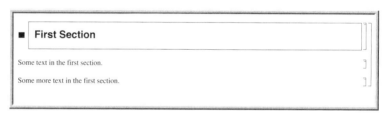

This is what happens when the setting is made for the "`Section`" style.

In the standard notebook front end, you can check and set options at any level by using the Option Inspector menu item. If you do not set an option at a particular level, then its value will always be inherited from the level above. Thus, for example, if a particular cell does not set the `CellFrame` option, then the value used will be inherited from its setting for the style of the cell or for the whole notebook that contains the cell.

As a result, if you set `CellFrame->True` at the level of a whole notebook, then all the cells in the notebook will have frames drawn around them—unless the style of a particular cell, or the cell itself, explicitly overrides this setting.

- Choose the basic default styles for a notebook
- Choose the styles for screen and printing style environments
- Edit specific styles for the notebook

Ways to set up styles in a notebook.

Depending on what you intend to use your *Mathematica* notebook for, you may want to choose different basic default styles for the notebook. In the standard notebook front end, you can do this using the Edit Style Sheet menu item.

"Report"	styles for everyday work and for reports
"Tutorial"	styles for tutorial-type material
"Book"	styles for books such as this one

Some typical choices of basic default styles.

With each choice of basic default styles, the styles that are provided will change. Thus, for example, only in the Book default styles is there a Box style which sets up the gray boxes used in this book.

Here is a notebook that uses Book default styles.

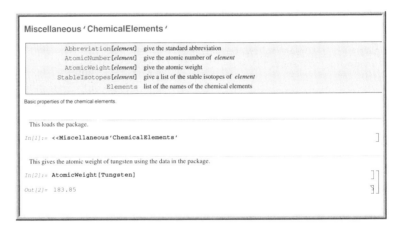

option	default value	
ScreenStyleEnvironment	"Working"	the style environment to use for display on the screen
PrintingStyleEnvironment	"Printout"	the style environment to use for printed output

Options for specifying style environments.

Within a particular set of basic default styles, *Mathematica* allows for two different style environments: one for display on the screen, and another for output to a printer. The existence of separate screen and printing style environments allows you to set up styles which are separately optimized both for low-resolution display on a screen, and high-resolution printing.

"Working"	on-screen working environment
"Presentation"	on-screen environment for presentations
"Condensed"	on-screen environment for maximum display density
"Printout"	paper printout environment

Some typical settings for style environments.

Here is a notebook with the usual
Working screen style environment.

$$\int \frac{\log(x)}{x^3 - 1}\,dx$$

$$-\frac{-\log(1-x)\log(x)-\mathrm{Li}_2(x)}{\left(1+\sqrt[3]{-1}\right)(1-(-1)^{2/3})} + \frac{-\log(x)\log\!\left(\sqrt[3]{-1}\,x+1\right)-\mathrm{Li}_2\!\left(-\sqrt[3]{-1}\,x\right)}{(1-(-1)^{2/3})\left(\sqrt[3]{-1}+(-1)^{2/3}\right)} + $$

$$\frac{-\log(x)\log(1-(-1)^{2/3}\,x)-\mathrm{Li}_2((-1)^{2/3}\,x)}{\left(1+\sqrt[3]{-1}\right)\left(-\sqrt[3]{-1}-(-1)^{2/3}\right)}$$

Here is the same notebook with the
Condensed screen style environment.

$$\int \frac{\log(x)}{x^3 - 1}\,dx$$

$$-\frac{-\log(1-x)\log(x)-\mathrm{Li}_2(x)}{\left(1+\sqrt[3]{-1}\right)(1-(-1)^{2/3})} + \frac{-\log(x)\log\!\left(\sqrt[3]{-1}\,x+1\right)-\mathrm{Li}_2\!\left(-\sqrt[3]{-1}\,x\right)}{(1-(-1)^{2/3})\left(\sqrt[3]{-1}+(-1)^{2/3}\right)} + \frac{-\log(x)\log(1-(-1)^{2/3}\,x)-\mathrm{Li}_2((-1)^{2/3}\,x)}{\left(1+\sqrt[3]{-1}\right)\left(-\sqrt[3]{-1}-(-1)^{2/3}\right)}$$

The way that *Mathematica* actually sets up the definitions for styles is by using *style definition cells*. These cells can either be given in separate *style definition notebooks*, or can be included in the options of a specific notebook. In either case, you can access style definitions by using the Edit Style Sheet menu item in the standard notebook front end.

| "*name*.nb" | get definitions from the specified notebook |
| {*cell*₁, *cell*₂, ... } | get definitions from the explicit cells given |

Settings for the StyleDefinitions option for a Notebook.

Here is an example of a typical style
definition cell.

Prototype for style: "Section":
Section

This is the expression corresponding to the cell. Any cell in Section style will inherit the option settings given here.

```
Cell[StyleData["Section"],NotebookDefault,
  CellFrame->False,
  CellDingbat->"\[GraySquare]",
  CellMargins->{{22, Inherited}, {Inherited, 20}},
  CellGroupingRules->{"SectionGrouping", 30},
  PageBreakBelow->False,
  CounterIncrements->"Section",
  CounterAssignments->{{"Subsection", 0}, {"Subsubsection", 0}},
  FontFamily->"Times",
  FontSize->18,
  FontWeight->"Bold"]
```

Cell[StyleData["*style*"], *options*]   a cell specifying option settings for a particular style

Cell[StyleData["*style*", "*env*"], *options*]

            a cell specifying additional options for a particular style environment

Expressions corresponding to style definition cells.

■ 2.11.9 Options for Cells

Mathematica provides a large number of options for cells. All of these options can be accessed through the Option Inspector menu item in the front end. They can be set either directly at the level of individual cells or at a higher level, to be inherited by individual cells.

option	typical default value	
CellDingbat	""	a dingbat to use to emphasize the cell
CellFrame	False	whether to draw a frame around the cell
Background	GrayLevel[1]	the background color for the cell
ShowCellBracket	True	whether to display the cell bracket
Magnification	1	the magnification at which to display the cell
CellOpen	True	whether to display the contents of the cell

Some basic cell display options.

This creates a cell in Section style with default settings for all options.

In[1]:= **CellPrint[Cell["A Heading", "Section"]]**

This creates a cell with dingbat and background options modified.

In[2]:= **CellPrint[Cell["A Heading", "Section",**
CellDingbat->"\[FilledCircle]", Background->GrayLevel[.7]]]

option	typical default value	
CellMargins	{{7, 0}, {4, 4}}	outer margins in printer's points to leave around the contents of the cell
CellFrameMargins	8	margins to leave inside the cell frame
CellElementSpacings	list of rules	details of the layout of cell elements
CellBaseline	Baseline	how to align the baseline of an inline cell with text around it

Options for cell positioning.

The option `CellMargins` allows you to specify both horizontal and vertical margins to put around a cell. You can set the horizontal margins interactively by using the margin stops in the ruler displayed when you choose the Show Ruler menu item in the front end.

Whenever an option can refer to all four edges of a cell, *Mathematica* follows the convention that the setting for the option takes the form {{*left*, *right*}, {*bottom*, *top*}}. By giving non-zero values for the *top* and *bottom* elements, `CellMargins` can specify gaps to leave above and below a particular cell. The values are always taken to be in printer's points.

This leaves 50 points of space on the left of the cell, and 20 points above and below.

In[3]:= `CellPrint[Cell["First text", "Text",`
`        CellMargins->{{50, 0}, {20, 20}}]]`

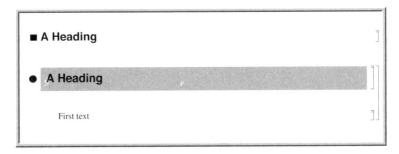

Almost every aspect of *Mathematica* notebooks can be controlled by some option or another. More detailed aspects are typically handled by "aggregate options" such as `CellElementSpacings`. The settings for these options are lists of *Mathematica* rules, which effectively give values for a sequence of suboptions. The names of these suboptions are usually strings rather than symbols.

This shows the settings for all the suboptions associated with `CellElementSpacings`.

In[4]:= `Options[SelectedNotebook[ ], CellElementSpacings]`

Out[4]= `{CellElementSpacings →`
`        {CellMinHeight → 12., ClosedCellHeight → 19.,`
`          ClosedGroupTopMargin → 4., GroupIconTopMargin →`
`          3., GroupIconBottomMargin → 12.}}`

Mathematica allows you to embed cells inside pieces of text. The option `CellBaseline` determines how such "inline cells" will be aligned vertically with respect to the text around them. In direct analogy with the option `GridBaseline` for a `GridBox`, the option `CellBaseline` specifies what aspect of the cell should be considered its baseline.

Here is a cell containing an inline formula. The baseline of the formula is aligned with the baseline of the text around it.

■ the $\frac{x}{y}$ fraction

Here is a cell in which the bottom of the formula is aligned with the baseline of the text around it.

■ the $\frac{x}{y}$ fraction

This alignment is specified using the `CellBaseline->Bottom` setting.

```
Cell[TextData[{
  "the ",
  Cell[BoxData[
   RowBox[{
     FractionBox["x", "y"], " "}]],
   CellBaseline->Bottom],
  "fraction "
}], "Section"]
```

option	typical default value	
CellLabel	""	a label for a cell
ShowCellLabel	True	whether to show the label for a cell
CellLabelAutoDelete	True	whether to delete the label if the cell is modified
CellTags	{ }	tags for a cell
ShowCellTags	False	whether to show tags for a cell
ConversionRules	{ }	rules for external conversions

Options for ancillary data associated with cells.

In addition to the actual contents of a cell, it is often useful to associate various kinds of ancillary data with cells.

In a standard *Mathematica* session, cells containing successive lines of kernel input and output are given labels of the form In[n]:= and Out[n]=. The option ShowCellLabel determines whether such labels should be displayed. CellLabelAutoDelete determines whether the label on a cell should be removed if the contents of the cell are modified. Doing this ensures that In[n]:= and Out[n]= labels are only associated with unmodified pieces of kernel input and output.

Cell tags are typically used to associate keywords or other attributes with cells, that can be searched for using functions like NotebookFind. Destinations for hyperlinks in *Mathematica* notebooks are usually implemented using cell tags.

The option ConversionRules allows you to give a list containing entries such as "TeX" -> *data* which specify how the contents of a cell should be converted to external formats. This is particularly relevant if you want to keep a copy of the original form of a cell that has been converted in *Mathematica* notebook format from some external format.

option	typical default value	
Deletable	True	whether to allow a cell to be deleted interactively with the front end
Copyable	True	whether to allow a cell to be copied
Selectable	True	whether to allow the contents of a cell to be selected
Editable	True	whether to allow the contents of a cell to be edited
CellEditDuplicate	False	whether to make a copy of a cell if its contents are edited
Active	False	whether buttons in the cell are active

Options for controlling interactive operations on cells.

The options `Deletable`, `Copyable`, `Selectable` and `Editable` allow you to control what interactive operations should be allowed on cells. By setting these options to `False` at the notebook level, you can protect all the cells in a notebook.

Even if you allow a particular cell to be edited, you can set `CellEditDuplicate->True` to get *Mathematica* to make a copy of the contents of the cell before they are actually changed. Styles for cells that contain output from *Mathematica* kernel evaluations usually make use of this option.

option	typical default value	
Evaluator	"Local"	the name of the kernel to use for evaluations
Evaluatable	False	whether to allow the contents of a cell to be evaluated
CellEvaluationDuplicate	False	whether to make a copy of a cell if it is evaluated
CellAutoOverwrite	False	whether to overwrite previous output when new output is generated
GeneratedCell	False	whether this cell was generated from the kernel
InitializationCell	False	whether this cell should automatically be evaluated when the notebook is opened

Options for evaluation.

Mathematica makes it possible to specify a different evaluator for each cell in a notebook. But most often, the `Evaluator` option is set only at the notebook level, typically using the Kernel menu item in the front end.

The option `CellAutoOverwrite` is typically set to `True` for styles that represent *Mathematica* output. Doing this means that when you re-evaluate a particular piece of input, *Mathematica* will automatically delete the output that was previously generated from that input, and will overwrite it with new output.

The option `GeneratedCell` is set whenever a cell is generated by an external request to the front end rather than by an interactive operation within the front end. Thus, for example, any cell obtained as output from a kernel evaluation, or created using a function like `CellPrint` or `NotebookWrite`, will have `GeneratedCell->True`.

option	typical default value	
PageBreakAbove	Automatic	whether to put a page break just above a particular cell
PageBreakWithin	False	whether to allow a page break within a particular cell
PageBreakBelow	Automatic	whether to put a page break just below a particular cell
GroupPageBreakWithin	False	whether to allow a page break within a particular group of cells

Options for controlling page breaks when cells are printed.

When you display a notebook on the screen, you can scroll continuously through it. But if you print the notebook out, you have to decide where page breaks will occur. A setting of Automatic for a page break option tells *Mathematica* to make a page break if necessary; True specifies that a page break should always be made, while False specifies that it should never be.

■ 2.11.10 Text and Font Options

option	typical default value	
PageWidth	WindowWidth	how wide to assume the page to be
TextAlignment	Left	how to align successive lines of text
TextJustification	0	how much to allow lines of text to be stretched to make them fit
Hyphenation	True	whether to allow hyphenation
ParagraphIndent	0	how many printer's points to indent the first line in each paragraph

General options for text formatting.

If you have a large block of text containing no explicit RETURN characters, then *Mathematica* will automatically break your text into a sequence of lines. The option PageWidth specifies how long each line should be allowed to be.

`WindowWidth`	the width of the window on the screen
`PaperWidth`	the width of the page as it would be printed
`Infinity`	an infinite width (no linebreaking)
n	explicit width given in printer's points

Settings for the `PageWidth` option in cells and notebooks.

The option `TextAlignment` allows you to specify how you want successive lines of text to be aligned. Since *Mathematica* normally breaks text only at space or punctuation characters, it is common to end up with lines of different lengths. Normally the variation in lengths will give your text a ragged boundary. But *Mathematica* allows you to adjust the spaces in successive lines of text so as to make the lines more nearly equal in length. The setting for `TextJustification` gives the fraction of extra space which *Mathematica* is allowed to add. `TextJustification->1` leads to "full justification" in which all complete lines of text are adjusted to be exactly the same length.

`Left`	aligned on the left
`Right`	aligned on the right
`Center`	centered
x	aligned at a position x running from −1 to +1 across the page

Settings for the `TextAlignment` option.

Here is text with
`TextAlignment->Left` and
`TextJustification->0`.

Like other objects in *Mathematica*, the cells in a notebook, and in fact the whole notebook itself, are all ultimately represented as *Mathematica* expressions. With the standard notebook front end, you can use the command Show Expression to see the text of the *Mathematica* expression that corresponds to any particular cell.

With `TextAlignment->Center` the text is centered.

Like other objects in *Mathematica*, the cells in a notebook, and in fact the whole notebook itself, are all ultimately represented as *Mathematica* expressions. With the standard notebook front end, you can use the command Show Expression to see the text of the *Mathematica* expression that corresponds to any particular cell.

`TextJustification->1` adjusts word spacing so that both the left and right edges line up.

Like other objects in *Mathematica*, the cells in a notebook, and in fact the whole notebook itself, are all ultimately represented as *Mathematica* expressions. With the standard notebook front end, you can use the command Show Expression to see the text of the *Mathematica* expression that corresponds to any particular cell.

`TextJustification->0.5` reduces the degree of raggedness, but does not force the left and right edges to be precisely lined up.

Like other objects in *Mathematica*, the cells in a notebook, and in fact the whole notebook itself, are all ultimately represented as *Mathematica* expressions. With the standard notebook front end, you can use the command Show Expression to see the text of the *Mathematica* expression that corresponds to any particular cell.

When you enter a block of text in a *Mathematica* notebook, *Mathematica* will treat any explicit RETURN characters that you type as paragraph breaks. The option `ParagraphIndent` allows you to specify how much you want to indent the first line in each paragraph. By giving a negative setting for `ParagraphIndent`, you can make the first line stick out to the left relative to subsequent lines.

`LineSpacing->{c, 0}`	leave space so that the total height of each line is c times the height of its contents
`LineSpacing->{0, n}`	make the total height of each line exactly n printer's points
`LineSpacing->{c, n}`	make the total height c times the height of the contents plus n printer's points
`ParagraphSpacing->{c, 0}`	leave an extra space of c times the height of the font before the beginning of each paragraph
`ParagraphSpacing->{0, n}`	leave an extra space of exactly n printer's points before the beginning of each paragraph
`ParagraphSpacing->{c, n}`	leave an extra space of c times the height of the font plus n printer's points

Options for spacing between lines of text.

Here is some text with the default setting `LineSpacing->{1, 1}`, which inserts just 1 printer's point of extra space between successive lines.

> Like other objects in *Mathematica*, the cells in a notebook, and in fact the whole notebook itself, are all ultimately represented as *Mathematica* expressions. With the standard notebook front end, you can use the command Show Expression to see the text of the *Mathematica* expression that corresponds to any particular cell.

With `LineSpacing->{1, 5}` the text is "looser".

> Like other objects in *Mathematica*, the cells in a notebook, and in fact the whole notebook itself, are all ultimately represented as *Mathematica* expressions. With the standard notebook front end, you can use the command Show Expression to see the text of the *Mathematica* expression that corresponds to any particular cell.

`LineSpacing->{2, 0}` makes the text double-spaced.

> Like other objects in *Mathematica*, the cells in a notebook, and in fact the whole notebook itself, are all ultimately represented as *Mathematica* expressions. With the standard notebook front end, you can use the command Show Expression to see the text of the *Mathematica* expression that corresponds to any particular cell.

With `LineSpacing->{1, -2}` the text is tight.

> Like other objects in *Mathematica*, the cells in a notebook, and in fact the whole notebook itself, are all ultimately represented as *Mathematica* expressions. With the standard notebook front end, you can use the command Show Expression to see the text of the *Mathematica* expression that corresponds to any particular cell.

option	typical default value	
FontFamily	"Courier"	the family of font to use
FontSubstitutions	{ }	a list of substitutions to try for font family names
FontSize	12	the maximum height of characters in printer's points
FontWeight	"Bold"	the weight of characters to use
FontSlant	"Plain"	the slant of characters to use
FontTracking	"Plain"	the horizontal compression or expansion of characters
FontColor	GrayLevel[0]	the color of characters
Background	GrayLevel[1]	the color of the background for each character

Options for fonts.

"Courier"	text like this
"Times"	text like this
"Helvetica"	text like this

Some typical font family names.

FontWeight->"Plain"	text like this
FontWeight->"Bold"	**text like this**
FontWeight->"ExtraBold"	**text like this**
FontSlant->"Oblique"	*text like this*

Some settings of font options.

Mathematica allows you to specify the font that you want to use in considerable detail. Sometimes, however, the particular combination of font families and variations that you request may not be available on your computer system. In such cases, *Mathematica* will try to find the closest approximation it can. There are various additional options, such as FontPostScriptName, that you can set to help *Mathematica* find an appropriate font. In addition, you can set FontSubstitutions to be a list of rules that give replacements to try for font family names.

There are a great many fonts available for ordinary text. But for special technical characters, and even for Greek letters, far fewer fonts are available. The *Mathematica* system includes fonts that were built to support all of the various special characters that are used by *Mathematica*. There are three versions of these fonts: ordinary (like Times), monospaced (like Courier), and sans serif (like Helvetica).

For a given text font, *Mathematica* tries to choose the special character font that matches it best. You can help *Mathematica* to make this choice by giving rules for "FontSerifed" and "FontMonospaced" in the setting for the FontProperties option. You can also give rules for "FontEncoding" to specify explicitly from what font each character is to be taken.

■ 2.11.11 Advanced Topic: Options for Expression Input and Output

option	typical default value	
AutoIndent	Automatic	whether to indent after an explicit RETURN character is entered
DelimiterFlashTime	0.3	the time in seconds to flash a delimiter when a matching one is entered
ShowAutoStyles	True	whether to show automatic style variations for syntactic and other constructs
ShowCursorTracker	True	whether an elliptical spot should appear momentarily to guide the eye if the cursor position jumps
ShowSpecialCharacters	True	whether to replace \[*Name*] by a special character as soon as the] is entered
ShowStringCharacters	False	whether to display " when a string is entered
SingleLetterItalics	False	whether to put single-letter symbol names in italics
ZeroWidthTimes	False	whether to represent multiplication by a zero width character
InputAliases	{}	additional ⠆*name*⠆ aliases to allow
InputAutoReplacements	{"->" -> "→", ... }	strings to automatically replace on input
AutoItalicWords	{"Mathematica", ... }	words to automatically put in italics
LanguageCategory	Automatic	what category of language to assume a cell contains for spell checking and hyphenation

Options associated with the interactive entering of expressions.

The options `SingleLetterItalics` and `ZeroWidthTimes` are typically set whenever a cell uses `TraditionalForm`.

Here is an expression entered with default options for a `StandardForm` input cell.

$$x^6 + 6 x^5 y + 15 x^4 y^2 + 20 x^3 y^3 + 15 x^2 y^4 + 6 x y^5 + y^6$$

Here is the same expression entered in a cell with `SingleLetterItalics->True` and `ZeroWidthTimes->True`.

$$x^6 + 6x^5 y + 15x^4 y^2 + 20x^3 y^3 + 15x^2 y^4 + 6xy^5 + y^6$$

Built into *Mathematica* are a large number of aliases for common special characters. `InputAliases` allows you to add your own aliases for further special characters or for any other kind of *Mathematica* input. A rule of the form *"name"->expr* specifies that ⁚*name*⁚ should immediately be replaced on input by *expr*.

Aliases are delimited by explicit ESC characters. The option `InputAutoReplacements` allows you to specify that certain kinds of input sequences should be immediately replaced even when they have no explicit delimiters. By default, for example, `->` is immediately replaced by →. You can give a rule of the form *"seq"->"rhs"* to specify that whenever *seq* appears as a token in your input, it should immediately be replaced by *rhs*.

`"NaturalLanguage"`	human natural language such as English
`"Mathematica"`	*Mathematica* input
`"Formula"`	mathematical formula
`None`	do no spell checking or hyphenation

Settings for `LanguageCategory` to control spell checking and hyphenation.

The option `LanguageCategory` allows you to tell *Mathematica* what type of contents it should assume cells have. This determines how spelling and structure should be checked, and how hyphenation should be done.

option	typical default value	
StructuredSelection	False	whether to allow only complete subexpressions to be selected
DragAndDrop	False	whether to allow drag-and-drop editing

Options associated with interactive manipulation of expressions.

Mathematica normally allows you to select any part of an expression that you see on the screen. Occasionally, however, you may find it useful to get *Mathematica* to allow only selections which correspond to complete subexpressions. You can do this by setting the option StructuredSelection->True.

Here is an expression with a piece selected.

$$(-1+x)\ (1+x)\ (1-x+x^2-x^3+x^4)\ (1+x+x^2+x^3+x^4)$$

With StructuredSelection->True only complete subexpressions can ever be selected.

$$(-1+x)\ (1+x)\ (1-x+x^2-x^3+x^4)\ (1+x+x^2+x^3+x^4)$$

$$(-1+x)\ (1+x)\ (1-x+x^2-x^3+x^4)\ (1+x+x^2+x^3+x^4)$$

$$(-1+x)\ (1+x)\ (1-x+x^2-x^3+x^4)\ (1+x+x^2+x^3+x^4)$$

GridBox[*data*, *opts*]	give options that apply to a particular grid box
StyleBox[*boxes*, *opts*]	give options that apply to all boxes in *boxes*
Cell[*contents*, *opts*]	give options that apply to all boxes in *contents*
Cell[*contents*, GridBoxOptions->*opts*]	give default options settings for all GridBox objects in *contents*

Examples of specifying options for the display of expressions.

As discussed in Section 2.9, *Mathematica* provides many options for specifying how expressions should be displayed. By using StyleBox[*boxes*, *opts*] you can apply such options to collections of boxes. But *Mathematica* is set up so that any option that you can give to a StyleBox can also be given to a complete Cell object, or even a complete Notebook. Thus, for example, options like Background and LineIndent can be given to complete cells as well as to individual StyleBox objects.

There are some options that apply only to a particular type of box, such as GridBox. Usually these options are best given separately in each GridBox where they are needed. But sometimes you may want to specify default settings to be inherited by all GridBox objects that appear in a particular cell.

You can do this by giving these default settings as the value of the option `GridBoxOptions` for the whole cell.

For each box type named *XXXBox*, *Mathematica* provides a cell option *XXXBoxOptions* that allows you to specify the default options settings for that type of box.

■ 2.11.12 Options for Graphics Cells

option	typical default value	
AspectRatioFixed	True	whether to keep a fixed aspect ratio if the image is resized
ImageSize	{288, 288}	the absolute width and height of the image in printer's points
ImageMargins	{{0, 0}, {0, 0}}	the widths of margins in printer's points to leave around the image

Options for displaying images in notebooks.

Here is a graphic displayed in a notebook.

With the default setting `AspectRatioFixed->True` resizing the graphic does not change its shape.

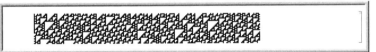

If you set `AspectRatioFixed->False` then you can change the shape.

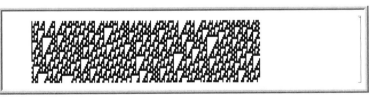

Mathematica allows you to specify the final size of a graphic by setting the `ImageSize` option in kernel graphics functions such as `Plot` and `Display`. Once a graphic is in a notebook, you can then typically resize or move it just by using the mouse.

- Use the Animate Selected Graphics menu item in the front end.

- Use the kernel command `SelectionAnimate[obj]`.

Ways to generate animations in a notebook.

Mathematica generates animated graphics by taking a sequence of graphics cells, and then treating them like frames in a movie. The option `AnimationDisplayTime` specifies how long a particular cell should be displayed as part of the movie.

option	typical default value	
`AnimationDisplayTime`	0.1	minimum time in seconds to display this cell during an animation
`AnimationDirection`	Forward	which direction to run an animation starting with this cell

Options for animations.

■ 2.11.13 Options for Notebooks

- Use the Option Inspector menu to change options interactively.

- Use `SetOptions[obj, options]` from the kernel.

- Use `NotebookCreate[options]` to create a new notebook with specified options.

Ways to change the overall options for a notebook.

This creates a notebook displayed in a 40 × 30 window with a thin frame.

```
In[1]:= NotebookCreate[WindowFrame->"ThinFrame",
                       WindowSize->{40, 30}]
```

option	typical default value	
StyleDefinitions	"DefaultStyles.nb"	the basic style sheet to use for the notebook
ScreenStyleEnvironment	"Working"	the style environment to use for screen display
PrintingStyleEnvironment	"Printout"	the style environment to use for printing

Style options for a notebook.

In giving style definitions for a particular notebook, *Mathematica* allows you either to reference another notebook, or explicitly to include the Notebook expression that defines the styles.

option	typical default value	
CellGrouping	Automatic	how to group cells in the notebook
ShowPageBreaks	False	whether to show where page breaks would occur if the notebook were printed
NotebookAutoSave	False	whether to automatically save the notebook after each piece of output

General options for notebooks.

With CellGrouping->Automatic, cells are automatically grouped based on their style.

With CellGrouping->Manual, you have to group cells by hand.

option	typical default value	
DefaultNewCellStyle	"Input"	the default style for new cells created in the notebook
DefaultDuplicateCellStyle	"Input"	the default style for cells created by automatic duplication of existing cells

Options specifying default styles for cells created in a notebook.

Mathematica allows you to take any cell option and set it at the notebook level, thereby specifying a global default for that option throughout the notebook.

option	typical default value	
Editable	True	whether to allow cells in the notebook to be edited
Selectable	True	whether to allow cells to be selected
Deletable	True	whether to allow cells to be deleted
ShowSelection	True	whether to show the current selection highlighted
Background	GrayLevel[1]	what background color to use for the notebook
Magnification	1	at what magnification to display the notebook
PageWidth	WindowWidth	how wide to allow the contents of cells to be

A few cell options that are often set at the notebook level.

Here is a notebook with the
Background option set at the notebook
level.

Here is some text.

option	typical default value	
Visible	True	whether the window should be visible on the screen
WindowSize	{Automatic, Automatic}	the width and height of the window in printer's points
WindowMargins	Automatic	the margins to leave around the window when it is displayed on the screen
WindowFrame	"Normal"	the type of frame to draw around the window
WindowElements	{"StatusArea", ... }	elements to include in the window
WindowTitle	Automatic	what title should be displayed for the window
WindowToolbars	{ }	toolbars to display at the top of the window
WindowMovable	True	whether to allow the window to be moved around on the screen
WindowFloating	False	whether the window should always float on top of other windows
WindowClickSelect	True	whether the window should become selected if you click in it

Characteristics of the notebook window.

WindowSize allows you to specify how large you want a window to be; WindowMargins allows you to specify where you want the window to be placed on your screen. The setting WindowMargins->{{*left*, *right*}, {*bottom*, *top*}} gives the margins in printer's points to leave around your window on the screen. Often only two of the margins will be set explicitly; the others will be Automatic, indicating that these margins will be determined from the particular size of screen that you use.

`"Normal"`	an ordinary window
`"Palette"`	a palette window
`"ModelessDialog"`	a modeless dialog box window
`"ModalDialog"`	a modal dialog box window
`"MovableModalDialog"`	a modal dialog box window that can be moved around the screen
`"ThinFrame"`	an ordinary window with a thin frame
`"Frameless"`	an ordinary window with no frame at all
`"Generic"`	a window with a generic border, as used for the examples in this book

Typical possible settings for `WindowFrame`.

Mathematica allows many different types of windows. The details of how particular windows are rendered may differ slightly from one computer system to another, but their general form is always the same. `WindowFrame` specifies the type of frame to draw around the window. `WindowElements` gives a list of specific elements to include in the window.

`"StatusArea"`	an area used to display status messages, such as those from `ButtonNote` options
`"MagnificationPopUp"`	a pop-up menu of common magnifications
`"HorizontalScrollBar"`	a scroll bar for horizontal motion
`"VerticalScrollBar"`	a scroll bar for vertical motion

Some typical possible entries in the `WindowElements` list.

Here is a window with a status area and horizontal scroll bar, but no magnification pop-up or vertical scroll bar.

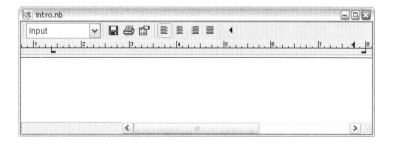

`"RulerBar"`	a ruler showing margin settings
`"EditBar"`	buttons for common editing operations

Some typical possible entries in the `WindowToolbars` list.

Here is a window with ruler and edit toolbars.

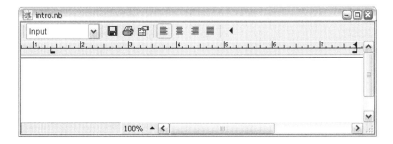

■ 2.11.14 Advanced Topic: Global Options for the Front End

In the standard notebook front end, *Mathematica* allows you to set a large number of global options. The values of all these options are by default saved in a "preferences file", and are automatically reused when you run *Mathematica* again.

style definitions	default style definitions to use for new notebooks
file locations	directories for finding notebooks and system files
data export options	how to export data in various formats
character encoding options	how to encode special characters
language options	what language to use for text
message options	how to handle messages generated by *Mathematica*
menu settings	items displayed in modifiable menus
dialog settings	choices made in dialog boxes
system configuration	private options for specific computer systems

Some typical categories of global options for the front end.

As discussed on page 592, you can access global front end options from the kernel by using `Options[$FrontEnd, `*name*`]`. But more often, you will want to access these options interactively using the Option Inspector in the front end.

2.12 Files and Streams

■ 2.12.1 Reading and Writing *Mathematica* Files

Particularly if you use a text-based *Mathematica* interface, you will often need to read and write files containing definitions and results from *Mathematica*. Section 1.11.1 gave a general discussion of how to do this. This section gives some more details.

`<<`*file* or `Get["`*file*`"]`	read in a file of *Mathematica* input, and return the last expression in the file
`!!`*file*	display the contents of a file

Reading files.

This shows the contents of the file factors.

```
In[1]:= !!factors
(* Factors of x^20 - 1 *)
  (-1 + x)*(1 + x)*(1 + x^2)*(1 - x + x^2 - x^3 + x^4)*
  (1 + x + x^2 + x^3 + x^4)*(1 - x^2 + x^4 - x^6 + x^8)
```

This reads in the file, and returns the last expression in it.

$$In[2]:= \texttt{<<factors}$$

$$Out[2]= (-1+x)(1+x)(1+x^2)(1-x+x^2-x^3+x^4)$$
$$(1+x+x^2+x^3+x^4)(1-x^2+x^4-x^6+x^8)$$

If *Mathematica* cannot find the file you ask it to read, it prints a message, then returns the symbol $Failed.

```
In[3]:= <<faxors
```

Get::noopen: Cannot open faxors.

$$Out[3]= \texttt{\$Failed}$$

Mathematica input files can contain any number of expressions. Each expression, however, must start on a new line. The expressions may however continue for as many lines as necessary. Just as in a standard interactive *Mathematica* session, the expressions are processed as soon as they are complete. Note, however, that in a file, unlike an interactive session, you can insert a blank line at any point without effect.

When you read in a file with `<<`*file*, *Mathematica* returns the last expression it evaluates in the file. You can avoid getting any visible result from reading a file by ending the last expression in the file with a semicolon, or by explicitly adding `Null` after that expression.

If *Mathematica* encounters a syntax error while reading a file, it reports the error, skips the remainder of the file, then returns `$Failed`. If the syntax error occurs in the middle of a package which uses `BeginPackage` and other context manipulation functions, then *Mathematica* tries to restore the context to what it was before the package was read.

---

expr >> *file*   or   Put[*expr*, "*file*"]

                       write an expression to a file

expr >>> *file*   or   PutAppend[*expr*, "*file*"]

                       append an expression to a file

Writing expressions to files.

This writes an expression to the file tmp.	*In[4]:=* **Factor[x^6 - 1] >> tmp**
Here are the contents of the file.	*In[5]:=* **!!tmp**
	(-1 + x)*(1 + x)*(1 - x + x^2)*(1 + x + x^2)
This appends another expression to the same file.	*In[6]:=* **Factor[x^8 - 1] >>> tmp**
Both expressions are now in the file.	*In[7]:=* **!!tmp**
	(-1 + x)*(1 + x)*(1 - x + x^2)*(1 + x + x^2)
	(-1 + x)*(1 + x)*(1 + x^2)*(1 + x^4)

When you use *expr* >>> *file*, *Mathematica* appends each new expression you give to the end of your file. If you use *expr* >> *file*, however, then *Mathematica* instead wipes out anything that was in the file before, and then puts *expr* into the file.

When you use either >> or >>> to write expressions to files, the expressions are usually given in *Mathematica* input format, so that you can read them back into *Mathematica*. Sometimes, however, you may want to save expressions in other formats. You can do this by explicitly wrapping a format directive such as OutputForm around the expression you write out.

This writes an expression to the file tmp in output format.	*In[8]:=* **OutputForm[Factor[x^6 - 1]] >> tmp**
The expression in tmp is now in output format.	*In[9]:=* **!!tmp**
	$(-1 + x) (1 + x) (1 - x + x^2) (1 + x + x^2)$

One of the most common reasons for using files is to save definitions of *Mathematica* objects, to be able to read them in again in a subsequent *Mathematica* session. The operators >> and >>> allow you to save *Mathematica* expressions in files. You can use the function Save to save complete definitions of *Mathematica* objects, in a form suitable for execution in subsequent *Mathematica* sessions.

Save["*file*", *symbol*]	save the complete definitions for a symbol in a file
Save["*file*", "*form*"]	save definitions for symbols whose names match the string pattern *form*
Save["*file*", "*context`*"]	save definitions for all symbols in the specified context
Save["*file*", {*object*$_1$, *object*$_2$, ... }]	save definitions for several objects

Writing out definitions.

This assigns a value to the symbol a.	*In[10]:=* **a = 2 - x^2**
	Out[10]= $2 - x^2$
You can use Save to write the definition of a to a file.	*In[11]:=* **Save["afile", a]**
Here is the definition of a that was saved in the file.	*In[12]:=* **!!afile**
	a = 2 - x^2

When you define a new object in *Mathematica*, your definition will often depend on other objects that you defined before. If you are going to be able to reconstruct the definition of your new object in a subsequent *Mathematica* session, it is important that you store not only its own definition, but also the definitions of other objects on which it depends. The function Save looks through the definitions of the objects you ask it to save, and automatically also saves all definitions of other objects on which it can see that these depend. However, in order to avoid saving a large amount of unnecessary material, Save never includes definitions for symbols that have the attribute Protected. It assumes that the definitions for these symbols are also built in. Nevertheless, with such definitions taken care of, it should always be the case that reading the output generated by Save back into a new *Mathematica* session will set up the definitions of your objects exactly as you had them before.

This defines a function f which depends on the symbol a defined above.	*In[13]:=* **f[z_] := a^2 - 2**
This saves the complete definition of f in a file.	*In[14]:=* **Save["ffile", f]**
The file contains not only the definition of f itself, but also the definition of the symbol a on which f depends.	*In[15]:=* **!!ffile**
	f[z_] := a^2 - 2
	a = 2 - x^2

The function Save makes use of the output forms Definition and FullDefinition, which print as definitions of *Mathematica* symbols. In some cases, you may find it convenient to use these output forms directly.

The output form Definition[*f*] prints as the sequence of definitions that have been made for *f*.	*In[16]:=* **Definition[f]** *Out[16]=* f[z_] := a^2 - 2
FullDefinition[*f*] includes definitions of the objects on which *f* depends.	*In[17]:=* **FullDefinition[f]** *Out[17]=* f[z_] := a^2 - 2 a = 2 - x^2

When you create files for input to *Mathematica*, you usually want them to contain only "plain text", which can be read or modified directly. Sometimes, however, you may want the contents of a file to be "encoded" so that they cannot be read or modified directly as plain text, but can be loaded into *Mathematica*. You can create encoded files using the *Mathematica* function Encode.

Encode["*source*", "*dest*"]	write an encoded version of the file *source* to the file *dest*
<<*dest*	read in an encoded file
Encode["*source*", "*dest*", "*key*"]	
	encode with the specified key
Get["*dest*", "*key*"]	read in a file that was encoded with a key
Encode["*source*", "*dest*", MachineID -> "*ID*"]	
	create an encoded file which can only be read on a machine with a particular ID

Creating and reading encoded files.

This writes an expression in plain text to the file tmp.	*In[18]:=* **Factor[x^2 - 1] >> tmp**
This writes an encoded version of the file tmp to the file tmp.x.	*In[19]:=* **Encode["tmp", "tmp.x"]**
Here are the contents of the encoded file. The only recognizable part is the special *Mathematica* comment at the beginning.	*In[20]:=* **!!tmp.x** (*!1N!*)mcm _QZ9tcI1cfre*Wo8:) P
Even though the file is encoded, you can still read it into *Mathematica* using the << operator.	*In[21]:=* **<<tmp.x** *Out[21]=* (-1 + x) (1 + x)

DumpSave["*file*.mx", *symbol*]	save definitions for a symbol in internal *Mathematica* format
DumpSave["*file*.mx", "*context*`"]	save definitions for all symbols in a context
DumpSave["*file*.mx", {*object*₁, *object*₂, ... }]	save definitions for several symbols or contexts
DumpSave["*package*`", *objects*]	save definitions in a file with a specially chosen name

Saving definitions in internal *Mathematica* format.

If you have to read in very large or complicated definitions, you will often find it more efficient to store these definitions in internal *Mathematica* format, rather than as text. You can do this using DumpSave.

This saves the definition for f in internal *Mathematica* format.	`In[22]:=` **DumpSave["ffile.mx", f]** `Out[22]=` {f}
You can still use << to read the definition in.	`In[23]:=` **<<ffile.mx**

<< recognizes when a file contains definitions in internal *Mathematica* format, and operates accordingly. One subtlety is that the internal *Mathematica* format differs from one computer system to another. As a result, .mx files created on one computer cannot typically be read on another.

If you use DumpSave["*package*`", ...] then *Mathematica* will write out definitions to a file with a name like *package*.mx/*system*/*package*.mx, where *system* identifies your type of computer system.

This creates a file with a name that reflects the name of the computer system being used.	`In[24]:=` **DumpSave["gffile`", f]**   `Out[24]=` {f}
<< automatically picks out the file with the appropriate name for your computer system.	`In[25]:=` **<<gffile`**

DumpSave["*file*.mx"]	save all definitions in your current *Mathematica* session
DumpSave["*package*`"]	save all definitions in a file with a specially chosen name

Saving the complete state of a *Mathematica* session.

■ 2.12.2 External Programs

On most computer systems, you can execute external programs or commands from within *Mathematica*. Often you will want to take expressions you have generated in *Mathematica*, and send them to an external program, or take results from external programs, and read them into *Mathematica*.

Mathematica supports two basic forms of communication with external programs: *structured* and *unstructured*.

Structured communication	use *MathLink* to exchange expressions with *MathLink*-compatible external programs
Unstructured communication	use file reading and writing operations to exchange ordinary text

Two kinds of communication with external programs in *Mathematica*.

The idea of structured communication is to exchange complete *Mathematica* expressions to external programs which are specially set up to handle such objects. The basis for structured communication is the *MathLink* system, discussed in Section 2.13.

Unstructured communication consists in sending and receiving ordinary text from external programs. The basic idea is to treat an external program very much like a file, and to support the same kinds of reading and writing operations.

expr >> "!*command*"	send the text of an expression to an external program
<< "!*command*"	read in text from an external program as *Mathematica* input

Reading and writing to external programs.

In general, wherever you might use an ordinary file name, *Mathematica* allows you instead to give a *pipe*, written as an external command, prefaced by an exclamation point. When you use the pipe, *Mathematica* will execute the external command, and send or receive text from it.

This sends the result from FactorInteger to the external program lpr. On many Unix systems, this program generates a printout.

In[1]:= **FactorInteger[2^31 - 1] >> !lpr**

This executes the external command echo $TERM, then reads the result as *Mathematica* input.

In[2]:= **<<"!echo $TERM"**

Out[2]= dumb

One point to notice is that you can get away with dropping the double quotes around the name of a pipe on the right-hand side of << or >> if the name does not contain any spaces or other special characters.

Pipes in *Mathematica* provide a very general mechanism for unstructured communication with external programs. On many computer systems, *Mathematica* pipes are implemented using pipe mechanisms in the underlying operating system; in some cases, however, other interprocess communication mechanisms are used. One restriction of unstructured communication in *Mathematica* is that a given pipe can only be used for input or for output, and not for both at the same time. In order to do genuine two-way communication, you need to use *MathLink*.

Even with unstructured communication, you can nevertheless set up somewhat more complicated arrangements by using temporary files. The basic idea is to write data to a file, then to read it as needed.

`OpenTemporary[ ]`	open a temporary file with a unique name

Opening a temporary file.

Particularly when you work with temporary files, you may find it useful to be able to execute external commands which do not explicitly send or receive data from *Mathematica*. You can do this using the *Mathematica* function Run.

`Run["command", arg₁, ... ]`	run an external command from within *Mathematica*

Running external commands without input or output.

This executes the external Unix command `date`. The returned value is an "exit code" from the operating system.

```
In[3]:= Run["date"]

Sat Jun 28 01:19:18 CDT 2003

Out[3]= 0
```

Note that when you use Run, you must not preface commands with exclamation points. Run simply takes the textual forms of the arguments you specify, then joins them together with spaces in between, and executes the resulting string as an external command.

It is important to realize that Run never "captures" any of the output from an external command. As a result, where this output goes is purely determined by your operating system. Similarly, Run does not supply input to external commands. This means that the commands can get input through any mechanism provided by your operating system. Sometimes external commands may be able to access the same input and output streams that are used by *Mathematica* itself. In some cases, this may be what you want. But particularly if you are using *Mathematica* with a front end, this can cause considerable trouble.

`!command`	intercept a line of *Mathematica* input, and run it as an external command

Shell escapes in *Mathematica*.

If you use *Mathematica* with a text-based interface, there is usually a special mechanism for executing external commands. With such an interface, *Mathematica* takes any line of input that starts with an exclamation point, and executes the text on the remainder of the line as an external command.

The way *Mathematica* uses !*command* is typical of the way "shell escapes" work in programs running under the Unix operating system. In most versions of *Mathematica*, you will be able to start an interactive shell from *Mathematica* simply by typing a single exclamation point on its own on a line.

This line is taken as a "shell escape", and executes the Unix command date.

```
In[4]:= !date

Sat Jun 28 01:19:18 CDT 2003

Out[4]= 0
```

`RunThrough["command", expr]`	run *command*, using *expr* as input, and reading the output back into *Mathematica*

Running *Mathematica* expressions through external programs.

As discussed above, << and >> cannot be used to both send and receive data from an external program at the same time. Nevertheless, by using temporary files, you can effectively both send and receive data from an external program while still using unstructured communication.

The function `RunThrough` writes the text of an expression to a temporary file, then feeds this file as input to an external program, and captures the output as input to *Mathematica*. Note that in `RunThrough`, like `Run`, you should not preface the names of external commands with exclamation points.

This feeds the expression 789 to the external program cat, which in this case simply echoes the text of the expression. The output from cat is then read back into *Mathematica*.

```
In[5]:= RunThrough["cat", 789]

Out[5]= 789
```

■ 2.12.3 Advanced Topic: Streams and Low-Level Input and Output

Files and pipes are both examples of general *Mathematica* objects known as *streams*. A stream in *Mathematica* is a source of input or output. There are many operations that you can perform on streams.

You can think of >> and << as "high-level" *Mathematica* input-output functions. They are based on a set of lower-level input-output primitives that work directly with streams. By using these primitives, you can exercise more control over exactly how *Mathematica* does input and output. You will often need to do this, for example, if you write *Mathematica* programs which store and retrieve intermediate data from files or pipes.

The basic low-level scheme for writing output to a stream in *Mathematica* is as follows. First, you call `OpenWrite` or `OpenAppend` to "open the stream", telling *Mathematica* that you want to write output to a particular file or external program, and in what form the output should be written. Having opened a stream, you can then call `Write` or `WriteString` to write a sequence of expressions or strings to the stream. When you have finished, you call `Close` to "close the stream".

`"name"`	a file, specified by name
`"!name"`	a command, specified by name
`InputStream["name", n]`	an input stream
`OutputStream["name", n]`	an output stream

Streams in *Mathematica*.

When you open a file or a pipe, *Mathematica* creates a "stream object" that specifies the open stream associated with the file or pipe. In general, the stream object contains the name of the file or the external command used in a pipe, together with a unique number.

The reason that the stream object needs to include a unique number is that in general you can have several streams connected to the same file or external program at the same time. For example, you may start several different instances of the same external program, each connected to a different stream.

Nevertheless, when you have opened a stream, you can still refer to it using a simple file name or external command name so long as there is only one stream associated with this object.

This opens an output stream to the file tmp.	`In[1]:= stmp = OpenWrite["tmp"]`
	
	`Out[1]= OutputStream[tmp, 6]`

This writes a sequence of expressions to the file.	`In[2]:= Write[stmp, a, b, c]`
Since you only have one stream associated with file tmp, you can refer to it simply by giving the name of the file.	`In[3]:= Write["tmp", x]`

This closes the stream.	`In[4]:= Close[stmp]`
	
	`Out[4]= tmp`

Here is what was written to the file.	`In[5]:= !!tmp`
	
	`abc`
	`x`

OpenWrite["*file*"]	open an output stream to a file, wiping out the previous contents of the file
OpenAppend["*file*"]	open an output stream to a file, appending to what was already in the file
OpenWrite["!*command*"]	open an output stream to an external command
Write[*stream*, *expr*$_1$, *expr*$_2$, ...]	write a sequence of expressions to a stream, ending the output with a newline (line feed)
WriteString[*stream*, *str*$_1$, *str*$_2$, ...]	write a sequence of character strings to a stream, with no extra newlines
Display[*stream*, *graphics*]	write graphics or sound output to a stream, in PostScript form
Close[*stream*]	tell *Mathematica* that you are finished with a stream

Low-level output functions.

When you call Write[*stream*, *expr*], it writes an expression to the specified stream. The default is to write the expression in *Mathematica* input form. If you call Write with a sequence of expressions, it will write these expressions one after another to the stream. In general, it leaves no space between the successive expressions. However, when it has finished writing all the expressions, Write always ends its output with a newline.

This re-opens the file tmp.	*In[6]:=* **stmp = OpenWrite["tmp"]**
	Out[6]= OutputStream[tmp, 10]
This writes a sequence of expressions to the file, then closes the file.	*In[7]:=* **Write[stmp, a^2, 1 + b^2]; Write[stmp, c^3]; Close[stmp]**
	Out[7]= tmp
All the expressions are written in input form. The expressions from a single Write are put on the same line.	*In[8]:=* **!!tmp**
	a^21 + b^2
	c^3

Write provides a way of writing out complete *Mathematica* expressions. Sometimes, however, you may want to write out less structured data. WriteString allows you to write out any character string. Unlike Write, WriteString adds no newlines or other characters.

This opens the stream.	*In[9]:=* **stmp = OpenWrite["tmp"]**
	Out[9]= OutputStream[tmp, 13]
This writes two strings to the stream.	*In[10]:=* **WriteString[stmp, "Arbitrary output.\n", "More output."]**

This writes another string, then closes the stream.

```
In[11]:= WriteString[stmp, "  Second line.\n"]; Close[stmp]

Out[11]= tmp
```

Here are the contents of the file. The strings were written exactly as specified, including only the newlines that were explicitly given.

```
In[12]:= !!tmp

Arbitrary output.
More output.  Second line.
```

Write[{*stream*₁, *stream*₂, ... }, *expr*₁, ...]
> write expressions to a list of streams

WriteString[{*stream*₁, *stream*₂, ... }, *str*₁, ...]
> write strings to a list of streams

Writing output to lists of streams.

An important feature of the functions Write and WriteString is that they allow you to write output not just to a single stream, but also to a list of streams.

In using *Mathematica*, it is often convenient to define a *channel* which consists of a list of streams. You can then simply tell *Mathematica* to write to the channel, and have it automatically write the same object to several streams.

In a standard interactive *Mathematica* session, there are several output channels that are usually defined. These specify where particular kinds of output should be sent. Thus, for example, $Output specifies where standard output should go, while $Messages specifies where messages should go. The function Print then works essentially by calling Write with the $Output channel. Message works in the same way by calling Write with the $Messages channel. Page 705 lists the channels used in a typical *Mathematica* session.

Note that when you run *Mathematica* through *MathLink*, a different approach is usually used. All output is typically written to a single *MathLink* link, but each piece of output appears in a "packet" which indicates what type it is.

In most cases, the names of files or external commands that you use in *Mathematica* correspond exactly with those used by your computer's operating system. On some systems, however, *Mathematica* supports various streams with special names.

"stdout"	standard output
"stderr"	standard error

Special streams used on some computer systems.

The special stream `"stdout"` allows you to give output to the "standard output" provided by the operating system. Note however that you can use this stream only with simple text-based interfaces to *Mathematica*. If your interaction with *Mathematica* is more complicated, then this stream will not work, and trying to use it may cause considerable trouble.

option name	default value	
FormatType	InputForm	the default output format to use
PageWidth	78	the width of the page in characters
NumberMarks	$NumberMarks	whether to include ` marks in approximate numbers
CharacterEncoding	$CharacterEncoding	encoding to be used for special characters

Some options for output streams.

You can associate a number of options with output streams. You can specify these options when you first open a stream using `OpenWrite` or `OpenAppend`.

This opens a stream, specifying that the default output format used should be `OutputForm`.

In[13]:= `stmp = OpenWrite["tmp", FormatType -> OutputForm]`

Out[13]= `OutputStream[tmp, 16]`

This writes expressions to the stream, then closes the stream.

In[14]:= `Write[stmp, x^2 + y^2, "    ", z^2]; Close[stmp]`

Out[14]= `tmp`

The expressions were written to the stream in `OutputForm`.

In[15]:= `!!tmp`

```
 2    2     2
x  + y     z
```

Note that you can always override the output format specified for a particular stream by wrapping a particular expression you write to the stream with an explicit *Mathematica* format directive, such as `OutputForm` or `TeXForm`.

The option `PageWidth` gives the width of the page available for textual output from *Mathematica*. All lines of output are broken so that they fit in this width. If you do not want any lines to be broken, you can set `PageWidth -> Infinity`. Usually, however, you will want to set `PageWidth` to the value appropriate for your particular output device. On many systems, you will have to run an external program to find out what this value is. Using `SetOptions`, you can make the default rule for `PageWidth` be, for example, `PageWidth :> <<"!devicewidth"`, so that an external program is run automatically to find the value of the option.

This opens a stream, specifying that the page width is 20 characters.

In[16]:= `stmp = OpenWrite["tmp", PageWidth -> 20]`

Out[16]= `OutputStream[tmp, 19]`

This writes out an expression, then closes the stream.	*In[17]:=* **Write[stmp, Expand[(1 + x)^5]]; Close[stmp]** *Out[17]=* tmp
The lines in the expression written out are all broken so as to be at most 20 characters long.	*In[18]:=* **!!tmp** 1 + 5*x + 10*x^2 + 10*x^3 + 5*x^4 + x^5

The option CharacterEncoding allows you to specify a character encoding that will be used for all strings containing special characters which are sent to a particular output stream, whether by Write or WriteString. You will typically need to use CharacterEncoding if you want to modify an international character set, or prevent a particular output device from receiving characters that it cannot handle.

Options[*stream*]   find the options that have been set for a stream SetOptions[*stream*, *opt$_1$* -> *val$_1$*, ...]   reset options for an open stream

Manipulating options of streams.

This opens a stream with the default settings for options.	*In[19]:=* **stmp = OpenWrite["tmp"]** *Out[19]=* OutputStream[tmp, 22]
This changes the FormatType option for the open stream.	*In[20]:=* **SetOptions[stmp, FormatType -> TeXForm];**

Options shows the options you have set for the open stream.	*In[21]:=* **Options[stmp]**
	
	Out[21]= {DOSTextFormat → True, FormatType → TeXForm,
	    PageWidth → 78, PageHeight → 22, TotalWidth → ∞,
	    TotalHeight → ∞, CharacterEncoding :→ ASCII,
	    NumberMarks :→ $NumberMarks}

This closes the stream again.	*In[22]:=* **Close[stmp]** *Out[22]=* tmp

Options[$Output]   find the options set for all streams in the channel $Output SetOptions[$Output, *opt$_1$* -> *val$_1$*, ...]   set options for all streams in the channel $Output

Manipulating options for the standard output channel.

At every point in your session, *Mathematica* maintains a list Streams[ ] of all the input and output streams that are currently open, together with their options. In some cases, you may find it useful to look at this list directly. *Mathematica* will not, however, allow you to modify the list, except indirectly through OpenRead and so on.

■ 2.12.4 Naming and Finding Files

The precise details of the naming of files differ from one computer system to another. Nevertheless, *Mathematica* provides some fairly general mechanisms that work on all systems.

As mentioned in Section 1.11.2, *Mathematica* assumes that all your files are arranged in a hierarchy of *directories*. To find a particular file, *Mathematica* must know both what the name of the file is, and what sequence of directories it is in.

At any given time, however, you have a *current working directory*, and you can refer to files or other directories by specifying where they are relative to this directory. Typically you can refer to files or directories that are actually *in* this directory simply by giving their names, with no directory information.

`Directory[ ]`	your current working directory
`SetDirectory["`*dir*`"]`	set your current working directory
`ResetDirectory[ ]`	revert to your previous working directory

Manipulating directories.

This gives a string representing your current working directory.	`In[1]:= Directory[ ]` `Out[1]= /users/sw`
This sets your current working directory to be the Packages subdirectory.	`In[2]:= SetDirectory["Packages"]` `Out[2]= /users/sw/Packages`
Now your current working directory is different.	`In[3]:= Directory[ ]` `Out[3]= /users/sw/Packages`
This reverts to your previous working directory.	`In[4]:= ResetDirectory[ ]` `Out[4]= /users/sw`

When you call `SetDirectory`, you can give any directory name that is recognized by your operating system. Thus, for example, on Unix-based systems, you can specify a directory one level up in the directory hierarchy using the notation `..`, and you can specify your "home" directory as `~`.

Whenever you go to a new directory using `SetDirectory`, *Mathematica* always remembers what the previous directory was. You can return to this previous directory using `ResetDirectory`. In general, *Mathematica* maintains a stack of directories, given by `DirectoryStack[ ]`. Every time you call `SetDirectory`, it adds a new directory to the stack, and every time you call `ResetDirectory` it removes a directory from the stack.

ParentDirectory[ ]	the parent of your current working directory
$InitialDirectory	the initial directory when *Mathematica* was started
$HomeDirectory	your home directory, if this is defined
+ $BaseDirectory	the base directory for system-wide files to be loaded by *Mathematica*
+ $UserBaseDirectory	the base directory for user-specific files to be loaded by *Mathematica*
+ $InstallationDirectory	the top-level directory in which your *Mathematica* installation resides

Special directories.

Whenever you ask for a particular file, *Mathematica* in general goes through several steps to try and find the file you want. The first step is to use whatever standard mechanisms exist in your operating system or shell.

Mathematica scans the full name you give for a file, and looks to see whether it contains any of the "metacharacters" *, $, ~, ?, [, ", \ and '. If it finds such characters, then it passes the full name to your operating system or shell for interpretation. This means that if you are using a Unix-based system, then constructions like *name** and $*VAR* will be expanded at this point. But in general, *Mathematica* takes whatever was returned by your operating system or shell, and treats this as the full file name.

For output files, this is the end of the processing that *Mathematica* does. If *Mathematica* cannot find a unique file with the name you specified, then it will proceed to create the file.

If you are trying to get input from a file, however, then there is another round of processing that *Mathematica* does. What happens is that *Mathematica* looks at the value of the Path option for the function you are using to determine the names of directories relative to which it should search for the file. The default setting for the Path option is the global variable $Path.

Get["*file*", Path -> {"*dir₁*", "*dir₂*", ... }]	get a file, searching for it relative to the directories *dir_i*
$Path	default list of directories relative to which to search for input files

Search path for files.

In general, the global variable $Path is defined to be a list of strings, with each string representing a directory. Every time you ask for an input file, what *Mathematica* effectively does is temporarily to make each of these directories in turn your current working directory, and then from that directory to try and find the file you have requested.

Here is a typical setting for $Path. The current directory (.) and your home directory (~) are listed first.

```
In[5]:= $Path
Out[5]= {., ~, /users/math/bin, /users/math/Packages}
```

FileNames[ ]	list all files in your current working directory
FileNames["*form*"]	list all files in your current working directory whose names match the string pattern *form*
FileNames[{"*form*$_1$", "*form*$_2$", ... }]	list all files whose names match any of the *form*$_i$
FileNames[*forms*, {"*dir*$_1$", "*dir*$_2$", ... }]	give the full names of all files whose names match *forms* in any of the directories *dir*$_i$
FileNames[*forms*, *dirs*, *n*]	include files that are in subdirectories up to *n* levels down
FileNames[*forms*, *dirs*, Infinity]	include files in all subdirectories
FileNames[*forms*, $Path, Infinity]	give all files whose names match *forms* in any subdirectory of the directories in $Path

Getting lists of files in particular directories.

Here is a list of all files in the current working directory whose names end with .m.

```
In[6]:= FileNames["*.m"]
Out[6]= {alpha.m, control.m, signals.m, test.m}
```

This lists files whose names start with a in the current directory, and in subdirectories with names that start with P.

```
In[7]:= FileNames["a*", {".", "P*"}]
Out[7]= {alpha.m, Packages/astrodata, Packages/astro.m,
           Previous/atmp}
```

FileNames returns a list of strings corresponding to file names. When it returns a file that is not in your current directory, it gives the name of the file relative to the current directory. Note that all names are given in the format appropriate for the particular computer system on which they were generated.

DirectoryName["*file*"]	extract the directory name from a file name
ToFileName["*directory*", "*name*"]	assemble a full file name from a directory name and a file name
ParentDirectory["*directory*"]	give the parent of a directory
ToFileName[{"*dir₁*", "*dir₂*", ... }, "*name*"]	assemble a full file name from a hierarchy of directory names
ToFileName[{"*dir₁*", "*dir₂*", ... }]	assemble a single directory name from a hierarchy of directory names

Manipulating file names.

You should realize that different computer systems may give file names in different ways. Thus, for example, Windows systems typically give names in the form *dir*:*dir*\\#dir\\#name, Unix systems in the form *dir/dir/name* and Macintosh systems in the form :*dir*:*dir*:*name*. The function ToFileName assembles file names in the appropriate way for the particular computer system you are using.

This gives the directory portion of the file name.	*In[8]:=* **DirectoryName["Packages/Math/test.m"]** *Out[8]=* Packages/Math/
This constructs the full name of another file in the same directory as test.m.	*In[9]:=* **ToFileName[%, "abc.m"]** *Out[9]=* Packages/Math/abc.m

If you want to set up a collection of related files, it is often convenient to be able to refer to one file when you are reading another one. The global variable $Input gives the name of the file from which input is currently being taken. Using DirectoryName and ToFileName you can then conveniently specify the names of other related files.

$Input	the name of the file or stream from which input is currently being taken

Finding out how to refer to a file currently being read by *Mathematica*.

■ 2.12.5 Files for Packages

When you create or use *Mathematica* packages, you will often want to refer to files in a system-independent way. You can use contexts to do this.

The basic idea is that on every computer system there is a convention about how files corresponding to *Mathematica* contexts should be named. Then, when you refer to a file using a context, the particular version of *Mathematica* you are using converts the context name to the file name appropriate for the computer system you are on.

`<<`*context*`	read in the file corresponding to the specified context

Using contexts to specify files.

This reads in one of the standard packages that come with *Mathematica*.

`In[1]:= <<Graphics`Colors` `

name`.mx`	file in DumpSave format
name`.mx/$SystemID/`*name*`.mx`	file in DumpSave format for your computer system
name`.m`	file in *Mathematica* source format
name`/init.m`	initialization file for a particular directory
dir`/...`	files in other directories specified by `$Path`

The typical sequence of files looked for by `<<`*name*`.

Mathematica is set up so that `<<`*name*` will automatically try to load the appropriate version of a file. It will first try to load a *name*`.mx` file that is optimized for your particular computer system. If it finds no such file, then it will try to load a *name*`.m` file containing ordinary system-independent *Mathematica* input.

If *name* is a directory, then *Mathematica* will try to load the initialization file `init.m` in that directory. The purpose of the `init.m` file is to provide a convenient way to set up *Mathematica* packages that involve many separate files. The idea is to allow you to give just the command `<<`*name*`, but then to load `init.m` to initialize the whole package, reading in whatever other files are necessary.

This reads in the file `Graphics/init.m`, which initializes all standard *Mathematica* graphics packages.

`In[2]:= <<Graphics` `

■ 2.12.6 Manipulating Files and Directories

CopyFile["*file*₁", "*file*₂"]	copy *file*₁ to *file*₂
RenameFile["*file*₁", "*file*₂"]	give *file*₁ the name *file*₂
DeleteFile["*file*"]	delete a file
FileByteCount["*file*"]	give the number of bytes in a file
FileDate["*file*"]	give the modification date for a file
SetFileDate["*file*"]	set the modification date for a file to be the current date
FileType["*file*"]	give the type of a file as File, Directory or None

Functions for manipulating files.

Different operating systems have different commands for manipulating files. *Mathematica* provides a simple set of file manipulation functions, intended to work in the same way under all operating systems.

Notice that CopyFile and RenameFile give the final file the same modification date as the original one. FileDate returns modification dates in the {*year*, *month*, *day*, *hour*, *minute*, *second*} format used by Date.

CreateDirectory["*name*"]	create a new directory
DeleteDirectory["*name*"]	delete an empty directory
DeleteDirectory["*name*", DeleteContents -> True]	
	delete a directory and all files and directories it contains
RenameDirectory["*name*₁", "*name*₂"]	
	rename a directory
CopyDirectory["*name*₁", "*name*₂"]	
	copy a directory and all the files in it

Functions for manipulating directories.

■ 2.12.7 Importing and Exporting Files

Import["*file*", "List"]	import a one-dimensional list of data from a file
Export["*file*", *list*, "List"]	export *list* to a file as a one-dimensional list of data
Import["*file*", "Table"]	import a two-dimensional table of data from a file
Export["*file*", *list*, "Table"]	export *list* to a file as a two-dimensional table of data
+ Import["*file*", "CSV"]	import data in comma-separated format
+ Export["*file*", *list*, "CSV"]	export data in comma-separated format

Importing and exporting lists and tables of data.

This exports a list of data to the file out1.dat.	*In[1]:=* **Export["out1.dat", {6.7, 8.2, -5.3}, "List"]** *Out[1]=* out1.dat

Here are the contents of the file.	*In[2]:=* **!!out1.dat**
	Out[2]= 6.7
	         8.2
	        -5.3

This imports the contents back into *Mathematica*.	*In[3]:=* **Import["out1.dat", "List"]** *Out[3]=* {6.7, 8.2, -5.3}

If you want to use data purely within *Mathematica*, then the best way to keep it in a file is usually as a complete *Mathematica* expression, with all its structure preserved, as discussed on page 623. But if you want to exchange data with other programs, it is often more convenient to have the data in a simple list or table format.

This exports a two-dimensional array of data.	*In[4]:=* **Export["out2.dat", {{5.6 10^12, 7.2 10^12}, {3, 5}}, "Table"]** *Out[4]=* out2.dat
When necessary, numbers are written in C or Fortran-like "E" notation.	*In[5]:=* **!!out2.dat** 5.6e12 7.2e12 3 5
This imports the array back into *Mathematica*.	*In[6]:=* **Import["out2.dat", "Table"]** *Out[6]=* $\left\{\left\{5.6\times10^{12}, 7.2\times10^{12}\right\}, \{3, 5\}\right\}$

If you have a file in which each line consists of a single number, then you can use Import["*file*", "List"] to import the contents of the file as a list of numbers. If each line consists of a sequence of numbers separated by tabs or spaces, then Import["*file*", "Table"] will yield a list of lists of numbers. If the file contains items that are not numbers, then these are returned as *Mathematica* strings.

This exports a mixture of textual and numerical data.

```
In[7]:= Export["out3.dat", {{"first", 3.4}, {"second", 7.8}}]
Out[7]= out3.dat
```

Here is the exported data.

```
In[8]:= !!out3.dat
first    3.4
second   7.8
```

This imports the data back into *Mathematica*.

```
In[9]:= Import["out3.dat", "Table"]
Out[9]= {{first, 3.4}, {second, 7.8}}
```

With InputForm, you can explicitly see the strings.

```
In[10]:= InputForm[%]
Out[10]//InputForm= {{"first", 3.4}, {"second", 7.8}}
```

Import["*file*", "List"]	treat each line as a separate numerical or other data item
Import["*file*", "Table"]	treat each element on each line as a separate numerical or other data item
Import["*file*", "Text"]	treat the whole file as a single string of text
Import["*file*", "Lines"]	treat each line as a string of text
Import["*file*", "Words"]	treat each separated word as a string of text

Importing files in different formats.

This creates a file with two lines of text.

```
In[11]:= Export["out4.dat",
            {"The first line.", "The second line."}, "Lines"]
Out[11]= out4.dat
```

Here are the contents of the file.

```
In[12]:= !!out4.dat
The first line.
The second line.
```

This imports the whole file as a single string.

```
In[13]:= Import["out4.dat", "Text"]//InputForm
Out[13]//InputForm= "The first line.\nThe second line."
```

This imports the file as a list of lines of text.

```
In[14]:= Import["out4.dat", "Lines"]//InputForm
Out[14]//InputForm= {"The first line.", "The second line."}
```

This imports the file as a list of words separated by white space.

```
In[15]:= Import["out4.dat", "Words"]//InputForm
Out[15]//InputForm=
            {"The", "first", "line.", "The", "second", "line."}
```

■ 2.12.8 Reading Textual Data

With <<, you can read files which contain *Mathematica* expressions given in input form. Sometimes, however, you may instead need to read files of *data* in other formats. For example, you may have data generated by an external program which consists of a sequence of numbers separated by spaces. This data cannot be read directly as *Mathematica* input. However, the function ReadList can take such data from a file or input stream, and convert it to a *Mathematica* list.

ReadList["*file*", Number]	read a sequence of numbers from a file, and put them in a *Mathematica* list

Reading numbers from a file.

Here is a file of numbers.

```
In[1]:= !!numbers

11.1   22.2   33.3
44.4   55.5   66.6
```

This reads all the numbers in the file, and returns a list of them.

```
In[2]:= ReadList["numbers", Number]

Out[2]= {11.1, 22.2, 33.3, 44.4, 55.5, 66.6}
```

ReadList["*file*", {Number, Number}]	read numbers from a file, putting each successive pair into a separate list
ReadList["*file*", Table[Number, {*n*}]]	put each successive block of *n* numbers in a separate list
ReadList["*file*", Number, RecordLists -> True]	put all the numbers on each line of the file into a separate list

Reading blocks of numbers.

This puts each successive pair of numbers from the file into a separate list.

```
In[3]:= ReadList["numbers", {Number, Number}]

Out[3]= {{11.1, 22.2}, {33.3, 44.4}, {55.5, 66.6}}
```

This makes each line in the file into a separate list.

```
In[4]:= ReadList["numbers", Number, RecordLists -> True]

Out[4]= {{11.1, 22.2, 33.3}, {44.4, 55.5, 66.6}}
```

ReadList can handle numbers which are given in Fortran-like "E" notation. Thus, for example, ReadList will read 2.5E+5 as 2.5×10^5. Note that ReadList can handle numbers with any number of digits of precision.

Here is a file containing numbers in Fortran-like "E" notation.

In[5]:= **!!bignum**

```
4.5E-5      7.8E4
2.5E2      -8.9
```

ReadList can handle numbers in this form.

In[6]:= **ReadList["bignum", Number]**

Out[6]= {0.000045, 78000., 250., -8.9}

ReadList["*file*", *type*]	read a sequence of objects of a particular type
ReadList["*file*", *type*, *n*]	read at most *n* objects

Reading objects of various types.

ReadList can read not only numbers, but also a variety of other types of object. Each type of object is specified by a symbol such as Number.

Here is a file containing text.

In[7]:= **!!strings**

```
Here is text.
And more text.
```

This produces a list of the characters in the file, each given as a one-character string.

In[8]:= **ReadList["strings", Character]**

Out[8]= {H, e, r, e, , i, s, , t, e, x, t, ., ,
            , A, n, d, , m, o, r, e, , t, e, x, t, .,
            }

Here are the integer codes corresponding to each of the bytes in the file.

In[9]:= **ReadList["strings", Byte]**

Out[9]= {72, 101, 114, 101, 32, 105, 115, 32, 116, 101,
            120, 116, 46, 32, 10, 65, 110, 100, 32, 109,
            111, 114, 101, 32, 116, 101, 120, 116, 46, 10}

This puts the data from each line in the file into a separate list.

In[10]:= **ReadList["strings", Byte, RecordLists -> True]**

Out[10]= {{72, 101, 114, 101, 32, 105, 115, 32, 116, 101,
            120, 116, 46, 32}, {65, 110, 100, 32, 109,
            111, 114, 101, 32, 116, 101, 120, 116, 46}}

Byte	single byte of data, returned as an integer
Character	single character, returned as a one-character string
Real	approximate number in Fortran-like notation
Number	exact or approximate number in Fortran-like notation
Word	sequence of characters delimited by word separators
Record	sequence of characters delimited by record separators
String	string terminated by a newline
Expression	complete *Mathematica* expression
Hold[Expression]	complete *Mathematica* expression, returned inside Hold

Types of objects to read.

This returns a list of the "words" in the file strings.

```
In[11]:= ReadList["strings", Word]
Out[11]= {Here, is, text., And, more, text.}
```

ReadList allows you to read "words" from a file. It considers a "word" to be any sequence of characters delimited by word separators. You can set the option WordSeparators to specify the strings you want to treat as word separators. The default is to include spaces and tabs, but not to include, for example, standard punctuation characters. Note that in all cases successive words can be separated by any number of word separators. These separators are never taken to be part of the actual words returned by ReadList.

option name	default value	
RecordLists	False	whether to make a separate list for the objects in each record
RecordSeparators	{"\n"}	separators for records
WordSeparators	{" ", "\t"}	separators for words
NullRecords	False	whether to keep zero-length records
NullWords	False	whether to keep zero-length words
TokenWords	{}	words to take as tokens

Options for ReadList.

This reads the text in the file strings as a sequence of words, using the letter e and . as word separators.

```
In[12]:= ReadList["strings", Word, WordSeparators -> {"e", "."}]

Out[12]= {ll, r, is t, xt, , And mor, t, xt}
```

Mathematica considers any data file to consist of a sequence of *records*. By default, each line is considered to be a separate record. In general, you can set the option RecordSeparators to give a list of separators for records. Note that words can never cross record separators. As with word separators, any number of record separators can exist between successive records, and these separators are not considered to be part of the records themselves.

By default, each line of the file is considered to be a record.

```
In[13]:= ReadList["strings", Record] // InputForm

Out[13]//InputForm= {"Here is text. ", "And more text."}
```

Here is a file containing three "sentences" ending with periods.

```
In[14]:= !!sentences

Here is text. And more.
And a second line.
```

This allows both periods and newlines as record separators.

```
In[15]:= ReadList["sentences", Record,
                        RecordSeparators -> {".", "\n"}]

Out[15]= {Here is text, And more, And a second line}
```

This puts the words in each "sentence" into a separate list.

```
In[16]:= ReadList["sentences", Word, RecordLists -> True,
                        RecordSeparators -> {".", "\n"}]

Out[16]= {{Here, is, text},
                {And, more}, {And, a, second, line}}
```

ReadList["*file*", Record, RecordSeparators -> { }]
> read the whole of a file as a single string

ReadList["*file*", Record, RecordSeparators -> {{"*lsep*$_1$", ... }, {"*rsep*$_1$", ... }}]
> make a list of those parts of a file which lie between the *lsep*$_i$ and the *rsep*$_i$

Settings for the RecordSeparators option.

Here is a file containing some text.

```
In[17]:= !!source

f[x] (: function f :)

g[x] (: function g :)
```

This reads all the text in the file source, and returns it as a single string.

```
In[18]:= InputForm[
                ReadList["source", Record, RecordSeparators -> { }]
                ]

Out[18]//InputForm=
                {"f[x] (: function f :)\ng[x] (: function g :)\n"}
```

This gives a list of the parts of the file that lie between (: and :) separators.	*In[19]:=* **ReadList["source", Record,** 　　　　　　　　**RecordSeparators -> {{"(: "}, {" :)"}}]** *Out[19]=* {function f, function g}
By choosing appropriate separators, you can pick out specific parts of files.	*In[20]:=* **ReadList["source", Record,** 　　　**RecordSeparators ->** 　　　　　　　**{{"(: function ", "["}, {" :)", "]"}}]** *Out[20]=* {x, f, x, g}

Mathematica usually allows any number of appropriate separators to appear between successive records or words. Sometimes, however, when several separators are present, you may want to assume that a "null record" or "null word" appears between each pair of adjacent separators. You can do this by setting the options **NullRecords -> True** or **NullWords -> True**.

Here is a file containing "words" separated by colons.	*In[21]:=* **!!words** first:second::fourth:::seventh
Here the repeated colons are treated as single separators.	*In[22]:=* **ReadList["words", Word, WordSeparators -> {":"}]** *Out[22]=* {first, second, fourth, seventh}
Now repeated colons are taken to have null words in between.	*In[23]:=* **ReadList["words", Word, WordSeparators -> {":"},** 　　　　　　　　　**NullWords -> True]** *Out[23]=* {first, second, , fourth, , , seventh}

In most cases, you want words to be delimited by separators which are not themselves considered as words. Sometimes, however, it is convenient to allow words to be delimited by special "token words", which are themselves words. You can give a list of such token words as a setting for the option **TokenWords**.

Here is some text.	*In[24]:=* **!!language** 22*a*b+56*c+13*a*d
This reads the text, using the specified token words to delimit words in the text.	*In[25]:=* **ReadList["language", Word, TokenWords -> {"+", "*"}]** *Out[25]=* {22, *, a, *, b, +, 56, *, c, +, 13, *, a, *, d}

You can use **ReadList** to read *Mathematica* expressions from files. In general, each expression must end with a newline, although a single expression may go on for several lines.

Here is a file containing text that can be used as *Mathematica* input.	*In[26]:=* **!!exprs** x + y + z 2^8
This reads the text in exprs as *Mathematica* expressions.	*In[27]:=* **ReadList["exprs", Expression]** *Out[27]=* {x + y + z, 256}
This prevents the expressions from being evaluated.	*In[28]:=* **ReadList["exprs", Hold[Expression]]** *Out[28]=* {Hold[x + y + z], Hold[2^8]}

ReadList can insert the objects it reads into any *Mathematica* expression. The second argument to ReadList can consist of any expression containing symbols such as Number and Word specifying objects to read. Thus, for example, ReadList["*file*", {Number, Number}] inserts successive pairs of numbers that it reads into lists. Similarly, ReadList["*file*", Hold[Expression]] puts expressions that it reads inside Hold.

If ReadList reaches the end of your file before it has finished reading a particular set of objects you have asked for, then it inserts the special symbol EndOfFile in place of the objects it has not yet read.

Here is a file of numbers.	*In[29]:=* **!!numbers**
	11.1 22.2 33.3 44.4 55.5 66.6
The symbol EndOfFile appears in place of numbers that were needed after the end of the file was reached.	*In[30]:=* **ReadList["numbers", {Number, Number, Number, Number}]**
	Out[30]= {{11.1, 22.2, 33.3, 44.4}, {55.5, 66.6, EndOfFile, EndOfFile}}

ReadList["!*command*", *type*]	execute a command, and read its output
ReadList[*stream*, *type*]	read any input stream

Reading from commands and streams.

This executes the Unix command date, and reads its output as a string.	*In[31]:=* **ReadList["!date", String]**
	Out[31]= {Sat Jun 28 01:19:37 CDT 2003}

OpenRead["*file*"]	open a file for reading
OpenRead["!*command*"]	open a pipe for reading
Read[*stream*, *type*]	read an object of the specified type from a stream
Skip[*stream*, *type*]	skip over an object of the specified type in an input stream
Skip[*stream*, *type*, *n*]	skip over *n* objects of the specified type in an input stream
Close[*stream*]	close an input stream

Functions for reading from input streams.

ReadList allows you to read *all* the data in a particular file or input stream. Sometimes, however, you want to get data a piece at a time, perhaps doing tests to find out what kind of data to expect next.

When you read individual pieces of data from a file, *Mathematica* always remembers the "current point" that you are at in the file. When you call OpenRead, *Mathematica* sets up an input stream from a file, and makes your current point the beginning of the file. Every time you read an object from the file using Read, *Mathematica* sets your current point to be just after the object you have read. Using Skip, you can advance the current point past a sequence of objects without actually reading the objects.

Here is a file of numbers.	*In[32]:=* `!!numbers`
	`11.1   22.2    33.3` `44.4   55.5    66.6`
This opens an input stream from the file.	*In[33]:=* `snum = OpenRead["numbers"]`
	Out[33]= `InputStream[numbers, 49]`
This reads the first number from the file.	*In[34]:=* `Read[snum, Number]`
	Out[34]= `11.1`
This reads the second pair of numbers.	*In[35]:=* `Read[snum, {Number, Number}]`
	Out[35]= `{22.2, 33.3}`
This skips the next number.	*In[36]:=* `Skip[snum, Number]`
And this reads the remaining numbers.	*In[37]:=* `ReadList[snum, Number]`
	Out[37]= `{55.5, 66.6}`
This closes the input stream.	*In[38]:=* `Close[snum]`
	Out[38]= `numbers`

You can use the options WordSeparators and RecordSeparators in Read and Skip just as you do in ReadList.

Note that if you try to read past the end of file, Read returns the symbol EndOfFile.

■ 2.12.9 Searching Files

FindList["*file*", "*text*"]	get a list of all the lines in the file that contain the specified text
FindList["*file*", "*text*", *n*]	get a list of the first *n* lines that contain the specified text
FindList["*file*", {"*text*₁", "*text*₂", ... }]	
	get lines that contain any of the *text*ᵢ

Finding lines that contain specified text.

Here is a file containing some text.	*In[1]:=* `!!textfile`

	`Here is the first line of text.`
	`And the second.`
	`And the third. Here is the end.`

This returns a list of all the lines in the file containing the text is.	`In[2]:= FindList["textfile", "is"]`
	`Out[2]= {Here is the first line of text.,`
	`            And the third. Here is the end.}`

The text fourth appears nowhere in the file.	`In[3]:= FindList["textfile", "fourth"]`
	`Out[3]= {}`

By default, `FindList` scans successive lines of a file, and returns those lines which contain the text you specify. In general, however, you can get `FindList` to scan successive *records*, and return complete records which contain specified text. As in `ReadList`, the option `RecordSeparators` allows you to tell *Mathematica* what strings you want to consider as record separators. Note that by giving a pair of lists as the setting for `RecordSeparators`, you can specify different left and right separators. By doing this, you can make `FindList` search only for text which is between specific pairs of separators.

This finds all "sentences" ending with a period which contain And.	`In[4]:= FindList["textfile", "And", RecordSeparators -> {"."}]`
	`Out[4]= {`
	`            And the second,`
	`            And the third}`

option name	default value	
RecordSeparators	{"\n"}	separators for records
AnchoredSearch	False	whether to require the text searched for to be at the beginning of a record
WordSeparators	{" ", "\t"}	separators for words
WordSearch	False	whether to require that the text searched for appear as a word
IgnoreCase	False	whether to treat lower- and upper-case letters as equivalent

Options for `FindList`.

This finds only the occurrence of Here which is at the beginning of a line in the file.	`In[5]:= FindList["textfile", "Here", AnchoredSearch -> True]`
	`Out[5]= {Here is the first line of text.}`

In general, `FindList` finds text that appears anywhere inside a record. By setting the option `WordSearch -> True`, however, you can tell `FindList` to require that the text it is looking for appears as a separate *word* in the record. The option `WordSeparators` specifies the list of separators for words.

The text th does appear in the file, but not as a word. As a result, the `FindList` fails.	`In[6]:= FindList["textfile", "th", WordSearch -> True]`
	`Out[6]= {}`

> FindList[{"*file*₁", "*file*₂", ... }, "*text*"]
>   search for occurrences of the text in any of the *file*ᵢ

Searching in multiple files.

This searches for third in two copies   *In[7]:=* **FindList[{"textfile", "textfile"}, "third"]**
of textfile.
                                             Out[7]= {And the third. Here is the end.,
                                                        And the third. Here is the end.}

It is often useful to call FindList on lists of files generated by functions such as FileNames.

> FindList["!*command*", ...]   run an external command, and find text in its output

Finding text in the output from an external program.

This runs the external Unix command   *In[8]:=* **!date**
date.
                                          Sat Jun 28 01:19:40 CDT 2003

                                          Out[8]= 0

This finds the time-of-day field in the   *In[9]:=* **FindList["!date", ":", RecordSeparators -> {" "}]**
date.
                                          Out[9]= {01:19:40}

> OpenRead["*file*"]   open a file for reading
>
> OpenRead["!*command*"]   open a pipe for reading
>
> Find[*stream*, *text*]   find the next occurrence of *text*
>
> Close[*stream*]   close an input stream

Finding successive occurrences of text.

FindList works by making one pass through a particular file, looking for occurrences of the text you specify. Sometimes, however, you may want to search incrementally for successive occurrences of a piece of text. You can do this using Find.

In order to use Find, you first explicitly have to open an input stream using OpenRead. Then, every time you call Find on this stream, it will search for the text you specify, and make the current point in the file be just after the record it finds. As a result, you can call Find several times to find successive pieces of text.

This opens an input stream for   *In[10]:=* **stext = OpenRead["textfile"]**
textfile.
                                   Out[10]= InputStream[textfile, 24]

This finds the first line containing And.	*In[11]:=* **Find[stext, "And"]**
	Out[11]= And the second.
Calling Find again gives you the next line containing And.	*In[12]:=* **Find[stext, "And"]**
	Out[12]= And the third. Here is the end.
This closes the input stream.	*In[13]:=* **Close[stext]**
	Out[13]= textfile

Once you have an input stream, you can mix calls to Find, Skip and Read. If you ever call FindList or ReadList, *Mathematica* will immediately read to the end of the input stream.

This opens the input stream.	*In[14]:=* **stext = OpenRead["textfile"]**
	Out[14]= InputStream[textfile, 29]
This finds the first line which contains second, and leaves the current point in the file at the beginning of the next line.	*In[15]:=* **Find[stext, "second"]**
	Out[15]= And the second.
Read can then read the word that appears at the beginning of the line.	*In[16]:=* **Read[stext, Word]**
	Out[16]= And
This skips over the next three words.	*In[17]:=* **Skip[stext, Word, 3]**
Mathematica finds is in the remaining text, and prints the entire record as output.	*In[18]:=* **Find[stext, "is"]**
	Out[18]= And the third. Here is the end.
This closes the input stream.	*In[19]:=* **Close[stext]**
	Out[19]= textfile

StreamPosition[*stream*]	find the position of the current point in an open stream
SetStreamPosition[*stream*, *n*]	set the position of the current point
SetStreamPosition[*stream*, 0]	set the current point to the beginning of a stream
SetStreamPosition[*stream*, Infinity]	set the current point to the end of a stream

Finding and setting the current point in a stream.

Functions like Read, Skip and Find usually operate on streams in an entirely sequential fashion. Each time one of the functions is called, the current point in the stream moves on.

Sometimes, you may need to know where the current point in a stream is, and be able to reset it. On most computer systems, StreamPosition returns the position of the current point as an integer giving the number of bytes from the beginning of the stream.

This opens the stream.	*In[20]:=* **stext = OpenRead["textfile"]**
	Out[20]= InputStream[textfile, 35]
When you first open the file, the current point is at the beginning, and StreamPosition returns 0.	*In[21]:=* **StreamPosition[stext]**
	Out[21]= 0
This reads the first line in the file.	*In[22]:=* **Read[stext, Record]**
	Out[22]= Here is the first line of text.
Now the current point has advanced.	*In[23]:=* **StreamPosition[stext]**
	Out[23]= 31
This sets the stream position back.	*In[24]:=* **SetStreamPosition[stext, 5]**
	Out[24]= 5
Now Read returns the remainder of the first line.	*In[25]:=* **Read[stext, Record]**
	Out[25]= is the first line of text.
This closes the stream.	*In[26]:=* **Close[stext]**
	Out[26]= textfile

■ 2.12.10 Searching and Reading Strings

Functions like Read and Find are most often used for processing text and data from external files. In some cases, however, you may find it convenient to use these same functions to process strings within *Mathematica*. You can do this by using the function StringToStream, which opens an input stream that takes characters not from an external file, but instead from a *Mathematica* string.

StringToStream["*string*"]	open an input stream for reading from a string
Close[*stream*]	close an input stream

Treating strings as input streams.

This opens an input stream for reading from the string.	*In[1]:=* **str = StringToStream["A string of words."]**
	Out[1]= InputStream[String, 6]
This reads the first "word" from the string.	*In[2]:=* **Read[str, Word]**
	Out[2]= A
This reads the remaining words from the string.	*In[3]:=* **ReadList[str, Word]**
	Out[3]= {string, of, words.}

This closes the input stream.   *In[4]:=* `Close[str]`

                                                 Out[4]= String

Input streams associated with strings work just like those with files. At any given time, there is a current position in the stream, which advances when you use functions like Read. The current position is given as the number of bytes from the beginning of the string by the function `StreamPosition[`*stream*`]`. You can explicitly set the current position using `SetStreamPosition[`*stream*`, n]`.

Here is an input stream associated with a string.

In[5]:= `str = StringToStream["123 456 789"]`

Out[5]= InputStream[String, 12]

The current position is initially 0 bytes from the beginning of the string.

In[6]:= `StreamPosition[str]`

Out[6]= 0

This reads a number from the stream.

In[7]:= `Read[str, Number]`

Out[7]= 123

The current position is now 3 bytes from the beginning of the string.

In[8]:= `StreamPosition[str]`

Out[8]= 3

This sets the current position to be 1 byte from the beginning of the string.

In[9]:= `SetStreamPosition[str, 1]`

Out[9]= 1

If you now read a number from the string, you get the 23 part of 123.

In[10]:= `Read[str, Number]`

Out[10]= 23

This sets the current position to the end of the string.

In[11]:= `SetStreamPosition[str, Infinity]`

Out[11]= 11

If you now try to read from the stream, you will always get EndOfFile.

In[12]:= `Read[str, Number]`

Out[12]= EndOfFile

This closes the stream.

In[13]:= `Close[str]`

Out[13]= String

Particularly when you are processing large volumes of textual data, it is common to read fairly long strings into *Mathematica*, then to use `StringToStream` to allow further processing of these strings within *Mathematica*. Once you have created an input stream using `StringToStream`, you can read and search the string using any of the functions discussed for files above.

This puts the whole contents of textfile into a string.

In[14]:= `s = First[ ReadList["textfile", Record,`
                     `RecordSeparators -> {}] ]`

Out[14]= Here is the first line of text.
           And the second.
           And the third. Here is the end.

This opens an input stream for the string.

In[15]:= `str = StringToStream[s]`

Out[15]= InputStream[String, 24]

This gives the lines of text in the string that contain is.

In[16]:= **FindList[str, "is"]**

Out[16]= {Here is the first line of text.,
            And the third. Here is the end.}

This resets the current position back to the beginning of the string.

In[17]:= **SetStreamPosition[str, 0]**

Out[17]= 0

This finds the first occurrence of the in the string, and leaves the current point just after it.

In[18]:= **Find[str, "the", RecordSeparators -> {" "}]**

Out[18]= the

This reads the "word" which appears immediately after the.

In[19]:= **Read[str, Word]**

Out[19]= first

This closes the input stream.

In[20]:= **Close[str]**

Out[20]= String

2.13 *MathLink* and External Program Communication

■ 2.13.1 How *MathLink* Is Used

Most of this book has been concerned with how human users interact with *Mathematica*. *MathLink* provides a mechanism through which *programs* rather than human users can interact with *Mathematica*.

- Calling functions in an external program from within *Mathematica*.
- Calling *Mathematica* from within an external program.
- Setting up alternative front ends to *Mathematica*.
- Exchanging data between *Mathematica* and external programs.
- Exchanging data between concurrent *Mathematica* processes.

Some typical uses of *MathLink*.

MathLink provides a general interface for external programs to communicate with *Mathematica*. Many standard software systems now have *MathLink* compatibility either built in or available in add-on modules.

In addition, the *MathLink* Developer Kit bundled with most versions of *Mathematica* provides the tools you need to create your own *MathLink*-compatible programs.

Once you have a *MathLink*-compatible program, you can transparently establish a link between it and *Mathematica*.

The link can either be on a single computer, or it can be over a network, potentially with a different type of computer at each end.

- Implementing inner loops in a low-level language.
- Handling large volumes of data external to *Mathematica*.
- Sending *Mathematica* graphics or other data for special processing.
- Connecting to a system with an existing user interface.

A few uses of *MathLink*-compatible programs.

MathLink-compatible programs range from very simple to very complex. A minimal *MathLink*-compatible program is just a few lines long. But it is also possible to build very large and sophisticated *MathLink*-compatible programs. Indeed, the *Mathematica* notebook front end is one example of a sophisticated *MathLink*-compatible program.

> ■ *MathLink* is a mechanism for exchanging *Mathematica* expressions between programs.

The basic idea of *MathLink*.

Much of the power of *MathLink* comes from its use of *Mathematica* expressions. The basic idea is that *MathLink* provides a way to exchange *Mathematica* expressions between programs, and such expressions can represent absolutely any kind of data.

> ■ An array of numbers.
>
> ■ A collection of geometrical objects.
>
> ■ A sequence of commands.
>
> ■ A stream of text.
>
> ■ Records in a database.
>
> ■ The cells of a *Mathematica* notebook.

A few examples of data represented by *Mathematica* expressions in *MathLink*.

The *MathLink* library consists of a collection of routines that allow external programs to send and receive *Mathematica* expressions.

The *MathLink* Developer Kit provides utilities for incorporating these routines into external programs. Utilities are included for a variety of languages, although in this chapter we discuss mainly the case of C.

An important feature of the *MathLink* library is that it is completely platform independent: it can transparently use any interprogram communication mechanism that exists on your computer system.

■ 2.13.2 Installing Existing *MathLink*-Compatible Programs

One of the most common uses of *MathLink* is to allow you to call functions in an external program from within *Mathematica*. Once the external program has been set up, all you need do to be able to use it is to "install" it in your current *Mathematica* session.

Install["*prog*"]	install a *MathLink*-compatible external program
Uninstall[*link*]	uninstall the program

Setting up external programs with functions to be called from within *Mathematica*.

This installs a *MathLink*-compatible external program called `bitprog`.	*In[1]:=* **Install["bitprog"]** *Out[1]=* LinkObject[bitprog, 4, 4]
BitShift is one of the functions inside `bitprog`.	*In[2]:=* **BitShift[111, 3]** *Out[2]=* 13
You can use it just as you would a function within *Mathematica*.	*In[3]:=* **Table[BitShift[111, i], {i, 30, 35}]** *Out[3]=* {0, 0, 111, 55, 27, 13}

When you have a package written in the *Mathematica* language a single version will run unchanged on any computer system. But external programs typically need to be compiled separately for every different type of computer.

Mathematica has a convention of keeping versions of external programs in directories that are named after the types of computers on which they will run. And assuming that this convention has been followed, Install["*prog*"] should always install the version of *prog* appropriate for the particular kind of computer that you are currently using.

Install["*name*`"]	install a program found anywhere on $Path

Using context names to specify programs to install.

When you ask to read in a *Mathematica* language file using <<*name*`, *Mathematica* will automatically search all directories in the list $Path in order to find a file with the appropriate name. Similarly, if you use Install["*name*`"] *Mathematica* will automatically search all directories in $Path in order to find an external program with the name *name*.exe. Install["*name*`"] allows you to install programs that are stored in a central directory without explicitly having to specify their location.

■ 2.13.3 Setting Up External Functions to Be Called from *Mathematica*

If you have a function defined in an external program, then what you need to do in order to make it possible to call the function from within *Mathematica* is to add appropriate *MathLink* code that passes arguments to the function, and takes back the results it produces.

In simple cases, you can generate the necessary code just by giving an appropriate *MathLink template* for each external function.

```
:Begin:
:Function:     f
:Pattern:      f[x_Integer, y_Integer]
:Arguments:    {x, y}
:ArgumentTypes: {Integer, Integer}
:ReturnType:   Integer
:End:
```

A file `f.tm` containing a *MathLink* template for an external function `f`.

`:Begin:`	begin the template for a particular function
`:Function:`	the name of the function in the external program
`:Pattern:`	the pattern to be defined to call the function
`:Arguments:`	the arguments to the function
`:ArgumentTypes:`	the types of the arguments to the function
`:ReturnType:`	the type of the value returned by the function
`:End:`	end the template for a particular function
`:Evaluate:`	*Mathematica* input to evaluate when the function is installed

The elements of a *MathLink* template.

Once you have constructed a *MathLink* template for a particular external function, you have to combine this template with the actual source code for the function. Assuming that the source code is written in the C programming language, you can do this just by adding a line to include the standard *MathLink* header file, and then inserting a small `main` program.

Include the standard *MathLink* header file.	`#include "mathlink.h"`

Here is the actual source code for the function `f`.	`int f(int x, int y) {`
	`    return x+y;`
	`}`

This sets up the external program to be ready to take requests from *Mathematica*.	`int main(int argc, char *argv[]) {`
	`    return MLMain(argc, argv);`
	`}`

A file `f.c` containing C source code.

Note that the form of `main` required on different systems may be slightly different. The release notes included in the *MathLink* Developer Kit on your particular computer system should give the appropriate form.

`mcc`	preprocess and compile *MathLink* source files
`mprep`	preprocess *MathLink* source files

Typical external programs for processing *MathLink* source files.

MathLink templates are conventionally put in files with names of the form *file*.`tm`. Such files can also contain C source code, interspersed between templates for different functions.

Once you have set up the appropriate files, you then need to process the *MathLink* template information, and compile all of your source code. Typically you do this by running various external programs, but the details will depend on your computer system.

Under Unix, for example, the *MathLink* Developer Kit includes a program named `mcc` which will preprocess *MathLink* templates in any file whose name ends with `.tm`, and then call `cc` on the resulting C source code. `mcc` will pass command-line options and other files directly to `cc`.

This preprocesses `f.tm`, then compiles the resulting C source file together with the file `f.c`.	`mcc -o f.exe f.tm f.c`

This installs the binary in the current *Mathematica* session.	`In[1]:= Install["f.exe"]` `Out[1]= LinkObject[f.exe, 4, 4]`
Now f[x, y] calls the external function f(int x, int y) and adds two integers together.	`In[2]:= f[6, 9]` `Out[2]= 15`
The external program handles only machine integers, so this gives a peculiar result.	`In[3]:= f[2^31-1, 5]` `Out[3]= -2147483644`

On systems other than Unix, the *MathLink* Developer Kit typically includes a program named `mprep`, which you have to call directly, giving as input all of the `.tm` files that you want to preprocess. `mprep` will generate C source code as output, which you can then feed to a C compiler.

Install["*prog*"]	install an external program
Uninstall[*link*]	uninstall an external program
Links["*prog*"]	show active links associated with "*prog*"
Links[ ]	show all active links
LinkPatterns[*link*]	show patterns that can be evaluated on a particular link

Handling links to external programs.

This finds the link to the `f.exe` program.

```
In[4]:= Links["f.exe"]
Out[4]= {LinkObject[f.exe, 4, 4]}
```

This shows the *Mathematica* patterns that can be evaluated using the link.

```
In[5]:= LinkPatterns[%[[1]]]
Out[5]= {f[x_Integer, y_Integer]}
```

Install sets up the actual function `f` to execute an appropriate `ExternalCall` function.

```
In[6]:= ?f
Global`f
f[x_Integer, y_Integer] := ExternalCall[
        LinkObject["f.exe", 4, 4], CallPacket[0, {x, y}]]
```

When a *MathLink* template file is processed, two basic things are done. First, the `:Pattern:` and `:Arguments:` specifications are used to generate a *Mathematica* definition that calls an external function via *MathLink*. And second, the `:Function:`, `:ArgumentTypes:` and `:ReturnType:` specifications are used to generate C source code that calls your function within the external program.

	:Begin:	
This gives the name of the actual C function to call in the external program.	:Function:	prog_add
This gives the *Mathematica* pattern for which a definition should be set up.	:Pattern:	SkewAdd[x_Integer, y_Integer:1]
The values of the two list elements are the actual arguments to be passed to the external function.	:Arguments:	{x, If[x > 1, y, y + x - 2]}
This specifies that the arguments should be passed as integers to the C function.	:ArgumentTypes:	{Integer, Integer}
This specifies that the return value from the C function will be an integer.	:ReturnType:	Integer
	:End:	

Both the :`Pattern`: and :`Arguments`: specifications in a *MathLink* template can be any *Mathematica* expressions. Whatever you give as the :`Arguments`: specification will be evaluated every time you call the external function. The result of the evaluation will be used as the list of arguments to pass to the function.

Sometimes you may want to set up *Mathematica* expressions that should be evaluated not when an external function is called, but instead only when the external function is first installed.

You can do this by inserting :`Evaluate`: specifications in your *MathLink* template. The expression you give after :`Evaluate`: can go on for several lines: it is assumed to end when there is first a blank line, or a line that does not begin with spaces or tabs.

This specifies that a usage message for SkewAdd should be set up when the external program is installed.	`:Evaluate:    SkewAdd::usage = "SkewAdd[x, y] performs` `            a skew addition in an external program."`

When an external program is installed, the specifications in its *MathLink* template file are used in the order they were given. This means that any expressions given in :`Evaluate`: specifications that appear before :`Begin`: will have been evaluated before definitions for the external function are set up.

Here are *Mathematica* expressions to be evaluated before the definitions for external functions are set up.	`:Evaluate:    BeginPackage["XPack`"]` `:Evaluate: XF1::usage = "XF1[x, y] is one external function."` `:Evaluate: XF2::usage = "XF2[x] is another external function."` `:Evaluate: Begin["`Private`"]`

This specifies that the function XF1 in *Mathematica* should be set up to call the function f in the external C program.	`:Begin:`
	`:Function:       f`
	`:Pattern:        XF1[x_Integer, y_Integer]`
	`:Arguments:      {x, y}`
	`:ArgumentTypes:  {Integer, Integer}`
	`:ReturnType:     Integer`
	`:End:`

This specifies that XF2 in *Mathematica* should call g. Its argument and return value are taken to be approximate real numbers.	`:Begin:`
	`:Function:       g`
	`:Pattern:        XF2[x_?NumberQ]`
	`:Arguments:      {x}`
	`:ArgumentTypes:  {Real}`
	`:ReturnType:     Real`
	`:End:`

These *Mathematica* expressions are evaluated after the definitions for the external functions. They end the special context used for the definitions.	`:Evaluate:    End[ ]` `:Evaluate:    EndPackage[ ]`

Here is the actual source code for the function f. There is no need for the arguments of this function to have the same names as their *Mathematica* counterparts.	```int f(int i, int j) { return i + j; }```
Here is the actual source code for g. Numbers that you give in *Mathematica* will automatically be converted into C `double` types before being passed to g.	```double g(double x) { return x*x; }```

By using `:Evaluate:` specifications, you can evaluate *Mathematica* expressions when an external program is first installed. You can also execute code inside the external program at this time simply by inserting the code in `main()` before the call to `MLMain()`. This is sometimes useful if you need to initialize the external program before any functions in it are used.

> `MLEvaluateString(stdlink, "string")`   evaluate a string as *Mathematica* input

Executing a command in *Mathematica* from within an external program.

	```int diff(int i, int j) {```
This evaluates a *Mathematica* Print function if i < j.	``` if (i < j) MLEvaluateString(stdlink, "Print[\"negative\"]");```
	``` return i - j; }```

This installs an external program containing the diff function defined above.	*In[7]:=* **Install["diffprog"]** *Out[7]=* LinkObject[diffprog, 5, 5]
Calling diff causes Print to be executed.	*In[8]:=* **diff[4, 7]** negative *Out[8]=* -3

Note that any results generated in the evaluation requested by `MLEvaluateString()` are ignored. To make use of such results requires full two-way communication between *Mathematica* and external programs, as discussed on page 687.

■ 2.13.4 Handling Lists, Arrays and Other Expressions

MathLink allows you to exchange data of any type with external programs. For more common types of data, you simply need to give appropriate :`ArgumentTypes`: or :`ReturnType`: specifications in your *MathLink* template file.

Mathematica specification		C specification
Integer	integer	int
Real	floating-point number	double
IntegerList	list of integers	int *, long
RealList	list of floating-point numbers	double *, long
String	character string	char *
Symbol	symbol name	char *
Manual	call *MathLink* routines directly	void

Basic type specifications.

Here is the *MathLink* template for a function that takes a list of integers as its argument.

```
:Begin:
:Function:       h
:Pattern:        h[a_List]
:Arguments:      {a}
:ArgumentTypes:  {IntegerList}
:ReturnType:     Integer
:End:
```

Here is the C source code for the function. Note the extra argument alen which is used to pass the length of the list.

```
int h(int *a, long alen) {

    int i, tot=0;

    for(i=0; i<alen; i++)
        tot += a[i];

    return tot;
}
```

This installs an external program containing the specifications for the function h.

```
In[1]:= Install["hprog"]

Out[1]= LinkObject[hprog, 4, 4]
```

| This calls the external code. | *In[2]:=* **h[{3, 5, 6}]** |
| | *Out[2]=* 14 |

| This does not match the pattern h[a_List] so does not call the external code. | *In[3]:=* **h[67]** |
| | *Out[3]=* h[67] |

| The pattern is matched, but the elements in the list are of the wrong type for the external code, so $Failed is returned. | *In[4]:=* **h[{a, b, c}]** |
| | *Out[4]=* $Failed |

You can mix basic types of arguments in any way you want. Whenever you use `IntegerList` or `RealList`, however, you have to include an extra argument in your C program to represent the length of the list.

| Here is an :ArgumentTypes: specification. | :ArgumentTypes: {IntegerList, RealList, Integer} |
| Here is a possible corresponding C function declaration. | void f(int *a, long alen, double *b, long blen, int c) |

Note that when a list is passed to a C program by *MathLink* its first element is assumed to be at position 0, as is standard in C, rather than at position 1, as is standard in *Mathematica*.

In addition, following C standards, character strings specified by `String` are passed as `char *` objects, terminated by \0 null bytes. Page 679 discusses how to handle special characters.

`MLPutInteger(stdlink, int i)`	put a single integer
`MLPutReal(stdlink, double x)`	put a single floating-point number

`MLPutIntegerList(stdlink, int *a, long n)`
                  put a list of n integers starting from location a

`MLPutRealList(stdlink, double *a, long n)`
                  put a list of n floating-point numbers starting from location a

`MLPutIntegerArray(stdlink, int *a, long *dims, NULL, long d)`
                  put an array of integers to form a depth d list with dimensions *dims*

`MLPutRealArray(stdlink, double *a, long *dims, NULL, long d)`
                  put an array of floating-point numbers

`MLPutString(stdlink, char *s)`	put a character string
`MLPutSymbol(stdlink, char *s)`	put a character string as a symbol name

`MLPutFunction(stdlink, char *s, long n)`
                  begin putting a function with head s and n arguments

MathLink functions for sending data to *Mathematica*.

When you use a *MathLink* template file, what `mprep` and `mcc` actually do is to create a C program that includes explicit calls to *MathLink* library functions. If you want to understand how *MathLink* works, you can look at the source code of this program. Note when you use `mcc`, you typically need to give a `-g` option, otherwise the source code that is generated is automatically deleted.

If your external function just returns a single integer or floating-point number, then you can specify this just by giving `Integer` or `Real` as the `:ReturnType:` in your *MathLink* template file. But because of the way memory allocation and deallocation work in C, you cannot directly give `:ReturnType:` specifications such as `IntegerList` or `RealList`. And instead, to return such structures, you must explicitly call *MathLink* library functions within your C program, and give `Manual` as the `:ReturnType:` specification.

| Here is the *MathLink* template for a function that takes an integer as an argument, and returns its value using explicit *MathLink* functions. | ```
:Begin:
:Function:      bits
:Pattern:       bits[i_Integer]
:Arguments:     {i}
:ArgumentTypes: {Integer}
:ReturnType:    Manual
:End:
``` |
| The function is declared as void. | ```
void bits(int i) {

    int a[32], k;
``` |
| This puts values into the C array a. | ```
    for(k=0; k<32; k++) {
        a[k] = i%2;
        i >>= 1;
        if (i==0) break;
    }

    if (k<32) k++;
``` |
| This sends k elements of the array a back to *Mathematica*. | ```
    MLPutIntegerList(stdlink, a, k);
    return ;
}
``` |

This installs the program containing the external function bits.	*In[5]:=* **Install["bitsprog"]** *Out[5]=* LinkObject[bitsprog, 5, 5]
The external function now returns a list of bits.	*In[6]:=* **bits[14]** *Out[6]=* {0, 1, 1, 1}

If you declare an array in C as int $a[n1][n2][n3]$ then you can use MLPutIntegerArray() to send it to *Mathematica* as a depth 3 list.

	`. . .`
Here is a declaration for a 3-dimensional C array.	`int a[8][16][100];`
This sets up the array `dims` and initializes it to the dimensions of `a`.	`long dims[] = {8, 16, 100};`
	`. . .`
This sends the 3-dimensional array `a` to *Mathematica*, creating a depth 3 list.	`MLPutIntegerArray(stdlink, a, dims, NULL, 3);`
	`. . .`

You can use *MathLink* functions to create absolutely any *Mathematica* expression. The basic idea is to call a sequence of *MathLink* functions that correspond directly to the `FullForm` representation of the *Mathematica* expression.

This sets up the *Mathematica* function `Plus` with 2 arguments.	`MLPutFunction(stdlink, "Plus", 2);`
This specifies that the first argument is the integer 77.	`MLPutInteger(stdlink, 77);`
And this specifies that the second argument is the symbol `x`.	`MLPutSymbol(stdlink, "x");`

In general, you first call `MLPutFunction()`, giving the head of the *Mathematica* function you want to create, and the number of arguments it has. Then you call other *MathLink* functions to fill in each of these arguments in turn. Section 2.1 discusses the general structure of *Mathematica* expressions and the notion of heads.

This creates a *Mathematica* list with 2 elements.	`MLPutFunction(stdlink, "List", 2);`
The first element of the list is a list of 10 integers from the C array `r`.	`MLPutIntegerList(stdlink, r, 10);`
The second element of the main list is itself a list with 2 elements.	`MLPutFunction(stdlink, "List", 2);`
The first element of this sublist is a floating-point number.	`MLPutReal(stdlink, 4.5);`
The second element is an integer.	`MLPutInteger(stdlink, 11);`

`MLPutIntegerArray()` and `MLPutRealArray()` allow you to send arrays which are laid out in memory in the one-dimensional way that C pre-allocates them. But if you create arrays during the execution of a C program, it is more common to set them up as nested collections of pointers. You can send such arrays to *Mathematica* by using a sequence of `MLPutFunction()` calls, ending with an `MLPutIntegerList()` call.

	`. . .`
This declares a to be a nested list of lists of lists of integers.	`int ***a;`
	`. . .`
This creates a *Mathematica* list with n1 elements.	`MLPutFunction(stdlink, "List", n1);`
	`for (i=0; i<n1; i++) {`
This creates a sublist with n2 elements.	`    MLPutFunction(stdlink, "List", n2);`
	`    for (j=0; j<n2; j++) {`
This writes out lists of integers.	`        MLPutIntegerList(stdlink, a[i][j], n3);`
	`    }`
	`}`
	`. . .`

It is important to realize that any expression you create using *MathLink* functions will be evaluated as soon as it is sent to *Mathematica*. This means, for example, that if you wanted to transpose an array that you were sending back to *Mathematica*, all you would need to do is to wrap a `Transpose` around the expression representing the array. You can then do this simply by calling `MLPutFunction(stdlink, "Transpose", 1);` just before you start creating the expression that represents the array.

The idea of post-processing data that you send back to *Mathematica* has many uses. One example is as a way of sending lists whose length you do not know in advance.

This creates a list in *Mathematica* by explicitly appending successive elements.	*In[7]:=* `t = {}; Do[t = Append[t, i^2], {i, 5}]; t`
	Out[7]= `{1, 4, 9, 16, 25}`
This creates a list in which each successive element is in a nested sublist.	*In[8]:=* `t = {}; Do[t = {t, i^2}, {i, 5}]; t`
	Out[8]= `{{{{{{}, 1}, 4}, 9}, 16}, 25}`
Flatten flattens out the list.	*In[9]:=* `Flatten[t]`
	Out[9]= `{1, 4, 9, 16, 25}`

Sequence automatically flattens itself.

```
In[10]:= {Sequence[1, Sequence[4, Sequence[ ]]]}
Out[10]= {1, 4}
```

In order to call MLPutIntegerList(), you need to know the length of the list you want to send. But by creating a sequence of nested Sequence objects, you can avoid having to know the length of your whole list in advance.

This sets up the List around your result.	`MLPutFunction(stdlink, "List", 1);`
	`while(condition) {` *generate an element*
Create the next level Sequence object.	`MLPutFunction(stdlink, "Sequence", 2);`
Put the element.	`MLPutInteger(stdlink, i);`
	`}`
This closes off your last Sequence object.	`MLPutFunction(stdlink, "Sequence", 0);`

`MLGetInteger(stdlink, int *i)`	get an integer, storing it at address i
`MLGetReal(stdlink, double *x)`	get a floating-point number, storing it at address x

Basic functions for explicitly getting data from *Mathematica*.

Just as *MathLink* provides functions like MLPutInteger() to send data from an external program into *Mathematica*, so also *MathLink* provides functions like MLGetInteger() that allow you to get data from *Mathematica* into an external program.

The list that you give for :ArgumentTypes: in a *MathLink* template can end with Manual, indicating that after other arguments have been received, you will call *MathLink* functions to get additional expressions.

	:Begin:	
	:Function:	f
The function f in *Mathematica* takes 3 arguments.	:Pattern:	f[i_Integer, x_Real, y_Real]
All these arguments are passed directly to the external program.	:Arguments:	{i, x, y}
Only the first argument is sent directly to the external function.	:ArgumentTypes:	{Integer, Manual}
	:ReturnType:	Real
	:End:	

```
The external function only takes one        double f(int i) {
explicit argument.

This declares the variables x and y.            double x, y;

MLGetReal() explicitly gets data from           MLGetReal(stdlink, &x);
the link.                                       MLGetReal(stdlink, &y);

                                                return i+x+y;
                                            }
```

MathLink functions such as MLGetInteger(*link*, *pi*) work much like standard C library functions such as fscanf(*fp*, "%d", *pi*). The first argument specifies the link from which to get data. The last argument gives the address at which the data that is obtained should be stored.

MLCheckFunction(stdlink, "*name*", long *n*)

                        check the head of a function and store how many arguments it has

---

Getting a function via *MathLink*.

| | ```
:Begin:
:Function:      f
``` |
| The function f in *Mathematica* takes a list of integers as an argument. | ```
:Pattern:       f[a:{___Integer}]
``` |
| The list is passed directly to the external program. | ```
:Arguments:     {a}
``` |
| The argument is to be retrieved manually by the external program. | ```
:ArgumentTypes:  {Manual}
``` |
| | ```
:ReturnType:    Integer
:End:
``` |
| The external function takes no explicit arguments. | ```
int f(void) {
``` |
| This declares local variables. | ```
    long n, i;
    int a[MAX];
``` |
| This checks that the function being sent is a list, and stores how many elements it has in n. | ```
    MLCheckFunction(stdlink, "List", &n);
``` |
| This gets each element in the list, storing it in a[i]. | ```
    for (i=0; i<n; i++)
        MLGetInteger(stdlink, a+i);
``` |
| | ```
    ...
}
``` |

In simple cases, it is usually possible to ensure on the *Mathematica* side that the data you send to an external program has the structure that is expected. But in general the return value from MLCheckFunction() will be non-zero only if the data consists of a function with the name you specify.

Note that if you want to get a nested collection of lists or other objects, you can do this by making an appropriate sequence of calls to MLCheckFunction().

```
MLGetIntegerList(stdlink, int **a, long *n)
                              get a list of integers, allocating the memory needed to
                              store it

MLGetRealList(stdlink, double **a, long *n)
                              get a list of floating-point numbers
```

```
MLDisownIntegerList(stdlink, int *a, long n)
                              disown the memory associated with a list of integers

MLDisownRealList(stdlink, double *a, long n)
                              disown the memory associated with a list of floating-point
                              numbers
```

Getting lists of numbers.

When an external program gets data from *Mathematica*, it must set up a place to store the data. If the data consists of a single integer, as in MLGetInteger(stdlink, &n), then it suffices just to have declared this integer using int n.

But when the data consists of a list of integers of potentially any length, memory must be allocated to store this list at the time when the external program is actually called.

MLGetIntegerList(stdlink, &a, &n) will automatically do this allocation, setting *a* to be a pointer to the result. Note that memory allocated by functions like MLGetIntegerList() is always in a special reserved area, so you cannot modify or free it directly.

Here is an external program that will be sent a list of integers.	`int f(void) {`
This declares local variables. a is an array of integers.	`long n;` `int *a;`
This gets a list of integers, making a be a pointer to the result.	`MLGetIntegerList(stdlink, &a, &n);`
	`. . .`
This disowns the memory used to store the list of integers.	`MLDisownIntegerList(stdlink, a, n);`
	`. . .` `}`

If you use `IntegerList` as an `:ArgumentTypes:` specification, then *MathLink* will automatically disown the memory used for the list after your external function exits. But if you get a list of integers explicitly using `MLGetIntegerList()`, then you must not forget to disown the memory used to store the list after you have finished with it.

`MLGetIntegerArray(stdlink, int **a, long **dims, char ***heads, long *d)`
get an array of integers of any depth

`MLGetRealArray(stdlink, double **a, long **dims, char ***heads, long *d)`
get an array of floating-point numbers of any depth

`MLDisownIntegerArray(stdlink, int *a, long *dims, char **heads, long d)`
disown memory associated with an integer array

`MLDisownRealArray(stdlink, double *a, long *dims, char **heads, long d)`
disown memory associated with a floating-point array

Getting arrays of numbers.

`MLGetIntegerList()` extracts a one-dimensional array of integers from a single *Mathematica* list. `MLGetIntegerArray()` extracts an array of integers from a collection of lists or other *Mathematica* functions nested to any depth.

The name of the *Mathematica* function at level i in the structure is stored as a string in *heads*[i]. The size of the structure at level i is stored in *dims*[i], while the total depth is stored in d.

If you pass a list of complex numbers to your external program, then `MLGetRealArray()` will create a two-dimensional array containing a sequence of pairs of real and imaginary parts. In this case, *heads*[0] will be "List" while *heads*[1] will be "Complex".

Note that you can conveniently exchange arbitrary-precision numbers with external programs by converting them to lists of digits in *Mathematica* using `IntegerDigits` and `RealDigits`.

`MLGetString(stdlink, char **s)`   get a character string

`MLGetSymbol(stdlink, char **s)`   get a symbol name

`MLDisownString(stdlink, char *s)`
disown memory associated with a character string

`MLDisownSymbol(stdlink, char *s)`
disown memory associated with a symbol name

Getting character strings and symbol names.

If you use `String` as an `:ArgumentTypes:` specification, then *MathLink* will automatically disown the memory that is used to store the string after your function exits. This means that if you want to continue to refer to the string, you must allocate memory for it, and explicitly copy each character in it.

If you get a string using `MLGetString()`, however, then *MathLink* will not automatically disown the memory used for the string when your function exits. As a result, you can continue referring to the string. When you no longer need the string, you must nevertheless explicitly call `MLDisownString()` in order to disown the memory associated with it.

`MLGetFunction(stdlink, char **s, long *n)`
> begin getting a function, storing the name of the head in *s* and the number of arguments in *n*

`MLDisownSymbol(stdlink, char *s)`
> disown memory associated with a function name

Getting an arbitrary function.

If you know what function to expect in your external program, then it is usually simpler to call `MLCheckFunction()`. But if you do not know what function to expect, you have no choice but to call `MLGetFunction()`. If you do this, you need to be sure to call `MLDisownSymbol()` to disown the memory associated with the name of the function that is found by `MLGetFunction()`.

■ 2.13.5 Special Topic: Portability of *MathLink* Programs

The *Mathematica* side of a *MathLink* connection is set up to work exactly the same on all computer systems. But inevitably there are differences between external programs on different computer systems.

For a start, different computer systems almost always require different executable binaries. When you call `Install["prog"]`, therefore, you must be sure that *prog* corresponds to a program that can be executed on your particular computer system.

Install["*file*"]	try to execute *file* directly
Install["*file*", LinkProtocol->"*type*"]	
	use the specified protocol for low-level data transport
$SystemID	identify the type of computer system being used
Install["*dir*"]	try to execute a file with a name of the form *dir*/$SystemID/*dir*

Installing programs on different computer systems.

Mathematica follows the convention that if *prog* is an ordinary file, then Install["*prog*"] will just try to execute it. But if *prog* is a directory, then *Mathematica* will look for a subdirectory of that directory whose name agrees with the current value of $SystemID, and will then try to execute a file named *prog* within that subdirectory.

mcc -o *prog* ...	put compiled code in the file *prog* in the current directory
mcc -xo *prog* ...	put compiled code in *prog*/$SystemID/*prog*

Typical Unix commands for compiling external programs.

Even though the executable binary of an external program is inevitably different on different computer systems, it can still be the case that the source code in a language such as C from which this binary is obtained can be essentially the same.

But to achieve portability in your C source code there are several points that you need to watch.

For a start, you should never make use of extra features of the C language or C run-time libraries that happen to be provided on a particular system, but are not part of standard C. In addition, you should try to avoid dealing with segmented or otherwise special memory models.

The include file mathlink.h contains standard C prototypes for all the functions in the *MathLink* library. If your compiler does not support such prototypes, you can ignore them by giving the directive #define MLPROTOTYPES 0 before #include "mathlink.h". But assuming that it does support prototypes, your compiler will always be able to check that the calls you make to functions in the *MathLink* library have arguments of appropriate types.

MLPutInteger()	MLGetInteger()	default integer of type int; sometimes 16 bits, sometimes 32 bits
MLPutShortInteger()	MLGetShortInteger()	short integer of type short; usually 16 bits
MLPutLongInteger()	MLGetLongInteger()	long integer of type long; usually 32 bits
MLPutReal()	MLGetReal()	default real number of type double; usually at least 64 bits
MLPutFloat()	MLGetFloat()	single-precision floating-point number of type float; often 32 bits
MLPutDouble()	MLGetDouble()	double-precision floating-point number of type double; usually at least 64 bits

MathLink functions that use specific C types.

On some computer systems and with some compilers, a C language int may be equivalent to a long. But the standard for the C language equally well allows int to be equivalent to short. And if you are going to call *MathLink* library functions in a portable way, it is essential that you use the same types as they do.

Once you have passed your data into the *MathLink* library functions, these functions then take care of all further issues associated with differences between data representations on different computer systems. Thus, for example, *MathLink* automatically swaps bytes when it sends data between big and little endian machines, and converts floating-point formats losing as little precision as possible.

MLPutString(stdlink, char *s)　　put a string without special characters

MLPutUnicodeString(stdlink, unsigned short *s, long *n*)
　　　　　　　　　　　put a string encoded in terms of 16-bit Unicode characters

MLPutByteString(stdlink, unsigned char *s, long *n*)
　　　　　　　　　　　put a string containing only 8-bit character codes

---

MLGetString(stdlink, char **s)　　get a string without special characters

MLGetUnicodeString(stdlink, unsigned short **s, long *n*)
　　　　　　　　　　　get a string encoded in terms of 16-bit Unicode characters

MLGetByteString(stdlink, unsigned char **s, long *n*, long *spec*)
　　　　　　　　　　　get a string containing only 8-bit character codes, using
　　　　　　　　　　　spec as the code for all 16-bit characters

Manipulating general strings.

In simple C programs, it is typical to use strings that contain only ordinary ASCII characters. But in *Mathematica* it is possible to have strings containing all sorts of special characters. These characters are specified within *Mathematica* using Unicode character codes, as discussed on page 420.

C language `char *` strings typically use only 8 bits to store the code for each character. Unicode character codes, however, require 16 bits. As a result, the functions `MLPutUnicodeString()` and `MLGetUnicodeString()` work with arrays of `unsigned short` integers.

If you know that your program will not have to handle special characters, then you may find it convenient to use `MLPutByteString()` and `MLGetByteString()`. These functions represent all characters directly using 8-bit character codes. If a special character is sent from *Mathematica*, then it will be converted by `MLGetByteString()` to a fixed code that you specify.

■ **main() may need to be different on different computer systems**

A point to watch in creating portable *MathLink* programs.

Computer systems and compilers that have C run-time libraries based on the Unix model allow *MathLink* programs to have a main program of the form `main(argc, argv)` which simply calls `MLMain(argc, argv)`.

Some computer systems or compilers may however require main programs of a different form. You should realize that you can do whatever initialization you want inside `main()` before calling `MLMain()`. Once you have called `MLMain()`, however, your program will effectively go into an infinite loop, responding to requests from *Mathematica* until the link to it is closed.

■ 2.13.6 Using *MathLink* to Communicate between *Mathematica* Sessions

LinkCreate["*name*"]	create a link for another program to connect to
LinkConnect["*name*"]	connect to a link created by another program
LinkClose[*link*]	close a *MathLink* connection
LinkWrite[*link*, *expr*]	write an expression to a *MathLink* connection
LinkRead[*link*]	read an expression from a *MathLink* connection
LinkRead[*link*, Hold]	read an expression and immediately wrap it with Hold
LinkReadyQ[*link*]	find out whether there is data ready to be read from a link

MathLink connections between *Mathematica* sessions.

	Session A
This starts up a link on port number 8000.	*In[1]:=* **link = LinkCreate["8000"]**
	Out[1]= LinkObject[8000@frog.wolfram.com, 4, 4]

	Session B
This connects to the link on port 8000.	*In[1]:=* **Link = LinkConnect["8000"]**
	Out[1]= LinkObject["8000@frog.wolfram.com", 4, 4]

	Session A
This evaluates 15! and writes it to the link.	*In[2]:=* **LinkWrite[link, 15!]**

	Session B
This reads from the link, getting the 15! that was sent.	*In[2]:=* **LinkRead[link]**
	Out[2]= 1307674368000
This writes data back on the link.	*In[3]:=* **LinkWrite[link, N[%^6]]**

	Session A
And this reads the data written in session B.	*In[3]:=* **LinkRead[link]**
	Out[3]= 5.00032×10^{72}

One use of *MathLink* connections between *Mathematica* sessions is simply as a way to transfer data without using intermediate files.

Another use is as a way to dispatch different parts of a computation to different sessions.

	Session A
This writes the expression 2 + 2 without evaluating it.	*In[4]:=* `LinkWrite[link, Unevaluated[2 + 2]]`

	Session B
This reads the expression from the link, immediately wrapping it in Hold.	*In[4]:=* `LinkRead[link, Hold]`
	Out[4]= Hold[2 + 2]
This evaluates the expression.	*In[5]:=* `ReleaseHold[%]`
	Out[5]= 4

When you call LinkWrite, it writes an expression to the *MathLink* connection and immediately returns. But when you call LinkRead, it will not return until it has read a complete expression from the *MathLink* connection.

You can tell whether anything is ready to be read by calling LinkReadyQ[*link*]. If LinkReadyQ returns True, then you can safely call LinkRead and expect immediately to start reading an expression. But if LinkReadyQ returns False, then LinkRead would block until an expression for it to read had been written by a LinkWrite in your other *Mathematica* session.

	Session A
There is nothing waiting to be read on the link, so if LinkRead were to be called, it would block.	*In[5]:=* `LinkReadyQ[link]`
	Out[5]= False

	Session B
This writes an expression to the link.	*In[6]:=* `LinkWrite[link, x + y]`

	Session A
Now there is an expression waiting to be read on the link.	*In[6]:=* `LinkReadyQ[link]`
	Out[6]= True
LinkRead can thus be called without fear of blocking.	*In[7]:=* `LinkRead[link]`
	Out[7]= x + y

LinkCreate[ ]	pick any unused port on your computer
LinkCreate["*number*"]	use a specific port
LinkConnect["*number*"]	connect to a port on the same computer
LinkConnect["*number@host*"]	connect a port on another computer

Ways to set up *MathLink* links.

MathLink can use whatever mechanism for interprogram communication your computer system supports. In setting up connections between concurrent *Mathematica* sessions, the most common mechanism is internet TCP ports.

Most computer systems have a few thousand possible numbered ports, some of which are typically allocated to standard system services.

You can use any of the unallocated ports for *MathLink* connections.

This finds an unallocated port on frog.wolfram.com.

```
Session on frog.wolfram.com
In[8]:= link = LinkCreate[ ]
Out[8]= LinkObject["2981@frog.wolfram.com", 5, 5]
```

This connects to the port on frog.wolfram.com.

```
Session on toad.wolfram.com
In[7]:= link = LinkConnect["2981@frog.wolfram.com"]
Out[7]= LinkObject["2981@frog.wolfram.com", 5, 5]
```

This sends the current machine name over the link.

```
In[8]:= LinkWrite[link, $MachineName]
```

This reads the expression written on toad.

```
Session on frog.wolfram.com
In[9]:= LinkRead[link]
Out[9]= toad
```

By using internet ports for *MathLink* connections, you can easily transfer data between *Mathematica* sessions on different machines. All that is needed is that an internet connection exists between the machines.

Note that because *MathLink* is completely system independent, the computers at each end of a *MathLink* connection do not have to be of the same type. *MathLink* nevertheless notices when they are, and optimizes data transmission in this case.

■ 2.13.7 Calling Subsidiary *Mathematica* Processes

LinkLaunch["*prog*"]	start an external program and open a connection to it

Connecting to a subsidiary program via *MathLink*.

This starts a subsidiary *Mathematica* process on the computer system used here.

```
In[1]:= link = LinkLaunch["math -mathlink"]
Out[1]= LinkObject[math -mathlink, 4, 4]
```

Here is a packet representing the first input prompt from the subsidiary *Mathematica* process.

```
In[2]:= LinkRead[link]
Out[2]= InputNamePacket[In[1]:= ]
```

This writes a packet representing text to enter in the subsidiary *Mathematica* process.

```
In[3]:= LinkWrite[link, EnterTextPacket["10!"]]
```

Here is a packet representing the output prompt from the subsidiary *Mathematica* process.

```
In[4]:= LinkRead[link]
Out[4]= OutputNamePacket[Out[1]= ]
```

And here is the actual result from the computation.

```
In[5]:= LinkRead[link]
Out[5]= ReturnTextPacket[3628800]
```

The basic way that the various different objects involved in a *Mathematica* session are kept organized is by using *MathLink packets*. A *MathLink* packet is simply an expression with a definite head that indicates its role or meaning.

EnterTextPacket["*input*"]	text to enter corresponding to an input line
ReturnTextPacket["*output*"]	text returned corresponding to an output line
InputNamePacket["*name*"]	text returned for the name of an input line
OutputNamePacket["*name*"]	text returned for the name of an output line

Basic packets used in *Mathematica* sessions.

The fact that LinkRead returns an InputNamePacket indicates that the subsidiary *Mathematica* is now ready for new input.

```
In[6]:= LinkRead[link]
Out[6]= InputNamePacket[In[2]:= ]
```

This enters two Print commands as input.

```
In[7]:= LinkWrite[link, EnterTextPacket["Print[a]; Print[b];"]]
```

Here is the text from the first Print.	*In[8]:=* **LinkRead[link]**
	Out[8]= TextPacket[a]
And here is the text from the second Print.	*In[9]:=* **LinkRead[link]**
	Out[9]= TextPacket[b]
No output line is generated, so the new packet is an InputNamePacket.	*In[10]:=* **LinkRead[link]**
	Out[10]= InputNamePacket[In[3]:=]

TextPacket["*string*"]	text from Print etc.
MessagePacket[*symb*, "*tag*"]	a message name
DisplayPacket["*string*"]	parts of PostScript graphics
DisplayEndPacket["*string*"]	the end of PostScript graphics

Some additional packets generated in *Mathematica* sessions.

If you enter input to *Mathematica* using EnterTextPacket["*input*"], then *Mathematica* will automatically generate a string version of your output, and will respond with ReturnTextPacket["*output*"]. But if you instead enter input using EnterExpressionPacket[*expr*] then *Mathematica* will respond with ReturnExpressionPacket[*expr*] and will not turn your output into a string.

EnterExpressionPacket[*expr*]	an expression to enter corresponding to an input line
ReturnExpressionPacket[*expr*]	an expression returned corresponding to an output line

Packets for representing input and output lines using expressions.

This enters an expression into the subsidiary *Mathematica* session without evaluating it.	*In[11]:=* **LinkWrite[link, Unevaluated[EnterExpressionPacket[** **Factor[x^6 - 1]]]]**
Here are the next 3 packets that come back from the subsidiary *Mathematica* session.	*In[12]:=* **Table[LinkRead[link], {3}]**

	Out[12]= {OutputNamePacket[Out[3]=],
	        ReturnExpressionPacket[
	        $(-1 + x) (1 + x) (1 - x - x^2) (1 + x + x^2)$],
	        InputNamePacket[In[4]:=]}

InputNamePacket and OutputNamePacket packets are often convenient for making it possible to tell the current state of a subsidiary *Mathematica* session. But you can suppress the generation of these packets by calling the subsidiary *Mathematica* session with a string such as "math -mathlink -batchoutput".

Even if you suppress the explicit generation of InputNamePacket and OutputNamePacket packets, *Mathematica* will still process any input that you give with EnterTextPacket or EnterExpressionPacket as if you were entering an input line. This means for example that *Mathematica* will call $Pre and $Post, and will assign values to In[$Line] and Out[$Line].

EvaluatePacket[*expr*]	an expression to be sent purely for evaluation
ReturnPacket[*expr*]	an expression returned from an evaluation

Evaluating expressions without explicit input and output lines.

This sends an EvaluatePacket. The Unevaluated prevents evaluation before the packet is sent.	*In[13]:=* **LinkWrite[link, Unevaluated[EvaluatePacket[10!]]]**
The result is a pure ReturnPacket.	*In[14]:=* **LinkRead[link]**
	Out[14]= ReturnPacket[3628800]
This sends an EvaluatePacket requesting evaluation of Print[x].	*In[15]:=* **LinkWrite[link, Unevaluated[EvaluatePacket[Print[x]]]]**
The first packet to come back is a TextPacket representing text generated by the Print.	*In[16]:=* **LinkRead[link]**
	Out[16]= TextPacket[x]
After that, the actual result of the Print is returned.	*In[17]:=* **LinkRead[link]**
	Out[17]= ReturnPacket[Null]

In most cases, it is reasonable to assume that sending an EvaluatePacket to *Mathematica* will simply cause *Mathematica* to do a computation and to return various other packets, ending with a ReturnPacket. However, if the computation involves a function like Input, then *Mathematica* will have to request additional input before it can proceed with the computation.

This sends a packet whose evaluation involves an Input function.	*In[18]:=* **LinkWrite[link,** **Unevaluated[EvaluatePacket[2 + Input["data ="]]]]**
What comes back is an InputPacket which indicates that further input is required.	*In[19]:=* **LinkRead[link]**
	Out[19]= InputPacket[data =]
There is nothing more to be read on the link at this point.	*In[20]:=* **LinkReadyQ[link]**
	Out[20]= False
This enters more input.	*In[21]:=* **LinkWrite[link, EnterTextPacket["x + y"]]**
Now the Input function can be evaluated, and a ReturnPacket is generated.	*In[22]:=* **LinkRead[link]**
	Out[22]= ReturnPacket[2 + x + y]

LinkInterrupt[*link*]	send an interrupt to a *MathLink*-compatible program

Interrupting a *MathLink*-compatible program.

This sends a very time-consuming calculation to the subsidiary process.

```
In[23]:= LinkWrite[link,
              EnterTextPacket["FactorInteger[2^777-1]"]]
```

The calculation is still going on.

```
In[24]:= LinkReadyQ[link]
Out[24]= False
```

This sends an interrupt.

```
In[25]:= LinkInterrupt[link]
```

Now the subsidiary process has stopped, and is sending back an interrupt menu.

```
In[26]:= LinkRead[link]
Out[26]= MenuPacket[1, Interrupt> ]
```

■ 2.13.8 Special Topic: Communication with *Mathematica* Front Ends

The *Mathematica* kernel uses *MathLink* to communicate with *Mathematica* front ends. If you start a *Mathematica* kernel from within a front end, therefore, the kernel will be controlled through a *MathLink* connection to this front end.

$ParentLink	the *MathLink* connection to use for kernel input and output

The link to the front end for a particular kernel.

The global variable $ParentLink specifies the *MathLink* connection that a particular kernel will use for input and output.

It is sometimes useful to reset $ParentLink in the middle of a *Mathematica* session, thereby effectively changing the front end to which the kernel is connected.

Session A

This creates a link on port 8000.

```
In[1]:= link = LinkCreate["8000"]
Out[1]= LinkObject[8000@frog.wolfram.com, 4, 4]
```

Session B

This connects to the link opened in session A.

```
In[1]:= LinkConnect["8000"]
Out[1]= LinkObject[8000@frog.wolfram.com, 4, 4]
```

This tells session B that it should use session A as a front end.

```
In[2]:= $ParentLink = %
```

	Session A
Session A now acts as a front end to session B and gets all output from it.	*In[2]:=* **Table[LinkRead[link], {4}]**
	Out[2]= {ResumePacket[LinkObject[ParentLink, 1, 1]], OutputNamePacket[Out[2]=], ReturnTextPacket[LinkObject[8000@frog.wolfram.com, 4, 4]], InputNamePacket[In[3]:=]}
This releases session B again.	*In[3]:=* **LinkWrite[link, EnterTextPacket["$ParentLink=."]]**

Much like the *Mathematica* kernel, the standard notebook front end for *Mathematica* is set up to handle a certain set of *MathLink* packets.

Usually it is best to use functions like NotebookWrite and FrontEndExecute if you want to control the *Mathematica* front end from the kernel. But in some cases you may find it convenient to send packets directly to the front end using LinkWrite.

■ 2.13.9 Two-Way Communication with External Programs

When you install a *MathLink*-compatible external program using Install, the program is set up to behave somewhat like a simplified *Mathematica* kernel. Every time you call a function in the external program, a CallPacket is sent to the program, and the program responds by sending back a result wrapped in a ReturnPacket.

This installs an external program, returning the LinkObject used for the connection to that program.	*In[1]:=* **link = Install["bitsprog"]** *Out[1]=* LinkObject[bitsprog, 4, 4]
The function ExternalCall sends a CallPacket to the external program.	*In[2]:=* **?bits** Global`bits bits[i_Integer] := ExternalCall[LinkObject["bitsprog", 4, 4], CallPacket[0, {i}]]
You can send the CallPacket explicitly using LinkWrite. The first argument of the CallPacket specifies which function in the external program to call.	*In[3]:=* **LinkWrite[link, CallPacket[0, {67}]]**
Here is the response to the CallPacket from the external program.	*In[4]:=* **LinkRead[link]** *Out[4]=* {1, 1, 0, 0, 0, 0, 1}

If you use Install several times on a single external program, *Mathematica* will open several *MathLink* connections to the program. Each connection will however always correspond to a unique LinkObject. Note that on some computer systems, you may need to make an explicit copy of the file containing the external program in order to be able to call it multiple times.

$CurrentLink	the *MathLink* connection to the external program currently being run

Identifying different instances of a single external program.

This gives $CurrentLink as an argument to addto.

```
:Begin:
:Function:        addto

:Pattern:         addto[$CurrentLink, n_Integer]

:Arguments:       {n}
:ArgumentTypes:  {Integer}
:ReturnType:      Integer
:End:
```

This zeros the global variable counter every time the program is started.

```
int counter = 0;

int addto(int n) {
    counter += n;
    return counter;
}
```

This installs one instance of the external program containing addto.

In[5]:= **ct1 = Install["addtoprog"]**

Out[5]= LinkObject[addtoprog, 5, 5]

This installs another instance.

In[6]:= **ct2 = Install["addtoprog"]**

Out[6]= LinkObject[addtoprog, 6, 6]

This adds 10 to the counter in the first instance of the external program.

In[7]:= **addto[ct1, 10]**

Out[7]= 10

This adds 15 to the counter in the second instance of the external program.

In[8]:= **addto[ct2, 15]**

Out[8]= 15

This operates on the first instance of the program again.

In[9]:= **addto[ct1, 20]**

Out[9]= 30

If an external program maintains information about its state then you can use different instances of the program to represent different states. $CurrentLink then provides a way to refer to each instance of the program.

The value of $CurrentLink is temporarily set every time a particular instance of the program is called, as well as when each instance of the program is first installed.

> `MLEvaluateString(stdlink, "`*string*`")`
>
> send input to *Mathematica* but return no results

Sending a string for evaluation by *Mathematica*.

The two-way nature of *MathLink* connections allows you not only to have *Mathematica* call an external program, but also to have that external program call back to *Mathematica*.

In the simplest case, you can use the *MathLink* function `MLEvaluateString()` to send a string to *Mathematica*. *Mathematica* will evaluate this string, producing whatever effects the string specifies, but it will not return any results from the evaluation back to the external program.

To get results back you need explicitly to send an `EvaluatePacket` to *Mathematica*, and then read the contents of the `ReturnPacket` that comes back.

	`. . .`
This starts an `EvaluatePacket`.	`MLPutFunction(stdlink, "EvaluatePacket", 1);`
This constructs the expression `Factorial[7]` or `7!`.	`MLPutFunction(stdlink, "Factorial", 1);` `MLPutInteger(stdlink, 7);`
This specifies that the packet you are constructing is finished.	`MLEndPacket(stdlink);`
This checks the `ReturnPacket` that comes back.	`MLCheckFunction(stdlink, "ReturnPacket", &n);`
This extracts the integer result for `7!` from the packet.	`MLGetInteger(stdlink, &ans);`
	`. . .`

> `MLEndPacket(stdlink)` specify that a packet is finished and ready to be sent to *Mathematica*

Sending a packet to *Mathematica*.

When you can send *Mathematica* an `EvaluatePacket[`*input*`]`, it may in general produce many packets in response, but the final packet should be `ReturnPacket[`*output*`]`. Page 695 will discuss how to handle sequences of packets and expressions whose structure you do not know in advance.

■ 2.13.10 Special Topic: Running Programs on Remote Computers

MathLink allows you to call an external program from within *Mathematica* even when that program is running on a remote computer. Typically, you need to start the program directly from the operating system on the remote computer. But then you can connect to it using commands within your *Mathematica* session.

	Operating system on `toad.wolfram.com`
This starts the program `fprog` and tells it to create a new link.	`fprog -linkcreate`
The program responds with the specification of the link it has created.	`Link created on: 2976@toad.wolfram.com`

	Mathematica session on `frog.wolfram.com`
This connects to the link that has been created.	`In[1]:= Install[LinkConnect["2976@toad.wolfram.com"]]`
	`Out[1]= LinkObject[2976@toad.wolfram.com, 1]`
This now executes code in the external program on `toad.wolfram.com`.	`In[2]:= f[16]`
	`Out[2]= 561243`

External programs that are created using `mcc` or `mprep` always contain the code that is needed to set up *MathLink* connections. If you start such programs directly from your operating system, they will prompt you to specify what kind of connection you want. Alternatively, if your operating system supports it, you can also give this information as a command-line argument to the external program.

prog `-linkcreate`	operating system command to run a program and have it create a link
`Install[LinkConnect["`*port@host*`"]]`	*Mathematica* command to connect to the external program

Running an external program on a remote computer.

■ 2.13.11 Special Topic: Running External Programs under a Debugger

MathLink allows you to run external programs under whatever debugger is provided in your software environment.

MathLink-compatible programs are typically set up to take arguments, usually on the command line, which specify what *MathLink* connections they should use.

In debugger:	`run -linkcreate`
In *Mathematica*:	`Install[LinkConnect["port"]]`

Running an external program under a debugger.

Note that in order to get a version of an external program that can be run under a debugger, you may need to specify -g or other flags when you compile the program.

	Debugger
Set a breakpoint in the C function f.	*(debug)* **break f** Breakpoint set: f: line 1
Start the external program.	*(debug)* **run -linkcreate**
The program responds with what port it is listening on.	Link created on: 2981@frog.wolfram.com

	Mathematica session
This connects to the program running under the debugger.	*In[1]:=* **Install[LinkConnect["2981@frog.wolfram.com"]]** *Out[1]=* LinkObject[2981@frog.wolfram.com, 1]
This calls a function which executes code in the external program.	*In[2]:=* **f[16]**

	Debugger
The external program stops at the breakpoint.	*(debug)* Breakpoint: f(16)
This tells the debugger to continue.	*(debug)* **continue**

	Mathematica session
Now f returns.	*Out[2]=* 561243

■ 2.13.12 Manipulating Expressions in External Programs

Mathematica expressions provide a very general way to handle all kinds of data, and you may sometimes want to use such expressions inside your external programs. A language like C, however, offers no direct way to store general *Mathematica* expressions. But it is nevertheless possible to do this by using the *loopback links* provided by the *MathLink* library. A loopback link is a local *MathLink* connection inside your external program, to which you can write expressions that can later be read back.

MLINK MLLoopbackOpen(stdenv, long *errno)
                              open a loopback link

     void MLClose(MLINK *link*)   close a link

---

  int MLTransferExpression(MLINK *dest*, MLINK *src*)
                                get an expression from *src* and put it onto *dest*

Functions for manipulating loopback links.

	. . .
This opens a loopback link.	`ml = MLLoopbackOpen(stdenv, &errno);`

This puts the expression Power[x, 3] onto the loopback link.	`MLPutFunction(ml, "Power", 2);`
	`  MLPutSymbol(ml, "x");`
	`  MLPutInteger(ml, 3);`

	. . .

This gets the expression back from the loopback link.	`MLGetFunction(ml, &head, &n);`
	`  MLGetSymbol(ml, &sname);`
	`  MLGetInteger(ml, &k);`

	. . .
This closes the loopback link again.	`MLClose(ml);`

You can use `MLTransferExpression()` to take an expression that you get via `stdlink` from *Mathematica*, and save it in a local loopback link for later processing.

You can also use `MLTransferExpression()` to take an expression that you have built up on a local loopback link, and transfer it back to *Mathematica* via `stdlink`.

...

This puts 21! onto a local loopback link.	`MLPutFunction(ml, "Factorial", 1);` `MLPutInteger(ml, 21);`
This sends the head `FactorInteger` to *Mathematica*.	`MLPutFunction(stdlink, "FactorInteger", 1);`
This transfers the 21! from the loopback link to `stdlink`.	`MLTransferExpression(stdlink, ml);`

You can put any sequence of expressions onto a loopback link. Usually you get the expressions off the link in the same order as you put them on.

And once you have got an expression off the link it is usually no longer saved. But by using `MLCreateMark()` you can mark a particular position in a sequence of expressions on a link, forcing *MathLink* to save every expression after the mark so that you can go back to it later.

`MLMARK MLCreateMark(MLINK `*link*`)`	create a mark at the current position in a sequence of expressions on a link
`MLSeekMark(MLINK `*link*`, MLMARK `*mark*`, long `*n*`)`	go back to a position *n* expressions after the specified mark on a link
`MLDestroyMark(MLINK `*link*`, MLMARK `*mark*`)`	destroy a mark in a link

Setting up marks in *MathLink* links.

	`. . .`
This puts the integer 45 onto a loopback link.	`MLPutInteger(ml, 45);`
This puts 33 onto the link.	`MLPutInteger(ml, 33);`
And this puts 76.	`MLPutInteger(ml, 76);`
This will read 45 from the link. The 45 will no longer be saved.	`MLGetInteger(ml, &i);`
This creates a mark at the current position on the link.	`mark = MLCreateMark(ml);`
This will now read 33.	`MLGetInteger(ml, &i);`
And this will read 76.	`MLGetInteger(ml, &i);`
This goes back to the position of the mark.	`MLSeekMark(ml, mark, 0);`
Now this will read 33 again.	`MLGetInteger(ml, &i);`
It is important to destroy marks when you have finished with them, so no unnecessary expressions will be saved.	`MLDestroyMark(ml, mark);`

The way the *MathLink* library is implemented, it is very efficient to open and close loopback links, and to create and destroy marks in them. The only point to remember is that as soon as you create a mark on a particular link, *MathLink* will save subsequent expressions that are put on that link, and will go on doing this until the mark is destroyed.

`int MLGetNext(MLINK `*`link`*`)`	find the type of the next object on a link
`int MLGetArgCount(MLINK `*`link`*`, long *`*`n`*`)`	store in *n* the number of arguments for a function on a link
`int MLGetSymbol(MLINK `*`link`*`, char **`*`name`*`)`	get the name of a symbol
`int MLGetInteger(MLINK `*`link`*`, int *`*`i`*`)`	get a machine integer
`int MLGetReal(MLINK `*`link`*`, double *`*`x`*`)`	get a machine floating-point number
`int MLGetString(MLINK `*`link`*`, char **`*`string`*`)`	get a character string

Functions for getting pieces of expressions from a link.

MLTKFUNC	composite function—head and arguments
MLTKSYM	*Mathematica* symbol
MLTKINT	integer
MLTKREAL	floating-point number
MLTKSTR	character string

Constants returned by MLGetNext().

| | ```
switch(MLGetNext(ml)) {
``` |
| This reads a composite function. | ```
  case MLTKFUNC:
  MLGetArgCount(ml, &n);
``` *recurse for head* ```
  for (i = 0; i < n; i++) {
``` *recurse for each argument* ```
  }
  ...
``` |
| This reads a single symbol. | ```
  case MLTKSYM:
  MLGetSymbol(ml, &name);
  ...
``` |
| This reads a machine integer. | ```
  case MLTKINT:
  MLGetInteger(ml, &i);
  ...
``` |
| | ```
}
``` |

By using `MLGetNext()` it is straightforward to write programs that can read any expression. The way *MathLink* works, the head and arguments of a function appear as successive expressions on the link, which you read one after another.

Note that if you know that the head of a function will be a symbol, then you can use `MLGetFunction()` instead of `MLGetNext()`. In this case, however, you still need to call `MLDisownSymbol()` to disown the memory used to store the symbol name.
```

int MLPutNext(MLINK *link*, int *type*)	prepare to put an object of the specified type on a link
int MLPutArgCount(MLINK *link*, long *n*)	give the number of arguments for a composite function
int MLPutSymbol(MLINK *link*, char **name*)	put a symbol on the link
int MLPutInteger(MLINK *link*, int *i*)	put a machine integer
int MLPutReal(MLINK *link*, double *x*)	put a machine floating-point number
int MLPutString(MLINK *link*, char **string*)	put a character string

Functions for putting pieces of expressions onto a link.

MLPutNext() specifies types of expressions using constants such as MLTKFUNC from the mathlink.h header file—just like MLGetNext().

■ 2.13.13 Advanced Topic: Error and Interrupt Handling

When you are putting and getting data via *MathLink* various kinds of errors can occur. Whenever any error occurs, *MathLink* goes into a completely inactive state, and all *MathLink* functions you call will return 0 immediately.

long MLError(MLINK *link*)	return a number identifying the current error, or 0 if none has occurred
char *MLErrorMessage(MLINK *link*)	return a character string describing the current error
int MLClearError(MLINK *link*)	clear the current error, returning *MathLink* if possible to an active state

Handling errors in *MathLink* programs.

When you do complicated operations, it is often convenient to check for errors only at the end. If you find that an error occurred, you must then call MLClearError() to activate *MathLink* again.

---

int MLNewPacket(MLINK *link*)   skip to the end of the current packet

---

Clearing out the remains of a packet.

After an error, it is common to want to discard the remainder of the packet or expression that you are currently processing. You can do this using MLNewPacket().

In some cases, you may want to set it up so that if an error occurs while you are processing particular data, you can then later go back and reprocess the data in a different way. You can do this by calling MLCreateMark() to create a mark before you first process the data, and then calling MLSeekMark() to seek back to the mark if you need to reprocess the data. You should not forgot to call MLDestroyMark() when you have finally finished with the data—otherwise *MathLink* will continue to store it.

---

int MLAbort   a global variable set when a program set up by Install is
                sent an abort interrupt

Aborting an external program.

If you interrupt *Mathematica* while it is in the middle of executing an external function, it will typically give you the opportunity to try to abort the external function. If you choose to do this, what will happen is that the global variable MLAbort will be set to 1 inside your external program.

MathLink cannot automatically back out of an external function call that has been made. So if you have a function that can take a long time, you should explicitly check MLAbort every so often, returning from the function if you find that the variable has been set.

■ 2.13.14 Running *Mathematica* from Within an External Program

To run *Mathematica* from within an external program requires making use of many general features of *MathLink*. The first issue is how to establish a *MathLink* connection to *Mathematica*.

When you use *MathLink* templates to create external programs that can be called from *Mathematica*, source code to establish a *MathLink* connection is automatically generated, and all you have to do in your external program is to call MLMain(*argc, argv*). But in general you need to call several functions to establish a *MathLink* connection.

`MLENV MLInitialize(0)`	initialize *MathLink* library functions
`MLINK MLOpenArgv(MLENV` *env*`, char **`*argv0*`, char **`*argv1*`, long *`*errno*`)`	
	open a *MathLink* connection taking parameters from an `argv` array
`MLINK MLOpenString(MLENV` *env*`, char *`*string*`, long *`*errno*`)`	
	open a *MathLink* connection taking parameters from a single character string
`int MLActivate(MLINK` *link*`)`	activate a *MathLink* connection, waiting for the program at the other end to respond
`void MLClose(MLINK` *link*`)`	close a *MathLink* connection
`void MLDeinitialize(MLENV` *env*`)`	
	deinitialize *MathLink* library functions

Opening and closing *MathLink* connections.

Include the standard *MathLink* header file.	`#include "mathlink.h"`
	`int main(int argc, char *argv[]) {`
	`    MLENV env;`
	`    MLINK link;`
	`    long errno;`
This initializes *MathLink* library functions.	`    env = MLInitialize(0);`
This opens a *MathLink* connection, using the same arguments as were passed to the main program.	`    link = MLOpenArgv(env, argv, argv+argc, &errno);`
This activates the connection, waiting for the other program to respond.	`    MLActivate(link);`
	`    ...`
	`}`

Often the `argv` that you pass to `MLOpenArgv()` will come directly from the `argv` that is passed to `main()` when your whole program is started. Note that `MLOpenArgv()` takes pointers to the beginning and end of the `argv` array. By not using `argc` directly it avoids having to know the size of an `int`.

The elements in the `argv` array are character strings which mirror the arguments and options used in the *Mathematica* functions `LinkLaunch`, `LinkCreate` and `LinkConnect`.

`"-linklaunch"`	operate like `LinkLaunch["`*name*`"]`
`"-linkcreate"`	operate like `LinkCreate["`*name*`"]`
`"-linkconnect"`	operate like `LinkConnect["`*name*`"]`
`"-linkname"`, *"name"*	give the name to use
`"-linkprotocol"`, *"protocol"*	give the link protocol to use (`tcp`, `pipes`, etc.)

Possible elements of the `argv` array passed to `MLOpenArgv()`.

As an alternative to `MLOpenArgv()` you can use `MLOpenString()`, which takes parameters concatenated into a single character string with spaces in between.

Once you have successfully opened a *MathLink* connection to the *Mathematica* kernel, you can then use standard *MathLink* functions to exchange data with it.

`int MLEndPacket(MLINK `*link*`)`	indicate the end of a packet
`int MLNextPacket(MLINK `*link*`)`	find the head of the next packet
`int MLNewPacket(MLINK `*link*`)`	skip to the end of the current packet

Functions often used in communicating with the *Mathematica* kernel.

Once you have sent all the pieces of a packet using `MLPutFunction()` etc., *MathLink* requires you to call `MLEndPacket()` to ensure synchronization and consistency.

One of the main issues in writing an external program which communicates directly with the *Mathematica* kernel is handling all the various kinds of packets that the kernel can generate.

The function `MLNextPacket()` finds the head of the next packet that comes from the kernel, and returns a constant that indicates the type of the packet.

Mathematica packet	constant	
ReturnPacket[*expr*]	RETURNPKT	result from a computation
ReturnTextPacket["*string*"]	RETURNTEXTPKT	textual form of a result
InputNamePacket["*name*"]	INPUTNAMEPKT	name of an input line
OutputNamePacket["*name*"]	OUTPUTNAMEPKT	name of an output line
TextPacket["*string*"]	TEXTPKT	textual output from functions like Print
MessagePacket[*symb*, "*tag*"]	MESSAGEPKT	name of a message generated by *Mathematica*
DisplayPacket["*string*"]	DISPLAYPKT	part of PostScript graphics
DisplayEndPacket["*string*"]	DISPLAYENDPKT	end of PostScript graphics
InputPacket["*prompt*"]	INPUTPKT	request for a response to an Input function
CallPacket[*i*, *list*]	CALLPKT	request for a call to an external function

Some packets recognized by MLNextPacket().

This keeps on reading data from a link, discarding it until an error or a ReturnPacket is found.

```
while ((p = MLNextPacket(link)) && p != RETURNPKT)
    MLNewPacket(link);
```

If you want to write a complete front end to *Mathematica*, you will need to handle all of the possible types of packets that the kernel can generate. Typically you can do this by setting up an appropriate switch on the value returned by MLNextPacket().

The *MathLink* Developer Kit contains sample source code for several simple but complete front ends.

int MLReady(MLINK *link*)	test whether there is data waiting to be read on a link
int MLFlush(MLINK *link*)	flush out buffers containing data waiting to be sent on a link

Flow of data on links.

One feature of more sophisticated external programs such as front ends is that they may need to perform operations while they are waiting for data to be sent to them by *Mathematica*. When you call a standard *MathLink* library function such as MLNextPacket() your program will normally block until all the data needed by this function is available.

You can avoid blocking by repeatedly calling MLReady(), and only calling functions like MLNextPacket() when MLReady() no longer returns 0. MLReady() is the analog of the *Mathematica* function LinkReadyQ.

Note that *MathLink* sometimes buffers the data that you tell it to send. To make sure that all necessary data has been sent you should call MLFlush(). Only after doing this does it make sense to call MLReady() and wait for data to be sent back.

2.14 Global Aspects of *Mathematica* Sessions

■ 2.14.1 The Main Loop

In any interactive session, *Mathematica* effectively operates in a loop. It waits for your input, processes the input, prints the result, then goes back to waiting for input again. As part of this "main loop", *Mathematica* maintains and uses various global objects. You will often find it useful to work with these objects.

You should realize, however, that if you use *Mathematica* through a special front end, your front end may set up its own main loop, and what is said in this section may not apply.

$\text{In}[n]$	the expression on the nth input line
$\text{InString}[n]$	the textual form of the nth input line
$\%n$ or $\text{Out}[n]$	the expression on the nth output line
$\text{Out}[\{n_1, n_2, \ldots\}]$	a list of output expressions
$\%\% \ldots \%$ (n times) or $\text{Out}[-n]$	the expression on the nth previous output line
$\text{MessageList}[n]$	a list of messages produced while processing the nth line
$\text{\$Line}$	the current line number (resettable)

Input and output expressions.

In a standard interactive session, there is a sequence of input and output lines. *Mathematica* stores the values of the expressions on these lines in $\text{In}[n]$ and $\text{Out}[n]$.

As indicated by the usual $\text{In}[n]\text{:=}$ prompt, the input expressions are stored with delayed assignments. This means that whenever you ask for $\text{In}[n]$, the input expression will always be re-evaluated in your current environment.

This assigns a value to x.	`In[1]:= x = 7` `Out[1]= 7`
Now the value for x is used.	`In[2]:= x - x^2 + 5x - 1` `Out[2]= -8`
This removes the value assigned to x.	`In[3]:= x =.`
This is re-evaluated in your current environment, where there is no value assigned to x.	`In[4]:= In[2]` $Out[4]= -1 + 6\,x - x^2$

This gives the textual form of the second input line, appropriate for editing or other textual manipulation.

```
In[5]:= InString[2] // InputForm
Out[5]//InputForm= "x - x^2 + 5x - 1"
```

$HistoryLength	the number of previous lines of input and output to keep

Specifying the length of session history to keep.

Mathematica by default stores *all* your input and output lines for the duration of the session. In a very long session, this may take up a large amount of computer memory. You can nevertheless get rid of the input and output lines by explicitly clearing the values of In and Out, using Unprotect[In, Out], followed by Clear[In, Out]. You can also tell *Mathematica* to keep only a limited number of lines of history by setting the global variable $HistoryLength .

Note that at any point in a session, you can reset the line number counter $Line, so that for example new lines are numbered so as to overwrite previous ones.

$PreRead	a function applied to each input string before being fed to *Mathematica*
$Pre	a function applied to each input expression before evaluation
$Post	a function applied to each expression after evaluation
$PrePrint	a function applied after Out[*n*] is assigned, but before the result is printed
$SyntaxHandler	a function applied to any input line that yields a syntax error

Global functions used in the main loop.

Mathematica provides a variety of "hooks" that allow you to insert functions to be applied to expressions at various stages in the main loop. Thus, for example, any function you assign as the value of the global variable $Pre will automatically be applied before evaluation to any expression you give as input.

For a particular input line, the standard main loop begins by getting a text string of input. Particularly if you need to deal with special characters, you may want to modify this text string before it is further processed by *Mathematica*. You can do this by assigning a function as the value of the global variable $PreRead. This function will be applied to the text string, and the result will be used as the actual input string for the particular input line.

This tells *Mathematica* to replace << ... >> by { ... } in every input string.	`In[6]:= $PreRead = StringReplace[#, {"<<" -> "{", ">>" -> "}"}]&`
	
	`Out[6]= StringReplace[#1, {<< → {, >> → }}] &`

You can now enter braces as double angle brackets.	`In[7]:= <<4, 5, 6>>`
	
	`Out[7]= {4, 5, 6}`

You can remove the value for $PreRead like this, at least so long as your definition for $PreRead does not modify this very input string.	`In[8]:= $PreRead =.`

Once any `$PreRead` processing on an input string is finished, the string is read by *Mathematica*. At this point, *Mathematica* may find that there is a syntax error in the string. If this happens, then *Mathematica* calls whatever function you have specified as the value of `$SyntaxHandler`. It supplies two arguments: the input string, and the character position at which the syntax error was detected. With `$SyntaxHandler` you can, for example, generate an analysis of the syntax error, or call an editor. If your function returns a string, then *Mathematica* will use this string as a new input string.

This specifies what *Mathematica* should do when it gets a syntax error.	`In[9]:= $SyntaxHandler =`
	`        (Print[StringForm["Error at char `1` in `2`",`
	`                          #2, #1]]; $Failed)&`
	
	`Out[9]= (Print[Error at char #2 in #1]; $Failed) &`

This input generates a syntax error.	`In[10]:= 3 +/+ 5`
	`Syntax::sntxf: "3 +" cannot be followed by "/+ 5".`
	
	`Error at char 4 in 3 +/+ 5`

Once *Mathematica* has successfully read an input expression, it then evaluates this expression. Before doing the evaluation, *Mathematica* applies any function you have specified as the value of `$Pre`, and after the evaluation, it applies any function specified as the value of `$Post`. Note that unless the `$Pre` function holds its arguments unevaluated, the function will have exactly the same effect as `$Post`.

`$Post` allows you to specify arbitrary "post processing" to be done on results obtained from *Mathematica*. Thus, for example, to make *Mathematica* get a numerical approximation to every result it generates, all you need do is to set `$Post = N`.

This tells *Mathematica* to apply N to every result it generates.	`In[10]:= $Post = N`
	
	`Out[10]= N`

Now *Mathematica* gets a numerical approximation to anything you type in.	`In[11]:= Sqrt[7]` `Out[11]= 2.64575`
This removes the post-processing function you specified.	`In[12]:= $Post =.`

As soon as *Mathematica* has generated a result, and applied any `$Post` function you have specified, it takes the result, and assigns it as the value of `Out[$Line]`. The next step is for *Mathematica* to print the result. However, before doing this, it applies any function you have specified as the value of $PrePrint.

This tells *Mathematica* to shorten all output to two lines.

In[13]:= **$PrePrint = Short[#, 2]& ;**

Only a two-line version of the output is now shown.

In[14]:= **Expand[(x + y)^40]**

Out[14]= $x^{40} + 40\,x^{39}\,y + 780\,x^{38}\,y^2 +$
$\ll 35 \gg + 780\,x^2\,y^{38} + 40\,x\,y^{39} + y^{40}$

This removes the value you assigned to $PrePrint.

In[15]:= **$PrePrint =.**

There are various kinds of output generated in a typical *Mathematica* session. In general, each kind of output is sent to a definite *output channel*, as discussed on page 633. Associated with each output channel, there is a global variable which gives a list of the output streams to be included in that output channel.

$Output	standard output and text generated by Print
$Echo	an echo of each input line (as stored in InString[n])
$Urgent	input prompts and other urgent output
$Messages	standard messages and output generated by Message
$Display	graphics output generated by the default $DisplayFunction
$SoundDisplay	sound output generated by the default $SoundDisplayFunction

Output channels in a standard *Mathematica* session.

By modifying the list of streams in a given output channel, you can redirect or copy particular kinds of *Mathematica* output. Thus, for example, by opening an output stream to a file, and including that stream in the $Echo list, you can get each piece of input you give to *Mathematica* saved in a file.

Streams[ ]	list of all open streams
Streams["*name*"]	list of all open streams with the specified name
$Input	the name of the current input stream

Open streams in a *Mathematica* session.

The function Streams shows you all the input, output and other streams that are open at a particular point in a *Mathematica* session. The variable $Input gives the name of the current stream from which *Mathematica* input is being taken at a particular point. $Input is reset, for example, during the execution of a Get command.

$MessagePrePrint	a function to be applied to expressions that are given in messages
$Language	list of default languages to use for messages

Parameters for messages.

There are various global parameters which determine the form of messages generated by *Mathematica*.

As discussed in Section 2.9.21, typical messages include a sequence of expressions which are combined with the text of the message through StringForm. $MessagePrePrint gives a function to be applied to the expressions before they are printed. The default value of $MessagePrePrint is Short.

As discussed in Section 2.9.22, *Mathematica* allows you to specify the language in which you want messages to be produced. In a particular *Mathematica* session, you can assign a list of language names as the value of $Language.

Exit[ ] or Quit[ ]	terminate your *Mathematica* session
$Epilog	a global variable to be evaluated before termination

Terminating *Mathematica* sessions.

Mathematica will continue in its main loop until you explicitly tell it to exit. Most *Mathematica* interfaces provide special ways to do this. Nevertheless, you can always do it by explicitly calling Exit or Quit.

Mathematica allows you to give a value to the global variable $Epilog to specify operations to perform just before *Mathematica* actually exits. In this way, you can for example make *Mathematica* always save certain objects before exiting.

$IgnoreEOF	whether to ignore the end-of-file character

A global variable that determines the treatment of end-of-file characters.

As discussed in Section 2.8.5, *Mathematica* usually does not treat special characters in a special way. There is one potential exception, however. With the default setting $IgnoreEOF = False, *Mathematica* recognizes end-of-file characters. If *Mathematica* receives an end-of-file character as the only thing on a particular input line in a standard interactive *Mathematica* session, then it will exit the session.

Exactly how you enter an end-of-file character depends on the computer system you are using. Under Unix, for example, you typically press CONTROL-D.

Note that if you use *Mathematica* in a "batch mode", with all its input coming from a file, then it will automatically exit when it reaches the end of the file, regardless of the value of $IgnoreEOF.

■ 2.14.2 Dialogs

Within a standard interactive session, you can create "subsessions" or *dialogs* using the *Mathematica* command `Dialog`. Dialogs are often useful if you want to interact with *Mathematica* while it is in the middle of doing a calculation. As mentioned in Section 2.6.11, `TraceDialog` for example automatically calls `Dialog` at specified points in the evaluation of a particular expression. In addition, if you interrupt *Mathematica* during a computation, you can typically "inspect" its state using a dialog.

`Dialog[ ]`	initiate a *Mathematica* dialog
`Dialog[expr]`	initiate a dialog with *expr* as the current value of %
`Return[ ]`	return from a dialog, taking the current value of % as the return value
`Return[expr]`	return from a dialog, taking *expr* as the return value

Initiating and returning from dialogs.

This initiates a dialog.	*In[1]:=* **Dialog[ ]**
You can do computations in a dialog just as you would in any *Mathematica* session.	*In[2]:=* **2^41** *Out[2]=* 2199023255552
You can use `Return` to exit from a dialog.	*In[3]:=* **Return[ ]** *Out[1]=* 2199023255552

When you exit a dialog, you can return a value for the dialog using `Return[expr]`. If you do not want to return a value, and you have set `$IgnoreEOF = False`, then you can also exit a dialog simply by giving an end-of-file character, at least on systems with text-based interfaces.

To evaluate this expression, *Mathematica* initiates a dialog.	*In[2]:=* **1 + Dialog[ ]^2**
The value a + b returned from the dialog is now inserted in the original expression.	*In[3]:=* **Return[a + b]** *Out[2]=* $1 + (a+b)^2$

In starting a dialog, you will often find it useful to have some "initial expression". If you use `Dialog[expr]`, then *Mathematica* will start a dialog, using *expr* as the initial expression, accessible for example as the value of %.

This first starts a dialog with initial expression a^2.	*In[3]:=* **Map[Dialog, {a^2, b + c}]** *Out[4]=* a^2
% is the initial expression in the dialog.	*In[5]:=* **%^2 + 1** *Out[5]=* $1 + a^4$
This returns a value from the first dialog, and starts the second dialog, with initial expression b + c.	*In[6]:=* **Return[%]** *Out[4]=* $b + c$
This returns a value from the second dialog. The final result is the original expression, with values from the two dialogs inserted.	*In[5]:=* **Return[444]** *Out[3]=* $\{1 + a^4, 444\}$

Dialog effectively works by running a subsidiary version of the standard *Mathematica* main loop. Each dialog you start effectively "inherits" various values from the overall main loop. Some of the values are, however, local to the dialog, so their original values are restored when you exit the dialog.

Thus, for example, dialogs inherit the current line number $Line when they start. This means that the lines in a dialog have numbers that follow the sequence used in the main loop. Nevertheless, the value of $Line is local to the dialog. As a result, when you exit the dialog, the value of $Line reverts to what it was in the main loop.

If you start a dialog on line 10 of your *Mathematica* session, then the first line of the dialog will be labeled *In[11]*. Successive lines of the dialog will be labeled *In[12]*, *In[13]* and so on. Then, when you exit the dialog, the next line in your main loop will be labeled *In[11]*. At this point, you can still refer to results generated within the dialog as *Out[11]*, *Out[12]* and so on. These results will be overwritten, however, when you reach lines *In[12]*, *In[13]*, and so on in the main loop.

In a standard *Mathematica* session, you can tell whether you are in a dialog by seeing whether your input and output lines are indented. If you call a dialog from within a dialog, you will get two levels of indentation. In general, the indentation you get inside d nested dialogs is determined by the output form of the object **DialogIndent[d]**. By defining the format for this object, you can specify how dialogs should be indicated in your *Mathematica* session.

DialogSymbols :> {$x, y, \ldots$}	symbols whose values should be treated as local to the dialog
DialogSymbols :> {$x = x_0, y = y_0, \ldots$}	symbols with initial values
DialogProlog :> *expr*	an expression to evaluate before starting the dialog

Options for **Dialog**.

Whatever setting you give for DialogSymbols, Dialog will always treat the values of $Line, $Epilog and $MessageList as local. Note that if you give a value for $Epilog, it will automatically be evaluated when you exit the dialog.

When you call Dialog, its first step is to localize the values of variables. Then it evaluates any expression you have set for the option DialogProlog. If you have given an explicit argument to the Dialog function, this is then evaluated next. Finally, the actual dialog is started.

When you exit the dialog, you can explicitly specify the return value using Return[*expr*]. If you do not do this, the return value will be taken to be the last value generated in the dialog.

■ 2.14.3 Date and Time Functions

Date[ ]	give the current local date and time in the form *{year, month, day, hour, minute, second}*
Date[z]	give the current date and time in time zone *z*
TimeZone[ ]	give the time zone assumed by your computer system

Finding the date and time.

This gives the current date and time.

In[1]:= **Date[ ]**

Out[1]= {2003, 6, 28, 1, 20, 53.518907}

The *Mathematica* Date function returns whatever your computer system gives as the current date and time. It assumes that any corrections for daylight saving time and so on have already been done by your computer system. In addition, it assumes that your computer system has been set for the appropriate time zone.

The function TimeZone[ ] returns the current time zone assumed by your computer system. The time zone is given as the number of hours which must be added to Greenwich mean time (GMT) to obtain the correct local time. Thus, for example, U.S. eastern standard time (EST) corresponds to time zone -5. Note that daylight saving time corrections must be included in the time zone, so U.S. eastern daylight time (EDT) corresponds to time zone -4.

This gives the current time zone assumed by your computer system.

In[2]:= **TimeZone[ ]**

Out[2]= -5.

This gives the current date and time in time zone +9, the time zone for Japan.

In[3]:= **Date[9]**

Out[3]= {2003, 6, 28, 15, 20, 53.862027}

AbsoluteTime[ ]	total number of seconds since the beginning of January 1, 1900
SessionTime[ ]	total number of seconds elapsed since the beginning of your current *Mathematica* session
TimeUsed[ ]	total number of seconds of CPU time used in your current *Mathematica* session
$TimeUnit	the minimum time interval recorded on your computer system

Time functions.

You should realize that on any computer system, there is a certain "granularity" in the times that can be measured. This granularity is given as the value of the global variable $TimeUnit. Typically it is either about $\frac{1}{100}$ or $\frac{1}{1000}$ of a second.

Pause[*n*]	pause for at least *n* seconds

Pausing during a calculation.

This gives various time functions.

```
In[4]:= {AbsoluteTime[ ], SessionTime[ ], TimeUsed[ ]}

Out[4]= {3.265752053952846 × 10^9, 1.845655, 0.26}
```

This pauses for 10 seconds, then re-evaluates the time functions. Note that TimeUsed[ ] is not affected by the pause.

```
In[5]:= Pause[10]; {AbsoluteTime[ ], SessionTime[ ],
                                            TimeUsed[ ]}

Out[5]= {3.265752064079360 × 10^9, 11.972179, 0.26}
```

FromDate[*date*]	convert from date to absolute time
ToDate[*time*]	convert from absolute time to date

Converting between dates and absolute times.

This sets d to be the current date.

```
In[6]:= d = Date[ ]

Out[6]= {2003, 6, 28, 1, 21, 4.162634}
```

This adds one month to the current date.

```
In[7]:= Date[ ] + {0, 1, 0, 0, 0, 0}

Out[7]= {2003, 7, 28, 1, 21, 4.282415}
```

This gives the number of seconds in the additional month.	*In[8]:=* **FromDate[%] - FromDate[d]**	
	Out[8]= $2.592000119781 \times 10^6$	

Timing[*expr*]	evaluate *expr*, and return a list of the CPU time needed, together with the result obtained	
+ AbsoluteTiming[*expr*]	evaluate *expr*, giving the absolute time taken	

Timing *Mathematica* operations.

Timing allows you to measure the CPU time, corresponding to the increase in TimeUsed, associated with the evaluation of a single *Mathematica* expression. Note that only CPU time associated with the actual evaluation of the expression within the *Mathematica* kernel is included. The time needed to format the expression for output, and any time associated with external programs, is not included.

AbsoluteTiming allows you to measure absolute total elapsed time. You should realize, however, that the time reported for a particular calculation by both AbsoluteTiming and Timing depends on many factors.

First, the time depends in detail on the computer system you are using. It depends not only on instruction times, but also on memory caching, as well as on the details of the optimization done in compiling the parts of the internal code of *Mathematica* used in the calculation.

The time also depends on the precise state of your *Mathematica* session when the calculation was done. Many of the internal optimizations used by *Mathematica* depend on details of preceding calculations. For example, *Mathematica* often uses previous results it has obtained, and avoids unnecessarily re-evaluating expressions. In addition, some *Mathematica* functions build internal tables when they are first called in a particular way, so that if they are called in that way again, they run much faster. For all of these kinds of reasons, it is often the case that a particular calculation may not take the same amount of time if you run it at different points in the same *Mathematica* session.

This gives the CPU time needed for the calculation. The semicolon causes the result of the calculation to be given as Null.	*In[9]:=* **Timing[100000!;]** *Out[9]=* {0.51 Second, Null}
Now *Mathematica* has built internal tables for factorial functions, and the calculation takes no measurable CPU time.	*In[10]:=* **Timing[100000!;]** *Out[10]=* {0. Second, Null}
However, some absolute time does elapse.	*In[11]:=* **AbsoluteTiming[100000!;]** *Out[11]=* {0.000083 Second, Null}

Note that the results you get from Timing are only accurate to the timing granularity $TimeUnit of your computer system. Thus, for example, a timing reported as 0 could in fact be as much as $TimeUnit.

TimeConstrained[*expr*, *t*]	try to evaluate *expr*, aborting the calculation after *t* seconds
TimeConstrained[*expr*, *t*, *failexpr*]	return *failexpr* if the time constraint is not met

Time-constrained calculation.

When you use *Mathematica* interactively, it is quite common to try doing a calculation, but to abort the calculation if it seems to be taking too long. You can emulate this behavior inside a program by using TimeConstrained. TimeConstrained tries to evaluate a particular expression for a specified amount of time. If it does not succeed, then it aborts the evaluation, and returns either $Aborted, or an expression you specify.

You can use TimeConstrained, for example, to have *Mathematica* try a particular approach to a problem for a certain amount of time, and then to switch to another approach if the first one has not yet succeeded. You should realize however that TimeConstrained may overrun the time you specify if *Mathematica* cannot be interrupted during a particular part of a calculation. In addition, you should realize that because different computer systems run at different speeds, programs that use TimeConstrained will often give different results on different systems.

■ 2.14.4 Memory Management

MemoryInUse[ ]	number of bytes of memory currently being used by *Mathematica*
MaxMemoryUsed[ ]	maximum number of bytes of memory used by *Mathematica* in this session

Finding memory usage.

Particularly for symbolic computations, memory is usually the primary resource which limits the size of computations you can do. If a computation runs slowly, you can always potentially let it run longer. But if the computation generates intermediate expressions which simply cannot fit in the memory of your computer system, then you cannot proceed with the computation.

Mathematica is careful about the way it uses memory. Every time an intermediate expression you have generated is no longer needed, *Mathematica* immediately reclaims the memory allocated to it. This means that at any point in a session, *Mathematica* stores only those expressions that are actually needed; it does not keep unnecessary objects which have to be "garbage collected" later.

This gives the number of bytes of memory currently being used by *Mathematica*.

```
In[1]:= MemoryInUse[ ]
Out[1]= 947712
```

This generates a 10000-element list.	*In[2]:=* **Range[10000] // Short**
	Out[2]= {1, 2, 3, 4, 5, 6, 7, 8, «9985», 9994, 9995, 9996, 9997, 9998, 9999, 10000}
Additional memory is needed to store the list.	*In[3]:=* **MemoryInUse[ ]**
	Out[3]= 989616
This list is kept because it is the value of Out[2]. If you clear Out[2], the list is no longer needed.	*In[4]:=* **Unprotect[Out]; Out[2]=.**
The memory in use goes down again.	*In[5]:=* **MemoryInUse[ ]**
	Out[5]= 954408
This shows the maximum memory needed at any point in the session.	*In[6]:=* **MaxMemoryUsed[ ]**
	Out[6]= 1467536

One issue that often comes up is exactly how much memory *Mathematica* can actually use on a particular computer system. Usually there is a certain amount of memory available for *all* processes running on the computer at a particular time. Sometimes this amount of memory is equal to the physical number of bytes of RAM in the computer. Often, it includes a certain amount of "virtual memory", obtained by swapping data on and off a mass storage device.

When *Mathematica* runs, it needs space both for data and for code. The complete code of *Mathematica* is typically several megabytes in size. For any particular calculation, only a small fraction of this code is usually used. However, in trying to work out the total amount of space available for *Mathematica* data, you should not forget what is needed for *Mathematica* code. In addition, you must include the space that is taken up by other processes running in the computer. If there are fewer jobs running, you will usually find that your job can use more memory.

It is also worth realizing that the time needed to do a calculation can depend very greatly on how much physical memory you have. Although virtual memory allows you in principle to use large amounts of memory space, it is usually hundreds or even thousands of times slower to access than physical memory. As a result, if your calculation becomes so large that it needs to make use of virtual memory, it may run *much* more slowly.

MemoryConstrained[*expr*, *b*]	try to evaluate *expr*, aborting if more than *b* additional bytes of memory are requested
MemoryConstrained[*expr*, *b*, *failexpr*]	return *failexpr* if the memory constraint is not met

Memory-constrained computation.

MemoryConstrained works much like TimeConstrained. If more than the specified amount of memory is requested, MemoryConstrained attempts to abort your computation. As with

`TimeConstrained`, there may be some overshoot in the actual amount of memory used before the computation is aborted.

`ByteCount[`*expr*`]`	the maximum number of bytes of memory needed to store *expr*
`LeafCount[`*expr*`]`	the number of terminal nodes in the expression tree for *expr*

Finding the size of expressions.

Although you may find `ByteCount` useful in estimating how large an expression of a particular kind you can handle, you should realize that the specific results given by `ByteCount` can differ substantially from one version of *Mathematica* to another.

Another important point is that `ByteCount` always gives you the *maximum* amount of memory needed to store a particular expression. Often *Mathematica* will actually use a much smaller amount of memory to store the expression. The main issue is how many of the subexpressions in the expression can be *shared*.

In an expression like `f[1 + x, 1 + x]`, the two subexpressions `1 + x` are identical, but they may or may not actually be stored in the same piece of computer memory. `ByteCount` gives you the number of bytes needed to store expressions with the assumption that no subexpressions are shared. You should realize that the sharing of subexpressions is often destroyed as soon as you use an operation like the `/.` operator.

Nevertheless, you can explicitly tell *Mathematica* to share subexpressions using the function `Share`. In this way, you can significantly reduce the actual amount of memory needed to store a particular expression.

`Share[`*expr*`]`	share common subexpressions in the storage of *expr*
`Share[ ]`	share common subexpressions throughout memory

Optimizing memory usage.

On most computer systems, the memory used by a running program is divided into two parts: memory explicitly allocated by the program, and "stack space". Every time an internal routine is called in the program, a certain amount of stack space is used to store parameters associated with the call. On many computer systems, the maximum amount of stack space that can be used by a program must be specified in advance. If the specified stack space limit is exceeded, the program usually just exits.

In *Mathematica*, one of the primary uses of stack space is in handling the calling of one *Mathematica* function by another. All such calls are explicitly recorded in the *Mathematica* `Stack` discussed in Section 2.6.12. You can control the size of this stack by setting the global parameter $RecursionLimit. You should be sure that this parameter is set small enough that you do not run out of stack space on your particular computer system.

■ 2.14.5 Advanced Topic: Global System Information

In order to write the most general *Mathematica* programs you will sometimes need to find out global information about the setup under which your program is being run.

Thus, for example, to tell whether your program should be calling functions like NotebookWrite, you need to find out whether the program is being run in a *Mathematica* session that is using the notebook front end. You can do this by testing the global variable $Notebooks.

$Notebooks	whether a notebook front end is being used

Determining whether a notebook front end is being used.

Mathematica is usually used interactively, but it can also operate in a batch mode—say taking input from a file and writing output to a file. In such a case, a program cannot for example expect to get interactive input from the user.

$BatchInput	whether input is being given in batch mode
$BatchOutput	whether output should be given in batch mode, without labeling, etc.

Variables specifying batch mode operation.

The *Mathematica* kernel is a process that runs under the operating system on your computer. Within *Mathematica* there are several global variables that allow you to find the characteristics of this process and its environment.

$CommandLine	the original command line used to invoke the *Mathematica* kernel
$ParentLink	the *MathLink* LinkObject specifying the program that invoked the kernel (or Null if the kernel was invoked directly)
$ProcessID	the ID assigned to the *Mathematica* kernel process by the operating system
$ParentProcessID	the ID of the process that invoked the *Mathematica* kernel
$UserName	the login name of the user running the *Mathematica* kernel
Environment["*var*"]	the value of a variable defined by the operating system

Variables associated with the *Mathematica* kernel process.

If you have a variable such as x in a particular *Mathematica* session, you may or may not want that variable to be the same as an x in another *Mathematica* session. In order to make it possible to maintain distinct objects in different sessions, *Mathematica* supports the variable $SessionID, which uses information such as starting time, process ID and machine ID to try to give a different value for every single *Mathematica* session, whether it is run on the same computer or a different one.

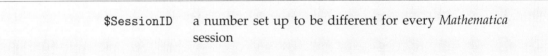

$SessionID	a number set up to be different for every *Mathematica* session

A unique number different for every *Mathematica* session.

Mathematica provides various global variables that allow you to tell which version of the kernel you are running. This is important if you write programs that make use of features that are, say, new in Version 5. You can then check $VersionNumber to find out if these features will be available.

$Version	a string giving the complete version of *Mathematica* in use
$VersionNumber	the *Mathematica* kernel version number (e.g. 5.0)
$ReleaseNumber	the release number for your version of the *Mathematica* kernel on your particular computer system
$CreationDate	the date, in Date format, on which your particular *Mathematica* release was created
$InstallationDate	the date on which your copy of *Mathematica* was installed
$ProductInformation	a list of detailed product information

Variables specifying the version of *Mathematica* used.

Mathematica itself is set up to be as independent of the details of the particular computer system on which it is run as possible. However, if you want to access external aspects of your computer system, then you will often need to find out its characteristics.

$System	a full string describing the computer system in use
$SystemID	a short string specifying the computer system in use
$ProcessorType	the architecture of the processor in your computer system
$MachineType	the general type of your computer system
$ByteOrdering	the native byte ordering convention on your computer system
$OperatingSystem	the basic operating system in use
$SystemCharacterEncoding	the default raw character encoding used by your operating system

Variables specifying the characteristics of your computer system.

Mathematica uses the values of $SystemID to label directories that contain versions of files for different computer systems, as discussed on pages 627 and 677. Computer systems for which $SystemID is the same will normally be binary compatible.

$OperatingSystem has values such as "Unix" and "MacOS". By testing $OperatingSystem you can determine whether a particular external program is likely to be available on your computer system.

This gives some characteristics of the computer system used to generate the examples for this book.

```
In[1]:= {$System, $ProcessorType, $OperatingSystem}

Out[1]= {Linux, x86, Unix}
```

`$MachineName`	the name of the computer on which *Mathematica* is running
`$MachineDomain`	the network domain for the computer
`$MachineID`	the unique ID assigned by *Mathematica* to the computer

Variables identifying the computer on which *Mathematica* is running.

`$LicenseID`	the ID for the license under which *Mathematica* is running
`$LicenseExpirationDate`	the date on which the license expires
`$NetworkLicense`	whether this is a network license
`$LicenseServer`	the full name of the machine serving the license
`$LicenseProcesses`	the number of *Mathematica* processes currently being run under the license
`$MaxLicenseProcesses`	the maximum number of processes provided by the license
`$PasswordFile`	password file used when the kernel was started

Variables associated with license management.

Part 3

Part 1 described how to do basic mathematics with Mathematica. For many kinds of calculations, you will need to know nothing more. But if you do want to use more advanced mathematics, this part discusses how to do it in Mathematica.

This part goes through the various mathematical functions and methods that are built into Mathematica. Some calculations can be done just by using these built-in mathematical capabilities. For many specific calculations, however, you will need to use application packages that have been written in Mathematica. These packages build on the mathematical capabilities discussed in this part, but add new functions for doing special kinds of calculations.

Much of what is said in this part assumes a knowledge of mathematics at an advanced undergraduate level. If you do not understand a particular section, then you can probably assume that you will not need to use that section.

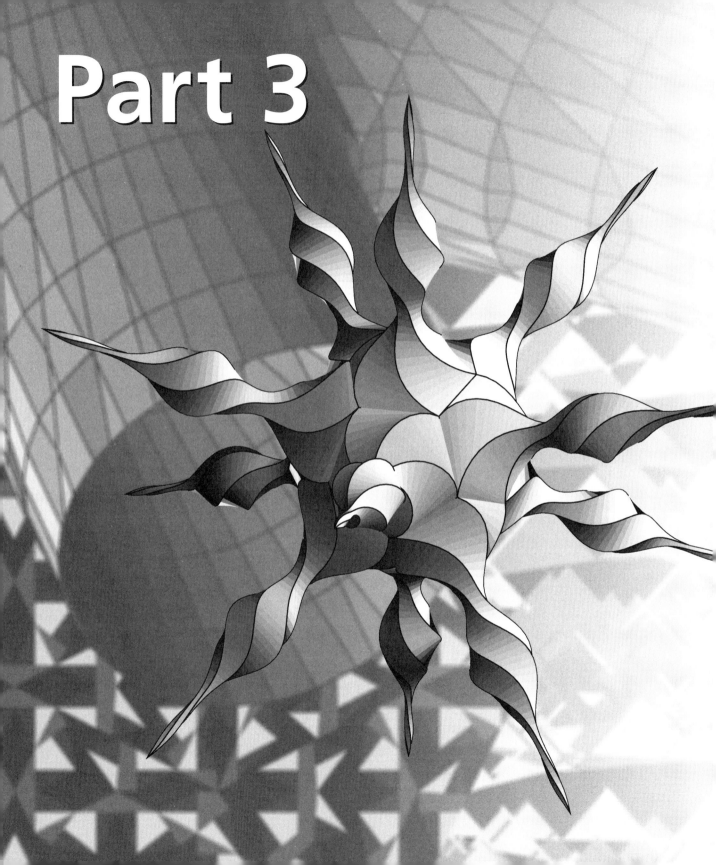

Part 3

Advanced Mathematics in *Mathematica*

3.1 Numbers

■ 3.1.1 Types of Numbers

Four underlying types of numbers are built into *Mathematica*.

Integer	arbitrary-length exact integer
Rational	*integer*/*integer* in lowest terms
Real	approximate real number, with any specified precision
Complex	complex number of the form *number* + *number* I

Intrinsic types of numbers in *Mathematica*.

Rational numbers always consist of a ratio of two integers, reduced to lowest terms.

$In[1]:=$ **12344/2222**

$$Out[1]= \frac{6172}{1111}$$

Approximate real numbers are distinguished by the presence of an explicit decimal point.

$In[2]:=$ **5456.**

$Out[2]=$ 5456.

An approximate real number can have any number of digits.

$In[3]:=$ **4.54543523454543523453452345234543**

$Out[3]=$ 4.54543523454543523453452345234523454

Complex numbers can have integer or rational components.

$In[4]:=$ **4 + 7/8 I**

$$Out[4]= 4 + \frac{7i}{8}$$

They can also have approximate real number components.

$In[5]:=$ **4 + 5.6 I**

$Out[5]=$ 4 + 5.6 i

123	an exact integer
123.	an approximate real number
123.0000000000000	an approximate real number with a certain precision
123. + 0. I	a complex number with approximate real number components

Several versions of the number 123.

You can distinguish different types of numbers in *Mathematica* by looking at their heads. (Although numbers in *Mathematica* have heads like other expressions, they do not have explicit elements which you can extract.)

The object 123 is taken to be an exact integer, with head Integer.

```
In[6]:= Head[123]
Out[6]= Integer
```

The presence of an explicit decimal point makes *Mathematica* treat 123. as an approximate real number, with head Real.

```
In[7]:= Head[123.]
Out[7]= Real
```

NumberQ[*x*]	test whether *x* is any kind of number
IntegerQ[*x*]	test whether *x* is an integer
EvenQ[*x*]	test whether *x* is even
OddQ[*x*]	test whether *x* is odd
PrimeQ[*x*]	test whether *x* is a prime integer
Head[*x*]===*type*	test the type of a number

Tests for different types of numbers.

NumberQ[*x*] tests for any kind of number.

```
In[8]:= NumberQ[5.6]
Out[8]= True
```

5. is treated as a Real, so IntegerQ gives False.

```
In[9]:= IntegerQ[5.]
Out[9]= False
```

If you use complex numbers extensively, there is one subtlety you should be aware of. When you enter a number like 123., *Mathematica* treats it as an approximate real number, but assumes that its imaginary part is exactly zero. Sometimes you may want to enter approximate complex numbers with imaginary parts that are zero, but only to a certain precision.

When the imaginary part is the exact integer 0, *Mathematica* simplifies complex numbers to real ones.

```
In[10]:= Head[ 123 + 0 I ]
Out[10]= Integer
```

Here the imaginary part is only zero to a certain precision, so *Mathematica* retains the complex number form.

```
In[11]:= Head[ 123. + 0. I ]
Out[11]= Complex
```

The distinction between complex numbers whose imaginary parts are exactly zero, or are only zero to a certain precision, may seem like a pedantic one. However, when we discuss, for example, the interpretation of powers and roots of complex numbers in Section 3.2.7, the distinction will become significant.

One way to find out the type of a number in *Mathematica* is just to pick out its head using Head[*expr*]. For many purposes, however, it is better to use functions like IntegerQ which explicitly test for particular types. Functions like this are set up to return True if their argument is manifestly of the required type, and to return False otherwise. As a result, IntegerQ[x] will give False, unless x has an explicit integer value.

■ 3.1.2 Numeric Quantities

NumberQ[*expr*]	test whether *expr* is explicitly a number
NumericQ[*expr*]	test whether *expr* has a numerical value

Testing for numeric quantities.

Pi is a symbol, so Pi + 3 is not explicitly a number.	*In[1]:=* **NumberQ[Pi + 3]** *Out[1]=* False
It does however have a numerical value.	*In[2]:=* **NumericQ[Pi + 3]** *Out[2]=* True
This finds the explicit numerical value of Pi + 3.	*In[3]:=* **N[Pi + 3]** *Out[3]=* 6.14159

Mathematica knows that constants such as Pi are numeric quantities. It also knows that standard mathematical functions such as Log and Sin have numerical values when their arguments are numerical.

Log[2 + x] contains x, and is therefore not a numeric quantity.	*In[4]:=* **{NumericQ[Log[2]], NumericQ[Log[2 + x]]}** *Out[4]=* {True, False}
Many functions implicitly use the numerical values of numeric quantities.	*In[5]:=* **Min[Exp[2], Log[2], Sqrt[2]]** *Out[5]=* Log[2]

In general, *Mathematica* assumes that any function which has the attribute NumericFunction will yield numerical values when its arguments are numerical. All standard mathematical functions in *Mathematica* already have this attribute. But when you define your own functions, you can explicitly set the attribute to tell *Mathematica* to assume that these functions will have numerical values when their arguments are numerical.

■ 3.1.3 Digits in Numbers

IntegerDigits[n]	a list of the decimal digits in the integer n
IntegerDigits[n, b]	the digits of n in base b
IntegerDigits[n, b, *len*]	the list of digits padded on the left with zeros to give total length *len*
IntegerExponent[n, b]	the number of zeros at the end of n in base b
RealDigits[x]	a list of the decimal digits in the approximate real number x, together with the number of digits to the left of the decimal point
RealDigits[x, b]	the digits of x in base b
RealDigits[x, b, *len*]	the first *len* digits of x in base b
RealDigits[x, b, *len*, n]	the first *len* digits starting with the coefficient of b^n
FromDigits[*list*]	reconstruct a number from its decimal digit sequence
FromDigits[*list*, b]	reconstruct a number from its digits sequence in base b

Converting between numbers and lists of digits.

Here is the list of base 16 digits for an integer.

```
In[1]:= IntegerDigits[1234135634, 16]
Out[1]= {4, 9, 8, 15, 6, 10, 5, 2}
```

This gives a list of digits, together with the number of digits that appear to the left of the decimal point.

```
In[2]:= RealDigits[123.4567890123456]
Out[2]= {{1, 2, 3, 4, 5, 6, 7, 8, 9, 0, 1, 2, 3, 4, 5, 6}, 3}
```

Here is the binary digit sequence for 56, padded with zeros so that it is of total length 8.

```
In[3]:= IntegerDigits[56, 2, 8]
Out[3]= {0, 0, 1, 1, 1, 0, 0, 0}
```

This reconstructs the original number from its binary digit sequence.

```
In[4]:= FromDigits[%, 2]
Out[4]= 56
```

b^^$nnnn$	a number in base b
BaseForm[x, b]	print with x in base b

Numbers in other bases.

When the base is larger than 10, extra digits are represented by letters a–z.

The number 100101_2 in base 2 is 37 in base 10.	`In[5]:= 2^^100101` `Out[5]= 37`

This prints 37 in base 2.	`In[6]:= BaseForm[37, 2]` `Out[6]//BaseForm= 100101`$_2$

Here is a number in base 16.	`In[7]:= 16^^ffffaa00` `Out[7]= 4294945280`

You can do computations with numbers in base 16. Here the result is given in base 10.	`In[8]:= 16^^fffaa2 + 16^^ff - 1` `Out[8]= 16776096`

This gives the result in base 16.	`In[9]:= BaseForm[%, 16]` `Out[9]//BaseForm= fffba0`$_{16}$

You can give approximate real numbers, as well as integers, in other bases.	`In[10]:= 2^^101.100101` `Out[10]= 5.57813`

Here are the first few digits of $\sqrt{2}$ in octal.	`In[11]:= BaseForm[N[Sqrt[2], 30], 8]` `Out[11]//BaseForm= 1.32404746317716746220426276611546`7_8

This gives an explicit list of the first 15 octal digits.	`In[12]:= RealDigits[Sqrt[2], 8, 15]` `Out[12]= {{1, 3, 2, 4, 0, 4, 7, 4, 6, 3, 1, 7, 7, 1, 7}, 1}`

This gives 15 octal digits starting with the coefficient of 8^{-10}.	`In[13]:= RealDigits[Sqrt[2], 8, 15, -10]` `Out[13]= {{1, 7, 7, 1, 6, 7, 4, 6, 2, 2, 0, 4, 2, 6, 3}, -9}`

Section 2.9.7 describes how to print numbers in various formats. If you want to create your own formats, you will often need to use MantissaExponent to separate the pieces of real numbers.

MantissaExponent[x]	give a list containing the mantissa and exponent of x
MantissaExponent[x, b]	give the mantissa and exponent in base b

Separating the mantissa and exponent of numbers.

This gives a list in which the mantissa and exponent of the number are separated.	`In[14]:= MantissaExponent[3.45 10^125]` `Out[14]= {0.345, 126}`

◼ 3.1.4 Numerical Precision

As discussed in Section 1.1.2, *Mathematica* can handle approximate real numbers with any number of digits. In general, the *precision* of an approximate real number is the effective number of decimal digits in it which are treated as significant for computations. The *accuracy* is the effective number of these digits which appear to the right of the decimal point. Note that to achieve full consistency in the treatment of numbers, precision and accuracy often have values that do not correspond to integer numbers of digits.

Precision[x]	the total number of significant decimal digits in x
Accuracy[x]	the number of significant decimal digits to the right of the decimal point in x

Precision and accuracy of real numbers.

This generates a number with 30-digit precision.

```
In[1]:= x = N[Pi^10, 30]
Out[1]= 93648.0747476083020973716690 1849
```

This gives the precision of the number.

```
In[2]:= Precision[x]
Out[2]= 30.
```

The accuracy is lower since only some of the digits are to the right of the decimal point.

```
In[3]:= Accuracy[x]
Out[3]= 25.0285
```

This number has all its digits to the right of the decimal point.

```
In[4]:= x / 10^6
Out[4]= 0.0936480747476083020973716690 1849
```

Now the accuracy is larger than the precision.

```
In[5]:= {Precision[%], Accuracy[%]}
Out[5]= {30., 31.0285}
```

An approximate real number always has some uncertainty in its value, associated with digits beyond those known. One can think of precision as providing a measure of the relative size of this uncertainty. Accuracy gives a measure of the absolute size of the uncertainty.

Mathematica is set up so that if a number x has uncertainty δ, then its true value can lie anywhere in an interval of size δ from $x - \delta/2$ to $x + \delta/2$. An approximate number with accuracy a is defined to have uncertainty 10^{-a}, while a non-zero approximate number with precision p is defined to have uncertainty $|x|10^{-p}$.

Precision[x]	$-\log_{10}(\delta/|x|)$
Accuracy[x]	$-\log_{10}(\delta)$

Definitions of precision and accuracy in terms of uncertainty.

Adding or subtracting a quantity smaller than the uncertainty has no visible effect.

```
In[6]:= {x - 10^-26, x, x + 10^-26}

Out[6]= {93648.0474760830209737166901849,
         93648.0474760830209737166901849,
         93648.0474760830209737166901849}
```

N[$expr$, n]	evaluate $expr$ to n-digit precision using arbitrary-precision numbers
N[$expr$]	evaluate $expr$ numerically using machine-precision numbers

Numerical evaluation with arbitrary-precision and machine-precision numbers.

Mathematica distinguishes two kinds of approximate real numbers: *arbitrary-precision* numbers, and *machine-precision* numbers or *machine numbers*. Arbitrary-precision numbers can contain any number of digits, and maintain information on their precision. Machine numbers, on the other hand, always contain the same number of digits, and maintain no information on their precision.

Here is a machine-number approximation to π.

```
In[7]:= N[Pi]

Out[7]= 3.14159
```

These are both arbitrary-precision numbers.

```
In[8]:= {N[Pi, 4], N[Pi, 20]}

Out[8]= {3.142, 3.1415926535897932385}
```

As discussed in more detail below, machine numbers work by making direct use of the numerical capabilities of your underlying computer system. As a result, computations with them can often be done more quickly. They are however much less flexible than arbitrary-precision numbers, and difficult numerical analysis can be needed to determine whether results obtained with them are correct.

+ MachinePrecision	the precision specification used to indicate machine numbers
$MachinePrecision	the effective precision for machine numbers on your computer system
MachineNumberQ[x]	test whether x is a machine number

Machine numbers.

This returns the symbol MachinePrecision to indicate a machine number.	*In[9]:=* **Precision[N[Pi]]** *Out[9]=* MachinePrecision
On this computer, machine numbers have slightly less than 16 decimal digits.	*In[10]:=* **\$MachinePrecision** *Out[10]=* 15.9546

When you enter an approximate real number, *Mathematica* has to decide whether to treat it as a machine number or an arbitrary-precision number. Unless you specify otherwise, then if you give less than \$MachinePrecision digits, *Mathematica* will treat the number as machine precision, and if you give more digits, it will treat the number as arbitrary precision.

123.4	a machine-precision number
123.45678901234567890	an arbitrary-precision number on some computer systems
123.45678901234567890`	a machine-precision number on all computer systems
123.456`200	an arbitrary-precision number with 200 digits of precision
123.456``200	an arbitrary-precision number with 200 digits of accuracy
1.234*^6	a machine-precision number in scientific notation (1.234×10^6)
1.234`200*^6	a number in scientific notation with 200 digits of precision
2^^101.111`200	a number in base 2 with 200 binary digits of precision
2^^101.111`200*^6	a number in base 2 scientific notation $(101.111_2 \times 2^6)$

Input forms for numbers.

When *Mathematica* prints out numbers, it usually tries to give them in a form that will be as easy as possible to read. But if you want to take numbers that are printed out by *Mathematica*, and then later use them as input to *Mathematica*, you need to make sure that no information gets lost.

In standard output form, *Mathematica* prints a number like this to six digits.	*In[11]:=* **N[Pi]** *Out[11]=* 3.14159
In input form, *Mathematica* prints all the digits it knows.	*In[12]:=* **InputForm[%]** *Out[12]//InputForm=* 3.141592653589793
Here is an arbitrary-precision number in standard output form.	*In[13]:=* **N[Pi, 20]** *Out[13]=* 3.1415926535897932385

In input form, *Mathematica* explicitly indicates the precision of the number, and gives extra digits to make sure the number can be reconstructed correctly.

```
In[14]:= InputForm[%]
Out[14]//InputForm= 3.1415926535897932384626433832795028842`20.
```

This makes *Mathematica* not explicitly indicate precision.

```
In[15]:= InputForm[%, NumberMarks->False]
Out[15]//InputForm= 3.1415926535897932385
```

InputForm[*expr*, NumberMarks->True]
                                use ` marks in all approximate numbers

InputForm[*expr*, NumberMarks->Automatic]
                                use ` only in arbitrary-precision numbers

InputForm[*expr*, NumberMarks->False]
                                never use ` marks

Controlling printing of numbers.

The default setting for the NumberMarks option, both in InputForm and in functions such as ToString and OpenWrite is given by the value of $NumberMarks. By resetting $NumberMarks, therefore, you can globally change the way that numbers are printed in InputForm.

This makes *Mathematica* by default always include number marks in input form.

```
In[16]:= $NumberMarks = True
Out[16]= True
```

Even a machine-precision number is now printed with an explicit number mark.

```
In[17]:= InputForm[N[Pi]]
Out[17]//InputForm= 3.141592653589793`
```

Even with no number marks, InputForm still uses *^ for scientific notation.

```
In[18]:= InputForm[N[Exp[600], 20], NumberMarks->False]
Out[18]//InputForm= 3.7730203009299398234*^260
```

In doing numerical computations, it is inevitable that you will sometimes end up with results that are less precise than you want. Particularly when you get numerical results that are very close to zero, you may well want to *assume* that the results should be exactly zero. The function Chop allows you to replace approximate real numbers that are close to zero by the exact integer 0.

Chop[*expr*]   replace all approximate real numbers in *expr* with magnitude less than 10^{-10} by 0

Chop[*expr*, *dx*]   replace numbers with magnitude less than *dx* by 0

Removing numbers close to zero.

| This computation gives a small imaginary part. | $In[19]:=$ **Exp[N[2 Pi I]]** |
| | $Out[19]=$ $1. - 2.44921 \times 10^{-16}$ i |

| You can get rid of the imaginary part using Chop. | $In[20]:=$ **Chop[%]** |
| | $Out[20]=$ $1.$ |

■ 3.1.5 Arbitrary-Precision Numbers

When you do calculations with arbitrary-precision numbers, *Mathematica* keeps track of precision at all points. In general, *Mathematica* tries to give you results which have the highest possible precision, given the precision of the input you provided.

Mathematica treats arbitrary-precision numbers as representing the values of quantities where a certain number of digits are known, and the rest are unknown. In general, an arbitrary-precision number x is taken to have Precision[x] digits which are known exactly, followed by an infinite number of digits which are completely unknown.

| This computes π to 10-digit precision. | $In[1]:=$ **N[Pi, 10]** |
| | $Out[1]=$ 3.141592654 |

After a certain point, all digits are indeterminate.	$In[2]:=$ **RealDigits[%, 10, 13]**
	$Out[2]=$ {{3, 1, 4, 1, 5, 9, 2, 6, 5, 3,
	5, Indeterminate, Indeterminate}, 1}

When you do a computation, *Mathematica* keeps track of which digits in your result could be affected by unknown digits in your input. It sets the precision of your result so that no affected digits are ever included. This procedure ensures that all digits returned by *Mathematica* are correct, whatever the values of the unknown digits may be.

| This evaluates $\Gamma(1/7)$ to 30-digit precision. | $In[3]:=$ **N[Gamma[1/7], 30]** |
| | $Out[3]=$ $6.54806294024782443771409334943$ |

| The result has a precision of exactly 30 digits. | $In[4]:=$ **Precision[%]** |
| | $Out[4]=$ $30.$ |

| If you give input only to a few digits of precision, *Mathematica* cannot give you such high-precision output. | $In[5]:=$ **N[Gamma[0.142], 30]** |
| | $Out[5]=$ 6.58965 |

| If you want *Mathematica* to assume that the argument is *exactly* 142/1000, then you have to say so explicitly. | $In[6]:=$ **N[Gamma[142/1000], 30]** |
| | $Out[6]=$ $6.58964729492039788328481917496$ |

In many computations, the precision of the results you get progressively degrades as a result of "roundoff error". A typical case of this occurs if you subtract two numbers that are close together. The result you get depends on high-order digits in each number, and typically has far fewer digits of precision than either of the original numbers.

Both input numbers have a precision of around 20 digits, but the result has much lower precision.

```
In[7]:= 1.1111111111111111111 -
        1.1111111111111111000

Out[7]= 1.1 × 10^-18
```

Adding extra digits in one number but not the other is not sufficient to allow extra digits to be found in the result.

```
In[8]:= 1.111111111111111111345 -
        1.1111111111111111000

Out[8]= 1.1 × 10^-18
```

The precision of the output from a function can depend in a complicated way on the precision of the input. Functions that vary rapidly typically give less precise output, since the variation of the output associated with uncertainties in the input is larger. Functions that are close to constants can actually give output that is more precise than their input.

Functions like Sin that vary rapidly typically give output that is less precise than their input.

```
In[9]:= Sin[111111111.0000000000000000]

Out[9]= -0.2975351033349432
```

Here is e^{-40} evaluated to 20-digit precision.

```
In[10]:= N[Exp[-40], 20]

Out[10]= 4.2483542552915889953 × 10^-18
```

The result you get by adding the exact integer 1 has a higher precision.

```
In[11]:= 1 + %

Out[11]= 1.0000000000000000042483542552915889953
```

It is worth realizing that different ways of doing the same calculation can end up giving you results with very different precisions. Typically, if you once lose precision in a calculation, it is essentially impossible to regain it; in losing precision, you are effectively losing information about your result.

Here is a 40-digit number that is close to 1.

```
In[12]:= x = N[1 - 10^-30, 40]

Out[12]= 0.99999999999999999999999999990000000000
```

Adding 1 to it gives another 40-digit number.

```
In[13]:= 1 + x

Out[13]= 1.9999999999999999999999999999000000000
```

The original precision has been maintained.

```
In[14]:= Precision[%]

Out[14]= 40.301
```

This way of computing 1 + x loses precision.

```
In[15]:= (x^2 - 1) / (x - 1)

Out[15]= 2.000000000
```

The result obtained in this way has quite low precision.

```
In[16]:= Precision[%]

Out[16]= 9.69897
```

The fact that different ways of doing the same calculation can give you different numerical answers means, among other things, that comparisons between approximate real numbers must be treated with care. In testing whether two real numbers are "equal", *Mathematica* effectively finds their difference, and tests whether the result is "consistent with zero" to the precision given.

These numbers are equal to the precision given.	`In[17]:=` **3 == 3.000000000000000000**
	`Out[17]=` True

The internal algorithms that *Mathematica* uses to evaluate mathematical functions are set up to maintain as much precision as possible. In most cases, built-in *Mathematica* functions will give you results that have as much precision as can be justified on the basis of your input. In some cases, however, it is simply impractical to do this, and *Mathematica* will give you results that have lower precision. If you give higher-precision input, *Mathematica* will use higher precision in its internal calculations, and you will usually be able to get a higher-precision result.

N[*expr*]	evaluate *expr* numerically to machine precision
N[*expr*, *n*]	evaluate *expr* numerically trying to get a result with *n* digits of precision

Numerical evaluation.

If you start with an expression that contains only integers and other exact numeric quantities, then N[*expr*, *n*] will in almost all cases succeed in giving you a result to *n* digits of precision. You should realize, however, that to do this *Mathematica* sometimes has to perform internal intermediate calculations to much higher precision.

The global variable $MaxExtraPrecision specifies how many additional digits should be allowed in such intermediate calculations.

variable	default value	
$MaxExtraPrecision	50	maximum additional precision to use

Controlling precision in intermediate calculations.

Mathematica automatically increases the precision that it uses internally in order to get the correct answer here.	`In[18]:=` **N[Sin[10^40], 30]**
	`Out[18]=` -0.569633400953636327308034181574

Using the default setting $MaxExtraPrecision=50 *Mathematica* cannot get the correct answer here.	`In[19]:=` **N[Sin[10^100], 30]**
	N::meprec: Internal precision limit $MaxExtraPrecision = 50. reached while evaluating Sin[10000000000000000000<<71>>00000000000].
	`Out[19]=` 0.

This tells *Mathematica* that it can use more digits in its internal calculations.	`In[20]:=` **$MaxExtraPrecision = 200**
	`Out[20]=` 200

Now it gets the correct answer.	*In[21]:=* **N[Sin[10^100], 30]**
	Out[21]= -0.37237612366127668826208669553
This resets $MaxExtraPrecision to its default value.	*In[22]:=* **$MaxExtraPrecision = 50**
	Out[22]= 50

Even when you are doing computations that give exact results, *Mathematica* still occasionally uses approximate numbers for some of its internal calculations, so that the value of $MaxExtraPrecision can thus have an effect.

Mathematica works this out using bounds from approximate numbers.	*In[23]:=* **Sin[Exp[100]] > 0**
	Out[23]= True

With the default value of $MaxExtraPrecision, *Mathematica* cannot work this out.	*In[24]:=* **Sin[Exp[200]] > 0**
	N::meprec: Internal precision limit $MaxExtraPrecision =
	200
	50. reached while evaluating -Sin[E].
	Out[24]= $Sin[e^{200}] > 0$

Temporarily resetting $MaxExtraPrecision allows *Mathematica* to get the result.	*In[25]:=* **Block[{$MaxExtraPrecision = 100},**
	Sin[Exp[200]] > 0]
	Out[25]= False

In doing calculations that degrade precision, it is possible to end up with numbers that have no significant digits at all. But even in such cases, *Mathematica* still maintains information on the accuracy of the numbers. Given a number with no significant digits, but accuracy *a*, *Mathematica* can then still tell that the actual value of the number must be in the range $\{-10^{-a}, +10^{-a}\}/2$. *Mathematica* by default prints such numbers in the form $0. \times 10^e$.

Here is a number with 20-digit precision.	*In[26]:=* **x = N[Exp[50], 20]**
	Out[26]= $5.1847055285870724641 \times 10^{21}$

Here there are no significant digits left.	*In[27]:=* **Sin[x]/x**
	Out[27]= $0. \times 10^{-22}$

But *Mathematica* still keeps track of the accuracy of the result.	*In[28]:=* **Accuracy[%]**
	Out[28]= 21.7147

Adding this to an exact 1 gives a number with quite high precision.	*In[29]:=* **1 + %**
	Out[29]= 22.7147

One subtlety in characterizing numbers by their precision is that any number that is consistent with zero must be treated as having zero precision. The reason for this is that such a number has no digits that can be recognized as significant, since all its known digits are just zero.

This gives a number whose value is consistent with zero.	*In[30]:=* **d = N[Pi, 20] - Pi**
	Out[30]= $-0. \times 10^{-20}$

The number has no recognizable significant digits of precision.	*In[31]:=* **Precision[d]**
	Out[31]= 0.
But it still has a definite accuracy, that characterizes the uncertainty in it.	*In[32]:=* **Accuracy[d]**
	Out[32]= 19.2089

If you do computations whose results are likely to be near zero, it can be convenient to specify the accuracy, rather than the precision, that you want to get.

N[*expr*, *p*]	evaluate *expr* to precision *p*
+ N[*expr*, {*p*, *a*}]	evaluate *expr* to at most precision *p* and accuracy *a*
+ N[*expr*, {Infinity, *a*}]	evaluate *expr* to any precision but to accuracy *a*

Specifying accuracy as well as precision.

Here is a symbolic expression.	*In[33]:=* **u = ArcTan[1/3] - ArcCot[3]**
	Out[33]= $-\text{ArcCot}[3] + \text{ArcTan}\left[\dfrac{1}{3}\right]$
This shows that the expression is equivalent to zero.	*In[34]:=* **FullSimplify[u]**
	Out[34]= 0
N cannot guarantee to get a result to precision 20.	*In[35]:=* **N[u, 20]**

```
N::meprec: Internal precision limit $MaxExtraPrecision =
                                               1
    50. reached while evaluating -ArcCot[3] + ArcTan[-].
                                               3
```

Out[35]= $0. \times 10^{-71}$

But it can get a result to accuracy 20.	*In[36]:=* **N[u, {Infinity, 20}]**
	Out[36]= $0. \times 10^{-21}$

When *Mathematica* works out the potential effect of unknown digits in arbitrary-precision numbers, it assumes by default that these digits are completely independent in different numbers. While this assumption will never yield too high a precision in a result, it may lead to unnecessary loss of precision.

In particular, if two numbers are generated in the same way in a computation, some of their unknown digits may be equal. Then, when these numbers are, for example, subtracted, the unknown digits may cancel. By assuming that the unknown digits are always independent, however, *Mathematica* will miss such cancellations.

Here is a number computed to 20-digit precision.	*In[37]:=* **d = N[3^-30, 20]**
	Out[37]= $4.8569357496188611379 \times 10^{-15}$

The quantity 1 + d has about 34-digit precision.

In[38]:= **Precision[1 + d]**

Out[38]= 34.3136

This quantity still has the same precision, since *Mathematica* assumes that the unknown digits in each number d are independent.

In[39]:= **Precision[(1 + d) - d]**

Out[39]= 34.0126

Numerical algorithms sometimes rely on cancellations between unknown digits in different numbers yielding results of higher precision. If you can be sure that certain unknown digits will eventually cancel, then you can explicitly introduce fixed digits in place of the unknown ones. You can carry these fixed digits through your computation, then let them cancel, and get a result of higher precision.

SetPrecision[x, n]	create a number with n decimal digits of precision, padding with base-2 zeros if necessary
SetAccuracy[x, n]	create a number with n decimal digits of accuracy

Functions for modifying precision and accuracy.

This introduces 10 more digits in d.

In[40]:= **d = SetPrecision[d, 30]**

Out[40]= $4.85693574961886113790624266497 \times 10^{-15}$

The digits that were added cancel out here.

In[41]:= **(1 + d) - d**

Out[41]= 1.0000000000000000000000000000000000000000000

The precision of the result is now about 44 digits, rather than 34.

In[42]:= **Precision[%]**

Out[42]= 44.0126

SetPrecision works by adding digits which are zero in base 2. Sometimes, *Mathematica* stores slightly more digits in an arbitrary-precision number than it displays, and in such cases, **SetPrecision** will use these extra digits before introducing zeros.

This creates a number with a precision of 40 decimal digits. The extra digits come from conversion to base 10.

In[43]:= **SetPrecision[0.400000000000000, 40]**

Out[43]= 0.4000000000000000222044604925031308084726

variable	default value	
~ $MaxPrecision	Infinity	maximum total precision to be used
~ $MinPrecision	-Infinity	minimum precision to be used

Global precision control parameters.

By making the global assignment $MinPrecision = *n*, you can effectively apply SetPrecision[*expr, n*] at every step in a computation. This means that even when the number of correct digits in an arbitrary-precision number drops below *n*, the number will always be padded to have *n* digits.

If you set $MaxPrecision = *n* as well as $MinPrecision = *n*, then you can force all arbitrary-precision numbers to have a fixed precision of *n* digits. In effect, what this does is to make *Mathematica* treat arbitrary-precision numbers in much the same way as it treats machine numbers—but with more digits of precision.

Fixed-precision computation can make some calculations more efficient, but without careful analysis you can never be sure how many digits are correct in the results you get.

Here is a small number with 20-digit precision.	*In[44]:=* **k = N[Exp[-60], 20]** *Out[44]=* $8.7565107626965203385 \times 10^{-27}$
With *Mathematica*'s usual arithmetic, this works fine.	*In[45]:=* **Evaluate[1 + k] - 1** *Out[45]=* $8.7565107626965203385 \times 10^{-27}$
This tells *Mathematica* to use fixed-precision arithmetic.	*In[46]:=* **$MinPrecision = $MaxPrecision = 20** *Out[46]=* 20
The first few digits are correct, but the rest are wrong.	*In[47]:=* **Evaluate[1 + k] - 1** *Out[47]=* $8.7565107626963908935 \times 10^{-27}$

■ 3.1.6 Machine-Precision Numbers

Whenever machine-precision numbers appear in a calculation, the whole calculation is typically done in machine precision. *Mathematica* will then give machine-precision numbers as the result.

Whenever the input contains any machine-precision numbers, *Mathematica* does the computation to machine precision.	*In[1]:=* **1.4444444444444444444 ^ 5.7** *Out[1]=* 8.13382
Zeta[5.6] yields a machine-precision result, so the N is irrelevant.	*In[2]:=* **N[Zeta[5.6], 30]** *Out[2]=* 1.02338
This gives a higher-precision result.	*In[3]:=* **N[Zeta[56/10], 30]** *Out[3]=* 1.02337547922702991086041788103

When you do calculations with arbitrary-precision numbers, as discussed in the previous section, *Mathematica* always keeps track of the precision of your results, and gives only those digits which are known to be correct, given the precision of your input. When you do calculations with machine-precision numbers, however, *Mathematica* always gives you a machine-precision result, whether or not all the digits in the result can, in fact, be determined to be correct on the basis of your input.

This subtracts two machine-precision numbers.

In[4]:= **diff = 1.11111111 - 1.11111000**

Out[4]= 1.11×10^{-6}

The result is taken to have machine precision.

In[5]:= **Precision[diff]**

Out[5]= MachinePrecision

Here are all the digits in the result.

In[6]:= **InputForm[diff]**

Out[6]//InputForm= 1.1099999999153454*^-6

The fact that you can get spurious digits in machine-precision numerical calculations with *Mathematica* is in many respects quite unsatisfactory. The ultimate reason, however, that *Mathematica* uses fixed precision for these calculations is a matter of computational efficiency.

Mathematica is usually set up to insulate you as much as possible from the details of the computer system you are using. In dealing with machine-precision numbers, you would lose too much, however, if *Mathematica* did not make use of some specific features of your computer.

The important point is that almost all computers have special hardware or microcode for doing floating-point calculations to a particular fixed precision. *Mathematica* makes use of these features when doing machine-precision numerical calculations.

The typical arrangement is that all machine-precision numbers in *Mathematica* are represented as "double-precision floating-point numbers" in the underlying computer system. On most current computers, such numbers contain a total of 64 binary bits, typically yielding 16 decimal digits of mantissa.

The main advantage of using the built-in floating-point capabilities of your computer is speed. Arbitrary-precision numerical calculations, which do not make such direct use of these capabilities, are usually many times slower than machine-precision calculations.

There are several disadvantages of using built-in floating-point capabilities. One already mentioned is that it forces all numbers to have a fixed precision, independent of what precision can be justified for them.

A second disadvantage is that the treatment of machine-precision numbers can vary slightly from one computer system to another. In working with machine-precision numbers, *Mathematica* is at the mercy of the floating-point arithmetic system of each particular computer. If floating-point arithmetic is done differently on two computers, you may get slightly different results for machine-precision *Mathematica* calculations on those computers.

$MachinePrecision	the number of decimal digits of precision
$MachineEpsilon	the minimum positive machine-precision number which can be added to 1.0 to give a result distinguishable from 1.0
$MaxMachineNumber	the maximum machine-precision number
$MinMachineNumber	the minimum positive machine-precision number
$MaxNumber	the maximum magnitude of an arbitrary-precision number
$MinNumber	the minimum magnitude of a positive arbitrary-precision number

Properties of numbers on a particular computer system.

Since machine-precision numbers on any particular computer system are represented by a definite number of binary bits, numbers which are too close together will have the same bit pattern, and so cannot be distinguished. The parameter $MachineEpsilon gives the distance between 1.0 and the closest number which has a distinct binary representation.

This gives the value of $MachineEpsilon for the computer system on which these examples are run.

```
In[7]:= $MachineEpsilon
```
$$Out[7]= 2.22045 \times 10^{-16}$$

Although this prints as 1., *Mathematica* knows that the result is larger than 1.

```
In[8]:= 1. + $MachineEpsilon
```
$$Out[8]= 1.$$

Subtracting 1 gives $MachineEpsilon.

```
In[9]:= % - 1.
```
$$Out[9]= 2.22045 \times 10^{-16}$$

This again prints as 1.

```
In[10]:= 1. + $MachineEpsilon/2
```
$$Out[10]= 1.$$

In this case, however, subtracting 1 yields 0, since 1 + $MachineEpsilon/2 is not distinguished from 1. to machine precision.

```
In[11]:= % - 1.
```
$$Out[11]= 0.$$

Machine numbers have not only limited precision, but also limited magnitude. If you generate a number which lies outside the range specified by $MinMachineNumber and $MaxMachineNumber, *Mathematica* will automatically convert the number to arbitrary-precision form.

This is the maximum machine-precision number which can be handled on the computer system used for this example.

```
In[12]:= $MaxMachineNumber
```
$$Out[12]= 1.79769 \times 10^{308}$$

Mathematica automatically converts the result of this computation to arbitrary precision.

```
In[13]:= Exp[1000.]
```

$$Out[13]=\ 1.970071114017 \times 10^{434}$$

■ 3.1.7 Advanced Topic: Interval Arithmetic

Interval[{*min*, *max*}]   the interval from *min* to *max*

Interval[{*min*$_1$, *max*$_1$}, {*min*$_2$, *max*$_2$}, ...]

the union of intervals from *min*$_1$ to *max*$_1$, *min*$_2$ to *max*$_2$, ...

Representations of real intervals.

This represents all numbers between −2 and +5.

```
In[1]:= Interval[{-2, 5}]
```

$$Out[1]=\ Interval[\{-2, 5\}]$$

The square of any number between −2 and +5 is always between 0 and 25.

```
In[2]:= Interval[{-2, 5}]^2
```

$$Out[2]=\ Interval[\{0, 25\}]$$

Taking the reciprocal gives two distinct intervals.

```
In[3]:= 1/Interval[{-2, 5}]
```

$$Out[3]=\ Interval\left[\left\{-\infty,\ -\frac{1}{2}\right\},\ \left\{\frac{1}{5},\ \infty\right\}\right]$$

Abs folds the intervals back together again.

```
In[4]:= Abs[%]
```

$$Out[4]=\ Interval\left[\left\{\frac{1}{5},\ \infty\right\}\right]$$

You can use intervals in many kinds of functions.

```
In[5]:= Solve[3 x + 2 == Interval[{-2, 5}], x]
```

$$Out[5]=\ \left\{\left\{x \to Interval\left[\left\{-\frac{4}{3},\ 1\right\}\right]\right\}\right\}$$

Some functions automatically generate intervals.	*In[6]:=* **Limit[Sin[1/x], x -> 0]**
	Out[6]= Interval[{-1, 1}]

> **IntervalUnion[***interval*$_1$**,** *interval*$_2$**,** ... **]**
> find the union of several intervals
>
> **IntervalIntersection[***interval*$_1$**,** *interval*$_2$**,** ... **]**
> find the intersection of several intervals
>
> **IntervalMemberQ[***interval***,** *x***]**   test whether the point *x* lies within an interval
>
> **IntervalMemberQ[***interval*$_1$**,** *interval*$_2$**]**
> test whether *interval*$_2$ lies completely within *interval*$_1$

Operations on intervals.

This finds the overlap of the two intervals.	*In[7]:=* **IntervalIntersection[Interval[{3, 7}], Interval[{-2, 5}]]**
	Out[7]= Interval[{3, 5}]
You can use Max and Min to find the end points of intervals.	*In[8]:=* **Max[%]**
	Out[8]= 5
This finds out which of a list of intervals contains the point 7.	*In[9]:=* **IntervalMemberQ[** **Table[Interval[{i, i+1}], {i, 1, 20, 3}], 7]**
	Out[9]= {False, False, True, False, False, False, False}

You can use intervals not only with exact quantities but also with approximate numbers. Even with machine-precision numbers, *Mathematica* always tries to do rounding in such a way as to preserve the validity of results.

This shows explicitly the interval treated by *Mathematica* as the machine-precision number 0.	*In[10]:=* **Interval[0.]**
	Out[10]= Interval$\left[\left\{-2.22507 \times 10^{-308}, 2.22507 \times 10^{-308}\right\}\right]$
This shows the corresponding interval around 100., shifted back to zero.	*In[11]:=* **Interval[100.] - 100**
	Out[11]= Interval$\left[\left\{-1.42109 \times 10^{-14}, 1.42109 \times 10^{-14}\right\}\right]$
The same kind of thing works with numbers of any precision.	*In[12]:=* **Interval[N[Pi, 50]] - Pi**
	Out[12]= Interval$\left[\left\{-1. \times 10^{-49}, 1. \times 10^{-49}\right\}\right]$
With ordinary machine-precision arithmetic, this computation gives an incorrect result.	*In[13]:=* **Sin[N[Pi]]**
	Out[13]= 1.22461×10^{-16}
The interval generated here, however, includes the correct value of 0.	*In[14]:=* **Sin[Interval[N[Pi]]]**
	Out[14]= Interval$\left[\left\{-3.21629 \times 10^{-16}, 5.6655 \times 10^{-16}\right\}\right]$

■ 3.1.8 Advanced Topic: Indeterminate and Infinite Results

If you type in an expression like 0/0, *Mathematica* prints a message, and returns the result Indeterminate.

```
In[1]:= 0/0
                            1
Power::infy: Infinite expression - encountered.
                            0
Infinity::indet:
    Indeterminate expression 0 ComplexInfinity encountered.

Out[1]= Indeterminate
```

An expression like 0/0 is an example of an *indeterminate numerical result*. If you type in 0/0, there is no way for *Mathematica* to know what answer you want. If you got 0/0 by taking the limit of x/x as $x \to 0$, then you might want the answer 1. On the other hand, if you got 0/0 instead as the limit of $2x/x$, then you probably want the answer 2. The expression 0/0 on its own does not contain enough information to choose between these and other cases. As a result, its value must be considered indeterminate.

Whenever an indeterminate result is produced in an arithmetic computation, *Mathematica* prints a warning message, and then returns Indeterminate as the result of the computation. If you ever try to use Indeterminate in an arithmetic computation, you always get the result Indeterminate. A single indeterminate expression effectively "poisons" any arithmetic computation. (The symbol Indeterminate plays a role in *Mathematica* similar to the "not a number" object in the IEEE Floating Point Standard.)

The usual laws of arithmetic simplification are suspended in the case of Indeterminate.

```
In[2]:= Indeterminate - Indeterminate
Out[2]= Indeterminate
```

Indeterminate "poisons" any arithmetic computation, and leads to an indeterminate result.

```
In[3]:= 2 Indeterminate - 7
Out[3]= Indeterminate
```

When you do arithmetic computations inside *Mathematica* programs, it is often important to be able to tell whether indeterminate results were generated in the computations. You can do this by using the function Check discussed on page 481 to test whether any warning messages associated with indeterminate results were produced.

You can use Check inside a program to test whether warning messages are generated in a computation.

```
In[4]:= Check[(7 - 7)/(8 - 8), meaningless]
                            1
Power::infy: Infinite expression - encountered.
                            0
Infinity::indet:
    Indeterminate expression 0 ComplexInfinity encountered.

Out[4]= meaningless
```

`Indeterminate`	an indeterminate numerical result
`Infinity`	a positive infinite quantity
`-Infinity`	a negative infinite quantity (`DirectedInfinity[-1]`)
`DirectedInfinity[r]`	an infinite quantity with complex direction *r*
`ComplexInfinity`	an infinite quantity with an undetermined direction
`DirectedInfinity[ ]`	equivalent to `ComplexInfinity`

Indeterminate and infinite quantities.

There are many situations where it is convenient to be able to do calculations with infinite quantities. The symbol `Infinity` in *Mathematica* represents a positive infinite quantity. You can use it to specify such things as limits of sums and integrals. You can also do some arithmetic calculations with it.

Here is an integral with an infinite limit.

In[5]:= `Integrate[1/x^3, {x, 1, Infinity}]`

Out[5]= $\dfrac{1}{2}$

Mathematica knows that $1/\infty = 0$.

In[6]:= `1/Infinity`

Out[6]= 0

If you try to find the difference between two infinite quantities, you get an indeterminate result.

In[7]:= `Infinity - Infinity`

`Infinity::indet:`
    `Indeterminate expression -Infinity + Infinity`
      `encountered.`

Out[7]= `Indeterminate`

There are a number of subtle points that arise in handling infinite quantities. One of them concerns the "direction" of an infinite quantity. When you do an infinite integral, you typically think of performing the integration along a path in the complex plane that goes to infinity in some direction. In this case, it is important to distinguish different versions of infinity that correspond to different directions in the complex plane. $+\infty$ and $-\infty$ are two examples, but for some purposes one also needs $i\infty$ and so on.

In *Mathematica*, infinite quantities can have a "direction", specified by a complex number. When you type in the symbol `Infinity`, representing a positive infinite quantity, this is converted internally to the form `DirectedInfinity[1]`, which represents an infinite quantity in the +1 direction. Similarly, `-Infinity` becomes `DirectedInfinity[-1]`, and `I Infinity` becomes `DirectedInfinity[I]`. Although the `DirectedInfinity` form is always used internally, the standard output format for `DirectedInfinity[r]` is *r* `Infinity`.

`Infinity` is converted internally to `DirectedInfinity[1]`.

In[8]:= `Infinity // FullForm`

Out[8]//FullForm= `DirectedInfinity[1]`

Although the notion of a "directed infinity" is often useful, it is not always available. If you type in 1/0, you get an infinite result, but there is no way to determine the "direction" of the infinity. *Mathematica* represents the result of 1/0 as DirectedInfinity[ ]. In standard output form, this undirected infinity is printed out as ComplexInfinity.

1/0 gives an undirected form of infinity.

In[9]:= **1/0**

Power::infy: Infinite expression $\frac{1}{0}$ encountered.

Out[9]= ComplexInfinity

■ 3.1.9 Advanced Topic: Controlling Numerical Evaluation

NHoldAll	prevent any arguments of a function from being affected by N
NHoldFirst	prevent the first argument from being affected
NHoldRest	prevent all but the first argument from being affected

Attributes for controlling numerical evaluation.

Usually N goes inside functions and gets applied to each of their arguments.

In[1]:= **N[f[2/3, Pi]]**

Out[1]= f[0.666667, 3.14159]

This tells *Mathematica* not to apply N to the first argument of f.

In[2]:= **SetAttributes[f, NHoldFirst]**

Now the first argument of f is left in its exact form.

In[3]:= **N[f[2/3, Pi]]**

Out[3]= $f\left[\frac{2}{3}, 3.14159\right]$

3.2 Mathematical Functions

■ 3.2.1 Naming Conventions

Mathematical functions in *Mathematica* are given names according to definite rules. As with most *Mathematica* functions, the names are usually complete English words, fully spelled out. For a few very common functions, *Mathematica* uses the traditional abbreviations. Thus the modulo function, for example, is Mod, not Modulo.

Mathematical functions that are usually referred to by a person's name have names in *Mathematica* of the form *PersonSymbol*. Thus, for example, the Legendre polynomials $P_n(x)$ are denoted LegendreP[n, x]. Although this convention does lead to longer function names, it avoids any ambiguity or confusion.

When the standard notation for a mathematical function involves both subscripts and superscripts, the subscripts are given *before* the superscripts in the *Mathematica* form. Thus, for example, the associated Legendre polynomials $P_n^m(x)$ are denoted LegendreP[n, m, x].

■ 3.2.2 Numerical Functions

IntegerPart[x]	integer part of x
FractionalPart[x]	fractional part of x
Round[x]	integer $\langle x \rangle$ closest to x
Floor[x]	greatest integer $\lfloor x \rfloor$ not larger than x
Ceiling[x]	least integer $\lceil x \rceil$ not smaller than x
Sign[x]	1 for $x > 0$, -1 for $x < 0$
UnitStep[x]	1 for $x \geq 0$, 0 for $x < 0$
Abs[x]	absolute value $|x|$ of x
Max[x_1, x_2, ...] or Max[{x_1, x_2, ... }, ...]	the maximum of x_1, x_2, ...
Min[x_1, x_2, ...] or Min[{x_1, x_2, ... }, ...]	the minimum of x_1, x_2, ...

Some numerical functions of real variables.

x	IntegerPart[x]	FractionalPart[x]	Round[x]	Floor[x]	Ceiling[x]
2.4	2	0.4	2	2	3
2.5	2	0.5	2	2	3
2.6	2	0.6	3	2	3
-2.4	-2	-0.4	-2	-3	-2
-2.5	-2	-0.5	-2	-3	-2
-2.6	-2	-0.6	-3	-3	-2

Extracting integer and fractional parts.

IntegerPart[x] and FractionalPart[x] can be thought of as extracting digits to the left and right of the decimal point. Round[x] is often used for forcing numbers that are close to integers to be exactly integers. Floor[x] and Ceiling[x] often arise in working out how many elements there will be in sequences of numbers with non-integer spacings.

$x + I\, y$	the complex number $x + iy$
Re[z]	the real part $\mathrm{Re}\, z$
Im[z]	the imaginary part $\mathrm{Im}\, z$
Conjugate[z]	the complex conjugate z^* or $\bar{z}$
Abs[z]	the absolute value $|z|$
Arg[z]	the argument ϕ such that $z = |z|e^{i\phi}$

Numerical functions of complex variables.

Rationalize[x]	a rational number approximation to x
Rationalize[x, dx]	a rational approximation within tolerance dx

Finding rational approximations.

■ 3.2.3 Pseudorandom Numbers

Random[ ]	a pseudorandom real between 0 and 1
Random[Real, *xmax*]	a pseudorandom real between 0 and *xmax*
Random[Real, {*xmin*, *xmax*}]	a pseudorandom real between *xmin* and *xmax*
Random[Complex]	a pseudorandom complex number in the unit square
Random[Complex, {*zmin*, *zmax*}]	a pseudorandom complex number in the rectangle defined by *zmin* and *zmax*
Random[*type*, *range*, *n*]	an *n*-digit pseudorandom number
Random[Integer]	0 or 1 with probability $\frac{1}{2}$
Random[Integer, {*imin*, *imax*}]	a pseudorandom integer between *imin* and *imax*, inclusive
SeedRandom[ ]	reseed the pseudorandom generator, with the time of day
SeedRandom[*s*]	reseed with the integer *s*
$RandomState	the current state of the pseudorandom generator

Pseudorandom number generation.

This gives a list of 3 pseudorandom numbers.

```
In[1]:= Table[Random[ ], {3}]
Out[1]= {0.0560708, 0.6303, 0.359894}
```

Here is a 30-digit pseudorandom real number in the range 0 to 1.

```
In[2]:= Random[Real, {0, 1}, 30]
Out[2]= 0.748823044099679773836330229338
```

This gives a list of 8 pseudorandom integers between 100 and 200 (inclusive).

```
In[3]:= Table[Random[Integer, {100, 200}], {8}]
Out[3]= {120, 108, 109, 147, 146, 189, 188, 187}
```

If you call Random[ ] repeatedly, you should get a "typical" sequence of numbers, with no particular pattern. There are many ways to use such numbers.

One common way to use pseudorandom numbers is in making numerical tests of hypotheses. For example, if you believe that two symbolic expressions are mathematically equal, you can test this by plugging in "typical" numerical values for symbolic parameters, and then comparing the numerical results. (If you do this, you should be careful about numerical accuracy problems and about functions of complex variables that may not have unique values.)

Here is a symbolic equation.	*In[4]:=* `Sin[Cos[x]] == Cos[Sin[x]]`
	Out[4]= $\text{Sin}[\text{Cos}[x]] == \text{Cos}[\text{Sin}[x]]$
Substituting in a random numerical value shows that the equation is not always True.	*In[5]:=* `% /. x -> Random[ ]`
	Out[5]= `False`

Other common uses of pseudorandom numbers include simulating probabilistic processes, and sampling large spaces of possibilities. The pseudorandom numbers that *Mathematica* generates are always uniformly distributed over the range you specify.

`Random` is unlike almost any other *Mathematica* function in that every time you call it, you potentially get a different result. If you use `Random` in a calculation, therefore, you may get different answers on different occasions.

The sequences that you get from `Random[ ]` are not in most senses "truly random", although they should be "random enough" for practical purposes. The sequences are in fact produced by applying a definite mathematical algorithm, starting from a particular "seed". If you give the same seed, then you get the same sequence.

When *Mathematica* starts up, it takes the time of day (measured in small fractions of a second) as the seed for the pseudorandom number generator. Two different *Mathematica* sessions will therefore almost always give different sequences of pseudorandom numbers.

If you want to make sure that you always get the same sequence of pseudorandom numbers, you can explicitly give a seed for the pseudorandom generator, using `SeedRandom`.

This reseeds the pseudorandom generator.	*In[6]:=* `SeedRandom[143]`
Here are three pseudorandom numbers.	*In[7]:=* `Table[Random[ ], {3}]`
	Out[7]= `{0.952312, 0.93591, 0.813754}`
If you reseed the pseudorandom generator with the same seed, you get the same sequence of pseudorandom numbers.	*In[8]:=* `SeedRandom[143]; Table[Random[ ], {3}]`
	Out[8]= `{0.952312, 0.93591, 0.813754}`

Every single time `Random` is called, the internal state of the pseudorandom generator that it uses is changed. This means that calls to `Random` made in subsidiary calculations will have an effect on the numbers returned by `Random` in your main calculation. To avoid any problems associated with this, you can save the value of `$RandomState` before you do subsidiary calculations, and then restore it afterwards.

By localizing the value of `$RandomState` using `Block`, the internal state of the pseudorandom generator is restored after generating the first list.	*In[9]:=* `{Block[{$RandomState}, {Random[ ], Random[ ]}],` `{Random[ ], Random[ ]}}`
	Out[9]= `{{0.1169, 0.783447}, {0.1169, 0.783447}}`

■ 3.2.4 Integer and Number-Theoretical Functions

Mod[k, n]	k modulo n (remainder from dividing k by n)
Quotient[m, n]	the quotient of m and n (integer part of m/n)
GCD[n_1, n_2, ...]	the greatest common divisor of n_1, n_2, ...
LCM[n_1, n_2, ...]	the least common multiple of n_1, n_2, ...
KroneckerDelta[n_1, n_2, ...]	the Kronecker delta $\delta_{n_1 n_2 \ldots}$ equal to 1 if all the n_i are equal, and 0 otherwise
IntegerDigits[n, b]	the digits of n in base b
IntegerExponent[n, b]	the highest power of b that divides n

Some integer functions.

The remainder on dividing 17 by 3.	*In[1]:=* **Mod[17, 3]**
	Out[1]= 2
The integer part of 17/3.	*In[2]:=* **Quotient[17, 3]**
	Out[2]= 5
Mod also works with real numbers.	*In[3]:=* **Mod[5.6, 1.2]**
	Out[3]= 0.8
The result from Mod always has the same sign as the second argument.	*In[4]:=* **Mod[-5.6, 1.2]**
	Out[4]= 0.4

For any integers a and b, it is always true that b*Quotient[a, b] + Mod[a, b] is equal to a.

Mod[k, n]	result in the range 0 to $n - 1$
Mod[k, n, 1]	result in the range 1 to n
Mod[k, n, $-n/2$]	result in the range $\lceil -n/2 \rceil$ to $\lfloor +n/2 \rfloor$
Mod[k, n, d]	result in the range d to $d + n - 1$

Integer remainders with offsets.

Particularly when you are using Mod to get indices for parts of objects, you will often find it convenient to specify an offset.

This effectively extracts the 18th part of the list, with the list treated cyclically.	*In[5]:=* **Part[{a, b, c}, Mod[18, 3, 1]]**
	Out[5]= c

The **greatest common divisor** function GCD[n_1, n_2, ...] gives the largest integer that divides all the n_i exactly. When you enter a ratio of two integers, *Mathematica* effectively uses GCD to cancel out common factors, and give a rational number in lowest terms.

The **least common multiple** function LCM[n_1, n_2, ...] gives the smallest integer that contains all the factors of each of the n_i.

The largest integer that divides both 24 and 15 is 3.	*In[6]:=* **GCD[24, 15]**
	Out[6]= 3

The **Kronecker delta** or **Kronecker symbol** KroneckerDelta[n_1, n_2, ...] is equal to 1 if all the n_i are equal, and is 0 otherwise. $\delta_{n_1 n_2 ...}$ can be thought of as a totally symmetric tensor.

This gives a totally symmetric tensor of rank 3.	*In[7]:=* **Array[KroneckerDelta, {3, 3, 3}]**
	Out[7]= {{{1, 0, 0}, {0, 0, 0}, {0, 0, 0}},
	{{0, 0, 0}, {0, 1, 0}, {0, 0, 0}},
	{{0, 0, 0}, {0, 0, 0}, {0, 0, 1}}}

FactorInteger[n]	a list of the prime factors of n, and their exponents
Divisors[n]	a list of the integers that divide n
Prime[k]	the kth prime number
PrimePi[x]	the number of primes less than or equal to x
PrimeQ[n]	give True if n is a prime, and False otherwise
FactorInteger[n, GaussianIntegers->True]	a list of the Gaussian prime factors of the Gaussian integer n, and their exponents
PrimeQ[n, GaussianIntegers->True]	give True if n is a Gaussian prime, and False otherwise

Integer factoring and related functions.

This gives the factors of 24 as 2^3, 3^1. The first element in each list is the factor; the second is its exponent.	*In[8]:=* **FactorInteger[24]**
	Out[8]= {{2, 3}, {3, 1}}
Here are the factors of a larger integer.	*In[9]:=* **FactorInteger[111111111111111111]**
	Out[9]= {{3, 2}, {7, 1}, {11, 1}, {13, 1},
	{19, 1}, {37, 1}, {52579, 1}, {333667, 1}}

You should realize that according to current mathematical thinking, integer factoring is a fundamentally difficult computational problem. As a result, you can easily type in an integer that *Mathematica* will not be able to factor in anything short of an astronomical length of time. But as long as the integers you give are less than about 50 digits long, FactorInteger should have no trouble. And in special cases it will be able to deal with much longer integers. (You can make some factoring problems go faster by setting the option `FactorComplete->False`, so that `FactorInteger[n]` tries to pull out only easy factors from *n*.)

Here is a rather special long integer.

In[10]:= **30!**

Out[10]= 265252859812191058636308480000000

Mathematica can easily factor this special integer.

In[11]:= **FactorInteger[%]**

Out[11]= {{2, 26}, {3, 14}, {5, 7}, {7, 4}, {11, 2},
{13, 2}, {17, 1}, {19, 1}, {23, 1}, {29, 1}}

Although *Mathematica* may not be able to factor a large integer, it can often still test whether or not the integer is a prime. In addition, *Mathematica* has a fast way of finding the kth prime number.

It is often much faster to test whether a number is prime than to factor it.

In[12]:= **PrimeQ[234242423]**

Out[12]= False

Here is a plot of the first 100 primes.

In[13]:= **ListPlot[Table[Prime[n], {n, 100}]]**

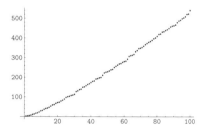

This is the millionth prime.

In[14]:= **Prime[1000000]**

Out[14]= 15485863

Particularly in number theory, it is often more important to know the distribution of primes than their actual values. The function `PrimePi[x]` gives the number of primes $\pi(x)$ that are less than or equal to *x*.

This gives the number of primes less than a billion.

In[15]:= **PrimePi[10^9]**

Out[15]= 50847534

By default, `FactorInteger` allows only real integers. But with the option setting `GaussianIntegers -> True`, it also handles **Gaussian integers**, which are complex numbers with integer real and imaginary parts. Just as it is possible to factor uniquely in terms of real primes, it is also possible to factor uniquely in terms of Gaussian primes. There is nevertheless some potential ambiguity in the choice of Gaussian primes. In *Mathematica*, they are always chosen to have positive real parts, and non-negative imaginary parts, except for a possible initial factor of -1 or $\pm i$.

Over the Gaussian integers, 2 can be factored as $(-i)(1 + i)^2$.

In[16]:= **FactorInteger[2, GaussianIntegers -> True]**

Out[16]= {{-i, 1}, {1 + i, 2}}

Here are the factors of a Gaussian integer.

In[17]:= `FactorInteger[111 + 78 I, GaussianIntegers -> True]`

Out[17]= `{{2 + i, 1}, {3, 1}, {20 + 3 i, 1}}`

PowerMod[*a*, *b*, *n*]	the power a^b modulo n
EulerPhi[*n*]	the Euler totient function $\phi(n)$
MoebiusMu[*n*]	the Möbius function $\mu(n)$
DivisorSigma[*k*, *n*]	the divisor function $\sigma_k(n)$
JacobiSymbol[*n*, *m*]	the Jacobi symbol $\left(\frac{n}{m}\right)$
ExtendedGCD[n_1, n_2, ...]	the extended gcd of n_1, n_2, ...
MultiplicativeOrder[*k*, *n*]	the multiplicative order of k modulo n
MultiplicativeOrder[*k*, *n*, {r_1, r_2, ... }]	
	the generalized multiplicative order with residues r_i
CarmichaelLambda[*n*]	the Carmichael function $\lambda(n)$
LatticeReduce[{v_1, v_2, ... }]	the reduced lattice basis for the set of integer vectors v_i

Some functions from number theory.

The **modular power function** PowerMod[*a*, *b*, *n*] gives exactly the same results as Mod[*a*^*b*, *n*] for $b > 0$. PowerMod is much more efficient, however, because it avoids generating the full form of *a*^*b*.

You can use PowerMod not only to find positive modular powers, but also to find **modular inverses**. For negative *b*, PowerMod[*a*, *b*, *n*] gives, if possible, an integer k such that $ka^{-b} \equiv 1$ mod n. (Whenever such an integer exists, it is guaranteed to be unique modulo n.) If no such integer k exists, *Mathematica* leaves PowerMod unevaluated.

PowerMod is equivalent to using Power, then Mod, but is much more efficient.

In[18]:= `PowerMod[2, 13451, 3]`

Out[18]= `2`

This gives the modular inverse of 3 modulo 7.

In[19]:= `PowerMod[3, -1, 7]`

Out[19]= `5`

Multiplying the inverse by 3 modulo 7 gives 1, as expected.

In[20]:= `Mod[3 %, 7]`

Out[20]= `1`

The **Euler totient function** $\phi(n)$ gives the number of integers less than n that are relatively prime to n. An important relation (Fermat's Little Theorem) is that $a^{\phi(n)} \equiv 1$ mod n for all a relatively prime to n.

The **Möbius function** $\mu(n)$ is defined to be $(-1)^k$ if n is a product of k distinct primes, and 0 if n contains a squared factor (other than 1). An important relation is the Möbius inversion formula, which states that if $g(n) = \sum_{d|n} f(d)$ for all n, then $f(n) = \sum_{d|n} \mu(d)g(n/d)$, where the sums are over all positive integers d that divide n.

The **divisor function** $\sigma_k(n)$ is the sum of the kth powers of the divisors of n. The function $\sigma_0(n)$ gives the total number of divisors of n, and is often denoted $d(n)$. The function $\sigma_1(n)$, equal to the sum of the divisors of n, is often denoted $\sigma(n)$.

For prime n, $\phi(n) = n - 1$.	*In[21]:=* **EulerPhi[17]**
	Out[21]= 16
The result is 1, as guaranteed by Fermat's Little Theorem.	*In[22]:=* **PowerMod[3, %, 17]**
	Out[22]= 1
This gives a list of all the divisors of 24.	*In[23]:=* **Divisors[24]**
	Out[23]= {1, 2, 3, 4, 6, 8, 12, 24}
$\sigma_0(n)$ gives the total number of distinct divisors of 24.	*In[24]:=* **DivisorSigma[0, 24]**
	Out[24]= 8

The **Jacobi symbol** JacobiSymbol[n, m] reduces to the **Legendre symbol** $\left(\frac{n}{m}\right)$ when m is an odd prime. The Legendre symbol is equal to zero if n is divisible by m, otherwise it is equal to 1 if n is a quadratic residue modulo the prime m, and to -1 if it is not. An integer n relatively prime to m is said to be a quadratic residue modulo m if there exists an integer k such that $k^2 \equiv n \bmod m$. The full Jacobi symbol is a product of the Legendre symbols $\left(\frac{n}{p_i}\right)$ for each of the prime factors p_i such that $m = \prod_i p_i$.

The **extended gcd** ExtendedGCD[n_1, n_2, ...] gives a list $\{g, \{r_1, r_2, ... \}\}$ where g is the greatest common divisor of the n_i, and the r_i are integers such that $g = r_1 n_1 + r_2 n_2 + ...$. The extended gcd is important in finding integer solutions to linear Diophantine equations.

The first number in the list is the gcd of 105 and 196.	*In[25]:=* **ExtendedGCD[105, 196]**
	Out[25]= {7, {-13, 7}}
The second pair of numbers satisfies $g = rm + sn$.	*In[26]:=* **-13 105 + 7 196**
	Out[26]= 7

The **multiplicative order function** MultiplicativeOrder[k, n] gives the smallest integer m such that $k^m \equiv 1 \bmod n$. The function is sometimes known as the **index** or **discrete log** of k. The notation $\mathrm{ord}_n(k)$ is occasionally used.

The **generalized multiplicative order function** MultiplicativeOrder[k, n, $\{r_1, r_2, ... \}$] gives the smallest integer m such that $k^m \equiv r_i \bmod n$ for some i. MultiplicativeOrder[k, n, {-1, 1}] is sometimes known as the **suborder function** of k modulo n, denoted $\mathrm{sord}_n(k)$.

The **Carmichael function** or **least universal exponent** $\lambda(n)$ gives the smallest integer m such that $k^m \equiv 1 \bmod n$ for all integers k relatively prime to n.

The lattice reduction function LatticeReduce[{v_1, v_2, ... }] is used in several kinds of modern algorithms. The basic idea is to think of the vectors v_k of integers as defining a mathematical *lattice*. Any vector representing a point in the lattice can be written as a linear combination of the form $\sum c_k v_k$, where the c_k are integers. For a particular lattice, there are many possible choices of the "basis vectors" v_k. What LatticeReduce does is to find a reduced set of basis vectors $\bar{v}_k$ for the lattice, with certain special properties.

Three unit vectors along the three coordinate axes already form a reduced basis.	`In[27]:= LatticeReduce[{{1,0,0},{0,1,0},{0,0,1}}]`
	
	`Out[27]= {{1, 0, 0}, {0, 1, 0}, {0, 0, 1}}`

This gives the reduced basis for a lattice in four-dimensional space specified by three vectors.	`In[28]:= LatticeReduce[{{1,0,0,12345}, {0,1,0,12435},`
	`                      {0,0,1,12354}}]`
	
	`Out[28]= {{-1, 0, 1, 9}, {9, 1, -10, 0}, {85, -143, 59, 6}}`

Notice that in the last example, LatticeReduce replaces vectors that are nearly parallel by vectors that are more perpendicular. In the process, it finds some quite short basis vectors.

ContinuedFraction[x, n]	generate the first n terms in the continued fraction representation of x
FromContinuedFraction[*list*]	reconstruct a number from its continued fraction representation
Rationalize[x, dx]	find a rational approximation to x with tolerance dx

Continued fractions.

This generates the first 10 terms in the continued fraction representation for π.	`In[29]:= ContinuedFraction[Pi, 10]`
	
	`Out[29]= {3, 7, 15, 1, 292, 1, 1, 1, 2, 1}`

This reconstructs the number represented by the list of continued fraction terms.	`In[30]:= FromContinuedFraction[%]` `Out[30]= `$\dfrac{1146408}{364913}$

The result is close to π.	`In[31]:= N[%]`
	
	`Out[31]= 3.14159`

This gives directly a rational approximation to π.	`In[32]:= Rationalize[Pi, 1/1000]` `Out[32]= `$\dfrac{201}{64}$

Continued fractions appear in many number-theoretical settings. Rational numbers have terminating continued fraction representations. Quadratic irrational numbers have continued fraction representations that become repetitive.

ContinuedFraction[*x*]	the complete continued fraction representation for a rational or quadratic irrational number
RealDigits[*x*]	the complete digit sequence for a rational number
RealDigits[*x*, *b*]	the complete digit sequence in base *b*

Complete representations for numbers.

The continued fraction representation of $\sqrt{79}$ starts with the term 8, then involves a sequence of terms that repeat forever.

In[33]:= **ContinuedFraction[Sqrt[79]]**

Out[33]= {8, {1, 7, 1, 16}}

This reconstructs $\sqrt{79}$ from its continued fraction representation.

In[34]:= **FromContinuedFraction[%]**

Out[34]= $\sqrt{79}$

This shows the recurring sequence of decimal digits in 3/7.

In[35]:= **RealDigits[3/7]**

Out[35]= {{{4, 2, 8, 5, 7, 1}}, 0}

FromDigits reconstructs the original number.

In[36]:= **FromDigits[%]**

Out[36]= $\dfrac{3}{7}$

DigitCount[*n*, *b*, *d*]	the number of *d* digits in the base *b* representation of *n*

Digit count function.

Here are the digits in the base 2 representation of the number 77.

In[37]:= **IntegerDigits[77, 2]**

Out[37]= {1, 0, 0, 1, 1, 0, 1}

This directly computes the number of ones in the base 2 representation.

In[38]:= **DigitCount[77, 2, 1]**

Out[38]= 4

The plot of the digit count function is self-similar.

In[39]:= `ListPlot[Table[DigitCount[n, 2, 1], {n, 128}],`
            `PlotJoined->True]`

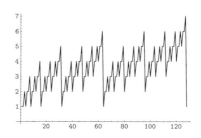

BitAnd[n_1, n_2, ...]	bitwise AND of the integers n_i
BitOr[n_1, n_2, ...]	bitwise OR of the integers n_i
BitXor[n_1, n_2, ...]	bitwise XOR of the integers n_i
BitNot[n]	bitwise NOT of the integer n

Bitwise operations.

Bitwise operations act on integers represented as binary bits. BitAnd[n_1, n_2, ...] yields the integer whose binary bit representation has ones at positions where the binary bit representations of all of the n_i have ones. BitOr[n_1, n_2, ...] yields the integer with ones at positions where any of the n_i have ones. BitXor[n_1, n_2] yields the integer with ones at positions where n_1 or n_2 but not both have ones. BitXor[n_1, n_2, ...] has ones where an odd number of the n_i have ones.

This finds the bitwise AND of the numbers 23 and 29 entered in base 2.

In[40]:= `BaseForm[BitAnd[2^^10111, 2^^11101], 2]`

Out[40]//BaseForm= 10101_2

Bitwise operations are used in various combinatorial algorithms. They are also commonly used in manipulating bitfields in low-level computer languages. In such languages, however, integers normally have a limited number of digits, typically a multiple of 8. Bitwise operations in *Mathematica* in effect allow integers to have an unlimited number of digits. When an integer is negative, it is taken to be represented in two's complement form, with an infinite sequence of ones on the left. This allows BitNot[n] to be equivalent simply to $-1 - n$.

■ 3.2.5 Combinatorial Functions

$n!$	factorial $n(n-1)(n-2) \times \ldots \times 1$
$n!!$	double factorial $n(n-2)(n-4) \times \ldots$
Binomial[n, m]	binomial coefficient $\binom{n}{m} = n!/[m!(n-m)!]$
Multinomial[n_1, n_2, ...]	multinomial coefficient $(n_1 + n_2 + \ldots)!/(n_1!n_2!\ldots)$
Fibonacci[n]	Fibonacci number F_n
Fibonacci[n, x]	Fibonacci polynomial $F_n(x)$
HarmonicNumber[n]	harmonic number H_n
HarmonicNumber[n, r]	harmonic number $H_n^{(r)}$ of order r
BernoulliB[n]	Bernoulli number B_n
BernoulliB[n, x]	Bernoulli polynomial $B_n(x)$
EulerE[n]	Euler number E_n
EulerE[n, x]	Euler polynomial $E_n(x)$
StirlingS1[n, m]	Stirling number of the first kind $S_n^{(m)}$
StirlingS2[n, m]	Stirling number of the second kind $\mathcal{S}_n^{(m)}$
PartitionsP[n]	the number $p(n)$ of unrestricted partitions of the integer n
PartitionsQ[n]	the number $q(n)$ of partitions of n into distinct parts
Signature[{i_1, i_2, ... }]	the signature of a permutation

Combinatorial functions.

The **factorial function** $n!$ gives the number of ways of ordering n objects. For non-integer n, the numerical value of $n!$ is obtained from the gamma function, discussed in Section 3.2.10.

The **binomial coefficient** Binomial[n, m] can be written as $\binom{n}{m} = n!/[m!(n-m)!]$. It gives the number of ways of choosing m objects from a collection of n objects, without regard to order. The **Catalan numbers**, which appear in various tree enumeration problems, are given in terms of binomial coefficients as $c_n = \binom{2n}{n}/(n+1)$.

The **multinomial coefficient** Multinomial[n_1, n_2, ...], denoted $(N; n_1, n_2, ..., n_m) = N!/(n_1!n_2!...n_m!)$, gives the number of ways of partitioning N distinct objects into m sets of sizes n_i (with $N = \sum_{i=1}^{m} n_i$).

Mathematica gives the exact integer result for the factorial of an integer.	`In[1]:= 30!`
	
	`Out[1]= 265252859812191058636308480000000`

For non-integers, *Mathematica* evaluates factorials using the gamma function.	`In[2]:= 3.6!`
	
	`Out[2]= 13.3813`

Mathematica can give symbolic results for some binomial coefficients.	`In[3]:= Binomial[n, 2]`
	
	`Out[3]= ` $\frac{1}{2}$ `(-1 + n) n`

This gives the number of ways of partitioning $6 + 5 = 11$ objects into sets containing 6 and 5 objects.	`In[4]:= Multinomial[6, 5]`
	
	`Out[4]= 462`

The result is the same as $\binom{11}{6}$.	`In[5]:= Binomial[11, 6]`
	
	`Out[5]= 462`

The **Fibonacci numbers** Fibonacci[n] satisfy the recurrence relation $F_n = F_{n-1} + F_{n-2}$ with $F_1 = F_2 = 1$. They appear in a wide range of discrete mathematical problems. For large n, F_n/F_{n-1} approaches the golden ratio.

The **Fibonacci polynomials** Fibonacci[n, x] appear as the coefficients of t^n in the expansion of $t/(1 - xt - t^2) = \sum_{n=0}^{\infty} F_n(x)t^n$.

The **harmonic numbers** HarmonicNumber[n] are given by $H_n = \sum_{i=1}^{n} 1/i$; the harmonic numbers of order r HarmonicNumber[n, r] are given by $H_n^{(r)} = \sum_{i=1}^{n} 1/i^r$. Harmonic numbers appear in many combinatorial estimation problems, often playing the role of discrete analogs of logarithms.

The **Bernoulli polynomials** BernoulliB[n, x] satisfy the generating function relation $te^{xt}/(e^t - 1) = \sum_{n=0}^{\infty} B_n(x)t^n/n!$. The **Bernoulli numbers** BernoulliB[n] are given by $B_n = B_n(0)$. The B_n appear as the coefficients of the terms in the Euler-Maclaurin summation formula for approximating integrals.

Numerical values for Bernoulli numbers are needed in many numerical algorithms. You can always get these numerical values by first finding exact rational results using BernoulliB[n], and then applying N.

The **Euler polynomials** EulerE[n, x] have generating function $2e^{xt}/(e^t + 1) = \sum_{n=0}^{\infty} E_n(x)t^n/n!$, and the **Euler numbers** EulerE[n] are given by $E_n = 2^n E_n(\frac{1}{2})$. The Euler numbers are related to the **Genocchi numbers** by $G_n = 2^{2-2n} n E_{2n-1}$.

This gives the second Bernoulli polynomial $B_2(x)$.	`In[6]:= BernoulliB[2, x]` `Out[6]= ` $\frac{1}{6}$ `- x + x`^{2}

You can also get Bernoulli polynomials by explicitly computing the power series for the generating function.

$In[7]:=$ **Series[t Exp[x t]/(Exp[t] - 1), {t, 0, 4}]**

$Out[7]=$ $1 + \left(-\dfrac{1}{2} + x\right) t + \left(\dfrac{1}{12} - \dfrac{x}{2} + \dfrac{x^2}{2}\right) t^2 + \left(\dfrac{x}{12} - \dfrac{x^2}{4} + \dfrac{x^3}{6}\right) t^3 +$

$\left(-\dfrac{1}{720} + \dfrac{x^2}{24} - \dfrac{x^3}{12} + \dfrac{x^4}{24}\right) t^4 + O[t]^5$

BernoulliB[n] gives exact rational-number results for Bernoulli numbers.

$In[8]:=$ **BernoulliB[20]**

$Out[8]=$ $-\dfrac{174611}{330}$

Stirling numbers show up in many combinatorial enumeration problems. For **Stirling numbers of the first kind** StirlingS1[n, m], $(-1)^{n-m} S_n^{(m)}$ gives the number of permutations of n elements which contain exactly m cycles. These Stirling numbers satisfy the generating function relation $x(x - 1)...(x - n + 1) = \sum_{m=0}^{n} S_n^{(m)} x^m$. Note that some definitions of the $S_n^{(m)}$ differ by a factor $(-1)^{n-m}$ from what is used in *Mathematica*.

Stirling numbers of the second kind StirlingS2[n, m] give the number of ways of partitioning a set of n elements into m non-empty subsets. They satisfy the relation $x^n = \sum_{m=0}^{n} S_n^{(m)} x(x-1)...(x-m+1)$.

The **partition function** PartitionsP[n] gives the number of ways of writing the integer n as a sum of positive integers, without regard to order. PartitionsQ[n] gives the number of ways of writing n as a sum of positive integers, with the constraint that all the integers in each sum are distinct.

This gives a table of Stirling numbers of the first kind.

$In[9]:=$ **Table[StirlingS1[5, i], {i, 5}]**

$Out[9]=$ {24, -50, 35, -10, 1}

The Stirling numbers appear as coefficients in this product.

$In[10]:=$ **Expand[Product[x - i, {i, 0, 4}]]**

$Out[10]=$ $24 x - 50 x^2 + 35 x^3 - 10 x^4 + x^5$

This gives the number of partitions of 100, with and without the constraint that the terms should be distinct.

$In[11]:=$ **{PartitionsQ[100], PartitionsP[100]}**

$Out[11]=$ {444793, 190569292}

The partition function $p(n)$ increases asymptotically like $e^{\sqrt{n}}$. Note that you cannot simply use Plot to generate a plot of a function like PartitionsP because the function can only be evaluated with integer arguments.

$In[12]:=$ **ListPlot[Table[**
              N[Log[PartitionsP[n]]], {n, 100}]]

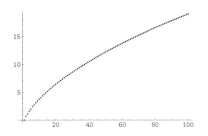

The functions in this section allow you to *enumerate* various kinds of combinatorial objects. Functions like `Permutations` allow you instead to *generate* lists of various combinations of elements.

The **signature function** `Signature[{`i_1, i_2, ... `}]` gives the signature of a permutation. It is equal to $+1$ for even permutations (composed of an even number of transpositions), and to -1 for odd permutations. The signature function can be thought of as a totally antisymmetric tensor, **Levi-Civita symbol** or **epsilon symbol**.

`ClebschGordan[{`j_1, m_1`}, {`j_2, m_2`}, {`j, m`}]`
Clebsch-Gordan coefficient

`ThreeJSymbol[{`j_1, m_1`}, {`j_2, m_2`}, {`j_3, m_3`}]`
Wigner 3-j symbol

`SixJSymbol[{`j_1, j_2, j_3`}, {`j_4, j_5, j_6`}]`
Racah 6-j symbol

Rotational coupling coefficients.

Clebsch-Gordan coefficients and *n*-j symbols arise in the study of angular momenta in quantum mechanics, and in other applications of the rotation group. The **Clebsch-Gordan coefficients** `ClebschGordan[{`j_1, m_1`}, {`j_2, m_2`}, {`j, m`}]` give the coefficients in the expansion of the quantum mechanical angular momentum state $|j, m\rangle$ in terms of products of states $|j_1, m_1\rangle |j_2, m_2\rangle$.

The **3-j symbols** or **Wigner coefficients** `ThreeJSymbol[{`j_1, m_1`}, {`j_2, m_2`}, {`j_3, m_3`}]` are a more symmetrical form of Clebsch-Gordan coefficients. In *Mathematica*, the Clebsch-Gordan coefficients are given in terms of 3-j symbols by $C^{j_1 j_2 j_3}_{m_1 m_2 m_3} = (-1)^{m_3+j_1-j_2} \sqrt{2j_3 + 1} \begin{pmatrix} j_1 & j_2 & j_3 \\ m_1 & m_2 & -m_3 \end{pmatrix}$.

The **6-j symbols** `SixJSymbol[{`j_1, j_2, j_3`}, {`j_4, j_5, j_6`}]` give the couplings of three quantum mechanical angular momentum states. The **Racah coefficients** are related by a phase to the 6-j symbols.

You can give symbolic parameters in 3-j symbols.	$In[13]:=$ `ThreeJSymbol[{j, m}, {j+1/2, -m-1/2}, {1/2, 1/2}]`
	$Out[13]= -\dfrac{(-1)^{-j+m} \sqrt{1+j+m}}{\sqrt{2}\,\sqrt{1+j}\,\sqrt{1+2j}}$

■ 3.2.6 Elementary Transcendental Functions

Exp[z]	exponential function e^z
Log[z]	logarithm $\log_e(z)$
Log[b, z]	logarithm $\log_b(z)$ to base b
Sin[z], Cos[z], Tan[z], Csc[z], Sec[z], Cot[z]	trigonometric functions (with arguments in radians)
ArcSin[z], ArcCos[z], ArcTan[z], ArcCsc[z], ArcSec[z], ArcCot[z]	inverse trigonometric functions (giving results in radians)
ArcTan[x, y]	the argument of $x + iy$
Sinh[z], Cosh[z], Tanh[z], Csch[z], Sech[z], Coth[z]	hyperbolic functions
ArcSinh[z], ArcCosh[z], ArcTanh[z], ArcCsch[z], ArcSech[z], ArcCoth[z]	inverse hyperbolic functions

Elementary transcendental functions.

Mathematica gives exact results for logarithms whenever it can. Here is $\log_2 1024$.

```
In[1]:= Log[2, 1024]
Out[1]= 10
```

You can find the numerical values of mathematical functions to any precision.

```
In[2]:= N[Log[2], 40]
Out[2]= 0.6931471805599453094172321214581765680755
```

This gives a complex number result.

```
In[3]:= N[ Log[-2] ]
Out[3]= 0.693147 + 3.14159 i
```

Mathematica can evaluate logarithms with complex arguments.

```
In[4]:= N[ Log[2 + 8 I] ]
Out[4]= 2.10975 + 1.32582 i
```

The arguments of trigonometric functions are always given in radians.

```
In[5]:= Sin[Pi/2]
Out[5]= 1
```

You can convert from degrees by explicitly multiplying by the constant Degree.

```
In[6]:= N[ Sin[30 Degree] ]
Out[6]= 0.5
```

Here is a plot of the hyperbolic tangent function. It has a characteristic "sigmoidal" form.

$In[7]:=$ **Plot[Tanh[x], {x, -8, 8}]**

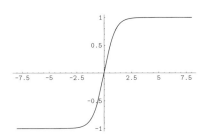

There are a number of additional trigonometric and hyperbolic functions that are sometimes used. The **versine** function is defined as $\mathrm{vers}(z) = 1 - \cos(z)$. The **haversine** is simply $\mathrm{hav}(z) = \frac{1}{2}\mathrm{vers}(z)$. The complex exponential e^{ix} is sometimes written as $\mathrm{cis}(x)$. The **gudermannian function** is defined as $\mathrm{gd}(z) = 2\tan^{-1}(e^z) - \frac{\pi}{2}$. The **inverse gudermannian** is $\mathrm{gd}^{-1}(z) = \log[\sec(z) + \tan(z)]$. The gudermannian satisfies such relations as $\sinh(z) = \tan[\mathrm{gd}(x)]$.

■ 3.2.7 Functions That Do Not Have Unique Values

When you ask for the square root s of a number a, you are effectively asking for the solution to the equation $s^2 = a$. This equation, however, in general has two different solutions. Both $s = 2$ and $s = -2$ are, for example, solutions to the equation $s^2 = 4$. When you evaluate the "function" $\sqrt{4}$, however, you usually want to get a single number, and so you have to choose one of these two solutions. A standard choice is that $\sqrt{x}$ should be positive for $x > 0$. This is what the *Mathematica* function Sqrt[x] does.

The need to make one choice from two solutions means that Sqrt[x] cannot be a true *inverse function* for x^2. Taking a number, squaring it, and then taking the square root can give you a different number than you started with.

$\sqrt{4}$ gives +2, not −2.

$In[1]:=$ **Sqrt[4]**
$Out[1]=$ 2

Squaring and taking the square root does not necessarily give you the number you started with.

$In[2]:=$ **Sqrt[(-2)^2]**
$Out[2]=$ 2

When you evaluate $\sqrt{-2i}$, there are again two possible answers: $-1 + i$ and $1 - i$. In this case, however, it is less clear which one to choose.

There is in fact no way to choose $\sqrt{z}$ so that it is continuous for all complex values of z. There has to be a "branch cut"—a line in the complex plane across which the function $\sqrt{z}$ is discontinuous. *Mathematica* adopts the usual convention of taking the branch cut for $\sqrt{z}$ to be along the negative real axis.

This gives $1 - i$, not $-1 + i$.

```
In[3]:= N[ Sqrt[-2 I] ]
Out[3]= 1. - 1. i
```

The branch cut in Sqrt along the negative real axis means that values of Sqrt[z] with z just above and below the axis are very different.

```
In[4]:= {Sqrt[-2 + 0.1 I], Sqrt[-2 - 0.1 I]}
Out[4]= {0.0353443 + 1.41466 i, 0.0353443 - 1.41466 i}
```

Their squares are nevertheless close.

```
In[5]:= %^2
Out[5]= {-2. + 0.1 i, -2. - 0.1 i}
```

The discontinuity along the negative real axis is quite clear in this three-dimensional picture of the imaginary part of the square root function.

```
In[6]:= Plot3D[ Im[Sqrt[x + I y]], {x, -4, 4}, {y, -4, 4} ]
```

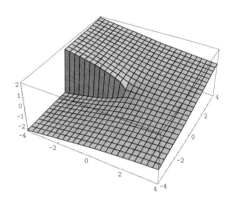

When you find an nth root using $z^{1/n}$, there are, in principle, n possible results. To get a single value, you have to choose a particular *principal root*. There is absolutely no guarantee that taking the nth root of an nth power will leave you with the same number.

This takes the tenth power of a complex number. The result is unique.

```
In[7]:= (2.5 + I)^10
Out[7]= -15781.2 - 12335.8 i
```

There are ten possible tenth roots. *Mathematica* chooses one of them. In this case it is not the number whose tenth power you took.

```
In[8]:= %^(1/10)
Out[8]= 2.61033 - 0.660446 i
```

There are many mathematical functions which, like roots, essentially give solutions to equations. The logarithm function and the inverse trigonometric functions are examples. In almost all cases, there are many possible solutions to the equations. Unique "principal" values nevertheless have to be chosen for the functions. The choices cannot be made continuous over the whole complex plane. Instead, lines of discontinuity, or branch cuts, must occur. The positions of these branch cuts are often quite arbitrary. *Mathematica* makes the most standard mathematical choices for them.

Sqrt[z] and z^s	$(-\infty, 0)$ for $\text{Re}\, s > 0$, $(-\infty, 0]$ for $\text{Re}\, s \leq 0$ (s not an integer)
Exp[z]	none
Log[z]	$(-\infty, 0]$
trigonometric functions	none
ArcSin[z] and ArcCos[z]	$(-\infty, -1)$ and $(+1, +\infty)$
ArcTan[z]	$(-i\infty, -i]$ and $[i, i\infty)$
ArcCsc[z] and ArcSec[z]	$(-1, +1)$
ArcCot[z]	$[-i, +i]$
hyperbolic functions	none
ArcSinh[z]	$(-i\infty, -i)$ and $(+i, +i\infty)$
ArcCosh[z]	$(-\infty, +1)$
ArcTanh[z]	$(-\infty, -1]$ and $[+1, +\infty)$
ArcCsch[z]	$(-i, i)$
ArcSech[z]	$(-\infty, 0]$ and $(+1, +\infty)$
ArcCoth[z]	$[-1, +1]$

Some branch-cut discontinuities in the complex plane.

ArcSin is a multiple-valued function, so there is no guarantee that it always gives the "inverse" of Sin.

```
In[9]:= ArcSin[Sin[4.5]]
Out[9]= -1.35841
```

Values of ArcSin[z] on opposite sides of the branch cut can be very different.

```
In[10]:= {ArcSin[2 + 0.1 I], ArcSin[2 - 0.1 I]}
Out[10]= {1.51316 + 1.31888 i, 1.51316 - 1.31888 i}
```

A three-dimensional picture, showing the two branch cuts for the function $\sin^{-1}(z)$.

In[11]:= `Plot3D[ Im[ArcSin[x + I y]], {x, -4, 4}, {y, -4, 4}]`

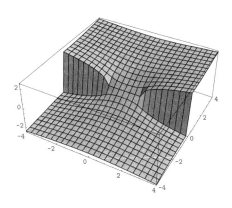

■ 3.2.8 Mathematical Constants

I	$i = \sqrt{-1}$
Infinity	∞
Pi	$\pi \simeq 3.14159$
Degree	$\pi/180$: degrees to radians conversion factor
GoldenRatio	$\phi = (1 + \sqrt{5})/2 \simeq 1.61803$
E	$e \simeq 2.71828$
EulerGamma	Euler's constant $\gamma \simeq 0.577216$
Catalan	Catalan's constant $\simeq 0.915966$
Khinchin	Khinchin's constant $\simeq 2.68545$
Glaisher	Glaisher's constant $\simeq 1.28243$

Mathematical constants.

Euler's constant `EulerGamma` is given by the limit $\gamma = \lim_{m\to\infty}\left(\sum_{k=1}^{m} \frac{1}{k} - \log m\right)$. It appears in many integrals, and asymptotic formulas. It is sometimes known as the **Euler-Mascheroni constant**, and denoted C.

Catalan's constant `Catalan` is given by the sum $\sum_{k=0}^{\infty}(-1)^k(2k + 1)^{-2}$. It often appears in asymptotic estimates of combinatorial functions.

Khinchin's constant Khinchin (sometimes called Khintchine's constant) is given by $\prod_{s=1}^{\infty}(1 + \frac{1}{s(s+2)})^{\log_2 s}$. It gives the geometric mean of the terms in the continued fraction representation for a typical real number.

Glaisher's constant Glaisher A (sometimes called the Glaisher-Kinkelin constant) satisfies $\log(A) = \frac{1}{12} - \zeta'(-1)$, where ζ is the Riemann zeta function. It appears in various sums and integrals, particularly those involving gamma and zeta functions.

Mathematical constants can be
evaluated to arbitrary precision.

```
In[1]:= N[EulerGamma, 40]
```
```
Out[1]= 0.5772156649015328606065120900824024310422
```

Exact computations can also be done
with them.

```
In[2]:= IntegerPart[GoldenRatio^100]
```
```
Out[2]= 792070839848372253126
```

■ 3.2.9 Orthogonal Polynomials

LegendreP[n, x]	Legendre polynomials $P_n(x)$
LegendreP[n, m, x]	associated Legendre polynomials $P_n^m(x)$
SphericalHarmonicY[l, m, θ, ϕ]	spherical harmonics $Y_l^m(\theta,\phi)$
GegenbauerC[n, m, x]	Gegenbauer polynomials $C_n^{(m)}(x)$
ChebyshevT[n, x], ChebyshevU[n, x]	Chebyshev polynomials $T_n(x)$ and $U_n(x)$ of the first and second kinds
HermiteH[n, x]	Hermite polynomials $H_n(x)$
LaguerreL[n, x]	Laguerre polynomials $L_n(x)$
LaguerreL[n, a, x]	generalized Laguerre polynomials $L_n^a(x)$
JacobiP[n, a, b, x]	Jacobi polynomials $P_n^{(a,b)}(x)$

Orthogonal polynomials.

Legendre polynomials LegendreP[n, x] arise in studies of systems with three-dimensional spherical symmetry. They satisfy the differential equation $(1 - x^2)y'' - 2xy' + n(n + 1)y = 0$, and the orthogonality relation $\int_{-1}^{1} P_m(x)P_n(x)\,dx = 0$ for $m \neq n$.

The **associated Legendre polynomials** LegendreP[n, m, x] are obtained from derivatives of the Legendre polynomials according to $P_n^m(x) = (-1)^m(1 - x^2)^{m/2}\,d^m[P_n(x)]/dx^m$. Notice that for odd integers $m \leq n$, the $P_n^m(x)$ contain powers of $\sqrt{1 - x^2}$, and are therefore not strictly polynomials. The $P_n^m(x)$ reduce to $P_n(x)$ when $m = 0$.

The **spherical harmonics** SphericalHarmonicY[l, m, θ, ϕ] are related to associated Legendre polynomials. They satisfy the orthogonality relation $\int Y_l^m(\theta,\phi)\bar{Y}_{l'}^{m'}(\theta,\phi)\,d\omega = 0$ for $l \neq l'$ or $m \neq m'$, where $d\omega$ represents integration over the surface of the unit sphere.

This gives the algebraic form of the Legendre polynomial $P_8(x)$.

    In[1]:= **LegendreP[8, x]**

$$Out[1]= \frac{35}{128} - \frac{315\,x^2}{32} + \frac{3465\,x^4}{64} - \frac{3003\,x^6}{32} + \frac{6435\,x^8}{128}$$

The integral $\int_{-1}^{1} P_7(x)\,P_8(x)\,dx$ gives zero by virtue of the orthogonality of the Legendre polynomials.

    In[2]:= **Integrate[LegendreP[7,x] LegendreP[8,x], {x, -1, 1}]**
    Out[2]= 0

Integrating the square of a single Legendre polynomial gives a non-zero result.

    In[3]:= **Integrate[LegendreP[8, x]^2, {x, -1, 1}]**

$$Out[3]= \frac{2}{17}$$

High-degree Legendre polynomials oscillate rapidly.

    In[4]:= **Plot[LegendreP[10, x], {x, -1, 1}]**

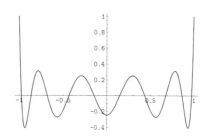

The associated Legendre "polynomials" involve fractional powers.

    In[5]:= **LegendreP[8, 3, x]**

$$Out[5]= -\frac{3465}{8}\sqrt{\frac{-1-x}{-1+x}}\,(-1+x)^2\,(1+x)\,(3\,x - 26\,x^3 + 39\,x^5)$$

Section 3.2.10 discusses the generalization of Legendre polynomials to Legendre functions, which can have non-integer degrees.

    In[6]:= **LegendreP[8.1, 0]**
    Out[6]= 0.268502

Gegenbauer polynomials GegenbauerC[n, m, x] can be viewed as generalizations of the Legendre polynomials to systems with ($m + 2$)-dimensional spherical symmetry. They are sometimes known as **ultraspherical polynomials**.

GegenbauerC[n, 0, x] is always equal to zero. GegenbauerC[n, x] is however given by the limit $\lim_{m\to 0} C_n^{(m)}(x)/m$. This form is sometimes denoted $C_n^{(0)}(x)$.

Series of Chebyshev polynomials are often used in making numerical approximations to functions. The **Chebyshev polynomials of the first kind** ChebyshevT[n, x] are defined by $T_n(\cos\theta) = \cos(n\theta)$. They are normalized so that $T_n(1) = 1$. They satisfy the orthogonality relation $\int_{-1}^{1} T_m(x)T_n(x)(1 -$

$x^2)^{-1/2}\,dx\,=\,0$ for $m \neq n$. The $T_n(x)$ also satisfy an orthogonality relation under summation at discrete points in x corresponding to the roots of $T_n(x)$.

The **Chebyshev polynomials of the second kind** ChebyshevU[n, z] are defined by $U_n(\cos\theta) = \sin[(n+1)\theta]/\sin\theta$. With this definition, $U_n(1) = n + 1$. The U_n satisfy the orthogonality relation $\int_{-1}^{1} U_m(x)U_n(x)(1-x^2)^{1/2}\,dx = 0$ for $m \neq n$.

The name "Chebyshev" is a transliteration from the Cyrillic alphabet; several other spellings, such as "Tschebyscheff", are sometimes used.

Hermite polynomials HermiteH[n, x] arise as the quantum-mechanical wave functions for a harmonic oscillator. They satisfy the differential equation $y'' - 2xy' + 2ny = 0$, and the orthogonality relation $\int_{-\infty}^{\infty} H_m(x)H_n(x)e^{-x^2}\,dx = 0$ for $m \neq n$. An alternative form of Hermite polynomials sometimes used is $He_n(x) = 2^{-n/2}H_n(x/\sqrt{2})$ (a different overall normalization of the $He_n(x)$ is also sometimes used).

The Hermite polynomials are related to the **parabolic cylinder functions** or **Weber functions** $D_n(x)$ by $D_n(x) = 2^{-n/2}e^{-x^2/4}H_n(x/\sqrt{2})$.

This gives the density for an excited state of a quantum-mechanical harmonic oscillator. The average of the wiggles is roughly the classical physics result.

In[7]:= **Plot[(HermiteH[6, x] Exp[-x^2/2])^2, {x, -6, 6}]**

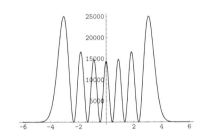

Generalized Laguerre polynomials LaguerreL[n, a, x] are related to hydrogen atom wave functions in quantum mechanics. They satisfy the differential equation $xy'' + (a + 1 - x)y' + ny = 0$, and the orthogonality relation $\int_0^{\infty} L_m^a(x)L_n^a(x)x^a e^{-x}\,dx = 0$ for $m \neq n$. The **Laguerre polynomials** LaguerreL[n, x] correspond to the special case $a = 0$.

Jacobi polynomials JacobiP[n, a, b, x] occur in studies of the rotation group, particularly in quantum mechanics. They satisfy the orthogonality relation $\int_{-1}^{1} P_m^{(a,b)}(x)P_n^{(a,b)}(x)(1-x)^a(1+x)^b\,dx = 0$ for $m \neq n$. Legendre, Gegenbauer and Chebyshev polynomials can all be viewed as special cases of Jacobi polynomials. The Jacobi polynomials are sometimes given in the alternative form $G_n(p, q, x) = n!\,\Gamma(n+p)/\Gamma(2n+p)\,P_n^{(p-q,q-1)}(2x-1)$.

You can get formulas for generalized Laguerre polynomials with arbitrary values of a.

In[8]:= **LaguerreL[2, a, x]**

Out[8]= $\dfrac{1}{2}\,(2 + 3\,a + a^2 - 4\,x - 2\,a\,x + x^2)$

■ 3.2.10 Special Functions

Mathematica includes all the common special functions of mathematical physics found in standard handbooks. We will discuss each of the various classes of functions in turn.

One point you should realize is that in the technical literature there are often several conflicting definitions of any particular special function. When you use a special function in *Mathematica*, therefore, you should be sure to look at the definition given here to confirm that it is exactly what you want.

Mathematica gives exact results for some values of special functions.	`In[1]:= Gamma[15/2]` $$Out[1]= \frac{135135 \sqrt{\pi}}{128}$$
No exact result is known here.	`In[2]:= Gamma[15/7]` $$Out[2]= \text{Gamma}\left[\frac{15}{7}\right]$$
A numerical result, to arbitrary precision, can nevertheless be found.	`In[3]:= N[%, 40]` $Out[3]= 1.069071500448624397994137689702693267367$
You can give complex arguments to special functions.	`In[4]:= Gamma[3 + 4I] //N` $Out[4]= 0.00522554 - 0.172547\,\mathrm{i}$
Special functions automatically get applied to each element in a list.	`In[5]:= Gamma[{3/2, 5/2, 7/2}]` $$Out[5]= \left\{\frac{\sqrt{\pi}}{2}, \frac{3\sqrt{\pi}}{4}, \frac{15\sqrt{\pi}}{8}\right\}$$
Mathematica knows analytical properties of special functions, such as derivatives.	`In[6]:= D[Gamma[x], {x, 2}]` $Out[6]= \text{Gamma}[x]\,\text{PolyGamma}[0, x]^2 + \text{Gamma}[x]\,\text{PolyGamma}[1, x]$
You can use FindRoot to find roots of special functions.	`In[7]:= FindRoot[ BesselJ[0, x], {x, 1} ]` $Out[7]= \{x \to 2.40483\}$

Special functions in *Mathematica* can usually be evaluated for arbitrary complex values of their arguments. Often, however, the defining relations given below apply only for some special choices of arguments. In these cases, the full function corresponds to a suitable extension or "analytic continuation" of these defining relations. Thus, for example, integral representations of functions are valid only when the integral exists, but the functions themselves can usually be defined elsewhere by analytic continuation.

As a simple example of how the domain of a function can be extended, consider the function represented by the sum $\sum_{k=0}^{\infty} x^k$. This sum converges only when $|x| < 1$. Nevertheless, it is easy to show analytically that for any x, the complete function is equal to $1/(1 - x)$. Using this form, you can easily find a value of the function for any x, at least so long as $x \neq 1$.

Gamma and Related Functions

Beta[a, b]	Euler beta function $B(a,b)$
Beta[z, a, b]	incomplete beta function $B_z(a,b)$
BetaRegularized[z, a, b]	regularized incomplete beta function $I(z,a,b)$
Gamma[z]	Euler gamma function $\Gamma(z)$
Gamma[a, z]	incomplete gamma function $\Gamma(a,z)$
Gamma[a, z_0, z_1]	generalized incomplete gamma function $\Gamma(a,z_0) - \Gamma(a,z_1)$
GammaRegularized[a, z]	regularized incomplete gamma function $Q(a,z)$
InverseBetaRegularized[s, a, b]	inverse beta function
InverseGammaRegularized[a, s]	inverse gamma function
Pochhammer[a, n]	Pochhammer symbol $(a)_n$
PolyGamma[z]	digamma function $\psi(z)$
PolyGamma[n, z]	n^{th} derivative of the digamma function $\psi^{(n)}(z)$

Gamma and related functions.

The **Euler gamma function** Gamma[z] is defined by the integral $\Gamma(z) = \int_0^\infty t^{z-1}e^{-t}dt$. For positive integer n, $\Gamma(n) = (n-1)!$. $\Gamma(z)$ can be viewed as a generalization of the factorial function, valid for complex arguments z.

There are some computations, particularly in number theory, where the logarithm of the gamma function often appears. For positive real arguments, you can evaluate this simply as Log[Gamma[z]]. For complex arguments, however, this form yields spurious discontinuities. *Mathematica* therefore includes the separate function LogGamma[z], which yields the **logarithm of the gamma function** with a single branch cut along the negative real axis.

The **Euler beta function** Beta[a, b] is $B(a,b) = \Gamma(a)\Gamma(b)/\Gamma(a+b) = \int_0^1 t^{a-1}(1-t)^{b-1}dt$.

The **Pochhammer symbol** or **rising factorial** Pochhammer[a, n] is $(a)_n = a(a+1)...(a+n-1) = \Gamma(a+n)/\Gamma(a)$. It often appears in series expansions for hypergeometric functions. Note that the Pochhammer symbol has a definite value even when the gamma functions which appear in its definition are infinite.

The **incomplete gamma function** Gamma[a, z] is defined by the integral $\Gamma(a,z) = \int_z^\infty t^{a-1}e^{-t}dt$. *Mathematica* includes a generalized incomplete gamma function Gamma[a, z_0, z_1] defined as $\int_{z_0}^{z_1} t^{a-1}e^{-t}dt$.

The alternative incomplete gamma function $\gamma(a, z)$ can therefore be obtained in *Mathematica* as `Gamma[a, 0, z]`.

The **incomplete beta function** `Beta[z, a, b]` is given by $B_z(a,b) = \int_0^z t^{a-1}(1-t)^{b-1}dt$. Notice that in the incomplete beta function, the parameter z is an *upper* limit of integration, and appears as the *first* argument of the function. In the incomplete gamma function, on the other hand, z is a *lower* limit of integration, and appears as the *second* argument of the function.

In certain cases, it is convenient not to compute the incomplete beta and gamma functions on their own, but instead to compute *regularized forms* in which these functions are divided by complete beta and gamma functions. *Mathematica* includes the **regularized incomplete beta function** `BetaRegularized[z, a, b]` defined for most arguments by $I(z,a,b) = B(z,a,b)/B(a,b)$, but taking into account singular cases. *Mathematica* also includes the **regularized incomplete gamma function** `GammaRegularized[a, z]` defined by $Q(a,z) = \Gamma(a,z)/\Gamma(a)$, with singular cases taken into account.

The incomplete beta and gamma functions, and their inverses, are common in statistics. The **inverse beta function** `InverseBetaRegularized[s, a, b]` is the solution for z in $s = I(z,a,b)$. The **inverse gamma function** `InverseGammaRegularized[a, s]` is similarly the solution for z in $s = Q(a,z)$.

Derivatives of the gamma function often appear in summing rational series. The **digamma function** `PolyGamma[z]` is the logarithmic derivative of the gamma function, given by $\psi(z) = \Gamma'(z)/\Gamma(z)$. For integer arguments, the digamma function satisfies the relation $\psi(n) = -\gamma + H_{n-1}$, where γ is Euler's constant (`EulerGamma` in *Mathematica*) and H_n are the harmonic numbers.

The **polygamma functions** `PolyGamma[n, z]` are given by $\psi^{(n)}(z) = d^n\psi(z)/dz^n$. Notice that the digamma function corresponds to $\psi^{(0)}(z)$. The general form $\psi^{(n)}(z)$ is the $(n+1)^{\text{th}}$, not the nth, logarithmic derivative of the gamma function. The polygamma functions satisfy the relation $\psi^{(n)}(z) = (-1)^{n+1}n! \sum_{k=0}^{\infty} 1/(z+k)^{n+1}$.

Many exact results for gamma and polygamma functions are built into *Mathematica*.

```
In[1]:= PolyGamma[6]
```

$$Out[1]= \frac{137}{60} - \text{EulerGamma}$$

Here is a contour plot of the gamma function in the complex plane.

```
In[2]:= ContourPlot[ Abs[Gamma[x + I y]], {x, -3, 3},
                {y, -2, 2}, PlotPoints->50 ]
```

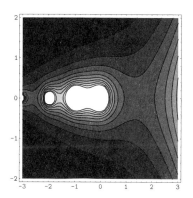

Zeta and Related Functions

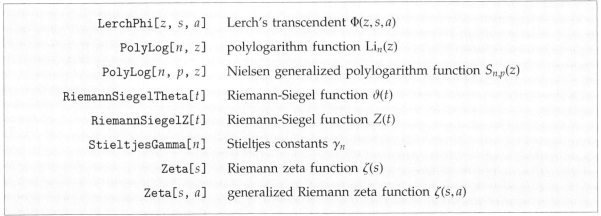

LerchPhi[z, s, a]	Lerch's transcendent $\Phi(z,s,a)$
PolyLog[n, z]	polylogarithm function $\text{Li}_n(z)$
PolyLog[n, p, z]	Nielsen generalized polylogarithm function $S_{n,p}(z)$
RiemannSiegelTheta[t]	Riemann-Siegel function $\vartheta(t)$
RiemannSiegelZ[t]	Riemann-Siegel function $Z(t)$
StieltjesGamma[n]	Stieltjes constants γ_n
Zeta[s]	Riemann zeta function $\zeta(s)$
Zeta[s, a]	generalized Riemann zeta function $\zeta(s,a)$

Zeta and related functions.

The **Riemann zeta function** Zeta[s] is defined by the relation $\zeta(s) = \sum_{k=1}^{\infty} k^{-s}$ (for $s > 1$). Zeta functions with integer arguments arise in evaluating various sums and integrals. *Mathematica* gives exact results when possible for zeta functions with integer arguments.

There is an analytic continuation of $\zeta(s)$ for arbitrary complex $s \neq 1$. The zeta function for complex arguments is central to number-theoretical studies of the distribution of primes. Of particular importance are the values on the critical line $\text{Re}\, s = \frac{1}{2}$.

In studying $\zeta(\frac{1}{2} + it)$, it is often convenient to define the two analytic **Riemann-Siegel functions** RiemannSiegelZ[t] and RiemannSiegelTheta[z] according to $Z(t) = e^{i\vartheta(t)}\zeta(\frac{1}{2} + it)$ and $\vartheta(t) = \text{Im} \log \Gamma(\frac{1}{4} + it/2) - t\log(\pi)/2$ (for t real). Note that the Riemann-Siegel functions are both real as long as t is real.

The **Stieltjes constants** StieltjesGamma[n] are generalizations of Euler's constant which appear in the series expansion of $\zeta(s)$ around its pole at $s = 1$; the coefficient of $(1-s)^n$ is $\gamma_n/n!$. Euler's constant is γ_0.

The **generalized Riemann zeta function** or **Hurwitz zeta function** Zeta[s, a] is given by $\zeta(s,a) = \sum_{k=0}^{\infty}(k + a)^{-s}$, where any term with $k + a = 0$ is excluded.

Mathematica gives exact results for $\zeta(2n)$.

```
In[1]:= Zeta[6]
```

$$Out[1]= \frac{\pi^6}{945}$$

Here is a three-dimensional picture of the Riemann zeta function in the complex plane.

`In[2]:= Plot3D[ Abs[ Zeta[x + I y] ], {x, -3, 3}, {y, 2, 35}]`

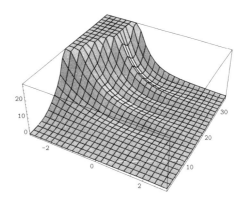

This is a plot of the absolute value of the Riemann zeta function on the critical line $\mathrm{Re}\,z = \frac{1}{2}$. You can see the first few zeros of the zeta function.

`In[3]:= Plot[ Abs[ Zeta[ 1/2 + I y ] ], {y, 0, 40} ]`

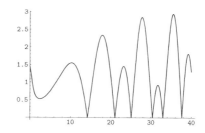

The **polylogarithm functions** `PolyLog[n, z]` are given by $\mathrm{Li}_n(z) = \sum_{k=1}^{\infty} z^k/k^n$. The polylogarithm function is sometimes known as **Jonquière's function**. The **dilogarithm** `PolyLog[2, z]` satisfies $\mathrm{Li}_2(z) = \int_z^0 \log(1-t)/t\,dt$. Sometimes $\mathrm{Li}_2(1-z)$ is known as **Spence's integral**. The **Nielsen generalized polylogarithm functions** or **hyperlogarithms** `PolyLog[n, p, z]` are given by $S_{n,p}(z) = (-1)^{n+p-1}/((n-1)!p!) \int_0^1 \log^{n-1}(t)\log^p(1-zt)/t\,dt$. Polylogarithm functions appear in Feynman diagram integrals in elementary particle physics, as well as in algebraic K-theory.

The **Lerch transcendent** `LerchPhi[z, s, a]` is a generalization of the zeta and polylogarithm functions, given by $\Phi(z,s,a) = \sum_{k=0}^{\infty} z^k/(a+k)^s$, where any term with $a + k = 0$ is excluded. Many sums of reciprocal powers can be expressed in terms of the Lerch transcendent. For example, the **Catalan beta function** $\beta(s) = \sum_{k=0}^{\infty}(-1)^k(2k+1)^{-s}$ can be obtained as $2^{-s}\Phi(-1,s,\frac{1}{2})$.

The Lerch transcendent is related to integrals of the **Fermi-Dirac** distribution in statistical mechanics by $\int_0^{\infty} k^s/(e^{k-\mu}+1)\,dk = e^{\mu}\Gamma(s+1)\Phi(-e^{\mu},s+1,1)$.

The Lerch transcendent can also be used to evaluate **Dirichlet *L*-series** which appear in number theory. The basic *L*-series has the form $L(s,\chi) = \sum_{k=1}^{\infty}\chi(k)k^{-s}$, where the "character" $\chi(k)$ is an integer function with period m. *L*-series of this kind can be written as sums of Lerch functions with z a power of $e^{2\pi i/m}$.

LerchPhi[z, s, a, DoublyInfinite->True] gives the doubly infinite sum $\sum_{k=-\infty}^{\infty} z^k/(a+k)^s$.

Exponential Integral and Related Functions

CosIntegral[z]	cosine integral function $Ci(z)$
CoshIntegral[z]	hyperbolic cosine integral function $Chi(z)$
ExpIntegralE[n, z]	exponential integral $E_n(z)$
ExpIntegralEi[z]	exponential integral $Ei(z)$
LogIntegral[z]	logarithmic integral $li(z)$
SinIntegral[z]	sine integral function $Si(z)$
SinhIntegral[z]	hyperbolic sine integral function $Shi(z)$

Exponential integral and related functions.

Mathematica has two forms of exponential integral: ExpIntegralE and ExpIntegralEi.

The **exponential integral function** ExpIntegralE[n, z] is defined by $E_n(z) = \int_1^\infty e^{-zt}/t^n \, dt$.

The second **exponential integral function** ExpIntegralEi[z] is defined by $Ei(z) = -\int_{-z}^\infty e^{-t}/t \, dt$ (for $z > 0$), where the principal value of the integral is taken.

The **logarithmic integral function** LogIntegral[z] is given by $li(z) = \int_0^z dt/\log t$ (for $z > 1$), where the principal value of the integral is taken. $li(z)$ is central to the study of the distribution of primes in number theory. The logarithmic integral function is sometimes also denoted by $Li(z)$. In some number-theoretical applications, $li(z)$ is defined as $\int_2^z dt/\log t$, with no principal value taken. This differs from the definition used in *Mathematica* by the constant $li(2)$.

The **sine and cosine integral functions** SinIntegral[z] and CosIntegral[z] are defined by $Si(z) = \int_0^z \sin(t)/t \, dt$ and $Ci(z) = -\int_z^\infty \cos(t)/t \, dt$. The **hyperbolic sine and cosine integral functions** SinhIntegral[z] and CoshIntegral[z] are defined by $Shi(z) = \int_0^z \sinh(t)/t \, dt$ and $Chi(z) = \gamma + \log(z) + \int_0^z (\cosh(t) - 1)/t \, dt$.

Error Function and Related Functions

Erf[z]	error function erf(z)
Erf[z_0, z_1]	generalized error function erf(z_1) $-$ erf(z_0)
Erfc[z]	complementary error function erfc(z)
Erfi[z]	imaginary error function erfi(z)
FresnelC[z]	Fresnel integral $C(z)$
FresnelS[z]	Fresnel integral $S(z)$
InverseErf[s]	inverse error function
InverseErfc[s]	inverse complementary error function

Error function and related functions.

The **error function** Erf[z] is the integral of the Gaussian distribution, given by erf(z) = $2/\sqrt{\pi} \int_0^z e^{-t^2} dt$. The **complementary error function** Erfc[z] is given simply by erfc(z) = $1 -$ erf(z). The **imaginary error function** Erfi[z] is given by erfi(z) = erf(iz)$/i$. The generalized error function Erf[z_0, z_1] is defined by the integral $2/\sqrt{\pi} \int_{z_0}^{z_1} e^{-t^2} dt$. The error function is central to many calculations in statistics.

The **inverse error function** InverseErf[s] is defined as the solution for z in the equation $s =$ erf(z). The inverse error function appears in computing confidence intervals in statistics as well as in some algorithms for generating Gaussian random numbers.

Closely related to the error function are the **Fresnel integrals** FresnelC[z] defined by $C(z) = \int_0^z \cos\left(\pi t^2/2\right) dt$ and FresnelS[z] defined by $S(z) = \int_0^z \sin\left(\pi t^2/2\right) dt$. Fresnel integrals occur in diffraction theory.

Bessel and Related Functions

AiryAi[z] and AiryBi[z]	Airy functions Ai(z) and Bi(z)
AiryAiPrime[z] and AiryBiPrime[z]	derivatives of Airy functions Ai$'$(z) and Bi$'$(z)
BesselJ[n, z] and BesselY[n, z]	Bessel functions $J_n(z)$ and $Y_n(z)$
BesselI[n, z] and BesselK[n, z]	modified Bessel functions $I_n(z)$ and $K_n(z)$
StruveH[n, z] and StruveL[n, z]	Struve function $\mathbf{H}_n(z)$ and modified Struve function $\mathbf{L}_n(z)$

Bessel and related functions.

The **Bessel functions** BesselJ[n, z] and BesselY[n, z] are linearly independent solutions to the differential equation $z^2 y'' + z y' + (z^2 - n^2)y = 0$. For integer n, the $J_n(z)$ are regular at $z = 0$, while the $Y_n(z)$ have a logarithmic divergence at $z = 0$.

Bessel functions arise in solving differential equations for systems with cylindrical symmetry.

$J_n(z)$ is often called the **Bessel function of the first kind**, or simply *the* Bessel function. $Y_n(z)$ is referred to as the **Bessel function of the second kind**, the **Weber function**, or the **Neumann function** (denoted $N_n(z)$).

The **Hankel functions** (or **Bessel functions of the third kind**) $H_n^{(1,2)}(z) = J_n(z) \pm i Y_n(z)$ give an alternative pair of solutions to the Bessel differential equation.

In studying systems with spherical symmetry, **spherical Bessel functions** arise, defined by $f_n(z) = \sqrt{\pi/2z}\, F_{n+\frac{1}{2}}(z)$, where f and F can be j and J, y and Y, or h^i and H^i. For integer n, *Mathematica* gives exact algebraic formulas for spherical Bessel functions.

The **modified Bessel functions** BesselI[n, z] and BesselK[n, z] are solutions to the differential equation $z^2 y'' + z y' - (z^2 + n^2)y = 0$. For integer n, $I_n(z)$ is regular at $z = 0$; $K_n(z)$ always has a logarithmic divergence at $z = 0$. The $I_n(z)$ are sometimes known as **hyperbolic Bessel functions**.

Particularly in electrical engineering, one often defines the **Kelvin functions**, according to $\mathrm{ber}_n(z) + i\,\mathrm{bei}_n(z) = e^{n\pi i} J_n(z e^{-\pi i/4})$, $\mathrm{ker}_n(z) + i\,\mathrm{kei}_n(z) = e^{-n\pi i/2} K_n(z e^{\pi i/4})$.

The **Airy functions** AiryAi[z] and AiryBi[z] are the two independent solutions Ai(z) and Bi(z) to the differential equation $y'' - zy = 0$. Ai(z) tends to zero for large positive z, while Bi(z) increases unboundedly. The Airy functions are related to modified Bessel functions with one-third-integer orders. The Airy functions often appear as the solutions to boundary value problems in electromagnetic theory and quantum mechanics. In many cases the **derivatives of the Airy functions** AiryAiPrime[z] and AiryBiPrime[z] also appear.

The **Struve function** StruveH[n, z] appears in the solution of the inhomogeneous Bessel equation which for integer n has the form $z^2 y'' + z y' + (z^2 - n^2)y = \frac{2}{\pi}\frac{z^{n+1}}{(2n-1)!!}$; the general solution to this equation consists of a linear combination of Bessel functions with the Struve function $\mathbf{H}_n(z)$ added. The **modified Struve function** StruveL[n, z] is given in terms of the ordinary Struve function by $\mathbf{L}_n(z) = -i e^{-in\pi/2}\mathbf{H}_n(z)$. Struve functions appear particularly in electromagnetic theory.

Here is a plot of $J_0(\sqrt{x})$. This is a curve that an idealized chain hanging from one end can form when you wiggle it.

In[1]:= **Plot[BesselJ[0, Sqrt[x]], {x, 0, 50}]**

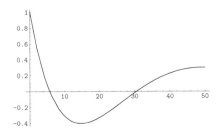

Mathematica generates explicit formulas for half-integer-order Bessel functions.

$In[2]:=$ **BesselK[3/2, x]**

$$Out[2]= \frac{e^{-x}\sqrt{\frac{\pi}{2}}\left(1+\frac{1}{x}\right)}{\sqrt{x}}$$

The Airy function plotted here gives the quantum-mechanical amplitude for a particle in a potential that increases linearly from left to right. The amplitude is exponentially damped in the classically inaccessible region on the right.

$In[3]:=$ **Plot[AiryAi[x], {x, -10, 10}]**

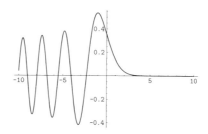

Legendre and Related Functions

LegendreP[n, z]	Legendre functions of the first kind $P_n(z)$
LegendreP[n, m, z]	associated Legendre functions of the first kind $P_n^m(z)$
LegendreQ[n, z]	Legendre functions of the second kind $Q_n(z)$
LegendreQ[n, m, z]	associated Legendre functions of the second kind $Q_n^m(z)$

Legendre and related functions.

The **Legendre functions** and **associated Legendre functions** satisfy the differential equation $(1-z^2)y'' - 2zy' + [n(n+1) - m^2/(1-z^2)]y = 0$. The **Legendre functions of the first kind**, LegendreP[n, z] and LegendreP[n, m, z], reduce to Legendre polynomials when n and m are integers. The **Legendre functions of the second kind** LegendreQ[n, z] and LegendreQ[n, m, z] give the second linearly independent solution to the differential equation. For integer m they have logarithmic singularities at $z = \pm1$. The $P_n(z)$ and $Q_n(z)$ solve the differential equation with $m = 0$.

Legendre functions arise in studies of quantum-mechanical scattering processes.

LegendreP[n, m, z] or LegendreP[n, m, 1, z]
type 1 function containing $(1 - z^2)^{m/2}$

LegendreP[n, m, 2, z]   type 2 function containing $((1 + z)/(1 - z))^{m/2}$

LegendreP[n, m, 3, z]   type 3 function containing $((1 + z)/(-1 + z))^{m/2}$

Types of Legendre functions. Analogous types exist for LegendreQ.

Legendre functions of type 1 are defined only when z lies inside the unit circle in the complex plane. **Legendre functions of type 2** have the same numerical values as type 1 inside the unit circle, but are also defined outside. The type 2 functions have branch cuts from $-\infty$ to -1 and from $+1$ to $+\infty$. **Legendre functions of type 3**, sometimes denoted $\mathcal{P}_n^m(z)$ and $\mathcal{Q}_n^m(z)$, have a single branch cut from $-\infty$ to $+1$.

Toroidal functions or **ring functions**, which arise in studying systems with toroidal symmetry, can be expressed in terms of the Legendre functions $P_{\nu-\frac{1}{2}}^{\mu}(\cosh\eta)$ and $Q_{\nu-\frac{1}{2}}^{\mu}(\cosh\eta)$.

Conical functions can be expressed in terms of $P_{-\frac{1}{2}+ip}^{\mu}(\cos\theta)$ and $Q_{-\frac{1}{2}+ip}^{\mu}(\cos\theta)$.

When you use the function LegendreP[n, x] with an integer n, you get a Legendre polynomial. If you take n to be an arbitrary complex number, you get, in general, a Legendre function.

In the same way, you can use the functions GegenbauerC and so on with arbitrary complex indices to get **Gegenbauer functions**, **Chebyshev functions**, **Hermite functions**, **Jacobi functions** and **Laguerre functions**. Unlike for associated Legendre functions, however, there is no need to distinguish different types in such cases.

Confluent Hypergeometric Functions

HypergeometricOF1[a, z]   hypergeometric function $_0F_1(;a;z)$

HypergeometricOF1Regularized[a, z]
regularized hypergeometric function $_0F_1(;a;z)/\Gamma(a)$

Hypergeometric1F1[a, b, z]   Kummer confluent hypergeometric function $_1F_1(a;b;z)$

Hypergeometric1F1Regularized[a, b, z]
regularized confluent hypergeometric function
$_1F_1(a;b;z)/\Gamma(b)$

HypergeometricU[a, b, z]   confluent hypergeometric function $U(a,b,z)$

Confluent hypergeometric functions.

Many of the special functions that we have discussed so far can be viewed as special cases of the **confluent hypergeometric function** Hypergeometric1F1[a, b, z].

The confluent hypergeometric function can be obtained from the series expansion $_1F_1(a;b;z) = 1 + az/b + a(a+1)/b(b+1) \, z^2/2! + \cdots = \sum_{k=0}^{\infty} (a)_k/(b)_k \, z^k/k!$. Some special results are obtained when a and b are both integers. If $a < 0$, and either $b > 0$ or $b < a$, the series yields a polynomial with a finite number of terms.

If b is zero or a negative integer, then $_1F_1(a;b;z)$ itself is infinite. But the **regularized confluent hypergeometric function** Hypergeometric1F1Regularized[a, b, z] given by $_1F_1(a;b;z)/\Gamma(b)$ has a finite value in all cases.

Among the functions that can be obtained from $_1F_1$ are the Bessel functions, error function, incomplete gamma function, and Hermite and Laguerre polynomials.

The function $_1F_1(a;b;z)$ is sometimes denoted $\Phi(a;b;z)$ or $M(a,b,z)$. It is often known as the **Kummer function**.

The $_1F_1$ function can be written in the integral representation $_1F_1(a;b;z) = \Gamma(b)/[\Gamma(b-a)\Gamma(a)] \int_0^1 e^{zt} t^{a-1} (1-t)^{b-a-1} \, dt$.

The $_1F_1$ confluent hypergeometric function is a solution to Kummer's differential equation $zy'' + (b-z)y' - ay = 0$, with the boundary conditions $_1F_1(a;b;0) = 1$ and $\partial[_1F_1(a;b;z)]/\partial z|_{z=0} = a/b$.

The function HypergeometricU[a, b, z] gives a second linearly independent solution to Kummer's equation. For Re $b > 1$ this function behaves like z^{1-b} for small z. It has a branch cut along the negative real axis in the complex z plane.

The function $U(a,b,z)$ has the integral representation $U(a,b,z) = 1/\Gamma(a) \int_0^{\infty} e^{-zt} t^{a-1} (1+t)^{b-a-1} \, dt$.

$U(a,b,z)$, like $_1F_1(a;b;z)$, is sometimes known as the **Kummer function**. The U function is sometimes denoted by Ψ.

The **Whittaker functions** give an alternative pair of solutions to Kummer's differential equation. The Whittaker function $M_{\kappa,\mu}$ is related to $_1F_1$ by $M_{\kappa,\mu}(z) = e^{-z/2} z^{1/2+\mu} {_1F_1}(\frac{1}{2} + \mu - \kappa; 1 + 2\mu; z)$. The second Whittaker function $W_{\kappa,\mu}$ obeys the same relation, with $_1F_1$ replaced by U.

The **parabolic cylinder functions** are related to Whittaker functions by $D_\nu(z) = 2^{1/4+\nu/2} z^{-1/2} \times W_{\frac{1}{4}+\frac{\nu}{2},-\frac{1}{4}}(z^2/2)$. For integer ν, the parabolic cylinder functions reduce to Hermite polynomials.

The **Coulomb wave functions** are also special cases of the confluent hypergeometric function. Coulomb wave functions give solutions to the radial Schrödinger equation in the Coulomb potential of a point nucleus. The regular Coulomb wave function is given by $F_L(\eta,\rho) = C_L(\eta)\rho^{L+1} e^{-i\rho} {_1F_1}(L + 1 - i\eta; 2L + 2; 2i\rho)$, where $C_L(\eta) = 2^L e^{-\pi\eta/2} |\Gamma(L + 1 + i\eta)|/\Gamma(2L + 2)$.

Other special cases of the confluent hypergeometric function include the **Toronto functions** $T(m, n, r)$, **Poisson-Charlier polynomials** $\rho_n(\nu, x)$, **Cunningham functions** $\omega_{n,m}(x)$ and **Bateman functions** $k_\nu(x)$.

A limiting form of the confluent hypergeometric function which often appears is `HypergeometricOF1[a, z]`. This function is obtained as the limit $_0F_1(;a;z) = \lim_{q\to\infty} {_1F_1}(q;a;z/q)$.

The $_0F_1$ function has the series expansion $_0F_1(;a;z) = \sum_{k=0}^{\infty} 1/(a)_k\, z^k/k!$ and satisfies the differential equation $zy'' + ay' - y = 0$.

Bessel functions of the first kind can be expressed in terms of the $_0F_1$ function.

Hypergeometric Functions and Generalizations

`Hypergeometric2F1[a, b, c, z]`	hypergeometric function $_2F_1(a,b;c;z)$
`Hypergeometric2F1Regularized[a, b, c, z]`	
	regularized hypergeometric function $_2F_1(a,b;c;z)/\Gamma(c)$
`HypergeometricPFQ[{a_1, ... , a_p}, {b_1, ... , b_q}, z]`	
	generalized hypergeometric function $_pF_q(\mathbf{a};\mathbf{b};z)$
`HypergeometricPFQRegularized[{a_1, ... , a_p}, {b_1, ... , b_q}, z]`	
	regularized generalized hypergeometric function
`MeijerG[{{a_1, ... , a_n}, {a_{n+1}, ... , a_p}}, {{b_1, ... , b_m}, {b_{m+1}, ... , b_q}}, z]`	
	Meijer G function
`AppellF1[a, b_1, b_2, c, x, y]`	Appell hypergeometric function of two variables $F_1(a;b_1,b_2;c;x,y)$

Hypergeometric functions and generalizations.

The **hypergeometric function** `Hypergeometric2F1[a, b, c, z]` has series expansion $_2F_1(a,b;c;z) = \sum_{k=0}^{\infty} (a)_k(b)_k/(c)_k\, z^k/k!$. The function is a solution of the hypergeometric differential equation $z(1 - z)y'' + [c - (a + b + 1)z]y' - aby = 0$.

The hypergeometric function can also be written as an integral: $_2F_1(a,b;c;z) = \Gamma(c)/[\Gamma(b)\Gamma(c - b)] \times \int_0^1 t^{b-1}(1 - t)^{c-b-1}(1 - tz)^{-a}\, dt$.

The hypergeometric function is also sometimes denoted by F, and is known as the **Gauss series** or the **Kummer series**.

The Legendre functions, and the functions which give generalizations of other orthogonal polynomials, can be expressed in terms of the hypergeometric function. Complete elliptic integrals can also be expressed in terms of the $_2F_1$ function.

The **Riemann P function**, which gives solutions to Riemann's differential equation, is also a $_2F_1$ function.

The **generalized hypergeometric function** or **Barnes extended hypergeometric function** HypergeometricPFQ[{a_1, ... , a_p}, {b_1, ... , b_q}, z] has series expansion $_pF_q(\mathbf{a};\mathbf{b};z) = \sum_{k=0}^{\infty}(a_1)_k...(a_p)_k/[(b_1)_k...(b_q)_k]\,z^k/k!$.

The **Meijer G function** MeijerG[{{a_1,...,a_n}, {a_{n+1},...,a_p}}, {{b_1,...,b_m}, {b_{m+1},...,b_q}}, z] is defined by the contour integral representation $G_{pq}^{mn}\left(z\,|\,{a_1,..,a_p \atop b_1,..,b_q}\right) = \frac{1}{2\pi i}\int \Gamma(1-a_1-s)...\Gamma(1-a_n-s)\times\Gamma(b_1+s)...\Gamma(b_m+s)/(\Gamma(a_{n+1}+s)...\Gamma(a_p+s)\Gamma(1-b_{m+1}-s)...\Gamma(1-b_q-s))\,z^{-s}ds$, where the contour of integration is set up to lie between the poles of $\Gamma(1-a_i-s)$ and the poles of $\Gamma(b_i+s)$. MeijerG is a very general function whose special cases cover most of the functions discussed in the past few sections.

The **Appell hypergeometric function of two variables** AppellF1[a, b_1, b_2, c, x, y] has series expansion $F_1(a;b_1,b_2;c;x,y) = \sum_{m=0}^{\infty}\sum_{n=0}^{\infty}(a)_{m+n}(b_1)_m(b_2)_n/(m!n!(c)_{m+n})x^m y^n$. This function appears for example in integrating cubic polynomials to arbitrary powers.

The Product Log Function

ProductLog[z]	product log function $W(z)$

The product log function.

The **product log function** gives the solution for w in $z = we^w$. The function can be viewed as a generalization of a logarithm. It can be used to represent solutions to a variety of transcendental equations. The **tree generating function** for counting distinct oriented trees is related to the product log by $T(z) = -W(-z)$.

■ 3.2.11 Elliptic Integrals and Elliptic Functions

Even more so than for other special functions, you need to be very careful about the arguments you give to elliptic integrals and elliptic functions. There are several incompatible conventions in common use, and often these conventions are distinguished only by the specific names given to arguments or by the presence of separators other than commas between arguments.

- Amplitude ϕ (used by *Mathematica*, in radians)

- Argument u (used by *Mathematica*): related to amplitude by $\phi = \mathrm{am}(u)$

- Delta amplitude $\Delta(\phi)$: $\Delta(\phi) = \sqrt{1 - m\sin^2(\phi)}$

- Coordinate x: $x = \sin(\phi)$

- Characteristic n (used by *Mathematica* in elliptic integrals of the third kind)

- Parameter m (used by *Mathematica*): preceded by |, as in $I(\phi|m)$

- Complementary parameter m_1: $m_1 = 1 - m$

- Modulus k: preceded by comma, as in $I(\phi, k)$; $m = k^2$

- Modular angle α: preceded by \, as in $I(\phi\backslash\alpha)$; $m = \sin^2(\alpha)$

- Nome q: preceded by comma in θ functions; $q = \exp[-\pi K(1 - m)/K(m)] = \exp(i\pi\omega'/\omega)$

- Invariants g_2, g_3 (used by *Mathematica*)

- Half-periods ω, ω': $g_2 = 60 \sum'_{r,s} w^{-4}$, $g_3 = 140 \sum'_{r,s} w^{-6}$, where $w = 2r\omega + 2s\omega'$

- Ratio of periods τ: $\tau = \omega'/\omega$

- Discriminant Δ: $\Delta = g_2^3 - 27g_3^2$

- Parameters of curve a, b (used by *Mathematica*)

- Coordinate y (used by *Mathematica*): related by $y^2 = x^3 + ax^2 + bx$

Common argument conventions for elliptic integrals and elliptic functions.

`JacobiAmplitude[u, m]`	give the amplitude ϕ corresponding to argument u and parameter m
`EllipticNomeQ[m]`	give the nome q corresponding to parameter m
`InverseEllipticNomeQ[q]`	give the parameter m corresponding to nome q
`WeierstrassInvariants[{ω, ω'}]`	give the invariants $\{g_2, g_3\}$ corresponding to the half-periods $\{\omega, \omega'\}$
`WeierstrassHalfPeriods[{g_2, g_3}]`	give the half-periods $\{\omega, \omega'\}$ corresponding to the invariants $\{g_2, g_3\}$

Converting between different argument conventions.

Elliptic Integrals

EllipticK[*m*]	complete elliptic integral of the first kind $K(m)$
EllipticF[ϕ, *m*]	elliptic integral of the first kind $F(\phi \| m)$
EllipticE[*m*]	complete elliptic integral of the second kind $E(m)$
EllipticE[ϕ, *m*]	elliptic integral of the second kind $E(\phi \| m)$
EllipticPi[*n*, *m*]	complete elliptic integral of the third kind $\Pi(n \| m)$
EllipticPi[*n*, ϕ, *m*]	elliptic integral of the third kind $\Pi(n; \phi \| m)$
JacobiZeta[ϕ, *m*]	Jacobi zeta function $Z(\phi \| m)$

Elliptic integrals.

Integrals of the form $\int R(x, y)\, dx$, where R is a rational function, and y^2 is a cubic or quartic polynomial in x, are known as **elliptic integrals**. Any elliptic integral can be expressed in terms of the three standard kinds of **Legendre-Jacobi elliptic integrals**.

The **elliptic integral of the first kind** EllipticF[ϕ, *m*] is given for $-\pi/2 < \phi < \pi/2$ by $F(\phi \| m) = \int_0^\phi [1 - m \sin^2(\theta)]^{-1/2}\, d\theta = \int_0^{\sin(\phi)} [(1 - t^2)(1 - mt^2)]^{-1/2}\, dt$. This elliptic integral arises in solving the equations of motion for a simple pendulum. It is sometimes known as an **incomplete elliptic integral of the first kind**.

Note that the arguments of the elliptic integrals are sometimes given in the opposite order from what is used in *Mathematica*.

The **complete elliptic integral of the first kind** EllipticK[*m*] is given by $K(m) = F(\frac{\pi}{2} \| m)$. Note that K is used to denote the *complete* elliptic integral of the first kind, while F is used for its incomplete form. In many applications, the parameter m is not given explicitly, and $K(m)$ is denoted simply by K. The **complementary complete elliptic integral of the first kind** $K'(m)$ is given by $K(1 - m)$. It is often denoted K'. K and iK' give the "real" and "imaginary" quarter-periods of the corresponding Jacobi elliptic functions discussed below.

The **elliptic integral of the second kind** EllipticE[ϕ, *m*] is given for $-\pi/2 < \phi < \pi/2$ by $E(\phi \| m) = \int_0^\phi [1 - m \sin^2(\theta)]^{1/2}\, d\theta = \int_0^{\sin(\phi)} (1 - t^2)^{-1/2}(1 - mt^2)^{1/2}\, dt$.

The **complete elliptic integral of the second kind** EllipticE[*m*] is given by $E(m) = E(\frac{\pi}{2} \| m)$. It is often denoted E. The complementary form is $E'(m) = E(1 - m)$.

The **Jacobi zeta function** JacobiZeta[ϕ, *m*] is given by $Z(\phi \| m) = E(\phi \| m) - E(m)F(\phi \| m)/K(m)$.

The **Heuman lambda function** is given by $\Lambda_0(\phi \| m) = F(\phi \| 1 - m)/K(1 - m) + \frac{2}{\pi}K(m)Z(\phi \| 1 - m)$.

The **elliptic integral of the third kind** EllipticPi[n, ϕ, m] is given by $\Pi(n; \phi \mid m) = \int_0^\phi (1 - n \sin^2(\theta))^{-1}[1 - m \sin^2(\theta)]^{-1/2} d\theta$.

The **complete elliptic integral of the third kind** EllipticPi[n, m] is given by $\Pi(n \mid m) = \Pi(n; \frac{\pi}{2} \mid m)$.

Here is a plot of the complete elliptic integral of the second kind $E(m)$.	*In[1]:=* **Plot[EllipticE[m], {m, 0, 1}]**

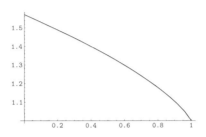

Here is $K(\alpha)$ with $\alpha = 30°$.	*In[2]:=* **EllipticK[Sin[30 Degree]^2] // N**
	Out[2]= 1.68575

The elliptic integrals have a complicated structure in the complex plane.	*In[3]:=* **Plot3D[Im[EllipticF[px + I py, 2]],** **{px, 0.5, 2.5}, {py, -1, 1}, PlotPoints->60]**

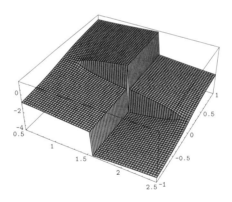

Elliptic Functions

JacobiAmplitude[u, m]	amplitude function am($u\|m$)
JacobiSN[u, m], JacobiCN[u, m], etc.	Jacobi elliptic functions sn($u\|m$), etc.
InverseJacobiSN[v, m], InverseJacobiCN[v, m], etc.	inverse Jacobi elliptic functions sn$^{-1}(v\|m)$, etc.
EllipticTheta[a, u, q]	theta functions $\vartheta_a(u, q)$ ($a = 1, ..., 4$)
EllipticThetaPrime[a, u, q]	derivatives of theta functions $\vartheta'_a(u, q)$ ($a = 1, ..., 4$)
WeierstrassP[u, $\{g_2, g_3\}$]	Weierstrass elliptic function $\wp(u; g_2, g_3)$
WeierstrassPPrime[u, $\{g_2, g_3\}$]	derivative of Weierstrass elliptic function $\wp'(u; g_2, g_3)$
InverseWeierstrassP[p, $\{g_2, g_3\}$]	inverse Weierstrass elliptic function
WeierstrassSigma[u, $\{g_2, g_3\}$]	Weierstrass sigma function $\sigma(u; g_2, g_3)$
WeierstrassZeta[u, $\{g_2, g_3\}$]	Weierstrass zeta function $\zeta(u; g_2, g_3)$

Elliptic and related functions.

Rational functions involving square roots of quadratic forms can be integrated in terms of inverse trigonometric functions. The trigonometric functions can thus be defined as inverses of the functions obtained from these integrals.

By analogy, **elliptic functions** are defined as inverses of the functions obtained from elliptic integrals.

The **amplitude** for Jacobi elliptic functions JacobiAmplitude[u, m] is the inverse of the elliptic integral of the first kind. If $u = F(\phi\,|\,m)$, then $\phi = $ am($u\,|\,m$). In working with Jacobi elliptic functions, the argument m is often dropped, so am($u\,|\,m$) is written as am(u).

The **Jacobi elliptic functions** JacobiSN[u, m] and JacobiCN[u, m] are given respectively by sn(u) = sin(ϕ) and cn(u) = cos(ϕ), where $\phi = $ am($u\,|\,m$). In addition, JacobiDN[u, m] is given by dn(u) = $\sqrt{1 - m\sin^2(\phi)}$ = $\Delta(\phi)$.

There are a total of twelve Jacobi elliptic functions JacobiPQ[u, m], with the letters P and Q chosen from the set S, C, D and N. Each Jacobi elliptic function JacobiPQ[u, m] satisfies the relation pq(u) = pn(u)/qn(u), where for these purposes nn(u) = 1.

There are many relations between the Jacobi elliptic functions, somewhat analogous to those between trigonometric functions. In limiting cases, in fact, the Jacobi elliptic functions reduce to trigonometric functions. So, for example, $\mathrm{sn}(u\,|\,0) = \sin(u)$, $\mathrm{sn}(u\,|\,1) = \tanh(u)$, $\mathrm{cn}(u\,|\,0) = \cos(u)$, $\mathrm{cn}(u\,|\,1) = \mathrm{sech}(u)$, $\mathrm{dn}(u\,|\,0) = 1$ and $\mathrm{dn}(u\,|\,1) = \mathrm{sech}(u)$.

The notation $\mathrm{Pq}(u)$ is often used for the integrals $\int_0^u \mathrm{pq}^2(t)\,dt$. These integrals can be expressed in terms of the Jacobi zeta function defined above.

One of the most important properties of elliptic functions is that they are *doubly periodic* in the complex values of their arguments. Ordinary trigonometric functions are singly periodic, in the sense that $f(z + s\omega) = f(z)$ for any integer s. The elliptic functions are doubly periodic, so that $f(z + r\omega + s\omega') = f(z)$ for any pair of integers r and s.

The Jacobi elliptic functions $\mathrm{sn}(u\,|\,m)$, etc. are doubly periodic in the complex u plane. Their periods include $\omega = 4K(m)$ and $\omega' = 4iK(1 - m)$, where K is the complete elliptic integral of the first kind.

The choice of p and q in the notation $\mathrm{pq}(u\,|\,m)$ for Jacobi elliptic functions can be understood in terms of the values of the functions at the quarter periods K and iK'.

This shows two complete periods in each direction of the absolute value of the Jacobi elliptic function $\mathrm{sn}(u\,|\,\tfrac{1}{3})$.

```
In[1]:= ContourPlot[Abs[JacobiSN[ux + I uy, 1/3]],
            {ux, 0, 4 EllipticK[1/3]},
            {uy, 0, 4 EllipticK[2/3]},
            PlotPoints->40 ]
```

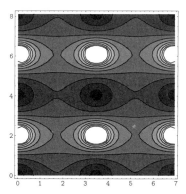

Also built into *Mathematica* are the **inverse Jacobi elliptic functions** InverseJacobiSN[v, m], InverseJacobiCN[v, m], etc. The inverse function $\mathrm{sn}^{-1}(v\,|\,m)$, for example, gives the value of u for which $v = \mathrm{sn}(u\,|\,m)$. The inverse Jacobi elliptic functions are related to elliptic integrals.

The four **theta functions** $\vartheta_a(u, q)$ are obtained from EllipticTheta[a, u, q] by taking a to be 1, 2, 3 or 4. The functions are defined by: $\vartheta_1(u, q) = 2q^{1/4} \sum_{n=0}^{\infty}(-1)^n q^{n(n+1)} \sin[(2n + 1)u]$, $\vartheta_2(u, q) = 2q^{1/4} \sum_{n=0}^{\infty} q^{n(n+1)} \cos[(2n + 1)u]$, $\vartheta_3(u, q) = 1 + 2 \sum_{n=1}^{\infty} q^{n^2} \cos(2nu)$, $\vartheta_4(u, q) = 1 + 2 \sum_{n=1}^{\infty}(-1)^n q^{n^2} \cos(2nu)$. The theta functions are often written as $\vartheta_a(u)$ with the parameter q not explicitly given. The theta functions are sometimes written in the form $\vartheta(u\,|\,m)$, where m is related to q by $q = \exp[-\pi K(1-m)/K(m)]$. In addition, q is sometimes replaced by τ, given by $q = e^{i\pi\tau}$. All the theta functions satisfy a diffusion-like differential equation $\partial^2\vartheta(u, \tau)/\partial u^2 = 4\pi i\, \partial\vartheta(u, \tau)/\partial\tau$.

The Jacobi elliptic functions can be expressed as ratios of the theta functions.

An alternative notation for theta functions is $\Theta(u \mid m) = \vartheta_4(v \mid m)$, $\Theta_1(u \mid m) = \vartheta_3(v \mid m)$, $\mathrm{H}(u \mid m) = \vartheta_1(v)$, $\mathrm{H}_1(u \mid m) = \vartheta_2(v)$, where $v = \pi u/2K(m)$.

The **Neville theta functions** can be defined in terms of the theta functions as $\vartheta_s(u) = 2K(m)\vartheta_1(v \mid m)/\pi\vartheta_1'(0 \mid m)$, $\vartheta_c(u) = \vartheta_2(v \mid m)/\vartheta_2(0 \mid m)$, $\vartheta_d(u) = \vartheta_3(v \mid m)/\vartheta_3(0 \mid m)$, $\vartheta_n(u) = \vartheta_4(v \mid m)/\vartheta_4(0 \mid m)$, where $v = \pi u/2K(m)$. The Jacobi elliptic functions can be represented as ratios of the Neville theta functions.

The **Weierstrass elliptic function** `WeierstrassP[`u`, {`g_2`, `g_3`}]` can be considered as the inverse of an elliptic integral. The Weierstrass function $\wp(u; g_2, g_3)$ gives the value of x for which $u = \int_\infty^x (4t^3 - g_2 t - g_3)^{-1/2} \, dt$. The function `WeierstrassPPrime[`$u$`, {`$g_2$`, `$g_3$`}]` is given by $\wp'(u; g_2, g_3) = \frac{\partial}{\partial u}\wp(u; g_2, g_3)$.

The Weierstrass functions are also sometimes written in terms of their *fundamental half-periods* ω and ω', obtained from the invariants g_2 and g_3 using `WeierstrassHalfPeriods[{`g_2`, `g_3`}]`.

The function `InverseWeierstrassP[`p`, {`g_2`, `g_3`}]` finds one of the two values of u for which $p = \wp(u; g_2, g_3)$. This value always lies in the parallelogram defined by the complex number half-periods ω and ω'.

`InverseWeierstrassP[{`p`, `q`}, {`g_2`, `g_3`}]` finds the unique value of u for which $p = \wp(u; g_2, g_3)$ and $q = \wp'(u; g_2, g_3)$. In order for any such value of u to exist, p and q must be related by $q^2 = 4p^3 - g_2 p - g_3$.

The **Weierstrass zeta function** `WeierstrassZeta[`u`, {`g_2`, `g_3`}]` and **Weierstrass sigma function** `WeierstrassSigma[`u`, {`g_2`, `g_3`}]` are related to the Weierstrass elliptic functions by $\zeta'(z; g_2, g_3) = -\wp(z; g_2, g_3)$ and $\sigma'(z; g_2, g_3)/\sigma(z; g_2, g_3) = \zeta(z; g_2, g_3)$.

The Weierstrass zeta and sigma functions are not strictly elliptic functions since they are not periodic.

Elliptic Modular Functions

`DedekindEta[`τ`]`	Dedekind eta function $\eta(\tau)$
`KleinInvariantJ[`τ`]`	Klein invariant modular function $J(\tau)$
`ModularLambda[`τ`]`	modular lambda function $\lambda(\tau)$

Elliptic modular functions.

The **modular lambda function** `ModularLambda[`τ`]` relates the ratio of half-periods $\tau = \omega'/\omega$ to the parameter according to $m = \lambda(\tau)$.

The **Klein invariant modular function** `KleinInvariantJ[`τ`]` and the **Dedekind eta function** `DedekindEta[`τ`]` satisfy the relations $\Delta = g_2^3/J(\tau) = (2\pi)^{12}\eta^{24}(\tau)$.

Modular elliptic functions are defined to be invariant under certain fractional linear transformations of their arguments. Thus for example $\lambda(\tau)$ is invariant under any combination of the transformations $\tau \to \tau + 2$ and $\tau \to \tau/(1 - 2\tau)$.

Generalized Elliptic Integrals and Functions

ArithmeticGeometricMean[a, b]	the arithmetic-geometric mean of a and b
EllipticExp[u, {a, b}]	generalized exponential associated with the elliptic curve $y^2 = x^3 + ax^2 + bx$
EllipticLog[{x, y}, {a, b}]	generalized logarithm associated with the elliptic curve $y^2 = x^3 + ax^2 + bx$

Generalized elliptic integrals and functions.

The definitions for elliptic integrals and functions given above are based on traditional usage. For modern algebraic geometry, it is convenient to use slightly more general definitions.

The function EllipticLog[{x, y}, {a, b}] is defined as the value of the integral $\frac{1}{2} \int_{\infty}^{x} (t^3 + at^2 + bt)^{-1/2} dt$, where the sign of the square root is specified by giving the value of y such that $y = \sqrt{x^3 + ax^2 + bx}$. Integrals of the form $\int_{\infty}^{x} (t^2 + at)^{-1/2} dt$ can be expressed in terms of the ordinary logarithm (and inverse trigonometric functions). You can think of EllipticLog as giving a generalization of this, where the polynomial under the square root is now of degree three.

The function EllipticExp[u, {a, b}] is the inverse of EllipticLog. It returns the list $\{x, y\}$ that appears in EllipticLog. EllipticExp is an elliptic function, doubly periodic in the complex u plane.

ArithmeticGeometricMean[a, b] gives the **arithmetic-geometric mean** (**AGM**) of two numbers a and b. This quantity is central to many numerical algorithms for computing elliptic integrals and other functions. For positive reals a and b the AGM is obtained by starting with $a_0 = a$, $b_0 = b$, then iterating the transformation $a_{n+1} = \frac{1}{2}(a_n + b_n)$, $b_{n+1} = \sqrt{a_n b_n}$ until $a_n = b_n$ to the precision required.

■ 3.2.12 Mathieu and Related Functions

MathieuC[a, q, z]	even Mathieu functions with characteristic value a and parameter q
MathieuS[b, q, z]	odd Mathieu function with characteristic value b and parameter q
MathieuCPrime[a, q, z] and MathieuSPrime[b, q, z]	z derivatives of Mathieu functions
MathieuCharacteristicA[r, q]	characteristic value a_r for even Mathieu functions with characteristic exponent r and parameter q
MathieuCharacteristicB[r, q]	characteristic value b_r for odd Mathieu functions with characteristic exponent r and parameter q
MathieuCharacteristicExponent[a, q]	characteristic exponent r for Mathieu functions with characteristic value a and parameter q

Mathieu and related functions.

The **Mathieu functions** MathieuC[a, q, z] and MathieuS[a, q, z] are solutions to the equation $y'' + [a - 2q\cos(2z)]y = 0$. This equation appears in many physical situations that involve elliptical shapes or periodic potentials. The function MathieuC is defined to be even in z, while MathieuS is odd.

When $q = 0$ the Mathieu functions are simply $\cos(\sqrt{a}z)$ and $\sin(\sqrt{a}z)$. For non-zero q, the Mathieu functions are only periodic in z for certain values of a. Such **Mathieu characteristic values** are given by MathieuCharacteristicA[r, q] and MathieuCharacteristicB[r, q] with r an integer or rational number. These values are often denoted by a_r and b_r.

For integer r, the even and odd Mathieu functions with characteristic values a_r and b_r are often denoted $ce_r(z, q)$ and $se_r(z, q)$, respectively. Note the reversed order of the arguments z and q.

According to Floquet's Theorem any Mathieu function can be written in the form $e^{irz}f(z)$, where $f(z)$ has period 2π and r is the **Mathieu characteristic exponent** MathieuCharacteristicExponent[a, q]. When the characteristic exponent r is an integer or rational number, the Mathieu function is therefore periodic. In general, however, when r is not a real integer, a_r and b_r turn out to be equal.

This shows the first five characteristic values a_r as functions of q.

In[1]:= **Plot[Evaluate[Table[MathieuCharacteristicA[r, q],**
{r, 0, 4}]], {q, 0, 15}]

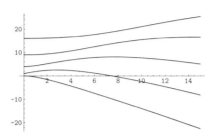

■ 3.2.13 Working with Special Functions

automatic evaluation	exact results for specific arguments
N[*expr*, *n*]	numerical approximations to any precision
D[*expr*, *x*]	exact results for derivatives
N[D[*expr*, *x*]]	numerical approximations to derivatives
Series[*expr*, {*x*, x_0, *n*}]	series expansions
Integrate[*expr*, *x*]	exact results for integrals
NIntegrate[*expr*, *x*]	numerical approximations to integrals
FindRoot[*expr*==0, {*x*, x_0}]	numerical approximations to roots

Some common operations on special functions.

Most special functions have simpler forms when given certain specific arguments. *Mathematica* will automatically simplify special functions in such cases.

Mathematica automatically writes this in terms of standard mathematical constants.

In[1]:= **PolyLog[2, 1/2]**

$$Out[1]= \frac{\pi^2}{12} - \frac{\mathrm{Log}[2]^2}{2}$$

Here again *Mathematica* reduces a special case of the Airy function to an expression involving gamma functions.	$In[2]:=$ **AiryAi[0]** $$Out[2]= \frac{1}{3^{2/3} \text{Gamma}\left[\frac{2}{3}\right]}$$

For most choices of arguments, no exact reductions of special functions are possible. But in such cases, *Mathematica* allows you to find numerical approximations to any degree of precision. The algorithms that are built into *Mathematica* cover essentially all values of parameters—real and complex—for which the special functions are defined.

There is no exact result known here.	$In[3]:=$ **AiryAi[1]** $Out[3]=$ AiryAi[1]

This gives a numerical approximation to 40 digits of precision.	$In[4]:=$ **N[AiryAi[1], 40]** $Out[4]=$ 0.1352924163128814155241474235154663061749

The result here is a huge complex number, but *Mathematica* can still find it.	$In[5]:=$ **N[AiryAi[1000 I]]** $Out[5]=$ $-4.78026663777 \times 10^{6472} + 3.6749209072 \times 10^{6472}$ i

Most special functions have derivatives that can be expressed in terms of elementary functions or other special functions. But even in cases where this is not so, you can still use N to find numerical approximations to derivatives.

This derivative comes out in terms of elementary functions.	$In[6]:=$ **D[FresnelS[x], x]** $$Out[6]= \text{Sin}\left[\frac{\pi x^2}{2}\right]$$

This evaluates the derivative of the gamma function at the point 3.	$In[7]:=$ **Gamma'[3]** $$Out[7]= 2\left(\frac{3}{2} - \text{EulerGamma}\right)$$

There is no exact formula for this derivative of the zeta function.	$In[8]:=$ **Zeta'[Pi]** $Out[8]=$ Zeta$'$ [π]

Applying N gives a numerical approximation.	$In[9]:=$ **N[%]** $Out[9]=$ -0.167603

Mathematica incorporates a vast amount of knowledge about special functions—including essentially all the results that have been derived over the years. You access this knowledge whenever you do operations on special functions in *Mathematica*.

Here is a series expansion for a Fresnel function.	$In[10]:=$ **Series[FresnelS[x], {x, 0, 15}]** $$Out[10]= \frac{\pi x^3}{6} - \frac{\pi^3 x^7}{336} + \frac{\pi^5 x^{11}}{42240} - \frac{\pi^7 x^{15}}{9676800} + O[x]^{16}$$

Mathematica knows how to do a vast range of integrals involving special functions.	$In[11]:=$ **Integrate[AiryAi[x]^2, {x, 0, Infinity}]**
	$Out[11]= \dfrac{1}{3^{2/3} \operatorname{Gamma}\left[\frac{1}{3}\right]^2}$

One feature of working with special functions is that there are a large number of relations between different functions, and these relations can often be used in simplifying expressions.

FullSimplify[*expr*]	try to simplify *expr* using a range of transformation rules

Simplifying expressions involving special functions.

This uses the reflection formula for the gamma function.	$In[12]:=$ **FullSimplify[Gamma[x] Gamma[1 - x]]**
	$Out[12]= \pi \operatorname{Csc}[\pi x]$
This makes use of a representation for Chebyshev polynomials.	$In[13]:=$ **FullSimplify[ChebyshevT[n, z] - k Cos[n ArcCos[z]]]**
	$Out[13]= -(-1+k) \operatorname{Cos}[n \operatorname{ArcCos}[z]]$
The Airy functions are related to Bessel functions.	$In[14]:=$ **FullSimplify[3 AiryAi[1] + Sqrt[3] AiryBi[1]]**
	$Out[14]= 2 \operatorname{BesselI}\left[-\dfrac{1}{3}, \dfrac{2}{3}\right]$

FunctionExpand[*expr*]	try to expand out special functions

Manipulating expressions involving special functions.

This expands out the PolyGamma, yielding a function with a simpler argument.	$In[15]:=$ **FunctionExpand[PolyGamma[2, 2 + x]]**
	$Out[15]= 2\left(\dfrac{1}{x^3} + \dfrac{1}{(1+x)^3}\right) + \operatorname{PolyGamma}[2, x]$
Here is an example involving Bessel functions.	$In[16]:=$ **FunctionExpand[BesselY[n, I x]]**
	$Out[16]= -\dfrac{2 (i x)^{-n} x^n \operatorname{BesselK}[n, x]}{\pi} + \operatorname{BesselI}[n, x]$ $(-(i x)^{-n} x^n + (i x)^n x^{-n} \operatorname{Cos}[n \pi]) \operatorname{Csc}[n \pi]$
In this case the final result does not even involve PolyGamma.	$In[17]:=$ **FunctionExpand[Im[PolyGamma[0, 3 I]]]**
	$Out[17]= \dfrac{1}{6} + \dfrac{1}{2} \pi \operatorname{Coth}[3 \pi]$

This finds an expression for the second derivative of the zeta function at zero.

$In[18]:=$ **FunctionExpand[Zeta''[0]]**

$$Out[18]= \frac{\text{EulerGamma}^2}{2} - \frac{\pi^2}{24} - \frac{1}{2} (\text{Log}[2] + \text{Log}[\pi])^2 + \text{StieltjesGamma}[1]$$

■ 3.2.14 Statistical Distributions and Related Functions

There are standard *Mathematica* packages for evaluating functions related to common statistical distributions. *Mathematica* represents the statistical distributions themselves in the symbolic form *name*[*param*$_1$, *param*$_2$, ...], where the *param*$_i$ are parameters for the distributions. Functions such as Mean, which give properties of statistical distributions, take the symbolic representation of the distribution as an argument.

BetaDistribution[α, β]	continuous beta distribution
CauchyDistribution[a, b]	Cauchy distribution with location parameter a and scale parameter b
ChiSquareDistribution[n]	chi-square distribution with n degrees of freedom
ExponentialDistribution[λ]	exponential distribution with scale parameter λ
ExtremeValueDistribution[α, β]	extreme value (Fisher-Tippett) distribution
FRatioDistribution[n_1, n_2]	*F*-ratio distribution with n_1 numerator and n_2 denominator degrees of freedom
GammaDistribution[α, λ]	gamma distribution with shape parameter α and scale parameter λ
NormalDistribution[μ, σ]	normal (Gaussian) distribution with mean μ and standard deviation σ
LaplaceDistribution[μ, β]	Laplace (double exponential) distribution with mean μ and variance parameter β
LogNormalDistribution[μ, σ]	lognormal distribution with mean parameter μ and variance parameter σ
LogisticDistribution[μ, β]	logistic distribution with mean μ and variance parameter β
RayleighDistribution[σ]	Rayleigh distribution
StudentTDistribution[n]	Student *t* distribution with n degrees of freedom
UniformDistribution[*min*, *max*]	uniform distribution on the interval {*min*, *max*}
WeibullDistribution[α, β]	Weibull distribution

Statistical distributions from the package Statistics`ContinuousDistributions`.

Most of the continuous statistical distributions commonly used are derived from the **normal** or **Gaussian distribution** NormalDistribution[μ, σ]. This distribution has probability density $1/(\sqrt{2\pi}\sigma) \exp[-(x - \mu)^2/(2\sigma^2)]$. If you take random variables that follow any distribution with bounded variance, then the Central Limit Theorem shows that the mean of a large number of these variables always approaches a normal distribution.

The **logarithmic normal distribution** or **lognormal distribution** LogNormalDistribution[μ, σ] is the distribution followed by the exponential of a normal-distributed random variable. This distribution arises when many independent random variables are combined in a multiplicative fashion.

The **chi-square distribution** ChiSquareDistribution[n] is the distribution of the quantity $\sum_{i=1}^{n} x_i^2$, where the x_i are random variables which follow a normal distribution with mean zero and unit variance. The chi-square distribution gives the distribution of variances of samples from a normal distribution.

The **Student t distribution** StudentTDistribution[n] is the distribution followed by the ratio of a variable that follows the normal distribution to the square root of one that follows the chi-square distribution with n degrees of freedom. The t distribution characterizes the uncertainty in a mean when both the mean and variance are obtained from data.

The **F-ratio distribution**, **F-distribution** or **variance ratio distribution** FRatioDistribution[n_1, n_2] is the distribution of the ratio of two chi-square variables with n_1 and n_2 degrees of freedom. The *F*-ratio distribution is used in the analysis of variance for comparing variances from different models.

The **extreme value distribution** ExtremeValueDistribution[α, β] is the limiting distribution for the smallest or largest values in large samples drawn from a variety of distributions, including the normal distribution.

PDF[*dist*, *x*]	probability density function (frequency function) at *x*
CDF[*dist*, *x*]	cumulative distribution function at *x*
Quantile[*dist*, *q*]	q^{th} quantile
Mean[*dist*]	mean
Variance[*dist*]	variance
StandardDeviation[*dist*]	standard deviation
Skewness[*dist*]	coefficient of skewness
Kurtosis[*dist*]	coefficient of kurtosis
CharacteristicFunction[*dist*, *t*]	characteristic function $\phi(t)$
Random[*dist*]	pseudorandom number with specified distribution

Functions of statistical distributions.

The **cumulative distribution function** (cdf) CDF[*dist*, *x*] is given by the integral of the **probability density function** for the distribution up to the point *x*. For the normal distribution, the cdf is usually denoted $\Phi(x)$. Cumulative distribution functions are used in evaluating probabilities for statistical hypotheses. For discrete distributions, the cdf is given by the sum of the probabilities up to the point *x*. The cdf is sometimes called simply the **distribution function**. The cdf at a particular point *x* for a given distribution is often denoted $P(x \,|\, \theta_1, \theta_2, ...)$, where the θ_i are parameters of the distribution. The **upper tail area** is given in terms of the cdf by $Q(x \,|\, \theta_i) = 1 - P(x \,|\, \theta_i)$. Thus, for example, the upper tail area for a chi-square distribution with *v* degrees of freedom is denoted $Q(\chi^2 \,|\, v)$ and is given by 1 - CDF[ChiSquareDistribution[*nu*], *chi2*].

The **quantile** Quantile[*dist*, *q*] is effectively the inverse of the cdf. It gives the value of *x* at which CDF[*dist*, *x*] reaches *q*. The median is given by Quantile[*dist*, 1/2]; quartiles, deciles and percentiles can also be expressed as quantiles. Quantiles are used in constructing confidence intervals for statistical parameter estimates.

The characteristic function CharacteristicFunction[*dist*, *t*] is given by $\phi(t) = \int p(x) \exp(itx)\, dx$, where $p(x)$ is the probability density for a distribution. The nth **central moment** of a distribution is given by the nth derivative $i^{-n}\phi^{(n)}(0)$.

Random[*dist*] gives pseudorandom numbers that follow the specified distribution. The numbers can be seeded as discussed in Section 3.2.3.

This loads the package which defines continuous statistical distributions.	*In[1]:=* **<<Statistics`ContinuousDistributions`**
This represents a normal distribution with mean zero and unit variance.	*In[2]:=* **ndist = NormalDistribution[0, 1]**
	Out[2]= NormalDistribution[0, 1]
Here is a symbolic result for the cumulative distribution function of the normal distribution.	*In[3]:=* **CDF[ndist, x]**
	Out[3]= $\dfrac{1}{2}\left(1 + \text{Erf}\left[\dfrac{x}{\sqrt{2}}\right]\right)$
This gives the value of *x* at which the cdf of the normal distribution reaches the value 0.9.	*In[4]:=* **Quantile[ndist, 0.9] // N**
	Out[4]= 1.28155
Here is a list of five normal-distributed pseudorandom numbers.	*In[5]:=* **Table[Random[ndist], {5}]**
	Out[5]= {-1.63994, 0.987641, -0.475946, -0.598517, -1.04913}

BernoulliDistribution[p]	discrete Bernoulli distribution with mean p
BinomialDistribution[n, p]	binomial distribution for n trials with probability p
DiscreteUniformDistribution[n]	discrete uniform distribution with n states
GeometricDistribution[p]	discrete geometric distribution with mean $1/p - 1$
HypergeometricDistribution[n, n_{succ}, n_{tot}]	
	hypergeometric distribution for n trials with n_{succ} successes in a population of size n_{tot}
NegativeBinomialDistribution[r, p]	negative binomial distribution for failure count r and probability p
PoissonDistribution[mu]	Poisson distribution with mean μ

Statistical distributions from the package Statistics`DiscreteDistributions`.

Most of the common discrete statistical distributions can be derived by considering a sequence of "trials", each with two possible outcomes, say "success" and "failure".

The **Bernoulli distribution** BernoulliDistribution[p] is the probability distribution for a single trial in which success, corresponding to value 1, occurs with probability p, and failure, corresponding to value 0, occurs with probability $1 - p$.

The **binomial distribution** BinomialDistribution[n, p] is the distribution of the number of successes that occur in n independent trials when the probability for success in an individual trial is p. The distribution is given by $\binom{n}{k}p^k(1 - p)^{n-k}$.

The **negative binomial distribution** NegativeBinomialDistribution[r, p] gives the distribution of the number of failures that occur in a sequence of trials before r successes have occurred, given that the probability for success in each individual trial is p.

The **geometric distribution** GeometricDistribution[p] gives the distribution of the total number of trials before the first success occurs in a sequence of trials where the probability for success in each individual trial is p.

The **hypergeometric distribution** HypergeometricDistribution[n, n_{succ}, n_{tot}] is used in place of the binomial distribution for experiments in which the n trials correspond to sampling without replacement from a population of size n_{tot} with n_{succ} potential successes.

The **discrete uniform distribution** DiscreteUniformDistribution[n] represents an experiment with n outcomes that occur with equal probabilities.

3.3 Algebraic Manipulation

■ 3.3.1 Structural Operations on Polynomials

Expand[*poly*]	expand out products and powers
Factor[*poly*]	factor completely
FactorTerms[*poly*]	pull out any overall numerical factor
FactorTerms[*poly*, {*x*, *y*, ... }]	pull out any overall factor that does not depend on *x*, *y*, ...
Collect[*poly*, *x*]	arrange a polynomial as a sum of powers of *x*
Collect[*poly*, {*x*, *y*, ... }]	arrange a polynomial as a sum of powers of *x*, *y*, ...

Structural operations on polynomials.

Here is a polynomial in one variable.

$In[1]:=$ **(2 + 4 x^2)^2 (x - 1)^3**

$Out[1]=$ $(-1 + x)^3 (2 + 4 x^2)^2$

Expand expands out products and powers, writing the polynomial as a simple sum of terms.

$In[2]:=$ **t = Expand[%]**

$Out[2]=$ $-4 + 12 x - 28 x^2 + 52 x^3 - 64 x^4 + 64 x^5 - 48 x^6 + 16 x^7$

Factor performs complete factoring of the polynomial.

$In[3]:=$ **Factor[t]**

$Out[3]=$ $4 (-1 + x)^3 (1 + 2 x^2)^2$

FactorTerms pulls out the overall numerical factor from t.

$In[4]:=$ **FactorTerms[t]**

$Out[4]=$ $4 (-1 + 3 x - 7 x^2 + 13 x^3 - 16 x^4 + 16 x^5 - 12 x^6 + 4 x^7)$

There are several ways to write any polynomial. The functions Expand, FactorTerms and Factor give three common ways. Expand writes a polynomial as a simple sum of terms, with all products expanded out. FactorTerms pulls out common factors from each term. Factor does complete factoring, writing the polynomial as a product of terms, each of as low degree as possible.

When you have a polynomial in more than one variable, you can put the polynomial in different forms by essentially choosing different variables to be "dominant". Collect[*poly*, *x*] takes a polynomial in several variables and rewrites it as a sum of terms containing different powers of the "dominant variable" *x*.

Here is a polynomial in two variables.

$In[5]:=$ **Expand[(1 + 2x + y)^3]**

$Out[5]=$ $1 + 6 x + 12 x^2 + 8 x^3 + 3 y + 12 x y + 12 x^2 y + 3 y^2 + 6 x y^2 + y^3$

Collect reorganizes the polynomial so that x is the "dominant variable".

$In[6]:=$ **Collect[%, x]**

$Out[6]=$ $1 + 8\,x^3 + 3\,y + 3\,y^2 + y^3 + x^2\,(12 + 12\,y) + x\,(6 + 12\,y + 6\,y^2)$

If you specify a list of variables, Collect will effectively write the expression as a polynomial in these variables.

$In[7]:=$ **Collect[Expand[(1 + x + 2y + 3z)^3], {x, y}]**

$Out[7]=$ $1 + x^3 + 8\,y^3 + 9\,z + 27\,z^2 + 27\,z^3 + x^2\,(3 + 6\,y + 9\,z) +$
$\qquad y^2\,(12 + 36\,z) + y\,(6 + 36\,z + 54\,z^2) +$
$\qquad x\,(3 + 12\,y^2 + 18\,z + 27\,z^2 + y\,(12 + 36\,z))$

Expand[*poly*, *patt*]	expand out *poly* avoiding those parts which do not contain terms matching *patt*

Controlling polynomial expansion.

This avoids expanding parts which do not contain x.

$In[8]:=$ **Expand[(x + 1)^2 (y + 1)^2, x]**

$Out[8]=$ $(1 + y)^2 + 2\,x\,(1 + y)^2 + x^2\,(1 + y)^2$

This avoids expanding parts which do not contain objects matching b[_].

$In[9]:=$ **Expand[(a[1] + a[2] + 1)^2 (1 + b[1])^2, b[_]]**

$Out[9]=$ $(1 + a[1] + a[2])^2 +$
$\qquad 2\,(1 + a[1] + a[2])^2\,b[1] + (1 + a[1] + a[2])^2\,b[1]^2$

PowerExpand[*expr*]	expand out $(ab)^c$ and $(a^b)^c$ in *expr*

Expanding powers.

Mathematica does not automatically expand out expressions of the form $(a\,b)\hat{\,}c$ except when c is an integer. In general it is only correct to do this expansion if a and b are positive reals. Nevertheless, the function PowerExpand does the expansion, effectively assuming that a and b are indeed positive reals.

Mathematica does not automatically expand out this expression.

$In[10]:=$ **(x y)^n**

$Out[10]=$ $(x\,y)^n$

PowerExpand does the expansion, effectively assuming that x and y are positive reals.

$In[11]:=$ **PowerExpand[%]**

$Out[11]=$ $x^n\,y^n$

Log is not automatically expanded out.

$In[12]:=$ **Log[%]**

$Out[12]=$ $Log[x^n\,y^n]$

PowerExpand does the expansion.

$In[13]:=$ **PowerExpand[%]**

$Out[13]=$ $n\,Log[x] + n\,Log[y]$

Collect[*poly, patt*]	collect separately terms involving each object that matches *patt*
Collect[*poly, patt, h*]	apply *h* to each final coefficient obtained

Ways of collecting terms.

Here is an expression involving various functions f.

In[14]:= t = 3 + x f[1] + x^2 f[1] + y f[2]^2 + z f[2]^2

Out[14]= $3 + x f[1] + x^2 f[1] + y f[2]^2 + z f[2]^2$

This collects terms that match f[_].

In[15]:= Collect[t, f[_]]

Out[15]= $3 + (x + x^2) f[1] + (y + z) f[2]^2$

This applies Factor to each coefficient obtained.

In[16]:= Collect[t, f[_], Factor]

Out[16]= $3 + x (1 + x) f[1] + (y + z) f[2]^2$

■ 3.3.2 Finding the Structure of a Polynomial

PolynomialQ[*expr, x*]	test whether *expr* is a polynomial in *x*
PolynomialQ[*expr*, {$x_1, x_2, \ldots$}]	test whether *expr* is a polynomial in the x_i
Variables[*poly*]	a list of the variables in *poly*
Exponent[*poly, x*]	the maximum exponent with which *x* appears in *poly*
Coefficient[*poly, expr*]	the coefficient of *expr* in *poly*
Coefficient[*poly, expr, n*]	the coefficient of *expr^n* in *poly*
Coefficient[*poly, expr, 0*]	the term in *poly* independent of *expr*
CoefficientList[*poly*, {$x_1, x_2, \ldots$}]	generate an array of the coefficients of the x_i in *poly*

Finding the structure of polynomials written in expanded form.

Here is a polynomial in two variables.

In[1]:= t = (1 + x)^3 (1 - y - x)^2

Out[1]= $(1 + x)^3 (1 - x - y)^2$

This is the polynomial in expanded form.

In[2]:= Expand[t]

Out[2]= $1 + x - 2x^2 - 2x^3 + x^4 + x^5 - 2y - 4xy + 4x^3 y + 2x^4 y + y^2 + 3xy^2 + 3x^2 y^2 + x^3 y^2$

PolynomialQ reports that t is a polynomial in x.

```
In[3]:= PolynomialQ[t, x]
Out[3]= True
```

This expression, however, is not a polynomial in x.

```
In[4]:= PolynomialQ[x + Sin[x], x]
Out[4]= False
```

Variables gives a list of the variables in the polynomial t.

```
In[5]:= Variables[t]
Out[5]= {x, y}
```

This gives the maximum exponent with which x appears in the polynomial t. For a polynomial in one variable, Exponent gives the degree of the polynomial.

```
In[6]:= Exponent[t, x]
Out[6]= 5
```

Coefficient[*poly*, *expr*] gives the total coefficient with which *expr* appears in *poly*. In this case, the result is a sum of two terms.

```
In[7]:= Coefficient[t, x^2]
```
$$Out[7]= -2 + 3\,y^2$$

This is equivalent to Coefficient[t, x^2].

```
In[8]:= Coefficient[t, x, 2]
```
$$Out[8]= -2 + 3\,y^2$$

This picks out the coefficient of x^0 in t.

```
In[9]:= Coefficient[t, x, 0]
```
$$Out[9]= 1 - 2\,y + y^2$$

CoefficientList gives a list of the coefficients of each power of x, starting with x^0.

```
In[10]:= CoefficientList[1 + 3x^2 + 4x^4, x]
Out[10]= {1, 0, 3, 0, 4}
```

For multivariate polynomials, CoefficientList gives an array of the coefficients for each power of each variable.

```
In[11]:= CoefficientList[t, {x, y}]
Out[11]= {{1, -2, 1}, {1, -4, 3}, {-2, 0, 3},
          {-2, 4, 1}, {1, 2, 0}, {1, 0, 0}}
```

It is important to notice that the functions in this section will work even on polynomials that are not explicitly given in expanded form.

Many of the functions also work on expressions that are not strictly polynomials.

Without giving specific integer values to a, b and c, this expression cannot strictly be considered a polynomial.

```
In[12]:= x^a + x^b + y^c
```
$$Out[12]= x^a + x^b + y^c$$

Exponent[*expr*, x] still gives the maximum exponent of x in *expr*, but here has to write the result in symbolic form.

```
In[13]:= Exponent[%, x]
Out[13]= Max[0, a, b]
```

■ 3.3.3 Structural Operations on Rational Expressions

For ordinary polynomials, Factor and Expand give the most important forms. For rational expressions, there are many different forms that can be useful.

ExpandNumerator[*expr*]	expand numerators only
ExpandDenominator[*expr*]	expand denominators only
Expand[*expr*]	expand numerators, dividing the denominator into each term
ExpandAll[*expr*]	expand numerators and denominators completely

Different kinds of expansion for rational expressions.

Here is a rational expression.

$In[1]:=$ **t = (1 + x)^2 / (1 - x) + 3 x^2 / (1 + x)^2 + (2 - x)^2**

$Out[1]= (2 - x)^2 + \dfrac{3 x^2}{(1 + x)^2} + \dfrac{(1 + x)^2}{1 - x}$

ExpandNumerator writes the numerator of each term in expanded form.

$In[2]:=$ **ExpandNumerator[t]**

$Out[2]= 4 - 4 x + x^2 + \dfrac{3 x^2}{(1 + x)^2} + \dfrac{1 + 2 x + x^2}{1 - x}$

Expand expands the numerator of each term, and divides all the terms by the appropriate denominators.

$In[3]:=$ **Expand[t]**

$Out[3]= 4 + \dfrac{1}{1 - x} - 4 x + \dfrac{2 x}{1 - x} + x^2 + \dfrac{x^2}{1 - x} + \dfrac{3 x^2}{(1 + x)^2}$

ExpandDenominator expands out the denominator of each term.

$In[4]:=$ **ExpandDenominator[t]**

$Out[4]= (2 - x)^2 + \dfrac{(1 + x)^2}{1 - x} + \dfrac{3 x^2}{1 + 2 x + x^2}$

ExpandAll does all possible expansions in the numerator and denominator of each term.

$In[5]:=$ **ExpandAll[t]**

$Out[5]= 4 + \dfrac{1}{1 - x} - 4 x + \dfrac{2 x}{1 - x} + x^2 + \dfrac{x^2}{1 - x} + \dfrac{3 x^2}{1 + 2 x + x^2}$

ExpandAll[*expr*, *patt*], etc.	avoid expanding parts which contain no terms matching *patt*

Controlling expansion.

This avoids expanding the term which does not contain z.

$In[6]:=$ **ExpandAll[(x + 1)^2/y^2 + (z + 1)^2/z^2, z]**

$Out[6]= 1 + \dfrac{(1 + x)^2}{y^2} + \dfrac{1}{z^2} + \dfrac{2}{z}$

Together[*expr*]	combine all terms over a common denominator
Apart[*expr*]	write an expression as a sum of terms with simple denominators
Cancel[*expr*]	cancel common factors between numerators and denominators
Factor[*expr*]	perform a complete factoring

Structural operations on rational expressions.

Here is a rational expression.

$In[7]:=$ **u = (-4x + x^2)/(-x + x^2) + (-4 + 3x + x^2)/(-1 + x^2)**

$$Out[7]= \frac{-4x+x^2}{-x+x^2} + \frac{-4+3x+x^2}{-1+x^2}$$

Together puts all terms over a common denominator.

$In[8]:=$ **Together[u]**

$$Out[8]= \frac{2\,(\,{-}4+x^2)}{(-1+x)\,(1+x)}$$

You can use Factor to factor the numerator and denominator of the resulting expression.

$In[9]:=$ **Factor[%]**

$$Out[9]= \frac{2\,(-2+x)\,(2+x)}{(-1+x)\,(1+x)}$$

Apart writes the expression as a sum of terms, with each term having as simple a denominator as possible.

$In[10]:=$ **Apart[u]**

$$Out[10]= 2 - \frac{3}{-1+x} + \frac{3}{1+x}$$

Cancel cancels any common factors between numerators and denominators.

$In[11]:=$ **Cancel[u]**

$$Out[11]= \frac{-4+x}{-1+x} + \frac{4+x}{1+x}$$

Factor first puts all terms over a common denominator, then factors the result.

$In[12]:=$ **Factor[%]**

$$Out[12]= \frac{2\,(-2+x)\,(2+x)}{(-1+x)\,(1+x)}$$

In mathematical terms, Apart decomposes a rational expression into "partial fractions".

In expressions with several variables, you can use Apart[*expr*, *var*] to do partial fraction decompositions with respect to different variables.

Here is a rational expression in two variables.

$In[13]:=$ **v = (x^2+y^2)/(x + x y)**

$$Out[13]= \frac{x^2+y^2}{x+x\,y}$$

This gives the partial fraction decomposition with respect to x.	$In[14]:=$ **Apart[v, x]**
	$Out[14]=$ $\dfrac{x}{1+y} + \dfrac{y^2}{x(1+y)}$
Here is the partial fraction decomposition with respect to y.	$In[15]:=$ **Apart[v, y]**
	$Out[15]=$ $-\dfrac{1}{x} + \dfrac{y}{x} + \dfrac{1+x^2}{x(1+y)}$

■ 3.3.4 Algebraic Operations on Polynomials

For many kinds of practical calculations, the only operations you will need to perform on polynomials are essentially the structural ones discussed in the preceding sections.

If you do more advanced algebra with polynomials, however, you will have to use the algebraic operations discussed in this section.

You should realize that most of the operations discussed in this section work only on ordinary polynomials, with integer exponents and rational-number coefficients for each term.

PolynomialQuotient[$poly_1$, $poly_2$, x]	find the result of dividing the polynomial $poly_1$ in x by $poly_2$, dropping any remainder term
PolynomialRemainder[$poly_1$, $poly_2$, x]	find the remainder from dividing the polynomial $poly_1$ in x by $poly_2$
PolynomialGCD[$poly_1$, $poly_2$]	find the greatest common divisor of two polynomials
PolynomialLCM[$poly_1$, $poly_2$]	find the least common multiple of two polynomials
PolynomialMod[$poly$, m]	reduce the polynomial $poly$ modulo m
Resultant[$poly_1$, $poly_2$, x]	find the resultant of two polynomials
Subresultants[$poly_1$, $poly_2$, x]	find the principal subresultant coefficients of two polynomials
GroebnerBasis[{$poly_1$, $poly_2$, ... }, {x_1, x_2, ... }]	find the Gröbner basis for the polynomials $poly_i$
GroebnerBasis[{$poly_1$, $poly_2$, ... }, {x_1, x_2, ... }, {y_1, y_2, ... }]	find the Gröbner basis eliminating the y_i
PolynomialReduce[$poly$, {$poly_1$, $poly_2$, ... }, {x_1, x_2, ... }]	find a minimal representation of $poly$ in terms of the $poly_i$

Reduction of polynomials.

Given two polynomials $p(x)$ and $q(x)$, one can always uniquely write $\frac{p(x)}{q(x)} = a(x) + \frac{b(x)}{q(x)}$, where the degree of $b(x)$ is less than the degree of $q(x)$. `PolynomialQuotient` gives the quotient $a(x)$, and `PolynomialRemainder` gives the remainder $b(x)$.

This gives the remainder from dividing x^2 by $1 + x$.	*In[1]:=* **PolynomialRemainder[x^2, x+1, x]** *Out[1]=* 1
Here is the quotient of x^2 and $x + 1$, with the remainder dropped.	*In[2]:=* **PolynomialQuotient[x^2, x+1, x]** *Out[2]=* -1 + x
This gives back the original expression.	*In[3]:=* **Simplify[(x+1) % + %%]** *Out[3]=* x^2
Here the result depends on whether the polynomials are considered to be in x or y.	*In[4]:=* **{PolynomialRemainder[x+y, x-y, x],** 　　　　　　　　**PolynomialRemainder[x+y, x-y, y]}** *Out[4]=* {2 y, 2 x}

`PolynomialGCD[poly₁, poly₂]` finds the highest degree polynomial that divides the $poly_i$ exactly. It gives the analog for polynomials of the integer function GCD.

PolynomialGCD gives the greatest common divisor of the two polynomials.	*In[5]:=* **PolynomialGCD[(1-x)^2 (1+x) (2+x), (1-x) (2+x) (3+x)]** *Out[5]=* (-1 + x) (2 + x)

`PolynomialMod` is essentially the analog for polynomials of the function Mod for integers. When the modulus m is an integer, `PolynomialMod[poly, m]` simply reduces each coefficient in *poly* modulo the integer m. If m is a polynomial, then `PolynomialMod[poly, m]` effectively tries to get as low degree a polynomial as possible by subtracting from *poly* appropriate multiples $q\ m$ of m. The multiplier q can itself be a polynomial, but its degree is always less than the degree of *poly*. `PolynomialMod` yields a final polynomial whose degree and leading coefficient are both as small as possible.

This reduces x^2 modulo $x + 1$. The result is simply the remainder from dividing the polynomials.	*In[6]:=* **PolynomialMod[x^2, x+1]** *Out[6]=* 1
In this case, PolynomialMod and PolynomialRemainder do not give the same result.	*In[7]:=* **{PolynomialMod[x^2, a x + 1],** 　　　　　　**PolynomialRemainder[x^2, a x + 1, x]}** *Out[7]=* $\left\{ x^2, \dfrac{1}{a^2} \right\}$

The main difference between `PolynomialMod` and `PolynomialRemainder` is that while the former works simply by multiplying and subtracting polynomials, the latter uses division in getting its results. In addition, `PolynomialMod` allows reduction by several moduli at the same time. A typical case is reduction modulo both a polynomial and an integer.

This reduces the polynomial $x^2 + 1$ modulo both $x + 1$ and 2.	*In[8]:=* **PolynomialMod[x^2 + 1, {x + 1, 2}]** *Out[8]=* 0

The function $\mathtt{Resultant}[poly_1, poly_2, x]$ is used in a number of classical algebraic algorithms. The resultant of two polynomials a and b, both with leading coefficient one, is given by the product of all the differences $a_i - b_j$ between the roots of the polynomials. It turns out that for any pair of polynomials, the resultant is always a polynomial in their coefficients. By looking at when the resultant is zero, one can tell for what values of their parameters two polynomials have a common root. Two polynomials with leading coefficient one have k common roots if exactly the first k elements in the list $\mathtt{Subresultants}[poly_1, poly_2, x]$ are zero.

Here is the resultant with respect to y of two polynomials in x and y. The original polynomials have a common root in y only for values of x at which the resultant vanishes.

In[9]:= **Resultant[(x-y)^2-2, y^2-3, y]**

Out[9]= $1 - 10\,x^2 + x^4$

Gröbner bases appear in many modern algebraic algorithms and applications. The function $\mathtt{GroebnerBasis}[\{poly_1, poly_2, \dots\}, \{x_1, x_2, \dots\}]$ takes a set of polynomials, and reduces this set to a canonical form from which many properties can conveniently be deduced. An important feature is that the set of polynomials obtained from $\mathtt{GroebnerBasis}$ always has exactly the same collection of common roots as the original set.

The $(x + y)^2$ is effectively redundant, and so does not appear in the Gröbner basis.

In[10]:= **GroebnerBasis[{(x+y), (x+y)^2}, {x, y}]**

Out[10]= $\{x + y\}$

The polynomial 1 has no roots, showing that the original polynomials have no common roots.

In[11]:= **GroebnerBasis[{x+y,x^2-1,y^2-2x}, {x, y}]**

Out[11]= $\{1\}$

The polynomials are effectively unwound here, and can now be seen to have exactly five common roots.

In[12]:= **GroebnerBasis[{x y^2+2 x y+x^2+1, x y+y^2+1}, {x, y}]**

Out[12]= $\{1 + y^2 - y^3 - y^4 - y^5, \; x + y^2 + y^3 + y^4\}$

$\mathtt{PolynomialReduce}[poly, \{p_1, p_2, \dots\}, \{x_1, x_2, \dots\}]$ yields a list $\{\{a_1, a_2, \dots\}, b\}$ of polynomials with the property that b is minimal and $a_1\,p_1 + a_2\,p_2 + \dots + b$ is exactly *poly*.

This writes $x^2 + y^2$ in terms of $x - y$ and $y + a$, leaving a remainder that depends only on a.

In[13]:= **PolynomialReduce[x^2 + y^2, {x - y, y + a}, {x, y}]**

Out[13]= $\{\{x + y, -2\,a + 2\,y\}, \, 2\,a^2\}$

Factor[*poly*]	factor a polynomial
FactorSquareFree[*poly*]	write a polynomial as a product of powers of square-free factors
FactorTerms[*poly*, *x*]	factor out terms that do not depend on *x*
FactorList[*poly*], FactorSquareFreeList[*poly*], FactorTermsList[*poly*] give results as lists of factors	

Functions for factoring polynomials.

Factor, FactorTerms and FactorSquareFree perform various degrees of factoring on polynomials. Factor does full factoring over the integers. FactorTerms extracts the "content" of the polynomial. FactorSquareFree pulls out any multiple factors that appear.

Here is a polynomial, in expanded form.

$In[14]:=$ **t = Expand[2 (1 + x)^2 (2 + x) (3 + x)]**

$Out[14]=$ $12 + 34\,x + 34\,x^2 + 14\,x^3 + 2\,x^4$

FactorTerms pulls out only the factor of 2 that does not depend on x.

$In[15]:=$ **FactorTerms[t, x]**

$Out[15]=$ $2\,(6 + 17\,x + 17\,x^2 + 7\,x^3 + x^4)$

FactorSquareFree factors out the 2 and the term (1 + x)^2, but leaves the rest unfactored.

$In[16]:=$ **FactorSquareFree[t]**

$Out[16]=$ $2\,(1 + x)^2\,(6 + 5\,x + x^2)$

Factor does full factoring, recovering the original form.

$In[17]:=$ **Factor[t]**

$Out[17]=$ $2\,(1 + x)^2\,(2 + x)\,(3 + x)$

Particularly when you write programs that work with polynomials, you will often find it convenient to pick out pieces of polynomials in a standard form. The function FactorList gives a list of all the factors of a polynomial, together with their exponents. The first element of the list is always the overall numerical factor for the polynomial.

The form that FactorList returns is the analog for polynomials of the form produced by FactorInteger for integers.

Here is a list of the factors of the polynomial in the previous set of examples. Each element of the list gives the factor, together with its exponent.

$In[18]:=$ **FactorList[t]**

$Out[18]=$ $\{\{2, 1\}, \{1 + x, 2\}, \{2 + x, 1\}, \{3 + x, 1\}\}$

> Factor[*poly*, GaussianIntegers -> True]
> factor a polynomial, allowing coefficients that are Gaussian integers

Factoring polynomials with complex coefficients.

Factor and related functions usually handle only polynomials with ordinary integer or rational-number coefficients. If you set the option GaussianIntegers -> True, however, then Factor will allow polynomials with coefficients that are complex numbers with rational real and imaginary parts. This often allows more extensive factorization to be performed.

This polynomial is irreducible when only ordinary integers are allowed.

$In[19]:=$ **Factor[1 + x^2]**

$Out[19]=$ $1 + x^2$

When Gaussian integer coefficients are allowed, the polynomial factors.

$In[20]:=$ **Factor[1 + x^2, GaussianIntegers -> True]**

$Out[20]=$ $(-i + x)(i + x)$

> Cyclotomic[*n*, *x*]   give the cyclotomic polynomial of order *n* in *x*

Cyclotomic polynomials.

Cyclotomic polynomials arise as "elementary polynomials" in various algebraic algorithms. The cyclotomic polynomials are defined by $C_n(x) = \prod_k (x - e^{2\pi i k/n})$, where k runs over all positive integers less than n that are relatively prime to n.

This is the cyclotomic polynomial $C_6(x)$.

$In[21]:=$ **Cyclotomic[6, x]**

$Out[21]=$ $1 - x + x^2$

$C_6(x)$ appears in the factors of $x^6 - 1$.

$In[22]:=$ **Factor[x^6 - 1]**

$Out[22]=$ $(-1 + x)(1 + x)(1 - x + x^2)(1 + x + x^2)$

> Decompose[*poly*, *x*]   decompose *poly*, if possible, into a composition of a list of simpler polynomials

Decomposing polynomials.

Factorization is one important way of breaking down polynomials into simpler parts. Another, quite different, way is *decomposition*. When one factors a polynomial $P(x)$, one writes it as a product $p_1(x)p_2(x)...$ of polynomials $p_i(x)$. Decomposing a polynomial $Q(x)$ consists of writing it as a *composition* of polynomials of the form $q_1(q_2(...(x)...))$.

Here is a simple example of Decompose. The original polynomial $x^4 + x^2 + 1$ can be written as the polynomial $\bar{x}^2 + \bar{x} + 1$, where $\bar{x}$ is the polynomial x^2.

```
In[23]:= Decompose[x^4 + x^2 + 1, x]
```

$Out[23]= \{1 + x + x^2, x^2\}$

Here are two polynomial functions.

```
In[24]:= ( q1[x_] = 1 - 2x + x^4 ;
            q2[x_] = 5x + x^3 ; )
```

This gives the composition of the two functions.

```
In[25]:= Expand[ q1[ q2[ x ] ] ]
```

$Out[25]= 1 - 10x - 2x^3 + 625x^4 + 500x^6 + 150x^8 + 20x^{10} + x^{12}$

Decompose recovers the original functions.

```
In[26]:= Decompose[%, x]
```

$Out[26]= \{1 - 2x + x^4, 5x + x^3\}$

Decompose[*poly*, *x*] is set up to give a list of polynomials in *x*, which, if composed, reproduce the original polynomial. The original polynomial can contain variables other than *x*, but the sequence of polynomials that Decompose produces are all intended to be considered as functions of *x*.

Unlike factoring, the decomposition of polynomials is not completely unique. For example, the two sets of polynomials p_i and q_i, related by $q_1(x) = p_1(x - a)$ and $q_2(x) = p_2(x) + a$ give the same result on composition, so that $p_1(p_2(x)) = q_1(q_2(x))$. *Mathematica* follows the convention of absorbing any constant terms into the first polynomial in the list produced by Decompose.

InterpolatingPolynomial[$\{f_1, f_2, \dots \}$, x]
  give a polynomial in x which is equal to f_i when x is the integer i

InterpolatingPolynomial[$\{\{x_1, f_1\}, \{x_2, f_2\}, \dots \}$, x]
  give a polynomial in x which is equal to f_i when x is x_i

Generating interpolating polynomials.

This yields a quadratic polynomial which goes through the specified three points.

```
In[27]:= InterpolatingPolynomial[{{-1, 4}, {0, 2}, {1, 6}}, x]
```

$Out[27]= 4 + (1 + x) (-2 + 3x)$

When x is 0, the polynomial has value 2.

```
In[28]:= % /. x -> 0
```

$Out[28]= 2$

■ 3.3.5 Polynomials Modulo Primes

Mathematica can work with polynomials whose coefficients are in the finite field Z_p of integers modulo a prime p.

`PolynomialMod[`*poly*`, `*p*`]`	reduce the coefficients in a polynomial modulo p
`Expand[`*poly*`, Modulus -> `*p*`]`	expand *poly* modulo p
`Factor[`*poly*`, Modulus -> `*p*`]`	factor *poly* modulo p
`PolynomialGCD[`*poly*$_1$`, `*poly*$_2$`, Modulus -> `*p*`]`	find the GCD of the *poly*$_i$ modulo p
`GroebnerBasis[`*polys*`, `*vars*`, Modulus -> `*p*`]`	find the Gröbner basis modulo p

Functions for manipulating polynomials over finite fields.

Here is an ordinary polynomial.

```
In[1]:= Expand[ (1 + x)^6 ]
Out[1]= 1 + 6 x + 15 x^2 + 20 x^3 + 15 x^4 + 6 x^5 + x^6
```

This reduces the coefficients modulo 2.

```
In[2]:= PolynomialMod[%, 2]
Out[2]= 1 + x^2 + x^4 + x^6
```

Here are the factors of the resulting polynomial over the integers.

```
In[3]:= Factor[%]
Out[3]= (1 + x^2) (1 + x^4)
```

If you work modulo 2, further factoring becomes possible.

```
In[4]:= Factor[%, Modulus->2]
Out[4]= (1 + x)^6
```

■ 3.3.6 Advanced Topic: Polynomials over Algebraic Number Fields

Functions like `Factor` usually assume that all coefficients in the polynomials they produce must involve only rational numbers. But by setting the option `Extension` you can extend the domain of coefficients that will be allowed.

`Factor[`*poly*`, Extension->{`a_1`, `a_2`, ... }]`	factor *poly* allowing coefficients that are rational combinations of the a_i

Factoring polynomials over algebraic number fields.

Allowing only rational number coefficients, this polynomial cannot be factored.

In[1]:= **Factor[1 + x^4]**

Out[1]= $1 + x^4$

With coefficients that can involve $\sqrt{2}$, the polynomial can now be factored.

In[2]:= **Factor[1 + x^4, Extension -> {Sqrt[2]}]**

Out[2]= $-\left(-1 + \sqrt{2}\ x - x^2\right)\left(1 + \sqrt{2}\ x + x^2\right)$

The polynomial can also be factored if one allows coefficients involving $\sqrt{-1}$.

In[3]:= **Factor[1 + x^4, Extension -> {Sqrt[-1]}]**

Out[3]= $(-i + x^2)(i + x^2)$

GaussianIntegers->True is equivalent to Extension->Sqrt[-1].

In[4]:= **Factor[1 + x^4, GaussianIntegers -> True]**

Out[4]= $(-i + x^2)(i + x^2)$

If one allows coefficients that involve both $\sqrt{2}$ and $\sqrt{-1}$ the polynomial can be factored completely.

In[5]:= **Factor[1 + x^4, Extension -> {Sqrt[2], Sqrt[-1]}]**

Out[5]= $\dfrac{1}{4}\left(\sqrt{2} - (1 + i)\,x\right)\left(\sqrt{2} - (1 - i)\,x\right)$
$\left(\sqrt{2} + (1 - i)\,x\right)\left(\sqrt{2} + (1 + i)\,x\right)$

Expand gives the original polynomial back again.

In[6]:= **Expand[%]**

Out[6]= $1 + x^4$

Factor[*poly*, Extension->Automatic]
        factor *poly* allowing algebraic numbers in *poly* to appear in coefficients

---

Factoring polynomials with algebraic number coefficients.

Here is a polynomial with a coefficient involving $\sqrt{2}$.

In[7]:= **t = Expand[(Sqrt[2] + x)^2]**

Out[7]= $2 + 2\sqrt{2}\ x + x^2$

By default, Factor will not factor this polynomial.

In[8]:= **Factor[t]**

Out[8]= $2 + 2\sqrt{2}\ x + x^2$

But now the field of coefficients is extended by including $\sqrt{2}$, and the polynomial is factored.

In[9]:= **Factor[t, Extension -> Automatic]**

Out[9]= $\left(\sqrt{2} + x\right)^2$

Other polynomial functions work much like Factor. By default, they treat algebraic number coefficients just like independent symbolic variables. But with the option Extension->Automatic they perform operations on these coefficients.

By default, Cancel does not reduce these polynomials.

In[10]:= **Cancel[t / (x^2 - 2)]**

Out[10]= $\dfrac{2 + 2\sqrt{2}\ x + x^2}{-2 + x^2}$

But now it does.

In[11]:= `Cancel[t / (x^2 - 2), Extension->Automatic]`

Out[11]= $\dfrac{-\sqrt{2} - x}{\sqrt{2} - x}$

By default, `PolynomialLCM` pulls out no common factors.

In[12]:= `PolynomialLCM[t, x^2 - 2]`

Out[12]= $(-2 + x^2)\left(2 + 2\sqrt{2}\,x + x^2\right)$

But now it does.

In[13]:= `PolynomialLCM[t, x^2 - 2, Extension->Automatic]`

Out[13]= $-2\sqrt{2} - 2x + \sqrt{2}\,x^2 + x^3$

■ 3.3.7 Trigonometric Expressions

`TrigExpand[`*expr*`]`	expand trigonometric expressions out into a sum of terms
`TrigFactor[`*expr*`]`	factor trigonometric expressions into products of terms
`TrigFactorList[`*expr*`]`	give terms and their exponents in a list
`TrigReduce[`*expr*`]`	reduce trigonometric expressions using multiple angles

Functions for manipulating trigonometric expressions.

This expands out a trigonometric expression.

In[1]:= `TrigExpand[Sin[2 x] Cos[2 y]]`

Out[1]= $2\,\text{Cos}[x]\,\text{Cos}[y]^2\,\text{Sin}[x] - 2\,\text{Cos}[x]\,\text{Sin}[x]\,\text{Sin}[y]^2$

This factors the expression.

In[2]:= `TrigFactor[%]`

Out[2]= $2\,\text{Cos}[x]\,\text{Sin}[x]\,(\text{Cos}[y] - \text{Sin}[y])\,(\text{Cos}[y] + \text{Sin}[y])$

And this reduces the expression to a form linear in the trigonometric functions.

In[3]:= `TrigReduce[%]`

Out[3]= $\dfrac{1}{2}\,(\text{Sin}[2x - 2y] + \text{Sin}[2x + 2y])$

`TrigExpand` works on hyperbolic as well as circular functions.

In[4]:= `TrigExpand[Tanh[x + y]]`

Out[4]= $\dfrac{\text{Cosh}[y]\,\text{Sinh}[x]}{\text{Cosh}[x]\,\text{Cosh}[y] + \text{Sinh}[x]\,\text{Sinh}[y]} + \dfrac{\text{Cosh}[x]\,\text{Sinh}[y]}{\text{Cosh}[x]\,\text{Cosh}[y] + \text{Sinh}[x]\,\text{Sinh}[y]}$

`TrigReduce` reproduces the original form again.

In[5]:= `TrigReduce[%]`

Out[5]= $\text{Tanh}[x + y]$

Mathematica automatically uses functions like Tan whenever it can.

In[6]:= `Sin[x]^2/Cos[x]`

Out[6]= $\text{Sin}[x]\,\text{Tan}[x]$

With `TrigFactorList`, however, you can see the parts of functions like Tan.

```
In[7]:= TrigFactorList[%]
Out[7]= {{1, 1}, {Sin[x], 2}, {Cos[x], -1}}
```

`TrigToExp[`*expr*`]`	write trigonometric functions in terms of exponentials
`ExpToTrig[`*expr*`]`	write exponentials in terms of trigonometric functions

Converting to and from exponentials.

`TrigToExp` writes trigonometric functions in terms of exponentials.

```
In[8]:= TrigToExp[Tan[x]]
```

$$Out[8]= \frac{\mathring{\imath}\,(e^{-i\,x} - e^{i\,x})}{e^{-i\,x} + e^{i\,x}}$$

`ExpToTrig` does the reverse, getting rid of explicit complex numbers whenever possible.

```
In[9]:= ExpToTrig[%]
Out[9]= Tan[x]
```

`ExpToTrig` deals with hyperbolic as well as circular functions.

```
In[10]:= ExpToTrig[Exp[x] - Exp[-x]]
Out[10]= 2 Sinh[x]
```

You can also use `ExpToTrig` on purely numerical expressions.

```
In[11]:= ExpToTrig[(-1)^(1/17)]
```

$$Out[11]= \text{Cos}\left[\frac{\pi}{17}\right] + \mathring{\imath}\,\text{Sin}\left[\frac{\pi}{17}\right]$$

■ 3.3.8 Expressions Involving Complex Variables

Mathematica usually pays no attention to whether variables like x stand for real or complex numbers. Sometimes, however, you may want to make transformations which are appropriate only if particular variables are assumed to be either real or complex.

The function `ComplexExpand` expands out algebraic and trigonometric expressions, making definite assumptions about the variables that appear.

`ComplexExpand[`*expr*`]`	expand *expr* assuming that all variables are real
`ComplexExpand[`*expr*`, {`x_1`, `x_2`, ... }]`	expand *expr* assuming that the x_i are complex

Expanding complex expressions.

This expands the expression, assuming that x and y are both real.

```
In[1]:= ComplexExpand[Tan[x + I y]]
```

$$Out[1]= \frac{\text{Sin}[2\,x]}{\text{Cos}[2\,x] + \text{Cosh}[2\,y]} + \frac{\mathring{\imath}\,\text{Sinh}[2\,y]}{\text{Cos}[2\,x] + \text{Cosh}[2\,y]}$$

In this case, a is assumed to be real, but x is assumed to be complex, and is broken into explicit real and imaginary parts.	*In[2]:=* `ComplexExpand[a + x^2, {x}]`
	Out[2]= $a - Im[x]^2 + 2 i Im[x] Re[x] + Re[x]^2$

With several complex variables, you quickly get quite complicated results.	*In[3]:=* `ComplexExpand[Sin[x] Exp[y], {x, y}]`
	Out[3]= $e^{Re[y]} Cos[Im[y]] Cosh[Im[x]] Sin[Re[x]] -$ $e^{Re[y]} Cos[Re[x]] Sin[Im[y]] Sinh[Im[x]] +$ $i (e^{Re[y]} Cosh[Im[x]] Sin[Im[y]] Sin[Re[x]] +$ $e^{Re[y]} Cos[Im[y]] Cos[Re[x]] Sinh[Im[x]])$

There are several ways to write a complex variable *z* in terms of real parameters. As above, for example, *z* can be written in the "Cartesian form" `Re[z] + I Im[z]`. But it can equally well be written in the "polar form" `Abs[z] Exp[I Arg[z]]`.

The option `TargetFunctions` in `ComplexExpand` allows you to specify how complex variables should be written. `TargetFunctions` can be set to a list of functions from the set {`Re`, `Im`, `Abs`, `Arg`, `Conjugate`, `Sign`}. `ComplexExpand` will try to give results in terms of whichever of these functions you request. The default is typically to give results in terms of `Re` and `Im`.

This gives an expansion in Cartesian form.	*In[4]:=* `ComplexExpand[Re[z^2], {z}]`
	Out[4]= $-Im[z]^2 + Re[z]^2$

Here is an expansion in polar form.	*In[5]:=* `ComplexExpand[Re[z^2], {z},` `            TargetFunctions -> {Abs, Arg}]`
	Out[5]= $Abs[z]^2 Cos[Arg[z]]^2 - Abs[z]^2 Sin[Arg[z]]^2$

Here is another form of expansion.	*In[6]:=* `ComplexExpand[Re[z^2], {z}, TargetFunctions -> Conjugate]`
	Out[6]= $\dfrac{z^2}{2} + \dfrac{Conjugate[z]^2}{2}$

■ 3.3.9 Simplification

`Simplify[`*expr*`]`	try various algebraic and trigonometric transformations to simplify an expression
`FullSimplify[`*expr*`]`	try a much wider range of transformations

Simplifying expressions.

Mathematica does not automatically simplify an algebraic expression like this.	*In[1]:=* `(1 - x)/(1 - x^2)`
	Out[1]= $\dfrac{1 - x}{1 - x^2}$

Simplify performs the simplification.	*In[2]:=* **Simplify[%]**
	Out[2]= $\dfrac{1}{1+x}$
Simplify performs standard algebraic and trigonometric simplifications.	*In[3]:=* **Simplify[Sin[x]^2 + Cos[x]^2]**
	Out[3]= 1
It does not, however, do more sophisticated transformations that involve, for example, special functions.	*In[4]:=* **Simplify[Gamma[1+n]/n]**
	Out[4]= $\dfrac{\text{Gamma}[1+n]}{n}$
FullSimplify does perform such transformations.	*In[5]:=* **FullSimplify[%]**
	Out[5]= Gamma[n]

FullSimplify[*expr*, ExcludedForms -> *pattern*]
             try to simplify *expr*, without touching subexpressions that match *pattern*

Controlling simplification.

Here is an expression involving trigonometric functions and square roots.	*In[6]:=* **t = (1 - Sin[x]^2) Sqrt[Expand[(1 + Sqrt[2])^20]]**
	Out[6]= $\sqrt{22619537 + 15994428\sqrt{2}}\ \left(1 - \text{Sin}[x]^2\right)$
By default, FullSimplify will try to simplify everything.	*In[7]:=* **FullSimplify[t]**
	Out[7]= $\left(3363 + 2378\sqrt{2}\right)\text{Cos}[x]^2$
This makes FullSimplify avoid simplifying the square roots.	*In[8]:=* **FullSimplify[t, ExcludedForms->Sqrt[_]]**
	Out[8]= $\sqrt{22619537 + 15994428\sqrt{2}}\ \text{Cos}[x]^2$

FullSimplify[*expr*, TimeConstraint->*t*]
             try to simplify *expr*, working for at most *t* seconds on each transformation

FullSimplify[*expr*, TransformationFunctions -> {f_1, f_2, ... }]
             use only the functions f_i in trying to transform parts of *expr*

FullSimplify[*expr*, TransformationFunctions -> {Automatic, f_1, f_2, ... }]
             use built-in transformations as well as the f_i

Simplify[*expr*, ComplexityFunction->*c*] and **FullSimplify[*expr*, ComplexityFunction->*c*]**
             simplify using *c* to determine what form is considered simplest

Further control of simplification.

In both `Simplify` and `FullSimplify` there is always an issue of what counts as the "simplest" form of an expression. You can use the option `ComplexityFunction -> c` to provide a function to determine this. The function will be applied to each candidate form of the expression, and the one that gives the smallest numerical value will be considered simplest.

With its default definition of simplicity, `Simplify` leaves this unchanged.	`In[9]:= Simplify[4 Log[10]]`
	
	 `Out[9]= 4 Log[10]`

This now tries to minimize the number of elements in the expression.	`In[10]:= Simplify[4 Log[10], ComplexityFunction -> LeafCount]`
	
	 `Out[10]= Log[10000]`

■ 3.3.10 Using Assumptions

Mathematica normally makes as few assumptions as possible about the objects you ask it to manipulate. This means that the results it gives are as general as possible. But sometimes these results are considerably more complicated than they would be if more assumptions were made.

`Refine[`*expr*`, `*assum*`]`	refine *expr* using assumptions
`Simplify[`*expr*`, `*assum*`]`	simplify with assumptions
`FullSimplify[`*expr*`, `*assum*`]`	full simplify with assumptions
`FunctionExpand[`*expr*`, `*assum*`]`	function expand with assumptions

Doing operations with assumptions.

`Simplify` by default does essentially nothing with this expression.	`In[1]:= Simplify[1/Sqrt[x] - Sqrt[1/x]]` $Out[1]= -\sqrt{\dfrac{1}{x}} + \dfrac{1}{\sqrt{x}}$
The reason is that its value is quite different for different choices of *x*.	`In[2]:= % /. x -> {-3, -2, -1, 1, 2, 3}` $Out[2]= \left\{-\dfrac{2 \, \mathbb{i}}{\sqrt{3}}, -\mathbb{i} \sqrt{2}, -2 \, \mathbb{i}, 0, 0, 0\right\}$
With the assumption $x > 0$, `Simplify` can immediately reduce the expression to 0.	`In[3]:= Simplify[1/Sqrt[x] - Sqrt[1/x], x > 0]` `Out[3]= 0`
Without making assumptions about *x* and *y*, nothing can be done.	`In[4]:= FunctionExpand[Log[x y]]` `Out[4]= Log[x y]`
If *x* and *y* are both assumed positive, the log can be expanded.	`In[5]:= FunctionExpand[Log[x y], x > 0 && y > 0]` `Out[5]= Log[x] + Log[y]`

By applying `Simplify` and `FullSimplify` with appropriate assumptions to equations and inequalities you can in effect establish a vast range of theorems.

Without making assumptions about x the truth or falsity of this equation cannot be determined.	*In[6]:=* `Simplify[Abs[x] == x]` *Out[6]=* `x == Abs[x]`

Now `Simplify` can prove that the equation is true.	*In[7]:=* `Simplify[Abs[x] == x, x > 0]` *Out[7]=* `True`

This establishes the standard result that the arithmetic mean is larger than the geometric one.	*In[8]:=* `Simplify[(x + y)/2 >= Sqrt[x y], x >= 0 && y >= 0]` *Out[8]=* `True`

This proves that erf(x) lies in the range $(0, 1)$ for all positive arguments.	*In[9]:=* `FullSimplify[0 < Erf[x] < 1, x > 0]` *Out[9]=* `True`

`Simplify` and `FullSimplify` always try to find the simplest forms of expressions. Sometimes, however, you may just want *Mathematica* to follow its ordinary evaluation process, but with certain assumptions made. You can do this using `Refine`. The way it works is that `Refine[`*expr*`, `*assum*`]` performs the same transformations as *Mathematica* would perform automatically if the variables in *expr* were replaced by numerical expressions satisfying the assumptions *assum*.

There is no simpler form that `Simplify` can find.	*In[10]:=* `Simplify[Log[x], x < 0]` *Out[10]=* `Log[x]`

`Refine` just evaluates `Log[x]` as it would for any explicit negative number x.	*In[11]:=* `Refine[Log[x], x < 0]` *Out[11]=* `i π + Log[-x]`

An important class of assumptions are those which assert that some object is an element of a particular domain. You can set up such assumptions using $x \in dom$, where the $\in$ character can be entered as `:el:` or `\[Element]`.

$x \in dom$ or `Element[`x`, `dom`]`	assert that x is an element of the domain *dom*
$\{x_1, x_2, \dots \} \in dom$	assert that all the x_i are elements of the domain *dom*
$patt \in dom$	assert that any expression which matches *patt* is an element of the domain *dom*

Asserting that objects are elements of domains.

This confirms that π is an element of the domain of real numbers.	*In[12]:=* `Pi ∈ Reals` *Out[12]=* `True`

These numbers are all elements of the domain of algebraic numbers.	*In[13]:=* `{1, Sqrt[2], 3 + Sqrt[5]} ∈ Algebraics` *Out[13]=* `True`

Mathematica knows that π is not an algebraic number.

```
In[14]:= Pi ∈ Algebraics
Out[14]= False
```

Current mathematics has not established whether $e + \pi$ is an algebraic number or not.

```
In[15]:= E + Pi ∈ Algebraics
Out[15]= e + π ∈ Algebraics
```

This represents the assertion that the symbol x is an element of the domain of real numbers.

```
In[16]:= x ∈ Reals
Out[16]= x ∈ Reals
```

Complexes	the domain of complex numbers $\mathbb{C}$
Reals	the domain of real numbers $\mathbb{R}$
Algebraics	the domain of algebraic numbers $\mathbb{A}$
Rationals	the domain of rational numbers $\mathbb{Q}$
Integers	the domain of integers $\mathbb{Z}$
Primes	the domain of primes $\mathbb{P}$
Booleans	the domain of booleans (True and False) $\mathbb{B}$

Domains supported by *Mathematica*.

If n is assumed to be an integer, $\sin(n\pi)$ is zero.

```
In[17]:= Simplify[Sin[n Pi], n ∈ Integers]
Out[17]= 0
```

This establishes the theorem $\cosh(x) \geq 1$ if x is assumed to be a real number.

```
In[18]:= Simplify[Cosh[x] >= 1, x ∈ Reals]
Out[18]= True
```

If you say that a variable satisfies an inequality, *Mathematica* will automatically assume that it is real.

```
In[19]:= Simplify[x ∈ Reals, x > 0]
Out[19]= True
```

By using `Simplify`, `FullSimplify` and `FunctionExpand` with assumptions you can access many of *Mathematica*'s vast collection of mathematical facts.

This uses the periodicity of the tangent function.

```
In[20]:= Simplify[Tan[x + Pi k], k ∈ Integers]
Out[20]= Tan[x]
```

The assumption $k/2 \in$ Integers implies that k must be even.

```
In[21]:= Simplify[Tan[x + Pi k/2], k/2 ∈ Integers]
Out[21]= Tan[x]
```

Mathematica knows that $\log(x) < \exp(x)$ for positive x.

```
In[22]:= Simplify[Log[x] < Exp[x], x > 0]
Out[22]= True
```

FullSimplify accesses knowledge
about special functions.

```
In[23]:= FullSimplify[Im[BesselJ[0, x]], x ∈ Reals]
Out[23]= 0
```

Mathematica knows about discrete mathematics and number theory as well as continuous mathematics.

This uses Wilson's Theorem to simplify
the result.

```
In[24]:= FunctionExpand[Mod[(p - 1)!, p], p ∈ Primes]
Out[24]= -1 + p
```

This uses the multiplicative property of
the Euler phi function.

```
In[25]:= FunctionExpand[EulerPhi[m n], {m, n} ∈ Integers &&
                           GCD[m, n] == 1]

Out[25]= EulerPhi[m] EulerPhi[n]
```

In something like Simplify[*expr*, *assum*] or Refine[*expr*, *assum*] you explicitly give the assumptions you want to use. But sometimes you may want to specify one set of assumptions to use in a whole collection of operations. You can do this by using Assuming.

+	Assuming[*assum*, *expr*]	use assumptions *assum* in the evaluation of *expr*
+	$Assumptions	the default assumptions to use

Specifying assumptions with larger scopes.

This tells Simplify to use the default
assumption x > 0.

```
In[26]:= Assuming[x > 0, Simplify[Sqrt[x^2]]]
Out[26]= x
```

This combines the two assumptions
given.

```
In[27]:= Assuming[x > 0,
               Assuming[x ∈ Integers, Refine[Floor[Sqrt[x^2]]]]]
Out[27]= x
```

Functions like Simplify and Refine take the option Assumptions, which specifies what default assumptions they should use. By default, the setting for this option is Assumptions :> $Assumptions. The way Assuming then works is to assign a local value to $Assumptions, much as in Block.

In addition to Simplify and Refine, a number of other functions take Assumptions options, and thus can have assumptions specified for them by Assuming. Examples are FunctionExpand, Integrate, Limit, LaplaceTransform.

The assumption is automatically used
in Integrate.

```
In[28]:= Assuming[n > 0, 1 + Integrate[x^n, {x, 0, 1}]^2]
```
$$Out[28]= 1 + \frac{1}{(1 + n)^2}$$

3.4 Manipulating Equations and Inequalities

■ 3.4.1 The Representation of Equations and Solutions

Mathematica treats equations as logical statements. If you type in an equation like x^2 + 3x == 2, *Mathematica* interprets this as a logical statement which asserts that x^2 + 3x is equal to 2. If you have assigned an explicit value to x, say x = 4, then *Mathematica* can explicitly determine that the logical statement x^2 + 3x == 2 is False.

If you have not assigned any explicit value to x, however, *Mathematica* cannot work out whether x^2 + 3x == 2 is True or False. As a result, it leaves the equation in the symbolic form x^2 + 3x == 2.

You can manipulate symbolic equations in *Mathematica* in many ways. One common goal is to rearrange the equations so as to "solve" for a particular set of variables.

Here is a symbolic equation.	*In[1]:=* **x^2 + 3x == 2**
	Out[1]= $3x + x^2 == 2$

You can use the function Reduce to reduce the equation so as to give "solutions" for x. The result, like the original equation, can be viewed as a logical statement.	*In[2]:=* **Reduce[%, x]**
	Out[2]= $x == \frac{1}{2}\left(-3 - \sqrt{17}\right)$ || $x == \frac{1}{2}\left(-3 + \sqrt{17}\right)$

The quadratic equation x^2 + 3x == 2 can be thought of as an implicit statement about the value of x. As shown in the example above, you can use the function Reduce to get a more explicit statement about the value of x. The expression produced by Reduce has the form x == r_1 \|\| x == r_2. This expression is again a logical statement, which asserts that either x is equal to r_1, or x is equal to r_2. The values of x that are consistent with this statement are exactly the same as the ones that are consistent with the original quadratic equation. For many purposes, however, the form that Reduce gives is much more useful than the original equation.

You can combine and manipulate equations just like other logical statements. You can use logical connectives such as \|\| and && to specify alternative or simultaneous conditions. You can use functions like LogicalExpand, as well as FullSimplify, to simplify collections of equations.

For many purposes, you will find it convenient to manipulate equations simply as logical statements. Sometimes, however, you will actually want to use explicit solutions to equations in other calculations. In such cases, it is convenient to convert equations that are stated in the form *lhs* == *rhs* into transformation rules of the form *lhs* -> *rhs*. Once you have the solutions to an equation in the form of explicit transformation rules, you can substitute the solutions into expressions by using the /. operator.

Reduce produces a logical statement about the values of x corresponding to the roots of the quadratic equation.	*In[3]:=* **Reduce[x^2 + 3x == 2, x]**
	Out[3]= $x == \frac{1}{2}\left(-3 - \sqrt{17}\right)$ || $x == \frac{1}{2}\left(-3 + \sqrt{17}\right)$

ToRules converts the logical statement into an explicit list of transformation rules.

$In[4]:=$ **{ToRules[%]}**

$Out[4]=$ $\left\{\left\{x \to \frac{1}{2}\left(-3-\sqrt{17}\right)\right\}, \left\{x \to \frac{1}{2}\left(-3+\sqrt{17}\right)\right\}\right\}$

You can now use the transformation rules to substitute the solutions for x into expressions involving x.

$In[5]:=$ **x^2 + a x /. %**

$Out[5]=$ $\left\{\frac{1}{4}\left(-3-\sqrt{17}\right)^2 + \frac{1}{2}\left(-3-\sqrt{17}\right)a,\right.$

$\left.\frac{1}{4}\left(-3+\sqrt{17}\right)^2 + \frac{1}{2}\left(-3+\sqrt{17}\right)a\right\}$

The function Solve produces transformation rules for solutions directly.

$In[6]:=$ **Solve[x^2 + 3x == 2, x]**

$Out[6]=$ $\left\{\left\{x \to \frac{1}{2}\left(-3-\sqrt{17}\right)\right\}, \left\{x \to \frac{1}{2}\left(-3+\sqrt{17}\right)\right\}\right\}$

■ 3.4.2 Equations in One Variable

The main equations that Solve and related *Mathematica* functions deal with are *polynomial equations*.

It is easy to solve a linear equation in x.

$In[1]:=$ **Solve[a x + b == c , x]**

$Out[1]=$ $\left\{\left\{x \to \frac{-b+c}{a}\right\}\right\}$

One can also solve quadratic equations just by applying a simple formula.

$In[2]:=$ **Solve[x^2 + a x + 2 == 0 , x]**

$Out[2]=$ $\left\{\left\{x \to \frac{1}{2}\left(-a-\sqrt{-8+a^2}\right)\right\}, \left\{x \to \frac{1}{2}\left(-a+\sqrt{-8+a^2}\right)\right\}\right\}$

Mathematica can also find exact solutions to cubic equations. Here is the first solution to a comparatively simple cubic equation.

$In[3]:=$ **Solve[x^3 + 34 x + 1 == 0 , x] [[1]]**

$Out[3]=$ $\left\{x \to -34\left(\frac{2}{3\left(-9+\sqrt{471729}\right)}\right)^{1/3} + \right.$

$\left.\frac{\left(\frac{1}{2}\left(-9+\sqrt{471729}\right)\right)^{1/3}}{3^{2/3}}\right\}$

For cubic and quartic equations the results are often complicated, but for all equations with degrees up to four *Mathematica* is always able to give explicit formulas for the solutions.

An important feature of these formulas is that they involve only *radicals*: arithmetic combinations of square roots, cube roots and higher roots.

It is a fundamental mathematical fact, however, that for equations of degree five or higher, it is no longer possible in general to give explicit formulas for solutions in terms of radicals.

There are some specific equations for which this is still possible, but in the vast majority of cases it is not.

This constructs a degree six polynomial.

$In[4]:=$ **Expand[Product[x^2 - 2 i, {i, 3}]]**

$Out[4]=$ $-48 + 44 x^2 - 12 x^4 + x^6$

For a polynomial that factors in the way this one does, it is straightforward for Solve to find the roots.

In[5]:= **Solve[% == 0, x]**

Out[5]= $\{\{x \to -2\}, \{x \to 2\}, \{x \to -\sqrt{2}\},$
$\{x \to \sqrt{2}\}, \{x \to -\sqrt{6}\}, \{x \to \sqrt{6}\}\}$

This constructs a polynomial of degree eight.

In[6]:= **Expand[x^2 - 2 /. x -> x^2 - 3 /. x -> x^2 - 5]**

Out[6]= $482 - 440\,x^2 + 144\,x^4 - 20\,x^6 + x^8$

The polynomial does not factor, but it can be decomposed into nested polynomials, so Solve can again find explicit formulas for the roots.

In[7]:= **Solve[% == 0, x]**

Out[7]= $\{\{x \to -\sqrt{5 - \sqrt{3 - \sqrt{2}}}\}, \{x \to \sqrt{5 - \sqrt{3 - \sqrt{2}}}\},$

$\{x \to -\sqrt{5 + \sqrt{3 - \sqrt{2}}}\}, \{x \to \sqrt{5 + \sqrt{3 - \sqrt{2}}}\},$

$\{x \to -\sqrt{5 - \sqrt{3 + \sqrt{2}}}\}, \{x \to \sqrt{5 - \sqrt{3 + \sqrt{2}}}\},$

$\{x \to -\sqrt{5 + \sqrt{3 + \sqrt{2}}}\}, \{x \to \sqrt{5 + \sqrt{3 + \sqrt{2}}}\}\}$

Root[*f*, *k*]	the kth root of the equation *f*[*x*] == 0

Implicit representation for roots.

No explicit formulas for the solution to this equation can be given in terms of radicals, so *Mathematica* uses an implicit symbolic representation.

In[8]:= **Solve[x^5 - x + 11 == 0, x]**

Out[8]= $\{\{x \to \text{Root}[11 - \#1 + \#1^5 \,\&, 1]\},$
$\{x \to \text{Root}[11 - \#1 + \#1^5 \,\&, 2]\},$
$\{x \to \text{Root}[11 - \#1 + \#1^5 \,\&, 3]\},$
$\{x \to \text{Root}[11 - \#1 + \#1^5 \,\&, 4]\},$
$\{x \to \text{Root}[11 - \#1 + \#1^5 \,\&, 5]\}\}$

This finds a numerical approximation to each root.

In[9]:= **N[%]**

Out[9]= $\{\{x \to -1.66149\}, \{x \to -0.46194 - 1.565\,i\},$
$\{x \to -0.46194 + 1.565\,i\}, \{x \to 1.29268 - 0.903032\,i\},$
$\{x \to 1.29268 + 0.903032\,i\}\}$

If what you want in the end is a numerical solution, it is usually much faster to use NSolve from the outset.

In[10]:= **NSolve[x^5 - x + 11 == 0, x]**

Out[10]= $\{\{x \to -1.66149\}, \{x \to -0.46194 - 1.565\,i\},$
$\{x \to -0.46194 + 1.565\,i\}, \{x \to 1.29268 - 0.903032\,i\},$
$\{x \to 1.29268 + 0.903032\,i\}\}$

Root objects provide an exact, though implicit, representation for the roots of a polynomial. You can work with them much as you would work with Sqrt[2] or any other expression that represents an exact numerical quantity.

Here is the Root object representing the first root of the polynomial discussed above.

$In[11]:=$ **r = Root[#^5 - # + 11 &, 1]**

$Out[11]=$ $\text{Root}\left[11 - \#1 + \#1^5 \,\&,\, 1\right]$

This is a numerical approximation to its value.

$In[12]:=$ **N[r]**

$Out[12]=$ -1.66149

Round does an exact computation to find the closest integer to the root.

$In[13]:=$ **Round[r]**

$Out[13]=$ -2

If you substitute the root into the original polynomial, and then simplify the result, you get zero.

$In[14]:=$ **FullSimplify[x^5 - x + 11 /. x -> r]**

$Out[14]=$ 0

This finds the product of all the roots of the original polynomial.

$In[15]:=$ **FullSimplify[**
             Product[Root[11 - # + #^5 &, k], {k, 5}]]

$Out[15]=$ -11

The complex conjugate of the third root is the second root.

$In[16]:=$ **Conjugate[Root[11 - # + #^5 &, 3]]**

$Out[16]=$ $\text{Root}\left[11 - \#1 + \#1^5 \,\&,\, 2\right]$

If the only symbolic parameter that exists in an equation is the variable that you are solving for, then all the solutions to the equation will just be numbers. But if there are other symbolic parameters in the equation, then the solutions will typically be functions of these parameters.

The solution to this equation can again be represented by Root objects, but now each Root object involves the parameter a.

$In[17]:=$ **Solve[x^5 + x + a == 0, x]**

$Out[17]=$ $\left\{\left\{x \to \text{Root}\left[a + \#1 + \#1^5 \,\&,\, 1\right]\right\},\right.$
          $\left\{x \to \text{Root}\left[a + \#1 + \#1^5 \,\&,\, 2\right]\right\},$
          $\left\{x \to \text{Root}\left[a + \#1 + \#1^5 \,\&,\, 3\right]\right\},$
          $\left\{x \to \text{Root}\left[a + \#1 + \#1^5 \,\&,\, 4\right]\right\},$
          $\left.\left\{x \to \text{Root}\left[a + \#1 + \#1^5 \,\&,\, 5\right]\right\}\right\}$

When a is replaced with 1, the Root objects can be simplified, and some are given as explicit radicals.

$In[18]:=$ **Simplify[% /. a -> 1]**

$Out[18]=$ $\left\{\left\{x \to \text{Root}\left[1 - \#1^2 + \#1^3 \,\&,\, 1\right]\right\},\, \left\{x \to -\frac{1}{2}\, i\, \left(-i + \sqrt{3}\,\right)\right\},\right.$

$\left\{x \to \frac{1}{2}\, i\, \left(i + \sqrt{3}\,\right)\right\},\, \left\{x \to \text{Root}\left[1 - \#1^2 + \#1^3 \,\&,\, 2\right]\right\},$

$\left.\left\{x \to \text{Root}\left[1 - \#1^2 + \#1^3 \,\&,\, 3\right]\right\}\right\}$

This shows the behavior of the first root as a function of a.

$In[19]:=$ **Plot[Root[#^5 + # + a &, 1], {a, -2, 2}]**

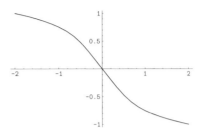

This finds the derivative of the first root with respect to a.

$In[20]:=$ **D[Root[#^5 + # + a &, 1], a]**

$$Out[20]= -\frac{1}{1 + 5\,\text{Root}\left[a + \#1 + \#1^5\,\&,\,1\right]^4}$$

If you give `Solve` any n^{th}-degree polynomial equation, then it will always return exactly n solutions, although some of these may be represented by `Root` objects. If there are degenerate solutions, then the number of times that each particular solution appears will be equal to its multiplicity.

Solve gives two identical solutions to this equation.

$In[21]:=$ **Solve[(x - 1)^2 == 0, x]**

$Out[21]=$ $\{\{x \to 1\},\ \{x \to 1\}\}$

Here are the first four solutions to a tenth degree equation. The solutions come in pairs.

$In[22]:=$ **Take[Solve[(x^5 - x + 11)^2 == 0, x], 4]**

$$Out[22]= \left\{\left\{x \to \text{Root}\left[11 - \#1 + \#1^5\,\&,\,1\right]\right\},\right.$$
$$\left\{x \to \text{Root}\left[11 - \#1 + \#1^5\,\&,\,1\right]\right\},$$
$$\left\{x \to \text{Root}\left[11 - \#1 + \#1^5\,\&,\,2\right]\right\},$$
$$\left.\left\{x \to \text{Root}\left[11 - \#1 + \#1^5\,\&,\,2\right]\right\}\right\}$$

Mathematica also knows how to solve equations which are not explicitly in the form of polynomials.

Here is an equation involving square roots.

$In[23]:=$ **Solve[Sqrt[x] + Sqrt[1 + x] == a, x]**

$$Out[23]= \left\{\left\{x \to \frac{1 - 2\,a^2 + a^4}{4\,a^2}\right\}\right\}$$

And here is one involving logarithms.

$In[24]:=$ **Solve[Log[x] + Log[1 - x] == a, x]**

$$Out[24]= \left\{\left\{x \to \frac{1}{2}\left(1 - \sqrt{1 - 4\,e^a}\right)\right\},\ \left\{x \to \frac{1}{2}\left(1 + \sqrt{1 - 4\,e^a}\right)\right\}\right\}$$

So long as it can reduce an equation to some kind of polynomial form, *Mathematica* will always be able to represent its solution in terms of `Root` objects. However, with more general equations, involving say transcendental functions, there is no systematic way to use `Root` objects, or even necessarily to find numerical approximations.

Here is a simple transcendental equation for x.

$In[25]:=$ **Solve[ArcSin[x] == a, x]**

$Out[25]=$ $\{\{x \to \text{Sin}[a]\}\}$

There is no solution to this equation in terms of standard functions.

```
In[26]:= Solve[Cos[x] == x, x]

Solve::tdep:
    The equations appear to involve the variables to be
      solved for in an essentially non-algebraic way.

Out[26]= Solve[Cos[x] == x, x]
```

Mathematica can nevertheless find a numerical solution even in this case.

```
In[27]:= FindRoot[Cos[x] == x, {x, 0}]

Out[27]= {x → 0.739085}
```

Polynomial equations in one variable only ever have a finite number of solutions. But transcendental equations often have an infinite number. Typically the reason for this is that functions like `Sin` in effect have infinitely many possible inverses. With the default option setting `InverseFunctions->True`, `Solve` will nevertheless assume that there is a definite inverse for any such function. `Solve` may then be able to return particular solutions in terms of this inverse function.

Mathematica returns a particular solution in terms of `ArcSin`, but prints a warning indicating that other solutions are lost.

```
In[28]:= Solve[Sin[x] == a, x]

Solve::ifun:
    Inverse functions are being used by Solve, so some
      solutions may not be found; use Reduce for complete
      solution information.

Out[28]= {{x → ArcSin[a]}}
```

Here the answer comes out in terms of `ProductLog`.

```
In[29]:= Solve[Exp[x] + x + 1 == 0, x]

InverseFunction::ifun:
    Inverse functions are being used. Values may be lost
      for multivalued inverses.

Solve::ifun:
    Inverse functions are being used by Solve, so some
      solutions may not be found; use Reduce for complete
      solution information.
```

$$Out[29]= \left\{\left\{x \to -1 - \text{ProductLog}\left[\frac{1}{e}\right]\right\}\right\}$$

If you ask `Solve` to solve an equation involving an arbitrary function like `f`, it will by default try to construct a formal solution in terms of inverse functions.

`Solve` by default uses a formal inverse for the function `f`.

```
In[30]:= Solve[f[x] == a, x]

InverseFunction::ifun:
    Inverse functions are being used. Values may be lost
      for multivalued inverses.
```

$$Out[30]= \{\{x \to f^{(-1)}[a]\}\}$$

This is the structure of the inverse function.

```
In[31]:= InputForm[%]

Out[31]//InputForm= {{x -> InverseFunction[f, 1, 1][a]}}
```

InverseFunction[*f*]	the inverse function of *f*
InverseFunction[*f*, *k*, *n*]	the inverse function of the *n*-argument function *f* with respect to its kth argument

Inverse functions.

This returns an explicit inverse function.

In[32]:= **InverseFunction[Tan]**

Out[32]= ArcTan

Mathematica can do formal operations on inverse functions.

In[33]:= **D[InverseFunction[f][x^2], x]**

$$Out[33]= \frac{2\,x}{f'\,[f^{(-1)}\,[x^2]]}$$

While Solve can only give specific solutions to an equation, Reduce can give a representation of a whole solution set. For transcendental equations, it often ends up introducing new parameters, say with values ranging over all possible integers.

This is a complete representation of the solution set.

In[34]:= **Reduce[Sin[x] == a, x]**

Out[34]= C[1] $\in$ Integers && (x == π - ArcSin[a] + 2 π C[1] ||
                x == ArcSin[a] + 2 π C[1])

Here again is a representation of the general solution.

In[35]:= **Reduce[Exp[x] + x + 1 == 0, x]**

$$Out[35]= C[1] \in \text{Integers \&\& } x == -1 - \text{ProductLog}\left[C[1],\,\frac{1}{e}\right]$$

As discussed at more length in Section 3.4.9, Reduce allows you to restrict the domains of variables. Sometimes this will let you generate definite solutions to transcendental equations—or show that they do not exist.

With the domain of x restricted, this yields definite solutions.

In[36]:= **Reduce[{Sin[x] == 1/2, Abs[x] < 4}, x]**

$$Out[36]= x == -\frac{7\,\pi}{6} \,||\, x == \frac{\pi}{6} \,||\, x == \frac{5\,\pi}{6}$$

With x constrained to be real, only one solution is possible.

In[37]:= **Reduce[Exp[x] + x + 1 == 0, x, Reals]**

$$Out[37]= x == -1 - \text{ProductLog}\left[\frac{1}{e}\right]$$

Reduce knows there can be no solution here.

In[38]:= **Reduce[{Sin[x] == x, x > 1}, x]**

Out[38]= False

■ 3.4.3 Advanced Topic: Algebraic Numbers

`Root[f, k]`	the kth root of the polynomial equation $f[x] == 0$

The representation of algebraic numbers.

When you enter a Root object, the polynomial that appears in it is automatically reduced to a minimal form.

$In[1]:=$ `Root[24 - 2 # + 4 #^5 &, 1]`

$Out[1]=$ $\text{Root}\left[12 - \#1 + 2\,\#1^5 \,\&,\, 1\right]$

This extracts the pure function which represents the polynomial, and applies it to x.

$In[2]:=$ `First[%][x]`

$Out[2]=$ $12 - x + 2\,x^5$

Root objects are the way that *Mathematica* represents *algebraic numbers*. Algebraic numbers have the property that when you perform algebraic operations on them, you always get a single algebraic number as the result.

Here is the square root of an algebraic number.

$In[3]:=$ `Sqrt[Root[2 - # + #^5 &, 1]]`

$Out[3]=$ $\sqrt{\text{Root}\left[2 - \#1 + \#1^5 \,\&,\, 1\right]}$

RootReduce reduces this to a single Root object.

$In[4]:=$ `RootReduce[%]`

$Out[4]=$ $\text{Root}\left[2 - \#1^2 + \#1^{10} \,\&,\, 6\right]$

Here is a more complicated expression involving an algebraic number.

$In[5]:=$ `Sqrt[2] + Root[2 - # + #^5 &, 1]^2`

$Out[5]=$ $\sqrt{2} + \text{Root}\left[2 - \#1 + \#1^5 \,\&,\, 1\right]^2$

Again this can be reduced to a single Root object, albeit a fairly complicated one.

$In[6]:=$ `RootReduce[%]`

$Out[6]=$ $\text{Root}\big[14 - 72\,\#1 + 25\,\#1^2 - 144\,\#1^3 - $
$\qquad 88\,\#1^4 - 8\,\#1^5 + 62\,\#1^6 - 14\,\#1^8 + \#1^{10} \,\&,\, 2\big]$

`RootReduce[`*expr*`]`	attempt to reduce *expr* to a single Root object
`ToRadicals[`*expr*`]`	attempt to transform Root objects to explicit radicals

Operations on algebraic numbers.

In this simple case the Root object is automatically expressed in terms of radicals.

$In[7]:=$ `Root[#^2 - # - 1 &, 1]`

$Out[7]=$ $\dfrac{1}{2}\left(1 - \sqrt{5}\right)$

When cubic polynomials are involved, Root objects are not automatically expressed in terms of radicals.

$In[8]:=$ `Root[#^3 - 2 &, 1]`

$Out[8]=$ $\text{Root}\left[-2 + \#1^3 \,\&,\, 1\right]$

ToRadicals attempts to express all Root objects in terms of radicals.	*In[9]:=* **ToRadicals[%]**
	Out[9]= $2^{1/3}$

If `Solve` and `ToRadicals` do not succeed in expressing the solution to a particular polynomial equation in terms of radicals, then it is a good guess that this fundamentally cannot be done. However, you should realize that there are some special cases in which a reduction to radicals is in principle possible, but *Mathematica* cannot find it. The simplest example is the equation $x^5 + 20x + 32 = 0$, but here the solution in terms of radicals is very complicated. The equation $x^6 - 9x^4 - 4x^3 + 27x^2 - 36x - 23$ is another example, where now $x = 2^{\frac{1}{3}} + 3^{\frac{1}{2}}$ is a solution.

This gives a Root object involving a degree six polynomial.	*In[10]:=* **RootReduce[2^(1/3) + Sqrt[3]]**
	Out[10]= $\text{Root}\left[-23 - 36\,\#1 + 27\,\#1^2 - 4\,\#1^3 - 9\,\#1^4 + \#1^6 \,\&,\, 2\right]$

Even though a simple form in terms of radicals does exist, ToRadicals does not find it.	*In[11]:=* **ToRadicals[%]**
	Out[11]= $\text{Root}\left[-23 - 36\,\#1 + 27\,\#1^2 - 4\,\#1^3 - 9\,\#1^4 + \#1^6 \,\&,\, 2\right]$

Beyond degree four, most polynomials do not have roots that can be expressed at all in terms of radicals. However, for degree five it turns out that the roots can always be expressed in terms of elliptic or hypergeometric functions. The results, however, are typically much too complicated to be useful in practice.

RootSum[*f*, *form*]	the sum of *form*[*x*] for all *x* satisfying the polynomial equation *f*[*x*] == 0
Normal[*expr*]	the form of *expr* with RootSum replaced by explicit sums of Root objects

Sums of roots.

This computes the sum of the reciprocals of the roots of $1 + 2x + x^5$.	*In[12]:=* **RootSum[(1 + 2 # + #^5)&, (1/#)&]**
	Out[12]= -2

Now no explicit result can be given in terms of radicals.	*In[13]:=* **RootSum[(1 + 2 # + #^5)&, (# Log[1 + #])&]**
	Out[13]= $\text{RootSum}\left[1 + 2\,\#1 + \#1^5 \,\&,\, \text{Log}[1 + \#1]\,\#1\,\&\right]$

This expands the RootSum into a explicit sum involving Root objects.

$In[14]:=$ **Normal[%]**

$Out[14]=$ $\text{Log}\left[1 + \text{Root}\left[1 + 2\,\#1 + \#1^5 \,\&,\, 1\right]\right]$
$\qquad \text{Root}\left[1 + 2\,\#1 + \#1^5 \,\&,\, 1\right] +$
$\qquad \text{Log}\left[1 + \text{Root}\left[1 + 2\,\#1 + \#1^5 \,\&,\, 2\right]\right]$
$\qquad \text{Root}\left[1 + 2\,\#1 + \#1^5 \,\&,\, 2\right] +$
$\qquad \text{Log}\left[1 + \text{Root}\left[1 + 2\,\#1 + \#1^5 \,\&,\, 3\right]\right]$
$\qquad \text{Root}\left[1 + 2\,\#1 + \#1^5 \,\&,\, 3\right] +$
$\qquad \text{Log}\left[1 + \text{Root}\left[1 + 2\,\#1 + \#1^5 \,\&,\, 4\right]\right]$
$\qquad \text{Root}\left[1 + 2\,\#1 + \#1^5 \,\&,\, 4\right] +$
$\qquad \text{Log}\left[1 + \text{Root}\left[1 + 2\,\#1 + \#1^5 \,\&,\, 5\right]\right]$
$\qquad \text{Root}\left[1 + 2\,\#1 + \#1^5 \,\&,\, 5\right]$

■ 3.4.4 Simultaneous Equations

You can give Solve a list of simultaneous equations to solve. Solve can find explicit solutions for a large class of simultaneous polynomial equations.

Here is a simple linear equation with two unknowns.

$In[1]:=$ **Solve[{ a x + b y == 1, x - y == 2 } , {x, y}]**

$Out[1]=$ $\left\{\left\{x \to -\dfrac{-1 - 2\,b}{a + b},\, y \to -\dfrac{-1 + 2\,a}{a + b}\right\}\right\}$

Here is a more complicated example. The result is a list of solutions, with each solution consisting of a list of transformation rules for the variables.

$In[2]:=$ **Solve[{x^2 + y^2 == 1, x + y == a}, {x, y}]**

$Out[2]=$ $\left\{\left\{x \to \dfrac{1}{2}\left(a - \sqrt{2 - a^2}\right),\, y \to \dfrac{1}{2}\left(a + \sqrt{2 - a^2}\right)\right\},\right.$
$\qquad \left.\left\{x \to \dfrac{a}{2} + \dfrac{\sqrt{2 - a^2}}{2},\, y \to \dfrac{1}{2}\left(a - \sqrt{2 - a^2}\right)\right\}\right\}$

You can use the list of solutions with the /. operator.

$In[3]:=$ **x^3 + y^4 /. % /. a -> 0.7**

$Out[3]=$ $\{0.846577, 0.901873\}$

Even when Solve cannot find explicit solutions, it often can "unwind" simultaneous equations to produce a symbolic result in terms of Root objects.

$In[4]:=$ **First[Solve[{x^2 + y^3 == x y, x + y + x y == 1},**
$\qquad\qquad$ **{x, y}]]**

$Out[4]=$ $\left\{x \to \right.$
$\qquad \dfrac{1}{2}\left(1 - \text{Root}\left[1 - 3\,\#1 + \#1^2 + 2\,\#1^3 + 2\,\#1^4 + \#1^5 \,\&,\, 1\right]^2 - \right.$
$\qquad\quad \text{Root}\left[1 - 3\,\#1 + \#1^2 + 2\,\#1^3 + 2\,\#1^4 + \#1^5 \,\&,\, 1\right]^3 -$
$\qquad\quad \left.\text{Root}\left[1 - 3\,\#1 + \#1^2 + 2\,\#1^3 + 2\,\#1^4 + \#1^5 \,\&,\, 1\right]^4\right),$
$\qquad \left.y \to \text{Root}\left[1 - 3\,\#1 + \#1^2 + 2\,\#1^3 + 2\,\#1^4 + \#1^5 \,\&,\, 1\right]\right\}$

You can then use N to get a numerical result.

$In[5]:=$ **N[%]**

$Out[5]=$ $\{x \to -3.4875,\, y \to -1.80402\}$

The variables that you use in Solve do not need to be single symbols. Often when you set up large collections of simultaneous equations, you will want to use expressions like $a[i]$ as variables.

Here is a list of three equations for the $a[i]$.

```
In[6]:= Table[ 2 a[i] + a[i-1] == a[i+1], {i, 3} ]
Out[6]= {a[0] + 2 a[1] == a[2],
         a[1] + 2 a[2] == a[3], a[2] + 2 a[3] == a[4]}
```

This solves for some of the $a[i]$.

```
In[7]:= Solve[ % , {a[1], a[2], a[3]} ]
```

$$Out[7]= \left\{\left\{a[1] \to -\frac{1}{12}\,(5\,a[0] - a[4]),\right.\right.$$
$$a[2] \to -\frac{1}{6}\,(-a[0] - a[4]),$$
$$\left.\left.a[3] \to -\frac{1}{12}\,(a[0] - 5\,a[4])\right\}\right\}$$

Solve[*eqns*, {x_1, x_2, ... }]	solve *eqns* for the specific objects x_i
Solve[*eqns*]	try to solve *eqns* for all the objects that appear in them

Solving simultaneous equations.

If you do not explicitly specify objects to solve for, Solve will try to solve for all the variables.

```
In[8]:= Solve[ { x + y == 1, x - 3 y == 2 } ]
```

$$Out[8]= \left\{\left\{x \to \frac{5}{4}, y \to -\frac{1}{4}\right\}\right\}$$

- Solve[{*lhs*$_1$==*rhs*$_1$, *lhs*$_2$==*rhs*$_2$, ... }, *vars*]
- Solve[*lhs*$_1$==*rhs*$_1$ && *lhs*$_2$==*rhs*$_2$ && ... , *vars*]
- Solve[{*lhs*$_1$, *lhs*$_2$, ... } == {*rhs*$_1$, *rhs*$_2$, ... }, *vars*]

Ways to present simultaneous equations to Solve.

If you construct simultaneous equations from matrices, you typically get equations between lists of expressions.

```
In[9]:= {{3,1},{2,-5}}.{x,y}=={7,8}
Out[9]= {3 x + y, 2 x - 5 y} == {7, 8}
```

Solve converts equations involving lists to lists of equations.

```
In[10]:= Solve[%, {x, y}]
```

$$Out[10]= \left\{\left\{x \to \frac{43}{17}, y \to -\frac{10}{17}\right\}\right\}$$

You can use LogicalExpand to do the conversion explicitly.

```
In[11]:= LogicalExpand[%%]
Out[11]= 2 x - 5 y == 8 && 3 x + y == 7
```

In some kinds of computations, it is convenient to work with arrays of coefficients instead of explicit equations. You can construct such arrays from equations by using CoefficientArrays.

■ 3.4.5 Generic and Non-Generic Solutions

If you have an equation like 2 x == 0, it is perfectly clear that the only possible solution is x -> 0. However, if you have an equation like a x == 0, things are not so clear. If a is not equal to zero, then x -> 0 is again the only solution. However, if a is in fact equal to zero, then *any* value of x is a solution. You can see this by using Reduce.

Solve implicitly assumes that the parameter a does not have the special value 0.	*In[1]:=* **Solve[a x == 0 , x]** *Out[1]=* {{x → 0}}
Reduce, on the other hand, gives you all the possibilities, without assuming anything about the value of a.	*In[2]:=* **Reduce[a x == 0 , x]** *Out[2]=* a == 0 || x == 0

A basic difference between Reduce and Solve is that Reduce gives *all* the possible solutions to a set of equations, while Solve gives only the *generic* ones. Solutions are considered "generic" if they involve conditions only on the variables that you explicitly solve for, and not on other parameters in the equations. Reduce and Solve also differ in that Reduce always returns combinations of equations, while Solve gives results in the form of transformation rules.

Solve[*eqns*, *vars*]	find generic solutions to equations
Reduce[*eqns*, *vars*]	reduce equations, maintaining all solutions

Solving equations.

This is the solution to an arbitrary linear equation given by Solve.	*In[3]:=* **Solve[a x + b == 0, x]** *Out[3]=* $\left\{\left\{x \to -\dfrac{b}{a}\right\}\right\}$
Reduce gives the full version, which includes the possibility a==b==0. In reading the output, note that && has higher precedence than ||.	*In[4]:=* **Reduce[a x + b == 0, x]** *Out[4]=* b == 0 && a == 0 || a ≠ 0 && x == $-\dfrac{b}{a}$
Here is the full solution to a general quadratic equation. There are three alternatives. If a is non-zero, then there are two solutions for x, given by the standard quadratic formula. If a is zero, however, the equation reduces to a linear one. Finally, if a, b and c are all zero, there is no restriction on x.	*In[5]:=* **Reduce[a x^2 + b x + c == 0, x]** *Out[5]=* a ≠ 0 && $\left(x == \dfrac{-b - \sqrt{b^2 - 4\,a\,c}}{2\,a} \;\middle|\middle|\; x == \dfrac{-b + \sqrt{b^2 - 4\,a\,c}}{2\,a}\right) \;\middle|\middle|$ a == 0 && b ≠ 0 && x == $-\dfrac{c}{b}$ || c == 0 && b == 0 && a == 0

When you have several simultaneous equations, Reduce can show you under what conditions the equations have solutions. Solve shows you whether there are any generic solutions.

This shows there can never be any solution to these equations.	*In[6]:=* **Reduce[{x == 1, x == 2}, x]** *Out[6]=* False
There is a solution to these equations, but only when a has the special value 1.	*In[7]:=* **Reduce[{x == 1, x == a}, x]** *Out[7]=* a == 1 && x == 1
The solution is not generic, and is rejected by Solve.	*In[8]:=* **Solve[{x == 1, x == a}, x]** *Out[8]=* {}
But if a is constrained to have value 1, then Solve again returns a solution.	*In[9]:=* **Solve[{x == 1, x == a, a == 1}, x]** *Out[9]=* {{x → 1}}
This equation is true for any value of x.	*In[10]:=* **Reduce[x == x , x]** *Out[10]=* True
This is the kind of result Solve returns when you give an equation that is always true.	*In[11]:=* **Solve[x == x , x]** *Out[11]=* {{}}

When you work with systems of linear equations, you can use Solve to get generic solutions, and Reduce to find out for what values of parameters solutions exist.

Here is a matrix whose i,j^{th} element is $i + j$.	*In[12]:=* **m = Table[i + j, {i, 3}, {j, 3}]** *Out[12]=* {{2, 3, 4}, {3, 4, 5}, {4, 5, 6}}
The matrix has determinant zero.	*In[13]:=* **Det[m]** *Out[13]=* 0
This makes a set of three simultaneous equations.	*In[14]:=* **eqn = m . {x, y, z} == {a, b, c}** *Out[14]=* {2 x + 3 y + 4 z, 3 x + 4 y + 5 z, 4 x + 5 y + 6 z} == {a, b, c}
Solve reports that there are no generic solutions.	*In[15]:=* **Solve[eqn, {x, y, z}]** *Out[15]=* {}
Reduce, however, shows that there *would* be a solution if the parameters satisfied the special condition a == 2b - c.	*In[16]:=* **Reduce[eqn, {x, y, z}]** *Out[16]=* a == 2 b - c && y == -6 b + 5 c - 2 x && z == 5 b - 4 c + x

For nonlinear equations, the conditions for the existence of solutions can be much more complicated.

Here is a very simple pair of nonlinear equations.	*In[17]:=* **eqn = {x y == a, x^2 y^2 == b}** *Out[17]=* {x y == a, $x^2 y^2$ == b}
Solve shows that the equations have no generic solutions.	*In[18]:=* **Solve[eqn, {x, y}]** *Out[18]=* {}

Reduce gives the complete conditions for a solution to exist.

$In[19]:=$ **Reduce[eqn, {x, y}]**

$Out[19]=$ $b == 0$ && $a == 0$ && $x == 0$ ||

$$\left(a == -\sqrt{b} \ || \ a == \sqrt{b}\right) \ \&\& \ x \neq 0 \ \&\& \ y == \frac{a}{x}$$

■ 3.4.6 Eliminating Variables

When you write down a set of simultaneous equations in *Mathematica*, you are specifying a collection of constraints between variables. When you use `Solve`, you are finding values for some of the variables in terms of others, subject to the constraints represented by the equations.

`Solve[`*eqns*`, `*vars*`, `*elims*`]`	find solutions for *vars*, eliminating the variables *elims*
`Eliminate[`*eqns*`, `*elims*`]`	rearrange equations to eliminate the variables *elims*

Eliminating variables.

Here are two equations involving x, y and the "parameters" a and b.

$In[1]:=$ **eqn = {x + y == 6a + 3b, y == 9a + 2 x}**

$Out[1]=$ $\{x + y == 6\,a + 3\,b, \ y == 9\,a + 2\,x\}$

If you solve for both x and y, you get results in terms of a and b.

$In[2]:=$ **Solve[eqn, {x, y}]**

$Out[2]=$ $\{\{x \rightarrow -a + b, \ y \rightarrow 7\,a + 2\,b\}\}$

Similarly, if you solve for x and a, you get results in terms of y and b.

$In[3]:=$ **Solve[eqn, {x, a}]**

$Out[3]=$ $\left\{\left\{x \rightarrow -\frac{1}{7}\,(-9\,b + y), \ a \rightarrow -\frac{1}{7}\,(2\,b - y)\right\}\right\}$

If you only want to solve for x, however, you have to specify whether you want to eliminate y or a or b. This eliminates y, and so gives the result in terms of a and b.

$In[4]:=$ **Solve[eqn, x, y]**

$Out[4]=$ $\{\{x \rightarrow -a + b\}\}$

If you eliminate a, then you get a result in terms of y and b.

$In[5]:=$ **Solve[eqn, x, a]**

$Out[5]=$ $\left\{\left\{x \rightarrow -\frac{1}{7}\,(-9\,b + y)\right\}\right\}$

In some cases, you may want to construct explicitly equations in which variables have been eliminated. You can do this using `Eliminate`.

This combines the two equations in the list eqn, by eliminating the variable a.

$In[6]:=$ **Eliminate[eqn, a]**

$Out[6]=$ $9\,b - y == 7\,x$

This is what you get if you eliminate y instead of a.

$In[7]:=$ **Eliminate[eqn, y]**

$Out[7]=$ $b - x == a$

As a more sophisticated example of Eliminate, consider the problem of writing $x^5 + y^5$ in terms of the "symmetric polynomials" $x + y$ and xy.

To solve the problem, we simply have to write f in terms of a and b, eliminating the original variables x and y.

$In[8]:=$ **Eliminate[{f == x^5 + y^5, a == x + y, b == x y},**
$\qquad\qquad$ **{x, y}]**

$Out[8]=$ $f == a^5 - 5 a^3 b + 5 a b^2$

In dealing with sets of equations, it is common to consider some of the objects that appear as true "variables", and others as "parameters". In some cases, you may need to know for what values of parameters a particular relation between the variables is *always* satisfied.

SolveAlways[*eqns*, *vars*]	solve for the values of parameters for which the *eqns* are satisfied for all values of the *vars*

Solving for parameters that make relations always true.

This finds the values of parameters that make the equation hold for all x.

$In[9]:=$ **SolveAlways[a + b x + c x^2 == (1 + x)^2, x]**

$Out[9]=$ $\{\{a \to 1, b \to 2, c \to 1\}\}$

This equates two series.

$In[10]:=$ **Series[a Cos[x] + b Cos[2x] + Cos[3x], {x, 0, 3}] ==**
$\qquad\qquad$ **Series[Cosh[x], {x, 0, 3}]**

$Out[10]=$ $(1 + a + b) + \left(-\dfrac{9}{2} - \dfrac{a}{2} - 2 b\right) x^2 + O[x]^4 == 1 + \dfrac{x^2}{2} + O[x]^4$

This finds values of the undetermined coefficients.

$In[11]:=$ **SolveAlways[%, x]**

$Out[11]=$ $\left\{\left\{a \to \dfrac{10}{3}, b \to -\dfrac{10}{3}\right\}\right\}$

■ 3.4.7 Solving Logical Combinations of Equations

When you give a list of equations to Solve, it assumes that you want all the equations to be satisfied simultaneously. It is also possible to give Solve more complicated logical combinations of equations.

Solve assumes that the equations x + y == 1 and x − y == 2 are simultaneously valid.

$In[1]:=$ **Solve[{x + y == 1, x − y == 2}, {x, y}]**

$Out[1]=$ $\left\{\left\{x \to \dfrac{3}{2}, y \to -\dfrac{1}{2}\right\}\right\}$

Here is an alternative form, using the logical connective && explicitly.

$In[2]:=$ **Solve[x + y == 1 && x − y == 2, {x, y}]**

$Out[2]=$ $\left\{\left\{x \to \dfrac{3}{2}, y \to -\dfrac{1}{2}\right\}\right\}$

This specifies that *either* x + y == 1 *or* x − y == 2. Solve gives two solutions for x, corresponding to these two possibilities.

$In[3]:=$ **Solve[x + y == 1 || x − y == 2, x]**

$Out[3]=$ $\{\{x \to 1 - y\}, \{x \to 2 + y\}\}$

Solve gives three solutions to this equation.

In[4]:= **Solve[x^3 == x, x]**

Out[4]= {{x → -1}, {x → 0}, {x → 1}}

If you explicitly include the assertion that x != 0, one of the previous solutions is suppressed.

In[5]:= **Solve[x^3 == x && x != 0, x]**

Out[5]= {{x → -1}, {x → 1}}

Here is a slightly more complicated example. Note that the precedence of || is lower than the precedence of &&, so the equation is interpreted as (x^3 == x && x != 1) || x^2 == 2, not x^3 == x && (x != 1 || x^2 == 2).

In[6]:= **Solve[x^3 == x && x != 1 || x^2 == 2 , x]**

Out[6]= $\left\{\{x → -1\}, \{x → 0\}, \left\{x → -\sqrt{2}\right\}, \left\{x → \sqrt{2}\right\}\right\}$

When you use Solve, the final results you get are in the form of transformation rules. If you use Reduce or Eliminate, on the other hand, then your results are logical statements, which you can manipulate further.

This gives a logical statement representing the solutions of the equation x^2 == x.

In[7]:= **Reduce[x^2 == x, x]**

Out[7]= x == 0 || x == 1

This finds values of x which satisfy x^5 == x but do not satisfy the statement representing the solutions of x^2 == x.

In[8]:= **Reduce[x^5 == x && !%, x]**

Out[8]= x == -1 || x == -i || x == i

The logical statements produced by Reduce can be thought of as representations of the solution set for your equations. The logical connectives &&, || and so on then correspond to operations on these sets.

eqns$_1$ || *eqns*$_2$	union of solution sets
eqns$_1$ && *eqns*$_2$	intersection of solution sets
!*eqns*	complement of a solution set
Implies[*eqns*$_1$**, ***eqns*$_2$**]**	the part of *eqns*$_1$ that contains *eqns*$_2$

Operations on solution sets.

You may often find it convenient to use special notations for logical connectives, as discussed on page 1001.

The input uses special notations for Implies and Or.

In[9]:= **Reduce[x^2 == 1 ⇒ (x == 1 ∨ x == -1), x]**

Out[9]= True

+■ 3.4.8 Inequalities

Just as the *equation* x^2 + 3x == 2 asserts that x^2 + 3x is equal to 2, so also the *inequality* x^2 + 3x > 2 asserts that x^2 + 3x is greater than 2. In *Mathematica*, Reduce works not only on equations, but also on inequalities.

+ Reduce[{*ineq*$_1$, *ineq*$_2$, ... }, x]	reduce a collection of inequalities in x

Manipulating univariate inequalities.

This pair of inequalities reduces to a single inequality.

```
In[1]:= Reduce[{0 < x < 2, 1 < x < 4}, x]
Out[1]= 1 < x < 2
```

These inequalities can never simultaneously be satisfied.

```
In[2]:= Reduce[{x < 1, x > 3}, x]
Out[2]= False
```

When applied to an equation, Reduce[*eqn*, x] tries to get a result consisting of simple equations for x of the form x == r_1, ... When applied to an inequality, Reduce[*ineq*, x] does the exactly analogous thing, and tries to get a result consisting of simple inequalities for x of the form $l_1 < x < r_1$, ...

This reduces a quadratic equation to two simple equations for x.

```
In[3]:= Reduce[x^2 + 3x == 2, x]
```
$$Out[3]= \ x == \frac{1}{2}\left(-3 - \sqrt{17}\right) \ || \ x == \frac{1}{2}\left(-3 + \sqrt{17}\right)$$

This reduces a quadratic inequality to two simple inequalities for x.

```
In[4]:= Reduce[x^2 + 3x > 2, x]
```
$$Out[4]= \ x < \frac{1}{2}\left(-3 - \sqrt{17}\right) \ || \ x > \frac{1}{2}\left(-3 + \sqrt{17}\right)$$

You can think of the result generated by Reduce[*ineq*, x] as representing a series of intervals, described by inequalities. Since the graph of a polynomial of degree n can go up and down as many as n times, a polynomial inequality of degree n can give rise to as many as $n/2 + 1$ distinct intervals.

This inequality yields three distinct intervals.

```
In[5]:= Reduce[(x - 1)(x - 2)(x - 3)(x - 4) > 0, x]
Out[5]= x < 1 || 2 < x < 3 || x > 4
```

The ends of the intervals are at roots and poles.

```
In[6]:= Reduce[1 < (x^2 + 3x)/(x + 1) < 2, x]
```
$$Out[6]= \ -1 - \sqrt{2} < x < -2 \ || \ -1 + \sqrt{2} < x < 1$$

Solving this inequality requires introducing ProductLog.

```
In[7]:= Reduce[x - 2 < Log[x] < x, x]
```
$$Out[7]= \ -\text{ProductLog}\left[-\frac{1}{e^2}\right] < x < -\text{ProductLog}\left[-1, -\frac{1}{e^2}\right]$$

Transcendental functions like sin(x) have graphs that go up and down infinitely many times, so that infinitely many intervals can be generated.

The second inequality allows only finitely many intervals.

```
In[8]:= Reduce[{Sin[x] > 0, 0 < x < 20}, x]
```
$$Out[8]= \ 0 < x < \pi \ || \ 2\pi < x < 3\pi \ || \ 4\pi < x < 5\pi \ || \ 6\pi < x < 20$$

This is how `Reduce` represents infinitely many intervals.

$In[9]:=$ `Reduce[{Sin[x] > 0, 0 < x}, x]`

$Out[9]=$ C[1] $\in$ Integers &&
$(0 < x < \pi$ || C[1] ≥ 1 && 2π C[1] $< x < \pi + 2\pi$ C[1])

Fairly simple inputs can give fairly complicated results.

$In[10]:=$ `Reduce[{Sin[x]^2 + Sin[3x] > 0, x^2 + 2 < 20}, x]`

$Out[10]=$ $-3\sqrt{2} < x < -\pi$ ||

$2\,\mathrm{ArcTan}\left[\frac{1}{3}\left(-4 - \sqrt{7}\right)\right] < x < 2\,\mathrm{ArcTan}\left[\frac{1}{3}\left(-4 + \sqrt{7}\right)\right]$ ||

$0 < x < \dfrac{\pi}{2}$ || $\dfrac{\pi}{2} < x < \pi$ ||

$2\pi + 2\,\mathrm{ArcTan}\left[\frac{1}{3}\left(-4 - \sqrt{7}\right)\right] < x < 3\sqrt{2}$

If you have inequalities that involve `<=` as well as `<`, there may be isolated points where the inequalities can be satisfied. `Reduce` represents such points by giving equations.

This inequality can be satisfied at just two isolated points.

$In[11]:=$ `Reduce[(x^2 - 3x + 1)^2 <= 0, x]`

$Out[11]=$ $x == \dfrac{1}{2}\left(3 - \sqrt{5}\right)$ || $x == \dfrac{1}{2}\left(3 + \sqrt{5}\right)$

This yields both intervals and isolated points.

$In[12]:=$ `Reduce[{Max[Sin[2x], Cos[3x]] <= 0, 0 < x < 10}, x]`

$Out[12]=$ $x == \dfrac{\pi}{2}$ || $\dfrac{5\pi}{6} \leq x \leq \pi$ ||

$\dfrac{3\pi}{2} \leq x \leq \dfrac{11\pi}{6}$ || $x == \dfrac{5\pi}{2}$ || $\dfrac{17\pi}{6} \leq x \leq 3\pi$

┌──┐
│ ⊹ `Reduce[{`*ineq*$_1$ *ineq*$_2$`, ... }, {`x_1, x_2`, ... }]` │
│   reduce a collection of inequalities in several variables │
└──┘

Multivariate inequalities.

For inequalities involving several variables, `Reduce` in effect yields nested collections of interval specifications, in which later variables have bounds that depend on earlier variables.

This represents the unit disk as nested inequalities for x and y.

$In[13]:=$ `Reduce[x^2 + y^2 < 1, {x, y}]`

$Out[13]=$ $-1 < x < 1$ && $-\sqrt{1 - x^2} < y < \sqrt{1 - x^2}$

In geometrical terms, any linear inequality divides space into two halves. Lists of linear inequalities thus define polyhedra, sometimes bounded, sometimes not. `Reduce` represents such polyhedra in terms of nested inequalities. The corners of the polyhedra always appear among the endpoints of these inequalities.

This defines a triangular region in the plane.

$In[14]:=$ `Reduce[{x > 0, y > 0, x + y < 1}, {x, y}]`

$Out[14]=$ $0 < x < 1$ && $0 < y < 1 - x$

Even a single triangle may need to be described as two components.

$In[15]:=$ **Reduce[{x > y - 1, y > 0, x + y < 1}, {x, y}]**

$Out[15]=$ $-1 < x \le 0$ && $0 < y < 1 + x$ || $0 < x < 1$ && $0 < y < 1 - x$

Lists of inequalities in general represent regions of overlap between geometrical objects. Often the description of these can be quite complicated.

This represents the part of the unit disk on one side of a line.

$In[16]:=$ **Reduce[{x^2 + y^2 < 1, x + 3y > 2}, {x, y}]**

$Out[16]=$ $\frac{1}{10}\left(2 - 3\sqrt{6}\right) < x < \frac{1}{10}\left(2 + 3\sqrt{6}\right)$ && $\frac{2-x}{3} < y < \sqrt{1-x^2}$

Here is the intersection between two disks.

$In[17]:=$ **Reduce[{(x - 1)^2 + y^2 < 2, x^2 + y^2 < 2}, {x, y}]**

$Out[17]=$ $1 - \sqrt{2} < x \le \frac{1}{2}$ && $-\sqrt{1 + 2x - x^2} < y < \sqrt{1 + 2x - x^2}$ ||

$\frac{1}{2} < x < \sqrt{2}$ && $-\sqrt{2 - x^2} < y < \sqrt{2 - x^2}$

If the disks are too far apart, there is no intersection.

$In[18]:=$ **Reduce[{(x - 4)^2 + y^2 < 2, x^2 + y^2 < 2}, {x, y}]**

$Out[18]=$ False

Here is an example involving a transcendental inequality.

$In[19]:=$ **Reduce[{Sin[x y] > 1/2, x^2 + y^2 < 3/2}, {x, y}]**

$Out[19]=$ $-\sqrt{\frac{3}{4} + \frac{1}{12}\sqrt{81 - 4\pi^2}} < x <$

$-\frac{1}{2}\sqrt{\frac{1}{3}\left(9 - \sqrt{81 - 4\pi^2}\right)}$ && $-\frac{\sqrt{3 - 2x^2}}{\sqrt{2}} < y < \frac{\pi}{6x}$ ||

$\frac{1}{2}\sqrt{\frac{1}{3}\left(9 - \sqrt{81 - 4\pi^2}\right)} < x < \sqrt{\frac{3}{4} + \frac{1}{12}\sqrt{81 - 4\pi^2}}$ &&

$\frac{\pi}{6x} < y < \frac{\sqrt{3 - 2x^2}}{\sqrt{2}}$

If you have inequalities that involve parameters, Reduce automatically handles the different cases that can occur, just as it does for equations.

The form of the intervals depends on the value of a.

$In[20]:=$ **Reduce[(x - 1)(x - a) > 0, x]**

$Out[20]=$ $a \le 1$ && $(x < a$ || $x > 1)$ || $a > 1$ && $(x < 1$ || $x > a)$

One gets a hyperbolic or an elliptical region, depending on the value of a.

In[21]:= **Reduce[x^2 + a y^2 < 1, {x, y}]**

Out[21]= $y \in \text{Reals \&\&}$

$$\left(a < 0 \,\&\&\, \left(x \le -1 \,\&\&\, \left(y < -\sqrt{\frac{1-x^2}{a}} \,||\, y > \sqrt{\frac{1-x^2}{a}}\right) \,||\, \right.\right.$$

$$-1 < x < 1 \,|| $$

$$\left.x \ge 1 \,\&\&\, \left(y < -\sqrt{\frac{1-x^2}{a}} \,||\, y > \sqrt{\frac{1-x^2}{a}}\right)\right) \,|| $$

$$a == 0 \,\&\&\, -1 < x < 1 \,||\, a > 0 \,\&\&\, -1 < x < 1 \,\&\&$$

$$\left.-\sqrt{\frac{1-x^2}{a}} < y < \sqrt{\frac{1-x^2}{a}}\right)$$

Reduce tries to give you a complete description of the region defined by a set of inequalities. Sometimes, however, you may just want to find individual instances of values of variables that satisfy the inequalities. You can do this using FindInstance.

+	FindInstance[*ineqs*, {x_1, x_2, ... }]	try to find an instance of the x_i satisfying *ineqs*
+	FindInstance[*ineqs*, *vars*, *n*]	try to find *n* instances

Finding individual points that satisfy inequalities.

This finds a specific instance that satisfies the inequalities.

In[22]:= **FindInstance[{Sin[x y] > 1/2, x^2 + y^2 < 3/2}, {x, y}]**

Out[22]= $\left\{\left\{x \to -\frac{118}{151},\, y \to -\frac{149}{185}\right\}\right\}$

This shows that there is no way to satisfy the inequalities.

In[23]:= **FindInstance[{Sin[x y] > 1/2, x^2 + y^2 < 1/4}, {x, y}]**

Out[23]= {}

FindInstance is in some ways an analog for inequalities of Solve for equations. For like Solve, it returns a list of rules giving specific values for variables. But while for equations these values can generically give an accurate representation of all solutions, for inequalities they can only correspond to isolated sample points within the regions described by the inequalities.

Every time you call FindInstance with specific input, it will give the same output. And when there are instances that correspond to special, limiting, points of some kind, it will preferentially return these. But in general, the distribution of instances returned by FindInstance will typically seem somewhat random. Each instance is, however, in effect a constructive proof that the inequalities you have given can in fact be satisfied.

If you ask for one point in the unit disk, FindInstance gives the origin.

In[24]:= **FindInstance[x^2 + y^2 <= 1, {x, y}]**

Out[24]= {{x → 0, y → 0}}

This finds 500 points in the unit disk.

In[25]:= **FindInstance[x^2 + y^2 <= 1, {x, y}, 500];**

Their distribution seems somewhat random.

In[26]:= **ListPlot[{x, y} /. %, AspectRatio->Automatic]**

+■ 3.4.9 Equations and Inequalities over Domains

Mathematica normally assumes that variables which appear in equations can stand for arbitrary complex numbers. But when you use Reduce, you can explicitly tell *Mathematica* that the variables stand for objects in more restricted domains.

+ Reduce[*expr*, *vars*, *dom*]	reduce *eqns* over the domain *dom*
Complexes	complex numbers $\mathbb{C}$
Reals	real numbers $\mathbb{R}$
Integers	integers $\mathbb{Z}$

Solving over domains.

Reduce by default assumes that x can be complex, and gives all five complex solutions.

In[1]:= **Reduce[x^6 - x^4 - 4x^2 + 4 == 0, x]**

Out[1]= $x == -1 \;||\; x == 1 \;||\; x == -\sqrt{2} \;||$
$\qquad x == -i\sqrt{2} \;||\; x == i\sqrt{2} \;||\; x == \sqrt{2}$

But here it assumes that x is real, and gives only the real solutions.

In[2]:= **Reduce[x^6 - x^4 - 4x^2 + 4 == 0, x, Reals]**

Out[2]= $x == -1 \;||\; x == 1 \;||\; x == -\sqrt{2} \;||\; x == \sqrt{2}$

And here it assumes that x is an integer, and gives only the integer solutions.

In[3]:= **Reduce[x^6 - x^4 - 4x^2 + 4 == 0, x, Integers]**

Out[3]= $x == -1 \;||\; x == 1$

A single polynomial equation in one variable will always have a finite set of discrete solutions. And in such a case one can think of Reduce[*eqns*, *vars*, *dom*] as just filtering the solutions by selecting the ones that happen to lie in the domain *dom*.

But as soon as there are more variables, things can become more complicated, with solutions to equations corresponding to parametric curves or surfaces in which the values of some variables can depend on the values of others. Often this dependence can be described by some collection of equations or inequalities, but the form of these can change significantly when one goes from one domain to another.

This gives solutions over the complex numbers as simple formulas.	$In[4]:=$ **Reduce[x^2 + y^2 == 1, {x, y}]**
	$Out[4]=$ $y == -\sqrt{1 - x^2} \;\|\|\; y == \sqrt{1 - x^2}$

To represent solutions over the reals requires introducing an inequality.	$In[5]:=$ **Reduce[x^2 + y^2 == 1, {x, y}, Reals]**
	$Out[5]=$ $-1 \le x \le 1 \;\&\&\; \left(y == -\sqrt{1 - x^2} \;\|\|\; y == \sqrt{1 - x^2}\right)$

Over the integers, the solution can be represented as equations for discrete points.	$In[6]:=$ **Reduce[x^2 + y^2 == 1, {x, y}, Integers]**
	$Out[6]=$ $x == -1 \;\&\&\; y == 0 \;\|\|\; x == 0 \;\&\&\; y == -1 \;\|\|$
	$\quad\quad x == 0 \;\&\&\; y == 1 \;\|\|\; x == 1 \;\&\&\; y == 0$

If your input involves only equations, then Reduce will by default assume that all variables are complex. But if your input involves inequalities, then Reduce will assume that any algebraic variables appearing in them are real, since inequalities can only compare real quantities.

Since the variables appear in an inequality, they are assumed to be real.	$In[7]:=$ **Reduce[{x + y + z == 1, x^2 + y^2 + z^2 < 1}, {x, y, z}]**
	$Out[7]=$ $-\dfrac{1}{3} < x < 1 \;\&\&\; \dfrac{1 - x}{2} - \dfrac{1}{2}\sqrt{1 + 2x - 3x^2} <$
	$\quad\quad y < \dfrac{1 - x}{2} + \dfrac{1}{2}\sqrt{1 + 2x - 3x^2} \;\&\&\; z == 1 - x - y$

Complexes	*polynomial* != 0, x_i == Root[...]
Reals	Root[...] < x_i < Root[...], x_i == Root[...]
Integers	arbitrarily complicated

Schematic building blocks for solutions to polynomial equations and inequalities.

For systems of polynomials over real and complex domains, the solutions always consist of a finite number of components, within which the values of variables are given by algebraic numbers or functions.

Here the components are distinguished by equations and inequations on x.	$In[8]:=$ **Reduce[x y^3 + y == 1, {x, y}, Complexes]**
	$Out[8]=$ $x == 0 \;\&\&\; y == 1 \;\|\|$
	$\quad\quad x \neq 0 \;\&\&\; \left(y == \text{Root}\left[-1 + \#1 + x\,\#1^3 \,\&, 1\right] \;\|\|\right.$
	$\quad\quad\quad y == \text{Root}\left[-1 + \#1 + x\,\#1^3 \,\&, 2\right] \;\|\|$
	$\quad\quad\quad \left. y == \text{Root}\left[-1 + \#1 + x\,\#1^3 \,\&, 3\right]\right)$

And here the components are distinguished by inequalities on x.

$In[9]:=$ `Reduce[x y^3 + y == 1, {x, y}, Reals]`

$Out[9]=$ $x < -\dfrac{4}{27}$ && $y ==$ Root$\left[-1 + \#1 + x\,\#1^3\,\&,\,1\right]$ ||

$\quad x == -\dfrac{4}{27}$ && $\left(y == -3 \;||\; y == \dfrac{3}{2}\right)$ ||

$\quad -\dfrac{4}{27} < x < 0$ && $\left(y ==$ Root$\left[-1 + \#1 + x\,\#1^3\,\&,\,1\right]$ ||

$\qquad y ==$ Root$\left[-1 + \#1 + x\,\#1^3\,\&,\,2\right]$ ||

$\qquad y ==$ Root$\left[-1 + \#1 + x\,\#1^3\,\&,\,3\right]\right)$ ||

$\qquad x \geq 0$ && $y ==$ Root$\left[-1 + \#1 + x\,\#1^3\,\&,\,1\right]$

While in principle `Reduce` can always find the complete solution to any collection of polynomial equations and inequalities with real or complex variables, the results are often very complicated, with the number of components typically growing exponentially as the number of variables increases.

With 3 variables, the solution here already involves 8 components.

$In[10]:=$ `Reduce[x^2 == y^2 == z^2 == 1, {x, y, z}]`

$Out[10]=$ $z == -1$ && $y == -1$ && $x == -1$ || $z == -1$ && $y == -1$ && $x == 1$ ||

$\quad z == -1$ && $y == 1$ && $x == -1$ || $z == -1$ && $y == 1$ && $x == 1$ ||

$\quad z == 1$ && $y == -1$ && $x == -1$ || $z == 1$ && $y == -1$ && $x == 1$ ||

$\quad z == 1$ && $y == 1$ && $x == -1$ || $z == 1$ && $y == 1$ && $x == 1$

As soon as one introduces functions like `Sin` or `Exp`, even equations in single real or complex variables can have solutions with an infinite number of components. `Reduce` labels these components by introducing additional parameters. By default, the nth parameter in a given solution will be named `C[n]`. In general you can specify that it should be named $f[n]$ by giving the option setting `GeneratedParameters -> f`.

The components here are labeled by the integer parameter c_1.

$In[11]:=$ `Reduce[Exp[x] == 2, x,`
$\qquad\qquad\qquad\qquad$ `GeneratedParameters -> (Subscript[c, #]&)]`

$Out[11]=$ $c_1 \in$ Integers && $x ==$ Log$[2] + 2\,\mathbb{i}\,\pi\,c_1$

`Reduce` can handle equations not only over real and complex variables, but also over integers. Solving such *Diophantine equations* can often be a very difficult problem.

Describing the solution to this equation over the reals is straightforward.

$In[12]:=$ `Reduce[x y == 8, {x, y}, Reals]`

$Out[12]=$ $(x < 0 \;||\; x > 0)$ && $y == \dfrac{8}{x}$

The solution over the integers involves the divisors of 8.

$In[13]:=$ `Reduce[x y == 8, {x, y}, Integers]`

$Out[13]=$ $x == -8$ && $y == -1$ || $x == -4$ && $y == -2$ ||

$\quad x == -2$ && $y == -4$ || $x == -1$ && $y == -8$ || $x == 1$ && $y == 8$ ||

$\quad x == 2$ && $y == 4$ || $x == 4$ && $y == 2$ || $x == 8$ && $y == 1$

Solving an equation like this effectively requires factoring a large number.

$In[14]:=$ `Reduce[{x y == 7777777, x > y > 0}, {x, y}, Integers]`

$Out[14]=$ $x == 4649$ && $y == 1673$ || $x == 32543$ && $y == 239$ ||

$\quad x == 1111111$ && $y == 7$ || $x == 7777777$ && $y == 1$

Reduce can solve any system of linear equations or inequalities over the integers. With *m* linear equations in *n* variables, *n − m* parameters typically need to be introduced. But with inequalities, a much larger number of parameters may be needed.

Three parameters are needed here, even though there are only two variables.

$In[15]:=$ **Reduce[{3x - 2y > 1, x > 0, y > 0}, {x, y}, Integers]**

$Out[15]=$ $(C[1] \mid C[2] \mid C[3]) \in$ Integers &&
$\qquad$ $C[1] \geq 0$ && $C[2] \geq 0$ && $C[3] \geq 0$ &&
$\qquad$ $(x == 2 + 2 C[1] + C[2] + C[3]$ && $y == 2 + 3 C[1] + C[2]$ ||
$\qquad\qquad$ $x == 2 + 2 C[1] + C[2] + C[3]$ && $y == 1 + 3 C[1] + C[2])$

With two variables, Reduce can solve any quadratic equation over the integers. The result can be a Fibonacci-like sequence, represented in terms of powers of quadratic irrationals.

Here is the solution to a Pell equation.

$In[16]:=$ **Reduce[{x^2 == 13 y^2 + 1, x > 0, y > 0}, {x, y}, Integers]**

$Out[16]=$ $C[1] \in$ Integers && $C[1] \geq 1$ &&

$$x == \frac{1}{2}\left(\left(649 - 180\sqrt{13}\right)^{C[1]} + \left(649 + 180\sqrt{13}\right)^{C[1]}\right) \&\&$$

$$y == -\frac{\left(649 - 180\sqrt{13}\right)^{C[1]} - \left(649 + 180\sqrt{13}\right)^{C[1]}}{2\sqrt{13}}$$

The actual values for specific C[1] as integers, as they should be.

$In[17]:=$ **FullSimplify[% /. Table[{C[1] -> i}, {i, 4}]]**

$Out[17]=$ $\{x == 649$ && $y == 180,\ x == 842401$ && $y == 233640,$
$\qquad$ $x == 1093435849$ && $y == 303264540,$
$\qquad$ $x == 1419278889601$ && $y == 393637139280\}$

Reduce can handle many specific classes of equations over the integers.

Here Reduce finds the solution to a Thue equation.

$In[18]:=$ **Reduce[x^3 - 4 x y^2 + y^3 == 1, {x, y}, Integers]**

$Out[18]=$ $x == -2$ && $y == 1$ || $x == 0$ && $y == 1$ || $x == 1$ && $y == 0$ ||
$\qquad$ $x == 1$ && $y == 4$ || $x == 2$ && $y == 1$ || $x == 508$ && $y == 273$

Changing the right-hand side to 3, the equation now has no solution.

$In[19]:=$ **Reduce[x^3 - 4 x y^2 + y^3 == 3, {x, y}, Integers]**

$Out[19]=$ False

Equations over the integers sometimes have seemingly quite random collections of solutions. And even small changes in equations can often lead them to have no solutions at all.

For polynomial equations over real and complex numbers, there is a definite *decision procedure* for determining whether or not any solution exists. But for polynomial equations over the integers, the unsolvability of Hilbert's Tenth Problem demonstrates that there can never be any such general procedure.

For specific classes of equations, however, procedures can be found, and indeed many are implemented in Reduce. But handling different classes of equations can often seem to require whole different branches of number theory, and quite different kinds of computations. And in fact it is known that there are *universal* integer polynomial equations, for which filling in some variables can make solutions for other variables correspond to the output of absolutely any possible program. This then means that for such equations there can never in general be any closed-form solution built from fixed elements like algebraic functions.

If one includes functions like `Sin`, then even for equations involving real and complex numbers the same issues can arise.

Reduce here effectively has to solve an equation over the integers.

$In[20]:=$ `Reduce[Sin[Pi x]^2 + Sin[Pi y]^2 +`
            `(x^2 + y^2 - 25)^2 == 0, {x, y}, Reals]`

$Out[20]=$ x == -5 && y == 0 || x == -4 && (y == -3 || y == 3) ||
            x == -3 && (y == -4 || y == 4) ||
            x == 0 && (y == -5 || y == 5) ||
            x == 3 && (y == -4 || y == 4) ||
            x == 4 && (y == -3 || y == 3) || x == 5 && y == 0

+ `Reduce[eqns, vars, Modulus->n]`	find solutions modulo n

Handling equations involving integers modulo n.

Since there are only ever a finite number of possible solutions for integer equations modulo n, `Reduce` can systematically find them.

This finds all solutions modulo 4.

$In[21]:=$ `Reduce[x^5 == y^4 + x y + 1, {x, y}, Modulus -> 4]`

$Out[21]=$ x == 1 && y == 0 || x == 1 && y == 3 || x == 2 && y == 1 ||
            x == 2 && y == 3 || x == 3 && y == 2 || x == 3 && y == 3

+ `Reduce[expr, vars, dom]`	specify a default domain for all variables
+ `Reduce[{expr`$_1$`, ... , x`$_1 \in$`dom`$_1$`, ... }, vars]`	explicitly specify individual domains for variables

Different ways to specify domains for variables.

This assumes that x is an integer, but y is a real.

$In[22]:=$ `Reduce[{x^2 + 2y^2 == 1, x ∈ Integers, y ∈ Reals}, {x, y}]`

$Out[22]=$ x == -1 && y == 0 ||

$$x == 0 \text{ \&\& } \left(y == -\frac{1}{\sqrt{2}} \ || \ y == \frac{1}{\sqrt{2}} \right) || \ x == 1 \text{ \&\& } y == 0$$

`Reduce` normally treats complex variables as single objects. But in dealing with functions that are not analytic or have branch cuts, it sometimes has to break them into pairs of real variables `Re[z]` and `Im[z]`.

The result involves separate real and imaginary parts.

$In[23]:=$ `Reduce[Abs[z] == 1, z]`

$Out[23]=$ -1 ≤ Re[z] ≤ 1 &&

$$\left(\text{Im}[z] == -\sqrt{1 - \text{Re}[z]^2} \ || \ \text{Im}[z] == \sqrt{1 - \text{Re}[z]^2} \right)$$

Here again there is a separate
condition on the imaginary part.

$In[24]:=$ **Reduce[Log[z] == a, {a, z}]**

$Out[24]=$ $-\pi < \text{Im}[a] \leq \pi \,\&\&\, z == e^a$

Reduce by default assumes that variables that appear algebraically in inequalities are real. But you can override this by explicitly specifying **Complexes** as the default domain. It is often useful in such cases to be able to specify that certain variables are still real.

Reduce by default assumes that x is a
real.

$In[25]:=$ **Reduce[x^2 < 1, x]**

$Out[25]=$ $-1 < x < 1$

This forces Reduce to consider the case
where x can be complex.

$In[26]:=$ **Reduce[x^2 < 1, x, Complexes]**

$Out[26]=$ $-1 < \text{Re}[x] < 0 \,\&\&\, \text{Im}[x] == 0 \,||$
$\text{Re}[x] == 0 \,||\, 0 < \text{Re}[x] < 1 \,\&\&\, \text{Im}[x] == 0$

Since x does not appear algebraically,
Reduce immediately assumes that it
can be complex.

$In[27]:=$ **Reduce[Abs[x] < 1, x]**

$Out[27]=$ $-1 < \text{Re}[x] < 1 \,\&\&\, -\sqrt{1 - \text{Re}[x]^2} < \text{Im}[x] < \sqrt{1 - \text{Re}[x]^2}$

Here x is a real, but y can be complex.

$In[28]:=$ **Reduce[{Abs[y] < Abs[x], x ∈ Reals}, {x, y}]**

$Out[28]=$ $x < 0 \,\&\&\, -\sqrt{x^2} < \text{Re}[y] < \sqrt{x^2} \,\&\&$
$-\sqrt{x^2 - \text{Re}[y]^2} < \text{Im}[y] < \sqrt{x^2 - \text{Re}[y]^2} \,||$
$x > 0 \,\&\&\, -\sqrt{x^2} < \text{Re}[y] < \sqrt{x^2} \,\&\&$
$-\sqrt{x^2 - \text{Re}[y]^2} < \text{Im}[y] < \sqrt{x^2 - \text{Re}[y]^2}$

+ FindInstance[*expr*, {x_1, x_2, ... }, *dom*]	try to find an instance of the x_i in *dom* satisfying *expr*
+ FindInstance[*expr*, *vars*, *dom*, *n*]	try to find *n* instances
Complexes	the domain of complex numbers $\mathbb{C}$
Reals	the domain of real numbers $\mathbb{R}$
Integers	the domain of integers $\mathbb{Z}$
Booleans	the domain of booleans (True and False) $\mathbb{B}$

Finding particular solutions in domains.

Reduce always returns a complete representation of the solution to a system of equations or inequalities. Sometimes, however, you may just want to find particular sample solutions. You can do this using **FindInstance**.

If `FindInstance[`*expr*`, `*vars*`, `*dom*`]` returns `{}` then this means that *Mathematica* has effectively proved that *expr* cannot be satisfied for any values of variables in the specified domain. When *expr* can be satisfied, `FindInstance` will normally pick quite arbitrarily among values that do this, as discussed for inequalities on page 838.

Particularly for integer equations, `FindInstance` can often find particular solutions to equations even when `Reduce` cannot find a complete solution. In such cases it usually returns one of the smallest solutions to the equations.

This finds the smallest integer point on an elliptic curve.	`In[29]:=` **FindInstance[{x^2 == y^3 + 12, x > 0, y > 0},** **{x, y}, Integers]**
	`Out[29]=` $\{\{x \to 47,\ y \to 13\}\}$

One feature of `FindInstance` is that it also works with Boolean expressions whose variables can have values `True` or `False`. You can use `FindInstance` to determine whether a particular expression is *satisfiable*, so that there is some choice of truth values for its variables that makes the expression `True`.

This expression cannot be satisfied for any choice of p and q.	`In[30]:=` **FindInstance[p && ! (p || ! q), {p, q}, Booleans]**
	`Out[30]=` `{}`
But this can.	`In[31]:=` **FindInstance[p && ! (! p || ! q), {p, q}, Booleans]**
	`Out[31]=` $\{\{p \to \text{True},\ q \to \text{True}\}\}$

+■ 3.4.10 Advanced Topic: The Representation of Solution Sets

One can think of any combination of equations or inequalities as implicitly defining a region in some kind of space. The fundamental function of `Reduce` is to turn this type of implicit description into an explicit one.

An implicit description in terms of equations or inequalities is sufficient if one just wants to test whether a point specified by values of variables is in the region. But to understand the structure of the region, or to generate points in it, one typically needs a more explicit description, of the kind obtained from `Reduce`.

Here are inequalities that implicitly define a semicircular region.	`In[1]:=` **semi = x > 0 && x^2 + y^2 < 1**
	`Out[1]=` $x > 0 \ \&\&\ x^2 + y^2 < 1$
This shows that the point $(1/2, 1/2)$ lies in the region.	`In[2]:=` **semi /. { x -> 1/2, y -> 1/2 }**
	`Out[2]=` `True`
Reduce gives a more explicit representation of the region.	`In[3]:=` **Reduce[semi, {x, y}]**
	`Out[3]=` $0 < x < 1 \ \&\&\ -\sqrt{1 - x^2} < y < \sqrt{1 - x^2}$

If we pick a value for x consistent with the first inequality, we then immediately get an explicit inequality for y.

$In[4]:= \% /. x \to 1/2$

$Out[4]= -\frac{\sqrt{3}}{2} < y < \frac{\sqrt{3}}{2}$

$Reduce[expr, \{x_1, x_2, \dots \}]$ is set up to describe regions by first giving fixed conditions for x_1, then giving conditions for x_2 that depend on x_1, then conditions for x_3 that depend on x_1 and x_2, and so on. This structure has the feature that it allows one to pick points by successively choosing values for each of the x_i in turn—in much the same way as when one uses iterators in functions like Table.

This gives a representation for the region in which one first picks a value for y, then x.

$In[5]:= Reduce[semi, \{y, x\}]$

$Out[5]= -1 < y < 1 \text{ \&\& } 0 < x < \sqrt{1 - y^2}$

In some simple cases the region defined by a system of equations or inequalities will end up having only one component. In such cases, the output from Reduce will be of the form e_1 && e_2 && … where each of the e_i is an equation or inequality involving variables up to x_i.

In most cases, however, there will be several components, represented by output containing forms such as $u_1 \mid\mid u_2 \mid\mid \dots$. Reduce typically tries to minimize the number of components used in describing a region. But in some cases multiple parametrizations may be needed to cover a single connected component, and each one of these will appear as a separate component in the output from Reduce.

In representing solution sets, it is common to find that several components can be described together by using forms such as … && ($u_1 \mid\mid u_2$) && … . Reduce by default does this so as to return its results as compactly as possible. You can use LogicalExpand to generate an expanded form in which each component appears separately.

In generating the most compact results, Reduce sometimes ends up making conditions on later variables x_i depend on more of the earlier x_i than is strictly necessary. You can force Reduce to generate results in which a particular x_i only has minimal dependence on earlier x_i by giving the option Backsubstitution->True. Usually this will lead to much larger output, although sometimes it may be easier to interpret.

By default, Reduce expresses the condition on y in terms of x.

$In[6]:= Reduce[x^2 + y == 4 \text{ \&\& } x^3 - 4y == 8, \{x, y\}]$

$Out[6]= \left(x == 2 \mid\mid x == -3 - i\sqrt{3} \mid\mid x == -3 + i\sqrt{3}\right) \text{ \&\& } y == 4 - x^2$

Backsubstituting allows conditions for y to be given without involving x.

$In[7]:= Reduce[x^2 + y == 4 \text{ \&\& } x^3 - 4y == 8, \{x, y\},$
$\qquad\qquad\qquad Backsubstitution \to True]$

$Out[7]= x == 2 \text{ \&\& } y == 0 \mid\mid$
$\qquad x == -i\left(-3\,i + \sqrt{3}\right) \text{ \&\& } y == -2\,i\left(-i + 3\sqrt{3}\right) \mid\mid$
$\qquad x == i\left(3\,i + \sqrt{3}\right) \text{ \&\& } y == 2\,i\left(i + 3\sqrt{3}\right)$

> + `CylindricalDecomposition[`*expr*`, {`x_1`, `x_2`, ... }]`
>
> generate the cylindrical algebraic decomposition of *expr*

Cylindrical algebraic decomposition.

For polynomial equations or inequalities over the reals, the structure of the result returned by `Reduce` is typically a *cylindrical algebraic decomposition* or *CAD*. Sometimes `Reduce` can yield a simpler form. But in all cases you can get the complete CAD by using `CylindricalDecomposition`.

+■ 3.4.11 Advanced Topic: Quantifiers

In a statement like `x^4 + x^2 > 0`, *Mathematica* treats the variable x as having a definite, though unspecified, value. Sometimes, however, it is useful to be able to make statements about whole collections of possible values for x. You can do this using *quantifiers*.

+ `ForAll[`x`, `*expr*`]`	*expr* holds for all values of x
+ `ForAll[{`x_1`, `x_2`, ... }, `*expr*`]`	*expr* holds for all values of all the x_i
+ `ForAll[{`x_1`, `x_2`, ... }, `*cond*`, `*expr*`]`	*expr* holds for all x_i satisfying *cond*
+ `Exists[`x`, `*expr*`]`	there exists a value of x for which *expr* holds
+ `Exists[{`x_1`, `x_2`, ... }, `*expr*`]`	there exist values of the x_i for which *expr* holds
+ `Exists[{`x_1`, ... }, `*cond*`, `*expr*`]`	there exist values of the x_i satisfying *cond* for which *expr* holds

The structure of quantifiers.

You can work with quantifiers in *Mathematica* much as you work with equations, inequalities or logical connectives. In most cases, the quantifiers will not immediately be changed by evaluation. But they can be simplified or reduced by functions like `FullSimplify` and `Reduce`.

This asserts that an x exists that makes the inequality true. The output here is just a formatted version of the input.

In[1]:= `Exists[x, x^4 + x^2 > 0]`

Out[1]= $\exists_x \ x^2 + x^4 > 0$

`FullSimplify` establishes that the assertion is true.

In[2]:= `FullSimplify[%]`

Out[2]= `True`

This gives `False`, since the inequality fails when x is zero.

In[3]:= `FullSimplify[ForAll[x, x^4 + x^2 > 0]]`

Out[3]= `False`

Mathematica supports a version of the standard notation for quantifiers used in predicate logic and pure mathematics. You can input ∀ as \[ForAll] or :fa:, and you can input ∃ as \[Exists] or :ex:. To make the notation precise, however, *Mathematica* makes the quantified variable a subscript. The conditions on the variable can also be given in the subscript, separated by a comma.

$\forall_x\ expr$	ForAll[x, *expr*]
$\forall_{\{x_1,x_2,\ldots\}}\ expr$	ForAll[{x_1, x_2, ... }, *expr*]
$\forall_{x,cond}\ expr$	ForAll[x, *cond*, *expr*]
$\exists_x\ expr$	Exists[x, *expr*]
$\exists_{\{x_1,x_2,\ldots\}}\ expr$	Exists[{x_1, x_2, ... }, *expr*]
$\exists_{x,cond}\ expr$	Exists[x, *cond*, *expr*]

Notation for quantifiers.

Given a statement that involves quantifiers, there are certain important cases where it is possible to resolve it into an equivalent statement in which the quantifiers have been eliminated. Somewhat like solving an equation, such quantifier elimination turns an implicit statement about what is true for all x or for some x into an explicit statement about the conditions under which this holds.

+	Resolve[*expr*]	attempt to eliminate quantifiers from *expr*
+	Resolve[*expr*, *dom*]	attempt to eliminate quantifiers with all variables assumed to be in domain *dom*

Quantifier elimination.

This shows that an x exists that makes the equation true.

In[4]:= **Resolve[Exists[x, x^2 == x^3]]**

Out[4]= True

This shows that the equations can only be satisfied if c obeys a certain condition.

In[5]:= **Resolve[Exists[x, x^2 == c && x^3 == c + 1]]**

Out[5]= $-1-2\,c-c^2+c^3 == 0$

Resolve can always eliminate quantifiers from any collection of polynomial equations and inequations over complex numbers, and from any collection of polynomial equations and inequalities over real numbers. It can also eliminate quantifiers from Boolean expressions.

This finds the conditions for a quadratic form over the reals to be positive.

In[6]:= `Resolve[ForAll[x, a x^2 + b x + c > 0], Reals]`

Out[6]= $c > 0$ &&

$$\left(b < 0 \,\&\&\, a > \frac{b^2}{4\,c} \mid\mid b == 0 \,\&\&\, a \geq 0 \mid\mid b > 0 \,\&\&\, a > \frac{b^2}{4\,c} \right)$$

This shows that there is a way of assigning truth values to p and q that makes the expression true.

In[7]:= `Resolve[Exists[{p, q}, p || q && ! q], Booleans]`

Out[7]= `True`

You can also use quantifiers with Reduce. If you give Reduce a collection of equations or inequalities, then it will try to produce a detailed representation of the complete solution set. But sometimes you may want to address a more global question, such as whether the solution set covers all values of *x*, or whether it covers none of these values. Quantifiers provide a convenient way to specify such questions.

This gives the complete structure of the solution set.

In[8]:= `Reduce[x^2 + x + c == 0, {c, x}, Reals]`

Out[8]= $c < \dfrac{1}{4}$ &&

$$\left(x == -\frac{1}{2} - \frac{1}{2}\sqrt{1 - 4\,c} \mid\mid x == -\frac{1}{2} + \frac{1}{2}\sqrt{1 - 4\,c} \right) \mid\mid$$

$$c == \frac{1}{4} \,\&\&\, x == -\frac{1}{2}$$

This instead just gives the condition for a solution to exist.

In[9]:= `Reduce[Exists[x, x^2 + x + c == 0], {c}, Reals]`

Out[9]= $c \leq \dfrac{1}{4}$

It is possible to formulate a great many mathematical questions in terms of quantifiers.

This finds the conditions for a circle to be contained within an arbitrary conic section.

In[10]:= `Reduce[ForAll[{x, y}, x^2 + y^2 < 1, a x^2 + b y^2 < c],`
`            {a, b, c}, Reals]`

Out[10]= $a \leq 0$ && $(b \leq 0 \,\&\&\, c > 0 \mid\mid b > 0 \,\&\&\, c \geq b)$ ||
      $a > 0$ && $(b < a \,\&\&\, c \geq a \mid\mid b \geq a \,\&\&\, c \geq b)$

This finds the conditions for a line to intersect a circle.

In[11]:= `Reduce[Exists[{x, y}, x^2 + y^2 < 1, r x + s y == 1],`
`            {r, s}, Reals]`

Out[11]= $r < -1$ ||
      $-1 \leq r \leq 1$ && $\left(s < -\sqrt{1 - r^2} \mid\mid s > \sqrt{1 - r^2} \right)$ || $r > 1$

This defines q to be a general monic quartic.

In[12]:= `q[x_] := x^4 + b x^3 + c x^2 + d x + e`

This finds the condition for all pairs of roots to the quartic to be equal.

In[13]:= `Reduce[ForAll[{x, y}, q[x] == 0 && q[y] == 0, x == y],`
`            {b, c, d, e}]`

Out[13]= $c == \dfrac{3\,b^2}{8}$ && $d == \dfrac{b^3}{16}$ && $e == \dfrac{b^4}{256}$ ||
      $b == 0$ && $c == 0$ && $d == 0$ && $e == 0$

Although quantifier elimination over the integers is in general a computationally impossible problem, *Mathematica* can do it in specific cases.

This shows that $\sqrt{2}$ cannot be a rational number.

$In[14]:=$ **Resolve[Exists[{x, y}, x^2 == 2 y^2 && y > 0], Integers]**

$Out[14]=$ False

$\sqrt{9/4}$ is, though.

$In[15]:=$ **Resolve[Exists[{x, y}, 4 x^2 == 9 y^2 && y > 0], Integers]**

$Out[15]=$ True

■ 3.4.12 Minimization and Maximization

+ Minimize[*expr*, {x_1, x_2, ... }]	minimize *expr*
+ Minimize[{*expr*, *cons*}, {x_1, x_2, ... }]	
	minimize *expr* subject to the constraints *cons*
+ Maximize[*expr*, {x_1, x_2, ... }]	maximize *expr*
+ Maximize[{*expr*, *cons*}, {x_1, x_2, ... }]	
	maximize *expr* subject to the constraints *cons*

Minimization and maximization.

`Minimize` and `Maximize` yield lists giving the value attained at the minimum or maximum, together with rules specifying where the minimum or maximum occurs.

This finds the minimum of a quadratic function.

$In[1]:=$ **Minimize[x^2 - 3x + 6, x]**

$Out[1]= \left\{ \dfrac{15}{4}, \left\{ x \to \dfrac{3}{2} \right\} \right\}$

Applying the rule for x gives the value at the minimum.

$In[2]:=$ **x^2 - 3x + 6 /. Last[%]**

$Out[2]= \dfrac{15}{4}$

This maximizes with respect to x and y.

$In[3]:=$ **Maximize[5 x y - x^4 - y^4, {x, y}]**

$Out[3]= \left\{ \dfrac{25}{8}, \left\{ x \to -\dfrac{\sqrt{5}}{2}, y \to -\dfrac{\sqrt{5}}{2} \right\} \right\}$

`Minimize[`*expr*`, `*x*`]` minimizes *expr* allowing *x* to range over all possible values from $-\infty$ to $+\infty$. `Minimize[{`*expr*`, `*cons*`}, `*x*`]` minimizes *expr* subject to the constraints *cons* being satisfied. The constraints can consist of any combination of equations and inequalities.

This finds the minimum subject to the constraint $x \geq 3$.

$In[4]:=$ **Minimize[{x^2 - 3x + 6, x >= 3}, x]**

$Out[4]= \{6, \{x \to 3\}\}$

This finds the maximum within the unit circle.	$In[5]:=$ **Maximize[{5 x y - x^4 - y^4, x^2 + y^2 <= 1}, {x, y}]**
	$Out[5]= \left\{2, \left\{x \to -\dfrac{1}{\sqrt{2}}, y \to -\dfrac{1}{\sqrt{2}}\right\}\right\}$

This finds the maximum within an ellipse. The result is fairly complicated.	$In[6]:=$ **Maximize[{5 x y - x^4 - y^4, x^2 + 2y^2 <= 1}, {x, y}]**
	$Out[6]= \left\{-\text{Root}\left[-811219 + 320160\,\#1 + \right.\right.$
	$\qquad 274624\,\#1^2 - 170240\,\#1^3 + 25600\,\#1^4 \,\&, 1\right],$
	$\qquad \left\{x \to \text{Root}\left[25 - 102\,\#1^2 + 122\,\#1^4 - 70\,\#1^6 + 50\,\#1^8 \,\&, 2\right],\right.$
	$\qquad y \to \text{Root}\left[\vphantom{\#1^8}\right.$
	$\qquad\qquad \left.\left.\left. 25 - 264\,\#1^2 + 848\,\#1^4 - 1040\,\#1^6 + 800\,\#1^8 \,\&, 1\right]\right\}\right\}$

This finds the maximum along a line.	$In[7]:=$ **Maximize[{5 x y - x^4 - y^4, x + y == 1}, {x, y}]**
	$Out[7]= \left\{\dfrac{9}{8}, \left\{x \to \dfrac{1}{2}, y \to \dfrac{1}{2}\right\}\right\}$

Minimize and **Maximize** can solve any *linear programming* problem in which both the objective function *expr* and the constraints *cons* involve the variables x_i only linearly.

Here is a typical linear programming problem.	$In[8]:=$ **Minimize[{x + 3 y, x - 3 y <= 7 && x + 2y >= 10}, {x, y}]**
	$Out[8]= \left\{\dfrac{53}{5}, \left\{x \to \dfrac{44}{5}, y \to \dfrac{3}{5}\right\}\right\}$

They can also in principle solve any *polynomial programming* problem in which the objective function and the constraints involve arbitrary polynomial functions of the variables. There are many important geometrical and other problems that can be formulated in this way.

This solves the simple geometrical problem of maximizing the area of a rectangle with fixed perimeter.	$In[9]:=$ **Maximize[{x y, x + y == 1}, {x, y}]**
	$Out[9]= \left\{\dfrac{1}{4}, \left\{x \to \dfrac{1}{2}, y \to \dfrac{1}{2}\right\}\right\}$

This finds the maximal volume of a cuboid that fits inside the unit sphere.	$In[10]:=$ **Maximize[{8 x y z, x^2 + y^2 + z^2 <= 1}, {x, y, z}]**
	$Out[10]= \left\{\dfrac{8}{3\sqrt{3}}, \left\{x \to -\dfrac{1}{\sqrt{3}}, y \to -\dfrac{1}{\sqrt{3}}, z \to \dfrac{1}{\sqrt{3}}\right\}\right\}$

An important feature of **Minimize** and **Maximize** is that they always find *global* minima and maxima. Often functions will have various local minima and maxima at which derivatives vanish. But **Minimize** and **Maximize** use global methods to find absolute minima or maxima, not just local extrema.

Here is a function with many local maxima and minima.

$In[11]:=$ **Plot[x + 2 Sin[x], {x, -10, 10}]**

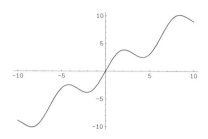

Maximize finds the global maximum.

$In[12]:=$ **Maximize[{x + 2 Sin[x], -10 <= x <= 10}, x]**

$Out[12]= \left\{\sqrt{3} + \frac{8\pi}{3}, \left\{x \rightarrow \frac{8\pi}{3}\right\}\right\}$

If you give functions that are unbounded, Minimize and Maximize will return $-\infty$ and $+\infty$ as the minima and maxima. And if you give constraints that can never be satisfied, they will return $+\infty$ and $-\infty$ as the minima and maxima, and Indeterminate as the values of variables.

One subtle issue is that Minimize and Maximize allow both *non-strict* inequalities of the form $x <= v$, and *strict* ones of the form $x < v$. With non-strict inequalities there is no problem with a minimum or maximum lying exactly on the boundary $x \rightarrow v$. But with strict inequalities, a minimum or maximum must in principle be at least infinitesimally inside the boundary.

With a strict inequality, *Mathematica* prints a warning, then returns the point on the boundary.

$In[13]:=$ **Minimize[{x^2 - 3x + 6, x > 3}, x]**

Minimize::wksol :
    Warning: There is no minimum in the region described by
    the constraints; returning a result on the boundary.

$Out[13]=$ {6, {x → 3}}

Minimize and Maximize normally assume that all variables you give are real. But by giving a constraint such as $x \in$ Integers you can specify that a variable must in fact be an integer.

This does maximization only over integer values of x and y.

$In[14]:=$ **Maximize[{x y, x^2 + y^2 < 120 &&**
                    (x | y) ∈ Integers}, {x, y}]

$Out[14]=$ {56, {x → -8, y → -7}}

3.5 Calculus

■ 3.5.1 Differentiation

D[*f*, *x*]	partial derivative $\frac{\partial}{\partial x} f$
D[*f*, x_1, x_2, ...]	multiple derivative $\frac{\partial}{\partial x_1} \frac{\partial}{\partial x_2} ... f$
D[*f*, {*x*, *n*}]	n^{th} derivative $\frac{\partial^n}{\partial x^n} f$
D[*f*, *x*, NonConstants -> {v_1, v_2, ... }]	$\frac{\partial}{\partial x} f$ with the v_i taken to depend on *x*

Partial differentiation operations.

This gives $\frac{\partial}{\partial x} x^n$.

```
In[1]:= D[x^n, x]
Out[1]= n x^{-1+n}
```

This gives the third derivative.

```
In[2]:= D[x^n, {x, 3}]
Out[2]= (-2 + n) (-1 + n) n x^{-3+n}
```

You can differentiate with respect to any expression that does not involve explicit mathematical operations.

```
In[3]:= D[ x[1]^2 + x[2]^2, x[1] ]
Out[3]= 2 x[1]
```

D does *partial differentiation*. It assumes here that y is independent of x.

```
In[4]:= D[x^2 + y^2, x]
Out[4]= 2 x
```

If y does in fact depend on x, you can use the explicit functional form y[x]. Section 3.5.4 describes how objects like y'[x] work.

```
In[5]:= D[x^2 + y[x]^2, x]
Out[5]= 2 x + 2 y[x] y'[x]
```

Instead of giving an explicit function y[x], you can tell D that y *implicitly* depends on x.
D[y, x, NonConstants->{y}] then represents $\frac{\partial y}{\partial x}$, with y implicitly depending on x.

```
In[6]:= D[x^2 + y^2, x, NonConstants -> {y}]
Out[6]= 2 x + 2 y D[y, x, NonConstants → {y}]
```

■ 3.5.2 Total Derivatives

Dt[*f*]	total differential df
Dt[*f*, *x*]	total derivative $\frac{df}{dx}$
Dt[*f*, x_1, x_2, ...]	multiple total derivative $\frac{d}{dx_1} \frac{d}{dx_2} ... f$
Dt[*f*, *x*, Constants -> {c_1, c_2, ... }]	total derivative with c_i constant (i.e., $dc_i = 0$)
y/: Dt[*y*, *x*] = 0	set $\frac{dy}{dx} = 0$
SetAttributes[*c*, Constant]	define c to be a constant in all cases

Total differentiation operations.

When you find the derivative of some expression f with respect to x, you are effectively finding out how fast f changes as you vary x. Often f will depend not only on x, but also on other variables, say y and z. The results that you get then depend on how you assume that y and z vary as you change x.

There are two common cases. Either y and z are assumed to stay fixed when x changes, or they are allowed to vary with x. In a standard *partial derivative* $\frac{\partial f}{\partial x}$, all variables other than x are assumed fixed. On the other hand, in the *total derivative* $\frac{df}{dx}$, all variables are allowed to change with x.

In *Mathematica*, D[*f*, *x*] gives a partial derivative, with all other variables assumed independent of x. Dt[*f*, *x*] gives a total derivative, in which all variables are assumed to depend on x. In both cases, you can add an argument to give more information on dependencies.

This gives the *partial derivative* $\frac{\partial}{\partial x}(x^2 + y^2)$. y is assumed to be independent of x.	*In[1]:=* **D[x^2 + y^2, x]** *Out[1]=* 2 x
This gives the *total derivative* $\frac{d}{dx}(x^2 + y^2)$. Now y is assumed to depend on x.	*In[2]:=* **Dt[x^2 + y^2, x]** *Out[2]=* 2 x + 2 y Dt[y, x]
You can make a replacement for $\frac{dy}{dx}$.	*In[3]:=* **% /. Dt[y, x] -> yp** *Out[3]=* 2 x + 2 y yp
You can also make an explicit definition for $\frac{dy}{dx}$. You need to use y/: to make sure that the definition is associated with y.	*In[4]:=* **y/: Dt[y, x] = 0** *Out[4]=* 0
With this definition made, Dt treats y as independent of x.	*In[5]:=* **Dt[x^2 + y^2 + z^2, x]** *Out[5]=* 2 x + 2 z Dt[z, x]
This removes your definition for the derivative of y.	*In[6]:=* **Clear[y]**

This takes the total derivative, with z held fixed.

In[7]:= **Dt[x^2 + y^2 + z^2, x, Constants->{z}]**

Out[7]= $2 x + 2 y \, Dt[y, x, Constants \rightarrow \{z\}]$

This specifies that c is a constant under differentiation.

In[8]:= **SetAttributes[c, Constant]**

The variable c is taken as a constant.

In[9]:= **Dt[a^2 + c x^2, x]**

Out[9]= $2 c x + 2 a \, Dt[a, x]$

The *function* c is also assumed to be a constant.

In[10]:= **Dt[a^2 + c[x] x^2, x]**

Out[10]= $2 x c[x] + 2 a \, Dt[a, x]$

This gives the total differential $d(x^2 + cy^2)$.

In[11]:= **Dt[x^2 + c y^2]**

Out[11]= $2 x \, Dt[x] + 2 c y \, Dt[y]$

You can make replacements and assignments for total differentials.

In[12]:= **% /. Dt[y] -> dy**

Out[12]= $2 c \, dy \, y + 2 x \, Dt[x]$

■ 3.5.3 Derivatives of Unknown Functions

Differentiating a known function gives an explicit result.

In[1]:= **D[Log[x]^2, x]**

Out[1]= $\dfrac{2 \, Log[x]}{x}$

Differentiating an unknown function f gives a result in terms of f′.

In[2]:= **D[f[x]^2, x]**

Out[2]= $2 \, f[x] \, f'[x]$

Mathematica applies the chain rule for differentiation, and leaves the result in terms of f′.

In[3]:= **D[x f[x^2], x]**

Out[3]= $f[x^2] + 2 x^2 \, f'[x^2]$

Differentiating again gives a result in terms of f, f′ and f′′.

In[4]:= **D[%, x]**

Out[4]= $6 x \, f'[x^2] + 4 x^3 \, f''[x^2]$

When a function has more than one argument, superscripts are used to indicate how many times each argument is being differentiated.

In[5]:= **D[g[x^2, y^2], x]**

Out[5]= $2 x \, g^{(1,0)}[x^2, y^2]$

This represents $\frac{\partial}{\partial x}\frac{\partial}{\partial x}\frac{\partial}{\partial y}g(x,y)$. *Mathematica* assumes that the order in which derivatives are taken with respect to different variables is irrelevant.

In[6]:= **D[g[x, y], x, x, y]**

Out[6]= $g^{(2,1)}[x, y]$

You can find the value of the derivative
when $x = 0$ by replacing x with 0.

```
In[7]:= % /. x->0

Out[7]= g^(2,1) [0, y]
```

$f'[x]$	first derivative of a function of one variable
$f^{(n)}[x]$	n^{th} derivative of a function of one variable
$f^{(n_1,n_2,\dots)}[x]$	derivative of a function of several variables, n_i times with respect to variable i

Output forms for derivatives of unknown functions.

■ 3.5.4 Advanced Topic: The Representation of Derivatives

Derivatives in *Mathematica* work essentially the same as in standard mathematics. The usual mathematical notation, however, often hides many details. To understand how derivatives are represented in *Mathematica*, we must look at these details.

The standard mathematical notation $f'(0)$ is really a shorthand for $\frac{d}{dt}f(t)|_{t=0}$, where t is a "dummy variable". Similarly, $f'(x^2)$ is a shorthand for $\frac{d}{dt}f(t)|_{t=x^2}$. As suggested by the notation f', the object $\frac{d}{dt}f(t)$ can in fact be viewed as a "pure function", to be evaluated with a particular choice of its parameter t. You can think of the operation of differentiation as acting on a *function f*, to give a new *function*, usually called f'.

With functions of more than one argument, the simple notation based on primes breaks down. You cannot tell for example whether $g'(0, 1)$ stands for $\frac{d}{dt}g(t, 1)|_{t=0}$ or $\frac{d}{dt}g(0, t)|_{t=1}$, and for almost any g, these will have totally different values. Once again, however, t is just a dummy variable, whose sole purpose is to show with respect to which "slot" g is to be differentiated.

In *Mathematica*, as in some branches of mathematics, it is convenient to think about a kind of differentiation that acts on *functions*, rather than expressions. We need an operation that takes the function f, and gives us the *derivative function f'*. Operations such as this that act on *functions*, rather than variables, are known in mathematics as *functionals*.

The object f' in *Mathematica* is the result of applying the differentiation functional to the function f. The full form of f' is in fact Derivative[1][f]. Derivative[1] is the *Mathematica* differentiation functional.

The arguments in the functional Derivative[n_1, n_2, ...] specify how many times to differentiate with respect to each "slot" of the function on which it acts. By using functionals to represent differentiation, *Mathematica* avoids any need to introduce explicit "dummy variables".

This is the full form of the derivative
of the function f.

```
In[1]:= f' // FullForm

Out[1]//FullForm= Derivative[1][f]
```

Here an argument x is supplied.	*In[2]:=* **f'[x] // FullForm**
	Out[2]//FullForm= Derivative[1][f][x]
This is the second derivative.	*In[3]:=* **f''[x] // FullForm**
	Out[3]//FullForm= Derivative[2][f][x]
This gives a derivative of the function g with respect to its second "slot".	*In[4]:=* **D[g[x, y], y]**
	Out[4]= $g^{(0,1)}[x, y]$
Here is the full form.	*In[5]:=* **% // FullForm**
	Out[5]//FullForm= Derivative[0, 1][g][x, y]
Here is the second derivative with respect to the variable y, which appears in the second slot of g.	*In[6]:=* **D[g[x, y], {y, 2}] // FullForm**
	Out[6]//FullForm= Derivative[0, 2][g][x, y]
This is a mixed derivative.	*In[7]:=* **D[g[x, y], x, y, y] // FullForm**
	Out[7]//FullForm= Derivative[1, 2][g][x, y]
Since **Derivative** only specifies how many times to differentiate with respect to each slot, the order of the derivatives is irrelevant.	*In[8]:=* **D[g[x, y], y, y, x] // FullForm**
	Out[8]//FullForm= Derivative[1, 2][g][x, y]
Here is a more complicated case, in which both arguments of g depend on the differentiation variable.	*In[9]:=* **D[g[x, x], x]**
	Out[9]= $g^{(0,1)}[x, x] + g^{(1,0)}[x, x]$
This is the full form of the result.	*In[10]:=* **% // FullForm**
	Out[10]//FullForm= Plus[Derivative[0, 1][g][x, x], Derivative[1, 0][g][x, x]]

The object **f'** behaves essentially like any other function in *Mathematica*. You can evaluate the function with any argument, and you can use standard *Mathematica* **/.** operations to change the argument. (This would not be possible if explicit dummy variables had been introduced in the course of the differentiation.)

This is the *Mathematica* representation of the derivative of a function f, evaluated at the origin.	*In[11]:=* **f'[0] // FullForm**
	Out[11]//FullForm= Derivative[1][f][0]
The result of this derivative involves f' evaluated with the argument x^2.	*In[12]:=* **D[f[x^2], x]**
	Out[12]= $2 x f'[x^2]$
You can evaluate the result at the point $x = 2$ by using the standard *Mathematica* replacement operation.	*In[13]:=* **% /. x->2**
	Out[13]= $4 f'[4]$

There is some slight subtlety when you need to deduce the value of **f'** based on definitions for objects like **f[x_]**.

Here is a definition for a function h.	*In[14]:=* **h[x_] := x^4**
When you take the derivative of h[x], *Mathematica* first evaluates h[x], then differentiates the result.	*In[15]:=* **D[h[x], x]** *Out[15]=* $4 x^3$
You can get the same result by applying the function h' to the argument x.	*In[16]:=* **h'[x]** *Out[16]=* $4 x^3$
Here is the function h' on its own.	*In[17]:=* **h'** *Out[17]=* $4 \#1^3$ &

The function f' is completely determined by the form of the function f. Definitions for objects like f[x_] do not immediately apply however to expressions like f'[x]. The problem is that f'[x] has the full form Derivative[1][f][x], which nowhere contains anything that explicitly matches the pattern f[x_]. In addition, for many purposes it is convenient to have a representation of the function f' itself, without necessarily applying it to any arguments.

What *Mathematica* does is to try and find the explicit form of a *pure function* which represents the object f'. When *Mathematica* gets an expression like Derivative[1][f], it effectively converts it to the explicit form D[f[#], #]& and then tries to evaluate the derivative. In the explicit form, *Mathematica* can immediately use values that have been defined for objects like f[x_]. If *Mathematica* succeeds in doing the derivative, it returns the explicit pure-function result. If it does not succeed, it leaves the derivative in the original f' form.

This gives the derivative of Tan in pure-function form.	*In[18]:=* **Tan'** *Out[18]=* $\text{Sec}[\#1]^2$ &
Here is the result of applying the pure function to the specific argument y.	*In[19]:=* **%[y]** *Out[19]=* $\text{Sec}[y]^2$

■ 3.5.5 Defining Derivatives

You can define the derivative in *Mathematica* of a function f of one argument simply by an assignment like f'[x_] = fp[x].

This defines the derivative of $f(x)$ to be $fp(x)$. In this case, you could have used = instead of :=.	*In[1]:=* **f'[x_] := fp[x]**
The rule for f'[x_] is used to evaluate this derivative.	*In[2]:=* **D[f[x^2], x]** *Out[2]=* $2 x \, fp[x^2]$
Differentiating again gives derivatives of *fp*.	*In[3]:=* **D[%, x]** *Out[3]=* $2 \, fp[x^2] + 4 x^2 \, fp'[x^2]$

| This defines a value for the derivative of *g* at the origin. | *In[4]:=* **g'[0] = g0** |
| | *Out[4]=* g0 |

| The value for g'[0] is used. | *In[5]:=* **D[g[x]^2, x] /. x->0** |
| | *Out[5]=* 2 g0 g[0] |

| This defines the second derivative of g, with any argument. | *In[6]:=* **g''[x_] = gpp[x]** |
| | *Out[6]=* gpp[x] |

| The value defined for the second derivative is used. | *In[7]:=* **D[g[x]^2, {x, 2}]** |
| | *Out[7]=* $2\,g[x]\,gpp[x] + 2\,g'[x]^2$ |

To define derivatives of functions with several arguments, you have to use the general representation of derivatives in *Mathematica*.

$f'[x\_] := rhs$ define the first derivative of *f*

$\text{Derivative}[n][f][x\_] := rhs$ define the nth derivative of *f*

$\text{Derivative}[m, n, \ldots][g][x\_, \_, \ldots] := rhs$
       define derivatives of *g* with respect to various arguments

Defining derivatives.

| This defines the second derivative of g with respect to its second argument. | *In[8]:=* **Derivative[0, 2][g][x_, y_] := g2p[x, y]** |

| This uses the definition just given. | *In[9]:=* **D[g[a^2, x^2], x, x]** |
| | *Out[9]=* $4\,x^2\,g2p[a^2, x^2] + 2\,g^{(0,1)}[a^2, x^2]$ |

■ 3.5.6 Indefinite Integrals

The *Mathematica* function Integrate[*f*, *x*] gives you the *indefinite integral* $\int f\,dx$. You can think of the operation of indefinite integration as being an inverse of differentiation. If you take the result from Integrate[*f*, *x*], and then differentiate it, you always get a result that is mathematically equal to the original expression *f*.

In general, however, there is a whole family of results which have the property that their derivative is *f*. Integrate[*f*, *x*] gives you *an* expression whose derivative is *f*. You can get other expressions by adding an arbitrary constant of integration, or indeed by adding any function that is constant except at discrete points.

If you fill in explicit limits for your integral, any such constants of integration must cancel out. But even though the indefinite integral can have arbitrary constants added, it is still often very convenient to manipulate it without filling in the limits.

Mathematica applies standard rules to find indefinite integrals.

$In[1]:=$ **Integrate[x^2, x]**

$Out[1]=$ $\dfrac{x^3}{3}$

You can add an arbitrary constant to the indefinite integral, and still get the same derivative. Integrate simply gives you *an* expression with the required derivative.

$In[2]:=$ **D[% + c, x]**

$Out[2]=$ x^2

This gives the indefinite integral $\int \frac{dx}{x^2-1}$.

$In[3]:=$ **Integrate[1/(x^2 - 1), x]**

$Out[3]=$ $\dfrac{1}{2} \text{Log}[-1 + x] - \dfrac{1}{2} \text{Log}[1 + x]$

Differentiating should give the original function back again.

$In[4]:=$ **D[%, x]**

$Out[4]=$ $\dfrac{1}{2(-1+x)} - \dfrac{1}{2(1+x)}$

You need to manipulate it to get it back into the original form.

$In[5]:=$ **Simplify[%]**

$Out[5]=$ $\dfrac{1}{-1+x^2}$

The Integrate function assumes that any object that does not explicitly contain the integration variable is independent of it, and can be treated as a constant. As a result, Integrate is like an inverse of the *partial differentiation* function D.

The variable a is assumed to be independent of x.

$In[6]:=$ **Integrate[a x^2, x]**

$Out[6]=$ $\dfrac{a\,x^3}{3}$

The integration variable can be any expression that does not involve explicit mathematical operations.

$In[7]:=$ **Integrate[x b[x]^2, b[x]]**

$Out[7]=$ $\dfrac{1}{3} x\,b[x]^3$

Another assumption that Integrate implicitly makes is that all the symbolic quantities in your integrand have "generic" values. Thus, for example, *Mathematica* will tell you that $\int x^n\,dx$ is $\frac{x^{n+1}}{n+1}$ even though this is not true in the special case $n = -1$.

Mathematica gives the standard result for this integral, implicitly assuming that n is not equal to -1.

$In[8]:=$ **Integrate[x^n, x]**

$Out[8]=$ $\dfrac{x^{1+n}}{1+n}$

If you specifically give an exponent of -1, *Mathematica* produces a different result.

$In[9]:=$ **Integrate[x^-1, x]**

$Out[9]=$ $\text{Log}[x]$

You should realize that the result for any particular integral can often be written in many different forms. *Mathematica* tries to give you the most convenient form, following principles such as avoiding explicit complex numbers unless your input already contains them.

This integral is given in terms of ArcTan.

In[10]:= `Integrate[1/(1 + a x^2), x]`

$$Out[10]= \frac{\text{ArcTan}\left[\sqrt{a}\ x\right]}{\sqrt{a}}$$

This integral is given in terms of ArcTanh.

In[11]:= `Integrate[1/(1 - b x^2), x]`

$$Out[11]= \frac{\text{ArcTanh}\left[\sqrt{b}\ x\right]}{\sqrt{b}}$$

This is mathematically equal to the first integral, but is given in a somewhat different form.

In[12]:= `% /. b -> -a`

$$Out[12]= \frac{\text{ArcTanh}\left[\sqrt{-a}\ x\right]}{\sqrt{-a}}$$

The derivative is still correct.

In[13]:= `D[%, x]`

$$Out[13]= \frac{1}{1 + a\,x^2}$$

Even though they look quite different, both `ArcTan[x]` and `-ArcTan[1/x]` are indefinite integrals of $1/(1 + x^2)$.

In[14]:= `Simplify[D[{ArcTan[x], -ArcTan[1/x]}, x]]`

$$Out[14]= \left\{\frac{1}{1 + x^2}, \frac{1}{1 + x^2}\right\}$$

Integrate chooses to use the simpler of the two forms.

In[15]:= `Integrate[1/(1 + x^2), x]`

Out[15]= `ArcTan[x]`

■ 3.5.7 Integrals That Can and Cannot Be Done

Evaluating integrals is much more difficult than evaluating derivatives. For derivatives, there is a systematic procedure based on the chain rule that effectively allows any derivative to be worked out. But for integrals, there is no such systematic procedure.

One of the main problems is that it is difficult to know what kinds of functions will be needed to evaluate a particular integral. When you work out a derivative, you always end up with functions that are of the same kind or simpler than the ones you started with. But when you work out integrals, you often end up needing to use functions that are much more complicated than the ones you started with.

This integral can be evaluated using the same kind of functions that appeared in the input.

In[1]:= `Integrate[Log[x]^2, x]`

$$Out[1]= x\left(2 - 2\,\text{Log}[x] + \text{Log}[x]^2\right)$$

But for this integral the special function `LogIntegral` is needed.

In[2]:= `Integrate[Log[Log[x]], x]`

Out[2]= `x Log[Log[x]] - LogIntegral[x]`

It is not difficult to find integrals that require all sorts of functions.

In[3]:= `Integrate[Sin[x^2], x]`

$$Out[3]= \sqrt{\frac{\pi}{2}}\ \text{FresnelS}\left[\sqrt{\frac{2}{\pi}}\ x\right]$$

Simple-looking integrals can give remarkably complicated results. Often it is convenient to apply Simplify to your answers.

```
In[4]:= Simplify[ Integrate[Log[x] Exp[-x^2], x] ]
```

$$Out[4]= -x \, \text{HypergeometricPFQ}\left[\left\{\frac{1}{2}, \frac{1}{2}\right\}, \left\{\frac{3}{2}, \frac{3}{2}\right\}, -x^2\right] + \frac{1}{2} \sqrt{\pi} \, \text{Erf}[x] \, \text{Log}[x]$$

This integral involves an incomplete gamma function. Note that the power is carefully set up to allow any complex value of x.

```
In[5]:= Integrate[Exp[-x^a], x]
```

$$Out[5]= -\frac{x \, (x^a)^{-1/a} \, \text{Gamma}\left[\frac{1}{a}, x^a\right]}{a}$$

Mathematica includes a very wide range of mathematical functions, and by using these functions a great many integrals can be done. But it is still possible to find even fairly simple-looking integrals that just cannot be done in terms of any standard mathematical functions.

Here is a fairly simple-looking integral that cannot be done in terms of any standard mathematical functions.

```
In[6]:= Integrate[Sin[x]/Log[x], x]
```

$$Out[6]= \int \frac{\text{Sin}[x]}{\text{Log}[x]} \, dx$$

The main point of being able to do an integral in terms of standard mathematical functions is that it lets one use the known properties of these functions to evaluate or manipulate the result one gets.

In the most convenient cases, integrals can be done purely in terms of elementary functions such as exponentials, logarithms and trigonometric functions. In fact, if you give an integrand that involves only such elementary functions, then one of the important capabilities of Integrate is that if the corresponding integral can be expressed in terms of elementary functions, then Integrate will essentially always succeed in finding it.

Integrals of rational functions are straightforward to evaluate, and always come out in terms of rational functions, logarithms and inverse trigonometric functions.

```
In[7]:= Integrate[x/((x - 1)(x + 2)), x]
```

$$Out[7]= \frac{1}{3} \, \text{Log}[-1 + x] + \frac{2}{3} \, \text{Log}[2 + x]$$

The integral here is still of the same form, but now involves an implicit sum over the roots of a polynomial.

```
In[8]:= Integrate[1/(1 + 2 x + x^3), x]
```

$$Out[8]= \text{RootSum}\left[1 + 2\#1 + \#1^3 \, \&, \frac{\text{Log}[x - \#1]}{2 + 3\#1^2} \, \&\right]$$

This finds numerical approximations to all the root objects.

```
In[9]:= N[%]
```

$$Out[9]= (-0.19108 - 0.088541 \, i)$$
$$\text{Log}[(-0.226699 - 1.46771 \, i) + x] -$$
$$(0.19108 - 0.088541 \, i)$$
$$\text{Log}[(-0.226699 + 1.46771 \, i) + x] +$$
$$0.38216 \, \text{Log}[0.453398 + x]$$

Integrals of trigonometric functions usually come out in terms of other trigonometric functions.

```
In[10]:= Integrate[Sin[x]^3 Cos[x]^2, x]
```

$$Out[10]= \frac{1}{30} \, \text{Cos}[x]^3 \, (-7 + 3 \, \text{Cos}[2 x])$$

This is a fairly simple integral involving algebraic functions.

In[11]:= **Integrate[Sqrt[x] Sqrt[1 + x], x]**

Out[11]= $\frac{1}{4} \left(\sqrt{x} \sqrt{1+x} \ (1+2\,x) - \text{ArcSinh}\left[\sqrt{x}\right] \right)$

Here is an integral involving nested square roots.

In[12]:= **Integrate[Sqrt[x + Sqrt[x]], x]**

Out[12]= $\left(\sqrt{\sqrt{x}+x} \ \left(\sqrt{1+\sqrt{x}} \ x^{1/4} \ (-3 + 2\sqrt{x} + 8\,x) + \right.\right.$
$\left.\left. 3\,\text{ArcSinh}[x^{1/4}] \right) \right) \Big/ \left(12 \sqrt{1+\sqrt{x}} \ x^{1/4} \right)$

By nesting elementary functions you sometimes get integrals that can be done in terms of elementary functions.

In[13]:= **Integrate[Cos[Log[x]], x]**

Out[13]= $\frac{1}{2}\,x\,(\text{Cos}[\text{Log}[x]] + \text{Sin}[\text{Log}[x]])$

But more often other kinds of functions are needed.

In[14]:= **Integrate[Log[Cos[x]], x]**

Out[14]= $\frac{\mathbb{i}\,x^2}{2} - x\,\text{Log}[1 + e^{2\,\mathbb{i}\,x}] +$
$x\,\text{Log}[\text{Cos}[x]] + \frac{1}{2}\,\mathbb{i}\,\text{PolyLog}[2, -e^{2\,\mathbb{i}\,x}]$

Integrals like this typically come out in terms of elliptic functions.

In[15]:= **Integrate[Sqrt[Cos[x]], x]**

Out[15]= $2\,\text{EllipticE}\left[\frac{x}{2}, 2\right]$

But occasionally one can get results in terms of elementary functions alone.

In[16]:= **Integrate[Sqrt[Tan[x]], x]**

Out[16]= $\frac{1}{2\sqrt{2}} \left(-2\,\text{ArcTan}\left[1 - \sqrt{2}\ \sqrt{\text{Tan}[x]}\right] + \right.$
$2\,\text{ArcTan}\left[1 + \sqrt{2}\ \sqrt{\text{Tan}[x]}\right] +$
$\text{Log}\left[-1 + \sqrt{2}\ \sqrt{\text{Tan}[x]} - \text{Tan}[x]\right] -$
$\left.\text{Log}\left[1 + \sqrt{2}\ \sqrt{\text{Tan}[x]} + \text{Tan}[x]\right] \right)$

Beyond working with elementary functions, Integrate includes a large number of algorithms for dealing with special functions. Sometimes it uses a direct generalization of the procedure for elementary functions. But more often its strategy is first to try to write the integrand in a form that can be integrated in terms of certain sophisticated special functions, and then having done this to try to find reductions of these sophisticated functions to more familiar functions.

To integrate this Bessel function requires a generalized hypergeometric function.

In[17]:= **Integrate[BesselJ[0, x], x]**

Out[17]= $x\,\text{HypergeometricPFQ}\left[\left\{\frac{1}{2}\right\}, \left\{1, \frac{3}{2}\right\}, -\frac{x^2}{4}\right]$

To integrate an elliptic integral also requires a generalized hypergeometric function.

In[18]:= **Integrate[EllipticK[x], x]**

Out[18]= $\frac{1}{2}\,\pi\,x\,\text{HypergeometricPFQ}\left[\left\{\frac{1}{2}, \frac{1}{2}\right\}, \{2\}, x\right]$

Sometimes the integrals can be reduced to more familiar forms.

In[19]:= **Integrate[x^3 BesselJ[0, x], x]**

Out[19]= $-x^2\,(-2\,\text{BesselJ}[2, x] + x\,\text{BesselJ}[3, x])$

A large book of integral tables will list perhaps a few thousand indefinite integrals. *Mathematica* can do essentially all of these integrals. And because it contains general algorithms rather than just specific cases, *Mathematica* can actually do a vastly wider range of integrals.

You could expect to find this integral in any large book of integral tables.	*In[20]:=* **Integrate[Log[1 - x]/x, x]** *Out[20]=* -PolyLog[2, x]

To do this integral, however, requires a more general algorithm, rather than just a direct table lookup.

$$In[21]:= \textbf{Integrate[Log[1 + 3 x + x^2]/x, x]}$$

$$Out[21]= -\text{Log}[x]\,\text{Log}\left[1 - \frac{2\,x}{-3 + \sqrt{5}}\right] -$$

$$\text{Log}[x]\,\text{Log}\left[1 + \frac{2\,x}{3 + \sqrt{5}}\right] + \text{Log}[x]\,\text{Log}[1 + 3\,x + x^2] -$$

$$\text{PolyLog}\left[2, \frac{2\,x}{-3 + \sqrt{5}}\right] - \text{PolyLog}\left[2, -\frac{2\,x}{3 + \sqrt{5}}\right]$$

Particularly if you introduce new mathematical functions of your own, you may want to teach *Mathematica* new kinds of integrals. You can do this by making appropriate definitions for Integrate.

In the case of differentiation, the chain rule allows one to reduce all derivatives to a standard form, represented in *Mathematica* using Derivative. But for integration, no such similar standard form exists, and as a result you often have to make definitions for several different versions of the same integral. Changes of variables and other transformations can rarely be done automatically by Integrate.

This integral cannot be done in terms of any of the standard mathematical functions built into *Mathematica*.	*In[22]:=* **Integrate[Sin[Sin[x]], x]** *Out[22]=* $\int \text{Sin}[\text{Sin}[x]]\,dx$

Before you add your own rules for integration, you have to remove write protection.	*In[23]:=* **Unprotect[Integrate]** *Out[23]=* {Integrate}

You can set up your own rule to define the integral to be, say, a "Jones" function.	*In[24]:=* **Integrate[Sin[Sin[a_. + b_. x_]], x_] := Jones[a, x]/b**

Now *Mathematica* can do integrals that give Jones functions.	*In[25]:=* **Integrate[Sin[Sin[3x]], x]** *Out[25]=* $\frac{1}{3}$ Jones[0, x]

As it turns out, the integral $\int \sin(\sin(x))\,dx$ can in principle be represented as an infinite sum of $_2F_1$ hypergeometric functions, or as a suitably generalized Kampé de Fériet hypergeometric function of two variables.

■ 3.5.8 Definite Integrals

Integrate[f, x]	the indefinite integral $\int f\, dx$
Integrate[f, {x, xmin, xmax}]	the definite integral $\int_{xmin}^{xmax} f\, dx$
Integrate[f, {x, xmin, xmax}, {y, ymin, ymax}]	
	the multiple integral $\int_{xmin}^{xmax} dx \int_{ymin}^{ymax} dy\, f$

Integration functions.

Here is the integral $\int_a^b x^2\, dx$.

$In[1]:=$ **Integrate[x^2, {x, a, b}]**

$Out[1]=$ $\dfrac{1}{3}\,(-a^3 + b^3)$

This gives the multiple integral $\int_0^a dx \int_0^b dy\,(x^2 + y^2)$.

$In[2]:=$ **Integrate[x^2 + y^2, {x, 0, a}, {y, 0, b}]**

$Out[2]=$ $\dfrac{1}{3}\,a\,b\,(a^2 + b^2)$

The y integral is done first. Its limits can depend on the value of x. This ordering is the same as is used in functions like Sum and Table.

$In[3]:=$ **Integrate[x^2 + y^2, {x, 0, a}, {y, 0, x}]**

$Out[3]=$ $\dfrac{a^4}{3}$

In simple cases, definite integrals can be done by finding indefinite forms and then computing appropriate limits. But there is a vast range of integrals for which the indefinite form cannot be expressed in terms of standard mathematical functions, but the definite form still can be.

This indefinite integral cannot be done in terms of standard mathematical functions.

$In[4]:=$ **Integrate[Cos[Sin[x]], x]**

$Out[4]=$ $\int \mathrm{Cos}[\mathrm{Sin}[x]]\, dx$

This definite integral, however, can be done in terms of a Bessel function.

$In[5]:=$ **Integrate[Cos[Sin[x]], {x, 0, 2Pi}]**

$Out[5]=$ $2\pi\, \mathrm{BesselJ}[0, 1]$

Here is an integral where the indefinite form can be found, but it is much more efficient to work out the definite form directly.

$In[6]:=$ **Integrate[Log[x] Exp[-x^2], {x, 0, Infinity}]**

$Out[6]=$ $-\dfrac{1}{4}\,\sqrt{\pi}\,(\mathrm{EulerGamma} + \mathrm{Log}[4])$

Just because an integrand may contain special functions, it does not mean that the definite integral will necessarily be complicated.

$In[7]:=$ **Integrate[BesselK[0, x]^2, {x, 0, Infinity}]**

$Out[7]=$ $\dfrac{\pi^2}{4}$

Special functions nevertheless occur in this result.

$In[8]:=$ **Integrate[BesselK[0, x] BesselJ[0, x], {x, 0, Infinity}]**

$Out[8]=$ $\dfrac{\mathrm{Gamma}\left[\frac{1}{4}\right]^2}{4\sqrt{2\pi}}$

The integrand here is simple, but the definite integral is not.

$In[9]:=$ **Integrate[Sin[x^2] Exp[-x], {x, 0, Infinity}]**

$Out[9]= \frac{1}{2\sqrt{2}}\left(-\sqrt{2}\ \text{HypergeometricPFQ}\left[\{1\}, \left\{\frac{3}{4}, \frac{5}{4}\right\}, -\frac{1}{64}\right] + \sqrt{\pi}\left(\cos\left[\frac{1}{4}\right] + \sin\left[\frac{1}{4}\right]\right)\right)$

Even when you can find the indefinite form of an integral, you will often not get the correct answer for the definite integral if you just subtract the values of the limits at each end point. The problem is that within the domain of integration there may be singularities whose effects are ignored if you follow this procedure.

Here is the indefinite integral of $1/x^2$.

$In[10]:=$ **Integrate[1/x^2, x]**

$Out[10]= -\frac{1}{x}$

This subtracts the limits at each end point.

$In[11]:=$ **Limit[%, x->2] - Limit[%, x->-2]**

$Out[11]= -1$

The true definite integral is divergent because of the double pole at $x = 0$.

$In[12]:=$ **Integrate[1/x^2, {x, -2, 2}]**

$Out[12]= \infty$

Here is a more subtle example, involving branch cuts rather than poles.

$In[13]:=$ **Integrate[1/(1 + a Sin[x]), x]**

$Out[13]= \frac{2\ \text{ArcTan}\left[\frac{a+\text{Tan}\left[\frac{x}{2}\right]}{\sqrt{1-a^2}}\right]}{\sqrt{1-a^2}}$

Taking limits in the indefinite integral gives 0.

$In[14]:=$ **Limit[%, x -> 2Pi] - Limit[%, x -> 0]**

$Out[14]= 0$

The definite integral, however, gives the correct result which depends on a.

$In[15]:=$ **Integrate[1/(1 + a Sin[x]), {x, 0, 2Pi}]**

$Out[15]= \frac{4\pi}{\sqrt{4 - 4a^2}}$

Integrate[f, {x, $xmin$, $xmax$}, PrincipalValue -> True]
　　　　the Cauchy principal value of a definite integral

Principal value integrals.

Here is the indefinite integral of $1/x$.

$In[16]:=$ **Integrate[1/x, x]**

$Out[16]= \text{Log}[x]$

Substituting in the limits -1 and $+2$ yields a strange result involving $i\pi$.

$In[17]:=$ **Limit[%, x -> 2] - Limit[%, x -> -1]**

$Out[17]= -i\pi + \text{Log}[2]$

The ordinary Riemann definite integral is divergent.	*In[18]:=* **Integrate[1/x, {x, -1, 2}]**

Integrate::idiv:

$$\text{Integral of } \frac{1}{x} \text{ does not converge on } \{-1, 2\}.$$

$$Out[18]= \int_{-1}^{2} \frac{1}{x} \, dx$$

The Cauchy principal value, however, is finite.	*In[19]:=* **Integrate[1/x, {x, -1, 2}, PrincipalValue->True]**
	Out[19]= Log[2]

When parameters appear in an indefinite integral, it is essentially always possible to get results that are correct for almost all values of these parameters. But for definite integrals this is no longer the case. The most common problem is that a definite integral may converge only when the parameters that appear in it satisfy certain specific conditions.

This indefinite integral is correct for all $n \neq -1$.	*In[20]:=* **Integrate[x^n, x]**

$$Out[20]= \frac{x^{1+n}}{1+n}$$

For the definite integral, however, n must satisfy a condition in order for the integral to be convergent.	*In[21]:=* **Integrate[x^n, {x, 0, 1}]**

$$Out[21]= \text{If}\left[\text{Re}[n] > -1, \frac{1}{1+n}, \right.$$
$$\left. \text{Integrate}[x^n, \{x, 0, 1\}, \text{Assumptions} \to \text{Re}[n] \leq -1]\right]$$

If n is replaced by 2, the condition is satisfied.	*In[22]:=* **% /. n -> 2**

$$Out[22]= \frac{1}{3}$$

option name	default value	
GenerateConditions	Automatic	whether to generate explicit conditions
Assumptions	{}	what relations about parameters to assume

Options for Integrate.

With the assumption $n > 2$, the result is always $1/(1 + n)$.	*In[23]:=* **Integrate[x^n, {x, 0, 1}, Assumptions -> (n > 2)]**

$$Out[23]= \frac{1}{1+n}$$

Even when a definite integral is convergent, the presence of singularities on the integration path can lead to discontinuous changes when the parameters vary. Sometimes a single formula containing functions like Sign can be used to summarize the result. In other cases, however, an explicit If is more convenient.

The If here gives the condition for the integral to be convergent.

$In[24]:=$ **Integrate[Sin[a x]/x, {x, 0, Infinity}]**

$Out[24]=$ $\text{If}\left[\text{Im}[a] == 0, \frac{1}{2}\pi\,\text{Sign}[a], \text{Integrate}\left[\frac{\text{Sin}[a\,x]}{x}, \{x, 0, \infty\}, \text{Assumptions} \rightarrow \text{Im}[a] \neq 0\right]\right]$

Here is the result assuming that a is real.

$In[25]:=$ **Integrate[Sin[a x]/x, {x, 0, Infinity},**
                    Assumptions -> Im[a] == 0]

$Out[25]=$ $\frac{1}{2}\pi\,\text{Sign}[a]$

The result is discontinuous as a function of a. The discontinuity can be traced to the essential singularity of $\sin(x)$ at $x = \infty$.

$In[26]:=$ **Plot[%, {a, -5, 5}]**

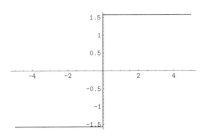

There is no convenient way to represent this answer in terms of Sign, so *Mathematica* generates an explicit If.

$In[27]:=$ **Integrate[Sin[x] BesselJ[0, a x]/x, {x, 0, Infinity},**
                    Assumptions -> Im[a] == 0]

$Out[27]=$ $\text{If}\left[a^2 > 1, \frac{a\,\text{ArcSin}\left[\frac{1}{a}\right]}{\text{Abs}[a]}, \frac{\pi}{2}\right]$

Here is a plot of the resulting function of a.

$In[28]:=$ **Plot[Evaluate[%], {a, -5, 5}]**

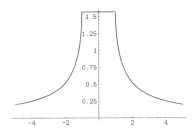

■ 3.5.9 Manipulating Integrals in Symbolic Form

When *Mathematica* cannot give you an explicit result for an integral, it leaves the integral in a symbolic form. It is often useful to manipulate this symbolic form.

Mathematica cannot give an explicit result for this integral, so it leaves the integral in symbolic form.

$In[1]:=$ **Integrate[x^2 f[x], x]**

$Out[1]=$ $\int x^2 f[x] dx$

Differentiating the symbolic form gives the integrand back again.

$In[2]:=$ **D[%, x]**

$Out[2]=$ $x^2 f[x]$

Here is a definite integral which cannot be done explicitly.

$In[3]:=$ **Integrate[f[x], {x, a[x], b[x]}]**

$Out[3]=$ $\int_{a[x]}^{b[x]} f[x] dx$

This gives the derivative of the definite integral.

$In[4]:=$ **D[%, x]**

$Out[4]=$ $-f[a[x]] a'[x] + f[b[x]] b'[x]$

Here is a definite integral with end points that do not explicitly depend on x.

$In[5]:=$ **defint = Integrate[f[x], {x, a, b}]**

$Out[5]=$ $\int_a^b f[x] dx$

The partial derivative of this with respect to u is zero.

$In[6]:=$ **D[defint, u]**

$Out[6]=$ 0

There is a non-trivial total derivative, however.

$In[7]:=$ **Dt[defint, u]**

$Out[7]=$ $-Dt[a, u] f[a] + Dt[b, u] f[b]$

■ 3.5.10 Differential Equations

As discussed in Section 1.5.9, you can use the *Mathematica* function DSolve to find symbolic solutions to ordinary and partial differential equations.

Solving a differential equation consists essentially in finding the form of an unknown function. In *Mathematica*, unknown functions are represented by expressions like y[x]. The derivatives of such functions are represented by y'[x], y''[x] and so on.

The *Mathematica* function DSolve returns as its result a list of rules for functions. There is a question of how these functions are represented. If you ask DSolve to solve for y[x], then DSolve will indeed return a rule for y[x]. In some cases, this rule may be all you need. But this rule, on its own, does not give values for y'[x] or even y[0]. In many cases, therefore, it is better to ask DSolve to solve not for y[x], but instead for y itself. In this case, what DSolve will return is a rule which gives y as a pure function, in the sense discussed in Section 2.2.5.

If you ask DSolve to solve for y[x], it will give a rule specifically for y[x].

$In[1]:=$ **DSolve[y'[x] + y[x] == 1, y[x], x]**

$Out[1]=$ $\{\{y[x] \rightarrow 1 + e^{-x} C[1]\}\}$

The rule applies only to y[x] itself, and not, for example, to objects like y[0] or y'[x].

$In[2]:=$ **y[x] + 2y'[x] + y[0] /. %**

$Out[2]=$ $\{1 + e^{-x} C[1] + y[0] + 2 y'[x]\}$

If you ask DSolve to solve for y, it gives a rule for the object y on its own as a pure function.

$In[3]:=$ **DSolve[y'[x] + y[x] == 1, y, x]**

$Out[3]=$ $\{\{y \rightarrow \text{Function}[\{x\}, 1 + e^{-x} C[1]]\}\}$

Now the rule applies to all occurrences of y.

$In[4]:=$ **y[x] + 2y'[x] + y[0] /. %**

$Out[4]=$ $\{2 + C[1] - e^{-x} C[1]\}$

Substituting the solution into the original equation yields True.

$In[5]:=$ **y'[x] + y[x] == 1 /. %%**

$Out[5]=$ $\{\text{True}\}$

DSolve[*eqn*, y[x], x]	solve a differential equation for $y[x]$
DSolve[*eqn*, y, x]	solve a differential equation for the function y

Getting solutions to differential equations in different forms.

In standard mathematical notation, one typically represents solutions to differential equations by explicitly introducing "dummy variables" to represent the arguments of the functions that appear. If all you need is a symbolic form for the solution, then introducing such dummy variables may be convenient. However, if you actually intend to use the solution in a variety of other computations, then you will usually find it better to get the solution in pure-function form, without dummy variables. Notice that this form, while easy to represent in *Mathematica*, has no direct analog in standard mathematical notation.

DSolve[{*eqn*$_1$, *eqn*$_2$, ... }, {y_1, y_2, ... }, x] solve a list of differential equations

Solving simultaneous differential equations.

This solves two simultaneous differential equations.

$In[6]:=$ **DSolve[{y[x] == -z'[x], z[x] == -y'[x]}, {y, z}, x]**

$Out[6]=$ $\left\{\left\{z \rightarrow \text{Function}\left[\{x\}, \right.\right.\right.$

$\left. \frac{1}{2} e^{-x} (1 + e^{2x}) C[1] - \frac{1}{2} e^{-x} (-1 + e^{2x}) C[2]\right],$

$y \rightarrow \text{Function}\left[\{x\}, -\frac{1}{2} e^{-x} (-1 + e^{2x}) C[1] + \right.$

$\left.\left.\left. \frac{1}{2} e^{-x} (1 + e^{2x}) C[2]\right]\right\}\right\}$

Mathematica returns two distinct solutions for y in this case.	*In[7]:=* **DSolve[y[x] y'[x] == 1, y, x]** $$Out[7]= \left\{\left\{y \to \text{Function}\left[\{x\}, -\sqrt{2}\ \sqrt{x + C[1]}\ \right]\right\},\right.$$ $$\left.\left\{y \to \text{Function}\left[\{x\}, \sqrt{2}\ \sqrt{x + C[1]}\ \right]\right\}\right\}$$

You can add constraints and boundary conditions for differential equations by explicitly giving additional equations such as $y[0] == 0$.

This asks for a solution which satisfies the condition $y[0] == 1$.	*In[8]:=* **DSolve[{y'[x] == a y[x], y[0] == 1}, y[x], x]** $$Out[8]= \{\{y[x] \to e^{a\,x}\}\}$$

If you ask *Mathematica* to solve a set of differential equations and you do not give any constraints or boundary conditions, then *Mathematica* will try to find a *general solution* to your equations. This general solution will involve various undetermined constants. One new constant is introduced for each order of derivative in each equation you give.

The default is that these constants are named C[*n*], where the index *n* starts at 1 for each invocation of DSolve. You can override this choice, by explicitly giving a setting for the option GeneratedParameters. Any function you give is applied to each successive index value *n* to get the constants to use for each invocation of DSolve.

The general solution to this fourth-order equation involves four undetermined constants.	*In[9]:=* **DSolve[y''''[x] == y[x], y[x], x]** $$Out[9]= \{\{y[x] \to e^x\ C[1] + e^{-x}\ C[3] + C[2]\ \text{Cos}[x] + C[4]\ \text{Sin}[x]\}\}$$

Each independent initial or boundary condition you give reduces the number of undetermined constants by one.	*In[10]:=* **DSolve[{y''''[x] == y[x], y[0] == y'[0] == 0}, y[x], x]** $$Out[10]= \{\{y[x] \to$$ $$e^{-x}\ (C[3] + e^{2\,x}\ C[3] - e^{2\,x}\ C[4] - 2\ e^x\ C[3]\ \text{Cos}[x] +$$ $$e^x\ C[4]\ \text{Cos}[x] + e^x\ C[4]\ \text{Sin}[x])\}\}$$

You should realize that finding exact formulas for the solutions to differential equations is a difficult matter. In fact, there are only fairly few kinds of equations for which such formulas can be found, at least in terms of standard mathematical functions.

The most widely investigated differential equations are linear ones, in which the functions you are solving for, as well as their derivatives, appear only linearly.

This is a homogeneous first-order linear differential equation, and its solution is quite simple.	*In[11]:=* **DSolve[y'[x] - x y[x] == 0, y[x], x]** $$Out[11]= \left\{\left\{y[x] \to e^{\frac{x^2}{2}}\ C[1]\right\}\right\}$$

Making the equation inhomogeneous leads to a significantly more complicated solution.	*In[12]:=* **DSolve[y'[x] - x y[x] == 1, y[x], x]** $$Out[12]= \left\{\left\{y[x] \to e^{\frac{x^2}{2}}\ C[1] + e^{\frac{x^2}{2}}\ \sqrt{\frac{\pi}{2}}\ \text{Erf}\left[\frac{x}{\sqrt{2}}\right]\right\}\right\}$$

If you have only a single linear differential equation, and it involves only a first derivative of the function you are solving for, then it turns out that the solution can always be found just by doing integrals.

But as soon as you have more than one differential equation, or more than a first-order derivative, this is no longer true. However, some simple second-order linear differential equations can nevertheless be solved using various special functions from Section 3.2.10. Indeed, historically many of these special functions were first introduced specifically in order to represent the solutions to such equations.

This is Airy's equation, which is solved in terms of Airy functions.

```
In[13]:= DSolve[y''[x] - x y[x] == 0, y[x], x]
```

$$Out[13]= \{\{y[x] \to \text{AiryAi}[x]\ C[1] + \text{AiryBi}[x]\ C[2]\}\}$$

This equation comes out in terms of Bessel functions.

```
In[14]:= DSolve[y''[x] - Exp[x] y[x] == 0, y[x], x]
```

$$Out[14]= \{\{y[x] \to \text{BesselI}\left[0,\ 2\sqrt{\mathbb{e}^x}\ \right] C[1] + 2\,\text{BesselK}\left[0,\ 2\sqrt{\mathbb{e}^x}\ \right] C[2]\}\}$$

This requires Mathieu functions.

```
In[15]:= DSolve[y''[x] + Cos[x] y[x] == 0, y, x]
```

$$Out[15]= \left\{\left\{y \to \text{Function}\left[\{x\},\ C[1]\ \text{MathieuC}\left[0,\ -2,\ \frac{x}{2}\right] + C[2]\ \text{MathieuS}\left[0,\ -2,\ \frac{x}{2}\right]\right]\right\}\right\}$$

Occasionally second-order linear equations can be solved using only elementary functions.

```
In[16]:= DSolve[x^2 y''[x] + y[x] == 0, y[x], x]
```

$$Out[16]= \left\{\left\{y[x] \to \sqrt{x}\ C[1]\ \text{Cos}\left[\frac{1}{2}\sqrt{3}\ \text{Log}[x]\right] + \sqrt{x}\ C[2]\ \text{Sin}\left[\frac{1}{2}\sqrt{3}\ \text{Log}[x]\right]\right\}\right\}$$

Beyond second order, the kinds of functions needed to solve even fairly simple linear differential equations become extremely complicated. At third order, the generalized Meijer G function `MeijerG` can sometimes be used, but at fourth order and beyond absolutely no standard mathematical functions are typically adequate, except in very special cases.

Here is a third-order linear differential equation which can be solved in terms of generalized hypergeometric functions.

```
In[17]:= DSolve[y'''[x] + x y[x] == 0, y[x], x]
```

$$Out[17]= \left\{\left\{y[x] \to C[1]\ \text{HypergeometricPFQ}\left[\{\},\ \left\{\frac{1}{2},\ \frac{3}{4}\right\},\ -\frac{x^4}{64}\right] + \frac{x\,C[2]\ \text{HypergeometricPFQ}\left[\{\},\ \left\{\frac{3}{4},\ \frac{5}{4}\right\},\ -\frac{x^4}{64}\right]}{2\sqrt{2}} + \frac{1}{8}\ x^2\,C[3]\ \text{HypergeometricPFQ}\left[\{\},\ \left\{\frac{5}{4},\ \frac{3}{2}\right\},\ -\frac{x^4}{64}\right]\right\}\right\}$$

This requires more general Meijer G functions.

```
In[18]:= DSolve[y'''[x] + Exp[x] y[x] == 0, y[x], x]
```

$$Out[18]= \{\{y[x] \to C[1]\ \text{HypergeometricPFQ}[\{\},\ \{1,\ 1\},\ -\mathbb{e}^x] + C[2]\ \text{MeijerG}[\{\{\},\ \{\}\},\ \{\{0,\ 0\},\ \{0\}\},\ -\mathbb{e}^x] + C[3]\ \text{MeijerG}[\{\{\},\ \{\}\},\ \{\{0,\ 0,\ 0\},\ \{\}\},\ \mathbb{e}^x]\}\}$$

For nonlinear differential equations, only rather special cases can usually ever be solved in terms of standard mathematical functions. Nevertheless, `DSolve` includes fairly general procedures which allow it to handle almost all nonlinear differential equations whose solutions are found in standard reference books.

First-order nonlinear differential equations in which x does not appear on its own are fairly easy to solve.

```
In[19]:= DSolve[y'[x] - y[x]^2 == 0, y[x], x]
```

$$Out[19]= \left\{\left\{y[x] \to \frac{1}{-x - C[1]}\right\}\right\}$$

This Riccati equation already gives a significantly more complicated solution.

```
In[20]:= DSolve[y'[x] - y[x]^2 == x, y[x], x] // FullSimplify
```

$$Out[20]= \Bigg\{\Bigg\{y[x] \to$$

$$\left(\sqrt{x}\left(-\text{BesselJ}\left[-\frac{2}{3}, \frac{2x^{3/2}}{3}\right] + \text{BesselJ}\left[\frac{2}{3}, \frac{2x^{3/2}}{3}\right]\right)$$

$$C[1]\right)\Bigg/\left(\text{BesselJ}\left[\frac{1}{3}, \frac{2x^{3/2}}{3}\right] +\right.$$

$$\left.\text{BesselJ}\left[-\frac{1}{3}, \frac{2x^{3/2}}{3}\right]C[1]\right)\Bigg\}\Bigg\}$$

This Bernoulli equation, however, has a fairly simple solution.

```
In[21]:= DSolve[y'[x] - x y[x]^2 - y[x] == 0, y[x], x]
```

$$Out[21]= \left\{\left\{y[x] \to -\frac{e^x}{-e^x + e^x x - C[1]}\right\}\right\}$$

This Abel equation can be solved but only implicitly.

```
In[22]:= DSolve[y'[x] + x y[x]^3 + y[x]^2 == 0, y[x], x]
```

```
Solve::tdep:
    The equations appear to involve the variables to be
      solved for in an essentially non-algebraic way.
```

$$Out[22]= \text{Solve}\Bigg[\frac{1}{2}\Bigg(\frac{2\,\text{ArcTanh}\left[\frac{-1-2x\,y[x]}{\sqrt{5}}\right]}{\sqrt{5}} +$$

$$\text{Log}\left[\frac{-1 - x\,y[x]\,(-1 - x\,y[x])}{x^2\,y[x]^2}\right]\Bigg) ==$$

$$C[1] - \text{Log}[x], y[x]\Bigg]$$

Beyond ordinary differential equations, one can consider *differential-algebraic equations* that involve a mixture of differential and algebraic equations.

This solves a differential-algebraic equation.

```
In[23]:= DSolve[{y'[x] + 3z'[x] == 4 y[x] + 1/x, y[x] + z[x] == 1},
                 {y[x], z[x]}, x]
```

$$Out[23]= \Bigg\{\Bigg\{y[x] \to \frac{3}{2} + \frac{1}{18}$$

$$(-e^{-2x}\,C[1] - 9\,e^{-2x}\,(3\,e^{2x} + \text{ExpIntegralEi}[2x])),$$

$$z[x] \to -\frac{1}{2} + \frac{1}{18}\,(e^{-2x}\,C[1] +$$

$$9\,e^{-2x}\,(3\,e^{2x} + \text{ExpIntegralEi}[2x]))\Bigg\}\Bigg\}$$

> DSolve[*eqn*, y[x_1, x_2, ...], {x_1, x_2, ... }]
> solve a partial differential equation for y[x_1, x_2, ...]
>
> DSolve[*eqn*, y, {x_1, x_2, ... }]   solve a partial differential equation for the function y

Solving partial differential equations.

DSolve is set up to handle not only *ordinary differential equations* in which just a single independent variable appears, but also *partial differential equations* in which two or more independent variables appear.

This finds the general solution to a simple partial differential equation with two independent variables.

$In[24]:=$ **DSolve[D[y[x1, x2], x1] + D[y[x1, x2], x2] == 1/(x1 x2),**
      y[x1, x2], {x1, x2}]

$Out[24]=$ $\left\{\left\{y[x1, x2] \to \dfrac{1}{x1 - x2}(-\text{Log}[x1] + \text{Log}[x2] + \right.\right.$
      $\left.\left. x1\,C[1][-x1 + x2] - x2\,C[1][-x1 + x2])\right\}\right\}$

Here is the result represented as a pure function.

$In[25]:=$ **DSolve[D[y[x1, x2], x1] + D[y[x1, x2], x2] == 1/(x1 x2),**
      y, {x1, x2}]

$Out[25]=$ $\left\{\left\{y \to \text{Function}\left[\{x1, x2\}, \dfrac{1}{x1 - x2}(-\text{Log}[x1] + \text{Log}[x2] + \right.\right.\right.$
      $\left.\left.\left. x1\,C[1][-x1 + x2] - x2\,C[1][-x1 + x2])\right]\right\}\right\}$

The basic mathematics of partial differential equations is considerably more complicated than that of ordinary differential equations. One feature is that whereas the general solution to an ordinary differential equation involves only arbitrary *constants*, the general solution to a partial differential equation, if it can be found at all, must involve arbitrary *functions*. Indeed, with m independent variables, arbitrary functions of $m - 1$ arguments appear. DSolve by default names these functions C[n].

Here is a simple PDE involving three independent variables.

$In[26]:=$ **(D[#, x1] + D[#, x2] + D[#, x3])& [y[x1, x2, x3]] == 0**

$Out[26]=$ $y^{(0,0,1)}[x1, x2, x3] + y^{(0,1,0)}[x1, x2, x3] + $
      $y^{(1,0,0)}[x1, x2, x3] == 0$

The solution involves an arbitrary function of two variables.

$In[27]:=$ **DSolve[%, y[x1, x2, x3], {x1, x2, x3}]**

$Out[27]=$ {{y[x1, x2, x3] $\to$ C[1][-x1 + x2, -x1 + x3]}}

Here is the one-dimensional wave equation.

$In[28]:=$ **(c^2 D[#, x, x] - D[#, t, t])& [y[x, t]] == 0**

$Out[28]=$ $-y^{(0,2)}[x, t] + c^2\,y^{(2,0)}[x, t] == 0$

The solution to this second-order equation involves two arbitrary functions.

$In[29]:=$ **DSolve[%, y[x, t], {x, t}]**

$Out[29]=$ $\left\{\left\{y[x, t] \to C[1]\left[t - \dfrac{\sqrt{c^2}\,x}{c^2}\right] + C[2]\left[t + \dfrac{\sqrt{c^2}\,x}{c^2}\right]\right\}\right\}$

For an ordinary differential equation, it is guaranteed that a general solution must exist, with the property that adding initial or boundary conditions simply corresponds to forcing specific choices for arbitrary constants in the solution. But for partial differential equations this is no longer true. Indeed, it is only for linear partial differential and a few other special types that such general solutions exist.

Other partial differential equations can be solved only when specific initial or boundary values are given, and in the vast majority of cases no solutions can be found as exact formulas in terms of standard mathematical functions.

Since y and its derivatives appear only linearly here, a general solution exists.

$In[30]:=$ **DSolve[x1 D[y[x1, x2], x1] + x2 D[y[x1, x2], x2]**
$\qquad\qquad$ **== Exp[x1 x2], y[x1, x2], {x1, x2}]**

$Out[30]=$ $\left\{\left\{ y[x1, x2] \rightarrow \right.\right.$
$\qquad\qquad \dfrac{1}{2} \left(\text{ExpIntegralEi}[x1\,x2] + 2\,C[1]\left[\dfrac{x2}{x1}\right] \right) \Big\}\Big\}$

This weakly nonlinear PDE turns out to have a general solution.

$In[31]:=$ **DSolve[D[y[x1, x2], x1] + D[y[x1, x2], x2]**
$\qquad\qquad$ **== Exp[y[x1, x2]], y[x1, x2], {x1, x2}]**

$Out[31]=$ $\{\{y[x1, x2] \rightarrow -\text{Log}[-x1 - C[1][-x1 + x2]]\}\}$

Here is a nonlinear PDE which has no general solution.

$In[32]:=$ **DSolve[D[y[x1, x2], x1] D[y[x1, x2], x2] == a,**
$\qquad\qquad$ **y[x1, x2], {x1, x2}]**

$Out[32]=$ $\text{DSolve}[y^{(0,1)}[x1, x2]\,y^{(1,0)}[x1, x2] == a,$
$\qquad\qquad y[x1, x2], \{x1, x2\}]$

■ 3.5.11 Integral Transforms and Related Operations

Laplace Transforms

LaplaceTransform[*expr*, *t*, *s*]	the Laplace transform of *expr*
InverseLaplaceTransform[*expr*, *s*, *t*]	the inverse Laplace transform of *expr*

One-dimensional Laplace transforms.

The Laplace transform of a function $f(t)$ is given by $\int_0^\infty f(t)e^{-st}\,dt$. The inverse Laplace transform of $F(s)$ is given for suitable γ by $\frac{1}{2\pi i}\int_{\gamma-i\infty}^{\gamma+i\infty} F(s)e^{st}\,ds$.

Here is a simple Laplace transform.

$In[1]:=$ **LaplaceTransform[t^4 Sin[t], t, s]**

$Out[1]=$ $\dfrac{24\,(1 + 5\,s^2\,(-2 + s^2))}{(1 + s^2)^5}$

Here is the inverse.	*In[2]:=* `InverseLaplaceTransform[%, s, t]`
	Out[2]= $t^4 \sin[t]$
Even simple transforms often involve special functions.	*In[3]:=* `LaplaceTransform[1/(1 + t^2), t, s]`
	Out[3]= $\text{CosIntegral}[s] \sin[s] +$ $\frac{1}{2} \cos[s] \, (\pi - 2 \, \text{SinIntegral}[s])$
Here the result involves a Meijer G function.	*In[4]:=* `LaplaceTransform[1/(1 + t^3), t, s]`
	Out[4]= $\dfrac{\text{MeijerG}\left[\left\{\left\{\frac{2}{3}\right\}, \{\}\right\}, \left\{\left\{0, \frac{1}{3}, \frac{2}{3}, \frac{2}{3}\right\}, \{\}\right\}, \frac{s^3}{27}\right]}{2 \sqrt{3}\, \pi}$
The Laplace transform of a Bessel function involves a hypergeometric function.	*In[5]:=* `LaplaceTransform[BesselJ[n, t], t, s]`
	Out[5]= $\dfrac{\left(s + \sqrt{1 + s^2}\,\right)^{-n}}{\sqrt{1 + s^2}}$

Laplace transforms have the property that they turn integration and differentiation into essentially algebraic operations. They are therefore commonly used in studying systems governed by differential equations.

Integration becomes multiplication by $1/s$ when one does a Laplace transform.	*In[6]:=* `LaplaceTransform[Integrate[f[u], {u, 0, t}], t, s]`
	Out[6]= $\dfrac{\text{LaplaceTransform}[f[t], t, s]}{s}$

`LaplaceTransform[`*expr*`, {`t_1`, `t_2`, ... }, {`s_1`, `s_2`, ... }]`
    the multidimensional Laplace transform of *expr*

`InverseLaplaceTransform[`*expr*`, {`s_1`, `s_2`, ... }, {`t_1`, `t_2`, ... }]`
    the multidimensional inverse Laplace transform
    of *expr*

Multidimensional Laplace transforms.

Fourier Transforms

`FourierTransform[`*expr*`, `t`, `ω`]`   the Fourier transform of *expr*

`InverseFourierTransform[`*expr*`, `ω`, `t`]`   the inverse Fourier transform of *expr*

One-dimensional Fourier transforms.

Here is a Fourier transform.

$In[1]:=$ **FourierTransform[1/(1 + t^4), t, ω]**

$Out[1]= \left(\frac{1}{4} + \frac{\mathbb{i}}{4}\right) e^{-\frac{(1+\mathbb{i})\omega}{\sqrt{2}}} \sqrt{\pi} \left(e^{\sqrt{2}\,\omega}\left(-\mathbb{i} + e^{\mathbb{i}\sqrt{2}\,\omega}\right) \text{UnitStep}[-\omega] +\right.$
$\left.\left(1 - \mathbb{i}\,e^{\mathbb{i}\sqrt{2}\,\omega}\right) \text{UnitStep}[\omega]\right)$

This finds the inverse.

$In[2]:=$ **InverseFourierTransform[%, ω, t]**

$Out[2]= \dfrac{1}{1 + t^4}$

In *Mathematica* the Fourier transform of a function $f(t)$ is by default defined to be $\frac{1}{\sqrt{2\pi}} \int_{-\infty}^{\infty} f(t)\,e^{i\omega t}\,dt$. The inverse Fourier transform of $F(\omega)$ is similarly defined as $\frac{1}{\sqrt{2\pi}} \int_{-\infty}^{\infty} F(\omega)\,e^{-i\omega t}\,d\omega$.

In different scientific and technical fields different conventions are often used for defining Fourier transforms. The option `FourierParameters` in *Mathematica* allows you to choose any of these conventions you want.

common convention	setting	Fourier transform	inverse Fourier transform
Mathematica default	{0, 1}	$\frac{1}{\sqrt{2\pi}} \int_{-\infty}^{\infty} f(t)\,e^{i\omega t}\,dt$	$\frac{1}{\sqrt{2\pi}} \int_{-\infty}^{\infty} F(\omega)\,e^{-i\omega t}\,d\omega$
pure mathematics	{1, -1}	$\int_{-\infty}^{\infty} f(t)\,e^{-i\omega t}\,dt$	$\frac{1}{2\pi} \int_{-\infty}^{\infty} F(\omega)\,e^{i\omega t}\,d\omega$
classical physics	{-1, 1}	$\frac{1}{2\pi} \int_{-\infty}^{\infty} f(t)\,e^{i\omega t}\,dt$	$\int_{-\infty}^{\infty} F(\omega)\,e^{-i\omega t}\,d\omega$
modern physics	{0, 1}	$\frac{1}{\sqrt{2\pi}} \int_{-\infty}^{\infty} f(t)\,e^{i\omega t}\,dt$	$\frac{1}{\sqrt{2\pi}} \int_{-\infty}^{\infty} F(\omega)\,e^{-i\omega t}\,d\omega$
systems engineering	{1, -1}	$\int_{-\infty}^{\infty} f(t)\,e^{-i\omega t}\,dt$	$\frac{1}{2\pi} \int_{-\infty}^{\infty} F(\omega)\,e^{i\omega t}\,d\omega$
signal processing	{0, -2 Pi}	$\int_{-\infty}^{\infty} f(t)\,e^{-2\pi i\omega t}\,dt$	$\int_{-\infty}^{\infty} F(\omega)\,e^{2\pi i\omega t}\,d\omega$
general case	{a, b}	$\sqrt{\frac{\lvert b\rvert}{(2\pi)^{1-a}}} \int_{-\infty}^{\infty} f(t)\,e^{ib\omega t}\,dt$	$\sqrt{\frac{\lvert b\rvert}{(2\pi)^{1+a}}} \int_{-\infty}^{\infty} F(\omega)\,e^{-ib\omega t}\,d\omega$

Typical settings for `FourierParameters` with various conventions.

Here is a Fourier transform with the default choice of parameters.

$In[3]:=$ **FourierTransform[Exp[-t^2], t, ω]**

$Out[3]= \dfrac{e^{-\frac{\omega^2}{4}}}{\sqrt{2}}$

Here is the same Fourier transform with the choice of parameters typically used in signal processing.

$In[4]:=$ **FourierTransform[Exp[-t^2], t, ω,**
                 FourierParameters->{0, -2 Pi}]

$Out[4]= e^{-\pi^2 \omega^2} \sqrt{\pi}$

FourierSinTransform[*expr*, *t*, ω]	Fourier sine transform
FourierCosTransform[*expr*, *t*, ω]	Fourier cosine transform
InverseFourierSinTransform[*expr*, ω, *t*]	
	inverse Fourier sine transform
InverseFourierCosTransform[*expr*, ω, *t*]	
	inverse Fourier cosine transform

Fourier sine and cosine transforms.

In some applications of Fourier transforms, it is convenient to avoid ever introducing complex exponentials. Fourier sine and cosine transforms correspond to integrating respectively with $\sin(\omega t)$ and $\cos(\omega t)$ instead of $\exp(i\omega t)$, and using limits 0 and ∞ rather than $-\infty$ and ∞.

Here are the Fourier sine and cosine transforms of e^{-t}.

```
In[5]:= {FourierSinTransform[Exp[-t], t, ω],
                FourierCosTransform[Exp[-t], t, ω]}
```

$$Out[5]= \left\{ \frac{\sqrt{\frac{2}{\pi}}\,\omega}{1+\omega^2}, \frac{\sqrt{\frac{2}{\pi}}}{1+\omega^2} \right\}$$

FourierTransform[*expr*, {t_1, t_2, ... }, {ω_1, ω_2, ... }]	
	the multidimensional Fourier transform of *expr*
InverseFourierTransform[*expr*, {ω_1, ω_2, ... }, {t_1, t_2, ... }]	
	the multidimensional inverse Fourier transform of *expr*
FourierSinTransform[*expr*, {t_1, t_2, ... }, {ω_1, ω_2, ... }], FourierCosTransform[*expr*, {t_1, t_2, ... }, {ω_1, ω_2, ... }]	
	the multidimensional sine and cosine Fourier transforms of *expr*
InverseFourierSinTransform[*expr*, {ω_1, ω_2, ... }, {t_1, t_2, ... }], InverseFourierCosTransform[*expr*, {ω_1, ω_2, ... }, {t_1, t_2, ... }]	
	the multidimensional inverse Fourier sine and cosine transforms of *expr*

Multidimensional Fourier transforms.

This evaluates a two-dimensional Fourier transform.

```
In[6]:= FourierTransform[(u v)^2 Exp[-u^2-v^2], {u, v}, {a, b}]
```

$$Out[6]= \frac{1}{32} (-2+a^2)(-2+b^2)\,e^{-\frac{1}{4}(a^2+b^2)}$$

This inverts the transform. $In[7]:=$ **InverseFourierTransform[%, {a, b}, {u, v}]**

$Out[7]=$ $e^{-u^2-v^2} u^2 v^2$

Z Transforms

ZTransform[*expr*, *n*, *z*]	Z transform of *expr*
InverseZTransform[*expr*, *z*, *n*]	inverse Z transform of *expr*

Z transforms.

The Z transform of a function $f(n)$ is given by $\sum_{n=0}^{\infty} f(n)z^{-n}$. The inverse Z transform of $F(z)$ is given by the contour integral $\frac{1}{2\pi i} \oint F(z)z^{n-1} dz$. Z transforms are effectively discrete analogs of Laplace transforms. They are widely used for solving difference equations, especially in digital signal processing and control theory. They can be thought of as producing generating functions, of the kind commonly used in combinatorics and number theory.

This computes the Z transform of 2^{-n}. $In[1]:=$ **ZTransform[2^-n, n, z]**

$$Out[1]= \frac{2z}{-1+2z}$$

Here is the inverse Z transform. $In[2]:=$ **InverseZTransform[%, z, n]**

$Out[2]=$ 2^{-n}

The generating function for $1/n!$ is an $In[3]:=$ **ZTransform[1/n!, n, z]**
exponential function.
$Out[3]=$ $e^{\frac{1}{z}}$

■ 3.5.12 Generalized Functions and Related Objects

In many practical situations it is convenient to consider limits in which a fixed amount of something is concentrated into an infinitesimal region. Ordinary mathematical functions of the kind normally encountered in calculus cannot readily represent such limits. However, it is possible to introduce *generalized functions* or *distributions* which can represent these limits in integrals and other types of calculations.

DiracDelta[*x*]	Dirac delta function $\delta(x)$
UnitStep[*x*]	unit step function, equal to 0 for $x < 0$ and 1 for $x > 0$

Dirac delta and unit step functions.

Here is a function concentrated around $x = 0$.

$In[1]:=$ **Plot[Sqrt[50/Pi] Exp[-50 x^2], {x, -2, 2}, PlotRange->All]**

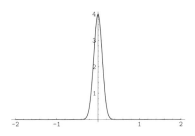

As n gets larger, the functions become progressively more concentrated.

$In[2]:=$ **Plot[Evaluate[Sqrt[n/Pi] Exp[-n x^2] /. n -> {1, 10, 100}], {x, -2, 2}, PlotRange->All];**

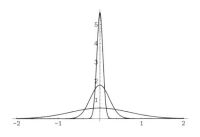

For any $n > 0$, their integrals are nevertheless always equal to 1.

$In[3]:=$ **Integrate[Sqrt[n/Pi] Exp[-n x^2], {x, -Infinity, Infinity}, Assumptions -> n > 0]**

$Out[3]=$ 1

The limit of the functions for infinite n is effectively a Dirac delta function, whose integral is again 1.

$In[4]:=$ **Integrate[DiracDelta[x], {x, -Infinity, Infinity}]**

$Out[4]=$ 1

DiracDelta evaluates to 0 at all real points except $x = 0$.

$In[5]:=$ **Table[DiracDelta[x], {x, -3, 3}]**

$Out[5]=$ {0, 0, 0, DiracDelta[0], 0, 0, 0}

Inserting a delta function in an integral effectively causes the integrand to be sampled at discrete points where the argument of the delta function vanishes.

This samples the function f with argument 2.

$In[6]:=$ **Integrate[DiracDelta[x - 2] f[x], {x, -4, 4}]**

$Out[6]=$ f[2]

Here is a slightly more complicated example.

$In[7]:=$ **Integrate[DiracDelta[x^2 - x - 1], {x, 0, 2}]**

$Out[7]=$ $\dfrac{1}{\sqrt{5}}$

This effectively counts the number of zeros of cos(*x*) in the region of integration.

In[8]:= `Integrate[DiracDelta[Cos[x]], {x, -30, 30}]`

Out[8]= 20

The **unit step function** `UnitStep[x]` is effectively the indefinite integral of the delta function. It is sometimes known as the **Heaviside function**, and is variously denoted $H(x)$, $\theta(x)$, $\mu(x)$, and $U(x)$. It does not need to be considered as a generalized function, though it has a discontinuity at $x = 0$. The unit step function is often used in setting up piecewise continuous functions, and in representing signals and other quantities that become non-zero only beyond some point.

The indefinite integral of the delta function is the unit step function.

In[9]:= `Integrate[DiracDelta[x], x]`

Out[9]= `UnitStep[x]`

This generates a square wave.

In[10]:= `Plot[UnitStep[Sin[x]], {x, 0, 30}]`

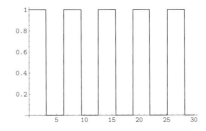

Here is the integral of the square wave.

In[11]:= `Integrate[UnitStep[Sin[x]], {x, 0, 30}]`

Out[11]= 5π

The value of the integral depends on whether *a* lies in the interval $(-2, 2)$.

In[12]:= `Integrate[f[x] DiracDelta[x - a], {x, -2, 2}]`

Out[12]= `f[a] UnitStep[2 - a] UnitStep[2 + a]`

`DiracDelta` and `UnitStep` often arise in doing integral transforms.

The Fourier transform of a constant function is a delta function.

In[13]:= `FourierTransform[1, t, ω]`

Out[13]= $\sqrt{2\pi}$ `DiracDelta[ω]`

The Fourier transform of cos(*t*) involves the sum of two delta functions.

In[14]:= `FourierTransform[Cos[t], t, ω]`

Out[14]= $\sqrt{\dfrac{\pi}{2}}$ `DiracDelta[-1 + ω]` $+ \sqrt{\dfrac{\pi}{2}}$ `DiracDelta[1 + ω]`

Dirac delta functions can be used in `DSolve` to find the impulse response or Green's function of systems represented by linear and certain other differential equations.

This finds the behavior of a harmonic oscillator subjected to an impulse at $t = 0$.

In[15]:= `DSolve[{x''[t] + r x[t] == DiracDelta[t],`
`                x[0]==0, x'[0]==1}, x[t], t]`

Out[15]= $\left\{\left\{x[t] \rightarrow \dfrac{\text{Sin}\left[\sqrt{r}\ t\right]\text{UnitStep[t]}}{\sqrt{r}}\right\}\right\}$

DiracDelta[x_1, x_2, ...]	multidimensional Dirac delta function equal to 0 unless all the x_i are zero
UnitStep[x_1, x_2, ...]	multidimensional unit step function, equal to 0 if any of the x_i are negative

Multidimensional Dirac delta and unit step functions.

Related to the multidimensional Dirac delta function are two integer functions: discrete delta and Kronecker delta. Discrete delta $\delta(n_1, n_2, ...)$ is 1 if all the $n_i = 0$, and is zero otherwise. Kronecker delta $\delta_{n_1 n_2 ...}$ is 1 if all the n_i are equal, and is zero otherwise.

DiscreteDelta[n_1, n_2, ...]	discrete delta $\delta(n_1, n_2, ...)$
KroneckerDelta[n_1, n_2, ...]	Kronecker delta $\delta_{n_1 n_2 ...}$

Integer delta functions.

3.6 Series, Limits and Residues

■ 3.6.1 Making Power Series Expansions

`Series[expr, {x, x0, n}]`	find the power series expansion of *expr* about the point $x = x_0$ to order at most $(x - x_0)^n$
`Series[expr, {x, x0, nx}, {y, y0, ny}]`	find series expansions with respect to y then x

Functions for creating power series.

Here is the power series expansion for exp(x) about the point $x = 0$ to order x^4.

$In[1]:=$ **Series[Exp[x], {x, 0, 4}]**

$Out[1]=$ $1 + x + \dfrac{x^2}{2} + \dfrac{x^3}{6} + \dfrac{x^4}{24} + O[x]^5$

Here is the series expansion of exp(x) about the point $x = 1$.

$In[2]:=$ **Series[Exp[x], {x, 1, 4}]**

$Out[2]=$ $e + e (x - 1) + \dfrac{1}{2} e (x - 1)^2 +$

$\dfrac{1}{6} e (x - 1)^3 + \dfrac{1}{24} e (x - 1)^4 + O[x - 1]^5$

If *Mathematica* does not know the series expansion of a particular function, it writes the result symbolically in terms of derivatives.

$In[3]:=$ **Series[f[x], {x, 0, 3}]**

$Out[3]=$ $f[0] + f'[0] x + \dfrac{1}{2} f''[0] x^2 + \dfrac{1}{6} f^{(3)}[0] x^3 + O[x]^4$

In mathematical terms, `Series` can be viewed as a way of constructing Taylor series for functions.

The standard formula for the Taylor series expansion about the point $x = x_0$ of a function $g(x)$ with k^{th} derivative $g^{(k)}(x)$ is $g(x) = \sum_{k=0}^{\infty} g^{(k)}(x_0) \dfrac{(x-x_0)^k}{k!}$. Whenever this formula applies, it gives the same results as `Series`. (For common functions, `Series` nevertheless internally uses somewhat more efficient algorithms.)

`Series` can also generate some power series that involve fractional and negative powers, not directly covered by the standard Taylor series formula.

Here is a power series that contains negative powers of x.

$In[4]:=$ **Series[Exp[x]/x^2, {x, 0, 4}]**

$Out[4]=$ $\dfrac{1}{x^2} + \dfrac{1}{x} + \dfrac{1}{2} + \dfrac{x}{6} + \dfrac{x^2}{24} + \dfrac{x^3}{120} + \dfrac{x^4}{720} + O[x]^5$

Here is a power series involving fractional powers of x.

$In[5]:=$ **Series[Exp[Sqrt[x]], {x, 0, 2}]**

$Out[5]=$ $1 + \sqrt{x} + \dfrac{x}{2} + \dfrac{x^{3/2}}{6} + \dfrac{x^2}{24} + O[x]^{5/2}$

Series can also handle series that involve logarithmic terms.

$In[6]:=$ **Series[Exp[2x] Log[x], {x, 0, 2}]**

$Out[6]=$ $\text{Log}[x] + 2\,\text{Log}[x]\,x + 2\,\text{Log}[x]\,x^2 + O[x]^3$

There are, of course, mathematical functions for which no standard power series exist. *Mathematica* recognizes many such cases.

Series sees that $\exp(\frac{1}{x})$ has an essential singularity at $x = 0$, and does not produce a power series.

$In[7]:=$ **Series[Exp[1/x], {x, 0, 2}]**

Series::esss:

$\qquad$ Essential singularity encountered in $\text{Exp}[\overset{1}{\underset{x}{-}} + O[x]^3\,]$.

$Out[7]=$ $e^{\frac{1}{x}}$

Series can nevertheless give you the power series for $\exp(\frac{1}{x})$ about the point $x = \infty$.

$In[8]:=$ **Series[Exp[1/x], {x, Infinity, 3}]**

$Out[8]=$ $1 + \dfrac{1}{x} + \dfrac{1}{2}\left(\dfrac{1}{x}\right)^2 + \dfrac{1}{6}\left(\dfrac{1}{x}\right)^3 + O\left[\dfrac{1}{x}\right]^4$

Especially when negative powers occur, there is some subtlety in exactly how many terms of a particular power series the function Series will generate.

One way to understand what happens is to think of the analogy between power series taken to a certain order, and real numbers taken to a certain precision. Power series are "approximate formulas" in much the same sense as finite-precision real numbers are approximate numbers.

The procedure that Series follows in constructing a power series is largely analogous to the procedure that N follows in constructing a real-number approximation. Both functions effectively start by replacing the smallest pieces of your expression by finite-order, or finite-precision, approximations, and then evaluating the resulting expression. If there are, for example, cancellations, this procedure may give a final result whose order or precision is less than the order or precision that you originally asked for. Like N, however, Series has some ability to retry its computations so as to get results to the order you ask for. In cases where it does not succeed, you can usually still get results to a particular order by asking for a higher order than you need.

Series compensates for cancellations in this computation, and succeeds in giving you a result to order x^3.

$In[9]:=$ **Series[Sin[x]/x^2, {x, 0, 3}]**

$Out[9]=$ $\dfrac{1}{x} - \dfrac{x}{6} + \dfrac{x^3}{120} + O[x]^4$

When you make a power series expansion in a variable x, *Mathematica* assumes that all objects that do not explicitly contain x are in fact independent of x. Series thus does partial derivatives (effectively using D) to build up Taylor series.

Both a and n are assumed to be independent of x.

$In[10]:=$ **Series[(a + x)^n , {x, 0, 2}]**

$Out[10]=$ $a^n + a^{-1+n}\,n\,x + \left(-\dfrac{1}{2}\,a^{-2+n}\,n + \dfrac{1}{2}\,a^{-2+n}\,n^2\right)x^2 + O[x]^3$

a[x] is now given as an explicit function of x.	*In[11]:=* **Series[(a[x] + x)^n, {x, 0, 2}]**

$$Out[11]= a[0]^n + n\,a[0]^{-1+n}\,(1 + a'[0])\,x + $$
$$\left(\frac{1}{2}\,(-1+n)\,n\,a[0]^{-2+n}\,(1 + a'[0])^2 + \right.$$
$$\left. \frac{1}{2}\,n\,a[0]^{-1+n}\,a''[0]\right)x^2 + O[x]^3$$

You can use **Series** to generate power series in a sequence of different variables. **Series** works like **Integrate**, **Sum** and so on, and expands first with respect to the last variable you specify.

Series performs a series expansion successively with respect to each variable. The result in this case is a series in x, whose coefficients are series in y.	*In[12]:=* **Series[Exp[x y], {x, 0, 3}, {y, 0, 3}]**

$$Out[12]= 1 + \left(y + O[y]^4\right)x + $$
$$\left(\frac{y^2}{2} + O[y]^4\right)x^2 + \left(\frac{y^3}{6} + O[y]^4\right)x^3 + O[x]^4$$

■ 3.6.2 Advanced Topic: The Representation of Power Series

Power series are represented in *Mathematica* as **SeriesData** objects.

The power series is printed out as a sum of terms, ending with O[x] raised to a power.	*In[1]:=* **Series[Cos[x], {x, 0, 4}]**

$$Out[1]= 1 - \frac{x^2}{2} + \frac{x^4}{24} + O[x]^5$$

Internally, however, the series is stored as a SeriesData object.	*In[2]:=* **InputForm[%]**

Out[2]//InputForm= SeriesData[x, 0, {1, 0, -1/2, 0, 1/24}, 0, 5, 1]

By using **SeriesData** objects, rather than ordinary expressions, to represent power series, *Mathematica* can keep track of the order and expansion point, and do operations on the power series appropriately. You should not normally need to know the internal structure of **SeriesData** objects.

You can recognize a power series that is printed out in standard output form by the presence of an O[x] term. This term mimics the standard mathematical notation $O(x)$, and represents omitted terms of order x. For various reasons of consistency, *Mathematica* uses the notation O[x]^n for omitted terms of order x^n, corresponding to the mathematical notation $O(x)^n$, rather than the slightly more familiar, though equivalent, form $O(x^n)$.

Any time that an object like O[x] appears in a sum of terms, *Mathematica* will in fact convert the whole sum into a power series.

The presence of O[x] makes *Mathematica* convert the whole sum to a power series.	*In[3]:=* **a x + Exp[x] + O[x]^3**

$$Out[3]= 1 + (1 + a)\,x + \frac{x^2}{2} + O[x]^3$$

■ 3.6.3 Operations on Power Series

Mathematica allows you to perform many operations on power series. In all cases, *Mathematica* gives results only to as many terms as can be justified from the accuracy of your input.

Here is a power series accurate to fourth order in x.

$In[1]:=$ **Series[Exp[x], {x, 0, 4}]**

$Out[1]= 1 + x + \dfrac{x^2}{2} + \dfrac{x^3}{6} + \dfrac{x^4}{24} + O[x]^5$

When you square the power series, you get another power series, also accurate to fourth order.

$In[2]:=$ **%^2**

$Out[2]= 1 + 2x + 2x^2 + \dfrac{4x^3}{3} + \dfrac{2x^4}{3} + O[x]^5$

Taking the logarithm gives you the result $2x$, but only to order x^4.

$In[3]:=$ **Log[%]**

$Out[3]= 2x + O[x]^5$

Mathematica keeps track of the orders of power series in much the same way as it keeps track of the precision of approximate real numbers. Just as with numerical calculations, there are operations on power series which can increase, or decrease, the precision (or order) of your results.

Here is a power series accurate to order x^{10}.

$In[4]:=$ **Series[Cos[x], {x, 0, 10}]**

$Out[4]= 1 - \dfrac{x^2}{2} + \dfrac{x^4}{24} - \dfrac{x^6}{720} + \dfrac{x^8}{40320} - \dfrac{x^{10}}{3628800} + O[x]^{11}$

This gives a power series that is accurate only to order x^6.

$In[5]:=$ **1 / (1 - %)**

$Out[5]= \dfrac{2}{x^2} + \dfrac{1}{6} + \dfrac{x^2}{120} + \dfrac{x^4}{3024} + \dfrac{x^6}{86400} + O[x]^7$

Mathematica also allows you to do calculus with power series.

Here is a power series for $\tan(x)$.

$In[6]:=$ **Series[Tan[x], {x, 0, 10}]**

$Out[6]= x + \dfrac{x^3}{3} + \dfrac{2x^5}{15} + \dfrac{17x^7}{315} + \dfrac{62x^9}{2835} + O[x]^{11}$

Here is its derivative with respect to x.

$In[7]:=$ **D[%, x]**

$Out[7]= 1 + x^2 + \dfrac{2x^4}{3} + \dfrac{17x^6}{45} + \dfrac{62x^8}{315} + O[x]^{10}$

Integrating with respect to x gives back the original power series.

$In[8]:=$ **Integrate[%, x]**

$Out[8]= x + \dfrac{x^3}{3} + \dfrac{2x^5}{15} + \dfrac{17x^7}{315} + \dfrac{62x^9}{2835} + O[x]^{11}$

When you perform an operation that involves both a normal expression and a power series, *Mathematica* "absorbs" the normal expression into the power series whenever possible.

The 1 is automatically absorbed into the power series.

$In[9]:=$ **1 + Series[Exp[x], {x, 0, 4}]**

$Out[9]= 2 + x + \dfrac{x^2}{2} + \dfrac{x^3}{6} + \dfrac{x^4}{24} + O[x]^5$

The x^2 is also absorbed into the power series.

In[10]:= **% + x^2**

Out[10]= $2 + x + \dfrac{3\,x^2}{2} + \dfrac{x^3}{6} + \dfrac{x^4}{24} + O[x]^5$

If you add Sin[x], *Mathematica* generates the appropriate power series for Sin[x], and combines it with the power series you have.

In[11]:= **% + Sin[x]**

Out[11]= $2 + 2\,x + \dfrac{3\,x^2}{2} + \dfrac{x^4}{24} + O[x]^5$

Mathematica also absorbs expressions that multiply power series. The symbol a is assumed to be independent of x.

In[12]:= **(a + x) %^2**

Out[12]= $4\,a + (4 + 8\,a)\,x + (8 + 10\,a)\,x^2 +$
$\qquad (10 + 6\,a)\,x^3 + \left(6 + \dfrac{29\,a}{12}\right)x^4 + O[x]^5$

Mathematica knows how to apply a wide variety of functions to power series. However, if you apply an arbitrary function to a power series, it is impossible for *Mathematica* to give you anything but a symbolic result.

Mathematica does not know how to apply the function f to a power series, so it just leaves the symbolic result.

In[13]:= **f[Series[Exp[x], {x, 0, 3}]]**

Out[13]= $f\left[1 + x + \dfrac{x^2}{2} + \dfrac{x^3}{6} + O[x]^4\right]$

■ 3.6.4 Advanced Topic: Composition and Inversion of Power Series

When you manipulate power series, it is sometimes convenient to think of the series as representing *functions*, which you can, for example, compose or invert.

ComposeSeries[*series*$_1$, *series*$_2$, ...]	compose power series
InverseSeries[*series*, *x*]	invert a power series

Composition and inversion of power series.

Here is the power series for exp(*x*) to order x^5.

In[1]:= **Series[Exp[x], {x, 0, 5}]**

Out[1]= $1 + x + \dfrac{x^2}{2} + \dfrac{x^3}{6} + \dfrac{x^4}{24} + \dfrac{x^5}{120} + O[x]^6$

This replaces the variable *x* in the power series for exp(*x*) by a power series for sin(*x*).

In[2]:= **ComposeSeries[%, Series[Sin[x], {x, 0, 5}]]**

Out[2]= $1 + x + \dfrac{x^2}{2} - \dfrac{x^4}{8} - \dfrac{x^5}{15} + O[x]^6$

The result is the power series for exp(sin(*x*)).

In[3]:= **Series[Exp[Sin[x]], {x, 0, 5}]**

Out[3]= $1 + x + \dfrac{x^2}{2} - \dfrac{x^4}{8} - \dfrac{x^5}{15} + O[x]^6$

If you have a power series for a function $f(y)$, then it is often possible to get a power series approximation to the solution for y in the equation $f(y) = x$. This power series effectively gives the inverse function $f^{-1}(x)$ such that $f(f^{-1}(x)) = x$. The operation of finding the power series for an inverse function is sometimes known as *reversion* of power series.

Here is the series for $\sin(y)$.

$In[4]:=$ **Series[Sin[y], {y, 0, 5}]**

$Out[4]= y - \dfrac{y^3}{6} + \dfrac{y^5}{120} + O[y]^6$

Inverting the series gives the series for $\sin^{-1}(x)$.

$In[5]:=$ **InverseSeries[%, x]**

$Out[5]= x + \dfrac{x^3}{6} + \dfrac{3 x^5}{40} + O[x]^6$

Composing the two series gives the identity function.

$In[6]:=$ **ComposeSeries[%, %%]**

$Out[6]= y + O[y]^6$

■ 3.6.5 Converting Power Series to Normal Expressions

$\text{Normal}[\textit{expr}]$	convert a power series to a normal expression

Converting power series to normal expressions.

As discussed above, power series in *Mathematica* are represented in a special internal form, which keeps track of such attributes as their expansion order.

For some purposes, you may want to convert power series to normal expressions. From a mathematical point of view, this corresponds to truncating the power series, and assuming that all higher-order terms are zero.

This generates a power series, with four terms.

$In[1]:=$ **t = Series[ArcTan[x], {x, 0, 8}]**

$Out[1]= x - \dfrac{x^3}{3} + \dfrac{x^5}{5} - \dfrac{x^7}{7} + O[x]^9$

Squaring the power series gives you another power series, with the appropriate number of terms.

$In[2]:=$ **t^2**

$Out[2]= x^2 - \dfrac{2 x^4}{3} + \dfrac{23 x^6}{45} - \dfrac{44 x^8}{105} + O[x]^{10}$

Normal truncates the power series, giving a normal expression.

$In[3]:=$ **Normal[%]**

$Out[3]= x^2 - \dfrac{2 x^4}{3} + \dfrac{23 x^6}{45} - \dfrac{44 x^8}{105}$

You can now apply standard algebraic operations.

$In[4]:=$ **Factor[%]**

$Out[4]= -\dfrac{1}{315} x^2 (-315 + 210 x^2 - 161 x^4 + 132 x^6)$

`SeriesCoefficient[`*series*`, `*n*`]`	give the coefficient of the nth order term in a power series

Extracting coefficients of terms in power series.

This gives the coefficient of x^7 in the original power series.

`In[5]:= SeriesCoefficient[t, 7]`

$$Out[5]= \; -\frac{1}{7}$$

■ 3.6.6 Solving Equations Involving Power Series

`LogicalExpand[`*series*$_1$ `== `*series*$_2$`]`	give the equations obtained by equating corresponding coefficients in the power series
`Solve[`*series*$_1$ `== `*series*$_2$`, {`a_1`, `a_2`, ... }]`	solve for coefficients in power series

Solving equations involving power series.

Here is a power series.

`In[1]:= y = 1 + Sum[a[i] x^i, {i, 3}] + O[x]^4`

$$Out[1]= \; 1 + a[1]\,x + a[2]\,x^2 + a[3]\,x^3 + O[x]^4$$

This gives an equation involving the power series.

`In[2]:= D[y, x]^2 - y == x`

$$Out[2]= \; \left(-1 + a[1]^2\right) + (-a[1] + 4\,a[1]\,a[2])\,x +$$
$$\left(-a[2] + 4\,a[2]^2 + 6\,a[1]\,a[3]\right)x^2 + O[x]^3 == x$$

`LogicalExpand` generates a sequence of equations for each power of x.

`In[3]:= LogicalExpand[ % ]`

$$Out[3]= \; -1 + a[1]^2 == 0 \;\&\&\; -1 - a[1] + 4\,a[1]\,a[2] == 0 \;\&\&$$
$$-a[2] + 4\,a[2]^2 + 6\,a[1]\,a[3] == 0$$

This solves the equations for the coefficients a[i]. You can also feed equations involving power series directly to `Solve`.

`In[4]:= Solve[ % ]`

$$Out[4]= \; \left\{\left\{a[3] \to -\frac{1}{12}, a[1] \to 1, a[2] \to \frac{1}{2}\right\},\right.$$
$$\left.\{a[3] \to 0, a[1] \to -1, a[2] \to 0\}\right\}$$

Some equations involving power series can also be solved using the `InverseSeries` function discussed on page 888.

■ 3.6.7 Summation of Series

Sum[*expr*, {*n*, *nmin*, *nmax*}]	find the sum of *expr* as *n* goes from *nmin* to *nmax*

Evaluating sums.

Mathematica recognizes this as the power series expansion of e^x.

$In[1]:=$ **Sum[x^n/n!, {n, 0, Infinity}]**

$Out[1]=$ e^x

This sum comes out in terms of a Bessel function.

$In[2]:=$ **Sum[x^n/(n!^2), {n, 0, Infinity}]**

$Out[2]=$ $\mathtt{BesselI}\left[0, 2\sqrt{x}\right]$

Here is another sum that can be done in terms of common special functions.

$In[3]:=$ **Sum[n! x^n/(2n)!, {n, 1, Infinity}]**

$Out[3]=$ $\dfrac{1}{2} e^{x/4} \sqrt{\pi} \sqrt{x} \, \mathtt{Erf}\left[\dfrac{\sqrt{x}}{2}\right]$

Generalized hypergeometric functions are not uncommon in sums.

$In[4]:=$ **Sum[x^n/(n!^4), {n, 0, Infinity}]**

$Out[4]=$ $\mathtt{HypergeometricPFQ}[\{\}, \{1, 1, 1\}, x]$

There are many analogies between sums and integrals. And just as it is possible to have indefinite integrals, so indefinite sums can be set up by using symbolic variables as upper limits.

This is effectively an indefinite sum.

$In[5]:=$ **Sum[k, {k, 0, n}]**

$Out[5]=$ $\dfrac{1}{2} n (1 + n)$

This sum comes out in terms of incomplete gamma functions.

$In[6]:=$ **Sum[x^k/k!, {k, 0, n}]**

$Out[6]=$ $\dfrac{e^x (1 + n) \, \mathtt{Gamma}[1 + n, x]}{\mathtt{Gamma}[2 + n]}$

This sum involves polygamma functions.

$In[7]:=$ **Sum[1/(k+1)^4, {k, 0, n}]**

$Out[7]=$ $\dfrac{\pi^4}{90} - \dfrac{1}{6} \mathtt{PolyGamma}[3, 2 + n]$

Taking the difference between results for successive values of *n* gives back the original summand.

$In[8]:=$ **FullSimplify[% - (% /. n->n-1)]**

$Out[8]=$ $\dfrac{1}{(1 + n)^4}$

Mathematica can do essentially all sums that are found in books of tables. Just as with indefinite integrals, indefinite sums of expressions involving simple functions tend to give answers that involve more complicated functions. Definite sums, like definite integrals, often, however, come out in terms of simpler functions.

This indefinite sum gives a quite complicated result.

$In[9]:=$ **Sum[Binomial[2k, k]/3^(2k), {k, 0, n}]**

$Out[9]=$ $\dfrac{3}{\sqrt{5}}$ -

$$\left(\left(\frac{9}{4}\right)^{-1-n} \text{Gamma}\left[\frac{3}{2}+n\right] \text{Hypergeometric2F1}\left[1, \frac{3}{2}+n,\right.\right.$$

$$\left.\left. 2+n, \frac{4}{9}\right]\right) \bigg/ \left(\sqrt{\pi}\ \text{Gamma}[2+n]\right)$$

The definite form is much simpler.

$In[10]:=$ **Sum[Binomial[2k, k]/3^(2k), {k, 0, Infinity}]**

$Out[10]=$ $\dfrac{3}{\sqrt{5}}$

Here is a slightly more complicated definite sum.

$In[11]:=$ **Sum[PolyGamma[k]/k^2, {k, 1, Infinity}]**

$Out[11]=$ $\dfrac{1}{6}$ $(-\text{EulerGamma}\ \pi^2 + 6\ \text{Zeta}[3])$

■ 3.6.8 Solving Recurrence Equations

If you represent the nth term in a sequence as $a[n]$, you can use a *recurrence equation* to specify how it is related to other terms in the sequence.

RSolve takes recurrence equations and solves them to get explicit formulas for $a[n]$.

This solves a simple recurrence equation.

$In[1]:=$ **RSolve[{a[n] == 2 a[n-1], a[1] == 1}, a[n], n]**

$Out[1]=$ $\{\{a[n] \to 2^{-1+n}\}\}$

This takes the solution and makes an explicit table of the first ten $a[n]$.

$In[2]:=$ **Table[a[n] /. First[%], {n, 10}]**

$Out[2]=$ $\{1, 2, 4, 8, 16, 32, 64, 128, 256, 512\}$

RSolve[*eqn*, $a[n]$, n]	solve a recurrence equation

Solving a recurrence equation.

This solves a recurrence equation for a geometric series.

$In[3]:=$ **RSolve[{a[n] == r a[n-1] + 1, a[1] == 1}, a[n], n]**

$Out[3]=$ $\left\{\left\{a[n] \to \dfrac{-1+r^n}{-1+r}\right\}\right\}$

This gives the same result.

$In[4]:=$ **RSolve[{a[n+1] == r a[n] + 1, a[1] == 1}, a[n], n]**

$Out[4]=$ $\left\{\left\{a[n] \to \dfrac{-1+r^n}{-1+r}\right\}\right\}$

This gives an algebraic solution to the Fibonacci recurrence equation.

$In[5]:=$ **RSolve[{a[n] == a[n-1] + a[n-2], a[1] == a[2] == 1}, a[n], n]**

$Out[5]=$ $\left\{\left\{a[n] \to -\dfrac{\left(-5+\sqrt{5}\right)\left(-\left(\frac{1}{2}-\frac{\sqrt{5}}{2}\right)^n+\left(\frac{1}{2}+\frac{\sqrt{5}}{2}\right)^n\right)}{5\left(-1+\sqrt{5}\right)}\right\}\right\}$

RSolve can be thought of as a discrete analog of DSolve. Many of the same functions generated in solving differential equations also appear in finding symbolic solutions to recurrence equations.

This generates a gamma function, which generalizes the factorial.	$In[6]:=$ **RSolve[{a[n] == n a[n-1], a[1] == 1}, a[n], n]** $Out[6]=$ {{a[n] → Gamma[1 + n]}}

This second-order recurrence equation comes out in terms of Bessel functions.	$In[7]:=$ **RSolve[{a[n + 1] == n a[n] + a[n - 1],**
	                a[1] == 0, a[2] == 1}, a[n], n]
	
	$Out[7]=$ {{a[n] → (BesselI[n, -2] BesselK[1, 2] -
	             BesselI[1, -2] BesselK[n, 2]) /
	             (BesselI[2, -2] BesselK[1, 2] -
	             BesselI[1, -2] BesselK[2, 2])}}

RSolve does not require you to specify explicit values for terms such as a[1]. Like DSolve, it automatically introduces undetermined constants C[*i*] to give a general solution.

This gives a general solution with one undetermined constant.	$In[8]:=$ **RSolve[a[n] == n a[n-1], a[n], n]** $Out[8]=$ {{a[n] → C[1] Gamma[1 + n]}}

RSolve can solve equations that do not depend only linearly on *a*[*n*]. For nonlinear equations, however, there are sometimes several distinct solutions that must be given. Just as for differential equations, it is a difficult matter to find symbolic solutions to recurrence equations, and standard mathematical functions only cover a limited set of cases.

Here is the general solution to a nonlinear recurrence equation.	$In[9]:=$ **RSolve[{a[n] == a[n + 1] a[n - 1]}, a[n], n]** $Out[9]=$ $\left\{\left\{a[n] \to e^{C[1] \cos\left[\frac{n\pi}{3}\right] + C[2] \sin\left[\frac{n\pi}{3}\right]}\right\}\right\}$

This gives two distinct solutions.	$In[10]:=$ **RSolve[a[n] == (a[n + 1] a[n - 1])^2, a[n], n]** $Out[10]=$ $\left\{\left\{a[n] \to e^{C[2] \cos\left[n \arctan\left[\sqrt{15}\right]\right] + C[1] \sin\left[n \arctan\left[\sqrt{15}\right]\right]}\right\},\right.$ $\left.\left\{a[n] \to e^{\frac{2 i \pi}{3} + C[2] \cos\left[n \arctan\left[\sqrt{15}\right]\right] + C[1] \sin\left[n \arctan\left[\sqrt{15}\right]\right]}\right\}\right\}$

RSolve can solve not only ordinary *difference equations* in which the arguments of *a* differ by integers, but also *q-difference equations* in which the arguments of *a* are related by multiplicative factors.

This solves the *q*-difference analog of the factorial equation.	$In[11]:=$ **RSolve[a[q n] == n a[n], a[n], n]** $Out[11]=$ $\left\{\left\{a[n] \to n^{\frac{1}{2}\left(-1 + \frac{\text{Log}[n]}{\text{Log}[q]}\right)} C[1]\right\}\right\}$

Here is a second-order *q*-difference equation.	$In[12]:=$ **RSolve[a[n] == a[q n] + a[n/q], a[n], n]** $Out[12]=$ $\left\{\left\{a[n] \to C[1] \cos\left[\frac{\pi \text{Log}[n]}{3 \text{Log}[q]}\right] + C[2] \sin\left[\frac{\pi \text{Log}[n]}{3 \text{Log}[q]}\right]\right\}\right\}$

+ RSolve[{*eqn*$_1$, *eqn*$_2$, ... }, {*a*$_1$[*n*], *a*$_2$[*n*], ... }, *n*]
        solve a coupled system of recurrence equations

Solving systems of recurrence equations.

This solves a system of two coupled recurrence equations.

$In[13]:=$ **RSolve[{a[n] == b[n - 1] + n, b[n] == a[n - 1] - n, a[1] == b[1] == 1}, {a[n], b[n]}, n]**

$Out[13]= \left\{ \left\{ a[n] \rightarrow \frac{1}{4} \left(4 + 3\,(-1)^n + (-1)^{2\,n} + 2\,(-1)^{2\,n}\,n \right), \right. \right.$

$\left. \left. b[n] \rightarrow \frac{1}{4} \left(4 - 3\,(-1)^n - (-1)^{2\,n} - 2\,(-1)^{2\,n}\,n \right) \right\} \right\}$

+ **RSolve[*eqns*, *a*[n_1, n_2, ...], {n_1, n_2, ... }]** solve partial recurrence equations

Solving partial recurrence equations.

Just as one can set up partial differential equations that involve functions of several variables, so one can also set up partial recurrence equations that involve multidimensional sequences. Just as in the differential equations case, general solutions to partial recurrence equations can involve undetermined functions.

This gives the general solution to a simple partial recurrence equation.

$In[14]:=$ **RSolve[a[i + 1, j + 1] == i j a[i, j], a[i, j], {i, j}]**

$Out[14]= \left\{ \left\{ a[i, j] \rightarrow \frac{\text{Gamma}[i]\,\text{Gamma}[j]\,C[1][i - j]}{\text{Gamma}[1 - i + j]} \right\} \right\}$

■ 3.6.9 Finding Limits

In doing many kinds of calculations, you need to evaluate expressions when variables take on particular values. In many cases, you can do this simply by applying transformation rules for the variables using the /. operator.

You can get the value of $\cos(x^2)$ at 0 just by explicitly replacing x with 0, and then evaluating the result.

$In[1]:=$ **Cos[x^2] /. x -> 0**

$Out[1]=$ 1

In some cases, however, you have to be more careful.

Consider, for example, finding the value of the expression $\frac{\sin(x)}{x}$ when $x = 0$. If you simply replace x by 0 in this expression, you get the indeterminate result $\frac{0}{0}$. To find the correct value of $\frac{\sin(x)}{x}$ when $x = 0$, you need to take the *limit*.

Limit[*expr*, x -> x_0]   find the limit of *expr* when x approaches x_0

Finding limits.

This gives the correct value for the limit of $\frac{\sin(x)}{x}$ as $x \rightarrow 0$.

$In[2]:=$ **Limit[Sin[x]/x, x -> 0]**

$Out[2]=$ 1

No finite limit exists in this case.

```
In[3]:= Limit[ Sin[x]/x^2, x -> 0 ]
Out[3]= ∞
```

Limit can find this limit, even though you cannot get an ordinary power series for $x \log(x)$ at $x = 0$.

```
In[4]:= Limit[ x Log[x], x -> 0 ]
Out[4]= 0
```

The same is true here.

```
In[5]:= Limit[ ( 1 + 2 x ) ^ (1/x), x -> 0 ]
Out[5]= e^2
```

The value of Sign[x] at $x=0$ is 0.

```
In[6]:= Sign[0]
Out[6]= 0
```

Its *limit*, however, is 1. The limit is by default taken from above.

```
In[7]:= Limit[Sign[x], x -> 0]
Out[7]= 1
```

Not all functions have definite limits at particular points. For example, the function $\sin(1/x)$ oscillates infinitely often near $x = 0$, so it has no definite limit there. Nevertheless, at least so long as x remains real, the values of the function near $x = 0$ always lie between -1 and 1. Limit represents values with bounded variation using Interval objects. In general, Interval[{$xmin$, $xmax$}] represents an uncertain value which lies somewhere in the interval $xmin$ to $xmax$.

Limit returns an Interval object, representing the range of possible values of $\sin(1/x)$ near its essential singularity at $x = 0$.

```
In[8]:= Limit[ Sin[1/x], x -> 0 ]
Out[8]= Interval[{-1, 1}]
```

Mathematica can do arithmetic with Interval objects.

```
In[9]:= (1 + %)^3
Out[9]= Interval[{0, 8}]
```

Mathematica represents this limit symbolically in terms of an Interval object.

```
In[10]:= Limit[ Exp[Sin[x]], x -> Infinity ]
```

$$Out[10]= \text{Interval}\left[\left\{\frac{1}{e}, e\right\}\right]$$

Some functions may have different limits at particular points, depending on the direction from which you approach those points. You can use the Direction option for Limit to specify the direction you want.

Limit[*expr*, x -> x_0, Direction -> 1]
                             find the limit as x approaches x_0 from below

Limit[*expr*, x -> x_0, Direction -> -1]
                             find the limit as x approaches x_0 from above

Directional limits.

The function $1/x$ has a different limiting value at $x = 0$, depending on whether you approach from above or below.

$In[11]:=$ **Plot[1/x, {x, -1, 1}]**

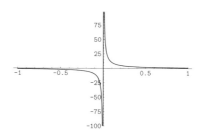

Approaching from below gives a limiting value of $-\infty$.

$In[12]:=$ **Limit[1/x, x -> 0, Direction -> 1]**

$Out[12]=$ $-\infty$

Approaching from above gives a limiting value of ∞.

$In[13]:=$ **Limit[1/x, x -> 0, Direction -> -1]**

$Out[13]=$ ∞

Limit makes no assumptions about functions like f[x] about which it does not have definite knowledge. As a result, Limit remains unevaluated in most cases involving symbolic functions.

Limit has no definite knowledge about f, so it leaves this limit unevaluated.

$In[14]:=$ **Limit[x f[x], x -> 0]**

$Out[14]=$ Limit[x f[x], $x \to 0$]

■ 3.6.10 Residues

Limit[*expr*, $x \to x_0$] tells you what the value of *expr* is when x tends to x_0. When this value is infinite, it is often useful instead to know the *residue* of *expr* when x equals x_0. The residue is given by the coefficient of $(x - x_0)^{-1}$ in the power series expansion of *expr* about the point x_0.

Residue[*expr*, {x, x_0}]	the residue of *expr* when x equals x_0

Computing residues.

The residue here is equal to 1.

$In[1]:=$ **Residue[1/x, {x, 0}]**

$Out[1]=$ 1

The residue here is zero.

$In[2]:=$ **Residue[1/x^2, {x, 0}]**

$Out[2]=$ 0

3.7 Linear Algebra

■ 3.7.1 Constructing Matrices

Table[f, {i, m}, {j, n}]	build an $m \times n$ matrix where f is a function of i and j that gives the value of the i, jth entry
Array[f, {m, n}]	build an $m \times n$ matrix whose i, jth entry is $f[i, j]$
DiagonalMatrix[$list$]	generate a diagonal matrix with the elements of $list$ on the diagonal
IdentityMatrix[n]	generate an $n \times n$ identity matrix
+ Normal[SparseArray[{{i_1, j_1}->v_1, {i_2, j_2}->v_2, ... }, {m, n}]]	make a matrix with non-zero values v_k at positions {i_k, j_k}

Functions for constructing matrices.

This generates a 2×2 matrix whose i, jth entry is a[i, j].

```
In[1]:= Table[a[i, j], {i, 2}, {j, 2}]
Out[1]= {{a[1, 1], a[1, 2]}, {a[2, 1], a[2, 2]}}
```

Here is another way to produce the same matrix.

```
In[2]:= Array[a, {2, 2}]
Out[2]= {{a[1, 1], a[1, 2]}, {a[2, 1], a[2, 2]}}
```

DiagonalMatrix makes a matrix with zeros everywhere except on the leading diagonal.

```
In[3]:= DiagonalMatrix[{a, b, c}]
Out[3]= {{a, 0, 0}, {0, b, 0}, {0, 0, c}}
```

IdentityMatrix[n] produces an $n \times n$ identity matrix.

```
In[4]:= IdentityMatrix[3]
Out[4]= {{1, 0, 0}, {0, 1, 0}, {0, 0, 1}}
```

This makes a 3×4 matrix with two non-zero values filled in.

```
In[5]:= Normal[SparseArray[{{2, 3}->a, {3, 2}->b}, {3, 4}]]
Out[5]= {{0, 0, 0, 0}, {0, 0, a, 0}, {0, b, 0, 0}}
```

MatrixForm prints the matrix in a two-dimensional form.

```
In[6]:= MatrixForm[%]
```

$$Out[6]//MatrixForm= \begin{pmatrix} 0 & 0 & 0 & 0 \\ 0 & 0 & a & 0 \\ 0 & b & 0 & 0 \end{pmatrix}$$

Table[0, {*m*}, {*n*}]	a zero matrix
Table[Random[ ], {*m*}, {*n*}]	a matrix with random numerical entries
Table[If[*i* >= *j*, 1, 0], {*i*, *m*}, {*j*, *n*}]	a lower-triangular matrix

Constructing special types of matrices with `Table`.

Table evaluates Random[ ] separately for each element, to give a different pseudorandom number in each case.

```
In[7]:= Table[Random[ ], {2}, {2}]
```
```
Out[7]= {{0.0560708, 0.6303}, {0.359894, 0.871377}}
```

+ SparseArray[{}, {*n*, *n*}]	a zero matrix
+ SparseArray[{*i*_, *i*_} -> 1, {*n*, *n*}]	an *n* × *n* identity matrix
+ SparseArray[{*i*_, *j*_} /; *i* >= *j* -> 1, {*n*, *n*}]	a lower-triangular matrix

Constructing special types of matrices with `SparseArray`.

This sets up a general lower-triangular matrix.

```
In[8]:= SparseArray[{i_, j_}/;i>=j -> f[i, j], {3, 3}] // MatrixForm
```

$$Out[8]//MatrixForm= \begin{pmatrix} f[1, 1] & 0 & 0 \\ f[2, 1] & f[2, 2] & 0 \\ f[3, 1] & f[3, 2] & f[3, 3] \end{pmatrix}$$

■ 3.7.2 Getting and Setting Pieces of Matrices

$m[[i, j]]$	the i,j^{th} entry
$m[[i]]$	the ith row
$m[[\text{All}, i]]$	the ith column
$\text{Take}[m, \{i_0, i_1\}, \{j_0, j_1\}]$	the submatrix with rows i_0 through i_1 and columns j_0 through j_1
$m[[\{i_1, \ldots, i_r\}, \{j_1, \ldots, j_s\}]]$	the $r \times s$ submatrix with elements having row indices i_k and column indices j_k
$\text{Tr}[m, \text{List}]$	elements on the diagonal
$\text{ArrayRules}[m]$	positions of non-zero elements

Ways to get pieces of matrices.

Matrices in *Mathematica* are represented as lists of lists. You can use all the standard *Mathematica* list-manipulation operations on matrices.

Here is a sample 3×3 matrix.

```
In[1]:= t = Array[a, {3, 3}]

Out[1]= {{a[1, 1], a[1, 2], a[1, 3]},
         {a[2, 1], a[2, 2], a[2, 3]},
         {a[3, 1], a[3, 2], a[3, 3]}}
```

This picks out the second row of the matrix.

```
In[2]:= t[[2]]

Out[2]= {a[2, 1], a[2, 2], a[2, 3]}
```

Here is the second column of the matrix.

```
In[3]:= t[[All, 2]]

Out[3]= {a[1, 2], a[2, 2], a[3, 2]}
```

This picks out a submatrix.

```
In[4]:= Take[t, {1, 2}, {2, 3}]

Out[4]= {{a[1, 2], a[1, 3]}, {a[2, 2], a[2, 3]}}
```

$m = \{\{a_{11},\, a_{12},\, \dots\,\},\, \{a_{21},\, a_{22},\, \dots\,\},\, \dots\,\}$
        assign m to be a matrix

$m[[i,\, j]] = v$ reset element $\{i,\, j\}$ to be v

$m[[i]] = v$ reset all elements in row i to be v

$m[[i]] = \{v_1,\, v_2,\, \dots\,\}$ reset elements in row i to be $\{v_1,\, v_2,\, \dots\,\}$

$m[[\text{All},\, j]] = v$ reset all elements in column j to be v

$m[[\text{All},\, j]] = \{v_1,\, v_2,\, \dots\,\}$ reset elements in column j to be $\{v_1,\, v_2,\, \dots\,\}$

Resetting parts of matrices.

Here is a 2×2 matrix.	`In[5]:= m = {{a, b}, {c, d}}` `Out[5]= {{a, b}, {c, d}}`
This resets the 2, 2 element to be x, then shows the whole matrix.	`In[6]:= m[[2, 2]] = x; m` `Out[6]= {{a, b}, {c, x}}`
This resets all elements in the second column to be z.	`In[7]:= m[[All, 2]] = z; m` `Out[7]= {{a, z}, {c, z}}`
This separately resets the two elements in the second column.	`In[8]:= m[[All, 2]] = {i, j}; m` `Out[8]= {{a, i}, {c, j}}`
This increments all the values in the second column.	`In[9]:= m[[All, 2]]++; m` `Out[9]= {{a, 1 + i}, {c, 1 + j}}`

■ 3.7.3 Scalars, Vectors and Matrices

Mathematica represents matrices and vectors using lists. Anything that is not a list *Mathematica* considers as a scalar.

A vector in *Mathematica* consists of a list of scalars. A matrix consists of a list of vectors, representing each of its rows. In order to be a valid matrix, all the rows must be the same length, so that the elements of the matrix effectively form a rectangular array.

VectorQ[*expr*]	give True if *expr* has the form of a vector, and False otherwise
MatrixQ[*expr*]	give True if *expr* has the form of a matrix, and False otherwise
Dimensions[*expr*]	a list of the dimensions of a vector or matrix

Functions for testing the structure of vectors and matrices.

The list {a, b, c} has the form of a vector.

```
In[1]:= VectorQ[ {a, b, c} ]
Out[1]= True
```

Anything that is not manifestly a list is treated as a scalar, so applying VectorQ gives False.

```
In[2]:= VectorQ[ x + y ]
Out[2]= False
```

This is a 2 × 3 matrix.

```
In[3]:= Dimensions[ {{a, b, c}, {ap, bp, cp}} ]
Out[3]= {2, 3}
```

For a vector, Dimensions gives a list with a single element equal to the result from Length.

```
In[4]:= Dimensions[ {a, b, c} ]
Out[4]= {3}
```

This object does not count as a matrix because its rows are of different lengths.

```
In[5]:= MatrixQ[ {{a, b, c}, {ap, bp}} ]
Out[5]= False
```

■ 3.7.4 Operations on Scalars, Vectors and Matrices

Most mathematical functions in *Mathematica* are set up to apply themselves separately to each element in a list. This is true in particular of all functions that carry the attribute Listable.

A consequence is that most mathematical functions are applied element by element to matrices and vectors.

The Log applies itself separately to each element in the vector.

```
In[1]:= Log[ {a, b, c} ]
Out[1]= {Log[a], Log[b], Log[c]}
```

The same is true for a matrix, or, for that matter, for any nested list.

```
In[2]:= Log[ {{a, b}, {c, d}} ]
Out[2]= {{Log[a], Log[b]}, {Log[c], Log[d]}}
```

The differentiation function D also applies separately to each element in a list.

```
In[3]:= D[ {x, x^2, x^3}, x ]
Out[3]= {1, 2x, 3x^2}
```

The sum of two vectors is carried out element by element.

```
In[4]:= {a, b} + {ap, bp}
Out[4]= {a + ap, b + bp}
```

If you try to add two vectors with different lengths, you get an error.	$In[5]:=$ **{a, b, c} + {ap, bp}**
	
	Thread::tdlen:
	    Objects of unequal length in {a, b, c} + {ap, bp}
	      cannot be combined.
	
	$Out[5]=$ {ap, bp} + {a, b, c}

This adds the scalar 1 to each element of the vector.	$In[6]:=$ **1 + {a, b}** $Out[6]=$ {1 + a, 1 + b}
Any object that is not manifestly a list is treated as a scalar. Here c is treated as a scalar, and added separately to each element in the vector.	$In[7]:=$ **{a, b} + c** $Out[7]=$ {a + c, b + c}
This multiplies each element in the vector by the scalar k.	$In[8]:=$ **k {a, b}** $Out[8]=$ {a k, b k}

It is important to realize that *Mathematica* treats an object as a vector in a particular operation only if the object is explicitly a list at the time when the operation is done. If the object is not explicitly a list, *Mathematica* always treats it as a scalar. This means that you can get different results, depending on whether you assign a particular object to be a list before or after you do a particular operation.

The object p is treated as a scalar, and added separately to each element in the vector.	$In[9]:=$ **{a, b} + p** $Out[9]=$ {a + p, b + p}
This is what happens if you now replace p by the list {c, d}.	$In[10]:=$ **% /. p -> {c, d}** $Out[10]=$ {{a + c, a + d}, {b + c, b + d}}
You would have got a different result if you had replaced p by {c, d} before you did the first operation.	$In[11]:=$ **{a, b} + {c, d}** $Out[11]=$ {a + c, b + d}

■ 3.7.5 Multiplying Vectors and Matrices

$c\,v,\ c\,m,$ etc.	multiply each element by a scalar
$v.v,\ v.m,\ m.v,\ m.m,$ etc.	vector and matrix multiplication
$\mathtt{Cross}[v,\ v]$	vector cross product (also input as $v \times v$)
$\mathtt{Outer}[\mathtt{Times},\ t,\ u]$	outer product

Different kinds of vector and matrix multiplication.

This multiplies each element of the vector by the scalar k.	$In[1]:=$ **k {a, b, c}** $Out[1]=$ {a k, b k, c k}

The "dot" operator gives the scalar product of two vectors.	*In[2]:=* **{a, b, c} . {ap, bp, cp}** *Out[2]=* a ap + b bp + c cp
You can also use dot to multiply a matrix by a vector.	*In[3]:=* **{{a, b}, {c, d}} . {x, y}** *Out[3]=* {a x + b y, c x + d y}
Dot is also the notation for matrix multiplication in *Mathematica*.	*In[4]:=* **{{a, b}, {c, d}} . {{1, 2}, {3, 4}}** *Out[4]=* {{a + 3 b, 2 a + 4 b}, {c + 3 d, 2 c + 4 d}}

It is important to realize that you can use "dot" for both left- and right-multiplication of vectors by matrices. *Mathematica* makes no distinction between "row" and "column" vectors. Dot carries out whatever operation is possible. (In formal terms, $a.b$ contracts the last index of the tensor a with the first index of b.)

Here are definitions for a matrix m and a vector v.	*In[5]:=* **m = {{a, b}, {c, d}} ; v = {x, y}** *Out[5]=* {x, y}
This left-multiplies the vector v by m. The object v is effectively treated as a column vector in this case.	*In[6]:=* **m . v** *Out[6]=* {a x + b y, c x + d y}
You can also use dot to right-multiply v by m. Now v is effectively treated as a row vector.	*In[7]:=* **v . m** *Out[7]=* {a x + c y, b x + d y}
You can multiply m by v on both sides, to get a scalar.	*In[8]:=* **v . m . v** *Out[8]=* x (a x + c y) + y (b x + d y)

For some purposes, you may need to represent vectors and matrices symbolically, without explicitly giving their elements. You can use dot to represent multiplication of such symbolic objects.

Dot effectively acts here as a non-commutative form of multiplication.	*In[9]:=* **a . b . a** *Out[9]=* a.b.a
It is, nevertheless, associative.	*In[10]:=* **(a . b) . (a . b)** *Out[10]=* a.b.a.b
Dot products of sums are not automatically expanded out.	*In[11]:=* **(a + b) . c . (d + e)** *Out[11]=* (a + b).c.(d + e)
You can apply the distributive law in this case using the function Distribute, as discussed on page 255.	*In[12]:=* **Distribute[%]** *Out[12]=* a.c.d + a.c.e + b.c.d + b.c.e

The "dot" operator gives "inner products" of vectors, matrices, and so on. In more advanced calculations, you may also need to construct outer or Kronecker products of vectors and matrices. You can use the general function Outer to do this.

The outer product of two vectors is a matrix.

In[13]:= **Outer[Times, {a, b}, {c, d}]**

Out[13]= {{a c, a d}, {b c, b d}}

The outer product of a matrix and a vector is a rank three tensor.

In[14]:= **Outer[Times, {{1, 2}, {3, 4}}, {x, y, z}]**

Out[14]= {{{x, y, z}, {2 x, 2 y, 2 z}},
          {{3 x, 3 y, 3 z}, {4 x, 4 y, 4 z}}}

Outer products will be discussed in more detail in Section 3.7.11.

■ 3.7.6 Matrix Inversion

Inverse[m]	find the inverse of a square matrix

Matrix inversion.

Here is a simple 2×2 matrix.

In[1]:= **m = {{a, b}, {c, d}}**

Out[1]= {{a, b}, {c, d}}

This gives the inverse of m. In producing this formula, *Mathematica* implicitly assumes that the determinant a d – b c is non-zero.

In[2]:= **Inverse[m]**

$$Out[2]= \left\{\left\{\frac{d}{-b c + a d}, -\frac{b}{-b c + a d}\right\}, \left\{-\frac{c}{-b c + a d}, \frac{a}{-b c + a d}\right\}\right\}$$

Multiplying the inverse by the original matrix should give the identity matrix.

In[3]:= **% . m**

$$Out[3]= \left\{\left\{-\frac{b c}{-b c + a d} + \frac{a d}{-b c + a d}, 0\right\},$$
$$\left\{0, -\frac{b c}{-b c + a d} + \frac{a d}{-b c + a d}\right\}\right\}$$

You have to use Together to clear the denominators, and get back a standard identity matrix.

In[4]:= **Together[%]**

Out[4]= {{1, 0}, {0, 1}}

Here is a matrix of rational numbers.

In[5]:= **hb = Table[1/(i + j), {i, 4}, {j, 4}]**

$$Out[5]= \left\{\left\{\frac{1}{2}, \frac{1}{3}, \frac{1}{4}, \frac{1}{5}\right\}, \left\{\frac{1}{3}, \frac{1}{4}, \frac{1}{5}, \frac{1}{6}\right\},$$
$$\left\{\frac{1}{4}, \frac{1}{5}, \frac{1}{6}, \frac{1}{7}\right\}, \left\{\frac{1}{5}, \frac{1}{6}, \frac{1}{7}, \frac{1}{8}\right\}\right\}$$

Mathematica finds the exact inverse of the matrix.

In[6]:= **Inverse[hb]**

Out[6]= {{200, -1200, 2100, -1120},
         {-1200, 8100, -15120, 8400},
         {2100, -15120, 29400, -16800},
         {-1120, 8400, -16800, 9800}}

Multiplying by the original matrix gives the identity matrix.

In[7]:= **% . hb**

Out[7]= {{1, 0, 0, 0}, {0, 1, 0, 0}, {0, 0, 1, 0}, {0, 0, 0, 1}}

If you try to invert a singular matrix, *Mathematica* prints a warning message, and returns the inverse undone.

```
In[8]:= Inverse[ {{1, 2}, {1, 2}} ]
```
Inverse::sing: Matrix {{1, 2}, {1, 2}} is singular.
```
Out[8]= Inverse[{{1, 2}, {1, 2}}]
```

If you give a matrix with exact symbolic or numerical entries, *Mathematica* gives the exact inverse. If, on the other hand, some of the entries in your matrix are approximate real numbers, then *Mathematica* finds an approximate numerical result.

Here is a matrix containing approximate real numbers.

```
In[9]:= m = {{1.2, 5.7}, {4.2, 5.6}}
```
```
Out[9]= {{1.2, 5.7}, {4.2, 5.6}}
```

This finds the numerical inverse.

```
In[10]:= Inverse[ % ]
```
```
Out[10]= {{-0.325203, 0.33101}, {0.243902, -0.0696864}}
```

Multiplying by the original matrix gives you an identity matrix with small numerical errors.

```
In[11]:= % . m
```
$$Out[11]= \left\{\left\{1., -1.25442 \times 10^{-16}\right\}, \left\{1.00831 \times 10^{-17}, 1.\right\}\right\}$$

You can get rid of the small off-diagonal terms using Chop.

```
In[12]:= Chop[ % ]
```
```
Out[12]= {{1., 0}, {0, 1.}}
```

When you try to invert a matrix with exact numerical entries, *Mathematica* can always tell whether or not the matrix is singular. When you invert an approximate numerical matrix, *Mathematica* can usually not tell for certain whether or not the matrix is singular: all it can tell is for example that the determinant is small compared to the entries of the matrix. When *Mathematica* suspects that you are trying to invert a singular numerical matrix, it prints a warning.

Mathematica prints a warning if you invert a numerical matrix that it suspects is singular.

```
In[13]:= Inverse[ {{1., 2.}, {1., 2.}} ]
```
Inverse::sing: Matrix {{1., 2.}, {1., 2.}} is singular.
```
Out[13]= Inverse[{{1., 2.}, {1., 2.}}]
```

If you work with high-precision approximate numbers, *Mathematica* will keep track of the precision of matrix inverses that you generate.

This generates a 6×6 numerical matrix with entries of 20-digit precision.

```
In[14]:= m = N [ Table[ GCD[i, j] + 1, {i, 6}, {j, 6} ], 20 ] ;
```

This takes the matrix, multiplies it by its inverse, and shows the first row of the result.

```
In[15]:= (m . Inverse[m]) [[1]]
```
$$Out[15]= \left\{1.000000000000000000, 0. \times 10^{-19}, \right.$$
$$\left. 0. \times 10^{-19}, 0. \times 10^{-20}, 0. \times 10^{-20}, 0. \times 10^{-20}\right\}$$

This generates a 20-digit numerical approximation to a 6×6 Hilbert matrix. Hilbert matrices are notoriously hard to invert numerically.

```
In[16]:= m = N[Table[1/(i + j - 1), {i, 6}, {j, 6}], 20] ;
```

The result is still correct, but the zeros now have lower accuracy.

$In[17]:=$ `(m . Inverse[m]) [[1]]`

$Out[17]=$ $\{1.000000000000000, -0. \times 10^{-15},$
$\qquad\qquad 0. \times 10^{-14}, -0. \times 10^{-14}, 0. \times 10^{-14}, -0. \times 10^{-14}\}$

Inverse works only on square matrices. Section 3.7.10 discusses the function `PseudoInverse`, which can also be used with non-square matrices.

■ 3.7.7 Basic Matrix Operations

Transpose[m]	transpose
Inverse[m]	matrix inverse
Det[m]	determinant
Minors[m]	matrix of minors
Minors[m, k]	k^{th} minors
Tr[m]	trace
+ CharacteristicPolynomial[m, x]	characteristic polynomial

Some basic matrix operations.

Transposing a matrix interchanges the rows and columns in the matrix. If you transpose an $m \times n$ matrix, you get an $n \times m$ matrix as the result.

Transposing a 2×3 matrix gives a 3×2 result.

$In[1]:=$ **Transpose[{{a, b, c}, {ap, bp, cp}}]**

$Out[1]=$ `{{a, ap}, {b, bp}, {c, cp}}`

Det[m] gives the determinant of a square matrix m. **Minors[m]** is the matrix whose $(i, j)^{th}$ element gives the determinant of the submatrix obtained by deleting the $(n - i + 1)^{th}$ row and the $(n - j + 1)^{th}$ column of m. The $(i, j)^{th}$ cofactor of m is $(-1)^{i+j}$ times the $(n - i + 1, n - j + 1)^{th}$ element of the matrix of minors.

Minors[m, k] gives the determinants of the $k \times k$ submatrices obtained by picking each possible set of k rows and k columns from m. Note that you can apply **Minors** to rectangular, as well as square, matrices.

Here is the determinant of a simple 2×2 matrix.

$In[2]:=$ **Det[{{a, b}, {c, d}}]**

$Out[2]=$ `-b c + a d`

This generates a 3×3 matrix, whose i, j^{th} entry is a[i, j].

```
In[3]:= m = Array[a, {3, 3}]
Out[3]= {{a[1, 1], a[1, 2], a[1, 3]},
         {a[2, 1], a[2, 2], a[2, 3]},
         {a[3, 1], a[3, 2], a[3, 3]}}
```

Here is the determinant of m.

```
In[4]:= Det[ m ]
Out[4]= -a[1, 3] a[2, 2] a[3, 1] + a[1, 2] a[2, 3] a[3, 1] +
         a[1, 3] a[2, 1] a[3, 2] - a[1, 1] a[2, 3] a[3, 2] -
         a[1, 2] a[2, 1] a[3, 3] + a[1, 1] a[2, 2] a[3, 3]
```

The *trace* or *spur* of a matrix Tr[m] is the sum of the terms on the leading diagonal.

This finds the trace of a simple 2×2 matrix.

```
In[5]:= Tr[{{a, b}, {c, d}}]
Out[5]= a + d
```

MatrixPower[m, n]	n^{th} matrix power
MatrixExp[m]	matrix exponential

Powers and exponentials of matrices.

Here is a 2×2 matrix.

```
In[6]:= m = {{0.4, 0.6}, {0.525, 0.475}}
Out[6]= {{0.4, 0.6}, {0.525, 0.475}}
```

This gives the third matrix power of m.

```
In[7]:= MatrixPower[m, 3]
Out[7]= {{0.465625, 0.534375}, {0.467578, 0.532422}}
```

It is equivalent to multiplying three copies of the matrix.

```
In[8]:= m . m . m
Out[8]= {{0.465625, 0.534375}, {0.467578, 0.532422}}
```

Here is the millionth matrix power.

```
In[9]:= MatrixPower[m, 10^6]
Out[9]= {{0.466667, 0.533333}, {0.466667, 0.533333}}
```

This gives the matrix exponential of m.

```
In[10]:= MatrixExp[m]
Out[10]= {{1.7392, 0.979085}, {0.8567, 1.86158}}
```

Here is an approximation to the exponential of m, based on a power series approximation.

```
In[11]:= Sum[MatrixPower[m, i]/i!, {i, 0, 5}]
Out[11]= {{1.73844, 0.978224}, {0.855946, 1.86072}}
```

■ 3.7.8 Solving Linear Systems

Many calculations involve solving systems of linear equations. In many cases, you will find it convenient to write down the equations explicitly, and then solve them using Solve.

In some cases, however, you may prefer to convert the system of linear equations into a matrix equation, and then apply matrix manipulation operations to solve it. This approach is often useful when the system of equations arises as part of a general algorithm, and you do not know in advance how many variables will be involved.

A system of linear equations can be stated in matrix form as **m.x = b**, where **x** is the vector of variables.

Note that if your system of equations is sparse, so that most of the entries in the matrix **m** are zero, then it is best to represent the matrix as a SparseArray object. As discussed on page 922, you can convert from symbolic equations to SparseArray objects using CoefficientArrays. All the functions described in this section work on SparseArray objects as well as ordinary matrices.

LinearSolve[m, b]	a vector x which solves the matrix equation $m.x == b$
NullSpace[m]	a list of basis vectors whose linear combinations satisfy the matrix equation $m.x == 0$
MatrixRank[m]	the number of linearly independent rows of m
RowReduce[m]	a simplified form of m obtained by making linear combinations of rows

Solving and analyzing linear systems.

Here is a 2×2 matrix.

In[1]:= m = {{1, 5}, {2, 1}}

Out[1]= {{1, 5}, {2, 1}}

This gives two linear equations.

In[2]:= m . {x, y} == {a, b}

Out[2]= {x + 5 y, 2 x + y} == {a, b}

You can use Solve directly to solve these equations.

In[3]:= Solve[%, {x, y}]

Out[3]= $\left\{\left\{x \to -\frac{1}{9} (a - 5 b), y \to -\frac{1}{9} (-2 a + b)\right\}\right\}$

You can also get the vector of solutions by calling LinearSolve. The result is equivalent to the one you get from Solve.

In[4]:= LinearSolve[m, {a, b}]

Out[4]= $\left\{\frac{1}{9} (-a + 5 b), \frac{1}{9} (2 a - b)\right\}$

Another way to solve the equations is to invert the matrix m, and then multiply {a, b} by the inverse. This is not as efficient as using LinearSolve.

In[5]:= **Inverse[m] . {a, b}**

Out[5]= $\left\{ -\dfrac{a}{9} + \dfrac{5\,b}{9},\ \dfrac{2\,a}{9} - \dfrac{b}{9} \right\}$

RowReduce performs a version of Gaussian elimination and can also be used to solve the equations.

In[6]:= **RowReduce[{{1, 5, a}, {2, 1, b}}]**

Out[6]= $\left\{ \left\{ 1,\ 0,\ \dfrac{1}{9}\,(-a + 5\,b) \right\},\ \left\{ 0,\ 1,\ \dfrac{1}{9}\,(2\,a - b) \right\} \right\}$

If you have a square matrix **m** with a non-zero determinant, then you can always find a unique solution to the matrix equation **m.x = b** for any **b**. If, however, the matrix **m** has determinant zero, then there may be either no vector, or an infinite number of vectors **x** which satisfy **m.x = b** for a particular **b**. This occurs when the linear equations embodied in **m** are not independent.

When **m** has determinant zero, it is nevertheless always possible to find non-zero vectors **x** that satisfy **m.x = 0**. The set of vectors **x** satisfying this equation form the *null space* or *kernel* of the matrix **m**. Any of these vectors can be expressed as a linear combination of a particular set of basis vectors, which can be obtained using NullSpace[*m*].

Here is a simple matrix, corresponding to two identical linear equations.

In[7]:= **m = {{1, 2}, {1, 2}}**

Out[7]= {{1, 2}, {1, 2}}

The matrix has determinant zero.

In[8]:= **Det[m]**

Out[8]= 0

LinearSolve cannot find a solution to the equation **m.x = b** in this case.

In[9]:= **LinearSolve[m, {a, b}]**

LinearSolve::nosol:
    Linear equation encountered which has no solution.

Out[9]= LinearSolve[{{1, 2}, {1, 2}}, {a, b}]

There is a single basis vector for the null space of m.

In[10]:= **NullSpace[m]**

Out[10]= {{-2, 1}}

Multiplying the basis vector for the null space by m gives the zero vector.

In[11]:= **m . %[[1]]**

Out[11]= {0, 0}

There is only 1 linearly independent row in m.

In[12]:= **MatrixRank[m]**

Out[12]= 1

NullSpace and MatrixRank have to determine whether particular combinations of matrix elements are zero. For approximate numerical matrices, the Tolerance option can be used to specify how close to zero is considered good enough. For exact symbolic matrices, you may sometimes need to specify something like ZeroTest->(FullSimplify[#]==0&) to force more to be done to test whether symbolic expressions are zero.

Here is a simple symbolic matrix with determinant zero.

In[13]:= **m = {{a, b, c}, {2 a, 2 b, 2 c}, {3 a, 3 b, 3 c}}**

Out[13]= {{a, b, c}, {2a, 2b, 2c}, {3a, 3b, 3c}}

The basis for the null space of m
contains two vectors.

In[14]:= **NullSpace[m]**

$Out[14]= \left\{\left\{-\frac{c}{a}, 0, 1\right\}, \left\{-\frac{b}{a}, 1, 0\right\}\right\}$

Multiplying m by any linear
combination of these vectors gives
zero.

In[15]:= **Simplify[m . (x %[[1]] + y %[[2]])]**

Out[15]= {0, 0, 0}

An important feature of functions like LinearSolve and NullSpace is that they work with *rectangular*, as well as *square*, matrices.

When you represent a system of linear equations by a matrix equation of the form **m.x = b**, the number of columns in **m** gives the number of variables, and the number of rows gives the number of equations. There are a number of cases.

Underdetermined	number of equations less than the number of variables; no solutions or many solutions may exist
Overdetermined	number of equations more than the number of variables; solutions may or may not exist
Nonsingular	number of independent equations equal to the number of variables, and determinant non-zero; a unique solution exists
Consistent	at least one solution exists
Inconsistent	no solutions exist

Classes of linear systems represented by rectangular matrices.

This asks for the solution to the
inconsistent set of equations $x = 1$ and
$x = 0$.

In[16]:= **LinearSolve[{{1}, {1}}, {1, 0}]**

LinearSolve::nosol:
    Linear equation encountered which has no solution.

Out[16]= LinearSolve[{{1}, {1}}, {1, 0}]

This matrix represents two equations,
for three variables.

In[17]:= **m = {{1, 3, 4}, {2, 1, 3}}**

Out[17]= {{1, 3, 4}, {2, 1, 3}}

LinearSolve gives one of the possible
solutions to this underdetermined set
of equations.

In[18]:= **v = LinearSolve[m, {1, 1}]**

$Out[18]= \left\{\frac{2}{5}, \frac{1}{5}, 0\right\}$

When a matrix represents an
underdetermined system of equations,
the matrix has a non-trivial null space.
In this case, the null space is spanned
by a single vector.

In[19]:= **NullSpace[m]**

Out[19]= {{-1, -1, 1}}

If you take the solution you get from LinearSolve, and add any linear combination of the basis vectors for the null space, you still get a solution.

`In[20]:= m . (v + 4 %[[1]])`

`Out[20]= {1, 1}`

The number of independent equations is the *rank* of the matrix `MatrixRank[m]`. The number of redundant equations is `Length[NullSpace[m]]`. Note that the sum of these quantities is always equal to the number of columns in *m*.

+	LinearSolve[*m*] generate a function for solving equations of the form *m* . *x* == *b*

Generating `LinearSolveFunction` objects.

In some applications, you will want to solve equations of the form **m.x** = **b** many times with the same **m**, but different **b**. You can do this efficiently in *Mathematica* by using `LinearSolve[m]` to create a single `LinearSolveFunction` that you can apply to as many vectors as you want.

This creates a LinearSolveFunction.

`In[21]:= f = LinearSolve[{{1, 4}, {2, 3}}]`

`Out[21]= LinearSolveFunction[{2, 2}, <>]`

You can apply this to a vector.

`In[22]:= f[{5, 7}]`

$$Out[22]= \left\{ \frac{13}{5}, \frac{3}{5} \right\}$$

You get the same result by giving the vector as an explicit argument to LinearSolve.

`In[23]:= LinearSolve[{{1, 4}, {2, 3}}, {5, 7}]`

$$Out[23]= \left\{ \frac{13}{5}, \frac{3}{5} \right\}$$

But you can apply f to any vector you want.

`In[24]:= f[{-5, 9}]`

$$Out[24]= \left\{ \frac{51}{5}, -\frac{19}{5} \right\}$$

3.7.9 Eigenvalues and Eigenvectors

Eigenvalues[*m*]	a list of the eigenvalues of *m*
Eigenvectors[*m*]	a list of the eigenvectors of *m*
Eigensystem[*m*]	a list of the form {*eigenvalues*, *eigenvectors*}
Eigenvalues[N[*m*]], etc.	numerical eigenvalues
Eigenvalues[N[*m*, *p*]], etc.	numerical eigenvalues, starting with *p*-digit precision
+ CharacteristicPolynomial[*m*, *x*]	the characteristic polynomial of *m*

Eigenvalues and eigenvectors.

The eigenvalues of a matrix **m** are the values λ_i for which one can find non-zero vectors $\mathbf{v}_i$ such that $\mathbf{m}.\mathbf{v}_i = \lambda_i \mathbf{v}_i$. The eigenvectors are the vectors $\mathbf{v}_i$.

The *characteristic polynomial* `CharacteristicPolynomial[m, x]` for an $n \times n$ matrix is given by `Det[m - x IdentityMatrix[n]]`. The eigenvalues are the roots of this polynomial.

Finding the eigenvalues of an $n \times n$ matrix in general involves solving an nth-degree polynomial equation. For $n \geq 5$, therefore, the results cannot in general be expressed purely in terms of explicit radicals. `Root` objects can nevertheless always be used, although except for fairly sparse or otherwise simple matrices the expressions obtained are often unmanageably complex.

Even for a matrix as simple as this, the explicit form of the eigenvalues is quite complicated.	`In[1]:= Eigenvalues[ {{a, b}, {-b, 2a}} ]` $Out[1]= \left\{ \frac{1}{2} \left(3a - \sqrt{a^2 - 4b^2} \right), \frac{1}{2} \left(3a + \sqrt{a^2 - 4b^2} \right) \right\}$

If you give a matrix of approximate real numbers, *Mathematica* will find the approximate numerical eigenvalues and eigenvectors.

Here is a 2×2 numerical matrix.	`In[2]:= m = {{2.3, 4.5}, {6.7, -1.2}}`
	
	`Out[2]= {{2.3, 4.5}, {6.7, -1.2}}`

The matrix has two eigenvalues, in this case both real.	`In[3]:= Eigenvalues[ m ]`
	
	`Out[3]= {6.31303, -5.21303}`

Here are the two eigenvectors of m.	`In[4]:= Eigenvectors[ m ]`
	
	`Out[4]= {{0.746335, 0.66557}, {-0.513839, 0.857886}}`

Eigensystem computes the eigenvalues and eigenvectors at the same time. The assignment sets vals to the list of eigenvalues, and vecs to the list of eigenvectors.	`In[5]:= {vals, vecs} = Eigensystem[m]`
	
	`Out[5]= {{6.31303, -5.21303},`
	`        {{0.746335, 0.66557}, {-0.513839, 0.857886}}}`

This verifies that the first eigenvalue and eigenvector satisfy the appropriate condition.	`In[6]:= m . vecs[[1]] == vals[[1]] vecs[[1]]`
	
	`Out[6]= True`

This finds the eigenvalues of a random 4×4 matrix. For non-symmetric matrices, the eigenvalues can have imaginary parts.	`In[7]:= Eigenvalues[ Table[Random[ ], {4}, {4}] ]`
	
	`Out[7]= {2.30022, 0.319764 + 0.547199 i,`
	`        0.319764 - 0.547199 i, 0.449291}`

The function `Eigenvalues` always gives you a list of n eigenvalues for an $n \times n$ matrix. The eigenvalues correspond to the roots of the characteristic polynomial for the matrix, and may not necessarily be distinct. `Eigenvectors`, on the other hand, gives a list of eigenvectors which are guaranteed to be independent. If the number of such eigenvectors is less than n, then `Eigenvectors` appends zero vectors to the list it returns, so that the total length of the list is always n.

Here is a 3×3 matrix.	`In[8]:= mz = {{0, 1, 0}, {0, 0, 1}, {0, 0, 0}}`
	
	`Out[8]= {{0, 1, 0}, {0, 0, 1}, {0, 0, 0}}`

The matrix has three eigenvalues, all equal to zero.

```
In[9]:= Eigenvalues[mz]
Out[9]= {0, 0, 0}
```

There is, however, only one independent eigenvector for the matrix. Eigenvectors appends two zero vectors to give a total of three vectors in this case.

```
In[10]:= Eigenvectors[mz]
Out[10]= {{1, 0, 0}, {0, 0, 0}, {0, 0, 0}}
```

+	Eigenvalues[m, k]	the largest k eigenvalues of m
+	Eigenvectors[m, k]	the corresponding eigenvectors of m
+	Eigenvalues[m, $-k$]	the smallest k eigenvalues of m
+	Eigenvectors[m, $-k$]	the corresponding eigenvectors of m

Finding largest and smallest eigenvalues.

Eigenvalues sorts numeric eigenvalues so that the ones with large absolute value come first. In many situations, you may be interested only in the largest or smallest eigenvalues of a matrix. You can get these efficiently using Eigenvalues[m, k] and Eigenvalues[m, $-k$].

This computes the exact eigenvalues of an integer matrix.

```
In[11]:= Eigenvalues[{{1, 2}, {3, 4}}]
```
$$Out[11]= \left\{ \frac{1}{2} \left(5 + \sqrt{33} \right), \frac{1}{2} \left(5 - \sqrt{33} \right) \right\}$$

The eigenvalues are sorted in decreasing order of size.

```
In[12]:= N[%]
Out[12]= {5.37228, -0.372281}
```

This gives the three eigenvalues with largest absolute value.

```
In[13]:= Eigenvalues[Table[N[Tan[i/j]], {i, 10}, {j, 10}], 3]
Out[13]= {10.044, 2.94396 + 6.03728 i, 2.94396 - 6.03728 i}
```

+	Eigenvalues[{m, a}]	the generalized eigenvalues of m with respect to a
+	Eigenvectors[{m, a}]	the generalized eigenvectors of m
+	CharacteristicPolynomial[{m, a}, x]	the generalized characteristic polynomial of m

Generalized eigenvalues and eigenvectors.

The generalized eigenvalues for a matrix **m** with respect to a matrix **a** are defined to be those λ_i for which $\mathbf{m}.\mathbf{v}_i = \lambda_i \mathbf{a}.\mathbf{v}_i$.

The generalized eigenvalues correspond to zeros of the generalized characteristic polynomial Det[*m* - *x* *a*].

Note that while ordinary matrix eigenvalues always have definite values, some generalized eigenvalues will always be Indeterminate if the generalized characteristic polynomial vanishes, which happens if **m** and **a** share a null space. Note also that generalized eigenvalues can be infinite.

These two matrices share a one-dimensional null space, so one generalized eigenvalue is Indeterminate.	*In[14]:=* **Eigenvalues[{{{1.5, 0}, {0, 0}}, {{2, 0}, {1, 0}}}]** *Out[14]=* {0., Indeterminate}

■ 3.7.10 Advanced Matrix Operations

+	SingularValueList[*m*]	the list of non-zero singular values of *m*
+	SingularValueList[*m*, *k*]	the *k* largest singular values of *m*
+	SingularValueList[{*m*, *a*}]	the generalized singular values of *m* with respect to *a*
+	Norm[*m*, *p*]	the *p*-norm of *m*

Finding singular values and norms of matrices.

The *singular values* of a matrix **m** are the square roots of the eigenvalues of **m.m***, where $*$ denotes Hermitian transpose. The number of such singular values is the smaller dimension of the matrix. SingularValueList sorts the singular values from largest to smallest. Very small singular values are usually numerically meaningless. With the option setting Tolerance -> *t*, SingularValueList drops singular values that are less than a fraction *t* of the largest singular value. For approximate numerical matrices, the tolerance is by default slightly greater than zero.

If you multiply the vector for each point in a unit sphere in *n*-dimensional space by an $m \times n$ matrix **m**, then you get an *m*-dimensional ellipsoid, whose principal axes have lengths given by the singular values of **m**.

The *2-norm* of a matrix Norm[*m*, 2] is the largest principal axis of the ellipsoid, equal to the largest singular value of the matrix. This is also the maximum 2-norm length of **m**.*v* for any possible unit vector *v*.

The *p-norm* of a matrix Norm[*m*, *p*] is in general the maximum *p*-norm length of **m**.*v* that can be attained. The cases most often considered are $p = 1$, $p = 2$ and $p = \infty$. Also sometimes considered is the Frobenius norm, whose square is the trace of **m.m***.

| LUDecomposition[*m*] | the LU decomposition |
| CholeskyDecomposition[*m*] | the Cholesky decomposition |

Decomposing matrices into triangular forms.

When you create a `LinearSolveFunction` using `LinearSolve[`*m*`]`, this often works by decomposing the matrix *m* into triangular forms, and sometimes it is useful to be able to get such forms explicitly.

LU decomposition effectively factors any square matrix into a product of lower- and upper-triangular matrices. *Cholesky decomposition* effectively factors any Hermitian positive-definite matrix into a product of a lower-triangular matrix and its Hermitian conjugate, which can be viewed as the analog of finding a square root of a matrix.

PseudoInverse[*m*]	the pseudoinverse
QRDecomposition[*m*]	the QR decomposition
SingularValueDecomposition[*m*]	the singular value decomposition
SingularValueDecomposition[{*m*, *a*}]	the generalized singular value decomposition

Orthogonal decompositions of matrices.

The standard definition for the inverse of a matrix fails if the matrix is not square or is singular. The *pseudoinverse* $\mathbf{m}^{(-1)}$ of a matrix **m** can however still be defined. It is set up to minimize the sum of the squares of all entries in $\mathbf{m}.\mathbf{m}^{(-1)} - \mathbf{I}$, where **I** is the identity matrix. The pseudoinverse is sometimes known as the generalized inverse, or the Moore-Penrose inverse. It is particularly used in doing problems related to least-squares fitting.

QR decomposition writes any matrix **m** as a product $\mathbf{q}^*\mathbf{r}$, where **q** is an orthonormal matrix, $*$ denotes Hermitian transpose, and **r** is a triangular matrix, in which all entries below the leading diagonal are zero.

Singular value decomposition, or *SVD*, is an underlying element in many numerical matrix algorithms. The basic idea is to write any matrix **m** in the form $\mathbf{usv}^*$, where **s** is a matrix with the singular values of **m** on its diagonal, **u** and **v** are orthonormal matrices, and $\mathbf{v}^*$ is the Hermitian transpose of **v**.

JordanDecomposition[m]	the Jordan decomposition
SchurDecomposition[m]	the Schur decomposition
+ SchurDecomposition[{m, a}]	the generalized Schur decomposition

Functions related to eigenvalue problems.

Most matrices can be reduced to a diagonal matrix of eigenvalues by applying a matrix of their eigenvectors as a similarity transformation. But even when there are not enough eigenvectors to do this, one can still reduce a matrix to a *Jordan form* in which there are both eigenvalues and Jordan blocks on the diagonal. *Jordan decomposition* in general writes any matrix in the form as $\mathbf{sjs}^{-1}$.

Numerically more stable is the *Schur decomposition*, which writes any matrix **m** in the form $\mathbf{qtq}^*$, where **q** is an orthonormal matrix, and **t** is block upper triangular.

◼ 3.7.11 Advanced Topic: Tensors

Tensors are mathematical objects that give generalizations of vectors and matrices. In *Mathematica*, a tensor is represented as a set of lists, nested to a certain number of levels. The nesting level is the *rank* of the tensor.

rank 0	scalar
rank 1	vector
rank 2	matrix
rank k	rank k tensor

Interpretations of nested lists.

A tensor of rank k is essentially a k-dimensional table of values. To be a true rank k tensor, it must be possible to arrange the elements in the table in a k-dimensional cuboidal array. There can be no holes or protrusions in the cuboid.

The *indices* that specify a particular element in the tensor correspond to the coordinates in the cuboid. The *dimensions* of the tensor correspond to the side lengths of the cuboid.

One simple way that a rank k tensor can arise is in giving a table of values for a function of k variables. In physics, the tensors that occur typically have indices which run over the possible directions in space or spacetime. Notice, however, that there is no built-in notion of covariant and contravariant tensor indices in *Mathematica*: you have to set these up explicitly using metric tensors.

Table[f, {i_1, n_1}, {i_2, n_2}, ... , {i_k, n_k}]

create an $n_1 \times n_2 \times ... \times n_k$ tensor whose elements are the values of f

Array[a, {n_1, n_2, ... , n_k}]

create an $n_1 \times n_2 \times ... \times n_k$ tensor with elements given by applying a to each set of indices

ArrayQ[t, n]   test whether t is a tensor of rank n

Dimensions[t]   give a list of the dimensions of a tensor

ArrayDepth[t]   find the rank of a tensor

MatrixForm[t]   print with the elements of t arranged in a two-dimensional array

Functions for creating and testing the structure of tensors.

Here is a $2 \times 3 \times 2$ tensor.

```
In[1]:= t = Table[i1+i2 i3, {i1, 2}, {i2, 3}, {i3, 2}]

Out[1]= {{{2, 3}, {3, 5}, {4, 7}}, {{3, 4}, {4, 6}, {5, 8}}}
```

This is another way to produce the same tensor.

```
In[2]:= Array[(#1 + #2 #3)&, {2, 3, 2}]

Out[2]= {{{2, 3}, {3, 5}, {4, 7}}, {{3, 4}, {4, 6}, {5, 8}}}
```

MatrixForm displays the elements of the tensor in a two-dimensional array. You can think of the array as being a 2×3 matrix of column vectors.

```
In[3]:= MatrixForm[ t ]
```

$$Out[3]//MatrixForm= \begin{pmatrix} \binom{2}{3} & \binom{3}{5} & \binom{4}{7} \\ \binom{3}{4} & \binom{4}{6} & \binom{5}{8} \end{pmatrix}$$

Dimensions gives the dimensions of the tensor.

```
In[4]:= Dimensions[ t ]

Out[4]= {2, 3, 2}
```

Here is the 111 element of the tensor.

```
In[5]:= t[[1, 1, 1]]

Out[5]= 2
```

ArrayDepth gives the rank of the tensor.

```
In[6]:= ArrayDepth[ t ]

Out[6]= 3
```

The rank of a tensor is equal to the number of indices needed to specify each element. You can pick out subtensors by using a smaller number of indices.

Transpose[t]	transpose the first two indices in a tensor
Transpose[t, {p_1, p_2, ... }]	transpose the indices in a tensor so that the kth becomes the $p_k{}^{\text{th}}$
Tr[t, f]	form the generalized trace of the tensor t
Outer[f, t_1, t_2]	form the generalized outer product of the tensors t_1 and t_2 with "multiplication operator" f
t_1 . t_2	form the dot product of t_1 and t_2 (last index of t_1 contracted with first index of t_2)
Inner[f, t_1, t_2, g]	form the generalized inner product, with "multiplication operator" f and "addition operator" g

Tensor manipulation operations.

You can think of a rank k tensor as having k "slots" into which you insert indices. Applying Transpose is effectively a way of reordering these slots. If you think of the elements of a tensor as forming a k-dimensional cuboid, you can view Transpose as effectively rotating (and possibly reflecting) the cuboid.

In the most general case, Transpose allows you to specify an arbitrary reordering to apply to the indices of a tensor. The function Transpose[T, {p_1, p_2, ... , p_k}], gives you a new tensor T' such that the value of $T'_{i_1 i_2 ... i_k}$ is given by $T_{i_{p_1} i_{p_2} ... i_{p_k}}$.

If you originally had an $n_{p_1} \times n_{p_2} \times ... \times n_{p_k}$ tensor, then by applying Transpose, you will get an $n_1 \times n_2 \times ... \times n_k$ tensor.

Here is a matrix that you can also think of as a 2×3 tensor.	*In[7]:=* **m = {{a, b, c}, {ap, bp, cp}}** *Out[7]=* {{a, b, c}, {ap, bp, cp}}
Applying Transpose gives you a 3×2 tensor. Transpose effectively interchanges the two "slots" for tensor indices.	*In[8]:=* **mt = Transpose[m]** *Out[8]=* {{a, ap}, {b, bp}, {c, cp}}
The element m[[2, 3]] in the original tensor becomes the element m[[3, 2]] in the transposed tensor.	*In[9]:=* **{ m[[2, 3]], mt[[3, 2]] }** *Out[9]=* {cp, cp}
This produces a $2 \times 3 \times 1 \times 2$ tensor.	*In[10]:=* **t = Array[a, {2, 3, 1, 2}]** *Out[10]=* {{{{a[1, 1, 1, 1], a[1, 1, 1, 2]}}, {{a[1, 2, 1, 1], a[1, 2, 1, 2]}}, {{a[1, 3, 1, 1], a[1, 3, 1, 2]}}}, {{{a[2, 1, 1, 1], a[2, 1, 1, 2]}}, {{a[2, 2, 1, 1], a[2, 2, 1, 2]}}, {{a[2, 3, 1, 1], a[2, 3, 1, 2]}}}}

This transposes the first two levels of t.	*In[11]:=* **tt1 = Transpose[t]**

Out[11]= {{{{a[1, 1, 1, 1], a[1, 1, 1, 2]}},
　　　　{{a[2, 1, 1, 1], a[2, 1, 1, 2]}}},
　　　{{{a[1, 2, 1, 1], a[1, 2, 1, 2]}},
　　　　{{a[2, 2, 1, 1], a[2, 2, 1, 2]}}},
　　　{{{a[1, 3, 1, 1], a[1, 3, 1, 2]}},
　　　　{{a[2, 3, 1, 1], a[2, 3, 1, 2]}}}}

The result is a $3 \times 2 \times 1 \times 2$ tensor.	*In[12]:=* **Dimensions[tt1]**

Out[12]= {3, 2, 1, 2}

If you have a tensor that contains lists of the same length at different levels, then you can use Transpose to effectively collapse different levels.

This collapses all three levels, giving a list of the elements on the "main diagonal".	*In[13]:=* **Transpose[Array[a, {3, 3, 3}], {1, 1, 1}]**

Out[13]= {a[1, 1, 1], a[2, 2, 2], a[3, 3, 3]}

This collapses only the first two levels.	*In[14]:=* **Transpose[Array[a, {2, 2, 2}], {1, 1}]**

Out[14]= {{a[1, 1, 1], a[1, 1, 2]}, {a[2, 2, 1], a[2, 2, 2]}}

You can also use Tr to extract diagonal elements of a tensor.

This forms the ordinary trace of a rank 3 tensor.	*In[15]:=* **Tr[Array[a, {3, 3, 3}]]**

Out[15]= a[1, 1, 1] + a[2, 2, 2] + a[3, 3, 3]

Here is a generalized trace, with elements combined into a list.	*In[16]:=* **Tr[Array[a, {3, 3, 3}], List]**

Out[16]= {a[1, 1, 1], a[2, 2, 2], a[3, 3, 3]}

This combines diagonal elements only down to level 2.	*In[17]:=* **Tr[Array[a, {3, 3, 3}], List, 2]**

Out[17]= {{a[1, 1, 1], a[1, 1, 2], a[1, 1, 3]},
　　　{a[2, 2, 1], a[2, 2, 2], a[2, 2, 3]},
　　　{a[3, 3, 1], a[3, 3, 2], a[3, 3, 3]}}

Outer products, and their generalizations, are a way of building higher-rank tensors from lower-rank ones. Outer products are also sometimes known as direct, tensor or Kronecker products.

From a structural point of view, the tensor you get from Outer[*f*, *t*, *u*] has a copy of the structure of *u* inserted at the "position" of each element in *t*. The elements in the resulting structure are obtained by combining elements of *t* and *u* using the function *f*.

This gives the "outer f" of two vectors. The result is a matrix.	*In[18]:=* **Outer[f, {a, b}, {ap, bp}]**

Out[18]= {{f[a, ap], f[a, bp]}, {f[b, ap], f[b, bp]}}

If you take the "outer f" of a length 3 vector with a length 2 vector, you get a 3×2 matrix.	*In[19]:=* **Outer[f, {a, b, c}, {ap, bp}]**

Out[19]= {{f[a, ap], f[a, bp]},
　　　{f[b, ap], f[b, bp]}, {f[c, ap], f[c, bp]}}

The result of taking the "outer f" of a 2×2 matrix and a length 3 vector is a $2 \times 2 \times 3$ tensor.	`In[20]:=` **`Outer[ f, {{m11, m12}, {m21, m22}}, {a, b, c} ]`**

```
Out[20]= {{{f[m11, a], f[m11, b], f[m11, c]},
           {f[m12, a], f[m12, b], f[m12, c]}},
          {{f[m21, a], f[m21, b], f[m21, c]},
           {f[m22, a], f[m22, b], f[m22, c]}}}
```

Here are the dimensions of the tensor.	`In[21]:=` **`Dimensions[ % ]`**

```
Out[21]= {2, 2, 3}
```

If you take the generalized outer product of an $m_1 \times m_2 \times \ldots \times m_r$ tensor and an $n_1 \times n_2 \times \ldots \times n_s$ tensor, you get an $m_1 \times \ldots \times m_r \times n_1 \times \ldots \times n_s$ tensor. If the original tensors have ranks r and s, your result will be a rank $r + s$ tensor.

In terms of indices, the result of applying `Outer` to two tensors $T_{i_1 i_2 \ldots i_r}$ and $U_{j_1 j_2 \ldots j_s}$ is the tensor $V_{i_1 i_2 \ldots i_r j_1 j_2 \ldots j_s}$ with elements $f[T_{i_1 i_2 \ldots i_r}, U_{j_1 j_2 \ldots j_s}]$.

In doing standard tensor calculations, the most common function f to use in `Outer` is `Times`, corresponding to the standard outer product.

Particularly in doing combinatorial calculations, however, it is often convenient to take f to be `List`. Using `Outer`, you can then get combinations of all possible elements in one tensor, with all possible elements in the other.

In constructing `Outer[f, t, u]` you effectively insert a copy of u at every point in t. To form `Inner[f, t, u]`, you effectively combine and collapse the last dimension of t and the first dimension of u. The idea is to take an $m_1 \times m_2 \times \ldots \times m_r$ tensor and an $n_1 \times n_2 \times \ldots \times n_s$ tensor, with $m_r = n_1$, and get an $m_1 \times m_2 \times \ldots \times m_{r-1} \times n_2 \times \ldots \times n_s$ tensor as the result.

The simplest examples are with vectors. If you apply `Inner` to two vectors of equal length, you get a scalar. `Inner[f, v_1, v_2, g]` gives a generalization of the usual scalar product, with f playing the role of multiplication, and g playing the role of addition.

This gives a generalization of the standard scalar product of two vectors.	`In[22]:=` **`Inner[f, {a, b, c}, {ap, bp, cp}, g]`**

```
Out[22]= g[f[a, ap], f[b, bp], f[c, cp]]
```

This gives a generalization of a matrix product.	`In[23]:=` **`Inner[f, {{1, 2}, {3, 4}}, {{a, b}, {c, d}}, g]`**

```
Out[23]= {{g[f[1, a], f[2, c]], g[f[1, b], f[2, d]]},
          {g[f[3, a], f[4, c]], g[f[3, b], f[4, d]]}}
```

Here is a $3 \times 2 \times 2$ tensor.	`In[24]:=` **`a = Array[1&, {3, 2, 2}]`**

```
Out[24]= {{{1, 1}, {1, 1}}, {{1, 1}, {1, 1}}, {{1, 1}, {1, 1}}}
```

Here is a $2 \times 3 \times 1$ tensor.	`In[25]:=` **`b = Array[2&, {2, 3, 1}]`**

```
Out[25]= {{{2}, {2}, {2}}, {{2}, {2}, {2}}}
```

This gives a $3 \times 2 \times 3 \times 1$ tensor.	`In[26]:=` **`a . b`**

```
Out[26]= {{{{4}, {4}, {4}}, {{4}, {4}, {4}}},
          {{{4}, {4}, {4}}, {{4}, {4}, {4}}},
          {{{4}, {4}, {4}}, {{4}, {4}, {4}}}}
```

Here are the dimensions of the result.
```
In[27]:= Dimensions[ % ]

Out[27]= {3, 2, 3, 1}
```

You can think of `Inner` as performing a "contraction" of the last index of one tensor with the first index of another. If you want to perform contractions across other pairs of indices, you can do so by first transposing the appropriate indices into the first or last position, then applying `Inner`, and then transposing the result back.

In many applications of tensors, you need to insert signs to implement antisymmetry. The function `Signature[{$i_1$, $i_2$, ... }]`, which gives the signature of a permutation, is often useful for this purpose.

`Outer[f, $t_1$, $t_2$, ... ]`	form a generalized outer product by combining the lowest-level elements of t_1, t_2, ...
`Outer[f, $t_1$, $t_2$, ... , n]`	treat only sublists at level n as separate elements
`Outer[f, $t_1$, $t_2$, ... , $n_1$, $n_2$, ... ]`	treat only sublists at level n_i in t_i as separate elements
`Inner[f, $t_1$, $t_2$, g]`	form a generalized inner product using the lowest-level elements of t_1
`Inner[f, $t_1$, $t_2$, g, n]`	treat only sublists at level n in t_1 as separate elements

Treating only certain sublists in tensors as separate elements.

Here every single symbol is treated as a separate element.
```
In[28]:= Outer[f, {{i, j}, {k, l}}, {x, y}]

Out[28]= {{{f[i, x], f[i, y]}, {f[j, x], f[j, y]}},
          {{f[k, x], f[k, y]}, {f[l, x], f[l, y]}}}
```

But here only sublists at level 1 are treated as separate elements.
```
In[29]:= Outer[f, {{i, j}, {k, l}}, {x, y}, 1]

Out[29]= {{f[{i, j}, x], f[{i, j}, y]},
          {f[{k, l}, x], f[{k, l}, y]}}
```

■ 3.7.12 Sparse Arrays

Many large-scale applications of linear algebra involve matrices that have many elements, but comparatively few that are non-zero. You can represent such sparse matrices efficiently in *Mathematica* using `SparseArray` objects, as discussed in Section 2.4.5. `SparseArray` objects work by having lists of rules that specify where non-zero values appear.

> SparseArray[*list*]   a SparseArray version of an ordinary list
>
> SparseArray[{{i_1, j_1} -> v_1, {i_2, j_2} -> v_2, ... }, {m, n}]
>   an $m \times n$ sparse array with element {i_k, j_k} having value v_k
>
> SparseArray[{{i_1, j_1}, {i_2, j_2}, ... } -> {v_1, v_2, ... }, {m, n}]
>   the same sparse array
>
> ---
>
> Normal[*array*]   the ordinary list corresponding to a SparseArray

Specifying sparse arrays.

As discussed in Section 2.4.5, you can use patterns to specify collections of elements in sparse arrays. You can also have sparse arrays that correspond to tensors of any rank.

This makes a 50 × 50 sparse numerical matrix, with 148 non-zero elements.

```
In[1]:= m = SparseArray[{{30, _} -> 11.5, {_, 30} -> 21.5,
                         {i_, i_} -> i}, {50, 50}]

Out[1]= SparseArray[<148>, {50, 50}]
```

This shows a visual representation of the matrix elements.

```
In[2]:= ListDensityPlot[-m]
```

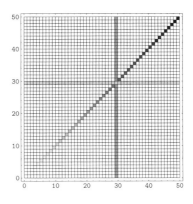

Here are the four largest eigenvalues of the matrix.

```
In[3]:= Eigenvalues[m, 4]

Out[3]= {129.846, -92.6878, 12.8319, 2.42012}
```

Dot gives a SparseArray result.

```
In[4]:= m . m

Out[4]= SparseArray[<2500>, {50, 50}]
```

You can extract parts just like in an ordinary array.

```
In[5]:= %[[20, 20]]

Out[5]= 647.25
```

You can apply most standard structural operations directly to SparseArray objects, just as you would to ordinary lists. When the results are sparse, they typically return SparseArray objects.

Dimensions[*m*]	the dimensions of an array
ArrayRules[*m*]	the rules for non-zero elements in an array
m[[*i*, *j*]]	element *i*, *j*
m[[*i*]]	the ith row
m[[All, *j*]]	the ith column
m[[*i*, *j*]] = *v*	reset element *i*, *j*

A few structural operations that can be done directly on SparseArray objects.

This gives the first column of m. It has only 2 non-zero elements.	*In[6]:=* **m[[All, 1]]** *Out[6]=* SparseArray[<2>, {50}]
This adds 3 to each element in the first column of m.	*In[7]:=* **m[[All, 1]] = 3 + m[[All, 1]]** *Out[7]=* SparseArray[<2>, {50}, 3]
Now all the elements in the first column are non-zero.	*In[8]:=* **m[[All, 1]]** *Out[8]=* SparseArray[<50>, {50}]
This gives the rules for the non-zero elements on the second row.	*In[9]:=* **ArrayRules[m[[2]]]** *Out[9]=* {{1} → 3, {2} → 2, {30} → 21.5, {_} → 0}

SparseArray[*rules*]	generate a sparse array from rules
CoefficientArrays[{*eqns*$_1$, *eqns*$_2$, ... }, {*x*$_1$, *x*$_2$, ... }]	get arrays of coefficients from equations
Import["*file*.mtx"]	import a sparse array from a file

Typical ways to get sparse arrays.

This generates a tridiagonal random matrix.	*In[10]:=* **SparseArray[{i_, j_} /; Abs[i-j] <= 1 :> Random[],** **{100, 100}]** *Out[10]=* SparseArray[<298>, {100, 100}]
Even the tenth power of the matrix is still fairly sparse.	*In[11]:=* **MatrixPower[%, 10]** *Out[11]=* SparseArray[<1990>, {100, 100}]
This extracts the coefficients as sparse arrays.	*In[12]:=* **s = CoefficientArrays[{c + x - z == 0, x + 2 y + z == 0},** **{x, y, z}]** *Out[12]=* {SparseArray[<1>, {2}], SparseArray[<5>, {2, 3}]}

Here are the corresponding ordinary arrays.	*In[13]:=* **Normal[%]**
	Out[13]= {{c, 0}, {{1, 0, -1}, {1, 2, 1}}}
This reproduces the original forms.	*In[14]:=* **s[[1]] + s[[2]] . {x, y, z}**
	Out[14]= {c + x - z, x + 2 y + z}

CoefficientArrays can handle general polynomial equations.	*In[15]:=* **s = CoefficientArrays[**
	        {c + x^2 - z == 0, x^2 + 2 y + z^2 == 0},
	                              {x, y, z}]

	Out[15]= {SparseArray[<1>, {2}], SparseArray[<2>, {2, 3}], SparseArray[<3>, {2, 3, 3}]}
The coefficients of the quadratic part are given in a rank 3 tensor.	*In[16]:=* **Normal[%]**

	Out[16]= {{c, 0}, {{0, 0, -1}, {0, 2, 0}},
	         {{{1, 0, 0}, {0, 0, 0}, {0, 0, 0}},
	          {{1, 0, 0}, {0, 0, 0}, {0, 0, 1}}}}

This reproduces the original forms.	*In[17]:=* **s[[1]] + s[[2]] . {x, y, z} + s[[3]] . {x, y, z} . {x, y, z}**
	Out[17]= {c + x^2 - z, x^2 + 2 y + z^2}

For machine-precision numerical sparse matrices, *Mathematica* supports standard file formats such as Matrix Market (.mtx) and Harwell-Boeing. You can import and export matrices in these formats using Import and Export.

3.8 Numerical Operations on Data

■ 3.8.1 Basic Statistics

Mean[*list*]	mean (average)
Median[*list*]	median (central value)
Max[*list*]	maximum value
Variance[*list*]	variance
StandardDeviation[*list*]	standard deviation
Quantile[*list*, *q*]	q^{th} quantile
Total[*list*]	total

Basic descriptive statistics operations.

Given a list with n elements x_i, the **mean** Mean[*list*] is defined to be $\mu(x) = \bar{x} = \sum x_i/n$.

The **variance** Variance[*list*] is defined to be $\text{var}(x) = \sigma^2(x) = \sum (x_i - \mu(x))^2/n$.

The **standard deviation** StandardDeviation[*list*] is defined to be $\sigma(x) = \sqrt{\text{var}(x)}$.

If the elements in *list* are thought of as being selected at random according to some probability distribution, then the mean gives an estimate of where the center of the distribution is located, while the standard deviation gives an estimate of how wide the dispersion in the distribution is.

The **median** Median[*list*] effectively gives the value at the halfway point in the sorted list Sort[*list*]. It is often considered a more robust measure of the center of a distribution than the mean, since it depends less on outlying values.

The qth **quantile** Quantile[*list*, *q*] effectively gives the value that is q of the way through the sorted list Sort[*list*].

For a list of length n, *Mathematica* defines Quantile[*list*, *q*] to be Sort[*list*][[Ceiling[n q]]].

There are, however, about ten other definitions of quantile in use, all potentially giving slightly different results. *Mathematica* covers the common cases by introducing four *quantile parameters* in the form Quantile[*list*, *q*, {{*a*, *b*}, {*c*, *d*}}]. The parameters *a* and *b* in effect define where in the list should be considered a fraction q of the way through. If this corresponds to an integer position, then the element at that position is taken to be the qth quantile. If it is not an integer position, then a linear combination of the elements on either side is used, as specified by *c* and *d*.

The position in a sorted list s for the qth quantile is taken to be $k = a + (n + b) q$. If k is an integer, then the quantile is s_k. Otherwise, it is $s_{\lfloor k \rfloor} + (s_{\lceil k \rceil} - s_{\lfloor k \rfloor})(c + d(k - \lfloor k \rfloor))$, with the indices taken to be 1 or n if they are out of range.

{{0, 0}, {1, 0}}	inverse empirical CDF (default)
{{0, 0}, {0, 1}}	linear interpolation (California method)
{{1/2, 0}, {0, 0}}	element numbered closest to qn
{{1/2, 0}, {0, 1}}	linear interpolation (hydrologist method)
{{0, 1}, {0, 1}}	mean-based estimate (Weibull method)
{{1, -1}, {0, 1}}	mode-based estimate
{{1/3, 1/3}, {0, 1}}	median-based estimate
{{3/8, 1/4}, {0, 1}}	normal distribution estimate

Common choices for quantile parameters.

Whenever $d = 0$, the value of the qth quantile is always equal to some actual element in *list*, so that the result changes discontinuously as q varies. For $d = 1$, the qth quantile interpolates linearly between successive elements in *list*. Median is defined to use such an interpolation.

Note that Quantile[*list*, q] yields **quartiles** when $q = m/4$ and **percentiles** when $q = m/100$.

+	Mean[{x_1, x_2, ... }] the mean of the x_i
+	Mean[{{x_1, y_1, ... }, {x_2, y_2, ... }, ... }] a list of the means of the x_i, y_i, ...

Handling multidimensional data.

Sometimes each item in your data may involve a list of values. The basic statistics functions in *Mathematica* automatically apply to all corresponding elements in these lists.

This separately finds the mean of each "column" of data.

In[1]:= **Mean[{{x1, y1}, {x2, y2}, {x3, y3}}]**

$$Out[1]= \left\{ \frac{1}{3} \, (x1 + x2 + x3), \, \frac{1}{3} \, (y1 + y2 + y3) \right\}$$

Note that you can extract the elements in the ith "column" of a multidimensional list using *list*[[All, i]].

The standard set of packages distributed with *Mathematica* includes several for doing more sophisticated statistical analyses, as mentioned on page 109.

■ 3.8.2 Curve Fitting

There are many situations where one wants to find a formula that best fits a given set of data. One way to do this in *Mathematica* is to use Fit.

Fit[$\{f_1, f_2, \ldots\}$, $\{fun_1, fun_2, \ldots\}$, x]	find a linear combination of the *fun*$_i$ that best fits the values f_i

Basic linear fits.

Here is a table of the first 20 primes.

$In[1]:=$ **fp = Table[Prime[x], {x, 20}]**

$Out[1]=$ {2, 3, 5, 7, 11, 13, 17, 19, 23, 29,
           31, 37, 41, 43, 47, 53, 59, 61, 67, 71}

Here is a plot of this "data".

$In[2]:=$ **gp = ListPlot[fp]**

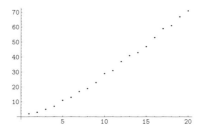

This gives a linear fit to the list of primes. The result is the best linear combination of the functions 1 and x.

$In[3]:=$ **Fit[fp, {1, x}, x]**

$Out[3]=$ $-7.67368 + 3.77368\, x$

Here is a plot of the fit.   *In[4]:=* **Plot[%, {x, 0, 20}]**

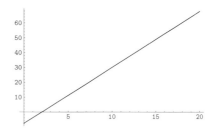

Here is the fit superimposed on the   *In[5]:=* **Show[%, gp]**
original data.

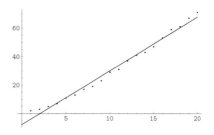

This gives a quadratic fit to the data.   *In[6]:=* **Fit[fp, {1, x, x^2}, x]**

Out[6]= $-1.92368 + 2.2055\,x + 0.0746753\,x^2$

Here is a plot of the quadratic fit.   *In[7]:=* **Plot[%, {x, 0, 20}]**

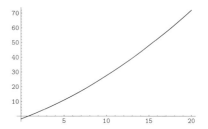

This shows the fit superimposed on the original data. The quadratic fit is better than the linear one.

$In[8]:=$ **Show[%, gp]**

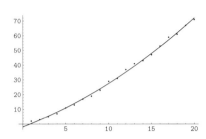

$\{f_1, f_2, \dots\}$	data points obtained when a single coordinate takes on values 1, 2, …
$\{\{x_1, f_1\}, \{x_2, f_2\}, \dots\}$	data points obtained when a single coordinate takes on values $x_1, x_2, \dots$
$\{\{x_1, y_1, \dots, f_1\}, \{x_2, y_2, \dots, f_2\}, \dots\}$	data points obtained with values $x_i, y_i, \dots$ of a sequence of coordinates

Ways of specifying data.

If you give data in the form $\{f_1, f_2, \dots\}$ then Fit will assume that the successive f_i correspond to values of a function at successive integer points 1, 2, … . But you can also give Fit data that corresponds to the values of a function at arbitrary points, in one or more dimensions.

Fit[$data$, $\{fun_1, fun_2, \dots\}$, $\{x, y, \dots\}$]	
	fit to a function of several variables

Multivariate fits.

This gives a table of the values of x, y and $1 + 5x - xy$. You need to use Flatten to get it in the right form for Fit.

$In[9]:=$ **Flatten[Table[{x, y, 1 + 5x - x y},**
{x, 0, 1, 0.4}, {y, 0, 1, 0.4}], 1]

$Out[9]=$ {{0, 0, 1}, {0, 0.4, 1}, {0, 0.8, 1},
{0.4, 0, 3.}, {0.4, 0.4, 2.84}, {0.4, 0.8, 2.68},
{0.8, 0, 5.}, {0.8, 0.4, 4.68}, {0.8, 0.8, 4.36}}

This produces a fit to a function of two variables.

$In[10]:=$ **Fit[% , {1, x, y, x y}, {x, y}]**

$Out[10]=$ $1. + 5. x + 4.53999 \times 10^{-15} y - 1. x y$

Fit takes a list of functions, and uses a definite and efficient procedure to find what linear combination of these functions gives the best least-squares fit to your data. Sometimes, however, you may want to find a *nonlinear fit* that does not just consist of a linear combination of specified functions. You can do this using FindFit, which takes a function of any form, and then searches for values of parameters that yield the best fit to your data.

+ FindFit[*data*, *form*, {*par*$_1$, *par*$_2$, ... }, *x*]

search for values of the *par*$_i$ that make *form* best fit *data*

+ FindFit[*data*, *form*, *pars*, {*x*, *y*, ... }]

fit multivariate data

Searching for general fits to data.

This fits the list of primes to a simple linear combination of terms.	*In[11]:=* **FindFit[fp, a + b x + c Exp[x], {a, b, c}, x]**
	Out[11]= $\{$a $\to$ -6.78932, b $\to$ 3.64309, c $\to$ 1.26883 $\times 10^{-8}\}$
The result is the same as from Fit.	*In[12]:=* **Fit[fp, {1, x, Exp[x]}, x]**
	Out[12]= $-6.78932 + 1.26883 \times 10^{-8}\, e^x + 3.64309\, x$
This fits to a nonlinear form, which cannot be handled by Fit.	*In[13]:=* **FindFit[fp, a x Log[b + c x], {a, b, c}, x]**
	Out[13]= $\{$a $\to$ 1.42076, b $\to$ 1.65558, c $\to$ 0.534645$\}$

By default, both Fit and FindFit produce *least-squares* fits, which are defined to minimize the quantity $\chi^2 = \sum_i |r_i|^2$, where the r_i are residuals giving the difference between each original data point and its fitted value. One can, however, also consider fits based on other norms. If you set the option NormFunction -> u, then FindFit will attempt to find the fit that minimizes the quantity $u[r]$, where r is the list of residuals. The default is NormFunction -> Norm, corresponding to a least-squares fit.

This uses the ∞-norm, which minimizes the maximum distance between the fit and the data. The result is slightly different from least-squares.	*In[14]:=* **FindFit[fp, a x Log[b + c x], {a, b, c}, x,** **NormFunction -> (Norm[#, Infinity] &)]**
	Out[14]= $\{$a $\to$ 1.15077, b $\to$ 1.0023, c $\to$ 1.04686$\}$

FindFit works by searching for values of parameters that yield the best fit. Sometimes you may have to tell it where to start in doing this search. You can do this by giving parameters in the form {{a, a_0}, {b, b_0}, ... }. FindFit also has various options that you can set to control how it does its search.

option name	default value	
+ NormFunction	Norm	the norm to use
AccuracyGoal	Automatic	number of digits of accuracy to try to get
PrecisionGoal	Automatic	number of digits of precision to try to get
WorkingPrecision	MachinePrecision	precision to use in internal computations
MaxIterations	100	maximum number of iterations to use
+ StepMonitor	None	expression to evaluate whenever a step is taken
+ EvaluationMonitor	None	expression to evaluate whenever *form* is evaluated
Method	Automatic	method to use

Options for `FindFit`.

■ 3.8.3 Approximate Functions and Interpolation

In many kinds of numerical computations, it is convenient to introduce *approximate functions*. Approximate functions can be thought of as generalizations of ordinary approximate real numbers. While an approximate real number gives the value to a certain precision of a single numerical quantity, an approximate function gives the value to a certain precision of a quantity which depends on one or more parameters. *Mathematica* uses approximate functions, for example, to represent numerical solutions to differential equations obtained with `NDSolve`, as discussed in Section 1.6.4.

Approximate functions in *Mathematica* are represented by `InterpolatingFunction` objects. These objects work like the pure functions discussed in Section 2.2.5. The basic idea is that when given a particular argument, an `InterpolatingFunction` object finds the approximate function value that corresponds to that argument.

The `InterpolatingFunction` object contains a representation of the approximate function based on interpolation. Typically it contains values and possibly derivatives at a sequence of points. It effectively assumes that the function varies smoothly between these points. As a result, when you ask for the value of the function with a particular argument, the `InterpolatingFunction` object can interpolate to find an approximation to the value you want.

Interpolation[{f_1, f_2, ... }]	construct an approximate function with values f_i at successive integers
Interpolation[{{x_1, f_1}, {x_2, f_2}, ... }]	construct an approximate function with values f_i at points x_i

Constructing approximate functions.

Here is a table of the values of the sine function.

```
In[1]:= Table[{x, Sin[x]}, {x, 0, 2, 0.25}]

Out[1]= {{0, 0}, {0.25, 0.247404}, {0.5, 0.479426},
         {0.75, 0.681639}, {1., 0.841471}, {1.25, 0.948985},
         {1.5, 0.997495}, {1.75, 0.983986}, {2., 0.909297}}
```

This constructs an approximate function which represents these values.

```
In[2]:= sin = Interpolation[%]

Out[2]= InterpolatingFunction[{{0., 2.}}, <>]
```

The approximate function reproduces each of the values in the original table.

```
In[3]:= sin[0.25]

Out[3]= 0.247404
```

It also allows you to get approximate values at other points.

```
In[4]:= sin[0.3]

Out[4]= 0.2955
```

In this case the interpolation is a fairly good approximation to the true sine function.

```
In[5]:= Sin[0.3]

Out[5]= 0.29552
```

You can work with approximate functions much as you would with any other *Mathematica* functions. You can plot approximate functions, or perform numerical operations such as integration or root finding.

If you give a non-numerical argument, the approximate function is left in symbolic form.

```
In[6]:= sin[x]

Out[6]= InterpolatingFunction[{{0., 2.}}, <>][x]
```

Here is a numerical integral of the approximate function.

```
In[7]:= NIntegrate[sin[x]^2, {x, 0, Pi/2}]

Out[7]= 0.78531
```

Here is the same numerical integral for the true sine function.

```
In[8]:= NIntegrate[Sin[x]^2, {x, 0, Pi/2}]

Out[8]= 0.785398
```

A plot of the approximate function is essentially indistinguishable from the true sine function.

In[9]:= **Plot[sin[x], {x, 0, 2}]**

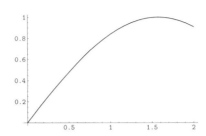

If you differentiate an approximate function, *Mathematica* will return another approximate function that represents the derivative.

This finds the derivative of the approximate sine function, and evaluates it at $\pi/6$.

In[10]:= **sin'[Pi/6]**

Out[10]= 0.865372

The result is close to the exact one.

In[11]:= **N[Cos[Pi/6]]**

Out[11]= 0.866025

InterpolatingFunction objects contain all the information *Mathematica* needs about approximate functions. In standard *Mathematica* output format, however, only the part that gives the domain of the InterpolatingFunction object is printed explicitly. The lists of actual parameters used in the InterpolatingFunction object are shown only in iconic form.

In standard output format, the only part of an InterpolatingFunction object printed explicitly is its domain.

In[12]:= **sin**

Out[12]= InterpolatingFunction[{{0., 2.}}, <>]

If you ask for a value outside of the domain, *Mathematica* prints a warning, then uses extrapolation to find a result.

In[13]:= **sin[3]**

InterpolatingFunction::dmval:
    Input value {3} lies outside the range of data in the
        interpolating function. Extrapolation will be used.

Out[13]= 0.0155471

The more information you give about the function you are trying to approximate, the better the approximation *Mathematica* constructs can be. You can, for example, specify not only values of the function at a sequence of points, but also derivatives.

Interpolation[{{x_1, {f_1, df_1, ddf_1, ... }}, ... }]
                                       construct an approximate function with specified derivatives
                                       at points x_i

Constructing approximate functions with specified derivatives.

Interpolation works by fitting polynomial curves between the points you specify. You can use the option InterpolationOrder to specify the degree of these polynomial curves. The default setting is InterpolationOrder -> 3, yielding cubic curves.

This makes a table of values of the cosine function.	*In[14]:=* **tab = Table[{x, Cos[x]}, {x, 0, 6}]** ;
This creates an approximate function using linear interpolation between the values in the table.	*In[15]:=* **Interpolation[tab, InterpolationOrder -> 1]** *Out[15]=* InterpolatingFunction[{{0, 6}}, <>]
The approximate function consists of a collection of straight-line segments.	*In[16]:=* **Plot[%[x], {x, 0, 6}]**

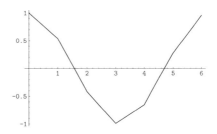

With the default setting InterpolationOrder -> 3, cubic curves are used, and the function looks smooth.

In[17]:= **Plot[Evaluate[Interpolation[tab]][x], {x, 0, 6}]**

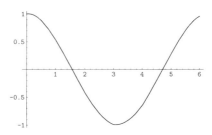

Increasing the setting for InterpolationOrder typically leads to smoother approximate functions. However, if you increase the setting too much, spurious wiggles may develop.

> ListInterpolation[{{f_{11}, f_{12}, ... }, {f_{21}, ... }, ... }]
> construct an approximate function from a two-dimensional grid of values at integer points
>
> ListInterpolation[*list*, {{*xmin*, *xmax*}, {*ymin*, *ymax*}}]
> assume the values are from an evenly spaced grid with the specified domain
>
> ListInterpolation[*list*, {{x_1, x_2, ... }, {y_1, y_2, ... }}]
> assume the values are from a grid with the specified grid lines

Interpolating multidimensional arrays of data.

This interpolates an array of values from integer grid points.

```
In[18]:= ListInterpolation[
              Table[1.5/(x^2 + y^3), {x, 10}, {y, 15}]]

Out[18]= InterpolatingFunction[{{1., 10.}, {1., 15.}}, <>]
```

Here is the value at a particular position.

```
In[19]:= %[6.5, 7.2]

Out[19]= 0.00360759
```

Here is another array of values.

```
In[20]:= tab = Table[1.5/(x^2 + y^3),
                {x, 5.5, 7.2, .2}, {y, 2.3, 8.9, .1}] ;
```

To interpolate this array you explicitly have to tell *Mathematica* the domain it covers.

```
In[21]:= ListInterpolation[tab, {{5.5, 7.2}, {2.3, 8.9}}]

Out[21]= InterpolatingFunction[{{5.5, 7.2}, {2.3, 8.9}}, <>]
```

ListInterpolation works for arrays of any dimension, and in each case it produces an InterpolatingFunction object which takes the appropriate number of arguments.

This interpolates a three-dimensional array.

```
In[22]:= ListInterpolation[
              Array[#1^2 + #2^2 - #3^2 &, {10, 10, 10}]] ;
```

The resulting InterpolatingFunction object takes three arguments.

```
In[23]:= %[3.4, 7.8, 2.6]

Out[23]= 65.64
```

Mathematica can handle not only purely numerical approximate functions, but also ones which involve symbolic parameters.

This generates an InterpolatingFunction that depends on the parameters a and b.

```
In[24]:= sfun = ListInterpolation[{1 + a, 2, 3, 4 + b, 5}]

Out[24]= InterpolatingFunction[{{1, 5}}, <>]
```

This shows how the interpolated value at 2.2 depends on the parameters.

```
In[25]:= sfun[2.2] // Simplify

Out[25]= 2.2 - 0.048 a - 0.032 b
```

With the default setting for InterpolationOrder used, the value at this point no longer depends on a.

```
In[26]:= sfun[3.8] // Simplify

Out[26]= 3.8 + 0.864 b
```

In working with approximate functions, you can quite often end up with complicated combinations of `InterpolatingFunction` objects. You can always tell *Mathematica* to produce a single `InterpolatingFunction` object valid over a particular domain by using `FunctionInterpolation`.

This generates a new `InterpolatingFunction` object valid in the domain 0 to 1.	`In[27]:= FunctionInterpolation[x + sin[x^2], {x, 0, 1}]`
	
	`Out[27]= InterpolatingFunction[{{0., 1.}}, <>]`

This generates a nested `InterpolatingFunction` object.	`In[28]:= ListInterpolation[{3, 4, 5, sin[a], 6}]`
	
	`Out[28]= InterpolatingFunction[{{1, 5}}, <>]`

This produces a pure two-dimensional `InterpolatingFunction` object.	`In[29]:= FunctionInterpolation[a^2 + %[x], {x, 1, 3}, {a, 0, 1.5}]`
	
	`Out[29]= InterpolatingFunction[{{1., 3.}, {0., 1.5}}, <>]`

`FunctionInterpolation[`*expr*`, {`*x*`, `*xmin*`, `*xmax*`}]`
  construct an approximate function by evaluating *expr* with *x* ranging from *xmin* to *xmax*

`FunctionInterpolation[`*expr*`, {`*x*`, `*xmin*`, `*xmax*`}, {`*y*`, `*ymin*`, `*ymax*`}, ... ]`
  construct a higher-dimensional approximate function

Constructing approximate functions by evaluating expressions.

■ 3.8.4 Fourier Transforms

A common operation in analyzing various kinds of data is to find the Fourier transform, or spectrum, of a list of values. The idea is typically to pick out components of the data with particular frequencies, or ranges of frequencies.

`Fourier[{`u_1`, `u_2`, ... , `u_n`}]`   Fourier transform

`InverseFourier[{`v_1`, `v_2`, ... , `v_n`}]`   inverse Fourier transform

Fourier transforms.

Here is some data, corresponding to a square pulse.	`In[1]:= {-1, -1, -1, -1, 1, 1, 1, 1}`
	
	`Out[1]= {-1, -1, -1, -1, 1, 1, 1, 1}`

Here is the Fourier transform of the data. It involves complex numbers.	`In[2]:= Fourier[%]`
	
	`Out[2]= {0. + 0. i, -0.707107 - 1.70711 i,`
	`0. + 0. i, -0.707107 - 0.292893 i,`
	`0. + 0. i, -0.707107 + 0.292893 i,`
	`0. + 0. i, -0.707107 + 1.70711 i}`

Here is the inverse Fourier transform.

```
In[3]:= InverseFourier[%]
Out[3]= {-1., -1., -1., -1., 1., 1., 1., 1.}
```

Fourier works whether or not your list of data has a length which is a power of two.

```
In[4]:= Fourier[{1, -1, 1}]
Out[4]= {0.57735 + 0. i, 0.57735 - 1. i, 0.57735 + 1. i}
```

This generates a length-200 list containing a periodic signal with random noise added.

```
In[5]:= data = Table[ N[Sin[30 2 Pi n/200] + (Random[ ] - 1/2)],
                {n, 200} ] ;
```

The data looks fairly random if you plot it directly.

```
In[6]:= ListPlot[ data, PlotJoined -> True ]
```

The Fourier transform, however, shows a strong peak at $30 + 1$, and a symmetric peak at $201 - 30$, reflecting the frequency component of the original signal near $30/200$.

```
In[7]:= ListPlot[ Abs[Fourier[data]], PlotJoined -> True,
                PlotRange -> All ]
```

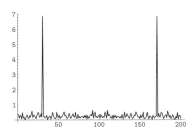

In *Mathematica*, the discrete Fourier transform v_s of a list u_r of length n is by default defined to be $\frac{1}{\sqrt{n}} \sum_{r=1}^{n} u_r e^{2\pi i (r-1)(s-1)/n}$. Notice that the zero frequency term appears at position 1 in the resulting list.

The inverse discrete Fourier transform u_r of a list v_s of length n is by default defined to be $\frac{1}{\sqrt{n}} \sum_{s=1}^{n} v_s e^{-2\pi i (r-1)(s-1)/n}$.

In different scientific and technical fields different conventions are often used for defining discrete Fourier transforms. The option FourierParameters in *Mathematica* allows you to choose any of these conventions you want.

common convention	setting	discrete Fourier transform	inverse discrete Fourier transform
Mathematica default	{0, 1}	$\frac{1}{n^{1/2}} \sum_{r=1}^{n} u_r e^{2\pi i(r-1)(s-1)/n}$	$\frac{1}{n^{1/2}} \sum_{s=1}^{n} v_s e^{-2\pi i(r-1)(s-1)/n}$
data analysis	{-1, 1}	$\frac{1}{n} \sum_{r=1}^{n} u_r e^{2\pi i(r-1)(s-1)/n}$	$\sum_{s=1}^{n} v_s e^{-2\pi i(r-1)(s-1)/n}$
signal processing	{1, -1}	$\sum_{r=1}^{n} u_r e^{-2\pi i(r-1)(s-1)/n}$	$\frac{1}{n} \sum_{s=1}^{n} v_s e^{2\pi i(r-1)(s-1)/n}$
general case	{a, b}	$\frac{1}{n^{(1-a)/2}} \sum_{r=1}^{n} u_r e^{2\pi ib(r-1)(s-1)/n}$	$\frac{1}{n^{(1+a)/2}} \sum_{s=1}^{n} v_s e^{-2\pi ib(r-1)(s-1)/n}$

Typical settings for `FourierParameters` with various conventions.

`Fourier[{{`u_{11}`, `u_{12}`, ... }, {`u_{21}`, `u_{22}`, ... }, ... }]`

two-dimensional Fourier transform

Two-dimensional Fourier transform.

Mathematica can find Fourier transforms for data in any number of dimensions. In n dimensions, the data is specified by a list nested n levels deep. Two-dimensional Fourier transforms are often used in image processing.

■ 3.8.5 Convolutions and Correlations

Convolution and correlation are central to many kinds of operations on lists of data. They are used in such areas as signal and image processing, statistical data analysis, approximations to partial differential equations, as well as operations on digit sequences and power series.

In both convolution and correlation the basic idea is to combine a kernel list with successive sublists of a list of data. The *convolution* of a kernel K_r with a list u_s has the general form $\sum_r K_r u_{s-r}$, while the *correlation* has the general form $\sum_r K_r u_{s+r}$.

`ListConvolve[`*kernel*`, `*list*`]` form the convolution of *kernel* with *list*

`ListCorrelate[`*kernel*`, `*list*`]` form the correlation of *kernel* with *list*

Convolution and correlation of lists.

This forms the convolution of the kernel {x, y} with a list of data.

In[1]:= `ListConvolve[{x,y}, {a,b,c,d,e}]`

Out[1]= {b x + a y, c x + b y, d x + c y, e x + d y}

This forms the correlation.

In[2]:= `ListCorrelate[{x,y}, {a,b,c,d,e}]`

Out[2]= {a x + b y, b x + c y, c x + d y, d x + e y}

In this case reversing the kernel gives exactly the same result as ListConvolve.

In[3]:= **ListCorrelate[{y, x}, {a,b,c,d,e}]**

Out[3]= {b x + a y, c x + b y, d x + c y, e x + d y}

This forms successive differences of the data.

In[4]:= **ListCorrelate[{-1,1}, {a,b,c,d,e}]**

Out[4]= {-a + b, -b + c, -c + d, -d + e}

In forming sublists to combine with a kernel, there is always an issue of what to do at the ends of the list of data. By default, ListConvolve and ListCorrelate never form sublists which would "overhang" the ends of the list of data. This means that the output you get is normally shorter than the original list of data.

With an input list of length 6, the output is in this case of length 4.

In[5]:= **ListCorrelate[{1,1,1}, Range[6]]**

Out[5]= {6, 9, 12, 15}

In practice one often wants to get output that is as long as the original list of data. To do this requires including sublists that overhang one or both ends of the list of data. The additional elements needed to form these sublists must be filled in with some kind of "padding". By default, *Mathematica* takes copies of the original list to provide the padding, thus effectively treating the list as being cyclic.

ListCorrelate[*kernel*, *list*]	do not allow overhangs on either side (result shorter than *list*)
ListCorrelate[*kernel*, *list*, 1]	allow an overhang on the right (result same length as *list*)
ListCorrelate[*kernel*, *list*, -1]	allow an overhang on the left (result same length as *list*)
ListCorrelate[*kernel*, *list*, {-1, 1}]	allow overhangs on both sides (result longer than *list*)
ListCorrelate[*kernel*, *list*, {k_L, k_R}]	allow particular overhangs on left and right

Controlling how the ends of the list of data are treated.

The default involves no overhangs.

In[6]:= **ListCorrelate[{x, y}, {a, b, c, d}]**

Out[6]= {a x + b y, b x + c y, c x + d y}

The last term in the last element now comes from the beginning of the list.

In[7]:= **ListCorrelate[{x, y}, {a, b, c, d}, 1]**

Out[7]= {a x + b y, b x + c y, c x + d y, d x + a y}

Now the first term of the first element and the last term of the last element both involve wraparound.

In[8]:= **ListCorrelate[{x, y}, {a, b, c, d}, {-1, 1}]**

Out[8]= {d x + a y, a x + b y, b x + c y, c x + d y, d x + a y}

In the general case ListCorrelate[*kernel*, *list*, {k_L, k_R}] is set up so that in the first element of the result, the first element of *list* appears multiplied by the element at position k_L in *kernel*, and in the last element of the result, the last element of *list* appears multiplied by the element at position

k_R in *kernel*. The default case in which no overhang is allowed on either side thus corresponds to
ListCorrelate[*kernel*, *list*, {1, -1}].

With a kernel of length 3, alignments
{-1, 2} always make the first and last
elements of the result the same.

In[9]:= **ListCorrelate[{x, y, z}, {a, b, c, d}, {-1, 2}]**

Out[9]= {c x + d y + a z, d x + a y + b z,
        a x + b y + c z, b x + c y + d z, c x + d y + a z}

For many kinds of data, it is convenient to assume not that the data is cyclic, but rather that it is
padded at either end by some fixed element, often 0, or by some sequence of elements.

ListCorrelate[*kernel*, *list*, *klist*, *p*]   pad with element *p*

ListCorrelate[*kernel*, *list*, *klist*, {p_1, p_2, ... }]
                          pad with cyclic repetitions of the p_i

ListCorrelate[*kernel*, *list*, *klist*, *list*]   pad with cyclic repetitions of the original data

ListCorrelate[*kernel*, *list*, *klist*, {}]   include no padding

---

Controlling the padding for a list of data.

This pads with element p.

In[10]:= **ListCorrelate[{x, y}, {a, b, c, d}, {-1, 1}, p]**

Out[10]= {p x + a y, a x + b y, b x + c y, c x + d y, d x + p y}

A common case is to pad with zero.

In[11]:= **ListCorrelate[{x, y}, {a, b, c, d}, {-1, 1}, 0]**

Out[11]= {a y, a x + b y, b x + c y, c x + d y, d x}

In this case q appears at one end, and
p at the other.

In[12]:= **ListCorrelate[{x, y}, {a, b, c, d}, {-1, 1}, {p, q}]**

Out[12]= {q x + a y, a x + b y, b x + c y, c x + d y, d x + p y}

Different choices of kernel allow ListConvolve and ListCorrelate to be used for different kinds
of computations.

This finds a moving average of data.

In[13]:= **ListCorrelate[{1,1,1}/3, {a,b,c,d,e}, {-1,1}]**

Out[13]= $\{ \frac{a}{3} + \frac{d}{3} + \frac{e}{3}, \frac{a}{3} + \frac{b}{3} + \frac{e}{3}, \frac{a}{3} + \frac{b}{3} + \frac{c}{3},$
$\frac{b}{3} + \frac{c}{3} + \frac{d}{3}, \frac{c}{3} + \frac{d}{3} + \frac{e}{3}, \frac{a}{3} + \frac{d}{3} + \frac{e}{3}, \frac{a}{3} + \frac{b}{3} + \frac{e}{3}\}$

Here is a Gaussian kernel.

In[14]:= **kern = Table[Exp[-n^2/100]/Sqrt[2. Pi], {n, -10, 10}] ;**

This generates some "data".

In[15]:= **data = Table[BesselJ[1, x] + 0.2 Random[ ], {x, 0, 10, .1}] ;**

Here is a plot of the data. $In[16]:=$ **ListPlot[data];**

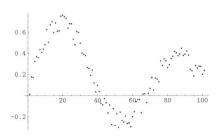

This convolves the kernel with the $In[17]:=$ **ListConvolve[kern, data, {-1, 1}] ;**
data.

The result is a smoothed version of the $In[18]:=$ **ListPlot[%]**
data.

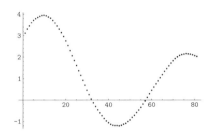

You can use **ListConvolve** and **ListCorrelate** to handle symbolic as well as numerical data.

This forms the convolution of two $In[19]:=$ **ListConvolve[{a,b,c}, {u,v,w}, {1, -1}, 0]**
symbolic lists.
                                              $Out[19]=$ {a u, b u + a v, c u + b v + a w, c v + b w, c w}

The result corresponds exactly with the $In[20]:=$ **Expand[(a + b x + c x^2)(u + v x + w x^2)]**
coefficients in the expanded form of
this product of polynomials. $Out[20]=$ a u + b u x + a v x + c u x^2 +
                                                        b v x^2 + a w x^2 + c v x^3 + b w x^3 + c w x^4

ListConvolve and **ListCorrelate** work on data in any number of dimensions.

This imports image data from a file. $In[21]:=$ **g = ReadList["fish.data", Number, RecordLists->True];**

Here is the image.

In[22]:= **Show[Graphics[Raster[g], AspectRatio->Automatic]]**

This convolves the data with a
two-dimensional kernel.

In[23]:= **ListConvolve[{{1,1,1},{1,-8,1},{1,1,1}}, g] ;**

This shows the image corresponding to
the data.

In[24]:= **Show[Graphics[Raster[%], AspectRatio->Automatic]]**

RotateLeft[*list*, {d_1, d_2, ... }], RotateRight[*list*, {d_1, d_2, ... }]
    rotate elements cyclically by d_i positions at level *i*

PadLeft[*list*, {n_1, n_2, ... }], PadRight[*list*, {n_1, n_2, ... }]
    pad with zeros to create an $n_1 \times n_2 \times ...$ array

Take[*list*, m_1, m_2, ...], Drop[*list*, m_1, m_2, ...]
    take or drop m_i elements at level *i*

Other functions for manipulating multidimensional data.

3.8.6 Cellular Automata

Cellular automata provide a convenient way to represent many kinds of systems in which the values of cells in an array are updated in discrete steps according to a local rule.

CellularAutomaton[*rnum*, *init*, *t*]	evolve rule *rnum* from *init* for *t* steps

Generating a cellular automaton evolution.

This starts with the list given, then evolves rule 30 for four steps.

```
In[1]:= CellularAutomaton[30, {0, 0, 0, 1, 0, 0, 0}, 4]
Out[1]= {{0, 0, 0, 1, 0, 0, 0},
         {0, 0, 1, 1, 1, 0, 0}, {0, 1, 1, 0, 0, 1, 0},
         {1, 1, 0, 1, 1, 1, 1}, {0, 0, 0, 1, 0, 0, 0}}
```

This defines a simple function for displaying cellular automaton evolution.

```
In[2]:= CAPlot[data_] := ListDensityPlot[Reverse[Max[data] - data],
            AspectRatio->Automatic, Mesh->False, FrameTicks->None]
```

This shows 100 steps of rule 30 evolution from random initial conditions.

```
In[3]:= CAPlot[CellularAutomaton[30, Table[Random[Integer], {250}],
            100]]
```

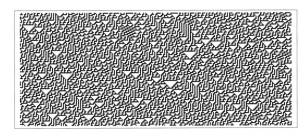

{a_1, a_2, ... }	explicit list of values a_i
{{a_1, a_2, ... }, b}	values a_i superimposed on a b background
{{a_1, a_2, ... }, *blist*}	values a_i superimposed on a background of repetitions of *blist*
{{{a_{11}, a_{12}, ... }, {d_1}}, ... }, *blist*	values a_{ij} at offsets d_i

Ways of specifying initial conditions for one-dimensional cellular automata.

If you give an explicit list of initial values, CellularAutomaton will take the elements in this list to correspond to all the cells in the system, arranged cyclically.

The right neighbor of the cell at the end is the cell at the beginning.

In[4]:= `CellularAutomaton[30, {1, 0, 0, 0, 0}, 1]`

Out[4]= `{{1, 0, 0, 0, 0}, {1, 1, 0, 0, 1}}`

It is often convenient to set up initial conditions in which there is a small "seed" region, superimposed on a constant "background". By default, `CellularAutomaton` automatically fills in enough background to cover the size of the pattern that can be produced in the number of steps of evolution you specify.

This shows rule 30 evolving from an initial condition containing a single black cell.

In[5]:= `CAPlot[CellularAutomaton[30, {{1}, 0}, 100]]`

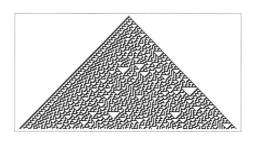

This shows rule 30 evolving from an initial condition consisting of a {1,1} seed on a background of repeated {1,0,1,1} blocks.

In[6]:= `CAPlot[CellularAutomaton[30, {{1, 1}, {1, 0, 1, 1}}, 100]]`

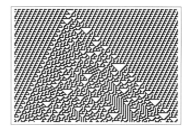

Particularly in studying interactions between structures, you may sometimes want to specify initial conditions for cellular automata in which certain blocks are placed at particular offsets.

This sets up an initial condition with black cells at offsets ±40.

In[7]:= `CAPlot[CellularAutomaton[30,`
`{{{ {1}, {-40} }, {{1}, {40}}}, 0}, 100]]`

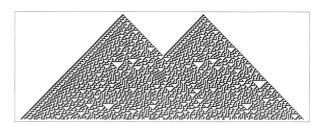

n	$k = 2$, $r = 1$, elementary rule
$\{n, k\}$	general nearest-neighbor rule with k colors
$\{n, k, r\}$	general rule with k colors and range r
$\{n, \{k, 1\}\}$	k-color nearest-neighbor totalistic rule
$\{n, \{k, 1\}, r\}$	k-color range r totalistic rule
$\{n, \{k, \{wt_1, wt_2, \ldots ,\}\}, r\}$	rule in which neighbor i is assigned weight wt_i
$\{n, kspec, \{\{off_1\}, \{off_2\}, \ldots , \{off_s\}\}\}$	rule with neighbors at specified offsets
$\{fun, \{\}, rspec\}$	rule obtained by applying function fun to each neighbor list

Specifying rules for one-dimensional cellular automata.

In the simplest cases, a cellular automaton allows k possible values or "colors" for each cell, and has rules that involve up to r neighbors on each side. The digits of the "rule number" n then specify what the color of a new cell should be for each possible configuration of the neighborhood.

This evolves a single neighborhood for 1 step.

```
In[8]:= CellularAutomaton[30, {1,1,0}, 1]
Out[8]= {{1, 1, 0}, {1, 0, 0}}
```

Here are the 8 possible neighborhoods for a $k = 2$, $r = 1$ cellular automaton.

```
In[9]:= Table[IntegerDigits[i,2,3],{i,7,0,-1}]
Out[9]= {{1, 1, 1}, {1, 1, 0}, {1, 0, 1}, {1, 0, 0},
         {0, 1, 1}, {0, 1, 0}, {0, 0, 1}, {0, 0, 0}}
```

This shows the new color of the center cell for each of the 8 neighborhoods.

```
In[10]:= Map[CellularAutomaton[30, #, 1][[2,2]]&, %]
Out[10]= {0, 0, 0, 1, 1, 1, 1, 0}
```

For rule 30, this sequence corresponds to the base-2 digits of the number 30.

```
In[11]:= FromDigits[%, 2]
Out[11]= 30
```

This runs the general $k = 3$, $r = 1$ rule with rule number 921408.

```
In[12]:= CAPlot[CellularAutomaton[{921408, 3, 1}, {{1}, 0}, 100]]
```

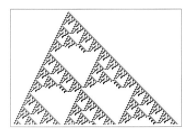

For a general cellular automaton rule, each digit of the rule number specifies what color a different possible neighborhood of $2r + 1$ cells should yield. To find out which digit corresponds to which neighborhood, one effectively treats the cells in a neighborhood as digits in a number. For an $r = 1$ cellular automaton, the number is obtained from the list of elements *neig* in the neighborhood by *neig* . {k^2, k, 1}.

It is sometimes convenient to consider *totalistic* cellular automata, in which the new value of a cell depends only on the total of the values in its neighborhood. One can specify totalistic cellular automata by rule numbers or "codes" in which each digit refers to neighborhoods with a given total value, obtained for example from *neig* . {1, 1, 1}.

In general, `CellularAutomaton` allows one to specify rules using any sequence of weights. Another choice sometimes convenient is {k, 1, k}, which yields outer totalistic rules.

This runs the $k = 3$, $r = 1$ totalistic rule   *In[13]:=* **CAPlot[CellularAutomaton[{867, {3, 1}, 1}, {{1}, 0}, 100]]**
with code number 867.

Rules with range r involve all cells with offsets $-r$ through $+r$. Sometimes it is convenient to think about rules that involve only cells with specific offsets. You can do this by replacing a single r with a list of offsets.

Any $k = 2$ cellular automaton rule can be thought of as corresponding to a Boolean function. In the simplest case, basic Boolean functions like `And` or `Nor` take two arguments. These are conveniently specified in a cellular automaton rule as being at offsets {{0}, {1}}. Note that for compatibility with handling higher-dimensional cellular automata, offsets must always be given in lists, even for one-dimensional cellular automata.

This generates the truth table for   *In[14]:=* **Map[CellularAutomaton[{7, 2, {{0}, {1}}}, #, 1][[2, 2]] &,**
2-cell-neighborhood rule number 7,   **{{1, 1}, {1, 0}, {0, 1}, {0, 0}}]**
which turns out to be the Boolean
function Nand.   *Out[14]=* {0, 1, 1, 1}

Rule numbers provide a highly compact way to specify cellular automaton rules. But sometimes it is more convenient to specify rules by giving an explicit function that should be applied to each possible neighborhood.

This runs an additive cellular automaton whose rule adds all values in each neighborhood modulo 4.

In[15]:= **CAPlot[CellularAutomaton[**
{Mod[Apply[Plus, #], 4]&, {}, 1}, {{1}, 0}, 100]]

The function is given a second argument, equal to the step number.

In[16]:= **CAPlot[CellularAutomaton[**
{Mod[Apply[Plus, #] + #2, 4]&, {}, 1}, {{1}, 0}, 100]]

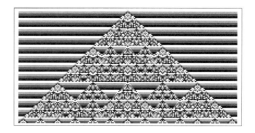

When you specify rules by functions, the values of cells need not be integers.

In[17]:= **CAPlot[CellularAutomaton[**
{Mod[1/2 Apply[Plus, #], 1] &, {}, 1}, {{1}, 0}, 100]]

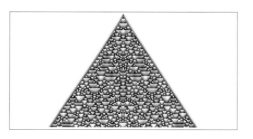

They can even be symbolic.

In[18]:= **Simplify[CellularAutomaton[{Mod[Apply[Plus, #], 2] &,**
{}, 1}, {{a}, 0}, 2], a ∈ Integers]

Out[18]= {{0, 0, a, 0, 0},
      {0, Mod[a, 2], Mod[a, 2], Mod[a, 2], 0},
      {Mod[Mod[a, 2], 2], 0,
       Mod[3 Mod[a, 2], 2], 0, Mod[Mod[a, 2], 2]}}

+	CellularAutomaton[*rnum*, *init*, *t*]	evolve for *t* steps, keeping all steps
+	CellularAutomaton[*rnum*, *init*, *t*, -1]	evolve for *t* steps, keeping only the last step
+	CellularAutomaton[*rnum*, *init*, *t*, {*spec*$_t$}]	keep only steps specified by *spec*$_t$

Selecting which steps to keep.

This runs rule 30 for 5 steps, keeping only the last step.

In[19]:= **CellularAutomaton[30, {{1}, 0}, 5, -1]**

Out[19]= {{1, 1, 0, 1, 1, 1, 1, 0, 1, 1, 1}}

This keeps the last 2 steps.

In[20]:= **CellularAutomaton[30, {{1}, 0}, 5, -2]**

Out[20]= {{0, 1, 1, 0, 0, 1, 0, 0, 0, 1, 0},
{1, 1, 0, 1, 1, 1, 1, 0, 1, 1, 1}}

The step specification *spec*$_t$ works very much like taking elements from a list with Take. One difference, though, is that the initial condition for the cellular automaton is considered to be step 0. Note that any step specification of the form { ... } must be enclosed in an additional list.

All	all steps 0 through *t* (default)
u	steps 0 through *u*
-*u*	the last *u* steps
{*u*}	step *u*
{*u*$_1$, *u*$_2$}	steps *u*$_1$ through *u*$_2$
{*u*$_1$, *u*$_2$, *d*}	steps *u*$_1$, *u*$_1$ + *d*, ...

Cellular automaton step specifications.

This evolves for 100 steps, but keeps only every other step.

In[21]:= **CAPlot[CellularAutomaton[30, {{1}, 0}, 100, {{1, -1, 2}}]]**

+	CellularAutomaton[*rnum*, *init*, *t*]	keep all steps, and all relevant cells
+	CellularAutomaton[*rnum*, *init*, *t*, {*spec_t*, *spec_x*}]	keep only specified steps and cells

Selecting steps and cells to keep.

Much as you can specify which steps to keep in a cellular automaton evolution, so also you can specify which cells to keep. If you give an initial condition such as {a_1, a_2, ... }, *blist*, then a_i is taken to have offset 0 for the purpose of specifying which cells to keep.

All	all cells that can be affected by the specified initial condition
Automatic	all cells in the region that differs from the background (default)
0	cell aligned with beginning of *aspec*
x	cells at offsets up to x on the right
$-x$	cells at offsets up to x on the left
{x}	cell at offset x to the right
{$-x$}	cell at offset x to the left
{x_1, x_2}	cells at offsets x_1 through x_2
{x_1, x_2, dx}	cells x_1, $x_1 + dx$, ...

Cellular automaton cell specifications.

This keeps all steps, but drops cells at offsets more than 20 on the left.

```
In[22]:= CAPlot[CellularAutomaton[30, {{1}, 0}, 100,
                    {All, {-20, 100}}]]
```

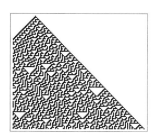

This keeps just the center column of cells.

```
In[23]:= CellularAutomaton[30, {{1}, 0}, 20, {All, {0}}]

Out[23]= {{1}, {1}, {0}, {1}, {1}, {1},
          {0}, {0}, {1}, {1}, {0}, {0}, {0},
          {1}, {0}, {1}, {1}, {0}, {0}, {1}, {0}}
```

If you give an initial condition such as $\{\{a_1, a_2, \dots\}, blist\}$, then `CellularAutomaton` will always effectively do the cellular automaton as if there were an infinite number of cells. By using a $spec_x$ such as $\{x_1, x_2\}$ you can tell `CellularAutomaton` to include only cells at specific offsets x_1 through x_2 in its output. `CellularAutomaton` by default includes cells out just far enough that their values never simply stay the same as in the background *blist*.

In general, given a cellular automaton rule with range r, cells out to distance $r\,t$ on each side could in principle be affected in the evolution of the system. With $spec_x$ being `All`, all these cells are included; with the default setting of `Automatic`, cells whose values effectively stay the same as in *blist* are trimmed off.

By default, only the parts that are not constant black are kept.

```
In[24]:= CAPlot[CellularAutomaton[225, {{1}, 0}, 100]]
```

Using `All` for $spec_x$ includes all cells that could be affected by a cellular automaton with this range.

```
In[25]:= CAPlot[CellularAutomaton[225, {{1}, 0}, 100, {All, All}]]
```

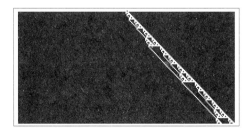

`CellularAutomaton` generalizes quite directly to any number of dimensions.

$\{n, k, \{r_1, r_2, \ldots, r_d\}\}$	d-dimensional rule with $(2r_1 + 1) \times (2r_2 + 1) \times \ldots \times (2r_d + 1)$ neighborhood
$\{n, \{k, 1\}, \{1, 1\}\}$	two-dimensional 9-neighbor totalistic rule
$\{n, \{k, \{\{0, 1, 0\}, \{1, 1, 1\}, \{0, 1, 0\}\}\}, \{1, 1\}\}$	
	two-dimensional 5-neighbor totalistic rule
$\{n, \{k, \{\{0, k, 0\}, \{k, 1, k\}, \{0, k, 0\}\}\}, \{1, 1\}\}$	
	two-dimensional 5-neighbor outer totalistic rule
$\{n + k\text{\textasciicircum}5\ (k - 1), \{k, \{\{0, 1, 0\}, \{1, 4\ k + 1, 1\}, \{0, 1, 0\}\}\}, \{1, 1\}\}$	
	two-dimensional 5-neighbor growth rule

Higher-dimensional rule specifications.

This is the rule specification for the two-dimensional 9-neighbor totalistic cellular automaton with code 797.

```
In[26]:= code797 = {797, {2, 1}, {1, 1}};
```

This gives steps 0 and 1 in its evolution.

```
In[27]:= CellularAutomaton[code797, {{{1}}, 0}, 1]
Out[27]= {{{0, 0, 0}, {0, 1, 0}, {0, 0, 0}},
          {{0, 0, 0}, {0, 0, 0}, {0, 0, 0}}}
```

This shows step 70 in the evolution.

```
In[28]:= CAPlot[First[CellularAutomaton[code797, {{{1}}, 0},
                                         70, -1]]]
```

This shows all steps in a slice along the x axis.

```
In[29]:= CAPlot[Map[First,
                CellularAutomaton[code797, {{{1}}, 0}, 70,
                                  {All, {0}, All}]]]
```

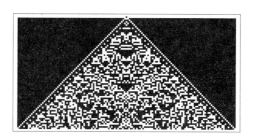

3.9 Numerical Operations on Functions

■ 3.9.1 Numerical Mathematics in *Mathematica*

One of the important features of *Mathematica* is its ability to give you exact, symbolic, results for computations. There are, however, computations where it is just mathematically impossible to get exact "closed form" results. In such cases, you can still often get approximate numerical results.

There is no "closed form" result for $\int_0^1 \sin(\sin(x)) \, dx$. *Mathematica* returns the integral in symbolic form.

```
In[1]:= Integrate[Sin[Sin[x]], {x, 0, 1}]
```

$$Out[1]= \int_0^1 \text{Sin}[\text{Sin}[x]] \, dx$$

You can now take the symbolic form of the integral, and ask for its approximate numerical value.

```
In[2]:= N[%]
```

```
Out[2]= 0.430606
```

When *Mathematica* cannot find an explicit result for something like a definite integral, it returns a symbolic form. You can take this symbolic form, and try to get an approximate numerical value by applying N.

By giving a second argument to N, you can specify the numerical precision to use.

```
In[3]:= N[ Integrate[Sin[Sin[x]], {x, 0, 1}], 40 ]
```

```
Out[3]= 0.4306061031206906049123773552484657864336
```

If you want to evaluate an integral numerically in *Mathematica*, then using Integrate and applying N to the result is not the most efficient way to do it. It is better instead to use the function NIntegrate, which immediately gives a numerical answer, without first trying to get an exact, symbolic, result. You should realize that even when Integrate does not in the end manage to give you an exact result, it may spend a lot of time trying to do so.

NIntegrate evaluates numerical integrals directly, without first trying to get a symbolic result.

```
In[4]:= NIntegrate[ Sin[Sin[x]], {x, 0, 1} ]
```

```
Out[4]= 0.430606
```

Integrate	NIntegrate	definite integrals
Sum	NSum	sums
Product	NProduct	products
Solve	NSolve	solutions of algebraic equations
DSolve	NDSolve	solutions of differential equations
Maximize	NMaximize	maximization

Symbolic and numerical versions of some *Mathematica* functions.

■ 3.9.2 The Uncertainties of Numerical Mathematics

Mathematica does operations like numerical integration very differently from the way it does their symbolic counterparts.

When you do a symbolic integral, *Mathematica* takes the functional form of the integrand you have given, and applies a sequence of exact symbolic transformation rules to it, to try and evaluate the integral.

When you do a numerical integral, however, *Mathematica* does not look directly at the functional form of the integrand you have given. Instead, it simply finds a sequence of numerical values of the integrand at particular points, then takes these values and tries to deduce from them a good approximation to the integral.

An important point to realize is that when *Mathematica* does a numerical integral, the *only* information it has about your integrand is a sequence of numerical values for it. To get a definite result for the integral, *Mathematica* then effectively has to make certain assumptions about the smoothness and other properties of your integrand. If you give a sufficiently pathological integrand, these assumptions may not be valid, and as a result, *Mathematica* may simply give you the wrong answer for the integral.

This problem may occur, for example, if you try to integrate numerically a function which has a very thin spike at a particular position. *Mathematica* samples your function at a number of points, and then assumes that the function varies smoothly between these points. As a result, if none of the sample points come close to the spike, then the spike will go undetected, and its contribution to the numerical integral will not be correctly included.

Here is a plot of the function $\exp(-x^2)$.   *In[1]:=* **Plot[Exp[-x^2], {x, -10, 10}, PlotRange->All]**

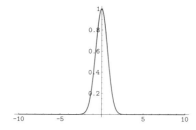

NIntegrate gives the correct answer for the numerical integral of this function from -10 to $+10$.

In[2]:= **NIntegrate[Exp[-x^2], {x, -10, 10}]**

Out[2]= 1.77245

If, however, you ask for the integral from -1000 to 1000, NIntegrate will miss the peak near $x = 0$, and give the wrong answer.

```
In[3]:= NIntegrate[Exp[-x^2], {x, -1000, 1000}]
```

NIntegrate::ploss:
    Numerical integration stopping due to loss of
    precision. Achieved neither the requested
    PrecisionGoal nor AccuracyGoal; suspect one of the
    following: highly oscillatory integrand or the true
    value of the integral is 0. If your integrand is
    oscillatory try using the option Method->Oscillatory
    in NIntegrate.

```
Out[3]= 1.34946 × 10^-26
```

Although NIntegrate follows the principle of looking only at the numerical values of your integrand, it nevertheless tries to make the best possible use of the information that it can get. Thus, for example, if NIntegrate notices that the estimated error in the integral in a particular region is large, it will take more samples in that region. In this way, NIntegrate tries to "adapt" its operation to the particular integrand you have given.

The kind of adaptive procedure that NIntegrate uses is similar, at least in spirit, to what Plot does in trying to draw smooth curves for functions. In both cases, *Mathematica* tries to go on taking more samples in a particular region until it has effectively found a smooth approximation to the function in that region.

The kinds of problems that can appear in numerical integration can also arise in doing other numerical operations on functions.

For example, if you ask for a numerical approximation to the sum of an infinite series, *Mathematica* samples a certain number of terms in the series, and then does an extrapolation to estimate the contributions of other terms. If you insert large terms far out in the series, they may not be detected when the extrapolation is done, and the result you get for the sum may be incorrect.

A similar problem arises when you try to find a numerical approximation to the minimum of a function. *Mathematica* samples only a finite number of values, then effectively assumes that the actual function interpolates smoothly between these values. If in fact the function has a sharp dip in a particular region, then *Mathematica* may miss this dip, and you may get the wrong answer for the minimum.

If you work only with numerical values of functions, there is simply no way to avoid the kinds of problems we have been discussing. Exact symbolic computation, of course, allows you to get around these problems.

In many calculations, it is therefore worthwhile to go as far as you can symbolically, and then resort to numerical methods only at the very end. This gives you the best chance of avoiding the problems that can arise in purely numerical computations.

■ 3.9.3 Numerical Integration

N[Integrate[*expr*, {*x*, *xmin*, *xmax*}]]	try to perform an integral exactly, then find numerical approximations to the parts that remain
NIntegrate[*expr*, {*x*, *xmin*, *xmax*}]	find a numerical approximation to an integral
NIntegrate[*expr*, {*x*, *xmin*, *xmax*}, {*y*, *ymin*, *ymax*}, ...]	multidimensional numerical integral $\int_{xmin}^{xmax} dx \int_{ymin}^{ymax} dy \dots expr$
NIntegrate[*expr*, {*x*, *xmin*, x_1, x_2, ... , *xmax*}]	do a numerical integral along a line, starting at *xmin*, going through the points x_i, and ending at *xmax*

Numerical integration functions.

This finds a numerical approximation to the integral $\int_0^\infty e^{-x^3}\, dx$.

```
In[1]:= NIntegrate[Exp[-x^3], {x, 0, Infinity}]
Out[1]= 0.89298
```

Here is the numerical value of the double integral $\int_{-1}^1 dx \int_{-1}^1 dy\,(x^2 + y^2)$.

```
In[2]:= NIntegrate[x^2 + y^2, {x, -1, 1}, {y, -1, 1}]
Out[2]= 2.66667
```

An important feature of NIntegrate is its ability to deal with functions that "blow up" at known points. NIntegrate automatically checks for such problems at the end points of the integration region.

The function $1/\sqrt{x}$ blows up at $x = 0$, but NIntegrate still succeeds in getting the correct value for the integral.

```
In[3]:= NIntegrate[1/Sqrt[x], {x, 0, 1}]
Out[3]= 2.
```

Mathematica can find the integral of $1/\sqrt{x}$ exactly.

```
In[4]:= Integrate[1/Sqrt[x], {x, 0, 1}]
Out[4]= 2
```

NIntegrate detects that the singularity in $1/x$ at $x = 0$ is not integrable.

```
In[5]:= NIntegrate[1/x, {x, 0, 1}]
```

NIntegrate::slwcon:
    Numerical integration converging too slowly; suspect
      one of the following: singularity, value of the
      integration being 0, oscillatory integrand, or
      insufficient WorkingPrecision. If your integrand is
      oscillatory try using the option Method->Oscillatory
      in NIntegrate.

NIntegrate::ncvb:
    NIntegrate failed to converge to prescribed accuracy
      after 7 recursive bisections in x near x =
                        -57
        4.36999 10   .

```
Out[5]= 23953.1
```

NIntegrate does not automatically look for singularities except at the end points of your integration region. When other singularities are present, NIntegrate may not give you the right answer for the integral. Nevertheless, in following its adaptive procedure, NIntegrate will often detect the presence of potentially singular behavior, and will warn you about it.

NIntegrate does not handle the singularity in $1/\sqrt{|x|}$ in the middle of the integration region. However, it warns you of a possible problem. In this case, the final result is numerically quite close to the correct answer.

```
In[6]:= NIntegrate[1/Sqrt[Abs[x]], {x, -1, 2}]

NIntegrate::slwcon:
   Numerical integration converging too slowly; suspect
    one of the following: singularity, value of the
    integration being 0, oscillatory integrand, or
    insufficient WorkingPrecision. If your integrand is
    oscillatory try using the option Method->Oscillatory
    in NIntegrate.

NIntegrate::ncvb:
   NIntegrate failed to converge to prescribed accuracy
    after 7 recursive bisections in x near x =
    -0.00390625.

Out[6]= 4.79343
```

If you know that your integrand has singularities at particular points, you can explicitly tell NIntegrate to deal with them. NIntegrate[*expr*, {x, *xmin*, x_1, x_2, ... , *xmax*}] integrates *expr* from *xmin* to *xmax*, looking for possible singularities at each of the intermediate points x_i.

This again gives the integral $\int_{-1}^{2} 1/\sqrt{|x|} \, dx$, but now explicitly deals with the singularity at $x = 0$.

```
In[7]:= NIntegrate[1/Sqrt[Abs[x]], {x, -1, 0, 2}]

Out[7]= 4.82843
```

You can also use the list of intermediate points x_i in NIntegrate to specify an integration contour to follow in the complex plane. The contour is taken to consist of a sequence of line segments, starting at *xmin*, going through each of the x_i, and ending at *xmax*.

This integrates $1/x$ around a closed contour in the complex plane, going from -1, through the points $-i$, 1 and i, then back to -1.

```
In[8]:= NIntegrate[1/x, {x, -1, -I, 1, I, -1}]

Out[8]= 1.11022 × 10^-16 + 6.28319 i
```

The integral gives $2\pi i$, as expected from Cauchy's Theorem.

```
In[9]:= N[ 2 Pi I ]

Out[9]= 0. + 6.28319 i
```

option name	default value	
MinRecursion	0	minimum number of recursive subdivisions of the integration region
MaxRecursion	6	maximum number of recursive subdivisions of the integration region
SingularityDepth	4	number of recursive subdivisions to use before doing a change of variables at the end points
MaxPoints	Automatic	maximum total number of times to sample the integrand

Special options for NIntegrate.

When NIntegrate tries to evaluate a numerical integral, it samples the integrand at a sequence of points. If it finds that the integrand changes rapidly in a particular region, then it recursively takes more sample points in that region. The parameters MinRecursion and MaxRecursion specify the minimum and maximum number of levels of recursive subdivision to use. Increasing the value of MinRecursion guarantees that NIntegrate will use a larger number of sample points. MaxRecursion limits the number of sample points which NIntegrate will ever try to use. Increasing MinRecursion or MaxRecursion will make NIntegrate work more slowly. SingularityDepth specifies how many levels of recursive subdivision NIntegrate should try before it concludes that the integrand is "blowing up" at one of the endpoints, and does a change of variables.

With the default settings for all options, NIntegrate misses the peak in $\exp(-x^2)$ near $x = 0$, and gives the wrong answer for the integral.

```
In[10]:= NIntegrate[Exp[-x^2], {x, -1000, 1000}]

NIntegrate::ploss:
   Numerical integration stopping due to loss of
     precision. Achieved neither the requested
     PrecisionGoal nor AccuracyGoal; suspect one of the
     following: highly oscillatory integrand or the true
     value of the integral is 0. If your integrand is
     oscillatory try using the option Method->Oscillatory
     in NIntegrate.

Out[10]= 1.34946 × 10^{-26}
```

With the option MinRecursion->3, NIntegrate samples enough points that it notices the peak around $x = 0$. With the default setting of MaxRecursion, however, NIntegrate cannot use enough sample points to be able to expect an accurate answer.

```
In[11]:= NIntegrate[Exp[-x^2], {x, -1000, 1000},
                                  MinRecursion->3]

NIntegrate::ncvb:
   NIntegrate failed to converge to prescribed accuracy
     after 7 recursive bisections in x near x = 7.8125.

Out[11]= 0.99187
```

With this setting of MaxRecursion, NIntegrate can get an accurate answer for the integral.

```
In[12]:= NIntegrate[Exp[-x^2], {x, -1000, 1000},
                        MinRecursion->3, MaxRecursion->10]
```

```
Out[12]= 1.77245
```

Another way to solve the problem is to make NIntegrate break the integration region into several pieces, with a small piece that explicitly covers the neighborhood of the peak.

```
In[13]:= NIntegrate[Exp[-x^2], {x, -1000, -10, 10, 1000}]
```

```
Out[13]= 1.77245
```

For integrals in many dimensions, it can take a long time for NIntegrate to get a precise answer. However, by setting the option MaxPoints, you can tell NIntegrate to give you just a rough estimate, sampling the integrand only a limited number of times.

This gives an estimate of the volume of the unit sphere in three dimensions.

```
In[14]:= NIntegrate[If[x^2 + y^2 + z^2 < 1, 1, 0], {x, -1, 1},
                        {y, -1, 1}, {z, -1, 1}, MaxPoints->10000]
```

```
Out[14]= 4.18106
```

Here is the precise result.

```
In[15]:= N[4/3 Pi]
```

```
Out[15]= 4.18879
```

■ 3.9.4 Numerical Evaluation of Sums and Products

NSum[f, {i, $imin$, $imax$}]	find a numerical approximation to the sum $\sum_{i=imin}^{imax} f$
NSum[f, {i, $imin$, $imax$, di}]	use step di in the sum
NProduct[f, {i, $imin$, $imax$}]	find a numerical approximation to the product $\prod_{i=imin}^{imax} f$

Numerical sums and products.

This gives a numerical approximation to $\sum_{i=1}^{\infty} \frac{1}{i^3 + i!}$.

```
In[1]:= NSum[1/(i^3 + i!), {i, 1, Infinity}]
```

```
Out[1]= 0.64703
```

There is no exact result for this sum, so *Mathematica* leaves it in a symbolic form.

```
In[2]:= Sum[1/(i^3 + i!), {i, 1, Infinity}]
```

$$Out[2]= \sum_{i=1}^{\infty} \frac{1}{i^3 + i!}$$

You can apply N explicitly to get a numerical result.	*In[3]:=* **N[%]**	
	Out[3]= 0.64703	

The way NSum works is to include a certain number of terms explicitly, and then to try and estimate the contribution of the remaining ones. There are two approaches to estimating this contribution. The first uses the Euler-Maclaurin method, and is based on approximating the sum by an integral. The second method, known as the Wynn epsilon method, samples a number of additional terms in the sum, and then tries to fit them to a polynomial multiplied by a decaying exponential.

option name	default value	
Method	Automatic	Integrate (Euler-Maclaurin method) or Fit (Wynn epsilon method)
NSumTerms	15	number of terms to include explicitly
NSumExtraTerms	12	number of terms to use for extrapolation in the Wynn epsilon method

Special options for NSum.

If you do not explicitly specify the method to use, NSum will try to choose between the methods it knows. In any case, some implicit assumptions about the functions you are summing have to be made. If these assumptions are not correct, you may get inaccurate answers.

The most common place to use NSum is in evaluating sums with infinite limits. You can, however, also use it for sums with finite limits. By making implicit assumptions about the objects you are evaluating, NSum can often avoid doing as many function evaluations as an explicit Sum computation would require.

This finds the numerical value of $\sum_{n=0}^{100} e^{-n}$ by extrapolation techniques.	*In[4]:=* **NSum[Exp[-n], {n, 0, 100}]**	
	Out[4]= 1.58198	

You can also get the result, albeit much less efficiently, by constructing the symbolic form of the sum, then evaluating it numerically.	*In[5]:=* **Sum[Exp[-n], {n, 0, 100}] //N**	
	Out[5]= 1.58198	

NProduct works in essentially the same way as NSum, with analogous options.

■ 3.9.5 Numerical Solution of Polynomial Equations

When Solve cannot find explicit solutions to polynomial equations, it returns a symbolic form of the result in terms of Root objects.

In[1]:= `Solve[x^5 + 7x + 1 == 0, x]`

$Out[1]=$ $\{\{x \rightarrow \text{Root}[1 + 7\,\#1 + \#1^5 \,\&,\, 1]\},$
$\{x \rightarrow \text{Root}[1 + 7\,\#1 + \#1^5 \,\&,\, 2]\},$
$\{x \rightarrow \text{Root}[1 + 7\,\#1 + \#1^5 \,\&,\, 3]\},$
$\{x \rightarrow \text{Root}[1 + 7\,\#1 + \#1^5 \,\&,\, 4]\},$
$\{x \rightarrow \text{Root}[1 + 7\,\#1 + \#1^5 \,\&,\, 5]\}\}$

You can get numerical solutions by applying N.

In[2]:= `N[%]`

$Out[2]=$ $\{\{x \rightarrow -0.142849\}, \{x \rightarrow -1.11308 - 1.15173\,i\},$
$\{x \rightarrow -1.11308 + 1.15173\,i\},$
$\{x \rightarrow 1.1845 - 1.15139\,i\}, \{x \rightarrow 1.1845 + 1.15139\,i\}\}$

This gives the numerical solutions to 25-digit precision.

In[3]:= `N[%%, 25]`

$Out[3]=$ $\{\{x \rightarrow -0.1428486455250044341134116\},$
$\{x \rightarrow -1.113077976547710735600398 -$
$1.151734362151674305046770\,i\},$
$\{x \rightarrow -1.113077976547710735600398 +$
$1.151734362151674305046770\,i\},$
$\{x \rightarrow 1.184502299310212952657104 -$
$1.151390075408837074699147\,i\},$
$\{x \rightarrow 1.184502299310212952657104 +$
$1.151390075408837074699147\,i\}\}$

You can use NSolve to get numerical solutions to polynomial equations directly, without first trying to find exact results.

In[4]:= `NSolve[x^7 + x + 1 == 0, x]`

$Out[4]=$ $\{\{x \rightarrow -0.796544\}, \{x \rightarrow -0.705298 - 0.637624\,i\},$
$\{x \rightarrow -0.705298 + 0.637624\,i\},$
$\{x \rightarrow 0.123762 - 1.05665\,i\},$
$\{x \rightarrow 0.123762 + 1.05665\,i\},$
$\{x \rightarrow 0.979808 - 0.516677\,i\},$
$\{x \rightarrow 0.979808 + 0.516677\,i\}\}$

NSolve[*poly*==0, *x*]	get approximate numerical solutions to a polynomial equation
NSolve[*poly*==0, *x*, *n*]	get solutions to *n*-digit precision

Numerical solution of polynomial equations.

NSolve will always give you the complete set of numerical solutions to any polynomial equation in one variable.

You can also get numerical solutions to sets of simultaneous polynomial equations. You can use Solve to "unwind" the simultaneous equations, and then apply N to get numerical results.

Solve writes the solution in terms of roots of a polynomial in one variable.

$In[5]:=$ **First[**
           Solve[{x^2 + y^2 == 1, x^3 + y^3 == 2}, {x, y}]]

$Out[5]=$ $\left\{x \rightarrow \frac{1}{3} \text{Root}\left[3 + 3\,\#1^2 - 4\,\#1^3 - 3\,\#1^4 + 2\,\#1^6\,\&,\,1\right]\right.$
           $\left(-3 - 6\,\text{Root}\left[3 + 3\,\#1^2 - 4\,\#1^3 - 3\,\#1^4 + 2\,\#1^6\,\&,\,1\right] -\right.$
           $\text{Root}\left[3 + 3\,\#1^2 - 4\,\#1^3 - 3\,\#1^4 + 2\,\#1^6\,\&,\,1\right]^2 +$
           $4\,\text{Root}\left[3 + 3\,\#1^2 - 4\,\#1^3 - 3\,\#1^4 + 2\,\#1^6\,\&,\,1\right]^3 +$
           $\left.2\,\text{Root}\left[3 + 3\,\#1^2 - 4\,\#1^3 - 3\,\#1^4 + 2\,\#1^6\,\&,\,1\right]^4\right),$
           $\left.y \rightarrow \text{Root}\left[3 + 3\,\#1^2 - 4\,\#1^3 - 3\,\#1^4 + 2\,\#1^6\,\&,\,1\right]\right\}$

You can apply N to get a numerical result.

$In[6]:=$ **N[%]**

$Out[6]=$ $\{x \rightarrow -1.09791 + 0.839887\,\mathbb{i},\ y \rightarrow -1.09791 - 0.839887\,\mathbb{i}\}$

■ 3.9.6 Numerical Root Finding

NSolve gives you a general way to find numerical approximations to the solutions of polynomial equations. Finding numerical solutions to more general equations, however, can be much more diffi-cult, as discussed in Section 3.4.2. FindRoot gives you a way to search for a numerical solution to an arbitrary equation, or set of equations.

FindRoot[*lhs*==*rhs*, {*x*, x_0}]	search for a numerical solution to the equation *lhs*==*rhs*, starting with $x = x_0$
FindRoot[{*eqn*$_1$, *eqn*$_2$, ... }, {{*x*, x_0}, {*y*, y_0}, ... }]	search for a numerical solution to the simultaneous equations *eqn*$_i$

Numerical root finding.

The curves for $\cos(x)$ and x intersect at one point.

$In[1]:=$ **Plot[{Cos[x], x}, {x, -1, 1}]**

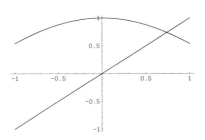

This finds a numerical approximation to the value of *x* at which the intersection occurs. The 0 tells FindRoot what value of *x* to try first.

```
In[2]:= FindRoot[Cos[x] == x, {x, 0}]

Out[2]- {x → 0.739085}
```

In trying to find a solution to your equation, FindRoot starts at the point you specify, and then progressively tries to get closer and closer to a solution. Even if your equations have several solutions, FindRoot always returns the first solution it finds. Which solution this is will depend on what starting point you chose. If you start sufficiently close to a particular solution, FindRoot will usually return that solution.

The equation $\sin(x) = 0$ has an infinite number of solutions of the form $x = n\pi$. If you start sufficiently close to a particular solution, FindRoot will give you that solution.

```
In[3]:= FindRoot[Sin[x] == 0, {x, 3}]

Out[3]= {x → 3.14159}
```

If you start with $x = 6$, you get a numerical approximation to the solution $x = 2\pi$.

```
In[4]:= FindRoot[Sin[x] == 0, {x, 6}]

Out[4]= {x → 6.28319}
```

If you want FindRoot to search for complex solutions, then you have to give a complex starting value.

```
In[5]:= FindRoot[Sin[x] == 2, {x, I}]

Out[5]= {x → 1.5708 + 1.31696 i}
```

This finds a zero of the Riemann zeta function.

```
In[6]:= FindRoot[Zeta[1/2 + I t] == 0, {t, 12}]

Out[6]= {t → 14.1347 - 9.35323 × 10⁻¹⁵ i}
```

This finds a solution to a set of simultaneous equations.

```
In[7]:= FindRoot[{Sin[x] == Cos[y], x + y == 1},
              {{x, 1}, {y, 1}}]

Out[7]= {x → -1.85619, y → 2.85619}
```

The variables used by FindRoot can have values that are lists. This allows you to find roots of functions that take vectors as arguments.

This is a way to solve a linear equation for the variable x.

```
In[8]:= FindRoot[{{1, 2}, {3, 4}} . x == {5, 6}, {x, {1, 1}}]

Out[8]= {x → {-4., 4.5}}
```

This finds a normalized eigenvector x and eigenvalue a.

```
In[9]:= FindRoot[{{{1, 2}, {3, 4}} . x == a x, x.x == 1},
              {{x, {1, 1}}, {a, 1}}]

Out[9]= {x → {0.415974, 0.909377}, a → 5.37228}
```

■ 3.9.7 Numerical Solution of Differential Equations

The function NDSolve discussed in Section 1.6.4 allows you to find numerical solutions to differential equations. NDSolve handles both single differential equations, and sets of simultaneous differential equations. It can handle a wide range of *ordinary differential equations* as well as some *partial differential equations*. In a system of ordinary differential equations there can be any number of unknown functions y_i, but all of these functions must depend on a single "independent variable" x, which is the same for each function. Partial differential equations involve two or more independent variables. NDSolve can also handle *differential-algebraic equations* that mix differential equations with algebraic ones.

NDSolve[{eqn_1, eqn_2, ... }, y, {x, $xmin$, $xmax$}]
           find a numerical solution for the function y with x in the
           range *xmin* to *xmax*

NDSolve[{eqn_1, eqn_2, ... }, {y_1, y_2, ... }, {x, $xmin$, $xmax$}]
           find numerical solutions for several functions y_i

---

Finding numerical solutions to ordinary differential equations.

NDSolve represents solutions for the functions y_i as InterpolatingFunction objects. The InterpolatingFunction objects provide approximations to the y_i over the range of values *xmin* to *xmax* for the independent variable x.

NDSolve finds solutions iteratively. It starts at a particular value of x, then takes a sequence of steps, trying eventually to cover the whole range *xmin* to *xmax*.

In order to get started, NDSolve has to be given appropriate initial or boundary conditions for the y_i and their derivatives. These conditions specify values for $y_i[x]$, and perhaps derivatives $y_i'[x]$, at particular points x. In general, at least for ordinary differential equations, the conditions you give can be at any x: NDSolve will automatically cover the range *xmin* to *xmax*.

This finds a solution for y with x in the range 0 to 2, using an initial condition for y[0].

```
In[1]:= NDSolve[{y'[x] == y[x], y[0] == 1}, y, {x, 0, 2}]
Out[1]= {{y → InterpolatingFunction[{{0., 2.}}, <>]}}
```

This still finds a solution with x in the range 0 to 2, but now the initial condition is for y[3].

```
In[2]:= NDSolve[{y'[x] == y[x], y[3] == 1}, y, {x, 0, 2}]
Out[2]= {{y → InterpolatingFunction[{{0., 2.}}, <>]}}
```

Here is a simple boundary value problem.

```
In[3]:= NDSolve[{y''[x] + x y[x] == 0, y[0] == 1, y[1] == -1},
                 y, {x, 0, 1}]
Out[3]= {{y → InterpolatingFunction[{{0., 1.}}, <>]}}
```

When you use NDSolve, the initial or boundary conditions you give must be sufficient to determine the solutions for the y_i completely. When you use DSolve to find symbolic solutions to differential equations, you can get away with specifying fewer initial conditions. The reason is that DSolve automatically inserts arbitrary constants C[i] to represent degrees of freedom associated with initial conditions that you have not specified explicitly. Since NDSolve must give a numerical solution, it cannot represent these kinds of additional degrees of freedom. As a result, you must explicitly give all the initial or boundary conditions that are needed to determine the solution.

In a typical case, if you have differential equations with up to n^{th} derivatives, then you need to give initial conditions for up to $(n-1)^{\text{th}}$ derivatives, or give boundary conditions at n points.

With a third-order equation, you need to give initial conditions for up to second derivatives.

```
In[4]:= NDSolve[
          { y'''[x] + 8 y''[x] + 17 y'[x] + 10 y[x] == 0,
            y[0] == 6, y'[0] == -20, y''[0] == 84},
            y, {x, 0, 1} ]
Out[4]= {{y → InterpolatingFunction[{{0., 1.}}, <>]}}
```

This plots the solution obtained.

```
In[5]:= Plot[Evaluate[ y[x] /. % ], {x, 0, 1}]
```

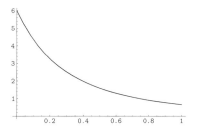

With a third-order equation, you can also give boundary conditions at three points.

```
In[6]:= NDSolve[
          { y'''[x] + Sin[x] == 0,
            y[0] == 4, y[1] == 7, y[2] == 0 }, y, {x, 0, 2}]
Out[6]= {{y → InterpolatingFunction[{{0., 2.}}, <>]}}
```

Mathematica allows you to use any appropriate linear combination of function values and derivatives as boundary conditions.

```
In[7]:= NDSolve[{ y''[x] + y[x] == 12 x,
            2 y[0] - y'[0] == -1, 2 y[1] + y'[1] == 9},
            y, {x, 0, 1}]
Out[7]= {{y → InterpolatingFunction[{{0., 1.}}, <>]}}
```

In most cases, all the initial conditions you give must involve the same value of x, say x_0. As a result, you can avoid giving both *xmin* and *xmax* explicitly. If you specify your range of x as $\{x, x_1\}$, then *Mathematica* will automatically generate a solution over the range x_0 to x_1.

This generates a solution over the range 0 to 2.

```
In[8]:= NDSolve[{y'[x] == y[x], y[0] == 1}, y, {x, 2}]
Out[8]= {{y → InterpolatingFunction[{{0., 2.}}, <>]}}
```

You can give initial conditions as equations of any kind. In some cases, these equations may have multiple solutions. In such cases, NDSolve will correspondingly generate multiple solutions.

The initial conditions in this case lead to multiple solutions.

```
In[9]:= NDSolve[{y'[x]^2 - y[x]^2 == 0, y[0]^2 == 4},
            y[x], {x, 1}]
Out[9]= {{y[x] → InterpolatingFunction[{{0., 1.}}, <>][x]},
          {y[x] → InterpolatingFunction[{{0., 1.}}, <>][x]},
          {y[x] → InterpolatingFunction[{{0., 1.}}, <>][x]},
          {y[x] → InterpolatingFunction[{{0., 1.}}, <>][x]}}
```

Here is a plot of all the solutions.   *In[10]:=* `Plot[Evaluate[ y[x] /. % ], {x, 0, 1}]`

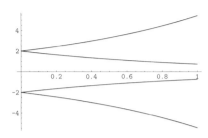

You can use `NDSolve` to solve systems of coupled differential equations.

This finds a numerical solution to a pair of coupled equations.

In[11]:= `sol = NDSolve[`
`        {x'[t] == -y[t] - x[t]^2, y'[t] == 2 x[t] - y[t],`
`         x[0] == y[0] == 1}, {x, y}, {t, 10}]`

Out[11]= `{{x → InterpolatingFunction[{{0., 10.}}, <>],`
`         y → InterpolatingFunction[{{0., 10.}}, <>]}}`

This plots the solution for y from these equations.

In[12]:= `Plot[Evaluate[y[t] /. sol], {t, 0, 10}]`

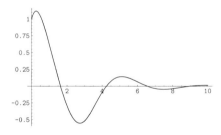

This generates a parametric plot using both x and y.

In[13]:= `ParametricPlot[Evaluate[{x[t], y[t]} /. sol],`
`                {t, 0, 10}, PlotRange -> All]`

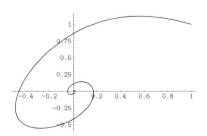

Unknown functions in differential equations do not necessarily have to be represented by single symbols. If you have a large number of unknown functions, you will often find it more convenient, for example, to give the functions names like $y[i]$.

This constructs a set of five coupled differential equations and initial conditions.	`In[14]:= eqns = Join[`
	`    Table[ y[i]'[x] == y[i-1][x] - y[i][x], {i, 2, 4} ],`
	`    {y[1]'[x] == -y[1][x], y[5]'[x] == y[4][x],`
	`                              y[1][0] == 1},`
	`    Table[ y[i][0] == 0, {i, 2, 5}]`
	`    ]`

`Out[14]= {y[2]'[x] == y[1][x] - y[2][x],`
`           y[3]'[x] == y[2][x] - y[3][x],`
`           y[4]'[x] == y[3][x] - y[4][x], y[1]'[x] == -y[1][x],`
`           y[5]'[x] == y[4][x], y[1][0] == 1, y[2][0] == 0,`
`           y[3][0] == 0, y[4][0] == 0, y[5][0] == 0}`

This solves the equations.	`In[15]:= NDSolve[eqns, Table[y[i], {i, 5}], {x, 10}]`

`Out[15]= {{y[1] → InterpolatingFunction[{{0., 10.}}, <>],`
`           y[2] → InterpolatingFunction[{{0., 10.}}, <>],`
`           y[3] → InterpolatingFunction[{{0., 10.}}, <>],`
`           y[4] → InterpolatingFunction[{{0., 10.}}, <>],`
`           y[5] → InterpolatingFunction[{{0., 10.}}, <>]}}`

Here is a plot of the solutions.	`In[16]:= Plot[ Evaluate[Table[y[i][x], {i, 5}] /. %],` `                              {x, 0, 10} ]`

NDSolve can handle functions whose values are lists or arrays. If you give initial conditions like $y[0] == \{v_1, v_2, \ldots, v_n\}]$, then NDSolve will assume that y is a function whose values are lists of length n.

This solves a system of four coupled differential equations.	`In[17]:= NDSolve[{y''[x] == -Table[Random[], {4}, {4}] . y[x],` `                 y[0] == y'[0] == Table[1, {4}]}, y, {x, 0, 8}]`

`Out[17]= {{y → InterpolatingFunction[{{0., 8.}}, <>]}}`

Here are the solutions.

```
In[18]:= With[{s = y[x] /. First[%]},
            Plot[{s[[1]], s[[2]], s[[3]], s[[4]]}, {x, 0, 8},
              PlotRange -> All]]
```

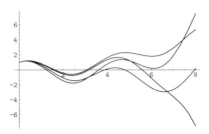

option name	default value	
MaxSteps	Automatic	maximum number of steps in x to take
StartingStepSize	Automatic	starting size of step in x to use
MaxStepSize	Infinity	maximum size of step in x to use
NormFunction	Automatic	the norm to use for error estimation

Special options for NDSolve.

NDSolve has many methods for solving equations, but essentially all of them at some level work by taking a sequence of steps in the independent variable x, and using an adaptive procedure to determine the size of these steps. In general, if the solution appears to be varying rapidly in a particular region, then NDSolve will reduce the step size or change the method so as to be able to track the solution better.

This solves a differential equation in which the derivative has a discontinuity.

```
In[19]:= NDSolve[
            {y'[x] == If[x < 0, 1/(x-1), 1/(x+1)],
              y[-5] == 5},
            y, {x, -5, 5}]

Out[19]= {{y → InterpolatingFunction[{{-5., 5.}}, <>]}}
```

NDSolve reduced the step size around $x = 0$ so as to reproduce the kink accurately.

In[20]:= **Plot[Evaluate[y[x] /. %], {x, -5, 5}]**

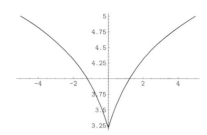

Through its adaptive procedure, NDSolve is able to solve "stiff" differential equations in which there are several components which vary with x at very different rates.

In these equations, y varies much more rapidly than z.

In[21]:= **sol = NDSolve[**
{y'[x] == -40 y[x], z'[x] == -z[x]/10,
y[0] == z[0] == 1},
{y, z}, {x, 0, 1}]

Out[21]= {{y → InterpolatingFunction[{{0., 1.}}, <>],
z → InterpolatingFunction[{{0., 1.}}, <>]}}

NDSolve nevertheless tracks both components successfully.

In[22]:= **Plot[Evaluate[{y[x], z[x]} /. sol], {x, 0, 1},**
PlotRange -> All]

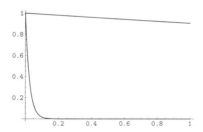

NDSolve follows the general procedure of reducing step size until it tracks solutions accurately. There is a problem, however, when the true solution has a singularity. In this case, NDSolve might go on reducing the step size forever, and never terminate. To avoid this problem, the option MaxSteps specifies the maximum number of steps that NDSolve will ever take in attempting to find a solution. For ordinary differential equations the default setting is MaxSteps -> 10000.

NDSolve stops after taking 10000 steps.

In[23]:= **NDSolve[{y'[x] == -1/x^2, y[-1] == -1}, y[x], {x, -1, 0}]**

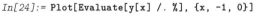

NDSolve::mxst:
  Maximum number of 10000 steps reached at the point x
                        -172
      == -1.00413 10   .

Out[23]= $\{\{y[x] \rightarrow \text{InterpolatingFunction}[$
           $\{\{-1., -1.00413 \times 10^{-172}\}\}, <>][x]\}\}$

There is in fact a singularity in the solution at $x = 0$.

In[24]:= **Plot[Evaluate[y[x] /. %], {x, -1, 0}]**

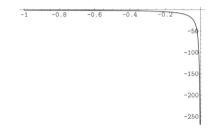

The default setting for MaxSteps should be sufficient for most equations with smooth solutions. When solutions have a complicated structure, however, you may occasionally have to choose larger settings for MaxSteps. With the setting MaxSteps -> Infinity there is no upper limit on the number of steps used.

To take the solution to the Lorenz equations this far, you need to remove the default bound on MaxSteps.

In[25]:= **NDSolve[{x'[t] == -3 (x[t] - y[t]),**
                  y'[t] == -x[t] z[t] + 26.5 x[t] - y[t],
                  z'[t] == x[t] y[t] - z[t],
                  x[0] == z[0] == 0, y[0] == 1},
              {x, y, z}, {t, 0, 200}, MaxSteps->Infinity]

Out[25]= $\{\{x \rightarrow \text{InterpolatingFunction}[\{\{0., 200.\}\}, <>],$
           $y \rightarrow \text{InterpolatingFunction}[\{\{0., 200.\}\}, <>],$
           $z \rightarrow \text{InterpolatingFunction}[\{\{0., 200.\}\}, <>]\}\}$

Here is a parametric plot of the solution in three dimensions.

In[26]:= `ParametricPlot3D[Evaluate[{x[t], y[t], z[t]} /. %],`
`{t, 0, 200}, PlotPoints -> 10000]`

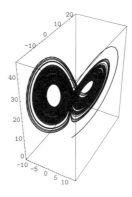

When `NDSolve` solves a particular set of differential equations, it always tries to choose a step size appropriate for those equations. In some cases, the very first step that `NDSolve` makes may be too large, and it may miss an important feature in the solution. To avoid this problem, you can explicitly set the option `StartingStepSize` to specify the size to use for the first step.

`NDSolve[{`eqn_1`, `eqn_2`, ... }, `y`, {`x`, `$xmin$`, `$xmax$`}]`
 find a numerical solution for y with x in the range $xmin$ to $xmax$

`NDSolve[{`eqn_1`, `eqn_2`, ... }, {`y_1`, `y_2`, ... }, {`x`, `$xmin$`, `$xmax$`}]`
 find numerical solutions for all the y_i

Finding numerical solutions to differential-algebraic equations.

The equations you give to `NDSolve` do not necessarily all have to involve derivatives; they can also just be algebraic. You can use `NDSolve` to solve many such *differential-algebraic equations*.

This solves a system of differential-algebraic equations.

In[27]:= `NDSolve[{x'[t] == y[t]^2 + x[t] y[t],`
`2 x[t]^2 + y[t]^2 == 1,`
`x[0] == 0, y[0] == 1}, {x, y}, {t, 0, 5}]`

Out[27]= `{{x → InterpolatingFunction[{{0., 5.}}, <>],`
`y → InterpolatingFunction[{{0., 5.}}, <>]}}`

Here is the solution.

In[28]:= `Plot[Evaluate[{x[t], y[t]} /. %], {t, 0, 5}]`

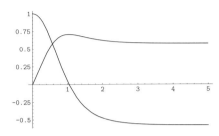

NDSolve[{eqn_1, eqn_2, ... }, u, {t, $tmin$, $tmax$}, {x, $xmin$, $xmax$}, ...]

  solve a system of partial differential equations for u

NDSolve[{eqn_1, eqn_2, ... }, {u_1, u_2, ... }, {t, $tmin$, $tmax$}, {x, $xmin$, $xmax$}, ...]

  solve a system of partial differential equations for several functions u_i

---

Finding numerical solutions to partial differential equations.

This finds a numerical solution to the wave equation. The result is a two-dimensional interpolating function.

In[29]:= `NDSolve[{D[u[t, x], t, t] == D[u[t, x], x, x],`
`    u[0, x] == Exp[-x^2], Derivative[1,0][u][0, x] == 0,`
`    u[t, -6] == u[t, 6]}, u, {t, 0, 6}, {x, -6, 6}]`

Out[29]= `{{u → InterpolatingFunction[`
`    {{0., 6.}, {..., -6., 6., ...}}, <>]}}`

This generates a plot of the result.

In[30]:= `Plot3D[Evaluate[u[t, x] /. First[%]],`
`    {t, 0, 6}, {x, -6, 6}, PlotPoints->50]`

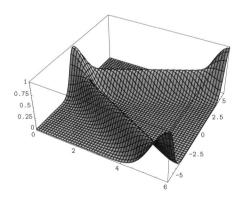

This finds a numerical solution to a
nonlinear wave equation.

```
In[31]:= NDSolve[
            {D[u[t, x], t, t] ==
                D[u[t, x], x, x] + (1 - u[t, x]^2)(1 + 2u[t, x]),
             u[0, x] == Exp[-x^2], Derivative[1, 0][u][0, x] == 0,
             u[t, -10] == u[t, 10]}, u, {t, 0, 10}, {x, -10, 10}]

Out[31]= {{u → InterpolatingFunction[
            {{0., 10.}, {..., -10., 10., ...}}, <>]}}
```

Here is a 3D plot of the result.

```
In[32]:= Plot3D[Evaluate[u[t, x] /. First[%]],
            {t, 0, 10}, {x, -10, 10}, PlotPoints->80]
```

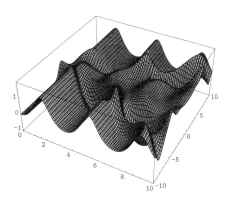

This is a higher-resolution density plot
of the solution.

```
In[33]:= DensityPlot[Evaluate[u[10 - t, x] /. First[%%]],
            {x, -10, 10}, {t, 0, 10},
            PlotPoints -> 200, Mesh -> False]
```

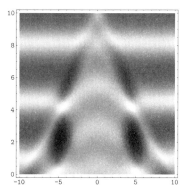

Here is a version of the equation in 2+1 dimensions.

```
In[34]:= eqn = D[u[t, x, y], t, t] == D[u[t, x, y], x, x] +
            D[u[t, x, y], y, y]/2 + (1 - u[t, x, y]^2)(1 + 2u[t, x, y])
```

$$Out[34]= u^{(2,0,0)}[t, x, y] == (1 + 2u[t, x, y])\left(1 - u[t, x, y]^2\right) +$$
$$\frac{1}{2} u^{(0,0,2)}[t, x, y] + u^{(0,2,0)}[t, x, y]$$

This solves the equation.

```
In[35]:= NDSolve[{eqn, u[0, x, y] == Exp[-(x^2 + y^2)],
            u[t, -5, y] == u[t, 5, y], u[t, x, -5] == u[t, x, 5],
            Derivative[1, 0, 0][u][0, x, y] == 0}, u,
            {t, 0, 4}, {x, -5, 5}, {y, -5, 5}]
```

```
Out[35]= {{u → InterpolatingFunction[
            {{0., 4.}, {..., -5., 5., ...},
             {..., -5., 5., ...}}, <>]}}
```

This generates an array of plots of the solution.

```
In[36]:= Show[GraphicsArray[
            Partition[
            Table[ Plot3D[Evaluate[u[t, x, y] /. First[%]],
                {x, -5, 5}, {y, -5, 5}, PlotRange -> All,
                PlotPoints -> 100, Mesh -> False,
                DisplayFunction -> Identity], {t, 1, 4}], 2]]]
```

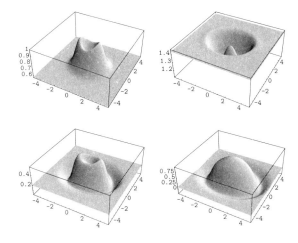

■ 3.9.8 Numerical Optimization

FindMinimum[*f*, {*x*, *x₀*}]	search for a local minimum in *f*, starting from the point $x = x_0$
FindMinimum[*f*, {{*x*, *x₀*}, {*y*, *y₀*}, ... }]	search for a local minimum in a function of several variables
FindMaximum[*f*, {*x*, *x₀*}]	search for a local maximum in *f*, starting from the point $x = x_0$
FindMaximum[*f*, {{*x*, *x₀*}, {*y*, *y₀*}, ... }]	search for a local maximum in a function of several variables

Searching for minima and maxima.

This finds the value of x which minimizes $\Gamma(x)$, starting from $x = 2$.	*In[1]:=* **FindMinimum[Gamma[x], {x, 2}]** *Out[1]=* {0.885603, {x → 1.46163}}
The last element of the list gives the value at which the minimum is achieved.	*In[2]:=* **Gamma[x] /. Last[%]** *Out[2]=* 0.885603

Like FindRoot, FindMinimum and FindMaximum work by starting from a point, then progressively searching for a minimum or maximum. But since they return a result as soon as they find anything, they may give only a local minimum or maximum of your function, not a global one.

This curve has two local minima.	*In[3]:=* **Plot[x^4 - 3x^2 + x, {x, -3, 2}]**

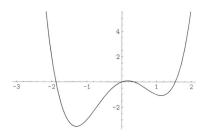

Starting at $x = 1$, you get the local minimum on the right.	*In[4]:=* **FindMinimum[x^4 - 3 x^2 + x, {x, 1}]** *Out[4]=* {-1.07023, {x → 1.1309}}
This gives the local minimum on the left, which in this case is also the global minimum.	*In[5]:=* **FindMinimum[x^4 - 3 x^2 + x, {x, -1}]** *Out[5]=* {-3.51391, {x → -1.30084}}

+ NMinimize[f, x]	try to find the global minimum of f
+ NMinimize[f, $\{x, y, ... \}$]	try to find the global minimum over several variables
+ NMaximize[f, x]	try to find the global maximum of f
+ NMaximize[f, $\{x, y, ... \}$]	try to find the global maximum over several variables

Finding global minima and maxima.

This immediately finds the global minimum.

In[6]:= **NMinimize[x^4 - 3x^2 + x, x]**

Out[6]= {-3.51391, {x → -1.30084}}

NMinimize and NMaximize are numerical analogs of Minimize and Maximize. But unlike Minimize and Maximize they usually cannot guarantee to find absolute global minima and maxima. Nevertheless, they typically work well when the function f is fairly smooth, and has a limited number of local minima and maxima.

+ NMinimize[$\{f, cons\}$, $\{x, y, ... \}$]	try to find the global minimum of f subject to constraints *cons*
+ NMaximize[$\{f, cons\}$, $\{x, y, ... \}$]	try to find the global maximum of f subject to constraints *cons*

Finding global minima and maxima subject to constraints.

With the constraint x > 0, NMinimize will give the local minimum on the right.

In[7]:= **NMinimize[{x^4 - 3x^2 + x, x > 0}, x]**

Out[7]= {-1.07023, {x → 1.1309}}

This finds the minimum of x + 2y within the unit circle.

In[8]:= **NMinimize[{x + 2y, x^2 + y^2 <= 1}, {x, y}]**

Out[8]= {-2.23607, {x → -0.447214, y → -0.894427}}

In this case Minimize can give an exact result.

In[9]:= **Minimize[{x + 2y, x^2 + y^2 <= 1}, {x, y}]**

Out[9]= $\left\{ -\sqrt{5}, \left\{ x \to -\dfrac{1}{\sqrt{5}}, y \to -\dfrac{2}{\sqrt{5}} \right\} \right\}$

But in this case it cannot.

In[10]:= **Minimize[{Cos[x + 2y], x^2 + y^2 <= 1}, {x, y}]**

Out[10]= Minimize[{Cos[x + 2 y], $x^2 + y^2 \le 1$}, {x, y}]

This gives a numerical approximation, effectively using NMinimize.

In[11]:= **N[%]**

Out[11]= {-0.617273, {x → 0.447214, y → 0.894427}}

If both the objective function *f* and the constraints *cons* are linear in all variables, then minimization and maximization correspond to a *linear programming problem*. Sometimes it is convenient to state such problems not in terms of explicit equations, but instead in terms of matrices and vectors.

LinearProgramming[*c*, *m*, *b*]	find the vector **x** which minimizes **c.x** subject to the constraints **m.x** ≥ **b** and **x** ≥ 0
+ LinearProgramming[*c*, *m*, *b*, *l*]	use the constraints **m.x** ≥ **b** and **x** ≥ *l*

Linear programming in matrix form.

Here is a linear programming problem in equation form.

In[12]:= **Minimize[{2x + 3y, x + 5y >= 10, x - y >= 2, x >= 1}, {x, y}]**

$$Out[12]= \left\{\frac{32}{3}, \left\{x \to \frac{10}{3}, y \to \frac{4}{3}\right\}\right\}$$

Here is the corresponding problem in matrix form.

In[13]:= **LinearProgramming[{2, 3}, {{1, 5}, {1, -1}, {1, 0}},**
                                                {10, 2, 1}]

$$Out[13]= \left\{\frac{10}{3}, \frac{4}{3}\right\}$$

You can specify a mixture of equality and inequality constraints by making the list *b* be a sequence of pairs $\{b_i, s_i\}$. If s_i is 1, then the ith constraint is $m_i \; . \; x \geq b_i$. If s_i is 0 then it is $m_i \; . \; x == b_i$, and if s_i is −1 then it is $m_i \; . \; x \leq b_i$.

This makes the first inequality use ≤.

In[14]:= **LinearProgramming[{2, 3}, {{1, 5}, {1, -1}, {1, 0}},**
                                                {{10, -1}, {2, 1}, {1, 1}}]

Out[14]= {2, 0}

In LinearProgramming[*c*, *m*, *b*, *l*], you can make *l* be a list of pairs $\{\{l_1, u_1\}, \{l_2, u_2\}, \dots \}$ representing lower and upper bounds on the x_i.

In doing large linear programming problems, it is often convenient to give the matrix *m* as a SparseArray object.

+ ■ 3.9.9 Advanced Topic: Controlling the Precision of Results

In doing numerical operations like NDSolve and NMinimize, *Mathematica* by default uses machine numbers. But by setting the option WorkingPrecision -> *n* you can tell it to use arbitrary-precision numbers with *n*-digit precision.

This does a machine-precision computation of a numerical integral.

In[1]:= **NIntegrate[Sin[Sin[x]], {x, 0, 1}]**

Out[1]= 0.430606

This does the computation with 30-digit arbitrary-precision numbers.

In[2]:= **NIntegrate[Sin[Sin[x]], {x, 0, 1}, WorkingPrecision -> 30]**

Out[2]= 0.430606103120690604912377

When you give a setting for WorkingPrecision, this typically defines an upper limit on the precision of the results from a computation. But within this constraint you can tell *Mathematica* how much precision and accuracy you want it to try to get. You should realize that for many kinds of numerical operations, increasing precision and accuracy goals by only a few digits can greatly increase the computation time required. Nevertheless, there are many cases where it is important to ensure that high precision and accuracy are obtained.

WorkingPrecision	the number of digits to use for computations
PrecisionGoal	the number of digits of precision to try to get
AccuracyGoal	the number of digits of accuracy to try to get

Options for controlling precision and accuracy.

This gives a result to 25-digit precision.

```
In[3]:= NIntegrate[Sin[Sin[x]], {x, 0, 1}, WorkingPrecision -> 30,
            PrecisionGoal -> 25]

Out[3]= 0.4306061031206906049123773552486
```

50-digit precision cannot be achieved with 30-digit working precision.

```
In[4]:= NIntegrate[Sin[Sin[x]], {x, 0, 1}, WorkingPrecision -> 30,
            PrecisionGoal -> 50]

NIntegrate::tmap:
    NIntegrate is unable to achieve the tolerances
     specified by the PrecisionGoal and AccuracyGoal
     options because the working precision is insufficient.
      Try increasing the setting of the WorkingPrecision
     option.

Out[4]= 0.4306061031206906049123773552486
```

Giving a particular setting for WorkingPrecision, each of the functions for numerical operations in *Mathematica* uses certain default settings for PrecisionGoal and AccuracyGoal. Typical is the case of NDSolve, in which these default settings are equal to half the setting given for WorkingPrecision.

The precision and accuracy goals normally apply both to the final results returned, and to various norms or error estimates for them. Functions for numerical operations in *Mathematica* typically try to refine their results until either the specified precision goal or accuracy goal is reached. If the setting for either of these goals is Infinity, then only the other goal is considered.

In doing ordinary numerical evaluation with N[*expr*, *n*], *Mathematica* automatically adjusts its internal computations to achieve *n*-digit precision in the result. But in doing numerical operations on functions, it is in practice usually necessary to specify WorkingPrecision and PrecisionGoal more explicitly.

▪ 3.9.10 Advanced Topic: Monitoring and Selecting Algorithms

Functions in *Mathematica* are carefully set up so that you normally do not have to know how they work inside. But particularly for numerical functions that use iterative algorithms, it is sometimes useful to be able to monitor the internal progress of these algorithms.

+	StepMonitor	an expression to evaluate whenever a successful step is taken
+	EvaluationMonitor	an expression to evaluate whenever functions from the input are evaluated

Options for monitoring progress of numerical functions.

This prints the value of x every time a step is taken.

```
In[1]:= FindRoot[Cos[x] == x, {x, 1}, StepMonitor :> Print[x]]
```

0.750364

0.739113

0.739085

0.739085

Out[1]= {x → 0.739085}

Note the importance of using *option :> expr* rather than *option -> expr*. You need a delayed rule *:>* to make *expr* be evaluated each time it is used, rather than just when the rule is given.

Reap and Sow provide a convenient way to make a list of the steps taken.

```
In[2]:= Reap[FindRoot[Cos[x] == x, {x, 1}, StepMonitor :> Sow[x]]]
```

Out[2]= {{x → 0.739085},
          {{0.750364, 0.739113, 0.739085, 0.739085}}}

This counts the steps.

```
In[3]:= Block[{ct = 0}, {FindRoot[Cos[x] == x, {x, 1},
                         StepMonitor :> ct++], ct}]
```

Out[3]= {{x → 0.739085}, 4}

To take a successful step towards an answer, iterative numerical algorithms sometimes have to do several evaluations of the functions they have been given. Sometimes this is because each step requires, say, estimating a derivative from differences between function values, and sometimes it is because several attempts are needed to achieve a successful step.

This shows the successful steps taken in reaching the answer.

```
In[4]:= Reap[FindRoot[Cos[x] == x, {x, 5}, StepMonitor :> Sow[x]]]
```

Out[4]= {{x → 0.739085},
          {{-0.741028, -0.285946, 0.526451, 0.751511,
            0.739119, 0.739085, 0.739085}}}

This shows every time the function was evaluated.

```
In[5]:= Reap[FindRoot[Cos[x] == x, {x, 5},
                      EvaluationMonitor :> Sow[x]]]

Out[5]= {{x → 0.739085},
         {{5., -109.821, -6.48206, -0.741028,
           3.80979, -0.285946, 1.44867, 0.526451,
           0.751511, 0.739119, 0.739085, 0.739085}}}
```

The pattern of evaluations done by algorithms in *Mathematica* can be quite complicated.

```
In[6]:= ListPlot[Reap[NIntegrate[1/Sqrt[x], {x, -1, 0, 1},
                      EvaluationMonitor :> Sow[x]]][[2, 1]]]
```

Method options.

Method -> Automatic	pick methods automatically (default)
Method -> "*name*"	specify an explicit method to use
Method -> {"*name*", {"par_1" -> val_1, ... }}	specify more details of a method

There are often several different methods known for doing particular types of numerical computations. Typically *Mathematica* supports most generally successful ones that have been discussed in the literature, as well as many that have not. For any specific problem, it goes to considerable effort to pick the best method automatically. But if you have sophisticated knowledge of a problem, or are studying numerical methods for their own sake, you may find it useful to tell *Mathematica* explicitly what method it should use. The Reference Guide lists some of the methods built into *Mathematica*; others are discussed in Section A.9.4 or in advanced or online documentation.

This solves a differential equation using method *m*, and returns the number of steps and evaluations needed.

```
In[7]:= try[m_] := Block[{s=e=0}, NDSolve[{y''[x] + Sin[y[x]] == 0,
               y'[0] == y[0] == 1}, y, {x, 0, 100}, StepMonitor :> s++,
               EvaluationMonitor :> e++, Method -> m]; {s, e}]
```

With the method selected automatically, this is the number of steps and evaluations that are needed.

```
In[8]:= try[Automatic]

Out[8]= {1118, 2329}
```

This shows what happens with several other possible methods. The Adams method that is selected automatically is the fastest.

```
In[9]:= try /@ {"Adams", "BDF", "ExplicitRungeKutta",
              "ImplicitRungeKutta", "Extrapolation"}

Out[9]= {{1118, 2329}, {2415, 2861},
         {474, 4749}, {277, 7200}, {83, 4650}}
```

This shows what happens with the explicit Runge-Kutta method when the difference order parameter is changed.

```
In[10]:= Table[try[{"ExplicitRungeKutta", "DifferenceOrder" -> n}],
               {n, 4, 9}]

Out[10]= {{3522, 14090}, {617, 4321}, {851, 6810},
          {474, 4742}, {291, 3785}, {289, 4626}}
```

■ 3.9.11 Advanced Topic: Functions with Sensitive Dependence on Their Input

Functions that are specified by simple algebraic formulas tend to be such that when their input is changed only slightly, their output also changes only slightly. But functions that are instead based on executing procedures quite often show almost arbitrarily sensitive dependence on their input. Typically the reason this happens is that the procedure "excavates" progressively less and less significant digits in the input.

This shows successive steps in a simple iterative procedure with input 0.1111.

```
In[1]:= NestList[FractionalPart[2 #]&, 0.1111, 10]

Out[1]= {0.1111, 0.2222, 0.4444, 0.8888, 0.7776,
         0.5552, 0.1104, 0.2208, 0.4416, 0.8832, 0.7664}
```

Here is the result with input 0.1112. Progressive divergence from the result with input 0.1111 is seen.

```
In[2]:= NestList[FractionalPart[2 #]&, 0.1112, 10]

Out[2]= {0.1112, 0.2224, 0.4448, 0.8896, 0.7792,
         0.5584, 0.1168, 0.2336, 0.4672, 0.9344, 0.8688}
```

The action of FractionalPart[2 x] is particularly simple in terms of the binary digits of the number x: it justs drops the first one, and shifts the remaining ones to the left. After several steps, this means that the results one gets are inevitably sensitive to digits that are far to the right, and have an extremely small effect on the original value of x.

This shows the shifting process achieved by FractionalPart[2 x] in the first 8 binary digits of x.

```
In[3]:= RealDigits[Take[%, 5], 2, 8, -1]

Out[3]= {{{0, 0, 0, 1, 1, 1, 0, 0}, 0},
         {{0, 0, 1, 1, 1, 0, 0, 1}, 0},
         {{0, 1, 1, 1, 0, 0, 1, 0}, 0},
         {{1, 1, 1, 0, 0, 1, 0, 0}, 0},
         {{1, 1, 0, 0, 0, 1, 1, 1}, 0}}
```

If you give input only to a particular precision, you are effectively specifying only a certain number of digits. And once all these digits have been "excavated" you can no longer get accurate results, since to do so would require knowing more digits of your original input. So long as you use arbitrary-precision numbers, *Mathematica* automatically keeps track of this kind of degradation in precision, indicating a number with no remaining significant digits by $0. \times 10^e$, as discussed on page 734.

Successive steps yield numbers of progressively lower precision, and eventually no precision at all.

In[4]:= `NestList[FractionalPart[40 #]&, N[1/9, 20], 20]`

Out[4]= $\{0.11111111111111111111, 0.4444444444444444444,$
$0.77777777777777778, 0.1111111111111111,$
$0.44444444444444, 0.777777777778, 0.11111111111,$
$0.444444444, 0.77777778, 0.111111, 0.4444,$
$0.778, 0.1, 0. \times 10^{-1}, 0. \times 10^{1}, 0. \times 10^{3},$
$0. \times 10^{4}, 0. \times 10^{6}, 0. \times 10^{7}, 0. \times 10^{9}, 0. \times 10^{11}\}$

This asks for the precision of each number. Zero precision indicates that there are no correct significant digits.

In[5]:= `Map[Precision, %]`

Out[5]= {20., 19., 17.641, 15.1938, 14.1938, 12.8348,
10.3876, 9.38764, 8.02862, 5.58146, 4.58146,
3.22244, 0.77528, 0., 0., 0., 0., 0., 0., 0., 0.}

This shows that the exact result is a periodic sequence.

In[6]:= `NestList[FractionalPart[40 #]&, 1/9, 10]`

Out[6]= $\left\{\dfrac{1}{9}, \dfrac{4}{9}, \dfrac{7}{9}, \dfrac{1}{9}, \dfrac{4}{9}, \dfrac{7}{9}, \dfrac{1}{9}, \dfrac{4}{9}, \dfrac{7}{9}, \dfrac{1}{9}, \dfrac{4}{9}\right\}$

It is important to realize that if you use approximate numbers of any kind, then in an example like the one above you will always eventually run out of precision. But so long as you use arbitrary-precision numbers, *Mathematica* will explicitly show you any decrease in precision that is occurring. However, if you use machine-precision numbers, then *Mathematica* will not keep track of precision, and you cannot tell when your results become meaningless.

If you use machine-precision numbers, *Mathematica* will no longer keep track of any degradation in precision.

In[7]:= `NestList[FractionalPart[40 #]&, N[1/9], 20]`

Out[7]= {0.111111, 0.444444, 0.777778, 0.111111,
0.444444, 0.777778, 0.111111, 0.444445, 0.77781,
0.112405, 0.496185, 0.847383, 0.89534, 0.813599,
0.543945, 0.757813, 0.3125, 0.5, 0., 0., 0.}

By iterating the operation `FractionalPart[2 x]` you extract successive binary digits in whatever number you start with. And if these digits are apparently random—as in a number like π—then the results will be correspondingly random. But if the digits have a simple pattern—as in any rational number—then the results you get will be correspondingly simple.

By iterating an operation such as `FractionalPart[3/2 x]` it turns out however to be possible to get seemingly random sequences even from very simple input. This is an example of a very general phenomenon first identified by me in the mid-1980s, which has nothing directly to do with sensitive dependence on input.

This generates a seemingly random sequence, even starting from simple input.

In[8]:= `NestList[FractionalPart[3/2 #]&, 1, 15]`

Out[8]= $\left\{1, \dfrac{1}{2}, \dfrac{3}{4}, \dfrac{1}{8}, \dfrac{3}{16}, \dfrac{9}{32}, \dfrac{27}{64}, \dfrac{81}{128}, \dfrac{243}{256}, \dfrac{217}{512},\right.$
$\left.\dfrac{651}{1024}, \dfrac{1953}{2048}, \dfrac{1763}{4096}, \dfrac{5289}{8192}, \dfrac{15867}{16384}, \dfrac{14833}{32768}\right\}$

After the values have been computed, one can safely find numerical approximations to them.

In[9]:= `N[%]`

Out[9]= {1., 0.5, 0.75, 0.125, 0.1875, 0.28125, 0.421875,
0.632813, 0.949219, 0.423828, 0.635742,
0.953613, 0.43042, 0.64563, 0.968445, 0.452667}

Here are the last 5 results after 1000 iterations, computed using exact numbers.

```
In[10]:= Take[N[NestList[FractionalPart[3/2 #]&, 1, 1000]], -5]
Out[10]= {0.0218439, 0.0327659,
            0.0491488, 0.0737233, 0.110585}
```

Using machine-precision numbers gives completely incorrect results.

```
In[11]:= Take[NestList[FractionalPart[3/2 #]&, 1., 1000], -5]
Out[11]= {0.670664, 0.0059966,
            0.0089949, 0.0134924, 0.0202385}
```

Many kinds of iterative procedures yield functions that depend sensitively on their input. Such functions also arise when one looks at solutions to differential equations. In effect, varying the independent parameter in the differential equation is a continuous analog of going from one step to the next in an iterative procedure.

This finds a solution to the Duffing equation with initial condition 1.

```
In[12]:= NDSolve[{x''[t] + 0.15 x'[t] - x[t] + x[t]^3 == 0.3 Cos[t],
              x[0] == -1, x'[0] == 1}, x, {t, 0, 50}]
Out[12]= {{x → InterpolatingFunction[{{0., 50.}}, <>]}}
```

Here is a plot of the solution.

```
In[13]:= Plot[Evaluate[x[t] /. %], {t, 0, 50}]
```

Here is the same equation with initial condition 1.001.

```
In[14]:= NDSolve[{x''[t] + 0.15 x'[t] - x[t] + x[t]^3 == 0.3 Cos[t],
              x[0] == -1, x'[0] == 1.001}, x, {t, 0, 50}]
Out[14]= {{x → InterpolatingFunction[{{0., 50.}}, <>]}}
```

The solution progressively diverges from the one shown above.

```
In[15]:= Plot[Evaluate[x[t] /. %], {t, 0, 50}]
```

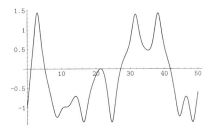

3.10 Mathematical and Other Notation

■ 3.10.1 Special Characters

Built into *Mathematica* are a large number of special characters intended for use in mathematical and other notation. Pages 1354–1401 give a complete listing.

Each special character is assigned a full name such as \[Infinity]. More common special characters are also assigned aliases, such as ⍞inf⍞, where ⍞ stands for the ESC key. You can set up additional aliases using the InputAliases notebook option discussed on page 613.

For special characters that are supported in standard dialects of TEX, *Mathematica* also allows you to use aliases based on TEX names. Thus, for example, you can enter \[Infinity] using the alias ⍞\infty⍞. *Mathematica* also supports aliases such as ⍞&infin⍞ based on names used in SGML and HTML.

Standard system software on many computer systems also supports special key combinations for entering certain special characters. On a Macintosh, for example, OPTION-5 will produce ∞ in most fonts. With the notebook front end *Mathematica* automatically allows you to use special key combinations when these are available, and with a text-based interface you can get *Mathematica* to accept such key combinations if you set an appropriate value for $CharacterEncoding.

- Use a full name such as \[Infinity]

- Use an alias such as ESC inf ESC

- Use a TEX alias such as ESC \infty ESC

- Use an SGML or HTML alias such as ESC &infin ESC

- Click on a button in a palette

- Use a special key combination supported by your computer system

---

Ways to enter special characters.

In a *Mathematica* notebook, you can use special characters just like you use standard keyboard characters. You can include special characters both in ordinary text and in input that you intend to give to *Mathematica*.

Some special characters are set up to have an immediate meaning to *Mathematica*. Thus, for example, π is taken to be the symbol Pi. Similarly, $\geq$ is taken to be the operator >=, while $\cup$ is equivalent to the function Union.

π and $\geq$ have immediate meanings in *Mathematica*.	`In[1]:= π ≥ 3`
	
	`Out[1]= True`

∪ or `\[Union]` is immediately interpreted as the `Union` function.	`In[2]:= {a, b, c} ∪ {c, d, e}`
	
	`Out[2]= {a, b, c, d, e}`

⊔ or `\[SquareUnion]` has no immediate meaning to *Mathematica*.	`In[3]:= {a, b, c} ⊔ {c, d, e}`
	
	`Out[3]= {a, b, c} ⊔ {c, d, e}`

Among ordinary characters such as E and i, some have an immediate meaning to *Mathematica*, but most do not. And the same is true of special characters.

Thus, for example, while π and ∞ have an immediate meaning to *Mathematica*, λ and $\mathcal{L}$ do not.

This allows you to set up your own definitions for λ and $\mathcal{L}$.

λ has no immediate meaning in *Mathematica*.	`In[4]:= λ[2] + λ[3]`
	
	`Out[4]= λ[2] + λ[3]`

This defines a meaning for λ.	`In[5]:= λ[x_] := `$\sqrt{x^2 - 1}$
Now *Mathematica* evaluates λ just as it would any other function.	`In[6]:= λ[2] + λ[3]` `Out[6]= `$2\sqrt{2} + \sqrt{3}$

Characters such as λ and $\mathcal{L}$ are treated by *Mathematica* as letters—just like ordinary keyboard letters like a or b.

But characters such as $\oplus$ and ⊔ are treated by *Mathematica* as *operators*. And although these particular characters are not assigned any built-in meaning by *Mathematica*, they are nevertheless required to follow a definite *syntax*.

⊔ is an infix operator.	`In[7]:= {a, b, c} ⊔ {c, d, e}`
	
	`Out[7]= {a, b, c} ⊔ {c, d, e}`

The definition assigns a meaning to the ⊔ operator.	`In[8]:= x_ ⊔ y_ := Join[x, y]`

Now ⊔ can be evaluated by *Mathematica*.	`In[9]:= {a, b, c} ⊔ {c, d, e}`
	
	`Out[9]= {a, b, c, c, d, e}`

The details of how input you give to *Mathematica* is interpreted depends on whether you are using `StandardForm` or `TraditionalForm`, and on what additional information you supply in `InterpretationBox` and similar constructs.

But unless you explicitly override its built-in rules by giving your own definitions for `MakeExpression`, *Mathematica* will always assign the same basic syntactic properties to any particular special character.

These properties not only affect the interpretation of the special characters in *Mathematica* input, but also determine the structure of expressions built with these special characters. They also affect various aspects of formatting; operators, for example, have extra space left around them, while letters do not.

Letters	a, E, π, Ξ, $\mathcal{L}$, etc.
Letter-like forms	∞, $\emptyset$, Υ, £, etc.
Operators	$\oplus$, ∂, $\approx$, $\rightleftharpoons$, etc.

Types of special characters.

In using special characters, it is important to make sure that you have the correct character for a particular purpose. There are quite a few examples of characters that look similar, yet are in fact quite different.

A common issue is operators whose forms are derived from letters. An example is $\sum$ or \[Sum], which looks very similar to Σ or \[CapitalSigma].

As is typical, however, the operator form $\sum$ is slightly less elaborate and more stylized than the letter form Σ. In addition, $\sum$ is an extensible character which grows depending on the summand, while Σ has a size determined only by the current font.

$\sum$ Σ	\[Sum], \[CapitalSigma]		μ μ	\[Micro], \[Mu]	
$\prod$ Π	\[Product], \[CapitalPi]		Å Å	\[Angstrom], \[CapitalARing]	
$\cup$ U	\[Union], keyboard U		$\emptyset$ Ø	\[EmptySet], \[CapitalOSlash]	
$\in$ ϵ	\[Element], \[Epsilon]		A A	\[CapitalAlpha], keyboard A	
d d	\[DifferentialD], keyboard d		i i	\[ImaginaryI], keyboard i	

Different characters that look similar.

In cases such as \[CapitalAlpha] versus A, both characters are letters. However, *Mathematica* treats these characters as different, and in some fonts, for example, they may look quite different.

The result contains four distinct characters.

```
In[10]:= Union[ {\[CapitalAlpha], A, A, \[Mu], \[Mu], \[Micro]} ]

Out[10]= {A, A, μ, μ}
```

Traditional mathematical notation occasionally uses ordinary letters as operators. An example is the d in a differential such as dx that appears in an integral.

To make *Mathematica* have a precise and consistent syntax, it is necessary at least in StandardForm to distinguish between an ordinary d and the $d\!\!\!\!\;$ used as a differential operator.

The way *Mathematica* does this is to use a special character ⅆ or \[DifferentialD] as the differential operator. This special character can be entered using the alias ⁚dd⁚.

Mathematica uses a special character for the differential operator, so there is no conflict with an ordinary d.	$In[11]:= \int x^{d} \, \mathrm{d}x$
	$Out[11]= \dfrac{x^{1+d}}{1+d}$

When letters and letter-like forms appear in *Mathematica* input, they are typically treated as names of symbols. But when operators appear, functions must be constructed that correspond to these operators. In almost all cases, what *Mathematica* does is to create a function whose name is the full name of the special character that appears as the operator.

Mathematica constructs a CirclePlus function to correspond to the operator ⊕, whose full name is \[CirclePlus].	$In[12]:=$ a ⊕ b ⊕ c // FullForm
	$Out[12]//FullForm=$ CirclePlus[a, b, c]

This constructs an And function, which happens to have built-in evaluation rules in *Mathematica*.	$In[13]:=$ a ∧ b ∧ c // FullForm
	$Out[13]//FullForm=$ And[a, b, c]

Following the correspondence between operator names and function names, special characters such as ∪ that represent built-in *Mathematica* functions have names that correspond to those functions. Thus, for example, ÷ is named \[Divide] to correspond to the built-in *Mathematica* function Divide, and ⇒ is named \[Implies] to correspond to the built-in function Implies.

In general, however, special characters in *Mathematica* are given names that are as generic as possible, so as not to prejudice different uses. Most often, characters are thus named mainly according to their appearance. The character ⊕ is therefore named \[CirclePlus], rather than, say, \[DirectSum], and ≈ is named \[TildeTilde] rather than, say, \[ApproximatelyEqual].

× ×	\[Times], \[Cross]		* *	\[Star], keyboard *
∧ ∧	\[And], \[Wedge]		\ \	\[Backslash], keyboard \
∨ ∨	\[Or], \[Vee]		· .	\[CenterDot], keyboard .
→ →	\[Rule], \[RightArrow]		∧ ^	\[Wedge], keyboard ^
⇒ ⇒	\[Implies], \[DoubleRightArrow]		∣ ∣	\[VerticalBar], keyboard	
= =	\[LongEqual], keyboard =		∣ ∣	\[VerticalSeparator], keyboard	

Different operator characters that look similar.

There are sometimes characters that look similar but which are used to represent different operators. An example is \[Times] and \[Cross]. \[Times] corresponds to the ordinary Times function for multiplication; \[Cross] corresponds to the Cross function for vector cross products. The × for \[Cross] is drawn slightly smaller than × for Times, corresponding to usual careful usage in mathematical typography.

The \[Times] operator represents ordinary multiplication.	*In[14]:=* **{5, 6, 7} \[Times] {2, 3, 1}** *Out[14]=* {10, 18, 7}
The \[Cross] operator represents vector cross products.	*In[15]:=* **{5, 6, 7} \[Cross] {2, 3, 1}** *Out[15]=* {-15, 9, 3}
The two operators display in a similar way—with \[Times] slightly larger than \[Cross].	*In[16]:=* **{a × b, a × b}** *Out[16]=* {a b, a × b}

In the example of \[And] and \[Wedge], the \[And] operator—which happens to be drawn slightly larger—corresponds to the built-in *Mathematica* function And, while the \[Wedge] operator has a generic name based on the appearance of the character and has no built-in meaning.

You can mix \[Wedge] and \[And] operators. Each has a definite precedence.	*In[17]:=* **a \[Wedge] b \[And] c \[Wedge] d // FullForm** *Out[17]//FullForm=* And[Wedge[a, b], Wedge[c, d]]

Some of the special characters commonly used as operators in mathematical notation look similar to ordinary keyboard characters. Thus, for example, ∧ or \[Wedge] looks similar to the ^ character on a standard keyboard.

Mathematica interprets a raw ^ as a power. But it interprets ∧ as a generic Wedge function. In cases such as this where there is a special character that looks similar to an ordinary keyboard character, the convention is to use the ordinary keyboard character as the alias for the special character. Thus, for example, ⁞^⁞ is the alias for \[Wedge].

The raw ^ is interpreted as a power, but the ⁞^⁞ is a generic wedge operator.	*In[18]:=* **{x ^ y, x ⁞^⁞ y}** *Out[18]=* {x^y, x ∧ y}

A related convention is that when a special character is used to represent an operator that can be typed using ordinary keyboard characters, those characters are used in the alias for the special character. Thus, for example, ⁞->⁞ is the alias for → or \[Rule], while ⁞&&⁞ is the alias for ∧ or \[And].

⁞->⁞ is the alias for \[Rule], and ⁞&&⁞ for \[And].	*In[19]:=* **{x ⁞->⁞ y, x ⁞&&⁞ y} // FullForm** *Out[19]//FullForm=* List[Rule[x, y], And[x, y]]

The most extreme case of characters that look alike but work differently occurs with vertical bars.

+ *form*	*character name*	*alias*	*interpretation*
$x \mid y$	keyboard |		Alternatives[x, y]
$x \mid y$	\[VerticalSeparator]	⦂|⦂	VerticalSeparator[x, y]
$x \mid y$	\[VerticalBar]	⦂␣|⦂	VerticalBar[x, y]
| x |	\[LeftBracketingBar]	⦂l|⦂	BracketingBar[x]
	\[RightBracketingBar]	⦂r|⦂	

Different types of vertical bars.

Notice that the alias for \[VerticalBar] is ⦂␣\|⦂, while the alias for the somewhat more common \[VerticalSeparator] is ⦂\|⦂. *Mathematica* often gives similar-looking characters similar aliases; it is a general convention that the aliases for the less commonly used characters are distinguished by having spaces at the beginning.

⦂*nnn*⦂	built-in alias for a common character
⦂␣*nnn*⦂	built-in alias for similar but less common character
⦂.*nnn*⦂	alias globally defined in a *Mathematica* session
⦂,*nnn*⦂	alias defined in a specific notebook

Conventions for special character aliases.

The notebook front end for *Mathematica* often allows you to set up your own aliases for special characters. If you want to, you can overwrite the built-in aliases. But the convention is to use aliases that begin with a dot or comma.

Note that whatever aliases you may use to enter special characters, the full names of the characters will always be used when the characters are stored in files.

■ 3.10.2 Names of Symbols and Mathematical Objects

Mathematica by default interprets any sequence of letters or letter-like forms as the name of a symbol.

All these are treated by *Mathematica* as symbols.	`In[1]:= {ξ, Σα, R∞, א, ℵ, ∠ABC, ■X, m…n}`
	`Out[1]= {ξ, Σα, R∞, א, ℵ, ∠ABC, ■X, m…n}`

form	character name	alias	interpretation
π	\[Pi]	⋮p⋮, ⋮pi⋮	equivalent to Pi
∞	\[Infinity]	⋮inf⋮	equivalent to Infinity
e	\[ExponentialE]	⋮ee⋮	equivalent to E
i	\[ImaginaryI]	⋮ii⋮	equivalent to I
j	\[ImaginaryJ]	⋮jj⋮	equivalent to I

Symbols with built-in meanings whose names do not start with capital English letters.

Essentially all symbols with built-in meanings in *Mathematica* have names that start with capital English letters. Among the exceptions are e and i, which correspond to E and I respectively.

Forms such as e are used for both input and output in `StandardForm`.	`In[2]:= {e ^ (2 π i), e ^ π}`
	`Out[2]= {1, eᵖⁱ}`

In `OutputForm` e is output as E.	`In[3]:= OutputForm[%]`
	`                     Pi`
	`Out[3]//OutputForm= {1, E  }`

In written material, it is standard to use very short names—often single letters—for most of the mathematical objects that one considers. But in *Mathematica*, it is usually better to use longer and more explicit names.

In written material you can always explain that a particular single-letter name means one thing in one place and another in another place. But in *Mathematica*, unless you use different contexts, a global symbol with a particular name will always be assumed to mean the same thing.

As a result, it is typically better to use longer names, which are more likely to be unique, and which describe more explicitly what they mean.

For variables to which no value will be assigned, or for local symbols, it is nevertheless convenient and appropriate to use short, often single-letter, names.

It is sensible to give the global function LagrangianL a long and explicit name. The local variables can be given short names.	`In[4]:= LagrangianL[φ_, μ_] = (□φ)² + μ² φ²`
	`Out[4]= μ² φ² + (□φ)²`

form	input	interpretation
x_n	x CTRL $\_$ n CTRL $\sqcup$ or $x\backslash\_n$	Subscript[x, n]
x_+	x CTRL $\_$ $+$ CTRL $\sqcup$ or $x\backslash\_+$	SubPlus[x]
x_-	x CTRL $\_$ $-$ CTRL $\sqcup$ or $x\backslash\_-$	SubMinus[x]
x_*	x CTRL $\_$ $*$ CTRL $\sqcup$ or $x\backslash\_*$	SubStar[x]
x^+	x CTRL $\wedge$ $+$ CTRL $\sqcup$ or $x\backslash\wedge+$	SuperPlus[x]
x^-	x CTRL $\wedge$ $-$ CTRL $\sqcup$ or $x\backslash\wedge-$	SuperMinus[x]
x^*	x CTRL $\wedge$ $*$ CTRL $\sqcup$ or $x\backslash\wedge*$	SuperStar[x]
$x^\dagger$	x CTRL $\wedge$ ⁝dg⁝ CTRL $\sqcup$ or $x\backslash\wedge\backslash$[Dagger]	SuperDagger[x]
$\bar{x}$	x CTRL $\&$ $\_$ CTRL $\sqcup$ or $x\backslash\&\_$	OverBar[x]
$\vec{x}$	x CTRL $\&$ ⁝vec⁝ CTRL $\sqcup$ or $x\backslash\&\backslash$[RightVector]	OverVector[x]
$\tilde{x}$	x CTRL $\&$ $\sim$ CTRL $\sqcup$ or $x\backslash\&\sim$	OverTilde[x]
$\hat{x}$	x CTRL $\&$ $\wedge$ CTRL $\sqcup$ or $x\backslash\&\wedge$	OverHat[x]
$\dot{x}$	x CTRL $\&$. CTRL $\sqcup$ or $x\backslash\&.$	OverDot[x]
$\underline{x}$	x CTRL $+$ $\_$ CTRL $\sqcup$ or $x\backslash+\_$	UnderBar[x]
x	StyleBox[x, FontWeight->"Bold"]	x

Creating objects with annotated names.

Note that with a notebook front end, you can typically change the style of text using menu items. Internally the result will be to insert StyleBox objects, but you do not need to do this explicitly.

option	typical default value	
SingleLetterItalics	Automatic	whether to use italics for single-letter symbol names

An option for cells in a notebook.

It is conventional in traditional mathematical notation that names consisting of single ordinary English letters are normally shown in italics, while other names are not. If you use TraditionalForm, then *Mathematica* will by default follow this convention. You can explicitly specify whether you want the convention followed by setting the SingleLetterItalics option for particular cells or cell styles.

■ 3.10.3 Letters and Letter-like Forms

Greek Letters

form	full name	aliases	form	full name	aliases
α	\[Alpha]	:a:, :alpha:	A	\[CapitalAlpha]	:A:, :Alpha:
β	\[Beta]	:b:, :beta:	B	\[CapitalBeta]	:B:, :Beta:
γ	\[Gamma]	:g:, :gamma:	Γ	\[CapitalGamma]	:G:, :Gamma:
δ	\[Delta]	:d:, :delta:	Δ	\[CapitalDelta]	:D:, :Delta:
ϵ	\[Epsilon]	:e:, :epsilon:	E	\[CapitalEpsilon]	:E:, :Epsilon:
ε	\[CurlyEpsilon]	:ce:, :cepsilon:			
ζ	\[Zeta]	:z:, :zeta:	Z	\[CapitalZeta]	:Z:, :Zeta:
η	\[Eta]	:h:, :et:, :eta:	H	\[CapitalEta]	:H:, :Et:, :Eta:
θ	\[Theta]	:q:, :th:, :theta:	Θ	\[CapitalTheta]	:Q:, :Th:, :Theta:
ϑ	\[CurlyTheta]	:cq:, :cth:, :ctheta:			
ι	\[Iota]	:i:, :iota:	I	\[CapitalIota]	:I:, :Iota:
κ	\[Kappa]	:k:, :kappa:	K	\[CapitalKappa]	:K:, :Kappa:
$\varkappa$	\[CurlyKappa]	:ck:, :ckappa:			
λ	\[Lambda]	:l:, :lambda:	Λ	\[CapitalLambda]	:L:, :Lambda:
μ	\[Mu]	:m:, :mu:	M	\[CapitalMu]	:M:, :Mu:
ν	\[Nu]	:n:, :nu:	N	\[CapitalNu]	:N:, :Nu:
ξ	\[Xi]	:x:, :xi:	Ξ	\[CapitalXi]	:X:, :Xi:
o	\[Omicron]	:om:, :omicron:	O	\[CapitalOmicron]	:Om:, :Omicron:
π	\[Pi]	:p:, :pi:	Π	\[CapitalPi]	:P:, :Pi:
ϖ	\[CurlyPi]	:cp:, :cpi:			
ρ	\[Rho]	:r:, :rho:	P	\[CapitalRho]	:R:, :Rho:
ϱ	\[CurlyRho]	:cr:, :crho:			
σ	\[Sigma]	:s:, :sigma:	Σ	\[CapitalSigma]	:S:, :Sigma:
ς	\[FinalSigma]	:fs:			
τ	\[Tau]	:t:, :tau:	T	\[CapitalTau]	:T:, :Tau:
υ	\[Upsilon]	:u:, :upsilon:	Υ	\[CapitalUpsilon]	:U:, :Upsilon:
			Υ	\[CurlyCapitalUpsilon]	:cU:, :cUpsilon:
ϕ	\[Phi]	:f:, :ph:, :phi:	Φ	\[CapitalPhi]	:F:, :Ph:, :Phi:
φ	\[CurlyPhi]	:j:, :cph:, :cphi:			
χ	\[Chi]	:c:, :ch:, :chi:	X	\[CapitalChi]	:C:, :Ch:, :Chi:
ψ	\[Psi]	:y:, :ps:, :psi:	Ψ	\[CapitalPsi]	:Y:, :Ps:, :Psi:
ω	\[Omega]	:o:, :w:, :omega:	Ω	\[CapitalOmega]	:O:, :W:, :Omega:
$\digamma$	\[Digamma]	:di:, :digamma:	F	\[CapitalDigamma]	:Di:, :Digamma:
$\varkoppa$	\[Koppa]	:ko:, :koppa:	Ϙ	\[CapitalKoppa]	:Ko:, :Koppa:
$\varstigma$	\[Stigma]	:sti:, :stigma:	Ϛ	\[CapitalStigma]	:Sti:, :Stigma:
$\sampi$	\[Sampi]	:sa:, :sampi:	Ϡ	\[CapitalSampi]	:Sa:, :Sampi:

The complete collection of Greek letters in *Mathematica*.

You can use Greek letters as the names of symbols. The only Greek letter with a built-in meaning in StandardForm is π, which *Mathematica* takes to stand for the symbol Pi.

Note that even though π on its own is assigned a built-in meaning, combinations such as $\pi 2$ or $x\pi$ have no built-in meanings.

The Greek letters Σ and Π look very much like the operators for sum and product. But as discussed above, these operators are different characters, entered as \[Sum] and \[Product] respectively.

Similarly, ϵ is different from the $\in$ operator \[Element], and μ is different from µ or \[Micro].

Some capital Greek letters such as \[CapitalAlpha] look essentially the same as capital English letters. *Mathematica* however treats them as different characters, and in TraditionalForm it uses \[CapitalBeta], for example, to denote the built-in function Beta.

Following common convention, lower-case Greek letters are rendered slightly slanted in the standard fonts provided with *Mathematica*, while capital Greek letters are unslanted.

Almost all Greek letters that do not look similar to English letters are widely used in science and mathematics. The **capital xi** Ξ is rare, though it is used to denote the cascade hyperon particles, the grand canonical partition function and regular language complexity. The **capital upsilon** Υ is also rare, though it is used to denote $b\bar{b}$ particles, as well as the vernal equinox.

Curly Greek letters are often assumed to have different meanings from their ordinary counterparts. Indeed, in pure mathematics a single formula can sometimes contain both curly and ordinary forms of a particular letter. The curly pi ϖ is rare, except in astronomy.

The **final sigma** ς is used for sigmas that appear at the ends of words in written Greek; it is not commonly used in technical notation.

The **digamma** $\digamma$, **koppa** $\koppa$, **stigma** ς and **sampi** $\sampi$ are archaic Greek letters. These letters provide a convenient extension to the usual set of Greek letters. They are sometimes needed in making correspondences with English letters. The digamma corresponds to an English w, and koppa to an English q. Digamma is occasionally used to denote the digamma function PolyGamma[x].

Variants of English Letters

form	full name	alias		form	full name	alias
l	\[ScriptL]	:scl:		ℂ	\[DoubleStruckCapitalC]	:dsC:
ℰ	\[ScriptCapitalE]	:scE:		ℝ	\[DoubleStruckCapitalR]	:dsR:
ℋ	\[ScriptCapitalH]	:scH:		ℚ	\[DoubleStruckCapitalQ]	:dsQ:
ℒ	\[ScriptCapitalL]	:scL:		ℤ	\[DoubleStruckCapitalZ]	:dsZ:
ℭ	\[GothicCapitalC]	:goC:		ℕ	\[DoubleStruckCapitalN]	:dsN:
ℌ	\[GothicCapitalH]	:goH:		ı	\[DotlessI]	
ℑ	\[GothicCapitalI]	:goI:		ȷ	\[DotlessJ]	
ℜ	\[GothicCapitalR]	:goR:		℘	\[WeierstrassP]	:wp:

Some commonly used variants of English letters.

By using menu items in the notebook front end, or explicit `StyleBox` objects, you can make changes in the font and style of ordinary text. However, such changes are usually discarded whenever you send input to the *Mathematica* kernel.

Script, gothic and double-struck characters are however treated as fundamentally different from their ordinary forms. This means that even though a C that is italic or a different size will be considered equivalent to an ordinary C when fed to the kernel, a double-struck ℂ will not.

Different styles and sizes of C are treated as the same by the kernel. But gothic and double-struck characters are treated as different.

```
In[1]:= C + 𝐶 + 𝐂 + ℭ + ℂ

Out[1]= 3 C + ℭ + ℂ
```

In standard mathematical notation, capital script and gothic letters are sometimes used interchangeably. The double-struck letters, sometimes called blackboard or openface letters, are conventionally used to denote specific sets. Thus, for example, ℂ conventionally denotes the set of complex numbers, and ℤ the set of integers.

Dotless i and j are not usually taken to be different in meaning from ordinary i and j; they are simply used when overscripts are being placed on the ordinary characters.

\[WeierstrassP] is a notation specifically used for the Weierstrass P function `WeierstrassP`.

full names	aliases	
\[ScriptA] – \[ScriptZ]	⫶sca⫶ – ⫶scz⫶	lower-case script letters
\[ScriptCapitalA] – \[ScriptCapitalZ]	⫶scA⫶ – ⫶scZ⫶	upper-case script letters
\[GothicA] – \[GothicZ]	⫶goa⫶ – ⫶goz⫶	lower-case gothic letters
\[GothicCapitalA] – \[GothicCapitalZ]	⫶goA⫶ – ⫶goZ⫶	upper-case gothic letters
\[DoubleStruckA] – \[DoubleStruckZ]	⫶dsa⫶ – ⫶dsz⫶	lower-case double-struck letters
\[DoubleStruckCapitalA] – \[DoubleStruckCapitalZ]	⫶dsA⫶ – ⫶dsZ⫶	upper-case double-struck letters

Complete alphabets of variant English letters.

Hebrew Letters

form	full name	alias		form	full name
ℵ	\[Aleph]	⫶al⫶		ℷ	\[Gimel]
ℶ	\[Bet]			ℸ	\[Dalet]

Hebrew characters.

Hebrew characters are used in mathematics in the theory of transfinite sets; $\aleph_0$ is for example used to denote the total number of integers.

Units and Letter-like Mathematical Symbols

form	full name	alias		form	full name	alias
μ	\[Micro]	:mi:		°	\[Degree]	:deg:
℧	\[Mho]	:mho:		∅	\[EmptySet]	:es:
Å	\[Angstrom]	:Ang:		∞	\[Infinity]	:inf:
ℏ	\[HBar]	:hb:		*e*	\[ExponentialE]	:ee:
¢	\[Cent]	:cent:		*i*	\[ImaginaryI]	:ii:
£	\[Sterling]			*j*	\[ImaginaryJ]	:jj:
€	\[Euro]			π	\[DoubledPi]	:pp:
¥	\[Yen]			γ	\[DoubledGamma]	:gg:

Units and letter-like mathematical symbols.

Mathematica treats ° or \[Degree] as the symbol Degree, so that, for example, 30° is equivalent to 30 Degree.

Note that μ, Å and ∅ are all distinct from the ordinary letters μ (\[Mu]), Å (\[CapitalARing]) and Ø (\[CapitalOSlash]).

Mathematica interprets ∞ as Infinity, *e* as E, and both *i* and *j* as I. The characters *e*, *i* and *j* are provided as alternatives to the usual upper-case letters E and I.

π and γ are not by default assigned meanings in StandardForm. You can therefore use π to represent a pi that will not automatically be treated as Pi. In TraditionalForm γ is interpreted as EulerGamma.

form	full name	alias		form	full name	alias
∂	\[PartialD]	:pd:		∇	\[Del]	:del:
d	\[DifferentialD]	:dd:		∑	\[Sum]	:sum:
D	\[CapitalDifferentialD]	:DD:		∏	\[Product]	:prod:

Operators that look like letters.

∇ is an operator while ℏ, ° and ¥ are ordinary symbols.

```
In[1]:= {∇ f, ℏ^2, 45°, 5000¥} // FullForm

Out[1]//FullForm= List[Del[f], Power[\[HBar], 2],
                    Times[45, Degree], Times[5000, \[Yen]]]
```

Shapes, Icons and Geometrical Constructs

form	full name	alias		form	full name	alias
▪	\[FilledVerySmallSquare]	:fvssq:		○	\[EmptySmallCircle]	:esci:
□	\[EmptySmallSquare]	:essq:		●	\[FilledSmallCircle]	:fsci:
▪	\[FilledSmallSquare]	:fssq:		◯	\[EmptyCircle]	:eci:
□	\[EmptySquare]	:esq:		⬤	\[GrayCircle]	:gci:
▦	\[GraySquare]	:gsq:		●	\[FilledCircle]	:fci:
■	\[FilledSquare]	:fsq:		△	\[EmptyUpTriangle]	
⬚	\[DottedSquare]			▲	\[FilledUpTriangle]	
▢	\[EmptyRectangle]			▽	\[EmptyDownTriangle]	
▪	\[FilledRectangle]			▼	\[FilledDownTriangle]	
◇	\[EmptyDiamond]			★	\[FivePointedStar]	:*5:
◆	\[FilledDiamond]			✶	\[SixPointedStar]	:*6:

Shapes.

Shapes are most often used as "dingbats" to emphasize pieces of text. But *Mathematica* treats them as letter-like forms, and also allows them to appear in the names of symbols.

In addition to shapes such as \[EmptySquare], there are characters such as \[Square] which are treated by *Mathematica* as operators rather than letter-like forms.

form	full name	alias		form	full name	aliases
✿	\[MathematicaIcon]	:math:		☺	\[HappySmiley]	:): , :-):
✺	\[KernelIcon]			☻	\[NeutralSmiley]	:-| :
♀	\[LightBulb]			☹	\[SadSmiley]	:-(:
⚠	\[WarningSign]			🤯	\[FreakedSmiley]	:-@:
⌚	\[WatchIcon]			𝔸	\[Wolf]	:wf: , :wolf:

Icons.

You can use icon characters just like any other letter-like forms.

In[1]:= **Expand[(θ + 𝔸)^4]**

Out[1]= $\theta^4 + 4\,\theta^3\,𝔸 + 6\,\theta^2\,𝔸^2 + 4\,\theta\,𝔸^3 + 𝔸^4$

form	full name		form	full name
∟	\[Angle]		⊀	\[SphericalAngle]
∟	\[RightAngle]		△	\[EmptyUpTriangle]
∡	\[MeasuredAngle]		⌀	\[Diameter]

Notation for geometrical constructs.

Since *Mathematica* treats characters like ∟ as letter-like forms, constructs like ∟BC are treated in *Mathematica* as single symbols.

Textual Elements

form	full name	alias		form	full name	alias
-	\[Dash]	:-:		′	\[Prime]	:':
—	\[LongDash]	:--:		″	\[DoublePrime]	:'':
•	\[Bullet]	:bu:		‵	\[ReversePrime]	:`:
¶	\[Paragraph]			‶	\[ReverseDoublePrime]	:``:
§	\[Section]			«	\[LeftGuillemet]	:g<<:
¿	\[DownQuestion]	:d?:		»	\[RightGuillemet]	:g>>:
¡	\[DownExclamation]	:d!:		…	\[Ellipsis]	:...:

Characters used for punctuation and annotation.

form	full name		form	full name	alias
©	\[Copyright]		†	\[Dagger]	:dg:
®	\[RegisteredTrademark]		‡	\[DoubleDagger]	:ddg:
™	\[Trademark]		♣	\[ClubSuit]	
♭	\[Flat]		◇	\[DiamondSuit]	
♮	\[Natural]		♡	\[HeartSuit]	
♯	\[Sharp]		♠	\[SpadeSuit]	

Other characters used in text.

form	full name	alias		form	full name	alias
-	\[HorizontalLine]	:hline:		‿	\[UnderParenthesis]	:u(:
'	\[VerticalLine]	:vline:		⁀	\[OverParenthesis]	:o(:
...	\[Ellipsis]	:...:		⎵	\[UnderBracket]	:u[:
⋯	\[CenterEllipsis]			⎴	\[OverBracket]	:o[:
⋮	\[VerticalEllipsis]			⏟	\[UnderBrace]	:u{:
⋰	\[AscendingEllipsis]			⏞	\[OverBrace]	:o{:
⋱	\[DescendingEllipsis]					

Characters used in building sequences and arrays.

The under and over braces grow to enclose the whole expression.

```
In[1]:= Underoverscript[Expand[(1 + x)^4],
                \[UnderBrace], \[OverBrace]]
```

$$Out[1]= \overbrace{1 + 4\,x + 6\,x^2 + 4\,x^3 + x^4}$$

Extended Latin Letters

Mathematica supports all the characters commonly used in Western European languages based on Latin scripts.

form	full name	alias	form	full name	alias
à	\[AGrave]	:a`:	À	\[CapitalAGrave]	:A`:
á	\[AAcute]	:a':	Á	\[CapitalAAcute]	:A':
â	\[AHat]	:a^:	Â	\[CapitalAHat]	:A^:
ã	\[ATilde]	:a~:	Ã	\[CapitalATilde]	:A~:
ä	\[ADoubleDot]	:a":	Ä	\[CapitalADoubleDot]	:A":
å	\[ARing]	:ao:	Å	\[CapitalARing]	:Ao:
ā	\[ABar]	:a-:	Ā	\[CapitalABar]	:A-:
ă	\[ACup]	:au:	Ă	\[CapitalACup]	:Au:
æ	\[AE]	:ae:	Æ	\[CapitalAE]	:AE:
ć	\[CAcute]	:c':	Ć	\[CapitalCAcute]	:C':
ç	\[CCedilla]	:c,:	Ç	\[CapitalCCedilla]	:C,:
č	\[CHacek]	:cv:	Č	\[CapitalCHacek]	:Cv:
è	\[EGrave]	:e`:	È	\[CapitalEGrave]	:E`:
é	\[EAcute]	:e':	É	\[CapitalEAcute]	:E':
ē	\[EBar]	:e-:	Ē	\[CapitalEBar]	:E-:
ê	\[EHat]	:e^:	Ê	\[CapitalEHat]	:E^:
ë	\[EDoubleDot]	:e":	Ë	\[CapitalEDoubleDot]	:E":
ě	\[ECup]	:eu:	Ě	\[CapitalECup]	:Eu:
ì	\[IGrave]	:i`:	Ì	\[CapitalIGrave]	:I`:
í	\[IAcute]	:i':	Í	\[CapitalIAcute]	:I':
î	\[IHat]	:i^:	Î	\[CapitalIHat]	:I^:
ï	\[IDoubleDot]	:i":	Ï	\[CapitalIDoubleDot]	:I":
ĭ	\[ICup]	:iu:	Ĭ	\[CapitalICup]	:Iu:
ð	\[Eth]	:d-:	Đ	\[CapitalEth]	:D-:
ł	\[LSlash]	:l/:	Ł	\[CapitalLSlash]	:L/:
ñ	\[NTilde]	:n~:	Ñ	\[CapitalNTilde]	:N~:
ò	\[OGrave]	:o`:	Ò	\[CapitalOGrave]	:O`:
ó	\[OAcute]	:o':	Ó	\[CapitalOAcute]	:O':
ô	\[OHat]	:o^:	Ô	\[CapitalOHat]	:O^:
õ	\[OTilde]	:o~:	Õ	\[CapitalOTilde]	:O~:
ö	\[ODoubleDot]	:o":	Ö	\[CapitalODoubleDot]	:O":
ő	\[ODoubleAcute]	:o'':	Ő	\[CapitalODoubleAcute]	:O'':
ø	\[OSlash]	:o/:	Ø	\[CapitalOSlash]	:O/:
š	\[SHacek]	:sv:	Š	\[CapitalSHacek]	:Sv:
ù	\[UGrave]	:u`:	Ù	\[CapitalUGrave]	:U`:
ú	\[UAcute]	:u':	Ú	\[CapitalUAcute]	:U':
û	\[UHat]	:u^:	Û	\[CapitalUHat]	:U^:
ü	\[UDoubleDot]	:u":	Ü	\[CapitalUDoubleDot]	:U":
ű	\[UDoubleAcute]	:u'':	Ű	\[CapitalUDoubleAcute]	:U'':
ý	\[YAcute]	:y':	Ý	\[CapitalYAcute]	:Y':
þ	\[Thorn]	:thn:	Þ	\[CapitalThorn]	:Thn:
ß	\[SZ]	:sz:, :ss:			

Variants of English letters.

Most of the characters shown are formed by adding diacritical marks to ordinary English letters. Exceptions include \[SZ] ß, used in German, and \[Thorn] þ and \[Eth] ð, used primarily in Old English.

You can make additional characters by explicitly adding diacritical marks yourself.

char CTRL-& *mark* CTRL-␣ or \(*char*\&*mark*\)	add a mark above a character
char CTRL-+ *mark* CTRL-␣ or \(*char*\+*mark*\)	add a mark below a character

Adding marks above and below characters.

form	alias	full name	
,	(keyboard character)	\[RawQuote]	acute accent
′	⦂′⦂	\[Prime]	acute accent
`	(keyboard character)	\[RawBackquote]	grave accent
\	⦂`⦂	\[ReversePrime]	grave accent
..	(keyboard characters)		umlaut or diaeresis
^	(keyboard character)	\[RawWedge]	circumflex or hat
○	⦂esc⦂	\[EmptySmallCircle]	ring
.	(keyboard character)	\[RawDot]	dot
~	(keyboard character)	\[RawTilde]	tilde
—	(keyboard character)	\[RawUnderscore]	bar or macron
ˇ	⦂hc⦂	\[Hacek]	hacek or check
˘	⦂bv⦂	\[Breve]	breve
⁀	⦂dbv⦂	\[DownBreve]	tie accent
″	⦂′′⦂	\[DoublePrime]	long umlaut
¸	⦂cd⦂	\[Cedilla]	cedilla

Diacritical marks to add to characters.

■ 3.10.4 Operators

Basic Mathematical Operators

form	full name	alias		form	full name	alias
×	\[Times]	:*:		×	\[Cross]	:cross:
÷	\[Divide]	:div:		±	\[PlusMinus]	:+-:
√	\[Sqrt]	:sqrt:		∓	\[MinusPlus]	:-+:

Some operators used in basic arithmetic and algebra.

Note that the × for \[Cross] is distinguished by being drawn slightly smaller than the × for \[Times].

$x \times y$	Times[x, y]	multiplication
$x \div y$	Divide[x, y]	division
$\sqrt{x}$	Sqrt[x]	square root
$x \times y$	Cross[x, y]	vector cross product
$\pm x$	PlusMinus[x]	(no built-in meaning)
$x \pm y$	PlusMinus[x, y]	(no built-in meaning)
$\mp x$	MinusPlus[x]	(no built-in meaning)
$x \mp y$	MinusPlus[x, y]	(no built-in meaning)

Interpretation of some operators in basic arithmetic and algebra.

Operators in Calculus

form	full name	alias		form	full name	alias
∇	\[Del]	:del:		∫	\[Integral]	:int:
∂	\[PartialD]	:pd:		∮	\[ContourIntegral]	:cint:
d	\[DifferentialD]	:dd:		∯	\[DoubleContourIntegral]	
Σ	\[Sum]	:sum:		∮	\[CounterClockwiseContourIntegral]	:cccint:
∏	\[Product]	:prod:		∮	\[ClockwiseContourIntegral]	:ccint:

Operators used in calculus.

~Logical and Other Connectives

form	full name	aliases		form	full name	alias
∧	\[And]	:&&:, :and:		⇒	\[Implies]	:=>:
∨	\[Or]	:||:, :or:		⥰	\[RoundImplies]	
¬	\[Not]	:!:, :not:		∴	\[Therefore]	:tf:
∈	\[Element]	:el:		∵	\[Because]	
∀	\[ForAll]	:fa:		⊢	\[RightTee]	
∃	\[Exists]	:ex:		⊣	\[LeftTee]	
∄	\[NotExists]	:!ex:		⊨	\[DoubleRightTee]	
⊻	\[Xor]	:xor:		⊨	\[DoubleLeftTee]	
⊼	\[Nand]	:nand:		∋	\[SuchThat]	:st:
⊽	\[Nor]	:nor:		|	\[VerticalSeparator]	:|:
				:	\[Colon]	:::

Operators used as logical connectives.

The operators $\wedge$, $\vee$ and $\neg$ are interpreted as corresponding to the built-in functions And, Or and Not, and are equivalent to the keyboard operators &&, || and !. The operators $\veebar$, $\barwedge$ and $\overline{\vee}$ correspond to the built-in functions Xor, Nand and Nor. Note that $\neg$ is a prefix operator.

$x \Rightarrow y$ and $x \Rrightarrow y$ are both taken to give the built-in function Implies[x, y]. $x \in y$ gives the built-in function Element[x, y].

This is interpreted using the built-in functions And and Implies.	$In[1]:=$ **3 < 4 ∧ x > 5 ⇒ y < 7**
	$Out[1]=$ Implies[x > 5, y < 7]

Mathematica supports most of the standard syntax used in mathematical logic. In *Mathematica*, however, the variables that appear in the quantifiers $\forall$, $\exists$ and $\nexists$ must appear as subscripts. If they appeared directly after the quantifier symbols then there could be a conflict with multiplication operations.

$\forall$ and $\exists$ are essentially prefix operators like ∂.	$In[2]:=$ **∀ₓ ∃ᵧ ϕ[x, y] // FullForm**
	$Out[2]//FullForm=$ ForAll[x, Exists[y, \[Phi][x, y]]]

Operators Used to Represent Actions

form	full name	alias		form	full name	alias
○	\[SmallCircle]	:sc:		∧	\[Wedge]	:^:
⊕	\[CirclePlus]	:c+:		∨	\[Vee]	:v:
⊖	\[CircleMinus]	:c-:		∪	\[Union]	:un:
⊗	\[CircleTimes]	:c*:		⊎	\[UnionPlus]	
⊙	\[CircleDot]	:c.:		∩	\[Intersection]	:inter:
◇	\[Diamond]	:dia:		⊓	\[SquareIntersection]	
·	\[CenterDot]	:.:		⊔	\[SquareUnion]	
*	\[Star]	:star:		∐	\[Coproduct]	:coprod:
≀	\[VerticalTilde]			⌢	\[Cap]	
\	\[Backslash]	:\:		⌣	\[Cup]	
				□	\[Square]	:sq:

Operators typically used to represent actions. All the operators except \[Square] are infix.

Following *Mathematica*'s usual convention, all the operators in the table above are interpreted to give functions whose names are exactly the names of the characters that appear in the operators.

The operators are interpreted as functions with corresponding names.

```
In[1]:= x ⊕ y ⌢ z // FullForm

Out[1]//FullForm= CirclePlus[x, Cap[y, z]]
```

All the operators in the table above, except for □, are infix, so that they must appear in between their operands.

Bracketing Operators

form	full name	alias		form	full name	alias
⌊	\[LeftFloor]	:lf:		⟨	\[LeftAngleBracket]	:<:
⌋	\[RightFloor]	:rf:		⟩	\[RightAngleBracket]	:>:
⌈	\[LeftCeiling]	:lc:		∤	\[LeftBracketingBar]	:l:
⌉	\[RightCeiling]	:rc:		∤	\[RightBracketingBar]	:r:
⟦	\[LeftDoubleBracket]	:[[:		∦	\[LeftDoubleBracketingBar]	:ll:
⟧	\[RightDoubleBracket]	:]]:		∦	\[RightDoubleBracketingBar]	:rll:

Characters used as bracketing operators.

$$\lfloor x \rfloor \qquad \text{Floor}[x]$$

$$\lceil x \rceil \qquad \text{Ceiling}[x]$$

$$m[\![i,j, \dots]\!] \qquad \text{Part}[m, i, j, \dots]$$

$$\langle x,y, \dots \rangle \qquad \text{AngleBracket}[x, y, \dots]$$

$$|x,y, \dots | \qquad \text{BracketingBar}[x, y, \dots]$$

$$\|x,y, \dots \| \qquad \text{DoubleBracketingBar}[x, y, \dots]$$

Interpretations of bracketing operators.

Operators Used to Represent Relations

form	full name	alias	form	full name	alias
==	\[Equal]	:==:	≠	\[NotEqual]	:!=:
=	\[LongEqual]	:l=:	≢	\[NotCongruent]	:!===:
≡	\[Congruent]	:===:	≁	\[NotTilde]	:!~:
∼	\[Tilde]	:~:	≉	\[NotTildeTilde]	:!~~:
≈	\[TildeTilde]	:~~:	≄	\[NotTildeEqual]	:!~=:
≃	\[TildeEqual]	:~=:	≇	\[NotTildeFullEqual]	:!~==:
≅	\[TildeFullEqual]	:~==:	≄	\[NotEqualTilde]	:!=~:
≊	\[EqualTilde]	:=~:	≠	\[NotHumpEqual]	:!h=:
≏	\[HumpEqual]	:h=:	≆	\[NotHumpDownHump]	
≎	\[HumpDownHump]		≭	\[NotCupCap]	
≍	\[CupCap]		∝	\[Proportional]	:prop:
≐	\[DotEqual]		∷	\[Proportion]	

Operators usually used to represent similarity or equivalence.

The special character == (or \[Equal]) is an alternative input form for ==.
≠ is used both for input and output.

```
In[1]:= {a == b, a == b, a != b, a ≠ b}

Out[1]= {a == b, a == b, a ≠ b, a ≠ b}
```

form	full name	alias	form	full name	alias
≥	\[GreaterEqual]	:>=:	≱	\[NotGreaterEqual]	:!>=:
≤	\[LessEqual]	:<=:	≰	\[NotLessEqual]	:!<=:
⩾	\[GreaterSlantEqual]	:>/:	⩾̸	\[NotGreaterSlantEqual]	:!>/:
⩽	\[LessSlantEqual]	:</:	⩽̸	\[NotLessSlantEqual]	:!</:
≧	\[GreaterFullEqual]		≧̸	\[NotGreaterFullEqual]	
≦	\[LessFullEqual]		≦̸	\[NotLessFullEqual]	
≳	\[GreaterTilde]	:>~:	≴	\[NotGreaterTilde]	:!>~:
≲	\[LessTilde]	:<~:	≴	\[NotLessTilde]	:!<~:
≫	\[GreaterGreater]		≫̸	\[NotGreaterGreater]	
≪	\[LessLess]		≪̸	\[NotLessLess]	
⋙	\[NestedGreaterGreater]		⋙̸	\[NotNestedGreaterGreater]	
⋘	\[NestedLessLess]		⋘̸	\[NotNestedLessLess]	
≷	\[GreaterLess]		≹	\[NotGreaterLess]	
≶	\[LessGreater]		≸	\[NotLessGreater]	
⋛	\[GreaterEqualLess]		≯	\[NotGreater]	:!>:
⋚	\[LessEqualGreater]		≮	\[NotLess]	:!<:

Operators usually used for ordering by magnitude.

form	full name	alias	form	full name	alias
⊂	\[Subset]	:sub:	⊄	\[NotSubset]	:!sub:
⊃	\[Superset]	:sup:	⊅	\[NotSuperset]	:!sup:
⊆	\[SubsetEqual]	:sub=:	⊈	\[NotSubsetEqual]	:!sub=:
⊇	\[SupersetEqual]	:sup=:	⊉	\[NotSupersetEqual]	:!sup=:
∈	\[Element]	:el:	∉	\[NotElement]	:!el:
∋	\[ReverseElement]	:mem:	∌	\[NotReverseElement]	:!mem:

Operators used for relations in sets.

form	full name		form	full name
≻	\[Succeeds]		⊁	\[NotSucceeds]
≺	\[Precedes]		⊀	\[NotPrecedes]
≽	\[SucceedsEqual]		⋡	\[NotSucceedsEqual]
≼	\[PrecedesEqual]		⋨	\[NotPrecedesTilde]
≽	\[SucceedsSlantEqual]		⋡	\[NotSucceedsSlantEqual]
≼	\[PrecedesSlantEqual]		⋠	\[NotPrecedesSlantEqual]
≿	\[SucceedsTilde]		⋩	\[NotSucceedsTilde]
≾	\[PrecedesTilde]		⋨	\[NotPrecedesEqual]
▷	\[RightTriangle]		⋫	\[NotRightTriangle]
◁	\[LeftTriangle]		⋪	\[NotLeftTriangle]
⊵	\[RightTriangleEqual]		⋭	\[NotRightTriangleEqual]
⊴	\[LeftTriangleEqual]		⋬	\[NotLeftTriangleEqual]
⧐	\[RightTriangleBar]		⧐̸	\[NotRightTriangleBar]
⧏	\[LeftTriangleBar]		⧏̸	\[NotLeftTriangleBar]
⊐	\[SquareSuperset]		⋣	\[NotSquareSuperset]
⊏	\[SquareSubset]		⋢	\[NotSquareSubset]
⊒	\[SquareSupersetEqual]		⋣	\[NotSquareSupersetEqual]
⊑	\[SquareSubsetEqual]		⋢	\[NotSquareSubsetEqual]

Operators usually used for other kinds of orderings.

form	full name	alias		form	full name	alias
∣	\[VerticalBar]	:␣|:		∤	\[NotVerticalBar]	:!|:
‖	\[DoubleVerticalBar]	:␣||:		∦	\[NotDoubleVerticalBar]	:!||:

Relational operators based on vertical bars.

Operators Based on Arrows and Vectors

Operators based on arrows are often used in pure mathematics and elsewhere to represent various kinds of transformations or changes.

$\rightarrow$ is equivalent to ->.

```
In[1]:= x + y /. x → 3
Out[1]= 3 + y
```

form	full name	alias		form	full name	alias
$\rightarrow$	\[Rule]	:->:		$\Rightarrow$	\[Implies]	:=>:
:$\rightarrow$	\[RuleDelayed]	::>:		$\Rightarrow$	\[RoundImplies]	

Arrow-like operators with built-in meanings in *Mathematica*.

form	full name	alias		form	full name
$\rightarrow$	\[RightArrow]	:_->:		$\uparrow$	\[UpArrow]
$\leftarrow$	\[LeftArrow]	:<-:		$\downarrow$	\[DownArrow]
$\leftrightarrow$	\[LeftRightArrow]	:<->:		$\updownarrow$	\[UpDownArrow]
$\longrightarrow$	\[LongRightArrow]	:-->:		$\uparrow$	\[UpTeeArrow]
$\longleftarrow$	\[LongLeftArrow]	:<--:		$\downarrow$	\[DownTeeArrow]
$\longleftrightarrow$	\[LongLeftRightArrow]	:<-->:		$\bar{\uparrow}$	\[UpArrowBar]
$\rightarrow$	\[ShortRightArrow]			$\downarrow$	\[DownArrowBar]
$\leftarrow$	\[ShortLeftArrow]			$\Uparrow$	\[DoubleUpArrow]
$\mapsto$	\[RightTeeArrow]			$\Downarrow$	\[DoubleDownArrow]
$\leftarrowtail$	\[LeftTeeArrow]			$\Updownarrow$	\[DoubleUpDownArrow]
$\rightarrowtail$	\[RightArrowBar]			$\rightleftarrows$	\[RightArrowLeftArrow]
$\leftarrowtail$	\[LeftArrowBar]			$\leftrightarrows$	\[LeftArrowRightArrow]
$\Rightarrow$	\[DoubleRightArrow]	:_=>:		$\updownarrows$	\[UpArrowDownArrow]
$\Leftarrow$	\[DoubleLeftArrow]	:_<=:		$\updownarrows$	\[DownArrowUpArrow]
$\Leftrightarrow$	\[DoubleLeftRightArrow]	:<=>:		$\searrow$	\[LowerRightArrow]
$\Longrightarrow$	\[DoubleLongRightArrow]	:==>:		$\swarrow$	\[LowerLeftArrow]
$\Longleftarrow$	\[DoubleLongLeftArrow]	:<==:		$\nwarrow$	\[UpperLeftArrow]
$\Longleftrightarrow$	\[DoubleLongLeftRightArrow]	:<==>:		$\nearrow$	\[UpperRightArrow]

Ordinary arrows.

form	full name	alias		form	full name
→	\[RightVector]	:vec:		↿	\[LeftUpVector]
←	\[LeftVector]			⇃	\[LeftDownVector]
↔	\[LeftRightVector]			⥮	\[LeftUpDownVector]
⇁	\[DownRightVector]			↾	\[RightUpVector]
↽	\[DownLeftVector]			⇂	\[RightDownVector]
⥯	\[DownLeftRightVector]			⥨	\[RightUpDownVector]
↦	\[RightTeeVector]			⥘	\[LeftUpTeeVector]
↤	\[LeftTeeVector]			⥙	\[LeftDownTeeVector]
↦	\[DownRightTeeVector]			⥚	\[RightUpTeeVector]
↤	\[DownLeftTeeVector]			⥛	\[RightDownTeeVector]
⇾	\[RightVectorBar]			⥔	\[LeftUpVectorBar]
⇽	\[LeftVectorBar]			⥕	\[LeftDownVectorBar]
⇾	\[DownRightVectorBar]			⥓	\[RightUpVectorBar]
⇽	\[DownLeftVectorBar]			⥖	\[RightDownVectorBar]
⇌	\[Equilibrium]	:equi:		⥮	\[UpEquilibrium]
⇋	\[ReverseEquilibrium]			⥯	\[ReverseUpEquilibrium]

Vectors and related arrows.

All the arrow and vector-like operators in *Mathematica* are infix.

In[2]:= **x ⇌ y ⥮ z**

Out[2]= x ⇌ y⥮z

form	full name	alias		form	full name
⊢	\[RightTee]	:rT:		⊨	\[DoubleRightTee]
⊣	\[LeftTee]	:lT:		⊨	\[DoubleLeftTee]
⊥	\[UpTee]	:uT:			
⊤	\[DownTee]	:dT:			

Tees.

■ 3.10.5 Structural Elements and Keyboard Characters

full name	alias		full name	alias
\[InvisibleComma]	⍽,⍽		\[AlignmentMarker]	⍽am⍽
\[InvisibleApplication]	⍽@⍽		\[NoBreak]	⍽nb⍽
\[InvisibleSpace]	⍽is⍽		\[Null]	⍽null⍽

Invisible characters.

In the input there is an invisible
comma between the 1 and 2.

```
In[1]:= m₁₂
Out[1]= m_{1,2}
```

Here there is an invisible space
between the x and y, interpreted as
multiplication.

```
In[2]:= FullForm[xy]
Out[2]//FullForm= Times[x, y]
```

\[Null] does not display, but can take
modifications such as superscripts.

```
In[3]:= \!\(f[x, \[Null]\^a]\)
Out[3]= f[x, ᵃ]
```

The \[AlignmentMarker] does not
display, but shows how to line up the
elements of the column.

```
In[4]:= GridBox[{{"b \[AlignmentMarker]+ c + d"},
                  {"a + b \[AlignmentMarker]+ c"}},
             ColumnAlignments->"\[AlignmentMarker]"] // DisplayForm
```

$$Out[4]//DisplayForm= \begin{array}{l} b + c + d \\ a + b + c \end{array}$$

full name	alias		full name	alias
\[VeryThinSpace]	⍽␣⍽		\[NegativeVeryThinSpace]	⍽-␣⍽
\[ThinSpace]	⍽␣␣⍽		\[NegativeThinSpace]	⍽-␣␣⍽
\[MediumSpace]	⍽␣␣␣⍽		\[NegativeMediumSpace]	⍽-␣␣␣⍽
\[ThickSpace]	⍽␣␣␣␣⍽		\[NegativeThickSpace]	⍽-␣␣␣␣⍽
\[InvisibleSpace]	⍽is⍽		\[NonBreakingSpace]	⍽nbs⍽
\[NewLine]			\[IndentingNewLine]	⍽nl⍽

Spacing and newline characters.

form	full name	alias	form	full name	alias
■	\[SelectionPlaceholder]	⍽spl⍽	□	\[Placeholder]	⍽pl⍽

Characters used in buttons.

In the buttons in a palette, you often want to set up a template with placeholders to indicate where expressions should be inserted. \[SelectionPlaceholder] marks the position where an expression that is currently selected should be inserted when the contents of the button are pasted. \[Placeholder] marks other positions where subsequent expressions can be inserted. The TAB key will take you from one such position to the next.

form	full name	alias		form	full name	alias
␣	\[SpaceIndicator]	:space:		⌣	\[RoundSpaceIndicator]	
↵	\[ReturnIndicator]	:ret:		CTRL	\[ControlKey]	:ctrl:
RET	\[ReturnKey]	:_ret:		CMD	\[CommandKey]	:cmd:
ENT	\[EnterKey]	:ent:		{	\[LeftModified]	:[:
ESC	\[EscapeKey]	:_esc:		]	\[RightModified]	:]:
:	\[AliasIndicator]	:esc:		⌘	\[CloverLeaf]	:cl:

Representations of keys on a keyboard.

In describing how to enter input into *Mathematica*, it is sometimes useful to give explicit representations for keys you should press. You can do this using characters like ↵ and ESC. Note that ␣ and ⌣ are actually treated as spacing characters by *Mathematica*.

This string shows how to type α².

```
In[5]:= "\[EscapeKey]a\[EscapeKey]
        \[ControlKey]\[LeftModified]^\[RightModified]2
        \[ControlKey]\[LeftModified]\[SpaceIndicator]\[RightModified]"
```

Out[5]= ESC a ESC CTRL{ ^ }2 CTRL{ ␣ }

form	full name		form	full name
⋱	\[Continuation]		■	\[SkeletonIndicator]
≪	\[LeftSkeleton]		▱	\[ErrorIndicator]
≫	\[RightSkeleton]			

Characters generated in *Mathematica* output.

Mathematica uses a \[Continuation] character to indicate that the number continues onto the next line.

```
In[6]:= 60!
```

Out[6]= 8320987112741390144276341183223364380754172606361⋱
        245952449277696409600000000000000

form	full name		form	full name
	\[RawTab]		/	\[RawSlash]
	\[NewLine]		:	\[RawColon]
	\[RawReturn]		;	\[RawSemicolon]
	\[RawSpace]		<	\[RawLess]
!	\[RawExclamation]		=	\[RawEqual]
"	\[RawDoubleQuote]		>	\[RawGreater]
#	\[RawNumberSign]		?	\[RawQuestion]
$	\[RawDollar]		@	\[RawAt]
%	\[RawPercent]		[	\[RawLeftBracket]
&	\[RawAmpersand]		\	\[RawBackslash]
'	\[RawQuote]		]	\[RawRightBracket]
(	\[RawLeftParenthesis]		^	\[RawWedge]
)	\[RawRightParenthesis]		_	\[RawUnderscore]
*	\[RawStar]		`	\[RawBackquote]
+	\[RawPlus]		{	\[RawLeftBrace]
,	\[RawComma]		|	\[RawVerticalBar]
−	\[RawDash]		}	\[RawRightBrace]
.	\[RawDot]		~	\[RawTilde]

Raw keyboard characters.

The fonts that are distributed with *Mathematica* contain their own renderings of many ordinary keyboard characters. The reason for this is that standard system fonts often do not contain appropriate renderings. For example, ^ and ~ are often drawn small and above the centerline, while for clarity in *Mathematica* they must be drawn larger and centered on the centerline.

Appendix

This appendix gives a definitive summary of the complete Mathematica system. Most of what it contains you will never need to know for any particular application of Mathematica.

You should realize that this appendix describes all the features of Mathematica, independent of their importance in typical usage.

Other parts of this book are organized along pedagogical lines, emphasizing important points, and giving details only when they are needed.

This appendix gives all the details of every feature. As a result, you will often find obscure details discussed alongside very common and important functions. Just remember that this appendix is intended for reference purposes, not for sequential reading. Do not be put off by the complexity of some of what you see; you will almost certainly never have to use it. But if you do end up having to use it, you will probably be happy that it is there.

By experimenting with Mathematica, you may find features that go beyond what is described in this appendix. You should not use any such features: there is no certainty that features which are not documented will continue to be supported in future versions of Mathematica.

Appendix

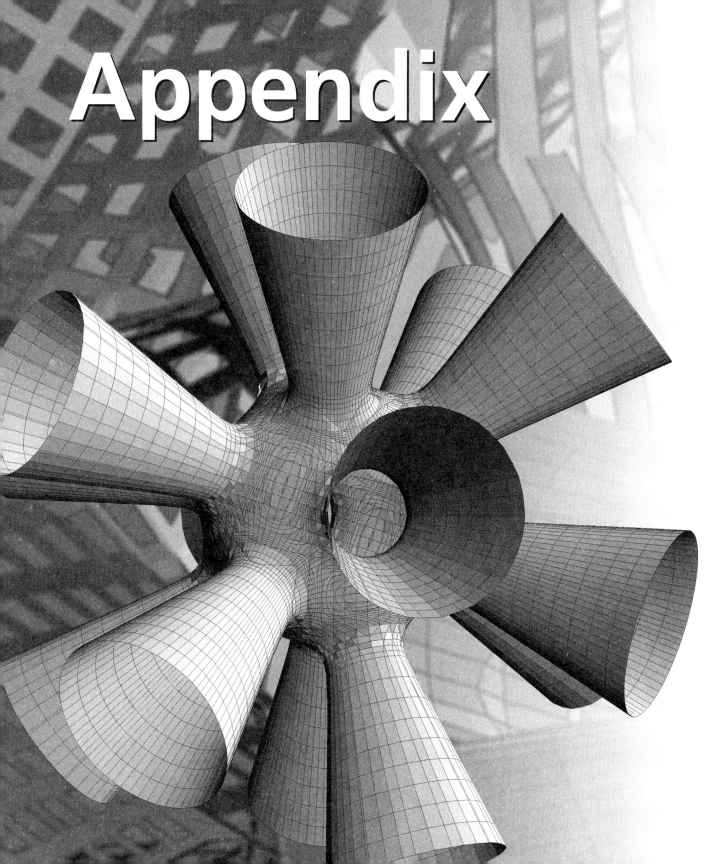

Mathematica Reference Guide

A.1 Basic Objects

■ A.1.1 Expressions

Expressions are the main type of data in *Mathematica*.

Expressions can be written in the form $h[e_1, e_2, \dots]$. The object h is known generically as the *head* of the expression. The e_i are termed the *elements* of the expression. Both the head and the elements may themselves be expressions.

The *parts* of an expression can be referred to by numerical indices. The head has index 0; element e_i has index i. Part[*expr*, i] or *expr*[[i]] gives the part of *expr* with index i. Negative indices count from the end.

Part[*expr*, i_1, i_2, $\dots$], *expr*[[i_1, i_2, $\dots$]] or Extract[*expr*, {i_1, i_2, $\dots$ }] gives the piece of *expr* found by successively extracting parts of subexpressions with indices i_1, i_2, $\dots$. If you think of expressions as trees, the indices specify which branch to take at each node as you descend from the root.

The pieces of an expression that are specified by giving a sequence of exactly n indices are defined to be at *level* n in the expression. You can use levels to determine the domain of application of functions like Map. Level 0 corresponds to the whole expression.

The *depth* of an expression is defined to be the maximum number of indices needed to specify any part of the expression, plus one. A negative level number $-n$ refers to all parts of an expression that have depth n.

■ A.1.2 Symbols

Symbols are the basic named objects in *Mathematica*.

The name of a symbol must be a sequence of letters, letter-like forms and digits, not starting with a digit. Upper- and lower-case letters are always distinguished in *Mathematica*.

aaaaa	user-defined symbol
Aaaaa	system-defined symbol
$Aaaa	global or internal system-defined symbol
aaaa$	symbol renamed in a scoping construct
aa$nn	unique local symbol generated in a module

Conventions for symbol names.

Essentially all system-defined symbols have names that contain only ordinary English letters, together with numbers and $. The exceptions are π, ∞, ℂ, ⅈ and ⅉ.

System-defined symbols conventionally have names that consist of one or more complete English words. The first letter of each word is capitalized, and the words are run together.

Once created, an ordinary symbol in *Mathematica* continues to exist unless it is explicitly removed using `Remove`. However, symbols created automatically in scoping constructs such as `Module` carry the attribute `Temporary` which specifies that they should automatically be removed as soon as they no longer appear in any expression.

When a new symbol is to be created, *Mathematica* first applies any value that has been assigned to `$NewSymbol` to strings giving the name of the symbol, and the context in which the symbol would be created.

If the message `General::newsym` is switched on, then *Mathematica* reports new symbols that are created. This message is switched off by default. Symbols created automatically in scoping constructs are not reported.

If the message `General::spell` is switched on, then *Mathematica* prints a warning if the name of a new symbol is close to the names of one or more existing symbols.

■ A.1.3 Contexts

The full name of any symbol in *Mathematica* consists of two parts: a *context*, and a *short name*. The full name is written in the form *context`name*. The context *context`* can contain the same characters as the short name. It may also contain any number of context mark characters `, and must end with a context mark.

At any point in a *Mathematica* session, there is a *current context* `$Context` and a *context search path* `$ContextPath` consisting of a list of contexts. Symbols in the current context, or in contexts on the context search path can be specified by giving only their short names.

name	search `$Context`, then `$ContextPath`; create in `$Context` if necessary
`*name*	search `$Context` only; create there if necessary
context`name	search *context* only; create there if necessary
`*context`name*	search `$Context`*context* only; create there if necessary

Contexts used for various specifications of symbols.

With *Mathematica* packages, it is conventional to associate contexts whose names correspond to the names of the packages. Packages typically use `BeginPackage` and `EndPackage` to define objects in the appropriate context, and to add the context to the global `$ContextPath`. `EndPackage` prints a warning about any symbols that were created in a package but which are "shadowed" by existing symbols on the context search path.

The context is included in the printed form of a symbol only if it would be needed to specify the symbol *at the time of printing*.

■ A.1.4 Atomic Objects

All expressions in *Mathematica* are ultimately made up from a small number of basic or atomic types of objects.

These objects have heads which are symbols that can be thought of as "tagging" their types. The objects contain "raw data", which can usually be accessed only by functions specific to the particular type of object. You can extract the head of the object using `Head`, but you cannot directly extract any of its other parts.

Symbol	symbol (extract name using `SymbolName`)
String	character string `"cccc"` (extract characters using `Characters`)
Integer	integer (extract digits using `IntegerDigits`)
Real	approximate real number (extract digits using `RealDigits`)
Rational	rational number (extract parts using `Numerator` and `Denominator`)
Complex	complex number (extract parts using `Re` and `Im`)

Atomic objects.

Atomic objects in *Mathematica* are considered to have depth 0 and yield `True` when tested with `AtomQ`.

As an optimization for some special kinds of computations, the raw data in *Mathematica* atomic objects can be given explicitly using `Raw[`*head*`, "`*hexstring*`"]`. The data is specified as a string of hexadecimal digits, corresponding to an array of bytes. When no special output form exists, `InputForm` prints special objects using `Raw`. *The behavior of* `Raw` *differs from one implementation of Mathematica to another; its general use is strongly discouraged.*

■ A.1.5 Numbers

Integer	integer *nnnn*
Real	approximate real number *nnn.nnn*
Rational	rational number *nnn/nnn*
Complex	complex number *nnn* + *nnn* I

Basic types of numbers.

All numbers in *Mathematica* can contain any number of digits. *Mathematica* does exact computations when possible with integers and rational numbers, and with complex numbers whose real and imaginary parts are integers or rational numbers.

There are two types of approximate real numbers in *Mathematica*: *arbitrary precision* and *machine precision*. In manipulating arbitrary-precision numbers, *Mathematica* always tries to modify the precision so as to ensure that all digits actually given are correct.

With machine-precision numbers, all computations are done to the same fixed precision, so some digits given may not be correct.

Unless otherwise specified, *Mathematica* treats as machine-precision numbers all approximate real numbers that lie between $MinMachineNumber and $MaxMachineNumber and that are input with less than $MachinePrecision digits.

In InputForm, *Mathematica* prints machine-precision numbers with $MachinePrecision digits, except when trailing digits are zero.

In any implementation of *Mathematica*, the magnitudes of numbers (except 0) must lie between $MinNumber and $MaxNumber. Numbers with magnitudes outside this range are represented by Underflow[ ] and Overflow[ ].

■ A.1.6 Character Strings

Character strings in *Mathematica* can contain any sequence of characters. They are input in the form "*ccccc*".

The individual characters can be printable ASCII (with character codes between 32 and 126), or in general any 8- or 16-bit characters. *Mathematica* uses the Unicode character encoding for 16-bit characters.

In input form, 16-bit characters are represented when possible in the form \[*name*], and otherwise as \:*nnnn*.

Null bytes can appear at any point within *Mathematica* strings.

A.2 Input Syntax

■ A.2.1 Entering Characters

+ ■ Enter it directly (e.g. +)

■ Enter it by full name (e.g. \[Alpha])

■ Enter it by alias (e.g. :a:) (notebook front end only)

■ Enter it by choosing from a palette (notebook front end only)

■ Enter it by character code (e.g. \053)

Typical ways to enter characters.

All printable ASCII characters can be entered directly. Those that are not alphanumeric are assigned explicit names in *Mathematica*, allowing them to be entered even on keyboards where they do not explicitly appear.

	\[RawSpace]	;	\[RawSemicolon]
!	\[RawExclamation]	<	\[RawLess]
"	\[RawDoubleQuote]	=	\[RawEqual]
#	\[RawNumberSign]	>	\[RawGreater]
$	\[RawDollar]	?	\[RawQuestion]
%	\[RawPercent]	@	\[RawAt]
&	\[RawAmpersand]	[	\[RawLeftBracket]
'	\[RawQuote]	\	\[RawBackslash]
(	\[RawLeftParenthesis]	]	\[RawRightBracket]
)	\[RawRightParenthesis]	^	\[RawWedge]
*	\[RawStar]	_	\[RawUnderscore]
+	\[RawPlus]	`	\[RawBackquote]
,	\[RawComma]	{	\[RawLeftBrace]
−	\[RawDash]	|	\[RawVerticalBar]
.	\[RawDot]	}	\[RawRightBrace]
/	\[RawSlash]	~	\[RawTilde]
:	\[RawColon]		

Full names for non-alphanumeric printable ASCII characters.

All characters which are entered into the *Mathematica* kernel are interpreted according to the setting for the `CharacterEncoding` option for the stream from which they came.

In the *Mathematica* front end, characters entered on the keyboard are interpreted according to the current setting of the `CharacterEncoding` option for the current notebook.

\[*Name*]	a character with the specified full name
nnn	a character with octal code *nnn*
\.*nn*	a character with hexadecimal code *nn*
\:*nnnn*	a character with hexadecimal code *nnnn*

Ways to enter characters.

Codes for characters can be generated using `ToCharacterCode`. The Unicode standard is followed, with various extensions.

8-bit characters have codes less than 256; 16-bit characters have codes between 256 and 65535. Approximately 750 characters are assigned explicit names in *Mathematica*. Other characters must be entered using their character codes.

\\	single backslash (decimal code 92)
\b	backspace or CONTROL-H (decimal code 8)
\t	tab or CONTROL-I (decimal code 9)
\n	newline or CONTROL-J (decimal code 10; full name \[NewLine])
\f	form feed or CONTROL-L (decimal code 12)
\r	carriage return or CONTROL-M (decimal code 13)
\000	null byte (code 0)

Some special 8-bit characters.

■ A.2.2 Types of Input Syntax

This appendix describes the standard input syntax used by *Mathematica*. This input syntax is the one used by default in `InputForm` and `StandardForm`. You can modify the syntax by making definitions for `MakeExpression[`*expr*`, `*form*`]`.

Options can be set to specify what form of input should be accepted by a particular cell in a notebook or from a particular stream.

The input syntax in `TraditionalForm`, for example, is different from that in `InputForm` and `StandardForm`.

In general, what input syntax does is to determine how a particular string or collection of boxes should be interpreted as an expression. When boxes are set up, say with the notebook front end, there can be hidden `InterpretationBox` or `TagBox` objects which modify the interpretation of the boxes.

■ A.2.3 Character Strings

"*characters*"	a character string
\"	a literal " in a character string
\\	a literal \ in a character string
\< ... \>	a substring in which newlines are interpreted literally
\!\(... \)	a substring representing two-dimensional boxes

Entering character strings.

Character strings can contain any sequence of 8- or 16-bit characters. Characters entered by name or character code are stored the same as if they were entered directly.

Single newlines followed by spaces or tabs are converted to a single space when a string is entered, unless these characters occur within \< ... \>, in which case they are left unchanged.

Within \!\(... \) any box structures represented using backslash sequences can be used.

■ A.2.4 Symbol Names and Contexts

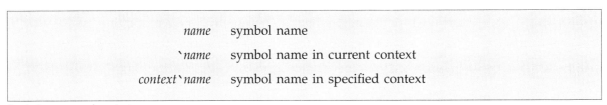

name	symbol name
`*name*	symbol name in current context
context`*name*	symbol name in specified context

Symbol names and contexts.

Symbol names and contexts can contain any characters that are treated by *Mathematica* as letters or letter-like forms. They can contain digits but cannot start with them.

■ A.2.5 Numbers

digits	integer
digits.*digits*	approximate number
base^^*digits*	integer in specified base
base^^*digits*.*digits*	approximate number in specified base
mantissa*^*n*	scientific notation ($mantissa \times 10^n$)
base^^*mantissa**^*n*	scientific notation in specified base ($mantissa \times base^n$)
number`	machine-precision approximate number
number`*s*	arbitrary-precision number with precision *s*
number``*s*	arbitrary-precision number with accuracy *s*

Input forms for numbers.

Numbers can be entered with the notation *base*^^*digits* in any base from 2 to 36. The base itself is given in decimal. For bases larger than 10, additional digits are chosen from the letters a–z or A–Z. Upper- and lower-case letters are equivalent for these purposes. Floating-point numbers can be specified by including . in the *digits* sequence.

In scientific notation, *mantissa* can contain ` marks. The exponent *n* must always be an integer, specified in decimal.

The precision or accuracy *s* can be any real number; it does not need to be an integer.

In the form *base*^^*number*`*s* the precision *s* is given in decimal, but it gives the effective number of digits of precision in the specified base, not in base 10.

An approximate number *x* is taken to be machine precision if the number of digits given in it is Ceiling[$MachinePrecision] + 1 or less. If more digits are given, then *x* is taken to be an arbitrary-precision number. The accuracy of *x* is taken to be the number of digits that appear to the right of the decimal point, while its precision is taken to be Log[10, Abs[*x*]] + Accuracy[*x*].

A number entered in the form 0``*s* is taken to have precision Indeterminate and accuracy *s*.

■ A.2.6 Bracketed Objects

Bracketed objects use explicit left and right delimiters to indicate their extent. They can appear anywhere within *Mathematica* input, and can be nested in any way.

The delimiters in bracketed objects are *matchfix operators*. But since these delimiters explicitly enclose all operands, no precedence need be assigned to such operators.

(* *any text* *)	comment
(*expr*)	parenthesization: grouping of input

Bracketed objects without comma-separated elements.

Comments can be nested, and can continue for any number of lines. They can contain any 8- or 16-bit characters.

Parentheses must enclose a single complete expression; neither (e, e) nor $(\ )$ are allowed.

$\{e_1, e_2, \ldots\}$	`List[`$e_1, e_2, \ldots$ `]`
$\langle e_1, e_2, \ldots \rangle$	`AngleBracket[`$e_1, e_2, \ldots$ `]`
$\lfloor expr \rfloor$	`Floor[`$expr$`]`
$\lceil expr \rceil$	`Ceiling[`$expr$`]`
$\lvert e_1, e_2, \ldots \rvert$	`BracketingBar[`$e_1, e_2, \ldots$ `]`
$\lVert e_1, e_2, \ldots \rVert$	`DoubleBracketingBar[`$e_1, e_2, \ldots$ `]`
\(*input*\)	input or grouping of boxes

Bracketed objects that allow comma-separated elements.

Throughout this book the notation ... is used to stand for any sequence of expressions.

$\{e_1, e_2, \ldots\}$ can include any number of elements, with successive elements separated by commas.

$\{\ \}$ is `List[ ]`, a list with zero elements.

$\langle e_1, e_2, \ldots \rangle$ can be entered as `\[LeftAngleBracket]` $e_1, e_2, \ldots$ `\[RightAngleBracket]`.

The character `\[InvisibleComma]` can be used interchangeably with ordinary commas; the only difference is that `\[InvisibleComma]` will not be displayed.

When the delimiters are special characters, it is a convention that they are named `\[Left`*Name*`]` and `\[Right`*Name*`]`.

`\( ... \)` is used to enter boxes using one-dimensional strings. Note that within the outermost `\( ... \)` in a piece of input the syntax used is slightly different from outside, as described on page 1036.

$h[e_1, e_2, \ldots]$	standard expression
$e[[i_1, i_2, \ldots]]$	$\text{Part}[e, i_1, i_2, \ldots]$
$e[\![\, i_1, i_2, \ldots \,]\!]$	$\text{Part}[e, i_1, i_2, \ldots]$

Bracketed objects with heads.

Bracketed objects with heads explicitly delimit all their operands except the head. A precedence must be assigned to define the extent of the head.

The precedence of $h[e]$ is high enough that $!h[e]$ is interpreted as $\text{Not}[h[e]]$. However, $h\_s[e]$ is interpreted as $(h\_s)[e]$.

■ A.2.7 Operator Input Forms

Characters that are not letters, letter-like forms or structural elements are treated by *Mathematica* as *operators*. *Mathematica* has built-in rules for interpreting all operators. The functions to which these operators correspond may or may not, however, have built-in evaluation or other rules. Cases in which built-in meanings are by default defined are indicated by ◁ in the tables below.

Operators that construct two-dimensional boxes—all of which have names beginning with back-slash—can only be used inside \(... \). The table below gives the interpretations of these operators within \!\(... \). Page 1037 gives interpretations when no \! is included.

expr and *expr*$_i$	any expression
symb	any symbol
patt	any pattern object
string and *string*$_i$	"*cccc*" or a sequence of letters, letter-like forms and digits
filename	like *string*, but can include additional characters described below
◁	built-in meanings exist

Objects used in the tables of operator input forms.

operator form	full form	grouping	
forms representing numbers (see page 1021)			◁
forms representing symbols (see page 1020)			◁
forms representing character strings (see page 1020)			◁
expr::*string*	MessageName[*expr*, "*string*"]		◁
expr::*string*$_1$::*string*$_2$	MessageName[*expr*, "*string*$_1$", "*string*$_2$"]		◁
forms containing # *(see page 1030)*			◁
forms containing % *(see page 1030)*			◁
forms containing _ *(see page 1030)*			◁
<< *filename*	Get["*filename*"]		◁
$\overset{expr_2}{expr_1}$	Overscript[*expr*$_1$, *expr*$_2$]	$\binom{e}{e}$	
expr$_1$ \& *expr*$_2$	Overscript[*expr*$_1$, *expr*$_2$]	$e\backslash\&(e\backslash\&e)$	
$\underset{expr_2}{expr_1}$	Underscript[*expr*$_1$, *expr*$_2$]	$\binom{e}{e}$	
expr$_1$ \+ *expr*$_2$	Underscript[*expr*$_1$, *expr*$_2$]	$e\backslash+(e\backslash+e)$	
$\overset{expr_3}{\underset{expr_2}{expr_1}}$	Underoverscript[*expr*$_1$, *expr*$_2$, *expr*$_3$]		
expr$_1$ \+ *expr*$_2$ \% *expr*$_3$	Underoverscript[*expr*$_1$, *expr*$_2$, *expr*$_3$]		
expr$_1$ \& *expr*$_2$ \% *expr*$_3$	Underoverscript[*expr*$_1$, *expr*$_3$, *expr*$_2$]		
expr$_{1\,expr_2}$	Subscript[*expr*$_1$, *expr*$_2$]	$e_{(e_e)}$	
expr$_1$ _ *expr*$_2$	Subscript[*expr*$_1$, *expr*$_2$]	$e\backslash\_(e\backslash\_e)$	
expr$_1$ _ *expr*$_2$ \% *expr*$_3$	Power[Subscript[*expr*$_1$, *expr*$_2$], *expr*$_3$]		◁
\!*boxes*	(interpreted version of *boxes*)		
expr$_1$?*expr*$_2$	PatternTest[*expr*$_1$, *expr*$_2$]		◁
expr$_1$[*expr*$_2$, ...]	*expr*$_1$[*expr*$_2$, ...]	$(e[e])[e]$	◁
expr$_1$[[*expr*$_2$, ...]]	Part[*expr*$_1$, *expr*$_2$, ...]	$(e[[e]])[[e]]$	◁
expr$_1$⟦*expr*$_2$, ... ⟧	Part[*expr*$_1$, *expr*$_2$, ...]	$(e⟦e⟧)⟦e⟧$	◁
expr$_{1\,⟦expr_2,...⟧}$	Part[*expr*$_1$, *expr*$_2$, ...]	$(e_{⟦e⟧})_{⟦e⟧}$	◁
*expr	(boxes constructed from *expr*)		
expr++	Increment[*expr*]		◁
expr--	Decrement[*expr*]		◁

Operator input forms, in order of decreasing precedence, part one.

operator form	full form	grouping	
`++`*expr*	`PreIncrement[`*expr*`]`		◁
`--`*expr*	`PreDecrement[`*expr*`]`		◁
expr$_1$ `@` *expr*$_2$	*expr*$_1$`[`*expr*$_2$`]`	e `@` (e `@` e)	◁
expr$_1$ *expr*$_2$ (invisible application, input as *expr*$_1$ `:@:` *expr*$_2$)			◁
	expr$_1$`[`*expr*$_2$`]`		
expr$_1$ `~` *expr*$_2$ `~` *expr*$_3$	*expr*$_2$`[`*expr*$_1$`, `*expr*$_3$`]`	(e `~` e `~` e) `~` e `~` e	◁
expr$_1$ `/@` *expr*$_2$	`Map[`*expr*$_1$`, `*expr*$_2$`]`	e `/@` (e `/@` e)	◁
expr$_1$ `//@` *expr*$_2$	`MapAll[`*expr*$_1$`, `*expr*$_2$`]`	e `//@` (e `//@` e)	◁
expr$_1$ `@@` *expr*$_2$	`Apply[`*expr*$_1$`, `*expr*$_2$`]`	e `@@` (e `@@` e)	◁
expr$_1$ `@@@` *expr*$_2$	`Apply[`*expr*$_1$`, `*expr*$_2$`, {1}]`	e `@@@` (e `@@@` e)	◁
expr`!`	`Factorial[`*expr*`]`		◁
expr`!!`	`Factorial2[`*expr*`]`		◁
expr`'`	`Derivative[1][`*expr*`]`		◁
expr`''` ... `'` (*n* times)	`Derivative[`*n*`][`*expr*`]`		◁
expr$_1$ `<>` *expr*$_2$ `<>` *expr*$_3$	`StringJoin[`*expr*$_1$`, `*expr*$_2$`, `*expr*$_3$`]`	e `<>` e `<>` e	◁
expr$_1$ `^` *expr*$_2$	`Power[`*expr*$_1$`, `*expr*$_2$`]`	e`^`(e`^`e)	◁
expr$_1$^{expr_2}	`Power[`*expr*$_1$`, `*expr*$_2$`]`	$e^{(e^e)}$	◁
expr$_{1\ expr_2}^{\ expr_3}$	`Power[Subscript[`*expr*$_1$`, `*expr*$_2$`], `*expr*$_3$`]`		◁
expr$_1$ `\^` *expr*$_2$ `\%` *expr*$_3$	`Power[Subscript[`*expr*$_1$`, `*expr*$_3$`], `*expr*$_2$`]`		◁
vertical arrow and vector operators			
$\sqrt{}$*expr*	`Sqrt[`*expr*`]`	$\sqrt{}$($\sqrt{}e$)	◁
`\@` *expr*	`Sqrt[`*expr*`]`	`\@`(`\@`e)	◁
`\@` *expr* `\%` *n*	`Power[`*expr*`, 1/`*n*`]`		◁
$\int$ *expr*$_1$ `d`*expr*$_2$	`Integrate[`*expr*$_1$`, `*expr*$_2$`]`	$\int$ ($\int$ e `d` e) `d` e	◁
$\int_{e_1}^{e_2} e_3\ \mathrm{d}e_4$	`Integrate[`e_3`, {`e_4`, `e_1`, `e_2`}]`	$\int$ ($\int$ e `d` e) `d` e	◁
other integration operators: see page 1031			
∂_{expr_1} *expr*$_2$	`D[`*expr*$_2$`, `*expr*$_1$`]`	∂_e (∂_e e)	◁
∇ *expr*	`Del[`*expr*`]`	∇ (∇ e)	
$\square$ *expr*	`Square[`*expr*`]`	$\square$ ($\square$ e)	
expr$_1$ `∘` *expr*$_2$ `∘` *expr*$_3$	`SmallCircle[`*expr*$_1$`, `*expr*$_2$`, `*expr*$_3$`]`	e `∘` e `∘` e	

Operator input forms, in order of decreasing precedence, part two.

operator form	full form	grouping	
$expr_1 \odot expr_2 \odot expr_3$	CircleDot[$expr_1$, $expr_2$, $expr_3$]	$e \odot e \odot e$	
$expr_1$ ** $expr_2$ ** $expr_3$	NonCommutativeMultiply[$expr_1$, $expr_2$, $expr_3$]	e ** e ** e	
$expr_1 \times expr_2 \times expr_3$	Cross[$expr_1$, $expr_2$, $expr_3$]	$e \times e \times e$	◁
$expr_1 \cdot expr_2 \cdot expr_3$	Dot[$expr_1$, $expr_2$, $expr_3$]	$e \cdot e \cdot e$	◁
$-expr$	Times[-1, $expr$]		◁
$+expr$	$expr$		◁
$\pm\, expr$	PlusMinus[$expr$]		
$\mp\, expr$	MinusPlus[$expr$]		
$expr_1$ / $expr_2$	$expr_1$ ($expr_2$)^-1	$(e\ /\ e)\ /\ e$	◁
$expr_1 \div expr_2$	Divide[$expr_1$, $expr_2$]	$(e \div e) \div e$	◁
$expr_1$ \/ $expr_2$	Divide[$expr_1$, $expr_2$]	$(e\backslash/e)\backslash/e$	◁
$expr_1 \backslash expr_2 \backslash expr_3$	Backslash[$expr_1$, $expr_2$, $expr_3$]	$e \backslash e \backslash e$	
$expr_1 \diamond expr_2 \diamond expr_3$	Diamond[$expr_1$, $expr_2$, $expr_3$]	$e \diamond e \diamond e$	
$expr_1 \wedge expr_2 \wedge expr_3$	Wedge[$expr_1$, $expr_2$, $expr_3$]	$e \wedge e \wedge e$	
$expr_1 \vee expr_2 \vee expr_3$	Vee[$expr_1$, $expr_2$, $expr_3$]	$e \vee e \vee e$	
$expr_1 \otimes expr_2 \otimes expr_3$	CircleTimes[$expr_1$, $expr_2$, $expr_3$]	$e \otimes e \otimes e$	
$expr_1 \cdot expr_2 \cdot expr_3$	CenterDot[$expr_1$, $expr_2$, $expr_3$]	$e \cdot e \cdot e$	
$expr_1\ expr_2\ expr_3$	Times[$expr_1$, $expr_2$, $expr_3$]	$e\ e\ e$	◁
$expr_1 * expr_2 * expr_3$	Times[$expr_1$, $expr_2$, $expr_3$]	$e * e * e$	◁
$expr_1 \times expr_2 \times expr_3$	Times[$expr_1$, $expr_2$, $expr_3$]	$e \times e \times e$	◁
$expr_1 * expr_2 * expr_3$	Star[$expr_1$, $expr_2$, $expr_3$]	$e * e * e$	
$\displaystyle\prod_{e_1=e_2}^{e_3} e_4$	Product[e_4, {e_1, e_2, e_3}]	$\prod (\prod e)$	◁
$expr_1 \wr expr_2 \wr expr_3$	VerticalTilde[$expr_1$, $expr_2$, $expr_3$]	$e \wr e \wr e$	
$expr_1 \sqcup expr_2 \sqcup expr_3$	Coproduct[$expr_1$, $expr_2$, $expr_3$]	$e \sqcup e \sqcup e$	
$expr_1 \frown expr_2 \frown expr_3$	Cap[$expr_1$, $expr_2$, $expr_3$]	$e \frown e \frown e$	
$expr_1 \smile expr_2 \smile expr_3$	Cup[$expr_1$, $expr_2$, $expr_3$]	$e \smile e \smile e$	
$expr_1 \oplus expr_2 \oplus expr_3$	CirclePlus[$expr_1$, $expr_2$, $expr_3$]	$e \oplus e \oplus e$	
$expr_1 \ominus expr_2$	CircleMinus[$expr_1$, $expr_2$]	$(e \ominus e) \ominus e$	

Operator input forms, in order of decreasing precedence, part three.

operator form	full form	grouping	
$\displaystyle\sum_{e_1=e_2}^{e_3} e_4$	$\texttt{Sum}[e_4,\ \{e_1,\ e_2,\ e_3\}]$	$\sum\ (\sum e)$	◁
$expr_1 + expr_2 + expr_3$	$\texttt{Plus}[expr_1,\ expr_2,\ expr_3]$	$e + e + e$	◁
$expr_1 - expr_2$	$expr_1 + (-1\ expr_2)$	$(e - e) - e$	◁
$expr_1 \pm expr_2$	$\texttt{PlusMinus}[expr_1,\ expr_2]$	$(e \pm e) \pm e$	
$expr_1 \mp expr_2$	$\texttt{MinusPlus}[expr_1,\ expr_2]$	$(e \mp e) \mp e$	
$expr_1 \cap expr_2$ *other intersection operators*	$\texttt{Intersection}[expr_1,\ expr_2]$	$e \cap e \cap e$	◁
$expr_1 \cup expr_2$ *other union operators*	$\texttt{Union}[expr_1,\ expr_2]$	$e \cup e \cup e$	◁
$expr_1 == expr_2$	$\texttt{Equal}[expr_1,\ expr_2]$	$e == e == e$	◁
$expr_1 == expr_2$	$\texttt{Equal}[expr_1,\ expr_2]$	$e == e == e$	◁
$expr_1 = expr_2$	$\texttt{Equal}[expr_1,\ expr_2]$	$e = e = e$	◁
$expr_1\ != expr_2$	$\texttt{Unequal}[expr_1,\ expr_2]$	$e\ != e\ != e$	◁
$expr_1 \neq expr_2$	$\texttt{Unequal}[expr_1,\ expr_2]$	$e \neq e \neq e$	◁
other equality and similarity operators			
$expr_1 > expr_2$	$\texttt{Greater}[expr_1,\ expr_2]$	$e > e > e$	◁
$expr_1 >= expr_2$	$\texttt{GreaterEqual}[expr_1,\ expr_2]$	$e >= e >= e$	◁
$expr_1 \geq expr_2$	$\texttt{GreaterEqual}[expr_1,\ expr_2]$	$e \geq e \geq e$	◁
$expr_1 \geqslant expr_2$	$\texttt{GreaterEqual}[expr_1,\ expr_2]$	$e \geqslant e \geqslant e$	◁
$expr_1 < expr_2$	$\texttt{Less}[expr_1,\ expr_2]$	$e < e < e$	◁
$expr_1 <= expr_2$	$\texttt{LessEqual}[expr_1,\ expr_2]$	$e <= e <= e$	◁
$expr_1 \leq expr_2$	$\texttt{LessEqual}[expr_1,\ expr_2]$	$e \leq e \leq e$	◁
$expr_1 \leqslant expr_2$	$\texttt{LessEqual}[expr_1,\ expr_2]$	$e \leqslant e \leqslant e$	◁
other ordering operators			
$expr_1 \mid expr_2$	$\texttt{VerticalBar}[expr_1,\ expr_2]$	$e \mid e \mid e$	
$expr_1 \nmid expr_2$	$\texttt{NotVerticalBar}[expr_1,\ expr_2]$	$e \nmid e \nmid e$	
$expr_1 \parallel expr_2$	$\texttt{DoubleVerticalBar}[expr_1,\ expr_2]$	$e \parallel e \parallel e$	
$expr_1 \nparallel expr_2$	$\texttt{NotDoubleVerticalBar}[expr_1,\ expr_2]$	$e \nparallel e \nparallel e$	
horizontal arrow and vector operators			
diagonal arrow operators			
$expr_1 === expr_2$	$\texttt{SameQ}[expr_1,\ expr_2]$	$e === e === e$	◁
$expr_1 =!= expr_2$	$\texttt{UnsameQ}[expr_1,\ expr_2]$	$e =!= e =!= e$	◁

Operator input forms, in order of decreasing precedence, part four.

operator form	full form	grouping	
$expr_1 \in expr_2$	Element[$expr_1$, $expr_2$]	$e \in e \in e$	◁
$expr_1 \notin expr_2$	NotElement[$expr_1$, $expr_2$]	$e \notin e \notin e$	◁
$expr_1 \subset expr_2$	Subset[$expr_1$, $expr_2$]	$e \subset e \subset e$	
$expr_1 \supset expr_2$	Superset[$expr_1$, $expr_2$]	$e \supset e \supset e$	
other set relation operators			
$\forall_{expr_1} expr_2$	ForAll[$expr_1$, $expr_2$]	$\forall_e (\forall_e e)$	◁
$\exists_{expr_1} expr_2$	Exists[$expr_1$, $expr_2$]	$\exists_e (\exists_e e)$	◁
$\nexists_{expr_1} expr_2$	NotExists[$expr_1$, $expr_2$]	$\nexists_e (\nexists_e e)$	
$!expr$	Not[$expr$]	$!(!e)$	◁
$\neg expr$	Not[$expr$]	$\neg (\neg e)$	◁
$expr_1$ && $expr_2$ && $expr_3$	And[$expr_1$, $expr_2$, $expr_3$]	e && e && e	◁
$expr_1 \wedge expr_2 \wedge expr_3$	And[$expr_1$, $expr_2$, $expr_3$]	$e \wedge e \wedge e$	◁
$expr_1 \bar{\wedge} expr_2 \bar{\wedge} expr_3$	Nand[$expr_1$, $expr_2$, $expr_3$]	$e \bar{\wedge} e \bar{\wedge} e$	◁
$expr_1 \veebar expr_2 \veebar expr_3$	Xor[$expr_1$, $expr_2$, $expr_3$]	$e \veebar e \veebar e$	◁
$expr_1$ || $expr_2$ || $expr_3$	Or[$expr_1$, $expr_2$, $expr_3$]	e || e || e	◁
$expr_1 \vee expr_2 \vee expr_3$	Or[$expr_1$, $expr_2$, $expr_3$]	$e \vee e \vee e$	◁
$expr_1 \bar{\vee} expr_2 \bar{\vee} expr_3$	Nor[$expr_1$, $expr_2$, $expr_3$]	$e \bar{\vee} e \bar{\vee} e$	◁
$expr_1 \Rightarrow expr_2$	Implies[$expr_1$, $expr_2$]	$e \Rightarrow (e \Rightarrow e)$	◁
$expr_1 \Rightarrow expr_2$	Implies[$expr_1$, $expr_2$]	$e \Rightarrow (e \Rightarrow e)$	◁
$expr_1 \vdash expr_2$	RightTee[$expr_1$, $expr_2$]	$e \vdash (e \vdash e)$	
$expr_1 \vDash expr_2$	DoubleRightTee[$expr_1$, $expr_2$]	$e \vDash (e \vDash e)$	
$expr_1 \dashv expr_2$	LeftTee[$expr_1$, $expr_2$]	$(e \dashv e) \dashv e$	
$expr_1 \Dashv expr_2$	DoubleLeftTee[$expr_1$, $expr_2$]	$(e \Dashv e) \Dashv e$	
$expr_1 \ni expr_2$	SuchThat[$expr_1$, $expr_2$]	$e \ni (e \ni e)$	
$expr..$	Repeated[$expr$]		◁
$expr...$	RepeatedNull[$expr$]		◁
$expr_1 \mid expr_2$	Alternatives[$expr_1$, $expr_2$]	$e \mid e \mid e$	◁
$symb:expr$	Pattern[$symb$, $expr$]		◁
$patt:expr$	Optional[$patt$, $expr$]		◁

Operator input forms, in order of decreasing precedence, part five.

operator form	full form	grouping	
$expr_1$ /; $expr_2$	`Condition[`$expr_1$`, `$expr_2$`]`	$(e/;e)/;e$	◁
$expr_1$ -> $expr_2$	`Rule[`$expr_1$`, `$expr_2$`]`	e -> $(e$ -> $e)$	◁
$expr_1$ → $expr_2$	`Rule[`$expr_1$`, `$expr_2$`]`	$e → (e → e)$	◁
$expr_1$:> $expr_2$	`RuleDelayed[`$expr_1$`, `$expr_2$`]`	e :> $(e$:> $e)$	◁
$expr_1$ ⧴ $expr_2$	`RuleDelayed[`$expr_1$`, `$expr_2$`]`	$e ⧴ (e ⧴ e)$	◁
$expr_1$ /. $expr_2$	`ReplaceAll[`$expr_1$`, `$expr_2$`]`	$(e /. e) /. e$	◁
$expr_1$ //. $expr_2$	`ReplaceRepeated[`$expr_1$`, `$expr_2$`]`	$(e //. e) //. e$	◁
$expr_1$ += $expr_2$	`AddTo[`$expr_1$`, `$expr_2$`]`	e += $(e$ += $e)$	◁
$expr_1$ -= $expr_2$	`SubtractFrom[`$expr_1$`, `$expr_2$`]`	e -= $(e$ -= $e)$	◁
$expr_1$ *= $expr_2$	`TimesBy[`$expr_1$`, `$expr_2$`]`	e *= $(e$ *= $e)$	◁
$expr_1$ /= $expr_2$	`DivideBy[`$expr_1$`, `$expr_2$`]`	e /= $(e$ /= $e)$	◁
$expr$ &	`Function[`$expr$`]`		◁
$expr_1$: $expr_2$	`Colon[`$expr_1$`, `$expr_2$`]`	$e : e : e$	
$expr_1$ // $expr_2$	$expr_2$`[`$expr_1$`]`	$(e // e) // e$	
$expr_1$ | $expr_2$	`VerticalSeparator[`$expr_1$`, `$expr_2$`]`	$e \mid e \mid e$	
$expr_1$ ∴ $expr_2$	`Therefore[`$expr_1$`, `$expr_2$`]`	$e ∴ (e ∴ e)$	
$expr_1$ ∵ $expr_2$	`Because[`$expr_1$`, `$expr_2$`]`	$(e ∵ e) ∵ e$	
$expr_1$ = $expr_2$	`Set[`$expr_1$`, `$expr_2$`]`	$e = (e = e)$	◁
$expr_1$:= $expr_2$	`SetDelayed[`$expr_1$`, `$expr_2$`]`	$e := (e := e)$	◁
$expr_1$ ^= $expr_2$	`UpSet[`$expr_1$`, `$expr_2$`]`	e ^= $(e$ ^= $e)$	◁
$expr_1$ ^:= $expr_2$	`UpSetDelayed[`$expr_1$`, `$expr_2$`]`	e ^:= $(e$ ^:= $e)$	◁
$symb$/: $expr_1$ = $expr_2$	`TagSet[`$symb$`, `$expr_1$`, `$expr_2$`]`		◁
$symb$/: $expr_1$:= $expr_2$	`TagSetDelayed[`$symb$`, `$expr_1$`, `$expr_2$`]`		◁
$expr$ =.	`Unset[`$expr$`]`		◁
$symb$/: $expr$ =.	`TagUnset[`$symb$`, `$expr$`]`		◁
$expr$ >> $filename$	`Put[`$expr$`, "`$filename$`"]`		◁
$expr$ >>> $filename$	`PutAppend[`$expr$`, "`$filename$`"]`		◁
$expr_1$;$expr_2$;$expr_3$	`CompoundExpression[`$expr_1$`, `$expr_2$`, `$expr_3$`]`		◁
$expr_1$;$expr_2$;	`CompoundExpression[`$expr_1$`, `$expr_2$`, Null]`		◁
$expr_1$ \\\` $expr_2$	`FormBox[`$expr_2$`, `$expr_1$`]`	$e \backslash\grave{} (e \backslash\grave{} e)$	◁

Operator input forms, in order of decreasing precedence, part six.

special input form	full form
#	Slot[1]
#*n*	Slot[*n*]
##	SlotSequence[1]
##*n*	SlotSequence[*n*]
%	Out[ ]
%%	Out[-2]
%% … % (*n* times)	Out[-*n*]
%*n*	Out[*n*]
_	Blank[ ]
_*expr*	Blank[*expr*]
__	BlankSequence[ ]
__*expr*	BlankSequence[*expr*]
___	BlankNullSequence[ ]
___*expr*	BlankNullSequence[*expr*]
_.	Optional[Blank[ ]]
*symb*_	Pattern[*symb*, Blank[ ]]
*symb*_*expr*	Pattern[*symb*, Blank[*expr*]]
*symb*__	Pattern[*symb*, BlankSequence[ ]]
*symb*__*expr*	Pattern[*symb*, BlankSequence[*expr*]]
*symb*___	Pattern[*symb*, BlankNullSequence[ ]]
*symb*___*expr*	Pattern[*symb*, BlankNullSequence[*expr*]]
*symb*_.	Optional[Pattern[*symb*, Blank[ ]]]

Additional input forms, in order of decreasing precedence.

Special Characters

Special characters that appear in operators usually have names that correspond to the names of the functions they represent. Thus the character ⊕ has name \[CirclePlus] and yields the function CirclePlus. Exceptions are \[GreaterSlantEqual], \[LessSlantEqual] and \[RoundImplies].

The delimiters in matchfix operators have names \[Left*Name*] and \[Right*Name*].

Pages 1354–1401 give a complete listing of special characters that appear in operators.

keyboard characters	special character	keyboard characters	special character
->	\[Rule] →	>=	\[GreaterEqual] ≥
:>	\[RuleDelayed] :→	>=	\[GreaterSlantEqual] ⩾
==	\[Equal] ==	<=	\[LessEqual] ≤
!=	\[NotEqual] ≠	<=	\[LessSlantEqual] ⩽

Keyboard and special characters with the same interpretations.

keyboard character	special character	keyboard character	special character
\[RawColon] :	\[Colon] :	\[RawDot] .	\[CenterDot] ·
\[RawTilde] ~	\[Tilde] ~	\[RawVerticalBar] |	\[VerticalBar] ❘
\[RawWedge] ^	\[Wedge] ∧	\[RawVerticalBar] |	\[VerticalSeparator] ❘
\[RawWedge] ^	\[And] ∧	\[RawVerticalBar] |	\[LeftBracketingBar] ❘
\[RawStar] *	\[Star] ⋆	\[RawDash] -	\[Dash] –
\[RawBackslash] \	\[Backslash] \	...	\[Ellipsis] …

Some keyboard and special characters with different interpretations.

Precedence and the Ordering of Input Forms

The tables of input forms are arranged in decreasing order of precedence. Input forms in the same box have the same precedence. Each page in the table begins a new box. As discussed in Section 2.1.3, precedence determines how *Mathematica* groups terms in input expressions. The general rule is that if $\otimes$ has higher precedence than $\oplus$, then $a \oplus b \otimes c$ is interpreted as $a \oplus (b \otimes c)$, and $a \otimes b \oplus c$ is interpreted as $(a \otimes b) \oplus c$.

Grouping of Input Forms

The third columns in the tables show how multiple occurrences of a single input form, or of several input forms with the same precedence, are grouped. For example, a/b/c is grouped as (a/b)/c ("left associative"), while a^b^c is grouped as a^(b^c) ("right associative"). No grouping is needed in an expression like a + b + c, since Plus is fully associative, as represented by the attribute Flat.

Precedence of Integration Operators

Forms such as $\int expr_1 \, \mathrm{d} \, expr_2$ have an "outer" precedence just below Power, as indicated in the table above, but an "inner" precedence just above $\sum$. The outer precedence determines when $expr_2$ needs to be parenthesized; the inner precedence determines when $expr_1$ needs to be parenthesized.

\[ContourIntegral], \[ClockwiseContourIntegral] and \[DoubleContourIntegral] work the same as \[Integral].

See page 1034 for two-dimensional input forms associated with integration operators.

Spaces and Multiplication

Spaces in *Mathematica* denote multiplication, just as they do in standard mathematical notation. In addition, *Mathematica* takes complete expressions that are adjacent, not necessarily separated by spaces, to be multiplied together.

- x y z ⟶ x*y*z
- 2x ⟶ 2*x
- 2(x+1) ⟶ 2*(x+1)
- c(x+1) ⟶ c*(x+1)
- (x+1)(y+2) ⟶ (x+1)*(y+2)
- x! y ⟶ x!*y
- x!y ⟶ x!*y

Alternative forms for multiplication.

An expression like x!y could potentially mean either (x!)*y or x*(!y). The first interpretation is chosen because Factorial has higher precedence than Not.

Spaces within single input forms are ignored. Thus, for example, a + b is equivalent to a+b. You will often want to insert spaces around lower precedence operators to improve readability.

You can give a "coefficient" for a symbol by preceding it with any sequence of digits. When you use numbers in bases larger than 10, the digits can include letters. (In bases other than 10, there must be a space between the end of the coefficient, and the beginning of the symbol name.)

- x^2y, like x^2 y, means (x^2) y
- x/2y, like x/2 y, means (x/2) y
- xy is a single symbol, not x*y

Some cases to be careful about.

Spaces to Avoid

You should avoid inserting any spaces between the different characters in composite operators such as /., =. and >=. Although in some cases such spaces are allowed, they are liable to lead to confusion.

Another case where spaces must be avoided is between the characters of the pattern object x_. If you type x _, *Mathematica* will interpret this as x*_, rather than the single named pattern object x_.

Similarly, you should not insert any spaces inside pattern objects like *x_*:*value*.

Spacing Characters

- Ordinary keyboard space (\[RawSpace])
- \[VeryThinSpace], \[ThinSpace], ..., \[ThickSpace]
- \[NegativeVeryThinSpace], \[NegativeThinSpace], ..., \[NegativeThickSpace]
- ␣ (\[SpaceIndicator])

Spacing characters equivalent to an ordinary keyboard space.

Relational Operators

Relational operators can be mixed. An expression like a > b >= c is converted to Inequality[a, Greater, b, GreaterEqual, c], which effectively evaluates as (a > b) && (b >= c). (The reason for the intermediate Inequality form is that it prevents objects from being evaluated twice when input like a > b >= c is processed.)

File Names

Any file name can be given in quotes after <<, >> and >>>. File names can also be given without quotes if they contain only alphanumeric characters, special characters and the characters `, /, ., \, !, -, _, :, $, *, ~ and ?, together with matched pairs of square brackets enclosing any characters other than spaces, tabs and newlines. Note that file names given without quotes can be followed only by spaces, tabs or newlines, or by the characters),], } as well as semicolon and comma.

■ A.2.8 Two-Dimensional Input Forms

x^y	`Power[x, y]`	$\int_{xmin}^{xmax} y\, dx$	`Integrate[y, {x, xmin, xmax}]`	
$\dfrac{x}{y}$	`Divide[x, y]`			
$\sqrt{x}$	`Sqrt[x]`	$\int_{xmin}^{xmax} y\, w\, \dfrac{dx}{z}$	`Integrate[y w/z, {x, xmin, xmax}]`	
$\sqrt[n]{x}$	`Power[x, 1/n]`			
$\begin{matrix} a_{11} & a_{12} & ... \\ a_{21} & a_{22} & ... \end{matrix}$	`{{a₁₁, a₁₂, …}, {a₂₁, a₂₂, …}}`	$\sum_{x=xmin}^{xmax} y$	`Sum[y, {x, xmin, xmax}]`	
$\partial_x y$	`D[y, x]`	$\prod_{x=xmin}^{xmax} y$	`Product[y, {x, xmin, xmax}]`	
$\partial_{x,...} y$	`D[y, x, ... ]`			

Two-dimensional input forms with built-in evaluation rules.

Any array of expressions represented by a `GridBox` is interpreted as a list of lists. Even if the `GridBox` has only one row, the interpretation is still $\{\{a_1, a_2, ... \}\}$.

In the form $\displaystyle\int_{xmin}^{xmax} y\, w\, \frac{dx}{z}$ the limits *xmin* and *xmax* can be omitted, as can *y* and *w*.

x_y	`Subscript[x, y]`	$\overset{y}{x}$	`Overscript[x, y]`	
x_+	`SubPlus[x]`	$\underset{y}{x}$	`Underscript[x, y]`	
x_-	`SubMinus[x]`			
x_*	`SubStar[x]`	$\bar{x}$	`OverBar[x]`	
		$\vec{x}$	`OverVector[x]`	
x^+	`SuperPlus[x]`	$\tilde{x}$	`OverTilde[x]`	
x^-	`SuperMinus[x]`	$\hat{x}$	`OverHat[x]`	
x^*	`SuperStar[x]`	$\dot{x}$	`OverDot[x]`	
$x^\dagger$	`SuperDagger[x]`			
		$\underline{x}$	`UnderBar[x]`	

Two-dimensional input forms without built-in evaluation rules.

There is no issue of precedence for forms such as $\sqrt{x}$ and $\hat{x}$ in which operands are effectively spanned by the operator. For forms such as x_y and $x^\dagger$ a left precedence does need to be specified, so such forms are included in the main table of precedences above.

■ A.2.9 Input of Boxes

- Use a palette
- Use control keys
- Use \!\(*input*\), together with [CTRL] [!]
- Use [CTRL] [*]

Ways to input boxes.

Control Keys

[CTRL] [1]	or	[CTRL] [!]	activate \! form
[CTRL] [2]	or	[CTRL] [@]	square root
[CTRL] [5]	or	[CTRL] [%]	switch to alternate position (e.g. subscript to superscript)
[CTRL] [6]	or	[CTRL] [^]	superscript
[CTRL] [7]	or	[CTRL] [&]	overscript
[CTRL] [8]	or	[CTRL] [*]	enter raw boxes
[CTRL] [9]	or	[CTRL] [(]	begin a new cell within an existing cell
[CTRL] [0]	or	[CTRL] [)]	end a new cell within an existing cell
[CTRL] [−]	or	[CTRL] [_]	subscript
[CTRL] [=]	or	[CTRL] [+]	underscript
[CTRL] [↵] (CONTROL-RETURN)			create a new row in a GridBox
		[CTRL] [,]	create a new column in a GridBox
		[CTRL] [.]	expand current selection
		[CTRL] [/]	fraction
[CTRL] [␣] (CONTROL-SPACE)			return from current position or state
[CTRL] [→], [CTRL] [←], [CTRL] [↑], [CTRL] [↓]			move an object by minimal increments on the screen

Standard control keys.

On English-language keyboards both forms will work where alternates are given. On other keyboards the first form should work but the second may not.

Boxes Constructed from Text

When textual input that you give is used to construct boxes, as in StandardForm or TraditionalForm cells in a notebook, the input is handled slightly differently from when it is fed directly to the kernel.

The input is broken into *tokens*, and then each token is included in the box structure as a separate character string. Thus, for example, xx+yyy is broken into the tokens "xx", "+", "yyy".

- symbol name (e.g. x123)
- number (e.g. 12.345)
- operator (e.g. +=)
- spacing (e.g. ␣)
- character string (e.g. "text")

Types of tokens in text used to construct boxes.

A RowBox is constructed to hold each operator and its operands. The nesting of RowBox objects is determined by the precedence of the operators in standard *Mathematica* syntax.

Note that spacing characters are not automatically discarded. Instead, each sequence of consecutive such characters is made into a separate token.

String-Based Input

\(... \)	input raw boxes
\!\(... \)	input and interpret boxes

Inputting raw and interpreted boxes.

Any textual input that you give between \(and \) is taken to specify boxes to construct. The boxes are only interpreted if you specify with \! that this should be done. Otherwise $x \text{\^{}} y$ is left for example as SuperscriptBox[x, y], and is not converted to Power[x, y].

Within the outermost \(... \), further \(... \) specify grouping and lead to the insertion of RowBox objects.

$\backslash(box_1, box_2, \dots \backslash)$	$\texttt{RowBox}[box_1, box_2, \dots \,]$
$box_1 \backslash \char`\^ box_2$	$\texttt{SuperscriptBox}[box_1, box_2]$
$box_1 \backslash\_ box_2$	$\texttt{SubscriptBox}[box_1, box_2]$
$box_1 \backslash\_ box_2 \backslash\% box_3$	$\texttt{SubsuperscriptBox}[box_1, box_2, box_3]$
$box_1 \backslash\& box_2$	$\texttt{OverscriptBox}[box_1, box_2]$
$box_1 \backslash + box_2$	$\texttt{UnderscriptBox}[box_1, box_2]$
$box_1 \backslash + box_2 \backslash\% box_3$	$\texttt{UnderoverscriptBox}[box_1, box_2, box_3]$
$box_1 \backslash / box_2$	$\texttt{FractionBox}[box_1, box_2]$
$\backslash@ box$	$\texttt{SqrtBox}[box]$
$form \backslash\char`\` box$	$\texttt{FormBox}[box, form]$
$\backslash* input$	construct box by interpreting *input*
$\backslash\_$	insert a space
$\backslash\texttt{n}$	insert a newline
$\backslash\texttt{t}$	indent at the beginning of a line

String-based ways of constructing raw boxes.

In string-based input between \(and \) spaces, tabs and newlines are discarded. \␣ can be used to insert a single space. Special spacing characters such as \[ThinSpace], \[ThickSpace] or \[NegativeThinSpace] are not discarded.

■ A.2.10 The Extent of Input Expressions

Mathematica will treat all input that you give on a single line as being part of the same expression.

Mathematica allows a single expression to continue for several lines. In general, it treats the input that you give on successive lines as belonging to the same expression whenever no complete expression would be formed without doing this.

Thus, for example, if one line ends with =, then *Mathematica* will assume that the expression must continue on the next line. It will do the same if for example parentheses or other matchfix operators remain open at the end of the line.

If at the end of a particular line the input you have given so far corresponds to a complete expression, then *Mathematica* will normally begin immediately to process that expression.

You can however explicitly tell *Mathematica* that a particular expression is incomplete by putting a \ or a ∴ (\[Continuation]) at the end of the line. *Mathematica* will then include the next line in the same expression, discarding any spaces or tabs that occur at the beginning of that line.

If you are using StandardForm input in a notebook front end, then *Mathematica* will also not treat an expression on a particular line as being complete if the line that follows it could not be complete without being combined with its predecessor. Thus, for example, if a line begins with an infix operator such as × or /, then *Mathematica* will combine this line with the previous one to try to obtain a complete expression. If a line begins with +, −, ±, or another operator that can be used both in infix or prefix form, then *Mathematica* will still combine the line with the previous one, but will issue a warning to say what it is doing.

■ A.2.11 Special Input

?*symbol*	get information
??*symbol*	get more information
?s_1 s_2 ...	get information on several objects
!*command*	execute an external command
!!*file*	display the contents of an external file

Special input lines.

In most implementations of *Mathematica*, you can give a line of special input anywhere in your input. The only constraint is that the special input must start at the beginning of a line.

Some implementations of *Mathematica* may not allow you to execute external commands using !*command*.

■ A.2.12 Front End Files

Notebook files as well as front end initialization files can contain a subset of standard *Mathematica* language syntax. This syntax includes:

■ Any *Mathematica* expression in FullForm.

■ Lists in {... } form. The operators ->, :> and &. Function slots in # form.

■ Special characters in \[*Name*], \:*xxxx* or \.*xx* form.

■ String representation of boxes involving \(, \) and other backslash operators.

■ *Mathematica* comments delimited by (* and *).

A.3 Some General Notations and Conventions

■ A.3.1 Function Names

The names of built-in functions follow some general guidelines.

- The name consists of complete English words, or standard mathematical abbreviations. American spelling is used.

- The first letter of each word is capitalized.

- Functions whose names end with `Q` usually "ask a question", and return either `True` or `False`.

- Mathematical functions that are named after people usually have names in *Mathematica* of the form *PersonSymbol*.

■ A.3.2 Function Arguments

The main expression or object on which a built-in function acts is usually given as the first argument to the function. Subsidiary parameters appear as subsequent arguments.

The following are exceptions:

- In functions like `Map` and `Apply`, the function to apply comes before the expression it is to be applied to.

- In scoping constructs such as `Module` and `Function`, local variables and parameter names come before bodies.

- In functions like `Write` and `Display`, the name of the file is given before the objects to be written to it.

For mathematical functions, arguments that are written as subscripts in standard mathematical notation are given before those that are written as superscripts.

■ A.3.3 Options

Some built-in functions can take *options*. Each option has a name, represented as a symbol, or in some cases a string. Options are set by giving rules of the form *name*->*value* or *name*:>*value*. Such rules must appear after all the other arguments in a function. Rules for different options can be given in any order. If you do not explicitly give a rule for a particular option, a default setting for that option is used.

Options[*f*]	give the default rules for all options associated with *f*
Options[*expr*]	give the options set in a particular expression
Options[*expr*, *name*]	give the setting for the option *name* in an expression
AbsoluteOptions[*expr*, *name*]	give the absolute setting for *name*, even if its actual setting is Automatic
SetOptions[*f*, *name*->*value*, ...]	set default rules for options associated with *f*

Operations on options.

■ A.3.4 Part Numbering

n	element *n* (starting at 1)
-*n*	element *n* from the end
0	head
All	all elements

Numbering of parts.

■ A.3.5 Sequence Specifications

All	all elements
None	no elements
n	elements 1 through *n*
-*n*	last *n* elements
{*n*}	element *n* only
{*m*, *n*}	elements *m* through *n* (inclusive)
{*m*, *n*, *s*}	elements *m* through *n* in steps of *s*

Specifications for sequences of parts.

The sequence specification {*m*, *n*, *s*} corresponds to elements *m*, *m* + *s*, *m* + 2*s*, ... , up to the largest element not greater than *n*.

Sequence specifications are used in the functions Drop, Ordering, StringDrop, StringTake, Take and Thread.

■ A.3.6 Level Specifications

n	levels 1 through n
Infinity	levels 1 through Infinity
$\{n\}$	level n only
$\{n_1, n_2\}$	levels n_1 through n_2
Heads -> True	include heads of expressions
Heads -> False	do not include heads of expressions

Level specifications.

The level in an expression corresponding to a non-negative integer n is defined to consist of parts specified by n indices. A negative level number $-n$ represents all parts of an expression that have depth n. The depth of an expression, Depth[*expr*], is the maximum number of indices needed to specify any part, plus one. Levels *do not* include heads of expressions, except with the option setting Heads -> True. Level 0 is the whole expression. Level -1 contains all symbols and other objects that have no subparts.

Ranges of levels specified by $\{n_1, n_2\}$ contain all parts that are neither above level n_1, nor below level n_2 in the tree. The n_i need not have the same sign. Thus, for example, $\{2, -2\}$ specifies subexpressions which occur anywhere below the top level, but above the leaves, of the expression tree.

Level specifications are used by functions such as Apply, Cases, Count, FreeQ, Level, Map, MapIndexed, Position, Replace and Scan. Note, however, that the default level specifications are not the same for all of these functions.

Functions with level specifications visit different subexpressions in an order that corresponds to depth-first traversal of the expression tree, with leaves visited before roots. The subexpressions visited have part specifications which occur in an order which is lexicographic, except that longer sequences appear before shorter ones.

■ A.3.7 Iterators

{imax}	iterate *imax* times
{i, imax}	*i* goes from 1 to *imax* in steps of 1
{i, imin, imax}	*i* goes from *imin* to *imax* in steps of 1
{i, imin, imax, di}	*i* goes from *imin* to *imax* in steps of *di*
{i, imin, imax}, *{j, jmin, jmax}*, ...	*i* goes from *imin* to *imax*, and for each value of *i*, *j* goes from *jmin* to *jmax*, etc.

Iterator notation.

Iterators are used in such functions as Sum, Table, Do and Range.

The iteration parameters *imin, imax* and *di* do not need to be integers. The variable *i* is given a sequence of values starting at *imin*, and increasing in steps of *di*, stopping when the next value of *i* would be greater than *imax*. The iteration parameters can be arbitrary symbolic expressions, so long as $(imax-imin)/di$ is a number.

When several iteration variables are used, the limits for the later ones can depend on the values of earlier ones.

The variable *i* can be any symbolic expression; it need not be a single symbol. The value of *i* is automatically set up to be local to the iteration function. This is effectively done by wrapping a Block construct containing *i* around the iteration function.

The procedure for evaluating iteration functions is described on page 1046.

■ A.3.8 Scoping Constructs

Function[{*x*, ... }, *body*]	local parameters
lhs -> *rhs* and *lhs* :> *rhs*	local pattern names
lhs = *rhs* and *lhs* := *rhs*	local pattern names
With[{*x* = x_0, ... }, *body*]	local constants
Module[{*x*, ... }, *body*]	local variables

Scoping constructs in *Mathematica*.

Scoping constructs allow the names of certain symbols to be local.

When nested scoping constructs are evaluated, new symbols are automatically generated in the inner scoping constructs so as to avoid name conflicts with symbols in outer scoping constructs.

In general, symbols with names of the form *xxx* are renamed *xxx*$.

When a transformation rule or definition is used, `ReplaceAll` (`/.`) is effectively used to replace the pattern names that appear on the right-hand side. Nevertheless, new symbols are generated when necessary to represent other objects that appear in scoping constructs on the right-hand side.

Each time it is evaluated, `Module` generates symbols with unique names of the form *xxx*$*nnn* as replacements for all local variables that appear in its body.

■ A.3.9 Ordering of Expressions

The canonical ordering of expressions used automatically with the attribute `Orderless` and in functions such as `Sort` satisfies the following rules:

- Integers, rational and approximate real numbers are ordered by their numerical values.

- Complex numbers are ordered by their real parts, and in the event of a tie, by the absolute values of their imaginary parts.

- Symbols are ordered according to their names, and in the event of a tie, by their contexts.

- Expressions are usually ordered by comparing their parts in a depth-first manner. Shorter expressions come first.

- Powers and products are treated specially, and are ordered to correspond to terms in a polynomial.

- Strings are ordered as they would be in a dictionary, with the upper-case versions of letters coming after lower-case ones. Ordinary letters appear first, followed in order by script, Gothic, double-struck, Greek and Hebrew. Mathematical operators appear in order of decreasing precedence.

■ A.3.10 Mathematical Functions

The mathematical functions such as `Log[`x`]` and `BesselJ[`n`, `x`]` that are built into *Mathematica* have a number of features in common.

- They carry the attribute `Listable`, so that they are automatically "threaded" over any lists that appear as arguments.

- They carry the attribute `NumericFunction`, so that they are assumed to give numerical values when their arguments are numerical.

- They give exact results in terms of integers, rational numbers and algebraic expressions in special cases.

- Except for functions whose arguments are always integers, mathematical functions in *Mathematica* can be evaluated to any numerical precision, with any complex numbers as arguments. If a function is undefined for a particular set of arguments, it is returned in symbolic form in this case.

- Numerical evaluation leads to results of a precision no higher than can be justified on the basis of the precision of the arguments. Thus N[Gamma[27/10], 100] yields a high-precision result, but N[Gamma[2.7], 100] cannot.

- When possible, symbolic derivatives, integrals and series expansions of built-in mathematical functions are evaluated in terms of other built-in functions.

■ A.3.11 Mathematical Constants

Mathematical constants such as E and Pi that are built into *Mathematica* have the following properties:

- They do not have values as such.

- They have numerical values that can be found to any precision.

- They are treated as numeric quantities in NumericQ and elsewhere.

- They carry the attribute Constant, and so are treated as constants in derivatives.

■ A.3.12 Protection

Mathematica allows you to make assignments that override the standard operation and meaning of built-in *Mathematica* objects.

To make it difficult to make such assignments by mistake, most built-in *Mathematica* objects have the attribute Protected. If you want to make an assignment for a built-in object, you must first remove this attribute. You can do this by calling the function Unprotect.

There are a few fundamental *Mathematica* objects to which you absolutely cannot assign your own values. These objects carry the attribute Locked, as well as Protected. The Locked attribute prevents you from changing any of the attributes, and thus from removing the Protected attribute.

■ A.3.13 String Patterns

Functions such as StringMatchQ, Names and Remove allow you to give *string patterns*. String patterns can contain *metacharacters*, which can stand for sequences of ordinary characters.

	*	zero or more characters
	@	one or more characters excluding upper-case letters
*	etc.	literal *, etc.

Metacharacters used in string patterns.

A.4 Evaluation

■ A.4.1 The Standard Evaluation Sequence

The following is the sequence of steps that *Mathematica* follows in evaluating an expression like $h[e_1, e_2, \dots]$. Every time the expression changes, *Mathematica* effectively starts the evaluation sequence over again.

- If the expression is a raw object (e.g., `Integer`, `String`, etc.), leave it unchanged.

- Evaluate the head h of the expression.

- Evaluate each element e_i of the expression in turn. If h is a symbol with attributes `HoldFirst`, `HoldRest`, `HoldAll` or `HoldAllComplete`, then skip evaluation of certain elements.

- Unless h has attribute `HoldAllComplete` strip the outermost of any `Unevaluated` wrappers that appear in the e_i.

- Unless h has attribute `SequenceHold`, flatten out all `Sequence` objects that appear among the e_i.

- If h has attribute `Flat`, then flatten out all nested expressions with head h.

- If h has attribute `Listable`, then thread through any e_i that are lists.

- If h has attribute `Orderless`, then sort the e_i into order.

- Unless h has attribute `HoldAllComplete`, use any applicable transformation rules associated with f that you have defined for objects of the form $h[\ f[e_1, \dots], \dots\ ]$.

- Use any built-in transformation rules associated with f for objects of the form $h[\ f[e_1, \dots], \dots\ ]$.

- Use any applicable transformation rules that you have defined for $h[e_1, e_2, \dots]$ or for $h[\ \dots\ ][\ \dots\ ]$.

- Use any built-in transformation rules for $h[e_1, e_2, \dots]$ or for $h[\ \dots\ ][\ \dots\ ]$.

■ A.4.2 Non-Standard Argument Evaluation

There are a number of built-in *Mathematica* functions that evaluate their arguments in special ways. The control structure `While` is an example. The symbol `While` has the attribute `HoldAll`. As a result, the arguments of `While` are not evaluated as part of the standard evaluation process. Instead, the internal code for `While` evaluates the arguments in a special way. In the case of `While`, the code evaluates the arguments repeatedly, so as to implement a loop.

Control structures	arguments evaluated in a sequence determined by control flow (e.g., `CompoundExpression`)
Conditionals	arguments evaluated only when they correspond to branches that are taken (e.g., `If`, `Which`)
Logical operations	arguments evaluated only when they are needed in determining the logical result (e.g., `And`, `Or`)
Iteration functions	first argument evaluated for each step in the iteration (e.g., `Do`, `Sum`, `Plot`)
Tracing functions	form never evaluated (e.g., `Trace`)
Assignments	first argument only partially evaluated (e.g., `Set`, `AddTo`)
Pure functions	function body not evaluated (e.g., `Function`)
Scoping constructs	variable specifications not evaluated (e.g., `Module`, `Block`)
Holding functions	argument maintained in unevaluated form (e.g., `Hold`, `HoldPattern`)

Built-in functions that evaluate their arguments in special ways.

Logical Operations

In an expression of the form $e_1 \&\& e_2 \&\& e_3$ the e_i are evaluated in order. As soon as any e_i is found to be `False`, evaluation is stopped, and the result `False` is returned. This means that you can use the e_i to represent different "branches" in a program, with a particular branch being evaluated only if certain conditions are met.

The `Or` function works much like `And`; it returns `True` as soon as it finds any argument that is `True`. `Xor`, on the other hand, always evaluates *all* its arguments.

Iteration Functions

An iteration function such as `Do[f, {i, imin, imax}]` is evaluated as follows:

■ The iteration specification is evaluated. If it is not found to be of the form {*i*, *imin*, *imax*}, the evaluation stops.

■ The value of the iteration variable *i* is made local, effectively using `Block`.

■ *imin* and *imax* are used to determine the sequence of values to be assigned to the iteration variable *i*.

- The iteration variable is successively set to each value, and f is evaluated in each case.

- The local values assigned to i are cleared.

If there are several iteration variables, the same procedure is followed for each variable in turn, for every value of all the preceding variables.

Unless otherwise specified, f is not evaluated until a specific value has been assigned to i, and is then evaluated for each value of i chosen. You can use `Evaluate[f]` to make f be evaluated immediately, rather than only after a specific value has been assigned to i.

Assignments

The left-hand sides of assignments are only partially evaluated.

- If the left-hand side is a symbol, no evaluation is performed.

- If the left-hand side is a function without hold attributes, the arguments of the function are evaluated, but the function itself is not evaluated.

The right-hand side is evaluated for immediate (=), but not for delayed (:=), assignments.

Any subexpression of the form `HoldPattern[`*expr*`]` that appears on the left-hand side of an assignment is not evaluated, but is replaced by the unevaluated form of *expr* before the assignment is done.

■ A.4.3 Overriding Non-Standard Argument Evaluation

$f[expr_1, \ldots, \texttt{Evaluate}[expr_n], \ldots]$	evaluates the argument $expr_n$, whether or not the attributes of f specify that it should be held

Overriding holding of arguments.

By using `Evaluate`, you can get any argument of a function evaluated immediately, even if the argument would usually be evaluated later under the control of the function.

■ A.4.4 Preventing Evaluation

Mathematica provides various functions which act as "wrappers" to prevent the expressions they contain from being evaluated.

Hold[*expr*]	treated as Hold[*expr*] in all cases
HoldComplete[*expr*]	treated as HoldComplete[*expr*] with upvalues disabled
HoldForm[*expr*]	treated as *expr* for printing
HoldPattern[*expr*]	treated as *expr* in rules, definitions and patterns
Unevaluated[*expr*]	treated as *expr* when arguments are passed to a function

Wrappers that prevent expressions from being evaluated.

■ A.4.5 Global Control of Evaluation

In the evaluation procedure described above, two basic kinds of steps are involved:

- Iteration: evaluate a particular expression until it no longer changes.

- Recursion: evaluate subsidiary expressions needed to find the value of a particular expression.

Iteration leads to evaluation chains in which successive expressions are obtained by the application of various transformation rules.

Trace shows evaluation chains as lists, and shows subsidiary evaluations corresponding to recursion in sublists.

The expressions associated with the sequence of subsidiary evaluations which lead to an expression currently being evaluated are given in the list returned by Stack[ ].

| $RecursionLimit | maximum recursion depth |
| $IterationLimit | maximum number of iterations |

Global variables controlling the evaluation of expressions.

■ A.4.6 Aborts

You can ask *Mathematica* to abort at any point in a computation, either by calling the function Abort[ ], or by typing appropriate interrupt keys.

When asked to abort, *Mathematica* will terminate the computation as quickly as possible. If the answer obtained would be incorrect or incomplete, then *Mathematica* returns $Aborted instead of giving that answer.

Aborts can be caught using CheckAbort, and can be postponed using AbortProtect.

A.5 Patterns and Transformation Rules

◼ A.5.1 Patterns

Patterns stand for classes of expressions. They contain *pattern objects* which represent sets of possible expressions.

_	any expression
*x*_	any expression, given the name *x*
x:*pattern*	a pattern, given the name *x*
pattern ? *test*	a pattern that yields True when *test* is applied to its value
_*h*	any expression with head *h*
*x*_*h*	any expression with head *h*, given the name *x*
__	any sequence of one or more expressions
___	any sequence of zero or more expressions
*x*__ and *x*___	sequences of expressions, given the name *x*
__*h* and ___*h*	sequences of expressions, each with head *h*
*x*__*h* and *x*___*h*	sequences of expressions with head *h*, given the name *x*
*x*_:*v*	an expression with default value *v*
*x*_*h*:*v*	an expression with head *h* and default value *v*
*x*_.	an expression with a globally defined default value
Optional[*x*_*h*]	an expression that must have head *h*, and has a globally defined default value
pattern..	a pattern repeated one or more times
pattern...	a pattern repeated zero or more times
*pattern*₁ | *pattern*₂ | ...	a pattern which matches at least one of the *pattern*ᵢ
pattern /; *cond*	a pattern for which *cond* evaluates to True
HoldPattern[*pattern*]	a pattern not evaluated
Verbatim[*expr*]	an expression to be matched verbatim

Pattern objects.

When several pattern objects with the same name occur in a single pattern, all the objects must stand for the same expression. Thus f[x_, x_] can stand for f[2, 2] but not f[2, 3].

In a pattern object such as _*h*, the head *h* can be any expression, but cannot itself be a pattern.

A pattern object such as x__ stands for a *sequence* of expressions. So, for example, f[x__] can stand for f[a, b, c], with x being Sequence[a, b, c]. If you use x, say in the result of a transformation rule, the sequence will be spliced into the function in which x appears. Thus g[u, x, u] would become g[u, a, b, c, u].

When the pattern objects x_:*v* and x_. appear as arguments of functions, they represent arguments which may be omitted. When the argument corresponding to x_:*v* is omitted, *x* is taken to have value *v*. When the argument corresponding to x_. is omitted, *x* is taken to have a *default value* that is associated with the function in which it appears. You can specify this default value by making assignments for Default[*f*] and so on.

Default[*f*]	default value for x_. when it appears as any argument of the function *f*
Default[*f*, *n*]	default value for x_. when it appears as the nth argument (negative *n* count from the end)
Default[*f*, *n*, *tot*]	default value for the nth argument when there are a total of *tot* arguments

Default values.

A pattern like f[x__, y__, z__] can match an expression like f[a, b, c, d, e] with several different choices of x, y and z. The choices with x and y of minimum length are tried first. In general, when there are multiple __ or ___ in a single function, the case that is tried first takes all the __ and ___ to stand for sequences of minimum length, except the last one, which stands for "the rest" of the arguments.

When x_:*v* or x_. are present, the case that is tried first is the one in which none of them correspond to omitted arguments. Cases in which later arguments are dropped are tried next.

Orderless	*f*[*x*, *y*] and *f*[*y*, *x*] are equivalent
Flat	*f*[*f*[*x*], *y*] and *f*[*x*, *y*] are equivalent
OneIdentity	*f*[*x*] and *x* are equivalent

Attributes used in matching patterns.

Pattern objects like $x\_$ can represent any sequence of arguments in a function f with attribute Flat. The value of x in this case is f applied to the sequence of arguments. If f has the attribute OneIdentity, then e is used instead of $f[e]$ when x corresponds to a sequence of just one argument.

■ A.5.2 Assignments

lhs = *rhs*	immediate assignment: *rhs* is evaluated at the time of assignment
lhs := *rhs*	delayed assignment: *rhs* is evaluated when the value of *lhs* is requested

The two basic types of assignment in *Mathematica*.

Assignments in *Mathematica* specify transformation rules for expressions. Every assignment that you make must be associated with a particular *Mathematica* symbol.

$f[args]$ = *rhs*	assignment is associated with f (downvalue)
t /: $f[args]$ = *rhs*	assignment is associated with t (upvalue)
$f[g[args]]$ ^= *rhs*	assignment is associated with g (upvalue)

Assignments associated with different symbols.

In the case of an assignment like $f[args]$ = *rhs*, *Mathematica* looks at f, then the head of f, then the head of that, and so on, until it finds a symbol with which to associate the assignment.

When you make an assignment like *lhs* ^= *rhs*, *Mathematica* will set up transformation rules associated with each distinct symbol that occurs either as an argument of *lhs*, or as the head of an argument of *lhs*.

The transformation rules associated with a particular symbol s are always stored in a definite order, and are tested in that order when they are used. Each time you make an assignment, the corresponding transformation rule is inserted at the end of the list of transformation rules associated with s, except in the following cases:

- The left-hand side of the transformation rule is identical to a transformation rule that has already been stored, and any /; conditions on the right-hand side are also identical. In this case, the new transformation rule is inserted in place of the old one.

- *Mathematica* determines that the new transformation rule is more specific than a rule already present, and would never be used if it were placed after this rule. In this case, the new rule is placed before the old one. Note that in many cases it is not possible to determine whether one rule is more specific than another; in such cases, the new rule is always inserted at the end.

■ A.5.3 Types of Values

Attributes[*f*]	attributes of *f*
DefaultValues[*f*]	default values for arguments of *f*
DownValues[*f*]	values for *f*[...], *f*[...][...], etc.
FormatValues[*f*]	print forms associated with *f*
Messages[*f*]	messages associated with *f*
NValues[*f*]	numerical values associated with *f*
Options[*f*]	defaults for options associated with *f*
OwnValues[*f*]	values for *f* itself
UpValues[*f*]	values for ... [... , *f*[...], ...]

Types of values associated with symbols.

■ A.5.4 Clearing and Removing Objects

expr =.	clear a value defined for *expr*
f /: *expr* =.	clear a value associated with *f* defined for *expr*
Clear[s_1, s_2, ...]	clear all values for the symbols s_i, except for attributes, messages and defaults
ClearAll[s_1, s_2, ...]	clear all values for the s_i, including attributes, messages and defaults
Remove[s_1, s_2, ...]	clear all values, and then remove the names of the s_i

Ways to clear and remove objects.

Clear, ClearAll and Remove can all take string patterns as arguments, to specify action on all symbols whose names match the string pattern.

Clear, ClearAll and Remove do nothing to symbols with the attribute Protected.

■ A.5.5 Transformation Rules

lhs -> *rhs*	immediate rule: *rhs* is evaluated when the rule is first given
lhs :> *rhs*	delayed rule: *rhs* is evaluated when the rule is used

The two basic types of transformation rules in *Mathematica*.

Replacements for pattern variables that appear in transformation rules are effectively done using ReplaceAll (the /. operator).

A.6 Files and Streams

■ A.6.1 File Names

name.m	*Mathematica* language source file
name.nb	*Mathematica* notebook file
name.ma	*Mathematica* notebook file from before Version 3
name.mx	*Mathematica* expression dump
name.exe	*MathLink* executable program
name.tm	*MathLink* template file
name.ml	*MathLink* stream file

Conventions for file names.

Most files used by *Mathematica* are completely system independent. .mx and .exe files are however system dependent. For these files, there is a convention that bundles of versions for different computer systems have names with forms such as *name*/$SystemID/*name*.

In general, when you refer to a file, *Mathematica* tries to resolve its name as follows:

■ If the name starts with !, *Mathematica* treats the remainder of the name as an external command, and uses a pipe to this command.

■ If the name contains metacharacters used by your operating system, then *Mathematica* passes the name directly to the operating system for interpretation.

■ Unless the file is to be used for input, no further processing on the name is done.

■ Unless the name given is an absolute file name under your operating system, *Mathematica* will search each of the directories specified in the list $Path.

■ If what is found is a directory rather than a file, then *Mathematica* will look for a file *name*/$SystemID/*name*.

For names of the form *name*` the following further translations are done in Get and related functions:

■ A file *name*.mx is used if it exists.

■ A file *name*.m is used if it exists.

■ If *name* is a directory, then the file *name*/init.m is used if it exists.

■ If name.mx is a directory, then *name*.mx/$SystemID/*name*.mx is used if it exists.

In Install, *name*` is taken to refer to a file or directory named *name*.exe.

■ A.6.2 Streams

InputStream["*name*", *n*]	input from a file or pipe
OutputStream["*name*", *n*]	output to a file or pipe

Types of streams.

option name	default value	
CharacterEncoding	$CharacterEncoding	
		encoding to use for special characters
DOSTextFormat	True	whether to output files with MS-DOS text-mode conventions
FormatType	InputForm	default format for expressions
PageWidth	78	number of characters per line
TotalWidth	Infinity	maximum number of characters in a single expression

Options for output streams.

You can test options for streams using Options, and reset them using SetOptions.

A.7 *Mathematica* Sessions

■ A.7.1 Command-Line Options and Environment Variables

`-pwfile`	*Mathematica* password file
`-pwpath`	path to search for a *Mathematica* password file
`-run`	*Mathematica* input to run (kernel only)
`-initfile`	*Mathematica* initialization file
`-initpath`	path to search for initialization files
`-noinit`	do not run initialization files
`-mathlink`	communicate only via *MathLink*

Typical command-line options for *Mathematica* executables.

If the *Mathematica* front end is called with a notebook file as a command-line argument, then this notebook will be made the initial selected notebook. Otherwise, a new notebook will be created for this purpose.

Mathematica kernels and front ends can also take additional command-line options specific to particular window environments.

`$MATHINIT`	command-line environment for the *Mathematica* front end, as well as *MathReader*
`$MATHKERNELINIT`	command-line environment for the *Mathematica* kernel
`$MATHEMATICA_BASE`	setting for `$BaseDirectory`
`$MATHEMATICA_USERBASE`	setting for `$UserBaseDirectory`

Environment variables.

If no command-line options are explicitly given, *Mathematica* will read the values of operating system environment variables, and will use these values like command lines.

■ A.7.2 Initialization

On startup, the *Mathematica* kernel does the following:

- Perform license management operations.

- Run *Mathematica* commands specified in any −runfirst options passed to the kernel executable.

- Run *Mathematica* commands specified in any −run options passed to the kernel executable.

- Run the *Mathematica* commands in the user-specific kernel init.m file.

- Run the *Mathematica* commands in the system-wide kernel init.m file.

- Load init.m and Kernel/init.m files in Autoload directories.

- Begin running the main loop.

■ A.7.3 The Main Loop

All *Mathematica* sessions repeatedly execute the following main loop:

- Read in input.

- Apply $PreRead function, if defined, to the input string.

- Print syntax warnings if necessary.

- Apply $SyntaxHandler function if there is a syntax error.

- Assign InString[n].

- Apply $Pre function, if defined, to the input expression.

- Assign In[n].

- Evaluate expression.

- Apply $Post function, if defined.

- Assign Out[n], stripping off any formatting wrappers.

- Apply $PrePrint function, if defined.

- Assign MessageList[n] and clear $MessageList.

- Print expression, if it is not Null.

- Increment $Line.

- Clear any pending aborts.

Note that if you call *Mathematica* via *MathLink* from within an external program, then you must effectively create your own main loop, which will usually differ from the one described above.

■ A.7.4 Messages

During a *Mathematica* session messages can be generated either by explicit calls to `Message`, or in the course of executing other built-in functions.

f::*name*::*lang*	a message in a specific language
f::*name*	a message in a default language
`General`::*name*	a general message with a given name

Message names.

If no language is specified for a particular message, text for the message is sought in each of the languages specified by `$Language`. If *f*::*name* is not defined, a definition for `General`::*name* is sought. If still no message is found, any value defined for `$NewMessage` is applied to *f* and "*name*".

`Off[`*message*`]` prevents a specified message from ever being printed. `Check` allows you to determine whether particular messages were generated during the evaluation of an expression. `$MessageList` and `MessageList[`*n*`]` record all the messages that were generated during the evaluation of a particular line in a *Mathematica* session.

Messages are specified as strings to be used as the first argument of `StringForm`. `$MessagePrePrint` is applied to each expression to be spliced into the string.

■ A.7.5 Termination

`Exit[ ]` or `Quit[ ]`	terminate *Mathematica*
`$Epilog`	symbol to evaluate before *Mathematica* exits
`$IgnoreEOF`	whether to exit an interactive *Mathematica* session when an end-of-file character is received
`end.m`	file to read when *Mathematica* terminates

Mathematica termination.

There are several ways to end a *Mathematica* session. If you are using *Mathematica* interactively, typing `Exit[ ]` or `Quit[ ]` on an input line will always terminate *Mathematica*.

If you are taking input for *Mathematica* from a file, *Mathematica* will exit when it reaches the end of the file. If you are using *Mathematica* interactively, it will still exit if it receives an end-of-file character (typically CTRL-d). You can stop *Mathematica* from doing this by setting `$IgnoreEOF=True`.

■ A.7.6 Network License Management

single-machine license	a process must always run on a specific machine
network license	a process can run on any machine on a network

Single-machine and network licenses.

Copies of *Mathematica* can be set up with either single-machine or network licenses. A network license is indicated by a line in the `mathpass` file starting with `!`*name*, where *name* is the name of the server machine for the network license.

Network licenses are controlled by the *Mathematica* license management program `mathlm`. This program must be running whenever a *Mathematica* with a network license is being used. Typically you will want to set up your system so that `mathlm` is started whenever the system boots.

- Type `.\mathlm` directly on the command line
- Add `mathlm` as a Windows service

Ways to start the network license manager under Microsoft Windows.

- Type `./mathlm` directly on the Unix command line
- Add a line to start `mathlm` in your central `/etc/rc.local` boot file
- Add a `crontab` entry to start `mathlm`

Ways to start the network license manager on Macintosh and Unix systems.

When `mathlm` is not started directly from a command line, it normally sets itself up as a background process, and continues running until it is explicitly terminated. Note that if one `mathlm` process is running, any other `mathlm` processes you try to start will automatically exit immediately.

-logfile *file*	write server messages to *file*
-pwfile *file*	use the specified `mathpass` file (default `./mathpass`)
-timeout *n*	suspend license from stopped *Mathematica* jobs after *n* hours (default infinity)
-restrict *file*	use the script contained in *file* to limit or deny access to specified users or machines
-install	install `mathlm` as a Windows service (Microsoft Windows only)
-uninstall *file*	uninstall `mathlm` as a Windows service (Microsoft Windows only)
-formatlog *string*	display server messages in a format specified by *string*
-localtime	use local time instead of the default Greenwich Mean Time in server messages
-trfile *file*	use the substitute text specified in *file* as the text of error messages,
-verbose *n*	print server messages to `stdout` with the level of verbosity determined by *n*, an integer between 1 and 4
-help	print the MathID and a list of all command-line options
-logginglevel *n*	control verbosity of messages to *logfile* with *n*, an integer between 1 and 4
-trlang *language*	use built-in translations, where *language* can be `english`, `french`, `german`, or `japanese`
-noremotemonitor	disable MonitorLM queries from hosts other than the MathLM server

Command-line options for `mathlm`.

You can use the `mathlm -restrict` *file* to tell the network license manager to authorize only certain sessions. The detailed syntax of a restriction script is explained in the *Network Mathematica System Administrator's Guide*.

`monitorlm`	a program to monitor network license activity

Monitoring network license activity.

You can use the program `monitorlm` to get information on current *Mathematica* license activity on your computer network.

`-server` *name*	report license activity on the server specified by *name*—this must be the first argument
`-template` *file*	use the format specified by *file* as a template for the output
`-output` *file*	write output to *file*
`-localtime`	use local time instead of the default Greenwich Mean Time
`-format` *format*	write output in the specified format, which can be `text`, `html`, `cgi`, or `file`

Command-line options for `monitorlm`.

A.8 *Mathematica* File Organization

■ A.8.1 *Mathematica* Distribution Files

A full *Mathematica* installation consists of something over 2200 separate files, arranged in a total of about 280 directories under the main installation directory. The location of the main installation directory is determined at install time. From within a *Mathematica* kernel, its name is given by the value of $InstallationDirectory.

```
C:\Program_Files\Wolfram_Research\Mathematica\5.0
                        Windows

/Applications/Mathematica 5.0.app
                        Macintosh

    /usr/local/mathematica    Unix
```

Default locations for the *Mathematica* installation directory.

The executable programs that launch *Mathematica* are typically in the main installation directory. Sometimes there may also be links to them, or scripts accessing them, in other locations. From within a *Mathematica* kernel, First[$CommandLine] gives the full name of the executable program corresponding to that kernel.

Mathematica	*Mathematica* front end
MathKernel	*Mathematica* kernel, usually with its own text-based interface
math	*Mathematica* kernel to be run in a terminal or shell
mcc	script for preprocessing and compiling *MathLink* C source files

Typical executable programs accessible from the installation directory.

The main installation directory has three standard subdirectories that contain material distributed with *Mathematica*. Under normal circumstances, none of the contents of these directories should ever be modified, except, for example, if you choose to edit a shared style sheet.

AddOns	bundled *Mathematica* add-ons
Documentation	*Mathematica* system documentation
SystemFiles	*Mathematica* system files

Top-level subdirectories of the main installation directory.

Particularly on Unix systems, *Mathematica* often has executable files for different computer architectures and systems stored in a single overall directory structure. Each system is in a subdirectory with a name given by $SystemID. Some resource directories may also contain files specific both to particular languages and particular computing environments. These files are given in subdirectories such as Japanese/Windows.

Kernel/Binaries/*system*	kernel binaries or elements for each computer system
Kernel/SystemResources/*system*	system-specific .mx files used by the kernel
Kernel/TextResources	message and text files used by the kernel
FrontEnd/Binaries/*system*	front end binaries or elements for each computer system
FrontEnd/SystemResources	files used by the front end in each window system environment
FrontEnd/TextResources	message and text files used by the front end
FrontEnd/StyleSheets	default notebook style sheets
FrontEnd/Palettes	default palette notebooks
Libraries/*system*	*MathLink* and other libraries used by the kernel and front end
Fonts	*Mathematica* fonts, often copied to a central directory
CharacterEncodings	specifications of character encodings
SpellingDictionaries	spelling dictionaries
SystemDocumentation/*env*	Unix man pages and other environment-specific documentation
Graphics/Binaries/*system*	PostScript interpreters and graphics programs
Graphics/SystemResources	PostScript definitions and other resources for graphics
Graphics/Packages	packages for setting up graphics

Typical subdirectories of the SystemFiles directory, part one.

Installation	various auxiliary programs used in installation, called automatically by the main installer program
IncludeFiles	files for inclusion in other programs
Java	files for the Java Runtime Environment (if needed)

Typical subdirectories of the `SystemFiles` directory, part two.

Bundled with versions of *Mathematica* are various standard add-on items. These are placed in the `AddOns` subdirectory of the main installation directory.

StandardPackages	standard add-on packages distributed with *Mathematica*
MathLink	*MathLink* development material
JLink	*J/Link* material
NETLink	*.NET/Link* material

Typical subdirectories of the `AddOns` directory.

The default contents of the *Mathematica* Help Browser are stored in the `Documentation` directory. `BrowserCategories` files in each subdirectory set up the categories used in the Help Browser. `BrowserIndex` files provide data for the master index.

RefGuide	reference guide and examples for built-in functions
MainBook	the complete text of this book
AddOns	documentation for standard add-on items
GettingStarted	introductory documentation, and demos
OtherInformation	additional information

Typical subdirectories of the `Documentation` directory.

■ A.8.2 Loadable Files

You can customize your *Mathematica* by adding files that can loaded into the system under different circumstances. Such files are conventionally placed in either system-wide or user-specific *base directories*.

$BaseDirectory	system-wide base directory for files to be loaded by *Mathematica*
$UserBaseDirectory	user-specific base directory for files to be loaded by *Mathematica*

Base directories for files to be loaded by *Mathematica*.

C:\Documents_and_Settings\All_Users\Application_Data\Mathematica	Windows
/Library/Mathematica	Macintosh
/usr/share/Mathematica	Unix

Typical values of $BaseDirectory.

C:\Documents_and_Settings*username*\Application_Data\Mathematica	Windows
~/Library/Mathematica	Macintosh
~/.Mathematica	Unix

Typical values of $UserBaseDirectory.

You can specify different locations for these directories by setting operating system environment variables when you launch *Mathematica,* as discussed on page 1055.

Applications	*Mathematica* application packages
Autoload	packages to be autoloaded on startup
FrontEnd	front end initialization files
Kernel	kernel initialization files
Licensing	license management files
SystemFiles	general system files

Typical subdirectories of *Mathematica* base directories.

Some files in base directories serve as configuration files, automatically used by the *Mathematica* kernel or front end.

`Kernel/init.m`	run when the kernel is started
`Kernel/end.m`	run when the kernel is terminated
`FrontEnd/init.m`	read when the front end is started
`SystemFiles/FrontEnd/StyleSheets/`	
	customized notebook style sheets
`SystemFiles/FrontEnd/Palettes/`	
	additional palettes to appear in the front end menu

Some typical kernel and front end configuration files.

Kernel configuration files can contain any *Mathematica* commands. These commands can test global variables such as $SystemID and $MachineName to determine what operations to perform. Front end configuration files can contain only certain special commands, as described on page 1038.

`Applications/`*name*`/`	named add-on applications
`Autoload/`*name*`/`	add-ons to be loaded automatically when *Mathematica* is started

Subdirectories under `$BaseDirectory` and `$UserBaseDirectory`.

With the default setting for the kernel $Path variable, an add-on can be loaded from within a *Mathematica* session simply by using the command <<*name*`. This will load the `init.m` file for the add-on, which should in turn be set up to load other necessary files or packages.

By placing an add-on under the `Autoload` subdirectory of $BaseDirectory or $UserBaseDirectory, you can have *Mathematica* automatically load the add-on whenever you start the kernel or the front end.

`init.m` or `Kernel/init.m`	an initialization file to be loaded by the kernel
`FrontEnd/init.m`	an initialization file to be loaded by the front end
`Documentation/`	documentation to be found by the front end

Typical possible contents of the directory for an add-on.

Note that with the default setting for the front end documentation path, all documentation in `Documentation` directories will automatically show up in the front end Help Browser.

A.9 Some Notes on Internal Implementation

■ A.9.1 Introduction

General issues about the internal implementation of *Mathematica* are discussed on pages 218–226. Given here are brief notes on particular features.

These notes apply to Version 5. Algorithms and other aspects of implementation are subject to change in future versions.

It should be emphasized that these notes give only a rough indication of basic methods and algorithms used. The actual implementation usually involves many substantial additional elements.

Thus, for example, the notes simply say that DSolve solves second-order linear differential equations using the Kovacic algorithm. But the internal code which achieves this is over 60 pages long, includes a number of other algorithms, and involves a great many subtleties.

■ A.9.2 Data Structures and Memory Management

A *Mathematica* expression internally consists of a contiguous array of pointers, the first to the head, and the rest to its successive elements.

Each expression contains a special form of hash code which is used both in pattern matching and evaluation.

For every symbol there is a central *symbol table entry* which stores all information about the symbol.

Most raw objects such as strings and numbers are allocated separately; unique copies are however maintained of small integers and of certain approximate numbers generated in computations.

Every piece of memory used by *Mathematica* maintains a count of how many times it is referenced. Memory is automatically freed when this count reaches zero.

The contiguous storage of elements in expressions reduces memory fragmentation and swapping. However, it can lead to the copying of a complete array of pointers when a single element in a long expression is modified. Many optimizations based on reference counts and pre-allocation are used to avoid such copying.

When appropriate, large lists and nested lists of numbers are automatically stored as packed arrays of machine-sized integers or real numbers. The *Mathematica* compiler is automatically used to compile complicated functions that will be repeatedly applied to such packed arrays. *MathLink*, DumpSave, Display, as well as various Import and Export formats, make external use of packed arrays.

■ A.9.3 Basic System Features

Mathematica is fundamentally an interpreter which scans through expressions calling internal code pointed to by the symbol table entries of heads that it encounters.

Any transformation rule—whether given as *x* -> *y* or in a definition—is automatically compiled into a form which allows for rapid pattern matching. Many different types of patterns are distinguished and are handled by special code.

A form of hashing that takes account of blanks and other features of patterns is used in pattern matching.

The internal code associated with pattern matching is approximately 250 pages long.

When a large number of definitions are given for a particular symbol, a hash table is automatically built using a version of Dispatch so that appropriate rules can quickly be found.

■ A.9.4 Numerical and Related Functions

Number representation and numerical evaluation

Large integers and high-precision approximate numbers are stored as arrays of base 2^{32} or 2^{64} digits, depending on the lengths of machine integers. ■ Precision is internally maintained as a floating-point number. ■ IntegerDigits, RealDigits and related base conversion functions use recursive divide-and-conquer algorithms. Similar algorithms are used for number input and output. ■ N uses an adaptive procedure to increase its internal working precision in order to achieve whatever overall precision is requested. ■ Floor, Ceiling and related functions use an adaptive procedure similar to N to generate exact results from exact input.

Basic arithmetic

Multiplication of large integers and high-precision approximate numbers is done using interleaved schoolbook, Karatsuba, three-way Toom-Cook and number-theoretic transform algorithms. ■ Machine-code optimization for specific architectures is achieved by using GMP. ■ Integer powers are found by a left-right binary decomposition algorithm. ■ Reciprocals and rational powers of approximate numbers use Newton's method. ■ Exact roots start from numerical estimates. ■ Significance arithmetic is used for all arithmetic with approximate numbers beyond machine precision.

Pseudorandom numbers

Random uses the Wolfram rule 30 cellular automaton generator for integers. ■ It uses a Marsaglia-Zaman subtract-with-borrow generator for real numbers.

Number-theoretical functions

GCD interleaves the HGCD algorithm, the Jebelean-Sorenson-Weber accelerated GCD algorithm, and a combination of Euclid's algorithm and an algorithm based on iterative removal of powers of 2. ■ PrimeQ first tests for divisibility using small primes, then uses the Miller-Rabin strong pseudoprime test base 2 and base 3, and then uses a Lucas test. ■ As of 1997, this procedure is known to be correct only for $n < 10^{16}$, and it is conceivable that for larger n it could claim a composite number to be prime. ■ The package NumberTheory`PrimeQ` contains a much slower algorithm which has been proved correct for all n. It can return an explicit certificate of primality. ■ FactorInteger switches between trial division, Pollard $p - 1$, Pollard rho and quadratic sieve algorithms. ■ The package NumberTheory`FactorIntegerECM` contains an elliptic curve algorithm suitable for factoring some very large integers. ■ Prime and PrimePi use sparse caching and sieving. For large n, the Lagarias-Miller-Odlyzko algorithm for PrimePi is used, based on asymptotic estimates of the density of primes, and is inverted to give Prime. ■ LatticeReduce uses the Lenstra-Lenstra-Lovasz lattice reduction algorithm. ■ To find a requested number of terms ContinuedFraction uses a modification of Lehmer's indirect method, with a self-restarting divide-and-conquer algorithm to reduce the numerical precision required at each step. ■ ContinuedFraction uses recurrence relations to find periodic continued fractions for quadratic irrationals. ■ FromContinuedFraction uses iterated matrix multiplication optimized by a divide-and-conquer method.

Combinatorial functions

Most combinatorial functions use sparse caching and recursion. ■ Factorial, Binomial and related functions use a divide-and-conquer algorithm to balance the number of digits in subproducts. ■ Fibonacci[n] uses an iterative method based on the binary digit sequence of n. ■ PartitionsP[n] uses Euler's pentagonal formula for small n, and the non-recursive Hardy-Ramanujan-Rademacher method for larger n. ■ ClebschGordan and related functions use generalized hypergeometric series.

Elementary transcendental functions

Exponential and trigonometric functions use Taylor series, stable recursion by argument doubling, and functional relations. ■ Log and inverse trigonometric functions use Taylor series and functional relations.

Mathematical constants

Values of constants are cached once computed. ■ Binary splitting is used to subdivide computations of constants. ■ Pi is computed using the Chudnovsky formula. ■ E is computed from its series expansion. ■ EulerGamma uses the Brent-McMillan algorithm. ■ Catalan is computed from a linearly convergent Ramanujan sum.

Special functions

For machine precision most special functions use *Mathematica*-derived rational minimax approximations. The notes that follow apply mainly to arbitrary precision. ▪ Orthogonal polynomials use stable recursion formulas for polynomial cases and hypergeometric functions in general. ▪ Gamma uses recursion, functional equations and the Binet asymptotic formula. ▪ Incomplete gamma and beta functions use hypergeometric series and continued fractions. ▪ PolyGamma uses Euler-Maclaurin summation, functional equations and recursion. ▪ PolyLog uses Euler-Maclaurin summation, expansions in terms of incomplete gamma functions and numerical quadrature. ▪ Zeta and related functions use Euler-Maclaurin summation and functional equations. Near the critical strip they also use the Riemann-Siegel formula. ▪ StieltjesGamma uses Keiper's algorithm based on numerical quadrature of an integral representation of the zeta function. ▪ The error function and functions related to exponential integrals are all evaluated using incomplete gamma functions. ▪ The inverse error functions use binomial search and a high-order generalized Newton's method. ▪ Bessel functions use series and asymptotic expansions. For integer orders, some also use stable forward recursion. ▪ The hypergeometric functions use functional equations, stable recurrence relations, series expansions and asymptotic series. Methods from NSum and NIntegrate are also sometimes used. ▪ ProductLog uses high-order Newton's method starting from rational approximations and asymptotic expansions. ▪ Elliptic integrals are evaluated using the descending Gauss transformation. ▪ Elliptic theta functions use series summation with recursive evaluation of series terms. ▪ Other elliptic functions mostly use arithmetic-geometric mean methods. ▪ Mathieu functions use Fourier series. The Mathieu characteristic functions use generalizations of Blanch's Newton method.

Numerical integration

With Method->Automatic, NIntegrate uses GaussKronrod in one dimension, and MultiDimensional otherwise. ▪ If an explicit setting for MaxPoints is given, NIntegrate by default uses Method->QuasiMonteCarlo. ▪ GaussKronrod: adaptive Gaussian quadrature with error estimation based on evaluation at Kronrod points. ▪ DoubleExponential: non-adaptive double-exponential quadrature. ▪ Trapezoidal: elementary trapezoidal method. ▪ Oscillatory: transformation to handle certain integrals containing trigonometric and Bessel functions. ▪ MultiDimensional: adaptive Genz-Malik algorithm. ▪ MonteCarlo: non-adaptive Monte Carlo. ▪ QuasiMonteCarlo: non-adaptive Halton-Hammersley-Wozniakowski algorithm.

Numerical sums and products

If the ratio test does not give 1, the Wynn epsilon algorithm is applied to a sequence of partial sums or products. ▪ Otherwise Euler-Maclaurin summation is used with Integrate or NIntegrate.

Numerical differential equations

For ordinary differential equations, NDSolve by default uses an LSODA approach, switching between a non-stiff Adams method and a stiff Gear backward differentiation formula method. ▪ For linear boundary value problems the Gel'fand-Lokutsiyevskii chasing method is used. ▪ Differential-algebraic equations use IDA, based on repeated BDF and Newton iteration methods. ▪ For $(n + 1)$-dimensional PDEs the method of lines is used. ▪ NDSolve supports explicit Method settings that cover most known methods from the literature. ▪ The code for NDSolve and related functions is about 1400 pages long.

Approximate equation solving and optimization

Polynomial root finding is done based on the Jenkins-Traub algorithm. ▪ For sparse linear systems, Solve and NSolve use several efficient numerical methods, mostly based on Gauss factoring with Markowitz products (approximately 250 pages of code). ▪ For systems of algebraic equations, NSolve computes a numerical Gröbner basis using an efficient monomial ordering, then uses eigensystem methods to extract numerical roots. ▪ FindRoot uses a damped Newton's method, the secant method and Brent's method. ▪ With Method->Automatic and two starting values, FindMinimum uses Brent's principal axis method. With one starting value for each variable, FindMinimum uses BFGS quasi-Newton methods, with a limited memory variant for large systems. ▪ If the function to be minimized is a sum of squares, FindMinimum uses the Levenberg-Marquardt method (Method->LevenbergMarquardt). ▪ LinearProgramming uses simplex and revised simplex methods, and with Method->"InteriorPoint" uses primal-dual interior point methods. ▪ For linear cases, NMinimize and NMaximize use the same methods as LinearProgramming. For nonlinear cases, they use Nelder-Mead methods, supplemented by differential evolution, especially when integer variables are present.

Data manipulation

`Fourier` uses the FFT algorithm with decomposition of the length into prime factors. When the prime factors are large, fast convolution methods are used to maintain $O(n \log(n))$ asymptotic complexity. ▪ For real input, `Fourier` uses a real transform method. ▪ `ListConvolve` and `ListCorrelate` use FFT algorithms when possible. For exact integer inputs, enough digits are computed to deduce exact integer results. ▪ `InterpolatingFunction` uses divided differences to construct Lagrange or Hermite interpolating polynomials. ▪ `Fit` works using singular value decomposition. `FindFit` uses the same method for the linear least-squares case, the Levenberg-Marquardt method for nonlinear least-squares, and general `FindMinimum` methods for other norms. ▪ `CellularAutomaton` uses bit-packed parallel operations with bit slicing. For elementary rules, absolutely optimal Boolean functions are used, while for totalistic rules, just-in-time-compiled bit-packed tables are used. In two dimensions, sparse bit-packed arrays are used when possible, with only active clusters updated.

Approximate numerical linear algebra

Machine-precision matrices are typically converted to a special internal representation for processing. ▪ `SparseArray` with rules involving patterns uses cylindrical algebraic decomposition to find connected array components. Sparse arrays are stored internally using compressed sparse row formats, generalized for tensors of arbitrary rank. ▪ For dense arrays, LAPACK algorithms extended for arbitrary precision are used when appropriate. ▪ BLAS technology is used to optimize for particular machine architectures. ▪ `LUDecomposition`, `Inverse`, `RowReduce` and `Det` use Gaussian elimination with partial pivoting. `LinearSolve` uses the same methods, together with iterative improvement for high-precision numbers. ▪ For sparse arrays, `LinearSolve` uses UMFPACK multifrontal direct solver methods and with `Method->"Krylov"` uses Krylov iterative methods preconditioned by an incomplete LU factorization. `Eigenvalues` and `Eigenvectors` use ARPACK Arnoldi methods. ▪ `SingularValueDecomposition` uses the QR algorithm with Givens rotations. `PseudoInverse`, `NullSpace` and `MatrixRank` are based on `SingularValueDecomposition`. ▪ `QRDecomposition` uses Householder transformations. ▪ `SchurDecomposition` uses QR iteration. ▪ `MatrixExp` uses Schur decomposition.

Exact numerical linear algebra

`Inverse` and `LinearSolve` use efficient row reduction based on numerical approximation. ▪ With `Modulus->`n, modular Gaussian elimination is used. ▪ `Det` uses modular methods and row reduction, constructing a result using the Chinese Remainder Theorem. ▪ `Eigenvalues` works by interpolating the characteristic polynomial. ▪ `MatrixExp` uses Putzer's method or Jordan decomposition.

▪ A.9.5 Algebra and Calculus

Polynomial manipulation

For univariate polynomials, `Factor` uses a variant of the Cantor-Zassenhaus algorithm to factor modulo a prime, then uses Hensel lifting and recombination to build up factors over the integers. ▪ Factoring over algebraic number fields is done by finding a primitive element over the rationals and then using Trager's algorithm. ▪ For multivariate polynomials `Factor` works by substituting appropriate choices of integers for all but one variable, then factoring the resulting univariate polynomials, and reconstructing multivariate factors using Wang's algorithm. ▪ The internal code for `Factor` exclusive of general polynomial manipulation is about 250 pages long. ▪ `FactorSquareFree` works by finding a derivative and then iteratively computing GCDs. ▪ `Resultant` uses either explicit subresultant polynomial remainder sequences or modular sequences accompanied by the Chinese Remainder Theorem. ▪ `Apart` uses either a version of the Padé technique or the method of undetermined coefficients. ▪ `PolynomialGCD` and `Together` usually use modular algorithms, including Zippel's sparse modular algorithm, but in some cases use subresultant polynomial remainder sequences. ▪ For multivariate polynomials the Chinese Remainder Theorem together with sparse interpolation are also used.

Symbolic linear algebra

`RowReduce`, `LinearSolve`, `NullSpace` and `MatrixRank` are based on Gaussian elimination. ▪ `Inverse` uses cofactor expansion and row reduction. Pivots are chosen heuristically by looking for simple expressions. ▪ `Det` uses direct cofactor expansion for small matrices, and Gaussian elimination for larger ones. ▪ `MatrixExp` finds eigenvalues and then uses Putzer's method. ▪ Zero testing for various functions is done using symbolic transformations and interval-based numerical approximations after random numerical values have been substituted for variables.

~Exact equation solving and reduction

For linear equations Gaussian elimination and other methods of linear algebra are used. ■ `Root` objects representing algebraic numbers are usually isolated and manipulated using validated numerical methods. With `ExactRootIsolation->True`, `Root` uses for real roots a continued fraction version of an algorithm based on Descartes' rule of signs, and for complex roots the Collins-Krandick algorithm. ■ For single polynomial equations, `Solve` uses explicit formulas up to degree four, attempts to reduce polynomials using `Factor` and `Decompose`, and recognizes cyclotomic and other special polynomials. ■ For systems of polynomial equations, `Solve` constructs a Gröbner basis. ■ `Solve` and `GroebnerBasis` use an efficient version of the Buchberger algorithm. ■ For non-polynomial equations, `Solve` attempts to change variables and add polynomial side conditions. ■ The code for `Solve` and related functions is about 500 pages long. ~■ For polynomial systems `Reduce` uses cylindrical algebraic decomposition for real domains and Gröbner basis methods for complex domains. ■ With algebraic functions, `Reduce` constructs equivalent purely polynomial systems. With transcendental functions, `Reduce` generates polynomial systems composed with transcendental conditions, then reduces these using functional relations and a database of inverse image information. ■ `CylindricalDecomposition` uses the Collins-Hong algorithm with Brown-McCallum projection for well-oriented sets and Hong projection for other sets. CAD construction is done by Strzebonski's genealogy-based method using validated numerics backed up by exact algebraic number computation. For zero-dimensional systems Gröbner basis methods are used. ■ For Diophantine systems, `Reduce` solves linear equations using Hermite normal form, and linear inequalities using Contejean-Devie methods. For univariate polynomial equations it uses an improved Cucker-Koiran-Smale method, while for bivariate quadratic equations, it uses Hardy-Muskat-Williams methods for ellipses, and classical techniques for Pell and other cases. `Reduce` includes specialized methods for about 25 classes of Diophantine equations, including the Tzanakis-de Weger algorithm for Thue equations. ■ With prime moduli, `Reduce` uses linear algebra for linear equations and Grobner bases over prime fields for polynomial equations. For composite moduli, it uses Hermite normal form and Gröbner bases over integers. ■ `Resolve` mainly uses an optimized subset of the methods from `Reduce`. ■ `Reduce` and related functions use about 350 pages of *Mathematica* code and 1400 pages of C code.

+Exact optimization

+For linear cases, `Minimize` and `Maximize` use exact linear programming methods. For polynomial cases they use cylindrical algebraic decomposition.

~Simplification

`FullSimplify` automatically applies about 40 types of general algebraic transformations, as well as about 400 types of rules for specific mathematical functions. ■ Generalized hypergeometric functions are simplified using about 70 pages of *Mathematica* transformation rules. These functions are fundamental to many calculus operations in *Mathematica*. ■ `FunctionExpand` uses an extension of Gauss's algorithm to expand trigonometric functions with arguments that are rational multiples of π. ■ `Simplify` and `FullSimplify` cache results when appropriate. ~■ When assumptions specify that variables are real, polynomial constraints are handled by cylindrical algebraic decomposition, while linear constraints are handled by the simplex algorithm or Loos-Weispfenning linear quantifier elimination. For strict polynomial inequalities, Strzebonski's generic CAD algorithm is used. ■ When assumptions involve equations among polynomials, Gröbner basis methods are used. ■ For non-algebraic functions, a database of relations is used to determine the domains of function values from the domains of their arguments. Polynomial-oriented algorithms are used whenever the resulting domains correspond to semi-algebraic sets. ■ For integer functions, several hundred theorems of number theory are used in the form of *Mathematica* rules.

Differentiation and integration

Differentiation uses caching to avoid recomputing partial results. ■ For indefinite integrals, an extended version of the Risch algorithm is used whenever both the integrand and integral can be expressed in terms of elementary functions, exponential integral functions, polylogarithms and other related functions. ■ For other indefinite integrals, heuristic simplification followed by pattern matching is used. ■ The algorithms in *Mathematica* cover all of the indefinite integrals in standard reference books such as Gradshteyn-Ryzhik. ■ Definite integrals that involve no singularities are mostly done by taking limits of the indefinite integrals. ■ Many other definite integrals are done using Marichev-Adamchik Mellin transform methods. The results are often initially expressed in terms of Meijer G functions, which are converted into hypergeometric functions using Slater's Theorem and then simplified. ■ `Integrate` uses about 500 pages of *Mathematica* code and 600 pages of C code.

Differential equations

Systems of linear equations with constant coefficients are solved using matrix exponentiation. ▪ Second-order linear equations with variable coefficients whose solutions can be expressed in terms of elementary functions and their integrals are solved using the Kovacic algorithm. ▪ Higher-order linear equations are solved using Abramov and Bronstein algorithms. ▪ Systems of linear equations with rational function coefficients whose solutions can be given as rational functions are solved using Abramov-Bronstein elimination algorithms. ▪ Linear equations with polynomial coefficients are solved in terms of special functions by using Mellin transforms. ▪ When possible, nonlinear equations are solved by symmetry reduction techniques. For first-order equations classical techniques are used; for second-order equations and systems integrating factor and Bocharov techniques are used. ▪ The algorithms in *Mathematica* cover most of the ordinary differential equations in standard reference books such as Kamke. ▪ For partial differential equations, separation of variables and symmetry reduction are used. ▪ For differential-algebraic equations, a method based on isolating singular parts by core nilpotent decomposition is used. ▪ DSolve uses about 300 pages of *Mathematica* code and 200 pages of C code.

Sums and products

Polynomial series are summed using Bernoulli and Euler polynomials. ▪ Series involving rational and factorial functions are summed using Adamchik techniques in terms of generalized hypergeometric functions, which are then simplified. ▪ Series involving polygamma functions are summed using integral representations. ▪ Dirichlet and related series are summed using pattern matching. ▪ For infinite series, d'Alembert and Raabe convergence tests are used. ▪ The algorithms in *Mathematica* cover at least 90% of the sums in standard reference books such as Gradshteyn-Ryzhik. ▪ Products are done primarily using pattern matching. ▪ Sum and Product use about 100 pages of *Mathematica* code.

Series and limits

Series works by recursively composing series expansions of functions with series expansions of their arguments. ▪ Limits are found from series and using other methods.

Recurrence equations

RSolve solves systems of linear equations with constant coefficients using matrix powers. ▪ Linear equations with polynomial coefficients whose solutions can be given as hypergeometric terms are solved using van Hoeij algorithms. ▪ Systems of linear equations with rational function coefficients whose solutions can be given as rational functions are solved using Abramov-Bronstein elimination algorithms. ▪ Nonlinear equations are solved by transformation of variables, Göktaş symmetry reduction methods or Germundsson trigonometric power methods. ▪ The algorithms in *Mathematica* cover most of the ordinary and *q*-difference equations ever discussed in the mathematical literature. ▪ For difference-algebraic equations, a method based on isolating singular parts by core nilpotent decomposition is used.

▪ A.9.6 Output and Interfacing

Graphics

Hidden-surface elimination for 3D graphics is done so as to be independent of display resolution. ▪ A custom-written PostScript interpreter is used to render graphics in the front end. ▪ Notebooks use a custom platform-independent bitmap image format.

Front end

The front end uses *MathLink* both for communication with the kernel, and for communication between its different internal components. ▪ All menu items and other functions in the front end are specified using *Mathematica* expressions. ▪ Configuration and preference files use *Mathematica* language format. ▪ The Help Browser is based on *Mathematica* notebooks generated from the same source code as this book.

Notebooks

Notebooks are represented as *Mathematica* expressions. ▪ Notebook files contain additional cached outline information in the form of *Mathematica* comments. This information makes possible efficient random access. ▪ Incremental saving of notebooks is done so as to minimize rewriting of data, moving data already written out whenever possible. ▪ Platform-independent double-buffering is used by default to minimize flicker when window contents are updated.

▪ Autoscrolling uses a control-theoretical mechanism to optimize smoothness and controllability. ▪ All special characters are platform-independently represented using Unicode. Mapping tables are set up for specific Kanji and other fonts. ▪ Spell checking and hyphenation are done using algorithms and a 100,000-word standard English dictionary, together with a 20,000-word technical dictionary, with 5000 *Mathematica* and other words added. Spelling correction is done using textual and phonetic metrics.

MathLink

In OSI terms, *MathLink* is a presentation-level protocol, which can be layered on top of any transport medium, both message-based and stream-based. ▪ *MathLink* encodes data in a compressed format when it determines that both ends of a link are on compatible computer systems. ▪ *MathLink* can transmit out-of-band data such as interrupts as well as *Mathematica* expressions. ▪ When possible *MathLink* is implemented using dynamically linked shared libraries.

Expression formatting

The front end uses a directed acyclic graph to represent the box structure of formatted expressions. ▪ Boxes are interpreted using a two-dimensional generalization of an operator precedence parser. ▪ Incremental parsing is used to minimize structure and display updating. ▪ Character spacing and positioning are determined from font data and operator tables. ▪ Line breaking is globally optimized throughout expressions, based on a method similar to the one used for text layout in TEX. ▪ During input, line breaking is set up so that small changes to expressions rarely cause large-scale reformatting; if the input needs to jump, an elliptical cursor tracker momentarily appears to guide the eye. ▪ Expression formatting uses about 2000 pages of C code.

A.10 Listing of Major Built-in *Mathematica* Objects

■ Introduction

This section gives an alphabetical list of built-in objects which are supported in *Mathematica* Version 5.

The list does not include objects such as `CirclePlus` that are associated with operators such as ⊕, but which have no built-in values.

The list also does not include objects that are defined in *Mathematica* packages, even those distributed as a standard part of the *Mathematica* system.

Note also that options which appear only in a single built-in *Mathematica* function are sometimes not given as separate entries in the list.

A few objects in the list, mostly ones related to external operations, are not available on some computer systems.

+■	object or feature completely new since Version 4.0
~■	object or feature whose functionality was extensively changed since Version 4.0

New and modified objects and features in the listing.

New in Version … indicates in what version of *Mathematica* a function first appeared.

Modified in Version … indicates in what version substantial changes of functionality were last made.

The internal code of *Mathematica* is continually improved and enhanced, and between each major version the code for a great many built-in functions is modified in some way or another. So even if an object is not indicated by +■, ~■ or *Modified in …* in this listing, it may well have been substantially enhanced in its efficiency or in the quality of results it gives.

This listing includes only standard built-in *Mathematica* objects that reside in the `System`` context. In a typical version of *Mathematica* there may be additional objects present both in the `System`` context, as well as in the `Developer`` and `Experimental`` contexts. For production work it is best to use only documented objects in the `System`` context, since the specifications of other objects may change in future versions. The online documentation for your version of *Mathematica* may contain information on `Developer`` and `Experimental`` objects. Further information is available at the Wolfram Research website.

System`	built-in objects given in this listing
Developer`	advanced objects intended for *Mathematica* developers
Experimental`	objects provided on an experimental basis

Contexts for built-in objects.

In many versions of *Mathematica*, you can access the text given in this section directly, typically using the Help Browser (see page 57). Typing ?*F* to the *Mathematica* kernel will also give you the main description of the object *F* from this section.

More information on related packages mentioned in this listing can be found using the Help Browser, or by looking at *Standard Add-on Packages* published by Wolfram Research. Note that the specifications of functions in packages are subject to incompatible changes in future versions of *Mathematica*.

There are a total of 1226 objects in this listing.

■ Conventions in This Listing

text in this style	literal *Mathematica* input that you type in as it is printed (e.g., function names)
text in this style	expressions that you fill in (e.g., function arguments)
object$_1$, *object*$_2$, ...	a sequence of any number of expressions
+	new since *Mathematica* Version 4.0
~	modified since *Mathematica* Version 4.0

Conventions used in the list of built-in objects.

Note that for items modified in Version 5 this listing makes no distinction between those new in Version 3 and those not.

■ Abort

Abort[ ] generates an interrupt to abort a computation.

You can call `Abort` anywhere within a computation. It has the same effect as an interactive interrupt in which you select the abort option. ■ You can use `Abort` as an "emergency stop" in a computation. ■ Once `Abort` has been called, *Mathematica* functions currently being evaluated return as quickly as possible. ■ In an interactive session, the final result from an aborted computation is `$Aborted`. ■ You can use `CheckAbort` to "catch" returns from an abort. ■ See page 371. ■ See also: `Throw`, `TimeConstrained`, `MemoryConstrained`, `Return`. ■ *New in Version 2.*

■ AbortProtect

AbortProtect[*expr*] evaluates *expr*, saving any aborts until the evaluation is complete.

Aborts that are generated during an `AbortProtect` take effect as soon as the execution of the `AbortProtect` is over. ■ `CheckAbort` can be used inside `AbortProtect` to catch and absorb any aborts that occur. ■ `AbortProtect` also protects against aborts generated by `TimeConstrained` and `MemoryConstrained`. ■ See page 371. ■ *New in Version 2.*

■ Abs

Abs[*z*] gives the absolute value of the real or complex number *z*.

For complex numbers z, `Abs[z]` gives the modulus $|z|$. ■ `Abs[z]` is left unevaluated if z is not a numeric quantity. ■ See pages 745 and 746. ■ See also: `Re`, `Im`, `Arg`, `Mod`, `ComplexExpand`, `Norm`. ■ *New in Version 1.*

■ AbsoluteDashing

AbsoluteDashing[{d_1, d_2, ... }] is a graphics directive which specifies that lines which follow are to be drawn dashed, with successive segments having absolute lengths d_1, d_2, ... (repeated cyclically).

The absolute lengths are measured in units of printer's points, approximately equal to $\frac{1}{72}$ of an inch. ■ `AbsoluteDashing[{ }]` specifies that lines should be solid. ■ `AbsoluteDashing` can be used in both two- and three-dimensional graphics. ■ See page 501. ■ See also: `AbsoluteThickness`, `Offset`, `Thickness`, `GrayLevel`, `Hue`, `RGBColor`. ■ *New in Version 2.*

■ AbsoluteOptions

AbsoluteOptions[*expr*] gives the absolute settings of options specified in an expression such as a graphics object.

AbsoluteOptions[*expr*, *name*] gives the absolute setting for the option *name*.

AbsoluteOptions[*expr*, {*name*$_1$, *name*$_2$, ... }] gives a list of the absolute settings for the options *name*$_i$.

AbsoluteOptions[*object*] gives the absolute settings for options associated with an external object such as a `NotebookObject`.

`AbsoluteOptions` gives the actual settings for options used internally by *Mathematica* when the setting given is `Automatic` or `All`. ■ `AbsoluteOptions` returns lists of rules, just like `Options`. ■ You can use `AbsoluteOptions` on graphics options such as `PlotRange` and `Ticks`. ■ If you ask for `AbsoluteOptions[NotebookObject[... ]`, *name*] the kernel will send a request to the front end to find the result. ■ See pages 145 and 490. ■ See also: `Options`, `FullGraphics`. ■ Related package: `Utilities`FilterOptions``. ■ *New in Version 4.*

■ **AbsolutePointSize**

AbsolutePointSize[*d*] is a graphics directive which specifies that points which follow are to be shown if possible as circular regions with absolute diameter *d*.

The absolute diameter is measured in units of printer's points, approximately equal to $\frac{1}{72}$ of an inch. ■ AbsolutePointSize can be used in both two- and three-dimensional graphics. ■ See page 500. ■ See also: Offset, PointSize, AbsoluteThickness, Thickness. ■ *New in Version 2; modified in Version 3.*

■ **AbsoluteThickness**

AbsoluteThickness[*d*] is a graphics directive which specifies that lines which follow are to be drawn with absolute thickness *d*.

The absolute thickness is measured in units of printer's points, approximately equal to $\frac{1}{72}$ of an inch. ■ AbsoluteThickness can be used in both two- and three-dimensional graphics. ■ See page 501. ■ See also: Offset, AbsoluteDashing, AbsolutePointSize, PointSize, Dashing. ■ *New in Version 2.*

■ **AbsoluteTime**

AbsoluteTime[ ] gives the total number of seconds since the beginning of January 1, 1900, in your time zone.

AbsoluteTime[ ] uses whatever date and time have been set on your computer system. It performs no corrections for time zones, daylight saving time, etc. ■ AbsoluteTime[*z*] gives the result for time zone *z*. This is inferred by knowing your local date and time, and local time zone. The time zone is given as the number of hours to be added to Greenwich mean time to obtain local time. ~■ AbsoluteTime[ ] is always accurate down to a granularity of $TimeUnit seconds, but on many systems is much more accurate. ■ There are 2208988800 seconds from the beginning of January 1, 1900 to the beginning of January 1, 1970 and 2840140800 seconds to the beginning of January 1, 1990. ■ See page 710. ■ See also: Date, SessionTime, TimeUsed, AbsoluteTiming, Timing, TimeZone, ToDate, FromDate. ■ Related package: Miscellaneous`Calendar`. ■ *New in Version 2.*

⁺■ **AbsoluteTiming**

AbsoluteTiming[*expr*] evaluates *expr*, returning a list of the absolute time that has elapsed, together with the result obtained.

AbsoluteTiming gives the absolute number of seconds of real time that have elapsed, multiplied by the symbol Second. ■ AbsoluteTiming has attribute HoldAll. ■ AbsoluteTiming[*expr*;] will give {*timing*, Null}. ■ First[AbsoluteTiming[*expr*;]] /. Second->1 yields just the number of seconds of time elapsed in the evaluation of *expr*. ■ AbsoluteTiming is always accurate down to a granularity of $TimeUnit seconds, but on many systems is much more accurate. ■ See page 711. ■ See also: Timing, TimeConstrained, SessionTime, AbsoluteTime. ■ *New in Version 5.0.*

■ **AccountingForm**

AccountingForm[*expr*] prints with all numbers in *expr* given in standard accounting notation.

AccountingForm[*expr*, *n*] prints with numbers given to *n*-digit precision.

AccountingForm never uses scientific notation. ■ AccountingForm uses parentheses to indicate negative numbers. ■ AccountingForm takes the same options as NumberForm, but uses a different default function for ExponentFunction, and a different default for NumberSigns. ■ AccountingForm acts as a "wrapper", which affects printing, but not evaluation. ■ See page 435. ■ See also: PaddedForm, NumberForm. ■ *New in Version 2.*

◼ Accuracy

Accuracy[x] gives the effective number of digits to the right of the decimal point in the number x.

+◾ Accuracy[x] gives a measure of the absolute uncertainty in the value of x. +◾ With uncertainty dx, Accuracy[x] is -Log[10, dx]. ◾ For exact numbers such as integers, Accuracy[x] is Infinity. ~◾ Accuracy[x] does not normally yield an integer result, and need not be positive. ~◾ For machine-precision numbers, Accuracy[x] gives the same as $MachinePrecision - Log[10, Abs[x]]. +◾ Accuracy[0.] is Log[10, $MinMachineNumber]. +◾ Numbers entered in the form *digits*`` *a* are taken to have accuracy *a*. ◾ If x is not a number, Accuracy[x] gives the minimum value of Accuracy for all the numbers that appear in x. ◾ See page 727. ◾ See also: Precision, N, Chop, SetAccuracy. ◾ *New in Version 1; modified in Version 5.0.*

◼ AccuracyGoal

AccuracyGoal is an option for various numerical operations which specifies how many effective digits of accuracy should be sought in the final result.

AccuracyGoal is an option for such functions as NIntegrate, NDSolve and FindRoot. ~◾ AccuracyGoal -> Automatic normally yields an accuracy goal equal to half the setting for WorkingPrecision. ◾ AccuracyGoal -> Infinity specifies that accuracy should not be used as the criterion for terminating the numerical procedure. PrecisionGoal is typically used in this case. ◾ Even though you may specify AccuracyGoal->n, the results you get may sometimes have much less than n-digit accuracy. ◾ In most cases, you must set WorkingPrecision to be at least as large as AccuracyGoal. ◾ AccuracyGoal effectively specifies the absolute error allowed in a numerical procedure. ◾ With AccuracyGoal->a and PrecisionGoal->p, *Mathematica* attempts to make the numerical error in a result of size x be less than $10^{-a} + |x|10^{-p}$. ◾ See page 976. ◾ See also: PrecisionGoal, WorkingPrecision. ◾ *New in Version 1; modified in Version 5.0.*

◼ Active

Active is an option for ButtonBox, Cell and Notebook which specifies whether a button should be active.

With Active->False the contents of a button can be edited. ◾ With Active->True a button will perform an action when it is clicked. ◾ Active cells are indicated by an A in their cell bracket. ◾ See page 607. ◾ See also: ButtonStyle, Evaluator. ◾ *New in Version 3.*

◼ AddTo

x += dx adds dx to x and returns the new value of x.

AddTo has the attribute HoldFirst. ◾ x += dx is equivalent to $x = x + dx$. ◾ See page 305. ◾ See also: Increment, PreIncrement, Set, PrependTo. ◾ *New in Version 1.*

■ AdjustmentBox

AdjustmentBox[*box*, *opts*] displays with the placement of *box* adjusted using the options given.

In the notebook front end, AdjustmentBox objects can typically be inserted and modified using CTRL ←, CTRL →, CTRL ↑ and CTRL ↓. These keys move your current selection by one pixel at the current screen magnification. ■ The following options can be given:

BoxMargins	{{*left*, *right*}, {*bottom*, *top*}}	margins to leave around the contents of the box
BoxBaselineShift	*up*	how much the baseline should be shifted relative to those of neighboring boxes

■ Horizontal motion specifications are in ems; vertical ones in x-heights. ■ Motion specifications can be either positive or negative numbers. ■ Positive margin specifications increase the spacing around *box*; negative ones decrease it. ■ Moving the baseline affects for example vertical alignment in a RowBox. ■ Top and bottom margins affect for example placement in a FractionBox or an OverscriptBox. ■ In StandardForm and InputForm input, AdjustmentBox is by default ignored, so that AdjustmentBox[*box*, *opts*] is interpreted just as *box* would be. ■ Inserting an explicit spacing character such as \[ThinSpace] can have the same effect for display as AdjustmentBox, but the spacing character by default affects interpretation. ■ AdjustmentBox[*box*, *opts*] uses the options given only to adjust the position of *box* itself. Unlike StyleBox, it does not propagate the options to subboxes. ■ See page 455. ■ See also: StyleBox, GridBox, ScriptBaselineShifts. ■ *New in Version 3.*

■ AiryAi

AiryAi[*z*] gives the Airy function Ai(*z*).

Mathematical function (see Section A.3.10). ■ The Airy function Ai(*z*) is a solution to the differential equation $y'' - xy = 0$. ■ Ai(*z*) tends to zero as $z \to \infty$. ■ AiryAi[*z*] is an entire function of *z* with no branch cut discontinuities. ■ See page 775. ■ See also: AiryAiPrime, AiryBi, AiryBiPrime. ■ *New in Version 1.*

■ AiryAiPrime

AiryAiPrime[*z*] gives the derivative of the Airy function Ai'(*z*).

Mathematical function (see Section A.3.10). ■ See notes for AiryAi. ■ See page 775. ■ See also: AiryBi, AiryBiPrime. ■ *New in Version 2.*

■ AiryBi

AiryBi[*z*] gives the Airy function Bi(*z*).

Mathematical function (see Section A.3.10). ■ The Airy function Bi(*z*) is a solution to the differential equation $y'' - xy = 0$. ■ Bi(*z*) increases exponentially as $z \to \infty$. ■ AiryBi[*z*] is an entire function of *z* with no branch cut discontinuities. ■ See page 775. ■ See also: AiryAi, AiryBiPrime. ■ *New in Version 2.*

■ AiryBiPrime

AiryBiPrime[*z*] gives the derivative of the Airy function Bi'(*z*).

Mathematical function (see Section A.3.10). ■ See notes for AiryBi. ■ See page 775. ■ See also: AiryAi, AiryAiPrime. ■ *New in Version 2.*

■ Algebraics

Algebraics represents the domain of algebraic numbers, as in $x \in$ **Algebraics**.

Algebraic numbers are defined to be numbers that solve polynomial equations with rational coefficients. ■ $x \in$ **Algebraics** evaluates immediately only for quantities x that are explicitly constructed from rational numbers, radicals and **Root** objects, or are known to be transcendental. ■ **Simplify[***expr* $\in$ **Algebraics]** can be used to try to determine whether an expression corresponds to an algebraic number. ■ **Algebraics** is output in **TraditionalForm** as $\mathbb{A}$. ■ See page 817. ■ See also: **Element, Simplify, Integers, Root, Extension, Reals**. ■ *New in Version 4.*

■ All

All is a setting used for certain options.

In **Part** and related functions, **All** specifies all parts at a particular level.

For example, **PlotRange -> All** specifies that all points are to be included in a plot. ■ See page 136. ■ See also: **Automatic, None, Part**. ■ *New in Version 1; modified in Version 4.0.*

■ Alternatives

$p_1 \mid p_2 \mid \ldots$ is a pattern object which represents any of the patterns p_i.

Example: **_Integer | _Real** represents an object with head either **Integer** or **Real**. ■ Unless the same set of pattern names appears in all of the p_i, you cannot use these pattern names on the right-hand side of transformation rules for the pattern. Thus, for example, you can use x in **a[x_] | b[x_]**, but you can use neither x nor y in **a[x_] | b[y_]**. ■ See page 269. ■ See also: **Optional**. ■ *New in Version 2.*

■ AmbientLight

AmbientLight is an option for **Graphics3D** and related functions that gives the level of simulated ambient illumination in a three-dimensional picture.

The setting for **AmbientLight** must be a **GrayLevel, Hue** or **RGBColor** directive. ■ See page 545. ■ See also: **Lighting, LightSources, SurfaceColor**. ■ *New in Version 1.*

■ AnchoredSearch

AnchoredSearch is an option for **Find** and **FindList** which specifies whether the text searched for must be at the beginning of a record.

With the default setting **RecordSeparators -> {"\n"}**, **AnchoredSearch -> True** specifies that the text must appear at the beginning of a line. ■ See page 651. ■ *New in Version 2.*

■ And

e_1 **&&** e_2 **&&** $\ldots$ is the logical AND function. It evaluates its arguments in order, giving **False** immediately if any of them are **False**, and **True** if they are all **True**.

And[e_1, e_2, $\ldots$ **]** can be input in **StandardForm** and **InputForm** as $e_1 \wedge e_2 \wedge \ldots$. The character $\wedge$ can be entered as :**&&**: :**and**: or **\[And]**. ■ **And** evaluates its arguments in a non-standard way (see page 1046). ■ **And** gives symbolic results when necessary, removing initial arguments that are **True**. ■ See page 87. ■ See also: **LogicalExpand, BitAnd, Nand**. ■ *New in Version 1; modified in Version 3.*

■ AnimationDirection

AnimationDirection is an option for **Cell** which specifies the direction to run an animation which starts with the cell.

The setting `AnimationDirection->Forward` specifies that the animation should run through successive selected graphics cells in the order that they appear in the notebook, and should then start again at the first cell. ■ `AnimationDirection->Backward` specifies that the reverse order should be used. ■ `AnimationDirection->ForwardBackward` specifies that the animation should run from the first cell to the last, and should then reverse back to the first cell again. ■ It is the setting of `AnimationDirection` for the first graphics cell in the sequence selected that determines the animation direction for the whole sequence. ■ See page 617. ■ See also: `AnimationDisplayTime`. ■ *New in Version 3.*

■ AnimationDisplayTime

AnimationDisplayTime is an option for **Cell** which specifies the minimum time in seconds for which a cell should be displayed in the course of an animation.

The default setting of `AnimationDisplayTime->0.1` specifies that the animation should be run as fast as your computer can. ■ See page 617. ■ See also: `AnimationDirection`. ■ *New in Version 3.*

■ Apart

Apart[*expr*] rewrites a rational expression as a sum of terms with minimal denominators.

Apart[*expr*, *var*] treats all variables other than *var* as constants.

Example: `Apart[(x^2+1)/(x-1)]` $\longrightarrow$ `1 + 2/(-1 + x) + x`. ■ Apart gives the partial fraction decomposition of a rational expression. ■ `Apart[`*expr*`, `*var*`]` writes *expr* as a polynomial in *var* together with a sum of ratios of polynomials, where the degree in *var* of each numerator polynomial is less than that of the corresponding denominator polynomial. ■ `Apart[(x + y)/(x - y), x]` $\longrightarrow$ `1 + (2*y)/(x - y)`. ■ `Apart[(x + y)/(x - y), y]` $\longrightarrow$ `-1 - (2*x)/(-x + y)`. ■ `Apart[`*expr*`, Trig -> True]` treats trigonometric functions as rational functions of exponentials, and manipulates them accordingly. ■ See page 802. ■ See also: `Together, Cancel, PolynomialQuotient`. ■ *New in Version 1.*

■ AppellF1

AppellF1[*a*, b_1, b_2, *c*, *x*, *y*] is the Appell hypergeometric function of two variables $F_1(a; b_1, b_2; c; x, y)$.

Mathematical function (see Section A.3.10). ■ $F_1(a; b_1, b_2; c; x, y)$ has series expansion $\sum_{m=0}^{\infty} \sum_{n=0}^{\infty} (a)_{m+n}(b_1)_m(b_2)_n/(m!n!(c)_{m+n})x^m y^n$. ■ $F_1(a; b_1, b_2; c; x, y)$ reduces to $_2F_1(a, b; c; z)$ when $x = 0$ or $y = 0$. ■ `AppellF1[`*a*, b_1, b_2, *c*, *x*, *y*`]` has singular lines in two-variable complex (x, y) space at $\text{Re}(x) = 1$ and $\text{Re}(y) = 1$, and has branch cut discontinuities along the rays from 1 to ∞ in *x* and *y*. ■ `FullSimplify` and `FunctionExpand` include transformation rules for `AppellF1`. ■ See page 780. ■ See also: `Hypergeometric2F1`. ■ *New in Version 4.*

■ Append

Append[*expr*, *elem*] gives *expr* with *elem* appended.

Examples: `Append[{a,b}, c]` $\longrightarrow$ `{a, b, c}`; `Append[f[a], b+c]` $\longrightarrow$ `f[a, b + c]`. ~■ In iteratively building a list, it is usually more efficient to use `Sow` and `Reap` than to use `Append[`*list*, *new*`]` at each step. +■ Append works on `SparseArray` objects, returning ordinary lists if necessary. ■ See pages 125 and 288. ■ See also: `Prepend, Insert, AppendTo, PadRight, Sow`. ■ *New in Version 1.*

■ AppendTo

`AppendTo[s, elem]` appends *elem* to the value of *s*, and resets *s* to the result.

`AppendTo[s, elem]` is equivalent to *s* = `Append[s, elem]`. ■ `AppendTo[s, elem]` does not evaluate *s*. ~■ You can use `AppendTo` repeatedly to build up a list, though `Sow` and `Reap` will usually be more efficient. +■ `AppendTo` works on `SparseArray` objects, returning ordinary lists if necessary. ■ See page 306. ■ See also: `PrependTo`, `Sow`. ■ *New in Version 1.*

■ Apply

`Apply[f, expr]` or *f* `@@` *expr* replaces the head of *expr* by *f*.

`Apply[f, expr, levelspec]` replaces heads in parts of *expr* specified by *levelspec*.

Examples: `Apply[f, {a, b, c}]` ⟶ `f[a, b, c]`; `Apply[Plus, g[a, b]]` ⟶ `a + b`. ■ Level specifications are described on page 1041. ■ The default value for *levelspec* in `Apply` is {0}. ■ *f* `@@@` *expr* is equivalent to `Apply[f, expr, {1}]`. ■ Examples: `Apply[f, {{a,b},{c,d}}]` ⟶ `f[{a, b}, {c, d}]`. ■ `Apply[f, {{a,b},{c,d}}, {1}]` ⟶ `{f[a, b], f[c, d]}`. ■ `Apply[f, {{{{a}}}}, -2]` ⟶ `{f[f[f[a]]]}`. +■ `Apply` operates on `SparseArray` objects just as it would on the corresponding ordinary lists. ■ See page 243. ■ See also: `Map`, `Scan`, `Level`, `Operate`, `MapThread`, `Total`. ■ *New in Version 1; modified in Version 4.0.*

■ ArcCos

`ArcCos[z]` gives the arc cosine $\cos^{-1}(z)$ of the complex number *z*.

Mathematical function (see Section A.3.10). ■ All results are given in radians. ■ For real *z* between −1 and 1, the results are always in the range 0 to π. ■ `ArcCos[z]` has branch cut discontinuities in the complex *z* plane running from −∞ to −1 and +1 to +∞. ■ See page 761. ■ *New in Version 1.*

■ ArcCosh

`ArcCosh[z]` gives the inverse hyperbolic cosine $\cosh^{-1}(z)$ of the complex number *z*.

Mathematical function (see Section A.3.10). ■ `ArcCosh[z]` has a branch cut discontinuity in the complex *z* plane running from −∞ to +1. ■ See page 761. ■ See also: `ArcSech`. ■ *New in Version 1.*

■ ArcCot

`ArcCot[z]` gives the arc cotangent $\cot^{-1}(z)$ of the complex number *z*.

Mathematical function (see Section A.3.10). ■ All results are given in radians. ■ For real *z*, the results are always in the range −π/2 to π/2, excluding 0. ■ `ArcCot[z]` has a branch cut discontinuity in the complex *z* plane running from −*i* to +*i*. ■ See page 761. ■ *New in Version 1.*

■ ArcCoth

`ArcCoth[z]` gives the inverse hyperbolic cotangent $\coth^{-1}(z)$ of the complex number *z*.

Mathematical function (see Section A.3.10). ■ `ArcCoth[z]` has a branch cut discontinuity in the complex *z* plane running from −1 to +1. ■ See page 761. ■ *New in Version 1.*

■ ArcCsc

`ArcCsc[z]` gives the arc cosecant $\csc^{-1}(z)$ of the complex number *z*.

Mathematical function (see Section A.3.10). ■ All results are given in radians. ■ For real *z* outside the interval −1 to 1, the results are always in the range −π/2 to π/2, excluding 0. ■ `ArcCsc[z]` has a branch cut discontinuity in the complex *z* plane running from −1 to +1. ■ See page 761. ■ *New in Version 1.*

■ ArcCsch

ArcCsch[z] gives the inverse hyperbolic cosecant $\mathrm{csch}^{-1}(z)$ of the complex number z.

Mathematical function (see Section A.3.10). ▪ ArcCsch[z] has a branch cut discontinuity in the complex z plane running from $-i$ to $+i$. ▪ See page 761. ▪ *New in Version 1.*

■ ArcSec

ArcSec[z] gives the arc secant $\sec^{-1}(z)$ of the complex number z.

Mathematical function (see Section A.3.10). ▪ All results are given in radians. ▪ For real z outside the interval -1 to 1, the results are always in the range 0 to π, excluding $\pi/2$. ▪ ArcSec[z] has a branch cut discontinuity in the complex z plane running from -1 to $+1$. ▪ See page 761. ▪ *New in Version 1.*

■ ArcSech

ArcSech[z] gives the inverse hyperbolic secant $\mathrm{sech}^{-1}(z)$ of the complex number z.

Mathematical function (see Section A.3.10). ▪ ArcSech[z] has branch cut discontinuities in the complex z plane running from $-\infty$ to 0 and $+1$ to $+\infty$. ▪ See page 761. ▪ *New in Version 1.*

■ ArcSin

ArcSin[z] gives the arc sine $\sin^{-1}(z)$ of the complex number z.

Mathematical function (see Section A.3.10). ▪ All results are given in radians. ▪ For real z between -1 and 1, the results are always in the range $-\pi/2$ to $\pi/2$. ▪ ArcSin[z] has branch cut discontinuities in the complex z plane running from $-\infty$ to -1 and $+1$ to $+\infty$. ▪ See page 761. ▪ *New in Version 1.*

■ ArcSinh

ArcSinh[z] gives the inverse hyperbolic sine $\sinh^{-1}(z)$ of the complex number z.

Mathematical function (see Section A.3.10). ▪ ArcSinh[z] has branch cut discontinuities in the complex z plane running from $-i\infty$ to $-i$ and $+i$ to $+i\infty$. ▪ See page 761. ▪ See also: ArcCsch. ▪ *New in Version 1.*

■ ArcTan

ArcTan[z] gives the arc tangent $\tan^{-1}(z)$ of the complex number z.

ArcTan[x, y] gives the arc tangent of $\frac{y}{x}$, taking into account which quadrant the point (x, y) is in.

Mathematical function (see Section A.3.10). ▪ All results are given in radians. ▪ For real z, the results are always in the range $-\pi/2$ to $\pi/2$. ▪ ArcTan[z] has branch cut discontinuities in the complex z plane running from $-i\infty$ to $-i$ and $+i$ to $+i\infty$. ▪ If x or y is complex, then ArcTan[x, y] gives $-i\,\log\!\left((x + iy)/\sqrt{x^2 + y^2}\right)$. When $x^2 + y^2 = 1$, ArcTan[x, y] gives the number ϕ such that $x = \cos\phi$ and $y = \sin\phi$. ▪ See page 761. ▪ See also: Arg. ▪ *New in Version 1.*

■ ArcTanh

ArcTanh[z] gives the hyperbolic arc tangent $\tanh^{-1}(z)$ of the complex number z.

Mathematical function (see Section A.3.10). ▪ See page 761. ▪ ArcTanh[z] has branch cut discontinuities in the complex z plane running from $-\infty$ to -1 and $+1$ to $+\infty$. ▪ See also: ArcCoth. ▪ *New in Version 1.*

■ Arg

Arg[z] gives the argument of the complex number *z*.

Mathematical function (see Section A.3.10). ■ **Arg[z]** is left unevaluated if *z* is not a numeric quantity. ■ **Arg[z]** gives the phase angle of *z* in radians. ■ The result from **Arg[z]** is always between $-\pi$ and $+\pi$. ■ **Arg[z]** has a branch cut discontinuity in the complex *z* plane running from $-\infty$ to 0. ■ See page 746. ■ See also: **ArcTan, Sign**. ■ *New in Version 1.*

■ ArithmeticGeometricMean

ArithmeticGeometricMean[*a*, *b*] gives the arithmetic-geometric mean of *a* and *b*.

See page 788. ■ *New in Version 1.*

■ Array

Array[*f*, *n*] generates a list of length *n*, with elements *f*[*i*].

Array[*f*, {n_1, n_2, ... }] generates an $n_1 \times n_2 \times ...$ array of nested lists, with elements *f*[i_1, i_2, ...].

Array[*f*, {n_1, n_2, ... }, {r_1, r_2, ... }] generates a list using the index origins r_i (default 1).

Array[*f*, *dims*, *origin*, *h*] uses head *h*, rather than **List**, for each level of the array.

Examples: **Array[f, 3]** $\longrightarrow$ **{f[1], f[2], f[3]}**.
■ **Array[f, {2, 3}]** $\longrightarrow$ **{{f[1, 1], f[1, 2], f[1, 3]}, {f[2, 1], f[2, 2], f[2, 3]}}** generates a 2×3 matrix.
■ **Array[#1^#2 &, {2, 2}]** $\longrightarrow$ **{{1, 1}, {2, 4}}**. ■ **Array[f, 3, 0]** $\longrightarrow$ **{f[0], f[1], f[2]}** generates an array with index origin 0. ■ **Array[f, 3, 1, Plus]** $\longrightarrow$ **f[1] + f[2] + f[3]**. ■ Note that the dimensions given to **Array** are *not* in standard *Mathematica* iterator notation. ■ See page 250. ■ See also: **Table, SparseArray**. ■ *New in Version 1; modified in Version 4.0.*

■ ArrayDepth

ArrayDepth[*expr*] gives the depth to which *expr* is a full array, with all the parts at a particular level being lists of the same length, or is a **SparseArray** object.

ArrayDepth[*list*] is equivalent to **Length[Dimensions[*list*]]**. ■ Examples: **ArrayDepth[{a,b}]** $\longrightarrow$ 1; **ArrayDepth[{a,{b}}]** $\longrightarrow$ 1. ■ See page 916. ■ See also: **Dimensions, Depth, ArrayQ, VectorQ, MatrixQ, PadLeft**. ■ *New in Version 5.0.*

■ ArrayQ

ArrayQ[*expr*] gives **True** if *expr* is a full array or a **SparseArray** object, and gives **False** otherwise.

ArrayQ[*expr*, *patt*] requires *expr* to be a full array with a depth that matches the pattern *patt*.

ArrayQ[*expr*, *patt*, *test*] requires also that *test* yield **True** when applied to each of the array elements in *expr*.

In a full array all parts at a particular level must be lists of the same length. ■ **ArrayQ[*expr*, 1|2]** tests whether *expr* is either a vector or a matrix. ■ **ArrayQ[*expr*, _, NumberQ]** tests whether *expr* is a numerical array at all levels. ■ See page 290. ■ See also: **ArrayDepth, MatrixQ, VectorQ, Dimensions**. ■ *New in Version 5.0.*

◼ ArrayRules

ArrayRules[SparseArray[...]] gives the rules {pos_1->val_1, pos_2->val_2, ... } specifying elements in a sparse array.

ArrayRules[*list*] gives rules for SparseArray[*list*].

The last element of ArrayRules[*s*] is always {_, _, ... } -> *def*, where *def* is the default value for unspecified elements in the sparse array. ▪ ArrayRules[*list*, *val*] takes the default value to be *val*. ▪ ArrayRules[*list*] assumes a default value of 0. ▪ See page 922. ▪ See also: Position, Normal. ▪ *New in Version 5.0.*

◼ AspectRatio

AspectRatio is an option for Show and related functions which specifies the ratio of height to width for a plot.

AspectRatio determines the scaling for the final image shape. ▪ AspectRatio -> Automatic determines the ratio of height to width from the actual coordinate values in the plot. ▪ The default value AspectRatio -> 1/GoldenRatio is used for two-dimensional plots. AspectRatio -> Automatic is used for three-dimensional plots. ▪ See page 509. ▪ See also: BoxRatios, PlotRegion. ▪ *New in Version 1.*

◼ AspectRatioFixed

AspectRatioFixed is an option for Cell which specifies whether graphics in the cell should be constrained to stay the same shape when they are interactively resized using the front end.

With AspectRatioFixed->False, the shape of an image is determined by the setting for ImageSize. ▪ See page 616. ▪ See also: ImageSize, AspectRatio. ▪ *New in Version 3.*

◼ Assuming

Assuming[*assum*, *expr*] evaluates *expr* with *assum* appended to $Assumptions, so that *assum* is included in the default assumptions used by functions such as Refine, Simplify and Integrate.

Assuming affects the default assumptions for all functions that have an Assumptions option. ▪ The assumptions can be equations, inequalities or domain specifications, or lists or logical combinations of these. ▪ Assumptions from nested invocations of Assuming are combined. ▪ Assuming[*assum*, *expr*] is effectively equivalent to Block[{$Assumptions = $Assumptions && *assum*}, *expr*]. ▪ Assuming converts lists of assumptions {a_1, a_2, ... } to a_1 && a_2 && ... . ▪ See page 818. ▪ See also: Block, Module, Refine, Reduce. ▪ *New in Version 5.0.*

◼ Assumptions

Assumptions is an option for functions such as Simplify, Refine and Integrate which specifies default assumptions to be made about symbolic quantities.

+▪ The default setting is Assumptions:>$Assumptions. ~▪ The assumptions can be equations, inequalities or domain specifications, or lists or logical combinations of these. +▪ Assuming modifies $Assumptions and so modifies the value of default settings for Assumptions options. ▪ $x \in$ Reals can be used to specify that x should be treated as a real variable. ▪ See page 867. ▪ See also: Assuming, $Assumptions, GenerateConditions, Integrate, Refine, Limit. ▪ *New in Version 3; modified in Version 5.0.*

▪ AtomQ

AtomQ[*expr*] yields True if *expr* is an expression which cannot be divided into subexpressions, and yields False otherwise.

You can use AtomQ in a recursive procedure to tell when you have reached the bottom of the tree corresponding to an expression. ▪ AtomQ gives True for symbols, numbers, strings and other raw objects, such as sparse arrays.
▪ AtomQ gives True on any object whose subparts cannot be accessed using functions like Map. ▪ See page 268.
▪ See also: NumberQ, Head, LeafCount, Length. ▪ *New in Version 1; modified in Version 5.0.*

▪ Attributes

Attributes[*symbol*] gives the list of attributes for a symbol.

The attributes of a symbol can be set by assigning a value to Attributes[*s*]. If a single attribute is assigned, it need not be in a list. ▪ Attributes[*s*] = {} clears all attributes of a symbol. ▪ Attributes[{s_1, s_2, ... }] gives a list of the attributes for each of the s_i. ▪ Attributes["*str*"] gives a list of the attributes for all symbols which match the string pattern *str*. ▪ Attributes[HoldPattern[*s*]] is treated as equivalent to Attributes[*s*]. ▪ Attributes for functions must be set before any definitions that involve the functions are given. ▪ The complete list of possible attributes for a symbol f is:

Constant	all derivatives of f are zero
Flat	f is associative
HoldAll	all the arguments of f are not evaluated
HoldAllComplete	the arguments of f are completely shielded from evaluation
HoldFirst	the first argument of f is not evaluated
HoldRest	all but the first argument of f are not evaluated
Listable	f is automatically "threaded" over lists
Locked	attributes of f cannot be changed
NHoldAll	the arguments of f are not affected by N
NHoldFirst	the first argument of f is not affected by N
NHoldRest	all but the first argument of f are not affected by N
NumericFunction	the value of f is assumed to be a number when its arguments are numbers
OneIdentity	$f[a]$, $f[f[a]]$, etc. are equivalent to a in pattern matching
Orderless	f is commutative
Protected	values of f cannot be changed
ReadProtected	values of f cannot be read
SequenceHold	Sequence objects in the arguments of f are not flattened out
Stub	Needs is automatically called if the symbol is ever input
Temporary	f is a local variable, removed when no longer used

▪ See page 328. ▪ See also: SetAttributes, ClearAttributes. ▪ *New in Version 1; modified in Version 3.*

■ AutoIndent

AutoIndent is an option for Cell which specifies what automatic indentation should be done at the beginning of a new line after an explicit return character has been entered.

Possible settings for AutoIndent are:

False	do no indentation
True	indent the same as the previous line
Automatic	indent according to the structure of the expression (default)

■ With AutoIndent->True, tabs or spaces used for indentation on the previous line are explicitly inserted at the beginning of the new line. ■ With AutoIndent->Automatic, line breaks are always indicated by an IndentingNewLine character even if they were originally entered using ↵ or \[NewLine]. ■ Indentation after an \[IndentingNewLine] is automatically redone every time an expression is displayed. ■ The amount of indentation after an IndentingNewLine is determined by the settings for the LineIndent and LineIndentMaxFraction options. ■ See page 613. ■ See also: LineIndent, ParagraphIndent, ShowAutoStyles. ■ *New in Version 3; modified in Version 4.0.*

■ AutoItalicWords

AutoItalicWords is an option for Cell which gives a list of words which should automatically be put in italics when they are entered.

Typical settings for AutoItalicWords include "Mathematica" and "MathLink". ■ AutoItalicWords affects only ordinary text strings, not elements of more general expressions. ■ See page 613. ■ See also: FontSlant, SingleLetterItalics. ■ *New in Version 3.*

■ Automatic

Automatic represents an option value that is to be chosen automatically by a built-in function.

See page 136. ■ See also: All, True. ■ *New in Version 1.*

■ AutoSpacing

AutoSpacing is an option for StyleBox and Cell which specifies whether spaces between successive characters should be adjusted automatically.

AutoSpacing->False leaves equal spaces between all characters. ■ AutoSpacing->True inserts additional space around lower-precedence operators. ■ AutoSpacing->False is in effect automatically used inside ordinary strings and comments. ■ See page 454. ■ See also: TextJustification. ■ *New in Version 3.*

■ Axes

Axes is an option for graphics functions that specifies whether axes should be drawn.

Axes -> True draws all axes. ■ Axes -> False draws no axes. ■ Axes -> {False, True} draws a y axis but no x axis in two dimensions. ■ In two dimensions, axes are drawn to cross at the position specified by the option AxesOrigin. ■ In three dimensions, axes are drawn on the edges of the bounding box specified by the option AxesEdge. ■ See pages 511 and 549. ■ See also: AxesLabel, Frame, GridLines, Boxed. ■ *New in Version 1.*

■ **AxesEdge**

> AxesEdge is an option for three-dimensional graphics functions that specifies on which edges of the bounding box axes should be drawn.
>
> AxesEdge->{{dir_y, dir_z}, {dir_x, dir_z}, {dir_x, dir_y}} specifies on which three edges of the bounding box axes are drawn. The dir_i must be either +1 or -1, and specify whether axes are drawn on the edge of the box with a larger or smaller value of coordinate i, respectively. ■ The default setting AxesEdge->Automatic chooses automatically on which exposed box edges axes should be drawn. ■ Any pair {dir_i, dir_j} in the setting for AxesEdge can be replaced by Automatic to specify that the position of the corresponding axis is to be chosen automatically. ■ Any pair {dir_i, dir_j} can be replaced by None, in which case the corresponding axis will not be drawn. ■ If you explicitly specify on which edge to draw an axis, the axis will be drawn on that edge, whether or not the edge is exposed with the view point you have chosen. ■ See page 551. ■ *New in Version 2.*

■ **AxesLabel**

> AxesLabel is an option for graphics functions that specifies labels for axes.
>
> AxesLabel -> None specifies that no labels should be given. ■ AxesLabel -> *label* specifies a label for the y axis of a two-dimensional plot, and the z axis of a three-dimensional plot. ■ AxesLabel -> {*xlabel*, *ylabel*, ... } specifies labels for different axes. ■ By default, axes labels in two-dimensional graphics are placed at the ends of the axes. In three-dimensional graphics, they are aligned with the middles of the axes. ■ Any expression can be specified as a label. It will be given in OutputForm. Arbitrary strings of text can be given as "*text*". ■ See pages 512 and 552. ■ See also: PlotLabel, FrameLabel. ■ *New in Version 1.*

■ **AxesOrigin**

> AxesOrigin is an option for two-dimensional graphics functions which specifies where any axes drawn should cross.
>
> AxesOrigin -> {x, y} specifies that the axes should cross at the point {x, y}. ■ AxesOrigin -> Automatic uses an internal algorithm to determine where the axes should cross. If the point {0, 0} is within, or close to, the plotting region, then it is usually chosen as the axis origin. ■ In contour and density plots, AxesOrigin -> Automatic puts axes outside the plotting area. ■ See page 512. ■ *New in Version 2.*

■ **AxesStyle**

> AxesStyle is an option for graphics functions which specifies how axes should be rendered.
>
> AxesStyle can be used in both two- and three-dimensional graphics. ■ AxesStyle -> *style* specifies that all axes are to be generated with the specified graphics directive, or list of graphics directives. ■ AxesStyle -> {{*xstyle*}, {*ystyle*}, ... } specifies that axes should use graphics directives *xstyle*, ... The styles must be enclosed in lists, perhaps of length one. ■ Styles can be specified using graphics directives such as Dashing, Hue and Thickness. ■ The default color of axes is specified by the option DefaultColor. ■ See pages 512 and 550. ■ See also: Prolog, Epilog, PlotStyle, FrameStyle. ■ *New in Version 2.*

■ **Background**

> Background is an option which specifies the background color to use.
>
> Background is an option for graphics functions, Text, Cell and ButtonBox. ■ The setting for Background in graphics functions must be a CMYKColor, GrayLevel, Hue or RGBColor directive. ■ The default setting in graphics functions is Background->Automatic, which produces a white background on most output devices. ■ In Text, Background->None draws no background rectangle around the text and Background->Automatic draws a background rectangle in the same color as the background for the whole plot. ■ In a cell, the background is used only for the region inside any cell frame. ■ See pages 504 and 604. ■ See also: Prolog, DefaultColor, PlotRegion, FontColor. ■ *New in Version 2; modified in Version 3.*

■ BaseForm

BaseForm[*expr*, *n*] prints with the numbers in *expr* given in base *n*.

The maximum allowed base is 36. For bases larger than 10, additional digits are chosen from the letters a–z. ■ You can enter a number in an arbitrary base using *base^^digits*. ■ When a number in an arbitrary base is given in scientific notation, the exponent is still given in base 10. ■ You can mix BaseForm with NumberForm and related functions. ■ BaseForm acts as a "wrapper", which affects printing, but not evaluation. ■ See pages 438 and 725. ■ See also: IntegerDigits, RealDigits. ■ *New in Version 1.*

■ Begin

Begin["*context`*"] resets the current context.

Begin resets the value of $Context. ■ The interpretation of symbol names depends on context. Begin thus affects the parsing of input expressions. ■ See page 398. ■ See also: BeginPackage, End, $ContextPath. ■ *New in Version 1.*

■ BeginPackage

BeginPackage["*context`*"] makes *context`* and System` the only active contexts.

BeginPackage["*context`*", {"*need₁`*", "*need₂`*", ... }] calls Needs on the *needᵢ*.

BeginPackage is typically used at the beginning of a *Mathematica* package. ■ BeginPackage resets the values of both $Context and $ContextPath. ■ The interpretation of symbol names depends on context. BeginPackage thus affects the parsing of input expressions. ■ See page 398. ■ See also: EndPackage. ■ *New in Version 1.*

■ BernoulliB

BernoulliB[*n*] gives the Bernoulli number B_n.

BernoulliB[*n*, *x*] gives the Bernoulli polynomial $B_n(x)$.

Mathematical function (see Section A.3.10). ■ The Bernoulli polynomials satisfy the generating function relation $te^{xt}/(e^t - 1) = \sum_{n=0}^{\infty} B_n(x)(t^n/n!)$. ■ The Bernoulli numbers are given by $B_n = B_n(0)$. ■ See page 757. ■ See also: EulerE. ■ *New in Version 1.*

■ BesselI

BesselI[*n*, *z*] gives the modified Bessel function of the first kind $I_n(z)$.

Mathematical function (see Section A.3.10). ■ $I_n(z)$ satisfies the differential equation $z^2 y'' + z y' - (z^2 + n^2)y = 0$. ■ BesselI[*n*, *z*] has a branch cut discontinuity in the complex *z* plane running from $-\infty$ to 0. ■ FullSimplify and FunctionExpand include transformation rules for BesselI. ■ See page 775. ■ See also: BesselK, AiryBi, BesselJ. ■ *New in Version 1.*

■ BesselJ

BesselJ[*n*, *z*] gives the Bessel function of the first kind $J_n(z)$.

Mathematical function (see Section A.3.10). ■ $J_n(z)$ satisfies the differential equation $z^2 y'' + z y' + (z^2 - n^2)y = 0$. ■ BesselJ[*n*, *z*] has a branch cut discontinuity in the complex *z* plane running from $-\infty$ to 0. ■ FullSimplify and FunctionExpand include transformation rules for BesselJ. ■ See page 775. ■ See also: BesselY, StruveH, BesselK. ■ Related package: NumericalMath`BesselZeros`. ■ *New in Version 1.*

■ BesselK

BesselK[n, z] gives the modified Bessel function of the second kind $K_n(z)$.

Mathematical function (see Section A.3.10). ■ $K_n(z)$ satisfies the differential equation $z^2 y'' + z y' - (z^2 + n^2)y = 0$. ■ BesselK[$n$, z] has a branch cut discontinuity in the complex z plane running from $-\infty$ to 0. ■ FullSimplify and FunctionExpand include transformation rules for BesselK. ■ See page 775. ■ See also: BesselI, AiryAi, BesselJ. ■ *New in Version 1.*

■ BesselY

BesselY[n, z] gives the Bessel function of the second kind $Y_n(z)$.

Mathematical function (see Section A.3.10). ■ $Y_n(z)$ satisfies the differential equation $z^2 y'' + z y' + (z^2 - n^2)y = 0$. ■ BesselY[$n$, z] has a branch cut discontinuity in the complex z plane running from $-\infty$ to 0. ■ FullSimplify and FunctionExpand include transformation rules for BesselY. ■ See page 775. ■ See also: BesselJ, StruveH, BesselI. ■ Related package: NumericalMath`BesselZeros`. ■ *New in Version 1.*

■ Beta

Beta[a, b] gives the Euler beta function B(a, b).

Beta[z, a, b] gives the incomplete beta function B$_z$(a, b).

Mathematical function (see Section A.3.10). ■ $B(a,b) = \Gamma(a)\Gamma(b)/\Gamma(a+b) = \int_0^1 t^{a-1}(1-t)^{b-1}dt$. ■ $B_z(a,b) = \int_0^z t^{a-1}(1-t)^{b-1}dt$. ■ Beta[$z$, a, b] has a branch cut discontinuity in the complex z plane running from $-\infty$ to 0. ■ Beta[z_0, z_1, a, b] gives the generalized incomplete beta function $\int_{z_0}^{z_1} t^{a-1}(1-t)^{b-1}dt$. ■ Note that the arguments in the incomplete form of Beta are arranged differently from those in the incomplete form of Gamma. ■ In TraditionalForm, Beta is output using \[CapitalBeta]. ■ See page 770. ■ See also: BetaRegularized, InverseBetaRegularized. ■ *New in Version 1.*

■ BetaRegularized

BetaRegularized[z, a, b] gives the regularized incomplete beta function $I_z(a, b)$.

Mathematical function (see Section A.3.10). ■ For non-singular cases, $I(z,a,b) = B(z,a,b)/B(a,b)$. ■ BetaRegularized[$z_0$, z_1, a, b] gives the generalized regularized incomplete beta function defined in non-singular cases as Beta[z_0, z_1, a, b]/Beta[a, b]. ■ Note that the arguments in BetaRegularized are arranged differently from those in GammaRegularized. ■ See page 770. ■ See also: Beta, InverseBetaRegularized. ■ *New in Version 2.*

■ Binomial

Binomial[n, m] gives the binomial coefficient $\binom{n}{m}$.

Integer mathematical function (see Section A.3.10). ■ Binomial is evaluated symbolically when possible. ■ Example: Binomial[x+2, x] $\longrightarrow$ ((1 + x) * (2 + x)) / 2. ■ In general, $\binom{n}{m}$ is defined by $\Gamma(n+1)/(\Gamma(m+1)\Gamma(n-m+1))$ or suitable limits of this. ■ See page 757. ■ Implementation notes: see page 1067. ■ See also: Multinomial, Pochhammer. ■ *New in Version 1.*

■ BitAnd

BitAnd[n_1, n_2, ...] gives the bitwise AND of the integers n_i.

Integer mathematical function (see Section A.3.10). ■ BitAnd[n_1, n_2, ...] yields the integer whose binary bit representation has ones at positions where the binary bit representations of all of the n_i have ones. ■ For negative integers BitAnd assumes a two's complement representation. ■ See page 756. ■ See also: BitOr, BitXor, BitNot, And, IntegerDigits, DigitCount, CellularAutomaton. ■ *New in Version 4.*

■ **BitNot**

BitNot[n] gives the bitwise NOT of the integer n.

Integer mathematical function (see Section A.3.10). ■ BitNot[n] turns ones into zeros and vice versa in the binary bit representation of n. ■ Integers are assumed to be represented in two's complement form, with an unlimited number of digits, so that BitNot[n] is simply equivalent to $-1-n$. ■ See page 756. ■ See also: BitAnd, BitOr, BitXor, Not. ■ *New in Version 4.*

■ **BitOr**

BitOr[n_1, n_2, ...] gives the bitwise OR of the integers n_i.

Integer mathematical function (see Section A.3.10). ■ BitOr[n_1, n_2, ...] yields the integer whose binary bit representation has ones at positions where the binary bit representations of any of the n_i have ones. ■ For negative integers BitOr assumes a two's complement representation. ■ See page 756. ■ See also: BitAnd, BitXor, BitNot, Or, IntegerDigits, CellularAutomaton. ■ *New in Version 4.*

■ **BitXor**

BitXor[n_1, n_2, ...] gives the bitwise XOR of the integers n_i.

Integer mathematical function (see Section A.3.10). ■ BitXor[n_1, n_2, ...] yields the integer whose binary bit representation has ones at positions where an odd number of the binary bit representations of the n_i have ones. ■ For negative integers BitXor assumes a two's complement representation. ■ See page 756. ■ See also: BitAnd, BitOr, BitNot, Xor, IntegerDigits, CellularAutomaton. ■ *New in Version 4.*

■ **Blank**

_ or Blank[ ] is a pattern object that can stand for any *Mathematica* expression.

_h or Blank[h] can stand for any expression with head h.

The head h in _h cannot itself contain pattern objects. ■ See page 259. ■ See also: Pattern, Optional, ForAll. ■ *New in Version 1.*

■ **BlankNullSequence**

___ (three _ characters) or BlankNullSequence[ ] is a pattern object that can stand for any sequence of zero or more *Mathematica* expressions.

___h or BlankNullSequence[h] can stand for any sequence of expressions, all of which have head h.

Blank sequences work slightly differently depending on whether or not the head of the expression in which they appear is a symbol with the attribute Flat. ■ Consider matching the pattern $f[a_1, a_2, ... , \_\_\_, c_1, ...]$ against the expression $f[a_1, a_2, ... , b_1, ... , c_1, ...]$. If f is a symbol with attribute Flat, then the ___ will be taken to stand for the expression $f[b_1, ...]$. If f is not a symbol with attribute Flat, then ___ will be taken to stand for the sequence of expressions $b_1, ... $. With a named pattern, such as $x\_\_\_$, x can be used only as an element in an expression. The sequence of expressions $b_1, ... $ is "spliced in" to replace x, thereby usually increasing the length of the expression. ■ If ___ matches a sequence of length more than one, then the sequence will be represented by a Sequence object. In most uses of ___, however, the Sequence object will automatically be spliced into another expression, and will never appear explicitly. ■ See page 273. ■ See also: Pattern, SlotSequence. ■ *New in Version 1.*

■ BlankSequence

__ (two _ characters) or BlankSequence[ ] is a pattern object that can stand for any sequence of one or more *Mathematica* expressions.

__*h* or BlankSequence[*h*] can stand for any sequence of one or more expressions, all of which have head *h*.

See notes for BlankNullSequence. ▪ See page 273. ▪ *New in Version 1.*

■ Block

Block[{*x*, *y*, ... }, *expr*] specifies that *expr* is to be evaluated with local values for the symbols *x*, *y*, ...

Block[{*x* = x_0, ... }, *expr*] defines initial local values for *x*, ...

Block allows you to set up an environment in which the values of variables can temporarily be changed. ▪ When you execute a block, values assigned to *x*, *y*, ... are cleared. When the execution of the block is finished, the original values of these symbols are restored. ▪ Block affects only the *values* of symbols, not their names. ▪ Initial values specified for *x*, *y*, ... are evaluated before *x*, *y*, ... are cleared. ▪ You can use Block[{*vars*}, *body* /; *cond*] as the right-hand side of a transformation rule with a condition attached. ▪ Block has attribute HoldAll. ▪ Block implements dynamic scoping of variables. ▪ Block is automatically used to localize values of iterators in iteration constructs such as Do, Sum and Table. ▪ See page 389. ▪ See also: Module, With, CompoundExpression. ▪ *New in Version 1.*

■ Booleans

Booleans represents the domain of booleans, as in *x* ∈ Booleans.

The domain of booleans is taken to consist of the symbols True and False. ▪ *x* ∈ Booleans evaluates immediately if *x* is explicitly True or False. ▪ Simplify[*expr* ∈ Booleans] can be used to try to determine whether an expression is boolean, with no undetermined variables. ▪ Boolean is output in TraditionalForm as 𝔹. ▪ See page 817. ▪ See also: Element, Simplify, True, False, Integers. ▪ *New in Version 4.*

■ Boxed

Boxed is an option for Graphics3D which specifies whether to draw the edges of the bounding box in a three-dimensional picture.

Boxed -> True draws the box; Boxed -> False does not. ▪ See pages 151 and 549. ▪ *New in Version 1.*

■ BoxRatios

BoxRatios is an option for Graphics3D and SurfaceGraphics which gives the ratios of side lengths for the bounding box of the three-dimensional picture.

BoxRatios -> {s_x, s_y, s_z} gives the side-length ratios. ▪ See page 531. ▪ *New in Version 1.*

■ BoxStyle

BoxStyle is an option for three-dimensional graphics functions which specifies how the bounding box should be rendered.

BoxStyle can be set to a list of graphics directives such as Dashing, Thickness, GrayLevel and RGBColor. ▪ See pages 503 and 550. ▪ See also: AxesStyle, Prolog, Epilog, DisplayFunction. ▪ *New in Version 2.*

■ Break

Break[ ] exits the nearest enclosing Do, For or While.

Break[ ] takes effect as soon as it is evaluated, even if it appears inside other functions. ■ After a Break the value Null is returned from the enclosing control structure. ■ The function of Break can also be achieved using Throw and Catch. ■ See page 353. ■ See also: Continue, Return, Goto, Abort. ■ *New in Version 1; modified in Version 3.*

■ ButtonBox

ButtonBox[*boxes*] represents a button in a notebook, displaying *boxes* and performing an action when it is clicked on.

The default action is to paste *boxes* at your current insertion point.

Other actions can be specified using options.

ButtonBox objects are used to implement palette buttons, hyperlinks and other active elements in notebooks.

ButtonBox objects are active when either they or the cell that contains them has the option Active->True.

When ButtonBox objects are active, they perform an action whenever they are clicked on. Otherwise, clicking on them simply selects them or their contents. ■ ButtonBox[*boxes*, ButtonStyle->"*style*"] takes the properties of the ButtonBox from the specified style. The style for a ButtonBox can specify both its appearance and its action. ■ The following options affecting button appearance can be given:

Background	Automatic	button background color
ButtonFrame	"Palette"	the type of frame for the button
ButtonExpandable	True	whether a button should expand to fill a position in a GridBox
ButtonMargins	3.0	the margin in printer's points around the contents of a button
ButtonMinHeight	1.0	the minimum total height of a button in units of font size

■ The following options affecting button action can be given:

Active	False	whether to make the button always active
ButtonData	Null	the second argument to supply to the button function
ButtonEvaluator	None	where to send the button function expression for evaluation
ButtonFunction	(pasting function)	the function to apply when the button is clicked
ButtonNote	None	what to display in the window status line when the cursor is over the button
ButtonSource	Automatic	where to get the first argument of the button function from

■ ButtonBox[...] is by default interpreted as Button[...] if it is given as input to the *Mathematica* kernel. ■ See pages 448 and 595. ■ See also: Dialog, Input. ■ *New in Version 3.*

■ ButtonData

ButtonData is an option for ButtonBox which specifies the second argument to give to the ButtonFunction for the button when the button is active and is clicked on.

The default is ButtonData->Automatic. ■ ButtonData provides a convenient way to associate additional data with a button that does not affect the display of the button. ■ See page 597. ■ See also: ButtonSource, ButtonNote, ButtonStyle. ■ *New in Version 3.*

■ ButtonEvaluator

ButtonEvaluator is an option for ButtonBox which specifies where the expression constructed from ButtonFunction should be sent for evaluation.

The default setting is ButtonEvaluator->None. ■ Possible settings are:

None	the front end
Automatic	the kernel used by default in the current notebook
"*name*"	a kernel referred to by a specific name

■ With ButtonEvaluator->Automatic the expression to be evaluated can contain any *Mathematica* objects. ■ With ButtonEvaluator->None the expression can contain only the specific notebook commands supported by the front end. All these commands are in the context FrontEnd`. Expressions intended for processing purely by the front end must be wrapped with FrontEndExecute. ■ See page 597. ■ See also: ButtonFunction, ButtonStyle, SelectionEvaluate, ButtonNotebook. ■ *New in Version 3.*

■ ButtonExpandable

ButtonExpandable is an option for ButtonBox which specifies whether the button should expand to fill any GridBox position in which it appears.

The default setting is ButtonExpandable->True. ■ This setting is usually used for all buttons that appear in palettes. ■ With ButtonExpandable->False the size of a button is determined purely by its contents, independent of its environment. ■ With ButtonExpandable->False, gutters will often be left between buttons in a GridBox. ■ See page 452. ■ See also: ButtonMargins, ButtonMinHeight, TextJustification. ■ *New in Version 3.*

■ ButtonFrame

ButtonFrame is an option for ButtonBox which specifies the type of frame to display around a button.

Typical settings supported include:

"Palette"	a button in a palette
"DialogBox"	a button in a dialog box
None	no frame

■ Button frames generated by ButtonFrame are set up to follow the conventions for particular computer systems. ■ A button with a particular setting for ButtonFrame may look slightly different on different computer systems. ■ See page 452. ■ See also: ButtonStyle, WindowFrame. ■ *New in Version 3.*

■ ButtonFunction

ButtonFunction is an option for ButtonBox which specifies the function to execute when the button is active and is clicked on.

The default setting for ButtonFunction causes the button to paste its contents at your current notebook selection. ■ ButtonFunction is used only with the setting Active->True either for the individual button, or for the cell which contains it. ■ With ButtonFunction->*f* the first argument supplied to *f* is specified by the setting for ButtonSource, and the second argument by the setting for ButtonData. ■ Standard *Mathematica* precedence rules require parentheses in ButtonFunction->(*body* &). ■ Settings for ButtonFunction are often inherited from button styles via the ButtonStyle option. ■ With the default setting ButtonEvaluator -> None the expression constructed from the button function is sent to the front end for evaluation. ■ See page 597. ■ See also: ButtonEvaluator, ButtonNote, NotebookApply, ButtonNotebook. ■ *New in Version 3.*

■ **ButtonMargins**

> ButtonMargins is an option for ButtonBox which specifies how much space in printer's points to leave around the contents of a button when the button is displayed.
>
> The default setting is ButtonMargins->3. ■ See page 452. ■ See also: ButtonExpandable, ButtonMinHeight. ■ *New in Version 3.*

■ **ButtonMinHeight**

> ButtonMinHeight is an option for ButtonBox which specifies the minimum total height in units of font size that should be allowed for the button.
>
> The default setting ButtonMinHeight->1 forces a button to have a total height which at least accommodates all the characters in the current font. ■ ButtonMinHeight->0 reduces the total height of a button as much as possible, allowing buttons containing characters such as x and X to be different heights. ■ See page 452. ■ See also: ButtonMargins, ButtonExpandable, RowMinHeight. ■ *New in Version 3.*

■ **ButtonNote**

> ButtonNote is an option for ButtonBox which specifies what should be displayed in the status line of the current notebook window when the button is active and the cursor is placed on top of it.
>
> The default is to display whatever setting is given for ButtonData. ■ Any expression can be specified as the setting for ButtonNote, though most windows will only allow a single character height to be displayed. ■ ButtonNote can be used to display keyboard equivalents for buttons in a palette. ■ See page 597. ■ See also: ButtonData, ButtonFunction, ButtonStyle. ■ *New in Version 3.*

■ **ButtonNotebook**

> ButtonNotebook[ ] gives the notebook, if any, that contains the button which initiated the current evaluation.
>
> ButtonNotebook returns a NotebookObject. ■ If a button in a palette initiates evaluation in another notebook, then ButtonNotebook[ ] will be the palette, but EvaluationNotebook[ ] will be the other notebook. ■ If the current evaluation was not initiated by a button, then ButtonNotebook[ ] will return $Failed. ■ See page 579. ■ See also: Notebooks, EvaluationNotebook, SelectedNotebook, InputNotebook. ■ *New in Version 3.*

■ **ButtonSource**

> ButtonSource is an option for ButtonBox which specifies the first argument to give to the ButtonFunction for the button when the button is active and is clicked on.
>
> The default is ButtonSource->Automatic. ■ Possible settings are:
>
> | | |
> |---|---|
> | Automatic | ButtonData if it is set, otherwise ButtonContents |
> | ButtonContents | the first argument of the ButtonBox |
> | ButtonData | the setting for the ButtonData option |
> | Cell | the whole cell in which the button appears |
> | CellContents | the contents of the cell in which the button appears |
> | Notebook | the whole notebook in which the button appears |
> | n | the expression n levels up from the button in the notebook |
>
> ■ See page 597. ■ See also: ButtonFunction, ButtonData, ButtonStyle, NotebookRead. ■ *New in Version 3.*

■ ButtonStyle

ButtonStyle is an option for ButtonBox which specifies the default properties for the button.

Typical styles defined in the standard notebook front end are:

"Paste"	paste the contents of the button (default)
"Evaluate"	paste then evaluate in place what has been pasted
"EvaluateCell"	paste then evaluate the whole cell
"CopyEvaluate"	copy the current selection into a new cell, then paste and evaluate in place
"CopyEvaluateCell"	copy the current selection into a new cell, then paste and evaluate the whole cell
"Hyperlink"	jump to a different location in the notebook

■ The properties specified by a button style can affect both the appearance and action of a button. ■ The properties can be overridden by explicit settings for ButtonBox options. ■ See page 595. ■ See also: ButtonFrame, ButtonFunction. ■ *New in Version 3.*

■ Byte

Byte represents a single byte of data in Read.

See page 646. ■ Related package: Utilities`BinaryFiles`. ■ *New in Version 1.*

■ ByteCount

ByteCount[*expr*] gives the number of bytes used internally by *Mathematica* to store *expr*.

ByteCount does not take account of any sharing of subexpressions. The results it gives assume that every part of the expression is stored separately. ByteCount will therefore often give an overestimate of the amount of memory currently needed to store a particular expression. When you manipulate the expression, however, subexpressions will often stop being shared, and the amount of memory needed will be close to the value returned by ByteCount. ■ See page 714. ■ See also: LeafCount, MemoryInUse, MaxMemoryUsed, Length, StringLength, Depth. ■ *New in Version 1.*

■ C

~ C[*i*] is the default form for the ith parameter or constant generated in representing the results of various symbolic computations.

+■ The C[*i*] are often used to parameterize families of solutions to equations. +■ In functions like DSolve, the C[*i*] can be thought of as corresponding to constants of integration. +■ In cases such as partial differential equations, the C[*i*] represent functions rather than variables. +■ C is the default setting for the option GeneratedParameters in such functions as DSolve, RSolve and Reduce. ■ See pages 93 and 871. ■ See also: GeneratedParameters, Unique. ■ *New in Version 2.*

■ Cancel

Cancel[*expr*] cancels out common factors in the numerator and denominator of *expr*.

Example: Cancel[(x^2-1)/(x-1)] $\longrightarrow$ 1 + x. ■ Cancel is Listable. ■ Cancel cancels out the greatest common divisor of the numerator and denominator. ■ Cancel[*expr*, Modulus->*p*] generates a result modulo *p*.
■ Cancel[*expr*, Extension->Automatic] allows operations to be performed on algebraic numbers in *expr*.
■ Cancel[*expr*, Trig -> True] treats trigonometric functions as rational functions of exponentials, and manipulates them accordingly. ■ See page 802. ■ See also: Apart, GCD. ■ *New in Version 1; modified in Version 3.*

■ **CarmichaelLambda**

> CarmichaelLambda[*n*] gives the Carmichael function $\lambda(n)$, defined as the smallest integer *m* such that $k^m \equiv 1 \bmod n$ for all *k* relatively prime to *n*.
>
> Integer mathematical function (see Section A.3.10). ▪ CarmichaelLambda returns unevaluated if there is no integer *m* satisfying the necessary conditions. ▪ See page 752. ▪ See also: MultiplicativeOrder, EulerPhi, RealDigits. ▪ *New in Version 4.*

■ **Cases**

> Cases[{e_1, e_2, ... }, *pattern*] gives a list of the e_i that match the pattern.
>
> Cases[{e_1, ... }, *pattern* -> *rhs*] gives a list of the values of *rhs* corresponding to the e_i that match the pattern.
>
> Cases[*expr*, *pattern*, *levspec*] gives a list of all parts of *expr* on levels specified by *levspec* which match the pattern.
>
> Cases[*expr*, *pattern* -> *rhs*, *levspec*] gives the values of *rhs* which match the pattern.
>
> Cases[*expr*, *pattern*, *levspec*, *n*] gives the first *n* parts in *expr* which match the pattern.
>
> Example: Cases[{2, x, 4}, _Integer] ⟶ {2, 4}. ▪ The first argument to Cases need not have head List. +▪ Cases[*expr*, *pattern* :> *rhs*] evaluates *rhs* only when the pattern is found. ▪ Level specifications are described on page 1041. ▪ See page 261. ▪ See also: Select, Position, ReplaceList, Collect, DeleteCases. ▪ Related package: Statistics`DataManipulation`. ▪ *New in Version 1.*

■ **Catalan**

> Catalan is Catalan's constant, with numerical value ≃ 0.915966.
>
> Mathematical constant (see Section A.3.11). ▪ Catalan's constant is given by the sum $\sum_{k=0}^{\infty}(-1)^k(2k+1)^{-2}$. ▪ See page 765. ▪ Implementation notes: see page 1067. ▪ *New in Version 1.*

■ **Catch**

> Catch[*expr*] returns the argument of the first Throw generated in the evaluation of *expr*.
>
> Catch[*expr*, *form*] returns *value* from the first Throw[*value*, *tag*] for which *form* matches *tag*.
>
> Catch[*expr*, *form*, *f*] returns *f*[*value*, *tag*].
>
> Catch[*expr*, ...] always returns the value of *expr* if no Throw was generated during the evaluation. ▪ *form* can be any expression, and is often a pattern. ▪ *tag* in Throw[*value*, *tag*] is re-evaluated every time it is compared to *form*. ▪ See page 350. ▪ See also: Check, CheckAbort, Reap. ▪ *New in Version 1; modified in Version 3.*

■ **Ceiling**

> Ceiling[*x*] gives the smallest integer greater than or equal to *x*.
>
> Mathematical function (see Section A.3.10). ▪ Examples: Ceiling[2.4] ⟶ 3; Ceiling[2.6] ⟶ 3; Ceiling[-2.4] ⟶ -2; Ceiling[-2.6] ⟶ -2. ▪ Ceiling[*x*] can be entered in StandardForm and InputForm as ⌈ *x* ⌉, :lc: *x* :rc: or \[LeftCeiling] *x* \[RightCeiling]. ▪ Ceiling[*x*] returns an integer when *x* is any numeric quantity, whether or not it is an explicit number. ▪ Example: Ceiling[Pi^2] ⟶ 10. ▪ For exact numeric quantities, Ceiling internally uses numerical approximations to establish its result. This process can be affected by the setting of the global variable $MaxExtraPrecision. ▪ See page 745. ▪ Implementation notes: see page 1067. ▪ See also: Floor, IntegerPart, Round, Chop. ▪ *New in Version 1; modified in Version 3.*

■ Cell

Cell[*contents*, "*style*"] represents a cell in a *Mathematica* notebook.

A *Mathematica* notebook consists of a list of cells. ■ You can see the form of a cell as an expression by using the Show Expression command in the standard *Mathematica* front end. ■ You can access cells in a notebook directly using the front end. You can also access the cells from the kernel using NotebookRead and NotebookWrite, or using Options and SetOptions on NotebookSelection[*obj*]. ■ The contents of cells can be the following:

"*text*"	plain text
TextData[{*text*$_1$, *text*$_2$, ... }]	general text objects
BoxData[*boxes*]	formatted *Mathematica* expressions
GraphicsData["*type*", *data*]	graphics or sounds
OutputFormData["*itext*", "*otext*"]	text as generated by InputForm and OutputForm
RawData["*data*"]	unformatted expressions
CellGroupData[{*cell*$_1$, *cell*$_2$, ... }, Open]	open group of cells
CellGroupData[{*cell*$_1$, *cell*$_2$, ... }, Closed]	closed group of cells
StyleData["*style*"]	sample cell for a particular style

■ In any given notebook, a collection of possible cell styles are defined, typically with names such as "Title", "Section", "Input" and "Output". ■ Cells can have many options, including:

Active	whether buttons in cell should be active
Background	the color of the background for the cell
Editable	whether to allow the contents of the cell to be edited
CellFrame	whether to draw a frame around the cell
CellTags	tags for the cell
FontSize	the default size of text in the cell
TextAlignment	how to align text in the cell

■ See page 599. ■ See also: Notebook, CellPrint. ■ *New in Version 3.*

■ CellAutoOverwrite

CellAutoOverwrite is an option for Cell which specifies whether new output obtained by evaluating this cell should overwrite old output.

Any sequence of cells with GeneratedCell->True which follow the given cell are assumed to correspond to output. ■ The output is deleted only when new output is ready to be inserted in its place. ■ CellAutoOverwrite is typically set for cells in "Output" style. ■ See page 608. ■ See also: GeneratedCell, CellEvaluationDuplicate, Deletable. ■ *New in Version 3.*

■ CellBaseline

CellBaseline is an option for Cell which specifies where the baseline of the cell should be assumed to be when it appears inside another cell.

CellBaseline is used to determine the vertical alignment of cells that are embedded in text, typically in TextData objects. ■ CellBaseline->*pos* specifies that position *pos* in the Cell should be assumed to be the baseline of the Cell and should therefore be aligned with baselines of other boxes. ■ Possible settings are:

Axis	axis of the expression in the cell
Baseline	baseline of the expression in the cell (default)
Bottom	bottom of the expression in the cell
Center	center of the expression in the cell
Top	top of the expression in the cell

■ See page 605. ■ See also: CellMargins, GridBaseline. ■ *New in Version 3.*

■ CellDingbat

CellDingbat is an option for Cell which specifies what dingbat to use to emphasize a cell.

The setting CellDingbat->"" displays no dingbat. ■ Dingbats are placed to the left of the main contents of a cell, aligned with the first line of the contents. ■ Dingbats are placed outside of any cell frame. ■ The setting for CellDingbat can be any string. A typical setting is "\[FilledSquare]". ■ CellDingbat is often set for styles of cells rather than for individual cells. ■ See page 604. ■ See also: CellFrame, Background. ■ *New in Version 3.*

■ CellEditDuplicate

CellEditDuplicate is an option for Cell which specifies whether the front end should make a copy of the cell before actually applying any changes in its contents that you request.

CellEditDuplicate is by default set to True for cells that are generated as *Mathematica* output. ■ New cells generated when CellEditDuplicate->True have styles specified by the setting for DefaultDuplicateCellStyle for the notebook. ■ CellEditDuplicate is typically set for styles of cells rather than for individual cells. ■ See page 607. ■ See also: CellEvaluationDuplicate, Editable. ■ *New in Version 3.*

■ CellEvaluationDuplicate

CellEvaluationDuplicate is an option for Cell which specifies whether the front end should make a copy of the cell before performing any evaluation of its contents that you request.

New cells generated when CellEvaluationDuplicate->True have styles specified by the setting for DefaultDuplicateCellStyle for the notebook. ■ CellEvaluationDuplicate is typically set for styles of cells rather than for individual cells. ■ See page 608. ■ See also: CellEditDuplicate, Evaluatable, CellAutoOverwrite. ■ *New in Version 3.*

■ CellFrame

CellFrame is an option for Cell which specifies whether a frame should be drawn around a cell.

The space left between the frame and the cell contents is determined by CellFrameMargins. ■ Dingbats go outside the frame. ■ See page 604. ■ See also: Background, CellDingbat, FrameBox. ■ *New in Version 3.*

■ CellFrameMargins

CellFrameMargins is an option for Cell which specifies the absolute margins in printer's points to leave inside a frame that is drawn around a cell.

Possible settings are:

dist	the same margins on all sides
{{*left*, *right*}, {*bottom*, *top*}}	different margins on different sides

■ See page 605. ■ See also: CellMargins. ■ *New in Version 3.*

■ CellGroupData

CellGroupData[{*cell*₁, *cell*₂, ... }, Open] represents an open group of cells in a notebook.

CellGroupData[{*cell*₁, *cell*₂, ... }, Closed] represents a closed group of cells.

When a group of cells is closed, only the first member of the group is visible. ■ When cells are entered into a notebook, they are automatically placed in groups unless CellGrouping->Manual is set. ■ See page 600. ■ See also: Cell, CellGrouping, CellOpen. ■ *New in Version 3.*

■ **CellGrouping**

> `CellGrouping` is an option for `Notebook` which specifies how cells in the notebook should be assembled into groups.

The default setting is typically `CellGrouping->Automatic`. ▪ With `CellGrouping->Automatic`, cells are automatically grouped in a hierarchical way based on their styles. ▪ With `CellGrouping->Manual`, cells must be grouped manually, either by setting up explicit `CellGroupData` expressions, or by using the Group Cells menu item in the notebook front end. ▪ See page 618. ▪ See also: `CellGroupData`. ▪ *New in Version 3.*

■ **CellLabel**

> `CellLabel` is an option for `Cell` which gives the label to use for a particular cell.

`CellLabel->""` specifies that no label should be used for a cell. ▪ Cell labels are displayed when the setting `ShowCellLabels->True` is made. ▪ Cell labels are typically generated automatically when cells appear as input or output to the *Mathematica* kernel. ▪ Cell labels are automatically deleted when a cell is modified if `CellLabelAutoDelete->True`. ▪ See page 607. ▪ See also: `CellTags`. ▪ *New in Version 3.*

■ **CellLabelAutoDelete**

> `CellLabelAutoDelete` is an option for `Cell` which specifies whether a label for the cell should be automatically deleted if the contents of the cell are modified or the notebook containing the cell is saved in a file.

Cell styles that represent *Mathematica* input and output typically have `CellLabelAutoDelete->True`. ▪ `CellLabelAutoDelete` is more often set for styles of cells than for individual cells. ▪ See page 607. ▪ See also: `CellLabel`, `ShowCellLabel`, `CellTags`, `CellAutoOverwrite`. ▪ *New in Version 3.*

■ **CellMargins**

> `CellMargins` is an option for `Cell` which specifies the absolute margins in printer's points to leave around a cell.

Possible settings are:

dist	the same margins on all sides
{{*left*, *right*}, {*bottom*, *top*}}	different margins on different sides

▪ The left margin gives the distance from the edge of the window to the left-hand side of the cell. ▪ The right margin gives the distance from the inside of the cell bracket to the right-hand side of the cell. ▪ The left and right margins can be set interactively in the front end using the Show Ruler ruler. ▪ The top and bottom margins determine the amount of space to leave above and below the cell. ▪ The margins go to the edge of any cell frame that is present. ▪ Cell dingbats are placed to the left of the left-hand side of the cell, and extend into the left cell margin. ▪ See page 605. ▪ See also: `CellFrameMargins`, `CellBaseline`, `ImageMargins`, `WindowMargins`. ▪ *New in Version 3.*

■ **CellOpen**

> `CellOpen` is an option for `Cell` which specifies whether the contents of a cell should be explicitly displayed.

With `CellOpen->False`, a small cell bracket is still shown to indicate the presence of a cell. ▪ Cells which are not open can still be evaluated automatically if you set `InitializationCell->True`. ▪ See page 604. ▪ See also: `Visible`, `CellGroupData`, `ConversionRules`. ▪ *New in Version 3.*

■ CellPrint

CellPrint[*cell*] inserts *cell* in a notebook immediately after the cell that is currently being evaluated.

CellPrint[{*cell*₁, *cell*₂, ... }] inserts a sequence of cells.

The *cell*ᵢ must all have head Cell. ■ CellPrint is a special case of NotebookWrite. ■ With a text-based front end, CellPrint[*cell*] does the same as applying Print to the contents of *cell*. ■ Cells generated by CellPrint by default have GeneratedCell->True. ■ See page 575. ■ See also: StylePrint, Print, NotebookWrite, NotebookPrint. ■ *New in Version 3.*

■ CellTags

CellTags is an option for Cell which gives a list of tags to associate with a cell.

Cell tags are typically used to allow searching for cells. ■ The tags are usually strings. ■ Cell tags are displayed when the setting ShowCellTags->True is made. ■ See page 607. ■ See also: CellLabel, ConversionRules. ■ *New in Version 3.*

■ CellularAutomaton

CellularAutomaton[*rnum*, *init*, *t*] generates a list representing the evolution of cellular automaton rule *rnum* from initial condition *init* for *t* steps.

CellularAutomaton[*rnum*, *init*, *t*, {*off*ₜ, *off*ₓ, ... }] keeps only the parts of the evolution list with the specified offsets.

Possible settings for *rnum* are:

n	$k = 2$, $r = 1$, elementary rule
$\{n, k\}$	general nearest-neighbor rule with k colors
$\{n, k, r\}$	general rule with k colors and range r
$\{n, k, \{r_1, r_2, \ldots, r_d\}\}$	d-dimensional rule with $(2r_1 + 1) \times (2r_2 + 1) \times \ldots \times (2r_d + 1)$ neighborhood
$\{n, k, \{\{off_1\}, \{off_2\}, \ldots, \{off_s\}\}\}$	rule with neighbors at specified offsets
$\{n, \{k, 1\}\}$	k-color nearest-neighbor totalistic rule
$\{n, \{k, 1\}, r\}$	k-color range r totalistic rule
$\{n, \{k, \{wt_1, wt_2, \ldots \}\}, rspec\}$	rule in which neighbor i is assigned weight wt_i
$\{fun, \{\}, rspec\}$	applies the function *fun* to each list of neighbors, with a second argument of the step number

■ CellularAutomaton[{n, k}, ...] is equivalent to CellularAutomaton[{n, {k, {k^2, k, 1}}}, ...]. ■ Common forms for 2D cellular automata include:

$\{n, \{k, 1\}, \{1, 1\}\}$	9-neighbor totalistic rule
$\{n, \{k, \{\{0, 1, 0\}, \{1, 1, 1\}, \{0, 1, 0\}\}\}, \{1, 1\}\}$	5-neighbor totalistic rule
$\{n, \{k, \{\{0, k, 0\}, \{k, 1, k\}, \{0, k, 0\}\}\}, \{1, 1\}\}$	5-neighbor outer totalistic rule
$\{n + k\text{^}5\ (k - 1), \{k, \{\{0, 1, 0\}, \{1, 4 k + 1, 1\}, \{0, 1, 0\}\}\}, \{1, 1\}\}$	5-neighbor growth rule

■ Normally, all elements in *init* and the evolution list are integers between 0 and $k - 1$. ■ But when a general function is used, the elements of *init* and the evolution list do not have to be integers. ■ The second argument passed to *fun* is the step number, starting at 0. ■ Initial conditions are constructed from *init* as follows:

$\{a_1, a_2, \ldots \}$	explicit list of values a_i, assumed cyclic
$\{\{a_1, a_2, \ldots \}, b\}$	values a_i superimposed on a b background
$\{\{a_1, a_2, \ldots \}, \{b_1, b_2, \ldots \}\}$	values a_i superimposed on a background of repetitions of $b_1, b_2, \ldots$

(continued)

⁺■ **CellularAutomaton** *(continued)*

$\{\{\{a_{11},\ a_{12},\ \ldots\ \},\ \textit{off}_1\},\ \{\{a_{21},\ \ldots\ \},\ \textit{off}_2\},\ \ldots\ \},\ \textit{bspec}\}$	values a_{ij} at offsets $\textit{off}_i$ on a background
$\{\{a_{11},\ a_{12},\ \ldots\ \},\ \{a_{21},\ \ldots\ \},\ \ldots\ \}$	explicit list of values in two dimensions
$\{\textit{aspec},\ \textit{bspec}\}$	values in d dimensions with d-dimensional padding

■ The first element of *aspec* is superimposed on the background at the first position in the positive direction in each coordinate relative to the origin. This means that *bspec*[[1, 1, ...]] is aligned with *aspec*[[1, 1, ...]]. ■ Time offsets $\textit{off}_t$ are specified as follows:

`All`	all steps 0 through t
u	steps 0 through u
`-1`	last step (step t)
$\{u\}$	step u
$\{u_1,\ u_2\}$	steps u_1 through u_2
$\{u_1,\ u_2,\ du\}$	steps $u_1,\ u_1 + du,\ \ldots$

■ CellularAutomaton[*rnum*, *init*, *t*] generates an evolution list of length $t + 1$. ■ The initial condition is taken to have offset 0. ■ Space offsets $\textit{off}_x$ are specified as follows:

`All`	all cells that can be affected by the specified initial condition
`Automatic`	all cells in the region that differs from the background
`0`	cell aligned with beginning of *aspec*
x	cells at offsets up to x on the right
$-x$	cells at offsets up to x on the left
$\{x\}$	cell at offset x to the right
$\{-x\}$	cell at offset x to the left
$\{x_1,\ x_2\}$	cells at offsets x_1 through x_2
$\{x_1,\ x_2,\ dx\}$	cells $x_1,\ x_1 + dx,\ \ldots$

■ In one dimension, the first element of *aspec* is taken by default to have space offset 0. ■ In any number of dimensions, *aspec*[[1, 1, 1, ...]] is taken by default to have space offset {0, 0, 0, ... }. ■ Each element of the evolution list produced by CellularAutomaton is always the same size. ■ With an initial condition specified by an *aspec* of width w, the region that can be affected after t steps by a cellular automaton with a rule of range r has width $w + 2rt$. ■ If no *bspec* background is specified, space offsets of All and Automatic will include every cell in *aspec*. ■ A space offset of All includes all cells that can be affected by the initial condition. ■ A space offset of Automatic can be used to trim off background from the sides of a cellular automaton pattern. ■ In working out how wide a region to keep, Automatic only looks at results on steps specified by $\textit{off}_t$. ■ See page 942. ■ Implementation notes: see page 1069. ■ See also: ListConvolve, Partition, BitXor. ■ *New in Version 4.2.*

■ **CForm**

CForm[*expr*] prints as a C language version of *expr*.

Standard arithmetic functions and certain control structures are translated. ■ No declarations are generated. ■ CForm acts as a "wrapper", which affects printing, but not evaluation. ■ See pages 213 and 425. ■ See also: FortranForm, Compile. ■ *New in Version 1.*

■ **Character**

Character represents a single character in Read.

See page 646. ■ Related package: Utilities`BinaryFiles`. ■ *New in Version 1.*

■ CharacterEncoding

CharacterEncoding is an option for input and output functions which specifies what raw character encoding should be used.

The default is CharacterEncoding:>$CharacterEncoding. ■ The possible settings for CharacterEncoding are the same as for $CharacterEncoding. ■ See pages 422 and 634. ■ See also: ToCharacterCode, FromCharacterCode, StringReplace, $SystemCharacterEncoding, ShowSpecialCharacters. ■ *New in Version 3.*

■ CharacteristicPolynomial

CharacteristicPolynomial[m, x] gives the characteristic polynomial for the matrix m.

m must be a square matrix. ■ It can contain numeric or symbolic entries. ■ See pages 905 and 910. ■ See also: Eigenvalues, Det. ■ *New in Version 5.0.*

■ CharacterRange

CharacterRange["c_1", "c_2"] yields a list of the characters in the range from "c_1" to "c_2".

Example: CharacterRange["A", "D"] $\longrightarrow$ {"A", "B", "C", "D"}. ■ CharacterRange["a", "z"] yields the English alphabet. ■ CharacterRange["0", "9"] yields a list of digits. ■ CharacterRange["c_1", "c_2"] gives the list of characters with character codes from ToCharacterCode["c_1"] to ToCharacterCode["c_2"]. ■ CharacterRange["b", "a"] gives { }. ■ See page 413. ■ See also: FromCharacterCode, Range, Sort, Symbol, Unique. ■ *New in Version 3.*

■ Characters

Characters["*string*"] gives a list of the characters in a string.

Each character is given as a length one string. ■ Characters handles both ordinary and special characters. ■ See page 412. ■ See also: StringJoin, StringLength, ToCharacterCode, StringToStream, CharacterRange. ■ *New in Version 1; modified in Version 3.*

■ ChebyshevT

ChebyshevT[n, x] gives the Chebyshev polynomial of the first kind $T_n(x)$.

Mathematical function (see Section A.3.10). ■ Explicit polynomials are given for integer n. ■ $T_n(\cos\theta) = \cos(n\theta)$. ■ ChebyshevT[$n$, z] has a branch cut discontinuity in the complex z plane running from $-\infty$ to -1. ■ See page 766. ■ See also: ChebyshevU. ■ *New in Version 1.*

■ ChebyshevU

ChebyshevU[n, x] gives the Chebyshev polynomial of the second kind $U_n(x)$.

Mathematical function (see Section A.3.10). ■ Explicit polynomials are given for integer n. ■ $U_n(\cos\theta) = \sin[(n+1)\theta]/\sin\theta$. ■ ChebyshevU[$n$, z] has a branch cut discontinuity in the complex z plane running from $-\infty$ to -1. ■ See page 766. ■ See also: ChebyshevT. ■ *New in Version 1.*

■ Check

Check[*expr*, *failexpr*] evaluates *expr*, and returns the result, unless messages were generated, in which case it evaluates and returns *failexpr*.

Check[*expr*, *failexpr*, s_1::t_1, s_2::t_2, ...] checks only for the specified messages.

Check has attribute HoldAll. ■ Check tests only for messages that are actually output. It does not test for messages that have been suppressed using Off. ■ See page 481. ■ See also: MessageList, $MessageList, Message, Indeterminate, TimeConstrained, CheckAbort. ■ *New in Version 1.*

■ CheckAbort

CheckAbort[*expr*, *failexpr*] evaluates *expr*, returning *failexpr* if an abort occurs.

CheckAbort absorbs any aborts it handles, and does not propagate them further. ■ CheckAbort works inside AbortProtect. ■ CheckAbort has attribute HoldAll. ■ See page 371. ■ See also: Catch, Check. ■ *New in Version 2.*

⁺■ CholeskyDecomposition

CholeskyDecomposition[*m*] gives the Cholesky decomposition of a matrix *m*.

The matrix *m* can be numerical or symbolic, but must be Hermitian and positive definite. ■ CholeskyDecomposition[*m*] yields an upper triangular matrix *u* so that Conjugate[Transpose[*u*]] . *u* == m. ■ See page 914. ■ See also: LUDecomposition, LinearSolve, LinearSolveFunction, FindMinimum. ■ *New in Version 5.0.*

■ Chop

Chop[*expr*] replaces approximate real numbers in *expr* that are close to zero by the exact integer 0.

Chop[*expr*, *delta*] replaces numbers smaller in absolute magnitude than *delta* by 0. ■ Chop uses a default tolerance of 10^{-10}. ■ Chop works on both Real and Complex numbers. ■ See page 730. ■ See also: Rationalize, Round. ■ *New in Version 1.*

■ Circle

Circle[{*x*, *y*}, *r*] is a two-dimensional graphics primitive that represents a circle of radius *r* centered at the point *x*, *y*.

Circle[{*x*, *y*}, {r_x, r_y}] yields an ellipse with semi-axes r_x and r_y.

Circle[{*x*, *y*}, *r*, {θ_1, θ_2}] represents a circular arc.

Angles are measured in radians counterclockwise from the positive *x* direction. ■ Circle[{*x*, *y*}, {r_x, r_y}, {θ_1, θ_2}] yields a segment of an ellipse obtained by transforming a circular arc with the specified starting and ending angles. ■ Scaled[{dr_x, dr_y}] or Scaled[{dr_x, dr_y}, {r_x, r_y}] can be used in the radius specification. The dr_i are in scaled coordinates, and the r_i are in ordinary coordinates. ■ Offset[{a_x, a_y}] can be used to specify radii in printer's points. ■ The thickness of the circle can be specified using the Thickness primitive. ■ See page 496. ■ See also: Disk. ■ *New in Version 2; modified in Version 3.*

■ Clear

Clear[*symbol*₁, *symbol*₂, ...] clears values and definitions for the *symbol*ᵢ.

Clear["*form*₁", "*form*₂", ...] clears values and definitions for all symbols whose names match any of the string patterns *form*ᵢ.

Clear does not clear attributes, messages, or defaults associated with symbols. ■ Clear["*form*"] allows metacharacters such as *, as specified on page 1044. ■ Clear["*context*`*"] clears all symbols in a particular context. ■ Clear is HoldAll. ■ Clear does not affect symbols with the attribute Protected. ■ See pages 110, 304, 403 and 1052. ■ See also: Remove. ■ *New in Version 1.*

■ ClearAll

ClearAll[$symb_1$, $symb_2$, ...] clears all values, definitions, attributes, messages and defaults associated with symbols.

ClearAll["$form_1$", "$form_2$", ...] clears all symbols whose names textually match any of the $form_i$.

See notes for Clear. ■ See pages 331 and 1052. ■ See also: Remove. ■ *New in Version 1.*

■ ClearAttributes

ClearAttributes[s, *attr*] removes *attr* from the list of attributes of the symbol s.

ClearAttributes modifies Attributes[s]. ■ ClearAttributes[s, {$attr_1$, $attr_2$, ... }] removes several attributes at a time. ■ ClearAttributes[{s_1, s_2, ... }, *attrs*] removes attributes from several symbols at a time. ■ ClearAttributes is HoldFirst. ■ ClearAttributes does not affect symbols with the attribute Locked. ■ See page 328. ■ See also: SetAttributes, Unprotect. ■ *New in Version 1.*

■ ClebschGordan

ClebschGordan[{j_1, m_1}, {j_2, m_2}, {j, m}] gives the Clebsch-Gordan coefficient for the decomposition of $|j, m\rangle$ in terms of $|j_1, m_1\rangle |j_2, m_2\rangle$.

The Clebsch-Gordan coefficients vanish except when $m = m_1 + m_2$ and the j_i satisfy a triangle inequality. ■ The parameters of ClebschGordan can be integers, half-integers or symbolic expressions. ■ *Mathematica* uses the standard conventions of Edmonds for the phase of the Clebsch-Gordan coefficients. ■ See page 760. ■ Implementation notes: see page 1067. ■ See also: ThreeJSymbol, SixJSymbol, SphericalHarmonicY. ■ *New in Version 2.*

■ ClipFill

ClipFill is an option for SurfaceGraphics that specifies how clipped parts of the surface are to be drawn.

ClipFill specifies what is to be shown in places where the surface would extend beyond the bounding box. ■ The possible settings are:

Automatic	show clipped areas like the rest of the surface
None	make holes in the surface where it would be clipped
color	show clipped areas with a particular color
{*bottom*, *top*}	use different specifications for bottom and top clipped areas

■ The colors for clipped areas can be specified by GrayLevel, Hue or RGBColor directives, or SurfaceColor objects. ■ See page 540. ■ *New in Version 1.*

■ Close

Close[*stream*] closes a stream.

The argument to Close can be an InputStream or OutputStream object. ■ If there is only one stream with a particular name, the argument to close can be "*name*". ■ See page 632. ■ See also: OpenAppend, SetOptions, Streams. ■ *New in Version 1.*

■ CMYKColor

CMYKColor[*cyan*, *magenta*, *yellow*, *black*] is a graphics directive which specifies that graphical objects which follow are to be displayed in the color given.

Color levels outside the range 0 to 1 will be clipped. ■ CMYKColor can be used to specify colors for color printing. ■ CMYKColor specifications are automatically converted to RGBColor when simulated lighting calculations are done. ■ See page 563. ■ See also: RGBColor, ColorOutput. ■ Related package: Graphics`Colors`. ■ *New in Version 2.*

■ Coefficient

Coefficient[*expr*, *form*] gives the coefficient of *form* in the polynomial *expr*.

Coefficient[*expr*, *form*, *n*] gives the coefficient of *form*^*n* in *expr*.

Coefficient picks only terms that contain the particular form specified. x^2 is not considered part of x^3. ■ *form* can be a product of powers. ■ Coefficient[*expr*, *form*, 0] picks out terms that are not proportional to *form*. ■ Coefficient works whether or not *expr* is explicitly given in expanded form. ■ See page 799. ■ See also: Exponent, CoefficientList, SeriesCoefficient. ■ *New in Version 1; modified in Version 3.*

■ CoefficientArrays

CoefficientArrays[*polys*, *vars*] gives the arrays of coefficients of the variables *vars* in the polynomials *polys*.

CoefficientArrays gives a list containing SparseArray objects, which can be converted to ordinary arrays using Normal. ■ If CoefficientArrays[*polys*, *vars*] gives $\{m_0, m_1, m_2, \ldots\}$, then *polys* can be reconstructed as $m_0 + m_1 \cdot vars + m_2 \cdot vars \cdot vars + \ldots$. ■ Any element of *polys* of the form *lhs* == *rhs* is taken to correspond to the polynomial *lhs* − *rhs*. ■ CoefficientArrays[*polys*, $\{form_1, form_2, \ldots\}$] takes all expressions in *polys* that match any of the $form_i$ to be variables. ■ CoefficientArrays[*polys*] is equivalent to CoefficientArrays[*polys*, Variables[*polys*]]. ■ The length of the list CoefficientArrays[*polys*, *vars*] is one more than the total degree of *polys*. ■ The m_i are sparse arrays with ranks $i + 1$. ■ The first element m_0 has the same length as the list *polys*. ■ If *polys* is a single polynomial rather than a list, m_0 is also not a list. ■ For linear equations, the solution to Thread[*polys*==0] is given by LinearSolve[m_1, $-m_0$]. ■ For nonlinear equations, the m_i are not unique. CoefficientArrays by default assigns non-zero coefficients only to monomials where the variables appear in the same order as *vars*. ■ CoefficientArrays[*polys*, *vars*, Symmetric->True] makes all the m_i symmetric in all their indices. The resulting arrays will generally be less sparse. ■ See page 922. ■ See also: CoefficientList, SparseArray, Solve. ■ *New in Version 5.0.*

■ CoefficientList

CoefficientList[*poly*, *var*] gives a list of coefficients of powers of *var* in *poly*, starting with power 0.

CoefficientList[*poly*, $\{var_1, var_2, \ldots\}$] gives an array of coefficients of the var_i.

Example: CoefficientList[x^2 + 2 x y - y, {x, y}] ⟶ {{0, -1}, {0, 2}, {1, 0}}. ■ The dimensions of the array returned by CoefficientList are determined by the values of the Exponent[*poly*, var_i]. ■ Terms that do not contain positive integer powers of a particular variable are included in the first element of the list for that variable. ■ CoefficientList always returns a full rectangular array. Combinations of powers that do not appear in *poly* give zeros in the array. ■ CoefficientList[0, *var*] gives {}. ■ CoefficientList works whether or not *poly* is explicitly given in expanded form. ■ See page 799. ■ See also: Series, CoefficientArrays, SeriesCoefficient, Coefficient, Collect, FactorList. ■ *New in Version 1; modified in Version 3.*

■ Collect

Collect[*expr*, *x*] collects together terms involving the same powers of objects matching *x*.

Collect[*expr*, {x_1, x_2, ... }] collects together terms that involve the same powers of objects matching x_1, x_2, ...

Collect[*expr*, *var*, *h*] applies *h* to the expression that forms the coefficient of each term obtained.

Collect[*expr*, *x*] effectively writes *expr* as a polynomial in *x* or a fractional power of *x*. ■ Examples:
Collect[x + n x + m, x] ⟶ m + (1 + n) x;
Collect[(1+x+y)^3, x] ⟶ $1 + x^3 + 3y + 3y^2 + y^3 + x^2 (3 + 3y) + x (3 + 6y + 3y^2)$. ■ Collect[*expr*, *x*, Simplify] can be used to simplify each coefficient separately. ■ See page 797. ■ See also: Series, CoefficientList, Together, Cases. ■ *New in Version 1; modified in Version 3.*

■ ColorFunction

ColorFunction is an option for various graphics functions which specifies a function to apply to *z* values to determine the color to use for a particular *x*, *y* region.

ColorFunction is an option for Plot3D, ListPlot3D, DensityPlot, ContourPlot, Raster and related functions. ■ With the default setting ColorFunctionScaling -> True, the arguments provided for the function specified by ColorFunction are always scaled to be in the range 0 to 1. ■ With ColorFunctionScaling -> False original unscaled values are used. ■ The function specified by ColorFunction must return a CMYKColor, GrayLevel, Hue or RGBColor directive. ■ ColorFunction -> Automatic yields a range of gray levels. ■ ColorFunction -> Hue yields a range of colors. ■ In three-dimensional graphics, ColorFunction is used only with the option setting Lighting -> False. ■ See page 517. ■ See also: ColorFunctionScaling, Lighting, ColorOutput. ■ *New in Version 2; modified in Version 4.0.*

■ ColorFunctionScaling

ColorFunctionScaling is an option for various graphics functions which specifies whether the values provided to a color function should be scaled to lie between 0 and 1.

The default setting for ColorFunctionScaling is True. ■ With ColorFunctionScaling -> False original unscaled values are fed to the color function. ■ See page 517. ■ See also: ColorFunction. ■ *New in Version 4.*

■ ColorOutput

ColorOutput is an option for graphics functions which specifies the type of color output to produce.

Possible settings are:

Automatic	use whatever color directives are given
None	convert to monochrome
CMYKColor	convert to CMYKColor
GrayLevel	convert to GrayLevel
RGBColor	convert to RGBColor
f	convert using the function *f*

■ *Mathematica* performs color conversions using approximations to typical primary display and printing colors. ■ See page 564. ■ *New in Version 2; modified in Version 3.*

■ ColumnAlignments

ColumnAlignments is an option for GridBox which specifies how entries in each column should be aligned.

The following settings can be given:

Center	centered (default)
Left	left justified (aligned on left edge)
Right	right justified (aligned on right edge)
"."	aligned at decimal points
"c"	aligned at the first occurrence of the character c
{pos_1, pos_2, ... }	separate settings for each column in the grid

■ Lists of settings are used cyclically if there are more columns in the grid than elements in the list. ■ With the setting ColumnAlignments->"c" a column will be right justified if the character c appears nowhere in it. ■ You can insert invisible \[AlignmentMarker] characters in the entries in a grid to specify how these entries should be aligned. ■ See page 449. ■ See also: RowAlignments, ColumnsEqual, TableAlignments, TextAlignment. ■ *New in Version 3.*

■ ColumnForm

ColumnForm[{e_1, e_2, ... }] prints as a column with e_1 above e_2, etc.

ColumnForm[*list*, *horiz*] specifies the horizontal alignment of each element.

ColumnForm[*list*, *horiz*, *vert*] also specifies the vertical alignment of the whole column.

Possible horizontal alignments are:

Center	centered
Left	left justified (default case)
Right	right justified

Possible vertical alignments are:

Above	the bottom element of the column is aligned with the baseline
Below	the top element is aligned with the baseline (default case)
Center	the column is centered on the baseline

■ The first argument of ColumnForm can have any head, not necessarily List. ■ ColumnForm acts as a "wrapper", which affects printing, but not evaluation. ■ See pages 416 and 437. ■ See also: TableForm, MatrixForm, SequenceForm, GridBox. ■ *New in Version 1.*

■ ColumnLines

ColumnLines is an option for GridBox which specifies whether lines should be drawn between adjacent columns.

The default setting is ColumnLines->False. ■ ColumnLines->{v_{12}, v_{23}, ... } specifies whether lines should be drawn between successive pairs of columns. The v_{ij} can be True or False. ■ If there are more columns than entries in the list, the last element is used repeatedly for remaining pairs of columns. ■ Lines can be drawn around the outside of a GridBox using FrameBox. ■ See page 446. ■ See also: RowLines, FrameBox, GridLines. ■ *New in Version 3.*

■ ColumnsEqual

ColumnsEqual is an option for GridBox which specifies whether all columns in the grid should be assigned equal width.

The default setting ColumnsEqual->False determines the width of each column from the widest entry in that column. ■ ColumnsEqual->True makes all columns the same width, with the width determined by the widest entry in the whole GridBox. ■ See page 449. ■ See also: ColumnWidths, ColumnAlignments, ColumnSpacings, RowsEqual, MatrixForm. ■ *New in Version 3.*

■ ColumnSpacings

ColumnSpacings is an option for GridBox which specifies the spaces in ems that should be inserted between adjacent columns.

The default setting is ColumnSpacings->0.8. ■ ColumnSpacings effectively specifies the minimum distance between entries in adjacent columns; individual entries will often not fill their columns and will therefore be further apart. ■ ColumnSpacings->n uses a column spacing equal to n times the current font size—usually about n times the width of an M in the current font. ■ ColumnSpacings->$\{s_{12}, s_{23}, \dots\}$ can be used to specify different spacings between different columns. If there are more columns than entries in this list, then the last element of the list is used repeatedly for the remaining columns. ■ See page 449. ■ See also: ColumnAlignments, ColumnWidths, ColumnsEqual, RowSpacings, TableSpacing. ■ *New in Version 3.*

■ ColumnWidths

ColumnWidths is an option for GridBox which specifies the widths of columns in ems.

The default setting is ColumnWidths->Automatic, specifying that all columns should be made wide enough to fit their contents without breaking onto multiple lines. ■ ColumnWidths->n uses column widths equal to n times the current font size—usually about n times the width of an M in the current font. ■ ColumnWidths->$\{w_1, w_2, \dots\}$ can be used to specify different widths for different columns. If there are more columns than entries in this list, then the last element of the list is used repeatedly for the remaining columns. ■ An explicit setting for ColumnWidths overrides ColumnsEqual->True. ■ See page 449. ■ See also: ColumnsEqual, ColumnSpacings. ■ *New in Version 3.*

■ Compile

Compile[$\{x_1, x_2, \dots\}$, *expr*] creates a compiled function which evaluates *expr* assuming numerical values of the x_i.

Compile[$\{\{x_1, t_1\}, \dots\}$, *expr*] assumes that x_i is of a type which matches t_i.

Compile[$\{\{x_1, t_1, n_1\}, \dots\}$, *expr*] assumes that x_i is a rank n_i array of objects each of a type which matches t_i.

Compile[*vars*, *expr*, $\{\{p_1, pt_1\}, \dots\}$] assumes that subexpressions in *expr* which match p_i are of types which match pt_i.

The types handled by Compile are:

_Integer	machine-size integer
_Real	machine-precision approximate real number (default)
_Complex	machine-precision approximate complex number
True | False	logical variable

(continued)

■ **Compile** *(continued)*

■ Nested lists given as input to a compiled function must be full arrays of numbers. ■ Compile handles numerical functions, matrix operations, procedural programming constructs, list manipulation functions, functional programming constructs, etc. ■ Compile generates a CompiledFunction object. ■ Compiled code does not handle numerical precision and local variables in the same way as ordinary *Mathematica* code. ■ If a compiled function cannot be evaluated with particular arguments using compiled code, ordinary *Mathematica* code is used instead. ■ Ordinary *Mathematica* code can be called from within compiled code. Results obtained from the *Mathematica* code are assumed to be approximate real numbers, unless specified otherwise by the third argument of Compile. ■ The number of times and the order in which objects are evaluated by Compile may be different from ordinary *Mathematica* code. ■ Compile has attribute HoldAll, and does not by default do any evaluation before compilation. ■ You can use Compile[... , Evaluate[*expr*]] to specify that *expr* should be evaluated symbolically before compilation. ■ See page 372. ■ See also: Dispatch, Function, InterpolatingFunction, CForm. ■ *New in Version 2; modified in Version 3.*

■ **Compiled**

Compiled is an option for various numerical and plotting functions which specifies whether the expressions they work with should automatically be compiled.

Compiled -> True automatically creates compiled functions. ■ You should set Compiled -> False if you need to use high-precision numbers. ■ See page 373. ■ *New in Version 2.*

■ **CompiledFunction**

CompiledFunction[*args*, *argregs*, *nregs*, *instr*, *func*] represents compiled code for evaluating a compiled function.

args is a list giving a pattern for the type of each argument to the function. The types are specified as in Compile. ■ *argregs* is a list of the registers into which actual argument values should be placed to evaluate the compiled code. ■ *nregs* is a list of the numbers of logical, integer, real, complex and tensor registers required in evaluating the compiled code. ■ *instr* is a list of actual compiled code instructions. ■ *func* is a *Mathematica* pure function to be used if no result can be obtained from the compiled code for any reason. ■ Compile generates a CompiledFunction object which can be executed by applying it to appropriate arguments. ■ CompiledFunction objects that are constructed explicitly can also be executed. Basic consistency checks are done when such objects are first evaluated by *Mathematica*. ■ The code in a CompiledFunction object is based on an idealized register machine. ■ See page 376. ■ See also: InterpolatingFunction. ■ *New in Version 2; modified in Version 4.0.*

■ **Complement**

Complement[*eall*, *e₁*, *e₂*, ...] gives the elements in *eall* which are not in any of the *eᵢ*.

The list returned by Complement is sorted into standard order. ■ Example: Complement[{a,b,c,d,e}, {a,c}, {d}] ⟶ {b, e}. ■ Complement[*eall*, *e₁*, ... , SameTest->*test*] applies *test* to each pair of elements in *eall* and the *eᵢ* to determine whether they should be considered the same. ■ See page 127. ■ See also: Intersection, Union. ■ *New in Version 1; modified in Version 3.*

■ **Complex**

Complex is the head used for complex numbers.

You can enter a complex number in the form $x + I\,y$. ■ _Complex can be used to stand for a complex number in a pattern. ■ You have to use Re and Im to extract parts of Complex numbers. ■ See page 722. ■ See also: Complexes, Real, Re, Im. ■ *New in Version 1.*

■ Complexes

Complexes represents the domain of complex numbers, as in $x \in$ Complexes.

$x \in$ Complexes evaluates immediately only if x is a numeric quantity. ■ Simplify[*expr* ∈ Complexes] can be used to try to determine whether an expression corresponds to a complex number. ■ The domain of real numbers is taken to be a subset of the domain of complex numbers. ■ Complexes is output in TraditionalForm as ℂ. ■ See pages 817 and 839. ■ See also: Element, Simplify, NumberQ, NumericQ, Complex, Reals. ■ Related package: Algebra`Quaternions`. ■ *New in Version 4.*

■ ComplexExpand

ComplexExpand[*expr*] expands *expr* assuming that all variables are real.

ComplexExpand[*expr*, {x_1, x_2, ... }] expands *expr* assuming that variables matching any of the x_i are complex.

Example: ComplexExpand[Sin[x + I y]] ⟶ Cosh[y] Sin[x] + i Cos[x] Sinh[y]. ■ The variables given in the second argument of ComplexExpand can be patterns. ■ Example: ComplexExpand[Sin[x], x] ⟶ Cosh[Im[x]] Sin[Re[x]] + i Cos[Re[x]] Sinh[Im[x]]. ■ The option TargetFunctions can be given as a list of functions from the set {Re, Im, Abs, Arg, Conjugate, Sign}. ComplexExpand will try to give results in terms of functions specified. ■ ComplexExpand[*expr*, *vars*, TargetFunctions -> {Abs, Arg}] converts to polar coordinates. ■ See page 812. ■ See also: GaussianIntegers, TrigToExp, ExpToTrig, TrigExpand, FunctionExpand. ■ *New in Version 2.*

■ ComplexInfinity

ComplexInfinity represents a quantity with infinite magnitude, but undetermined complex phase.

ComplexInfinity is converted to DirectedInfinity[ ]. ■ In OutputForm, DirectedInfinity[ ] is printed as ComplexInfinity. ■ See page 743. ■ See also: Infinity, Indeterminate. ■ *New in Version 1.*

■ ComplexityFunction

ComplexityFunction is an option for Simplify and FullSimplify which gives a function to rank the complexity of different forms of an expression.

With the default setting ComplexityFunction->Automatic, forms are ranked primarily according to their LeafCount, with corrections to treat integers with more digits as more complex. ■ Simplify[*expr*, ComplexityFunction->*f*] applies *f* to each intermediate expression generated by Simplify, treating the one which yields the smallest numerical value as simplest. ■ See page 815. ■ See also: Length, StringLength, TimeConstraint, ExcludedForms, TransformationFunctions. ■ *New in Version 3.*

■ ComposeList

ComposeList[{f_1, f_2, ... }, x] generates a list of the form {x, $f_1[x]$, $f_2[f_1[x]]$, ... }.

Example: ComposeList[{a, b, c}, x] ⟶ {x, a[x], b[a[x]], c[b[a[x]]]}. ■ See page 250. ■ See also: NestList, FoldList, NestWhileList. ■ *New in Version 2.*

■ ComposeSeries

ComposeSeries[*series*₁, *series*₂, ...] composes several power series.

ComposeSeries[*series*₁, *series*₂, ...] effectively replaces the variable in *series*₁ by *series*₂ and so on. ■ Two series can only meaningfully be composed when the point about which the first series is expanded corresponds to the limiting value of the second series at its expansion point. ■ See page 887. ■ See also: InverseSeries. ■ *New in Version 3.*

■ Composition

Composition[f_1, f_2, f_3, ...] represents a composition of the functions $f_1, f_2, f_3, \ldots$.

Composition allows you to build up compositions of functions which can later be applied to specific arguments. ■ Example: Composition[a, b, c][x] ⟶ a[b[c[x]]]. ■ Composition objects containing Identity or InverseFunction[f] are automatically simplified when possible. ■ Composition has the attributes Flat and OneIdentity. ■ a @ b @ c gives $a[b[c]]$. ■ a // b // c gives $c[b[a]]$. ■ See page 253. ■ See also: Nest, Function. ■ *New in Version 2.*

■ CompoundExpression

$expr_1$; $expr_2$; ... evaluates the $expr_i$ in turn, giving the last one as the result.

CompoundExpression evaluates its arguments in a sequence corresponding to the control flow. ■ The returned value can be the result of Return[$expr$]. ■ The evaluation of the $expr_i$ can be affected by Return, Throw and Goto. ■ $expr_1$; $expr_2$; returns value Null. If it is given as input, the resulting output will not be printed. Out[n] will nevertheless be assigned to be the value of $expr_2$. ■ See pages 43 and 1029. ■ See also: Block. ■ *New in Version 1.*

■ Condition

patt /; *test* is a pattern which matches only if the evaluation of *test* yields True.

lhs :> *rhs* /; *test* represents a rule which applies only if the evaluation of *test* yields True.

lhs := *rhs* /; *test* is a definition to be used only if *test* yields True.

Example: The pattern x_ /; x > 0 represents an expression which must be positive. ■ All pattern variables used in *test* must also appear in *patt*. ■ Example: f[x_] := fp[x] /; x > 1 defines a function in the case when $x > 1$. ■ *lhs* := Module[{*vars*}, *rhs* /; *test*] allows local variables to be shared between *test* and *rhs*. You can use the same construction with Block and With. ■ See pages 265 and 345. ■ See also: If, Switch, Which, PatternTest, Element. ■ *New in Version 1.*

■ Conjugate

Conjugate[z] gives the complex conjugate z^* of the complex number z.

Mathematical function (see Section A.3.10). ■ See page 746. ■ See also: ComplexExpand. ■ *New in Version 1.*

■ Constant

Constant is an attribute which indicates zero derivative of a symbol with respect to all parameters.

Constant is used by Dt. ■ Functions $f[\ldots]$ are taken to have zero total derivative if f has attribute Constant. ■ Mathematical constants such as Pi have attribute Constant. ■ See pages 329 and 854. ■ *New in Version 1.*

■ Constants

Constants is an option for Dt which gives a list of objects to be taken as constants.

If f appears in the list of Constants, then both Dt[f] and Dt[$f[\ldots]$] are taken to be zero. ■ See page 854. ■ See also: D. ■ *New in Version 1.*

■ Context

Context[ ] gives the current context.

Context[*symbol*] gives the context in which a symbol appears.

The current context is the value of $Context. ■ See page 394. ■ See also: Begin, $ContextPath, Remove. ■ *New in Version 1.*

▪ Contexts

Contexts[ ] gives a list of all contexts.

Contexts["*string*"] gives a list of the contexts which match the string.

The string can contain metacharacters such as * and @, as described on page 1044. ▪ See pages 394 and 403. ▪ See also: $Packages, $ContextPath. ▪ *New in Version 2.*

▪ Continue

Continue[ ] exits to the nearest enclosing Do, For or While in a procedural program.

Continue[ ] takes effect as soon as it is evaluated, even if it appears inside other functions. ▪ The function of Continue can also be achieved using Throw and Catch. ▪ See page 353. ▪ See also: Break, Goto. ▪ *New in Version 1; modified in Version 3.*

▪ ContinuedFraction

ContinuedFraction[x, n] generates a list of the first n terms in the continued fraction representation of x.

ContinuedFraction[x] generates a list of all terms that can be obtained given the precision of x.

The continued fraction representation $\{a_1, a_2, a_3, \dots\}$ corresponds to the expression $a_1 + 1/(a_2 + 1/(a_3 + \dots))$. ▪ x can be either an exact or an inexact number. ▪ Example: ContinuedFraction[Pi, 4] $\longrightarrow$ {3, 7, 15, 1}. ▪ For exact numbers, ContinuedFraction[x] can be used if x is rational, or is a quadratic irrational. ▪ For quadratic irrationals, ContinuedFraction[x] returns a result of the form $\{a_1, a_2, \dots, \{b_1, b_2, \dots \}\}$, corresponding to an infinite sequence of terms, starting with the a_i, and followed by cyclic repetitions of the b_i. ▪ Since the continued fraction representation for a rational number has only a limited number of terms, ContinuedFraction[x, n] may yield a list with less than n elements in this case. ▪ For terminating continued fractions, $\{\dots, k\}$ is always equivalent to $\{\dots, k\text{-}1, 1\}$; ContinuedFraction returns the first of these forms. ▪ FromContinuedFraction[*list*] reconstructs a number from the result of ContinuedFraction. ▪ See page 754. ▪ Implementation notes: see page 1067. ▪ See also: FromContinuedFraction, IntegerDigits, Rationalize, Khinchin, RealDigits. ▪ *New in Version 4.*

▪ ContourGraphics

ContourGraphics[*array*] is a representation of a contour plot.

array must be a rectangular array of real numbers, representing z values. ▪ The following options can be given:

AspectRatio	1	ratio of height to width
Axes	False	whether to draw axes
AxesLabel	None	axes labels
AxesOrigin	Automatic	where axes should cross
AxesStyle	Automatic	graphics directives to specify the style for axes
Background	Automatic	background color for the plot
ColorFunction	Automatic	function specifying the color of regions between contour lines
ColorFunctionScaling	True	whether to scale z values before applying a color function
ColorOutput	Automatic	type of color output to produce
ContourLines	True	whether to draw explicit contour lines
Contours	10	what contours to use
ContourShading	True	whether to shade the regions between contours
ContourStyle	Automatic	the style for contour lines
DefaultColor	Automatic	the default color for plot elements
DisplayFunction	$DisplayFunction	function for generating output
Epilog	{}	graphics primitives to be rendered after the main plot

(continued)

■ ContourGraphics *(continued)*

FormatType	$FormatType	the default format type for text
Frame	True	whether to put a frame around the plot
FrameLabel	None	frame labels
FrameStyle	Automatic	graphics directives giving the style for the frame
FrameTicks	Automatic	frame tick marks
ImageSize	Automatic	the absolute size at which to render the graphic in a notebook
MeshRange	Automatic	ranges of x and y coordinates
PlotLabel	None	a label for the plot
PlotRange	Automatic	range of z values to include
PlotRegion	Automatic	the final display region to be filled
Prolog	{}	graphics primitives to be rendered before the main plot
RotateLabel	True	whether to rotate y labels on the frame
TextStyle	$TextStyle	the default style for text
Ticks	Automatic	tick marks

■ ContourGraphics[g] converts DensityGraphics and SurfaceGraphics objects to ContourGraphics. The resulting graphics can be rendered using Show. ■ Graphics[ContourGraphics[...]] generates a representation in terms of an ordinary Graphics object. ■ ContourGraphics is generated by ContourPlot and ListContourPlot. ■ See page 517. ■ See also: ListContourPlot, DensityGraphics. ■ *New in Version 1.*

■ ContourLines

ContourLines is an option for contour plots which specifies whether to draw explicit contour lines.

ContourLines -> True draws contour lines. ContourLines -> False does not. ■ See page 519. ■ See also: ContourStyle, Contours. ■ *New in Version 2.*

■ ContourPlot

ContourPlot[f, {x, *xmin*, *xmax*}, {y, *ymin*, *ymax*}] generates a contour plot of f as a function of x and y.

ContourPlot evaluates its arguments in a non-standard way (see page 1046). You should use Evaluate to evaluate the function to be plotted if this can safely be done before specific numerical values are supplied. ■ ContourPlot has the same options as ContourGraphics, with the following additions:

Compiled	True	whether to compile the function to plot
PlotPoints	25	the number of points in each direction at which to sample the function

■ ContourPlot has the default option setting Frame -> True. ■ ContourPlot returns a ContourGraphics object, with the MeshRange option set. ■ See page 146. ■ See also: DensityPlot. ■ Related packages: Graphics`ContourPlot3D`, Graphics`ImplicitPlot`, Graphics`PlotField`, Graphics`ComplexMap`. ■ *New in Version 1.*

■ Contours

Contours is an option for ContourGraphics specifying the contours to use.

Contours -> n chooses n equally spaced contours between the minimum and maximum z values. ■ Contours -> {z_1, z_2, ... } specifies the explicit z values of contours to use. ■ See pages 147 and 519. ■ *New in Version 2.*

■ ContourShading

ContourShading is an option for contour plots which specifies whether the regions between contour lines should be shaded.

With ContourShading -> False, regions between contour lines are left blank. ■ With ContourShading -> True, regions are colored based on the setting for the option ColorFunction. The default is to color the regions with gray levels running from black to white with increasing height. ■ The value given as the argument for the ColorFunction function is the average of the values of the contour lines bounding a particular region. If ColorFunctionScaling -> True, it is scaled so as to lie between 0 and 1. ■ See page 519. ■ *New in Version 2.*

■ ContourStyle

ContourStyle is an option for contour plots that specifies the style in which contour lines should be drawn.

ContourStyle -> *style* specifies that all contour lines are to be generated with the specified graphics directive, or list of graphics directives. ■ ContourStyle -> {{$style_1$}, {$style_2$}, ... } specifies that successive contour lines should use graphics directives $style_1$, ... The styles must be enclosed in lists, perhaps of length one. ■ The $style_i$ are used cyclically. ■ Styles can be specified using graphics directives such as Dashing, Hue and Thickness. ■ See page 519. ■ See also: PlotStyle. ■ *New in Version 2.*

■ ConversionRules

ConversionRules is an option for Cell which can be set to a list of rules specifying how the contents of the cell are to be converted to external formats.

Typical elements in the list have the form "TeX" -> *data*. ■ Settings for ConversionRules do not affect the display of cells in the standard *Mathematica* notebook front end. ■ ConversionRules can be used to save the original form of a cell that has been converted from an external format. ■ See page 607. ■ See also: CellTags. ■ *New in Version 3.*

■ Copyable

Copyable is an option for Cell which specifies whether a cell can be copied interactively using the front end.

Even with the setting Copyable->False, the expression corresponding to a cell can still be read into the kernel using NotebookRead. ■ With Copyable->False set at the notebook level, no cells in the notebook can be copied interactively in the front end. ■ See page 607. ■ See also: Selectable, ReadProtected. ■ *New in Version 3.*

■ CopyDirectory

CopyDirectory["dir_1", "dir_2"] copies the directory dir_1 to dir_2.

dir_1 must already exist; dir_2 must not. ■ CopyDirectory copies all the files in dir_1 to dir_2. ■ CopyDirectory sets the modification dates for dir_2 and for all the files in it to be the same as those for dir_1. ■ CopyDirectory returns the full name of the directory it copies to, and $Failed if it cannot complete the copy. ■ See page 641. ■ See also: RenameDirectory, CreateDirectory, DeleteDirectory. ■ *New in Version 2.*

■ CopyFile

CopyFile["$file_1$", "$file_2$"] copies $file_1$ to $file_2$.

$file_1$ must already exist; $file_2$ must not. ■ CopyFile sets the modification date for $file_2$ to be the same as for $file_1$. ■ CopyFile returns the full name of the file it copies to, and $Failed if it cannot do the copy. ■ See page 641. ■ See also: RenameFile, DeleteFile, CopyDirectory. ■ *New in Version 2.*

■ Cos

Cos[z] gives the cosine of z.

Mathematical function (see Section A.3.10). ■ The argument of Cos is assumed to be in radians. (Multiply by Degree to convert from degrees.) ■ Cos is automatically evaluated when its argument is a simple rational multiple of π; for more complicated rational multiples, FunctionExpand can sometimes be used. ■ See page 761. ■ See also: ArcCos, Sec, TrigToExp, TrigExpand. ■ *New in Version 1.*

■ Cosh

Cosh[z] gives the hyperbolic cosine of z.

Mathematical function (see Section A.3.10). ■ $\cosh(z) = \frac{1}{2}(e^z + e^{-z})$. ■ See page 761. ■ See also: ArcCosh, Sech, TrigToExp, TrigExpand. ■ *New in Version 1.*

■ CoshIntegral

CoshIntegral[z] gives the hyperbolic cosine integral Chi(z).

Mathematical function (see Section A.3.10). ■ $\text{Chi}(z) = \gamma + \log(z) + \int_0^z (\cosh(t) - 1)/t\, dt$, where γ is Euler's constant. ■ CoshIntegral[z] has a branch cut discontinuity in the complex z plane running from $-\infty$ to 0. ■ See page 774. ■ See also: SinhIntegral. ■ *New in Version 3.*

■ CosIntegral

CosIntegral[z] gives the cosine integral function Ci(z).

Mathematical function (see Section A.3.10). ■ $\text{Ci}(z) = -\int_z^\infty \cos(t)/t\, dt$. ■ CosIntegral[z] has a branch cut discontinuity in the complex z plane running from $-\infty$ to 0. ■ See page 774. ■ See also: SinIntegral, ExpIntegralE, ExpIntegralEi, FresnelC. ■ *New in Version 2.*

■ Cot

Cot[z] gives the cotangent of z.

Mathematical function (see Section A.3.10). ■ The argument of Cot is assumed to be in radians. (Multiply by Degree to convert from degrees.) ■ $\cot(z) = 1/\tan(z)$. ■ Cos[z]/Sin[z] is automatically converted to Cot[z]. TrigFactorList[*expr*] does decomposition. ■ See page 761. ■ See also: ArcCot, TrigToExp, TrigExpand. ■ *New in Version 1.*

■ Coth

Coth[z] gives the hyperbolic cotangent of z.

Mathematical function (see Section A.3.10). ■ Cosh[z]/Sinh[z] is automatically converted to Coth[z]. TrigFactorList[*expr*] does decomposition. ■ See page 761. ■ See also: ArcCoth, TrigToExp, TrigExpand. ■ *New in Version 1.*

■ Count

Count[*list*, *pattern*] gives the number of elements in *list* that match *pattern*.

Count[*expr*, *pattern*, *levelspec*] gives the total number of subexpressions matching *pattern* that appear at the levels in *expr* specified by *levelspec*.

Level specifications are described on page 1041. ■ See page 261. ■ See also: FreeQ, MemberQ, Cases, Select, Position. ■ Related package: Statistics`DataManipulation`. ■ *New in Version 1.*

■ CreateDirectory

`CreateDirectory["`*dir*`"]` creates a directory.

CreateDirectory creates a subdirectory of your current working directory. ■ The directory created by CreateDirectory is initially empty. ■ CreateDirectory returns the full name of the directory it creates, and $Failed if it cannot create the directory. ■ CreateDirectory has attribute Listable. ■ See page 641. ■ See also: DeleteDirectory, RenameDirectory, CopyDirectory. ■ *New in Version 2.*

■ Cross

`Cross[`*a*`, `*b*`]` gives the vector cross product of *a* and *b*.

If *a* and *b* are lists of length 3, corresponding to vectors in three dimensions, then Cross[*a*, *b*] is also a list of length 3. ■ Cross[*a*, *b*] can be entered in StandardForm and InputForm as *a* × *b*, *a* :cross: *b* or *a* \[Cross] *b*. Note the difference between \[Cross] and \[Times]. ■ Cross is antisymmetric, so that Cross[*b*, *a*] is -Cross[*a*, *b*]. ■ In general, Cross[v_1, v_2, ... , v_{n-1}] is a totally antisymmetric product which takes vectors of length *n* and yields a vector of length *n* that is orthogonal to all of the v_i. ■ Cross[v_1, v_2, ...] gives the dual (Hodge star) of the wedge product of the v_i, viewed as one-forms in *n* dimensions. ■ See page 119. ■ See also: Dot, Signature, Outer. ■ *New in Version 3.*

■ Csc

`Csc[`*z*`]` gives the cosecant of *z*.

Mathematical function (see Section A.3.10). ■ The argument of Csc is assumed to be in radians. (Multiply by Degree to convert from degrees.) ■ $\csc(z) = 1/\sin(z)$. ■ 1/Sin[*z*] is automatically converted to Csc[*z*]. TrigFactorList[*expr*] does decomposition. ■ See page 761. ■ See also: ArcCsc, TrigToExp, TrigExpand. ■ *New in Version 1.*

■ Csch

`Csch[`*z*`]` gives the hyperbolic cosecant of *z*.

Mathematical function (see Section A.3.10). ■ $\operatorname{csch}(z) = 1/\sinh(z)$. ■ 1/Sinh[*z*] is automatically converted to Csch[*z*]. TrigFactorList[*expr*] does decomposition. ■ See page 761. ■ See also: ArcCsch, TrigToExp, TrigExpand. ■ *New in Version 1.*

■ Cuboid

`Cuboid[{`*xmin*`, `*ymin*`, `*zmin*`}]` is a three-dimensional graphics primitive that represents a unit cuboid, oriented parallel to the axes.

`Cuboid[{`*xmin*`, `*ymin*`, `*zmin*`}, {`*xmax*`, `*ymax*`, `*zmax*`}]` specifies a cuboid by giving the coordinates of opposite corners.

Each face of the cuboid (rectangular parallelepiped) is effectively a Polygon object. ■ You can specify how the faces and edges of the cuboid should be rendered using the same graphics directives as for polygons. ■ The coordinates of the corners of the cuboid can be given using Scaled. ■ See page 520. ■ See also: Polygon, Rectangle. ■ Related package: Graphics`Polyhedra`. ■ *New in Version 2.*

■ Cyclotomic

`Cyclotomic[`*n*`, `*x*`]` gives the cyclotomic polynomial of order *n* in *x*.

The cyclotomic polynomial $C_n(x)$ of order *n* is defined to be $\prod_k (x - e^{2\pi i k/n})$, where the product runs over integers *k* less than *n* that are relatively prime to *n*. ■ See page 807. ■ See also: Factor, Roots. ■ *New in Version 1.*

◼ CylindricalDecomposition

CylindricalDecomposition[*ineqs*, {x_1, x_2, ... }] finds a decomposition of the region represented by the inequalities *ineqs* into cylindrical parts whose directions correspond to the successive x_i.

Example: CylindricalDecomposition[x^2 + y^2 < 1, {x, y}] $\longrightarrow$ $-1 < x < 1$ && $-\sqrt{1-x^2} < y < \sqrt{1-x^2}$. ▪ CylindricalDecomposition assumes that all variables are real. ▪ Lists or logical combinations of inequalities can be given. ▪ CylindricalDecomposition returns inequalities whose bounds in general involve algebraic functions. ▪ See page 847. ▪ Implementation notes: see page 1070. ▪ See also: Reduce, Resolve, FindInstance, FullSimplify, GroebnerBasis. ▪ *New in Version 5.0.*

◼ D

D[*f*, *x*] gives the partial derivative $\partial f / \partial x$.

D[*f*, {*x*, *n*}] gives the multiple derivative $\partial^n f / \partial x^n$.

D[*f*, x_1, x_2, ...] gives $\partial/\partial x_1 \ \partial/\partial x_2 \ ... \ f$.

D[*f*, *x*] can be input as $\partial_x f$. The character ∂ is entered as :pd: or \[PartialD]. The variable *x* is entered as a subscript. ▪ All quantities that do not explicitly depend on the x_i are taken to have zero partial derivative. ▪ D[*f*, x_1, ... , NonConstants -> {v_1, ... }] specifies that the v_i implicitly depend on the x_i, so that they do not have zero partial derivative. ▪ The derivatives of built-in mathematical functions are evaluated when possible in terms of other built-in mathematical functions. ▪ Numerical approximations to derivatives can be found using N. ▪ D uses the chain rule to simplify derivatives of unknown functions. ▪ D[*f*, *x*, *y*] can be input as $\partial_{x,y} f$. The character \[InvisibleComma], entered as :,:, can be used instead of an ordinary comma. It does not display, but is still interpreted just like a comma. ▪ See page 853. ▪ Implementation notes: see page 1070. ▪ See also: Dt, Derivative, Maximize. ▪ Related packages: Calculus`VectorAnalysis`, NumericalMath`NLimit`. ▪ *New in Version 1; modified in Version 3.*

◼ Dashing

Dashing[{r_1, r_2, ... }] is a two-dimensional graphics directive which specifies that lines which follow are to be drawn dashed, with successive segments of lengths r_1, r_2, ... (repeated cyclically). The r_i is given as a fraction of the total width of the graph.

Dashing can be used in both two- and three-dimensional graphics. ▪ Dashing[{ }] specifies that lines should be solid. ▪ See page 501. ▪ See also: AbsoluteDashing, Thickness, GrayLevel, Hue, RGBColor, PlotStyle. ▪ *New in Version 1.*

◼ Date

Date[ ] gives the current local date and time in the form {*year*, *month*, *day*, *hour*, *minute*, *second*}.

Date[ ] uses whatever date and time have been set on your computer system. It performs no corrections for time zones, daylight saving time, etc. ▪ Date[*z*] gives the date in time zone *z*. This is inferred by knowing your local date and time, and local time zone. The time zone is given as the number of hours to be added to Greenwich mean time to obtain local time. ▪ All values returned by Date[ ] are integers, except the number of seconds. The number of seconds is never more accurate than $TimeUnit. ▪ You can compare two lists returned by Date using Order. ▪ See page 709. ▪ See also: AbsoluteTime, TimeZone, SessionTime, TimeUsed, ToDate, FromDate, FileDate, $CreationDate. ▪ Related package: Miscellaneous`Calendar`. ▪ *New in Version 2.*

■ **DeclarePackage**

DeclarePackage["*context*`", {"*name*$_1$", "*name*$_2$", ... }] declares that Needs["*context*`"] should automatically be executed if a symbol with any of the specified names is ever used.

You can use DeclarePackage to tell *Mathematica* automatically to load a particular package when any of the symbols defined in it are used. ■ DeclarePackage creates symbols with the attribute Stub in the specified context. ■ DeclarePackage prepends *context*` to $ContextPath. ■ See page 401. ■ See also: Needs, $NewSymbol. ■ *New in Version 2.*

■ **Decompose**

Decompose[*poly*, *x*] decomposes a polynomial, if possible, into a composition of simpler polynomials.

Decompose gives a list of the polynomials P_i which can be composed as $P_1(P_2(...(x)...))$ to give the original polynomial. ■ The set of polynomials P_i is not necessarily unique. ■ Decomposition is an operation which is independent of polynomial factorization. ■ See page 807. ■ See also: FactorList, Solve. ■ *New in Version 1.*

■ **Decrement**

x-- decreases the value of *x* by 1, returning the old value of *x*.

Decrement has attribute HoldFirst. ■ See page 305. ■ See also: PreDecrement, SubtractFrom, Set. ■ *New in Version 1.*

■ **DedekindEta**

DedekindEta[*τ*] gives the Dedekind eta modular elliptic function $\eta(\tau)$.

Mathematical function (see Section A.3.10). ■ DedekindEta is defined only in the upper half of the complex τ plane. It is not defined for real τ. ■ The argument τ is the ratio of Weierstrass half-periods ω'/ω. ■ DedekindEta satisfies $\Delta = (2\pi)^{12}\eta^{24}(\tau)$ where Δ is the discriminant, given in terms of Weierstrass invariants by $g_2^3 - 27g_3^2$. ■ See page 782 for a discussion of argument conventions for elliptic functions. ■ See page 787. ■ See also: ModularLambda, KleinInvariantJ, EllipticTheta, PartitionsP. ■ *New in Version 3.*

■ **Default**

Default[*f*], if defined, gives the default value for arguments of the function *f* obtained with a _. pattern object.

Default[*f*, *i*] gives the default value to use when _. appears as the ith argument of *f*.

Default[*f*, *i*, *n*] gives the default value for the ith argument out of a total of *n* arguments.

_. represents an optional argument to a function, with a default value specified by Default. ■ The necessary values for Default[*f*] must always be defined before _. is used as an argument of *f*. ■ Values defined for Default[*f*] are stored in DefaultValues[*f*]. ■ See page 1050. ■ See also: Options. ■ Related package: Utilities`FilterOptions`. ■ *New in Version 1.*

■ **DefaultColor**

DefaultColor is an option for graphics functions which specifies the default color to use for lines, points, etc.

The setting for DefaultColor must be a CMYKColor, GrayLevel, Hue or RGBColor directive. ■ The default setting is DefaultColor->Automatic, which gives a default color complementary to the background specified. ■ See page 504. ■ See also: Prolog, Background, FontColor, TextStyle. ■ *New in Version 2.*

■ DefaultDuplicateCellStyle

`DefaultDuplicateCellStyle` is an option for `Notebook` which specifies the default style to use for cells created by automatic duplication of other cells in the notebook.

A typical default setting for `DefaultDuplicateCellStyle` is `"Input"`. ■ `DefaultDuplicateCellStyle` determines the style for new cells created from cells with `CellEditDuplicate->True` or `CellEvaluationDuplicate->True`. ■ See page 619. ■ See also: `DefaultNewCellStyle`. ■ *New in Version 3.*

■ DefaultNewCellStyle

`DefaultNewCellStyle` is an option for `Notebook` which specifies the default style to use for new cells created in the notebook.

A typical default setting for `DefaultNewCellStyle` is `"Input"`. ■ `DefaultNewCellStyle` determines the style for new cells created interactively in the front end. ■ See page 619. ■ See also: `DefaultDuplicateCellStyle`. ■ *New in Version 3.*

■ Definition

`Definition[`*symbol*`]` prints as the definitions given for a symbol.

`Definition` has attribute `HoldAll`. ■ `Definition[`*symbol*`]` prints as all values and attributes defined for *symbol*. ■ `?s` uses `Definition`. ■ See page 625. ■ See also: `FullDefinition`, `Information`. ■ *New in Version 1.*

■ Degree

`Degree` gives the number of radians in one degree. It has a numerical value of $\frac{\pi}{180}$.

You can multiply by `Degree` to convert from degrees to radians. ■ Example: `30 Degree` represents $30°$. ■ `Degree` can be entered in `StandardForm` and `InputForm` as `°`, `:deg:` or `\[Degree]`. ■ `Degree` is printed in `StandardForm` as `°`. ■ See page 765. ■ *New in Version 1; modified in Version 3.*

■ Deletable

`Deletable` is an option for `Cell` which specifies whether the cell can be deleted interactively using the front end.

With the setting `Deletable->False` at the notebook level, you can prevent any cells in any notebook from being deleted. ■ See pages 448 and 607. ■ See also: `Editable`, `Selectable`. ■ *New in Version 3.*

■ Delete

`Delete[`*expr*, *n*`]` deletes the element at position *n* in *expr*. If *n* is negative, the position is counted from the end.

`Delete[`*expr*, `{`*i*, *j*, ... `}]` deletes the part at position `{`*i*, *j*, ... `}`.

`Delete[`*expr*, `{{`i_1, j_1, ... `}`, `{`i_2, j_2, ... `}`, ... `}]` deletes parts at several positions.

Example: `Delete[{a, b, c, d}, 3]` $\longrightarrow$ `{a, b, d}`. ■ `Delete[{a, b, c, d}, {{1}, {3}}]` $\longrightarrow$ `{b, d}`. ■ Deleting the head of a particular element in an expression is equivalent to applying `FlattenAt` to the expression at that point. ■ Example: `Delete[{a, {b}, c}, {2, 0}]` $\longrightarrow$ `{a, b, c}`. ■ Deleting the head of a whole expression makes the head be `Sequence`. ■ Example: `Delete[{a, b}, 0]` $\longrightarrow$ `Sequence[a, b]`. ■■ `Delete` works on `SparseArray` objects. ■ See pages 125 and 288. ■ See also: `Insert`, `MapAt`, `ReplacePart`, `FlattenAt`, `DeleteCases`, `Drop`, `StringDrop`. ■ *New in Version 2.*

■ DeleteCases

DeleteCases[*expr*, *pattern*] removes all elements of *expr* which match *pattern*.

DeleteCases[*expr*, *pattern*, *levspec*] removes all parts of *expr* on levels specified by *levspec* which match *pattern*.

DeleteCases[*expr*, *pattern*, *levspec*, *n*] removes the first *n* parts of *expr* which match *pattern*.

Example: DeleteCases[{1, a, 2, b}, _Integer] ⟶ {a, b}. ■ With the option Heads -> True, you can delete heads with DeleteCases. Deleting the head of a particular element in an expression is equivalent to applying FlattenAt to the expression at that point. ■ Example: DeleteCases[{1, f[2, 3], 4}, f, {2}, Heads -> True] ⟶ {1, 2, 3, 4}. ■ Level specifications are described on page 1041. ■ See page 262. ■ See also: Cases, ReplaceAll, Delete. ■ *New in Version 2; modified in Version 4.1.*

■ DeleteDirectory

DeleteDirectory["*dir*"] deletes the specified directory.

DeleteDirectory["*dir*", DeleteContents -> True] deletes *dir* and all files and directories that it contains. ■ DeleteDirectory["*dir*"] deletes the directory *dir* only if it contains no files. ■ DeleteDirectory returns Null if it succeeds in deleting a directory, and $Failed if it fails. ■ See page 641. ■ See also: CreateDirectory, DeleteFile. ■ *New in Version 2.*

■ DeleteFile

DeleteFile["*file*"] deletes a file.

DeleteFile[{"*file*$_1$", "*file*$_2$", ... }] deletes a list of files.

DeleteFile returns Null if it succeeds in deleting files, and $Failed if it fails. ■ See page 641. ■ See also: RenameFile, DeleteDirectory. ■ *New in Version 2.*

■ DelimiterFlashTime

DelimiterFlashTime is an option for cells and notebooks which specifies how long in seconds a delimiter should flash for when its matching delimiter is entered.

DelimiterFlashTime->0 makes delimiters not flash. ■ A typical default setting is DelimiterFlashTime->0.3, which makes matching delimiters flash for 0.3 seconds. ■ Delimiters include parentheses, brackets and braces, as well as [[,]] and (* and *), and paired special characters such as ⟨, ⟩. ■ If you enter an unpaired closing delimiter the standard *Mathematica* front end will beep. ■ You can use the front end menu item Check Balance to select ranges with balanced delimiters in an expressions. ■ You can set DelimiterFlashTime at the level of a single cell, a notebook, or the whole front end. ■ See page 613. ■ See also: ShowAutoStyles, SyntaxQ, ShowCursorTracker. ■ *New in Version 3.*

■ Denominator

Denominator[*expr*] gives the denominator of *expr*.

Denominator picks out terms which have superficially negative exponents. Numerator picks out all remaining terms. ■ An exponent is "superficially negative" if it has a negative number as a factor. ■ The standard representation of rational expressions as products of powers means that you cannot simply use Part to extract denominators. ■ Denominator can be used on rational numbers. ■ See page 74. ■ See also: ExpandDenominator, Rationals. ■ *New in Version 1.*

■ DensityGraphics

DensityGraphics[*array*] is a representation of a density plot.

array must be a rectangular array of real numbers, representing *z* values. ■ The following options can be given:

AspectRatio	1	ratio of height to width
Axes	False	whether to draw axes
AxesLabel	None	axes labels
AxesOrigin	Automatic	where axes should cross
AxesStyle	Automatic	graphics directives to specify the style for axes
Background	Automatic	background color for the plot
ColorFunction	Automatic	function specifying the color for each cell
ColorFunctionScaling	True	whether to scale *z* values before applying a color function
ColorOutput	Automatic	type of color output to produce
DefaultColor	Automatic	the default color for plot elements
DisplayFunction	$DisplayFunction	function for generating output
Epilog	{}	graphics primitives to be rendered after the main plot
FormatType	$FormatType	the default format type for text
Frame	True	whether to put a frame around the plot
FrameLabel	None	frame labels
FrameStyle	Automatic	graphics directives giving the style for the frame
FrameTicks	Automatic	frame tick marks
ImageSize	Automatic	the absolute size at which to render the graphic in a notebook
Mesh	True	whether to draw a mesh
MeshRange	Automatic	ranges of *x* and *y* coordinates
MeshStyle	Automatic	graphics directives to specify the style for mesh lines
PlotLabel	None	a label for the plot
PlotRange	Automatic	range of *z* values to include
PlotRegion	Automatic	the final display region to be filled
Prolog	{}	graphics primitives to be rendered before the main plot
RotateLabel	True	whether to rotate *y* labels on the frame
TextStyle	$TextStyle	the default style for text
Ticks	Automatic	tick marks

■ DensityGraphics can be displayed using Show. ■ DensityGraphics is generated by DensityPlot and ListDensityPlot. ■ DensityGraphics[*g*] converts ContourGraphics and SurfaceGraphics objects to DensityGraphics. The resulting graphics can be rendered using Show. ■ Graphics[DensityGraphics[...]] generates a representation in terms of an ordinary Graphics object. +■ SparseArray objects can be used in DensityGraphics. ■ See page 517. ■ See also: ListDensityPlot, ContourGraphics, Raster, RasterArray. ■ *New in Version 1.*

■ DensityPlot

DensityPlot[*f*, {*x*, *xmin*, *xmax*}, {*y*, *ymin*, *ymax*}] makes a density plot of *f* as a function of *x* and *y*.

DensityPlot evaluates its arguments in a non-standard way (see page 1046). You should use Evaluate to evaluate the function to be plotted if this can safely be done before specific numerical values are supplied. ■ DensityPlot has the same options as DensityGraphics, with the following additions:

Compiled	True	whether to compile the function to plot
PlotPoints	25	the number of points in each direction at which to sample the function

■ DensityPlot has the default option setting Frame -> True. ■ DensityPlot returns a DensityGraphics object, with the MeshRange option set. ■ See page 146. ■ See also: ContourPlot. ■ *New in Version 1.*

■ Depth

Depth[*expr*] gives the maximum number of indices needed to specify any part of *expr*, plus one.

Raw objects have depth 1. ■ The computation of Depth does not include heads of expressions. +■ Depth treats SparseArray objects just like the corresponding ordinary lists. ■ See page 239. ■ See also: ArrayDepth, Level, LeafCount, Length, Nest. ■ *New in Version 1; modified in Version 5.0.*

■ Derivative

f′ represents the derivative of a function *f* of one argument.

Derivative[n_1, n_2, ...][*f*] is the general form, representing a function obtained from *f* by differentiating n_1 times with respect to the first argument, n_2 times with respect to the second argument, and so on.

f′ is equivalent to Derivative[1][*f*]. ■ *f*′′ evaluates to Derivative[2][*f*]. ■ You can think of Derivative as a *functional operator* which acts on functions to give derivative functions. ■ Derivative is generated when you apply D to functions whose derivatives *Mathematica* does not know. ■ *Mathematica* attempts to convert Derivative[*n*][*f*] and so on to pure functions. Whenever Derivative[*n*][*f*] is generated, *Mathematica* rewrites it as D[*f*[#]&, {#, *n*}]. If *Mathematica* finds an explicit value for this derivative, it returns this value. Otherwise, it returns the original Derivative form. ■ Example: Cos′ $\longrightarrow$ -Sin[#1] &. ■ Derivative[-*n*][*f*] represents the nth indefinite integral of *f*. ■ Derivative[{n_1, n_2, ... }][*f*] represents the derivative of *f*[{x_1, x_2, ... }] taken n_i times with respect to x_i. In general, arguments given in lists in *f* can be handled by using a corresponding list structure in Derivative. ■ N[*f*′[*x*]] will give a numerical approximation to a derivative. ■ See page 856. ■ See also: D, Dt. ■ *New in Version 1; modified in Version 4.0.*

■ Det

Det[*m*] gives the determinant of the square matrix *m*.

Det[*m*, Modulus->*n*] computes the determinant modulo *n*. ■ See page 905. ■ Implementation notes: see page 1069. ■ See also: CharacteristicPolynomial, Minors, RowReduce, MatrixRank, NullSpace, Tr, Signature. ■ *New in Version 1.*

■ DiagonalMatrix

DiagonalMatrix[*list*] gives a matrix with the elements of *list* on the leading diagonal, and 0 elsewhere.

See page 896. ■ See also: IdentityMatrix, Tr, KroneckerDelta. ■ Related package: LinearAlgebra`MatrixManipulation`. ■ *New in Version 1.*

■ Dialog

Dialog[ ] initiates a dialog.

Dialog[*expr*] initiates a dialog with *expr* as the current value of %.

Dialog creates a dialog which consists of a sequence of input and output lines. ■ You can exit a dialog using Return. ■ With the global setting $IgnoreEOF = False, you can also exit a dialog by entering an end-of-file character. ■ If you exit with Return[*expr*], then *expr* is the value returned by the Dialog function. Otherwise, the value returned is the expression on the last output line in the dialog. ■ Dialog automatically localizes the values of $Line, $MessageList and $Epilog. ■ Dialog initially sets the local value of $Line to be equal to its global value. This means that the numbering of input and output lines in the dialog follows the sequence outside the dialog. When the dialog is exited, however, the numbering reverts to the sequence that would be followed if there had been no dialog. ■ Any local value assigned to $Epilog is evaluated when the dialog is exited. ■ The main loop within a dialog uses global variables such as $Pre and $Post. ■ The option DialogSymbols :> {*x*, *y*, ... } sets up local values for variables within the dialog. DialogSymbols :> {*x* = x_0, ... } defines initial values for the variables. ■ The option DialogProlog :> *expr* specifies an expression to evaluate before starting the dialog. ■ Dialog first localizes variables, then evaluates any expression specified by DialogProlog, then evaluates any argument you have given for Dialog. ■ See page 707. ■ See also: TraceDialog, Input, $Inspector, ButtonBox. ■ *New in Version 2.*

■ DialogProlog

DialogProlog is an option for Dialog which can give an expression to evaluate before the dialog starts.

You must use a delayed rule of the form DialogProlog :> *expr* to prevent *expr* from evaluating prematurely. ■ Expressions given by DialogProlog are evaluated after symbol values are localized, and before any expression given as the argument of Dialog is evaluated. ■ See page 708. ■ See also: $Epilog. ■ *New in Version 2.*

■ DialogSymbols

DialogSymbols is an option for Dialog which gives a list of symbols whose values should be localized in the dialog.

DialogSymbols :> {*x*, *y*, ... } specifies that *x*, *y*, ... should have local values for the duration of the dialog. ■ DialogSymbols :> {*x* = x_0, ... } defines initial values for variables. ■ In addition to any symbols you specify, Dialog always uses local values for $Epilog, $Line and $MessageList. ■ The DialogSymbols option sets up local values in a dialog in the same way that a Block enclosing the dialog would. ■ See page 708. ■ *New in Version 2.*

■ DigitBlock

DigitBlock is an option for NumberForm and related functions which specifies the maximum length of blocks of digits between breaks.

The default setting is DigitBlock -> Infinity, which specifies that no breaks should be inserted. ■ DigitBlock -> *n* inserts a break every *n* digits. ■ DigitBlock -> {*nleft*, *nright*} inserts a break every *nleft* digits to the left of the decimal point, and every *nright* digits to the right of the decimal point. ■ The setting for NumberSeparator determines what string should be used at each break. ■ See page 436. ■ *New in Version 1.*

■ DigitCount

DigitCount[*n*, *b*, *d*] gives the number of *d* digits in the base *b* representation of *n*.

DigitCount[*n*, *b*] gives a list of the numbers of 1, 2, ..., *b* − 1, 0 digits in the base *b* representation of *n*.

DigitCount[*n*] gives a list of the numbers of 1, 2, ..., 9, 0 digits in the base 10 representation of *n*.

DigitCount[*n*] is equivalent to DigitCount[*n*, 10, Mod[Range[10],10]]. ■ Integer mathematical function (see Section A.3.10). ■ See page 755. ■ See also: IntegerDigits, FromDigits, BitAnd, IntegerExponent. ■ *New in Version 4.*

■ DigitQ

DigitQ[*string*] yields True if all the characters in the string are digits in the range 0 through 9, and yields False otherwise.

See page 413. ■ See also: LetterQ, Number. ■ *New in Version 2.*

Dimensions

Dimensions[*expr*] gives a list of the dimensions of *expr*.

Dimensions[*expr*, *n*] gives a list of the dimensions of *expr* down to level *n*.

expr must be a *full array*, with all the pieces of *expr* at a particular level having the same length. (The elements of *expr* can then be thought of as filling up a hyper-rectangular region.) ▪ Each successive level in *expr* sampled by Dimensions must have the same head. ▪ Example: Dimensions[{{a,b,c},{d,e,f}}] ⟶ {2, 3}. ▪ For SparseArray objects, Dimensions yields the dimensions of the corresponding ordinary lists. ▪ See page 900. ▪ See also: ArrayDepth, VectorQ, MatrixQ. ▪ *New in Version 1; modified in Version 5.0.*

DiracDelta

DiracDelta[*x*] represents the Dirac delta function $\delta(x)$.

DiracDelta[x_1, x_2, ...] represents the multidimensional Dirac delta function $\delta(x_1, x_2, ...)$.

DiracDelta[*x*] returns 0 for all numeric *x* other than 0. ▪ DiracDelta can be used in integrals, integral transforms and differential equations. ▪ Some transformations are done automatically when DiracDelta appears in a product of terms. ▪ DiracDelta[x_1, x_2, ...] returns 0 if any of the x_i are numeric and not 0. ▪ DiracDelta has attribute Orderless. ▪ For exact numeric quantities, DiracDelta internally uses numerical approximations to establish its result. This process can be affected by the setting of the global variable $MaxExtraPrecision. ▪ See page 879. ▪ See also: UnitStep, If, PrincipalValue, Limit, KroneckerDelta. ▪ *New in Version 4.*

DirectedInfinity

DirectedInfinity[ ] represents an infinite numerical quantity whose direction in the complex plane is unknown.

DirectedInfinity[*z*] represents an infinite numerical quantity that is a positive real multiple of the complex number *z*.

You can think of DirectedInfinity[*z*] as representing a point in the complex plane reached by starting at the origin and going an infinite distance in the direction of the point *z*. ▪ The following conversions are made:

Infinity	DirectedInfinity[1]
-Infinity	DirectedInfinity[-1]
ComplexInfinity	DirectedInfinity[ ]

▪ Certain arithmetic operations are performed on DirectedInfinity quantities. ▪ In OutputForm, DirectedInfinity[*z*] is printed in terms of Infinity, and DirectedInfinity[ ] is printed as ComplexInfinity. ▪ See page 743. ▪ See also: Indeterminate. ▪ *New in Version 1.*

Directory

Directory[ ] gives the current working directory.

Directory returns the full name of the directory as a string. ▪ See page 636. ▪ See also: $Path, SetDirectory, ResetDirectory, ParentDirectory, $HomeDirectory, DirectoryName, FileNames. ▪ *New in Version 2.*

DirectoryName

DirectoryName["*name*"] extracts the directory name from the specification for a file.

DirectoryName works differently on different computer systems. ▪ DirectoryName["*directory*"] is normally equivalent to ParentDirectory["*directory*"]. ▪ DirectoryName["*name*", *n*] applies DirectoryName *n* times to *name*. ▪ DirectoryName yields output appropriate for use in SetDirectory and ToFileName. ▪ If *name* contains no directory specification, DirectoryName["*name*"] returns "". ▪ See page 639. ▪ See also: $Input, Directory. ▪ *New in Version 3.*

■ DirectoryStack

`DirectoryStack[ ]` gives the directory stack which represents the sequence of current directories used.

`DirectoryStack[ ]` returns a list of full names of directories. ■ Each call to `SetDirectory` prepends one element to the directory stack; each call to `ResetDirectory` drops one. ■ See page 636. ■ *New in Version 2.*

■ DiscreteDelta

`DiscreteDelta[`n_1`,` n_2`, ... ]` gives the discrete delta function $\delta(n_1, n_2, ...)$, equal to 1 if all the n_i are zero, and 0 otherwise.

`DiscreteDelta[0]` gives 1; `DiscreteDelta[`n`]` gives 0 for other numeric n. ■ `DiscreteDelta` has attribute `Orderless`. ■ See page 882. ■ See also: `IdentityMatrix`, `UnitStep`, `If`, `Signature`, `DiracDelta`. ■ *New in Version 4.*

■ Disk

`Disk[{`x`,` y`},` r`]` is a two-dimensional graphics primitive that represents a filled disk of radius r centered at the point x, y.

`Disk[{`x`,` y`}, {`r_x`,` r_y`}]` yields an elliptical disk with semi-axes r_x and r_y.

`Disk[{`x`,` y`},` r`, {`θ_1`,` θ_2`}]` represents a segment of a disk.

Angles are measured in radians counterclockwise from the positive x direction. ■ `Disk[{`x`,` y`}, {`r_x`,` r_y`}, {`θ_1`,` θ_2`}]` yields an elliptical disk segment obtained by transforming a circular disk segment with the specified starting and ending angles. ■ `Scaled` and `Offset` can be used in the radius specification (see notes for `Circle`). ■ See page 496. ■ See also: `Circle`, `Polygon`. ■ *New in Version 2.*

■ Dispatch

`Dispatch[{`*lhs*$_1$`->`*rhs*$_1$`,` *lhs*$_2$`->`*rhs*$_2$`, ... }]` generates an optimized dispatch table representation of a list of rules. The object produced by `Dispatch` can be used to give the rules in *expr /. rules.*

The use of `Dispatch` will never affect results that are obtained, but may make the application of long lists of rules much faster. ■ Lists of rules are usually scanned sequentially when you evaluate an expression like *expr /. rules*. Rules such as a[1]->a1 and a[2]->a2, which cannot simultaneously apply, need not both be scanned explicitly. `Dispatch` generates a dispatch table which uses hash codes to specify which sets of rules need actually be scanned for a particular input expression. ■ Lists of rules produced by assignments made with = and := are automatically optimized with dispatch tables when appropriate. ■ See page 302. ■ See also: `ReplaceAll`, `Compile`. ■ *New in Version 2.*

■ Display

`Display[`*channel*`,` *graphics*`]` writes graphics or sound to the specified output channel in *Mathematica* PostScript format.

`Display[`*channel*`,` *graphics*`, "`*format*`"]` writes graphics or sound in the specified format.

`Display[`*channel*`,` *expr*`, "`*format*`"]` writes boxes, cells or notebook expressions in the specified format.

The output channel can be a single file or pipe, or a list of them. ■ The *graphics* in `Display` can be `Graphics`, `Graphics3D`, `SurfaceGraphics`, `ContourGraphics`, `DensityGraphics` or `GraphicsArray`. ■ The *graphics* can also include `Sound`. ■ The *expr* in `Display` can be `Cell`, `Notebook` or any boxes, as generated by `ToBoxes[`*expr*`]`. ■ Any of the graphics formats specified for `Export` can be used. ■ The following options can be given:

`CharacterEncoding`	`{}`	the encoding to use for characters in text
`ImageOffset`	`{0, 0}`	offset of the image in the viewing area

(continued)

■ **Display** *(continued)*

ImageResolution	Automatic	resolution in dpi for the image
ImageRotated	False	whether to rotate the image to landscape mode
ImageSize	Automatic	absolute image size in printer's points

■ $DisplayFunction is usually given in terms of Display. ■ If any of the specified files or pipes in *channel* are not open, Display uses OpenWrite to open them, then closes these particular files or pipes when it has finished. ■ In many cases, Display calls the *Mathematica* notebook front end via *MathLink*. If the front end is not present, certain capabilities of Display may not be available. ■ When displaying text, Display may make use of fonts that are specifically installed for *Mathematica*. ■ See page 554. ■ See also: Export, Write, Show, DisplayString, HTMLSave. ■ *New in Version 1; modified in Version 3.*

■ **DisplayForm**

DisplayForm[*expr*] prints with boxes inside *expr* shown in explicit two-dimensional or other form.

In ordinary StandardForm output, boxes such as SubscriptBox are shown literally. In DisplayForm they are shown as explicit two-dimensional constructs. ■ Example: DisplayForm[SubscriptBox["x", "y"]] ⟶ x_y. ■ DisplayForm acts as a "wrapper", which affects printing, but not evaluation. ■ See page 445. ■ See also: FullForm, ToExpression, ToBoxes. ■ *New in Version 3.*

■ **DisplayFunction**

DisplayFunction is an option for graphics and sound functions that specifies the function to apply to graphics and sound objects in order to display them.

The default setting for DisplayFunction in graphics functions is $DisplayFunction, and in sound functions is $SoundDisplayFunction. ■ A typical setting is DisplayFunction->Display[*channel*, #]&. ■ Setting DisplayFunction->Identity will cause the objects to be returned, but no display to be generated. ■ See pages 134 and 553. ■ See also: Show. ■ *New in Version 1.*

■ **DisplayString**

DisplayString[*graphics*] generates a string giving graphics or sound in *Mathematica* PostScript format.

DisplayString[*graphics*, "*format*"] generates a string giving graphics or sound in the specified format.

DisplayString[*expr*, "*format*"] generates a string giving boxes, cells or notebook expressions in the specified format.

The options and *format* settings for DisplayString are the same as for Display. ■ See page 554. ■ See also: StringToStream. ■ *New in Version 3.*

■ **Distribute**

Distribute[*f*[x_1, x_2, ...]] distributes *f* over Plus appearing in any of the x_i.

Distribute[*expr*, *g*] distributes over *g*.

Distribute[*expr*, *g*, *f*] performs the distribution only if the head of *expr* is *f*.

Distribute effectively implements the distributive law for operators *f* and *g*. ■ Distribute explicitly constructs the complete result of a distribution; Expand, on the other hand, builds up results iteratively, simplifying at each stage. ■ Example: Distribute[f[a+b,c+d]] ⟶ f[a, c] + f[a, d] + f[b, c] + f[b, d]. ■ Distribute[f[a+b,g[x,y],c], g] ⟶ g[f[a + b, x, c], f[a + b, y, c]]. ■ Distribute[*expr*, *g*, *f*, *gp*, *fp*] gives *gp* and *fp* in place of *g* and *f* respectively in the result of the distribution. ■ See page 256. ■ See also: Expand, Thread, Outer, Inner. ■ *New in Version 1.*

■ Divide

x/*y* or Divide[*x*, *y*] is equivalent to *x y*^−1.

x/*y* is converted to *x y*^−1 on input. ■ Divide[*x*, *y*] can be entered in StandardForm and InputForm as *x* ÷ *y*, *x* :div: *y* or *x* \[Divide] *y*. ■ See page 29. ■ *New in Version 1; modified in Version 3.*

■ DivideBy

x /= *c* divides *x* by *c* and returns the new value of *x*.

DivideBy has the attribute HoldFirst. ■ *x* /= *c* is equivalent to *x* = *x*/*c*. ■ See page 305. ■ See also: TimesBy, SubtractFrom, Set. ■ *New in Version 1.*

■ Divisors

Divisors[*n*] gives a list of the integers that divide *n*.

Example: Divisors[12] ⟶ {1, 2, 3, 4, 6, 12}. ■ Divisors[*n*, GaussianIntegers -> True] includes divisors that are Gaussian integers. ■ See page 750. ■ See also: FactorInteger, EulerPhi. ■ *New in Version 1.*

■ DivisorSigma

DivisorSigma[*k*, *n*] gives the divisor function $\sigma_k(n)$.

Integer mathematical function (see Section A.3.10). ■ $\sigma_k(n)$ is the sum of the kth powers of the divisors of *n*. ■ DivisorSigma[*k*, *n*, GaussianIntegers -> True] includes divisors that are Gaussian integers. ■ See page 752. ■ See also: EulerPhi. ■ *New in Version 1.*

■ Do

Do[*expr*, {*imax*}] evaluates *expr imax* times.

Do[*expr*, {*i*, *imax*}] evaluates *expr* with the variable *i* successively taking on the values 1 through *imax* (in steps of 1).

Do[*expr*, {*i*, *imin*, *imax*}] starts with *i* = *imin*. Do[*expr*, {*i*, *imin*, *imax*, *di*}] uses steps *di*.

Do[*expr*, {*i*, *imin*, *imax*}, {*j*, *jmin*, *jmax*}, ...] evaluates *expr* looping over different values of *j*, etc. for each *i*.

Do uses the standard *Mathematica* iteration specification. ■ Do evaluates its arguments in a non-standard way (see page 1046). ■ You can use Return, Break, Continue and Throw inside Do. ■ Unless an explicit Return is used, the value returned by Do is Null. ■ See page 348. ■ See also: For, While, Table, Nest, NestWhile, Fold. ■ *New in Version 1.*

■ Dot

a.*b*.*c* or Dot[*a*, *b*, *c*] gives products of vectors, matrices and tensors.

a.*b* gives an explicit result when *a* and *b* are lists with appropriate dimensions. It contracts the last index in *a* with the first index in *b*. ■ Various applications of Dot:

{a_1, a_2} . {b_1, b_2}	scalar product of vectors
{a_1, a_2} . {{m_{11}, m_{12}}, {m_{21}, m_{22}}}	product of a vector and a matrix
{{m_{11}, m_{12}}, {m_{21}, m_{22}}} . {a_1, a_2}	product of a matrix and a vector
{{m_{11}, m_{12}}, {m_{21}, m_{22}}} . {{n_{11}, n_{12}}, {n_{21}, n_{22}}}	product of two matrices

■ Examples: {a, b} . {c, d} ⟶ a c + b d. ■ {{a, b}, {c, d}} . {x, y} ⟶ {a x + b y, c x + d y}. ■ The result of applying Dot to two tensors $T_{i_1 i_2 \dots i_n}$ and $U_{j_1 j_2 \dots j_m}$ is the tensor $\sum_k T_{i_1 i_2 \dots i_{n-1} k} U_{k j_2 \dots j_m}$. Applying Dot to a rank *n* tensor and a rank *m* tensor gives a rank *n* + *m* − 2 tensor. +■ Dot can be used on SparseArray objects, returning a SparseArray object when possible. ~■ When its arguments are not lists or sparse arrays, Dot remains unevaluated. It has the attribute Flat. ■ See pages 118 and 901. ■ See also: Inner, Cross, Outer, NonCommutativeMultiply, Norm. ■ Related package: Calculus`VectorAnalysis`. ■ *New in Version 1.*

■ DownValues

DownValues[*f*] gives a list of transformation rules corresponding to all downvalues defined for the symbol *f*.

You can specify the downvalues for *f* by making an assignment of the form DownValues[*f*] = *list*. ■ The list returned by DownValues has elements of the form HoldPattern[*lhs*] :> *rhs*. ■ See page 322. ■ See also: Set, UpValues. ■ *New in Version 2; modified in Version 3.*

■ DragAndDrop

DragAndDrop is an option for Cell which specifies whether to allow drag-and-drop editing on the contents of the cell.

With DragAndDrop->True, dragging an already-selected region cuts the region from its original location, and pastes it at the location you move to. ■ DragAndDrop is more often set as a global option in the front end, rather than as an option for individual cells. ■ See page 615. ■ See also: StructuredSelection. ■ *New in Version 3.*

■ Drop

Drop[*list*, *n*] gives *list* with its first *n* elements dropped.

Drop[*list*, -*n*] gives *list* with its last *n* elements dropped.

Drop[*list*, {*n*}] gives *list* with its *n*th element dropped.

Drop[*list*, {*m*, *n*}] gives *list* with elements *m* through *n* dropped.

Drop[*list*, {*m*, *n*, *s*}] gives *list* with elements *m* through *n* in steps of *s* dropped.

Drop[*list*, *seq*$_1$, *seq*$_2$, ...] gives a nested list in which elements specified by *seq*$_i$ have been dropped at level *i* in *list*.

Drop uses the standard *sequence specification* (see page 1040). ■ Examples: Drop[{a,b,c,d,e}, 2] ⟶ {c, d, e}. ■ Drop[{a,b,c,d,e}, -3] ⟶ {a, b}. ■ Drop[Range[7], {2, 5, 2}] ⟶ {1, 3, 5, 6, 7}. ■ Drop can be used on an object with any head, not necessarily List. ■ Drop[*list*, *seq*$_1$, *seq*$_2$] effectively drops all elements except those in a submatrix of *list*. ■ Example: Drop[{{a,b,c},{d,e,f}}, 1, -1] ⟶ {{d, e}}. +■ Drop works on SparseArray objects. ■ See pages 123 and 287. ■ See also: Rest, Most, StringDrop, Take, Cases. ■ Related package: LinearAlgebra`MatrixManipulation`. ■ *New in Version 1; modified in Version 4.*

■ DSolve

DSolve[*eqn*, *y*, *x*] solves a differential equation for the function *y*, with independent variable *x*.

DSolve[{*eqn*$_1$, *eqn*$_2$, ... }, {*y*$_1$, *y*$_2$, ... }, *x*] solves a list of differential equations.

DSolve[*eqn*, *y*, {*x*$_1$, *x*$_2$, ... }] solves a partial differential equation.

DSolve[*eqn*, *y*[*x*], *x*] gives solutions for *y*[*x*] rather than for the function *y* itself. ■ Example: DSolve[y'[x] == 2 a x, y[x], x] ⟶ {{y[x] → a x^2 + C[1]}}. ■ Differential equations must be stated in terms of derivatives such as *y*'[*x*], obtained with D, not total derivatives obtained with Dt. +■ The list of equations given to DSolve can include algebraic ones that do not involve derivatives. ~■ DSolve generates constants of integration indexed by successive integers. The option GeneratedParameters specifies the function to apply to each index. The default is GeneratedParameters->C, which yields constants of integration C[1], C[2], ... ~■ GeneratedParameters->(Module[{C}, C]&) guarantees that the constants of integration are unique, even across different invocations of DSolve. ■ For partial differential equations, DSolve generates arbitrary functions C[*n*][...].

(continued)

■ DSolve *(continued)*

■ Boundary conditions can be specified by giving equations such as y'[0] == b. ■ Solutions given by DSolve sometimes include integrals that cannot be carried out explicitly by Integrate. Dummy variables with local names are used in such integrals. ■ DSolve sometimes gives implicit solutions in terms of Solve. ■ DSolve can solve linear ordinary differential equations of any order with constant coefficients. It can solve also many linear equations up to second order with non-constant coefficients. ■ DSolve includes general procedures that handle a large fraction of the nonlinear ordinary differential equations whose solutions are given in standard reference books such as Kamke. ■ DSolve can find general solutions for linear and weakly nonlinear partial differential equations. Truly nonlinear partial differential equations usually admit no general solutions. +■ DSolve can handle not only pure differential equations but also differential-algebraic equations. ■ See page 869. ■ Implementation notes: see page 1071. ■ See also: NDSolve, Solve, RSolve. ■ Related packages: Calculus`VariationalMethods`, Calculus`VectorAnalysis`. ■ *New in Version 2; modified in Version 5.0.*

■ Dt

Dt[f, x] gives the total derivative df/dx.

Dt[f] gives the total differential df.

Dt[f, {x, n}] gives the multiple derivative $d^n f/dx^n$.

Dt[f, x_1, x_2, ...] gives $d/dx_1\ d/dx_2\ ... f$.

Dt[f, x_1, ... , Constants -> {c_1, ... }] specifies that the c_i are constants, which have zero total derivative. ■ Symbols with attribute Constant are taken to be constants, with zero total derivative. ■ If an object is specified to be a constant, then all functions with that object as a head are also taken to be constants. ■ All quantities not explicitly specified as constants are assumed to depend on the x_i. ■ Example: Dt[x y] $\longrightarrow$ y Dt[x] + x Dt[y]. ■ Dt[x y, Constants -> {x}] $\longrightarrow$ x Dt[y, Constants → {x}]. ■ You can specify total derivatives by assigning values to Dt[f], etc. ■ See page 854. ■ See also: D, Derivative. ■ *New in Version 1.*

■ DumpSave

DumpSave["*file*.mx", *symbol*] writes definitions associated with a symbol to a file in internal *Mathematica* format.

DumpSave["*file*.mx", "*context*`"] writes out definitions associated with all symbols in the specified context.

DumpSave["*file*.mx", {*object_1*, *object_2*, ... }] writes out definitions for several symbols or contexts.

DumpSave["*package*`", *objects*] chooses the name of the output file based on the computer system used.

DumpSave["*file*"] saves all definitions in the current session.

DumpSave writes out definitions in a binary format that is optimized for input by *Mathematica*. ■ Each file has a plain text header identifying its type and contents. ■ Files written by DumpSave can be read by Get. ■ Files written by DumpSave can only be read on the same type of computer system on which they were written. ■ DumpSave will not preserve open stream and link objects. ■ Files written by DumpSave conventionally have names that end with .mx. ■ DumpSave["*package*`", ...] writes a file with a name such as *package*.mx/$SystemID/*package*.mx. ■ You can use DumpSave["*file*", "*s*"] to write out the definition for the value of a symbol s itself. ■ DumpSave["*file*"] will save the definitions for all symbols in the current session. ■ You can typically read a dump file when you start *Mathematica* by using the initfile command-line option. ■ See page 627. ■ See also: Save, LinkWrite. ■ *New in Version 3.*

■ E

E is the exponential constant e (base of natural logarithms), with numerical value $\simeq 2.71828$.

Mathematical constant (see Section A.3.11). ■ E can be entered in StandardForm and InputForm as e, ⁝ee⁝ or \[ExponentialE]. ■ In StandardForm and TraditionalForm, E is printed as e. ■ See page 765. ■ Implementation notes: see page 1067. ■ See also: Exp. ■ *New in Version 1; modified in Version 3.*

■ EdgeForm

EdgeForm[g] is a three-dimensional graphics directive which specifies that edges of polygons are to be drawn using the graphics directive or list of graphics directives g.

EdgeForm[ ] draws no edges of polygons. ■ The directives RGBColor, CMYKColor, GrayLevel, Hue and Thickness can be used in EdgeForm. ■ EdgeForm does not affect the rendering of Line objects. ■ No lines are ever drawn when an edge is formed by one polygon intersecting another. ■ See page 528. ■ See also: FaceForm, Line. ■ *New in Version 1.*

■ Editable

Editable is an option for boxes, cells and notebooks which specifies whether their contents can be edited interactively using the front end.

Even with the setting Editable->False, the contents of an object can still be copied as a whole. ■ Editable is an option for InterpretationBox and TagBox, as well as for StyleBox. ■ Setting Editable->False effectively allows you to "write protect" elements of notebooks. ■ See pages 448 and 607. ■ See also: CellEditDuplicate, Selectable, Copyable, Protected. ■ *New in Version 3.*

■ Eigensystem

Eigensystem[m] gives a list {$values$, $vectors$} of the eigenvalues and eigenvectors of the square matrix m.

₊ Eigensystem[{m, a}] gives the generalized eigenvalues and eigenvectors of m with respect to a.

₊ Eigensystem[m, k] gives the eigenvalues and eigenvectors for the first k eigenvalues of m.

Eigensystem finds numerical eigenvalues and eigenvectors if m contains approximate real or complex numbers. ■ All the non-zero eigenvectors given are independent. If the number of eigenvectors is equal to the number of non-zero eigenvalues, then corresponding eigenvalues and eigenvectors are given in corresponding positions in their respective lists. ■ If there are more eigenvalues than independent eigenvectors, then each extra eigenvalue is paired with a vector of zeros. ■ Eigensystem[m, ZeroTest -> $test$] applies $test$ to determine whether expressions should be assumed to be zero. The default setting is ZeroTest -> Automatic. ■ The eigenvalues and eigenvectors satisfy the matrix equation m.Transpose[$vectors$] == Transpose[$vectors$].DiagonalMatrix[$values$]. ₊■ Generalized eigenvalues and eigenvectors satisfy m.Transpose[$vectors$] == a.Transpose[$vectors$].DiagonalMatrix[$values$]. ■ {$vals$, $vecs$} = Eigensystem[m] can be used to set $vals$ and $vecs$ to be the eigenvalues and eigenvectors respectively. ₊■ Eigensystem[m, $spec$] is equivalent to Take[Eigensystem[m], $spec$]. ₊■ SparseArray objects can be used in Eigensystem. ■ See notes for Eigenvalues. ■ See page 910. ■ See also: NullSpace, JordanDecomposition, SchurDecomposition, SingularValueDecomposition, QRDecomposition. ■ Related package: LinearAlgebra`Orthogonalization`. ■ *New in Version 1; modified in Version 5.0.*

■ Eigenvalues

Eigenvalues[*m*] gives a list of the eigenvalues of the square matrix *m*.

+ Eigenvalues[{*m*, *a*}] gives the generalized eigenvalues of *m* with respect to *a*.

+ Eigenvalues[*m*, *k*] gives the first *k* eigenvalues of *m*.

Eigenvalues finds numerical eigenvalues if *m* contains approximate real or complex numbers. ■ Repeated eigenvalues appear with their appropriate multiplicity. ■ An $n \times n$ matrix gives a list of exactly *n* eigenvalues, not necessarily distinct. +■ If they are numeric, eigenvalues are sorted in order of decreasing absolute value. ■ The eigenvalues of a matrix *m* are those λ for which $m \cdot v == \lambda v$ for some non-zero eigenvector *v*. +■ The generalized eigenvalues of *m* with respect to *a* are those λ for which $m \cdot v == \lambda a \cdot v$. +■ When matrices *m* and *a* have a dimension-*d* shared null space, then *d* of their generalized eigenvalues will be Indeterminate. +■ Ordinary eigenvalues are always finite; generalized eigenvalues can be infinite. +■ For numeric eigenvalues, Eigenvalues[*m*, *k*] gives the *k* that are largest in absolute value. +■ Eigenvalues[*m*, -*k*] gives the *k* that are smallest in absolute value. +■ Eigenvalues[*m*, *spec*] is always equivalent to Take[Eigenvalues[*m*], *spec*]. +■ The option settings Cubics->True and Quartics->True can be used to specify that explicit radicals should be generated for all cubics and quartics. +■ SparseArray objects can be used in Eigenvalues. ■ See page 910. ■ See also: SingularValueList, CharacteristicPolynomial, Det, Tr. ■ *New in Version 1; modified in Version 5.0.*

■ Eigenvectors

Eigenvectors[*m*] gives a list of the eigenvectors of the square matrix *m*.

+ Eigenvectors[{*m*, *a*}] gives the generalized eigenvectors of *m* with respect to *a*.

+ Eigenvectors[*m*, *k*] gives the first *k* eigenvectors of *m*.

Eigenvectors finds numerical eigenvectors if *m* contains approximate real or complex numbers. ■ Eigenvectors corresponding to degenerate eigenvalues are chosen to be linearly independent. ■ Eigenvectors are not normalized. ■ For an $n \times n$ matrix, Eigenvectors always returns a list of length *n*. The list contains each of the independent eigenvectors of the matrix, followed if necessary by an appropriate number of vectors of zeros. +■ Eigenvectors with numeric eigenvalues are sorted in order of decreasing absolute value of their eigenvalues. ■ Eigenvectors[*m*, ZeroTest -> *test*] applies *test* to determine whether expressions should be assumed to be zero. The default setting is ZeroTest -> Automatic. +■ Eigenvectors[*m*, *spec*] is equivalent to Take[Eigenvectors[*m*], *spec*]. +■ SparseArray objects can be used in Eigenvectors. ■ See notes for Eigenvalues. ■ See page 910. ■ See also: NullSpace. ■ Related package: LinearAlgebra`Orthogonalization`. ■ *New in Version 1; modified in Version 5.0.*

■ Element

Element[*x*, *dom*] or $x \in dom$ asserts that *x* is an element of the domain *dom*.

Element[{x_1, x_2, ... }, *dom*] asserts that all the x_i are elements of *dom*.

Element[*patt*, *dom*] asserts that any expression matching the pattern *patt* is an element of *dom*.

~■ $x \in dom$ can be entered as *x* :el: *dom* or *x* \[Element] *dom*. ■ Element can be used to set up assumptions in Simplify and related functions. ■ Possible domains are:

Algebraics	algebraic numbers
Booleans	True or False
Complexes	complex numbers
Integers	integers
Primes	prime numbers
Rationals	rational numbers
Reals	real numbers

(continued)

◾ Element *(continued)*

◾ $x \in dom$ if possible evaluates immediately when x is numeric. ◾ Examples: Pi $\in$ Algebraics $\longrightarrow$ False; Pi $\in$ Reals $\longrightarrow$ True. ◾ $(x_1 \mid x_2 \mid \dots)$ $\in dom$ is equivalent to $\{x_1, x_2, \dots\} \in dom$. ◾ $\{x_1, x_2, \dots\} \in dom$ evaluates to $(x_1 \mid x_2 \mid \dots) \in dom$ if its truth or falsity cannot immediately be determined. ◾ See pages 73 and 816. ◾ See also: Simplify, MemberQ, IntegerQ, Assumptions, Condition, PatternTest, Equal, Less. ◾ *New in Version 4; modified in Version 5.0.*

◾ Eliminate

Eliminate[*eqns*, *vars*] eliminates variables between a set of simultaneous equations.

Equations are given in the form *lhs* == *rhs*. ◾ Simultaneous equations can be combined either in a list or with &&. ◾ A single variable or a list of variables can be specified. ◾ Example: Eliminate[{x == 2 + y, y == z}, y] $\longrightarrow$ 2 + z == x. ◾ Variables can be any expressions. ◾ Eliminate works primarily with linear and polynomial equations. ◾ See page 832. ◾ See also: Reduce, SolveAlways, Solve, GroebnerBasis, Exists. ◾ *New in Version 1.*

◾ EllipticE

EllipticE[*m*] gives the complete elliptic integral $E(m)$.

EllipticE[ϕ, *m*] gives the elliptic integral of the second kind $E(\phi|m)$.

Mathematical function (see Section A.3.10). ◾ For $-\pi/2 < \phi < \pi/2$, $E(\phi|m) = \int_0^\phi (1 - m\sin^2(\theta))^{1/2}\, d\theta$. ◾ $E(m) = E(\frac{\pi}{2}|m)$. ◾ See page 782 for a discussion of argument conventions for elliptic integrals. ◾ EllipticE[*m*] has a branch cut discontinuity in the complex *m* plane running from 1 to ∞. ◾ EllipticE[ϕ, *m*] has a branch cut discontinuity running along the ray from $\csc^2(\phi)$ to infinity. ◾ See page 783. ◾ See also: JacobiZeta, JacobiAmplitude. ◾ *New in Version 1.*

◾ EllipticExp

EllipticExp[*u*, {*a*, *b*}] is the inverse for EllipticLog. It produces a list {*x*, *y*} such that *u* == EllipticLog[{*x*, *y*}, {*a*, *b*}].

EllipticExp gives the generalized exponential associated with the elliptic curve $y^2 = x^3 + ax^2 + bx$. ◾ EllipticExp is the basis for computing Weierstrass functions in *Mathematica*. ◾ See page 788. ◾ *New in Version 1.*

◾ EllipticF

EllipticF[ϕ, *m*] gives the elliptic integral of the first kind $F(\phi|m)$.

Mathematical function (see Section A.3.10). ◾ For $-\pi/2 < \phi < \pi/2$, $F(\phi|m) = \int_0^\phi (1 - m\sin^2(\theta))^{-1/2}\, d\theta$. ◾ The complete elliptic integral associated with EllipticF is EllipticK. ◾ EllipticF is the inverse of JacobiAmplitude. If $\phi = \mathrm{am}(u|m)$ then $u = F(\phi|m)$. ◾ EllipticF[ϕ, *m*] has a branch cut discontinuity running along the ray from $\csc^2(\phi)$ to infinity. ◾ See page 782 for a discussion of argument conventions for elliptic integrals. ◾ See page 783. ◾ See also: JacobiZeta, JacobiAmplitude. ◾ *New in Version 1.*

◾ EllipticK

EllipticK[*m*] gives the complete elliptic integral of the first kind $K(m)$.

Mathematical function (see Section A.3.10). ◾ EllipticK is given in terms of the incomplete elliptic integral of the first kind by $K(m) = F(\frac{\pi}{2}|m)$. ◾ See page 782 for a discussion of argument conventions for elliptic integrals. ◾ EllipticK[*m*] has a branch cut discontinuity in the complex *m* plane running from 1 to ∞. ◾ See page 783. ◾ See also: JacobiZeta, EllipticNomeQ. ◾ *New in Version 1.*

■ **EllipticLog**

`EllipticLog[{x, y}, {a, b}]` gives the generalized logarithm associated with the elliptic curve $y^2 = x^3 + ax^2 + bx$.

`EllipticLog[{x, y}, {a, b}]` is defined as the value of the integral $\frac{1}{2} \int_{\infty}^{x} (t^3 + at^2 + bt)^{-1/2} dt$, where the sign of the square root is specified by giving the value of y such that $y = \sqrt{x^3 + ax^2 + bx}$. ■ See page 788. ■ See also: `EllipticExp`. ■ *New in Version 1.*

■ **EllipticNomeQ**

`EllipticNomeQ[m]` gives the nome q corresponding to the parameter m in an elliptic function.

Mathematical function (see Section A.3.10). ■ `EllipticNomeQ` is related to `EllipticK` by $q(m) = \exp[-\pi K(1-m)/K(m)]$. ■ `EllipticNomeQ[m]` has a branch cut discontinuity in the complex m plane running from 1 to ∞. ■ See page 782. ■ See also: `InverseEllipticNomeQ`. ■ *New in Version 3.*

■ **EllipticPi**

`EllipticPi[n, m]` gives the complete elliptic integral of the third kind $\Pi(n|m)$.

`EllipticPi[n, $\phi$, m]` gives the incomplete elliptic integral $\Pi(n; \phi|m)$.

Mathematical function (see Section A.3.10). ■ $\Pi(n; \phi|m) = \int_{0}^{\phi} (1 - n \sin^2(\theta))^{-1}[1 - m \sin^2(\theta)]^{-1/2} d\theta$. ■ $\Pi(n|m) = \Pi(n; \frac{\pi}{2}|m)$. ■ See page 782 for a discussion of argument conventions for elliptic integrals. ■ See page 783. ■ *New in Version 1.*

■ **EllipticTheta**

`EllipticTheta[a, u, q]` gives the theta function $\vartheta_a(u, q)$ ($a = 1, ..., 4$).

Mathematical function (see Section A.3.10). ■ $\vartheta_1(u, q) = 2q^{1/4} \sum_{n=0}^{\infty} (-1)^n q^{n(n+1)} \sin((2n+1)u)$,

$\vartheta_2(u, q) = 2q^{1/4} \sum_{n=0}^{\infty} q^{n(n+1)} \cos((2n+1)u)$, $\vartheta_3(u, q) = 1 + 2 \sum_{n=1}^{\infty} q^{n^2} \cos(2nu)$, $\vartheta_4(u, q) = 1 + 2 \sum_{n=1}^{\infty} (-1)^n q^{n^2} \cos(2nu)$. ■ See page 782 for a discussion of argument conventions for elliptic and related functions. ■ See page 785. ■ See also: `ModularLambda`, `DedekindEta`, `KleinInvariantJ`. ■ *New in Version 1.*

■ **EllipticThetaPrime**

`EllipticThetaPrime[a, u, q]` gives the derivative with respect to u of the theta function $\vartheta_a(u, q)$ ($a = 1, ..., 4$).

See notes for `EllipticTheta`. ■ See page 785. ■ *New in Version 3.*

■ **Encode**

`Encode["source", "dest"]` writes an encoded version of the file *source* to the file *dest*.

`<<dest` decodes the file before reading its contents.

`Encode["source", "dest", "key"]` produces an encoded file which must be read in using `Get["dest", "key"]`.

Encoded files contain only printable ASCII characters. They begin with a special sequence which is recognized by `Get`. ■ On certain computer systems `Encode["source", "dest", MachineID->"ID"]` can be used to generate an encoded file which can be read in only on a computer with a particular `$MachineID`. ■ No function is provided in *Mathematica* to convert encoded files back to their original form. ■ See page 626. ■ See also: `ReadProtected`, `$MachineID`. ■ *New in Version 2.*

■ End

End[ ] returns the present context, and reverts to the previous one.

Every call to End must be balanced by an earlier call to Begin. ■ End[ ] resets the value of $Context. ■ End[ ] returns the present context name as a string of the form "*context*`". ■ End[ ] does not modify $ContextPath. ■ See page 398. ■ *New in Version 1.*

■ EndOfFile

EndOfFile is a symbol returned by Read when it reaches the end of a file.

Subsequent calls to Read will also give EndOfFile. ■ See page 649. ■ *New in Version 1.*

■ EndPackage

EndPackage[ ] restores $Context and $ContextPath to their values before the preceding BeginPackage, and prepends the current context to the list $ContextPath.

Every call to EndPackage must be balanced by an earlier call to BeginPackage. ■ EndPackage is typically used at the end of a *Mathematica* package. ■ EndPackage returns Null. ■ EndPackage resets the values of both $Context and $ContextPath. ■ See page 398. ■ *New in Version 1.*

■ EngineeringForm

EngineeringForm[*expr*] prints with all real numbers in *expr* given in engineering notation.

EngineeringForm[*expr*, *n*] prints with numbers given to *n*-digit precision.

In "engineering notation" the exponent is always arranged to be a multiple of 3. ■ EngineeringForm takes the same options as NumberForm, but uses a different default function for ExponentFunction. ■ You can mix EngineeringForm and BaseForm. ■ EngineeringForm acts as a "wrapper", which affects printing, but not evaluation. ■ See page 435. ■ See also: ScientificForm, NumberForm. ■ *New in Version 1.*

■ Environment

Environment["*var*"] gives the value of an operating system environment variable.

The values of environment variables are returned by Environment as strings. ■ Environment returns $Failed if it cannot find a value for the operating system variable you requested. ■ The behavior of Environment depends on the computer system you are using. ■ See page 716. ■ See also: Run, $CommandLine, $System. ■ *New in Version 1.*

■ Epilog

Epilog is an option for graphics functions which gives a list of graphics primitives to be rendered after the main part of the graphics is rendered.

In three-dimensional graphics, two-dimensional graphics primitives can be specified by the Epilog option. The graphics primitives are rendered in a 0,1 coordinate system. ■ See page 504. ■ See also: Prolog, AxesStyle, PlotStyle, DisplayFunction. ■ *New in Version 2.*

■ Equal

lhs == *rhs* returns True if *lhs* and *rhs* are identical.

lhs == *rhs* is used to represent a symbolic equation, to be manipulated using functions like Solve. ■ *lhs* == *rhs* returns True if *lhs* and *rhs* are identical expressions. ■ *lhs* == *rhs* returns False if *lhs* and *rhs* are determined to be unequal by comparisons between numbers or other raw data, such as strings. ■ Approximate numbers are considered equal if they differ in at most their last eight binary digits (roughly their last two decimal digits). ■ 2 == 2. gives True. ■ e_1 == e_2 == e_3 gives True if all the e_i are equal. ■ Equal[e] gives True. ■ For exact numeric quantities, Equal internally uses numerical approximations to establish inequality. This process can be affected by the setting of the global variable $MaxExtraPrecision. ■ In StandardForm and InputForm, *lhs* == *rhs* can be input as *lhs* \[Equal] *rhs* or *lhs* == *rhs*. +■ It can also be input as *lhs* \[LongEqual] *rhs* or *lhs* = *rhs*. ■ See page 86. ■ See also: SameQ, Unequal, KroneckerDelta, Order, Element. ■ *New in Version 1; modified in Version 4.1.*

■ Erf

Erf[z] gives the error function erf(z).

Erf[z_0, z_1] gives the generalized error function erf(z_1) − erf(z_0).

Mathematical function (see Section A.3.10). ■ Erf[z] is the integral of the Gaussian distribution, given by $\mathrm{erf}(z) = \frac{2}{\sqrt{\pi}} \int_0^z e^{-t^2} dt$. ■ Erf[$z_0$, z_1] is given by $\frac{2}{\sqrt{\pi}} \int_{z_0}^{z_1} e^{-t^2} dt$. ■ Erf[$z$] is an entire function of z with no branch cut discontinuities. ■ See page 775. ■ See also: InverseErf, Erfc, Erfi, ExpIntegralE, ExpIntegralEi, FresnelC, FresnelS. ■ Related package: Statistics`NormalDistribution`. ■ *New in Version 1.*

■ Erfc

Erfc[z] gives the complementary error function erfc(z).

Erfc[z] is given by erfc(z) = 1 − erf(z). ■ See notes for Erf. ■ See page 775. ■ See also: InverseErfc. ■ *New in Version 2.*

■ Erfi

Erfi[z] gives the imaginary error function erf(iz)/i.

See notes for Erf. ■ See page 775. ■ *New in Version 3.*

■ ErrorBox

ErrorBox[*boxes*] represents boxes that cannot be interpreted in input or output.

ErrorBox[*boxes*] typically displays as the raw form of *boxes* together with underlining that indicates parts that cannot be interpreted. ■ See page 447. ■ See also: TagBox, InterpretationBox, ToExpression. ■ *New in Version 3.*

■ EulerE

EulerE[n] gives the Euler number E_n.

EulerE[n, x] gives the Euler polynomial $E_n(x)$.

Mathematical function (see Section A.3.10). ■ The Euler polynomials satisfy the generating function relation $2e^{xt}/(e^t + 1) = \sum_{n=0}^{\infty} E_n(x)(t^n/n!)$. ■ The Euler numbers are given by $E_n = 2^n E_n(\frac{1}{2})$. ■ See page 757. ■ See also: BernoulliB. ■ *New in Version 1.*

■ **EulerGamma**

> EulerGamma is Euler's constant γ, with numerical value $\simeq 0.577216$.

Mathematical constant (see Section A.3.11). ▪ See page 765. ▪ Implementation notes: see page 1067. ▪ See also: PolyGamma, StieltjesGamma, HarmonicNumber. ▪ *New in Version 1.*

■ **EulerPhi**

> EulerPhi[*n*] gives the Euler totient function $\phi(n)$.

Integer mathematical function (see Section A.3.10). ▪ $\phi(n)$ gives the number of positive integers less than or equal to *n* which are relatively prime to *n*. ▪ See page 752. ▪ See also: FactorInteger, Divisors, MoebiusMu, MultiplicativeOrder, CarmichaelLambda, PowerMod. ▪ *New in Version 1.*

■ **Evaluatable**

> Evaluatable is an option for Cell which specifies whether a cell should be used as input to be evaluated by the *Mathematica* kernel.

With Evaluatable->True, typing SHIFT-RETURN in the front end when the cell is selected will cause the contents of the cell to be sent to the *Mathematica* kernel for evaluation. ▪ Evaluatable is more often set for styles of cells than for individual cells. ▪ See page 608. ▪ See also: Evaluator, InitializationCell, CellEvaluationDuplicate. ▪ *New in Version 3.*

■ **Evaluate**

> Evaluate[*expr*] causes *expr* to be evaluated even if it appears as the argument of a function whose attributes specify that it should be held unevaluated.

Example: Hold[Evaluate[1 + 1]] ⟶ Hold[2]. ▪ You can use Evaluate to override HoldFirst, etc. attributes of built-in functions. ▪ Evaluate only overrides HoldFirst, etc. attributes when it appears directly as the head of the function argument that would otherwise be held. ▪ See page 337. ▪ See also: ReleaseHold. ▪ *New in Version 2.*

⁺■ **EvaluationMonitor**

> EvaluationMonitor is an option for various numerical computation functions that gives an expression to evaluate whenever functions derived from the input are evaluated numerically.

The option setting is normally given as EvaluationMonitor :> *expr*. The :> is used instead of -> to avoid *expr* being immediately evaluated. ▪ Whenever *expr* is evaluated, all variables in the numerical computation are assigned their current values. Block[{*var*₁ = *val*₁, ... }, *expr*] is effectively used. ▪ See page 977. ▪ See also: StepMonitor, Sow, Print, Trace. ▪ *New in Version 5.0.*

■ **EvaluationNotebook**

> EvaluationNotebook[ ] gives the notebook in which this function is being evaluated.

EvaluationNotebook returns a NotebookObject. ▪ See page 579. ▪ See also: SelectedNotebook, InputNotebook, ButtonNotebook, Notebooks, SelectionMove. ▪ *New in Version 3.*

■ **Evaluator**

> Evaluator is an option for Cell which gives the name of the kernel to use to evaluate the contents of a cell.

The default setting is typically Evaluator->"Local". ▪ Evaluator is more often set at a global level or at the level of whole notebooks than at the level of individual cells. ▪ See page 608. ▪ See also: InitializationCell. ▪ *New in Version 3.*

■ EvenQ

EvenQ[*expr*] gives True if *expr* is an even integer, and False otherwise.

EvenQ[*expr*] returns False unless *expr* is manifestly an even integer (i.e., has head Integer, and is even). ■ You can use EvenQ[*x*] ^= True to override the normal operation of EvenQ, and effectively define *x* to be an even integer. ■ See pages 267 and 723. ■ See also: IntegerQ, OddQ, TrueQ. ■ *New in Version 1.*

■ ExcludedForms

ExcludedForms is an option for FullSimplify which can be set to a list of patterns for expressions that should not be touched if they are encountered at intermediate steps in the operation of FullSimplify.

The default setting for ExcludedForms is { }. ■ A setting such as Gamma[_] will cause FullSimplify to treat gamma functions as elementary objects which should not be transformed. ■ See page 814. ■ See also: TimeConstraint, ComplexityFunction, Simplify, TrigFactor. ■ *New in Version 3.*

⁺■ Exists

Exists[*x*, *expr*] represents the statement that there exists a value of *x* for which *expr* is True.

Exists[*x*, *cond*, *expr*] states that there exists an *x* satisfying the condition *cond* for which *expr* is True.

Exists[{x_1, x_2, ... }, *expr*] states that there exist values for all the x_i for which *expr* is True.

Exists[*x*, *expr*] can be entered as $\exists_x$ *expr*. The character $\exists$ can be entered as :ex: or \[Exists]. The variable *x* is given as a subscript. ■ Exists[*x*, *cond*, *expr*] can be entered as $\exists_{x,cond}$ *expr*. ■ In StandardForm, Exists[*x*, *expr*] is output as $\exists_x$ *expr*. ■ Exists[*x*, *cond*, *expr*] is output as $\exists_{x,cond}$ *expr*. ■ Exists can be used in such functions as Reduce, Resolve and FullSimplify. ■ The condition *cond* is often used to specify the domain of a variable, as in $x \in$ Integers. ■ Exists[*x*, *cond*, *expr*] is equivalent to Exists[*x*, *cond* && *expr*]. ■ Exists[{x_1, x_2, ... }, ...] is equivalent to $\exists_{x_1} \exists_{x_2}$ .... ■ The value of *x* in Exists[*x*, *expr*] is taken to be localized, as in Block. ■ See page 847. ■ See also: ForAll, FindInstance, Resolve, Reduce, Element, Eliminate. ■ *New in Version 5.0.*

■ Exit

Exit[ ] terminates a *Mathematica* kernel session.

Exit is a synonym for Quit. ■ Exit terminates the kernel session even if called from within Dialog. ■ On most computer systems, Exit[*n*] can be used to pass the integer exit code *n* to the operating system. ■ See pages 706 and 1057. ■ See also: Return, $IgnoreEOF. ■ *New in Version 1.*

■ Exp

Exp[*z*] is the exponential function.

Mathematical function (see Section A.3.10). ■ Exp[*z*] is converted to E^*z*. ■ See page 761. ■ See also: Power, E, ExpToTrig. ■ *New in Version 1.*

■ Expand

Expand[*expr*] expands out products and positive integer powers in *expr*.

Expand[*expr*, *patt*] leaves unexpanded any parts of *expr* that are free of the pattern *patt*.

Expand works only on positive integer powers. ■ Expand applies only to the top level in *expr*.
■ Expand[*expr*, Modulus->*p*] expands *expr* reducing the result modulo *p*. ■ See page 797. ■ See also: Distribute, Apart, Series, Factor, LogicalExpand, TrigExpand, PowerExpand, ExpandAll. ■ *New in Version 1; modified in Version 3.*

■ ExpandAll

ExpandAll[*expr*] expands out all products and integer powers in any part of *expr*.

ExpandAll[*expr*, *patt*] avoids expanding parts of *expr* that do not contain terms matching the pattern *patt*.

ExpandAll[*expr*] effectively maps Expand and ExpandDenominator onto every part of *expr*. ■ See page 801. ■ *New in Version 1.*

■ ExpandDenominator

ExpandDenominator[*expr*] expands out products and powers that appear as denominators in *expr*.

ExpandDenominator works only on negative integer powers. ■ ExpandDenominator applies only to the top level in *expr*. ■ See page 801. ■ See also: Expand, ExpandNumerator, ExpandAll, Together. ■ *New in Version 1.*

■ ExpandNumerator

ExpandNumerator[*expr*] expands out products and powers that appear in the numerator of *expr*.

ExpandNumerator works on terms that have positive integer exponents. ■ ExpandNumerator applies only to the top level in *expr*. ■ See page 801. ■ See also: Expand, ExpandDenominator, ExpandAll. ■ *New in Version 1.*

■ ExpIntegralE

ExpIntegralE[*n*, *z*] gives the exponential integral function $E_n(z)$.

Mathematical function (see Section A.3.10). ■ $E_n(z) = \int_1^\infty e^{-zt}/t^n \, dt$. ■ ExpIntegralE[*n*, *z*] has a branch cut discontinuity in the complex *z* plane running from $-\infty$ to 0. ■ See page 774. ■ See also: ExpIntegralEi, Erf, LogIntegral, SinIntegral, CosIntegral. ■ *New in Version 1.*

■ ExpIntegralEi

ExpIntegralEi[*z*] gives the exponential integral function Ei(*z*).

Mathematical function (see Section A.3.10). ■ $\mathrm{Ei}(z) = -\int_{-z}^\infty e^{-t}/t \, dt$, where the principal value of the integral is taken. ■ ExpIntegralEi[*z*] has a branch cut discontinuity in the complex *z* plane running from $-\infty$ to 0. ■ See page 774. ■ See also: ExpIntegralE, Erf, LogIntegral, SinIntegral, CosIntegral. ■ *New in Version 1.*

■ Exponent

Exponent[*expr*, *form*] gives the maximum power with which *form* appears in the expanded form of *expr*.

Exponent[*expr*, *form*, *h*] applies *h* to the set of exponents with which *form* appears in *expr*.

Example: Exponent[x^2 + a x^3, x] $\longrightarrow$ 3. ■ The default taken for *h* is Max. ■ Example: Exponent[x^2 + a x^3, x, List] $\longrightarrow$ {2, 3}. ■ *form* can be a product of terms. ■ Exponent works whether or not *expr* is explicitly given in expanded form. +■ Exponent[0, x] is -Infinity. ■ See page 799. ■ See also: Coefficient, Cases, IntegerExponent. ■ *New in Version 1; modified in Version 3.*

■ ExponentFunction

ExponentFunction is an option for NumberForm and related functions which determines the exponent to use in printing approximate real numbers.

Functions like NumberForm first find the exponent that would make exactly one digit appear to the left of the decimal point when the number is printed in scientific notation. Then they take this exponent and apply the function specified by ExponentFunction to it. If the value obtained from this function is an integer, it is used as the exponent of the number. If it is Null, then the number is printed without scientific notation. ■ The argument provided for the function specified by ExponentFunction is always an integer. ■ In NumberForm, the default setting for ExponentFunction never modifies the exponent, but returns Null for machine numbers with exponents between −5 and 5, and for high-precision numbers where insignificant zeros would have to be inserted if the number were not printed in scientific notation. ■ In ScientificForm, the default setting for ExponentFunction never returns Null. ■ In EngineeringForm, the default setting for ExponentFunction returns an exponent that is a multiple of 3. ■ In AccountingForm, the default setting for ExponentFunction always returns Null. ■ See page 436. ■ See also: NumberFormat. ■ *New in Version 2.*

■ Export

Export["*file.ext*", *expr*] exports data to a file, converting it to a format corresponding to the file extension *ext*.

Export["*file*", *expr*, "*format*"] exports data to a file, converting it to the specified format.

Export can handle numerical and textual data, graphics, sounds, material from notebooks, and general expressions in various formats. ~■ The following basic formats are supported for numerical and textual data:

"CSV"	comma-separated value tabular data (.csv)
"Lines"	list of strings to be placed on separate lines
"List"	list of numbers or strings to be placed on separate lines
"Table"	list of lists of numbers or strings to be placed in a two-dimensional array (.dat)
"Text"	single string of ordinary characters (.txt)
"TSV"	tab-separated value tabular data (.tsv)
"UnicodeText"	single string of 16-bit Unicode characters
"Words"	list of strings to be separated by spaces

~■ In "CSV", "List" and "Table" format, numbers are written in C or Fortran-like "E" notation when necessary. ~■ In "CSV" format, columns are separated by commas, unless other settings are specified using ConversionOptions. ■ In "Table" format, columns are separated by spaces. ■ Export["*file.txt*", *expr*] uses "Text" format. ■ Export["*file.dat*", *expr*] uses "Table" format. ~■ The following additional formats are also supported for numerical and textual data:

"FITS"	FITS astronomical data format (.fit, .fits)
"HDF"	Hierarchical Data Format (.hdf)
"MAT"	MAT matrix format (.mat)
"MTX"	Matrix Market format (.mtx)

■ All graphics formats in Export can handle any type of 2D or 3D *Mathematica* graphics. ■ They can also handle Notebook and Cell objects. ■ In some formats, lists of frames for animated graphics can be given. ■ The following options can be given when exporting graphics:

ImageResolution	Automatic	resolution in dpi for the image
ImageRotated	False	whether to rotate the image (landscape mode)
ImageSize	Automatic	absolute image size in printer's points

(continued)

~■ Export *(continued)*

~■ The following graphics formats are independent of the setting for `ImageResolution`:

"EPS"	Encapsulated PostScript (`.eps`)
"MPS"	*Mathematica* abbreviated PostScript (`.mps`)
"PDF"	Adobe Acrobat portable document format (`.pdf`)
"PICT"	Macintosh PICT
"SVG"	Scalable Vector Graphics (`.svg`)
"WMF"	Windows metafile format (`.wmf`)

~■ The following graphics formats depend on the setting for `ImageResolution`:

"BMP"	Microsoft bitmap format (`.bmp`)
"DICOM"	DICOM medical imaging format (`.dcm`, `.dic`)
"EPSI"	Encapsulated PostScript with device-independent preview (`.epsi`)
"EPSTIFF"	Encapsulated PostScript with TIFF preview
"GIF"	GIF and animated GIF (`.gif`)
"JPEG"	JPEG (`.jpg`, `.jpeg`)
"MGF"	*Mathematica* system-independent raster graphics format (`.mgf`)
"PBM"	portable bitmap format (`.pbm`)
"PGM"	portable graymap format (`.pgm`)
"PNG"	PNG format (`.png`)
"PNM"	portable anymap format (`.pnm`)
"PPM"	portable pixmap format (`.ppm`)
"TIFF"	TIFF (`.tif`, `.tiff`)
"XBitmap"	X window system bitmap (`.xbm`)

~■ The following three-dimensional graphics formats are supported:

"DXF"	AutoCAD drawing interchange format (`.dxf`)
"STL"	STL stereolithography format (`.stl`)

■ The following sound formats are supported:

"AIFF"	AIFF format (`.aif`, `.aiff`)
"AU"	μ law encoding (`.au`)
"SND"	sound file format (`.snd`)
"WAV"	Microsoft wave format (`.wav`)

~■ `Notebook` and `Cell` objects, as well as any box expression obtained from `ToBoxes`, can be exported in the following formats:

"HTML"	HTML (`.htm`, `.html`)
"NB"	*Mathematica* notebook format (`.nb`)
"TeX"	TEX (`.tex`)
"XHTML+MathML"	XHTML with MathML inclusions (`.xml`)

■ These formats generate markup material which maintains much of the document structure that exists within *Mathematica*. ■ With HTML and TEX formats, `Export` operates like `HTMLSave` and `TeXSave`. +■ The following XML formats are supported:

"ExpressionML"	format for *Mathematica* expressions
"MathML"	format for mathematical expressions (`.mml`)
"NotebookML"	format for notebook expressions (`.nbml`)
"SVG"	Scalable Vector Graphics format for graphics (`.svg`)
"XML"	format determined by content (`.xml`)

(continued)

~■ Export *(continued)*

~■ With format "MathML", box expressions are exported in terms of MathML presentation elements. Other expressions are if possible exported in TraditionalForm format. ~■ With format "XML", notebook or cell expressions, and notebook objects, are exported as NotebookML. SymbolicXML expressions are exported as general XML. Other expressions are exported as ExpressionML. +■ Arbitrary *Mathematica* expressions can be exported in the following formats:

"Dump"	internal binary format (.mx)
"Expression"	InputForm textual format (.m)
"ExpressionML"	XML-based ExpressionML format

■ Many details can be specified in the setting for ConversionOptions. ■ The following general options can be given:

ByteOrdering	$ByteOrdering	what byte order to use for binary data
CharacterEncoding	Automatic	the encoding to use for text characters
ConversionOptions	{}	private options for specific formats

■ Possible formats accepted by Export are given in the list $ExportFormats. ■ Export["!*prog*", *expr*, "*format*"] exports data to a pipe. ■ See pages 207, 567 and 642. ■ See also: Import, ExportString, $ExportFormats, Display, Write, Put, TeXSave, HTMLSave, MathMLForm, DumpSave. ■ *New in Version 4; modified in Version 5.0.*

~■ ExportString

ExportString[*expr*, "*format*"] generates a string corresponding to *expr* exported in the specified format.

Many graphics, sound and binary formats yield strings containing non-printable characters. ■ See notes for Export. ■ See page 567. ■ See also: ImportString, DisplayString. ■ *New in Version 4; modified in Version 5.0.*

■ Expression

Expression is a symbol that represents an ordinary *Mathematica* expression in Read and related functions.

See page 646. ■ See also: ToExpression. ■ *New in Version 1.*

■ ExpToTrig

ExpToTrig[*expr*] converts exponentials in *expr* to trigonometric functions.

ExpToTrig generates both circular and hyperbolic functions. ■ ExpToTrig tries when possible to give results that do not involve explicit complex numbers. ■ See page 812. ■ See also: TrigToExp, TrigReduce, ComplexExpand. ■ *New in Version 3.*

~■ ExtendedGCD

~ ExtendedGCD[n_1, n_2, ...] gives the extended greatest common divisor of the integers n_i.

Integer mathematical function (see Section A.3.10). ~■ ExtendedGCD[n_1, n_2, ...] returns a list {g, {r_1, r_2, ... }} where g is GCD[n_1, n_2, ...] and $g = r_1 n_1 + r_2 n_2 + ...$. ■ See page 752. ■ See also: GCD. ■ Related package: Algebra`PolynomialExtendedGCD`. ■ *New in Version 1; modified in Version 4.2.*

■ Extension

Extension is an option for Factor, PolynomialGCD and related functions which specifies what algebraic numbers to allow in the coefficients of resulting polynomials.

With the setting Extension->$\{a_1, a_2, \dots\}$ any rational combination of the a_i can appear. ■ The a_i must be exact numbers. They can involve I, n^{th} roots, and Root objects. ■ The a_i can be viewed as generators for the algebraic number field in which the coefficients are assumed to lie. ■ With the default setting Extension->None all coefficients are required to be rational numbers, and any algebraic numbers that appear in input polynomials are treated like independent variables. ■ Extension->Automatic includes any algebraic numbers from the input polynomials in the coefficient field. ■ Extension->$\{a_1, a_2, \dots\}$ includes both the a_i and any algebraic numbers from the input polynomials in the coefficient field. ■ GaussianIntegers->True is equivalent to Extension->I. ■ See page 809. ■ See also: Modulus, Algebraics. ■ *New in Version 3.*

■ Extract

Extract[*expr*, *list*] extracts the part of *expr* at the position specified by *list*.

Extract[*expr*, $\{list_1, list_2, \dots\}$] extracts a list of parts of *expr*.

Extract[*expr*, … , *h*] extracts parts of *expr*, wrapping each of them with head *h* before evaluation.

Extract[*expr*, $\{i, j, \dots\}$] is equivalent to Part[*expr*, *i*, *j*, …]. ■ The position specifications used by Extract have the same form as those returned by Position, and used in functions such as MapAt and ReplacePart. ■ You can use Extract[*expr*, … , Hold] to extract parts without evaluation. ■ If *expr* is a SparseArray object, Extract[*expr*, …] extracts parts in the corresponding ordinary array. ■ See page 286. ■ See also: Part, Take, PadLeft. ■ *New in Version 3.*

■ FaceForm

FaceForm[*gf*, *gb*] is a three-dimensional graphics directive which specifies that the front faces of polygons are to be drawn with the graphics primitive *gf*, and the back faces with *gb*.

The graphics specifications *gf* and *gb* must be CMYKColor, GrayLevel, Hue or RGBColor directives, or SurfaceColor objects. ■ Specifications given outside of FaceForm will apply both to the front and back faces of polygons. ■ The front face of a polygon is defined to be the one for which the corners as you specify them are in counterclockwise order (right-hand rule). ■ See page 529. ■ See also: EdgeForm. ■ *New in Version 1.*

■ FaceGrids

FaceGrids is an option for three-dimensional graphics functions that specifies grid lines to draw on the faces of the bounding box.

The following settings can be given for FaceGrids:

None	no grid lines drawn
All	grid lines drawn on all faces
$\{face_1, face_2, \dots\}$	grid lines drawn on the specified faces
$\{\{face_1, \{xgrid_1, ygrid_1\}\}, \dots\}$	details of grid lines specified

■ Faces are specified as $\{dir_x, dir_y, dir_z\}$, where two of the dir_i must be 0, and the third one must be +1 or −1. ■ Example: the *x*-*y* face with smallest *z* value is specified as $\{0, 0, -1\}$. ■ For each face, specifications $\{xgrid_i, ygrid_i\}$ can be given to determine the arrangement of grid lines. These specifications have the form described in the notes for GridLines. ■ See page 553. ■ See also: Ticks. ■ *New in Version 2.*

■ Factor

Factor[*poly*] factors a polynomial over the integers.

Factor[*poly*, Modulus->*p*] factors a polynomial modulo a prime *p*.

Factor[*poly*, Extension->{a_1, a_2, ... }] factors a polynomial allowing coefficients that are rational combinations of the algebraic numbers a_i.

Factor applies only to the top level in an expression. You may have to use Map, or apply Factor again, to reach other levels. ■ Factor[*poly*, GaussianIntegers->True] factors allowing Gaussian integer coefficients. ■ If any coefficients in *poly* are complex numbers, factoring is done allowing Gaussian integer coefficients. ■ The exponents of variables need not be positive integers. Factor can deal with exponents that are linear combinations of symbolic expressions. ■ When given a rational expression, Factor effectively first calls Together, then factors numerator and denominator. ■ With the default setting Extension->None, Factor[*poly*] will treat algebraic number coefficients in *poly* like independent variables. ■ Factor[*poly*, Extension->Automatic] will extend the domain of coefficients to include any algebraic numbers that appear in *poly*. ■ See page 797. ■ Implementation notes: see page 1069. ■ See also: FactorList, FactorTerms, FactorSquareFree, Solve, Expand, Simplify, FactorInteger, TrigFactor. ■ *New in Version 1; modified in Version 3.*

■ Factorial

n! gives the factorial of *n*.

Mathematical function (see Section A.3.10). ■ For non-integer *n*, the numerical value of *n*! is given by Gamma[1 + *n*]. ■ See page 757. ■ Implementation notes: see page 1067. ■ See also: Gamma, Binomial. ■ *New in Version 1.*

■ Factorial2

n!! gives the double factorial of *n*.

Mathematical function (see Section A.3.10). ■ $n!! = n(n-2)(n-4) \times ....$ ■ *n*!! is a product of even numbers for *n* even, and odd numbers for *n* odd. ■ See page 757. ■ See also: Gamma. ■ *New in Version 1.*

■ FactorInteger

FactorInteger[*n*] gives a list of the prime factors of the integer *n*, together with their exponents.

Example: FactorInteger[2434500] ⟶ {{2, 2}, {3, 2}, {5, 3}, {541, 1}}. ■ For negative numbers, the unit {-1, 1} is included in the list of factors. ■ FactorInteger also works on rational numbers. The prime factors of the denominator are given with negative exponents. ■ FactorInteger[*n*, GaussianIntegers->True] factors over Gaussian integers. +■ FactorInteger[*m* + I *m*] automatically works over the Gaussian integers. ■ When necessary, a unit of the form {-1, 1}, {I, 1} or {-I, 1} is included in the list of factors.
■ FactorInteger[*n*, FactorComplete->False] does fast but not necessarily complete factorization, and extracts only factors that are easy to find. ■ See page 750. ■ Implementation notes: see page 1067. ■ See also: IntegerExponent, Prime, PrimeQ, Divisors. ■ Related package: NumberTheory`FactorIntegerECM`. ■ *New in Version 1; modified in Version 5.0.*

■ FactorList

FactorList[*poly*] gives a list of the factors of a polynomial, together with their exponents.

The first element of the list is always the overall numerical factor. It is {1, 1} if there is no overall numerical factor. ■ Example: FactorList[3 (1+x)^2 (1-x)] ⟶ {{-3, 1}, {-1 + x, 1}, {1 + x, 2}}.
■ FactorList[*poly*, Modulus->*p*] factors modulo a prime *p*. ■ FactorList[*poly*, GaussianIntegers->True] allows Gaussian integer coefficients. ■ FactorList[*poly*, Extension->{a_1, a_2, ... }] allows coefficients that are arbitrary rational combinations of the a_i. ■ See page 806. ■ See also: FactorTermsList, TrigFactorList, CoefficientList, Factor. ■ *New in Version 1; modified in Version 3.*

■ **FactorSquareFree**

FactorSquareFree[*poly*] pulls out any multiple factors in a polynomial.

FactorSquareFree[*poly*, Modulus->*p*] pulls out multiple factors modulo a prime *p*.
■ FactorSquareFree[*poly*, Extension->Automatic] extends the coefficient field to include algebraic numbers that appear in the coefficients of *poly*. ■ See page 806. ■ *New in Version 1; modified in Version 3.* ■ See also: FactorSquareFreeList.

■ **FactorSquareFreeList**

FactorSquareFreeList[*poly*] gives a list of square-free factors of a polynomial, together with their exponents.

See page 806. ■ *New in Version 1.* ■ See also: FactorSquareFree.

■ **FactorTerms**

FactorTerms[*poly*] pulls out any overall numerical factor in *poly*.

FactorTerms[*poly*, *x*] pulls out any overall factor in *poly* that does not depend on *x*.

FactorTerms[*poly*, {x_1, x_2, ... }] pulls out any overall factor in *poly* that does not depend on any of the x_i.

Example: FactorTerms[3 - 3x^2] $\longrightarrow$ -3 (-1 + x²). ■ FactorTerms[*poly*, *x*] extracts the content of *poly* with respect to *x*. ■ See notes for Factor. ■ See page 797. ■ *New in Version 1.*

■ **FactorTermsList**

FactorTermsList[*poly*, {x_1, x_2, ... }] gives a list of factors of *poly*. The first element in the list is the overall numerical factor. The second element is a factor that does not depend on any of the x_i. Subsequent elements are factors which depend on progressively more of the x_i.

See notes for FactorTerms. ■ See page 806. ■ *New in Version 1.*

■ **False**

False is the symbol for the Boolean value false.

See page 85. ■ See also: TrueQ, True, Booleans. ■ *New in Version 1.*

■ **Fibonacci**

Fibonacci[*n*] gives the Fibonacci number F_n.

Fibonacci[*n*, *x*] gives the Fibonacci polynomial $F_n(x)$.

Integer mathematical function (see Section A.3.10). ■ The F_n satisfy the recurrence relation $F_n = F_{n-1} + F_{n-2}$ with $F_1 = F_2 = 1$. ■ For any complex value of *n* the F_n are given by the general formula $F_n = (\phi^n - (-\phi)^{-n})/\sqrt{5}$, where ϕ is the golden ratio. ■ The Fibonacci polynomial $F_n(x)$ is the coefficient of t^n in the expansion of $t/(1 - xt - t^2)$. ■ The Fibonacci polynomials satisfy the recurrence relation $F_n(x) = xF_{n-1}(x) + F_{n-2}(x)$. ■ FullSimplify and FunctionExpand include transformation rules for combinations of Fibonacci numbers with symbolic arguments when the arguments are specified to be integers using $n \in$ Integers. ■ See page 757. ■ Implementation notes: see page 1067. ■ See also: GoldenRatio. ■ *New in Version 3.*

■ FileByteCount

FileByteCount["*file*"] gives the number of bytes in a file.

If a particular file is moved from one computer system to another, the number of bytes in the file as reported by FileByteCount may change. ■ See page 641. ■ See also: StringLength, FileType. ■ Related package: Utilities`BinaryFiles`. ■ *New in Version 2.*

■ FileDate

FileDate["*file*"] gives the date and time at which a file was last modified.

FileDate returns the date and time in the format used by Date. ■ See page 641. ■ See also: SetFileDate, FromDate. ■ *New in Version 2.*

■ FileNames

FileNames[ ] lists all files in the current working directory.

FileNames["*form*"] lists all files in the current working directory whose names match the string pattern *form*.

FileNames[{"*form*$_1$", "*form*$_2$", ... }] lists all files whose names match any of the *form*$_i$.

FileNames[*forms*, {"*dir*$_1$", "*dir*$_2$", ... }] lists files with names matching *forms* in any of the directories *dir*$_i$.

FileNames[*forms*, *dirs*, *n*] includes files that are in subdirectories up to *n* levels down.

The string pattern "*form*" can contain the metacharacters specified on page 1044. ■ FileNames["*"] is equivalent to FileNames[ ]. ■ FileNames[*forms*, *dirs*, Infinity] looks for files in all subdirectories of the *dirs*. ■ The list of files returned by FileNames is sorted in the order generated by the function Sort. ■ FileNames[*forms*, *dirs*, *n*] includes names of directories only if they appear exactly at level *n*. ■ The *forms* can include relative or absolute directory specifications, in addition to names of files. ■ Setting the option IgnoreCase -> True makes FileNames treat lower- and upper-case letters in file names as equivalent. ■ On operating systems such as MS-DOS, FileNames always treats lower- and upper-case letters in file names as equivalent. ■ See page 638. ■ See also: Directory, FileType, Get. ■ Related package: Utilities`Package`. ■ *New in Version 2; modified in Version 4.0.*

■ FileType

FileType["*file*"] gives the type of a file, typically File, Directory or None.

FileType returns None if the file specified does not exist. ■ See page 641. ■ See also: FileNames, FileByteCount. ■ *New in Version 2.*

■ Find

Find[*stream*, "*text*"] finds the first line in an input stream that contains the specified string.

Find[*stream*, {"*text*$_1$", "*text*$_2$", ... }] finds the first line that contains any of the specified strings.

Find breaks the input stream into records, delimited by record separators, and scans each record for the strings you specify. ■ Find returns as a string the first record which contains the specified text. ■ If Find does not find any record which contains the specified text before it reaches the end of the file, it returns EndOfFile.

(continued)

■ **Find** *(continued)*

- The following options can be given:

AnchoredSearch	False	whether to require that the text searched for be at the beginning of a record
IgnoreCase	False	whether to treat lower- and upper-case as equivalent
RecordSeparators	{"\n"}	separators for records
WordSearch	False	whether to require that the text searched for appear as a word
WordSeparators	{" ", "\t"}	separators for words

- The first argument to Find can be InputStream["*name*", *n*], or simply "*name*" if there is only one open input stream with the specified name. ▪ You can open a file or pipe to get an InputStream object using OpenRead. ▪ Find does not close streams after it finishes reading from them. ▪ See page 652. ▪ See also: Read, Skip, StreamPosition, StringToStream, NotebookFind. ▪ *New in Version 2.*

⁺■ **FindFit**

FindFit[*data*, *expr*, *pars*, *vars*] finds numerical values of the parameters *pars* that make *expr* give a best fit to *data* as a function of *vars*.

The data can have the form $\{\{x_1, y_1, \dots, f_1\}, \{x_2, y_2, \dots, f_2\}, \dots\}$, where the number of coordinates $x, y, \dots$ is equal to the number of variables in the list *vars*.

The data can also be of the form $\{f_1, f_2, \dots\}$, with a single coordinate assumed to take values 1, 2, … .

FindFit returns a list of replacements for $par_1, par_2, \dots$. ▪ The expression *expr* must yield a numerical value when *pars* and *vars* are all numerical. ▪ The expression *expr* can depend either linearly or nonlinearly on the par_i. ▪ In the linear case, FindFit finds a globally optimal fit. ▪ In the nonlinear case, it finds in general only a locally optimal fit. ▪ FindFit[*data*, *expr*, $\{\{par_1, p_1\}, \{par_2, p_2\}, \dots\}$, *vars*] starts the search for a fit with $\{par_1 \rightarrow p_1, par_2 \rightarrow p_2, \dots\}$. ▪ FindFit by default finds a least-squares fit. ▪ The option NormFunction -> *f* specifies that the norm *f*[*residual*] should be minimized. ▪ The following options can be given:

AccuracyGoal	Automatic	the accuracy sought
EvaluationMonitor	None	expression to evaluate whenever *expr* is evaluated
MaxIterations	100	maximum number of iterations to use
Method	Automatic	method to use
NormFunction	Norm	the norm to minimize
PrecisionGoal	Automatic	the precision sought
StepMonitor	None	expression to evaluate whenever a step is taken
WorkingPrecision	MachinePrecision	the precision used in internal computations

- The default settings for AccuracyGoal and PrecisionGoal are WorkingPrecision/2. ▪ The settings for AccuracyGoal and PrecisionGoal specify the number of digits to seek in both the values of the parameters returned, and the value of the NormFunction. ▪ FindFit continues until either of the goals specified by AccuracyGoal or PrecisionGoal is achieved. ▪ Possible settings for Method are as for FindMinimum. ▪ See page 929. ▪ Implementation notes: see page 1069. ▪ See also: FindMinimum, Fit, NMinimize, Interpolation. ▪ Related packages: Statistics`NonlinearFit`, Statistics`LinearRegression`. ▪ *New in Version 5.0.*

+■ **FindInstance**

FindInstance[*expr*, *vars*] finds an instance of *vars* that makes the statement *expr* be True.

FindInstance[*expr*, *vars*, *dom*] finds an instance over the domain *dom*. Common choices of *dom* are Complexes, Reals, Integers and Booleans.

FindInstance[*expr*, *vars*, *dom*, *n*] finds *n* instances.

FindInstance[*expr*, {x_1, x_2, ... }] gives results in the same form as Solve: {{x_1 -> val_1, x_2 -> val_2, ... }} if an instance exists, and {} if it does not. ■ *expr* can contain equations, inequalities, domain specifications and quantifiers, in the same form as in Reduce. ■ With exact symbolic input, FindInstance gives exact results. ■ Even if two inputs define the same mathematical set, FindInstance may still pick different instances to return. ■ The instances returned by FindInstance typically correspond to special or interesting points in the set. ■ FindInstance[*expr*, *vars*] assumes by default that quantities appearing algebraically in inequalities are real, while all other quantities are complex. ■ FindInstance[*expr*, *vars*, Integers] finds solutions to Diophantine equations. ■ FindInstance[*expr*, *vars*, Booleans] solves Boolean satisfiability for *expr*. ■ FindInstance[*expr*, *vars*, Reals] assumes that not only *vars* but also all function values in *expr* are real. FindInstance[*expr* && *vars* ∈ Reals, *vars*] assumes only that the *vars* are real. ■ FindInstance may be able to find instances even if Reduce cannot give a complete reduction. ■ Every time you run FindInstance with a given input, it will return the same output. ■ Different settings for the option RandomSeed -> *n* may yield different collections of instances. ■ See pages 838 and 844. ■ See also: Solve, Reduce, FindRoot, Minimize, Random. ■ *New in Version 5.0.*

■ **FindList**

FindList["*file*", "*text*"] gives a list of lines in the file that contain the specified string.

FindList["*file*", {"*text₁*", "*text₂*", ... }] gives a list of all lines that contain any of the specified strings.

FindList[{"*file₁*", ... }, ...] gives a list of lines containing the specified strings in any of the *file_i*.

FindList[*files*, *text*, *n*] includes only the first *n* lines found.

FindList returns {} if it fails to find any record which contains the specified text. ■ If FindList opens a file or pipe, it closes it again when it has finished. ■ See notes for Find. ■ See page 650. ■ See also: ReadList. ■ *New in Version 2.*

+■ **FindMaximum**

FindMaximum[*f*, {*x*, x_0}] searches for a local maximum in *f*, starting from the point *x* = x_0.

FindMaximum[*f*, {{*x*, x_0}, {*y*, y_0}, ... }] searches for a local maximum in a function of several variables.

FindMaximum returns a list of the form {f_{max}, {*x*->x_{max}}}, where f_{max} is the maximum value of *f* found, and x_{max} is the value of *x* for which it is found. ■ See notes for FindMinimum. ■ See page 107. ■ See also: FindMinimum, NMaximize, Maximize, FindFit, LinearProgramming, D. ■ Related package: Statistics`NonlinearFit`. ■ *New in Version 5.0.*

■ **FindMinimum**

FindMinimum[*f*, {*x*, x_0}] searches for a local minimum in *f*, starting from the point *x*=x_0.

+ FindMinimum[*f*, {{*x*, x_0}, {*y*, y_0}, ... }] searches for a local minimum in a function of several variables.

(continued)

■ FindMinimum *(continued)*

▪ FindMinimum returns a list of the form $\{f_{min}, \{x\text{->}x_{min}\}\}$, where f_{min} is the minimum value of f found, and x_{min} is the value of x for which it is found. ＋▪ If the starting point for a variable is given as a list, the values of the variable are taken to be lists with the same dimensions. ▪ FindMinimum has attribute HoldAll. ～▪ FindMinimum[f, $\{x, x_0, x_1\}$] searches for a local minimum in f using x_0 and x_1 as the first two values of x, avoiding the use of derivatives. ▪ FindMinimum[f, $\{x, x_0, x_{min}, x_{max}\}$] searches for a local minimum, stopping the search if x ever gets outside the range x_{min} to x_{max}. ▪ The results found by FindMinimum may correspond only to local, but not global, minima. ～▪ The following options can be given:

AccuracyGoal	Automatic	the accuracy sought
Compiled	True	whether the function should be compiled
EvaluationMonitor	None	expression to evaluate whenever f is evaluated
Gradient	Automatic	the list of gradient functions $\{D[f, x], D[f, y], \dots \}$
MaxIterations	100	maximum number of iterations to use
Method	Automatic	method to use
PrecisionGoal	Automatic	the precision sought
StepMonitor	None	expression to evaluate whenever a step is taken
WorkingPrecision	MachinePrecision	the precision used in internal computations

～▪ The default settings for AccuracyGoal and PrecisionGoal are WorkingPrecision/2. ＋▪ The settings for AccuracyGoal and PrecisionGoal specify the number of digits to seek in both the value of the position of the minimum, and the value of the function at the minimum. ▪ FindMinimum continues until either of the goals specified by AccuracyGoal or PrecisionGoal is achieved. ～▪ Possible settings for Method include "ConjugateGradient", "Gradient", "LevenbergMarquardt", "Newton" and "QuasiNewton", with the default being Automatic. ▪ See page 973. ▪ Implementation notes: see page 1068. ▪ See also: FindMaximum, NMinimize, Minimize, FindFit, LinearProgramming, D, CholeskyDecomposition. ▪ *New in Version 1; modified in Version 5.0.*

～■ FindRoot

FindRoot[*lhs*==*rhs*, $\{x, x_0\}$] searches for a numerical solution to the equation *lhs*==*rhs*, starting with $x = x_0$.

FindRoot[$\{eqn_1, eqn_2, \dots \}$, $\{\{x, x_0\}, \{y, y_0\}, \dots \}$] searches for a numerical solution to the simultaneous equations eqn_i.

～▪ If the starting point for a variable is given as a list, the values of the variable are taken to be lists with the same dimensions. ▪ FindRoot returns a list of replacements for x, y, $\dots$, in the same form as obtained from Solve. ▪ FindRoot has attribute HoldAll. ～▪ FindRoot[*lhs*==*rhs*, $\{x, x_0, x_1\}$] searches for a solution using x_0 and x_1 as the first two values of x, avoiding the use of derivatives. ▪ FindRoot[*lhs*==*rhs*, $\{x, xstart, xmin, xmax\}$] searches for a solution, stopping the search if x ever gets outside the range $xmin$ to $xmax$. ▪ If you specify only one starting value of x, FindRoot searches for a solution using Newton methods. If you specify two starting values, FindRoot uses a variant of the secant method. ▪ If all equations and starting values are real, then FindRoot will search only for real roots. If any are complex, it will also search for complex roots. ▪ You can always tell FindRoot to search for complex roots by adding 0. I to the starting value. ＋▪ FindRoot[*expr*, $\dots$] will search for a root of the equation *expr*==0. ～▪ The following options can be given:

AccuracyGoal	Automatic	the accuracy sought
Compiled	True	whether the function should be compiled
EvaluationMonitor	None	expression to evaluate whenever equations are evaluated
Jacobian	Automatic	the Jacobian of the system
MaxIterations	100	maximum number of iterations to use
PrecisionGoal	Automatic	the precision sought
StepMonitor	None	expression to evaluate whenever a step is taken
WorkingPrecision	MachinePrecision	the precision to use in internal computations

(continued)

FindRoot *(continued)*

~■ The default settings for AccuracyGoal and PrecisionGoal are WorkingPrecision/2. +■ The setting for AccuracyGoal specifies the number of digits of accuracy to seek both in the value of the position of the root, and the value of the function at the root. +■ The setting for PrecisionGoal specifies the number of digits of precision to seek in the value of the position of the root. +■ FindRoot continues until either of the goals specified by AccuracyGoal or PrecisionGoal is achieved. ■ If FindRoot does not succeed in finding a solution to the accuracy you specify within MaxIterations steps, it returns the most recent approximation to a solution that it found. You can then apply FindRoot again, with this approximation as a starting point. ■ See page 960. ■ Implementation notes: see page 1068. ■ See also: NSolve, Solve, FindMinimum, FindInstance. ■ Related package: NumericalMath`InterpolateRoot`. ■ *New in Version 1; modified in Version 5.0.*

First

First[*expr*] gives the first element in *expr*.

First[*expr*] is equivalent to *expr*[[1]]. ■ See page 122. ■ See also: Part, Last, Rest, Take, Select. ■ *New in Version 1.*

Fit

Fit[*data*, *funs*, *vars*] finds a least-squares fit to a list of data as a linear combination of the functions *funs* of variables *vars*.

The data can have the form $\{\{x_1, y_1, \ldots, f_1\}, \{x_2, y_2, \ldots, f_2\}, \ldots\}$, where the number of coordinates $x, y, \ldots$ is equal to the number of variables in the list *vars*.

The data can also be of the form $\{f_1, f_2, \ldots\}$, with a single coordinate assumed to take values 1, 2, … .

The argument *funs* can be any list of functions that depend only on the objects *vars*.

Fit[$\{f_1, f_2, \ldots\}$, {1, x, x^2}, x] gives a quadratic fit to a sequence of values f_i. The result is of the form $a_0 + a_1 x + a_2 x^2$, where the a_i are real numbers. The successive values of x needed to obtain the f_i are assumed to be 1, 2, … . ■ Fit[$\{\{x_1, f_1\}, \{x_2, f_2\}, \ldots\}$, {1, x, x^2}, x] does a quadratic fit, assuming a sequence of x values x_i. ■ Fit[$\{\{x_1, y_1, f_1\}, \ldots\}$, {1, x, y}, {x, y}] finds a fit of the form $a_0 + a_1 x + a_2 y$. ■ Fit always finds the linear combination of the functions in the list *funs* that minimizes the sum of the squares of deviations from the values f_i. ■ Exact numbers given as input to Fit are converted to approximate numbers with machine precision. ■ See page 926. ■ Implementation notes: see page 1069. ■ See also: FindFit, Interpolation, InterpolatingPolynomial, Solve, PseudoInverse, QRDecomposition, FindMinimum. ■ Related packages: Statistics`LinearRegression`. ■ *New in Version 1.*

FixedPoint

FixedPoint[*f*, *expr*] starts with *expr*, then applies *f* repeatedly until the result no longer changes.

FixedPoint[*f*, *expr*, *n*] stops after at most *n* steps. ■ FixedPoint always returns the last result it gets. ■ You can use Throw to exit from FixedPoint before it is finished. ■ FixedPoint[*f*, *expr*] applies SameQ to successive pairs of results to determine whether a fixed point has been reached. ■ NestWhile[*f*, *expr*, *comp*, 2] uses a general comparison function. ■ See page 241. ■ See also: FixedPointList, NestWhile, Nest, ReplaceRepeated. ■ *New in Version 1; modified in Version 3.*

▪ FixedPointList

FixedPointList[*f*, *expr*] generates a list giving the results of applying *f* repeatedly, starting with *expr*, until the results no longer change.

See notes for FixedPoint. ▪ FixedPointList[*f*, *expr*] gives *expr* as the first element of the list it produces. ▪ The last two elements in the list produced by FixedPointList are always the same. ▪ See page 241. ▪ See also: NestWhileList, NestList, ComposeList. ▪ *New in Version 2.*

▪ Flat

Flat is an attribute that can be assigned to a symbol *f* to indicate that all expressions involving nested functions *f* should be flattened out. This property is accounted for in pattern matching.

Flat corresponds to the mathematical property of associativity. ▪ For a symbol *f* with attribute Flat, *f*[*f*[*a*, *b*], *f*[*c*]] is automatically reduced to *f*[*a*, *b*, *c*]. ▪ Functions like Plus, Times and Dot are Flat. ▪ For a Flat function *f*, the variables x and y in the pattern *f*[x_, y_] can correspond to any sequence of arguments. ▪ The Flat attribute must be assigned before defining any values for a Flat function. ▪ See page 329. ▪ See also: Orderless, OneIdentity. ▪ *New in Version 1.*

▪ Flatten

Flatten[*list*] flattens out nested lists.

Flatten[*list*, *n*] flattens to level *n*.

Flatten[*list*, *n*, *h*] flattens subexpressions with head *h*.

Example: Flatten[{a,{b,c},{d}}] ⟶ {a, b, c, d}. ▪ Flatten "unravels" lists, effectively just deleting inner braces. ▪ Flatten[*list*, *n*] effectively flattens the top level in *list* *n* times. ▪ Flatten[*f*[*e*, ...]] flattens out subexpressions with head *f*. +▪ Flatten flattens out levels in SparseArray objects just as in the corresponding ordinary arrays. ▪ See pages 130 and 255. ▪ See also: Partition, FlattenAt. ▪ *New in Version 1.*

▪ FlattenAt

FlattenAt[*list*, *n*] flattens out a sublist that appears as the nth element of *list*. If *n* is negative, the position is counted from the end.

FlattenAt[*expr*, {*i*, *j*, ... }] flattens out the part of *expr* at position {*i*, *j*, ... }.

FlattenAt[*expr*, {{*i*$_1$, *j*$_1$, ... }, {*i*$_2$, *j*$_2$, ... }, ... }] flattens out parts of *expr* at several positions.

Example: FlattenAt[{a, {b, c}, {d, e}}, 2] ⟶ {a, b, c, {d, e}}. ▪ See page 255. ▪ See also: DeleteCases, Flatten, Sequence, SlotSequence. ▪ *New in Version 2.*

▪ Floor

Floor[*x*] gives the greatest integer less than or equal to *x*.

Mathematical function (see Section A.3.10). ▪ Examples: Floor[2.4] ⟶ 2; Floor[2.6] ⟶ 2; Floor[-2.4] ⟶ -3; Floor[-2.6] ⟶ -3. ▪ Floor[*x*] can be entered in StandardForm and InputForm as ⌊ *x* ⌋, :lf: *x* :rf: or \[LeftFloor] *x* \[RightFloor]. ▪ Floor[*x*] returns an integer when *x* is any numeric quantity, whether or not it is an explicit number. ▪ Example: Floor[Pi^2] ⟶ 9. ▪ For exact numeric quantities, Floor internally uses numerical approximations to establish its result. This process can be affected by the setting of the global variable $MaxExtraPrecision. ▪ See page 745. ▪ Implementation notes: see page 1067. ▪ See also: Ceiling, Round, IntegerPart, Chop. ▪ *New in Version 1; modified in Version 3.*

■ Fold

Fold[*f*, *x*, *list*] gives the last element of FoldList[*f*, *x*, *list*].

Example: Fold[f, x, {a, b, c}] ⟶ f[f[f[x, a], b], c]. ■ You can use Throw to exit from Fold before it is finished. ■ See notes for FoldList. ■ See page 243. ■ See also: Nest. ■ *New in Version 2; modified in Version 3.*

■ FoldList

FoldList[*f*, *x*, {*a*, *b*, ... }] gives {*x*, *f*[*x*, *a*], *f*[*f*[*x*, *a*], *b*], ... }.

Example: FoldList[f, x, {a, b, c}] ⟶ {x, f[x, a], f[f[x, a], b], f[f[f[x, a], b], c]}. ■ FoldList[Plus, 0, *list*] generates cumulative sums of the elements in *list*. ■ Example: FoldList[Plus, 0, {a, b, c}] ⟶ {0, a, a + b, a + b + c}. ■ With a length *n* list, FoldList generates a list of length *n* + 1. ■ The head of *list* in FoldList[*f*, *x*, *list*] need not be List. ■ See page 243. ■ See also: Fold, NestList, ComposeList, Partition, MapIndexed. ■ *New in Version 2.*

■ FontColor

FontColor is an option for Cell, StyleBox and StyleForm which specifies the default color in which to render text.

The setting for FontColor must be a CMYKColor, GrayLevel, Hue or RGBColor directive. ■ See pages 444 and 612. ■ See also: Background, DefaultColor, FontWeight. ■ *New in Version 3.*

■ FontFamily

FontFamily is an option for Cell, StyleBox and StyleForm which specifies the font family in which text should be rendered.

The default is FontFamily->"Courier". Other common choices are "Times" and "Helvetica". ■ *Mathematica* will combine settings for FontFamily, FontWeight, FontSlant, FontTracking and sometimes FontSize to construct a complete name for the font you want. It will then use this name, together with any settings you have specified for FontPostScriptName and FontNativeName to try to locate an appropriate font on your particular computer system. ■ When generating PostScript output on a printer or otherwise, settings you give for FontPostScriptName are typically used in preference to other font specifications. ■ *Mathematica* will try making replacements for the font family name that you specify with the option FontSubstitutions. ■ *Mathematica* by default uses heuristics such as translating "Helvetica" to "Geneva" for appropriate computer systems. ■ See pages 444 and 612. ■ See also: StyleForm, TextStyle. ■ *New in Version 3.*

■ FontSize

FontSize is an option for Cell, StyleBox and StyleForm which specifies the default size in printer's points of the font in which to render text.

The size of a font is typically taken to be the distance from the top of the highest character to the bottom of the lowest character. ■ A printer's point is approximately $\frac{1}{72}$ of an inch. ■ Fonts with the same nominal point size may not look the same size to the eye. ■ See pages 444 and 612. ■ See also: FontWeight, FontTracking, ScriptMinSize, ScriptSizeMultipliers. ■ *New in Version 3.*

■ FontSlant

FontSlant is an option for Cell, StyleBox and StyleForm which specifies how slanted the characters should be in text in the cell.

Typical settings are "Plain", "Italic" and "Oblique". ■ With the "Oblique" setting, each character typically has the same basic form as with "Plain", but is slanted. With the "Italic" setting, the basic form is different. ■ See notes for FontFamily. ■ See pages 444 and 612. ■ See also: AutoItalicWords, SingleLetterItalics. ■ *New in Version 3.*

■ **FontSubstitutions**

FontSubstitutions is an option for Cell, StyleBox and StyleForm which gives a list of substitutions to try for font family names.

A typical setting is {"Geneva" -> "Helvetica"}. ■ FontSubstitutions is used only for FontFamily settings, and not for FontWeight, FontSlant and so on. ■ See page 612. ■ See also: FontFamily. ■ *New in Version 3.*

■ **FontTracking**

FontTracking is an option for Cell, StyleBox and StyleForm which specifies how condensed or expanded you want the font in which text is rendered to be.

Typical settings are "Condensed" and "Expanded". The default is "Plain". ■ For some fonts and on some computer systems, additional settings are supported, such as "Narrow", "Compressed", "SemiCondensed", "Extended" and "Wide". ■ See notes for FontFamily. ■ See page 612. ■ *New in Version 3.*

■ **FontWeight**

FontWeight is an option for Cell, StyleBox and StyleForm which specifies how heavy the characters in a font should be.

Typical settings are "Plain" and "Bold". ■ For some fonts and on some computer systems, additional settings are supported, such as "Thin", "Light", "Medium", "SemiBold", "Heavy", "Black" and "Fat". ■ See notes for FontFamily. ■ See pages 444 and 612. ■ *New in Version 3.*

■ **For**

For[*start*, *test*, *incr*, *body*] executes *start*, then repeatedly evaluates *body* and *incr* until *test* fails to give True.

For evaluates its arguments in a non-standard way. ■ For[*start*, *test*, *incr*] does the loop with a null body. ■ The sequence of evaluation is *test*, *body*, *incr*. The For exits as soon as *test* fails. ■ If Break[ ] is generated in the evaluation of *body*, the For loop exits. ■ Continue[ ] exits the evaluation of *body*, and continues the loop by evaluating *incr*. ■ Unless Return[*expr*] or Throw[*expr*] is generated, the final value returned by For is Null. ■ Example: For[tot=0; i=0, i < 3, i++, tot += f[i]]. Note that the roles of semicolon and comma are *reversed* relative to the C programming language. ■ See page 352. ■ See also: Do, While, Throw, NestWhile. ■ *New in Version 1.*

⁺■ **ForAll**

ForAll[*x*, *expr*] represents the statement that *expr* is True for all values of *x*.

ForAll[*x*, *cond*, *expr*] states that *expr* is True for all *x* satisfying the condition *cond*.

ForAll[{x_1, x_2, ... }, *expr*] states that *expr* is True for all values of all the x_i.

ForAll[*x*, *expr*] can be entered as $\forall_x$ *expr*. The character $\forall$ can be entered as ⸴fa⸴ or \[ForAll]. The variable *x* is given as a subscript. ■ ForAll[*x*, *cond*, *expr*] can be entered as $\forall_{x,cond}$ *expr*. ■ In StandardForm, ForAll[*x*, *expr*] is output as $\forall_x$ *expr*. ■ ForAll[*x*, *cond*, *expr*] is output as $\forall_{x,cond}$ *expr*. ■ ForAll can be used in such functions as Reduce, Resolve and FullSimplify. ■ The condition *cond* is often used to specify the domain of a variable, as in $x \in$ Integers. ■ ForAll[*x*, *cond*, *expr*] is equivalent to ForAll[*x*, Implies[*cond*, *expr*]]. ■ ForAll[{x_1, x_2, ... }, ...] is equivalent to $\forall_{x_1} \forall_{x_2}$ .... ■ The value of *x* in ForAll[*x*, *expr*] is taken to be localized, as in Block. ■ See page 847. ■ See also: Exists, Resolve, Reduce, Element, Blank, SolveAlways. ■ *New in Version 5.0.*

◼ Format

Format[*expr*] prints as the formatted form of *expr*.

Assigning values to Format[*expr*] defines print forms for expressions.

Format[*expr, form*] gives a format for the specified form of output.

◦◼ Standard forms for formatted output are:

CForm	C language input form
FortranForm	Fortran input form
InputForm	one-dimensional form suitable for direct keyboard input
MathMLForm	MathML form
OutputForm	character-based two-dimensional form
StandardForm	standard two-dimensional form
TeXForm	TEX input form
TraditionalForm	form approximating traditional mathematical notation

◼ You can add your own forms for formatted output. ◼ Example: Format[*s*] := *rhs* defines a symbol *s* to print like *rhs*. ◼ Format[*f*[...]] := *rhs* defines a function *f* to print like *rhs*. ◼ Definitions for Format are stored in the FormatValues of a symbol. ◼ If you specify a new output format for an expression by giving a definition for Format, there is no guarantee that *Mathematica* will be able to interpret this output format if it is used as input. ◼ Definitions given for Format are used before those given for MakeBoxes. ◼ See page 473. ◼ See also: ToString, ToBoxes, MakeBoxes, MakeExpression. ◼ *New in Version 1; modified in Version 4.1.*

◼ FormatType

FormatType is an option for output streams, graphics and functions such as Text which specifies the default format type to use when outputting expressions.

Standard values for FormatType are given in the notes for Format. ◼ SetOptions[*stream*, FormatType -> *type*] resets the format type for an open stream. ◼ For graphics functions the default option setting is FormatType :> $FormatType. ◼ For graphics functions box-based format types such as StandardForm and TraditionalForm can be used only when a notebook front end is present. ◼ See pages 556 and 634. ◼ See also: TextStyle, LanguageCategory. ◼ *New in Version 1; modified in Version 3.*

◼ FormBox

FormBox[*boxes, form*] displays as *boxes* but specifies that rules associated with *form* should be used to interpret *boxes* on input.

In InputForm and StandardForm \(*form*\`*input*\) yields FormBox[*input, form*]. ◼ \(\`*input*\) yields FormBox[*input*, RawForm]. ◼ See page 447. ◼ See also: TagBox, InterpretationBox, ToExpression, MakeExpression. ◼ *New in Version 3.*

◼ FortranForm

FortranForm[*expr*] prints as a Fortran language version of *expr*.

Standard arithmetic functions and certain control structures are translated. ◼ FortranForm acts as a "wrapper", which affects printing, but not evaluation. ◼ The width of output lines must be set explicitly by giving the option PageWidth -> *n* for the relevant output stream. ◼ SetOptions[$Output, PageWidth -> 72] uses a line width of 72 characters for standard *Mathematica* output. ◼ No declarations are generated. ◼ See pages 213 and 425. ◼ See also: CForm, Compile. ◼ *New in Version 1.*

■ Fourier

Fourier[*list*] finds the discrete Fourier transform of a list of complex numbers.

The discrete Fourier transform v_s of a list u_r of length n is by default defined to be $\frac{1}{\sqrt{n}} \sum_{r=1}^{n} u_r e^{2\pi i (r-1)(s-1)/n}$. ■ Note that the zero frequency term appears at position 1 in the resulting list. ■ Other definitions are used in some scientific and technical fields. ■ Different choices of definitions can be specified using the option FourierParameters. ■ With the setting FourierParameters -> {*a*, *b*} the discrete Fourier transform computed by Fourier is $\frac{1}{n^{(1-a)/2}} \sum_{r=1}^{n} u_r e^{2\pi i b(r-1)(s-1)/n}$. ■ Some common choices for {*a*, *b*} are {0, 1} (default), {-1, 1} (data analysis), {1, -1} (signal processing). ■ The setting $b = -1$ effectively corresponds to conjugating both input and output lists. ■ To ensure a unique inverse discrete Fourier transform, |*b*| must be relatively prime to n. ■ The list of data supplied to Fourier need not have a length equal to a power of two. ■ The *list* given in Fourier[*list*] can be nested to represent an array of data in any number of dimensions. ■ The array of data must be rectangular. ■ If the elements of *list* are exact numbers, Fourier begins by applying N to them. +■ Fourier can be used on SparseArray objects. ■ See page 935. ■ Implementation notes: see page 1069. ■ See also: InverseFourier, FourierTransform, Fit. ■ *New in Version 1; modified in Version 4.*

■ FourierCosTransform

FourierCosTransform[*expr*, *t*, ω] gives the symbolic Fourier cosine transform of *expr*.

FourierCosTransform[*expr*, {t_1, t_2, ... }, {ω_1, ω_2, ... }] gives the multidimensional Fourier cosine transform of *expr*.

The Fourier cosine transform of a function $f(t)$ is by default defined to be $\sqrt{\frac{2}{\pi}} \int_0^\infty f(t) \cos(\omega t)\, dt$. ■ Other definitions are used in some scientific and technical fields. ■ Different choices of definitions can be specified using the option FourierParameters. ■ With the setting FourierParameters->{*a*, *b*} the Fourier cosine transform computed by FourierCosTransform is $2\sqrt{\frac{|b|}{(2\pi)^{1-a}}} \int_0^\infty f(t) \cos(b\omega t)\, dt$. ■ See notes for FourierTransform. ■ See page 878. ■ See also: FourierSinTransform, FourierTransform, Fourier, InverseFourierCosTransform. ■ *New in Version 4.*

■ FourierSinTransform

FourierSinTransform[*expr*, *t*, ω] gives the symbolic Fourier sine transform of *expr*.

FourierSinTransform[*expr*, {t_1, t_2, ... }, {ω_1, ω_2, ... }] gives the multidimensional Fourier sine transform of *expr*.

The Fourier sine transform of a function $f(t)$ is by default defined to be $\sqrt{\frac{2}{\pi}} \int_0^\infty f(t) \sin(\omega t)\, dt$. ■ Other definitions are used in some scientific and technical fields. ■ Different choices of definitions can be specified using the option FourierParameters. ■ With the setting FourierParameters->{*a*, *b*} the Fourier sine transform computed by FourierSinTransform is $2\sqrt{\frac{|b|}{(2\pi)^{1-a}}} \int_0^\infty f(t) \sin(b\omega t)\, dt$. ■ See notes for FourierTransform. ■ See page 878. ■ See also: FourierCosTransform, FourierTransform, Fourier, InverseFourierSinTransform. ■ *New in Version 4.*

■ **FourierTransform**

FourierTransform[*expr*, *t*, ω] gives the symbolic Fourier transform of *expr*.

FourierTransform[*expr*, {t_1, t_2, ... }, {ω_1, ω_2, ... }] gives the multidimensional Fourier transform of *expr*.

The Fourier transform of a function $f(t)$ is by default defined to be $\frac{1}{\sqrt{2\pi}} \int_{-\infty}^{\infty} f(t)\,e^{i\omega t}\,dt$. ■ Other definitions are used in some scientific and technical fields. ■ Different choices of definitions can be specified using the option FourierParameters. ■ With the setting FourierParameters->{*a*, *b*} the Fourier transform computed by FourierTransform is $\sqrt{\frac{|b|}{(2\pi)^{1-a}}} \int_{-\infty}^{\infty} f(t)\,e^{ib\omega t}\,dt$. ■ Some common choices for {*a*, *b*} are {0, 1} (default; modern physics), {1, -1} (pure mathematics; systems engineering), {-1, 1} (classical physics), {0, -2 Pi} (signal processing). ■ Assumptions and other options to Integrate can also be given in FourierTransform. ■ FourierTransform[*expr*, *t*, ω] yields an expression depending on the continuous variable ω that represents the symbolic Fourier transform of *expr* with respect to the continuous variable *t*. Fourier[*list*] takes a finite list of numbers as input, and yields as output a list representing the discrete Fourier transform of the input. ■ In TraditionalForm, FourierTransform is output using $\mathcal{F}$. ■ See page 876. ■ See also: FourierSinTransform, FourierCosTransform, Fourier, InverseFourierTransform, LaplaceTransform, Integrate. ■ *New in Version 4.*

■ **FractionalPart**

FractionalPart[*x*] gives the fractional part of *x*.

Mathematical function (see Section A.3.10). ■ FractionalPart[*x*] in effect takes all digits to the right of the decimal point and drops the others. ■ Examples: FractionalPart[2.4] ⟶ 0.4; FractionalPart[2.6] ⟶ 0.6; FractionalPart[-2.4] ⟶ -0.4; FractionalPart[-2.6] ⟶ -0.6. ■ FractionalPart[*x*] + IntegerPart[*x*] is always exactly *x*. ■ FractionalPart[*x*] yields a result when *x* is any numeric quantity, whether or not it is an explicit number. ■ Example: FractionalPart[Pi^2] ⟶ $-9 + \pi^2$. ■ For exact numeric quantities, FractionalPart internally uses numerical approximations to establish its result. This process can be affected by the setting of the global variable $MaxExtraPrecision. ■ See page 745. ■ See also: IntegerPart, Mod. ■ *New in Version 3.*

■ **FractionBox**

FractionBox[*x*, *y*] represents $\frac{x}{y}$ in input and output.

Inside \(... \) FractionBox[*x*, *y*] can be input as *x* \/ *y*. ■ In a notebook a FractionBox can be created using [CTRL]/. [CTRL]␣ moves out of the fraction. ■ In StandardForm and InputForm, FractionBox[*x*, *y*] is interpreted on input as *x*/*y*. ■ The axis of FractionBox[*x*, *y*] is taken to go through the fraction line. ■ The baseline lies below the axis by the distance between the axis and the bottom of characters such as (in the current font. ■ The width of the fraction line can be given in x-heights as the setting for the SpanLineThickness option in StyleBox. ■ If FractionBox[*x*, *y*] does not fit on a single line, it is output as *x* / *y*. ■ In StandardForm, explicit FractionBox objects are output literally. You can use DisplayForm to see the display form of such objects. ■ See page 445. ■ See also: OverscriptBox, GridBox. ■ *New in Version 3.*

■ **Frame**

Frame is an option for two-dimensional graphics functions which specifies whether a frame should be drawn around the plot.

Frame -> True by default draws a frame with tick marks. If Ticks -> Automatic, setting Frame -> True suppresses tick marks on axes. ■ See pages 511 and 514. ■ See also: Boxed. ■ *New in Version 2.*

■ **FrameBox**

FrameBox[*box*] displays with a frame drawn around *box*.

In StandardForm and InputForm, FrameBox is by default ignored, so that FrameBox[*box*] is interpreted just as *box* would be. ■ In StandardForm, explicit FrameBox objects are output literally. You can use DisplayForm to see the display form of such objects. ■ See page 446. ■ See also: StyleBox, CellFrame, ColumnLines, RowLines. ■ *New in Version 3.*

■ **FrameLabel**

FrameLabel is an option for two-dimensional graphics functions that specifies labels to be placed on the edges of a frame around a plot.

FrameLabel -> None specifies that no labels should be given. ■ FrameLabel -> {*xmlabel*, *ymlabel*} specifies labels for the bottom and left-hand edges of the frame. ■ FrameLabel -> {*xmlabel*, *ymlabel*, *xplabel*, *yplabel*} specifies labels for each of the edges of the frame, ordered clockwise starting from the bottom edge. ■ Any expression can be specified as a label. It will be given in OutputForm. Arbitrary strings of text can be given as "*text*". ■ Labels for the vertical edges of the frame are by default written vertically. RotateLabel -> False specifies that they should be horizontal. ■ See page 514. ■ See also: AxesLabel, PlotLabel. ■ *New in Version 2.*

■ **FrameStyle**

FrameStyle is an option for two-dimensional graphics functions that specifies how the edges of a frame should be rendered.

FrameStyle -> *style* specifies that all edges of the frame are to be generated with the specified graphics directive, or list of graphics directives. ■ FrameStyle -> {{*xmstyle*}, {*ymstyle*}, ... } specifies that different edges of the frame should be generated with different styles. The edges are ordered clockwise starting from the bottom edge. All styles must be enclosed in lists, perhaps of length one. ■ Styles can be specified using graphics directives such as Dashing, Hue and Thickness. ■ The default color of frame edges is specified by the option DefaultColor. ■ See page 514. ■ See also: Prolog, Epilog, AxesStyle. ■ *New in Version 2.*

■ **FrameTicks**

FrameTicks is an option for two-dimensional graphics functions that specifies tick marks for the edges of a frame.

The following settings can be given for FrameTicks:

None	no tick marks drawn
Automatic	tick marks placed automatically
{*xmticks*, *ymticks*, ... }	tick mark options specified separately for each edge

■ When tick mark specifications are given separately for each edge, the edges are ordered clockwise starting from the bottom of the frame. ■ With the Automatic setting, tick marks are usually placed at points whose coordinates have the minimum number of digits in their decimal representation. ■ For each edge, tick marks can be specified as described in the notes for Ticks. ■ See page 514. ■ See also: Ticks, GridLines, FaceGrids. ■ *New in Version 2.*

■ **FreeQ**

FreeQ[*expr*, *form*] yields True if no subexpression in *expr* matches *form*, and yields False otherwise.

FreeQ[*expr*, *form*, *levelspec*] tests only those parts of *expr* on levels specified by *levelspec*.

form can be a pattern. ■ Example: FreeQ[f[x^2] + y^2, x^_] ⟶ False. ■ FreeQ looks at the heads of raw expressions, testing whether those heads match *form*. ■ See page 268. ■ See also: MemberQ, Count. ■ *New in Version 1.*

■ FresnelC

FresnelC[z] gives the Fresnel integral $C(z)$.

Mathematical function (see Section A.3.10). ■ FresnelC[z] is given by $\int_0^z \cos\left(\pi t^2/2\right) dt$. ■ FresnelC[z] is an entire function of z with no branch cut discontinuities. ■ See page 775. ■ See also: Erf, CosIntegral. ■ *New in Version 3.*

■ FresnelS

FresnelS[z] gives the Fresnel integral $S(z)$.

Mathematical function (see Section A.3.10). ■ FresnelS[z] is given by $\int_0^z \sin\left(\pi t^2/2\right) dt$. ■ FresnelS[z] is an entire function of z with no branch cut discontinuities. ■ See page 775. ■ See also: Erf, SinIntegral. ■ *New in Version 3.*

■ FromCharacterCode

FromCharacterCode[n] gives a string consisting of the character with integer code n.

FromCharacterCode[$\{n_1, n_2, \dots\}$] gives a string consisting of the sequence of characters with codes n_i.

FromCharacterCode[$\{\{n_{11}, n_{12}, \dots\}, \{n_{21}, \dots\}, \dots\}$] gives a list of strings.

FromCharacterCode[$\dots$, "*encoding*"] uses the specified character encoding.

The integer n must lie between 0 and 65535, as returned by ToCharacterCode. ■ For n between 0 and 127, FromCharacterCode returns ASCII characters. ■ For n between 129 and 255, it returns ISO Latin-1 characters. ■ For other n it returns characters specified by the standard *Mathematica* encoding based on Unicode. ■ InputForm[FromCharacterCode[n]] gives the full name assigned to a special character with character code n. ■ Whether a particular character generated by FromCharacterCode can be rendered on your output device will depend on what fonts and drivers you are using. ■ Encodings supported in FromCharacterCode[$\dots$, "*encoding*"] are listed in the notes for $CharacterEncoding. ■ See page 417. ■ See also: ToCharacterCode, CharacterRange, $CharacterEncoding. ■ Related package: Utilities`BinaryFiles`. ■ *New in Version 2; modified in Version 4.*

■ FromContinuedFraction

FromContinuedFraction[*list*] reconstructs a number from the list of its continued fraction terms.

FromContinuedFraction[$\{a_1, a_2, a_3, \dots\}$] returns $a_1 + 1/(a_2 + 1/(a_3 + \dots))$. ■ The a_i can be symbolic. ■ FromContinuedFraction[$\{a_1, a_2, \dots, \{b_1, b_2, \dots\}\}$] returns the exact number whose continued fraction terms start with the a_i, then consist of cyclic repetitions of the b_i. ■ FromContinuedFraction acts as the inverse of ContinuedFraction. ■ See page 754. ■ Implementation notes: see page 1067. ■ See also: ContinuedFraction, Rationalize, FromDigits, Fold. ■ *New in Version 4.*

■ FromDate

FromDate[*date*] converts a date of the form $\{y, m, d, h, m, s\}$ to an absolute number of seconds since the beginning of January 1, 1900.

FromDate converts between the forms returned by Date and AbsoluteTime. ■ FromDate assumes that both the date and the absolute time are to be given in the same time zone. ■ See page 710. ■ See also: ToDate. ■ Related package: Miscellaneous`Calendar`. ■ *New in Version 2.*

■ **FromDigits**

FromDigits[*list*] constructs an integer from the list of its decimal digits.

FromDigits[*list*, *b*] takes the digits to be given in base *b*.

Example: FromDigits[{3,7,4}] $\longrightarrow$ 374. ■ FromDigits is effectively the inverse of IntegerDigits.
■ FromDigits[{*list*, *n*}, *b*] takes *n* to be an exponent, while FromDigits[{{*list*, {*rep*}}, *n*}, *b*] takes *rep* to be repeated, so that FromDigits can also be used as the inverse of RealDigits. ■ Since IntegerDigits[*n*] discards the sign of *n*, FromDigits[IntegerDigits[*n*]] is Abs[*n*] not just *n*. ■ The digits in *list* and the base *b* need not be positive integers, and can be any expression. ■ If Indeterminate appears in *list*, it is assumed to signify unknown digits beyond the precision of an approximate real number. ■ See page 725. ■ See also: IntegerDigits, RealDigits, FromContinuedFraction, NumberForm, DigitCount. ■ *New in Version 3; modified in Version 4.0.*

■ **FrontEndExecute**

FrontEndExecute[*expr*] sends *expr* to be executed by the *Mathematica* front end.

FrontEndExecute[*expr*] sends *expr* to $FrontEnd via *MathLink* using LinkWrite. ■ The standard *Mathematica* front end can handle only specific notebook manipulation commands such as NotebookApply, NotebookLocate and SelectedNotebook. It uses the versions of these commands in the FrontEnd` context.
■ FrontEndExecute[FrontEndToken["*name*"]] executes named commands in the front end, typically corresponding to menu items. ■ See page 594. ■ See also: LinkWrite, ButtonEvaluator. ■ *New in Version 3.*

■ **FullDefinition**

FullDefinition[*symbol*] prints as the definitions given for *symbol*, and all symbols on which these depend.

FullDefinition has attribute HoldAll. ■ FullDefinition[*symbol*] recursively prints as all definitions for the *symbol*, and for the symbols that appear in these definitions, unless those symbols have the attribute Protected.
■ FullDefinition does not show rules associated with symbols that have attribute ReadProtected. ■ See page 625.
■ See also: Definition, Save, Information. ■ *New in Version 1.*

■ **FullForm**

FullForm[*expr*] prints as the full form of *expr*, with no special syntax.

Example: FullForm[a + b^2] $\longrightarrow$ Plus[a, Power[b, 2]]. ■ FullForm acts as a "wrapper", which affects printing, but not evaluation. ■ FullForm always effectively uses "PrintableASCII" as the setting for $CharacterEncoding.
■ See page 424. ■ See also: InputForm, TreeForm. ■ *New in Version 1; modified in Version 5.0.*

■ **FullGraphics**

FullGraphics[*g*] takes a graphics object, and generates a new one in which objects specified by graphics options are given as explicit lists of graphics primitives.

FullGraphics generates explicit graphics primitives for objects specified by options such as Axes, Ticks, etc. ■ See page 490. ■ See also: AbsoluteOptions. ■ *New in Version 2.*

■ FullSimplify

FullSimplify[*expr*] tries a wide range of transformations on *expr* involving elementary and special functions, and returns the simplest form it finds.

FullSimplify[*expr*, *assum*] does simplification using assumptions.

FullSimplify will always yield at least as simple a form as Simplify, but may take substantially longer. ~■ The following options can be given:

Assumptions	$Assumptions	default assumptions to append to *assum*
ComplexityFunction	Automatic	how to assess the complexity of each form generated
ExcludedForms	{ }	patterns specifying forms of subexpression that should not be touched
TimeConstraint	Infinity	for how many seconds to try doing any particular transformation
TransformationFunctions	Automatic	functions to try in transforming the expression

■ FullSimplify uses RootReduce on expressions that involve Root objects. ■ FullSimplify does transformations on most kinds of special functions. +■ You can specify default assumptions for FullSimplify using Assuming. ■ See notes for Simplify. ■ See pages 68 and 813. ■ Implementation notes: see page 1070. ■ See also: Simplify, Factor, Expand, PowerExpand, ComplexExpand, TrigExpand, Element, FunctionExpand, Assuming. ■ *New in Version 3; modified in Version 5.0.*

■ Function

Function[*body*] or *body*& is a pure function. The formal parameters are # (or #1), #2, etc.

Function[*x*, *body*] is a pure function with a single formal parameter *x*.

Function[{x_1, x_2, ... }, *body*] is a pure function with a list of formal parameters.

Example: (# + 1)&[x] ⟶ 1 + x. ■ Map[(# + 1)&, {x, y, z}] ⟶ {1 + x, 1 + y, 1 + z}. ■ When Function[*body*] or *body*& is applied to a set of arguments, # (or #1) is replaced by the first argument, #2 by the second, and so on. #0 is replaced by the function itself. ■ If there are more arguments supplied than #*i* in the function, the remaining arguments are ignored. ■ ## stands for the sequence of all arguments supplied. ■ ##*n* stands for arguments from number *n* on. ■ f[##, ##2]& [x, y, z] ⟶ f[x, y, z, y, z]. ■ Function is analogous to λ in LISP or formal logic. ■ Function has attribute HoldAll. The function body is evaluated only after the formal parameters have been replaced by arguments. ■ The named formal parameters x_i in Function[{x_1, ... }, *body*] are treated as local, and are renamed $x_i$$ when necessary to avoid confusion with actual arguments supplied to the function. ■ Function is treated as a scoping construct (see Section A.3.8). ■ Function[*params*, *body*, {$attr_1$, $attr_2$, ... }] represents a pure function that is to be treated as having attributes $attr_i$ for the purpose of evaluation. ■ See page 248. ■ See also: Apply, CompiledFunction. ■ *New in Version 1.*

■ FunctionExpand

FunctionExpand[*expr*] tries to expand out special and certain other functions in *expr*, when possible reducing compound arguments to simpler ones.

FunctionExpand[*expr*, *assum*] expands using assumptions.

FunctionExpand uses a large collection of rules. ■ FunctionExpand applies to certain trigonometric functions as well as special functions. ■ FunctionExpand is automatically called by FullSimplify. ■ Assumptions in FunctionExpand can be specified as in Simplify. ■ Example: FunctionExpand[*expr*, *x* ∈ Reals] performs expansion assuming that *x* is real. +■ FunctionExpand has the option Assumptions, specifying default assumptions to be appended to *assum*. +■ The default setting for the Assumptions option is $Assumptions. +■ You can specify default assumptions for FunctionExpand using Assuming. ■ See page 792. ■ Implementation notes: see page 1070. ■ See also: TrigExpand, TrigToExp, ComplexExpand, FullSimplify. ■ *New in Version 3; modified in Version 5.0.*

■ FunctionInterpolation

FunctionInterpolation[*expr*, {*x*, *xmin*, *xmax*}] evaluates *expr* with *x* running from *xmin* to *xmax* and constructs an InterpolatingFunction object which represents an approximate function corresponding to the result.

FunctionInterpolation[*expr*, {*x*, *xmin*, *xmax*}, {*y*, *ymin*, *ymax*}, ...] constructs an InterpolatingFunction object with several arguments.

You can use FunctionInterpolation to generate a single InterpolatingFunction object from an expression containing several such objects. ■ The option InterpolationPrecision specifies the precision of values to be returned by the InterpolatingFunction generated. ■ See notes for Interpolation. ■ See page 935. ■ See also: ListInterpolation, InterpolatingPolynomial, Table. ■ *New in Version 3.*

■ Gamma

Gamma[*z*] is the Euler gamma function $\Gamma(z)$.

Gamma[*a*, *z*] is the incomplete gamma function $\Gamma(a, z)$.

Gamma[*a*, z_0, z_1] is the generalized incomplete gamma function $\Gamma(a, z_0) - \Gamma(a, z_1)$.

Mathematical function (see Section A.3.10). ■ The gamma function satisfies $\Gamma(z) = \int_0^\infty t^{z-1} e^{-t} dt$. ■ The incomplete gamma function satisfies $\Gamma(a, z) = \int_z^\infty t^{a-1} e^{-t} dt$. ■ The generalized incomplete gamma function is given by the integral $\int_{z_0}^{z_1} t^{a-1} e^{-t} dt$. ■ Note that the arguments in the incomplete form of Gamma are arranged differently from those in the incomplete form of Beta. ■ Gamma[*z*] has no branch cut discontinuities. ■ Gamma[*a*, *z*] has a branch cut discontinuity in the complex *z* plane running from $-\infty$ to 0. ■ FullSimplify and FunctionExpand include transformation rules for Gamma. ■ See page 770. ■ Implementation notes: see page 1068. ■ See also: Factorial, LogGamma, GammaRegularized, InverseGammaRegularized, PolyGamma, RiemannSiegelTheta. ■ *New in Version 1.*

■ GammaRegularized

GammaRegularized[*a*, *z*] is the regularized incomplete gamma function $Q(a, z)$.

Mathematical function (see Section A.3.10). ■ In non-singular cases, $Q(a, z) = \Gamma(a, z)/\Gamma(a)$. ■ GammaRegularized[*a*, z_0, z_1] is the generalized regularized incomplete gamma function, defined in non-singular cases as Gamma[*a*, z_0, z_1]/Gamma[*a*]. ■ Note that the arguments in GammaRegularized are arranged differently from those in BetaRegularized. ■ See page 770. ■ See also: InverseGammaRegularized. ■ *New in Version 2.*

■ GaussianIntegers

GaussianIntegers is an option for FactorInteger, PrimeQ, Factor and related functions which specifies whether factorization should be done over Gaussian integers.

With GaussianIntegers -> False, factorization is done over the ordinary ring of integers $\mathbb{Z}$. ■ With GaussianIntegers -> True, factorization is done over the ring of integers with *i* adjoined $\mathbb{Z}[i]$. ■ Example: FactorInteger[13, GaussianIntegers -> True] $\longrightarrow$ {{-i, 1}, {2 + 3 i, 1}, {3 + 2 i, 1}}. ■ The Gaussian primes used when GaussianIntegers -> True are chosen to have both real and imaginary parts positive. ■ The first entry in the list given by FactorInteger with GaussianIntegers -> True may be -1 or -I. ■ See page 751. ■ See also: Extension, ComplexExpand. ■ *New in Version 2.*

■ GCD

GCD[n_1, n_2, ...] gives the greatest common divisor of the integers n_i.

Integer mathematical function (see Section A.3.10). ■ GCD[n_1, ...] gives the integer factors common to all the n_i. ■ GCD also works with rational numbers; GCD[r_1, r_2, ...] gives the greatest rational number r for which all the r_i/r are integers. ■ GCD has attributes Flat and Orderless. ■ See page 749. ■ See also: PolynomialGCD, Rational, LCM, ExtendedGCD. ■ *New in Version 1.*

■ GegenbauerC

GegenbauerC[n, m, x] gives the Gegenbauer polynomial $C_n^{(m)}(x)$.

GegenbauerC[n, x] gives the renormalized form $\lim_{m \to 0} C_n^{(m)}(x)/m$.

Mathematical function (see Section A.3.10). ■ Explicit polynomials are given for integer n and for any m. ■ $C_n^m(x)$ satisfies the differential equation $(1 - x^2)y'' - (2m + 1)xy' + n(n + 2m)y = 0$. ■ The Gegenbauer polynomials are orthogonal on the interval $(-1, 1)$ with weight function $(1 - x^2)^{m-1/2}$, corresponding to integration over a unit hypersphere. ■ GegenbauerC[n, 0, x] is always zero. ■ GegenbauerC[n, m, z] has a branch cut discontinuity in the complex z plane running from $-\infty$ to -1. ■ See page 766. ■ See also: LegendreP, ChebyshevT, ChebyshevU. ■ *New in Version 1.*

■ General

General is a symbol to which general system messages are attached.

When you refer to a message with name s::*tag* in On or Off, the text of the message is obtained from General::*tag* if no specific message named s::*tag* exists. ■ See page 480. ■ *New in Version 1.*

■ GenerateConditions

GenerateConditions is an option for Integrate that specifies whether explicit conditions on parameters should be generated in the results of definite integrals.

~■ The default setting is GenerateConditions->Automatic, which is equivalent to a setting of True for one-dimensional integrals. ■ See page 867. ■ See also: Assumptions. ■ *New in Version 3.*

■ GeneratedCell

GeneratedCell is an option for Cell which indicates whether the cell was generated from the kernel.

Cells created interactively using only operations in the front end have GeneratedCell->False. ■ The setting for GeneratedCell is used to determine which cells should be considered as *Mathematica* output. ■ See page 608. ■ See also: CellAutoOverwrite. ■ *New in Version 3.*

■ GeneratedParameters

GeneratedParameters is an option which specifies how parameters generated to represent the results of various symbolic operations should be named.

The typical default setting is GeneratedParameters->C. ■ The setting GeneratedParameters->f specifies that successive generated parameters should be named f[1], f[2], ... ■ In typical cases, the f[i] are used to parameterize families of solutions to equations. ■ The f[i] usually correspond to free parameters, but are also sometimes used to represent arbitrary functions. ■ The f[i] have indices that start at 1 for each invocation of a particular symbolic operation. ■ GeneratedParameters->(Module[{C}, C]&) guarantees that parameters are unique, even across different invocations of a function. ■ GeneratedParameters is an option to such functions as DSolve, RSolve and Reduce. ■ See page 841. ■ See also: C, Unique, Module. ■ *New in Version 5.0.*

■ Get

<<*name* reads in a file, evaluating each expression in it, and returning the last one.

On systems with graphical interfaces, there will usually be graphical tools for reading in files. ■ If *name* is the name of a *Mathematica* context, ending with a ` context mark character, then Get will process this name to find the file to read. ■ If *name* is the name of a file, any .m extension must be included explicitly. ■ Get can read .mx files of *Mathematica* definitions written by DumpSave. ■ <<"*name*" is equivalent to <<*name*. The double quotes can be omitted if the name is of the form specified on page 1033. ■ If a file with name *file*.mx is found to be a directory, Get will look for a file with a name like *file*.mx/$SystemID/*file*.mx. ■ If the file found by <<*name* is a directory, *Mathematica* will try to load the file init.m in that directory. ■ Get by default successively searches for files in the directories specified by the elements of $Path. ■ Get[*name*, Path->{"*dir*₁", "*dir*₂", ... }] successively searches for files in each of the *dir*ᵢ. ■ Syntax errors in *Mathematica* input files are reported in the standard form: *filename*: *line*: syntax error in *expr*. Get continues attempting to read a file even after a syntax error has been detected. However, if an error is detected, $Context and $ContextPath are reset to the values they had when Get was called. ■ During the execution of Get, the global variable $Input is set to the name of the file being read. ■ Get["*file*", "*key*"] reads a file which has been encoded using Encode["*source*", "*file*", "*key*"]. ■ See page 623. ■ See also: Read, Install, RunThrough, Put, Splice, FileNames, ToFileName, ToExpression, NotebookGet. ■ *New in Version 1; modified in Version 3.*

■ Glaisher

Glaisher is Glaisher's constant with numerical value ≃ 1.28243.

Mathematical constant (see Section A.3.11). ■ Glaisher's constant A satisfies $\log(A) = \frac{1}{12} - \zeta'(-1)$, where ζ is the Riemann zeta function. ■ See page 765. ■ See also: Zeta. ■ *New in Version 4.*

■ GoldenRatio

GoldenRatio is the golden ratio $\phi = (1 + \sqrt{5})/2$, with numerical value ≃ 1.61803.

Mathematical constant (see Section A.3.11). ■ See page 765. ■ See also: Fibonacci. ■ *New in Version 1.*

■ Goto

Goto[*tag*] scans for Label[*tag*], and transfers control to that point.

Goto first scans any compound expression in which it appears directly, then scans compound expressions which enclose this one. ■ See pages 353 and 354. ■ See also: Throw, Switch, Which. ■ *New in Version 1; modified in Version 3.*

■ Graphics

Graphics[*primitives*, *options*] represents a two-dimensional graphical image.

Graphics is displayed using Show. ■ The following graphics primitives can be used:

Circle[{*x*, *y*}, *r*]	circle
Disk[{*x*, *y*}, *r*]	filled disk
Line[{{*x*₁, *y*₁}, ... }]	line
Point[{*x*, *y*}]	point
Polygon[{{*x*₁, *y*₁}, ... }]	filled polygon
PostScript["*string*"]	PostScript code to include verbatim
Raster[*array*]	array of gray levels
RasterArray[*garray*]	array of colored cells
Rectangle[{*xmin*, *ymin*}, {*xmax*, *ymax*}]	filled rectangle
Text[*expr*, {*x*, *y*}]	text

(continued)

■ Graphics *(continued)*

- The sound primitives SampledSoundList and SampledSoundFunction can also be included. ■ The following graphics directives can be used:

AbsoluteDashing[{w_1, ... }]	absolute line dashing specification
AbsolutePointSize[d]	absolute point size specification
AbsoluteThickness[w]	absolute line thickness specification
CMYKColor[c, m, y, k]	color specification
Dashing[{w_1, ... }]	line dashing specification
GrayLevel[i]	intensity specification
Hue[h]	hue specification
PointSize[d]	point size specification
RGBColor[r, g, b]	color specification
Thickness[w]	line thickness specification

- The following options can be given:

AspectRatio	1/GoldenRatio	ratio of height to width
Axes	False	whether to draw axes
AxesLabel	None	axes labels
AxesOrigin	Automatic	where axes should cross
AxesStyle	Automatic	graphics directives to specify the style for axes
Background	Automatic	background color for the plot
ColorOutput	Automatic	type of color output to produce
DefaultColor	Automatic	the default color for plot elements
DisplayFunction	$DisplayFunction	function for generating output
Epilog	{}	graphics primitives to be rendered after the main plot
FormatType	$FormatType	the default format type for text
Frame	False	whether to put a frame around the plot
FrameLabel	None	frame labels
FrameStyle	Automatic	graphics directives giving the style for the frame
FrameTicks	Automatic	frame tick marks
GridLines	None	grid lines to draw
ImageSize	Automatic	the absolute size at which to render the graphic in a notebook
PlotLabel	None	a label for the plot
PlotRange	Automatic	range of values to include
PlotRegion	Automatic	the final display region to be filled
Prolog	{}	graphics primitives to be rendered before the main plot
RotateLabel	True	whether to rotate y labels on the frame
TextStyle	$TextStyle	the default style for text
Ticks	Automatic	tick marks

- Nested lists of graphics primitives can be given. Specifications such as GrayLevel remain in effect only until the end of the list which contains them. ■ Graphics[Graphics3D[...]] generates an ordinary 2D graphics object corresponding to 3D graphics. The same works for SurfaceGraphics, ContourGraphics and DensityGraphics. ■ The standard print form for Graphics[...] is -Graphics-. InputForm prints the explicit list of primitives. ■ See page 487. ■ See also: Plot, ListPlot, ParametricPlot. ■ Related package: Graphics`Graphics`. ■ *New in Version 1.*

■ **Graphics3D**

Graphics3D[*primitives*, *options*] represents a three-dimensional graphical image.

Graphics3D is displayed using Show. ■ The following graphics primitives can be used:

Cuboid[{*xmin*, *ymin*, *zmin*}, ...]	cuboid
Line[{{x_1, y_1, z_1}, ... }]	line
Point[{*x*, *y*, *z*}]	point
Polygon[{{x_1, y_1, z_1}, ... }]	polygon
Text[*expr*, {*x*, *y*, *z*}]	text

■ The sound primitives SampledSoundList and SampledSoundFunction can also be included. ■ The following graphics directives can be used:

AbsoluteDashing[{w_1, ... }]	absolute line dashing specification
AbsolutePointSize[*d*]	absolute point size specification
AbsoluteThickness[*w*]	absolute line thickness specification
CMYKColor[*c*, *m*, *y*, *k*]	color specification
Dashing[{w_1, ... }]	line dashing specification
EdgeForm[*spec*]	polygon edge specification
FaceForm[*spec*]	polygon face specification
GrayLevel[*i*]	gray-level specification
Hue[*h*]	hue specification
PointSize[*d*]	point size specification
RGBColor[*r*, *g*, *b*]	color specification
SurfaceColor[*spec*]	surface properties specification
Thickness[*w*]	line thickness specification

■ The following options can be given:

AmbientLight	GrayLevel[0]	ambient illumination level
AspectRatio	Automatic	ratio of height to width
Axes	False	whether to draw axes
AxesEdge	Automatic	on which edges to put axes
AxesLabel	None	axes labels
AxesStyle	Automatic	graphics directives to specify the style for axes
Background	Automatic	background color for the plot
Boxed	True	whether to draw the bounding box
BoxRatios	Automatic	bounding 3D box ratios
BoxStyle	Automatic	graphics directives to specify the style for the box
ColorOutput	Automatic	type of color output to produce
DefaultColor	Automatic	the default color for plot elements
DisplayFunction	$DisplayFunction	function for generating output
Epilog	{}	2D graphics primitives to be rendered after the main plot
FaceGrids	None	grid lines to draw on the bounding box
FormatType	$FormatType	the default format type for text
ImageSize	Automatic	the absolute size at which to render the graphic in a notebook
Lighting	True	whether to use simulated illumination
LightSources	(see below)	positions and colors of light sources
PlotLabel	None	a label for the plot
PlotRange	Automatic	range of values to include
PlotRegion	Automatic	the final display region to be filled
PolygonIntersections	True	whether to leave intersecting polygons unchanged
Prolog	{}	2D graphics primitives to be rendered before the main plot

(continued)

■ Graphics3D *(continued)*

RenderAll	True	whether to render all polygons
Shading	True	whether to shade polygons
SphericalRegion	False	whether to make the circumscribing sphere fit in final display area
TextStyle	$TextStyle	the default style for text
Ticks	Automatic	tick marks
ViewCenter	Automatic	point to put at the center of final display area
ViewPoint	{1.3, -2.4, 2.}	viewing position
ViewVertical	{0, 0, 1}	direction to make vertical

■ Nested lists of graphics primitives can be given. Specifications such as GrayLevel remain in effect only until the end of the list which contains them. ■ The standard print form for Graphics3D[...] is -Graphics3D-. InputForm prints the explicit list of primitives. ■ The default light sources used are {{{1,0,1}, RGBColor[1,0,0]}, {{1,1,1}, RGBColor[0,1,0]}, {{0,1,1}, RGBColor[0,0,1]}}. ■ Graphics3D[SurfaceGraphics[...]] can be used to convert a SurfaceGraphics object into Graphics3D representation. ■ Graphics[SurfaceGraphics[...]] generates a representation in terms of ordinary 2D graphics primitives. ■ See page 487. ■ See also: Plot3D, SurfaceGraphics, ParametricPlot3D. ■ Related packages: Graphics`Graphics3D`, Graphics`Shapes`, Graphics`Polyhedra`. ■ *New in Version 1.*

■ GraphicsArray

GraphicsArray[{g_1, g_2, ... }] represents a row of graphics objects.

GraphicsArray[{{g_{11}, g_{12}, ... }, ... }] represents a two-dimensional array of graphics objects.

You can display a GraphicsArray object using Show. ■ GraphicsArray sets up identical rectangular display areas for each of the graphics objects it contains. ■ GraphicsArray takes the same options as Graphics, with the defaults for Ticks and FrameTicks changed to None. ■ GraphicsArray takes the additional option GraphicsSpacing, which specifies the spacing between the rectangular areas containing each graphics object. The default setting is GraphicsSpacing -> 0.1. ■ The options DisplayFunction, ColorOutput and CharacterEncoding are ignored for graphics objects given inside GraphicsArray. ■ See pages 139 and 487. ■ See also: Rectangle, RasterArray, TableForm, GridBox. ■ *New in Version 2.*

■ GraphicsSpacing

GraphicsSpacing is an option for GraphicsArray which specifies the spacing between elements in the array.

GraphicsSpacing -> 0 inserts no horizontal or vertical spacing, so that all adjacent rectangular areas in the array are shown abutting. ■ GraphicsSpacing -> {h, v} specifies horizontal and vertical spacing to use. ■ GraphicsSpacing -> s is equivalent to GraphicsSpacing -> {s, s}. ■ The spacing is given in scaled coordinates, relative to each rectangular area in the array. ■ Example: a horizontal spacing of 0.1 yields an array in which the rectangular areas are separated horizontally by distances equal to 0.1 of their widths. ■ See page 141. ■ See also: TableSpacing. ■ *New in Version 2.*

■ GrayLevel

GrayLevel[*level*] is a graphics directive which specifies the gray-level intensity with which graphical objects that follow should be displayed.

The gray level must be a number between 0 and 1. ■ 0 represents black; 1 represents white. ■ On display devices with no native gray-level capability, dither patterns are typically used, as generated by the PostScript interpreter. ■ See page 499. ■ See also: RGBColor, Hue, Raster. ■ *New in Version 1.*

■ Greater

$x > y$ yields True if x is determined to be greater than y.

$x_1 > x_2 > x_3$ yields True if the x_i form a strictly decreasing sequence.

Greater gives True or False when its arguments are real numbers. ■ Greater does some simplification when its arguments are not numbers. ■ For exact numeric quantities, Greater internally uses numerical approximations to establish numerical ordering. This process can be affected by the setting of the global variable $MaxExtraPrecision. ■ See page 86. ■ See also: GreaterEqual, Less, Positive, Element. ■ *New in Version 1; modified in Version 3.*

■ GreaterEqual

$x >= y$ or $x \geq y$ yields True if x is determined to be greater than or equal to y.

$x_1 \geq x_2 \geq x_3$ yields True if the x_i form a non-increasing sequence.

$x \geq y$ can be entered as x :>=: y or x \[GreaterEqual] y. ■ GreaterEqual gives True or False when its arguments are real numbers. ■ GreaterEqual does some simplification when its arguments are not numbers. ■ For exact numeric quantities, GreaterEqual internally uses numerical approximations to establish numerical ordering. This process can be affected by the setting of the global variable $MaxExtraPrecision. ■ In StandardForm, GreaterEqual is printed using ≥. ■ $x \geqslant y$, entered as x :>/: y or x \[GreaterSlantEqual] y, can be used on input as an alternative to $x \geq y$. ■ See page 86. ■ See also: Greater, LessEqual, Element. ■ *New in Version 1; modified in Version 3.*

■ GridBaseline

GridBaseline is an option for GridBox which specifies where the baseline of the grid represented by the GridBox should be assumed to be.

GridBaseline determines how a GridBox will be positioned vertically with respect to other boxes, say in a RowBox. ■ GridBaseline->*pos* specifies that position *pos* in the GridBox should be assumed to be the baseline of the GridBox and should therefore be aligned with baselines of other boxes. ■ Possible settings are:

Axis	axis of the middle row in the grid (default)
Baseline	baseline of the middle row in the grid
Bottom	bottom of the whole grid
Center	halfway from top to bottom
Top	top of the whole grid

+■ A setting of {*pos*, {*i*, *j*}} specifies that the position *pos* in the *i*, *j* element of the GridBox should be assumed to be the baseline for the whole GridBox. ■ See page 449. ■ See also: RowAlignments, AdjustmentBox, CellBaseline. ■ *New in Version 3; modified in Version 5.0.*

■ GridBox

GridBox[{{*box*$_{11}$, *box*$_{12}$, ... }, {*box*$_{21}$, *box*$_{22}$, ... }, ... }] represents a two-dimensional grid of boxes or strings in input and output.

In a notebook, columns of a GridBox can be added using `CTRL`,] and rows using `CTRL`↵] (CONTROL-RETURN). ■ `CTRL`,] or a menu item can be used to start building a GridBox. ■ You can use tab to move from one entry in a GridBox to the next. `CTRL`␣] moves out of the whole GridBox. ■ In StandardForm and InputForm, GridBox[*list*] is interpreted as *list*. ■ You can place parentheses around a GridBox to make it look more like a matrix, but these are by default ignored when the GridBox is interpreted.

(continued)

■ GridBox *(continued)*

- The following options can be given:

ColumnAlignments	Center	how to align columns
ColumnLines	False	whether to draw lines between columns
ColumnsEqual	False	whether to make all columns equal width
ColumnSpacings	0.8	spacings between columns in ems
ColumnWidths	Automatic	actual widths of columns in ems
GridBaseline	Axis	the position of the baseline for the whole grid
GridDefaultElement	"\[Placeholder]"	what to insert when a new entry is created
RowAlignments	Baseline	how to align rows
RowLines	False	whether to draw lines between rows
RowMinHeight	1.0	the minimum total row height in x-heights
RowsEqual	False	whether to make all rows equal total height
RowSpacings	1.0	spacings between rows in x-heights

GridBox is a low-level construct that works only for two-dimensional arrays; TableForm and MatrixForm are higher-level constructs that can also be used for higher-dimensional arrays. ■ In StandardForm, explicit GridBox objects are output literally. You can use DisplayForm to see the display form of such objects. ■ See page 445. ■ See also: TableForm, MatrixForm, RowBox, OverscriptBox, UnderscriptBox, AdjustmentBox. ■ *New in Version 3.*

■ GridDefaultElement

GridDefaultElement is an option for GridBox which specifies what to insert when a new element is created interactively in a GridBox.

The default setting for GridDefaultElement is "\[Placeholder]" or "□". ■ When creating palettes, GridDefaultElement is typically set to ButtonBox["□"]. ■ The setting for GridDefaultElement is used to determine the contents of new columns or rows created with CTRL , or CTRL ↵ (CONTROL-RETURN). ■ See page 449. ■ *New in Version 3.*

■ GridLines

GridLines is an option for two-dimensional graphics functions that specifies grid lines.

The following settings can be given for GridLines:

None	no grid lines drawn
Automatic	grid lines placed automatically
{*xgrid*, *ygrid*}	grid lines specified separately in each direction

- With the Automatic setting, grid lines are usually placed at points whose coordinates have the minimum number of digits in their decimal representation. ■ For each direction, the following grid line options can be given:

None	no grid lines drawn
Automatic	grid line positions chosen automatically
{x_1, x_2, ... }	grid lines drawn at the specified positions
{{x_1, $style_1$}, ... }	grid lines with specified styles
func	a function to be applied to *xmin*, *xmax* to get the grid line option

- Grid line styles can involve graphics directives such as RGBColor and Thickness. ■ Grid lines are by default colored light blue. ■ The grid line function *func*[*xmin*, *xmax*] may return any other grid line option.
- AbsoluteOptions gives the explicit form of GridLines specifications when Automatic settings are used. ■ See pages 511 and 515. ■ See also: Ticks, FrameTicks, FaceGrids, ColumnLines, RowLines. ■ *New in Version 2.*

■ GroebnerBasis

GroebnerBasis[{$poly_1$, $poly_2$, ... }, {x_1, x_2, ... }] gives a list of polynomials that form a Gröbner basis for the set of polynomials $poly_i$.

GroebnerBasis[{$poly_1$, $poly_2$, ... }, {x_1, x_2, ... }, {y_1, y_2, ... }] finds a Gröbner basis in which the y_i have been eliminated.

The set of polynomials in a Gröbner basis have the same collection of roots as the original polynomials. ▪ For polynomials in one variable, GroebnerBasis reduces to PolynomialGCD. ▪ For linear functions in any number of variables, GroebnerBasis is equivalent to Gaussian elimination. ▪ The Gröbner basis in general depends on the ordering assigned to monomials. This ordering is affected by the ordering of the x_i. ▪ The following options can be given:

MonomialOrder	Lexicographic	the criterion used for ordering monomials
CoefficientDomain	Automatic	the type of objects assumed to be coefficients
Modulus	0	the modulus for numerical coefficients

▪ Possible settings for MonomialOrder are Lexicographic, DegreeLexicographic, DegreeReverseLexicographic or an explicit weight matrix. Monomials are specified for the purpose of MonomialOrder by lists of the exponents with which the x_i appear in them. ▪ The ordering of the x_i and the setting for MonomialOrder can substantially affect the efficiency of GroebnerBasis. ▪ Possible settings for CoefficientDomain are InexactNumbers, Rationals, RationalFunctions and Polynomials[x]. ▪ See page 803. ▪ Implementation notes: see page 1070. ▪ See also: PolynomialReduce, PolynomialGCD, Reduce, Solve, RowReduce, Eliminate, FindInstance, CylindricalDecomposition. ▪ *New in Version 2; modified in Version 3.*

■ GroupPageBreakWithin

GroupPageBreakWithin is an option for Cell which specifies whether a page break should be allowed within the group of cells if the notebook that contains the group is printed.

See page 609. ▪ See also: PageBreakWithin, ShowPageBreaks. ▪ *New in Version 3.*

■ HarmonicNumber

HarmonicNumber[n] gives the nth harmonic number H_n.

HarmonicNumber[n, r] gives the harmonic number $H_n^{(r)}$ of order r.

Mathematical function (see Section A.3.10). ▪ The harmonic numbers are given by $H_n^{(r)} = \sum_{i=1}^{n} 1/i^r$ with $H_n = H_n^{(1)}$. ▪ See page 757. ▪ See also: EulerGamma, PolyGamma, Zeta, Log. ▪ *New in Version 4.*

■ Head

Head[$expr$] gives the head of $expr$.

Examples: Head[f[x]] $\longrightarrow$ f; Head[a + b] $\longrightarrow$ Plus; Head[4] $\longrightarrow$ Integer; Head[x] $\longrightarrow$ Symbol. ▪ See page 231. ▪ *New in Version 1.*

■ Heads

Heads is an option for functions which use level specifications that specifies whether heads of expressions should be included.

Heads -> True treats heads just like other elements of expressions for the purpose of levels. ■ Heads -> False never includes heads as part of any level of an expression. ■ Most functions which use level specifications have the default setting Heads -> False. One exception is Position, for which the default is Heads -> True. ■ See page 238. ■ See also: Level. ■ *New in Version 2.*

■ HermiteH

HermiteH[*n*, *x*] gives the Hermite polynomial $H_n(x)$.

Mathematical function (see Section A.3.10). ■ Explicit polynomials are given for non-negative integers *n*. ■ The Hermite polynomials satisfy the differential equation $y'' - 2xy' + 2ny = 0$. ■ They are orthogonal polynomials with weight function e^{-x^2} in the interval $(-\infty, \infty)$. ■ HermiteH[*n*, *x*] is an entire function of *x* with no branch cut discontinuities. ■ See page 766. ■ See also: LaguerreL. ■ *New in Version 1.*

■ HiddenSurface

HiddenSurface is an option for **SurfaceGraphics** which specifies whether hidden surfaces are to be eliminated.

HiddenSurface -> True eliminates hidden surfaces. ■ See page 151. ■ See also: Shading. ■ *New in Version 1.*

■ Hold

Hold[*expr*] maintains *expr* in an unevaluated form.

Hold has attribute HoldAll, and performs no operation on its arguments. ■ Example: Hold[1+1] ⟶ Hold[1 + 1]. ■ Hold is removed by ReleaseHold. ■ Hold[e_1, e_2, ...] maintains a sequence of unevaluated expressions to which a function can be applied using Apply. ■ Even though *expr* itself is not evaluated, Hold[*expr*] may still evaluate if *expr* is of the form *f*[*args*], and upvalues for *f* have been defined. ■ See page 338. ■ See also: HoldPattern, HoldForm, HoldComplete, Unevaluated, HoldAll, Symbol. ■ *New in Version 1.*

■ HoldAll

HoldAll is an attribute which specifies that all arguments to a function are to be maintained in an unevaluated form.

You can use Evaluate to evaluate the arguments of a HoldAll function in a controlled way. ■ Even when a function has attribute HoldAll, Sequence objects that appear in its arguments are still by default flattened, Unevaluated wrappers are stripped, and upvalues associated with the arguments are used. ■ See pages 329 and 336. ■ See also: Unevaluated, Hold, NHoldAll, HoldAllComplete, SequenceHold, Extract. ■ *New in Version 1.*

■ HoldAllComplete

HoldAllComplete is an attribute which specifies that all arguments to a function are not to be modified or looked at in any way in the process of evaluation.

By setting the attribute HoldAllComplete you can effectively shield the arguments of a function from all aspects of the standard *Mathematica* evaluation process. ■ HoldAllComplete not only prevents arguments from being evaluated, but also prevents Sequence objects from being flattened, Unevaluated wrappers from being stripped, and upvalues associated with arguments from being used. ■ Evaluate cannot be used to override HoldAllComplete. ■ See pages 329 and 340. ■ See also: HoldComplete, HoldAll, SequenceHold, Extract. ■ *New in Version 3.*

■ HoldComplete

HoldComplete[*expr*] shields *expr* completely from the standard *Mathematica* evaluation process, preventing even upvalues associated with *expr* from being used.

HoldComplete has attribute HoldAllComplete, and performs no operations on its arguments. ■ HoldComplete is removed by ReleaseHold. ■ HoldComplete can be inserted as a wrapper by such functions as ToExpression and ReplacePart. ■ HoldComplete is generated by default by MakeExpression. ■ See pages 339 and 1048. ■ See also: Hold, HoldPattern, HoldForm, Unevaluated, HoldAllComplete, Symbol. ■ *New in Version 3.*

■ HoldFirst

HoldFirst is an attribute which specifies that the first argument to a function is to be maintained in an unevaluated form.

See pages 329 and 336. ■ *New in Version 1.*

■ HoldForm

HoldForm[*expr*] prints as the expression *expr*, with *expr* maintained in an unevaluated form.

HoldForm allows you to see the output form of an expression without evaluating the expression. ■ HoldForm has attribute HoldAll. ■ HoldForm is removed by ReleaseHold. ■ See pages 338 and 434. ■ See also: ToString, WriteString. ■ *New in Version 1.*

■ HoldPattern

HoldPattern[*expr*] is equivalent to *expr* for pattern matching, but maintains *expr* in an unevaluated form.

HoldPattern has attribute HoldAll. ■ The left-hand sides of rules are usually evaluated, as are parts of the left-hand sides of assignments. You can use HoldPattern to stop any part from being evaluated. ■ Example: *expr* /. HoldPattern[Integrate[y_, x_]] -> *rhs* transforms any subexpression of the form Integrate[y_, x_] in *expr*. Without the HoldPattern, the Integrate[y_, x_] in the rule would immediately be evaluated to give x_ y_, and the replacement would not work. ■ Example: f[HoldPattern[Integrate[y_, x_]]] := *value* can be used to make an assignment for expressions of the form f[Integrate[y_, x_]]. Without HoldPattern, the Integrate function would be evaluated at the time of assignment. ■ See page 340. ■ See also: Hold, Verbatim. ■ *New in Version 3.*

■ HoldRest

HoldRest is an attribute which specifies that all but the first argument to a function are to be maintained in an unevaluated form.

See pages 329 and 336. ■ *New in Version 1.*

■ HTMLSave

HTMLSave["*file*.html"] saves an HTML version of the currently selected notebook in the front end.

HTMLSave["*file*.html", "*source*.nb"] saves an HTML version of the notebook from the file *source*.nb.

HTMLSave["*file*.html", *notebook*] saves an HTML version of the notebook corresponding to the specified notebook object.

HTMLSave has options for specifying such features as how to include formulas, whether to make links for closed cell groups, and what correspondence to set up between notebook styles and HTML tags. ■ HTMLSave normally saves graphics in separate image files. +■ HTMLSave generates CSS style sheets to mimic notebook styles. ■ HTMLSave can often be accessed from an item in the Save As Special menu in the notebook front end. +■ The output from HTMLSave is compliant with XHTML 1.0. ■ See page 211. ■ See also: Export, MathMLForm, TeXSave, Display. ■ *New in Version 3; modified in Version 5.0.*

■ Hue

Hue[*h*] is a graphics directive which specifies that graphical objects which follow are to be displayed, if possible, in a color corresponding to hue *h*.

Hue[*h*, *s*, *b*] specifies colors in terms of hue, saturation and brightness.

The parameters *h*, *s* and *b* must all be between 0 and 1. Values of *s* and *b* outside this range are clipped. Values of *h* outside this range are treated cyclically. ■ As *h* varies from 0 to 1, the color corresponding to Hue[*h*] runs through red, yellow, green, cyan, blue, magenta, and back to red again. ■ Hue[*h*] is equivalent to Hue[*h*, 1, 1]. ■ On monochrome displays, a gray level based on the brightness value is used. ■ See page 499. ■ See also: RGBColor, GrayLevel, CMYKColor. ■ Related package: Graphics`Colors`. ■ *New in Version 2.*

■ Hypergeometric0F1

Hypergeometric0F1[*a*, *z*] is the confluent hypergeometric function $_0F_1(;a;z)$.

Mathematical function (see Section A.3.10). ■ The $_0F_1$ function has the series expansion $_0F_1(;a;z) = \sum_{k=0}^{\infty} 1/(a)_k \, z^k/k!$. ■ See page 778. ■ See also: Pochhammer, Hypergeometric1F1, HypergeometricPFQ, Hypergeometric0F1Regularized. ■ *New in Version 1.*

■ Hypergeometric0F1Regularized

Hypergeometric0F1Regularized[*a*, *z*] is the regularized confluent hypergeometric function $_0F_1(a;z)/\Gamma(a)$.

Mathematical function (see Section A.3.10). ■ Hypergeometric0F1Regularized[*a*, *z*] is finite for all finite values of *a* and *z*. ■ See notes for Hypergeometric0F1. ■ See page 778. ■ *New in Version 3.*

■ Hypergeometric1F1

Hypergeometric1F1[*a*, *b*, *z*] is the Kummer confluent hypergeometric function $_1F_1(a;b;z)$.

Mathematical function (see Section A.3.10). ■ The $_1F_1$ function has the series expansion $_1F_1(a;b;z) = \sum_{k=0}^{\infty} (a)_k/(b)_k \, z^k/k!$. ■ See page 778. ■ See also: HypergeometricU, Hypergeometric2F1, HypergeometricPFQ, Hypergeometric1F1Regularized. ■ *New in Version 1.*

■ Hypergeometric1F1Regularized

Hypergeometric1F1Regularized[*a*, *b*, *z*] is the regularized confluent hypergeometric function $_1F_1(a; b; z)/\Gamma(b)$.

Mathematical function (see Section A.3.10). ■ Hypergeometric1F1Regularized[*a*, *b*, *z*] is finite for all finite values of *a*, *b* and *z*. ■ See notes for Hypergeometric1F1. ■ See page 779. ■ *New in Version 3.*

■ Hypergeometric2F1

Hypergeometric2F1[*a*, *b*, *c*, *z*] is the hypergeometric function $_2F_1(a, b; c; z)$.

Mathematical function (see Section A.3.10). ■ The $_2F_1$ function has the series expansion $_2F_1(a, b; c; z) = \sum_{k=0}^{\infty} (a)_k (b)_k/(c)_k \; z^k/k!$. ■ Hypergeometric2F1[*a*, *b*, *c*, *z*] has a branch cut discontinuity in the complex *z* plane running from 1 to ∞. ■ FullSimplify and FunctionExpand include transformation rules for Hypergeometric2F1. ■ See page 780. ■ See also: AppellF1, Hypergeometric1F1, HypergeometricPFQ, Hypergeometric2F1Regularized. ■ *New in Version 1.*

■ Hypergeometric2F1Regularized

Hypergeometric2F1Regularized[*a*, *b*, *c*, *z*] is the regularized hypergeometric function $_2F_1(a, b; c; z)/\Gamma(c)$.

Mathematical function (see Section A.3.10). ■ Hypergeometric2F1Regularized[*a*, *b*, *c*, *z*] is finite for all finite values of *a*, *b*, *c* and *z* so long as |*z*| < 1. ■ See notes for Hypergeometric2F1. ■ See page 780. ■ *New in Version 3.*

■ HypergeometricPFQ

HypergeometricPFQ[{a_1, ... , a_p}, {b_1, ... , b_q}, *z*] is the generalized hypergeometric function $_pF_q(\mathbf{a}; \mathbf{b}; z)$.

Mathematical function (see Section A.3.10). ■ $_pF_q(\mathbf{a}; \mathbf{b}; z)$ has series expansion $\sum_{k=0}^{\infty} (a_1)_k ... (a_p)_k/(b_1)_k ... (b_q)_k \; z^k/k!$. ■ Hypergeometric0F1, Hypergeometric1F1, and Hypergeometric2F1 are special cases of HypergeometricPFQ. ■ In many special cases, HypergeometricPFQ is automatically converted to other functions. ■ For *p* = *q* + 1, HypergeometricPFQ[*alist*, *blist*, *z*] has a branch cut discontinuity in the complex *z* plane running from 1 to ∞. ■ FullSimplify and FunctionExpand include transformation rules for HypergeometricPFQ. ■ See page 780. ■ See also: MeijerG, Hypergeometric0F1, Hypergeometric1F1, Hypergeometric2F1, AppellF1, HypergeometricPFQRegularized. ■ *New in Version 3.*

■ HypergeometricPFQRegularized

HypergeometricPFQRegularized[{a_1, ... , a_p}, {b_1, ... , b_q}, *z*] is the regularized generalized hypergeometric function $_pF_q(\mathbf{a}; \mathbf{b}; z)/(\Gamma(b_1)...\Gamma(b_q))$.

Mathematical function (see Section A.3.10). ■ HypergeometricPFQRegularized is finite for all finite values of its arguments so long as *p* ≤ *q*. ■ See notes for HypergeometricPFQ. ■ See page 780. ■ *New in Version 3.*

■ HypergeometricU

HypergeometricU[*a*, *b*, *z*] is the confluent hypergeometric function $U(a, b, z)$.

Mathematical function (see Section A.3.10). ■ The function $U(a, b, z)$ has the integral representation $U(a, b, z) = 1/\Gamma(a) \int_0^{\infty} e^{-zt} t^{a-1} (1 + t)^{b-a-1} \, dt$. ■ HypergeometricU[*a*, *b*, *z*] has a branch cut discontinuity in the complex *z* plane running from −∞ to 0. ■ See page 778. ■ See also: Hypergeometric1F1, Hypergeometric0F1. ■ *New in Version 1.*

■ Hyphenation

Hyphenation is an option for Cell which specifies whether to allow hyphenation for words of text.

The choice of hyphenation points is based when possible on dictionaries and algorithms for the language in which the text is specified to be written. ■ See page 609. ■ See also: TextJustification, LanguageCategory. ■ *New in Version 4.*

■ I

I represents the imaginary unit $\sqrt{-1}$.

Numbers containing I are converted to the type Complex. ■ I can be entered in StandardForm and InputForm as i, ⁞ii⁞ or \[ImaginaryI]. ■ j, ⁞jj⁞ and \[ImaginaryJ] can also be used. ■ In StandardForm and TraditionalForm, I is output as i. ■ See page 765. ■ See also: Re, Im, ComplexExpand, GaussianIntegers. ■ *New in Version 1; modified in Version 3.*

■ Identity

Identity[*expr*] gives *expr* (the identity operation).

See page 253. ■ See also: Composition, Through, InverseFunction, Sequence, Hold. ■ *New in Version 1.*

■ IdentityMatrix

IdentityMatrix[*n*] gives the $n \times n$ identity matrix.

See page 896. ■ See also: DiagonalMatrix, KroneckerDelta, Table. ■ Related package: LinearAlgebra`MatrixManipulation`. ■ *New in Version 1.*

■ If

If[*condition*, *t*, *f*] gives *t* if *condition* evaluates to True, and *f* if it evaluates to False.

If[*condition*, *t*, *f*, *u*] gives *u* if *condition* evaluates to neither True nor False.

If evaluates only the argument determined by the value of the condition. ■ If[*condition*, *t*, *f*] is left unevaluated if *condition* evaluates to neither True nor False. ■ If[*condition*, *t*] gives Null if *condition* evaluates to False. ■ See page 345. ■ See also: Switch, Which, Condition, DiracDelta. ■ *New in Version 1.*

■ IgnoreCase

IgnoreCase is an option for string manipulation and searching functions which specifies whether lower- and upper-case letters should be treated as equivalent.

With the default setting IgnoreCase -> False, lower- and upper-case letters are treated as totally different. ■ With the setting IgnoreCase -> True, lower- and upper-case letters are treated as equivalent. ■ IgnoreCase is an option for StringPosition, StringReplace, StringMatchQ, Find and FindList. ■ IgnoreCase in no way affects the parsing of *Mathematica* expressions. ■ See page 410. ■ See also: ToUpperCase, ToLowerCase, SpellingCorrection. ■ *New in Version 2.*

■ Im

Im[*z*] gives the imaginary part of the complex number *z*.

Im[*expr*] is left unevaluated if *expr* is not a numeric quantity. ■ See page 746. ■ See also: Re, Abs, Arg, ComplexExpand. ■ *New in Version 1.*

ImageMargins

ImageMargins is an option for Cell which specifies the absolute margins in printer's points to leave around graphics in a cell.

Possible settings are:

dist	the same margins on all sides
{{*left*, *right*}, {*bottom*, *top*}}	different margins on different sides

■ ImageMargins represent space to be left inside whatever CellMargins are specified for a particular cell. ■ See page 616. ■ See also: ImageSize, CellMargins. ■ *New in Version 3.*

ImageResolution

ImageResolution is an option for Export and Display which specifies at what resolution bitmap images should be rendered.

ImageResolution->*r* specifies that a bitmap should be rendered at a resolution of *r* dpi. ■ ImageResolution is relevant only for bitmap graphics formats such as "TIFF", and not for resolution-independent formats such as "EPS". ■ The default setting ImageResolution->Automatic typically uses a resolution of 72 dpi for bitmap graphics formats. ■ See page 569. ■ See also: ImageSize. ■ *New in Version 3.*

ImageRotated

ImageRotated is an option for Export and Display which specifies whether images should be rotated into landscape mode.

The default setting for ImageRotated is False. ■ See page 569. ■ See also: ImageSize, RotateLabel. ■ *New in Version 3.*

ImageSize

ImageSize is an option for Export, Display and other graphics functions, as well as for Cell, which specifies the absolute size of an image to render.

ImageSize->*x* specifies that the image should have a width of *x* printer's points. ■ ImageSize->72 *xi* specifies that the image should have a width of *xi* inches. ■ ImageSize->{*x*, *y*} specifies that the image should be rendered within a region *x* printer's points wide by *y* printer's points high. ■ The image will fill the region only if its aspect ratio is exactly *y*/*x*. ■ In Display and other graphics functions, the default setting for ImageSize is Automatic. This specifies that when output is sent to the front end, the front end should determine the size of the image. When output is sent elsewhere, the effective default is 288, corresponding to 4 inches. ■ In the front end, the typical default setting for ImageSize is also 288, corresponding to 4 inches. ■ See page 616. ■ See also: ImageResolution, ImageMargins, AspectRatioFixed. ■ *New in Version 3.*

Implies

Implies[*p*, *q*] represents the logical implication $p \Rightarrow q$.

Implies[*p*, *q*] is equivalent to !*p* || *q*. ■ Implies[*p*, *q*] can be input in StandardForm and InputForm as $p \Rightarrow q$. The character $\Rightarrow$ can be entered as :=>: or \[Implies]. ■ See page 834. ■ See also: LogicalExpand, If. ■ *New in Version 1; modified in Version 3.*

~■ Import

Import["*file*.*ext*"] imports data from a file, assuming that it is in the format indicated by the file extension *ext*, and converts it to a *Mathematica* expression.

Import["*file*", "*format*"] imports data in the specified format from a file.

Import attempts to give a *Mathematica* expression whose meaning is as close as possible to the data in the external file. ■ Import can handle numerical and textual data, graphics, sounds, material from notebooks, and general expressions in various formats. ~■ The following basic formats are supported for textual and tabular data:

"CSV"	comma-separated value tabular data (.csv)
"Lines"	lines of text
"List"	lines consisting of numbers or strings
"Table"	two-dimensional array of numbers or strings
"Text"	string of ordinary characters
"TSV"	tab-separated value tabular data (.tsv)
"UnicodeText"	string of 16-bit Unicode characters
"Words"	words separated by spaces or newlines

■ "Text" and "UnicodeText" return single *Mathematica* strings. ■ "Lines" and "Words" return lists of *Mathematica* strings. ■ "List" returns a list of *Mathematica* numbers or strings. ~■ "Table", "CSV" and "TSV" return a list of lists of *Mathematica* numbers or strings. ~■ In "List", "Table", "CSV" and "TSV" formats, numbers can be read in C or Fortran-like "E" notation. ■ Numbers without explicit decimal points are returned as exact integers. ■ In "Table" format, columns can be separated by spaces or tabs. ■ In "Words" format, words can be separated by any form of white space. ~■ In "CSV" format, columns are taken to be separated by commas, unless other settings are specified using ConversionOptions. ■ Import["*file*.txt"] uses "Text" format. ■ Import["*file*.dat"] uses "Table" format. ■ Import["*file*.csv"] uses "CSV" format. ~■ The following additional formats are also supported for numerical data:

"FITS"	FITS astronomical data format (.fit, .fits)
"HarwellBoeing"	Harwell-Boeing matrix format
"HDF"	Hierarchical Data Format (.hdf)
"MAT"	MAT matrix format (.mat)
"MTX"	Matrix Market format (.mtx)
"SDTS"	SDTS spatial GIS data format (.ddf)

+■ When appropriate, numerical data is imported as SparseArray objects. +■ The following format yields a list of expressions suitable for input to NMinimize:

"MPS"	MPS Mathematical Programming System format (.mps)

■ Two-dimensional graphics formats are imported as Graphics objects; sound formats are imported as Sound objects. ■ Animated graphics are imported as lists of Graphics objects. ■ The following formats yield expressions of the form Graphics[*data*, *opts*]:

"EPS"	Encapsulated PostScript (.eps)
"EPSI"	Encapsulated PostScript with image preview (.epsi)
"EPSTIFF"	Encapsulated PostScript with TIFF preview
"MPS"	*Mathematica* abbreviated PostScript (.mps)

~■ The following formats yield expressions of the form Graphics[Raster[*data*], *opts*]:

"BMP"	Microsoft bitmap format (.bmp)
"DICOM"	DICOM medical imaging format (.dcm, .dic)
"GIF"	GIF and animated GIF (.gif)
"JPEG"	JPEG (.jpg, .jpeg)
"MGF"	*Mathematica* system-independent raster graphics format (.mgf)
"PBM"	portable bitmap format (.pbm)
"PGM"	portable graymap format (.pgm)

(continued)

~■ **Import** *(continued)*

"PNG"	PNG format (.png)
"PNM"	portable anymap format (.pnm)
"PPM"	portable pixmap format (.ppm)
"TIFF"	TIFF (.tif, .tiff)
"XBitmap"	X window system bitmap (.xbm)

■ Imported raster data normally consists of integers; ColorFunction is often used to specify a color map. ■ The following formats return objects of the form Graphics3D[*data*, *opts*]:

"DXF"	AutoCAD drawing interchange format (.dxf)
"STL"	STL stereolithography format (.stl)

■ The following formats yield expressions of the form Sound[SampledSoundList[*data*, *r*]]:

"AIFF"	AIFF format (.aif, .aiff)
"AU"	μ law encoding (.au)
"SND"	sound file format (.snd)
"WAV"	Microsoft wave format (.wav)

+■ The following gives a notebook expression Notebook[...] from a *Mathematica* notebook file:

"NB"	*Mathematica* notebook format (.nb)

~■ The following XML formats give various types of expressions:

"ExpressionML"	arbitrary expression
"MathML"	mathematical expression or boxes (.mml)
"NotebookML"	notebook expression (.nbml)
"SymbolicXML"	SymbolicXML expression
"XML"	determined by content (.xml)

~■ With format "MathML", MathML presentation elements are if possible imported as mathematical expressions using TraditionalForm interpretation rules. Otherwise, they are imported as box expressions. ~■ With format "SymbolicXML", XML data of any document type is imported as a SymbolicXML expression. ~■ With format "XML", Import will recognize MathML, NotebookML, and ExpressionML and interpret them accordingly. Other XML will be imported as SymbolicXML. +■ The following formats can be used for general expressions:

"Dump"	internal binary format (.mx)
"Expression"	InputForm textual format (.m)
"ExpressionML"	XML-based ExpressionML format

■ The following general options can be given:

ByteOrdering	$ByteOrdering	what byte order to use for binary data
CharacterEncoding	Automatic	the encoding to use for characters in text
ConversionOptions	{}	private options for specific formats
Path	$Path	the path to search for files

■ Possible formats accepted by Import are given in the list $ImportFormats. ■ Import["!*prog*", "*format*"] imports data from a pipe. ■ See pages 207, 570 and 642. ■ See also: Export, ImportString, $ImportFormats, ReadList. ■ *New in Version 4; modified in Version 5.0.*

~■ **ImportString**

ImportString["*data*", "*format*"] imports data in the specified format from a string.

See notes for Import. ■ See page 570. ■ See also: ExportString. ■ *New in Version 4; modified in Version 5.0.*

■ In

In[*n*] is a global object that is assigned to have a delayed value of the *n*th input line.

Typing In[*n*] causes the *n*th input line to be re-evaluated. ▪ In[ ] gives the last input line. ▪ In[-k] gives the input *k* lines back. ▪ See pages 48 and 702. ▪ See also: InString, Out, $Line, $HistoryLength. ▪ *New in Version 1.*

■ Increment

x++ increases the value of *x* by 1, returning the old value of *x*.

Increment has attribute HoldFirst. ▪ See page 305. ▪ See also: PreIncrement, AddTo, Set. ▪ *New in Version 1.*

■ Indeterminate

Indeterminate is a symbol that represents a numerical quantity whose magnitude cannot be determined.

Computations like 0/0 generate Indeterminate. ▪ A message is produced whenever an operation first yields Indeterminate as a result. ▪ See page 742. ▪ See also: DirectedInfinity, Check. ▪ *New in Version 1.*

■ Infinity

Infinity or ∞ is a symbol that represents a positive infinite quantity.

∞ can be entered as \[Infinity] or ⁝inf⁝. ▪ In StandardForm, Infinity is printed as ∞. ▪ Infinity is converted to DirectedInfinity[1]. ▪ Certain arithmetic operations work with Infinity. ▪ Example: 1/Infinity ⟶ 0. ▪ NumberQ[Infinity] yields False. ▪ See pages 743 and 765. ▪ See also: ComplexInfinity, Indeterminate. ▪ *New in Version 1; modified in Version 3.*

■ Infix

Infix[*f*[e_1, e_2, ...]] prints with *f*[e_1, e_2, ...] given in default infix form:
$e_1 \sim f \sim e_2 \sim f \sim e_3 \ldots$.

Infix[*expr*, *h*] prints with arguments separated by *h*: $e_1\ h\ e_2\ h\ e_3 \ldots$.

Infix[*expr*, *h*, *precedence*, *grouping*] can be used to specify how the output form should be parenthesized.
▪ Precedence levels are specified by integers. In OutputForm, some precedence levels are:

x . y . z	210
x y z	150
x + y + z	140
x == y	130
x = y	60

▪ Possible grouping (associativity) specifications are:

NonAssociative	not associative—always parenthesized
None	always associative—never parenthesized
Left	left associative (e.g., (*a*/*b*)/*c*)
Right	right associative (e.g., *a*^(*b*^*c*))

▪ See page 474. ▪ See also: Postfix, Prefix, PrecedenceForm. ▪ *New in Version 1.*

■ **Information**

> Information[*symbol*] prints information about a symbol.

Information[*symbol*] prints the same information as the input escape ??*symbol* would give. ■ Information has attribute HoldAll. ■ See pages 58 and 1038. ■ See also: Definition, Names, ValueQ, DownValues, UpValues. ■ *New in Version 1.*

■ **InitializationCell**

> InitializationCell is an option for Cell which specifies whether the cell should automatically be sent for evaluation by the *Mathematica* kernel when the notebook that contains it is opened.

See page 608. ■ See also: Evaluator. ■ *New in Version 3.*

■ **Inner**

> Inner[*f*, *list*₁, *list*₂, *g*] is a generalization of Dot in which *f* plays the role of multiplication and *g* of addition.

Example: Inner[f,{a,b},{x,y},g] ⟶ g[f[a, x], f[b, y]] .
■ Inner[f,{{a,b},{c,d}},{x,y},g] ⟶ {g[f[a, x], f[b, y]], g[f[c, x], f[d, y]]}. ■ Like Dot, Inner effectively contracts the last index of the first tensor with the first index of the second tensor. Applying Inner to a rank *r* tensor and a rank *s* tensor gives a rank $r + s - 2$ tensor. ■ Inner[*f*, *list*₁, *list*₂] uses Plus for *g*.
■ Inner[*f*, *list*₁, *list*₂, *g*, *n*] contracts index *n* of the first tensor with the first index of the second tensor. ■ The heads of *list*₁ and *list*₂ must be the same, but need not necessarily be List. ■ See page 917. ■ See also: Outer, Thread, MapThread, ListCorrelate. ■ *New in Version 1.*

■ **Input**

> Input[ ] interactively reads in one *Mathematica* expression.

> Input["*prompt*"] requests input, using the specified string as a prompt.

Input returns the expression it read. ■ The operation of Input may vary from one computer system to another. When a *Mathematica* front end is used, Input may work through a dialog box. ■ When no front end is used, Input reads from standard input. ■ If the standard input is a file, then Input returns EndOfFile if you try to read past the end of the file. ■ On most systems, Input[ ] uses ? as a prompt. ■ When Input is evaluated, *Mathematica* stops until the input has been read. ■ See page 478. ■ See also: InputString, Read, Get, Dialog, ButtonBox. ■ *New in Version 1.*

■ **InputAliases**

> InputAliases is an option for cells and notebooks which specifies additional ⦂*name*⦂ aliases to be allowed on input.

The setting InputAliases->{"*name*₁"->*expr*₁, ... } specifies that the ⦂*name*ᵢ⦂ should be replaced on input by the corresponding *expr*ᵢ. ■ The *expr*ᵢ should be strings or box expressions. ■ See page 613. ■ See also: InputAutoReplacements, $PreRead, Set. ■ *New in Version 4.*

■ InputAutoReplacements

InputAutoReplacements is an option for cells and notebooks which specifies strings of characters that should be replaced immediately on input.

The default setting of InputAutoReplacements for Input styles typically includes such rules as "->" -> "→". ■ In expression input, automatic replacements can be performed only on strings of characters that correspond to complete input tokens. ■ In textual input, automatic replacements can be performed on strings of alphanumeric characters delimited by spaces or other punctuation characters. ■ When material is copied from a notebook to the clipboard, replacements specified by ExportAutoReplacements are by default performed. Typically these replacements include ones that reverse the action of the replacements in InputAutoReplacements. ■ When material is pasted from the clipboard into a notebook, replacements specified by ImportAutoReplacements are by default performed. Typically these replacements are a subset of those given in InputAutoReplacements. ■ See page 613. ■ See also: InputAliases, $PreRead, Set. ■ *New in Version 4.*

■ InputForm

InputForm[*expr*] prints as a version of *expr* suitable for input to *Mathematica*.

Example: InputForm[x^2 + 1/a] ⟶ a^(-1) + x^2. ■ InputForm always produces one-dimensional output, suitable to be typed as lines of *Mathematica* input. ■ InputForm acts as a "wrapper", which affects printing, but not evaluation. ■ Put (>>) produces InputForm by default. ■ Short[InputForm[*expr*]] can be used, but may generate skeleton objects which cannot be given as *Mathematica* input. ■ The option NumberMarks can be used to specify whether ` marks should be used to indicate type, precision or accuracy of approximate numbers. ■ See page 424. ■ See also: OutputForm, FullForm, StandardForm. ■ *New in Version 1; modified in Version 3.*

■ InputNotebook

InputNotebook[ ] gives the current notebook into which keyboard input in the front end will be directed.

InputNotebook returns a NotebookObject. ■ If there is no current input notebook, InputNotebook[ ] will return $Failed. ■ The current input notebook is the notebook to which textual commands in the front end are normally directed. ■ A palette window can be a currently selected notebook but cannot normally be an input notebook. ■ See page 579. ■ See also: Notebooks, SelectedNotebook, EvaluationNotebook, ButtonNotebook. ■ *New in Version 3.*

■ InputStream

InputStream["*name*", *n*] is an object that represents an input stream for functions such as Read and Find.

OpenRead returns an InputStream object. ■ The serial number *n* is unique across all streams, regardless of their name. ■ StringToStream returns an object of the form InputStream[String, *n*]. ■ See page 631. ■ See also: $Input, Streams, OutputStream. ■ *New in Version 2.*

■ InputString

InputString[ ] interactively reads in a character string.

InputString["*prompt*"] requests input, using the specified string as a prompt.

See notes for Input. ■ See page 478. ■ *New in Version 1.*

■ Insert

Insert[*list*, *elem*, *n*] inserts *elem* at position *n* in *list*. If *n* is negative, the position is counted from the end.

Insert[*expr*, *elem*, {*i*, *j*, ... }] inserts *elem* at position {*i*, *j*, ... } in *expr*.

Insert[*expr*, *elem*, {{*i*₁, *j*₁, ... }, {*i*₂, *j*₂, ... }, ... }] inserts *elem* at several positions.

Examples: Insert[{a, b, c}, x, 2] ⟶ {a, x, b, c}.
■ Insert[{a, b, c}, x, {{1}, {-1}}] ⟶ {x, a, b, c, x}.
■ Insert[{{a, b}, {c, d}}, x, {2, 1}] ⟶ {{a, b}, {x, c, d}}. ■ *list* can have any head, not necessarily List. +■ Insert works on SparseArray objects by effectively inserting into the corresponding ordinary lists. ■ See pages 125 and 288. ■ See also: Prepend, Append, StringInsert, Take, Drop, Delete, ReplacePart, FlattenAt, Position, Sequence. ■ *New in Version 1.*

■ Install

Install["*name*"] starts a *MathLink*-compatible external program and installs *Mathematica* definitions to call functions in it.

The *Mathematica* definitions set up by Install are typically specified in the *MathLink* template file used to create the source code for the external program. ■ Install["*prog*"] will launch the specified program, then connect to it via *MathLink*. ■ If *prog* is a directory, Install["*prog*"] will try to execute *prog*/$SystemID/*prog*.
■ Install["*name*`"] searches all directories on $Path for a file or directory called *name*.exe. ■ Install[*link*] will take an existing LinkObject and set up what is needed to call functions in the program corresponding to that LinkObject. ■ Install returns a LinkObject representing the *MathLink* connection it is using.
■ LinkPatterns[*link*] gives a list of the patterns defined when the specified link was set up. ■ You can remove these definitions, and terminate the execution of the external program by calling Uninstall[*link*].
■ Install[LinkConnect["*port*"]] will install an external program that has created a link on the specified port. You can use this to call external programs that have been started in a debugger or on a remote computer system. ■ If you call Install["*command*"] multiple times with the same *command*, the later calls will overwrite definitions set up by earlier ones, unless the definitions depend on the values of global variables which have changed. ■ Install sets up definitions which send CallPacket objects to the external program whenever functions in it are called, and waits for results to be returned in ReturnPacket objects. ■ The external program can send EvaluatePacket objects back to *Mathematica* to request evaluations while the program is running. ■ See page 659. ■ See also: Get, Run, RunThrough, LinkLaunch, Uninstall, $CurrentLink. ■ *New in Version 2; modified in Version 3.*

■ InString

InString[*n*] is a global object that is assigned to be the text of the nth input line.

InString[*n*] gives the string that *Mathematica* read for the nth input line. The string includes all intermediate newlines in the input, but not the newline at the end. ■ The value of InString[*n*] is assigned after the input is verified to be syntactically correct, and after any function given as the value of $PreRead has been applied.
■ InString[ ] gives the text of the last input line. ■ InString[-*k*] gives the text of the input *k* lines back. ■ See pages 48 and 702. ■ See also: In, $SyntaxHandler. ■ *New in Version 2.*

■ Integer

Integer is the head used for integers.

_Integer can be used to stand for an integer in a pattern. ■ Integers can be of any length. ■ You can enter an integer in base *b* using *b*^^*digits*. The base must be less than 36. The letters are used in sequence to stand for digits 10 through 35. ■ See page 722. ■ See also: IntegerDigits, BaseForm, IntegerQ, Integers. ■ *New in Version 1.*

■ IntegerDigits

IntegerDigits[n] gives a list of the decimal digits in the integer n.

IntegerDigits[n, b] gives a list of the base-b digits in the integer n.

IntegerDigits[n, b, len] pads the list on the left with zeros to give a list of length len.

Examples: IntegerDigits[5810] ⟶ {5, 8, 1, 0}; IntegerDigits[5810, 16] ⟶ {1, 6, 11, 2}.
■ IntegerDigits[n] discards the sign of n. ■ If len is less than the number of digits in n then the len least significant digits are returned. +■ IntegerDigits[0] gives {0}. ■ FromDigits can be used as the inverse of IntegerDigits. ■ See page 725. ■ Implementation notes: see page 1067. ■ See also: DigitCount, RealDigits, BaseForm, NumberForm, FromDigits, IntegerExponent, IntegerPart, ContinuedFraction. ■ *New in Version 2; modified in Version 3.*

■ IntegerExponent

IntegerExponent[n, b] gives the highest power of b that divides n.

IntegerExponent[n] is equivalent to IntegerExponent[n, 10]. ■ IntegerExponent[n, b] gives the number of trailing zeros in the digits of n in base b. ■ See page 749. ■ See also: IntegerDigits, FactorInteger, MantissaExponent, DigitCount, Exponent. ■ *New in Version 4.*

■ IntegerPart

IntegerPart[x] gives the integer part of x.

Mathematical function (see Section A.3.10). ■ IntegerPart[x] in effect takes all digits to the left of the decimal point and drops the others. ■ Examples: IntegerPart[2.4] ⟶ 2; IntegerPart[2.6] ⟶ 2; IntegerPart[-2.4] ⟶ -2; IntegerPart[-2.6] ⟶ -2. ■ IntegerPart[x] + FractionalPart[x] is always exactly x. ■ IntegerPart[x] returns an integer when x is any numeric quantity, whether or not it is an explicit number. ■ Example: IntegerPart[Pi^2] ⟶ 9. ■ For exact numeric quantities, IntegerPart internally uses numerical approximations to establish its result. This process can be affected by the setting of the global variable $MaxExtraPrecision. ■ See page 745. ■ See also: FractionalPart, Round, Floor, Ceiling, Chop. ■ *New in Version 3.*

■ IntegerQ

IntegerQ[$expr$] gives True if $expr$ is an integer, and False otherwise.

IntegerQ[$expr$] returns False unless $expr$ is manifestly an integer (i.e., has head Integer). ■ Simplify[$expr$ ∈ Integers] can be used to try to determine whether an expression is mathematically equal to an integer. ■ See pages 267 and 723. ■ See also: EvenQ, OddQ, NumberQ, TrueQ, Element. ■ *New in Version 1.*

■ Integers

Integers represents the domain of integers, as in x ∈ Integers.

x ∈ Integers evaluates immediately only if x is a numeric quantity. ■ Simplify[$expr$ ∈ Integers] can be used to try to determine whether an expression is an integer. ■ IntegerQ[$expr$] tests only whether $expr$ is manifestly an integer (i.e., has head Integer). ■ Integers is output in TraditionalForm as ℤ. ■ See pages 73, 817 and 839. ■ See also: Element, Simplify, IntegerQ, Reals, Primes, Algebraics. ■ *New in Version 4.*

■ Integrate

Integrate[f, x] gives the indefinite integral $\int f\,dx$.

Integrate[f, {x, $xmin$, $xmax$}] gives the definite integral $\int_{xmin}^{xmax} f\,dx$.

Integrate[f, {x, $xmin$, $xmax$}, {y, $ymin$, $ymax$}] gives the multiple integral $\int_{xmin}^{xmax} dx \int_{ymin}^{ymax} dy\, f$.

Integrate[f, x] can be entered as $\int f\,dx$. ■ $\int$ can be entered as :int: or \[Integral]. ■ d is not an ordinary d; it is entered as :dd: or \[DifferentialD]. ■ Integrate[f, {x, $xmin$, $xmax$}] can be entered with $xmin$ as a subscript and $xmax$ as a superscript to $\int$. ■ Multiple integrals use a variant of the standard iterator notation. The first variable given corresponds to the outermost integral, and is done last. ■ Integrate can evaluate integrals of rational functions. It can also evaluate integrals that involve exponential, logarithmic, trigonometric and inverse trigonometric functions, so long as the result comes out in terms of the same set of functions. ■ Integrate can give results in terms of many special functions. ■ Integrate carries out some simplifications on integrals it cannot explicitly do. ■ You can get a numerical result by applying N to a definite integral. ■ You can assign values to patterns involving Integrate to give results for new classes of integrals. ■ The integration variable can be any expression. However, Integrate uses only its literal form. The object $d(x^n)$, for example, is not converted to $nx^{n-1}dx$. ■ For indefinite integrals, Integrate tries to find results that are correct for almost all values of parameters. ■ For definite integrals, the following options can be given:

Assumptions	$Assumptions	assumptions to make about parameters
GenerateConditions	Automatic	whether to generate answers that involve conditions on parameters
PrincipalValue	False	whether to find Cauchy principal values

■ Integrate can evaluate essentially all indefinite integrals and most definite integrals listed in standard books of tables. ■ In StandardForm, Integrate[f, x] is output as $\int f\,dx$. ■ See page 859. ■ Implementation notes: see page 1070. ■ See also: NIntegrate, DSolve, Sum, LaplaceTransform, FourierTransform. ■ *New in Version 1; modified in Version 5.0.*

■ InterpolatingFunction

InterpolatingFunction[*domain*, *table*] represents an approximate function whose values are found by interpolation.

InterpolatingFunction works like Function. ■ InterpolatingFunction[...][x] finds the value of an approximate function with a particular argument x. ■ In standard output format, only the *domain* element of an InterpolatingFunction object is printed explicitly. The remaining elements are indicated by <>. ■ *domain* specifies the domain of the data from which the InterpolatingFunction was constructed. ■ If you supply arguments outside of the domain, a warning is generated, and then an extrapolated value is returned.
■ InterpolatingFunction objects that take any number of real arguments may be constructed. ■ You can take derivatives of InterpolatingFunction objects using D and Derivative. ■ NDSolve returns its results in terms of InterpolatingFunction objects. ■ See page 930. ■ Implementation notes: see page 1069. ■ See also: Interpolation, CompiledFunction, FunctionInterpolation. ■ Related package: NumericalMath`SplineFit`. ■ *New in Version 2; modified in Version 3.*

■ InterpolatingPolynomial

InterpolatingPolynomial[*data*, *var*] gives a polynomial in the variable *var* which provides an exact fit to a list of data.

The data can have the forms $\{\{x_1, f_1\}, \{x_2, f_2\}, \dots \}$ or $\{f_1, f_2, \dots \}$, where in the second case, the x_i are taken to have values 1, 2, … .

The f_i can be replaced by $\{f_i, df_i, ddf_i, \dots \}$, specifying derivatives at the points x_i.

With a list of data of length n, InterpolatingPolynomial gives a polynomial of degree $n - 1$. ■ Example: InterpolatingPolynomial[{4, 5, 8}, x] $\longrightarrow 4 + (-1 + x)^2$. ■ InterpolatingPolynomial gives the interpolating polynomial in Newton form, suitable for numerical evaluation. ■ See page 808. ■ See also: Fit, Roots. ■ Related package: NumericalMath`PolynomialFit`. ■ *New in Version 2.*

■ Interpolation

Interpolation[*data*] constructs an InterpolatingFunction object which represents an approximate function that interpolates the data.

The data can have the forms $\{\{x_1, f_1\}, \{x_2, f_2\}, \dots \}$ or $\{f_1, f_2, \dots \}$, where in the second case, the x_i are taken to have values 1, 2, … .

Data can be given in the form $\{\{x_1, \{f_1, df_1, ddf_1, \dots \}\}, \dots \}$ to specify derivatives as well as values of the function at the points x_i. You can specify different numbers of derivatives at different points. ■ Function values and derivatives may be real or complex numbers, or arbitrary symbolic expressions. The x_i must be real numbers. ■ Multidimensional data can be given in the form $\{\{x_1, y_1, \dots, f_1\}, \dots \}$. Derivatives in this case can be given by replacing f_1 and so on by $\{f_1, \{dxf_1, dyf_1, \dots \}\}$. ■ Interpolation works by fitting polynomial curves between successive data points. ■ The degree of the polynomial curves is specified by the option InterpolationOrder. ■ The default setting is InterpolationOrder -> 3. ■ You can do linear interpolation by using the setting InterpolationOrder -> 1. ■ Interpolation[*data*] generates an InterpolatingFunction object which returns values with the same precision as those in *data*. ■ See page 931. ■ See also: ListInterpolation, FunctionInterpolation, InterpolatingPolynomial, Fit, Quantile. ■ Related packages: NumericalMath`SplineFit`, NumericalMath`PolynomialFit`, NumericalMath`Approximations`, DiscreteMath`ComputationalGeometry`. ■ *New in Version 2; modified in Version 3.*

■ InterpretationBox

InterpretationBox[*boxes*, *expr*] displays as *boxes* but is interpreted on input as *expr*.

InterpretationBox provides a way to store hidden information in *Mathematica* output. ■ InterpretationBox is generated sometimes in StandardForm output, and often in TraditionalForm output. ■ The following options can be given:

AutoDelete	False	whether to strip the InterpretationBox if *boxes* is modified
DeletionWarning	False	whether to issue a warning if *boxes* is deleted
Editable	False	whether to allow *boxes* to be edited
Selectable	True	whether to allow *boxes* to be selected

■ If you modify the displayed form of InterpretationBox[*boxes*, *expr*] only *boxes* will be modified, and there is no guarantee that correct correspondence with *expr* will be maintained. ■ InterpretationBox has attribute HoldComplete. ■ See page 447. ■ See also: TagBox, FormBox, ToExpression, ButtonBox. ■ *New in Version 3.*

■ **Interrupt**

> Interrupt[ ] generates an interrupt.

> You can call Interrupt anywhere within a computation. It has the same effect as an interactive interrupt at that point. ■ See page 371. ■ See also: Abort, TimeConstrained, MemoryConstrained, Throw, $Inspector, LinkInterrupt. ■ *New in Version 2.*

■ **Intersection**

> Intersection[*list*₁, *list*₂, ...] gives a sorted list of the elements common to all the *list*ᵢ.

> If the *list*ᵢ are considered as sets, Intersection gives their intersection. ■ Intersection[*list*₁, *list*₂, ...] can be input in StandardForm and InputForm as *list*₁ ∩ *list*₂ ∩ ... . The character ∩ can be entered as ⁚inter⁚ or \[Intersection]. ■ The *list*ᵢ must have the same head, but it need not be List.
> ■ Intersection[*list*₁, ... , SameTest->*test*] applies *test* to each pair of elements in the *list*ᵢ to determine whether they should be considered the same. ■ Intersection[*a*, *b*] can be entered in StandardForm and InputForm as *a* ∩ *b* or *a* \[Intersection] *b*. ■ See page 127. ■ See also: Union, Complement. ■ *New in Version 1; modified in Version 3.*

■ **Interval**

> Interval[{*min*, *max*}] represents the range of values between *min* and *max*.

> Interval[{*min*₁, *max*₁}, {*min*₂, *max*₂}, ...] represents the union of the ranges *min*₁ to *max*₁, *min*₂ to *max*₂, ...

> You can perform arithmetic and other operations on Interval objects. ■ Example: Interval[{1, 6}] + Interval[{0, 2}] ⟶ Interval[{1, 8}]. ■ Min[*interval*] and Max[*interval*] give the end points of an interval. ■ For approximate machine- or arbitrary-precision numbers *x*, Interval[*x*] yields an interval reflecting the uncertainty in *x*. ■ In operations on intervals that involve approximate numbers, *Mathematica* always rounds lower limits down and upper limits up. ■ Interval can be generated by functions such as Limit.
> ■ Relational operators such as Equal and Less yield explicit True or False results whenever they are given disjoint intervals. ■ See page 894. ■ See also: Range. ■ *New in Version 3.*

■ **IntervalIntersection**

> IntervalIntersection[*interval*₁, *interval*₂, ...] gives the interval representing all points common to each of the *interval*ᵢ.

> See page 741. ■ See also: Interval. ■ *New in Version 3.*

■ **IntervalMemberQ**

> IntervalMemberQ[*interval*, *x*] gives True if the number *x* lies within the specified interval, and False otherwise.

> IntervalMemberQ[*interval*₁, *interval*₂] gives True if *interval*₂ is completely contained within *interval*₁.

> IntervalMemberQ has attribute Listable. ■ See page 741. ■ See also: Interval, MemberQ. ■ *New in Version 3.*

■ **IntervalUnion**

> IntervalUnion[*interval*₁, *interval*₂, ...] gives the interval representing the set of all points in any of the *interval*ᵢ.

> See page 741. ■ See also: Interval. ■ *New in Version 3.*

■ Inverse

Inverse[*m*] gives the inverse of a square matrix *m*.

Inverse works on both symbolic and numerical matrices. ■ For matrices with approximate real or complex numbers, the inverse is generated to the maximum possible precision given the input. A warning is given for ill-conditioned matrices. ■ Inverse[*m*, Modulus->*n*] evaluates the inverse modulo *n*. ■ Inverse[*m*, ZeroTest -> *test*] evaluates *test*[*m*[[*i*, *j*]]] to determine whether matrix elements are zero. The default setting is ZeroTest -> (# == 0 &). ■ A Method option can also be given. Possible settings are as for LinearSolve. ■ See page 903. ■ Implementation notes: see page 1069. ■ See also: PseudoInverse, LinearSolve, RowReduce, NullSpace, LinearSolveFunction. ■ Related package: LinearAlgebra`Tridiagonal`. ■ *New in Version 1; modified in Version 3.*

■ InverseBetaRegularized

InverseBetaRegularized[*s*, *a*, *b*] gives the inverse of the regularized incomplete beta function.

Mathematical function (see Section A.3.10). ■ With the regularized incomplete beta function defined by $I(z,a,b) = B(z,a,b)/B(a,b)$, InverseBetaRegularized[*s*, *a*, *b*] is the solution for *z* in $s = I(z,a,b)$. ■ InverseBetaRegularized[z_0, *s*, *a*, *b*] gives the inverse of BetaRegularized[z_0, *z*, *a*, *b*]. ■ Note that the arguments of InverseBetaRegularized are arranged differently than in InverseGammaRegularized. ■ See page 770. ■ See also: InverseGammaRegularized, InverseErf. ■ *New in Version 3.*

■ InverseEllipticNomeQ

InverseEllipticNomeQ[*q*] gives the parameter *m* corresponding to the nome *q* in an elliptic function.

Mathematical function (see Section A.3.10). ■ InverseEllipticNomeQ[*q*] yields the unique value of the parameter *m* which makes EllipticNomeQ[*m*] equal to *q*. ■ The nome *q* must always satisfy $|q| < 1$. ■ See page 782. ■ See also: EllipticNomeQ. ■ *New in Version 3.*

■ InverseErf

InverseErf[*s*] gives the inverse error function obtained as the solution for *z* in $s = \mathrm{erf}(z)$.

Mathematical function (see Section A.3.10). ■ Explicit numerical values are given only for real values of *s* between −1 and +1. ■ InverseErf[z_0, *s*] gives the inverse of the generalized error function Erf[z_0, *z*]. ■ See page 775. ■ See also: Erf, InverseGammaRegularized, InverseBetaRegularized. ■ *New in Version 3.*

■ InverseErfc

InverseErfc[*s*] gives the inverse complementary error function obtained as the solution for *z* in $s = \mathrm{erfc}(z)$.

Mathematical function (see Section A.3.10). ■ Explicit numerical values are given only for real values of *s* between 0 and 2. ■ See page 775. ■ See also: Erfc, InverseGammaRegularized, InverseBetaRegularized. ■ *New in Version 3.*

■ InverseFourier

InverseFourier[*list*] finds the discrete inverse Fourier transform of a list of complex numbers.

The inverse Fourier transform u_r of a list v_s of length n is defined to be $\frac{1}{\sqrt{n}} \sum_{s=1}^{n} v_s e^{-2\pi i(r-1)(s-1)/n}$. ■ Note that the zero frequency term must appear at position 1 in the input list. ■ Other definitions are used in some scientific and technical fields. ■ Different choices of definitions can be specified using the option FourierParameters. ■ With the setting FourierParameters -> {*a*, *b*} the discrete Fourier transform computed by Fourier is $\frac{1}{n^{(1+a)/2}} \sum_{s=1}^{n} v_s e^{-2\pi i b(r-1)(s-1)/n}$. ■ Some common choices for {*a*, *b*} are {0, 1} (default), {-1, 1} (data analysis), {1, -1} (signal processing). ■ The setting $b = -1$ effectively corresponds to reversing both input and output lists. ■ To ensure a unique discrete Fourier transform, |*b*| must be relatively prime to n. ■ The list of data need not have a length equal to a power of two. ■ The *list* given in InverseFourier[*list*] can be nested to represent an array of data in any number of dimensions. ■ The array of data must be rectangular. ■ If the elements of *list* are exact numbers, InverseFourier begins by applying N to them. ■ See page 935. ■ See also: Fourier, InverseFourierTransform. ■ *New in Version 1; modified in Version 4.*

■ InverseFourierCosTransform

InverseFourierCosTransform[*expr*, ω, *t*] gives the symbolic inverse Fourier cosine transform of *expr*.

InverseFourierCosTransform[*expr*, {ω_1, ω_2, ... }, {t_1, t_2, ... }] gives the multidimensional inverse Fourier cosine transform of *expr*.

The inverse Fourier cosine transform of a function $F(\omega)$ is by default defined as $\sqrt{\frac{2}{\pi}} \int_0^\infty F(\omega) \cos(\omega t) \, d\omega$. ■ Other definitions are used in some scientific and technical fields. ■ Different choices of definitions can be specified using the option FourierParameters. ■ With the setting FourierParameters->{*a*, *b*} the inverse Fourier transform computed by InverseFourierCosTransform is $2\sqrt{\frac{|b|}{(2\pi)^{1+a}}} \int_0^\infty F(\omega) \cos(b\omega t) \, d\omega$. ■ See notes for InverseFourierTransform. ■ See page 878. ■ See also: InverseFourierSinTransform, FourierCosTransform, InverseFourierTransform, InverseFourier. ■ *New in Version 4.*

■ InverseFourierSinTransform

InverseFourierSinTransform[*expr*, ω, *t*] gives the symbolic inverse Fourier sine transform of *expr*.

InverseFourierSinTransform[*expr*, {ω_1, ω_2, ... }, {t_1, t_2, ... }] gives the multidimensional inverse Fourier sine transform of *expr*.

The inverse Fourier sine transform of a function $F(\omega)$ is by default defined as $\sqrt{\frac{2}{\pi}} \int_0^\infty F(\omega) \sin(\omega t) \, d\omega$. ■ Other definitions are used in some scientific and technical fields. ■ Different choices of definitions can be specified using the option FourierParameters. ■ With the setting FourierParameters->{*a*, *b*} the inverse Fourier transform computed by InverseFourierSinTransform is $2\sqrt{\frac{|b|}{(2\pi)^{1+a}}} \int_0^\infty F(\omega) \sin(b\omega t) \, d\omega$. ■ See notes for InverseFourierTransform. ■ See page 878. ■ See also: InverseFourierCosTransform, FourierSinTransform, InverseFourierTransform, InverseFourier. ■ *New in Version 4.*

■ InverseFourierTransform

InverseFourierTransform[*expr*, ω, *t*] gives the symbolic inverse Fourier transform of *expr*.

InverseFourierTransform[*expr*, {ω_1, ω_2, ... }, {t_1, t_2, ... }] gives the multidimensional inverse Fourier transform of *expr*.

The inverse Fourier transform of a function $F(\omega)$ is by default defined as $\frac{1}{\sqrt{2\pi}} \int_{-\infty}^{\infty} F(\omega) e^{-i\omega t} d\omega$. ■ Other definitions are used in some scientific and technical fields. ■ Different choices of definitions can be specified using the option FourierParameters. ■ With the setting FourierParameters->{*a*, *b*} the inverse Fourier transform computed by InverseFourierTransform is $\sqrt{\frac{|b|}{(2\pi)^{1+a}}} \int_{-\infty}^{\infty} F(\omega) e^{-ib\omega t} d\omega$. ■ Some common choices for {*a*, *b*} are {0, 1} (default; modern physics), {1, -1} (pure mathematics; systems engineering), {-1, 1} (classical physics), {0, -2 Pi} (signal processing). ■ Assumptions and other options to Integrate can also be given in InverseFourierTransform. ■ InverseFourierTransform[*expr*, ω, *t*] yields an expression depending on the continuous variable *t* that represents the symbolic inverse Fourier transform of *expr* with respect to the continuous variable ω. InverseFourier[*list*] takes a finite list of numbers as input, and yields as output a list representing the discrete inverse Fourier transform of the input. ■ In TraditionalForm, InverseFourierTransform is output using $\mathcal{F}^{-1}$. ■ See page 876. ■ See also: InverseFourierSinTransform, InverseFourierCosTransform, InverseFourier, FourierTransform, InverseLaplaceTransform, Integrate. ■ *New in Version 4.*

■ InverseFunction

InverseFunction[*f*] represents the inverse of the function *f*, defined so that InverseFunction[*f*][*y*] gives the value of *x* for which *f*[*x*] is equal to *y*.

For a function with several arguments, InverseFunction[*f*, *n*, *tot*] represents the inverse with respect to the nth argument when there are *tot* arguments in all.

In OutputForm and StandardForm, InverseFunction[*f*] is printed as $f^{(-1)}$. ■ As discussed in Section 3.2.7, many mathematical functions do not have unique inverses. In such cases, InverseFunction[*f*] can represent only one of the possible inverses for *f*. ■ Example: InverseFunction[Sin] $\longrightarrow$ ArcSin. ■ InverseFunction is generated by Solve when the option InverseFunctions is set to Automatic or True. ■ See pages 253 and 825. ■ See also: Solve, InverseSeries, Composition, Derivative. ■ *New in Version 2.*

■ InverseFunctions

InverseFunctions is an option for Solve and related functions which specifies whether inverse functions should be used.

Settings for InverseFunctions are:

True	always use inverse functions
Automatic	use inverse functions, printing a warning message (default)
False	never use inverse functions

■ Example: Solve[f[x] == a, x, InverseFunctions->True] $\longrightarrow$ {{x $\rightarrow$ f$^{(-1)}$[a]}}. ■ Inverse functions provide a way to get some, but not in general all, solutions to equations that involve functions which are more complicated than polynomials. ■ Solve[Sin[x] == a, x, InverseFunctions->True] $\longrightarrow$ {{x $\rightarrow$ ArcSin[a]}} gives a single solution in terms of ArcSin. In fact, there is an infinite number of solutions to the equation, differing by arbitrary multiples of 2π. Solve gives only one of these solutions. ■ When there are several simultaneous equations to be solved in terms of inverse functions, Solve may fail to find any solutions, even when one exists. ■ When inverse functions are allowed, Solve solves for *f*[*expr*] first, then applies InverseFunction[*f*] to the result, equates it to *expr*, and continues trying to solve for the remainder of the variables. ■ See page 824. ■ See also: FindRoot. ■ *New in Version 2.*

■ InverseGammaRegularized

`InverseGammaRegularized[a, s]` gives the inverse of the regularized incomplete gamma function.

Mathematical function (see Section A.3.10). ■ With the regularized incomplete gamma function defined by $Q(a, z) = \Gamma(a, z)/\Gamma(a)$, `InverseGammaRegularized[a, s]` is the solution for z in $s = Q(a, z)$. ■ `InverseGammaRegularized[a, z_0, s]` gives the inverse of `GammaRegularized[a, z_0, z]`. ■ Note that the arguments of `InverseGammaRegularized` are arranged differently than in `InverseBetaRegularized`. ■ See page 770. ■ See also: `InverseBetaRegularized, InverseErf`. ■ *New in Version 3.*

■ InverseJacobiSN, InverseJacobiCN, ...

`InverseJacobiSN[v, m]`, `InverseJacobiCN[v, m]`, etc. give the inverse Jacobi elliptic functions $\text{sn}^{-1}(v|m)$ etc.

There are a total of twelve functions, with names of the form `InverseJacobiPQ`, where P and Q can be any distinct pair of the letters S, C, D and N.

Mathematical functions (see Section A.3.10). ■ $\text{sn}^{-1}(v|m)$ gives the value of u for which $v = \text{sn}(u|m)$. ■ The inverse Jacobi elliptic functions are related to elliptic integrals. ■ See page 785. ■ *New in Version 1.*

■ InverseLaplaceTransform

`InverseLaplaceTransform[expr, s, t]` gives the inverse Laplace transform of *expr*.

`InverseLaplaceTransform[expr, {s_1, s_2, ... }, {t_1, t_2, ... }]` gives the multidimensional inverse Laplace transform of *expr*.

The inverse Laplace transform of a function $F(s)$ is defined to be $\frac{1}{2\pi i} \int_{\gamma - i\infty}^{\gamma + i\infty} F(s) e^{st} \, ds$, where γ is an arbitrary positive constant chosen so that the contour of integration lies to the right of all singularities in $F(s)$. ■ Assumptions and other options to `Integrate` can also be given in `InverseLaplaceTransform`. ■ In `TraditionalForm`, `InverseLaplaceTransform` is output using $\mathcal{L}^{-1}$. ■ See page 875. ■ See also: `LaplaceTransform`, `InverseFourierTransform, InverseZTransform, Integrate`. ■ *New in Version 4.*

■ InverseSeries

`InverseSeries[s, x]` takes the series *s* generated by `Series`, and gives a series for the inverse of the function represented by *s*.

`InverseSeries` performs "reversion" of series. ■ Given a series $s(y)$, `InverseSeries[s, x]` gives a series for y such that $s(y) = x$. ■ `InverseSeries` can be applied to any `SeriesData` object with the appropriate structure, whether or not it has been generated by `Series`. ■ See page 887. ■ See also: `Solve, InverseFunction`. ■ *New in Version 1.*

■ InverseWeierstrassP

`InverseWeierstrassP[p, {g_2, g_3}]` gives a value of u for which the Weierstrass function $\wp(u; g_2, g_3)$ is equal to p.

Mathematical function (see Section A.3.10). ■ The value of u returned always lies in the fundamental period parallelogram defined by the complex half-periods ω and ω'. ■ `InverseWeierstrassP[{p, q}, {g_2, g_3}]` finds the unique value of u for which $p = \wp(u; g_2, g_3)$ and $q = \wp'(u; g_2, g_3)$. For such a value to exist, p and q must be related by $q^2 = 4p^3 - g_2 p - g_3$. ■ See page 782 for a discussion of argument conventions for elliptic functions. ■ See page 785. ■ See also: `WeierstrassP, WeierstrassPPrime, WeierstrassHalfPeriods`. ■ *New in Version 3.*

■ InverseZTransform

`InverseZTransform[`*expr*`,` *z* `,` *n*`]` gives the inverse Z transform of *expr*.

The inverse Z transform of a function $F(z)$ is defined to be the contour integral $\frac{1}{2\pi i} \oint F(z) z^{n-1} \, dz$. ■ See page 879. ■ See also: `ZTransform`, `InverseLaplaceTransform`. ■ *New in Version 4.*

■ JacobiAmplitude

`JacobiAmplitude[`*u*`,` *m*`]` gives the amplitude am($u|m$) for Jacobi elliptic functions.

Mathematical function (see Section A.3.10). ■ `JacobiAmplitude[`*u*`,` *m*`]` converts from the argument u for an elliptic function to the amplitude ϕ. ■ `JacobiAmplitude` is the inverse of the elliptic integral of the first kind. If $u = F(\phi|m)$, then $\phi = \text{am}(u|m)$. ■ See page 785. ■ *New in Version 1.*

■ JacobiP

`JacobiP[`*n*`,` *a*`,` *b*`,` *x*`]` gives the Jacobi polynomial $P_n^{(a,b)}(x)$.

Mathematical function (see Section A.3.10). ■ Explicit polynomials are given when possible. ■ $P_n^{(a,b)}(x)$ satisfies the differential equation $(1 - x^2)y'' + (b - a - (a + b + 2)x)y' + n(n + a + b + 1)y = 0$. ■ The Jacobi polynomials are orthogonal with weight function $(1 - x)^a(1 + x)^b$. ■ `JacobiP[`*n*`,` *a*`,` *b*`,` *z*`]` has a branch cut discontinuity in the complex z plane running from $-\infty$ to -1. ■ See page 766. ■ See also: `LegendreP`, `ChebyshevT`, `ChebyshevU`, `GegenbauerC`. ■ *New in Version 1.*

■ JacobiSN, JacobiCN, ...

`JacobiSN[`*u*`,` *m*`]`, `JacobiCN[`*u*`,` *m*`]`, etc. give the Jacobi elliptic functions sn($u|m$), cn($u|m$), etc.

There are a total of twelve functions, with the names of the form `Jacobi`*PQ*, where *P* and *Q* can be any distinct pair of the letters S, C, D and N.

Mathematical functions (see Section A.3.10). ■ sn(u) = sin(ϕ), cn(u) = cos(ϕ) and dn(u) = $\sqrt{1 - m \sin^2(\phi)}$, where $\phi = \text{am}(u|m)$. ■ Other Jacobi elliptic functions can be found from the relation pq(u) = pr(u)/qr(u), where for these purposes pp(u) = 1. ■ See page 785. ■ See also: `InverseJacobiSN`. ■ *New in Version 1.*

■ JacobiSymbol

`JacobiSymbol[`*n*`,` *m*`]` gives the Jacobi symbol $\left(\frac{n}{m}\right)$.

Integer mathematical function (see Section A.3.10). ■ For prime m, the Jacobi symbol reduces to the Legendre symbol. The Legendre symbol is equal to ±1 depending on whether n is a quadratic residue modulo m. ■ See page 752. ■ See also: `FactorInteger`, `MoebiusMu`. ■ *New in Version 1.*

■ JacobiZeta

`JacobiZeta[`ϕ`,` *m*`]` gives the Jacobi zeta function $Z(\phi|m)$.

Mathematical function (see Section A.3.10). ■ The Jacobi zeta function is given in terms of elliptic integrals by $Z(\phi|m) = E(\phi|m) - E(m)F(\phi|m)/K(m)$. ■ Argument conventions for elliptic integrals are discussed on page 782. ■ See page 783. ■ See also: `EllipticE`, `EllipticF`, `EllipticK`. ■ *New in Version 2.*

■ Join

Join[*list₁*, *list₂*, ...] concatenates lists together. Join can be used on any set of expressions that have the same head.

+■ Join works on SparseArray objects by effectively concatenating the corresponding ordinary lists. ■ See page 126. ■ See also: Union, StringJoin, Append, Prepend, PadLeft. ■ *New in Version 1.*

■ JordanDecomposition

JordanDecomposition[*m*] yields the Jordan decomposition of a square matrix *m*. The result is a list {*s*, *j*} where *s* is a similarity matrix and *j* is the Jordan canonical form of *m*.

The original matrix *m* is equal to s . j . Inverse[s]. ■ The matrix *m* can be either numerical or symbolic. ■ See page 915. ■ See also: Eigensystem, SingularValueDecomposition, QRDecomposition, SchurDecomposition, MatrixExp. ■ *New in Version 3.*

■ Khinchin

Khinchin is Khinchin's constant, with numerical value $\simeq 2.68545$.

Mathematical constant (see Section A.3.11). ■ Khinchin's constant (sometimes called Khintchine's constant) is given by $\prod_{s=1}^{\infty}(1 + \frac{1}{s(s+2)})^{\log_2 s}$. ■ See page 765. ■ See also: ContinuedFraction. ■ *New in Version 4.*

■ KleinInvariantJ

KleinInvariantJ[τ] gives the Klein invariant modular elliptic function $J(\tau)$.

Mathematical function (see Section A.3.10). ■ The argument τ is the ratio of Weierstrass half-periods ω'/ω. ■ KleinInvariantJ is given in terms of Weierstrass invariants by $g_2^3/(g_2^3 - 27g_3^2)$. ■ $J(\tau)$ is invariant under any combination of the modular transformations $\tau \to \tau + 1$ and $\tau \to -1/\tau$. ■ See page 782 for a discussion of argument conventions for elliptic functions. ■ See page 787. ■ See also: ModularLambda, DedekindEta, WeierstrassInvariants, EllipticTheta. ■ *New in Version 3.*

■ KroneckerDelta

KroneckerDelta[n_1, n_2, ...] gives the Kronecker delta $\delta_{n_1 n_2 \dots}$, equal to 1 if all the n_i are equal, and 0 otherwise.

KroneckerDelta[0] gives 1; KroneckerDelta[*n*] gives 0 for other numeric *n*. ■ KroneckerDelta has attribute Orderless. ■ See page 749. ■ See also: DiscreteDelta, IdentityMatrix, Equal, UnitStep, If, Signature, DiracDelta. ■ *New in Version 4.*

■ Label

Label[*tag*] represents a point in a compound expression to which control can be transferred using Goto.

Label must appear as an explicit element of a CompoundExpression object. ■ Label has attribute HoldFirst. ■ See page 354. ■ See also: Catch. ■ *New in Version 1.*

■ LaguerreL

LaguerreL[n, x] gives the Laguerre polynomial $L_n(x)$.

LaguerreL[n, a, x] gives the generalized Laguerre polynomial $L_n^a(x)$.

Mathematical function (see Section A.3.10). ■ Explicit polynomials are given when possible. ■ $L_n(x) = L_n^0(x)$. ■ The Laguerre polynomials are orthogonal with weight function $x^a e^{-x}$. ■ They satisfy the differential equation $xy'' + (a + 1 - x)y' + ny = 0$. ■ LaguerreL[$n$, x] is an entire function of x with no branch cut discontinuities. ■ See page 766. ■ See also: HermiteH. ■ *New in Version 1.*

■ LanguageCategory

LanguageCategory is an option for Cell which determines in what category of language the contents of the cell should be assumed to be for purposes of spell checking and hyphenation.

Possible settings for LanguageCategory are:

"Formula"	mathematical formula
"Mathematica"	*Mathematica* input
"NaturalLanguage"	human natural language
None	do no spell checking or hyphenation

■ LanguageCategory is normally set to "NaturalLanguage" for text cells, and to "Mathematica" for input and output cells. ■ LanguageCategory is more often set at the level of styles than at the level of individual cells. ■ See page 613. ■ See also: $Language, Hyphenation, FormatType. ■ *New in Version 4.*

■ LaplaceTransform

LaplaceTransform[$expr$, t, s] gives the Laplace transform of $expr$.

LaplaceTransform[$expr$, {t_1, t_2, ... }, {s_1, s_2, ... }] gives the multidimensional Laplace transform of $expr$.

The Laplace transform of a function $f(t)$ is defined to be $\int_0^\infty f(t)e^{-st}\,dt$. ■ The lower limit of the integral is effectively taken to be 0_-, so that the Laplace transform of the Dirac delta function $\delta(t)$ is equal to 1. ■ Assumptions and other options to Integrate can also be given in LaplaceTransform. ■ In TraditionalForm, LaplaceTransform is output using $\mathcal{L}$. ■ See page 875. ■ See also: InverseLaplaceTransform, FourierTransform, ZTransform, Integrate. ■ *New in Version 4.*

■ Last

Last[$expr$] gives the last element in $expr$.

Last[$expr$] is equivalent to $expr$[[-1]]. ■ See page 122. ■ See also: Part, First, Take, Most. ■ *New in Version 1.*

■ LatticeReduce

LatticeReduce[{v_1, v_2, ... }] gives a reduced basis for the set of vectors v_i.

The elements of the v_i can be integers, Gaussian integers, or Gaussian rational numbers. ■ See page 752. ■ Implementation notes: see page 1067. ■ See also: Rationalize, ContinuedFraction. ■ Related package: NumberTheory`Recognize`. ■ *New in Version 1.*

■ LCM

LCM[n_1, n_2, ...] gives the least common multiple of the integers n_i.

Integer mathematical function (see Section A.3.10). ■ LCM also works with rational numbers; LCM[r_1, r_2, ...] gives the least rational number r for which all the r/r_i are integers. ■ LCM has attributes Flat and Orderless. ■ See page 749. ■ See also: GCD, PolynomialLCM. ■ *New in Version 1.*

■ LeafCount

LeafCount[$expr$] gives the total number of indivisible subexpressions in $expr$.

LeafCount gives a measure of the total "size" of an expression. ■ LeafCount counts the number of subexpressions in $expr$ which correspond to "leaves" on the expression tree. ■ Example: LeafCount[1 + a + b^2] ⟶ 6. ■ LeafCount is based on FullForm representation of expressions. ■ Numbers with heads Rational and Complex are treated as composite objects, just as in FullForm. ■ See page 714. ■ See also: ByteCount, Length, Depth, AtomQ. ■ *New in Version 1.*

■ LegendreP

LegendreP[n, x] gives the Legendre polynomial $P_n(x)$.

LegendreP[n, m, x] gives the associated Legendre polynomial $P_n^m(x)$.

Mathematical function (see Section A.3.10). ■ Explicit formulas are given for integer n and m. ■ The Legendre polynomials satisfy the differential equation $(1 - x^2)(d^2y/dx^2) - 2x(dy/dx) + n(n + 1)y = 0$. ■ The Legendre polynomials are orthogonal with unit weight function. ■ The associated Legendre polynomials are defined by $P_n^m(x) = (-1)^m(1 - x^2)^{m/2}(d^m/dx^m)P_n(x)$. ■ For arbitrary complex values of n, m and z, LegendreP[n, z] and LegendreP[n, m, z] give Legendre functions of the first kind. ■ LegendreP[n, m, a, z] gives Legendre functions of type a. The default is type 1. ~■ The symbolic form of type 1 involves $(1 - z^2)^{m/2}$, of type 2 involves $(1 + z)^{m/2}/(1 - z)^{m/2}$ and of type 3 involves $(1 + z)^{m/2}/(-1 + z)m/2$. ■ Type 1 is defined only for z within the unit circle in the complex plane. Type 2 represents an analytic continuation of type 1 outside the unit circle. ■ Type 2 functions have branch cuts from $-\infty$ to -1 and from $+1$ to $+\infty$ in the complex z plane. ■ Type 3 functions have a single branch cut from $-\infty$ to $+1$. ~■ LegendreP[n, m, a, z] is defined to be Hypergeometric2F1Regularized[-n,n+1,1-m,(1-z)/2] multiplied by $(1 + z)^{m/2}/(1 - z)^{m/2}$ for type 2 and by $(1 + z)^{m/2}/(-1 + z)^{m/2}$ for type 3. ■ See pages 766 and 777. ■ See also: SphericalHarmonicY. ■ *New in Version 1; modified in Version 5.0.*

■ LegendreQ

LegendreQ[n, z] gives the Legendre function of the second kind $Q_n(z)$.

LegendreQ[n, m, z] gives the associated Legendre function of the second kind $Q_n^m(z)$.

Mathematical function (see Section A.3.10). ■ For integer n and m, explicit formulas are generated. ■ The Legendre functions satisfy the differential equation $(1 - z^2)y'' - 2zy' + [n(n + 1) - m^2/(1 - z^2)]y = 0$. ■ LegendreQ[$n$, m, a, z] gives Legendre functions of type a. The default is type 1. ■ LegendreQ of types 1, 2 and 3 are defined in terms of LegendreP of these types, and have the same branch cut structure. ■ See page 777. ■ *New in Version 1; modified in Version 3.*

■ Length

Length[$expr$] gives the number of elements in $expr$.

See page 236. +■ When $expr$ is a SparseArray object, Length[$expr$] returns the length of corresponding ordinary list. ~■ Otherwise, Length[$expr$] returns 0 whenever AtomQ[$expr$] is True. ■ See also: LeafCount, ByteCount, Depth. ■ *New in Version 1; modified in Version 5.0.*

■ **LerchPhi**

LerchPhi[z, s, a] gives the Lerch transcendent $\Phi(z,s,a)$.

Mathematical function (see Section A.3.10). ■ $\Phi(z,s,a) = \sum_{k=0}^{\infty} z^k/(a+k)^s$, where any term with $k + a = 0$ is excluded. ■ LerchPhi[z, s, a, DoublyInfinite->True] gives the sum $\sum_{k=-\infty}^{\infty} z^k/(a+k)^s$. ■ LerchPhi is a generalization of Zeta and PolyLog. ■ See page 772. ■ Related package: NumberTheory`Ramanujan`. ■ *New in Version 1.*

■ **Less**

x < y yields True if x is determined to be less than y.

x_1 < x_2 < x_3 yields True if the x_i form a strictly increasing sequence.

Less gives True or False when its arguments are real numbers. ■ Less does some simplification when its arguments are not numbers. ■ For exact numeric quantities, Less internally uses numerical approximations to establish numerical ordering. This process can be affected by the setting of the global variable $MaxExtraPrecision. ■ See page 86. ■ See also: LessEqual, Greater, Positive, Element. ■ *New in Version 1; modified in Version 3.*

■ **LessEqual**

x <= y or $x \leq y$ yields True if x is determined to be less than or equal to y.

$x_1 \leq x_2 \leq x_3$ yields True if the x_i form a non-decreasing sequence.

$x \leq y$ can be entered as x :<=: y or x \[LessEqual] y. ■ LessEqual gives True or False when its arguments are real numbers. ■ LessEqual does some simplification when its arguments are not numbers. ■ For exact numeric quantities, LessEqual internally uses numerical approximations to establish numerical ordering. This process can be affected by the setting of the global variable $MaxExtraPrecision. ■ In StandardForm, LessEqual is printed using $\leq$. ■ $x \leqslant y$, entered as x :</: y or x \[LessSlantEqual] y, can be used on input as an alternative to $x \leq y$. ■ See page 86. ■ See also: Less, GreaterEqual, Element. ■ *New in Version 1; modified in Version 3.*

■ **LetterQ**

LetterQ[*string*] yields True if all the characters in the string are letters, and yields False otherwise.

LetterQ[*string*] by default gives False if *string* contains any space or punctuation characters. ■ LetterQ handles both ordinary and special characters. ■ LetterQ treats as letters all special characters explicitly listed as letters in the table on pages 1354–1401. ■ In general, LetterQ treats as letters all characters that appear as ordinary text in any language. ■ LetterQ treats as letters such special characters as α, $\mathbb{Z}$, $\mathcal{L}$ and æ. ■ LetterQ does not treat as letters $\emptyset$ (\[EmptySet]), $\hbar$ (\[HBar]), Å (\[Angstrom]) or $\sum$ (\[Sum]). ■ See page 413. ■ See also: DigitQ, UpperCaseQ, LowerCaseQ, CharacterRange. ■ *New in Version 2; modified in Version 3.*

■ **Level**

Level[*expr*, *levelspec*] gives a list of all subexpressions of *expr* on levels specified by *levelspec*.

Level[*expr*, *levelspec*, f] applies f to the list of subexpressions.

Level uses the standard level specification described on page 1041. ■ Level[*expr*, {-1}] gives a list of all "atomic" objects in *expr*. ■ Level traverses expressions in depth-first order, so that the subexpressions in the final list are ordered lexicographically by their indices. ■ See page 239. ■ See also: Apply, Map, Scan. ■ *New in Version 1.*

■ Lighting

Lighting is an option for **Graphics3D** and related functions that specifies whether to use simulated illumination in three-dimensional pictures.

Lighting -> True uses simulated illumination. The ambient light level is specified by the option AmbientLight. The option LightSources gives the positions and intensities of point light sources. ■ Lighting -> False uses no simulated illumination. In SurfaceGraphics, polygons are then shaded according to their height, or according to the ColorFunction option that is given. ■ See pages 526 and 544. ■ See also: Shading, ColorFunction, SurfaceColor. ■ *New in Version 1.*

■ LightSources

LightSources is an option for **Graphics3D** and related functions that specifies the properties of point light sources for simulated illumination.

The basic form is LightSources -> {s_1, s_2, ... }, where the s_i are the specifications for each light source. Each s_i has the form {*direction*, *color*}. The direction is specified as {x, y, z}, where the components are with respect to the final display area. The x and y are horizontal and vertical in the plane of the display; z is orthogonal to the display. Positive z is in front. Only the relative magnitude of the components is relevant; the overall normalization of the vector is ignored. The color can be specified by GrayLevel, Hue or RGBColor. ■ Simulated illumination determines the shading of polygons in three-dimensional pictures. ■ The shading of a particular polygon is computed as a sum of contributions from point light sources, plus a contribution from ambient light. ■ Surface properties of polygons are specified by SurfaceColor directives. ■ Light reflection properties assumed for polygons are described in the notes for SurfaceColor. ■ See page 545. ■ See also: AmbientLight. ■ *New in Version 1.*

■ Limit

Limit[*expr*, *x*->x_0] finds the limiting value of *expr* when x approaches x_0.

Example: Limit[Sin[x]/x, x->0] $\longrightarrow$ 1. ■ Limit[*expr*, *x*->x_0, Direction -> 1] computes the limit as x approaches x_0 from smaller values. Limit[*expr*, *x*->x_0, Direction -> -1] computes the limit as x approaches x_0 from larger values. ■ Limit returns Interval objects to represent ranges of possible values, for example at essential singularities. ■ Limit returns unevaluated when it encounters functions about which it has no specific information. Limit therefore by default makes no explicit assumptions about symbolic functions. ~■ Assumptions can be specified as a setting for the option Assumptions. ■ See page 893. ■ See also: Series, Residue. ■ Related package: NumericalMath`NLimit`. ■ *New in Version 1; modified in Version 5.0.*

■ LimitsPositioning

LimitsPositioning is an option for **UnderoverscriptBox** and related boxes which specifies whether to change the positioning of underscripts and overscripts in the way conventional for limits.

UnderoverscriptBox[x, y, z, LimitsPositioning->False] is always displayed with explicit underscripts and overscripts, as $\overset{z}{\underset{y}{x}}$. ■ UnderoverscriptBox[$x$, y, z, LimitsPositioning->True] is displayed as $\overset{z}{\underset{y}{x}}$ when large, and x_y^z when small. ■ The x_y^z form is used when the box appears in a subscript or other script, or inline in a piece of text. ■ With the default setting LimitsPositioning->Automatic the display of UnderoverscriptBox[x, y, z] depends on x. If x is \[Sum], \[Product] or another form conventionally displayed with limits, then LimitsPositioning->True is effectively used. Otherwise, LimitsPositioning->False is used. ■ LimitsPositioningTokens is a Cell option which can be set to a list of forms for which LimitsPositioning->True should be used. ■ See page 458. ■ See also: ScriptSizeMultipliers. ■ *New in Version 3.*

■ Line

Line[{pt_1, pt_2, ... }] is a graphics primitive which represents a line joining a sequence of points.

Line can be used in both Graphics and Graphics3D (two- and three-dimensional graphics). ■ The positions of points can be specified either in ordinary coordinates, as {x, y} or {x, y, z}, or in scaled coordinates as Scaled[{x, y}] or Scaled[{x, y, z}]. ■ Offset can be used to specify coordinates in two dimensions. ■ The line consists of a sequence of straight segments joining the specified points. ■ Line thickness can be specified using Thickness or AbsoluteThickness. ■ Line dashing can be specified using Dashing or AbsoluteDashing. ■ Line shading or coloring can be specified using CMYKColor, GrayLevel, Hue or RGBColor. ■ See pages 492 and 520. ■ See also: Polygon, PlotJoined. ■ Related packages: Graphics`Arrow`, Graphics`Spline`. ■ *New in Version 1; modified in Version 3.*

■ LinearProgramming

LinearProgramming[c, m, b] finds a vector x which minimizes the quantity $c.x$ subject to the constraints $m.x \geq b$ and $x \geq 0$.

+ **LinearProgramming[c, m, {{b_1, s_1}, {b_2, s_2}, ... }]** finds a vector x which minimizes $c.x$ subject to $x \geq 0$ and linear constraints specified by the matrix m and the pairs {b_i, s_i}. For each row m_i of m, the corresponding constraint is m_i . $x \geq b_i$ if s_i == 1, or m_i . $x == b_i$ if s_i == 0, or m_i . $x \leq b_i$ if s_i == -1.

+ **LinearProgramming[c, m, b, l]** minimizes $c.x$ subject to the constraints specified by m and b and $x \geq l$.

+ **LinearProgramming[c, m, b, {l_1, l_2, ... }]** minimizes $c.x$ subject to the constraints specified by m and b and $x_i \geq l_i$.

+ **LinearProgramming[c, m, b, {{l_1, u_1}, {l_2, u_2}, ... }]** minimizes $c.x$ subject to the constraints specified by m and b and $l_i \leq x_i \leq u_i$.

All entries in the vectors c and b and the matrix m must be real numbers. +■ The bounds l_i and u_i must be real numbers or Infinity or -Infinity. ■ LinearProgramming gives exact rational number results if its input is exact. +■ LinearProgramming returns unevaluated if no solution can be found. +■ LinearProgramming finds approximate numerical results if its input contains approximate numbers. The option Tolerance specifies the tolerance to be used for internal comparisons. The default is Tolerance->Automatic, which does exact comparisons for exact numbers, and uses tolerance 10^{-6} for approximate numbers. +■ SparseArray objects can be used in LinearProgramming. +■ With Method->"InteriorPoint", LinearProgramming uses interior point methods. ■ See page 975. ■ Implementation notes: see page 1068. ■ See also: NMinimize, Minimize. ■ *New in Version 2; modified in Version 5.0.*

■ LinearSolve

LinearSolve[m, b] finds an x which solves the matrix equation $m.x==b$.

+ **LinearSolve[m]** generates a **LinearSolveFunction[...]** which can be applied repeatedly to different b.

~■ LinearSolve works on both numerical and symbolic matrices, as well as SparseArray objects. ■ The argument b can be either a vector or a matrix. ■ The matrix m can be square or rectangular. +■ LinearSolve[m] and LinearSolveFunction[...] provide an efficient way to solve the same approximate numerical linear system many times. +■ LinearSolve[m, b] is equivalent to LinearSolve[m][b]. ■ For underdetermined systems, LinearSolve will return one of the possible solutions; Solve will return a general solution. ■ LinearSolve[m, b, Modulus -> n] takes the matrix equation to be modulo n. ■ LinearSolve[m, b, ZeroTest -> $test$] evaluates $test$[m[[i, j]]] to determine whether matrix elements are zero. The default setting is ZeroTest -> (# == 0 &). ~■ A Method option can also be given. Settings for exact and symbolic matrices include "CofactorExpansion", "DivisionFreeRowReduction" and "OneStepRowReduction". Settings for approximate numerical matrices include "Cholesky", and for sparse arrays "Multifrontal" and "Krylov". The default setting of Automatic switches between these methods depending on the matrix given. ■ See page 907. ■ Implementation notes: see page 1069. ■ See also: Inverse, PseudoInverse, Solve, NullSpace, CoefficientArrays, CholeskyDecomposition. ■ *New in Version 1; modified in Version 5.0.*

◼ LinearSolveFunction

LinearSolveFunction[*dimensions*, *data*] represents a function for providing solutions to a matrix equation.

LinearSolveFunction[...] is generated by LinearSolve[*m*]. ▪ LinearSolveFunction works like Function. ▪ LinearSolveFunction[...][*b*] finds the solution to the matrix equation *m* . *x* == *b* for the specific vector or matrix *b*. ▪ In standard output format, only the *dimensions* element of a LinearSolveFunction object is printed explicitly. The remaining elements are indicated by <>. ▪ *dimensions* specifies the dimensions of the matrix *m* from which the LinearSolveFunction was constructed. ▪ See page 252. ▪ See also: LinearSolve, Inverse, LUDecomposition, CholeskyDecomposition. ▪ *New in Version 5.0.*

◼ LineIndent

LineIndent is an option for Cell, StyleBox and StyleForm which specifies how many ems of indentation to add at the beginnings of lines for each level of nesting in an expression.

The typical default setting is LineIndent->1. ▪ The setting for LineIndent determines the amount of indentation that will be inserted after any explicit RETURN is entered when AutoIndent->True. ▪ See also: LineIndentMaxFraction, PageWidth. ▪ *New in Version 3.*

◼ LineIndentMaxFraction

LineIndentMaxFraction is an option for Cell, StyleBox and StyleForm which specifies the maximum fraction of the total page width to indent at the beginnings of lines.

The typical default setting is LineIndentMaxFraction->0.5. ▪ The setting for LineIndentMaxFraction is relevant in formatting deeply nested expressions. ▪ See also: LineIndent, PageWidth. ▪ *New in Version 3.*

◼ LineSpacing

LineSpacing is an option for Cell, StyleBox and StyleForm which specifies the spacing between successive lines of text.

LineSpacing->{*c*, 0} leaves space so that the total height of each line is *c* times the height of its contents. ▪ LineSpacing->{0, *n*} makes the total height of each line exactly *n* printer's points. ▪ LineSpacing->{*c*, *n*} makes the total height *c* times the height of the contents plus *n* printer's points. ▪ A typical default setting is LineSpacing->{1, 1}, which leaves space for the contents of the line, plus 1 printer's point (approximately $\frac{1}{72}$ of an inch) of extra space. ▪ LineSpacing->{2, 0} makes text "double spaced". ▪ LineSpacing-> {1, -*n*} tightens text by *n* printer's points. ▪ LineSpacing applies both to ordinary text and *Mathematica* expressions. ▪ In ordinary text, LineSpacing determines the spacing between lines produced by automatic linebreaking. For lines produced by explicit RETURN characters ParagraphSpacing is added. ▪ In *Mathematica* expressions, LineSpacing is used whether lines are produced by automatic linebreaking or by explicit RETURN characters. ▪ Extra space specified by LineSpacing is inserted equally above and below a line, except that no extra space is inserted before the first line or after the last line of an expression or cell. ▪ See page 611. ▪ See also: FontSize, ParagraphSpacing. ▪ *New in Version 3.*

◼ LinkClose

LinkClose[*link*] closes an open *MathLink* connection.

link must be an active LinkObject, as returned by functions like LinkLaunch and Links. ▪ Closing a *MathLink* connection does not necessarily terminate the program at the other end of the connection. ▪ See page 680. ▪ See also: LinkInterrupt, Close. ▪ *New in Version 3.*

■ LinkConnect

`LinkConnect["`*name*`"]` connects to a *MathLink* link created by another program.

`LinkConnect` by default operates with internet TCP links, with names of the form *port@host*. Ports are typically specified by numbers. ■ `LinkConnect` can connect to a port on a remote computer system. ■ On some computer systems, `LinkConnect[ ]` will bring up a port browser. ■ `LinkConnect` returns a `LinkObject`. ■ You can use `LinkConnect` with `LinkCreate` to set up peer-to-peer communication between two *Mathematica* processes. ■ `LinkConnect` can be used to connect to a link created by calling `LinkCreate` in another *Mathematica* process. ■ `LinkConnect` can be used to connect to an external program that has created a *MathLink* link by calling the appropriate *MathLink* library functions. ■ External programs built from *MathLink* templates using `mcc` and `mprep` can typically create *MathLink* links whenever they are given `-linkcreate` command-line arguments. ■ The option `LinkProtocol` specifies the underlying data transport protocol that `LinkConnect` should use. ■ `LinkConnect` internally calls a function analogous to the `MLOpenArgv()` function in the *MathLink* library. ■ Even though no program may yet be connected to the other end of the *MathLink* link, the function `LinkConnect` will return immediately and will not block. ■ See page 680. ■ See also: `LinkCreate`, `LinkLaunch`, `LinkClose`. ■ *New in Version 3.*

■ LinkCreate

`LinkCreate["`*name*`"]` creates a *MathLink* link with the specified name for another program to connect to.

`LinkCreate[ ]` picks an unused port on your computer system and creates a *MathLink* link on it.

`LinkCreate` returns a `LinkObject`. ■ You can use `LinkCreate` and `LinkConnect` to set up peer-to-peer communication between two *Mathematica* processes. ■ The option `LinkProtocol` specifies the underlying data transport protocol to use. ■ `LinkCreate` internally calls a function analogous to the `MLOpenArgv()` function in the *MathLink* library. ■ See page 680. ■ See also: `LinkConnect`, `LinkLaunch`, `LinkClose`. ■ *New in Version 3.*

■ LinkInterrupt

`LinkInterrupt[`*link*`]` sends an interrupt to the program at the other end of the specified *MathLink* connection.

link must be an active `LinkObject`, as returned by functions such as `LinkLaunch` or `Links`. ■ It is up to the external program to determine how it will handle the interrupt. ■ External programs created from *MathLink* templates will by default set the global variable `MLAbort` if they receive an abort. ■ See page 686. ■ See also: `Interrupt`, `LinkClose`. ■ *New in Version 3.*

■ LinkLaunch

`LinkLaunch["`*prog*`"]` starts the external program *prog* and opens a *MathLink* connection to it.

`LinkLaunch["`*prog*`"]` runs *prog* as a subsidiary or child process to your current *Mathematica* session. ■ You can use a command such as `LinkLaunch["math -mathlink"]` to launch a subsidiary *Mathematica* kernel process from within your *Mathematica* session. ■ On most computer systems calling `LinkLaunch["`*prog*`"]` multiple times with the same argument will start several *prog* processes running. ■ On some computer systems, `LinkLaunch[ ]` will bring up a program browser. ■ `LinkLaunch` returns a `LinkObject`. ■ The option `LinkProtocol` specifies the underlying data transport protocol to use. ■ `LinkLaunch` internally calls a function analogous to the `MLOpenArgv()` function in the *MathLink* library. ■ See page 683. ■ See also: `Install`, `LinkCreate`, `LinkConnect`, `LinkClose`. ■ *New in Version 3.*

■ LinkObject

LinkObject["*name*", *n*] is an object that represents an active *MathLink* connection for functions such as LinkRead and LinkWrite.

LinkConnect, LinkCreate, LinkLaunch and Install all return LinkObject objects. ■ The integer *n* is a serial number used to distinguish links with the same name. ■ *name* is typically the name of an external program, or an internet TCP specification of the form *port@host*. ■ See pages 659 and 687. ■ See also: Links, LinkReadyQ, InputStream. ■ *New in Version 3.*

■ LinkPatterns

LinkPatterns[*link*] gives a list of the patterns for which definitions were set up when the external program associated with the specified *MathLink* connection was installed.

Each element of the list returned by LinkPatterns is wrapped in HoldForm to prevent evaluation. ■ The patterns in LinkPatterns typically originate in :Pattern: specifications in the *MathLink* templates used to create source code for the external program. ■ Uninstall[*link*] calls Unset on the patterns in LinkPatterns[*link*]. ■ See page 662. ■ See also: Install. ■ *New in Version 3.*

■ LinkProtocol

LinkProtocol is an option to LinkLaunch, Install and related functions which specifies the underlying data transport protocol to use for a new *MathLink* link.

■ Typical settings for LinkProtocol are "SharedMemory" and "FileMap" (Windows), "Pipes" (Unix, Macintosh) and "TCPIP" (all systems). ■ See page 677. ■ *New in Version 3; modified in Version 5.0.*

■ LinkRead

LinkRead[*link*] reads one expression from the specified *MathLink* connection.

LinkRead[*link*, *h*] wraps *h* around the expression read before evaluating it.

link must be an active LinkObject, as returned by functions like LinkLaunch or Links. ■ LinkRead will wait until it has read a complete expression before returning. ■ You can test whether an expression is ready to be read from a particular link using LinkReadyQ. ■ You can use LinkRead[*link*, Hold] to get an expression from a link without evaluating it. ■ See page 680. ■ See also: LinkReadyQ, LinkWrite, Read. ■ *New in Version 3.*

■ LinkReadyQ

LinkReadyQ[*link*] tests whether there is an expression ready to read from the specified *MathLink* connection.

link must be an active LinkObject, as returned by functions like LinkLaunch or Links. ■ If LinkReadyQ[*link*] returns True, then LinkRead[*link*] will not block under any normal circumstances. ■ If LinkReadyQ[*link*] returns False, then LinkRead[*link*] will block, and will not return until something becomes available to read on *link*. ■ LinkReadyQ[*link*] tests whether there is any data to read; it cannot determine whether the data represents a complete expression. ■ LinkReadyQ corresponds to the *MathLink* library function MLReady(). ■ See page 680. ■ See also: LinkRead, LinkWrite, LinkInterrupt. ■ *New in Version 3.*

■ Links

Links[ ] gives a list of all *MathLink* connections that are currently open.

Links["*name*"] lists only links with the specified name.

Links returns a list of LinkObject objects. ■ See page 662. ■ See also: $ParentLink, $CurrentLink, Streams, LinkReadyQ, LinkLaunch, LinkClose. ■ *New in Version 3.*

■ LinkWrite

LinkWrite[*link*, *expr*] writes *expr* to the specified *MathLink* connection.

link must be an active LinkObject, as returned by functions like LinkLaunch or Links. ■ You can use LinkWrite[*link*, Unevaluated[*expr*]] to write *expr* to the link without evaluating it. ■ The head of *expr* will often be a packet which specifies how *expr* should be processed by the program which receives it. ■ When LinkWrite is used to send data to a *Mathematica* kernel, EnterTextPacket["*string*"] enters the text of an input line, and EvaluatePacket[*expr*] sends an expression for evaluation. ■ See page 680. ■ See also: LinkRead, Write, FrontEndExecute. ■ *New in Version 3.*

■ List

{e_1, e_2, ... } is a list of elements.

Lists are very general objects that represent collections of expressions. ■ Functions with attribute Listable are automatically "threaded" over lists, so that they act separately on each list element. Most built-in mathematical functions are Listable. ■ {*a*, *b*, *c*} represents a vector. ■ {{*a*, *b*}, {*c*, *d*}} represents a matrix. ■ Nested lists can be used to represent tensors. ■ See page 115. ■ See also: Sequence. ■ *New in Version 1.*

■ Listable

Listable is an attribute that can be assigned to a symbol *f* to indicate that the function *f* should automatically be threaded over lists that appear as its arguments.

Listable functions are effectively applied separately to each element in a list, or to corresponding elements in each list if there is more than one list. ■ Most built-in mathematical functions are Listable. ■ Example: Log is Listable. Log[{a,b,c}] ⟶ {Log[a], Log[b], Log[c]}. ■ All the arguments which are lists in a Listable function must be of the same length. ■ Arguments that are not lists are copied as many times as there are elements in the lists. ■ Example: Plus is Listable. {a, b, c} + x ⟶ {a + x, b + x, c + x}. ■ See page 329. ■ See also: Thread, Map, Sequence, SparseArray. ■ *New in Version 1.*

■ ListContourPlot

ListContourPlot[*array*] generates a contour plot from an array of height values.

ListContourPlot returns a ContourGraphics object. ■ ListContourPlot has the same options as ContourGraphics. ■ Successive rows of *array* are arranged up the page; successive columns across the page. ■ See notes for ContourGraphics. ■ See page 159. ■ *New in Version 1.*

■ ListConvolve

ListConvolve[*ker*, *list*] forms the convolution of the kernel *ker* with *list*.

ListConvolve[*ker*, *list*, *k*] forms the cyclic convolution in which the kth element of *ker* is aligned with each element in *list*.

ListConvolve[*ker*, *list*, {k_L, k_R}] forms the cyclic convolution whose first element contains *list*[[1]] *ker*[[k_L]] and whose last element contains *list*[[-1]] *ker*[[k_R]].

ListConvolve[*ker*, *list*, *klist*, *p*] forms the convolution in which *list* is padded at each end with repetitions of the element *p*.

ListConvolve[*ker*, *list*, *klist*, {p_1, p_2, ... }] forms the convolution in which *list* is padded at each end with cyclic repetitions of the p_i.

ListConvolve[*ker*, *list*, *klist*, *padding*, *g*, *h*] forms a generalized convolution in which *g* is used in place of Times and *h* in place of Plus.

ListConvolve[*ker*, *list*, *klist*, *padding*, *g*, *h*, *lev*] forms a convolution using elements at level *lev* in *ker* and *list*.

(continued)

■ **ListConvolve** *(continued)*

■ With kernel K_r and list a_s, ListConvolve[*ker*, *list*] computes $\sum_r K_r a_{s-r}$, where the limits of the sum are such that the kernel never overhangs either end of the list. ■ Example: ListConvolve[{x,y}, {a,b,c}] ⟶ {b x + a y, c x + b y}. ■ ListConvolve[*ker*, *list*] gives a result of length Length[*list*]-Length[*ker*]+1. ■ ListConvolve[*ker*, *list*] allows no overhangs and is equivalent to ListConvolve[*ker*, *list*, {-1, 1}]. ■ ListConvolve[*ker*, *list*, *k*] is equivalent to ListConvolve[*ker*, *list*, {*k*, *k*}]. ■ The values of k_L and k_R in ListConvolve[*ker*, *list*, {k_L, k_R}] determine the amount of overhang to allow at each end of *list*. ■ Common settings for {k_L, k_R} are:

{-1, 1}   no overhangs (default)
{-1, -1}   maximal overhang at the right-hand end
{1, 1}   maximal overhang at the left-hand end
{1, -1}   maximal overhangs at both beginning and end

■ Examples: ListConvolve[{x,y}, {a,b,c}, {1,1}] ⟶ {a x + c y, b x + a y, c x + b y}.
■ ListConvolve[{x,y}, {a,b,c}, {1,-1}] ⟶ {a x + c y, b x + a y, c x + b y, a x + c y}. ■ With maximal overhang at one end only, the result from ListConvolve is the same length as *list*.
■ ListConvolve[*ker*, *list*, {k_L, k_R}, *padlist*] effectively lays down repeated copies of *padlist*, then superimposes one copy of *list* on them and forms a convolution of the result. ■ Common settings for *padlist* are:

p pad with repetitions of a single element
{p_1, p_2, ... }   pad with cyclic repetitions of a sequence of elements
list   pad by treating *list* as cyclic (default)
{}   do no padding

■ ListConvolve works with multidimensional kernels and lists of data.
■ ListConvolve[*ker*, *list*, {{k_{L1}, k_{L2}, ... }, {k_{R1}, k_{R2}, ... }}] forms the cyclic convolution whose {1,1,... } element contains *ker*[[k_{L1}, k_{L2}, ...]] *list*[[1,1,...]] and whose {-1,-1,... } element contains *ker*[[k_{R1}, k_{R2}, ...]] *list*[[-1,-1,...]]. ■ {k_L, k_R} is taken to be equivalent to {{k_L, k_L, ... }, {k_R, k_R, ... }}.
■ When a function *h* is specified to use in place of Plus, explicit nested *h* expressions are generated with a depth equal to the depth of *ker*. ■ ListConvolve works with exact numbers and symbolic data as well as approximate numbers. ■ See page 937. ■ Implementation notes: see page 1069. ■ See also: ListCorrelate, Partition, Inner, CellularAutomaton, PadLeft. ■ *New in Version 4.*

■ **ListCorrelate**

ListCorrelate[*ker*, *list*] forms the correlation of the kernel *ker* with *list*.

ListCorrelate[*ker*, *list*, *k*] forms the cyclic correlation in which the kth element of *ker* is aligned with each element in *list*.

ListCorrelate[*ker*, *list*, {k_L, k_R}] forms the cyclic correlation whose first element contains *list*[[1]] *ker*[[k_L]] and whose last element contains *list*[[-1]] *ker*[[k_R]].

ListCorrelate[*ker*, *list*, *klist*, *p*] forms the correlation in which *list* is padded at each end with repetitions of the element *p*.

ListCorrelate[*ker*, *list*, *klist*, {p_1, p_2, ... }] forms the correlation in which *list* is padded at each end with cyclic repetitions of the p_i.

ListCorrelate[*ker*, *list*, *klist*, *padding*, *g*, *h*] forms a generalized correlation in which *g* is used in place of Times and *h* in place of Plus.

ListCorrelate[*ker*, *list*, *klist*, *padding*, *g*, *h*, *lev*] forms a correlation using elements at level *lev* in *ker* and *list*.

(continued)

■ ListCorrelate *(continued)*

■ With kernel K_r and list a_s, ListCorrelate[*ker*, *list*] computes $\sum_r K_r a_{s+r}$, where the limits of the sum are such that the kernel never overhangs either end of the list. ■ Example: ListCorrelate[{x,y}, {a,b,c}] $\longrightarrow$ {a x + b y, b x + c y}. ■ For a one-dimensional list ListCorrelate[*ker*, *list*] is equivalent to ListConvolve[Reverse[*ker*], *list*]. ■ For higher-dimensional lists, *ker* must be reversed at every level. ■ See notes for ListConvolve. ■ Settings for k_L and k_R are negated in ListConvolve relative to ListCorrelate. ■ Common settings for $\{k_L, k_R\}$ in ListCorrelate are:

{1, -1}	no overhangs (default)
{1, 1}	maximal overhang at the right-hand end
{-1, -1}	maximal overhang at the left-hand end
{-1, 1}	maximal overhangs at both beginning and end

■ See page 937. ■ Implementation notes: see page 1069. ■ See also: ListConvolve, Partition, Inner, CellularAutomaton, PadLeft. ■ *New in Version 4.*

■ ListDensityPlot

ListDensityPlot[*array*] generates a density plot from an array of height values.

ListDensityPlot returns a DensityGraphics object. ■ ListDensityPlot has the same options as DensityGraphics. ■ Successive rows of *array* are arranged up the page; successive columns across the page. ■ See notes for DensityGraphics. ■ See page 159. ■ *New in Version 1.*

■ ListInterpolation

ListInterpolation[*array*] constructs an InterpolatingFunction object which represents an approximate function that interpolates the array of values given.

ListInterpolation[*array*, {{*xmin*, *xmax*}, {*ymin*, *ymax*}, ... }] specifies the domain of the grid from which the values in *array* are assumed to come.

You can replace {*xmin*, *xmax*} etc. by explicit lists of positions for grid lines. The grid lines are otherwise assumed to be equally spaced. ■ ListInterpolation[*array*] assumes grid lines at integer positions in each direction. ■ *array* can be an array in any number of dimensions, corresponding to a list with any number of levels of nesting. ■ ListInterpolation[*array*, *domain*] generates an InterpolatingFunction object which returns values with the same precision as those in {*array*, *domain*}. ■ See notes for Interpolation. ■ See page 934. ■ See also: FunctionInterpolation, ListContourPlot, Quantile. ■ *New in Version 3.*

■ ListPlay

ListPlay[{a_1, a_2, ... }] plays a sound whose amplitude is given by the sequence of levels a_i.

ListPlay returns a Sound object. ■ The following options can be given:

DisplayFunction	$SoundDisplayFunction	function for generating output
Epilog	{}	sound or graphics to be used as an epilog
PlayRange	Automatic	the range of amplitude levels to include
Prolog	{}	sound or graphics to be used as a prolog
SampleDepth	8	how many bits to use to represent each amplitude level
SampleRate	8192	how many times per second amplitude samples should be generated

■ ListPlay[{$list_1$, $list_2$}] generates stereo sound. The left-hand channel is given first. ■ ListPlay[{$list_1$, $list_2$, ... }] generates sound on any number of channels. If the lists are of different lengths, silence is inserted at the ends of the shorter lists. ■ See page 172. ■ See also: Play, SampledSoundList, Show. ■ Related package: Miscellaneous`Audio`. ■ *New in Version 2.*

■ **ListPlot**

ListPlot[{y_1, y_2, ... }] plots a list of values. The x coordinates for each point are taken to be 1, 2, ...

ListPlot[{{x_1, y_1}, {x_2, y_2}, ... }] plots a list of values with specified x and y coordinates.

ListPlot returns a Graphics object. ■ ListPlot has the same options as Graphics, with the following additions:

PlotJoined   False   whether to draw a line joining the points
PlotStyle   Automatic   graphics directives to determine the style of the points or line

■ Setting PlotJoined -> True gives a line joining the points. ■ ListPlot has the default option setting Axes -> True. ■ See page 159. ■ See also: Plot, Fit. ■ Related packages: Graphics`MultipleListPlot`, Graphics`Graphics`. ■ *New in Version 1.*

■ **ListPlot3D**

ListPlot3D[*array*] generates a three-dimensional plot of a surface representing an array of height values.

ListPlot3D[*array*, *shades*] generates a plot with each element of the surface shaded according to the specification in *shades*.

ListPlot3D returns a SurfaceGraphics object. ■ ListPlot3D has the same options as SurfaceGraphics. ■ ListPlot3D has the default option setting Axes -> True. ■ *array* should be a rectangular array of real numbers, representing z values. There will be holes in the surface corresponding to any array elements that are not real numbers. ■ If *array* has dimensions $m \times n$, then *shades* must have dimensions $(m - 1) \times (n - 1)$. ■ The elements of *shades* must be either GrayLevel, Hue or RGBColor, or SurfaceColor objects. ■ See page 159. ■ See also: Plot3D. ■ Related packages: Graphics`Graphics3D`, DiscreteMath`ComputationalGeometry`. ■ *New in Version 1.*

■ **Locked**

Locked is an attribute which, once assigned, prevents modification of any attributes of a symbol.

See page 329. ■ See also: Protected, ReadProtected. ■ *New in Version 1.*

■ **Log**

Log[z] gives the natural logarithm of z (logarithm to base e).

Log[b, z] gives the logarithm to base b.

Mathematical function (see Section A.3.10). ■ Log gives exact rational number results when possible. ■ Log[z] has a branch cut discontinuity in the complex z plane running from $-\infty$ to 0. ■ See page 761. ■ See also: Exp, Power, Arg, MantissaExponent, ProductLog, HarmonicNumber. ■ *New in Version 1.*

■ **LogGamma**

LogGamma[z] gives the logarithm of the gamma function $\log \Gamma(z)$.

Mathematical function (see Section A.3.10). ■ Unlike Log[Gamma[z]], LogGamma[z] is analytic throughout the complex z plane, except for a branch cut discontinuity along the negative real axis. ■ See page 770. ■ *New in Version 2.*

■ LogicalExpand

LogicalExpand[*expr*] expands out expressions containing logical connectives such as && and ||.

LogicalExpand applies distributive laws for logical operations. ■ Example:
LogicalExpand[p && !(q || r)] ⟶ p && !q && !r. ■ LogicalExpand generates ORs of ANDs corresponding to disjunctive normal form, with some contractions. ■ See pages 87 and 889. ■ See also: Expand. ■ *New in Version 1.*

■ LogIntegral

LogIntegral[*z*] is the logarithmic integral function li(*z*).

Mathematical function (see Section A.3.10). ■ The logarithmic integral function is defined by $\text{li}(z) = \int_0^z dt/\log t$, where the principal value of the integral is taken. ■ LogIntegral[*z*] has a branch cut discontinuity in the complex *z* plane running from −∞ to +1. ■ See page 774. ■ See also: ExpIntegralE. ■ *New in Version 1.*

■ LowerCaseQ

LowerCaseQ[*string*] yields True if all the characters in the string are lower-case letters, and yields False otherwise.

LowerCaseQ treats both ordinary and special characters. ■ See page 413. ■ See also: UpperCaseQ, LetterQ, ToLowerCase, ToCharacterCode. ■ *New in Version 2; modified in Version 3.*

■ LUDecomposition

LUDecomposition[*m*] generates a representation of the LU decomposition of a square matrix *m*.

LUDecomposition returns a list of three elements. The first element is a combination of upper and lower triangular matrices, the second element is a vector specifying rows used for pivoting, and for approximate numerical matrices **m** the third element is an estimate of the $\mathbf{L}^\infty$ condition number of **m**. ■ See page 914. ■ Implementation notes: see page 1069. ■ See also: LinearSolveFunction, CholeskyDecomposition, QRDecomposition, SchurDecomposition. ■ Related package: LinearAlgebra`Orthogonalization`. ■ *New in Version 3.*

■ MachineNumberQ

MachineNumberQ[*expr*] returns True if *expr* is a machine-precision real or complex number, and returns False otherwise.

See page 728. ■ See also: Precision, NumberQ. ■ Related package: NumericalMath`ComputerArithmetic`. ■ *New in Version 2.*

+ ■ MachinePrecision

MachinePrecision is a symbol used to indicate machine-number precision.

The numerical value of MachinePrecision is $MachinePrecision. ■ Precision[1.] gives MachinePrecision. ■ MachinePrecision is the default specification for precision in N and other numerical functions. ■ Approximate real numbers are assumed to have precision specified by MachinePrecision if fewer than $MachinePrecision explicit digits are entered. ■ The option setting WorkingPrecision->MachinePrecision specifies that internal computations in numerical functions should be done with machine numbers. ■ MachinePrecision is treated as a numeric constant, with attribute Constant. ■ See page 728. ■ See also: $MachinePrecision, Precision. ■ *New in Version 5.0.*

■ Magnification

Magnification is an option for Cell which specifies at what magnification to display the cell.

Magnification is often set for styles of cells or whole notebooks instead of individual cells. ■ Magnification affects spaces between cells as well as individual cells. ■ See page 604. ■ *New in Version 3.*

■ MakeBoxes

MakeBoxes[*expr*, *form*] is the low-level function used in *Mathematica* sessions to convert expressions into boxes.

MakeBoxes does not evaluate *expr*. ■ *form* can be StandardForm, TraditionalForm, or any other output form. ■ You can give definitions for MakeBoxes[*expr*, *form*] to specify your own rules for how expressions should be converted to boxes. ■ MakeBoxes is not automatically called on the results it generates. This means that explicit MakeBoxes calls must typically be inserted into definitions that are given. ■ If you change the output format for an expression by giving a definition for MakeBoxes, there is no guarantee that output you get will subsequently be able to be interpreted by *Mathematica*. ■ Definitions you give for MakeBoxes will override built-in *Mathematica* rules for generating output. ■ See page 475. ■ See also: MakeExpression, ToBoxes, Format. ■ *New in Version 3.*

■ MakeExpression

MakeExpression[*boxes*, *form*] is the low-level function used in *Mathematica* sessions to construct expressions from boxes.

MakeExpression returns its result wrapped in HoldComplete. ■ *form* can be StandardForm, TraditionalForm, or other forms for which interpretation rules have been defined. ■ You can give definitions for MakeExpression[*expr*, *form*] to specify your own rules for how boxes should be converted to expressions. ■ MakeExpression is not automatically called on the results it generates. This means that explicit MakeExpression calls must typically be inserted into definitions for MakeExpression. ■ MakeExpression is used whenever boxes are supplied as input to *Mathematica*. ■ The boxes that are fed to MakeExpression are constructed from textual input by forming tokens, then grouping these according to standard *Mathematica* operator precedence rules, stripping out spacing characters. StyleBox and other objects not intended for interpretation are removed. ■ Definitions you give for MakeExpression will override built-in *Mathematica* rules for processing input. ■ Giving input prefaced by \! makes *Mathematica* effectively perform MakeExpression. ■ See page 475. ■ See also: MakeBoxes, ToExpression. ■ *New in Version 3.*

■ MantissaExponent

MantissaExponent[*x*] gives a list containing the mantissa and exponent of a number *x*.

MantissaExponent[*x*, *b*] gives the base-*b* mantissa and exponent of *x*.

Example: MantissaExponent[3.4 10^25] $\longrightarrow$ {0.34, 26}. ■ The mantissa always lies between $1/b$ and 1 or -1 and $-1/b$. ■ MantissaExponent works with exact as well as approximate numeric quantities. ■ Example: MantissaExponent[Exp[Pi], 2] $\longrightarrow$ $\left\{\frac{e^{\pi}}{32}, 5\right\}$. ■ See page 726. ■ See also: Log, RealDigits, IntegerExponent. ■ *New in Version 2; modified in Version 4.*

■ **Map**

Map[*f*, *expr*] or *f* /@ *expr* applies *f* to each element on the first level in *expr*.

Map[*f*, *expr*, *levelspec*] applies *f* to parts of *expr* specified by *levelspec*.

Examples: Map[f, {a, b, c}] ⟶ {f[a], f[b], f[c]}; Map[f, a + b + c] ⟶ f[a] + f[b] + f[c]. ▪ Level specifications are described on page 1041. ▪ The default value for *levelspec* in Map is {1}. ▪ Examples: Map[f, {{a,b},{c,d}}] ⟶ {f[{a, b}], f[{c, d}]}; Map[f, {{a,b},{c,d}}, 2] ⟶ {f[{f[a], f[b]}], f[{f[c], f[d]}]}; Map[f, {{a,b},{c,d}}, -1] ⟶ {f[{f[a], f[b]}], f[{f[c], f[d]}]}. ▪ If *expr* is a SparseArray object, Map[*f*, *expr*] applies *f* to the values or subarrays that appear in *expr*. ▪ See page 244. ▪ See also: Apply, Scan, MapAll, MapAt, MapIndexed, MapThread, Level, Operate. ▪ *New in Version 1.*

■ **MapAll**

MapAll[*f*, *expr*] or *f* //@ *expr* applies *f* to every subexpression in *expr*.

Example: MapAll[f, {{a,b},{c,d}}] ⟶ f[{f[{f[a], f[b]}], f[{f[c], f[d]}]}]. ▪ MapAll[*f*, *expr*] is equivalent to Map[*f*, *expr*, {0, Infinity}]. ▪ MapAll[*f*, *expr*, Heads -> True] applies *f* inside the heads of the parts of *expr*. ▪ See page 245. ▪ See also: ExpandAll, ReplaceAll. ▪ *New in Version 1.*

■ **MapAt**

MapAt[*f*, *expr*, *n*] applies *f* to the element at position *n* in *expr*. If *n* is negative, the position is counted from the end.

MapAt[*f*, *expr*, {*i*, *j*, ... }] applies *f* to the part of *expr* at position {*i*, *j*, ... }.

MapAt[*f*, *expr*, {{i_1, j_1, ... }, {i_2, j_2, ... }, ... }] applies *f* to parts of *expr* at several positions.

Example: MapAt[f, {a, b, c}, 2] ⟶ {a, f[b], c}.
▪ MapAt[f, {a, b, c, d}, {{1}, {4}}] ⟶ {f[a], b, c, f[d]}. ▪ MapAt[*f*, *expr*, {*i*, *j*, ... }] or MapAt[*f*, *expr*, {{*i*, *j*, ... }}] applies *f* to the part *expr*[[*i*, *j*, ...]].
▪ MapAt[*f*, *expr*, {{i_1, j_1, ... }, {i_2, j_2, ... }, ... }] applies *f* to parts *expr*[[i_1, j_1, ...]], *expr*[[i_2, j_2, ...]], ...
▪ The list of positions used by MapAt is in the same form as is returned by the function Position. ▪ MapAt applies *f* repeatedly to a particular part if that part is mentioned more than once in the list of positions. ▪ Example: MapAt[f, {a, b, c}, {{1}, {3}, {1}}] ⟶ {f[f[a]], b, f[c]}. ▪ See page 245. ▪ See also: ReplacePart, Delete, FlattenAt. ▪ *New in Version 1.*

■ **MapIndexed**

MapIndexed[*f*, *expr*] applies *f* to the elements of *expr*, giving the part specification of each element as a second argument to *f*.

MapIndexed[*f*, *expr*, *levspec*] applies *f* to all parts of *expr* on levels specified by *levspec*.

Example: MapIndexed[f, {a, b, c}] ⟶ {f[a, {1}], f[b, {2}], f[c, {3}]}. ▪ Level specifications are described on page 1041. ▪ The default value for *levelspec* in MapIndexed is {1}. ▪ Example: MapIndexed[f, {{a, b}, {c, d}}, Infinity] ⟶ {f[{f[a, {1, 1}], f[b, {1, 2}]}, {1}], f[{f[c, {2, 1}], f[d, {2, 2}]}, {2}]}. ▪ See page 246. ▪ See also: MapAt. ▪ *New in Version 2.*

◼ MapThread

MapThread[f, {{a_1, a_2, ... }, {b_1, b_2, ... }, ... }] gives
{$f[a_1$, b_1, ...], $f[a_2$, b_2, ...], ... }.

MapThread[f, {$expr_1$, $expr_2$, ... }, n] applies f to the parts of the $expr_i$ at level n.

Example: MapThread[f, {{a1, a2}, {b1, b2}}] ⟶ {f[a1, b1], f[a2, b2]}. ▪ MapThread[f, {{{a1, a2}}, {{b1, b2}}}] ⟶ {f[{a1, a2}, {b1, b2}]}. ▪ MapThread[f, {{{a1, a2}}, {{b1, b2}}}, 2] ⟶ {{f[a1, b1], f[a2, b2]}}. ▪ See page 247. ▪ See also: Map, Thread, Inner. ▪ *New in Version 2.*

◼ MatchLocalNames

MatchLocalNames is an option for Trace and related functions which specifies whether symbols such as x should match symbols with local names of the form $x\$nnn$.

The default setting is MatchLocalNames -> True. ▪ With the default setting, Trace[$expr$, x = rhs] will show assignments to local variables whose names are of the form $x\$nnn$.
▪ Trace[$expr$, x = rhs, MatchLocalNames->False] shows assignments only for the global symbol x. ▪ See page 365. ▪ *New in Version 2.*

◼ MatchQ

MatchQ[$expr$, $form$] returns True if the pattern $form$ matches $expr$, and returns False otherwise.

See page 268. ▪ See also: StringMatchQ. ▪ *New in Version 1.*

◼ MathieuC

MathieuC[a, q, z] gives the even Mathieu function with characteristic value a and parameter q.

Mathematical function (see Section A.3.10). ▪ The Mathieu functions satisfy the equation $y'' + (a - 2q\cos(2z))y = 0$. ▪ See page 789. ▪ See also: MathieuCPrime. ▪ *New in Version 3.*

◼ MathieuCharacteristicA

MathieuCharacteristicA[r, q] gives the characteristic value a_r for even Mathieu functions with characteristic exponent r and parameter q.

Mathematical function (see Section A.3.10). ▪ The characteristic value a_r gives the value of the parameter a in $y'' + (a - 2q\cos(2z))y = 0$ for which the solution has the form $e^{irz}f(z)$ where $f(z)$ is an even function of z with period 2π. ▪ See page 789. ▪ See also: MathieuCharacteristicB. ▪ *New in Version 3.*

◼ MathieuCharacteristicB

MathieuCharacteristicB[r, q] gives the characteristic value b_r for odd Mathieu functions with characteristic exponent r and parameter q.

Mathematical function (see Section A.3.10). ▪ The characteristic value b_r gives the value of the parameter a in $y'' + (a - 2q\cos(2z))y = 0$ for which the solution has the form $e^{irz}f(z)$ where $f(z)$ is an odd function of z with period 2π. ▪ When r is not a real integer, MathieuCharacteristicB gives the same results as MathieuCharacteristicA.
▪ See notes for MathieuCharacteristicA. ▪ See page 789. ▪ *New in Version 3.*

■ MathieuCharacteristicExponent

MathieuCharacteristicExponent[a, q] gives the characteristic exponent r for Mathieu functions with characteristic value a and parameter q.

Mathematical function (see Section A.3.10). ■ All Mathieu functions have the form $e^{irz}f(z)$ where $f(z)$ has period 2π and r is the Mathieu characteristic exponent. ■ See page 789. ■ *New in Version 3.*

■ MathieuCPrime

MathieuCPrime[a, q, z] gives the derivative with respect to z of the even Mathieu function with characteristic value a and parameter q.

Mathematical function (see Section A.3.10). ■ See page 789. ■ *New in Version 3.*

■ MathieuS

MathieuS[a, q, z] gives the odd Mathieu function with characteristic value a and parameter q.

Mathematical function (see Section A.3.10). ■ The Mathieu functions satisfy the equation $y'' + (a - 2q\cos(2z))y = 0$. ■ See page 789. ■ *New in Version 3.*

■ MathieuSPrime

MathieuSPrime[a, q, z] gives the derivative with respect to z of the odd Mathieu function with characteristic value a and parameter q.

Mathematical function (see Section A.3.10). ■ See page 789. ■ *New in Version 3.*

₊■ MathMLForm

MathMLForm[$expr$] prints as a MathML form of *expr*.

MathMLForm gives presentation MathML, although its output can normally be interpreted by *Mathematica*. ■ MathMLForm[$expr$] gives MathML for the TraditionalForm of *expr*. ■ MathMLForm[StandardForm[$expr$]] gives MathML for the StandardForm of *expr*. ■ MathMLForm acts as a "wrapper", which affects printing, but not evaluation. ■ MathMLForm gives special characters using HTML aliases. ■ See pages 211 and 425. ■ See also: HTMLSave, Export, TeXForm, Import. ■ *New in Version 4.1.*

■ MatrixExp

MatrixExp[mat] gives the matrix exponential of *mat*.

MatrixExp[mat] effectively evaluates the power series for the exponential function, with ordinary powers replaced by matrix powers. ■ MatrixExp works only on square matrices. ■ See page 906. ■ Implementation notes: see page 1069. ■ See also: MatrixPower, Dot, JordanDecomposition, QRDecomposition. ■ *New in Version 2.*

₋■ MatrixForm

MatrixForm[$list$] prints with the elements of *list* arranged in a regular array.

In StandardForm the array is shown enclosed in parentheses. ■ MatrixForm prints a single-level list in a column. It prints a two-level list in standard matrix form. More deeply nested lists are by default printed with successive dimensions alternating between rows and columns. ■ Elements in each column are by default centered. ₊■ MatrixForm prints SparseArray objects like the corresponding ordinary lists. ■ MatrixForm takes the same set of options as TableForm. ■ MatrixForm acts as a "wrapper", which affects printing, but not evaluation. ■ See page 439. ■ See also: TableForm, ColumnForm, GridBox, GraphicsArray. ■ *New in Version 1; modified in Version 5.0.*

■ **MatrixPower**

`MatrixPower[`*mat*`, `*n*`]` gives the nth matrix power of *mat*.

`MatrixPower[`*mat*`, `*n*`]` effectively evaluates the product of a matrix with itself *n* times. ■ When *n* is negative, `MatrixPower` finds powers of the inverse of *mat*. ■ `MatrixPower` works only on square matrices. +■ `MatrixPower` can be used on `SparseArray` objects. ■ See page 906. ■ See also: `Dot`, `MatrixExp`. ■ *New in Version 2.*

■ **MatrixQ**

~ `MatrixQ[`*expr*`]` gives `True` if *expr* is a list of lists or a two-dimensional `SparseArray` object that can represent a matrix, and gives `False` otherwise.

`MatrixQ[`*expr*`, `*test*`]` gives `True` only if *test* yields `True` when applied to each of the matrix elements in *expr*.

~■ `MatrixQ[`*expr*`]` gives `True` only if *expr* is a list, and each of its elements is a list of the same length, containing no elements that are themselves lists, or is a two-dimensional `SparseArray` object. ■ `MatrixQ[`*expr*`, NumberQ]` tests whether *expr* is a numerical matrix. ■ See pages 267 and 900. ■ See also: `VectorQ`, `ArrayQ`, `ArrayDepth`. ■ Related package: `LinearAlgebra`MatrixManipulation``. ■ *New in Version 1; modified in Version 2.*

+■ **MatrixRank**

`MatrixRank[`*m*`]` gives the rank of the matrix *m*.

`MatrixRank` works on both numerical and symbolic matrices. ■ The rank of a matrix is the number of linearly independent rows or columns. ■ `MatrixRank[`*m*`, Modulus->`*n*`]` finds the rank for integer matrices modulo *n*. ■ `MatrixRank[`*m*`, ZeroTest -> `*test*`]` evaluates *test*`[ `*m*`[[`*i*`, `*j*`]] ]` to determine whether matrix elements are zero. The default setting is `ZeroTest -> Automatic`. ■ `MatrixRank[`*m*`, Tolerance -> `*t*`]` gives the minimum rank with each element in a numerical matrix assumed to be correct only to within tolerance *t*. ■ See page 907. ■ Implementation notes: see page 1069. ■ See also: `NullSpace`, `Det`, `Eigensystem`, `RowReduce`, `SingularValueList`. ■ *New in Version 5.0.*

■ **Max**

`Max[`x_1`, `x_2`, ... ]` yields the numerically largest of the x_i.

`Max[{`x_1`, `x_2`, ... }, {`y_1`, ... }, ... ]` yields the largest element of any of the lists.

`Max` yields a definite result if all its arguments are real numbers. ■ In other cases, `Max` carries out some simplifications. ■ `Max[ ]` gives `-Infinity`. +■ `Max` works on `SparseArray` objects. ■ See page 745. ■ See also: `Min`, `Ordering`, `Maximize`, `FindMaximum`. ■ *New in Version 1.*

■ **MaxBend**

`MaxBend` is an option for `Plot` which measures the maximum bend angle between successive line segments on a curve.

`Plot` uses an adaptive algorithm to try and include enough sample points so that there are no bends larger than `MaxBend` between successive segments of the plot. ■ `Plot` will not, however, subdivide by a factor of more than `PlotDivision`. ■ Smaller settings for `MaxBend` will lead to smoother curves, based on more sample points. ■ See page 138. ■ *New in Version 1.*

◼ Maximize

Maximize[*f*, {*x*, *y*, ... }] maximizes *f* with respect to *x*, *y*, ...

Maximize[{*f*, *cons*}, {*x*, *y*, ... }] maximizes *f* subject to the constraints *cons*.

Maximize returns a list of the form {f_{max}, {x -> x_{max}, y -> y_{max}, ... }}. ▪ *cons* can contain equations, inequalities or logical combinations of these. ▪ If *f* and *cons* are linear or polynomial, Maximize will always find a global maximum. ▪ Maximize will return exact results if given exact input. ▪ If the maximum is achieved only infinitesimally outside the region defined by the constraints, or only asymptotically, Maximize will return the supremum and the closest specifiable point. ▪ By default, all variables are assumed to be real. ▪ $x \in$ Integers can be used to specify that a variable can take on only integer values. ▪ If the constraints cannot be satisfied, Maximize returns {-Infinity, {x -> Indeterminate, ... }}. ▪ See page 850. ▪ Implementation notes: see page 1070. ▪ See also: Minimize, NMaximize, FindMaximum, Max, D, LinearProgramming. ▪ *New in Version 5.0.*

◼ MaxMemoryUsed

MaxMemoryUsed[ ] gives the maximum number of bytes used to store all data for the current *Mathematica* session.

On most computer systems, MaxMemoryUsed[ ] will give results close to those obtained from external process status requests. ▪ MaxMemoryUsed[ ] will not typically account for code space, stack space or the effects of heap fragmentation. ▪ See page 712. ▪ See also: MemoryInUse, ByteCount. ▪ *New in Version 1.*

◼ Mean

Mean[*list*] gives the statistical mean of the elements in *list*.

Mean[*list*] is equivalent to Total[*list*]/Length[*list*]. ▪ Mean handles both numerical and symbolic data. ▪ Mean[{{x_1, y_1, ... }, {x_2, y_2, ... }, ... }] gives {Mean[{x_1, x_2, ... }], Mean[{y_1, y_2, ... }]}. ▪ Mean works with SparseArray objects. ▪ See pages 794 and 924. ▪ See also: Total, StandardDeviation, Variance, Median. ▪ Related packages: Statistics`DescriptiveStatistics`, Statistics`MultiDescriptiveStatistics`. ▪ *New in Version 5.0.*

◼ Median

Median[*list*] gives the median of the elements in *list*.

Median[*list*] gives the center element in the sorted version of *list*, or the average of the two center elements if *list* is of even length. ▪ Median[{{x_1, y_1, ... }, {x_2, y_2, ... }, ... }] gives {Median[{x_1, x_2, ... }], Median[{y_1, y_2, ... }]}. ▪ Median works with SparseArray objects. ▪ See page 924. ▪ See also: Mean, Quantile, Sort, Max, Ordering. ▪ Related packages: Statistics`DescriptiveStatistics`, Statistics`MultiDescriptiveStatistics`. ▪ *New in Version 5.0.*

◼ MeijerG

MeijerG[{{a_1, ... , a_n}, {a_{n+1}, ... , a_p}}, {{b_1, ... , b_m}, {b_{m+1}, ... , b_q}}, *z*] is the Meijer G function $G_{pq}^{mn}\left(z \mid {a_1,..,a_p \atop b_1,..,b_q}\right)$.

Mathematical function (see Section A.3.10). ▪ The generalized form MeijerG[*alist*, *blist*, *z*, *r*] is defined for real *r* by $r/(2\pi i) \int [\Gamma(1 - a_1 - rs)...\Gamma(1 - a_n - rs)\Gamma(b_1 + rs)...\Gamma(b_m + rs)]/[\Gamma(a_{n+1} + rs)...\Gamma(a_p + rs)\Gamma(1 - b_{m+1} - rs)...\Gamma(1 - b_q - rs)]z^{-s}ds$, where in the default case *r* = 1. ▪ In many special cases, MeijerG is automatically converted to other functions. ▪ See page 780. ▪ See also: HypergeometricPFQ. ▪ *New in Version 3.*

■ MemberQ

MemberQ[*list*, *form*] returns True if an element of *list* matches *form*, and False otherwise.

MemberQ[*list*, *form*, *levelspec*] tests all parts of *list* specified by *levelspec*.

form can be a pattern. ■ Example: MemberQ[{x^2, y^2}, x^_] ⟶ True. ■ The first argument of MemberQ can have any head, not necessarily List. ■ MemberQ[*list*, *form*] immediately tests whether any expression in *list* matches *form*; Element[*x*, *dom*] asserts that *x* is an element of the symbolic domain *dom*. ■ See page 268. ■ See also: FreeQ, Element, Count, Cases, IntervalMemberQ. ■ *New in Version 1.*

■ MemoryConstrained

MemoryConstrained[*expr*, *b*] evaluates *expr*, stopping if more than *b* bytes of memory are requested.

MemoryConstrained[*expr*, *b*, *failexpr*] returns *failexpr* if the memory constraint is not met.

MemoryConstrained generates an interrupt to stop the evaluation of *expr* if the amount of additional memory requested during the evaluation of *expr* exceeds *b* bytes. ■ MemoryConstrained evaluates *failexpr* only if the evaluation is aborted. ■ MemoryConstrained returns $Aborted if the evaluation is aborted and no *failexpr* is specified. ■ Aborts generated by MemoryConstrained are treated just like those generated by Abort, and can thus be overruled by AbortProtect. ■ See page 713. ■ See also: TimeConstrained, MaxMemoryUsed, $RecursionLimit, Abort. ■ *New in Version 1.*

■ MemoryInUse

MemoryInUse[ ] gives the number of bytes currently being used to store all data in the current *Mathematica* session.

See page 712. ■ See also: MaxMemoryUsed, ByteCount, Share. ■ Related package: Utilities`MemoryConserve`. ■ *New in Version 1.*

■ Mesh

Mesh is an option for SurfaceGraphics and DensityGraphics that specifies whether an explicit *x–y* mesh should be drawn.

See page 539. ■ See also: FaceGrids, Boxed. ■ *New in Version 1.*

■ MeshRange

MeshRange is an option for ListPlot3D, SurfaceGraphics, ListContourPlot, ListDensityPlot and related functions which specifies the range of *x* and *y* coordinates that correspond to the array of *z* values given.

MeshRange->{{*xmin*, *xmax*}, {*ymin*, *ymax*}} specifies ranges in *x* and *y*. Mesh lines are taken to be equally spaced. ■ MeshRange->Automatic takes *x* and *y* to be a grid of integers determined by indices in the array. ■ Settings for MeshRange are produced automatically by Plot3D, etc. for insertion into SurfaceGraphics etc. ■ MeshRange is used to determine tick values for surface, contour and density plots. ■ See page 539. ■ See also: PlotRange, PlotPoints. ■ *New in Version 2.*

■ MeshStyle

MeshStyle is an option for Plot3D, DensityPlot and related functions which specifies how mesh lines should be rendered.

MeshStyle can be set to a list of graphics directives including Dashing, Thickness, GrayLevel, Hue and RGBColor. ■ See pages 503 and 539. ■ See also: Mesh, AxesStyle, Prolog, Epilog, DisplayFunction. ■ *New in Version 2.*

■ Message

Message[*symbol*::*tag*] prints the message *symbol*::*tag* unless it has been switched off.

Message[*symbol*::*tag*, e_1, e_2, ...] prints a message, inserting the values of the e_i as needed.

Message generates output on the channel $Messages. ■ You can switch off a message using Off[*symbol*::*tag*]. You can switch on a message using On[*symbol*::*tag*]. ■ Between any two successive input lines, *Mathematica* prints a message with a particular name at most three times. On the last occurrence, it prints the message General::stop. ■ During the evaluation of a particular input line, names of messages associated with that input line are appended to the list $MessageList, wrapped with HoldForm. At the end of the evaluation of the nth input line, the value of $MessageList is assigned to MessageList[*n*]. ■ Message[*mname*, e_1, e_2, ...] is printed as StringForm[*mess*, e_1, e_2, ...] where *mess* is the value of the message *mname*. Entries of the form \`*i*\` in the string *mess* are replaced by the corresponding e_i. ■ Given a message specified as *symbol*::*tag*, Message first searches for messages *symbol*::*tag*::*lang*$_i$ for each of the languages in the list $Language. If it finds none of these, it then searches for the actual message *symbol*::*tag*. If it does not find this, it then performs the same search procedure for General::*tag*. If it still finds no message, it applies any value given for the global variable $NewMessage to *symbol* and "*tag*". ■ If you specify a message as *symbol*::*tag*::*lang*, then Message will search only for messages with the particular language *lang*. ■ See page 482. ■ See also: Print, CellPrint, Write, On, Off, Check, MessageList. ■ *New in Version 1.*

■ MessageList

MessageList[*n*] is a global object assigned to be a list of the names of messages generated during the processing of the nth input line.

Only messages that are actually output are included in the list MessageList[*n*]. ■ The message names in the list are wrapped with HoldForm. ■ MessageList[*n*] includes messages generated both by built-in functions and by explicit invocations of Message. ■ See pages 481 and 702. ■ See also: $MessageList. ■ *New in Version 2.*

■ MessageName

symbol::*tag* is a name for a message.

You can specify messages by defining values for *symbol*::*tag*. ■ *symbol*::*tag* is converted to MessageName[*symbol*, "*tag*"]. *tag* can contain any characters that can appear in symbol names. *symbol*::"*tag*" can also be used. ■ Assignments for *s*::*tag* are stored in the Messages value of the symbol *s*. ■ The following messages are typically defined for built-in functions:

f::template   a template showing a typical case of the function
f::usage   a description of how to use the function

■ ?*f* prints out the message *f*::usage. ■ When ?*form* finds more than one function, only the names of each function are printed. ■ You can switch on and off messages using On[*s*::*tag*] and Off[*s*::*tag*].
■ MessageName[*symbol*, "*tag*", "*lang*"] or *symbol*::*tag*::*lang* represents a message in a particular language. ■ See page 479. ■ See also: Message, MessageList, $MessageList. ■ *New in Version 1; modified in Version 4.*

■ Messages

Messages[*symbol*] gives all the messages assigned to a particular symbol.

Messages that have been switched off using Off are enclosed in $Off. ■ See page 479. ■ *New in Version 1.*

■ Min

Min[x_1, x_2, ...] yields the numerically smallest of the x_i.

Min[{x_1, x_2, ... }, {y_1, ... }, ...] yields the smallest element of any of the lists.

Min yields a definite result if all its arguments are real numbers. ■ In other cases, Min carries out some simplifications. ■ Min[ ] gives Infinity. +■ Min works on SparseArray objects. ■ See page 745. ■ See also: Max, Ordering, Minimize, FindMinimum. ■ *New in Version 1.*

+■ Minimize

Minimize[f, {x, y, ... }] minimizes f with respect to x, y, ...

Minimize[{f, *cons*}, {x, y, ... }] minimizes f subject to the constraints *cons*.

Minimize returns a list of the form {f_{min}, {x -> x_{min}, y -> y_{min}, ... }}. ■ *cons* can contain equations, inequalities or logical combinations of these. ■ If f and *cons* are linear or polynomial, Minimize will always find a global minimum. ■ Minimize will return exact results if given exact input. ■ If the minimum is achieved only infinitesimally outside the region defined by the constraints, or only asymptotically, Minimize will return the infimum and the closest specifiable point. ■ By default, all variables are assumed to be real. ■ x ∈ Integers can be used to specify that a variable can take on only integer values. ■ If the constraints cannot be satisfied, Minimize returns {+Infinity, {x -> Indeterminate, ... }}. ■ Even if the same minimum is achieved at several points, only one is returned. ■ See page 850. ■ Implementation notes: see page 1070. ■ See also: Maximize, NMinimize, FindMinimum, Min, D, FindInstance, LinearProgramming. ■ *New in Version 5.0.*

■ Minors

Minors[m] gives the minors of a matrix m.

Minors[m, k] gives k^{th} minors.

For an $n \times n$ matrix the $(i,j)^{\text{th}}$ element of Minors[m] gives the determinant of the matrix obtained by deleting the $(n - i + 1)^{\text{th}}$ row and the $(n - j + 1)^{\text{th}}$ column of m. ■ Map[Reverse, Minors[m], {0,1}] makes the $(i,j)^{\text{th}}$ element correspond to deleting the ith row and j^{th} column of m. ■ Minors[m] is equivalent to Minors[m, n-1]. ■ Minors[m, k] gives the determinants of the $k \times k$ submatrices obtained by picking each possible set of k rows and k columns from m. ■ Each element in the result corresponds to taking rows and columns with particular lists of positions. The ordering of the elements is such that reading across or down the final matrix the successive lists of positions appear in lexicographic order. ■ For an $n_1 \times n_2$ matrix Minors[m, k] gives a $\binom{n_1}{k} \times \binom{n_2}{k}$ matrix. ■ Minors[m, k, f] applies the function f rather than Det to each of the submatrices picked out. ■ See page 905. ■ See also: Det, Delete. ■ *New in Version 1; modified in Version 4.*

■ Minus

$-x$ is the arithmetic negation of x.

$-x$ is converted to Times[-1, x] on input. ■ See page 29. ■ See also: Subtract. ■ *New in Version 1.*

■ Mod

Mod[*m*, *n*] gives the remainder on division of *m* by *n*.

Mod[*m*, *n*, *d*] uses an offset *d*.

For integers *m* and *n* Mod[*m*, *n*] lies between 0 and *n* – 1. ■ Mod[*m*, *n*, 1] gives a result in the range 1 to *n*, suitable for use in functions such as Part. ■ Mod[*m*, *n*, *d*] gives a result *x* such that $d \leq x < d + n$ and *x* mod *n* = *m* mod *n*. ■ The sign of Mod[*m*, *n*] is always the same as the sign of *n*, at least so long as *m* and *n* are both real. ■ Mod[*m*, *n*] is equivalent to *m* – *n* Quotient[*m*, *n*]. ■ Mod[*m*, *n*, *d*] is equivalent to *m* – *n* Quotient[*m*, *n*, *d*]. ■ The arguments of Mod can be any numeric quantities, not necessarily integers. ■ Mod[*x*, 1] gives the fractional part of *x*. ■ For exact numeric quantities, Mod internally uses numerical approximations to establish its result. This process can be affected by the setting of the global variable $MaxExtraPrecision. ■ See page 749. ■ See also: PowerMod, Quotient, FractionalPart, MantissaExponent, PolynomialMod, PolynomialRemainder, Xor. ■ *New in Version 1; modified in Version 4.*

■ ModularLambda

ModularLambda[*τ*] gives the modular lambda elliptic function $\lambda(\tau)$.

Mathematical function (see Section A.3.10). ■ ModularLambda is defined only in the upper half of the complex *τ* plane. It is not defined for real *τ*. ■ The argument *τ* is the ratio of Weierstrass half-periods ω'/ω. ■ ModularLambda gives the parameter *m* for elliptic functions in terms of *τ* according to $m = \lambda(\tau)$. ■ ModularLambda is related to EllipticTheta by $\lambda(\tau) = \vartheta_2^4(0, q)/\vartheta_3^4(0, q)$ where the nome *q* is given by $e^{i\pi\tau}$. ■ $\lambda(\tau)$ is invariant under any combination of the modular transformations $\tau \to \tau + 2$ and $\tau \to \tau/(1 - 2\tau)$. ■ See page 782 for a discussion of argument conventions for elliptic functions. ■ See page 787. ■ See also: DedekindEta, KleinInvariantJ, WeierstrassHalfPeriods. ■ *New in Version 3.*

■ Module

Module[{*x*, *y*, ... }, *expr*] specifies that occurrences of the symbols *x*, *y*, ... in *expr* should be treated as local.

Module[{*x* = x_0, ... }, *expr*] defines initial values for *x*, ...

Module allows you to set up local variables with names that are local to the module. ■ Module creates new symbols to represent each of its local variables every time it is called. ■ Module creates a symbol with name *xxx*$*nnn* to represent a local variable with name *xxx*. The number *nnn* is the current value of $ModuleNumber. ■ The value of $ModuleNumber is incremented every time any module is used. ■ Before evaluating *expr*, Module substitutes new symbols for each of the local variables that appear anywhere in *expr* except as local variables in scoping constructs. ■ Symbols created by Module carry the attribute Temporary. ■ Symbols created by Module can be returned from modules. ■ You can use Module[{*vars*}, *body* /; *cond*] as the right-hand side of a transformation rule with a condition attached. ■ Module has attribute HoldAll. ■ Module is a scoping construct (see Section A.3.8). ■ Module constructs can be nested in any way. ■ Module implements lexical scoping. ■ See page 378. ■ See also: With, Block, Unique, GeneratedParameters. ■ *New in Version 2.*

■ Modulus

Modulus->*n* is an option that can be given in certain algebraic functions to specify that integers should be treated modulo *n*.

Equations for Modulus can be given in Solve and related functions.

Modulus appears as an option in Factor, PolynomialGCD and PolynomialLCM, as well as in linear algebra functions such as Inverse, LinearSolve and Det. ■ Arithmetic is usually done over the full ring $\mathbb{Z}$ of integers; setting the option Modulus specifies that arithmetic should instead be done in the finite ring $\mathbb{Z}_n$. ■ The setting Modulus -> 0 specifies the full ring $\mathbb{Z}$ of integers. ■ Some functions require that Modulus be set to a prime, or a power of a prime. $\mathbb{Z}_n$ is a finite field when *n* is prime. ■ See page 809. ■ See also: Extension. ■ *New in Version 1.*

■ MoebiusMu

MoebiusMu[*n*] gives the Möbius function $\mu(n)$.

Integer mathematical function (see Section A.3.10). ■ $\mu(n)$ is 1 if *n* is a product of an even number of distinct primes, −1 if it is a product of an odd number of primes, and 0 if it has a multiple prime factor. ■ See page 752. ■ See also: Divisors, FactorInteger, JacobiSymbol. ■ *New in Version 1.*

⁺■ Most

Most[*expr*] gives *expr* with the last element removed.

Example: Most[{a, b, c}] ⟶ {a, b}. ■ Most[*expr*] is equivalent to Drop[*expr*, -1]. ■ See page 123. ■ See also: Rest, Drop, Last, Part, Take. ■ *New in Version 5.0.*

■ Multinomial

Multinomial[n_1, n_2, ...] gives the multinomial coefficient $(n_1 + n_2 + ...)!/(n_1!n_2!...)$.

Integer mathematical function (see Section A.3.10). ■ The multinomial coefficient Multinomial[n_1, n_2, ...], denoted $(N; n_1, n_2, ..., n_m)$, gives the number of ways of partitioning N distinct objects into m sets, each of size n_i (with $N = \sum_{i=1}^{m} n_i$). ■ See page 757. ■ See also: Binomial. ■ *New in Version 1.*

■ MultiplicativeOrder

MultiplicativeOrder[*k*, *n*] gives the multiplicative order of *k* modulo *n*, defined as the smallest integer *m* such that $k^m \equiv 1$ mod *n*.

MultiplicativeOrder[*k*, *n*, {r_1, r_2, ... }] gives the generalized multiplicative order of *k* modulo *n*, defined as the smallest integer *m* such that $k^m \equiv r_i$ mod *n* for some *i*.

Integer mathematical function (see Section A.3.10). ■ MultiplicativeOrder returns unevaluated if there is no integer *m* satisfying the necessary conditions. ■ See page 752. ■ See also: EulerPhi, PowerMod, CarmichaelLambda, RealDigits. ■ *New in Version 4.*

⁻■ N

N[*expr*] gives the numerical value of *expr*.

N[*expr*, *n*] attempts to give a result with *n*-digit precision.

Unless numbers in *expr* are exact, or of sufficiently high precision, N[*expr*, *n*] may not be able to give results with *n*-digit precision. ■ N[*expr*, *n*] may internally do computations to more than *n* digits of precision. ■ $MaxExtraPrecision specifies the maximum number of extra digits of precision that will ever be used internally. ■ The precision *n* is given in decimal digits; it need not be an integer. ■ *n* must lie between $MinPrecision and $MaxPrecision. $MaxPrecision can be set to Infinity. ⁺■ *n* can be smaller than $MachinePrecision. ■ N[*expr*] gives a machine-precision number, so long as its magnitude is between $MinMachineNumber and $MaxMachineNumber. ⁺■ N[*expr*] is equivalent to N[*expr*, MachinePrecision]. ■ N[0] gives the number 0. with machine precision. ■ N converts all non-zero numbers to Real or Complex form. ■ N converts each successive argument of any function it encounters to numerical form, unless the head of the function has an attribute such as NHoldAll. ■ You can define numerical values of functions using N[*f*[*args*]] := *value* and N[*f*[*args*], *n*] := *value*. ⁺■ N[*expr*, {*p*, *a*}] attempts to generate a result with precision at most *p* and accuracy at most *a*. ⁺■ N[*expr*, {Infinity, *a*}] attempts to generate a result with accuracy *a*. ⁺■ N[*expr*, {Infinity, 1}] attempts to find a numerical approximation to the integer part of *expr*. ■ See pages 30, 33, 728 and 735. ■ Implementation notes: see page 1067. ■ See also: Chop, CompiledFunction, Rationalize, MachinePrecision, NHoldAll, RealDigits. ■ *New in Version 1; modified in Version 5.0.*

■ NameQ

NameQ["*string*"] yields True if there are any symbols whose names match the string pattern given, and yields False otherwise.

You can test for classes of symbol names using string patterns with metacharacters such as *, as specified on page 1044. ■ See page 403. ■ See also: Names. ■ *New in Version 1.*

■ Names

Names["*string*"] gives a list of the names of symbols which match the string.

Names["*string*", SpellingCorrection->True] includes names which match after spelling correction.

Names["*string*"] gives the same list of names as ?*string*. ■ Names returns a list of strings corresponding to the names of symbols. ■ The string can be a string pattern, with metacharacters such as * and @, as described on page 1044. ■ Names["*context*`*"] lists all symbols in the specified context. ■ With SpellingCorrection -> True, Names includes names which differ in a small fraction of their characters from those specifically requested. ■ With IgnoreCase -> True or SpellingCorrection -> True, Names treats lower- and upper-case letters as equivalent when matching names. ■ Names[ ] lists all names in all contexts. ■ See page 403. ■ See also: Information, Contexts, Unique, ValueQ, FileNames, NameQ. ■ *New in Version 1.*

⁺■ Nand

Nand[e_1, e_2, ...] is the logical NAND function. It evaluates its arguments in order, giving True immediately if any of them are False, and False if they are all True.

Nand[e_1, e_2, ...] can be input in StandardForm and InputForm as e_1 $\barwedge$ e_2 $\barwedge$ ... . The character $\barwedge$ can be entered as ⁚nand⁚ or \[Nand]. ■ Nand[e_1, e_2, ...] is equivalent to Not[And[e_1, e_2, ...]]. ■ Nand evaluates its arguments in a non-standard way (see page 1046). ■ Nand gives symbolic results when necessary, removing initial arguments that are True. ■ Nand is not Flat. ■ See page 87. ■ See also: LogicalExpand, And. ■ *New in Version 4.1.*

⁻■ NDSolve

NDSolve[*eqns*, y, {x, *xmin*, *xmax*}] finds a numerical solution to the ordinary differential equations *eqns* for the function y with the independent variable x in the range *xmin* to *xmax*.

NDSolve[*eqns*, y, {x, *xmin*, *xmax*}, {t, *tmin*, *tmax*}] finds a numerical solution to the partial differential equations *eqns*.

NDSolve[*eqns*, {y_1, y_2, ... }, {x, *xmin*, *xmax*}] finds numerical solutions for the functions y_i.

NDSolve gives results in terms of InterpolatingFunction objects. ■ NDSolve[*eqns*, $y[x]$, {x, *xmin*, *xmax*}] gives solutions for $y[x]$ rather than for the function y itself. ■ Differential equations must be stated in terms of derivatives such as $y'[x]$, obtained with D, not total derivatives obtained with Dt. ■ NDSolve solves a wide range of ordinary differential equations as well as many partial differential equations. ■ In ordinary differential equations the functions y_i must depend only on the single variable x. In partial differential equations they may depend on more than one variable. ■ The differential equations must contain enough initial or boundary conditions to determine the solutions for the y_i completely. ■ Initial and boundary conditions are typically stated in form $y[x_0] == c_0$, $y'[x_0] == dc_0$, etc., but may consist of more complicated equations. ⁺■ The c_0, dc_0, etc. can be lists, specifying that $y[x]$ is a function with vector or general list values. ⁺■ Periodic boundary conditions can be specified using $y[x_0] == y[x_1]$. ■ The point x_0 that appears in the initial or boundary conditions need not lie in the range *xmin* to *xmax* over which the solution is sought. ■ The differential equations in NDSolve can involve complex numbers. ⁺■ NDSolve can solve many differential-algebraic equations, in which some of the *eqns* are purely algebraic, or some of the variables are implicitly algebraic. ⁺■ The y_i can be functions of the dependent variables, and need not include all such variables.

(continued)

~■ **NDSolve** *(continued)*

~■ The following options can be given:

AccuracyGoal	Automatic	digits of absolute accuracy sought
Compiled	True	whether to compile the original equations
DependentVariables	Automatic	the list of all dependent variables
EvaluationMonitor	None	expression to evaluate whenever the function is evaluated
MaxStepFraction	1/10	maximum fraction of range to cover in each step
MaxSteps	10000	maximum number of steps to take
MaxStepSize	Infinity	maximum size of each step
Method	Automatic	method to use
NormFunction	Automatic	the norm to use for error estimation
PrecisionGoal	Automatic	digits of precision sought
StartingStepSize	Automatic	initial step size used
StepMonitor	None	expression to evaluate when a step is taken
WorkingPrecision	MachinePrecision	precision to use in internal computations

+■ NDSolve adapts its step size so that the estimated error in the solution is just within the tolerances specified by PrecisionGoal and AccuracyGoal. +■ The option NormFunction -> f specifies that the estimated errors for each of the y_i should be combined using $f[\{e_1, e_2, \dots \}]$. ~■ AccuracyGoal effectively specifies the absolute local error allowed at each step in finding a solution, while PrecisionGoal specifies the relative local error. ■ If solutions must be followed accurately when their values are close to zero, AccuracyGoal should be set larger, or to Infinity. ~■ The default setting of Automatic for AccuracyGoal and PrecisionGoal is equivalent to WorkingPrecision/2. +■ The setting for MaxStepFraction specifies the maximum step to be taken by NDSolve as a fraction of the range of values for each independent variable. +■ With DependentVariables->Automatic, NDSolve attempts to determine the dependent variables by analyzing the equations given. +■ Possible explicit settings for the Method option include:

"Adams"	predictor-corrector Adams method with orders 1 through 12
"BDF"	implicit backward differentiation formulas with orders 1 through 5
"ExplicitRungeKutta"	adaptive embedded pairs of 2(1) through 9(8) Runge-Kutta methods
"ImplicitRungeKutta"	families of arbitrary-order implicit Runge-Kutta methods
"SymplecticPartitionedRungeKutta"	interleaved Runge-Kutta methods for separable Hamiltonian systems

+■ With Method->{"*controller*", Method->"*submethod*"} or Method->{"*controller*", Method->{m_1, m_2, $\dots$ }} possible controller methods include:

"Composition"	compose a list of submethods
"DoubleStep"	adapt step size by the double-step method
"Extrapolation"	adapt order and step size using polynomial extrapolation
"FixedStep"	use a constant step size
"OrthogonalProjection"	project solutions to fulfill orthogonal constraints
"Projection"	project solutions to fulfill general constraints
"Splitting"	split equations and use different submethods
"StiffnessSwitching"	switch from explicit to implicit methods if stiffness is detected

+■ Methods used mainly as submethods include:

"ExplicitEuler"	forward Euler method
"ExplicitMidpoint"	midpoint rule method
"ExplicitModifiedMidpoint"	midpoint rule method with Gragg smoothing
"LinearlyImplicitEuler"	linearly implicit Euler method
"LinearlyImplicitMidpoint"	linearly implicit midpoint rule method
"LinearlyImplicitModifiedMidpoint"	linearly implicit Bader-smoothed midpoint rule method
"LocallyExact"	numerical approximation to locally exact symbolic solution

■ See page 961. ■ Implementation notes: see page 1068. ■ See also: DSolve, NIntegrate. ■ *New in Version 2; modified in Version 5.0.*

■ Needs

Needs["*context*`"] loads an appropriate file if the specified context is not already in $Packages.

Needs["*context*`", "*file*"] loads *file* if the specified context is not already in $Packages.

Needs["*context*`"] calls Get["*context*`"]. By convention, the file loaded in this way is the one which contains a package that defines *context*`. ■ Example: Needs["Collatz`"] typically reads in a file named Collatz.m. ■ See page 400. ■ See also: Get, DeclarePackage, FileNames. ■ Related package: Utilities`Package`. ■ *New in Version 1.*

■ Negative

Negative[*x*] gives True if *x* is a negative number.

Negative[*x*] gives False if *x* is manifestly a non-negative or complex numerical quantity. Otherwise, it remains unevaluated. ■ See also: NonNegative, Positive, Sign, Less, Simplify, Assumptions. ■ *New in Version 1.*

■ Nest

Nest[*f*, *expr*, *n*] gives an expression with *f* applied *n* times to *expr*.

Example: Nest[f, x, 3] ⟶ f[f[f[x]]]. ■ You can use Throw to exit from Nest before it is finished. ■ See page 241. ■ See also: NestList, NestWhile, Fold, Function, FixedPoint, Do. ■ *New in Version 1; modified in Version 3.*

■ NestList

NestList[*f*, *expr*, *n*] gives a list of the results of applying *f* to *expr* 0 through *n* times.

Example: NestList[f, x, 3] ⟶ {x, f[x], f[f[x]], f[f[f[x]]]}. ■ NestList[*f*, *expr*, *n*] gives a list of length *n* + 1. ■ See page 241. ■ See also: Nest, NestWhileList, FoldList, ComposeList. ■ *New in Version 1.*

■ NestWhile

NestWhile[*f*, *expr*, *test*] starts with *expr*, then repeatedly applies *f* until applying *test* to the result no longer yields True.

NestWhile[*f*, *expr*, *test*, *m*] supplies the most recent *m* results as arguments for *test* at each step.

NestWhile[*f*, *expr*, *test*, All] supplies all results so far as arguments for *test* at each step.

NestWhile[*f*, *expr*, *test*, *m*, *max*] applies *f* at most *max* times.

NestWhile[*f*, *expr*, *test*, *m*, *max*, *n*] applies *f* an extra *n* times.

NestWhile[*f*, *expr*, *test*, *m*, *max*, -*n*] returns the result found when *f* had been applied *n* fewer times.

NestWhile[*f*, *expr*, *test*] returns the first expression *f*[*f*[... *f*[*expr*]...]] to which applying *test* does not yield True. ■ If *test*[*expr*] does not yield True, NestWhile[*f*, *expr*, *test*] returns *expr*. ■ NestWhile[*f*, *expr*, *test*, *m*] at each step evaluates *test*[*res*$_1$, *res*$_2$, ... , *res*$_m$]. It does not put the results *res*$_i$ in a list. ■ The *res*$_i$ are given in the order they are generated, with the most recent coming last. ■ NestWhile[*f*, *expr*, *test*, *m*] does not start applying *test* until at least *m* results have been generated. ■ NestWhile[*f*, *expr*, *test*, {*mmin*, *m*}] does not start applying *test* until at least *mmin* results have been generated. At each step it then supplies as arguments to *test* as many recent results as possible, up to a maximum of *m*. ■ NestWhile[*f*, *expr*, *test*, *m*] is equivalent to NestWhile[*f*, *expr*, *test*, {*m*, *m*}]. ■ NestWhile[*f*, *expr*, UnsameQ, 2] is equivalent to FixedPoint[*f*, *expr*].

(continued)

■ **NestWhile** *(continued)*

- NestWhile[*f*, *expr*, *test*, All] is equivalent to NestWhile[*f*, *expr*, *test*, {1, Infinity}].
- NestWhile[*f*, *expr*, UnsameQ, All] goes on applying *f* until the same result first appears more than once.
- NestWhile[*f*, *expr*, *test*, *m*, *max*, *n*] applies *f* an additional *n* times after *test* fails, or *max* applications have already been performed. ■ NestWhile[*f*, *expr*, *test*, *m*, *max*, -*n*] is equivalent to Part[NestWhileList[*f*, *expr*, *test*, *m*, *max*], -*n*-1]. ■ NestWhile[*f*, *expr*, *test*, *m*, Infinity, -1] returns, if possible, the last expression in the sequence *expr*, *f*[*expr*], *f*[*f*[*expr*]], ... for which *test* yields True. ■ See page 242.
- See also: NestWhileList, FixedPoint, Nest, While. ■ *New in Version 4.*

■ **NestWhileList**

NestWhileList[*f*, *expr*, *test*] generates a list of the results of applying *f* repeatedly, starting with *expr*, and continuing until applying *test* to the result no longer yields True.

NestWhileList[*f*, *expr*, *test*, *m*] supplies the most recent *m* results as arguments for *test* at each step.

NestWhileList[*f*, *expr*, *test*, All] supplies all results so far as arguments for *test* at each step.

NestWhileList[*f*, *expr*, *test*, *m*, *max*] applies *f* at most *max* times.

The last element of the list returned by NestWhileList[*f*, *expr*, *test*] is always an expression to which applying *test* does not yield True. ■ NestWhileList[*f*, *expr*, *test*, *m*] at each step evaluates *test*[*res*$_1$, *res*$_2$, ... , *res*$_m$]. It does not put the results *res*$_i$ in a list. ■ The *res*$_i$ are given in the order they are generated, with the most recent coming last. ■ NestWhileList[*f*, *expr*, *test*, *m*] does not start applying *test* until at least *m* results have been generated. ■ NestWhileList[*f*, *expr*, *test*, {*mmin*, *m*}] does not start applying *test* until at least *mmin* results have been generated. At each step it then supplies as arguments to *test* as many recent results as possible, up to a maximum of *m*. ■ NestWhileList[*f*, *expr*, *test*, *m*] is equivalent to NestWhileList[*f*, *expr*, *test*, {*m*, *m*}].
- NestWhileList[*f*, *expr*, UnsameQ, 2] is equivalent to FixedPointList[*f*, *expr*].
- NestWhileList[*f*, *expr*, *test*, All] is equivalent to NestWhileList[*f*, *expr*, *test*, {1, Infinity}].
- NestWhileList[*f*, *expr*, UnsameQ, All] goes on applying *f* until the same result first appears more than once.
- NestWhileList[*f*, *expr*, *test*, *m*, *max*, *n*] applies *f* an extra *n* times, appending the results to the list generated.
- NestWhileList[*f*, *expr*, *test*, *m*, *max*, -*n*] drops the last *n* elements from the list generated. ■ See page 242.
- See also: NestWhile, FixedPointList, NestList, While. ■ *New in Version 4.*

■ **NHoldAll**

NHoldAll is an attribute which specifies that none of the arguments to a function should be affected by N.

NHoldAll, NHoldFirst and NHoldRest are useful in ensuring that arguments to functions are maintained as exact integers, rather than being converted by N to approximate numbers. ■ See page 329. ■ See also: NumericFunction, HoldAll. ■ *New in Version 3.*

■ **NHoldFirst**

NHoldFirst is an attribute which specifies that the first argument to a function should not be affected by N.

See page 329. ■ *New in Version 3.*

■ **NHoldRest**

NHoldRest is an attribute which specifies that all but the first argument to a function should not be affected by N.

See page 329. ■ *New in Version 3.*

■ **NIntegrate**

NIntegrate[*f*, {*x*, *xmin*, *xmax*}] gives a numerical approximation to the integral $\int_{xmin}^{xmax} f\, dx$.

Multidimensional integrals can be specified, as in Integrate. ■ NIntegrate tests for singularities at the end points of the integration range. ■ NIntegrate[*f*, {*x*, x_0, x_1, ... , x_k}] tests for singularities at each of the intermediate points x_i. If there are no singularities, the result is equivalent to an integral from x_0 to x_k. You can use complex numbers x_i to specify an integration contour in the complex plane. ~■ The following options can be given:

AccuracyGoal	Infinity	digits of absolute accuracy sought
Compiled	True	whether the integrand should be compiled
GaussPoints	Automatic	initial number of sample points
EvaluationMonitor	None	expression to evaluate whenever *expr* is evaluated
MaxPoints	Automatic	maximum total number of sample points
MaxRecursion	6	maximum number of recursive subdivisions
Method	Automatic	method to use
MinRecursion	0	minimum number of recursive subdivisions
PrecisionGoal	Automatic	digits of precision sought
SingularityDepth	4	number of recursive subdivisions before changing variables
WorkingPrecision	MachinePrecision	the precision used in internal computations

■ NIntegrate usually uses an adaptive algorithm, which recursively subdivides the integration region as needed. In one dimension, GaussPoints specifies the number of initial points to choose. The default setting for GaussPoints is Floor[WorkingPrecision/3]. In any number of dimensions, MinRecursion specifies the minimum number of recursive subdivisions to try. MaxRecursion gives the maximum number. ■ NIntegrate usually continues doing subdivisions until the error estimate it gets implies that the final result achieves either the AccuracyGoal or the PrecisionGoal specified. ■ The default setting for PrecisionGoal is usually equal to the setting for WorkingPrecision minus 10 digits. ■ If an explicit setting for MaxPoints is given, NIntegrate uses quasi Monte Carlo methods to get an estimate of the result, sampling at most the number of points specified. ■ The default setting for PrecisionGoal is taken to be 2 in this case. ■ You should realize that with sufficiently pathological functions, the algorithms used by NIntegrate can give wrong answers. In most cases, you can test the answer by looking at its sensitivity to changes in the setting of options for NIntegrate. ■ N[Integrate[...]] calls NIntegrate for integrals that cannot be done symbolically. ■ NIntegrate has attribute HoldAll. ■ Possible settings for Method are GaussKronrod, DoubleExponential, Trapezoidal, Oscillatory, MultiDimensional, MonteCarlo, and QuasiMonteCarlo. GaussKronrod and MultiDimensional are adaptive methods. MonteCarlo and QuasiMonteCarlo are randomized methods, appropriate for high-dimensional integrals. ■ See page 954. ■ Implementation notes: see page 1068. ■ See also: NDSolve, NSum. ■ Related packages: NumericalMath`ListIntegrate`, NumericalMath`CauchyPrincipalValue`, NumericalMath`GaussianQuadrature`. ■ *New in Version 1; modified in Version 5.0.*

■ **NMaximize**

NMaximize[*f*, {*x*, *y*, ... }] maximizes *f* numerically with respect to *x*, *y*, ...

NMaximize[{*f*, *cons*}, {*x*, *y*, ... }] maximizes *f* numerically subject to the constraints *cons*.

See notes for NMinimize. ■ See page 974. ■ See also: NMinimize, Maximize, FindMaximum. ■ *New in Version 5.0.*

NMinimize

NMinimize[*f*, {*x*, *y*, ... }] minimizes *f* numerically with respect to *x*, *y*, ...

NMinimize[{*f*, *cons*}, {*x*, *y*, ... }] minimizes *f* numerically subject to the constraints *cons*.

NMinimize returns a list of the form {f_{min}, {*x* -> x_{min}, *y* -> y_{min}, ... }}. ▪ *cons* can contain equations, inequalities or logical combinations of these. ▪ NMinimize always attempts to find a global minimum of *f* subject to the constraints given. ▪ Unless *f* and *cons* are both linear, NMinimize may sometimes find only a local minimum. ▪ By default, all variables are assumed to be real. ▪ $x \in$ Integers can be used to specify that a variable can take on only integer values. ▪ If NMinimize determines that the constraints cannot be satisfied, it returns {Infinity, {*x* -> Indeterminate, ... }}. ▪ The following options can be given:

AccuracyGoal	Automatic	the accuracy sought
EvaluationMonitor	None	expression to evaluation whenever *f* is evaluated
MaxIterations	100	maximum number of iterations to use
Method	Automatic	method to use
PrecisionGoal	Automatic	the precision sought
StepMonitor	None	expression to evaluate whenever a step is taken
WorkingPrecision	MachinePrecision	the precision used in internal computations

▪ The default settings for AccuracyGoal and PrecisionGoal are WorkingPrecision/2. ▪ The settings for AccuracyGoal and PrecisionGoal specify the number of digits to seek in both the value of the position of the maximum, and the value of the function at the minimum. ▪ NMinimize continues until either of the goals specified by AccuracyGoal or PrecisionGoal is achieved. ▪ Possible settings for the Method option include "NelderMead", "DifferentialEvolution", "SimulatedAnnealing" and "RandomSearch". ▪ See page 974. ▪ Implementation notes: see page 1068. ▪ See also: NMaximize, Minimize, FindMinimum, FindFit. ▪ *New in Version 5.0.*

NonCommutativeMultiply

a ** *b* ** *c* is a general associative, but non-commutative, form of multiplication.

NonCommutativeMultiply has attribute Flat. ▪ Instances of NonCommutativeMultiply are automatically flattened, but no other simplification is performed. ▪ You can use NonCommutativeMultiply as a generalization of ordinary multiplication for special mathematical objects. ▪ See page 1026. ▪ See also: Dot, Times, Cross. ▪ *New in Version 1.*

NonConstants

NonConstants is an option for D which gives a list of objects to be taken to depend implicitly on the differentiation variables.

If *c* does not appear in the list of NonConstants, then D[*c*, *x*] is taken to be 0 unless *c* and *x* are identical expressions. ▪ See page 853. ▪ See also: Dt. ▪ *New in Version 1.*

None

None is a setting used for certain options.

See also: All, Automatic. ▪ *New in Version 1.*

NonNegative

NonNegative[*x*] gives True if *x* is a non-negative number.

NonNegative[*x*] gives False if *x* is manifestly a negative or complex numerical quantity. Otherwise, it remains unevaluated. ▪ See also: Negative, Positive, Sign, Greater, Simplify, Assumptions. ▪ *New in Version 1.*

■ NonPositive

NonPositive[*x*] gives True if *x* is a non-positive number.

See notes for NonNegative. ▪ *New in Version 3.*

⁺■ Nor

Nor[*e*₁, *e*₂, ...] is the logical NOR function. It evaluates its arguments in order, giving False immediately if any of them are True, and True if they are all False.

Nor[*e*₁, *e*₂, ...] can be input in StandardForm and InputForm as *e*₁ $\bar{\vee}$ *e*₂ $\bar{\vee}$ ... . The character $\bar{\vee}$ can be entered as ⋮nor⋮ or \[Nor]. ▪ Nor[*e*₁, *e*₂, ...] is equivalent to Not[Or[*e*₁, *e*₂, ...]]. ▪ Nor evaluates its arguments in a non-standard way (see page 1046). ▪ Nor gives symbolic results when necessary, removing initial arguments that are False. ▪ Nor is not Flat. ▪ See page 87. ▪ See also: LogicalExpand, Or, Xor. ▪ *New in Version 4.1.*

⁺■ Norm

Norm[*expr*] gives the norm of a number or array.

Norm[*expr*, *p*] gives the *p*-norm.

For complex numbers, Norm[*z*] is Abs[*z*]. ▪ For vectors, Norm[*v*] is Sqrt[*v* . Conjugate[*v*]]. ▪ Norm[*v*, *p*] is Total[Abs[*v*^p]]^(1/*p*). ▪ Norm[*v*, Infinity] is the ∞-norm given by Max[Abs[*v*]]. ▪ For matrices, Norm[*m*] gives the maximum singular value of *m*. ▪ Norm can be used on SparseArray objects. ▪ See page 119. ▪ See also: Abs, Dot, Total, SingularValueList, Integrate. ▪ *New in Version 5.0.*

⁻■ Normal

Normal[*expr*] converts *expr* to a normal expression, from a variety of special forms.

Normal[*expr*] converts a power series to a normal expression by truncating higher-order terms. +▪ Normal[*expr*] converts SparseArray objects into ordinary arrays. ▪ Normal[*expr*] converts RootSum objects into explicit sums involving Root objects. ▪ When additional "data types" are introduced, Normal should be defined to convert them, when possible, to normal expressions. ▪ See page 888. ▪ See also: SeriesCoefficient. ▪ *New in Version 1.0; modified in Version 5.0.*

■ Not

!*expr* is the logical NOT function. It gives False if *expr* is True, and True if it is False.

Not[*expr*] can be input in StandardForm and InputForm as ¬*expr*. The character ¬ can be entered as ⋮!⋮, ⋮not⋮ or \[Not]. ▪ Not gives symbolic results when necessary, applying various simplification rules to them. ▪ If you are using *Mathematica* with a text-based front end, then you cannot use the notation !*expr* for Not[*expr*] if it appears at the very beginning of a line. In this case, !*expr* is interpreted as a shell escape. ▪ See page 87. ▪ See also: LogicalExpand, BitNot, Nand, Nor. ▪ *New in Version 1; modified in Version 3.*

■ Notebook

Notebook[{*cell*₁, *cell*₂, ... }] represents a notebook that can be manipulated by the *Mathematica* front end.

Notebook files contain explicit Notebook expressions written out in textual form. ▪ You can manipulate open notebooks in the front end using standard commands in the front end, and using the options inspector. ▪ Open notebooks in the front end are referred to in the kernel by NotebookObject constructs. You can use Options and SetOptions to look at and modify options for open notebooks. ▪ See page 576. ▪ See also: Cell. ▪ *New in Version 3.*

■ NotebookApply

NotebookApply[*notebook*, *data*] writes data into a notebook at the current selection, replacing the first selection placeholder in *data* by the current selection, and then setting the current selection to be just after the data written.

NotebookApply[*notebook*, *data*, *sel*] writes data into a notebook and then sets the current selection to be as specified by *sel*.

The first argument of NotebookApply is a NotebookObject. ■ NotebookApply does the same as NotebookWrite, except that it replaces the first selection placeholder in *data* by the current selection. ■ NotebookApply is often used in setting up actions for buttons in palettes. ■ Selection placeholders are represented by the character ■ or \[SelectionPlaceholder]. ■ Possible settings for *sel* are as in NotebookWrite. ■ See page 585. ■ See also: NotebookWrite, NotebookRead, SelectionMove, ButtonFunction. ■ *New in Version 3.*

■ NotebookAutoSave

NotebookAutoSave is an option for Notebook which specifies whether the notebook should automatically be saved after each piece of output generated by evaluation in it.

See page 618. ■ See also: NotebookSave. ■ *New in Version 3.*

■ NotebookClose

NotebookClose[*notebook*] closes the notebook corresponding to the specified notebook object.

NotebookClose will make a notebook disappear from your screen, and will invalidate all notebook objects which refer to that notebook. ■ See page 591. ■ See also: NotebookSave, Close. ■ *New in Version 3.*

■ NotebookCreate

NotebookCreate[ ] creates a new open notebook in the front end.

NotebookCreate[*options*] sets up the specified options for the new notebook.

NotebookCreate will by default create a notebook with name "Untitled-*n*". ■ Unless you set the option Visible->False, NotebookCreate will cause a new window to appear on your screen. ■ See page 591. ■ See also: NotebookOpen, NotebookClose. ■ *New in Version 3.*

■ NotebookDelete

NotebookDelete[*notebook*] deletes the current selection corresponding to the specified notebook object.

Using NotebookDelete in the kernel is equivalent to using the Clear command in the front end. ■ After NotebookDelete, the current selection becomes an insertion point at the position of the deleted material. ■ *notebook* must be a NotebookObject, as returned by NotebookOpen, etc. ■ See page 585. ■ See also: NotebookRead, NotebookWrite. ■ *New in Version 3.*

■ NotebookFind

NotebookFind[*notebook*, *data*] sets the current selection in the specified notebook object to be the next occurrence of *data*.

NotebookFind[*notebook*, *data*, Previous] sets the current selection to be the previous occurrence.

NotebookFind[*notebook*, *data*, All] sets the current selection to be all occurrences.

NotebookFind[*notebook*, *data*, *dir*, *elems*] searches the elements of cells specified by *elems*.

NotebookFind returns $Failed if the search it performs finds no occurrence of *data*. ▪ *notebook* must be a NotebookObject, as returned by NotebookOpen, etc. ▪ *data* can be a string, box expressions, or a complete cell. ▪ The possible elements are:

CellContents   contents of each cell, represented as a string
CellLabel   setting for the CellLabel option of each cell
CellStyle   name of style for each cell
CellTags   parts of the setting for the CellTags option for each cell
{*elem*₁, *elem*₂, ... }   list of different types of elements

▪ The default for *elems* is CellContents. ▪ Unless the option setting AutoScroll->False is given, the front end will scroll a notebook so that the result of NotebookFind is visible. ▪ The front end will also usually highlight the region corresponding to the result. ▪ See page 584. ▪ See also: NotebookLocate, SelectionMove, NotebookOpen, Find. ▪ *New in Version 3.*

■ NotebookGet

NotebookGet[*obj*] gets the expression corresponding to the notebook represented by the notebook object *obj*.

NotebookGet[ ] gets the expression corresponding to the currently selected notebook.

NotebookGet allows you to take a notebook that is open in the front end, and get the expression corresponding to it in the kernel. ▪ NotebookGet returns an expression with head Notebook. ▪ See page 578. ▪ See also: NotebookOpen, NotebookPut, Get. ▪ *New in Version 3.*

■ NotebookLocate

NotebookLocate["*tag*"] locates all cells with the specified tag in your currently selected notebook, selecting the cells and scrolling to the position of the first one.

NotebookLocate[{"*file*", "*tag*"}] if necessary opens the notebook stored in *file*, then locates cells with the specified tag.

NotebookLocate sets the current selection to contain all cells with the specified tag. ▪ If the cells are in closed groups, NotebookLocate will open all these groups. ▪ NotebookLocate is used for following hyperlinks within one notebook or between notebooks. ▪ NotebookLocate searches for tags in the list given as the setting for the CellTags option of each cell. ▪ See page 585. ▪ See also: NotebookFind, NotebookOpen, SetSelectedNotebook, ButtonBox. ▪ *New in Version 3.*

■ NotebookObject

NotebookObject[*fe*, *id*] is an object that represents an open notebook in the front end.

fe is a FrontEndObject which specifies the front end in which the notebook is open. ■ *id* is an integer that gives a unique serial number for this open notebook. ■ In StandardForm and OutputForm notebook objects are printed so as to indicate the current title of the window that would be used to display the notebook. ■ Functions such as NotebookPrint and NotebookClose take NotebookObject as their argument. ■ Within any open notebook, there is always a current selection. The current selection can be modified by applying functions such as SelectionMove to NotebookObject. ■ See page 579. ■ See also: NotebookSelection, NotebookOpen, Notebooks, SelectedNotebook. ■ *New in Version 3; modified in Version 4.*

■ NotebookOpen

NotebookOpen["*name*"] opens an existing notebook with the specified name, returning the corresponding notebook object.

NotebookOpen["*name*", *options*] opens a notebook using the options given.

NotebookOpen will usually cause a new notebook window to be opened on your screen. ■ NotebookOpen returns $Failed if it cannot open a notebook with the specified name. ■ NotebookOpen searches the directories specified by the NotebookPath global option for the front end. ■ With the option Visible->False set, NotebookOpen will return a NotebookObject, but will not cause a window to appear on your screen. ■ NotebookOpen initially sets the current selection to be before the first cell in the notebook. ■ See pages 578 and 591. ■ See also: NotebookCreate, NotebookLocate, NotebookSelection, OpenRead, Get, SetSelectedNotebook. ■ *New in Version 3.*

■ NotebookPrint

NotebookPrint[*notebook*] sends a notebook to your printer.

NotebookPrint[*notebook*, *stream*] sends a PostScript version of the notebook to the specified stream.

If *notebook* is a NotebookObject, then NotebookPrint will print the complete notebook. If it is a NotebookSelection, then NotebookPrint will print just the selection. ■ NotebookPrint uses the printing options set for the specified notebook, taking defaults from the global options set for the whole front end.
■ NotebookPrint[*notebook*, "*file*.ps"] saves the PostScript form of the notebook in a file.
■ NotebookPrint[*notebook*, "!*command*"] gives the PostScript form of the notebook as input to a command. ■ See page 591. ■ See also: NotebookSave, NotebookWrite, PrintingStyleEnvironment. ■ *New in Version 3.*

■ NotebookPut

NotebookPut[*expr*] creates a notebook corresponding to *expr* and makes it the currently selected notebook in the front end.

NotebookPut[*expr*, *obj*] replaces the notebook represented by the notebook object *obj* with one corresponding to *expr*.

NotebookPut allows you to take a notebook expression in the kernel and make it an open notebook in the front end. ■ *expr* must be a notebook expression with head Notebook. ■ NotebookPut returns a NotebookObject corresponding to the notebook it creates. ■ NotebookPut[*expr*, *obj*] overwrites whatever data was contained in the notebook represented by the notebook object *obj*. ■ See page 578. ■ See also: NotebookGet, NotebookCreate, Put.
■ *New in Version 3.*

■ NotebookRead

NotebookRead[*notebook*] gives the expression corresponding to the current selection in the specified notebook object.

NotebookRead is the basic way to get into the kernel pieces of notebooks that are being manipulated by the front end. ■ See page 585. ■ See also: Get, NotebookWrite, NotebookDelete, ButtonSource. ■ *New in Version 3.*

■ Notebooks

Notebooks[ ] gives a list of notebooks currently open in the front end.

Notebooks[ ] returns a list of NotebookObject constructs. ■ Notebooks[*fe*] gives a list of notebooks open in a specific front end, specified by a FrontEndObject. The default is $FrontEnd. ■ See page 579. ■ See also: SelectedNotebook, EvaluationNotebook, NotebookOpen, Streams. ■ *New in Version 3.*

■ NotebookSave

NotebookSave[*notebook*] saves the current version of a notebook in a file.

NotebookSave[*notebook*, "*file*"] saves the notebook in the specified file.

NotebookSave[*notebook*, *stream*] sends the expression corresponding to the current version of the notebook to the specified stream.

notebook must be a NotebookObject. ■ NotebookSave[*notebook*] saves the notebook in a file whose name is given by the notebook object *notebook*. ■ NotebookSave writes out the *Mathematica* expression corresponding to the notebook, together with *Mathematica* comments which make it easier for the front end to read the notebook in again. ■ See page 591. ■ See also: NotebookAutoSave, NotebookPrint. ■ *New in Version 3.*

■ NotebookSelection

NotebookSelection[*notebook*] represents the current selection in an open notebook in the front end.

NotebookSelection takes a NotebookObject as its argument. ■ You can use Options and SetOptions to read and write options associated with your current selection. ■ See page 591. ■ See also: SelectionMove. ■ *New in Version 3.*

■ NotebookWrite

NotebookWrite[*notebook*, *data*] writes data into a notebook at the current selection, setting the current selection to be just after the data written.

NotebookWrite[*notebook*, *data*, *sel*] writes data into a notebook setting the current selection to be as specified by *sel*.

The first argument of NotebookWrite is a NotebookObject. ■ NotebookWrite does essentially the same as a Paste operation in the front end: it replaces by *data* whatever the current selection in the notebook is. ■ NotebookWrite is the basic way to use the *Mathematica* kernel to modify the contents of notebooks that are being manipulated by the front end. ■ NotebookWrite automatically wraps Cell around the *data* you specify if this is necessary. ■ Possible settings for *sel* are:

After	place the current selection immediately after the data written
All	make the current selection be the data written
Before	place the current selection immediately before the data written
None	leave the current selection unchanged
Placeholder	make the current selection be the first placeholder in the data written

■ The default for *sel* is After, so that NotebookWrite[*obj*, *data*] can be called repeatedly to insert several pieces of data in sequence. ■ See page 585. ■ See also: NotebookApply, NotebookRead, NotebookDelete, SelectionMove. ■ *New in Version 3.*

■ **NProduct**

NProduct[f, {i, $imin$, $imax$}] gives a numerical approximation to the product $\prod_{i=imin}^{imax} f$.

NProduct[f, {i, $imin$, $imax$, di}] uses a step di in the product.

See notes for NSum. The options NSumExtraTerms and NSumTerms are replaced by NProductExtraFactors and NProductFactors. ■ See page 957. ■ Related package: NumericalMath`NLimit`. ■ *New in Version 1.*

■ **NSolve**

NSolve[lhs==rhs, var] gives a list of numerical approximations to the roots of a polynomial equation.

+ NSolve[{eqn_1, eqn_2, ... }, {var_1, var_2, ... }] solves a system of polynomial equations.

NSolve[$eqns$, $vars$, n] gives results to n-digit precision. ■ NSolve[$eqns$, $vars$] gives the same final result as N[Solve[$eqns$, $vars$]], apart from issues of numerical precision. ■ See page 959. ■ Implementation notes: see page 1068. ■ See also: Solve, FindRoot, NDSolve. ■ Related package: NumberTheory`Recognize`. ■ *New in Version 2; modified in Version 4.1.*

■ **NSum**

NSum[f, {i, $imin$, $imax$}] gives a numerical approximation to the sum $\sum_{i=imin}^{imax} f$.

NSum[f, {i, $imin$, $imax$, di}] uses a step di in the sum.

NSum can be used for sums with both finite and infinite limits. ■ NSum[f, {i, ... }, {j, ... }, ...] can be used to evaluate multidimensional sums. ~■ The following options can be given:

AccuracyGoal	Infinity	number of digits of final accuracy to try and get
Compiled	True	whether to compile the summand
EvaluationMonitor	None	expression to evaluate whenever f is evaluated
Method	Automatic	method to use: Integrate or Fit
NSumExtraTerms	12	maximum number of terms to use in extrapolation
NSumTerms	15	number of terms to use before extrapolation
PrecisionGoal	Automatic	number of digits of final precision to try and get
VerifyConvergence	True	whether to explicitly test for convergence
WorkingPrecision	MachinePrecision	the precision used in internal computations

■ NSum uses either the Euler-Maclaurin (Integrate) or Wynn epsilon (Fit) method. ■ With the Euler-Maclaurin method, the options AccuracyGoal and PrecisionGoal can be used to specify the accuracy and precision to try and get in the final answer. NSum stops when the error estimates it gets imply that either the accuracy or precision sought has been reached. ■ You should realize that with sufficiently pathological summands, the algorithms used by NSum can give wrong answers. In most cases, you can test the answer by looking at its sensitivity to changes in the setting of options for NSum. ■ VerifyConvergence is only used for sums with infinite limits. ■ N[Sum[...]] calls NSum. ■ NSum has attribute HoldAll. ■ See page 957. ■ Implementation notes: see page 1068. ■ See also: NProduct. ■ Related packages: NumericalMath`ListIntegrate`, NumericalMath`NLimit`. ■ *New in Version 1; modified in Version 5.0.*

■ **Null**

Null is a symbol used to indicate the absence of an expression or a result. When it appears as an output expression, no output is printed.

e_1; e_2; ... ; e_k; returns Null, and prints no output. ■ Expressions like $f[e_1, , e_2]$ are interpreted to have Null between each pair of adjacent commas. ■ *New in Version 1.*

■ NullRecords

NullRecords is an option for Read and related functions which specifies whether null records should be taken to exist between repeated record separators.

With the default setting NullRecords -> False, repeated record separators are treated like single record separators. ■ See page 646. ■ See also: WordSeparators. ■ *New in Version 2.*

■ NullSpace

NullSpace[*m*] gives a list of vectors that forms a basis for the null space of the matrix *m*.

NullSpace works on both numerical and symbolic matrices. ■ NullSpace[*m*, Modulus->*n*] finds null spaces for integer matrices modulo *n*. ■ NullSpace[*m*, ZeroTest -> *test*] evaluates *test*[*m*[[*i*, *j*]]] to determine whether matrix elements are zero. The default setting is ZeroTest -> Automatic. ■ A Method option can also be given. Possible settings are as for LinearSolve. ■ See page 907. ■ Implementation notes: see page 1069. ■ See also: MatrixRank, LinearSolve, RowReduce, SingularValueList. ■ *New in Version 1; modified in Version 3.*

■ NullWords

NullWords is an option for Read and related functions which specifies whether null words should be taken to exist between repeated word separators.

With the default setting NullWords -> False, repeated word separators are treated like single word separators. ■ See page 646. ■ See also: TokenWords, RecordSeparators. ■ *New in Version 2.*

■ Number

Number represents an exact integer or an approximate real number in Read.

An integer is returned if no explicit decimal point is present. ■ Approximate real numbers can be given in C or Fortran forms, such as 2.4E5 or -3.4e-4. ■ See page 646. ■ See also: Real, DigitQ. ■ *New in Version 1.*

■ NumberForm

NumberForm[*expr*, *n*] prints with approximate real numbers in *expr* given to *n*-digit precision.

NumberForm[*expr*, {*n*, *f*}] prints with approximate real numbers having *n* digits, with *f* digits to the right of the decimal point. ■ NumberForm works on integers as well as approximate real numbers. ~■ The following options can be given:

DigitBlock	Infinity	number of digits between breaks
ExponentFunction	Automatic	function to apply to exponents
NumberFormat	Automatic	function used to assemble mantissa, base, exponent
NumberMultiplier	"×"	string to use to indicate multiplication
NumberPadding	{"", ""}	strings to use for left and right padding
NumberPoint	"."	decimal point string
NumberSeparator	","	string to insert at breaks between blocks
NumberSigns	{"-", "+"}	strings to use for signs of negative and positive numbers
SignPadding	False	whether to insert padding after the sign

■ All options except ExponentFunction apply to integers as well as approximate real numbers. ■ You can mix NumberForm and BaseForm. ■ NumberForm acts as a "wrapper", which affects printing, but not evaluation. ■ See page 435. ■ See also: ScientificForm, EngineeringForm, AccountingForm, BaseForm, PaddedForm, N. ■ *New in Version 1; modified in Version 3.*

■ **NumberFormat**

NumberFormat is an option for NumberForm and related functions which specifies how the mantissa, base and exponent should be assembled into a final print form.

With the setting NumberFormat -> *f*, the function *f* is supplied with three arguments: the mantissa, base and exponent of each number to be printed. ■ The arguments are all given as strings. ■ When no exponent is to be printed, the third argument is given as "". ■ The function *f* must return the final format for the number. ■ See page 436. ■ See also: ExponentFunction. ■ *New in Version 2.*

■ **NumberMarks**

NumberMarks is an option for InputForm and related functions that specifies whether ` marks should be included in the printed forms of approximate numbers.

The default setting for NumberMarks is given by the value of $NumberMarks. ■ NumberMarks->True indicates that ` should be used in all approximate numbers, both machine-precision and arbitrary-precision ones. ■ NumberMarks -> Automatic indicates that ` should be used in arbitrary-precision but not machine-precision numbers. ■ NumberMarks -> False indicates that ` should never be used in outputting numbers. ■ Number marks are used to indicate the type of numbers, and their precision or accuracy. ■ The *^ form for scientific notation is always used in InputForm, and is independent of NumberMarks. ■ See page 730. ■ See also: NumberForm. ■ *New in Version 3.*

■ **NumberMultiplier**

NumberMultiplier is an option for NumberForm and related functions which gives the string to use as a multiplication sign in scientific notation.

The default is NumberMultiplier -> "\[Times]". ■ In OutputForm, \[Times] is rendered as x. ■ See page 436. ■ *New in Version 3.*

■ **NumberPadding**

NumberPadding is an option for NumberForm and related functions which gives strings to use as padding on the left- and right-hand sides of numbers.

NumberPadding -> {"*sleft*", "*sright*"} specifies strings to use for padding on the left and right. ■ In NumberForm, the default setting is NumberPadding -> {"", ""}. ■ In PaddedForm, the default setting is NumberPadding -> {" ", "0"}. ■ The strings specified as padding are inserted in place of digits. ■ See page 436. ■ See also: SignPadding. ■ *New in Version 2.*

■ **NumberPoint**

NumberPoint is an option for NumberForm and related functions which gives the string to use as a decimal point.

The default is NumberPoint -> ".". ■ See page 436. ■ *New in Version 1.*

■ **NumberQ**

NumberQ[*expr*] gives True if *expr* is a number, and False otherwise.

NumberQ[*expr*] returns False unless *expr* is manifestly a number (i.e., has head Complex, Integer, Rational or Real). ■ NumberQ[Infinity] gives False. ■ NumberQ[Overflow[ ]] and NumberQ[Underflow[ ]] give True. ■ You can use NumberQ[*x*] ^= True to override the normal operation of NumberQ, and effectively define *x* to be a number. ■ See pages 267 and 723. ■ See also: NumericQ, IntegerQ, MachineNumberQ, TrueQ, Complexes. ■ *New in Version 1; modified in Version 3.*

■ NumberSeparator

NumberSeparator is an option for NumberForm and related functions which gives the string to insert at breaks between digits.

NumberSeparator -> "*s*" specifies that the string *s* should be inserted at every break between digits specified by DigitBlock. ■ NumberSeparator -> {"*sleft*", "*sright*"} specifies different strings to be used on the left and right of the decimal point. ■ The default setting is NumberSeparator -> ",". ■ See page 436. ■ *New in Version 1.*

■ NumberSigns

NumberSigns is an option for NumberForm and related functions which gives strings to use as signs for negative and positive numbers.

NumberSigns -> {"*sneg*", "*spos*"} specifies that "*sneg*" should be given as the sign for negative numbers, and "*spos*" for positive numbers. ■ The default setting is NumberSigns -> {"-", ""}. ■ NumberSigns -> {{"*snleft*", "*snright*"}, {"*spleft*", "*spright*"}} specifies strings to put both on the left and right of numbers to specify their signs. ■ In AccountingForm, the default setting is NumberSigns -> {{"(", ")"}, ""}. ■ See page 436. ■ See also: SignPadding. ■ *New in Version 2.*

■ Numerator

Numerator[*expr*] gives the numerator of *expr*.

Numerator picks out terms which do not have superficially negative exponents. Denominator picks out the remaining terms. ■ An exponent is "superficially negative" if it has a negative number as a factor. ■ The standard representation of rational expressions as products of powers means that you cannot simply use Part to extract numerators. ■ Numerator can be used on rational numbers. ■ See page 74. ■ See also: ExpandNumerator. ■ *New in Version 1.*

■ NumericFunction

NumericFunction is an attribute that can be assigned to a symbol *f* to indicate that f[arg_1, arg_2, ...] should be considered a numeric quantity whenever all the arg_i are numeric quantities.

Most standard built-in mathematical functions have the attribute NumericFunction. ■ NumericQ checks the NumericFunction attribute of every function it encounters. ■ If you assign the attribute NumericFunction to a function that does not yield numerical values, then NumericQ will give misleading results. ■ See pages 329 and 724. ■ See also: NumericQ, NHoldAll. ■ *New in Version 3.*

■ NumericQ

NumericQ[*expr*] gives True if *expr* is a numeric quantity, and False otherwise.

An expression is considered a numeric quantity if it is either an explicit number or a mathematical constant such as Pi, or is a function that has attribute NumericFunction and all of whose arguments are numeric quantities. ■ In most cases, NumericQ[*expr*] gives True whenever N[*expr*] would yield an explicit number. ■ See page 724. ■ See also: NumberQ. ■ *New in Version 3.*

■ O

O[x]^n represents a term of order x^n.

O[x]^n is generated to represent omitted higher-order terms in power series.

O[x, x_0]^n represents a term of order $(x - x_0)^n$.

Normal can be used to truncate power series, and remove O terms. ■ See page 885. ■ See also: Series, SeriesData. ■ *New in Version 1.*

■ OddQ

OddQ[*expr*] gives True if *expr* is an odd integer, and False otherwise.

OddQ[*expr*] returns False unless *expr* is manifestly an odd integer (i.e., has head Integer, and is odd). ■ You can use OddQ[x] ^= True to override the normal operation of OddQ, and effectively define x to be an odd integer. ■ See pages 267 and 723. ■ See also: IntegerQ, EvenQ, TrueQ. ■ *New in Version 1.*

■ Off

Off[*symbol*::*tag*] switches off a message, so that it is no longer printed.

Off[*s*] switches off tracing messages associated with the symbol *s*.

Off[m_1, m_2, ...] switches off several messages.

Off[ ] switches off all tracing messages.

The *value* of *symbol*::*tag* is not affected by Off. ■ Off[*s*] is equivalent to Off[*s*::trace]. ■ Off[ ] is equivalent to Off[*s*::trace] for all symbols. ■ See pages 61 and 479. ■ See also: On, Message, Check. ■ *New in Version 1.*

■ Offset

Offset[{*dx*, *dy*}, *position*] gives the position of a graphical object obtained by starting at the specified position and then moving by absolute offset {*dx*, *dy*}.

Offset can be used to specify offsets in any two-dimensional graphics primitive. ■ *position* can be either {x, y} or Scaled[{x, y}, ...]. ■ The offset is measured in units of printer's points, approximately equal to $\frac{1}{72}$ of an inch. ■ Offset[{*dx*, *dy*}] can be used to specify an absolute radius in a Circle or Disk object. ■ See page 506. ■ See also: Scaled, AbsolutePointSize, AbsoluteThickness. ■ *New in Version 3.*

■ On

On[*symbol*::*tag*] switches on a message, so that it can be printed.

On[*s*] switches on tracing for the symbol *s*.

On[m_1, m_2, ...] switches on several messages.

On[ ] switches on tracing for all symbols.

When tracing is switched on, each evaluation of a symbol, on its own, or as a function, is printed, together with the result. ■ Note that the tracing information is printed when a function *returns*. As a result, traces of recursive functions appear in the opposite order from their calls. ■ On[*s*] is equivalent to On[*s*::trace]. ■ On[ ] is equivalent to On[*s*::trace] for all symbols. ■ See pages 61 and 479. ■ See also: Off, TracePrint. ■ *New in Version 1.*

■ OneIdentity

OneIdentity is an attribute that can be assigned to a symbol *f* to indicate that *f*[*x*], *f*[*f*[*x*]], etc. are all equivalent to *x* for the purpose of pattern matching.

+■ OneIdentity has an effect only if *f* has attribute Flat. ■ Functions like Plus and Times have the attribute OneIdentity. ■ The fact that Times has attribute OneIdentity allows a pattern like n_. x_ to match x. ■ See pages 271 and 329. ■ See also: Flat, Nest. ■ *New in Version 1.*

■ OpenAppend

OpenAppend["*file*"] opens a file to append output to it, and returns an OutputStream object.

The following options can be given:

CharacterEncoding	"ASCII"	what raw character encoding to use
FormatType	InputForm	default format for printing expressions
NameConversion	None	function for converting symbol names with special characters
NumberMarks	$NumberMarks	when to use ` marks in approximate numbers
PageWidth	78	number of character widths per line
TotalWidth	Infinity	maximum number of character widths for a single expression

■ On computer systems that support pipes, OpenAppend["!*command*"] runs the external program specified by *command*, and opens a pipe to send input to it. ■ If OpenRead does not succeed in opening a particular file or pipe, it generates a message, and returns $Failed. ■ OpenAppend resolves file names according to the procedure described in Section A.6.1. ■ OpenAppend returns OutputStream["*name*", *n*], where *name* is the full name of a file or command, and *n* is a serial number that is unique across all streams opened in the current *Mathematica* session. ■ SetOptions can be used to change the properties of an output stream, after it is already open. ■ Functions like Put and Write automatically open the files or pipes they need, if they are not already open. ■ Setting the option DOSTextFormat->True causes newlines specified by \n to be output as \r\n pairs, suitable for text-mode files on MS-DOS and related systems. ■ See page 632. ■ See also: Close, Put, Streams, LinkCreate. ■ *New in Version 1; modified in Version 3.*

■ OpenRead

OpenRead["*file*"] opens a file to read data from, and returns an InputStream object.

OpenRead prepares to read from a file, starting at the beginning of the file. ■ On systems that support pipes, OpenRead["!*command*"] runs the external program specified by *command*, and opens a pipe to get input from it. ■ If OpenRead does not succeed in opening a particular file or pipe, it generates a message, and returns $Failed. ■ OpenRead resolves file names according to the procedure described in Section A.6.1. ■ The function ReadList automatically opens files or pipes that it needs. ■ OpenRead returns InputStream["*name*", *n*], where *name* is the full name of a file or command, and *n* is a serial number that is unique across all streams opened in the current *Mathematica* session. ■ Setting the option DOSTextFormat->True causes all input to be treated as coming from a text-mode file on an MS-DOS or related system. This means that \r\n pairs are interpreted as single newlines, and [CTRL]-Z is interpreted as EndOfFile. ■ See page 649. ■ See also: Close, Read, ReadList, Streams, LinkCreate. ■ *New in Version 1; modified in Version 3.*

■ OpenTemporary

OpenTemporary[ ] opens a temporary file to which output can be written, and returns an OutputStream object.

OpenTemporary is often used in conjunction with Put and Get as a way of preparing data that is exchanged between *Mathematica* and external programs. ■ OpenTemporary always creates a new file, that does not already exist. ■ On Unix systems, OpenTemporary typically creates a file in the /tmp directory. ■ The global variable $TemporaryPrefix gives the base of the file name used by OpenTemporary. ■ See page 629. ■ See also: Close, Run. ■ *New in Version 1.*

■ **OpenWrite**

OpenWrite["*file*"] opens a file to write output to it, and returns an OutputStream object.

OpenWrite deletes any existing contents in a file, and prepares to write output starting at the beginning of the file.
- For output to pipes, OpenWrite and OpenAppend are equivalent. ■ See notes for OpenAppend. ■ See page 632.
- *New in Version 1.*

■ **Operate**

Operate[*p*, *f*[*x*, *y*]] gives *p*[*f*][*x*, *y*].

Operate[*p*, *expr*, *n*] applies *p* at level *n* in the head of *expr*.

Examples: Operate[p, f[x,y]] ⟶ p[f][x, y]; Operate[p, f[x][y][z], 1] ⟶ p[f[x][y]][z];
Operate[p, f[x][y][z], 2] ⟶ p[f[x]][y][z]. ■ Operate[*p*, *f*[*x*]] effectively applies the functional operator *p* to the function *f*. ■ Operate is essentially a generalization of Apply, which allows you to apply an operator to the head of an expression, rather than simply to replace the head. ■ See page 254. ■ See also: Through, Apply, Heads.
- *New in Version 1.*

■ **Optional**

p:*v* is a pattern object which represents an expression of the form *p*, which, if omitted, should be replaced by *v*.

Optional is used to specify "optional arguments" in functions represented by patterns. The pattern object *p* gives the form the argument should have, if it is present. The expression *v* gives the "default value" to use if the argument is absent. ■ Example: the pattern f[x_, y_:1] is matched by f[a], with x taking the value a, and y taking the value 1. It can also be matched by f[a, b], with y taking the value b. ■ The form *s*_:*v* is equivalent to Optional[*s*_, *v*]. This form is also equivalent to *s*:_:*v*. There is no syntactic ambiguity since *s* must be a symbol in this case. ■ The special form *s*_. is equivalent to Optional[*s*_] and can be used to represent function arguments which, if omitted, should be replaced by default values globally specified for the functions in which they occur. ■ Values for Default[*f*, ...] specify default values to be used when _. appears as an argument of *f*. Any assignments for Default[*f*, ...] must be made *before* _. first appears as an argument of *f*. ■ Optional[*s*_*h*] represents a function which can be omitted, but which, if present, must have head *h*. There is no simpler syntactic form for this case. ■ Functions with built-in default values include Plus, Times and Power. ■ See pages 274 and 1030. ■ See also: Alternatives. ■ *New in Version 1.*

■ **Options**

Options[*symbol*] gives the list of default options assigned to a symbol.

Options[*expr*] gives the options explicitly specified in a particular expression such as a graphics object.

Options[*stream*] or Options["*sname*"] gives options associated with a particular stream.

Options[*object*] gives options associated with an external object such as a NotebookObject.

Options[*obj*, *name*] gives the setting for the option *name*.

Options[*obj*, {*name*₁, *name*₂, ... }] gives a list of the settings for the options *name*ᵢ.

Many built-in functions allow you to give additional arguments that specify options with rules of the form *name* -> *value*. ■ Options[*f*] gives the list of rules to be used for the options associated with a function *f* if no explicit rules are given when the function is called. ■ Options always returns a list of transformation rules for option names. ■ You can assign a value to Options[*symbol*] to redefine all the default option settings for a function. ■ SetOptions[*symbol*, *name* -> *value*] can be used to specify individual default options. ■ You can use Options on InputStream and OutputStream objects. If there is only one stream with a particular name, you can give the name as a string as the argument of Options. ■ If you ask for Options[NotebookObject[...], *name*] the kernel will send a request to the front end to find the result. ■ Explicit values are found for options associated with cells even if these options are only set at the style, notebook or global level. ■ See pages 144 and 1040. ■ See also: AbsoluteOptions. ■ Related package: Utilities`FilterOptions`. ■ *New in Version 1; modified in Version 3.*

■ Or

e_1 || e_2 || ... is the logical OR function. It evaluates its arguments in order, giving True immediately if any of them are True, and False if they are all False.

Or[e_1, e_2, ...] can be input in StandardForm and InputForm as e_1 ∨ e_2 ∨ ... . The character ∨ can be entered as ⇥||⇥, ⇥or⇥ or \[Or]. ■ Or evaluates its arguments in a non-standard way (see page 1046). ■ Or gives symbolic results when necessary, removing initial arguments that are False. ■ See page 87. ■ See also: Xor, LogicalExpand, BitOr, Nor. ■ *New in Version 1; modified in Version 3.*

■ Order

Order[$expr_1$, $expr_2$] gives 1 if $expr_1$ is before $expr_2$ in canonical order, and −1 if $expr_1$ is after $expr_2$ in canonical order. It gives 0 if $expr_1$ is identical to $expr_2$.

Examples: Order[a, b] ⟶ 1; Order[b, a] ⟶ −1. ■ Order uses canonical order as described in the notes for Sort. ■ See page 255. ■ See also: Equal, SameQ, Sort. ■ *New in Version 1.*

■ OrderedQ

OrderedQ[h[e_1, e_2, ...]] gives True if the e_i are in canonical order, and False otherwise.

See notes for Order. ■ OrderedQ[{e, e}] gives True. ■ By default, OrderedQ uses canonical order as described in the notes for Sort. ■ OrderedQ[*list*, p] uses the function p to determine whether each pair of elements in *list* is in order. ■ See page 268. ■ See also: Signature, Sort. ■ *New in Version 1.*

⁺■ Ordering

Ordering[*list*] gives the positions in *list* at which each successive element of Sort[*list*] appears.

Ordering[*list*, n] gives the positions in *list* at which the first n elements of Sort[*list*] appear.

Ordering[*list*, −n] gives the positions of the last n elements of Sort[*list*].

Ordering[*list*, n, p] uses Sort[*list*, p].

Example: Ordering[{c, a, b}] ⟶ {2, 3, 1}. ■ In a numerical list Ordering[*list*, n] gives the positions of the n smallest elements. Ordering[*list*, −n] gives the positions of the n largest elements. ■ If there are several smallest elements in *list*, Ordering[*list*, 1] will give only the position of the one that appears first. ■ *list*[[Ordering[*list*]]] is the same as Sort[*list*]. ■ Ordering[*list*, *seq*] is equivalent to Take[Ordering[*list*], *seq*]. ■ Ordering[*list*, All, p] gives the position at which all elements of *list* appear in Sort[*list*, p]. ■ Ordering can be used on expressions with any head, not only List. ■ See page 129. ■ See also: Max, Min, Position, OrderedQ, Median. ■ *New in Version 4.1.*

■ Orderless

Orderless is an attribute that can be assigned to a symbol f to indicate that the elements e_i in expressions of the form f[e_1, e_2, ...] should automatically be sorted into canonical order. This property is accounted for in pattern matching.

The Orderless attribute for a function corresponds to the mathematical property of commutativity. ■ Functions with the Orderless attribute use canonical order as described in the notes for Sort. ■ For an object that represents a matrix or a tensor, the Orderless attribute represents symmetry among indices. ■ Functions like Plus and Times are Orderless. ■ In matching patterns with Orderless functions, all possible orders of arguments are tried. ■ The Orderless attribute must be assigned before defining any values for an Orderless function. ■ See page 329. ■ See also: Sort, Flat, OneIdentity. ■ *New in Version 1.*

■ Out

%*n* or Out[*n*] is a global object that is assigned to be the value produced on the nth output line.

% gives the last result generated.

%% gives the result before last. %% ... % (*k* times) gives the kth previous result.

Out[ ] is equivalent to %. ■ Out[-*k*] is equivalent to %% ... % (*k* times). ■ See page 702. ■ See also: In, $Line, $HistoryLength, MessageList. ■ *New in Version 1.*

■ Outer

Outer[*f*, *list*$_1$, *list*$_2$, ...] gives the generalized outer product of the *list*$_i$, forming all possible combinations of the lowest-level elements in each of them, and feeding them as arguments to *f*.

Outer[*f*, *list*$_1$, *list*$_2$, ... , *n*] treats as separate elements only sublists at level *n* in the *list*$_i$.

Outer[*f*, *list*$_1$, *list*$_2$, ... , *n*$_1$, *n*$_2$, ...] treats as separate elements only sublists at level *n*$_i$ in the corresponding *list*$_i$.

Example: Outer[f,{a,b},{x,y}] $\longrightarrow$ {{f[a, x], f[a, y]}, {f[b, x], f[b, y]}}. ■ Outer[Times, *list*$_1$, *list*$_2$] gives an outer product. ■ The result of applying Outer to the tensors $T_{i_1 i_2 \ldots i_r}$ and $U_{j_1 j_2 \ldots j_s}$ is the tensor $V_{i_1 i_2 \ldots i_r j_1 j_2 \ldots j_s}$ with elements $f[T_{i_1 i_2 \ldots i_r}, U_{j_1 j_2 \ldots j_s}]$. Applying Outer to two tensors of ranks *r* and *s* gives a tensor of rank *r* + *s*. ■ The heads of both *list*$_i$ must be the same, but need not necessarily be List. ■ The *list*$_i$ need not necessarily be cuboidal arrays. ■ The specifications *n*$_i$ of levels must be integers. ■ If only a single level specification is given, it is assumed to apply to all the *list*$_i$. If there are several *n*$_i$, but fewer than the number of *list*$_i$, all levels in the remaining *list*$_i$ will be used. +■ Outer can be used on SparseArray objects, returning a SparseArray object when possible. ■ See page 917. ■ See also: Inner, Distribute, Cross. ■ *New in Version 1; modified in Version 3.*

■ OutputForm

OutputForm[*expr*] prints as a two-dimensional representation of *expr* using only keyboard characters.

OutputForm is an approximation to StandardForm which uses only ordinary keyboard characters. ■ The OutputForm of many kinds of expressions is quite different from their internal representation. ■ OutputForm acts as a "wrapper", which affects printing, but not evaluation. ■ OutputForm cannot be used directly for input to *Mathematica*. ■ When possible, OutputForm uses approximations to special characters. Thus ≥ is given as >= and é as e'. ■ See page 424. ■ See also: StandardForm, TraditionalForm, InputForm, TeXForm, MathMLForm, Short, FullForm. ■ *New in Version 1; modified in Version 3.*

■ OutputStream

OutputStream["*name*", *n*] is an object that represents an output stream for functions such as Write.

OpenWrite and OpenAppend return OutputStream objects. ■ The serial number *n* is unique across all streams, regardless of their name. ■ See page 631. ■ See also: Streams, InputStream. ■ *New in Version 2.*

■ **OverscriptBox**

OverscriptBox[x, y] represents $\overset{y}{x}$ in input and output.

Inside \(... \) OverscriptBox[x, y] can be input as x \& y. ■ In a notebook an OverscriptBox can be created using [CTRL]7 or [CTRL]&. [CTRL]␣ moves out of the overscript position. ■ In StandardForm and InputForm, OverscriptBox[x, y] is interpreted on input as Overscript[x, y]. ■ The following special interpretations are made:

OverscriptBox[x, "_"]	OverBar[x]	$\bar{x}$
OverscriptBox[x, "→"]	OverVector[x]	$\vec{x}$
OverscriptBox[x, "~"]	OverTilde[x]	$\tilde{x}$
OverscriptBox[x, "^"]	OverHat[x]	$\hat{x}$
OverscriptBox[x, "."]	OverDot[x]	$\dot{x}$

■ For these special cases special input forms such as x\&_ can be used. ■ The baseline of OverscriptBox[x, y] is taken to be the baseline of x. ■ OverscriptBox[x, y] is usually output with y in a smaller font than x. ■ With the option setting LimitsPositioning->True y is placed in an overscript position when the whole OverscriptBox is displayed large, and in a superscript position when it is displayed smaller. ■ In StandardForm, explicit OverscriptBox objects are output literally. You can use DisplayForm to see the display form of such objects. ■ See page 445. ■ See also: UnderscriptBox, UnderoverscriptBox, SuperscriptBox, GridBox, FractionBox, ScriptSizeMultipliers. ■ *New in Version 3.*

■ **PaddedForm**

PaddedForm[*expr*, n] prints with all numbers in *expr* padded to leave room for a total of n digits.

PaddedForm[*expr*, {n, f}] prints with approximate real numbers having exactly f digits to the right of the decimal point.

By default, PaddedForm pads with spaces on the left to leave room for n digits. ■ PaddedForm pads with zeros on the right in approximate real numbers. ■ The length n specified in PaddedForm counts only digits, and not signs, breaks between digits, and so on. ■ PaddedForm takes the same options as NumberForm, but with some defaults different. ■ You can use PaddedForm to align columns of numbers. ■ PaddedForm acts as a "wrapper", which affects printing, but not evaluation. ■ See page 437. ■ See also: ColumnForm, TableForm. ■ *New in Version 2.*

■ **PadLeft**

PadLeft[*list*, n] makes a list of length n by padding *list* with zeros on the left.

PadLeft[*list*, n, x] pads by repeating the element x.

PadLeft[*list*, n, {x_1, x_2, ... }] pads by cyclically repeating the elements x_i.

PadLeft[*list*, n, *padding*, m] leaves a margin of m elements of padding on the right.

PadLeft[*list*, {n_1, n_2, ... }] makes a nested list with length n_i at level i.

(continued)

■ **PadLeft** *(continued)*

■ Example: PadLeft[{a,b,c}, 7] ⟶ {0, 0, 0, 0, a, b, c}. ~■ PadLeft[*list*, *n*, ...] always returns a list of length *n*, except in some special cases where *padding* is {}. ■ With padding $\{x_1, x_2, \dots, x_s\}$ cyclic repetitions of the x_i are effectively laid down and then the list is superimposed on top of them, with the last element of the list lying on an occurrence of x_s. ■ Examples: PadLeft[{a,b}, 7, {x,y,z}] ⟶ {z, x, y, z, x, a, b}.
■ PadLeft[{a,b}, 7, {x,y,z}, 2] ⟶ {y, z, x, a, b, x, y}. ■ PadLeft[*list*, *n*, *padding*, -*m*] truncates the last *m* elements of *list*. ■ A margin of Round[(*n*-Length[*list*])/2] effectively centers *list*. ■ PadLeft[*list*, *n*, *list*] effectively treats *list* as cyclic. ■ PadLeft[*list*, *n*, {*xlist*}] can be used to repeat an individual element that is itself a list. ■ Example: PadLeft[{a,b,c}, 5, {{u}}] ⟶ {{u}, {u}, a, b, c}. ■ PadLeft[{}, *n*, {x_1, x_2, ... }] repeats the sequence of x_i as many times as fits in a list of length *n*. ■ PadLeft[*list*, {n_1, n_2, ... }] creates a full array with dimensions {n_1, n_2, ... } even if *list* is ragged. ■ Negative n_i specify to pad on the right.
■ PadLeft[*list*, {n_1, n_2}, {{x_{11}, x_{12}, ... }, {x_{21}, ... }, ... }] pads by repeating the block of x_{ij}.
■ PadLeft[*list*, {n_1, n_2, ... }, *list*] effectively treats *list* as cyclic in every dimension.
■ PadLeft[*list*, {n_1, n_2, ... }, *padding*, {m_1, m_2, ... }] uses margin m_i at level *i*. ■ The object *list* need not have head List. +■ PadLeft can be used on SparseArray objects. ■ See page 294. ■ See also: PadRight, Join, Partition, ListCorrelate, RotateLeft. ■ *New in Version 4.*

■ **PadRight**

PadRight[*list*, *n*] makes a list of length *n* by padding *list* with zeros on the right.

PadRight[*list*, *n*, *x*] pads by repeating the element *x*.

PadRight[*list*, *n*, {x_1, x_2, ... }] pads by cyclically repeating the elements x_i.

PadRight[*list*, *n*, *padding*, *m*] leaves a margin of *m* elements of padding on the left.

PadRight[*list*, {n_1, n_2, ... }] makes a nested list with length n_i at level *i*.

PadRight[*list*, *n*, ...] always returns a list of length *n*. ■ Example: PadRight[{a,b,c}, 7] ⟶ {a, b, c, 0, 0, 0, 0}. ■ With padding {x_1, x_2, ... } cyclic repetitions of the x_i are effectively laid down and then the list is superimposed on top of them, with the first element of the list lying on an occurrence of x_1. ■ Examples: PadRight[{a,b}, 7, {x,y,z}] ⟶ {a, b, z, x, y, z, x}.
■ PadRight[{a,b}, 7, {x,y,z}, 2] ⟶ {y, z, a, b, z, x, y}. ■ See additional notes for PadLeft. ■ See page 294. ■ See also: PadLeft, Join, Partition, ListCorrelate, RotateRight. ■ *New in Version 4.*

■ **PageBreakAbove**

PageBreakAbove is an option for Cell which specifies whether a page break should be made immediately above the cell if the notebook that contains the cell is printed.

A setting of Automatic specifies that a page break should be made if necessary. ■ A setting of True specifies that a page break should always be made, while a setting of False specifies that it should never be made. ■ See page 609. ■ See also: PageBreakBelow, ShowPageBreaks. ■ *New in Version 3.*

■ **PageBreakBelow**

PageBreakBelow is an option for Cell which specifies whether a page break should be made immediately below the cell if the notebook that contains the cell is printed.

A setting of Automatic specifies that a page break should be made if necessary. ■ A setting of True specifies that a page break should always be made, while a setting of False specifies that it should never be made. ■ See page 609. ■ See also: PageBreakAbove, ShowPageBreaks. ■ *New in Version 3.*

■ **PageBreakWithin**

> PageBreakWithin is an option for Cell which specifies whether a page break should be allowed within the cell if the notebook that contains the cell is printed.
>
> See page 609. ■ See also: PageBreakAbove, GroupPageBreakWithin, ShowPageBreaks. ■ *New in Version 3.*

■ **PageWidth**

> PageWidth is an option for output streams and for cells which specifies how wide each line of text should be allowed to be.
>
> ~■ Possible settings for output streams are:
>
> Infinity   an infinite width (no linebreaking)
> *n*   explicit width in characters
>
> ■ SetOptions[*stream*, PageWidth -> *val*] resets the line width allowed for an open stream. ■ Possible settings for cells are:
>
> WindowWidth   the width of the window on the screen
> PaperWidth   the width of the page as it would be printed
> *n*   explicit width given in printer's points
>
> ■ PageWidth->WindowWidth allows each line to use the full width of the displayed window, taking into account settings for CellMargins. ■ See pages 609 and 634. ■ See also: TotalWidth, TextJustification, AutoIndent. ■ *New in Version 1; modified in Version 3.*

■ **ParagraphIndent**

> ParagraphIndent is an option for Cell which specifies how far in printer's points to indent the first line of each paragraph of text.
>
> A new paragraph is taken to start at the beginning of a cell, and after every explicit RETURN character in your text. ■ Negative settings for ParagraphIndent make the first line of each paragraph stick out to the left. ■ See page 609. ■ See also: AutoIndent, LineIndent, ParagraphSpacing. ■ *New in Version 3.*

■ **ParagraphSpacing**

> ParagraphSpacing is an option for Cell, StyleBox and StyleForm which specifies how much extra space to leave between successive paragraphs of text.
>
> ParagraphSpacing->{*c*, 0} leaves an extra space of *c* times the height of the font in the paragraph. ■ ParagraphSpacing->{0, *n*} leaves an extra space of exactly *n* printer's points. ■ ParagraphSpacing->{*c*, *n*} leaves an extra space of *c* times the height of the font plus *n* printer's points. ■ Paragraph breaks are taken to occur whenever an explicit RETURN character appears in a block of text. ■ ParagraphSpacing is added to LineSpacing to determine spacing between paragraphs. ■ A typical default setting is ParagraphSpacing->{0, 0}. ■ ParagraphSpacing applies only to ordinary text, not *Mathematica* expressions. ■ Extra space specified by ParagraphSpacing is inserted before the first line of each paragraph. No extra space is inserted if the paragraph is at the beginning of a cell or a string. ■ See page 611. ■ See also: LineSpacing, ParagraphIndent. ■ *New in Version 3.*

■ **ParametricPlot**

> ParametricPlot[{f_x, f_y}, {t, *tmin*, *tmax*}] produces a parametric plot with x and y coordinates f_x and f_y generated as a function of t.
>
> ParametricPlot[{{f_x, f_y}, {g_x, g_y}, ... }, {t, *tmin*, *tmax*}] plots several parametric curves.
>
> ParametricPlot evaluates its arguments in a non-standard way (see page 1046). You should use Evaluate to evaluate the function to be plotted if this can safely be done before specific numerical values are supplied. ■ The options that can be given for ParametricPlot are the same as for Plot. ■ ParametricPlot has the default option setting Axes -> True. ■ ParametricPlot returns a Graphics object. ■ See page 161. ■ See also: ContourPlot. ■ Related packages: Graphics`ImplicitPlot`, Graphics`PlotField`. ■ *New in Version 1.*

■ ParametricPlot3D

ParametricPlot3D[$\{f_x, f_y, f_z\}$, $\{t, tmin, tmax\}$] produces a three-dimensional space curve parametrized by a variable t which runs from $tmin$ to $tmax$.

ParametricPlot3D[$\{f_x, f_y, f_z\}$, $\{t, tmin, tmax\}$, $\{u, umin, umax\}$] produces a three-dimensional surface parametrized by t and u.

ParametricPlot3D[$\{f_x, f_y, f_z, s\}$, ...] shades the plot according to the color specification s.

ParametricPlot3D[$\{\{f_x, f_y, f_z\}, \{g_x, g_y, g_z\}, ... \}$, ...] plots several objects together.

ParametricPlot3D evaluates its arguments in a non-standard way (see page 1046). You should use Evaluate to evaluate the function to be plotted if this can safely be done before specific numerical values are supplied. ■ ParametricPlot3D has the same options as Graphics3D, with the following additions:

Compiled	True	whether to compile the function to plot
PlotPoints	Automatic	the number of sample points for each parameter

■ ParametricPlot3D has the default option setting Axes -> True. ~■ With the default setting
PlotPoints -> Automatic, ParametricPlot3D uses PlotPoints -> 75 for curves and PlotPoints -> {30, 30} for surfaces. ■ ParametricPlot3D returns a Graphics3D object. ■ See page 163. ■ Related packages:
Graphics`PlotField3D`, Graphics`ContourPlot3D`, Graphics`SurfaceOfRevolution`, Graphics`Shapes`. ■ *New in Version 2.*

■ ParentDirectory

ParentDirectory[ ] gives the parent of the current working directory.

ParentDirectory["*dir*"] gives the parent of the directory *dir*.

ParentDirectory returns the full name of the directory as a string. ■ ParentDirectory works only under operating systems which support hierarchical file systems. ■ See page 637. ■ See also: Directory, $HomeDirectory, DirectoryName. ■ *New in Version 2.*

■ Part

expr[[*i*]] or Part[*expr*, *i*] gives the ith part of *expr*.

expr[[-*i*]] counts from the end.

expr[[0]] gives the head of *expr*.

expr[[*i*, *j*, ...]] or Part[*expr*, *i*, *j*, ...] is equivalent to *expr*[[*i*]] [[*j*]] ... .

expr[[$\{i_1, i_2, ... \}$]] gives a list of the parts $i_1, i_2, ...$ of *expr*.

You can make an assignment like *t*[[*i*]] = *value* to modify part of an expression. ■ When *expr* is a list, *expr*[[$\{i_1, i_2, ... \}$]] gives a list of parts. In general, the head of *expr* is applied to the list of parts. ■ You can get a nested list of parts from *expr*[[*list*$_1$, *list*$_2$, ...]]. Each part has one index from each list. ■ If any of the *list*$_i$ are All, all parts at that level are kept. ■ *expr*[[All, *i*]] effectively gives the ith column in *expr*. ■ Notice that lists are used differently in Part than in functions like Extract, MapAt and Position. ■ *expr*[[Range[*i*, *j*]]] can be used to extract sequences of parts. +■ If *expr* is a SparseArray object, *expr*[[...]] gives the parts in the corresponding ordinary array. ■ In StandardForm and InputForm, *expr*[[*spec*]] can be input as *expr*⟦*spec*⟧. ■ ⟦ and ⟧ can be entered as :[[: and :]]: or \[LeftDoubleBracket] and \[RightDoubleBracket]. ■ In StandardForm, *expr*[[*spec*]] can be input as *expr*$_{[[spec]]}$ or *expr*$_{⟦spec⟧}$ ■ See pages 235 and 285. ■ See also: First, Head, Last, Extract, Position, ReplacePart, MapAt, Take, PadLeft. ■ Related package: LinearAlgebra`MatrixManipulation`. ■ *New in Version 1; modified in Version 5.0.*

■ Partition

Partition[*list*, *n*] partitions *list* into non-overlapping sublists of length *n*.

Partition[*list*, *n*, *d*] generates sublists with offset *d*.

Partition[*list*, {n_1, n_2, ... }] partitions a nested list into blocks of size $n_1 \times n_2 \times ...$.

Partition[*list*, {n_1, n_2, ... }, {d_1, d_2, ... }] uses offset d_i at level *i* in *list*.

Partition[*list*, *n*, *d*, {k_L, k_R}] specifies that the first element of *list* should appear at position k_L in the first sublist, and the last element of *list* should appear at or after position k_R in the last sublist. If additional elements are needed, Partition fills them in by treating *list* as cyclic.

Partition[*list*, *n*, *d*, {k_L, k_R}, *x*] pads if necessary by repeating the element *x*.

Partition[*list*, *n*, *d*, {k_L, k_R}, {x_1, x_2, ... }] pads if necessary by cyclically repeating the elements x_i.

Partition[*list*, *n*, *d*, {k_L, k_R}, {}] uses no padding, and so can yield sublists of different lengths.

Partition[*list*, *nlist*, *dlist*, {$klist_L$, $klist_R$}, *padlist*] specifies alignments and padding in a nested list.

Example: Partition[{a,b,c,d,e,f}, 2] ⟶ {{a, b}, {c, d}, {e, f}}. ■ All the sublists generated by Partition[*list*, *n*, *d*] are of length *n*. Some elements at the end of *list* may therefore not appear in any sublist. ■ The element e in Partition[{a,b,c,d,e}, 2] ⟶ {{a, b}, {c, d}} is dropped. ■ Partition[{a,b,c,d,e}, 3, 1] ⟶ {{a, b, c}, {b, c, d}, {c, d, e}} generates sublists with offset 1. ■ All elements of *list* appear in the sublists generated by Partition[*list*, *n*, 1]. ■ If *d* is greater than *n* in Partition[*list*, *n*, *d*], then elements in the middle of *list* are skipped. ■ Partition[*list*, 1, *d*] picks out elements in the same way as Take[*list*, {1, -1, *d*}]. ■ Partition[*list*, *n*, *d*, {k_L, k_R}] effectively allows sublists that have overhangs that extend past the beginning or end of *list*. ■ Partition[*list*, *n*, *d*, *k*] is equivalent to Partition[*list*, *n*, *d*, {*k*, *k*}]. ■ Common settings for {k_L, k_R} are:

{1, -1}	allow no overhangs
{1, 1}	allow maximal overhang at the end
{-1, -1}	allow maximal overhang at the beginning
{-1, 1}	allow maximal overhangs at both beginning and end

■ Example: Partition[{a,b,c,d},2,1,{-1,1}] ⟶ {{d, a}, {a, b}, {b, c}, {c, d}, {d, a}}. ■ Partition[*list*, *n*, *d*, {k_L, k_R}, *padlist*] effectively lays down repeated copies of *padlist*, then superimposes one copy of *list* on them, and partitions the result. ■ Common settings for *padlist* are:

x	pad with repetitions of a single element
{x_1, x_2, ... }	pad with cyclic repetitions of a sequence of elements
list	pad by treating *list* as cyclic (default)
{}	do no padding, potentially leaving sublists of different lengths

(continued)

■ **Partition** *(continued)*

- Example: `Partition[{a,b,c,d},2,1,{-1,1},{x,y}]` ⟶ `{{y, a}, {a, b}, {b, c}, {c, d}, {d, x}}`.
- `Partition[{a,b,c,d},2,1,{-1,1},{}]` ⟶ `{{a}, {a, b}, {b, c}, {c, d}, {d}}`. ■ If *list* has length s, then `Partition[`*list*`, n, d]` yields `Max[0, Floor[(s + d - n)/d]]` sublists. ■ `Partition[`*list*`, {`n_1, n_2, ... , n_r`}]` effectively replaces blocks of elements at level r in *list* by depth r nested lists of neighboring elements. ■ If no offsets are specified, the neighborhoods are adjacent and non-overlapping. ■ `Partition[`*list*`, {`n_1, n_2, ... `}, d]` uses offset d at every level. ■ `Partition[`*list*`, `*nlist*`, `*dlist*`, {{`k_{L1}, k_{L2}, ... `}, {`k_{R1}, k_{R2}, ... `}}]` specifies that element $\{1,1,...\}$ of *list* should appear at position $\{k_{L1}, k_{L2}, ...\}$ in the $\{1,1,...\}$ block of the result, while element $\{-1,-1,...\}$ of *list* should appear at or after position $\{k_{R1}, k_{R2}, ...\}$ in the $\{-1,-1,...\}$ block of the result. ■ $\{k_L, k_R\}$ is taken to be equivalent to $\{\{k_L, k_L, ...\}, \{k_R, k_R, ...\}\}$. ■ $\{\{k_1, k_2, ...\}\}$ is taken to be equivalent to $\{\{k_1, k_2, ...\}, \{k_1, k_2, ...\}\}$. ■ `Partition[`*list*`, {`$n_1$, n_2, ... , n_r`}, `*klist*`, `*padlist*`]` effectively makes a depth r array of copies of *padlist*, then superimposes *list* on them, and partitions the result. ■ If *list* has dimensions $\{s_1, s_2, ... , s_r\}$ then `Partition[`*list*`, {`n_1, n_2, ... , n_r`}]` will have dimensions $\{q_1, q_2, ... , q_r, n_1, n_2, ... , n_r\}$ where q_i is given by `Floor[`s_i/n_i`]`. ■ The object *list* need not have head `List`. ■ `Partition[f[a,b,c,d], 2]` ⟶ `f[f[a, b], f[c, d]]`. +■ Partition can be used on `SparseArray` objects. ■ See page 292. ■ See also: `Flatten`, `RotateLeft`, `Split`, `Take`, `PadLeft`, `ListConvolve`, `CellularAutomaton`. ■ *New in Version 1; modified in Version 4.*

■ **PartitionsP**

`PartitionsP[`n`]` gives the number $p(n)$ of unrestricted partitions of the integer n.

Integer mathematical function (see Section A.3.10). ■ See page 757. ■ Implementation notes: see page 1067. ■ See also: `PartitionsQ`, `DedekindEta`. ■ *New in Version 1.*

■ **PartitionsQ**

`PartitionsQ[`n`]` gives the number $q(n)$ of partitions of the integer n into distinct parts.

Integer mathematical function (see Section A.3.10). ■ See page 757. ■ See also: `PartitionsP`. ■ *New in Version 1.*

■ **Path**

`Path` is an option for `Get` and related functions which gives a list of directories to search in attempting to find an external file.

The default setting is `Path :> $Path`. ■ The possible settings for `Path` are the same as those for `$Path`. ■ See page 637. ■ See also: `$Path`, `SetDirectory`, `$Input`. ■ *New in Version 4.*

■ **Pattern**

s:*obj* represents the pattern object *obj*, assigned the name s.

The name s must be a symbol. ■ The object *obj* can be any pattern object. ■ When a transformation rule is used, any occurrence of s on the right-hand side is replaced by whatever expression it matched on the left-hand side. ■ The operator `:` has a comparatively low precedence. The expression `x:_+_` is thus interpreted as `x:(_+_)`, not `(x:_)+_`. ■ The form `s_` is equivalent to `s:_`. Similarly, `s_h` is equivalent to `s:_h`, `s__` to `s:__`, and so on. ■ See pages 263 and 1030. ■ *New in Version 1.*

■ **PatternTest**

p?*test* is a pattern object that stands for any expression which matches *p*, and on which the application of *test* gives `True`.

Any result for *test*[*pval*] other than `True` is taken to signify failure. ■ Example: `_?NumberQ` represents a number of any type. The `_` matches any expression, and `?NumberQ` restricts to any expression which gives `True` on application of the number test `NumberQ`. ■ The operator `?` has a high precedence. Thus `_^_?t` is `_^(_?t)` not `(_^_)?t`. ■ In a form such as `__?test` every element in the sequence matched by `__` must yield `True` when *test* is applied. ■ See page 269. ■ See also: `Condition`, `Element`. ■ *New in Version 1.*

■ **Pause**

`Pause[`*n*`]` pauses for at least *n* seconds.

Pause is accurate only down to a granularity of at least `$TimeUnit` seconds. ~■ The time elapsed during the execution of `Pause` is counted in `SessionTime` and `AbsoluteTiming`, but not in `TimeUsed` or `Timing`. ■ Under multitasking operating systems, there may be a delay of significantly more than *n* seconds when you execute `Pause[`*n*`]`. ■ See page 710. ■ *New in Version 2.*

■ **Permutations**

`Permutations[`*list*`]` generates a list of all possible permutations of the elements in *list*.

Example: `Permutations[{a,b,c}]` ⟶ `{{a, b, c}, {a, c, b}, {b, a, c}, {b, c, a}, {c, a, b}, {c, b, a}}`. ■ There are *n*! permutations of a list of *n* distinct elements. ■ Repeated elements are treated as identical. ■ The object *list* need not have head `List`. ■ See page 129. ■ See also: `Sort`, `Signature`, `Reverse`, `RotateLeft`. ■ Related packages: `DiscreteMath`Permutations``, `DiscreteMath`Combinatorica``. ■ *New in Version 1.*

■ **Pi**

`Pi` is π, with numerical value $\simeq 3.14159$.

Mathematical constant (see Section A.3.11). ■ `Pi` can be entered in `StandardForm` and `InputForm` as π, :`pi`:, :`p`: or `\[Pi]`. ■ In `StandardForm`, `Pi` is printed as π. ■ See page 765. ■ Implementation notes: see page 1067. ■ See also: `Degree`. ■ *New in Version 1; modified in Version 3.*

■ **Play**

`Play[`*f*`, {`*t*`, `*tmin*`, `*tmax*`}]` plays a sound whose amplitude is given by *f* as a function of time *t* in seconds between *tmin* and *tmax*.

Play evaluates its arguments in a non-standard way (see page 1046). ■ `Play[{`f_1`, `f_2`}, {`*t*`, `*tmin*`, `*tmax*`}]` produces stereo sound. The left-hand channel is given first. ■ `Play[{`f_1`, `f_2`, ... }, ... ]` generates sound output on any number of channels. ■ The following options can be given:

Compiled	True	whether to compile *f* for evaluation
DisplayFunction	$SoundDisplayFunction	function for generating output
Epilog	{}	sound or graphics to be used as an epilog
PlayRange	Automatic	the range of amplitude levels to include
Prolog	{}	sound or graphics to be used as a prolog
SampleDepth	8	how many bits to use to represent each amplitude level
SampleRate	8192	how many times per second amplitude samples should be generated

■ Play returns a Sound object. ■ See page 171. ■ See also: `ListPlay`, `SampledSoundFunction`, `Show`. ■ Related packages: `Miscellaneous`Audio``, `Miscellaneous`Music``. ■ *New in Version 2.*

■ PlayRange

PlayRange is an option for Play and related functions which specifies what range of sound amplitude levels should be included.

All amplitudes are scaled so that the amplitude levels to be included lie within the range that can be output. ■ Amplitude levels outside the range specified are clipped. ■ The possible settings for PlayRange are:

All	include all amplitude levels
Automatic	outlying levels are dropped
{*amin*, *amax*}	explicit amplitude limits

■ See page 172. ■ See also: SampleDepth. ■ *New in Version 2.*

■ Plot

Plot[*f*, {*x*, *xmin*, *xmax*}] generates a plot of *f* as a function of *x* from *xmin* to *xmax*.

Plot[{*f₁*, *f₂*, ... }, {*x*, *xmin*, *xmax*}] plots several functions f_i.

Plot evaluates its arguments in a non-standard way (see page 1046). You should use Evaluate to evaluate the function to be plotted if this can safely be done before specific numerical values are supplied. ■ Plot has the same options as Graphics, with the following additions:

Compiled	True	whether to compile the function to plot
MaxBend	10.	maximum bend between segments
PlotDivision	20.	maximum subdivision factor in sampling
PlotPoints	25	initial number of sample points
PlotStyle	Automatic	graphics directives to specify the style for each curve

■ Plot uses the default setting Axes -> True. ■ Plot initially evaluates *f* at a number of equally spaced sample points specified by PlotPoints. Then it uses an adaptive algorithm to choose additional sample points, attempting to produce a curve in which the bend between successive segments is less than MaxBend. It subdivides a given interval by a factor of at most PlotDivision. ■ You should realize that with the finite number of sample points used, it is possible for Plot to miss features in your function. To check your results, you should increase the setting for PlotPoints. ■ Plot returns a Graphics object. ■ See page 131. ■ See also: ListPlot, Graphics. ■ Related packages: Graphics`FilledPlot`, Graphics`Graphics`. ■ *New in Version 1.*

■ Plot3D

Plot3D[*f*, {*x*, *xmin*, *xmax*}, {*y*, *ymin*, *ymax*}] generates a three-dimensional plot of *f* as a function of *x* and *y*.

Plot3D[{*f*, *s*}, {*x*, *xmin*, *xmax*}, {*y*, *ymin*, *ymax*}] generates a three-dimensional plot in which the height of the surface is specified by *f*, and the shading is specified by *s*.

Plot3D evaluates its arguments in a non-standard way (see page 1046). You should use Evaluate to evaluate the function to be plotted if this can safely be done before specific numerical values are supplied. ■ Plot3D has the same options as SurfaceGraphics, with the following additions:

Compiled	True	whether to compile the function to plot
PlotPoints	25	the number of sample points in each direction

■ Plot3D has the default option setting Axes -> True. ■ Plot3D returns a SurfaceGraphics object. ■ The function *f* should give a real number for all values of *x* and *y* at which it is evaluated. There will be holes in the final surface at any values of *x* and *y* for which *f* does not yield a real number value. ■ If Lighting->False and no shading function *s* is specified, the surface is shaded according to height. The shading is determined by the option ColorFunction; the default is gray levels. ■ The shading function *s* must yield GrayLevel, Hue or RGBColor directives, or SurfaceColor objects. ■ Plot3D includes a setting for the MeshRange option in the SurfaceGraphics object it returns. ■ See page 149. ■ See also: ListPlot3D, ContourPlot, DensityPlot, Graphics3D. ■ *New in Version 1.*

■ PlotDivision

PlotDivision is an option for Plot which specifies the maximum amount of subdivision to be used in attempting to generate a smooth curve.

Plot initially uses PlotPoints equally spaced sample points. In attempting to generate curves with no bends larger than MaxBend, Plot subdivides by at most a factor of PlotDivision. ■ The finest resolution in Plot is of order 1/(PlotPoints PlotDivision). ■ See page 138. ■ See also: MaxBend. ■ *New in Version 1.*

■ PlotJoined

PlotJoined is an option for ListPlot that specifies whether the points plotted should be joined by a line.

The style of the line can be specified using the option PlotStyle. ■ See page 159. ■ See also: Line. ■ *New in Version 1.*

■ PlotLabel

PlotLabel is an option for graphics functions that specifies an overall label for a plot.

PlotLabel -> None specifies that no label should be given. ■ PlotLabel -> *label* specifies a label to give. ■ Any expression can be used as a label. It will be given in OutputForm. Arbitrary strings of text can be given as "*text*". ■ See page 511. ■ See also: AxesLabel. ■ Related package: Graphics`Legend`. ■ *New in Version 1.*

■ PlotPoints

PlotPoints is an option for plotting functions that specifies how many sample points to use.

The sample points are equally spaced. ■ In Plot, an adaptive procedure is used to choose more sample points. ■ With a single variable, PlotPoints -> n specifies the total number of sample points to use. ■ With two variables, PlotPoints -> n specifies that n points should be used in both x and y directions. ■ PlotPoints -> $\{n_x, n_y\}$ specifies different numbers of sample points for the x and y directions. ■ See page 138. ■ See also: PlotDivision. ■ *New in Version 1.*

■ PlotRange

PlotRange is an option for graphics functions that specifies what points to include in a plot.

PlotRange can be used for both two- and three-dimensional graphics. ■ The following settings can be used:

All	all points are included
Automatic	outlying points are dropped
{*min*, *max*}	explicit limits for y (2D) or z (3D)
{{*xmin*, *xmax*}, ... }	explicit limits

■ When no explicit limits are given for a particular coordinate, a setting of Automatic is assumed. ■ With the Automatic setting, the distribution of coordinate values is found, and any points sufficiently far out in the distribution are dropped. Such points are often produced as a result of singularities in functions being plotted. ■ A setting of the form {*min*, Automatic} specifies a particular minimum value for a coordinate, and a maximum value to be determined automatically. ■ AbsoluteOptions gives the explicit form of PlotRange specifications when Automatic settings are given. ■ See page 137. ■ See also: PlotRegion, AspectRatio, AbsoluteOptions. ■ *New in Version 1.*

■ PlotRegion

PlotRegion is an option for graphics functions that specifies what region of the final display area a plot should fill.

PlotRegion -> {{*sxmin*, *sxmax*}, {*symin*, *symax*}} specifies the region in scaled coordinates that the plot should fill in the final display area. ▪ The scaled coordinates run from 0 to 1 in each direction. ▪ The default setting PlotRegion -> {{0, 1}, {0, 1}} specifies that the plot should fill the whole display area. ▪ When the plot does not fill the whole display area, the remainder of the area is rendered according to the setting for the option Background. ▪ See page 507. ▪ See also: PlotRange, AspectRatio, Scaled, SphericalRegion. ▪ *New in Version 2.*

■ PlotStyle

PlotStyle is an option for Plot and ListPlot that specifies the style of lines or points to be plotted.

PlotStyle -> *style* specifies that all lines or points are to be generated with the specified graphics directive, or list of graphics directives. ▪ PlotStyle -> {{*style*$_1$}, {*style*$_2$}, ... } specifies that successive lines generated should use graphics directives *style*$_1$, ... The styles must be enclosed in lists, perhaps of length one. ▪ The *style*$_i$ are used cyclically. ▪ Styles can be specified using graphics directives such as Dashing, Hue and Thickness. ▪ See pages 138 and 503. ▪ See also: Graphics, TextStyle. ▪ *New in Version 1.*

■ Plus

$x + y + z$ represents a sum of terms.

Plus has attributes Flat, Orderless and OneIdentity. ▪ The default value for arguments of Plus, as used in x_. patterns, is 0. ▪ Plus[ ] is taken to be 0. ▪ Plus[x] is x. ▪ $x + 0$ evaluates to x, but $x + 0.0$ is left unchanged. ▪ Unlike other functions, Plus applies built-in rules before user-defined ones. As a result, it is not possible to make definitions such as 2+2=5. ▪ See page 29. ▪ See also: Minus, Subtract, AddTo, Increment, Total. ▪ *New in Version 1; modified in Version 3.*

■ Pochhammer

Pochhammer[a, n] gives the Pochhammer symbol $(a)_n$.

Mathematical function (see Section A.3.10). ▪ $(a)_n = a(a+1)...(a+n-1) = \Gamma(a+n)/\Gamma(a)$. ▪ See page 770. ▪ See also: Beta, Binomial, Gamma, Factorial, Hypergeometric0F1, Hypergeometric1F1, Hypergeometric2F1. ▪ *New in Version 1.*

■ Point

Point[*coords*] is a graphics primitive that represents a point.

The coordinates can be given either in the ordinary form {x, y} or {x, y, z} or in scaled form Scaled[{x, y}] or Scaled[{x, y, z}]. ▪ Offset can be used to specify coordinates in two dimensions. ▪ Points are rendered if possible as circular regions. Their diameters can be specified using the graphics primitive PointSize. ▪ Point diameters are not accounted for in hidden surface elimination for three-dimensional graphics. ▪ Shading and coloring of points can be specified using CMYKColor, GrayLevel, Hue or RGBColor. ▪ See pages 492 and 520. ▪ See also: Text. ▪ *New in Version 1; modified in Version 3.*

■ **PointSize**

PointSize[d] is a graphics directive which specifies that points which follow are to be shown if possible as circular regions with diameter d. The diameter d is given as a fraction of the total width of the graph.

PointSize can be used in both two- and three-dimensional graphics. ■ The initial default is PointSize[0.008] for two-dimensional graphics, and PointSize[0.01] for three-dimensional graphics. ■ See page 500. ■ See also: AbsolutePointSize, Thickness. ■ *New in Version 1.*

■ **PolyGamma**

PolyGamma[z] gives the digamma function $\psi(z)$.

PolyGamma[n, z] gives the nth derivative of the digamma function $\psi^{(n)}(z)$.

PolyGamma[z] is the logarithmic derivative of the gamma function, given by $\psi(z) = \Gamma'(z)/\Gamma(z)$. ■ PolyGamma[$n$, z] is given by $\psi^{(n)}(z) = d^n\psi(z)/dz^n$. ■ The digamma function is $\psi(z) = \psi^{(0)}(z)$; $\psi^{(n)}(z)$ is the $(n + 1)^{\text{th}}$ logarithmic derivative of the gamma function. ■ PolyGamma[z] and PolyGamma[n, z] are meromorphic functions of z with no branch cut discontinuities. ■ FullSimplify and FunctionExpand include transformation rules for PolyGamma. ■ See page 770. ■ Implementation notes: see page 1068. ■ See also: Gamma, LogGamma, EulerGamma. ■ *New in Version 1.*

■ **Polygon**

Polygon[{pt_1, pt_2, ... }] is a graphics primitive that represents a filled polygon.

Polygon can be used in both Graphics and Graphics3D (two- and three-dimensional graphics). ■ The positions of points can be specified either in ordinary coordinates as {x, y} or {x, y, z}, or in scaled coordinates as Scaled[{x, y}] or Scaled[{x, y, z}]. ■ Offset can be used to specify coordinates in two dimensions. ■ The boundary of the polygon is formed by joining the last point you specify to the first one. ■ In two dimensions, self-intersecting polygons are allowed. ■ In three dimensions, planar polygons that do not intersect themselves will be drawn exactly as you specify them. Other polygons will be broken into triangles. ■ You can use graphics directives such as GrayLevel and RGBColor to specify how polygons should be filled. ■ In three dimensions, the shading can be produced from simulated illumination. ■ In three-dimensional graphics, polygons are considered to have both a front and a back face. The sense of a polygon is defined in terms of its first three vertices. When taken in order, these vertices go in a *counterclockwise* direction when viewed from the *front*. (The frontward normal is thus obtained from a *right-hand* rule.) ■ You can use FaceForm to specify colors for the front and back faces of polygons. ■ In three-dimensional graphics, edges of polygons are shown as lines, with forms specified by the graphics directive EdgeForm. ■ See pages 492 and 520. ■ See also: Raster, Rectangle, Cuboid, SurfaceColor. ■ Related packages: Geometry`Polytopes`, Graphics`Polyhedra`. ■ *New in Version 1; modified in Version 3.*

■ **PolygonIntersections**

PolygonIntersections is an option for Graphics3D which specifies whether intersecting polygons should be left unchanged.

With the default setting PolygonIntersections -> True, Graphics3D objects are returned unchanged whether or not they contain intersecting polygons. ■ With the setting PolygonIntersections -> False, Graphics3D objects are modified by breaking polygons into smaller pieces which do not intersect each other. ■ PolygonIntersections -> False is useful in creating graphics objects which can be sent to certain external three-dimensional rendering programs. ■ See page 556. ■ See also: RenderAll. ■ *New in Version 2.*

■ PolyLog

PolyLog[n, z] gives the polylogarithm function $\mathrm{Li}_n(z)$.

PolyLog[n, p, z] gives the Nielsen generalized polylogarithm function $S_{n,p}(z)$.

Mathematical function (see Section A.3.10). ■ $\mathrm{Li}_n(z) = \sum_{k=1}^{\infty} z^k/k^n$.
■ $S_{n,p}(z) = (-1)^{n+p-1}/((n-1)!p!) \int_0^1 \log^{n-1}(t) \log^p(1-zt)/t\,dt$. ■ $S_{n-1,1}(z) = \mathrm{Li}_n(z)$. ■ PolyLog[$n$, z] has a branch cut discontinuity in the complex z plane running from 1 to ∞. ■ FullSimplify and FunctionExpand include transformation rules for PolyLog. ■ See page 772. ■ Implementation notes: see page 1068. ■ See also: Zeta, PolyGamma, LerchPhi. ■ *New in Version 1; modified in Version 4.*

■ PolynomialGCD

PolynomialGCD[$poly_1$, $poly_2$, ...] gives the greatest common divisor of the polynomials $poly_i$.

PolynomialGCD[$poly_1$, $poly_2$, ... , Modulus->p] evaluates the GCD modulo the prime p.

Example: PolynomialGCD[1 + x y, x + x^2 y] $\longrightarrow$ 1 + x y. ■ In PolynomialGCD[$poly_1$, $poly_2$, ...], all symbolic parameters are treated as variables. ■ PolynomialGCD[$poly_1$, $poly_2$, ...] will by default treat algebraic numbers that appear in the $poly_i$ as independent variables. ■ PolynomialGCD[$poly_1$, $poly_2$, ... , Extension->Automatic] extends the coefficient field to include algebraic numbers that appear in the $poly_i$. ■ See page 803. ■ See also: PolynomialLCM, PolynomialQuotient, GCD, Cancel, Together, PolynomialMod. ■ Related package: Algebra`PolynomialExtendedGCD`. ■ *New in Version 2; modified in Version 3.*

■ PolynomialLCM

PolynomialLCM[$poly_1$, $poly_2$, ...] gives the least common multiple of the polynomials $poly_i$.

PolynomialLCM[$poly_1$, $poly_2$, ... , Modulus->p] evaluates the LCM modulo the prime p.

Example: PolynomialLCM[1 + x y, x + x^2 y] $\longrightarrow$ x + x^2 y. ■ PolynomialLCM[$poly_1$, $poly_2$, ...] will by default treat algebraic numbers that appear in the $poly_i$ as independent variables.
■ PolynomialLCM[$poly_1$, $poly_2$, ... , Extension->Automatic] extends the coefficient field to include algebraic numbers that appear in the $poly_i$. ■ See page 803. ■ See also: PolynomialGCD, LCM. ■ *New in Version 2; modified in Version 3.*

■ PolynomialMod

PolynomialMod[$poly$, m] gives the polynomial $poly$ reduced modulo m.

PolynomialMod[$poly$, {m_1, m_2, ... }] reduces modulo all of the m_i.

PolynomialMod[$poly$, m] for integer m gives a polynomial in which all coefficients are reduced modulo m.
■ Example: PolynomialMod[3x^2 + 2x + 1, 2] $\longrightarrow$ 1 + x^2. ■ When m is a polynomial, PolynomialMod[$poly$, m] reduces $poly$ by subtracting polynomial multiples of m, to give a result with minimal degree and leading coefficient.
■ PolynomialMod gives results according to a definite convention; other conventions could yield results differing by multiples of m. ■ Unlike PolynomialRemainder, PolynomialMod never performs divisions in generating its results.
■ See page 803. ■ See also: PolynomialGCD, Mod, PolynomialRemainder, PolynomialReduce, GroebnerBasis.
■ Related package: Algebra`PolynomialPowerMod`. ■ *New in Version 2.*

■ PolynomialQ

PolynomialQ[$expr$, var] yields True if $expr$ is a polynomial in var, and yields False otherwise.

PolynomialQ[$expr$, {var_1, ... }] tests whether $expr$ is a polynomial in the var_i.

The var_i need not be symbols; PolynomialQ[f[a] + f[a]^2, f[a]] $\longrightarrow$ True. ■ See page 799. ■ See also: Collect, Series. ■ *New in Version 1.*

■ **PolynomialQuotient**

PolynomialQuotient[p, q, x] gives the quotient of p and q, treated as polynomials in x, with any remainder dropped.

See page 803. ■ See also: PolynomialRemainder, PolynomialReduce, PolynomialGCD, Apart, Cancel, Quotient. ■ *New in Version 1.*

■ **PolynomialReduce**

PolynomialReduce[*poly*, {*poly*$_1$, *poly*$_2$, ... }, {x_1, x_2, ... }] yields a list representing a reduction of *poly* in terms of the *poly*$_i$.

The list has the form {{a_1, a_2, ... }, b}, where b is minimal and a_1 *poly*$_1$ + a_2 *poly*$_2$ + ... + b is exactly *poly*.

The polynomial b has the property that none of its terms are divisible by leading terms of any of the *poly*$_i$. ■ If the *poly*$_i$ form a Gröbner basis then this property uniquely determines the remainder obtained from PolynomialReduce. ■ The following options can be given, as for GroebnerBasis:

MonomialOrder	Lexicographic	the criterion used for ordering monomials
CoefficientDomain	Rationals	the type of objects assumed to be coefficients
Modulus	0	the modulus for numerical coefficients

■ See page 803. ■ See also: GroebnerBasis, PolynomialRemainder, PolynomialMod. ■ Related package: Algebra`SymmetricPolynomials`. ■ *New in Version 3.*

■ **PolynomialRemainder**

PolynomialRemainder[p, q, x] gives the remainder from dividing p by q, treated as polynomials in x.

The degree of the result in x is guaranteed to be smaller than the degree of q. ■ Unlike PolynomialMod, PolynomialRemainder performs divisions in generating its results. ■ See page 803. ■ See also: PolynomialQuotient, Apart, Cancel, PolynomialMod, Mod, PolynomialReduce. ■ *New in Version 1.*

■ **Position**

Position[*expr*, *pattern*] gives a list of the positions at which objects matching *pattern* appear in *expr*.

Position[*expr*, *pattern*, *levspec*] finds only objects that appear on levels specified by *levspec*.

Position[*expr*, *pattern*, *levspec*, n] gives the positions of the first n objects found.

Example: Position[{1+x^2, 5, x^4}, x^_] ⟶ {{1, 2}, {3}}. ■ Position[*expr*, *pattern*] tests all the subparts of *expr* in turn to try and find ones that match *pattern*. ■ Position returns a list of positions in a form suitable for use in Extract, ReplacePart and MapAt. The form is different from the one used in Part. ■ The default level specification for Position is {0, Infinity}, with Heads -> True. ■ A part specification {} returned by Position represents the whole of *expr*. ■ Position[*list*, *pattern*, {1}, Heads -> False] finds positions only of objects that appear as complete elements of *list*. ■ Level specifications are described on page 1041. ■ See page 261. ■ See also: Cases, Count, StringPosition, Ordering, SparseArray, ReplaceList, Insert, Delete. ■ *New in Version 1.*

■ **Positive**

Positive[x] gives True if x is a positive number.

Positive[x] gives False if x is manifestly a negative numerical quantity, a complex numerical quantity, or zero. Otherwise, it remains unevaluated. ■ See also: Negative, NonNegative, Sign, Greater, Simplify, Assumptions. ■ *New in Version 1.*

■ Postfix

Postfix[$f[expr]$] prints with $f[expr]$ given in default postfix form: *expr // f*.

Postfix[$f[expr]$, h] prints as *exprh*.

Postfix[*expr*, *h*, *precedence*, *grouping*] can be used to specify how the output form should be parenthesized. ■ See the notes for Infix about precedence and grouping. ■ See page 474. ■ See also: Infix, Prefix. ■ *New in Version 1.*

■ PostScript

PostScript["*string*"] is a graphics primitive which gives PostScript code to include verbatim in graphics output.

Mathematica by default renders a point with coordinates 0 0 in the PostScript code at the bottom left-hand corner of your plot, and a point with coordinates 1 *r* at the top right-hand corner, where *r* is the aspect ratio of the whole plot. ■ You can specify a bounding box for the objects represented by your PostScript code by including a standard conforming PostScript comment of the form %%BoundingBox *pxmin pymin pxmax pymax*.
■ PostScript["*string*", {{*xmin*, *ymin*}, {*xmax*, *ymax*}}] then renders the point with coordinates *pxmin pymin* in the PostScript code at position {*xmin*, *ymin*} in the *Mathematica* graphic, and the point with coordinates *pxmax pymax* at position {*xmax*, *ymax*}. ■ *Mathematica* will transform graphics represented by a PostScript command to make it fill the specified rectangle. ■ After execution of PostScript code included by the PostScript command, all PostScript stacks must be restored to their original states. ■ The utility of the PostScript command depends on your PostScript interpreter's ability to process the PostScript commands you specify. ■ Display may or may not convert graphics produced by PostScript commands to other formats. ■ See page 554. ■ See also: Raster, RGBColor, Dashing, Thickness, PointSize, StyleForm. ■ *New in Version 2; modified in Version 3.*

■ Power

x^y gives x to the power y.

Mathematical function (see Section A.3.10). ■ Exact rational number results are given when possible for roots of the form $n^{1/m}$. ■ For complex numbers x and y, Power gives the principal value of $e^{y \log(x)}$. ■ (a b)^c is automatically converted to a^c b^c only if c is an integer. ■ (a^b)^c is automatically converted to a^(b c) only if c is an integer.
■ See page 29. ■ See also: Sqrt, Exp, PowerExpand, PowerMod, Log. ■ *New in Version 1.*

■ PowerExpand

PowerExpand[$expr$] expands all powers of products and powers.

Example: PowerExpand[Sqrt[x y]] $\longrightarrow \sqrt{x} \sqrt{y}$. ■ PowerExpand converts (a b)^c to a^c b^c, whatever the form of c is. ■ PowerExpand also converts (a^b)^c to a^(b c), whatever the form of c is. ■ The transformations made by PowerExpand are correct in general only if c is an integer or a and b are positive real numbers. ■ PowerExpand converts Log[a^b] to b Log[a]. ■ See page 798. ■ See also: Expand, Distribute, ComplexExpand, FullSimplify, FunctionExpand, Refine. ■ *New in Version 2; modified in Version 3.*

■ PowerMod

PowerMod[a, b, n] gives a^b mod n.

For negative b, PowerMod[a, b, n] gives modular inverses.

Integer mathematical function (see Section A.3.10). ■ For positive b, PowerMod[a, b, n] gives the same answers as Mod[a^b, n] but is much more efficient. ■ For negative b, PowerMod[a, b, n] gives the integer k such that $ka^{-b} \equiv 1$ mod n. If no such integer exists, PowerMod returns unevaluated. ■ See page 752. ■ See also: Mod, ExtendedGCD, MultiplicativeOrder, EulerPhi. ■ Related package: Algebra`PolynomialPowerMod`. ■ *New in Version 1.*

■ PrecedenceForm

PrecedenceForm[*expr*, *prec*] prints with *expr* parenthesized as it would be if it contained an operator with precedence *prec*.

prec must be an integer. See notes for Infix. ■ Example: a + PrecedenceForm[b c, 10] ⟶ a + (b c). ■ PrecedenceForm acts as a "wrapper", which affects printing, but not evaluation. ■ See page 474. ■ *New in Version 1.*

■ Precision

Precision[*x*] gives the effective number of digits of precision in the number *x*.

+■ Precision[*x*] gives a measure of the relative uncertainty in the value of *x*. +■ With absolute uncertainty *dx*, Precision[*x*] is -Log[10, *dx*/*x*]. ■ For exact numbers such as integers, Precision[*x*] is Infinity. +■ Precision[*x*] does not normally yield an integer result. +■ For machine-precision numbers Precision[*x*] yields MachinePrecision. +■ Numbers entered in the form *digits*`*p* are taken to have precision *p*. +■ Numbers such as 0``*a* whose overall scale cannot be determined are treated as having zero precision. +■ Numbers with zero precision are output in StandardForm as $0. \times 10^{-a}$, where *a* is their accuracy. ■ If *x* is not a number, Precision[*x*] gives the minimum value of Precision for all the numbers that appear in *x*. ■ See page 727. ■ See also: Accuracy, N, Chop, SetPrecision, MachineNumberQ. ■ *New in Version 1; modified in Version 5.0.*

■ PrecisionGoal

PrecisionGoal is an option for various numerical operations which specifies how many effective digits of precision should be sought in the final result.

PrecisionGoal is an option for such functions as NIntegrate and NDSolve. ~■ PrecisionGoal -> Automatic normally yields a precision goal equal to half the setting for WorkingPrecision. ■ PrecisionGoal -> Infinity specifies that precision should not be used as the criterion for terminating the numerical procedure. AccuracyGoal is typically used in this case. ■ Even though you may specify PrecisionGoal->*n*, the results you get may sometimes have much less than *n*-digit precision. ■ In most cases, you must set WorkingPrecision to be at least as large as PrecisionGoal. ■ PrecisionGoal effectively specifies the relative error allowed in a numerical procedure. ■ With PrecisionGoal->*p* and AccuracyGoal->*a*, *Mathematica* attempts to make the numerical error in a result of size *x* be less than $10^{-a} + |x| 10^{-p}$. ■ See pages 956 and 976. ■ See also: AccuracyGoal, WorkingPrecision. ■ *New in Version 2; modified in Version 5.0.*

■ PreDecrement

--*x* decreases the value of *x* by 1, returning the new value of *x*.

PreDecrement has attribute HoldFirst. ■ --*x* is equivalent to *x*=*x*-1. ■ See page 305. ■ See also: Decrement, SubtractFrom, Set. ■ *New in Version 1.*

■ Prefix

Prefix[*f*[*expr*]] prints with *f*[*expr*] given in default prefix form: *f* @ *expr*.

Prefix[*f*[*expr*], *h*] prints as *h*expr.

Prefix[*expr*, *h*, *precedence*, *grouping*] can be used to specify how the output form should be parenthesized. ■ See the notes for Infix about precedence and grouping. ■ See page 474. ■ See also: Infix, Postfix. ■ *New in Version 1.*

■ PreIncrement

++*x* increases the value of *x* by 1, returning the new value of *x*.

PreIncrement has attribute HoldFirst. ■ ++*x* is equivalent to *x*=*x*+1. ■ See page 305. ■ See also: Increment, AddTo, Set. ■ *New in Version 1.*

■ Prepend

Prepend[*expr*, *elem*] gives *expr* with *elem* prepended.

Examples: Prepend[{a,b}, x] ⟶ {x, a, b}; Prepend[f[a], x+y] ⟶ f[x + y, a]. +■ Prepend works on SparseArray objects, returning ordinary lists if necessary. ■ See pages 125 and 288. ■ See also: Append, Insert, PadRight. ■ *New in Version 1.*

■ PrependTo

PrependTo[*s*, *elem*] prepends *elem* to the value of *s*, and resets *s* to the result.

PrependTo[*s*, *elem*] is equivalent to *s* = Prepend[*s*, *elem*]. ■ PrependTo[*s*, *elem*] does not evaluate *s*. ~■ You can use PrependTo repeatedly to build up a list, though Sow and Reap will usually be more efficient. +■ PrependTo works on SparseArray objects, returning ordinary lists if necessary. ■ See page 306. ■ See also: AppendTo, Sow. ■ *New in Version 1.*

■ Prime

Prime[*n*] gives the nth prime number.

Prime[1] is 2. ■ On most computer systems, Prime[*n*] for *n* up to 10^8 can be obtained quite quickly. ■ See page 750. ■ Implementation notes: see page 1067. ■ See also: FactorInteger, PrimeQ, PrimePi, Primes. ■ Related package: NumberTheory`NumberTheoryFunctions`. ■ *New in Version 1.*

■ PrimePi

PrimePi[*x*] gives the number of primes $\pi(x)$ less than or equal to *x*.

The argument of PrimePi can be any positive real number. ■ PrimePi[1] gives 0. ■ See page 750. ■ Implementation notes: see page 1067. ■ See also: Prime, Zeta. ■ *New in Version 2.*

■ PrimeQ

PrimeQ[*expr*] yields True if *expr* is a prime number, and yields False otherwise.

PrimeQ[1] gives False. ■ PrimeQ[-*n*], where *n* is prime, gives True. ■ PrimeQ[*n*, GaussianIntegers->True] determines whether *n* is a Gaussian prime. +■ PrimeQ[*m* + I *m*] automatically works over the Gaussian integers. ■ Simplify[*expr* ∈ Primes] can be used to try to determine whether a symbolic expression is mathematically a prime. ■ See page 750. ■ Implementation notes: see page 1067. ■ See also: FactorInteger, Primes. ■ Related package: NumberTheory`PrimeQ`. ■ *New in Version 1.*

■ Primes

Primes represents the domain of prime numbers, as in *x* ∈ Primes.

x ∈ Primes evaluates only if *x* is a numeric quantity. ■ Simplify[*expr* ∈ Primes] can be used to try to determine whether an expression corresponds to a prime number. ■ The domain of primes is taken to be a subset of the domain of integers. ■ PrimeQ[*expr*] returns False unless *expr* explicitly has head Integer. ■ Primes is output in TraditionalForm as ℙ. ■ See pages 73 and 817. ■ See also: Element, Simplify, PrimeQ, Prime, Integers. ■ *New in Version 4.*

▪ PrincipalValue

PrincipalValue is an option for Integrate that specifies whether the Cauchy principal value should be found for a definite integral.

The default setting PrincipalValue->False computes ordinary Riemann integrals. ▪ Setting PrincipalValue->True gives finite answers for integrals that had single pole divergences with PrincipalValue->False. ▪ See page 866. ▪ See also: Residue, Limit, GenerateConditions, DiracDelta. ▪ Related package: NumericalMath`CauchyPrincipalValue`. ▪ *New in Version 3.*

▪ Print

Print[$expr_1$, $expr_2$, ...] prints the $expr_i$, followed by a newline (line feed).

Print sends its output to the channel $Output. ▪ Print uses the format type of $Output as its default format type. ▪ Print concatenates the output from each $expr_i$ together, effectively using SequenceForm. ▪ You can arrange to have expressions on several lines by using ColumnForm. ▪ See page 477. ▪ See also: CellPrint, Message, Put, Write, Reap. ▪ *New in Version 1.*

▪ PrintingStyleEnvironment

PrintingStyleEnvironment is an option for notebooks which specifies the style environment to be used in printing the notebook on paper.

See notes for ScreenStyleEnvironment. ▪ Style environments appropriate for printed output are typically substantially denser than those appropriate for on-screen display. ▪ See page 197. ▪ See also: ScreenStyleEnvironment, StyleDefinitions, NotebookPrint. ▪ *New in Version 3.*

▪ Product

Product[f, {i, $imax$}] evaluates the product $\prod_{i=1}^{imax} f$.

Product[f, {i, $imin$, $imax$}] starts with $i = imin$. Product[f, {i, $imin$, $imax$, di}] uses steps di.

Product[f, {i, $imin$, $imax$}, {j, $jmin$, $jmax$}, ...] evaluates the multiple product $\prod_{i=imin}^{imax} \prod_{j=jmin}^{jmax} \cdots f$.

Product[f, {i, $imax$}] can be entered as $\prod_i^{imax} f$. ▪ $\prod$ can be entered as ⁝prod⁝ or \[Product].

▪ Product[f, {i, $imin$, $imax$}] can be entered as $\prod_{i=imin}^{imax} f$. ▪ The limits should be underscripts and overscripts of $\prod$ in normal input, and subscripts and superscripts when embedded in other text. ▪ Product evaluates its arguments in a non-standard way (see page 1046). ▪ Product uses the standard *Mathematica* iteration specification. ▪ The iteration variable i is treated as local. ▪ In multiple products, the range of the outermost variable is given first. ▪ The limits of a product need not be numbers. They can be Infinity or symbolic expressions. ▪ If a product cannot be carried out explicitly by multiplying a finite number of terms, Product will attempt to find a symbolic result. In this case, f is first evaluated symbolically. ▪ Product can do essentially all products that are given in standard books of tables. ▪ Product is output in StandardForm using $\prod$. ▪ See page 83. ▪ Implementation notes: see page 1071. ▪ See also: Do, Sum, Table, NProduct, RSolve. ▪ *New in Version 1; modified in Version 3.*

■ ProductLog

ProductLog[z] gives the principal solution for w in $z = we^w$.

ProductLog[k, z] gives the kth solution.

Mathematical function (see Section A.3.10). ■ The solutions are ordered according to their imaginary parts. ■ For $z > -1/e$, ProductLog[z] is real. ■ ProductLog[z] satisfies the differential equation $dw/dz = w/(z(1 + w))$. ■ ProductLog[z] has a branch cut discontinuity in the complex z plane running from $-\infty$ to $-1/e$. ProductLog[k, z] for integer $k > 0$ has a branch cut discontinuity from $-\infty$ to 0. ■ See page 781. ■ See also: Log. ■ *New in Version 3.*

■ Prolog

Prolog is an option for graphics functions which gives a list of graphics primitives to be rendered before the main part of the graphics is rendered.

Graphics primitives specified by Prolog are rendered after axes, boxes and frames are rendered. ■ In three-dimensional graphics, two-dimensional graphics primitives can be specified by the Prolog option. The graphics primitives are rendered in a 0,1 coordinate system. ■ See page 504. ■ See also: Background, DefaultColor, Epilog, AxesStyle, PlotStyle, DisplayFunction. ■ *New in Version 2.*

■ Protect

Protect[s_1, s_2, ...] sets the attribute Protected for the symbols s_i.

Protect["$form_1$", "$form_2$", ...] protects all symbols whose names match any of the string patterns $form_i$.

Protect["$form$"] allows metacharacters such as *, as specified on page 1044. ■ Protect["$context$`*"] protects all symbols in a particular context. ■ See pages 321 and 1044. ■ See also: Unprotect. ■ *New in Version 1.*

■ Protected

Protected is an attribute which prevents any values associated with a symbol from being modified.

Many built-in *Mathematica* functions have the attribute Protected. ■ See page 329. ■ See also: Locked, ReadProtected, Editable. ■ *New in Version 1.*

■ PseudoInverse

PseudoInverse[m] finds the pseudoinverse of a rectangular matrix.

PseudoInverse works on both symbolic and numerical matrices. +■ For numerical matrices, PseudoInverse is based on SingularValueDecomposition. ■ PseudoInverse[m, Tolerance -> t] specifies that singular values smaller than t times the maximum singular value should be dropped. ■ With the default setting Tolerance->Automatic, singular values are dropped when they are less than 100 times 10^{-p}, where p is Precision[m]. ■ For non-singular square matrices **M**, the pseudoinverse $\mathbf{M}^{(-1)}$ is equivalent to the standard inverse. ■ See page 914. ■ See also: Inverse, SingularValueDecomposition, Fit, CholeskyDecomposition. ■ *New in Version 1; modified in Version 5.0.*

■ Put

expr >> *filename* writes *expr* to a file.

Put[*expr*$_1$, *expr*$_2$, ... , "*filename*"] writes a sequence of expressions *expr*$_i$ to a file.

On systems with advanced graphical interfaces, there will usually be graphical tools for saving expressions in files. ■ Put uses the format type InputForm by default. ■ Put starts writing output at the beginning of the file. It deletes whatever was previously in the file. ■ Put inserts a newline (line feed) at the end of its output. ■ *expr* >> *filename* is equivalent to *expr* >> "*filename*". The double quotes can be omitted if the file name is of the form specified on page 1033. ■ It is conventional to use names that end with .m for files containing *Mathematica* input. ■ See page 624. ■ See also: PutAppend, Save, Definition, DumpSave, Export, Get, NotebookPut. ■ *New in Version 1.*

■ PutAppend

expr >>> *filename* appends *expr* to a file.

PutAppend[*expr*$_1$, *expr*$_2$, ... , "*filename*"] appends a sequence of expressions *expr*$_i$ to a file.

PutAppend works the same as Put, except that it adds output to the end of the file, rather than replacing the complete contents of the file. ■ See page 624. ■ See also: Write. ■ *New in Version 1.*

■ QRDecomposition

QRDecomposition[*m*] yields the QR decomposition for a numerical matrix *m*. The result is a list {*q*, *r*}, where *q* is an orthogonal matrix and *r* is an upper triangular matrix.

The original matrix *m* is equal to Conjugate[Transpose[*q*]] . *r*. ■ For non-square matrices, *q* is row orthonormal. ■ The matrix *r* has zeros for all entries below the leading diagonal. ■ QRDecomposition[*m*, Pivoting -> True] yields a list {*q*, *r*, *p*} where *p* is a permutation matrix such that *m* . *p* is equal to Conjugate[Transpose[*q*]] . *r*. ■ See page 914. ■ Implementation notes: see page 1069. ■ See also: SchurDecomposition, LUDecomposition, SingularValueDecomposition, JordanDecomposition, CholeskyDecomposition. ■ Related package: LinearAlgebra`Orthogonalization`. ■ *New in Version 2.*

■ Quantile

Quantile[*list*, *q*] gives the *q*th quantile of *list*.

Quantile[*list*, {*q*$_1$, *q*$_2$, ... }] gives a list of quantiles *q*$_1$, *q*$_2$, ...

Quantile[*list*, *q*, {{*a*, *b*}, {*c*, *d*}}] uses the quantile definition specified by parameters *a*, *b*, *c*, *d*.

Quantile[*list*, *q*] gives Sort[*list*, Less][[Ceiling[*q* Length[*list*]]]]. ■ Quantile[{{*x*$_1$, *y*$_1$, ... }, {*x*$_2$, *y*$_2$, ... }, ... }, *q*] gives {Quantile[{*x*$_1$, *x*$_2$, ... }, *q*], Quantile[{*y*$_1$, *y*$_2$, ... }, *q*]}. ■ For a list of length *n*, Quantile[*list*, *q*, {{*a*, *b*}, {*c*, *d*}}] depends on *x* = *a* + (*n* + *b*) *q*. If *x* is an integer, the result is *s*[[*x*]], where *s* = Sort[*list*, Less]. Otherwise the result is *s*[[Floor[*x*]]] + (*s*[[Ceiling[*x*]]] − *s*[[Floor[*x*]]]) (*c* + *d* FractionalPart[*x*]), with the indices taken to be 1 or *n* if they are out of range. ■ The default choice of parameters is {{0, 0}, {1, 0}}. ■ Quantile[*list*, *q*] always gives a result equal to an element of *list*. ■ The same is true whenever *d* = 0. ■ When *d* = 1, Quantile is piecewise linear as a function of *q*. ■ Median[*list*] is equivalent to Quantile[*list*, 1/2, {{1/2, 0}, {0, 1}}]. ■ About ten different choices of parameters are in use in statistical work. ■ Quantile works with SparseArray objects. ■ See pages 794 and 924. ■ See also: Median, Ordering, Variance, Sort, ListInterpolation. ■ Related packages: Statistics`DescriptiveStatistics`, Statistics`MultiDescriptiveStatistics`. ■ *New in Version 5.0.*

■ Quit

Quit[ ] terminates a *Mathematica* kernel session.

+■ Quit[ ] quits only the *Mathematica* kernel, not the front end. +■ To quit a notebook front end, choose the Quit menu item. ■ All kernel definitions are lost when the kernel session terminates. ■ If you have kept the definitions in a file or in a notebook you can always re-enter them in a subsequent session. ■ Before terminating a kernel session, *Mathematica* executes any delayed value that has been assigned to the global variable $Epilog. Conventionally, this attempts to read in a file end.m of commands to be executed before termination. ■ On most computer systems, Quit[*n*] terminates the *Mathematica* kernel, passing the integer *n* as an exit code to the operating system. ■ Exit is a synonym for Quit. ■ See pages 706 and 1057. ■ See also: Return, $IgnoreEOF. ■ *New in Version 1.*

■ Quotient

Quotient[*m*, *n*] gives the integer quotient of *m* and *n*.

Quotient[*m*, *n*, *d*] uses an offset *d*.

Integer mathematical function (see Section A.3.10). ■ Quotient[*m*, *n*] is equivalent to Floor[*m*/*n*] for integers *m* and *n*. ■ Quotient[*m*, *n*, *d*] gives a result *x* such that $d \leq m - nx < d + n$. ■ n*Quotient[*m*, *n*, *d*] + Mod[*m*, *n*, *d*] is always equal to *m*. ■ See page 749. ■ See also: Mod, PolynomialQuotient. ■ *New in Version 1; modified in Version 4.*

■ RadicalBox

RadicalBox[*x*, *n*] represents $\sqrt[n]{x}$ in input and output.

Inside \(... \) RadicalBox[*x*, *n*] can be input as \@*x*\%*n*. ■ In a notebook a RadicalBox can be created using CTRL@ or CTRL2 , then using CTRL% to move to the index position. CTRL␣ moves out of the radical. ■ In StandardForm and InputForm, RadicalBox[*x*, *n*] is interpreted on input as *x*^(1/*n*). ■ The baseline of RadicalBox[*x*, *n*] is taken to be the baseline of *x*. ■ If RadicalBox[*x*, *n*] does not fit on a single line, it is output as *x* ^ (1/*n*). ■ In StandardForm, explicit RadicalBox objects are output literally. You can use DisplayForm to see the display form of such objects. ■ See page 445. ■ See also: SqrtBox, OverscriptBox, GridBox. ■ *New in Version 3.*

■ Random

Random[ ] gives a uniformly distributed pseudorandom Real in the range 0 to 1.

Random[*type*, *range*] gives a pseudorandom number of the specified type, lying in the specified range. Possible types are: Integer, Real and Complex. The default range is 0 to 1. You can give the range {*min*, *max*} explicitly; a range specification of *max* is equivalent to {0, *max*}.

Random[Integer] gives 0 or 1 with probability $\frac{1}{2}$. ■ Random[Complex] gives a pseudorandom complex number in the rectangle with corners 0 and 1 + *i*. ■ Random[Complex, {*zmin*, *zmax*}] uses the rectangle defined by *zmin* and *zmax*. ■ Random[Real, *range*, *n*] generates a pseudorandom real number with *n*-digit precision. Both leading and trailing digits may be chosen as 0. ■ Random gives a different sequence of pseudorandom numbers whenever you run *Mathematica*. You can start Random with a particular seed using SeedRandom. ■ See page 747. ■ Implementation notes: see page 1067. ■ See also: $RandomState, FindInstance. ■ Related packages: Statistics`ContinuousDistributions`, Statistics`DiscreteDistributions`. ■ *New in Version 1.*

■ Range

Range[*imax*] generates the list {1, 2, ... , *imax*}.

Range[*imin*, *imax*] generates the list {*imin*, ... , *imax*}. Range[*imin*, *imax*, *di*] uses step *di*.

Example: Range[4] ⟶ {1, 2, 3, 4}. ■ The arguments to Range need not be integers. ■ Range starts from *imin*, and successively adds increments of *di* until the result is greater than *imax*.
■ Range[0, 1, .3] ⟶ {0, 0.3, 0.6, 0.9}. ■ Range[x, x+2] ⟶ {x, 1 + x, 2 + x}. ■ Range uses the standard *Mathematica* iteration specification, as applied to a single variable. ■ See page 119. ■ See also: Table, Interval, CharacterRange. ■ *New in Version 1.*

■ Raster

Raster[{{a_{11}, a_{12}, ... }, ... }] is a two-dimensional graphics primitive which represents a rectangular array of gray cells.

Raster[*array*, ColorFunction -> *f*] specifies that each cell should be rendered using the graphics directives obtained by applying the function *f* to the scaled value of the cell. ■ Raster[*array*, ColorFunction -> Hue] generates an array in which cell values are specified by hues. ■ With the option ColorFunctionScaling -> False the original cell values a_{ij}, rather than scaled cell values, are fed to the color function. ■ With the default setting ColorFunctionScaling -> True cell values in Raster[*array*] outside the range 0 to 1 are clipped. ■ If *array* has dimensions {*m*, *n*}, then Raster[*array*] is assumed to occupy the rectangle Rectangle[{0, 0}, {*m*, *n*}].
■ Raster[*array*, {{*xmin*, *ymin*}, {*xmax*, *ymax*}}] specifies that the raster should be taken instead to fill the rectangle Rectangle[{*xmin*, *ymin*}, {*xmax*, *ymax*}]. ■ Scaled and Offset can be used to specify the coordinates for the rectangle. ■ Raster[*array*, *rect*, {*zmin*, *zmax*}] specifies that cell values should be scaled so that *zmin* corresponds to 0 and *zmax* corresponds to 1. Cell values outside this range are clipped. ▪■ *array* can be a SparseArray object. ■ See page 497. ■ See also: RasterArray, DensityGraphics, GraphicsArray. ■ *New in Version 2; modified in Version 4.*

■ RasterArray

RasterArray[{{g_{11}, g_{12}, ... }, ... }] is a two-dimensional graphics primitive which represents a rectangular array of cells colored according to the graphics directives g_{ij}.

Each of the g_{ij} must be GrayLevel, RGBColor or Hue. ■ If *array* has dimensions {*m*, *n*}, then RasterArray[*array*] is assumed to occupy the rectangle Rectangle[{0, 0}, {*m*, *n*}].
■ RasterArray[*array*, {{*xmin*, *ymin*}, {*xmax*, *ymax*}}] specifies that the raster should be taken instead to fill the rectangle Rectangle[{*xmin*, *ymin*}, {*xmax*, *ymax*}]. ■ Scaled and Offset can be used to specify the coordinates for the rectangle. ■ See page 497. ■ See also: Raster, GraphicsArray. ■ *New in Version 2; modified in Version 3.*

■ Rational

Rational is the head used for rational numbers.

You can enter a rational number in the form *n/m*. ■ The pattern object _Rational can be used to stand for a rational number. It cannot stand for a single integer. ■ You have to use Numerator and Denominator to extract parts of Rational numbers. ■ See page 722. ■ See also: Rationals, Integer, Numerator, Denominator. ■ *New in Version 1.*

■ Rationalize

Rationalize[x] takes Real numbers in x that are close to rationals, and converts them to exact Rational numbers.

Rationalize[x, dx] performs the conversion whenever the error made is smaller in magnitude than dx.

Example: Rationalize[3.78] $\longrightarrow$ 189/50. ■ Rationalize[x, dx] yields the rational number with the smallest denominator that lies within dx of x. ■ Rationalize[N[Pi]] $\longrightarrow$ 3.14159 does not give a rational number, since there is none "sufficiently close" to N[Pi]. ■ A rational number p/q is considered "sufficiently close" to a Real x if $|p/q - x| < c/q^2$, where c is chosen to be 10^{-4}. ■ Rationalize[x, 0] converts any x to rational form. ■ See page 746. ■ See also: Chop, Round, ContinuedFraction, LatticeReduce. ■ Related package: NumberTheory`Rationalize`. ■ *New in Version 1.*

■ Rationals

Rationals represents the domain of rational numbers, as in $x \in$ Rationals.

$x \in$ Rationals evaluates immediately only if x is a numeric quantity. ■ Simplify[$expr \in$ Rationals] can be used to try to determine whether an expression corresponds to a rational number. ■ The domain of integers is taken to be a subset of the domain of rationals. ■ Rationals is output in TraditionalForm as $\mathbb{Q}$. ■ See page 817. ■ See also: Element, Simplify, Algebraics, Integers, Rational, Denominator. ■ *New in Version 4.*

■ Raw

Raw[h, "*hexstring*"] constructs a raw data object with head h, and with contents corresponding to the binary bit pattern represented by the string *hexstring*, interpreted as a hexadecimal number.

Raw should be used only under very special circumstances. ■ It is possible to crash *Mathematica* by creating a fundamental *Mathematica* data object with Raw, and specifying illegal internal data for it. If you create an object with head Real, but with internal data incompatible with *Mathematica* Real numbers, you may end up crashing your whole *Mathematica* session. ■ Raw encodes data so that two hexadecimal digits represent one byte. Identical *hexstring* may lead to different internal data on different computer systems. ■ You cannot necessarily transport raw arrays of bytes from one type of computer to another without encountering byte swap incompatibilities. ■ See page 1016. ■ See also: Run. ■ Related package: Utilities`BinaryFiles`. ■ *New in Version 1.*

■ Re

Re[z] gives the real part of the complex number z.

Re[$expr$] is left unevaluated if *expr* is not a numeric quantity. ■ See page 746. ■ See also: Im, Abs, Arg, ComplexExpand. ■ *New in Version 1.*

■ Read

Read[*stream*] reads one expression from an input stream, and returns the expression.

Read[*stream*, *type*] reads one object of the specified type.

Read[*stream*, {*type*$_1$, *type*$_2$, ... }] reads a sequence of objects of the specified types.

Possible types to read are:

Byte	single byte, returned as an integer code
Character	single character, returned as a one-character string
Expression	complete *Mathematica* expression
Number	integer or an approximate number, given in "E" format

(continued)

■ **Read** *(continued)*

▪ Possible types to read are:

`Real`	approximate number, given in "E" format
`Record`	sequence of characters delimited by record separators
`String`	string terminated by a newline
`Word`	sequence of characters delimited by word separators

▪ Objects of type `Real` can be given in the scientific notation format used by languages such as C and Fortran, as well as in standard *Mathematica* format. A form like `2.e5` or `2E5` as well as `2*^5` can be used to represent the number 2×10^5. Objects read as type `Real` are always returned as approximate numbers. Objects read as type `Number` are returned as integers if they contain no explicit decimal points. ▪ The following options can be given:

`NullRecords`	`False`	whether to assume a null record between repeated record separators
`NullWords`	`False`	whether to assume a null word between repeated word separators
`RecordSeparators`	`{"\n"}`	separators allowed between records
`TokenWords`	`{}`	words taken as delimiters
`WordSeparators`	`{" ", "\t"}`	separators allowed between words

▪ Objects of type `String` must be terminated by newlines (`"\n"` characters). ▪ You can specify any nested list of types for `Read` to look for. Each successive object read will be placed in the next position in the list structure. A depth-first traversal of the list structure is used. ▪ Example: `Read[`*stream*`, {Number, Number}]` reads a pair of numbers from an input stream, and gives the result as a two-element list. ▪ `Read[`*stream*`, {{Number, Number}, {Number, Number}}]` reads a 2×2 matrix, going through each column, then each row. ▪ You can use `Read` to get objects to insert into any expression structure, not necessarily a list. Example: `Read[`*stream*`, Hold[Expression]]` gets an expression and places it inside `Hold`. ▪ The first argument to `Read` can be `InputStream["`*name*`", n]`, or simply `"`*name*`"` if there is only one open input stream with the specified name. ▪ You can open a file or pipe to get an `InputStream` object using `OpenRead`. ▪ There is always a "current point" maintained for any stream. When you read an object from a stream, the current point is left after the input you read. Successive calls to `Read` can therefore be used to read successive objects in a stream such as a file. ▪ `Read` returns `EndOfFile` for each object you try to read after you have reached the end of a file. ▪ `Read` returns `$Failed` if it cannot read an object of the type you requested. ▪ If there is a syntax error in a *Mathematica* expression that you try to read, then `Read` leaves the current point at the position of the error, and returns `$Failed`. ▪ See page 649. ▪ See also: `Input, Get, Skip, Find, StringToStream, LinkRead, Import`. ▪ *New in Version 1; modified in Version 3.*

■ **ReadList**

`ReadList["`*file*`"]` reads all the remaining expressions in a file, and returns a list of them.

`ReadList["`*file*`", `*type*`]` reads objects of the specified type from a file, until the end of the file is reached. The list of objects read is returned.

`ReadList["`*file*`", {`*type*₁*, *type*₂*, ... }]` reads objects with a sequence of types, until the end of the file is reached.

`ReadList["`*file*`", `*types*`, n]` reads only the first *n* objects of the specified types.

The option setting `RecordLists -> True` makes `ReadList` create separate sublists for objects that appear in separate records. ▪ With the default setting `RecordSeparators -> {"\n"}`, `RecordLists -> True` puts objects on separate lines into separate sublists. ▪ The option `RecordSeparators` gives a list of strings which are taken to delimit records. ▪ `ReadList` takes the same options as `Read`, with the addition of `RecordLists`. ▪ If *file* is not already open for reading, `ReadList` opens it, then closes it when it is finished. If the file is already open, `ReadList` does not close it at the end. ▪ `ReadList` prints a message if any of the objects remaining in the file are not of the specified types. ▪ `ReadList["`*file*`", {`*type*₁*, ... }]` looks for the sequence of *type*ᵢ in order. If the end of file is reached while part way through the sequence of *type*ᵢ, `EndOfFile` is returned in place of the elements in the sequence that have not yet been read. ▪ `ReadList[`*stream*`]` reads from an open input stream, as returned by `OpenRead`. ▪ See notes for `Read`. ▪ See page 644. ▪ See also: `Import, FindList`. ▪ *New in Version 1.*

■ ReadProtected

ReadProtected is an attribute which prevents values associated with a symbol from being seen.

Individual values associated with read-protected symbols can be used during evaluation. ■ Definition[*f*], ?*f*, and related functions give only the attributes for read-protected symbols *f*. ■ See page 329. ■ See also: Locked, Protected, Copyable. ■ *New in Version 1.*

■ Real

Real is the head used for real (floating-point) numbers.

_Real can be used to stand for a real number in a pattern. ■ You can enter a floating-point number of any length. ■ You can enter a number in scientific notation by using the form *mantissa**^*exponent*. ■ You can enter a floating-point number in base *b* using *b*^^*digits*. The base must be less than 36. The letters a–z or A–Z are used in sequence to stand for digits 10 through 35. ■ Real is also used to indicate an approximate real number in Read. ■ See page 722. ■ See also: RealDigits, BaseForm, Number, Reals. ■ *New in Version 1; modified in Version 3.*

■ RealDigits

RealDigits[*x*] gives a list of the digits in the approximate real number *x*, together with the number of digits that are to the left of the decimal point.

RealDigits[*x*, *b*] gives a list of base-*b* digits in *x*.

RealDigits[*x*, *b*, *len*] gives a list of *len* digits.

RealDigits[*x*, *b*, *len*, *n*] gives *len* digits starting with the coefficient of b^n.

RealDigits[*x*] normally returns a list of digits whose length is equal to Precision[*x*]. ■ RealDigits[*x*] and RealDigits[*x*, *b*] normally require that *x* be an approximate real number, returned for example by N. RealDigits[*x*, *b*, *len*] also works on exact numbers. ~■ For integers and rational numbers with terminating digit expansions, RealDigits[*x*] returns an ordinary list of digits. For rational numbers with non-terminating digit expansions it yields a list of the form {a_1, a_2, ... , {b_1, b_2, ... }} representing the digit sequence consisting of the a_i followed by infinite cyclic repetitions of the b_i. ■ If *len* is larger than Log[10, *b*] Precision[*x*], then remaining digits are filled in as Indeterminate. ■ RealDigits[*x*, *b*, *len*, *n*] starts with the digit which is the coefficient of b^n, truncating or padding with zeros as necessary. ■ RealDigits[*x*, *b*, *len*, -1] starts with the digit immediately to the right of the base-*b* decimal point in *x*. ■ The base *b* in RealDigits[*x*, *b*] need not be an integer. For any real *b* such that *b* > 1, RealDigits[*x*, *b*] successively finds the largest integer multiples of powers of *b* that can be removed while leaving a non-negative remainder. ■ RealDigits[*x*] discards the sign of *x*. ■ FromDigits can be used as the inverse of RealDigits. ■ See page 725. ■ Implementation notes: see page 1067. ■ See also: MantissaExponent, IntegerDigits, BaseForm, FromDigits, ContinuedFraction, MultiplicativeOrder. ■ *New in Version 2; modified in Version 4.*

■ Reals

Reals represents the domain of real numbers, as in *x* ∈ Reals.

x ∈ Reals evaluates immediately only if *x* is a numeric quantity. ■ Simplify[*expr* ∈ Reals] can be used to try to determine whether an expression corresponds to a real number. ■ Within Simplify and similar functions, objects that satisfy inequalities are always assumed to be real. ■ Reals is output in TraditionalForm as ℝ. ■ See pages 73, 817 and 839. ■ See also: Element, Simplify, Real, Integers, Complexes, Algebraics, ComplexExpand, PowerExpand. ■ *New in Version 4.*

⁺■ Reap

Reap[*expr*] gives the value of *expr* together with all expressions to which Sow has been applied during its evaluation.

Expressions sown using Sow[*e*] or Sow[*e*, *tag*$_i$] with different tags are given in different lists.

Reap[*expr*, *patt*] reaps only expressions sown with tags that match *patt*.

Reap[*expr*, {*patt*$_1$, *patt*$_2$, ... }] puts expressions associated with each of *patt*$_i$ in a separate list.

Reap[*expr*, *patt*, *f*] returns {*expr*, {*f*[*tag*$_1$, {*e*$_{11}$, *e*$_{12}$, ... }], ... }}.

Sow and Reap provide a convenient way to accumulate a list of intermediate results in a computation. ▪ Reap accumulates expressions in the order in which Sow is applied to them. ▪ Expressions sown with a particular tag are collected by the innermost Reap whose pattern matches the tag. ▪ Reap[*expr*] is equivalent to Reap[*expr*, _].
▪ Reap has attribute HoldFirst. ▪ See page 355. ▪ See also: Sow, Catch, AppendTo, Print. ▪ *New in Version 5.0.*

■ Record

Record represents a record in Read, Find and related functions.

The record is delimited by strings in the list given as the setting for RecordSeparators. ▪ See page 646. ▪ See also: Word. ▪ Related package: Utilities`BinaryFiles`. ▪ *New in Version 2.*

■ RecordLists

RecordLists is an option for ReadList which specifies whether objects from separate records should be returned in separate sublists.

With the default setting RecordSeparators -> {"\n"}, setting RecordLists -> True makes RecordLists return objects that appear on different lines in different sublists. ▪ With RecordLists -> False, ReadList returns a single list of all objects it reads. ▪ With RecordLists -> True, ReadList returns a list containing a sublist for each record.
▪ See page 644. ▪ *New in Version 2.*

■ RecordSeparators

RecordSeparators is an option for Read, Find and related functions which specifies the list of strings to be taken as delimiters for records.

The default setting is RecordSeparators -> {"\n"}. With this setting, each complete line of input is considered as a record. ▪ Strings used as record separators may contain several characters. ▪ With the option setting NullRecords -> False, any number of record separators may appear between any two successive records.
▪ RecordSeparators -> { } specifies that everything is to be included in a single record.
▪ RecordSeparators -> {{*lsep*$_1$, ... }, {*rsep*$_1$, ... }} specifies different left and right separators for records. When there are nested left and right separators, records are taken to be delimited by the innermost balanced pairs of separators. ▪ Example: with RecordSeparators -> {{"<"}, {">"}}, the records aaa and bbb are extracted from <x<aaa>yyy<<bbb>>>. ▪ Text that does not appear between left and right separators is discarded. ▪ See page 646.
▪ See also: WordSeparators. ▪ *New in Version 2.*

■ Rectangle

Rectangle[{*xmin*, *ymin*}, {*xmax*, *ymax*}] is a two-dimensional graphics primitive that represents a filled rectangle, oriented parallel to the axes.

Rectangle[{*xmin*, *ymin*}, {*xmax*, *ymax*}, *graphics*] gives a rectangle filled with the specified graphics.

Scaled and Offset can be used to specify the coordinates for the rectangle.
■ Rectangle[Scaled[{*xmin*, *ymin*}], Scaled[{*xmax*, *ymax*}]] yields a rectangle with corners specified by scaled coordinates. ■ Any combination of ordinary coordinates, as well as Scaled and Offset, can be used to specify the corners of the rectangle. ■ Rectangle[{*xmin*, *ymin*}, {*xmax*, *ymax*}] is equivalent to a suitable Polygon with four corners. ■ You can use graphics directives such as GrayLevel and RGBColor to specify how Rectangle[{*xmin*, *ymin*}, {*xmax*, *ymax*}] should be filled. ■ In Rectangle[{*xmin*, *ymin*}, {*xmax*, *ymax*}, *graphics*], *graphics* can be any graphics object. ■ The rectangle is taken as the complete display area in which the graphics object is rendered. ■ When rectangles overlap, their backgrounds are effectively taken to be transparent. ■ Fonts and absolute size specifications are not affected by the size of the rectangle in which the graphics are rendered. ■ The options DisplayFunction, ColorOutput and CharacterEncoding are ignored for graphics objects given inside Rectangle. ■ See page 492. ■ See also: Polygon, Raster, RasterArray, Cuboid, GraphicsArray. ■ *New in Version 1; modified in Version 3.*

■ Reduce

~ Reduce[*expr*, *vars*] reduces the statement *expr* by solving equations or inequalities for *vars* and eliminating quantifiers.

+ Reduce[*expr*, *vars*, *dom*] does the reduction over the domain *dom*. Common choices of *dom* are Reals, Integers and Complexes.

+■ The statement *expr* can be any logical combination of:

lhs == *rhs*	equations
lhs != *rhs*	inequations
lhs > *rhs* or *lhs* >= *rhs*	inequalities
expr ∈ *dom*	domain specifications
ForAll[*x*, *cond*, *expr*]	universal quantifiers
Exists[*x*, *cond*, *expr*]	existential quantifiers

+■ The result of Reduce[*expr*, *vars*] always describes exactly the same mathematical set as *expr*.
■ Reduce[{*expr*₁, *expr*₂, ... }, *vars*] is equivalent to Reduce[*expr*₁ && *expr*₂ && ... , *vars*]. +■ Reduce[*expr*, *vars*] assumes by default that quantities appearing algebraically in inequalities are real, while all other quantities are complex. +■ Reduce[*expr*, *vars*, *dom*] restricts all variables and parameters to belong to the domain *dom*. +■ If *dom* is Reals, or a subset such as Integers or Rationals, then all constants and function values are also restricted to be real. +■ Reduce[*expr* && *vars* ∈ Reals, *vars*, Complexes] performs reductions with variables assumed real, but function values allowed to be complex. +■ Reduce[*expr*, *vars*, Integers] reduces Diophantine equations over the integers. +■ Reduce[*expr*, {x_1, x_2, ... }, ...] effectively writes *expr* as a combination of conditions on x_1, x_2, ... , where each condition involves only the earlier x_i. +■ Algebraic variables in *expr* free of the x_i are treated as independent parameters. +■ Applying LogicalExpand to the results of Reduce[*expr*, ...] yields an expression of the form e_1 || e_2 || ... , where each of the e_i can be thought of as representing a separate component in the set defined by *expr*. +■ The e_i may not be disjoint, and may have different dimensions. After LogicalExpand, each of the e_i have the form *e* && *e* && ... . +■ Without LogicalExpand, Reduce by default returns a nested collection of conditions on the x_i, combined alternately by Or and And on successive levels. +■ When *expr* involves only polynomial equations and inequalities over real or complex domains then Reduce can always in principle solve directly for all the x_i. +■ When *expr* involves transcendental conditions or integer domains Reduce will often introduce additional parameters in its results. +■ When *expr* involves only polynomial conditions, Reduce[*expr*, *vars*, Reals] gives a cylindrical algebraic decomposition of *expr*.

(continued)

■ Reduce *(continued)*

+■ Reduce can give explicit representations for solutions to all linear equations and inequalities over the integers, and can solve a large fraction of Diophantine equations described in the literature. +■ When *expr* involves only polynomial conditions over real or complex domains, Reduce[*expr*, *vars*] will always eliminate quantifiers, so that quantified variables do not appear in the result. +■ The following options can be given:

Backsubstitution	False	whether to give results unwound by backsubstitution
Cubics	False	whether to use explicit radicals to solve all cubics
GeneratedParameters	C	how to name parameters that are generated
Modulus	0	modulus to assume for integers
Quartics	False	whether to use explicit radicals to solve all quartics

+■ Reduce[*expr*, $\{x_1, x_2, \dots\}$, Backsubstitution->True] yields a form in which values from equations generated for earlier x_i are backsubstituted so that the conditions for a particular x_i have only minimal dependence on earlier x_i. ■ See page 839. ■ Implementation notes: see page 1070. ■ See also: Solve, FindInstance, Roots, Eliminate, Resolve, LogicalExpand, ToRules, GroebnerBasis, Simplify. ■ *New in Version 1; modified in Version 5.0.*

+■ Refine

Refine[*expr*, *assum*] gives the form of *expr* that would be obtained if symbols in it were replaced by explicit numerical expressions satisfying the assumptions *assum*.

Refine[*expr*] uses default assumptions specified by any enclosing Assuming constructs.

Example: Refine[Sqrt[x^2], x > 0] $\longrightarrow$ x. ■ Assumptions can consist of equations, inequalities, domain specifications such as $x \in$ Integers, and logical combinations of these. ■ Example: Refine[Sqrt[x^2], x $\in$ Reals] $\longrightarrow$ Abs[x]. ■ Refine can be used on equations, inequalities and domain specifications. ■ Quantities that appear algebraically in inequalities are always assumed to be real. ■ Refine is one of the transformations tried by Simplify. ■ Refine has the option Assumptions, with default setting \$Assumptions. ■ Refine[*expr*, *a*, Assumptions->*b*] uses assumptions *a* && *b*. ■ See page 815. ■ See also: Simplify, PowerExpand, Assuming. ■ *New in Version 5.0.*

■ ReleaseHold

ReleaseHold[*expr*] removes Hold, HoldForm, HoldPattern and HoldComplete in *expr*.

Example: ReleaseHold[{2, Hold[1 + 1]}] $\longrightarrow$ {2, 2}. ■ ReleaseHold removes only one layer of Hold etc.; it does not remove inner occurrences in nested Hold etc. functions. ■ See page 339. ■ See also: Evaluate. ■ *New in Version 2.*

■ Remove

Remove[*symbol*$_1$, ...] removes symbols completely, so that their names are no longer recognized by *Mathematica*.

Remove["*form*$_1$", "*form*$_2$", ...] removes all symbols whose names match any of the string patterns *form*$_i$.

You can use Remove to get rid of symbols that you do not need, and which may shadow symbols in contexts later on your context path. ■ Remove["*form*"] allows metacharacters such as *, as specified on page 1044. ■ Remove["*context*`*"] removes all symbols in a particular context. ■ Remove does not affect symbols with the attribute Protected. ■ Once you have removed a symbol, you will never be able to refer to it again, unless you recreate it. ■ If you have an expression that contains a symbol which you remove, the removed symbol will be printed as Removed["*name*"], where its name is given in a string. ■ See pages 395, 403 and 1052. ■ See also: Clear. ■ *New in Version 1.*

■ **RenameDirectory**

RenameDirectory["*dir*₁", "*dir*₂"] renames the directory *dir*₁ to *dir*₂.

*dir*₁ must already exist; *dir*₂ must not. ■ RenameDirectory sets the modification date for *dir*₂ to be the same as for *dir*₁. ■ RenameDirectory returns the full new directory name, or $Failed if the directory cannot be renamed. ■ See page 641. ■ See also: CopyDirectory, CreateDirectory, DeleteDirectory. ■ *New in Version 2.*

■ **RenameFile**

RenameFile["*file*₁", "*file*₂"] renames *file*₁ to *file*₂.

*file*₁ must already exist; *file*₂ must not. ■ RenameFile sets the modification date for *file*₂ to be the same as for *file*₁. ■ RenameFile returns the full new file name, or $Failed if the file cannot be renamed. ■ See page 641. ■ See also: CopyFile, DeleteFile, RenameDirectory. ■ *New in Version 2.*

■ **RenderAll**

RenderAll is an option for Graphics3D which specifies whether or not PostScript should be generated for *all* polygons.

When RenderAll->False, PostScript will be generated only for those polygons or parts of polygons which are visible in the final picture. ■ If RenderAll->True, PostScript is generated for *all* polygons. The PostScript for polygons that are further back is given before the PostScript for those in front. If the PostScript is displayed incrementally, you can see the object being drawn from the back. ■ Setting RenderAll->False will usually lead to a smaller amount of PostScript code, but may take longer to run. ■ There may be slight differences in the images obtained with different settings for RenderAll, primarily as a result of different numerical roundoff in the PostScript code, and the rendering system. ■ See page 555. ■ See also: PolygonIntersections. ■ *New in Version 1.*

■ **Repeated**

p.. is a pattern object which represents a sequence of one or more expressions, each matching *p*.

p.. can appear as an argument of any function. It represents any sequence of arguments. ■ All the objects in the sequence represented by *p*.. must match *p*, but the objects need not be identical. ■ The expression *p* may, but need not, itself be a pattern object. ■ See pages 277 and 1028. ■ See also: RepeatedNull, BlankSequence. ■ *New in Version 1.*

■ **RepeatedNull**

p... is a pattern object which represents a sequence of zero or more expressions, each matching *p*.

See notes for Repeated. ■ See pages 277 and 1028. ■ *New in Version 1.*

■ **Replace**

Replace[*expr*, *rules*] applies a rule or list of rules in an attempt to transform the entire expression *expr*.

Replace[*expr*, *rules*, *levelspec*] applies rules to parts of *expr* specified by *levelspec*.

Examples: Replace[x^2, x^2 -> a] ⟶ a. ■ Replace[x + 1, x -> a] ⟶ 1 + x. ■ The rules must be of the form *lhs* -> *rhs* or *lhs* :> *rhs*. ■ A list of rules can be given. The rules are tried in order. The result of the first one that applies is returned. If none of the rules apply, the original *expr* is returned. ■ If the rules are given in nested lists, Replace is effectively mapped onto the inner lists. Thus Replace[*expr*, {{*r*₁₁, *r*₁₂}, {*r*₂₁, ... }, ... }] is equivalent to {Replace[*expr*, {*r*₁₁, *r*₁₂}], Replace[*expr*, {*r*₂₁, ... }], ... }. ■ Delayed rules defined with :> can contain /; conditions. ■ Level specifications are described on page 1041. ■ The default value for *levelspec* in Replace is {0}. ■ Replacements are performed to parts specified by *levelspec* even when those parts have Hold or related wrappers. ■ Replace takes a Heads option, with default setting Heads -> False. ■ See page 301. ■ See also: Rule, Set, ReplacePart, ReplaceList, StringReplace, PolynomialReduce. ■ *New in Version 1; modified in Version 4.*

■ ReplaceAll

expr /. rules applies a rule or list of rules in an attempt to transform each subpart of an expression *expr*.

Example: x + 2 /. x -> a ⟶ 2 + a. ■ `ReplaceAll` looks at each part of *expr*, tries all the *rules* on it, and then goes on to the next part of *expr*. The first rule that applies to a particular part is used; no further rules are tried on that part, or on any of its subparts. ■ `ReplaceAll` applies a particular rule only once to an expression. ■ Example: x /. x -> x + 1 ⟶ 1 + x. ■ See the notes on `Replace` for a description of how rules are applied to each part of *expr*. ■ *expr /. rules* returns *expr* if none of the rules apply. ■ See page 299. ■ See also: `Rule`, `Set`, `MapAll`, `ReplaceRepeated`, `TransformationFunctions`. ■ *New in Version 1.*

■ ReplaceList

`ReplaceList[`*expr*, *rules*`]` attempts to transform the entire expression *expr* by applying a rule or list of rules in all possible ways, and returns a list of the results obtained.

`ReplaceList[`*expr*, *rules*, *n*`]` gives a list of at most *n* results.

When no transformation is possible, `ReplaceList` returns {}. ■ See notes for `Replace`. ■ See pages 263 and 302. ■ See also: `Cases`, `StringPosition`, `Trace`, `Position`, `Split`. ■ *New in Version 3.*

■ ReplacePart

`ReplacePart[`*expr*, *new*, *n*`]` yields an expression in which the nth part of *expr* is replaced by *new*.

`ReplacePart[`*expr*, *new*, {*i*, *j*, ... }`]` replaces the part at position {*i*, *j*, ... }.

`ReplacePart[`*expr*, *new*, {{i_1, j_1, ... }, {i_2, j_2, ... }, ... }`]` replaces parts at several positions by *new*.

`ReplacePart[`*expr*, *new*, *pos*, *npos*`]` replaces parts at positions *pos* in *expr* by parts at positions *npos* in *new*.

Example: `ReplacePart[{a, b, c, d}, x, 3]` ⟶ {a, b, x, d}. ■ The list of positions used by `ReplacePart` is in the same form as is returned by the function `Position`. ■ `ReplacePart[`*expr*, `Hold[`*new*`]`, *pos*, 1`]` can be used to replace a part without evaluating it. ■ If *pos* and *npos* both specify multiple parts, each part in *pos* is replaced by the corresponding part in *npos*. +■ `ReplacePart` can be used on `SparseArray` objects. ■ See pages 235 and 288. ■ See also: `Part`, `Extract`, `MapAt`, `FlattenAt`, `Insert`, `Delete`, `Sequence`, `StringReplacePart`. ■ *New in Version 2; modified in Version 3.*

■ ReplaceRepeated

expr //. rules repeatedly performs replacements until *expr* no longer changes.

expr //. rules effectively applies /. repeatedly, until the results it gets no longer change. ■ It performs one complete pass over the expression using /., then carries out the next pass. ■ You should be very careful to avoid infinite loops when you use the //. operator. The command x //. x -> x + 1 will, for example, lead to an infinite loop. ■ `ReplaceRepeated` takes the option `MaxIterations`, which specifies the maximum number of times it will try to apply the rules you give. The default setting is `MaxIterations -> 65536`. With `MaxIterations -> Infinity` there is no limit. ■ See page 300. ■ See also: `ReplaceAll`, `Rule`, `Set`, `FixedPoint`. ■ *New in Version 1.*

■ ResetDirectory

ResetDirectory[ ] resets the current working directory to its previous value.

Successive calls to ResetDirectory yield earlier and earlier current directories. ■ ResetDirectory uses the directory stack given by DirectoryStack[ ]. ■ ResetDirectory removes the last element from the directory stack, and makes the second-to-last element current. ■ See page 636. ■ See also: SetDirectory, Directory, $Path. ■ *New in Version 2.*

■ Residue

Residue[*expr*, {*x*, x_0}] finds the residue of *expr* at the point $x = x_0$.

The residue is defined as the coefficient of $(x - x_0)$^-1 in the Laurent expansion of *expr*. ■ *Mathematica* can usually find residues at a point only when it can evaluate power series at that point. ■ See page 895. ■ See also: Series, Limit, PrincipalValue. ■ Related package: Algebra`RootIsolation`. ■ *New in Version 2.*

■ Resolve

Resolve[*expr*] attempts to resolve *expr* into a form that eliminates ForAll and Exists quantifiers.

Resolve[*expr*, *dom*] works over the domain *dom*. Common choices of *dom* are Complexes, Reals and Booleans.

Resolve is in effect automatically applied by Reduce. ■ *expr* can contain equations, inequalities, domain specifications and quantifiers, in the same form as in Reduce. ■ The result of Resolve[*expr*] always describes exactly the same mathematical set as *expr*, but without quantifiers. ■ Resolve[*expr*] assumes by default that quantities appearing algebraically in inequalities are real, while all other quantities are complex. ■ When a quantifier such as ForAll[*x*, ...] is eliminated the result will contain no mention of the localized variable *x*. ■ Resolve[*expr*] can in principle always eliminate quantifiers if *expr* contains only polynomial equations and inequalities over the reals or complexes. ■ See page 848. ■ Implementation notes: see page 1070. ■ See also: Reduce, FindInstance, Exists, ForAll. ■ *New in Version 5.0.*

■ Rest

Rest[*expr*] gives *expr* with the first element removed.

Example: Rest[{a, b, c}] ⟶ {b, c}. ■ Rest[*expr*] is equivalent to Drop[*expr*, 1]. ■ See page 123. ■ See also: Most, Drop, First, Part, Take. ■ *New in Version 1.*

■ Resultant

Resultant[$poly_1$, $poly_2$, *var*] computes the resultant of the polynomials $poly_1$ and $poly_2$ with respect to the variable *var*.

Resultant[$poly_1$, $poly_2$, *var*, Modulus->*p*] computes the resultant modulo the prime *p*.

The resultant of two polynomials *a* and *b*, both with leading coefficient one, is the product of all the differences $a_i - b_j$ between roots of the polynomials. The resultant is always a number or a polynomial. ■ See page 803. ■ See also: Subresultants, PolynomialGCD, Eliminate. ■ *New in Version 1.*

■ Return

Return[*expr*] returns the value *expr* from a function.

Return[ ] returns the value Null.

Return[*expr*] exits control structures within the definition of a function, and gives the value *expr* for the whole function. ■ Return takes effect as soon as it is evaluated, even if it appears inside other functions. ■ Return can be used inside functions like Scan. ■ See page 353. ■ See also: Break, Throw, Abort. ■ *New in Version 1.*

■ Reverse

Reverse[*expr*] reverses the order of the elements in *expr*.

Example: Reverse[{a, b, c}] ⟶ {c, b, a}. +■ Reverse works on SparseArray objects, reversing the elements in the corresponding ordinary array. ■ See page 127. ■ See also: Permutations, RotateLeft, RotateRight, StringReverse. ■ *New in Version 1.*

■ RGBColor

RGBColor[*red*, *green*, *blue*] is a graphics directive which specifies that graphical objects which follow are to be displayed, if possible, in the color given.

Red, green and blue color intensities outside the range 0 to 1 will be clipped. ■ On monochrome displays, a gray level based on the average of the color intensities is used. ■ See page 499. ■ See also: Hue, GrayLevel, CMYKColor, ColorOutput. ■ Related package: Graphics`Colors`. ■ *New in Version 1.*

■ RiemannSiegelTheta

RiemannSiegelTheta[*t*] gives the Riemann-Siegel function $\vartheta(t)$.

Mathematical function (see Section A.3.10). ■ $\vartheta(t) = \mathrm{Im}[\log \Gamma(\frac{1}{4} + i\frac{t}{2}) - t \log \pi/2]$ for real *t*. ■ $\vartheta(t)$ arises in the study of the Riemann zeta function on the critical line. It is closely related to the number of zeros of $\zeta(\frac{1}{2} + iu)$ for $0 < u < t$. ■ $\vartheta(t)$ is an analytic function of *t* except for branch cuts on the imaginary axis running from $\pm i/2$ to $\pm i\infty$. ■ See page 772. ■ See also: RiemannSiegelZ, Zeta. ■ *New in Version 2.*

■ RiemannSiegelZ

RiemannSiegelZ[*t*] gives the Riemann-Siegel function $Z(t)$.

Mathematical function (see Section A.3.10). ■ $Z(t) = e^{i\vartheta(t)}\zeta(\frac{1}{2} + it)$, where ϑ is the Riemann-Siegel theta function, and ζ is the Riemann zeta function. ■ $|Z(t)| = |\zeta(\frac{1}{2} + it)|$ for real *t*. ■ $Z(t)$ is an analytic function of *t* except for branch cuts on the imaginary axis running from $\pm i/2$ to $\pm i\infty$. ■ See page 772. ■ See also: RiemannSiegelTheta, Zeta. ■ *New in Version 2.*

■ Root

Root[*f*, *k*] represents the kth root of the polynomial equation $f[x] == 0$.

f must be a Function object such as (#^5 - 2 # + 1)&. ■ Root[*f*, *k*] is automatically reduced so that *f* has the smallest possible degree and smallest integer coefficients. ■ The ordering used by Root takes real roots to come before complex ones, and takes complex conjugate pairs of roots to be adjacent. ■ The coefficients in the polynomial $f[x]$ can involve symbolic parameters. ■ For linear and quadratic polynomials $f[x]$, Root[*f*, *k*] is automatically reduced to explicit rational or radical form. ■ N finds the approximate numerical value of a Root object. ■ Operations such as Abs, Re, Round and Less can be used on Root objects. ■ Root[*f*, *k*] is treated as a numeric quantity if *f* contains no symbolic parameters. ■ Root by default isolates the roots of a polynomial using approximate numerical methods. No cases are known where this approach fails. SetOptions[Root, ExactRootIsolation->True] will however make Root use much slower but fully rigorous methods. ■ See page 821. ■ See also: Solve, RootReduce, ToRadicals, RootSum, Extension, Algebraics. ■ Related package: Algebra`RootIsolation`. ■ *New in Version 3.*

■ RootReduce

RootReduce[*expr*] attempts to reduce *expr* to a single Root object.

If *expr* consists only of integers and Root objects combined using algebraic operations, then the result from RootReduce[*expr*] will always be a single Root object. ■ Simple Root objects may in turn automatically evaluate to rational expressions or combinations of radicals. ■ See page 826. ■ See also: FullSimplify, Solve, ToRadicals. ■ Related package: NumberTheory`PrimitiveElement`. ■ *New in Version 3.*

■ Roots

Roots[*lhs==rhs*, *var*] yields a disjunction of equations which represent the roots of a polynomial equation.

Roots uses Factor and Decompose in trying to find roots. ■ You can find numerical values of the roots by applying N. ■ Roots can take the following options:

Cubics	True	whether to generate explicit solutions for cubics
EquatedTo	Null	expression to which the variable solved for should be equated
Modulus	0	integer modulus
Multiplicity	1	multiplicity in final list of solutions
Quartics	True	whether to generate explicit solutions for quartics
Using	True	subsidiary equations to be solved

■ Roots is generated when Solve and related functions cannot produce explicit solutions. Options are often given in such cases. ■ Roots gives several identical equations when roots with multiplicity greater than one occur. ■ See page 819. ■ See also: Solve, NSolve, FindRoot, Reduce, ToRules, Root, Factor, Decompose, InterpolatingPolynomial. ■ Related package: Algebra`RootIsolation`. ■ *New in Version 1.*

■ RootSum

RootSum[*f*, *form*] represents the sum of *form*[*x*] for all *x* that satisfy the polynomial equation $f[x] == 0$.

f must be a Function object such as (#^5 - 2 # + 1)&. ■ *form* need not correspond to a polynomial function. ■ Normal[*expr*] expands RootSum objects into explicit sums involving Root objects. ■ *f* and *form* can contain symbolic parameters. ■ RootSum[*f*, *form*] is automatically simplified whenever *form* is a rational function. ■ RootSum is often generated in computing integrals of rational functions. ■ See page 827. ■ See also: Root. ■ Related package: Algebra`SymmetricPolynomials`. ■ *New in Version 3.*

■ RotateLabel

RotateLabel is an option for two-dimensional graphics functions which specifies whether labels on vertical frame axes should be rotated to be vertical.

For frame labels, the default is RotateLabel -> True. ■ With RotateLabel -> True, vertical frame axes labels read from bottom to top. ■ See page 514. ■ See also: Text, ImageRotated. ■ *New in Version 2.*

■ RotateLeft

RotateLeft[*expr*, *n*] cycles the elements in *expr* *n* positions to the left.

RotateLeft[*expr*] cycles one position to the left.

RotateLeft[*expr*, {*n*₁, *n*₂, ... }] cycles elements at successive levels n_i positions to the left.

Example: RotateLeft[{a, b, c}, 1] ⟶ {b, c, a}. ■ RotateLeft[*expr*, -*n*] rotates *n* positions to the right. +■ RotateLeft can be used on SparseArray objects. ■ See pages 127 and 130. ■ See also: RotateRight, Reverse, PadLeft. ■ *New in Version 1.*

■ **RotateRight**

RotateRight[*expr*, *n*] cycles the elements in *expr* *n* positions to the right.

RotateRight[*expr*] cycles one position to the right.

RotateRight[*expr*, {n_1, n_2, ... }] cycles elements at successive levels n_i positions to the right.

Example: RotateRight[{a, b, c}, 1] ⟶ {c, a, b}. ■ RotateRight[*expr*, -*n*] rotates *n* positions to the left. +■ RotateRight can be used on SparseArray objects. ■ See pages 127 and 130. ■ See also: RotateLeft, Reverse, PadRight. ■ *New in Version 1.*

■ **Round**

Round[*x*] gives the integer closest to *x*.

Mathematical function (see Section A.3.10). ■ Examples: Round[2.4] ⟶ 2; Round[2.6] ⟶ 3; Round[-2.4] ⟶ -2; Round[-2.6] ⟶ -3. ■ Round rounds numbers of the form *x*.5 toward the nearest even integer. ■ Round[*x*] returns an integer when *x* is any numeric quantity, whether or not it is an explicit number. ■ Example: Round[Pi^2] ⟶ 10. ■ For exact numeric quantities, Round internally uses numerical approximations to establish its result. This process can be affected by the setting of the global variable $MaxExtraPrecision. ■ See page 745. ■ See also: IntegerPart, Floor, Ceiling, Chop. ■ *New in Version 1; modified in Version 3.*

■ **RowAlignments**

RowAlignments is an option for GridBox which specifies how entries in each row should be aligned.

The following settings can be given:

Center	centered
Top	tops aligned
Bottom	bottoms aligned
Baseline	baselines aligned (default)
Axis	axes aligned
{pos_1, pos_2, ... }	separate settings for each row in the grid

■ Lists of settings are used cyclically if there are more rows in the grid than elements in the list. ■ See page 449.
■ See also: ColumnAlignments, RowsEqual, RowMinHeight, TableAlignments. ■ *New in Version 3.*

■ **RowBox**

RowBox[{box_1, box_2, ... }] represents a row of boxes or strings in input and output.

RowBox objects are generated automatically to correspond to each operator and its operands in input given as \(*input*\). ■ The default arrangement of RowBox objects in \(*input*\) is based on operator precedence. Additional \(... \) can be inserted like parentheses to specify different arrangements of RowBox objects. ■ The boxes or strings in a RowBox are output in a row with their baselines aligned. ■ In InputForm, RowBox objects are output using \(... \). ■ In StandardForm, explicit RowBox objects are output literally. You can use DisplayForm to see the display form of such objects. ■ See page 445. ■ See also: SequenceForm, GridBox, AdjustmentBox. ■ *New in Version 3.*

■ **RowLines**

RowLines is an option for GridBox which specifies whether lines should be drawn between adjacent rows.

The default setting is RowLines->False. ■ RowLines->{v_{12}, v_{23}, ... } specifies whether lines should be drawn between successive pairs of rows. The v_{ij} can be True or False. ■ If there are more rows than entries in the list, the last element is used repeatedly for remaining pairs of rows. ■ Lines can be drawn around the outside of a GridBox using FrameBox. ■ See page 446. ■ See also: ColumnLines, FrameBox, GridLines. ■ *New in Version 3.*

■ **RowMinHeight**

RowMinHeight is an option for GridBox which specifies the minimum total height in units of font size that should be allowed for each row.

The default setting RowMinHeight->1 forces each row to have a total height which at least accommodates all the characters in the current font. ■ RowMinHeight->0 reduces the total height of each entry as much as possible, allowing entries containing characters such as x and X to be different heights. ■ See page 449. ■ See also: RowSpacings, RowAlignments, RowsEqual, ButtonMinHeight. ■ *New in Version 3.*

■ **RowReduce**

RowReduce[m] gives the row-reduced form of the matrix m.

Example: RowReduce[{{3, 1, a}, {2, 1, b}}] $\longrightarrow$ {{1, 0, a-b}, {0, 1, -2a+3b}}. ■ RowReduce performs a version of Gaussian elimination, adding multiples of rows together so as to produce zero elements when possible. The final matrix is in reduced row echelon form. ■ If m is a non-degenerate square matrix, RowReduce[m] is IdentityMatrix[Length[m]]. ■ If m is a sufficiently non-degenerate rectangular matrix with k rows and more than k columns, then the first k columns of RowReduce[m] will form an identity matrix. ■ RowReduce works on both numerical and symbolic matrices. ■ RowReduce[m, Modulus -> n] performs row reduction modulo n. ■ RowReduce[m, ZeroTest -> *test*] evaluates *test*[m[[i, j]]] to determine whether matrix elements are zero. ■ See page 907. ■ Implementation notes: see page 1069. ■ See also: LinearSolve, Inverse, NullSpace, GroebnerBasis. ■ *New in Version 1; modified in Version 3.*

■ **RowsEqual**

RowsEqual is an option for GridBox which specifies whether all rows in the grid should be assigned equal total height.

The default setting RowsEqual->False determines the total height of each row from the entry in that row with the largest total height. ■ RowsEqual->True makes all rows the same total height, with the total height determined by the entry with the largest total height in the whole GridBox. ■ See page 449. ■ See also: RowAlignments, RowSpacings, RowMinHeight, ColumnsEqual, MatrixForm. ■ *New in Version 3.*

■ **RowSpacings**

RowSpacings is an option for GridBox which specifies the spaces in x-heights that should be inserted between successive rows.

The default setting is RowSpacings->1.0. ■ RowSpacings effectively specifies the minimum distance between entries in successive rows; individual entries will often not fill their rows and will therefore be further apart. ■ RowSpacings->n uses a column spacing equal to n times the height of an "x" character in the current font. ■ RowSpacings->{s_{12}, s_{23}, ... } can be used to specify different spacings between different rows. If there are more rows than entries in this list, then the last element of the list is used repeatedly for the remaining rows. ■ See page 449. ■ See also: RowAlignments, RowMinHeight, RowsEqual, ColumnSpacings, TableSpacing. ■ *New in Version 3.*

■ RSolve

RSolve[*eqn*, *a*[*n*], *n*] solves a recurrence equation for *a*[*n*].

RSolve[{*eqn*$_1$, *eqn*$_2$, ... }, {*a*$_1$[*n*], *a*$_2$[*n*], ... }, *n*] solves a system of recurrence equations.

RSolve[*eqn*, *a*[*n*$_1$, *n*$_2$, ...], {*n*$_1$, *n*$_2$, ... }] solves a partial recurrence equation.

RSolve[*eqn*, *a*, *n*] gives solutions for *a* as pure functions. ■ The equations can involve objects of the form *a*[*n+i*] where *i* is any fixed integer, or objects of the form *a*[*q*^*i* *n*]. ■ Equations such as *a*[0]==*val* can be given to specify end conditions. ■ If not enough end conditions are specified, RSolve will give general solutions in which undetermined constants are introduced. ■ The constants introduced by RSolve are indexed by successive integers. The option GeneratedParameters specifies the function to apply to each index. The default is GeneratedParameters->C, which yields constants C[1], C[2], ... ■ GeneratedParameters->(Module[{C}, C]&) guarantees that the constants of integration are unique, even across different invocations of RSolve. ■ For partial recurrence equations, RSolve generates arbitrary functions C[*n*][...]. ■ Solutions given by RSolve sometimes include sums that cannot be carried out explicitly by Sum. Dummy variables with local names are used in such sums. ■ RSolve sometimes gives implicit solutions in terms of Solve. ■ RSolve handles both ordinary difference equations and *q*-difference equations. ■ RSolve handles difference-algebraic equations as well as ordinary difference equations. ■ RSolve can solve linear recurrence equations of any order with constant coefficients. It can also solve many linear equations up to second order with non-constant coefficients, as well as many nonlinear equations. ■ See page 891. ■ Implementation notes: see page 1071. ■ See also: Sum, ZTransform, DSolve. ■ *New in Version 5.0.*

■ Rule

lhs -> *rhs* or *lhs* → *rhs* represents a rule that transforms *lhs* to *rhs*.

The character → can be entered as :->: or \[Rule]. ■ *lhs* -> *rhs* evaluates *rhs* immediately. ■ You can apply rules using Replace. ■ The assignment *lhs* = *rhs* specifies that the rule *lhs* -> *rhs* should be used whenever it applies. ■ *lhs* → *rhs* can be entered as *lhs* \[Rule] *rhs* or *lhs* :->: *rhs*. ■ In StandardForm, Rule is printed using →. ■ Rule is a scoping construct (see Section A.3.8). ■ Symbols that occur as pattern names in *lhs* are treated as local to the rule. This is true when the symbols appear on the right-hand side of /; conditions in *lhs*, and when the symbols appear anywhere in *rhs*, even inside other scoping constructs. ■ See pages 299 and 1052. ■ Implementation notes: see page 1066. ■ See also: Replace, Set, RuleDelayed, PolynomialReduce. ■ Related package: Utilities`FilterOptions`. ■ *New in Version 1; modified in Version 3.*

■ RuleDelayed

lhs :> *rhs* or *lhs* :→ *rhs* represents a rule that transforms *lhs* to *rhs*, evaluating *rhs* only after the rule is used.

The character :→ can be entered as ::>: or \[RuleDelayed]. ■ RuleDelayed has the attribute HoldRest. ■ You can apply rules using Replace. ■ The assignment *lhs* := *rhs* specifies that the rule *lhs* :> *rhs* should be used whenever it applies. ■ You can use Condition to specify when a particular rule applies. ■ *lhs* :→ *rhs* can be entered as *lhs* \[RuleDelayed] *rhs* or *lhs* ::>: *rhs*. ■ In StandardForm, RuleDelayed is printed using :→. ■ See notes for Rule. ■ See pages 299 and 1052. ■ See also: Replace, SetDelayed, Rule. ■ *New in Version 1; modified in Version 3.*

■ Run

Run[*expr*$_1$, *expr*$_2$, ...] generates the printed form of the expressions *expr*$_i$, separated by spaces, and runs it as an external, operating system, command.

Run is not available on all computer systems. ■ Run prints the *expr*$_i$ in InputForm format. ■ Run returns an integer which corresponds, when possible, to the exit code for the command returned by the operating system. ■ The command executed by Run cannot usually require interactive input. On most computer systems, it can, however, generate textual output. ■ You can enter the input line !*command* to execute an external command. ■ See page 629. ■ See also: Put, Splice. ■ *New in Version 1.*

■ RunThrough

RunThrough["*command*", *expr*] executes an external command, giving the printed form of *expr* as input, and taking the output, reading it as *Mathematica* input, and returning the result.

RunThrough is not available on all computer systems. ■ RunThrough writes the InputForm of *expr* on the standard input for *command*, then reads its standard output, and feeds it into *Mathematica*. ■ RunThrough starts *command*, then gives input to *command*, then terminates the input. ■ See page 630. ■ See also: Install, Put, Get, Splice. ■ *New in Version 1.*

■ SameQ

lhs === *rhs* yields True if the expression *lhs* is identical to *rhs*, and yields False otherwise.

SameQ requires exact correspondence between expressions, except that it considers Real numbers equal if their difference is less than the uncertainty of either of them. ■ 2 === 2. gives False. ■ e_1 === e_2 === e_3 gives True if all the e_i are identical. ■ See page 268. ■ See also: UnsameQ, Equal, Order. ■ *New in Version 1.*

■ SampleDepth

SampleDepth is an option for sound primitives which specifies how many bits should be used to encode sound amplitude levels.

The default setting is SampleDepth -> 8. ■ With the default setting, 256 distinct sound amplitudes are allowed. ■ See page 566. ■ See also: PlayRange, SampleRate. ■ *New in Version 2.*

■ SampledSoundFunction

SampledSoundFunction[*f*, *n*, *r*] is a sound primitive, which represents a sound whose amplitude sampled *r* times a second is generated by applying the function *f* to successive integers from 1 to *n*.

SampledSoundFunction[{f_1, f_2, ... }, *n*, *r*] yields sound on several channels. ■ SampledSoundFunction is generated by Play. ■ SampledSoundFunction primitives can appear inside Sound, Graphics and Graphics3D objects. ■ See page 566. ■ *New in Version 2.*

■ SampledSoundList

SampledSoundList[{a_1, a_2, ... }, *r*] is a sound primitive, which represents a sound whose amplitude has levels a_i sampled *r* times a second.

SampledSoundList[{$list_1$, $list_2$, ... }, *r*] yields sound on several channels. If the lists are of different lengths, silence is inserted at the ends of shorter lists. ■ SampledSoundList is generated by ListPlay. ■ SampledSoundList primitives can appear inside Sound, Graphics and Graphics3D objects. ■ See page 566. ■ *New in Version 2.*

■ SampleRate

SampleRate is an option for sound primitives which specifies the number of samples per second to generate for sounds.

The default setting is SampleRate -> 8192. ■ The highest frequency in hertz that can be present in a particular sound is equal to half the setting for SampleRate. ■ See page 172. ■ See also: SampleDepth. ■ *New in Version 2.*

■ Save

Save["*filename*", *symbol*] appends definitions associated with the specified symbol to a file.

Save["*filename*", "*form*"] appends definitions associated with all symbols whose names match the string pattern *form*.

Save["*filename*", "*context*`"] appends definitions associated with all symbols in the specified context.

Save["*filename*", {*object*$_1$, *object*$_2$, ... }] appends definitions associated with several objects.

Save uses FullDefinition to include subsidiary definitions. ■ Save writes out definitions in InputForm. ■ Save uses Names to find symbols whose names match a given string pattern. ■ You can use Save["*filename*", "s"] to write out the definition for the value of a symbol *s* itself. ■ See pages 204 and 625. ■ See also: PutAppend, Get, DumpSave. ■ *New in Version 1; modified in Version 3.*

■ Scaled

Scaled[{*x*, *y*, ... }] gives the position of a graphical object in terms of coordinates scaled to run from 0 to 1 across the whole plot in each direction.

Scaled[{*dx*, *dy*, ... }, {*x*$_0$, *y*$_0$, ... }] gives a position obtained by starting at ordinary coordinates {*x*$_0$, *y*$_0$, ... }, then moving by a scaled offset {*dx*, *dy*, ... }.

Scaled can be used to specify scaled coordinates in any two- or three-dimensional graphics primitive. ■ You can use Scaled to represent objects that occupy a fixed region in a plot, independent of the specific range of coordinates in the plot. ■ See pages 505 and 531. ■ See also: PlotRange, PlotRegion, Offset. ■ *New in Version 1.*

■ Scan

Scan[*f*, *expr*] evaluates *f* applied to each element of *expr* in turn.

Scan[*f*, *expr*, *levelspec*] applies *f* to parts of *expr* specified by *levelspec*.

Scan[*f*, *expr*] discards the results of applying *f* to the subexpressions in *expr*. Unlike Map, Scan does not build up a new expression to return. ■ You can use Return to exit from Scan. Return[*ret*] causes the final value of Scan to be *ret*. If no explicit return values are specified, the final result from Scan is Null. ■ You can also use Throw to exit from Scan. ■ Scan is useful in carrying out an operation on parts of expressions where the operation has a "side effect", such as making an assignment. ■ Level specifications are described on page 1041. ■ The default value for *levelspec* in Scan is {1}. +■ If *expr* is a SparseArray object, Scan[*f*, *expr*] applies *f* only to the values or subarrays that explicitly appear in *expr*. ■ See page 247. ■ See also: Apply, Map, Level, Sow. ■ *New in Version 1; modified in Version 3.*

■ SchurDecomposition

SchurDecomposition[*m*] yields the Schur decomposition for a numerical matrix *m*. The result is a list {*q*, *t*} where *q* is an orthonormal matrix and *t* is a block upper triangular matrix.

+ SchurDecomposition[{*m*, *a*}] gives the generalized Schur decomposition of *m* with respect to *a*.

The original matrix *m* is equal to *q* . *t* . Conjugate[Transpose[*q*]].
■ SchurDecomposition[*m*, Pivoting -> True] yields a list {*q*, *t*, *d*} where *d* is a permuted diagonal matrix such that *m* . *d* is equal to *d* . *q* . *t* . Conjugate[Transpose[*q*]]. +■ SchurDecomposition[{*m*, *a*}] yields a list of matrices {*q*, *s*, *p*, *t*} where *q* and *p* are orthonormal matrices, *s* and *t* are upper triangular matrices, such that *m* is given by *q* . *s* . Conjugate[Transpose[*p*]] and *a* is given by *q* . *t* . Conjugate[Transpose[*p*]]. ■ See page 915. ■ Implementation notes: see page 1069. ■ See also: QRDecomposition, LUDecomposition, SingularValueDecomposition, JordanDecomposition. ■ *New in Version 2; modified in Version 5.0.*

■ ScientificForm

ScientificForm[*expr*] prints with all real numbers in *expr* given in scientific notation.

ScientificForm[*expr*, *n*] prints with numbers given to *n*-digit precision.

ScientificForm takes the same options as NumberForm, but uses a different default function for ExponentFunction. ■ You can mix ScientificForm and BaseForm. ■ ScientificForm acts as a "wrapper", which affects printing, but not evaluation. ■ See page 435. ■ See also: EngineeringForm, NumberForm. ■ *New in Version 1.*

■ ScreenStyleEnvironment

ScreenStyleEnvironment is an option for notebooks which specifies the style environment to be used in displaying a notebook on the screen.

Style environments provided in typical style sheets include:

"Condensed"	environment for maximum display density
"Presentation"	environment for presentations
"Printout"	environment for paper printouts
"Working"	environment for typical on-screen working

■ See page 197. ■ See also: PrintingStyleEnvironment, StyleDefinitions. ■ *New in Version 3.*

■ ScriptBaselineShifts

ScriptBaselineShifts is an option for StyleBox which specifies the minimum distance in x-heights to shift subscripts and superscripts.

The setting ScriptBaselineShifts->{*sub*, *sup*} uses shift *sub* for subscripts and *sup* for superscripts. ■ A typical setting is ScriptBaselineShifts->{0.6, 0.9}. ■ The default setting ScriptBaselineShifts->{Automatic, Automatic} shifts subscripts and superscripts by a distance which depends on their height. ■ See page 457. ■ See also: AdjustmentBox, RowMinHeight, ScriptMinSize. ■ *New in Version 3.*

■ ScriptMinSize

ScriptMinSize is an option for StyleBox which specifies the minimum font size to use in rendering subscripts, etc.

Settings for ScriptMinSize are in units of printer's points. ■ ScriptMinSize is used for characters that appear in constructs such as subscripts, superscripts, underscripts, overscripts and built-up fractions. ■ ScriptMinSize is typically set larger in styles used for screen display than in those used for printing. ■ See page 457. ■ See also: ScriptSizeMultipliers, FontSize, ScriptBaselineShifts. ■ *New in Version 3.*

■ ScriptSizeMultipliers

ScriptSizeMultipliers is an option for StyleBox which specifies how much smaller to render each successive level of subscripts, etc.

ScriptSizeMultipliers is applied to FontSize for characters that appear in constructs such as subscripts, superscripts, underscripts, overscripts and built-up fractions. ■ The default setting for ScriptSizeMultipliers is 0.71, yielding approximately a factor 2 reduction in character area at each level. ■ ScriptSizeMultipliers -> {s_1, s_2, ... , s_n} uses multiplier s_i for level i, and multiplier s_n for levels n and beyond. ■ See page 457. ■ See also: ScriptMinSize, ScriptBaselineShifts. ■ *New in Version 3.*

■ Sec

Sec[*z*] gives the secant of *z*.

Mathematical function (see Section A.3.10). ■ The argument of Sec is assumed to be in radians. (Multiply by Degree to convert from degrees.) ■ sec(z) = 1/cos(z). ■ 1/Cos[*z*] is automatically converted to Sec[*z*]. TrigFactorList[*expr*] does decomposition. ■ See page 761. ■ See also: ArcSec, TrigToExp, TrigExpand. ■ *New in Version 1.*

■ Sech

Sech[*z*] gives the hyperbolic secant of *z*.

Mathematical function (see Section A.3.10). ■ sech(z) = 1/cosh(z). ■ 1/Cosh[*z*] is automatically converted to Sech[*z*]. TrigFactorList[*expr*] does decomposition. ■ See page 761. ■ See also: ArcSech, TrigToExp, TrigExpand. ■ *New in Version 1; modified in Version 3.*

■ SeedRandom

SeedRandom[*n*] resets the pseudorandom number generator, using the integer *n* as a seed.

SeedRandom[ ] resets the generator, using as a seed the time of day.

You can use SeedRandom[*n*] to make sure you get the same sequence of pseudorandom numbers on different occasions. ■ You can also use SeedRandom["*string*"], although the seed set in this way may be different on different computer systems. ■ See page 747. ■ See also: Random, $RandomState. ■ *New in Version 1.*

■ Select

Select[*list*, *crit*] picks out all elements e_i of *list* for which $crit[e_i]$ is True.

Select[*list*, *crit*, *n*] picks out the first *n* elements for which $crit[e_i]$ is True.

Example: Select[{1,4,2,7,6}, EvenQ] ⟶ {4, 2, 6}. ■ The object *list* can have any head, not necessarily List. +■ Select can be used on SparseArray objects. ■ See page 251. ■ See also: Cases, Take, Drop. ■ Related package: Statistics`DataManipulation`. ■ *New in Version 1.*

■ Selectable

Selectable is an option for boxes, cells and notebooks which specifies whether their contents can be selected interactively using the front end.

Even with the setting Selectable->False, an object can be selected as a whole. ■ With Selectable->False set at the notebook level, no cells in the notebook can be selected. ■ See pages 448 and 607. ■ See also: Editable, WindowClickSelect, StructuredSelection, ShowSelection. ■ *New in Version 3.*

■ SelectedNotebook

SelectedNotebook[ ] gives the currently selected notebook in the front end.

SelectedNotebook returns a NotebookObject. ■ The currently selected notebook will normally have its title bar highlighted. ■ The currently selected notebook is the one to which notebook-oriented menu commands in the front end will be directed. Textual commands are however directed to the input notebook. ■ A palette window can be a currently selected notebook but cannot normally be an input notebook. ■ See page 579. ■ See also: SetSelectedNotebook, Notebooks, InputNotebook, EvaluationNotebook, ButtonNotebook. ■ *New in Version 3.*

■ **SelectionAnimate**

SelectionAnimate[*notebook*] animates graphics in the current selection in a notebook.

SelectionAnimate[*notebook*, *t*] animates graphics for *t* seconds.

The first argument of SelectionAnimate is a NotebookObject. ■ The current selection for SelectionAnimate will typically be a cell group. ■ SelectionAnimate stops the animation as soon as you do any interactive operation in the front end, such as pressing a key or clicking the mouse. ■ The timing in SelectionAnimate does not count setup or initial rendering of frames. ■ See page 588. ■ See also: AnimationDisplayTime, SelectionEvaluate. ■ *New in Version 3.*

■ **SelectionCreateCell**

SelectionCreateCell[*notebook*] copies the contents of the current selection in a notebook into a new cell.

SelectionCreateCell[*notebook*, *sel*] sets the current selection after the copy to be as specified by *sel*.

The first argument of SelectionCreateCell is a NotebookObject. ■ If the current selection is a cell group, then SelectionCreateCell will create a new cell group. ■ Possible settings for *sel* are as in NotebookWrite. ■ The default for *sel* is After. ■ SelectionCreateCell[*notebook*, All] sets the current selection to be the whole of the newly created cell. ■ See page 588. ■ See also: SelectionEvaluateCreateCell, NotebookRead, NotebookWrite. ■ *New in Version 3.*

■ **SelectionEvaluate**

SelectionEvaluate[*notebook*] replaces the current selection in a notebook with the result obtained by evaluating the contents of the selection in the kernel.

SelectionEvaluate[*notebook*, *sel*] sets the current selection after the evaluation to be as specified by *sel*.

The first argument of SelectionEvaluate is a NotebookObject. ■ Possible settings for *sel* are as in NotebookWrite. ■ The default for *sel* is After. ■ Unless *sel* is None, the current selection after evaluation is complete will always be as specified by *sel*, even if you moved the selection interactively in the front end during the course of the evaluation. ■ See page 588. ■ See also: SelectionEvaluateCreateCell, NotebookRead, NotebookWrite, ButtonEvaluator, SelectionAnimate. ■ *New in Version 3.*

■ **SelectionEvaluateCreateCell**

SelectionEvaluateCreateCell[*notebook*] takes the current selection in a notebook and creates a new cell containing the result obtained by evaluating the contents of the selection using the kernel.

SelectionEvaluateCreateCell[*notebook*, *sel*] sets the current selection after the evaluation to be as specified by *sel*.

The first argument of SelectionEvaluateCreateCell is a NotebookObject. ■ Possible settings for *sel* are as in NotebookWrite. ■ The default for *sel* is After. ■ SelectionEvaluateCreateCell[*notebook*, All] sets the current selection to be the cell corresponding the result from the evaluation. ■ SelectionEvaluateCreateCell performs the same underlying operation as typing SHIFT-ENTER in the front end. It does not, however, have side effects such as incrementing $Line. ■ See page 588. ■ See also: SelectionEvaluate, SelectionCreateCell, NotebookRead, NotebookWrite. ■ *New in Version 3.*

■ **SelectionMove**

> SelectionMove[*obj*, *dir*, *unit*] moves the current selection in an open notebook in the front end in the direction *dir* by the specified unit.
>
> SelectionMove[*obj*, *dir*, *unit*, *n*] repeats the move *n* times.

The first argument of SelectionMove must be a NotebookObject. ■ Possible direction specifications are:

Next	make the selection be the next unit of the specified type
Previous	make the selection be the previous unit of the specified type
After	make the selection be just after the end of the present unit
Before	make the selection be just before the beginning of the present unit
All	make the selection be the whole of the present unit

■ Possible unit specifications are:

Character	individual character
Word	word or other token
Expression	complete subexpression
TextLine	line of text
CellContents	the contents of the cell
Cell	complete cell
CellGroup	cell group
EvaluationCell	cell associated with the current evaluation
ButtonCell	cell associated with any button that initiated the evaluation
GeneratedCell	cell generated by the current evaluation
Notebook	complete notebook

■ Unless the option setting AutoScroll->False is given, the front end will scroll a notebook so that the result of SelectionMove is visible. ■ The front end will also usually highlight the region corresponding to the result. ■ With direction specifications After and Before, SelectionMove will usually make the current selection be an insertion point between two units of the specified type. ■ SelectionMove returns $Failed if it cannot move the selection in the way you request. ■ The EvaluationCell defines the point after which output from the current evaluation will by default be placed. ■ A GeneratedCell corresponds to an element of the output. ■ See page 582. ■ See also: NotebookSelection, NotebookWrite, NotebookRead. ■ *New in Version 3.*

■ **Sequence**

> Sequence[*expr*₁, *expr*₂, ...] represents a sequence of arguments to be spliced automatically into any function.

Example: f[a, Sequence[b, c]] ⟶ f[a, b, c]. ■ Sequence objects will automatically be flattened out in all functions except those with attribute SequenceHold or HoldAllComplete. ■ See page 258. ■ See also: FlattenAt, BlankSequence, SlotSequence, List, Listable. ■ *New in Version 3.*

■ **SequenceForm**

> SequenceForm[*expr*₁, *expr*₂, ...] prints as the textual concatenation of the printed forms of the *expr*ᵢ.

Expressions printed by SequenceForm have their baselines aligned. ■ SequenceForm acts as a "wrapper", which affects printing, but not evaluation. ■ See page 434. ■ See also: RowBox, ColumnForm, TableForm. ■ *New in Version 1.*

■ SequenceHold

SequenceHold is an attribute which specifies that Sequence objects appearing in the arguments of a function should not automatically be flattened out.

The attribute HoldAllComplete prevents Sequence objects from being flattened out. ■ See pages 329 and 340. ■ See also: HoldAll, HoldAllComplete. ■ *New in Version 3.*

■ Series

Series[f, {x, x_0, n}] generates a power series expansion for f about the point $x = x_0$ to order $(x - x_0)^n$.

Series[f, {x, x_0, n_x}, {y, y_0, n_y}] successively finds series expansions with respect to y, then x.

Series can construct standard Taylor series, as well as certain expansions involving negative powers, fractional powers and logarithms. ■ Series detects certain essential singularities. ■ Series can expand about the point $x = \infty$. ■ Series[f, {x, 0, n}] constructs Taylor series for any function f according to the formula $f(0) + f'(0)x + f''(0)x^2/2 + \ldots f^{(n)}(0)x^n/n!$. ■ Series effectively evaluates partial derivatives using D. It assumes that different variables are independent. ■ The result of Series is usually a SeriesData object, which you can manipulate with other functions. ■ Normal[*series*] truncates a power series and converts it to a normal expression. ■ SeriesCoefficient[*series*, n] finds the coefficient of the nth order term. ■ See page 883. ■ Implementation notes: see page 1071. ■ See also: InverseSeries, ComposeSeries, Limit, Normal, InverseZTransform, RSolve. ■ Related packages: Calculus`Pade`, NumericalMath`Approximations`, NumericalMath`NSeries`. ■ *New in Version 1; modified in Version 3.*

■ SeriesCoefficient

SeriesCoefficient[*series*, n] finds the coefficient of the nth order term in a power series.

SeriesCoefficient[*series*, {n_1, n_2, ... }] finds a coefficient in a multivariate series.

■ See page 889. ■ See also: Coefficient, Normal, CoefficientList, CoefficientArrays. ■ *New in Version 3.*

■ SeriesData

SeriesData[x, x_0, {a_0, a_1, ... }, *nmin*, *nmax*, *den*] represents a power series in the variable x about the point x_0. The a_i are the coefficients in the power series. The powers of $(x-x_0)$ that appear are *nmin/den*, (*nmin*+1)/*den*, ... , *nmax/den*.

SeriesData objects are generated by Series. ■ SeriesData objects are printed as sums of the coefficients a_i, multiplied by powers of $x - x_0$. A SeriesData object representing a power series is printed with O[$x - x_0$]^p added, to represent omitted higher-order terms. ■ When you apply certain mathematical operations to SeriesData objects, new SeriesData objects truncated to the appropriate order are produced. ■ The operations you can perform on SeriesData objects include arithmetic ones, mathematical functions with built-in derivatives, and integration and differentiation. ■ Normal[*expr*] converts a SeriesData object into a normal expression, truncating omitted higher-order terms. ■ If the variable in a SeriesData object is itself a SeriesData object, then the composition of the SeriesData objects is computed. Substituting one series into another series with the same expansion parameter therefore automatically leads to composition of the series. Composition is only possible if the first term of the inner series involves a positive power of the variable. ■ InverseSeries can be applied to SeriesData objects to give series for inverse functions. ■ See page 885. ■ *New in Version 1.*

■ **SessionTime**

`SessionTime[ ]` gives the total number of seconds of real time that have elapsed since the beginning of your *Mathematica* session.

SessionTime starts counting time as soon as your operating system considers your *Mathematica* process to be executing. ■ SessionTime is accurate only down to a granularity of at least `$TimeUnit` seconds. ■ See page 710. ■ See also: `TimeUsed, AbsoluteTime, Date`. ■ *New in Version 2.*

■ **Set**

lhs = *rhs* evaluates *rhs* and assigns the result to be the value of *lhs*. From then on, *lhs* is replaced by *rhs* whenever it appears.

$\{l_1, l_2, \dots \}$ = $\{r_1, r_2, \dots \}$ evaluates the r_i, and assigns the results to be the values of the corresponding l_i.

lhs can be any expression, including a pattern. ■ `f[x_] = x^2` is a typical assignment for a pattern. Notice the presence of _ on the left-hand side, but not the right-hand side. ■ An assignment of the form *f[args]* = *rhs* sets up a transformation rule associated with the symbol *f*. ■ Different rules associated with a particular symbol are usually placed in the order that you give them. If a new rule that you give is determined to be *more specific* than existing rules, it is, however, placed before them. When the rules are used, they are tested in order. ■ New assignments with identical *lhs* overwrite old ones. ■ You can see all the assignments associated with a symbol *f* using `?f` or `Definition[f]`. ■ If you make assignments for functions that have attributes like `Flat` and `Orderless`, you must make sure to set these attributes before you make assignments for the functions. ■ Set has attribute `HoldFirst`. ■ If *lhs* is of the form *f[args]*, then *args* are evaluated. ■ There are some special functions for which an assignment to *s[f[args]]* is automatically associated with *f* rather than *s*. These functions include: `Attributes, Default, Format, MessageName, Messages, N` and `Options`. ■ When it appears in an unevaluated symbolic form, Set is treated as a scoping construct (see Section A.3.8). ■ *lhs* = *rhs* returns *rhs* even if for some reason the assignment specified cannot be performed. ■ Some global variables such as `$RecursionLimit` can only be assigned a certain range or class of values. ■ See pages 311 and 1051. ■ See also: `TagSet, Unset, Clear, HoldPattern, DownValues`. ■ *New in Version 1.*

■ **SetAccuracy**

`SetAccuracy[`*expr*`, `*a*`]` yields a version of *expr* in which all numbers have been set to have accuracy *a*.

When SetAccuracy is used to increase the accuracy of a number, the number is padded with zeros. The zeros are taken to be in base 2. In base 10, the additional digits are usually not zero. ■ SetAccuracy returns an arbitrary-precision number even if the number of significant digits obtained will be less than `$MachinePrecision`. ■ When *expr* contains machine-precision numbers, `SetAccuracy[`*expr*`, `*a*`]` can give results which differ from one computer system to another. ■ SetAccuracy will first expose any hidden extra digits in the internal binary representation of a number, and only after these are exhausted add trailing zeros. ■ `0.004``25` generates a number with all trailing digits zero and accuracy 25 on any computer system. ■ `SetAccuracy[`*expr*`, `*a*`]` does not modify *expr* itself. ■ See page 736. ■ See also: `N, Accuracy, SetPrecision`. ■ *New in Version 2.*

■ **SetAttributes**

`SetAttributes[`*s*`, `*attr*`]` adds *attr* to the list of attributes of the symbol *s*.

SetAttributes modifies `Attributes[`*s*`]`. ■ `SetAttributes[`*s*`, `$\{attr_1, attr_2, \dots \}$`]` sets several attributes at a time. ■ `SetAttributes[`$\{s_1, s_2, \dots \}$`, `*attrs*`]` sets attributes of several symbols at a time. ■ SetAttributes has the attribute `HoldFirst`. ■ See page 328. ■ See also: `ClearAttributes, Protect`. ■ *New in Version 1.*

■ **SetDelayed**

lhs := *rhs* assigns *rhs* to be the delayed value of *lhs*. *rhs* is maintained in an unevaluated form. When *lhs* appears, it is replaced by *rhs*, evaluated afresh each time.

See notes for Set. ■ SetDelayed has attribute HoldAll, rather than HoldFirst. ■ You can make assignments of the form *lhs* := *rhs* /; *test*, where *test* gives conditions for the applicability of each transformation rule. You can make several assignments with the same *lhs* but different forms of *test*. ■ *lhs* := *rhs* returns Null if the assignment specified can be performed, and returns $Failed otherwise. ■ See pages 311 and 1051. ■ See also: TagSetDelayed, Unset, Clear. ■ *New in Version 1.*

■ **SetDirectory**

SetDirectory["*dir*"] sets the current working directory.

SetDirectory sets the current working directory, then returns its full name. ■ SetDirectory prepends the current working directory to the directory stack given by DirectoryStack[ ]. ■ See page 636. ■ See also: ResetDirectory, Directory, DirectoryName, $Path. ■ *New in Version 2.*

■ **SetFileDate**

SetFileDate["*file*"] sets the modification date for a file to be the current date.

SetFileDate["*file*", *date*] sets the modification date to be the specified date. ■ The date must be given in the {*year*, *month*, *day*, *hour*, *minute*, *second*} format used by Date. ■ See page 641. ■ See also: FileDate. ■ Related package: Miscellaneous`Calendar`. ■ *New in Version 2.*

■ **SetOptions**

SetOptions[*s*, *name₁*->*value₁*, *name₂*->*value₂*, ...] sets the specified default options for a symbol *s*.

SetOptions[*stream*, ...] or SetOptions["*name*", ...] sets options associated with a particular stream.

SetOptions[*object*, ...] sets options associated with an external object such as a NotebookObject.

SetOptions is equivalent to an assignment which redefines certain elements of the list Options[*s*] of default options. ■ SetOptions can be used on Protected symbols. ■ SetOptions returns the new form of Options[*s*]. ■ You can use SetOptions on InputStream and OutputStream objects. If there is only one stream with a particular name, you can give the name as a string as the argument of Options. ■ SetOptions can be used on a list of streams, such as the value of $Output. ■ If you use SetOptions[NotebookObject[...], ...] the kernel will send a request to the front end which will immediately make the change specified. ■ See pages 144 and 1040. ■ *New in Version 1; modified in Version 3.*

■ **SetPrecision**

SetPrecision[*expr*, *p*] yields a version of *expr* in which all numbers have been set to have precision *p*.

When SetPrecision is used to increase the precision of a number, the number is padded with zeros. The zeros are taken to be in base 2. In base 10, the additional digits are usually not zero. ■ SetPrecision returns an arbitrary-precision number, even if the precision requested is less than $MachinePrecision. +■ SetPrecision[*expr*, MachinePrecision] converts all numbers in *expr* to machine precision. ■ If *expr* contains machine-precision numbers, SetPrecision[*expr*, *p*] can give results which differ from one computer system to another. ■ SetPrecision will first expose any hidden extra digits in the internal binary representation of a number, and only after these are exhausted add trailing zeros. ■ 0.004`25 generates a number with all trailing digits zero and precision 25 on any computer system. ■ SetPrecision[*expr*, *p*] does not modify *expr* itself. ■ See page 736. ■ See also: N, Precision, Chop, SetAccuracy, $MinPrecision, $NumberMarks. ■ *New in Version 2; modified in Version 5.0.*

■ SetSelectedNotebook

SetSelectedNotebook[*notebook*] makes the specified notebook be the currently selected one in the front end.

SetSelectedNotebook takes a NotebookObject as its argument. ▪ Setting a particular notebook to be the currently selected one typically makes it the top notebook displayed on the screen. ▪ Making a notebook the currently selected one does not affect the current selection within that notebook, or within other notebooks. ▪ See page 591. ▪ See also: SelectedNotebook, Notebooks, WindowClickSelect. ▪ *New in Version 3.*

■ SetStreamPosition

SetStreamPosition[*stream*, *n*] sets the current point in an open stream.

The integer *n* given to SetStreamPosition should usually be a value obtained from StreamPosition. ▪ SetStreamPosition[*stream*, 0] sets the current point to the beginning of a stream. ▪ SetStreamPosition[*stream*, Infinity] sets the current point to the end of a stream. ▪ See page 653. ▪ *New in Version 2.*

■ Shading

Shading is an option for SurfaceGraphics that specifies whether the surfaces should be shaded.

With Shading -> False, the surface will be white all over. So long as Mesh -> True, however, mesh lines will still be drawn. ▪ When Shading -> True, the actual shading used can either be determined by the height, or, when Lighting -> True, from simulated illumination. ▪ See page 151. ▪ See also: HiddenSurface, ClipFill. ▪ *New in Version 1.*

■ Shallow

Shallow[*expr*] prints as a shallow form of *expr*.

Shallow[*expr*, *depth*] prints with all parts of *expr* below the specified depth given in skeleton form.

Shallow[*expr*, {*depth*, *length*}] also gives parts whose lengths are above the specified limit in skeleton form.

Shallow[*expr*, {*depth*, *length*}, *form*] uses skeleton form for any parts which match the pattern *form*.

Omitted sequences of elements are given as Skeleton objects, which print in the form ≪*k*≫. ▪ In StandardForm, the characters used for this output are \[LeftSkeleton] and \[RightSkeleton]. ▪ Depth and length can be specified as Infinity. ▪ Shallow[*expr*] is equivalent to Shallow[*expr*, {4, 10}]. ▪ Shallow acts as a "wrapper", which affects printing, but not evaluation. ▪ Trying to feed ≪*k*≫ as obtained from Shallow back as input to *Mathematica* in StandardForm will generate an error. ▪ See page 431. ▪ See also: Short. ▪ *New in Version 2; modified in Version 3.*

■ Share

Share[*expr*] changes the way *expr* is stored internally, to try and minimize the amount of memory used.

Share[ ] tries to minimize the memory used to store all expressions.

Share works by sharing the storage of common subexpressions between different parts of an expression, or different expressions. ▪ Using Share will never affect the results you get from *Mathematica*. It may, however, reduce the amount of memory used, and in many cases also the amount of time taken. ▪ See page 714. ▪ See also: MemoryInUse, ByteCount. ▪ Related package: Utilities`MemoryConserve`. ▪ *New in Version 1.*

■ Short

Short[*expr*] prints as a short form of *expr*, less than about one line long.

Short[*expr*, *n*] prints as a form of *expr* about *n* lines long.

Short[*expr*] gives a "skeleton form" of *expr*, with omitted sequences of *k* elements indicated by ≪*k*≫. ■ In StandardForm, the characters used for this output are \[LeftSkeleton] and \[RightSkeleton]. ■ Omitted sequences of elements are printed as Skeleton objects. ■ Short prints long strings in skeleton form. ■ The number of lines specified need not be an integer. ■ Short can be used with InputForm and other formats as well as OutputForm. ■ Short acts as a "wrapper", which affects printing, but not evaluation. ■ Trying to feed ≪*k*≫ as obtained from Short back as input to *Mathematica* in StandardForm will generate an error. ■ Short is used to limit the length of output in standard *Mathematica* warning and other messages. ■ See page 431. ■ See also: Shallow, Format. ■ *New in Version 1; modified in Version 3.*

■ Show

Show[*graphics*, *options*] displays two- and three-dimensional graphics, using the options specified.

Show[g_1, g_2, ...] shows several plots combined.

Show can be used with Graphics, Graphics3D, SurfaceGraphics, ContourGraphics, DensityGraphics and GraphicsArray. ■ Options explicitly specified in Show override those included in the graphics expression. ■ When plots are combined, their lists of non-default options are concatenated. ■ Show is effectively the analog of Print for graphics. The option DisplayFunction determines the actual output mechanism used. ■ Functions like Plot automatically apply Show to the graphics expressions they generate. ■ See pages 139 and 487. ■ See also: Plot, etc., and Display. ■ *New in Version 1.*

■ ShowAutoStyles

ShowAutoStyles is an option for Cell which specifies whether styles that are specified to be automatically used for various syntactic and other constructs should be shown.

The default setting is ShowAutoStyles -> True. ■ Details of automatic styles can be specified in the setting for AutoStyleOptions. ■ For example, unmatched delimiters such as brackets are by default shown in purple. ■ See page 613. ■ See also: StyleBox, DelimiterFlashTime, ShowCursorTracker. ■ *New in Version 4.*

■ ShowCellBracket

ShowCellBracket is an option for Cell which specifies whether to display the bracket that indicates the extent of the cell.

ShowCellBracket is often set for styles of cells or whole notebooks instead of individual cells. ■ See page 604. ■ See also: CellFrame, ShowSelection. ■ *New in Version 3.*

■ ShowCellLabel

ShowCellLabel is an option for Cell which specifies whether to display the label for a cell.

ShowCellLabel is more often set for styles of cells than for individual cells. ■ With the setting CellLabelAutoDelete->True, the label for a cell is automatically deleted if the cell is modified. ■ See page 607. ■ See also: CellLabel, ShowCellTags. ■ *New in Version 3.*

■ ShowCellTags

ShowCellTags is an option for Cell which specifies whether to display tags for a cell.

ShowCellTags is more often set for styles of cells than for individual cells. ■ See also: CellTags, ShowCellLabel. ■ *New in Version 3.*

■ ShowCursorTracker

ShowCursorTracker is an option for Cell which specifies whether an elliptical spot should appear momentarily to guide the eye if the cursor position jumps.

The default setting is ShowCursorTracker -> True. ■ Line breaking is normally set up so that small changes to expressions in input cells rarely cause large-scale reformatting; the cursor tracker appears whenever reformatting is required that makes the cursor position jump. ■ The cursor tracker is intended to be sufficiently eye-catching to make the low-level human visual system cause an immediate shift in gaze. ■ See page 613. ■ See also: DelimiterFlashTime, ShowAutoStyles. ■ *New in Version 4.*

■ ShowPageBreaks

ShowPageBreaks is an option for Notebook which specifies whether to indicate in the on-screen display of a notebook where page breaks would occur if the notebook were printed.

ShowPageBreaks is often set using a menu item in the notebook front end. ■ See also: PageBreakWithin, ScreenStyleEnvironment. ■ *New in Version 3.*

■ ShowSelection

ShowSelection is an option for Cell which specifies whether to show the current selection highlighted.

ShowSelection is often set for styles of cells or whole notebooks instead of individual cells. ■ Settings for ShowSelection affect only how the selection is displayed, not where it is or how it works. ■ Setting ShowSelection->False is convenient if you want notebook operations to be performed invisibly. ■ See page 619. ■ See also: Selectable. ■ *New in Version 4.*

■ ShowSpecialCharacters

ShowSpecialCharacters is an option for Cell which specifies whether to replace \[*Name*], \:*nnnn*, etc. by explicit special characters.

With ShowSpecialCharacters->False special characters are always displayed by name when possible. ■ ShowSpecialCharacters is more often set at the level of styles or notebooks than at the level of individual cells. ■ See also: ShowStringCharacters, CharacterEncoding. ■ *New in Version 3.*

■ ShowStringCharacters

ShowStringCharacters is an option for Cell which specifies whether to display " when a string is entered.

ShowStringCharacters is typically set to False for output cells and True for input cells. ■ ShowStringCharacters is usually set at the level of styles or notebooks rather than at the level of individual cells. ■ See also: ShowSpecialCharacters. ■ *New in Version 3.*

■ Sign

Sign[x] gives -1, 0 or 1 depending on whether x is negative, zero, or positive.

For non-zero complex numbers z, Sign[z] is defined as z/Abs[z]. ■ Sign tries simple transformations in trying to determine the sign of symbolic expressions. ■ For exact numeric quantities, Sign internally uses numerical approximations to establish its result. This process can be affected by the setting of the global variable $MaxExtraPrecision. ■ See page 745. ■ See also: Abs, UnitStep, Positive, Negative, NonNegative, Greater, Simplify, Assumptions. ■ *New in Version 1; modified in Version 3.*

■ **Signature**

> Signature[*list*] gives the signature of the permutation needed to place the elements of *list* in canonical order.
>
> Examples: Signature[{a,b,c}] ⟶ 1; Signature[{a,c,b}] ⟶ -1. ■ The signature of the permutation is $(-1)^n$, where n is the number of transpositions of pairs of elements that must be composed to build up the permutation. ■ If any two elements of *list* are the same, Signature[*list*] gives 0. ■ See pages 757 and 920. ■ See also: Order, Sort, Cross, Minors, Det, KroneckerDelta. ■ Related package: DiscreteMath`Combinatorica`. ■ *New in Version 1.*

■ **SignPadding**

> SignPadding is an option for NumberForm and related functions which specifies whether padding should be inserted after signs.
>
> SignPadding -> True specifies that any padding that is needed should be inserted between the sign and the digits in a number. ■ SignPadding -> False specifies that the padding should be inserted before the sign. ■ See page 436. ■ See also: NumberPadding. ■ *New in Version 2.*

■ **Simplify**

> ~ Simplify[*expr*] performs a sequence of algebraic and other transformations on *expr*, and returns the simplest form it finds.
>
> Simplify[*expr*, *assum*] does simplification using assumptions.
>
> Simplify tries expanding, factoring and doing many other transformations on expressions, keeping track of the simplest form obtained. ~■ The following options can be given:

Assumptions	$Assumptions	default assumptions to append to *assum*
ComplexityFunction	Automatic	how to assess the complexity of each form generated
TimeConstraint	300	for how many seconds to try doing any particular transformation
TransformationFunctions	Automatic	functions to try in transforming the expression
Trig	True	whether to do trigonometric as well as algebraic transformations

> ■ Assumptions can consist of equations, inequalities, domain specifications such as $x \in$ Integers, and logical combinations of these. ■ Example: Simplify[Sqrt[x^2], x ∈ Reals] ⟶ Abs[x]. ■ Simplify can be used on equations, inequalities and domain specifications. ■ Example: Simplify[x^2 > 3, x > 2] ⟶ True. ~■ Quantities that appear algebraically in inequalities are always assumed to be real. ■ Example: Simplify[x ∈ Reals, x > 0] ⟶ True. ■ FullSimplify does more extensive simplification than Simplify. +■ You can specify default assumptions for Simplify using Assuming. ■ See pages 68, 72 and 813. ■ Implementation notes: see page 1070. ■ See also: FullSimplify, Refine, Factor, Expand, TrigExpand, PowerExpand, ComplexExpand, Element, FunctionExpand, Reduce, Assuming. ■ *New in Version 1; modified in Version 5.0.*

■ **Sin**

> Sin[*z*] gives the sine of *z*.
>
> Mathematical function (see Section A.3.10). ■ The argument of Sin is assumed to be in radians. (Multiply by Degree to convert from degrees.) ■ Sin is automatically evaluated when its argument is a simple rational multiple of π; for more complicated rational multiples, FunctionExpand can sometimes be used. ■ See page 761. ■ See also: ArcSin, Csc, TrigToExp, TrigExpand. ■ *New in Version 1.*

■ SingleLetterItalics

SingleLetterItalics is an option for Cell which specifies whether single-letter names should be displayed in italics.

SingleLetterItalics->True is typically set for cells that contain TraditionalForm expressions. ■ See page 613.
■ See also: AutoItalicWords, StyleBox. ■ *New in Version 3.*

⁺■ SingularValueDecomposition

SingularValueDecomposition[*m*] gives the singular value decomposition for a numerical matrix *m*. The result is a list of matrices {*u*, *w*, *v*}, where *w* is a diagonal matrix, and *m* can be written as *u* . *w* . Conjugate[Transpose[*v*]].

SingularValueDecomposition[{*m*, *a*}] gives the generalized singular value decomposition of *m* with respect to *a*.

SingularValueDecomposition[*m*, *k*] gives the singular value decomposition associated with the *k* largest singular values of *m*.

The matrix *m* may be rectangular. ■ The diagonal elements of *w* are the singular values of *m*.
■ SingularValueDecomposition sets to zero any singular values that would be dropped by SingularValueList.
■ The option Tolerance can be used as in SingularValueList to determine which singular values will be considered to be zero. ■ *u* and *v* are column orthonormal matrices, whose transposes can be considered as lists of orthonormal vectors. ■ SingularValueDecomposition[{*m*, *a*}] gives a list of matrices {{*u*, *ua*}, {*w*, *wa*}, *v*} such that *m* can be written as *u* . *w* . Conjugate[Transpose[*v*]] and *a* can be written as *ua* . *wa* . Conjugate[Transpose[*v*]]. ■ See page 914. ■ Implementation notes: see page 1069. ■ See also: SingularValueList, Norm, PseudoInverse, QRDecomposition. ■ Related packages: Statistics`LinearRegression`. ■ *New in Version 5.0.*

⁺■ SingularValueList

SingularValueList[*m*] gives a list of the non-zero singular values of a numerical matrix *m*.

SingularValueList[{*m*, *a*}] gives the generalized singular values of *m* with respect to *a*.

SingularValueList[*m*, *k*] gives the *k* largest singular values of *m*.

Singular values are sorted from largest to smallest. ■ Repeated singular values appear with their appropriate multiplicity. ■ By default, singular values are kept only when they are larger than 100 times 10^{-p}, where *p* is Precision[*m*]. ■ SingularValueList[*m*, Tolerance->*t*] keeps only singular values that are at least *t* times the largest singular value. ■ SingularValueList[*m*, Tolerance->0] returns all singular values. ■ The matrix *m* can be rectangular; the total number of singular values is always Min[Dimensions[*m*]]. ■ The singular values can be obtained from Sqrt[Eigenvalues[Conjugate[Transpose[*m*]] . *m*]]. ■ See page 913. ■ See also: SingularValueDecomposition, Norm, PseudoInverse, Eigenvalues, QRDecomposition, SchurDecomposition.
■ Related packages: Statistics`LinearRegression`. ■ *New in Version 5.0.*

■ Sinh

Sinh[*z*] gives the hyperbolic sine of *z*.

Mathematical function (see Section A.3.10). ■ See page 761. ■ See also: ArcSinh, Csch, TrigToExp, TrigExpand.
■ *New in Version 1.*

■ SinhIntegral

SinhIntegral[z] gives the hyperbolic sine integral function Shi(z).

Mathematical function (see Section A.3.10). ■ Shi(z) = $\int_0^z \sinh(t)/t\,dt$. ■ SinhIntegral[z] is an entire function of z with no branch cut discontinuities. ■ See page 774. ■ See also: CoshIntegral. ■ *New in Version 3.*

■ SinIntegral

SinIntegral[z] gives the sine integral function Si(z).

Mathematical function (see Section A.3.10). ■ Si(z) = $\int_0^z \sin(t)/t\,dt$. ■ SinIntegral[z] is an entire function of z with no branch cut discontinuities. ■ See page 774. ■ See also: CosIntegral, ExpIntegralE, ExpIntegralEi, FresnelS. ■ *New in Version 2.*

■ SixJSymbol

SixJSymbol[{j_1, j_2, j_3}, {j_4, j_5, j_6}] gives the values of the Racah 6-j symbol.

The 6-j symbols vanish except when certain triples of the j_i satisfy triangle inequalities. ■ The parameters of SixJSymbol can be integers, half-integers or symbolic expressions. ■ See page 760. ■ See also: ThreeJSymbol, ClebschGordan. ■ *New in Version 2.*

■ Skeleton

Skeleton[n] represents a sequence of n omitted elements in an expression printed with Short or Shallow.

The standard print form for Skeleton is ≪n≫.

In StandardForm, Skeleton is by default printed using \[LeftSkeleton] and \[RightSkeleton] characters. ■ You can reset the print form of Skeleton. ■ ≪n≫ indicates the presence of missing information, and so generates an error if you try to interpret it as *Mathematica* kernel input. ■ See also: Short, StringSkeleton, Shallow, TotalWidth. ■ *New in Version 1; modified in Version 3.*

■ Skip

Skip[*stream*, *type*] skips one object of the specified type in an input stream.

Skip[*stream*, *type*, n] skips n objects of the specified type.

Skip behaves like Read, except that it returns Null when it succeeds in skipping the specified objects, and $Failed otherwise. ■ See notes for Read. ■ See page 649. ■ See also: SetStreamPosition, Find. ■ *New in Version 2.*

■ Slot

represents the first argument supplied to a pure function.

#n represents the nth argument.

is used to represent arguments or formal parameters in pure functions of the form *body*& or Function[*body*]. ■ # is equivalent to Slot[1]. ■ #n is equivalent to Slot[n]. n must be a non-negative integer. ■ #0 gives the head of the function, i.e., the pure function itself. ■ See page 249. ■ *New in Version 1.*

■ SlotSequence

represents the sequence of arguments supplied to a pure function.

##n represents the sequence of arguments supplied to a pure function, starting with the nth argument.

is used to represent sequences of arguments in pure functions of the form *body*& or Function[*body*]. ■ ## is equivalent to SlotSequence[ ] or SlotSequence[1]. ■ ##n is equivalent to SlotSequence[n]. n must be a positive integer. ■ A sequence of arguments supplied to a pure function is "spliced" into the body of the function wherever ## and so on appear. ■ See page 249. ■ See also: Sequence. ■ *New in Version 1.*

■ Solve

Solve[*eqns*, *vars*] attempts to solve an equation or set of equations for the variables *vars*.

Solve[*eqns*, *vars*, *elims*] attempts to solve the equations for *vars*, eliminating the variables *elims*.

Equations are given in the form *lhs* == *rhs*. ■ Simultaneous equations can be combined either in a list or with &&. ■ A single variable or a list of variables can be specified. ■ Solve[*eqns*] tries to solve for all variables in *eqns*. ■ Example: Solve[3 x + 9 == 0, x]. ■ Solve gives solutions in terms of rules of the form $x \rightarrow sol$. ■ When there are several variables, the solution is given in terms of lists of rules: {$x \rightarrow s_x$, $y \rightarrow s_y$, ... }. ■ When there are several solutions, Solve gives a list of them. ■ When a particular root has multiplicity greater than one, Solve gives several copies of the corresponding solution. ■ Solve deals primarily with linear and polynomial equations. ■ The option InverseFunctions specifies whether Solve should use inverse functions to try and find solutions to more general equations. The default is InverseFunctions->Automatic. In this case, Solve can use inverse functions, but prints a warning message. See notes on InverseFunctions. ■ Solve gives generic solutions only. It discards solutions that are valid only when the parameters satisfy special conditions. Reduce gives the complete set of solutions. ■ Solve will not always be able to get explicit solutions to equations. It will give the explicit solutions it can, then give a symbolic representation of the remaining solutions in terms of Root objects. If there are sufficiently few symbolic parameters, you can then use N to get numerical approximations to the solutions. ■ Solve gives {} if there are no possible solutions to the equations. +■ Solve gives {{}} if all variables can have all possible values. ■ Solve[*eqns*, ... , Mode->Modular] solves equations with equality required only modulo an integer. You can specify a particular modulus to use by including the equation Modulus==p. If you do not include such an equation, Solve will attempt to solve for the possible moduli. ■ Solve uses special efficient techniques for handling sparse systems of linear equations with approximate numerical coefficients. ■ See page 829. ■ Implementation notes: see page 1070. ■ See also: Reduce, FindInstance, Eliminate, SolveAlways, Roots, NSolve, FindRoot, LinearSolve, RowReduce, GroebnerBasis, DSolve, Root, RSolve. ■ Related packages: Algebra`RootIsolation`, Graphics`ImplicitPlot`, Algebra`AlgebraicInequalities`. ■ *New in Version 1; modified in Version 3.*

■ SolveAlways

SolveAlways[*eqns*, *vars*] gives the values of parameters that make the equations *eqns* valid for all values of the variables *vars*.

Equations are given in the form *lhs* == *rhs*. ■ Simultaneous equations can be combined either in a list or with &&. ■ A single variable or a list of variables can be specified. ■ Example: SolveAlways[a x + b == 0, x] $\longrightarrow$ {{a $\rightarrow$ 0, b $\rightarrow$ 0}}. ■ SolveAlways works primarily with linear and polynomial equations. ■ SolveAlways produces relations between parameters that appear in *eqns*, but are not in the list of variables *vars*. ■ SolveAlways[*eqns*, *vars*] is equivalent to Solve[!Eliminate[!*eqns*, *vars*]]. ■ See page 833. ■ See also: Eliminate, Solve, Reduce, PolynomialReduce, ForAll. ■ *New in Version 1.*

■ **Sort**

Sort[*list*] sorts the elements of *list* into canonical order.

Sort[*list*, *p*] sorts using the ordering function *p*.

Example: Sort[{b, c, a}] ⟶ {a, b, c}. ■ The canonical ordering used by *Mathematica* is described on page 1043. ■ Sort[*list*, *p*] applies the function *p* to pairs of elements in *list* to determine whether they are in order. The default function *p* is OrderedQ[{#1, #2}]&. ■ Example: Sort[{4, 1, 3}, Greater] ⟶ {4, 3, 1}. ■ Sort can be used on expressions with any head, not only List. ■ See pages 127, 129 and 254. ■ See also: Ordering, Order, OrderedQ, Orderless, Median, Quantile. ■ *New in Version 1.*

■ **Sound**

Sound[*primitives*] represents a sound.

Any number of sound primitives or lists of sound primitives can be given. They are played in sequence. ■ Sound can be played using Show. ■ The following primitives can be used:

SampledSoundFunction[*f*, *n*, *r*]	amplitude levels generated by a function
SampledSoundList[{a_1, a_2, ... }, *r*]	amplitude levels given in a list

■ The standard print form for Sound[...] is -Sound-. InputForm prints the explicit list of primitives. ■ See page 565. ■ Related packages: Miscellaneous`Audio`, Miscellaneous`Music`. ■ *New in Version 2.*

⁺■ **Sow**

Sow[*e*] specifies that *e* should be collected by the nearest enclosing Reap.

Sow[*e*, *tag*] specifies that *e* should be collected by the nearest enclosing Reap whose pattern matches *tag*.

Sow[*e*, {tag_1, tag_2, ... }] specifies that *e* should be collected once for each pattern that matches a tag_i.

Sow[*e*, ...] returns *e*. ■ By having several identical tag_i, a single expression can be made to appear multiple times in a list returned by Reap. ■ Sow[*e*] is equivalent to Sow[*e*, None]. ■ Sow[*e*, {{*tag*}}] sows an expression with tag {*tag*}. ■ See page 355. ■ See also: Reap, Throw, AppendTo, EvaluationMonitor, StepMonitor, Scan. ■ *New in Version 5.0.*

⁺■ **SparseArray**

SparseArray[{pos_1->val_1, pos_2->val_2, ... }] yields a sparse array in which values val_i appear at positions pos_i.

SparseArray[{pos_1, pos_2, ... }->{val_1, val_2, ... }] yields the same sparse array.

SparseArray[*list*] yields a sparse array version of *list*.

SparseArray[*data*, {d_1, d_2, ... }] yields a sparse array representing a $d_1 \times d_2 \times ...$ array.

SparseArray[*data*, *dims*, *val*] yields a sparse array in which unspecified elements are taken to have value *val*.

(continued)

⁺■ **SparseArray** *(continued)*

■ By default, SparseArray takes unspecified elements to be 0. ■ SparseArray[*data*, ...] is always converted to an optimized standard form with structure SparseArray[Automatic, *dims*, *val*, ...]. ■ Normal[SparseArray[...]] gives the ordinary array corresponding to a sparse array object. ■ ArrayRules[SparseArray[...]] gives the list of rules {*pos*₁->*val*₁, *pos*₂->*val*₂, ... }. ■ The elements in SparseArray need not be numeric. ■ The position specifications pos_i can contain patterns. ■ Example: SparseArray[{{i_, i_}->1}, {*d*, *d*}] gives a $d \times d$ identity matrix. ■ With rules pos_i :> val_i the val_i are evaluated separately for each set of indices that match pos_i. ■ SparseArray[*list*] requires that *list* be a full array, with all parts at a particular level being lists of the same length. ■ The individual elements of a sparse array cannot themselves be lists. ■ SparseArray[*rules*] yields a sparse array with dimensions exactly large enough to include elements whose positions have been explicitly specified. ■ SparseArray[*rules*, Automatic, *val*] takes unspecified elements to have value *val*. ■ List and matrix operations are typically set up to work as they do on Normal[SparseArray[...]]. ■ Functions with attribute Listable are automatically threaded over the individual elements of the ordinary arrays represented by SparseArray objects. ■ Part extracts specified parts of the array represented by a SparseArray object, rather than parts of the SparseArray expression itself. ■ Functions like Map are automatically applied to components in a SparseArray object. ■ SparseArray is treated as a raw object by functions like AtomQ, and for purposes of pattern matching. ■ Dimensions gives the dimensions of a sparse array. ■ The standard output format for a sparse array specified by *n* rules is SparseArray[<n>, *dims*]. ■ See page 295. ■ Implementation notes: see page 1069. ■ See also: ArrayRules, Normal, Replace. ■ *New in Version 5.0.*

■ **SpellingCorrection**

SpellingCorrection is an option for StringMatchQ, Names and related functions which specifies whether strings should be considered to match even when a small fraction of the characters in them are different.

The default setting SpellingCorrection -> False requires exact matching. ■ ?*name* effectively uses SpellingCorrection -> True when it cannot find an exact match for *name*. ■ See page 412. ■ See also: IgnoreCase. ■ *New in Version 2.*

■ **SphericalHarmonicY**

SphericalHarmonicY[*l*, *m*, θ, ϕ] gives the spherical harmonic $Y_l^m(\theta, \phi)$.

Mathematical function (see Section A.3.10). ■ The spherical harmonics are orthogonal with respect to integration over the surface of the unit sphere. ■ For $l \geq 0$, $Y_l^m(\theta, \phi) = \sqrt{(2l+1)/(4\pi)}\sqrt{(l-m)!/(l+m)!}P_l^m(\cos(\theta))e^{im\phi}$ where P_l^m is the associated Legendre function. ■ For $l \leq -1$, $Y_l^m(\theta, \phi) = Y_{-(l+1)}^m(\theta, \phi)$. ■ See page 766. ■ See also: LegendreP, ClebschGordan. ■ *New in Version 1.*

■ **SphericalRegion**

SphericalRegion is an option for three-dimensional graphics functions which specifies whether the final image should be scaled so that a sphere drawn around the three-dimensional bounding box would fit in the display area specified.

SphericalRegion -> False scales three-dimensional images to be as large as possible, given the display area specified. ■ SphericalRegion -> True scales three-dimensional images so that a sphere drawn around the three-dimensional bounding box always fits in the display area specified. ■ The center of the sphere is taken to be at the center of the bounding box. The radius of the sphere is chosen so that the bounding box just fits within the sphere. ■ With SphericalRegion -> True, the image of a particular object remains consistent in size, regardless of the orientation of the object. ■ SphericalRegion -> True overrides any setting given for ViewCenter. ■ See page 536. ■ See also: PlotRegion, ViewPoint. ■ *New in Version 2.*

■ Splice

Splice["*file*"**]** splices *Mathematica* output into an external file. It takes text enclosed between **<*** and ***>** in the file, evaluates the text as *Mathematica* input, and replaces the text with the resulting *Mathematica* output.

Splice["*infile*", "*outfile*"] processes text from the file *infile*, and writes output into *outfile*. ∎ Splice["*file*"] takes files with names of the form *name*.m*x* and writes output in files with names *name*.*x*. ∎ Text in the input file not enclosed between <* and *> is copied without change to the output file. ∎ The default format for *Mathematica* output is determined by the extension of the input file name:

name.mc	CForm
name.mf	FortranForm
name.mtex	TeXForm

∎ The following options for Splice can be used:

Delimiters	{"<*", "*>"}	delimiters to search for
FormatType	Automatic	default format for *Mathematica* output
PageWidth	78	number of character widths per output line

∎ You can use pipes instead of files for input and output to Splice. ∎ See page 214. ∎ See also: RunThrough. ∎ *New in Version 1.*

■ Split

Split[*list***]** splits *list* into sublists consisting of runs of identical elements.

Split[*list***,** *test***]** treats pairs of adjacent elements as identical whenever applying the function *test* to them yields True.

Example: Split[{a, a, b, b, a, a, b}] ⟶ {{a, a}, {b, b}, {a, a}, {b}}. ∎ The default function used to test whether elements are identical is SameQ. ∎ Split can be used to perform run-length encoding. ∎ See page 292. ∎ See also: Partition, Union, Flatten, ReplaceList. ∎ *New in Version 3.*

■ Sqrt

Sqrt[*z***]** or **$\sqrt{z}$** gives the square root of *z*.

Mathematical function (see Section A.3.10). ∎ $\sqrt{z}$ can be entered using [CTRL]2 *z* [CTRL]_ or \(\@z\). ∎ Sqrt[*z*] is converted to *z*^(1/2). ∎ Sqrt[*z*^2] is not automatically converted to *z*. ∎ Sqrt[*a b*] is not automatically converted to Sqrt[*a*] Sqrt[*b*]. ∎ These conversions can be done using PowerExpand, but will typically be correct only for positive real arguments. ∎ In StandardForm, Sqrt[*z*] is printed as $\sqrt{z}$. ∎ $\sqrt{}$ *z* can also be used for input. The $\sqrt{}$ character is entered as :sqrt: or \[Sqrt]. ∎ See page 31. ∎ See also: Power, PowerExpand, SqrtBox. ∎ *New in Version 1; modified in Version 3.*

■ SqrtBox

SqrtBox[*x***]** represents **$\sqrt{x}$** in input and output.

Inside \(... \) SqrtBox[*x*] can be input as \@ *x*. ∎ In a notebook a SqrtBox can be created using [CTRL]2 or [CTRL]@. [CTRL]_ moves out from under the square root sign. ∎ In StandardForm and InputForm, SqrtBox[*x*] is interpreted on input as Sqrt[*x*]. ∎ The baseline of SqrtBox[*x*] is taken to be the baseline of *x*. ∎ If SqrtBox[*x*] does not fit on a single line, it is output as *x*^(1/2). ∎ In StandardForm, explicit SqrtBox objects are output literally. You can use DisplayForm to see the display form of such objects. ∎ See page 445. ∎ See also: RadicalBox, OverscriptBox. ∎ *New in Version 3.*

■ Stack

Stack[ ] shows the current evaluation stack, giving a list of the tags associated with evaluations that are currently being done.

Stack[*pattern*] gives a list of expressions currently being evaluated which match the pattern.

Stack[_] shows all expressions currently being evaluated. ■ You can call Stack from inside a dialog to see how the dialog was reached. ■ In the list returned by Stack[*pattern*], each expression is wrapped with HoldForm. ■ The maximum length of Stack[ ] is limited by $RecursionLimit. ■ Stack has attribute HoldFirst. ■ See page 367. ■ See also: Trace. ■ *New in Version 2.*

■ StackBegin

StackBegin[*expr*] evaluates *expr*, starting a fresh evaluation stack.

You can use StackBegin to prevent "outer" evaluations from appearing in the evaluation stack when you call Stack. ■ StackBegin has attribute HoldFirst. ■ A StackBegin is automatically done when the evaluation of each input line begins in an interactive *Mathematica* session. ■ See page 368. ■ See also: StackInhibit. ■ *New in Version 2.*

■ StackComplete

StackComplete[*expr*] evaluates *expr* with intermediate expressions in evaluation chains included on the stack.

Mathematica normally includes only the latest expression on each evaluation chain involved in the evaluation of a particular expression. Inside StackComplete, however, all preceding expressions on the evaluation chains are included. ■ StackComplete typically increases significantly the number of expressions kept on the evaluation stack. ■ See page 368. ■ See also: TraceBackward, TraceAbove. ■ *New in Version 2.*

■ StackInhibit

StackInhibit[*expr*] evaluates *expr* without modifying the evaluation stack.

You can use StackInhibit to prevent "innermost" evaluations from appearing in the evaluation stack when you look at it with Stack. ■ StackInhibit has attribute HoldFirst. ■ See page 368. ■ See also: StackBegin. ■ *New in Version 2.*

+ ■ StandardDeviation

StandardDeviation[*list*] gives the standard deviation of the elements in *list*.

StandardDeviation[*list*] is equivalent to Sqrt[Variance[*list*]]. ■ StandardDeviation handles both numerical and symbolic data. ■ StandardDeviation[{{x_1, y_1, ... }, {x_2, y_2, ... }, ... }] gives {StandardDeviation[{x_1, x_2, ... }], StandardDeviation[{y_1, y_2, ... }]}. ■ StandardDeviation works with SparseArray objects. ■ See pages 794 and 924. ■ See also: Variance, Mean, Quantile. ■ Related packages: Statistics`DescriptiveStatistics`, Statistics`MultiDescriptiveStatistics`. ■ *New in Version 5.0.*

■ StandardForm

StandardForm[*expr*] prints as the standard *Mathematica* two-dimensional representation of *expr*.

StandardForm generates output that gives a unique and unambiguous representation of *Mathematica* expressions, suitable for use as input. ■ StandardForm incorporates many aspects of traditional mathematical notation. ■ StandardForm is the standard format type used for both input and output of *Mathematica* expressions in notebooks. ■ StandardForm can be edited in the notebook front end. ■ StandardForm uses special characters as well as ordinary keyboard characters. ■ StandardForm is based on boxes. ■ The notebook front end contains menu items for conversion to and from StandardForm. ■ See page 424. ■ See also: TraditionalForm, OutputForm, InputForm, MakeExpression, ToBoxes. ■ *New in Version 3.*

■ StepMonitor

StepMonitor is an option for iterative numerical computation functions that gives an expression to evaluate whenever a step is taken by the numerical method used.

The option setting is normally given as StepMonitor :> *expr*. ■ The :> is used instead of -> to avoid *expr* being immediately evaluated. ■ Whenever *expr* is evaluated, all variables in the numerical computation are assigned their current values. ■ Block[{var_1 = val_1, ... }, *expr*] is effectively used. ■ See page 977. ■ See also: EvaluationMonitor, Sow, Print. ■ *New in Version 5.0.*

■ StieltjesGamma

StieltjesGamma[n] gives the Stieltjes constant γ_n.

Mathematical function (see Section A.3.10). ■ $\gamma_n/n!$ is the coefficient of $(1-s)^n$ in the Laurent expansion of $\zeta(s)$ about the point $s = 1$. ■ The γ_n are generalizations of Euler's constant; $\gamma = \gamma_0$. ■ See page 772. ■ Implementation notes: see page 1068. ■ See also: Zeta, EulerGamma. ■ *New in Version 3.*

■ StirlingS1

StirlingS1[n, m] gives the Stirling number of the first kind $S_n^{(m)}$.

Integer mathematical function (see Section A.3.10). ■ $(-1)^{n-m}S_n^{(m)}$ gives the number of permutations of n elements which contain exactly m cycles. ■ See page 757. ■ See also: StirlingS2. ■ *New in Version 1.*

■ StirlingS2

StirlingS2[n, m] gives the Stirling number of the second kind $S_n^{(m)}$.

Integer mathematical function (see Section A.3.10). ■ $S_n^{(m)}$ gives the number of ways of partitioning a set of n elements into m non-empty subsets. ■ See page 757. ■ See also: StirlingS1. ■ *New in Version 1.*

■ StreamPosition

StreamPosition[*stream*] returns an integer which specifies the position of the current point in an open stream.

On most computer systems, the integer returned by StreamPosition gives the position counting from the beginning of the file in bytes. ■ See page 653. ■ See also: SetStreamPosition. ■ *New in Version 2.*

■ Streams

Streams[ ] gives a list of all streams that are currently open.

Streams["*name*"] lists only streams with the specified name.

The list returned by Streams can contain InputStream and OutputStream objects. ■ See page 705. ■ See also: Links, OpenRead, OpenWrite, $Input, Options, SetOptions. ■ *New in Version 2.*

■ String

String is the head of a character string "*text*".

Strings can contain any sequence of ordinary or special characters. ■ *x*_String can be used as a pattern that represents a string. ■ String is used as a tag to indicate strings in Read, terminated by RecordSeparators characters. ■ In InputForm, special characters in strings are given as \[*Name*] or \:*code*. ■ Except when they are enclosed between \< and \>, newlines and any tabs which follow them are ignored when strings are input. ■ See page 406. ■ See also: ToExpression, ToString, SyntaxQ, Characters. ■ *New in Version 1; modified in Version 3.*

■ StringDrop

StringDrop["*string*", *n*] gives "*string*" with its first *n* characters dropped.

StringDrop["*string*", -*n*] gives "*string*" with its last *n* characters dropped.

StringDrop["*string*", {*n*}] gives "*string*" with its *n*th character dropped.

StringDrop["*string*", {*m*, *n*}] gives "*string*" with characters *m* through *n* dropped.

StringDrop uses the standard *sequence specification* (see page 1040). ■ Example:
StringDrop["abcdefgh", 2] ⟶ cdefgh. ■ StringDrop["*string*", {*m*, *n*, *s*}] drops characters *m* through *n* in steps of *s*. ■ See page 407. ■ See also: Drop, StringTake, StringPosition, StringReplacePart. ■ *New in Version 2; modified in Version 4.*

■ StringForm

StringForm["*controlstring*", *expr*₁, ...] prints as the text of the *controlstring*, with the printed forms of the *expr*ᵢ embedded.

`` `i` `` in the control string indicates a point at which to print *expr*ᵢ. ■ `` `` `` includes the next *expr*ᵢ not yet printed. +■ `` `.` `` prints a raw `` ` `` in the output string. ■ StringForm acts as a "wrapper", which affects printing, but not evaluation. ■ You can use StringForm to set up "formatted output". ■ Messages given as values for objects of the form *s*::*t* are used as control strings for StringForm. ■ See page 433. ■ See also: SequenceForm, ToString, Message. ■ *New in Version 1; modified in Version 5.0.*

■ StringInsert

StringInsert["*string*", "*snew*", *n*] yields a string with "*snew*" inserted starting at position *n* in "*string*".

StringInsert["*string*", "*snew*", -*n*] inserts at position *n* from the end of "*string*".

StringInsert["*string*", "*snew*", {*n*₁, *n*₂, ... }] inserts a copy of "*snew*" at each of the positions *n*ᵢ.

Example: StringInsert["abcdefg", "XYZ", 2] ⟶ aXYZbcdefg. ■ StringInsert["*string*", "*snew*", *n*] makes the first character of *snew* the *n*th character in the new string. ■ StringInsert["*string*", "*snew*", -*n*] makes the last character of *snew* the *n*th character from the end of the new string. ■ In StringInsert["*string*", "*snew*", {*n*₁, *n*₂, ... }] the *n*ᵢ are taken to refer to positions in "*string*" before any insertion is done. ■ See page 408. ■ See also: StringReplacePart, Insert, StringPosition. ■ *New in Version 2; modified in Version 3.*

■ StringJoin

"*s*₁" <> "*s*₂" <> ... , StringJoin["*s*₁", "*s*₂", ...] or StringJoin[{"*s*₁", "*s*₂", ... }] yields a string consisting of a concatenation of the *s*ᵢ.

Example: "the" <> " " <> "cat" ⟶ the cat. ■ StringJoin has attribute Flat. ■ When arguments are not strings, StringJoin is left in symbolic form. ■ See pages 407 and 412. ■ See also: Join, Characters, StringInsert, StringReplacePart. ■ *New in Version 1.*

■ StringLength

StringLength["*string*"] gives the number of characters in a string.

Example: StringLength["tiger"] ⟶ 5. ■ StringLength counts special characters such as α as single characters, even if their full names involve many characters. ■ See page 407. ■ See also: Length, Characters. ■ *New in Version 1; modified in Version 3.*

■ **StringMatchQ**

StringMatchQ["*string*", "*pattern*"] yields True if *string* matches the specified string pattern, and yields False otherwise.

The pattern string can contain literal characters, together with the metacharacters * and @ specified on page 1044. ■ Example: StringMatchQ["apppbb", "a*b"] ⟶ True. ■ Setting the option IgnoreCase -> True makes StringMatchQ treat lower- and upper-case letters as equivalent. ■ Setting the option SpellingCorrection -> True makes StringMatchQ allow strings to match even if a small fraction of their characters are different. ■ See page 411. ■ See also: StringPosition, Equal, Names, MatchQ. ■ *New in Version 1.*

■ **StringPosition**

StringPosition["*string*", "*sub*"] gives a list of the starting and ending character positions at which "*sub*" appears as a substring of "*string*".

StringPosition["*string*", "*sub*", k] includes only the first k occurrences of "*sub*".

StringPosition["*string*", {"*sub$_1$*", "*sub$_2$*", ... }] gives positions of all the "*sub$_i$*".

Example: StringPosition["abbaabbaa", "bb"] ⟶ {{2, 3}, {6, 7}}. ■ With the default option setting Overlaps -> True, StringPosition includes substrings that overlap. With the setting Overlaps -> False such substrings are excluded. ■ Setting the option IgnoreCase -> True makes StringPosition treat lower- and upper-case letters as equivalent. ■ Example: StringPosition["abAB", "a", IgnoreCase -> True] ⟶ {{1, 1}, {3, 3}}. ■ StringPosition returns sequence specifications in the form used by StringTake, StringDrop and StringReplacePart. ■ See page 409. ■ See also: Position, Characters, FindList, ReplaceList. ■ *New in Version 2.*

■ **StringReplace**

StringReplace["*string*", "s_1" -> "sp_1"] or
StringReplace["*string*", {"s_1" -> "sp_1", "s_2" -> "sp_2", ... }] replaces the "s_i" by "sp_i" whenever they appear as substrings of "*string*".

StringReplace goes through a string, testing substrings that start at each successive character position. On each substring, it tries in turn each of the transformation rules you have specified. If any of the rules apply, it replaces the substring, then continues to go through the string, starting at the character position after the end of the substring. ■ Delayed replacements of the form "s" :> *expr* can be given, so long as *expr* evaluates to a string every time the replacement is used. ■ Setting the option IgnoreCase -> True makes StringReplace treat lower- and upper-case letters as equivalent. ■ See page 410. ■ See also: Replace, StringReplacePart, StringPosition, ToLowerCase, ToUpperCase. ■ *New in Version 2; modified in Version 4.*

■ **StringReplacePart**

StringReplacePart["*string*", "*snew*", {m, n}] replaces the characters at positions m through n in "*string*" by "*snew*".

StringReplacePart["*string*", "*snew*", {{m_1, n_1}, {m_2, n_2}, ... }] inserts copies of "*snew*" at several positions.

StringReplacePart["*string*", {"*snew$_1$*", "*snew$_2$*", ... }, {{m_1, n_1}, {m_2, n_2}, ... }] replaces characters at positions m_i through n_i in "*string*" by "*snew$_i$*".

StringReplacePart uses position specifications in the form returned by StringPosition. ■ When a list of "*snew$_i$*" is given, its length must be the same as the length of the list of positions. ■ When multiple positions are given, all refer to the original "*string*", before any replacements have been done. ■ StringReplacePart[s, "", ...] can be used to delete substrings. ■ See page 409. ■ See also: StringInsert, StringDrop, StringReplace, StringJoin, ReplacePart. ■ *New in Version 3.*

■ **StringReverse**

StringReverse["*string*"] reverses the order of the characters in "*string*".

Example: StringReverse["abcde"] $\longrightarrow$ edcba. ■ See page 407. ■ See also: Reverse. ■ *New in Version 2.*

■ **StringSkeleton**

StringSkeleton[*n*] represents a sequence of *n* omitted characters in a string printed with Short.

The standard print form for StringSkeleton is an ellipsis.

You can reset the print form of StringSkeleton. ■ See also: Short, Skeleton, TotalWidth. ■ *New in Version 1.*

■ **StringTake**

StringTake["*string*", *n*] gives a string containing the first *n* characters in "*string*".

StringTake["*string*", -*n*] gives the last *n* characters in "*string*".

StringTake["*string*", {*n*}] gives the *n*th character in "*string*".

StringTake["*string*", {*m*, *n*}] gives characters *m* through *n* in "*string*".

StringTake uses the standard *sequence specification* (see page 1040). ■ Example: StringTake["abcdefg", 3] $\longrightarrow$ abc. ■ StringTake["*string*", {*m*, *n*, *s*}] gives characters *m* through *n* in steps of *s*. ■ See page 407. ■ See also: Take, StringDrop, StringPosition. ■ *New in Version 2; modified in Version 4.*

■ **StringToStream**

StringToStream["*string*"] opens an input stream for reading from a string.

StringToStream yields a stream of the form InputStream[String, *n*]. ■ Operations like Read and Find work on streams returned by StringToStream. ■ You must use Close to close streams created by StringToStream. ■ See page 654. ■ See also: Characters. ■ *New in Version 2.*

■ **StructuredSelection**

StructuredSelection is an option for Cell which specifies whether to allow only complete subexpressions in the cell to be selected interactively using the front end.

StructuredSelection is more often set at a global level than at the level of individual cells. ■ See page 615. ■ See also: Selectable, DragAndDrop. ■ *New in Version 3.*

■ **StruveH**

StruveH[*n*, *z*] gives the Struve function $\mathbf{H}_n(z)$.

Mathematical function (see Section A.3.10). ■ $\mathbf{H}_n(z)$ for integer *n* satisfies the differential equation $z^2 y'' + z y' + (z^2 - n^2) y = \frac{2}{\pi} \frac{z^{n+1}}{(2n-1)!!}$. ■ StruveH[*n*, *z*] has a branch cut discontinuity in the complex *z* plane running from $-\infty$ to 0. ■ See page 775. ■ See also: StruveL, BesselJ. ■ *New in Version 4.*

■ **StruveL**

StruveL[*n*, *z*] gives the modified Struve function $\mathbf{L}_n(z)$.

Mathematical function (see Section A.3.10). ■ $\mathbf{L}_n(z)$ for integer *n* is related to the ordinary Struve function by $\mathbf{L}_n(iz) = -ie^{-in\pi/2} \mathbf{H}_n(z)$. ■ StruveL[*n*, *z*] has a branch cut discontinuity in the complex *z* plane running from $-\infty$ to 0. ■ See page 775. ■ See also: StruveH, BesselJ. ■ *New in Version 4.*

■ Stub

Stub is an attribute which specifies that if a symbol is ever used, Needs should automatically be called on the context of the symbol.

Symbols with the Stub attribute are created by DeclarePackage. ■ A symbol is considered "used" if its name appears explicitly, not in the form of a string. ■ Names["*nameform*"] and Attributes["*nameform*"] do not constitute "uses" of a symbol. ■ See pages 329 and 402. ■ *New in Version 2.*

■ StyleBox

StyleBox[*boxes*, *options*] represents output in which *boxes* are shown with the specified option settings.

StyleBox[*boxes*, "*style*"] uses the option setting for the specified style in the current notebook.

You can use font options such as FontSize, FontWeight, FontSlant, FontFamily, FontColor and Background in StyleBox. ■ The following additional options can be given:

AutoSpacing	True	whether to adjust character spacings automatically
LineIndent	1.0	distance in ems to indent for each nesting level
LineIndentMaxFraction	0.5	maximum fraction of line width to indent
ScriptMinSize	4.0	the minimum point size to use for subscripts, etc.
ScriptSizeMultipliers	0.71	how much smaller to make each level of subscripts, etc.
ShowContents	True	whether to make *boxes* visible or just leave space for them
SpanLineThickness	Automatic	thickness in printer's points of fraction lines etc.
SpanMaxSize	Automatic	maximum size of expandable characters in units of font size
SpanMinSize	Automatic	minimum size of expandable characters in units of font size
SpanSymmetric	True	whether vertically expandable characters should be symmetric about the axis of the box they are in

■ In StandardForm and InputForm input, StyleBox is by default ignored, so that StyleBox[*box*, *spec*] is interpreted just as *box* would be. ■ When StyleBox objects are nested, the options of the innermost one control the display of particular boxes. ■ In StandardForm, explicit StyleBox objects are output literally. You can use DisplayForm to see the display form of such objects. ■ See page 446. ■ See also: StyleForm, AdjustmentBox, FrameBox, Cell, ShowAutoStyles. ■ *New in Version 3.*

■ StyleDefinitions

StyleDefinitions is an option for notebooks which gives definitions for the styles that can be used in a notebook.

StyleDefinitions->"*name*.nb" specifies that style definitions from the notebook *name*.nb should be used. ■ The standard notebook front end comes with a selection of style definition notebooks containing styles appropriate for particular purposes. ■ StyleDefinitions->Notebook[...] allows style definitions to be given explicitly. ■ The definition for a style named "s" is specified by the options for the first cell whose contents is StyleData["s"]. ■ See page 603. ■ See also: ScreenStyleEnvironment, PrintingStyleEnvironment. ■ *New in Version 3.*

◼ StyleForm

StyleForm[*expr*, *options*] prints using the specified style options.

StyleForm[*expr*, "*style*"] prints using the specified cell style in the current notebook.

You can use font options such as FontSize, FontWeight, FontSlant, FontFamily, FontColor and Background in StyleForm. ◼ Additional options can be given as in StyleBox. ◼ StyleForm acts as a "wrapper", which affects printing, but not evaluation. ◼ StyleForm can be used to specify the style for text in graphics. ◼ StyleForm[*expr*, "*style*"] will work only if the notebook front end is being used; StyleForm[*expr*, *options*] for many options will work in all cases. ◼ When StyleForm objects are nested, the options of the innermost one control the printing of a particular expression. ◼ See pages 443 and 558. ◼ See also: StylePrint, StyleBox, TextStyle, $TextStyle, FormatType, Cell. ◼ *New in Version 3.*

◼ StylePrint

StylePrint[*expr*, "*style*"] creates a new cell in the current notebook with the specified style, and prints *expr* into it.

StylePrint[*expr*] uses the default style for the current notebook.

◟◼ StylePrint creates a new cell immediately after the cell that is currently being evaluated. ◼ StylePrint[*expr*, "*style*", *opts*] can be used to specify options for the cell that is created. ◼ StylePrint is a special case of NotebookWrite. ◼ With a text-based front end, StylePrint does the same as Print. ◼ Cells generated by StylePrint by default have GeneratedCell->True and CellAutoOverwrite->True. ◼ StylePrint[*expr*, "*style*"] generates a whole cell with the specified style; Print[StyleForm[*expr*, "*style*"]] generates a cell with the default style but containing a StyleBox object. ◼ See pages 477 and 575. ◼ See also: CellPrint, Print, NotebookWrite, NotebookPrint, StyleForm. ◼ *New in Version 3.*

◼ Subresultants

Subresultants[*poly*$_1$, *poly*$_2$, *var*] generates a list of the principal subresultant coefficients of the polynomials *poly*$_1$ and *poly*$_2$ with respect to the variable *var*.

The first k subresultants of two polynomials a and b, both with leading coefficient one, are zero when a and b have k common roots. ◼ Subresultants returns a list whose length is Min[Exponent[*poly*$_1$, *var*], Exponent[*poly*$_2$, *var*]] + 1. ◼ See page 803. ◼ See also: Resultant, PolynomialGCD, Eliminate, Minors. ◼ *New in Version 4.*

◼ SubscriptBox

SubscriptBox[*x*, *y*] represents x_y in input and output.

Inside \(... \) SubscriptBox[*x*, *y*] can be input as *x* _ *y*. ◼ In a notebook a SubscriptBox can be created using CTRL - or CTRL _ . CTRL ␣ moves out of the subscript. ◼ In StandardForm and InputForm, SubscriptBox[*x*, *y*] is interpreted on input as Subscript[*x*, *y*]. ◼ The baseline of SubscriptBox[*x*, *y*] is taken to be the baseline of *x*. ◼ SubscriptBox[*x*, *y*] is usually output with *y* in a smaller font than *x*. ◼ In StandardForm, explicit SubscriptBox objects are output literally. You can use DisplayForm to see the display form of such objects. ◼ See page 445. ◼ See also: SuperscriptBox, SubsuperscriptBox, UnderscriptBox, ScriptSizeMultipliers. ◼ *New in Version 3.*

■ SubsuperscriptBox

SubsuperscriptBox[x, y, z] represents x_y^z .

SubsuperscriptBox[x, y, z] can be input as x _ y \% z when inside \\(... \\). ■ In a notebook a SubsuperscriptBox can be created by using [CTRL]-[-] or [CTRL]-[_] to move to the subscript, then [CTRL]-[%] to move to the superscript. [CTRL]-[␣] moves out of the subscript or superscript position. ■ In StandardForm and InputForm, SubsuperscriptBox[x, y, z] is interpreted on input as Power[Subscript[x, y], z]. ■ The baseline of SubsuperscriptBox[x, y, z] is taken to be the baseline of x. ■ SubsuperscriptBox[x, y, z] is usually output with y and z in a smaller font than x. ■ In StandardForm, explicit SubsuperscriptBox objects are output literally. You can use DisplayForm to see the display form of such objects. ■ See page 445. ■ See also: SubscriptBox, SuperscriptBox, UnderoverscriptBox. ■ *New in Version 3.*

■ Subtract

x − y is equivalent to x + (−1 ∗ y).

x − y is converted to x + (−1 ∗ y) on input. ■ See page 29. ■ See also: Minus, Decrement. ■ *New in Version 1.*

■ SubtractFrom

x −= dx subtracts dx from x and returns the new value of x.

SubtractFrom has the attribute HoldFirst. ■ x −= dx is equivalent to x = x − dx. ■ See page 305. ■ See also: Decrement, PreDecrement, Set. ■ *New in Version 1.*

■ Sum

Sum[f, {i, $imax$}] evaluates the sum $\sum_{i=1}^{imax} f$.

Sum[f, {i, $imin$, $imax$}] starts with i = $imin$. Sum[f, {i, $imin$, $imax$, di}] uses steps di.

Sum[f, {i, $imin$, $imax$}, {j, $jmin$, $jmax$}, ...] evaluates the multiple sum $\sum_{i=imin}^{imax} \sum_{j=jmin}^{jmax} ... f$.

Sum[f, {i, $imax$}] can be entered as $\sum_{i}^{imax} f$. ■ $\sum$ can be entered as :sum: or \\[Sum]. ■ Sum[f, {i, $imin$, $imax$}] can be entered as $\sum_{i=imin}^{imax} f$. ■ The limits should be underscripts and overscripts of $\sum$ in normal input, and subscripts and superscripts when embedded in other text. ■ Sum evaluates its arguments in a non-standard way (see page 1046). ■ Sum uses the standard *Mathematica* iteration specification. ■ The iteration variable i is treated as local. ■ In multiple sums, the range of the outermost variable is given first. ■ The limits of summation need not be numbers. They can be Infinity or symbolic expressions. ■ If a sum cannot be carried out explicitly by adding up a finite number of terms, Sum will attempt to find a symbolic result. In this case, f is first evaluated symbolically. ■ Sum can do essentially all sums that are given in standard books of tables. ■ Sum is output in StandardForm using $\sum$. ■ See pages 83 and 890. ■ Implementation notes: see page 1071. ■ See also: Do, Product, Table, NSum, ZTransform, Total, RSolve. ■ *New in Version 1; modified in Version 3.*

■ SuperscriptBox

SuperscriptBox[x, y] represents x^y in input and output.

Inside \\(... \\) SuperscriptBox[x, y] can be input as x \\^ y. ■ In a notebook a SuperscriptBox can be created using [CTRL]-[6] or [CTRL]-[^]. [CTRL]-[␣] moves out of the superscript. ■ In StandardForm and InputForm, SuperscriptBox[x, y] is interpreted on input as Power[x, y]. ■ The baseline of SuperscriptBox[x, y] is taken to be the baseline of x. ■ SuperscriptBox[x, y] is usually output with y in a smaller font than x. ■ In StandardForm, explicit SuperscriptBox objects are output literally. You can use DisplayForm to see the display form of such objects. ■ See page 445. ■ See also: SubscriptBox, SubsuperscriptBox, OverscriptBox, ScriptSizeMultipliers. ■ *New in Version 3.*

■ **SurfaceColor**

SurfaceColor[*dcol*] is a three-dimensional graphics directive which specifies that the polygons which follow should act as diffuse reflectors of light with a color given by *dcol*.

SurfaceColor[*dcol*, *scol*] specifies that a specular reflection component should be included, with a color given by *scol*.

SurfaceColor[*dcol*, *scol*, *n*] specifies that the reflection should occur with specular exponent *n*.

SurfaceColor directives give surface properties which determine the effect of simulated illumination on polygons. ■ SurfaceColor directives can appear inside FaceForm directives. ■ If no SurfaceColor directive is given, polygons are assumed to be white diffuse reflectors of light, obeying Lambert's law of reflection, so that the intensity of reflected light is $\cos(\alpha)$ times the intensity of incident light, where α is the angle between the direction of the incident light and the polygon normal. When $\alpha > 90°$, there is no reflected light. ■ SurfaceColor[GrayLevel[*a*]] specifies that polygons should act as diffuse reflectors, but with albedo *a*. The intensity of reflected light is therefore *a* times the intensity of the incident light, multiplied by $\cos(\alpha)$, and is of the same color. ■ SurfaceColor[RGBColor[*r*, *g*, *b*]] specifies that the red, green and blue components of the reflected light should be respectively *r*, *g* and *b* times those of the incident light, multiplied by $\cos(\alpha)$. ■ The second element in SurfaceColor[*dcol*, *scol*] specifies a specular reflection component. *scol* must be a GrayLevel, Hue or RGBColor specification. The color components of *scol* give the fractions of each color component in the incident intensity which are reflected in a specular way by the surface. ■ The parameter *n* gives the specular exponent. The intensity of specularly reflected light at angle θ from the mirror-reflection direction falls off like $\cos(\theta)^n$ as θ increases. It is zero when $\theta > 90°$. ■ For real materials, *n* is typically between about 1 and a few hundred. With a coarse polygonal mesh, however, values of *n* below 10 are usually most appropriate. The default value for *n* is 1. ■ *Mathematica* implements a version of the Phong lighting model, in which the intensity of reflected light is given schematically by $I_{in}(d\cos(\alpha) + s\cos(\theta)^n)$. ■ The intensity of light from diffuse and specular reflection is added linearly for each color component. The final color shown for a particular polygon is the sum of contributions from each light source, and from ambient light. ■ See page 546. ■ See also: Lighting, LightSources, AmbientLight. ■ *New in Version 2.*

■ **SurfaceGraphics**

SurfaceGraphics[*array*] is a representation of a three-dimensional plot of a surface, with heights of each point on a grid specified by values in *array*.

SurfaceGraphics[*array*, *shades*] represents a surface, whose parts are shaded according to the array *shades*.

SurfaceGraphics can be displayed using Show. ■ SurfaceGraphics has the same options as Graphics3D, with the following additions:

ClipFill	Automatic	how to draw clipped parts of the surface
ColorFunction	Automatic	function to determine color based on *z* value
ColorFunctionScaling	True	whether to scale *z* values before applying a color function
HiddenSurface	True	whether to eliminate hidden surfaces
Mesh	True	whether to draw a mesh on the surface
MeshRange	Automatic	the original range of *x*, *y* coordinates for the plot
MeshStyle	Automatic	graphics directives to specify the style for a mesh

■ SurfaceGraphics does not support the options PolygonIntersections and RenderAll available for Graphics3D. ■ For SurfaceGraphics, the default setting for BoxRatios is BoxRatios -> {1, 1, 0.4}. ■ *array* should be a rectangular array of real numbers, representing *z* values. There will be holes in the surface corresponding to any array elements that are not real numbers. ■ If *array* has dimensions $m \times n$, then *shades* must have dimensions $(m-1) \times (n-1)$. ■ The elements of *shades* must be GrayLevel, Hue or RGBColor directives, or SurfaceColor objects. ■ Graphics3D[SurfaceGraphics[...]] can be used to convert a SurfaceGraphics object into the more general Graphics3D representation. ■ SurfaceGraphics is generated by Plot3D and ListPlot3D. ■ See page 537. ■ See also: ListPlot3D, Plot3D, ContourGraphics, DensityGraphics. ■ *New in Version 1.*

■ Switch

Switch[*expr*, *form*₁, *value*₁, *form*₂, *value*₂, ...] evaluates *expr*, then compares it with each of the *form*ᵢ in turn, evaluating and returning the *value*ᵢ corresponding to the first match found.

Only the *value*ᵢ corresponding to the first *form*ᵢ that matches *expr* is evaluated. Each *form*ᵢ is evaluated only when the match is tried. ■ If the last *form*ᵢ is the pattern _, then the corresponding *value*ᵢ is always returned if this case is reached. ■ If none of the *form*ᵢ match *expr*, the Switch is returned unevaluated. ■ Switch has attribute HoldRest. ■ You can use Break, Return and Throw in Switch. ■ See page 345. ■ See also: If, Condition, Which. ■ *New in Version 1.*

■ Symbol

Symbol["*name*"] refers to a symbol with the specified name.

All symbols, whether explicitly entered using Symbol or not, have head Symbol. ■ *x*_Symbol can be used as a pattern to represent any symbol. ■ The string "*name*" in Symbol["*name*"] must be an appropriate name for a symbol. It can contain any letters, letter-like forms, or digits, but cannot start with a digit. ■ Symbol["*name*"] creates a new symbol if none exists with the specified name. ■ A symbol such as x has a name "x". ■ If Symbol["*name*"] creates a new symbol, it does so in the context specified by $Context. ■ See page 1016. ■ See also: SymbolName, ToExpression, Unique, Remove. ■ *New in Version 1.*

■ SymbolName

SymbolName[*symbol*] gives the name of the specified symbol.

Example: SymbolName[x] ⟶ "x". ■ SymbolName evaluates its input. ■ SymbolName always returns a string. ■ See page 402. ■ See also: ToString, Symbol. ■ *New in Version 3.*

■ SyntaxLength

SyntaxLength["*string*"] finds the number of characters starting at the beginning of a string that correspond to syntactically correct input for a single *Mathematica* expression.

SyntaxLength effectively returns the position of a syntax error, if one exists. ■ If SyntaxLength returns a position past the end of the string, it indicates that the string is syntactically correct as far as it goes, but needs to be continued in order to correspond to input for a complete *Mathematica* expression. ■ See page 466. ■ See also: SyntaxQ, $SyntaxHandler. ■ *New in Version 2.*

■ SyntaxQ

SyntaxQ["*string*"] returns True if the string corresponds to syntactically correct input for a single *Mathematica* expression, and returns False otherwise.

If SyntaxQ returns False, you can find the position of a syntax error using SyntaxLength. ■ See page 466. ■ See also: ToExpression, SyntaxLength, $SyntaxHandler, DelimiterFlashTime. ■ *New in Version 2.*

■ Table

Table[*expr*, {*imax*}] generates a list of *imax* copies of *expr*.

Table[*expr*, {*i*, *imax*}] generates a list of the values of *expr* when *i* runs from 1 to *imax*.

Table[*expr*, {*i*, *imin*, *imax*}] starts with *i* = *imin*.

Table[*expr*, {*i*, *imin*, *imax*, *di*}] uses steps *di*.

Table[*expr*, {*i*, *imin*, *imax*}, {*j*, *jmin*, *jmax*}, ...] gives a nested list. The list associated with *i* is outermost.

(continued)

■ Table *(continued)*

▪ Table evaluates its arguments in a non-standard way (see page 1046). ▪ Example: Table[f[i], {i, 4}] ⟶ {f[1], f[2], f[3], f[4]}. ▪ Table uses the standard *Mathematica* iteration specification. ▪ Example: Table[i-j, {i, 2}, {j, 2}] ⟶ {{0, -1}, {1, 0}}. ▪ You can use Table to build up vectors, matrices and tensors. ▪ See page 115. ▪ See also: Range, DiagonalMatrix, IdentityMatrix, Array, Do, Sum, Product, FunctionInterpolation, NestList, NestWhileList, SparseArray. ▪ Related package: LinearAlgebra`MatrixManipulation`. ▪ *New in Version 1.*

■ TableAlignments

TableAlignments is an option for TableForm and MatrixForm which specifies how entries in each dimension should be aligned.

TableAlignments -> {a_1, a_2, ... } specifies alignments for successive dimensions. ▪ For dimensions that are given as columns, possible alignments are Left, Center and Right. For dimensions that are given as rows, possible alignments are Bottom, Center and Top. ▪ The default setting TableAlignments -> Automatic uses Left for column alignment, and Bottom for row alignment. ▪ See page 442. ▪ See also: TableDirections, RowAlignments, ColumnAlignments. ▪ *New in Version 2.*

■ TableDepth

TableDepth is an option for TableForm and MatrixForm which specifies the maximum number of levels to be printed in tabular or matrix format.

TableForm[*list*, TableDepth -> n] prints elements in *list* below level n as ordinary lists, rather than arranging them in tabular form. ▪ With the default setting TableDepth -> Infinity, as many levels as possible are printed in tabular form. In TableForm, the levels printed need not consist of elements with the same list structure. In MatrixForm, they must. ▪ See page 442. ▪ See also: ArrayDepth. ▪ *New in Version 2.*

■ TableDirections

TableDirections is an option for TableForm and MatrixForm which specifies whether successive dimensions should be arranged as rows or columns.

TableDirections -> Column specifies that successive dimensions should be arranged alternately as columns and rows, with the first dimension arranged as columns. ▪ TableDirections -> Row takes the first dimension to be arranged as rows. ▪ TableDirections -> {dir_1, dir_2, ... } specifies explicitly whether each dimension should be arranged with Column or Row. ▪ See page 441. ▪ See also: TableSpacing. ▪ *New in Version 2.*

■ TableForm

TableForm[*list*] prints with the elements of *list* arranged in an array of rectangular cells.

The height of each row and the width of each column are determined by the maximum size of an element in the row or column. ▪ TableForm prints a single-level list in a column. It prints a two-level list as a two-dimensional table. More deeply nested lists are by default printed with successive dimensions alternating between rows and columns. ▪ Arrays in which all sublists at a particular level are not of the same length display as ragged tables. ▪ The following options can be given:

TableAlignments	Automatic	how to align entries in each dimension
TableDepth	Infinity	maximum number of levels to include
TableDirections	Column	whether to arrange dimensions as rows or columns
TableHeadings	None	how to label table entries
TableSpacing	Automatic	how many spaces to put between entries in each dimension

▪ TableForm acts as a "wrapper", which affects printing, but not evaluation. ▪ See page 439. ▪ See also: ColumnForm, MatrixForm, GridBox, GraphicsArray. ▪ *New in Version 1.*

■ TableHeadings

TableHeadings is an option for `TableForm` and `MatrixForm` which gives the labels to be printed for entries in each dimension of a table or matrix.

TableHeadings -> None gives no labels in any dimension. ■ TableHeadings -> Automatic gives successive integer labels for each entry in each dimension. ■ TableHeadings -> {{lab_{11}, lab_{12}, ... }, ... } gives explicit labels for each entry. ■ The labels can be strings or other *Mathematica* expressions. ■ The labels are placed as headings for rows or columns. ■ See page 442. ■ *New in Version 2.*

■ TableSpacing

TableSpacing is an option for `TableForm` and `MatrixForm` which specifies how many spaces should be left between each successive row or column.

TableSpacing -> {s_1, s_2, ... } specifies that s_i spaces should be left in dimension *i*. ■ For columns, the spaces are rendered as space characters. For rows, the spaces are rendered as blank lines. ■ For TableForm, TableSpacing -> Automatic yields spacings {1, 3, 0, 1, 0, 1, ... }. ■ See page 442. ■ See also: RowSpacings, ColumnSpacings, GraphicsSpacing. ■ *New in Version 2.*

■ TagBox

TagBox[*boxes*, *tag*] displays as *boxes* but maintains *tag* to guide the interpretation of *boxes* on input.

TagBox provides a way to store hidden information in *Mathematica* output. ■ TagBox is generated sometimes in StandardForm output, and often in TraditionalForm output. ■ By convention, *tag* is typically a symbol that corresponds to the head of the interpreted form of *boxes*. ■ The following options can be given:

AutoDelete	False	whether to strip the TagBox if *boxes* are modified
DeletionWarning	False	whether to issue a warning if *boxes* are deleted
Editable	True	whether to allow *boxes* to be edited
Selectable	True	whether to allow *boxes* to be selected
StripWrapperBoxes	False	whether to remove StyleBox etc. from within *boxes*

■ If you modify the displayed form of TagBox[*boxes*, *tag*] only *boxes* will be modified, and there is no guarantee that correct correspondence with *expr* will be maintained. ■ See page 447. ■ See also: InterpretationBox, FormBox, ToExpression. ■ *New in Version 3.*

■ TagSet

f / : *lhs* = *rhs* assigns *rhs* to be the value of *lhs*, and associates the assignment with the symbol *f*.

TagSet defines upvalues or downvalues as appropriate. ■ The symbol *f* in *f* / : *lhs* = *rhs* must appear in *lhs* as the head of *lhs*, the head of the head, one of the elements of *lhs*, or the head of one of the elements. ■ A common case is *f* / : *h*[*f*[*args*]] = *rhs*. ■ You can see all the rules associated with a particular symbol by typing ?*symbol*. ■ If *f* appears several times in *lhs*, then *f* / : *lhs* = *rhs* associates the assignment with each occurrence. ■ When it appears in symbolic form, TagSet is treated as a scoping construct (see Section A.3.8). ■ See pages 319 and 1051. ■ See also: Set, UpSet. ■ *New in Version 1.*

■ TagSetDelayed

f / : *lhs* := *rhs* assigns *rhs* to be the delayed value of *lhs*, and associates the assignment with the symbol *f*.

See notes for `TagSet` and `SetDelayed`. ■ See page 319. ■ *New in Version 1.*

■ TagUnset

f / : *lhs* =. removes any rules defined for *lhs*, associated with the symbol *f*.

Rules are removed only when their left-hand side is identical to *lhs*, and the tests in Condition given on the right-hand side are also identical. ■ See pages 1029 and 1052. ■ See also: Clear, Unset. ■ *New in Version 1.*

■ Take

Take[*list*, *n*] gives the first *n* elements of *list*.

Take[*list*, -*n*] gives the last *n* elements of *list*.

Take[*list*, {*m*, *n*}] gives elements *m* through *n* of *list*.

Take[*list*, {*m*, *n*, *s*}] gives elements *m* through *n* in steps of *s*.

Take[*list*, seq_1, seq_2, ...] gives a nested list in which elements specified by seq_i are taken at level *i* in *list*.

Take uses the standard *sequence specification* (see page 1040). ■ Examples: Take[{a,b,c,d,e}, 3] ⟶ {a, b, c}. ■ Take[{a,b,c,d,e}, -2] ⟶ {d, e}. ■ Take[Range[15], {3, 12, 4}] ⟶ {3, 7, 11}. ■ Take can be used on an object with any head, not necessarily List. ■ Take[*list*, seq_1, seq_2] effectively extracts a submatrix from *list*. ■ Example: Take[{{a,b,c},{d,e,f}}, -1, 2] ⟶ {{d, e}}. +■ Applying Take to a SparseArray object normally yields another SparseArray object. ■ See pages 123 and 287. ■ See also: Part, Drop, StringTake, Select, Cases, Partition, PadLeft. ■ Related package: LinearAlgebra`MatrixManipulation`. ■ *New in Version 1; modified in Version 4.*

■ Tan

Tan[*z*] gives the tangent of *z*.

Mathematical function (see Section A.3.10). ■ The argument of Tan is assumed to be in radians. (Multiply by Degree to convert from degrees.) ■ Sin[*z*]/Cos[*z*] is automatically converted to Tan[*z*]. TrigFactorList[*expr*] does decomposition. ■ Tan is automatically evaluated when its argument is a simple rational multiple of π; for more complicated rational multiples, FunctionExpand can sometimes be used. ■ See page 761. ■ See also: ArcTan, Cot, TrigToExp, TrigExpand. ■ *New in Version 1.*

■ Tanh

Tanh[*z*] gives the hyperbolic tangent of *z*.

Mathematical function (see Section A.3.10). ■ Sinh[*z*]/Cosh[*z*] is automatically converted to Tanh[*z*]. TrigFactorList[*expr*] does decomposition. ■ See page 761. ■ See also: ArcTanh, Coth, TrigToExp, TrigExpand. ■ *New in Version 1.*

■ Temporary

Temporary is an attribute assigned to symbols which are created as local variables by Module.

Symbols with attribute Temporary are automatically removed when they are no longer needed. ■ Symbols with attribute Temporary conventionally have names of the form *aaa*$*nnn*. ■ See pages 329 and 383. ■ See also: Module, Unique. ■ *New in Version 2.*

■ TeXForm

TeXForm[*expr*] prints as a TeX version of *expr*.

TeXForm produces plain TeX. Its output should be suitable for both LATEX and AMSTEX. ■ TeXForm acts as a "wrapper", which affects printing, but not evaluation. ■ TeXForm translates standard mathematical functions and operations. ■ Symbols with names like alpha and ALPHA that correspond to TeX symbols are translated into their corresponding TeX symbols. ■ Following standard mathematical conventions, single-character symbol names are given in italic font, while multiple character names are given in roman font. ■ All standard *Mathematica* box structures are translated by TeXForm. ■ *Mathematica* special characters are translated whenever possible to their TeX equivalents. ■ See pages 210 and 425. ■ See also: TeXSave, StandardForm, TraditionalForm, MathMLForm. ■ *New in Version 1; modified in Version 3.*

■ TeXSave

TeXSave["*file*.tex"] saves a TeX version of the currently selected notebook in the front end.

TeXSave["*file*.tex", "*source*.nb"] saves a TeX version of the notebook from the file *source*.nb.

TeXSave["*file*.tex", *notebook*] saves a TeX version of the notebook corresponding to the specified notebook object.

TeXSave has options for specifying such features as how to include graphics, what TeX style to use, and how each notebook style should be rendered in TeX. ■ TeXSave can often be accessed from an item in the Save As Special menu in the notebook front end. ■ See notes for TeXForm. ■ See page 210. ■ See also: TeXForm, MathMLForm. ■ *New in Version 3.*

■ Text

Text[*expr*, *coords*] is a graphics primitive that represents text corresponding to the printed form of *expr*, centered at the point specified by *coords*.

The *text* is printed by default in OutputForm. ■ Text can be used in both two- and three-dimensional graphics. ■ The coordinates can be specified either as $\{x, y, \ldots\}$ or as Scaled[$\{x, y, \ldots\}$]. ■ In two dimensions, coordinates can also be specified using Offset. ■ Text[*expr*, *coords*, *offset*] specifies an offset for the block of text relative to the coordinates given. Giving an offset $\{sdx, sdy\}$ specifies that the point $\{x, y\}$ should lie at relative coordinates $\{sdx, sdy\}$ within the bounding rectangle that encloses the text. Each relative coordinate runs from -1 to $+1$ across the bounding rectangle. ■ The offsets specified need not be in the range -1 to $+1$. ■ Here are sample offsets to use in two-dimensional graphics:

$\{0, 0\}$	text centered at $\{x, y\}$
$\{-1, 0\}$	left-hand end at $\{x, y\}$
$\{1, 0\}$	right-hand end at $\{x, y\}$
$\{0, -1\}$	centered above $\{x, y\}$
$\{0, 1\}$	centered below $\{x, y\}$

■ Text[*expr*, *coords*, *offset*, *dir*] specifies the orientation of the text is given by the direction vector *dir*. Possible values of *dir* are:

$\{1, 0\}$	ordinary horizontal text
$\{0, 1\}$	vertical text reading from bottom to top
$\{0, -1\}$	vertical text reading from top to bottom
$\{-1, 0\}$	horizontal upside-down text

(continued)

■ Text *(continued)*

▪ Text in three-dimensional graphics is placed at a position that corresponds to the projection of the point $\{x, y, z\}$ specified. Text is drawn in front of all other objects. ▪ The font or style for text can be specified using StyleForm or using the TextStyle option. If no such specifications are given, the font is determined from the setting for TextStyle for the whole plot, which is in turn by default given by the global variable $TextStyle. ▪ You can specify the color of text using CMYKColor, GrayLevel, Hue and RGBColor directives. ▪ The option CharacterEncoding for Display can be used to specify what raw character encoding to use for character strings in Text objects. ▪ The following options can be given:

Background	None	background color
FormatType	StandardForm	format type
TextStyle	Automatic	style specification

▪ See pages 492 and 560. ▪ See also: PlotLabel, AxesLabel, Cell. ▪ *New in Version 1; modified in Version 3.*

■ TextAlignment

TextAlignment is an option for Cell which specifies how successive lines of text should be aligned.

Possible settings are:

Left or -1	aligned on the left
Right or +1	aligned on the right
Center or 0	centered
x	lined up at position x across the page

▪ TextAlignment can be used both for ordinary text and for *Mathematica* expressions. ▪ See page 609. ▪ See also: TextJustification, ColumnAlignments, PageWidth. ▪ *New in Version 3.*

■ TextJustification

TextJustification is an option for Cell which specifies how much lines of text can be stretched in order to make them be the same length.

TextJustification->0 does no stretching, and leads to ragged text boundaries. ▪ TextJustification->1 does full justification, and forces all complete lines to be the same length. ▪ No stretching is done on lines that end with explicit RETURN characters. ▪ With settings for TextJustification between 0 and 1, partial justification is done. ▪ With TextJustification->*s*, *Mathematica* will take the amount by which each broken line is shorter than PageWidth, and then insert within the line a total amount of space equal to *s* times this. ▪ If TextJustification is not 0, the standard *Mathematica* front end will dynamically adjust the lengths of lines as you enter text. ▪ See page 609. ▪ See also: TextAlignment, Hyphenation, PageWidth, AutoSpacing, ButtonExpandable. ▪ *New in Version 3.*

■ TextStyle

TextStyle is an option for graphics functions and for Text which specifies the default style and font options with which text should be rendered.

The following forms of settings can be used:

"*style*"	a specific cell style
$\{opt_1 -> val_1, \dots\}$	a list of option settings
$\{$"*style*", $opt_1 -> val_1, \dots\}$	a style modified by option settings

▪ The options that can be given are as in StyleForm. ▪ "*style*" settings can only be used when a notebook front end is present. ▪ The default setting is TextStyle :> $TextStyle. ▪ The style specified by TextStyle in a graphics object is used by default for all text, including labels and tick marks. ▪ See page 556. ▪ See also: StyleForm, $TextStyle, PlotStyle, FormatType. ▪ *New in Version 3.*

■ Thickness

Thickness[r] is a graphics directive which specifies that lines which follow are to be drawn with a thickness r. The thickness r is given as a fraction of the total width of the graph.

Thickness can be used in both two- and three-dimensional graphics. ■ The initial default is Thickness[0.004] for two-dimensional graphics, and Thickness[0.001] for three-dimensional graphics ■ See page 501. ■ See also: AbsoluteThickness, PointSize, Dashing, PlotStyle. ■ *New in Version 1.*

■ Thread

Thread[$f[args]$] "threads" f over any lists that appear in *args*.

Thread[$f[args]$, h] threads f over any objects with head h that appear in *args*.

Thread[$f[args]$, h, n] threads f over objects with head h that appear in the first n *args*.

Thread[$f[args]$, h, $-n$] threads over the last n *args*.

Thread[$f[args]$, h, $\{m, n\}$] threads over arguments m through n.

Example: Thread[f[{a,b}, c, {d,e}]] ⟶ {f[a, c, d], f[b, c, e]}. ■ Functions with attribute Listable are automatically threaded over lists. ■ All the elements in the specified *args* whose heads are h must be of the same length. ■ Arguments that do not have head h are copied as many times as there are elements in the arguments that do have head h. ■ Thread uses the standard *sequence specification* (see page 1040). ■ See page 256. ■ See also: Distribute, Map, Inner, MapThread. ■ *New in Version 1.*

■ ThreeJSymbol

ThreeJSymbol[$\{j_1, m_1\}$, $\{j_2, m_2\}$, $\{j_3, m_3\}$] gives the values of the Wigner 3-j symbol.

The 3-j symbols vanish except when $m_1 + m_2 + m_3 = 0$ and the j_i satisfy a triangle inequality. ■ The parameters of ThreeJSymbol can be integers, half-integers or symbolic expressions. ■ The Clebsch-Gordan coefficients and 3-j symbols in *Mathematica* satisfy the relation $C^{j_1 j_2 j_3}_{m_1 m_2 m_3} = (-1)^{m_3 + j_1 - j_2} \sqrt{2j_3 + 1} \begin{pmatrix} j_1 & j_2 & j_3 \\ m_1 & m_2 & -m_3 \end{pmatrix}$. ■ See page 760. ■ See also: ClebschGordan, SixJSymbol, SphericalHarmonicY. ■ *New in Version 2.*

■ Through

Through[$p[f_1, f_2][x]$] gives $p[f_1[x], f_2[x]]$.

Through[*expr*, h] performs the transformation wherever h occurs in the head of *expr*.

Example: Through[(f + g)[x, y]] ⟶ f[x, y] + g[x, y]. ■ Through distributes operators that appear inside the heads of expressions. ■ See page 254. ■ See also: Operate. ■ *New in Version 1.*

■ Throw

Throw[*value*] stops evaluation and returns *value* as the value of the nearest enclosing Catch.

Throw[*value*, *tag*] is caught only by Catch[*expr*, *form*] where *form* is a pattern that matches *tag*.

You can use Throw and Catch to exit functions such as Nest, Fold, FixedPoint and Scan. ■ *tag* can be any expression. ■ *tag* in Throw[*value*, *tag*] is re-evaluated every time it is compared to *form* in Catch[*expr*, *form*]. ■ An error is generated and an unevaluated Throw is returned if there is no appropriate enclosing Catch to catch the Throw. ■ See page 350. ■ See also: Return, Goto, Interrupt, Abort, Sow. ■ *New in Version 1; modified in Version 3.*

■ Ticks

Ticks is an option for graphics functions that specifies tick marks for axes.

The following settings can be given for Ticks:

None	no tick marks drawn
Automatic	tick marks placed automatically
{*xticks*, *yticks*, ... }	tick mark options specified separately for each axis

■ With the Automatic setting, tick marks are usually placed at points whose coordinates have the minimum number of digits in their decimal representation. ■ For each axis, the following tick mark options can be given:

None	no tick marks drawn
Automatic	tick mark positions and labels chosen automatically
{x_1, x_2, ... }	tick marks drawn at the specified positions
{{x_1, *label*$_1$}, {x_2, *label*$_2$}, ... }	tick marks drawn with the specified labels
{{x_1, *label*$_1$, *len*$_1$},... }	tick marks with specified scaled length
{{x_1, *label*$_1$, {*plen*$_1$, *mlen*$_1$}}, ... }	tick marks with specified lengths in the positive and negative directions
{{x_1, *label*$_1$, *len*$_1$, *style*$_1$}, ... }	tick marks with specified styles
func	a function to be applied to *xmin*, *xmax* to get the tick mark option

■ If no explicit labels are given, the tick mark labels are given as the numerical values of the tick mark positions. ■ Any expression can be given as a tick mark label. The expressions are formatted in OutputForm. ■ Tick mark lengths are given as a fraction of the distance across the whole plot. ■ Tick mark styles can involve graphics directives such as RGBColor and Thickness. ■ The tick mark function *func*[*xmin*, *xmax*] may return any other tick mark option. ■ Ticks can be used in both two- and three-dimensional graphics. ■ AbsoluteOptions gives the explicit form of Ticks specifications when Automatic settings are given. ■ See pages 512 and 552. ■ See also: Axes, AxesLabel, FrameTicks, GridLines, MeshRange. ■ *New in Version 1.*

■ TimeConstrained

TimeConstrained[*expr*, *t*] evaluates *expr*, stopping after *t* seconds.

TimeConstrained[*expr*, *t*, *failexpr*] returns *failexpr* if the time constraint is not met.

TimeConstrained generates an interrupt to abort the evaluation of *expr* if the evaluation is not completed within the specified time. ■ TimeConstrained evaluates *failexpr* only if the evaluation is aborted. ■ TimeConstrained returns $Aborted if the evaluation is aborted and no *failexpr* is specified. ■ TimeConstrained is accurate only down to a granularity of at least $TimeUnit seconds. ■ Aborts generated by TimeConstrained are treated just like those generated by Abort, and can thus be overruled by AbortProtect. ■ See page 712. ■ See also: MemoryConstrained, AbsoluteTiming, Timing, $IterationLimit, $RecursionLimit, Pause, Abort, TimeConstraint. ■ *New in Version 1.*

■ TimeConstraint

TimeConstraint is an option for Simplify and FullSimplify which gives the maximum number of seconds for which to try any particular transformation on any subpart of an expression.

The default setting for TimeConstraint is 300 (corresponding to 5 minutes) in Simplify and Infinity in FullSimplify. ■ Settings for TimeConstraint give only the maximum time to be spent in doing a particular transformation on a particular subpart; the total time spent in processing the whole expression may be considerably larger. ■ Changing the setting for TimeConstraint will never affect the validity of a result obtained from Simplify or FullSimplify, but smaller settings may prevent the simplest possible form from being found. ■ Since different computer systems run at different speeds, the same setting for TimeConstraint can lead to different results on different systems. ■ See page 814. ■ See also: ExcludedForms, TimeConstrained, AbsoluteTiming. ■ *New in Version 3.*

■ Times

$x*y*z$, $x \times y \times z$ or $x\ y\ z$ represents a product of terms.

The character $\times$ is entered as :*: or \[Times]. It is not the same as \[Cross]. ■ Times has attributes Flat, Orderless and OneIdentity. ■ The default value for arguments of Times, as used in x_. patterns, is 1. ■ Times[ ] is taken to be 1. ■ Times[x] is x. ■ 0 x evaluates to 0, but 0.0 x is left unchanged. ■ Unlike other functions, Times applies built-in rules before user-defined ones. As a result, it is not possible to make definitions such as 2*2=5. ■ See page 29. ■ See also: Divide, NonCommutativeMultiply, Dot. ■ *New in Version 1; modified in Version 3.*

■ TimesBy

x *= c multiplies x by c and returns the new value of x.

TimesBy has the attribute HoldFirst. ■ x *= c is equivalent to $x = x*c$. ■ See page 305. ■ See also: DivideBy, AddTo, Set. ■ *New in Version 1.*

■ TimeUsed

TimeUsed[ ] gives the total number of seconds of CPU time used so far in the current *Mathematica* session.

TimeUsed records only CPU time actually used by the *Mathematica* kernel. It does not include time used by external processes called by the kernel. It also does not include time during pauses produced by Pause. ■ TimeUsed is accurate only down to a granularity of at least $TimeUnit seconds. ■ See page 710. ■ See also: Timing, SessionTime. ■ *New in Version 2.*

■ TimeZone

TimeZone[ ] gives the time zone set for your computer system.

The time zone gives the number of hours which must be added to Greenwich mean time (GMT) to obtain local time. ■ U.S. eastern standard time (EST) corresponds to time zone −5. ■ Daylight saving time corrections must be included in the time zone, so U.S. eastern daylight time (EDT) corresponds to time zone −4. ■ See page 709. ■ See also: Date, AbsoluteTime. ■ Related package: Miscellaneous`CityData`. ■ *New in Version 2.*

■ Timing

Timing[*expr*] evaluates *expr*, and returns a list of time used, together with the result obtained.

Timing gives the CPU time in seconds, multiplied by the symbol Second. ■ Timing has attribute HoldAll. ■ Timing[*expr*;] will give {*timing*, Null}. ■ First[Timing[*expr*;]] /. Second->1 yields just the number of seconds required for the evaluation of *expr*. ■ Timing is accurate only down to a granularity of at least $TimeUnit seconds. ■ Timing includes only CPU time spent in the *Mathematica* kernel. It does not include time spent in external processes connected via *MathLink* or otherwise. Nor does it include time spent in the *Mathematica* front end. ■ Timing[*expr*] includes only time spent in the evaluation of *expr*, and not, for example, in the formatting or printing of the result. ■ Timing should give accurate results on all operating systems where the running of processes is specifically scheduled by the operating system. ■ On early versions of Microsoft Windows and Mac OS where *Mathematica* must explicitly yield in order for other processes to run, Timing may substantially overestimate the time used within *Mathematica*. ■ See page 711. ■ See also: AbsoluteTiming, TimeUsed, TimeConstrained, SessionTime, AbsoluteTime. ■ *New in Version 1.*

■ ToBoxes

ToBoxes[*expr*] generates boxes corresponding to the printed form of *expr* in StandardForm.

ToBoxes[*expr*, *form*] gives the boxes corresponding to output in the specified form.

ToBoxes uses any relevant definitions given for Format and MakeBoxes. ■ You can see how box structures generated by ToBoxes would be displayed by using DisplayForm. ■ See page 428. ■ See also: ToString, ToExpression, MakeBoxes, HoldForm, DisplayForm. ■ *New in Version 3.*

■ ToCharacterCode

ToCharacterCode["*string*"] gives a list of the integer codes corresponding to the characters in a string.

ToCharacterCode["*string*", "*encoding*"] gives integer codes according to the specified encoding.

ToCharacterCode handles both ordinary and special characters. ■ ToCharacterCode["*string*"] returns standard internal character codes used by *Mathematica*, which are the same on all computer systems. ■ For characters on an ordinary American English keyboard, the character codes follow the ASCII standard. ■ For common European languages, they follow the ISO Latin-1 standard. ■ For other characters, they follow the Unicode standard. ■ *Mathematica* defines various additional characters in private Unicode space, with character codes between 64256 and 64300. ■ Character codes returned by ToCharacterCode["*string*"] lie between 0 and 65535. ■ Encodings supported in ToCharacterCode["*string*", "*encoding*"] are listed in the notes for \$CharacterEncoding. ■ If a particular character has no character code in a given encoding, ToCharacterCode returns None in place of a character code. ■ ToCharacterCode[{"s_1", "s_2", ... }] gives a list of the lists of integer codes for each of the s_i. ■ See page 417. ■ See also: FromCharacterCode, Characters, CharacterRange, \$CharacterEncoding, DigitQ, LetterQ, InputForm. ■ *New in Version 2; modified in Version 3.*

■ ToDate

ToDate[*time*] converts an absolute time in seconds since the beginning of January 1, 1900 to a date of the form {*y*, *m*, *d*, *h*, *m*, *s*}.

ToDate converts between the forms returned by AbsoluteTime and Date. ■ ToDate assumes that both the absolute time and the date are to be given in the same time zone. ■ See page 710. ■ See also: FromDate. ■ Related package: Miscellaneous`Calendar`. ■ *New in Version 2.*

■ ToExpression

ToExpression[*input*] gives the expression obtained by interpreting strings or boxes as *Mathematica* input.

ToExpression[*input*, *form*] uses interpretation rules corresponding to the specified form.

ToExpression[*input*, *form*, *h*] wraps the head *h* around the expression produced before evaluating it.

Example: ToExpression["1 + 1"] ⟶ 2. ■ *form* can be InputForm, StandardForm, TraditionalForm or MathMLForm. ■ ToExpression["*string*"] uses InputForm interpretation rules. ■ ToExpression[*boxes*] uses StandardForm interpretation rules. ■ ToExpression prints a message and returns \$Failed if it finds a syntax error. ToExpression does not call \$SyntaxHandler. ■ The input given in ToExpression can correspond to multiple *Mathematica* expressions. ToExpression processes each one in turn, just like Get. ■ ToExpression[*input*, *form*, Hold] can be used to convert input to an expression, but with the expression wrapped in Hold to prevent evaluation. ■ ToExpression uses any relevant definitions given for MakeExpression. ■ See page 428. ■ See also: Symbol, MakeExpression, ToString, ToBoxes, SyntaxQ, SyntaxLength, Read, Get. ■ *New in Version 1; modified in Version 4.1.*

■ ToFileName

ToFileName["*directory*", "*name*"] assembles a full file name from a directory name and a file name.

ToFileName[{*dir*$_1$, *dir*$_2$, ... }, *name*] assembles a full file name from a hierarchy of directory names.

ToFileName[{*dir*$_1$, *dir*$_2$, ... }] assembles a single directory name from a hierarchy of directory names.

ToFileName works differently on different computer systems. ▪ ToFileName just creates a file name; it does not actually search for the file specified. ▪ ToFileName["", "*name*"] gives "*name*". ▪ See page 639. ▪ See also: DirectoryName, Get, $Input. ▪ *New in Version 3.*

■ Together

Together[*expr*] puts terms in a sum over a common denominator, and cancels factors in the result.

Example: Together[1/x + 1/(1-x)] $\longrightarrow -\dfrac{1}{(-1+x)\,x}$. ▪ Together makes a sum of terms into a single rational function. ▪ The denominator of the result of Together is typically the lowest common multiple of the denominators of each of the terms in the sum. ▪ Together avoids expanding out denominators unless it is necessary. ▪ Together is effectively the inverse of Apart. ▪ Together[*expr*, Modulus->*p*] generates a result modulo *p*. ▪ Together[*expr*, Extension->Automatic] allows operations to be performed on algebraic numbers in *expr*. ▪ Together[*expr*, Trig -> True] treats trigonometric functions as rational functions of exponentials, and manipulates them accordingly. ▪ See page 802. ▪ See also: Cancel, Collect, Factor, PolynomialGCD. ▪ *New in Version 1; modified in Version 3.*

■ TokenWords

TokenWords is an option for Read and related functions which gives a list of token words to be used to delimit words.

The setting for TokenWords is a list of strings which are used as delimiters for words to be read. ▪ The delimiters specified by TokenWords are themselves returned as words. ▪ See page 646. ▪ See also: WordSeparators. ▪ *New in Version 2.*

■ ToLowerCase

ToLowerCase[*string*] yields a string in which all letters have been converted to lower case.

ToLowerCase handles both ordinary and special characters. ▪ Variant upper-case characters such as \[CurlyCapitalUpsilon] are converted to their non-variant lower-case forms. ▪ See page 413. ▪ See also: LowerCaseQ, ToUpperCase, StringReplace, IgnoreCase. ▪ *New in Version 2; modified in Version 3.*

■ ToRadicals

ToRadicals[*expr*] attempts to express all Root objects in *expr* in terms of radicals.

ToRadicals can always give expressions in terms of radicals when the highest degree of the polynomial that appears in any Root object is four. ▪ There are some cases in which expressions involving radicals can in principle be given, but ToRadicals cannot find them. +▪ If Root objects in *expr* contain parameters, ToRadicals[*expr*] may yield a result that is not equal to *expr* for all values of the parameters. ▪ See page 826. ▪ See also: Solve, NSolve, RootReduce, Roots. ▪ *New in Version 3.*

■ ToRules

ToRules[*eqns*] takes logical combinations of equations, in the form generated by Roots and Reduce, and converts them to lists of rules, of the form produced by Solve.

Example: {ToRules[x==1 || x==2]} ⟶ {{x → 1}, {x → 2}}. ■ ToRules discards nonequalities (!=), and thus gives only "generic" solutions. ■ See page 820. ■ *New in Version 1.*

■ ToString

ToString[*expr*] gives a string corresponding to the printed form of *expr* in OutputForm.

ToString[*expr*, *form*] gives the string corresponding to output in the specified form.

ToString supports the same set of options as OpenAppend, with default settings FormatType -> OutputForm, PageWidth -> Infinity, TotalWidth -> Infinity. ■ ToString uses any relevant definitions given for Format and MakeBoxes. ■ See page 428. ■ See also: ToBoxes, ToExpression, HoldForm, WriteString, SymbolName. ■ *New in Version 1; modified in Version 3.*

+■ Total

Total[*list*] gives the total of the elements in *list*.

Total[*list*, *n*] totals all elements down to level *n*.

Total[*list*] is equivalent to Apply[Plus, *list*]. ■ Total[$f[e_1, e_2, \dots]$, 1] gives the sum of the e_i for any head f. ■ Total is defined so that Total[{$\{x_1, y_1, \dots\}$, $\{x_2, y_2, \dots\}$, $\dots$}] gives {Total[$\{x_1, x_2, \dots\}$], Total[$\{y_1, y_2, \dots\}$]}. ■ Total[*list*, Method->"CompensatedSummation"] uses compensated summation to reduce numerical error in the result. ■ Total works with SparseArray objects. ■ See pages 109 and 924. ■ See also: Plus, Tr, Mean, Count, Norm, Sum, Max. ■ *New in Version 5.0.*

■ TotalWidth

TotalWidth is an option which can be set for output streams to specify the maximum total number of characters of text that should be printed for each output expression. Short forms of expressions are given if the number of characters needed to print the whole expression is too large.

TotalWidth bounds the actual numbers of characters generated. Line breaks are not counted. ■ TotalWidth -> Infinity allows expressions of any length to be printed. ■ SetOptions[*stream*, TotalWidth -> *n*] resets the total width allowed for an open stream. ■ See also: Short, Skeleton, PageWidth. ■ *New in Version 1.*

■ ToUpperCase

ToUpperCase[*string*] yields a string in which all letters have been converted to upper case.

ToUpperCase handles both ordinary and special characters. ■ Variant lower-case characters such as \[CurlyPhi] are converted to their non-variant upper-case forms. ■ See page 413. ■ See also: UpperCaseQ, ToLowerCase, StringReplace, IgnoreCase. ■ *New in Version 2; modified in Version 3.*

▓ Tr

Tr[*list*] finds the trace of the matrix or tensor *list*.

Tr[*list*, *f*] finds a generalized trace, combining terms with *f* instead of Plus.

Tr[*list*, *f*, *n*] goes down to level *n* in *list*.

Tr[*list*] sums the diagonal elements *list*[[*i*, *i*, ...]]. ▪ Tr works for rectangular as well as square matrices and tensors. +▪ Tr can be used on SparseArray objects. ▪ See page 905. ▪ See also: Total, Transpose, Det, DiagonalMatrix, Eigenvalues. ▪ *New in Version 4.*

▓ Trace

Trace[*expr*] generates a list of all expressions used in the evaluation of *expr*.

Trace[*expr*, *form*] includes only those expressions which match *form*.

Trace[*expr*, *s*] includes all evaluations which use transformation rules associated with the symbol *s*.

In general, *form* in Trace[*expr*, *form*] is compared both with each complete expression that is evaluated, and with the tag associated with any transformation rule used in the evaluation. ▪ Trace[*expr*, *lhs* -> *rhs*] picks out expressions which match *lhs*, then replaces them with *rhs* in the list returned. ▪ All expressions in the list returned by Trace are wrapped in HoldForm. ▪ Trace returns a set of nested lists. Each individual list corresponds to a single evaluation chain, which contains the sequence of forms found for a particular expression. The list has sublists which give the histories of subsidiary evaluations. ▪ Example: Trace[2 3 + 4] ⟶ {{2 3, 6}, 6 + 4, 10}. ▪ The following options can be given:

MatchLocalNames	True	whether to allow *x* to stand for *x*$*nnn*
TraceAbove	False	whether to show evaluation chains which contain the chain containing *form*
TraceBackward	False	whether to show expressions preceding *form* in the evaluation chain
TraceDepth	Infinity	how many levels of nested evaluations to include
TraceForward	False	whether to show expressions following *form* in the evaluation chain
TraceOff	None	forms within which to switch off tracing
TraceOn	_	forms within which to switch on tracing
TraceOriginal	False	whether to look at expressions before their heads and arguments are evaluated

▪ During the execution of Trace, the settings for the *form* argument, and for the options TraceOn and TraceOff, can be modified by resetting the values of the global variables $TracePattern, $TraceOn and $TraceOff, respectively. ▪ See page 356. ▪ See also: TraceDialog, TracePrint, TraceScan, EvaluationMonitor. ▪ *New in Version 2.*

▓ TraceAbove

TraceAbove is an option for Trace and related functions which specifies whether to include evaluation chains which contain the evaluation chain containing the pattern *form* sought.

TraceAbove -> True includes the first and last expressions in all evaluation chains within which the evaluation chain containing *form* occurs. ▪ TraceAbove -> All includes all expressions in these evaluation chains. ▪ TraceAbove -> {*backward*, *forward*} allows you to specify separately which expressions to include in the backward and forward directions. ▪ Using TraceAbove, you can see the complete paths by which expressions matching *form* arose during an evaluation. ▪ See page 363. ▪ See also: StackComplete. ▪ *New in Version 2.*

■ TraceBackward

TraceBackward is an option for Trace and related functions which specifies whether to include preceding expressions on the evaluation chain that contains the pattern *form* sought.

TraceBackward -> True includes the first expression on the evaluation chain that contains *form*. ■ TraceBackward -> All includes all expressions before *form* on the evaluation chain that contains *form*. ■ TraceBackward allows you to see the previous forms that an expression had during an evaluation. ■ See page 363. ■ See also: StackComplete. ■ *New in Version 2.*

■ TraceDepth

TraceDepth is an option for Trace and related functions which specifies the maximum nesting of evaluation chains that are to be included.

Setting TraceDepth -> *n* keeps only parts down to level *n* in nested lists generated by Trace. ■ By setting TraceDepth, you can make Trace and related functions skip over "inner" parts of a computation, making their operation more efficient. ■ See page 362. ■ See also: TraceOff. ■ *New in Version 2.*

■ TraceDialog

TraceDialog[*expr*] initiates a dialog for every expression used in the evaluation of *expr*.

TraceDialog[*expr*, *form*] initiates a dialog only for expressions which match *form*.

TraceDialog[*expr*, *s*] initiates dialogs only for expressions whose evaluations use transformation rules associated with the symbol *s*.

See notes for Trace. ■ The expression to be evaluated when a dialog is called is given as Out[$Line] of the dialog, wrapped in HoldForm. The expression can be seen by asking for % when the dialog is first started. ■ Any value returned from the dialog is discarded. ■ TraceDialog[*expr*] returns the result of evaluating *expr*. ■ See page 366. ■ *New in Version 2.*

■ TraceForward

TraceForward is an option for Trace and related functions which specifies whether to include later expressions on the evaluation chain that contains the pattern *form* sought.

TraceForward -> True includes the final expression on the evaluation chain that contains *form*. ■ TraceForward -> All includes all expressions after *form* on the evaluation chain that contains *form*. ■ TraceForward allows you to see the transformations performed on an expression generated during an evaluation. ■ See page 362. ■ *New in Version 2.*

■ TraceOff

TraceOff is an option for Trace and related functions which specifies forms inside which tracing should be switched off.

The setting for TraceOff gives a pattern which is compared with expressions to be evaluated. If the pattern matches the expression, then tracing will be switched off while that expression is being evaluated. The pattern is also tested against tags associated with the evaluation. ■ You can use TraceOff to avoid tracing inner parts of a computation. ■ The default setting TraceOff -> None never switches off tracing. ■ TraceOn will not work inside TraceOff. ■ During the execution of Trace, the settings for TraceOn and TraceOff can be modified by resetting the values of the global variables $TraceOn and $TraceOff. ■ See page 360. ■ See also: TraceDepth, TraceOn. ■ *New in Version 2.*

■ TraceOn

TraceOn is an option for Trace and related functions which specifies when tracing should be switched on.

With the setting TraceOn -> *patt*, Trace and related functions do not start tracing until they encounter expressions to evaluate which match the pattern *patt*. This pattern is also tested against tags associated with the evaluation. ■ TraceOff can be used within tracing switched on by TraceOn. ■ Once tracing has been switched off by TraceOff, however, TraceOn will not switch it on again. ■ During the execution of Trace, the settings for TraceOn and TraceOff can be modified by resetting the values of the global variables $TraceOn and $TraceOff. ■ See page 360. ■ See also: TraceOff. ■ *New in Version 2.*

■ TraceOriginal

TraceOriginal is an option for Trace and related functions which specifies whether to test the form of each expression before its head and arguments are evaluated.

With the default TraceOriginal -> False, the forms of expressions generated during an evaluation are tested only after their head and arguments have been evaluated. In addition, evaluation chains for expressions which do not change under evaluation are not included. ■ With TraceOriginal -> True, the forms before evaluation of the head and arguments are also tested, and evaluation chains for expressions which do not change under evaluation are included. ■ See page 364. ■ *New in Version 2.*

■ TracePrint

TracePrint[*expr*] prints all expressions used in the evaluation of *expr*.

TracePrint[*expr*, *form*] includes only those expressions which match *form*.

TracePrint[*expr*, *s*] includes all evaluations which use transformation rules associated with the symbol *s*.

See notes for Trace. ■ TracePrint indents its output in correspondence with the nesting levels for lists generated by Trace. ■ The indentation is done using the print form defined for the object Indent[*d*]. ■ TracePrint prints the forms of expressions before any of their elements are evaluated. ■ TracePrint does not support the TraceBackward option of Trace. ■ TracePrint yields only the forward part of the output specified by the option setting TraceAbove -> All. ■ TracePrint[*expr*] returns the result of evaluating *expr*. ■ See page 365. ■ *New in Version 2.*

■ TraceScan

TraceScan[*f*, *expr*] applies *f* to all expressions used in the evaluation of *expr*.

TraceScan[*f*, *expr*, *form*] includes only those expressions which match *form*.

TraceScan[*f*, *expr*, *s*] includes all evaluations which use transformation rules associated with the symbol *s*.

TraceScan[*f*, *expr*, *form*, *fp*] applies *f* before evaluation and *fp* after evaluation to expressions used in the evaluation of *expr*.

See notes for Trace. ■ All expressions are wrapped in HoldForm to prevent evaluation before *f* or *fp* are applied to them. ■ The function *fp* is given as arguments both the form before evaluation and the form after evaluation. ■ TraceScan[*f*, *expr*] returns the result of evaluating *expr*. ■ See page 366. ■ *New in Version 2.*

■ **TraditionalForm**

TraditionalForm[*expr*] prints as an approximation to the traditional mathematical notation for *expr*.

Output from TraditionalForm cannot necessarily be given as unique and unambiguous input to *Mathematica*. ■ TraditionalForm inserts invisible TagBox and InterpretationBox constructs into the box form of output it generates, to allow unique interpretation. ■ TraditionalForm can be edited in the notebook front end. ■ TraditionalForm uses special characters as well as ordinary keyboard characters. ■ TraditionalForm incorporates a large collection of rules for approximating traditional mathematical notation. ■ TraditionalForm prints functions in Global` context in the form $f(x)$. ■ ToExpression[*boxes*, TraditionalForm] will attempt to convert from TraditionalForm. ■ The notebook front end contains menu items for conversion to and from TraditionalForm. ■ See page 425. ■ See also: StandardForm, TeXForm, MakeExpression, ToBoxes, MathMLForm. ■ *New in Version 3.*

■ **TransformationFunctions**

TransformationFunctions is an option for Simplify and FullSimplify which gives the list of functions to apply to try to transform parts of an expression.

The default setting TransformationFunctions->Automatic uses a built-in collection of transformation functions. ■ TransformationFunctions->{f_1, f_2, ... } uses only the functions f_i. ■ TransformationFunctions->{Automatic, f_1, f_2, ... } uses built-in transformation functions together with the functions f_i. ■ See page 815. ■ See also: Simplify, FullSimplify, ReplaceAll, ExcludedForms, FunctionExpand. ■ *New in Version 4.*

■ **Transpose**

Transpose[*list*] transposes the first two levels in *list*.

Transpose[*list*, {n_1, n_2, ... }] transposes *list* so that the kth level in *list* is the $n_k{}^{\text{th}}$ level in the result.

Example: Transpose[{{a,b},{c,d}}] ⟶ {{a, c}, {b, d}}. ■ Transpose gives the usual transpose of a matrix. ■ Acting on a tensor $T_{i_1 i_2 i_3 ...}$ Transpose gives the tensor $T_{i_2 i_1 i_3 ...}$. ■ Transpose[*list*, {n_1, n_2, ... }] gives the tensor $T_{i_{n_1} i_{n_2} ...}$. ■ So long as the lengths of the lists at particular levels are the same, the specifications n_k do not necessarily have to be distinct. ■ Example: Transpose[Array[a, {3, 3}], {1, 1}] ⟶ {a[1, 1], a[2, 2], a[3, 3]}. ⁺■ Transpose works on SparseArray objects. ■ See page 905. ■ See also: Flatten, Thread, Tr. ■ Related package: LinearAlgebra`MatrixManipulation`. ■ *New in Version 1.*

■ **TreeForm**

TreeForm[*expr*] prints with different levels in *expr* shown at different depths.

See pages 236 and 237. ■ See also: FullForm, MatrixForm. ■ Related package: DiscreteMath`Tree`. ■ *New in Version 1.*

■ **TrigExpand**

TrigExpand[*expr*] expands out trigonometric functions in *expr*.

TrigExpand operates on both circular and hyperbolic functions. ■ TrigExpand splits up sums and integer multiples that appear in arguments of trigonometric functions, and then expands out products of trigonometric functions into sums of powers, using trigonometric identities when possible. ■ See page 811. ■ See also: TrigFactor, TrigReduce, TrigToExp, Expand, FunctionExpand, Simplify, FullSimplify. ■ *New in Version 3.*

■ TrigFactor

TrigFactor[*expr*] factors trigonometric functions in *expr*.

TrigFactor operates on both circular and hyperbolic functions. ■ TrigFactor splits up sums and integer multiples that appear in arguments of trigonometric functions, and then factors resulting polynomials in trigonometric functions, using trigonometric identities when possible. ■ See page 811. ■ See also: TrigExpand, TrigReduce, TrigToExp, Factor, Simplify, FullSimplify. ■ *New in Version 3.*

■ TrigFactorList

TrigFactorList[*expr*] factors trigonometric functions in *expr*, yielding a list of lists containing trigonometric monomials and exponents.

See notes for TrigFactor. ■ TrigFactorList tries to give results in terms of powers of Sin, Cos, Sinh and Cosh, explicitly decomposing functions like Tan. ■ See page 811. ■ See also: FactorList, TrigToExp. ■ *New in Version 3.*

■ TrigReduce

TrigReduce[*expr*] rewrites products and powers of trigonometric functions in *expr* in terms of trigonometric functions with combined arguments.

TrigReduce operates on both circular and hyperbolic functions. ■ Given a trigonometric polynomial, TrigReduce typically yields a linear expression involving trigonometric functions with more complicated arguments. ■ See page 811. ■ See also: TrigExpand, TrigFactor, TrigToExp, Simplify, FullSimplify. ■ *New in Version 3.*

■ TrigToExp

TrigToExp[*expr*] converts trigonometric functions in *expr* to exponentials.

TrigToExp operates on both circular and hyperbolic functions, and their inverses. ■ See page 812. ■ See also: ExpToTrig, TrigReduce, ComplexExpand. ■ *New in Version 3.*

■ True

True is the symbol for the Boolean value true.

See page 85. ■ See also: False, TrueQ, If, Booleans, ForAll. ■ *New in Version 1.*

■ TrueQ

TrueQ[*expr*] yields True if *expr* is True, and yields False otherwise.

Example: TrueQ[x==y] $\longrightarrow$ False. ■ You can use TrueQ to "assume" that a test fails when its outcome is not clear. ■ TrueQ[*expr*] is equivalent to If[*expr*, True, False, False]. ■ See page 346. ■ See also: If, Condition, SameQ. ■ *New in Version 1.*

■ UnderoverscriptBox

UnderoverscriptBox[*x*, *y*, *z*] represents $\overset{z}{\underset{y}{x}}$ in input and output.

Inside \(... \) UnderoverscriptBox[*x*, *y*, *z*] can be input as *x* \+ *y* \% *z*. ■ In a notebook an UnderoverscriptBox can be created by using CTRL+ to move to the underscript, then CTRL% to move to the overscript. CTRL␣ moves out of the underscript or overscript position. ■ In StandardForm and InputForm, UnderoverscriptBox[*x*, *y*, *z*] is interpreted on input as Underoverscript[*x*, *y*, *z*]. ■ See notes for UnderscriptBox and OverscriptBox. ■ See page 445. ■ See also: SubsuperscriptBox, GridBox, ColumnForm. ■ *New in Version 3.*

■ **UnderscriptBox**

UnderscriptBox[x, y] represents x in input and output.

Inside \(... \) UnderscriptBox[x, y] can be input as x \+ y. ■ In a notebook a UnderscriptBox can be created using [CTRL]+. [CTRL]␣ moves out of the underscript position. ■ In StandardForm and InputForm, UnderscriptBox[x, y] is interpreted on input as Underscript[x, y]. ■ UnderscriptBox[x, "_"] is interpreted as UnderBar[x] or $\underline{x}$. The input form x\&\%- can be used. ■ The baseline of UnderscriptBox[x, y] is taken to be the baseline of x. ■ UnderscriptBox[x, y] is usually output with y in a smaller font than x. ■ With the option setting LimitsPositioning->True y is placed in an underscript position when the whole UnderscriptBox is displayed large, and in a subscript position when it is displayed smaller. ■ In StandardForm, explicit UnderscriptBox objects are output literally. You can use DisplayForm to see the display form of such objects. ■ See page 445. ■ See also: OverscriptBox, UnderoverscriptBox, SubscriptBox, GridBox, ScriptSizeMultipliers. ■ *New in Version 3.*

■ **Unequal**

lhs != *rhs* or *lhs* ≠ *rhs* returns False if *lhs* and *rhs* are identical.

$x \neq y$ can be entered as x \[NotEqual] y or x :!=: y. ■ *lhs* ≠ *rhs* returns True if *lhs* and *rhs* are determined to be unequal by comparisons between numbers or other raw data, such as strings. ■ Approximate numbers are considered unequal if they differ beyond their last two decimal digits. ■ $e_1 \neq e_2 \neq e_3 \neq \ldots$ gives True only if none of the e_i are equal. $2 \neq 3 \neq 2 \longrightarrow$ False. ■ *lhs* ≠ *rhs* represents a symbolic condition that can be generated and manipulated by functions like Reduce and LogicalExpand. ■ Unequal[e] gives True. ■ For exact numeric quantities, Unequal internally uses numerical approximations to establish inequality. This process can be affected by the setting of the global variable $MaxExtraPrecision. ■ In StandardForm, Unequal is printed using ≠. ■ See page 86. ■ See also: Equal, UnsameQ, Order. ■ *New in Version 1; modified in Version 3.*

■ **Unevaluated**

Unevaluated[*expr*] represents the unevaluated form of *expr* when it appears as the argument to a function.

f[Unevaluated[*expr*]] effectively works by temporarily setting attributes so that f holds its argument unevaluated, then evaluating f[*expr*]. ■ Example: Length[Unevaluated[5+6]] $\longrightarrow$ 2. ■ See page 339. ■ See also: Hold, HoldFirst, ReplacePart. ■ *New in Version 2.*

■ **Uninstall**

Uninstall[*link*] terminates an external program started by Install, and removes *Mathematica* definitions set up by it.

The argument of Uninstall is a LinkObject representing a *MathLink* link as returned by Install. ■ Uninstall calls Unset to remove definitions set up by Install. ■ See page 659. ■ See also: Install, LinkClose, Close. ■ *New in Version 2; modified in Version 3.*

■ **Union**

Union[*list*$_1$, *list*$_2$, ...] gives a sorted list of all the distinct elements that appear in any of the *list*$_i$.

Union[*list*] gives a sorted version of a list, in which all duplicated elements have been dropped.

If the *list*$_i$ are considered as sets, Union gives their union. ■ Union[*list*$_1$, *list*$_2$, ...] can be input in StandardForm and InputForm as *list*$_1$ ∪ *list*$_2$ ∪ ... . The character ∪ can be entered as :un: or \[Union]. ■ The *list*$_i$ must have the same head, but it need not be List. ■ Union[*list*$_1$, ... , SameTest->*test*] applies *test* to each pair of elements in the *list*$_i$ to determine whether they should be considered the same. ■ See page 127. ■ See also: Join, Intersection, Complement, Split. ■ *New in Version 1; modified in Version 3.*

■ Unique

Unique[ ] generates a new symbol, whose name is of the form $nnn.

Unique[x] generates a new symbol, with a name of the form $x$nnn.

Unique[{x, y, ... }] generates a list of new symbols.

Unique["xxx"] generates a new symbol, with a name of the form $xxxnnn$.

Unique[x] numbers the symbols it creates using $ModuleNumber, and increments $ModuleNumber every time it is called. ■ Unique["xxx"] numbers the symbols it creates sequentially, starting at 1 for each string xxx. ■ Unique[$name$, {$attr_1$, $attr_2$, ... }] generates a symbol which has the attributes $attr_i$. ■ See page 382. ■ See also: Symbol, ToExpression, Names, GeneratedParameters, Module, CharacterRange. ■ *New in Version 1.*

■ UnitStep

UnitStep[x] represents the unit step function, equal to 0 for $x < 0$ and 1 for $x \geq 0$.

UnitStep[x_1, x_2, ...] represents the multidimensional unit step function which is 1 only if none of the x_i are negative.

Some transformations are done automatically when UnitStep appears in a product of terms. ■ UnitStep provides a convenient way to represent piecewise continuous functions. ■ UnitStep has attribute Orderless. ■ For exact numeric quantities, UnitStep internally uses numerical approximations to establish its result. This process can be affected by the setting of the global variable $MaxExtraPrecision. ■ See page 879. ■ See also: Sign, Positive, DiracDelta, DiscreteDelta, KroneckerDelta. ■ *New in Version 4.*

■ Unprotect

Unprotect[s_1, s_2, ...] removes the attribute Protected for the symbols s_i.

Unprotect["$form_1$", "$form_2$", ...] unprotects all symbols whose names textually match any of the $form_i$.

A typical sequence in adding your own rules for built-in functions is Unprotect[f]; *definition*; Protect[f]. ■ See notes for Protect. ■ See pages 321 and 1044. ■ See also: Protect, Locked, SetOptions. ■ *New in Version 1.*

■ UnsameQ

lhs =!= *rhs* yields True if the expression *lhs* is not identical to *rhs*, and yields False otherwise.

See notes for SameQ. ■ e_1 =!= e_2 =!= e_3 gives True if no two of the e_i are identical. ■ See page 268. ■ See also: Equal, Order. ■ *New in Version 2.*

■ Unset

lhs =. removes any rules defined for *lhs*.

Rules are removed only when their left-hand sides are identical to *lhs*, and the tests in Condition given on the right-hand side are also identical. ■ See pages 304 and 1052. ■ See also: Clear, TagUnset. ■ *New in Version 1.*

■ Update

Update[*symbol*] tells *Mathematica* that hidden changes have been made which could affect values associated with a symbol.

Update[ ] specifies that the value of any symbol could be affected.

Update manipulates internal optimization features of *Mathematica*. It should not need to be called except under special circumstances that rarely occur in practice. ■ One special circumstance is that changes in the value of one symbol can affect the value of another symbol by changing the outcome of Condition tests. In such cases, you may need to use Update on the symbol you think may be affected. ■ Using Update will never give you incorrect results, although it will slow down the operation of the system. ■ See page 370. ■ *New in Version 1.*

■ UpperCaseQ

UpperCaseQ[*string*] yields True if all the characters in the string are upper-case letters, and yields False otherwise.

UpperCaseQ treats both ordinary and special characters. ■ See page 413. ■ See also: LowerCaseQ, LetterQ, ToUpperCase, ToCharacterCode. ■ *New in Version 2; modified in Version 3.*

■ UpSet

lhs^=*rhs* assigns *rhs* to be the value of *lhs*, and associates the assignment with symbols that occur at level one in *lhs*.

f[*g*[*x*]]=*value* makes an assignment associated with *f*. *f*[*g*[*x*]]^=*value* makes an assignment associated instead with *g*. ■ UpSet associates an assignment with *all* the distinct symbols that occur either directly as arguments of *lhs*, or as the heads of arguments of *lhs*. ■ See pages 318 and 1051. ■ See also: TagSet, UpValues. ■ *New in Version 1.*

■ UpSetDelayed

lhs^:=*rhs* assigns *rhs* to be the delayed value of *lhs*, and associates the assignment with symbols that occur at level one in *lhs*.

See notes for UpSet and SetDelayed. ■ See pages 316 and 318. ■ *New in Version 1.*

■ UpValues

UpValues[*f*] gives a list of transformation rules corresponding to all upvalues defined for the symbol *f*.

You can specify the upvalues for *f* by making an assignment of the form UpValues[*f*] = *list*. ■ The list returned by UpValues has elements of the form HoldPattern[*lhs*] :> *rhs*. ■ See page 322. ■ See also: Set, DownValues, HoldAllComplete. ■ *New in Version 2; modified in Version 3.*

■ ValueQ

ValueQ[*expr*] gives True if a value has been defined for *expr*, and gives False otherwise.

ValueQ has attribute HoldFirst. ■ ValueQ gives False only if *expr* would not change if it were to be entered as *Mathematica* input. ■ See page 268. ■ See also: Information. ■ *New in Version 1.*

■ Variables

Variables[*poly*] gives a list of all independent variables in a polynomial.

See page 799. ■ See also: Coefficient. ■ *New in Version 1.*

⁺■ Variance

Variance[*list*] gives the statistical variance of the elements in *list*.

Variance[*list*] gives the unbiased estimate of variance. ■ Variance[*list*] is equivalent to Total[(*list*-Mean[*list*])^2]/(Length[*list*]-1). ■ Variance handles both numerical and symbolic data. ■ Variance[{{x_1, y_1, ... }, {x_2, y_2, ... }, ... }] gives {Variance[{x_1, x_2, ... }], Variance[{y_1, y_2, ... }]}. ■ Variance works with SparseArray objects. ■ See pages 794 and 924. ■ See also: StandardDeviation, Mean, Quantile. ■ Related packages: Statistics`DescriptiveStatistics`, Statistics`MultiDescriptiveStatistics`. ■ *New in Version 5.0.*

■ VectorQ

~ VectorQ[*expr*] gives True if *expr* is a list or a one-dimensional SparseArray object, none of whose elements are themselves lists, and gives False otherwise.

VectorQ[*expr*, *test*] gives True only if *test* yields True when applied to each of the elements in *expr*.

VectorQ[*expr*, NumberQ] tests whether *expr* is a vector of numbers. ■ See pages 267 and 900. ■ See also: MatrixQ, ArrayDepth. ■ *New in Version 1; modified in Version 2.*

■ Verbatim

Verbatim[*expr*] represents *expr* in pattern matching, requiring that *expr* be matched exactly as it appears, with no substitutions for blanks or other transformations.

Verbatim[x_] will match only the actual expression x_. ■ Verbatim is useful in setting up rules for transforming other transformation rules. ■ Verbatim[*expr*] does not maintain *expr* in an unevaluated form. ■ See page 278. ■ See also: HoldPattern. ■ *New in Version 3.*

■ ViewCenter

ViewCenter is an option for Graphics3D and SurfaceGraphics which gives the scaled coordinates of the point which appears at the center of the display area in the final plot.

With the default setting ViewCenter -> Automatic, the whole bounding box is centered in the final image area. ■ With the setting ViewCenter -> {1/2, 1/2, 1/2}, the center of the three-dimensional bounding box will be placed at the center of the final display area. ■ The setting for ViewCenter is given in scaled coordinates, which run from 0 to 1 across each dimension of the bounding box. ■ With SphericalRegion -> True, the circumscribing sphere is always centered, regardless of the setting for ViewCenter. ■ See page 533. ■ *New in Version 2.*

■ ViewPoint

ViewPoint is an option for Graphics3D and SurfaceGraphics which gives the point in space from which the objects plotted are to be viewed.

ViewPoint -> {*x*, *y*, *z*} gives the position of the view point relative to the center of the three-dimensional box that contains the object being plotted. ■ The view point is given in a special scaled coordinate system in which the longest side of the bounding box has length 1. The center of the bounding box is taken to have coordinates {0, 0, 0}.

(continued)

■ ViewPoint *(continued)*

    ■ Common settings for ViewPoint are:

{1.3, -2.4, 2}	default setting
{0, -2, 0}	directly in front
{0, -2, 2}	in front and up
{0, -2, -2}	in front and down
{-2, -2, 0}	left-hand corner
{2, -2, 0}	right-hand corner
{0, 0, 2}	directly above

    ■ Choosing ViewPoint further away from the object reduces the distortion associated with perspective. ■ The view point must lie outside the bounding box. ■ The coordinates of the corners of the bounding box in the special coordinate system used for ViewPoint are determined by the setting for the BoxRatios option. ■ See page 532. ■ See also: ViewCenter, ViewVertical, SphericalRegion. ■ Related package: Geometry`Rotations`. ■ *New in Version 1.*

■ ViewVertical

ViewVertical is an option for Graphics3D and SurfaceGraphics which specifies what direction in scaled coordinates should be vertical in the final image.

The default setting is ViewVertical -> {0, 0, 1}, which specifies that the z axis in your original coordinate system should end up vertical in the final image. ■ The setting for ViewVertical is given in scaled coordinates, which run from 0 to 1 across each dimension of the bounding box. ■ Only the direction of the vector specified by ViewVertical is important; its magnitude is irrelevant. ■ See page 533. ■ *New in Version 2.*

■ Visible

Visible is an option for Notebook which specifies whether the notebook should be explicitly displayed on the screen.

With Visible->False a notebook can still be manipulated from the kernel, but will not explicitly be displayed on the screen. ■ NotebookCreate[Visible->False] creates a new invisible window. ■ See page 620. ■ See also: Selectable, WindowFloating, CellOpen. ■ *New in Version 3.*

■ WeierstrassHalfPeriods

WeierstrassHalfPeriods[{g_2, g_3}] gives the half-periods {ω, ω'} for Weierstrass elliptic functions corresponding to the invariants {g_2, g_3}.

Mathematical function (see Section A.3.10). ■ The half-periods {ω, ω'} define the fundamental period parallelogram for the Weierstrass elliptic functions. ■ WeierstrassHalfPeriods is the inverse of WeierstrassInvariants. ■ See page 782. ■ See also: WeierstrassP, InverseWeierstrassP, ModularLambda. ■ *New in Version 3.*

■ WeierstrassInvariants

WeierstrassInvariants[{ω, ω'}] gives the invariants {g_2, g_3} for Weierstrass elliptic functions corresponding to the half-periods {ω, ω'}.

Mathematical function (see Section A.3.10). ■ WeierstrassInvariants is the inverse of WeierstrassHalfPeriods. ■ See page 782. ■ See also: WeierstrassP, InverseWeierstrassP, KleinInvariantJ. ■ *New in Version 3.*

■ WeierstrassP

WeierstrassP[u, {g_2, g_3}] gives the Weierstrass elliptic function $\wp(u;g_2,g_3)$.

Mathematical function (see Section A.3.10). ■ $\wp(u;g_2,g_3)$ gives the value of x for which $u = \int_{\infty}^{x}(4t^3 - g_2t - g_3)^{-1/2}\,dt$. ■ See page 782 for a discussion of argument conventions for elliptic functions. ■ See pages 785 and 787. ■ See also: InverseWeierstrassP. ■ *New in Version 1; modified in Version 3.*

■ WeierstrassPPrime

WeierstrassPPrime[u, {g_2, g_3}] gives the derivative of the Weierstrass elliptic function $\wp(u;g_2,g_3)$.

Mathematical function (see Section A.3.10). ■ $\wp'(u;g_2,g_3) = (\partial/\partial u)\wp(u;g_2,g_3)$. ■ See page 782 for a discussion of argument conventions for elliptic functions. ■ See pages 785 and 787. ■ *New in Version 1; modified in Version 3.*

■ WeierstrassSigma

WeierstrassSigma[u, {g_2, g_3}] gives the Weierstrass sigma function $\sigma(u;g_2,g_3)$.

Mathematical function (see Section A.3.10). ■ Related to WeierstrassZeta by the differential equation $\sigma'(z;g_2,g_3)/\sigma(z;g_2,g_3) = \zeta(z;g_2,g_3)$. ■ WeierstrassSigma is not periodic and is therefore not strictly an elliptic function. ■ See page 782 for a discussion of argument conventions for elliptic and related functions. ■ See page 785. ■ See also: WeierstrassZeta. ■ *New in Version 3.*

■ WeierstrassZeta

WeierstrassZeta[u, {g_2, g_3}] gives the Weierstrass zeta function $\zeta(u;g_2,g_3)$.

Mathematical function (see Section A.3.10). ■ Related to WeierstrassP by the differential equation $\zeta'(z;g_2,g_3) = -\wp(z;g_2,g_3)$. ■ WeierstrassZeta is not periodic and is therefore not strictly an elliptic function. ■ See page 782 for a discussion of argument conventions for elliptic and related functions. ■ See page 785. ■ See also: WeierstrassSigma. ■ *New in Version 3.*

■ Which

Which[$test_1$, $value_1$, $test_2$, $value_2$, ...] evaluates each of the $test_i$ in turn, returning the value of the $value_i$ corresponding to the first one that yields True.

Example: Which[1==2, x, 1==1, y] $\longrightarrow$ y. ■ Which has attribute HoldAll. ■ If any of the $test_i$ evaluated by Which give neither True nor False, then a Which object containing these remaining elements is returned unevaluated. ■ You can make Which return a "default value" by taking the last $test_i$ to be True. ■ If all the $test_i$ evaluate to False, Which returns Null. ■ See page 345. ■ See also: Switch, If. ■ *New in Version 1.*

■ While

While[$test$, $body$] evaluates $test$, then $body$, repetitively, until $test$ first fails to give True.

While[$test$] does the loop with a null body. ■ If Break[ ] is generated in the evaluation of $body$, the While loop exits. ■ Continue[ ] exits the evaluation of $body$, and continues the loop. ■ Unless Return[ ] or Throw[ ] are generated, the final value returned by While is Null. ■ Example: i=0; While[i < 0, tot += f[i]; i++]. Note that the roles of ; and , are *reversed* relative to the C programming language. ■ See page 352. ■ See also: Do, For, NestWhile, Nest, Fold, Select, Throw. ■ *New in Version 1.*

■ WindowClickSelect

WindowClickSelect is an option for Notebook which specifies whether the window for the notebook should become selected if you click on it.

With WindowClickSelect->True, clicking on the window corresponding to a notebook makes that notebook the currently selected one. ▪ WindowClickSelect affects selection of a window as a whole; Selectable affects only selection of the contents of a window. ▪ See page 620. ▪ See also: WindowFloating, SetSelectedNotebook. ▪ *New in Version 3.*

■ WindowElements

WindowElements is an option for Notebook which specifies the elements to include in the window used to display the notebook on the screen.

WindowElements is typically set to a list containing elements such as "HorizontalScrollBar", "MagnificationPopUp", "StatusArea" and "VerticalScrollBar". ▪ The details of particular elements may differ from one computer system to another. ▪ See page 620. ▪ See also: WindowToolbars, WindowTitle, WindowFrame. ▪ *New in Version 3.*

■ WindowFloating

WindowFloating is an option for Notebook which specifies whether the window for the notebook should float on top of other windows when it is displayed on the screen.

WindowFloating->True is often used for palettes. ▪ If there are several floating windows the most recently selected one goes on top. ▪ See page 620. ▪ See also: WindowClickSelect, Visible. ▪ *New in Version 3.*

■ WindowFrame

WindowFrame is an option for Notebook which specifies the type of frame to draw around the window in which the notebook is displayed on the screen.

Typical possible settings are:

"Frameless"	an ordinary window with no frame
"Generic"	a window with a generic border
"ModalDialog"	a modal dialog box window
"ModelessDialog"	a modeless dialog box window
"MovableModalDialog"	a movable modal dialog box window
"Normal"	an ordinary window
"Palette"	a palette window
"ThinFrame"	an ordinary window with a thin frame

▪ The details of how particular types of frames are rendered may differ from one computer system to another. ▪ Settings for WindowFrame affect only the appearance of a window, and not any of its other characteristics. ▪ See page 620. ▪ See also: WindowTitle, WindowElements, WindowToolbars. ▪ *New in Version 3.*

■ **WindowMargins**

WindowMargins is an option for Notebook which specifies what margins to leave around the window that is used to display the notebook on the screen.

WindowMargins->{{*left*, *right*}, {*bottom*, *top*}} specifies the distances from each edge of your screen to each edge of the window. ■ Typically only two distances are given explicitly; the others are Automatic, indicating that they should be determined from the size of the window. ■ Explicit distances are given in printer's points. ■ Negative values represent edges that are off the screen. ■ The settings for WindowMargins change whenever you move a window around interactively using the front end. ■ Window edges closer to the edges of the screen are typically assigned explicit margin distances; the others are set to Automatic. This allows the same setting for WindowMargins to work on screens of different sizes. ■ With WindowSize->{Automatic, Automatic} all four margin distances must be given explicitly. ■ With the default setting WindowMargins->Automatic, new windows are placed on your screen in such a way as to make as many window title bars as possible visible. ■ See page 620. ■ See also: WindowSize, WindowMovable. ■ *New in Version 3.*

■ **WindowMovable**

WindowMovable is an option for Notebook which specifies whether to allow the window for the notebook to be moved around interactively on the screen.

WindowMovable affects only interactive operations in the front end. ■ Even with WindowMovable->False, the WindowMargins option can still be reset from the kernel or option inspector menu. ■ See page 620. ■ See also: WindowMargins, Selectable. ■ *New in Version 3.*

■ **WindowSize**

WindowSize is an option for Notebook which specifies the size of window that should be used to display a notebook on the screen.

WindowSize->{*w*, *h*} gives the width and height of the window in printer's points. ■ Setting either width or height to Automatic causes the size of the window to be determined from the setting for WindowMargins and the size of your screen. ■ The setting for WindowSize changes whenever you resize a window interactively in the front end. ■ On most computer systems, the front end does not allow window sizes below a certain minimum value. ■ See page 620. ■ See also: WindowMargins. ■ *New in Version 3.*

■ **WindowTitle**

WindowTitle is an option for Notebook which specifies the title to give for the window used to display the notebook.

WindowTitle->Automatic makes the title be the name of the file in which the notebook is stored. ■ WindowTitle->None displays no title. ■ The title given for the window need have no connection with the name of the file in which the window is stored. ■ Not all settings for WindowFrame leave room for a title to be displayed. ■ See page 620. ■ See also: WindowElements. ■ *New in Version 3.*

■ **WindowToolbars**

WindowToolbars is an option for Notebook which specifies the toolbars to include at the top of the window used to display the notebook on the screen.

WindowToolbars gives a list of toolbars to include. Typical possible elements are:

"RulerBar"   a ruler showing margin settings
"EditBar"   buttons for common editing operations
"LinksBar"   buttons for hyperlink operations

▪ The detailed appearance and operation of toolbars differ from one computer system to another. ▪ Toolbars are always shown inside the main frame of the window. ▪ See page 620. ▪ See also: WindowElements, WindowFrame. ▪ *New in Version 3.*

■ **With**

With[{$x = x_0$, $y = y_0$, ... }, *expr*] specifies that in *expr* occurrences of the symbols x, y, ... should be replaced by x_0, y_0, ...

With allows you to define local constants. ▪ With replaces symbols in *expr* only when they do not occur as local variables inside scoping constructs. ▪ You can use With[{*vars*}, *body* /; *cond*] as the right-hand side of a transformation rule with a condition attached. ▪ With has attribute HoldAll. ▪ With is a scoping construct (see Section A.3.8). ▪ With constructs can be nested in any way. ▪ With implements read-only lexical variables. ▪ See page 380. ▪ See also: Module, Block, ReplaceAll. ▪ *New in Version 2.*

■ **Word**

Word represents a word in Read, Find and related functions.

Words are defined to be sequences of characters that lie between separators. The separators are strings given as the settings for WordSeparators and RecordSeparators. ▪ The default is for words to be delimited by "white space" consisting of spaces, tabs and newlines. ▪ See page 646. ▪ See also: Record. ▪ *New in Version 2.*

■ **WordSearch**

WordSearch is an option for Find and FindList which specifies whether the text searched for must appear as a word.

With the setting WordSearch -> True, the text must appear as a word, delimited by word or record separators, as specified by WordSeparators or RecordSeparators. ▪ See page 651. ▪ See also: AnchoredSearch. ▪ *New in Version 2.*

■ **WordSeparators**

WordSeparators is an option for Read, Find and related functions which specifies the list of strings to be taken as delimiters for words.

The default setting is WordSeparators -> {" ", "\t"}. ▪ Strings used as word separators may contain several characters. ▪ With the option setting NullWords -> False, any number of word separators may appear between any two successive words. ▪ WordSeparators -> {{$lsep_1$, ... }, {$rsep_1$, ... }} specifies different left and right separators for words. Words must have a left separator at the beginning, and a right separator at the end, and cannot contain any separators. ▪ Strings given as record separators are automatically taken as word separators. ▪ See page 646. ▪ See also: RecordSeparators, TokenWords. ▪ *New in Version 2.*

▪ WorkingPrecision

WorkingPrecision is an option for various numerical operations which specifies how many digits of precision should be maintained in internal computations.

WorkingPrecision is an option for such functions as NIntegrate and FindRoot. ▪ Setting WorkingPrecision->n causes all internal computations to be done to at most n-digit precision. +▪ Setting WorkingPrecision->MachinePrecision causes all internal computations to be done with machine numbers. ▪ Even if internal computations are done to n-digit precision, the final results you get may have much lower precision. ▪ See page 956. ▪ See also: AccuracyGoal, Precision, Accuracy, N. ▪ *New in Version 1; modified in Version 5.0.*

▪ Write

Write[*channel*, *expr*$_1$, *expr*$_2$, ...] writes the expressions *expr*$_i$ in sequence, followed by a newline, to the specified output channel.

The output channel can be a single file or pipe, or list of them, each specified by a string giving their name, or by an OutputStream object. ▪ Write is the basic *Mathematica* output function. Print and Message are defined in terms of it. ▪ If any of the specified files or pipes are not already open, Write calls OpenWrite to open them. ▪ Write does not close files and pipes after it finishes writing to them. ▪ By default, Write generates output in the form specified by the setting of the FormatType option for the output stream used. ▪ See page 632. ▪ See also: Print, Export, Display, Message, Read, LinkWrite. ▪ *New in Version 1.*

▪ WriteString

WriteString[*channel*, *expr*$_1$, *expr*$_2$, ...] converts the *expr*$_i$ to strings, and then writes them in sequence to the specified output channel.

WriteString uses the OutputForm of the *expr*$_i$. ~▪ WriteString allows you to create files which are effectively just streams of bytes. The files need to be opened with the options CharacterEncoding -> {} and DOSTextFormat -> False. ▪ WriteString does not put a newline at the end of the output it generates. ▪ See notes for Write. ▪ See page 632. ▪ *New in Version 1; modified in Version 5.0.*

▪ Xor

Xor[e_1, e_2, ...] is the logical XOR (exclusive OR) function.

It gives True if an odd number of the e_i are True, and the rest are False. It gives False if an even number of the e_i are True, and the rest are False.

+▪ Xor[e_1, e_2, ...] can be input in StandardForm and InputForm as $e_1 \veebar e_2 \veebar \ldots$. The character $\veebar$ can be entered as :xor: or \[Xor]. ▪ Xor gives symbolic results when necessary, applying various simplification rules to them. ▪ Unlike And and Nand, Or and Nor, Xor must always test all its arguments, and so is not a control structure, and does not have attribute HoldAll. ▪ See page 87. ▪ See also: LogicalExpand, Mod. ▪ *New in Version 1; modified in Version 4.1.*

▪ Zeta

Zeta[s] gives the Riemann zeta function $\zeta(s)$.

Zeta[s, a] gives the generalized Riemann zeta function $\zeta(s, a)$.

Mathematical function (see Section A.3.10). ▪ $\zeta(s) = \sum_{k=1}^{\infty} k^{-s}$. ▪ $\zeta(s, a) = \sum_{k=0}^{\infty} (k + a)^{-s}$, where any term with $k + a = 0$ is excluded. ▪ Zeta[s] has no branch cut discontinuities. ▪ FullSimplify and FunctionExpand include transformation rules for Zeta. ▪ See page 772. ▪ Implementation notes: see page 1068. ▪ See also: PolyLog, HarmonicNumber, LerchPhi, RiemannSiegelZ, StieltjesGamma, Glaisher, PrimePi. ▪ Related package: NumberTheory`Ramanujan`. ▪ *New in Version 1.*

■ ZTransform

ZTransform[*expr*, *n*, *z*] gives the Z transform of *expr*.

The Z transform of a function $f(n)$ is defined to be $\sum_{n=0}^{\infty} f(n)z^{-n}$. ■ See page 879. ■ See also: InverseZTransform, LaplaceTransform, Sum, Series, RSolve. ■ *New in Version 4.*

■ $Aborted

$Aborted is a special symbol that is returned as the result from a calculation that has been aborted.

See page 371. ■ See also: Abort, Interrupt. ■ *New in Version 2.*

⁺■ $Assumptions

$Assumptions is the default setting for the Assumptions option used in such functions as Simplify, Refine and Integrate.

The value of $Assumptions can be modified using Assuming. ■ The initial setting for $Assumptions is True. ■ See page 818. ■ See also: Assuming, Block. ■ *New in Version 5.0.*

⁺■ $BaseDirectory

$BaseDirectory gives the base directory in which system-wide files to be loaded by *Mathematica* are conventionally placed.

$BaseDirectory returns the full name of the directory as a string. ■ Typical values are:

C:\Documents_and_Settings\All_Users\Application_Data\Mathematica	Windows
/Library/Mathematica	Macintosh
/usr/share/Mathematica	Unix

■ The value of $UserBaseDirectory can be specified by setting the MATHEMATICA_USERBASE operating system environment variable when the *Mathematica* kernel is launched. It cannot be reset from inside the kernel. ■ Typical subdirectories of $BaseDirectory are:

Applications	*Mathematica* application packages
Autoload	packages to be autoloaded on startup
FrontEnd	front end initialization files
Kernel	kernel initialization files
Licensing	license management files
SystemFiles	general system files

■ These subdirectories are, if possible, created automatically the first time *Mathematica* is run. ■ Appropriate subdirectories are automatically included on $Path. ■ The subdirectories of $BaseDirectory are given in $Path after the corresponding ones of $UserBaseDirectory. ■ See pages 637 and 1064. ■ See also: $UserBaseDirectory, $InstallationDirectory, $InitialDirectory, $HomeDirectory. ■ *New in Version 5.0.*

■ $BatchInput

$BatchInput is True if input in the current session is being fed directly to the *Mathematica* kernel in batch mode.

$BatchInput is True if input is being taken from a file. ■ $BatchInput can be reset during a *Mathematica* session. ■ When $BatchInput is True, *Mathematica* terminates if it ever receives an interrupt, does not discard input when blank lines are given, and terminates when it receives end-of-file. ■ See page 715. ■ See also: $IgnoreEOF, $BatchOutput, $Linked, $Notebooks. ■ *New in Version 2.*

■ $BatchOutput

$BatchOutput is True if output in the current session is being sent in batch mode, suitable for reading by other programs.

The initial value of $BatchOutput is typically determined by a command-line option when the *Mathematica* session is started. ■ $BatchOutput cannot be reset during a *Mathematica* session. ■ When $BatchOutput is set to True, *Mathematica* generates all output in InputForm, with the PageWidth option effectively set to Infinity, does not give In and Out labels, and does not give any banner when it starts up. ■ See page 715. ■ See also: $BatchInput, $Linked, $CommandLine. ■ *New in Version 2.*

■ $ByteOrdering

$ByteOrdering gives the native ordering of bytes in binary data on your computer system.

Possible values of $ByteOrdering are +1 and −1. ■ +1 corresponds to big endian (appropriate for 680x0 and many other processors); −1 corresponds to little endian (appropriate for x86 processors). ■ +1 corresponds to having the most significant byte first; −1 to having the least significant byte first. ■ +1 is the order obtained from IntegerDigits[n, 256]. ■ $ByteOrdering gives the default setting for the ByteOrdering option in Import and Export. ■ See page 717. ■ See also: $ProcessorType. ■ *New in Version 4.*

■ $CharacterEncoding

$CharacterEncoding specifies the default raw character encoding to use for input and output functions.

The default setting for $CharacterEncoding is $SystemCharacterEncoding. ■ The setting $CharacterEncoding = None takes all special characters to be represented externally by printable ASCII sequences such as \[*Name*] and \:*xxxx*. ~■ Examples of other possible settings include:

"AdobeStandard"	Adobe standard PostScript font encoding
"ASCII"	full ASCII, with control characters
"EUC"	extended Unix code for Japanese
"ISOLatin1"	ISO 8859-1 standard
"ISOLatin2"	ISO 8859-2 standard
"ISOLatin3"	ISO 8859-3 standard
"ISOLatin4"	ISO 8859-4 standard
"ISOLatinCyrillic"	ISO 8859-5 standard
"MacintoshRoman"	Macintosh roman font encoding
"PrintableASCII"	printable ASCII
"ShiftJIS"	shift-JIS encoding of JIS X 0208-1990 and extensions

(continued)

■ $CharacterEncoding *(continued)*

"Symbol"	symbol font encoding
"Unicode"	raw 16-bit Unicode
"UTF8"	Unicode transformation format
"WindowsANSI"	Windows standard font encoding
"ZapfDingbats"	Zapf dingbats font encoding

■ With $CharacterEncoding = "*encoding*" characters that are included in the encoding can be input in their raw 8- or 16-bit form, and will be output in this form. ■ Unencoded characters can be input and will be output in standard \[*Name*] or \:*xxxx* form. ■ When using a text-based interface, resetting the value of $CharacterEncoding has an immediate effect on standard input and output in a *Mathematica* session. ■ When using the notebook front end, raw character encodings are normally handled automatically based on the fonts you use. Only raw 16-bit Unicode is ever sent through the *MathLink* connection to the kernel. ■ $CharacterEncoding can be set to a list of the form {*class*, {{n_1, "c_1"}, {n_2, "c_2"}, ... }}. The *class* defines the general form of encoding; the n_i give character codes for specific characters c_i. Possible settings for *class* include:

"7Bit"	characters 0–127 given as raw bytes; other characters unencoded
"8Bit"	characters 0–255 given as raw bytes; other characters unencoded
"16Bit"	full two-byte Unicode encoding
"ShiftJIS"	shift-JIS encoding

■ $CharacterEncoding affects the input and output of all characters, including those in symbol names and comments. ■ $CharacterEncoding also affects characters that appear in Text graphics primitives. ■ See page 420. ■ See also: CharacterEncoding, FromCharacterCode, ToCharacterCode, $SystemCharacterEncoding, $ByteOrdering. ■ *New in Version 3.*

■ $CommandLine

$CommandLine is a list of strings giving the elements of the original operating system command line with which *Mathematica* was invoked.

See page 716. ■ See also: Environment, $InstallationDirectory, $BatchInput, $BatchOutput, $Linked, In. ■ *New in Version 1.*

■ $Context

$Context is a global variable that gives the current context.

Contexts are specified by strings of the form "*name*`". ■ $Context is modified by Begin, BeginPackage, End and EndPackage. ■ $Context is a rough analog for *Mathematica* symbols of the current working directory for files in many operating systems. ■ See page 393. ■ See also: Context, $ContextPath. ■ *New in Version 1.*

■ $ContextPath

$ContextPath is a global variable that gives a list of contexts, after $Context, to search in trying to find a symbol that has been entered.

Each context is specified by a string of the form "*name*`". ■ The elements of $ContextPath are tested in order to try and find a context containing a particular symbol. ■ $ContextPath is modified by Begin, BeginPackage, End and EndPackage. ■ $ContextPath is a rough analog for *Mathematica* symbols of the "search path" for files in many operating systems. ■ See page 394. ■ *New in Version 1.*

■ **$CreationDate**

$CreationDate gives the date and time at which the particular release of the *Mathematica* kernel you are running was created.

$CreationDate is in the form {*year*, *month*, *day*, *hour*, *minute*, *second*} returned by Date. ▪ See page 717. ▪ See also: $VersionNumber, $ReleaseNumber, FileDate, $InstallationDate. ▪ *New in Version 2.*

■ **$CurrentLink**

$CurrentLink is the LinkObject representing the *MathLink* connection for an external program currently being installed or being called.

$CurrentLink is temporarily set by Install and by ExternalCall. ▪ You can use $CurrentLink to distinguish between several instances of an external program running at the same time. ▪ $CurrentLink can be included in :Pattern: and :Arguments: *MathLink* template specifications, and will be evaluated at the time when Install is called. ▪ See page 688. ▪ See also: $ParentLink, Links, $Input. ▪ *New in Version 3.*

■ **$Display**

$Display gives a list of files and pipes to be used with the default $DisplayFunction.

The initial setting of $Display is {}. ▪ See page 705. ▪ *New in Version 1.*

■ **$DisplayFunction**

$DisplayFunction gives the default setting for the option DisplayFunction in graphics functions.

The initial setting of $DisplayFunction is Display[$Display, #]&. ▪ $DisplayFunction is typically set to a procedure which performs the following: (1) open an output channel; (2) send a PostScript prolog to the output channel; (3) use Display to send PostScript graphics; (4) send PostScript epilog; (5) close the output channel and execute the external commands needed to produce actual display. ▪ See page 491. ▪ See also: Display, Put, Run, $SoundDisplayFunction. ▪ *New in Version 1.*

■ **$Echo**

$Echo gives a list of files and pipes to which all input is echoed.

You can use $Echo to keep a file of all your input commands. ▪ See page 705. ▪ *New in Version 1.*

■ **$Epilog**

$Epilog is a symbol whose value, if any, is evaluated when a dialog or a *Mathematica* session is terminated.

For *Mathematica* sessions, $Epilog is conventionally defined to read in a file named end.m. ▪ See page 706. ▪ See also: Exit, Quit, Dialog. ▪ *New in Version 1.*

■ **$ExportFormats**

$ExportFormats gives a list of export formats currently supported in your *Mathematica* system.

The strings that appear in $ExportFormats are the possible third arguments to Export. ▪ See page 208. ▪ See also: $ImportFormats, Export, $Packages. ▪ *New in Version 4.*

■ $Failed

$Failed is a special symbol returned by certain functions when they cannot do what they were asked to do.

Get returns $Failed when it cannot find the file or other object that was specified. ■ See page 623. ■ *New in Version 2.*

■ $FormatType

$FormatType gives the default format type to use for text that appears in graphics.

The default setting for the standard notebook front end is $FormatType = StandardForm. ■ The default setting for the text-based front end is $FormatType = OutputForm. ■ A common alternative setting is TraditionalForm. ■ Box-based format types such as StandardForm and TraditionalForm can be used only when a notebook front end is present. ■ $FormatType gives the default value for the FormatType option in graphics. ■ See page 556. ■ See also: $TextStyle, FormatType. ■ *New in Version 3.*

■ $FrontEnd

$FrontEnd is a global variable that specifies to what front end object, if any, the kernel is currently connected.

$FrontEnd is either a FrontEndObject, or Null. ■ You can use Options and SetOptions on $FrontEnd to read and set global options for the front end. ■ See page 592. ■ See also: $Notebooks. ■ *New in Version 3.*

■ $HistoryLength

$HistoryLength specifies the number of previous lines of input and output to keep in a *Mathematica* session.

The default setting for $HistoryLength is Infinity. ■ Values of In[n] and Out[n] corresponding to lines before those kept are explicitly cleared. ■ Using smaller values of $HistoryLength can save substantial amounts of memory in a *Mathematica* session. ■ See page 703. ■ See also: $Line. ■ *New in Version 3.*

■ $HomeDirectory

$HomeDirectory gives your "home" directory.

$HomeDirectory returns the full name of the directory as a string. ■ On multi-user operating systems, $HomeDirectory gives the main directory for the current user. ■ See page 637. ■ See also: Directory, ParentDirectory, $UserName, $UserBaseDirectory, $InstallationDirectory. ■ *New in Version 3.*

■ $IgnoreEOF

$IgnoreEOF specifies whether *Mathematica* should terminate when it receives an end-of-file character as input.

$IgnoreEOF defaults to False. ■ $IgnoreEOF is assumed to be False if the input to *Mathematica* comes from a file, rather than an interactive device. ■ See pages 706 and 1057. ■ See also: Exit, Quit, $BatchInput. ■ *New in Version 1.*

■ $ImportFormats

$ImportFormats gives a list of import formats currently supported in your *Mathematica* system.

The strings that appear in $ImportFormats are the possible second arguments to Import. ■ See page 208. ■ See also: $ExportFormats, Import, $Packages. ■ *New in Version 4.*

■ $InitialDirectory

$InitialDirectory gives the initial directory when the current *Mathematica* session was started.

$InitialDirectory returns the full name of the directory as a string. +■ If *Mathematica* is started from a shell or command line, $InitialDirectory gives the current operating system directory. +■ If *Mathematica* is started from a menu or icon, $InitialDirectory typically gives the user's home directory $HomeDirectory. ■ See page 637. ■ See also: Directory, $CommandLine, $HomeDirectory, $BaseDirectory, $InstallationDirectory. ■ *New in Version 3; modified in Version 5.0.*

■ $Input

$Input is a global variable whose value is the name of the stream from which input to *Mathematica* is currently being sought.

During the execution of <<*file*, $Input is set to "*file*". ■ During interactive input, $Input is "". ■ See pages 639 and 705. ■ See also: Get, Streams, DirectoryName, ToFileName, $BatchInput, $ParentLink. ■ *New in Version 2.*

■ $Inspector

$Inspector is a global variable which gives a function to apply when the inspector is invoked from an interrupt menu.

The argument supplied is the number of nested invocations of the inspector that are in use. ■ The default value of $Inspector is Dialog[ ]&. ■ See also: Interrupt. ■ *New in Version 2.*

■ $InstallationDate

$InstallationDate gives the date and time at which the copy of the *Mathematica* kernel you are running was installed.

$InstallationDate is in the form {*year*, *month*, *day*, *hour*, *minute*, *second*} returned by Date. ■ See page 717. ■ See also: $CreationDate, $InstallationDirectory. ■ *New in Version 3.*

■ $InstallationDirectory

$InstallationDirectory gives the top-level directory in which your *Mathematica* installation resides.

$InstallationDirectory returns the full name of the directory as a string. ■ Typical values are:

C:\Program_Files\Wolfram_Research\Mathematica\5.0   Windows
/Applications/Mathematica_5.0.app   Macintosh
/usr/local/mathematica   Unix

■ See page 637. ■ See also: $BaseDirectory, $HomeDirectory, $InitialDirectory, $InstallationDate. ■ *New in Version 5.0.*

■ $IterationLimit

$IterationLimit gives the maximum length of evaluation chain used in trying to evaluate any expression.

$IterationLimit limits the number of times *Mathematica* tries to re-evaluate a particular expression. ■ $IterationLimit gives an upper limit on the length of any list that can be generated by Trace. ■ See page 369. ■ See also: $RecursionLimit. ■ *New in Version 2.*

■ $Language

$Language is a list of strings which give the names of languages to use for messages.

All language names are conventionally given in English, and are capitalized, as in "French". ■ When a message with a name s::tag is requested either internally or through the Message function, *Mathematica* searches for messages with names s::tag::$lang_i$ corresponding to the entries "$lang_i$" in the list $Language. Only if it fails to find any of these messages will it use the message with the actual name s::tag. ■ See pages 483 and 706. ■ See also: MessageName, LanguageCategory. ■ *New in Version 2.*

■ $Line

$Line is a global variable that specifies the number of the current input line.

You can reset $Line. ■ See page 702. ■ See also: In, Out, $HistoryLength. ■ *New in Version 1.*

■ $Linked

$Linked is True if the *Mathematica* kernel is being run through *MathLink*.

$Linked is True when *Mathematica* is being run with a front end. ■ $Linked is typically False when *Mathematica* is being run with a text-based interface. ■ See also: $CommandLine, $BatchInput, $BatchOutput, $Notebooks. ■ *New in Version 2.*

■ $MachineDomain

$MachineDomain is a string which gives the name of the network domain for the computer on which *Mathematica* is being run, if such a name is defined.

$MachineDomain is "" if no name is defined. ■ See page 718. ■ See also: $MachineName, $MachineID. ■ *New in Version 3.*

■ $MachineEpsilon

$MachineEpsilon gives the smallest machine-precision number which can be added to 1.0 to give a result that is distinguishable from 1.0.

$MachineEpsilon is typically 2^{-n+1}, where n is the number of binary bits used in the internal representation of machine-precision floating-point numbers. ■ $MachineEpsilon measures the granularity of machine-precision numbers. ■ See page 739. ■ See also: $MachinePrecision, $MinMachineNumber, $MaxMachineNumber. ■ Related package: NumericalMath`ComputerArithmetic`. ■ *New in Version 2.*

■ $MachineID

$MachineID is a string which gives, if possible, a unique identification code for the computer on which *Mathematica* is being run.

On many computers, $MachineID is the MathID string printed by the external program mathinfo. ■ See page 718. ■ See also: $SystemID, $MachineName. ■ *New in Version 2.*

■ $MachineName

$MachineName is a string which gives the assigned name of the computer on which *Mathematica* is being run, if such a name is defined.

For many classes of computers, $MachineName is the network host name. ■ $MachineName is "" if no name is defined. ■ See page 718. ■ See also: $MachineDomain, $System, $MachineID. ■ *New in Version 2.*

■ $MachinePrecision

$MachinePrecision gives the number of decimal digits of precision used for machine-precision numbers.

~■ A typical value of $MachinePrecision is $53 \log_{10} 2$ or approximately 16. +■ $MachinePrecision is the numerical value of MachinePrecision. ■ See pages 728 and 739. ■ See also: MachinePrecision, $MachineEpsilon, $MinMachineNumber, $MaxMachineNumber. ■ Related package: NumericalMath`ComputerArithmetic`. ■ *New in Version 2; modified in Version 5.0.*

■ $MachineType

$MachineType is a string giving the general type of computer on which *Mathematica* is being run.

$MachineType is intended to reflect general families of hardware rather than specific models. ■ Typical values are "PC", "Macintosh", "Sun", "DEC" and "SGI". ■ Computers with the same $MachineType may not be binary compatible. ■ See page 717. ■ See also: $ProcessorType, $OperatingSystem, $System. ■ *New in Version 2.*

■ $MaxExtraPrecision

$MaxExtraPrecision gives the maximum number of extra digits of precision to be used in functions such as N.

The default value of $MaxExtraPrecision is 50. ■ You can use Block[{$MaxExtraPrecision = *n*}, *expr*] to reset the value of $MaxExtraPrecision temporarily during the evaluation of *expr*. ■ $MaxExtraPrecision is used implicitly in various exact numerical computations, including equality tests, comparisons and functions such as Round and Sign. ■ See page 733. ■ See also: $MaxPrecision. ■ *New in Version 3.*

■ $MaxMachineNumber

$MaxMachineNumber is the largest machine-precision number that can be used on a particular computer system.

Numbers larger than $MaxMachineNumber are always represented in arbitrary-precision form. ■ $MaxMachineNumber is typically 2^n, where *n* is the maximum exponent that can be used in the internal representation of machine-precision numbers. ■ See page 739. ■ See also: $MinMachineNumber, $MachineEpsilon, $MachinePrecision. ■ Related package: NumericalMath`ComputerArithmetic`. ■ *New in Version 2.*

■ $MaxNumber

$MaxNumber gives the magnitude of the maximum arbitrary-precision number that can be represented on a particular computer system.

A typical value for $MaxNumber is around $10^{323228010}$. ■ See page 739. ■ See also: $MaxPrecision, $MaxMachineNumber. ■ *New in Version 3.*

■ $MaxPrecision

$MaxPrecision gives the maximum number of digits of precision to be allowed in arbitrary-precision numbers.

~■ The default value of $MaxPrecision is Infinity. ■ $MaxPrecision = Infinity uses the maximum value possible on a particular computer system, given roughly by Log[10, $MaxNumber]. ■ $MaxPrecision is measured in decimal digits, and need not be an integer. ■ See page 736. ■ See also: $MinPrecision, $MaxExtraPrecision. ■ *New in Version 3; modified in Version 5.0.*

■ **$MessageList**

> $MessageList is a global variable that gives a list of the names of messages generated during the evaluation of the current input line.

Whenever a message is output, its name, wrapped with HoldForm is appended to $MessageList. ■ With the standard *Mathematica* main loop, $MessageList is reset to {} when the processing of a particular input line is complete. ■ You can reset $MessageList during a computation. ■ See page 481. ■ See also: MessageList, Check. ■ *New in Version 2.*

■ **$MessagePrePrint**

> $MessagePrePrint is a global variable whose value, if set, is applied to expressions before they are included in the text of messages.

The default value of $MessagePrePrint is Short. ■ $MessagePrePrint is applied after each expression is wrapped with HoldForm. ■ See pages 480 and 706. ■ See also: $PrePrint. ■ *New in Version 2.*

■ **$Messages**

> $Messages gives the list of files and pipes to which message output is sent.

Output from Message is always given on the $Messages channel. ■ See page 705. ■ *New in Version 1.*

■ **$MinMachineNumber**

> $MinMachineNumber is the smallest positive machine-precision number that can be used on a particular computer system.

+■ Accuracy[0.] yields Log[10, $MinMachineNumber]. ■ See notes for $MaxMachineNumber. ■ See page 739. ■ See also: $MinNumber. ■ Related package: NumericalMath`ComputerArithmetic`. ■ *New in Version 2.*

■ **$MinNumber**

> $MinNumber gives the magnitude of the minimum positive arbitrary-precision number that can be represented on a particular computer system.

A typical value for $MinNumber is around $10^{-323228015}$. ■ See page 739. ■ See also: $MinPrecision, $MinMachineNumber. ■ *New in Version 3.*

■ **$MinPrecision**

> $MinPrecision gives the minimum number of digits of precision to be allowed in arbitrary-precision numbers.

+■ The default value of $MinPrecision is -Infinity. ■ Positive values of $MinPrecision make *Mathematica* pad arbitrary-precision numbers with zero digits to achieve the specified nominal precision. The zero digits are taken to be in base 2, and may not correspond to zeros in base 10. ■ $MaxPrecision = $MinPrecision = n makes *Mathematica* do fixed-precision arithmetic. ■ $MinPrecision is measured in decimal digits, and need not be an integer. ■ See page 736. ■ See also: SetPrecision, $MinNumber. ■ *New in Version 3; modified in Version 5.0.*

■ **$ModuleNumber**

> $ModuleNumber gives the current serial number to be used for local variables that are created.

$ModuleNumber is incremented every time Module or Unique is called. ■ Every *Mathematica* session starts with $ModuleNumber set to 1. ■ You can reset $ModuleNumber to any positive integer, but if you do so, you run the risk of creating naming conflicts. ■ See page 381. ■ See also: $SessionID, Temporary. ■ *New in Version 2.*

■ $NewMessage

$NewMessage is a global variable which, if set, is applied to the symbol name and tag of messages that are requested but have not yet been defined.

$NewMessage is applied to the symbol name, tag and language of a message if an explicit language is specified. ▪ *Mathematica* looks for the value of *name*::*tag* or *name*::*tag*::*lang* after $NewMessage has been applied. ▪ You can set up $NewMessage to read the text of messages from files when they are first needed. ▪ A typical value for $NewMessage might be Function[ToExpression[FindList[*files*, ToString[MessageName[#1, #2]]]]]. ▪ See page 482. ▪ See also: $NewSymbol. ▪ *New in Version 2*.

■ $NewSymbol

$NewSymbol is a global variable which, if set, is applied to the name and context of each new symbol that *Mathematica* creates.

The name and context of the symbol are given as strings. ▪ $NewSymbol is applied before the symbol is actually created. If the action of $NewSymbol causes the symbol to be created, perhaps in a different context, then the symbol as created will be the one used. ▪ $NewSymbol is applied even if a symbol has already been created with a Stub attribute by DeclarePackage. ▪ $NewSymbol is not applied to symbols automatically created by scoping constructs such as Module. ▪ See page 405. ▪ See also: DeclarePackage, $NewMessage. ▪ *New in Version 2*.

■ $Notebooks

$Notebooks is True if *Mathematica* is being used with a notebook-based front end.

$Notebooks is automatically set by the front end when it starts the *Mathematica* kernel. ▪ See page 715. ▪ See also: $FrontEnd, $Linked, $BatchInput. ▪ *New in Version 2*.

■ $NumberMarks

$NumberMarks gives the default value for the option NumberMarks, which specifies whether ` marks should be included in the input form representations of approximate numbers.

The default setting for $NumberMarks is Automatic. ▪ $NumberMarks = True indicates that ` should by default be used in all approximate numbers, both machine-precision and arbitrary-precision ones. ▪ $NumberMarks = Automatic indicates that ` should by default be used in arbitrary-precision but not machine-precision numbers. ▪ $NumberMarks = False indicates that ` should by default never be used in outputting numbers. ▪ See page 730. ▪ See also: NumberForm, SetPrecision. ▪ *New in Version 3*.

■ $OperatingSystem

$OperatingSystem is a string giving the type of operating system under which *Mathematica* is being run.

Typical values for $OperatingSystem are "Windows98", "MacOS" and "Unix". ▪ You can use $OperatingSystem to get an idea of what external commands will be available from within *Mathematica*. ▪ $OperatingSystem typically has the same value for different versions or variants of a particular operating system. ▪ See page 717. ▪ See also: $MachineType, $System, $ProcessorType. ▪ *New in Version 2*.

■ $Output

$Output gives the list of files and pipes to which standard output from *Mathematica* is sent.

Output from Print is always given on the $Output channel. ▪ See page 705. ▪ See also: Streams. ▪ *New in Version 1*.

■ `$Packages`

`$Packages` gives a list of the contexts corresponding to all packages which have been loaded in your current *Mathematica* session.

`$Packages` is updated when `BeginPackage` is executed. ▪ `$Packages` is used by `Needs` to determine whether a particular package needs to be loaded explicitly. ▪ See page 397. ▪ See also: `Contexts`, `$ContextPath`, `DeclarePackage`, `$ExportFormats`. ▪ *New in Version 2.*

■ `$ParentLink`

`$ParentLink` is the *MathLink* `LinkObject` currently used for input and output by the *Mathematica* kernel in a particular session.

When the *Mathematica* kernel is started by a *Mathematica* front end, `$ParentLink` gives the *MathLink* connection between the front end and the kernel. ▪ You can reset `$ParentLink` in the middle of a *Mathematica* session to connect the kernel to a different front end. ▪ See page 686. ▪ See also: `$CurrentLink`, `Links`, `$Input`. ▪ *New in Version 3.*

■ `$ParentProcessID`

`$ParentProcessID` gives the ID assigned to the process which invokes the *Mathematica* kernel by the operating system under which it is run.

On operating systems where no process ID is assigned, `$ParentProcessID` is `None`. ▪ See page 716. ▪ See also: `$ParentLink`, `$ProcessID`, `$CommandLine`, `$UserName`, `Environment`. ▪ *New in Version 3.*

■ `$Path`

`$Path` gives the default list of directories to search in attempting to find an external file.

The structure of directory and file names may differ from one computer system to another. ▪ `$Path` is used both for files in `Get` and for external programs in `Install`. ▪ The setting for `$Path` can be overridden in specific functions using the `Path` option. ▪ The directory names are specified by strings. The full file names tested are of the form `ToFileName[`*directory*`,`*name*`]`. ▪ On most computer systems, the following special characters can be used in directory names:

`.`   the current directory
`..`   the directory one level up in the hierarchy
`~`   the user's home directory

▪ `$Path` can contain nested sublists. ▪ See page 637. ▪ See also: `Path`, `Directory`, `SetDirectory`, `Get`, `DirectoryName`, `$Input`. ▪ *New in Version 1.*

■ `$Post`

`$Post` is a global variable whose value, if set, is applied to every output expression.

See page 703. ▪ See also: `$Pre`, `$PrePrint`. ▪ *New in Version 1.*

■ `$Pre`

`$Pre` is a global variable whose value, if set, is applied to every input expression.

Unless `$Pre` is assigned to be a function which holds its arguments unevaluated, input expressions will be evaluated before `$Pre` is applied, so the effect of `$Pre` will be the same as `$Post`. ▪ `$Pre` is applied to expressions, while `$PreRead` is applied to strings which have not yet been parsed into expressions. ▪ See page 703. ▪ See also: `$Post`. ▪ *New in Version 1.*

■ $PrePrint

$PrePrint is a global variable whose value, if set, is applied to every expression before it is printed.

$PrePrint is applied after Out[*n*] is assigned, but before the output result is printed. ▪ See page 703. ▪ See also: $Post, $MessagePrePrint. ▪ *New in Version 1.*

■ $PreRead

$PreRead is a global variable whose value, if set, is applied to the text or box form of every input expression before it is fed to *Mathematica*.

$PreRead is always applied to each complete input string that will be fed to *Mathematica*. ▪ In multiline input with a text-based interface, $PreRead is typically applied to the input so far whenever each line is terminated. ▪ $PreRead is applied to all strings returned by a $SyntaxHandler function. ▪ $PreRead is applied before InString[*n*] is assigned. ▪ See page 703. ▪ See also: $Pre, StringReplace, ToExpression. ▪ *New in Version 2.*

■ $ProcessID

$ProcessID gives the ID assigned to the *Mathematica* kernel process by the operating system under which it is run.

On operating systems where no process ID is assigned, $ProcessID is None. ▪ See page 716. ▪ See also: $ParentProcessID, $UserName, Environment, $SessionID. ▪ *New in Version 3.*

■ $ProcessorType

$ProcessorType is a string giving the architecture of processor on which *Mathematica* is being run.

Typical values are "x86", "PowerPC", "SPARC", "MIPS", "PA-RISC" and "AXP". ▪ $ProcessorType specifies the basic instruction set used by the CPU of your computer. ▪ Computers with the same $ProcessorType may not be binary compatible. ▪ See page 717. ▪ See also: $MachineType, $OperatingSystem, $System. ▪ *New in Version 3.*

■ $ProductInformation

$ProductInformation is a list of rules giving detailed information about the software product to which the current kernel belongs.

Typical elements of $ProductInformation are "ProductIDName" -> "Mathematica" and "ProductVersion" -> *version*. ▪ See page 717. ▪ See also: $Version, $VersionNumber, $OperatingSystem, $System. ▪ *New in Version 4.2.*

■ $RandomState

$RandomState gives a representation of the internal state of the pseudorandom generator used by Random.

The value of $RandomState changes every time Random is called. ▪ You can use *s* = $RandomState to explicitly save the value of $RandomState, and $RandomState = *s* to restore. ▪ The value of $RandomState is always a long integer chosen from a certain large set of possibilities. You can assign $RandomState only to values in this set. ▪ You can use Block[{$RandomState}, *expr*] to localize the value of $RandomState during the evaluation of *expr*. ▪ See page 747. ▪ See also: SeedRandom. ▪ *New in Version 3.*

■ **$RecursionLimit**

$RecursionLimit gives the current limit on the number of levels of recursion that *Mathematica* can use.

$RecursionLimit=*n* sets the limit on the number of recursion levels that *Mathematica* can use to be *n*.
■ **$RecursionLimit=Infinity** removes any limit on the number of recursion levels. ■ **$RecursionLimit** gives the maximum length of the stack returned by **Stack[ ]**. ■ Each time the evaluation of a function requires the nested evaluation of the same or another function, one recursion level is used up. ■ On most computers, each level of recursion uses a certain amount of stack space. **$RecursionLimit** allows you to control the amount of stack space that *Mathematica* can use from within *Mathematica*. On some computer systems, your whole *Mathematica* session may crash if you allow it to use more stack space than the computer system allows. ■ **MemoryInUse** and related functions do not count stack space. ■ See page 369. ■ See also: **$IterationLimit, MemoryConstrained**. ■ *New in Version 1.*

■ **$ReleaseNumber**

$ReleaseNumber is an integer which gives the current *Mathematica* kernel release number, and increases in successive releases.

Each released revision of the *Mathematica* kernel for any particular computer system is assigned a new release number. ■ The same source code may yield releases with different numbers on different computer systems. ■ See page 717. ■ See also: **$VersionNumber**. ■ *New in Version 2.*

■ **$SessionID**

$SessionID is a number set up to be unique to a particular *Mathematica* session.

$SessionID should be different for different *Mathematica* sessions run either on the same computer or on different computers. ■ The value of **$SessionID** is based on **$MachineID**, as well as **AbsoluteTime[ ]** and operating system parameters such as the *Mathematica* process ID. ■ See pages 384 and 716. ■ See also: **$ModuleNumber, $ProcessID**. ■ *New in Version 2.*

■ **$SoundDisplayFunction**

$SoundDisplayFunction gives the default setting for the option **DisplayFunction** in sound functions.

The initial setting of **$SoundDisplayFunction** is **Display[$SoundDisplay, #]&**. ■ See page 567. ■ See also: **Play, ListPlay, Show, $DisplayFunction**. ■ *New in Version 2.*

■ **$SyntaxHandler**

$SyntaxHandler is a global variable which, if set, is applied to any input string that is found to contain a syntax error.

The arguments given to **$SyntaxHandler** are the complete input string and an integer specifying the character position at which the syntax error was detected. ■ The first character in the string is taken to have position 1. ■ Any string returned by **$SyntaxHandler** is used as a new version of the input string, and is fed to *Mathematica*. If the string does not end with a newline, *Mathematica* waits for input to complete the line. ■ If **$SyntaxHandler** returns **$Failed**, input to *Mathematica* is abandoned if possible. ■ Input is not assigned to **InString[***n***]** until after **$SyntaxHandler** is applied. ■ **$SyntaxHandler** is not called for input from files obtained using **Get**. ■ See page 703. ■ See also: **SyntaxLength, SyntaxQ**. ■ *New in Version 2.*

■ **$System**

> $System is a string describing the type of computer system on which *Mathematica* is being run.
>
> $System typically consists of words separated by spaces. ▪ Typical values are "Microsoft Windows", "Power Macintosh", "Linux" and "Solaris". ▪ $SystemID provides a more succinct version of the same information. ▪ See page 717. ▪ See also: $SystemID, $Version, $MachineType, $ProcessorType, $OperatingSystem. ▪ *New in Version 1.*

■ **$SystemCharacterEncoding**

> $SystemCharacterEncoding gives the default raw character encoding for the computer system on which *Mathematica* is being run.
>
> $SystemCharacterEncoding is used to determine the default value of $CharacterEncoding. ▪ The notebook front end handles raw character encodings independent of the kernel. ▪ The possible settings for $SystemCharacterEncoding are the same as for $CharacterEncoding. ▪ See page 420. ▪ See also: CharacterEncoding. ▪ *New in Version 3.*

■ **$SystemID**

> $SystemID is a short string that identifies the type of computer system on which *Mathematica* is being run.
>
> Computer systems with the same $SystemID should be binary compatible, so that the same external programs and .mx files can be used. ▪ Sometimes binary compatibility may only be complete when the same version of the operating system is used. ▪ $SystemID is used in naming directories generated by DumpSave and mcc. ▪ Values for $SystemID contain only alphanumeric characters and dashes. ▪ Typical values are "Windows", "PowerMac", "Linux" and "Solaris". ▪ See page 717. ▪ See also: $System, $Version, $MachineType, $OperatingSystem. ▪ *New in Version 3.*

■ **$TextStyle**

> $TextStyle gives the default style to use for text in graphics.
>
> The following forms of settings can be used:
>
> "*style*"   a specific cell style
> {*opt*$_1$->*val*$_1$, ... }   a list of option settings
> {"*style*", *opt*$_1$->*val*$_1$, ... }   a style modified by option settings
>
> ▪ The options that can be given are as in StyleForm. ▪ "*style*" settings can only be used when a notebook front end is present. ▪ $TextStyle gives the default value for the TextStyle option in graphics. ▪ See page 556. ▪ See also: $FormatType, TextStyle. ▪ *New in Version 3.*

■ **$TimeUnit**

> $TimeUnit gives the minimum time interval in seconds recorded on your computer system.
>
> ▪ Typical values for $TimeUnit are 1/100 and 1/1000. ▪ $TimeUnit determines the minimum granularity of measurement in functions like Timing and Date. ▪ In some functions the actual time granularity may be much smaller than $TimeUnit. ▪ See page 710. ▪ *New in Version 2.*

■ **$Urgent**

> $Urgent gives the list of files and pipes to which urgent output from *Mathematica* is sent.
>
> Urgent output includes input prompts, and results from ?*name* information requests. ▪ See page 705. ▪ *New in Version 1.*

+■ **$UserBaseDirectory**

> **$UserBaseDirectory** gives the base directory in which user-specific files to be loaded by *Mathematica* are conventionally placed.

> $UserBaseDirectory returns the full name of the directory as a string. ■ Typical values are:

> | | |
> |---|---|
> | C:\Documents␣ and␣ Settings*username* \Application␣ Data\Mathematica | Windows |
> | ~/Library/Mathematica | Macintosh |
> | ~/.Mathematica | Unix |

> ■ The value of $UserBaseDirectory can be specified by setting the MATHEMATICA_USERBASE operating system environment variable when the *Mathematica* kernel is launched. It cannot be reset from inside the kernel. ■ Typical subdirectories of $UserBaseDirectory are:

> | | |
> |---|---|
> | Applications | *Mathematica* application packages |
> | Autoload | packages to be autoloaded on startup |
> | FrontEnd | front end initialization files |
> | Kernel | kernel initialization files |
> | Licensing | license management files |
> | SystemFiles | general system files |

> ■ These subdirectories are, if possible, created automatically the first time *Mathematica* is run by a given user. ■ Appropriate subdirectories are automatically included on $Path. ■ The subdirectories of $UserBaseDirectory are given in $Path before the corresponding ones of $BaseDirectory. ■ See pages 637 and 1064. ■ See also: $BaseDirectory, $InitialDirectory, $HomeDirectory, $InstallationDirectory. ■ *New in Version 5.0.*

■ **$UserName**

> **$UserName** gives the login name of the user who invoked the *Mathematica* kernel, as recorded by the operating system.

> On Unix and similar operating systems, $UserName is derived from the UID associated with the *Mathematica* kernel process. ■ On operating systems where no login name can be found, $UserName is None. ■ See page 716. ■ See also: $HomeDirectory, Environment, $UserBaseDirectory. ■ *New in Version 3.*

■ **$Version**

> **$Version** is a string that represents the version of *Mathematica* you are running.

> See page 717. ■ See also: $System. ■ *New in Version 1.*

■ **$VersionNumber**

> **$VersionNumber** is a real number which gives the current *Mathematica* kernel version number, and increases in successive versions.

> To find out if you are running under Version 5 or above, you can use the test TrueQ[$VersionNumber >= 5.0]. ■ A version with a particular number is typically derived from the same source code on all computer systems. ■ See page 717. ■ See also: $ReleaseNumber. ■ *New in Version 2.*

A.11 Listing of C Functions in the *MathLink* Library

▓ Introduction

Listed here are functions provided in the *MathLink* Developer Kit.

These functions are declared in the file `mathlink.h`, which should be included in the source code for any *MathLink*-compatible program.

Unless you specify `#define MLPROTOTYPES 0` before `#include "mathlink.h"` the functions will be included with standard C prototypes.

The following special types are defined in `mathlink.h`:

■ `MLINK`: a *MathLink* link object (analogous to `LinkObject` in *Mathematica*)

■ `MLMARK`: a mark in a *MathLink* stream

■ `MLENV`: *MathLink* library environment

The following constants are set up when a *MathLink* template file is processed:

■ `MLINK stdlink`: the standard link that connects a program built from *MathLink* templates to *Mathematica*

■ `MLENV stdenv`: the standard *MathLink* environment in a program built from *MathLink* templates

All functions described here are C language functions. They can be called from other languages with appropriate wrappers.

The functions have the following general features:

■ Those which return `int` yield a non-zero value if they succeed; otherwise they return 0 and have no effect.

■ In a program set up using *MathLink* templates, the link to *Mathematica* is called `stdlink`.

■ Functions which put data to a link do not deallocate memory used to store the data.

■ Functions which get data from a link may allocate memory to store the data.

■ Functions which get data from a link will not return until the necessary data becomes available. A yield function can be registered to be called during the wait.

- ## MLAbort

    `int MLAbort` is a global variable set when a program created using `mcc` or `mprep` has been sent an abort interrupt.

    `LinkInterrupt[`*link*`]` can be used to send an abort interrupt from *Mathematica* to a program connected to a particular link. ▪ See page 697.

- ## MLActivate()

    `int MLActivate(MLINK `*link*`)` activates a *MathLink* connection, waiting for the program at the other end to respond.

    `MLActivate()` can be called only after `MLOpenArgv()` or `MLOpenString()`. ▪ See page 698.

- ## MLCheckFunction()

    `int MLCheckFunction(MLINK `*link*`, char *`*name*`, long *`*n*`)` checks that a function whose head is a symbol with the specified name is on *link*, and stores the number of the arguments of the function in *n*.

    `MLCheckFunction()` returns 0 if the current object on the link is not a function with a symbol as a head, or if the name of the symbol does not match *name*. ▪ See page 672. ▪ See also: `MLGetFunction`.

- ## MLClearError()

    `int MLClearError(MLINK `*link*`)` if possible clears any error on *link* and reactivates the link.

    `MLClearError()` returns 0 if it was unable to clear the error. This can happen if the error was for example the result of a link no longer being open. ▪ See page 696.

- ## MLClose()

    `void MLClose(MLINK `*link*`)` closes a *MathLink* connection.

    Calling `MLClose()` does not necessarily terminate a program at the other end of the link. ▪ Any data buffered in the link is sent when `MLClose()` is called. ▪ Programs should close all links they have opened before terminating. ▪ See pages 692 and 698. ▪ See also: `MLDeinitialize`.

- ## MLCreateMark()

    `MLMARK MLCreateMark(MLINK `*link*`)` creates a mark at the current position in a sequence of expressions on a link.

    Calling `MLCreateMark()` effectively starts recording all expressions received on the link. ▪ See page 693. ▪ See also: `MLLoopbackOpen`.

- ## MLDeinitialize()

    `void MLDeinitialize(MLENV `*env*`)` deinitializes functions in the *MathLink* library.

    An appropriate call to `MLDeinitialize()` is generated automatically when an external program is created from *MathLink* templates. ▪ Any external program that uses the *MathLink* library must call `MLDeinitialize()` before exiting. ▪ `MLClose()` must be called for all open links before calling `MLDeinitialize()`. ▪ See page 698.

- ## MLDestroyMark()

    int MLDestroyMark(MLINK *link*, MLMARK *mark*) destroys the specified mark on a link.

    Calling MLDestroyMark() disowns memory associated with the storage of expressions recorded after the mark.
    ▪ See page 693.

- ## MLDisownByteString()

    void MLDisownByteString(MLINK *link*, unsigned char *s*, long *n*) disowns memory allocated by MLGetByteString() to store the array of character codes *s*.

    See page 679. ▪ See also: MLDisownString.

- ## MLDisownIntegerArray()

    void MLDisownIntegerArray(MLINK *link*, int *a*, long *dims*, char **heads*, long *d*) disowns memory allocated by MLGetIntegerArray() to store the array *a*, its dimensions *dims* and the heads *heads*.

    See page 675.

- ## MLDisownIntegerList()

    void MLDisownIntegerList(MLINK *link*, int *a*, long *n*) disowns memory allocated by MLGetIntegerList() to store the array *a* of length *n*.

    See page 674.

- ## MLDisownRealArray()

    void MLDisownRealArray(MLINK *link*, double *a*, long *dims*, char **heads*, long *d*) disowns memory allocated by MLGetRealArray() to store the array *a*, its dimensions *dims* and the heads *heads*.

    See page 675.

- ## MLDisownRealList()

    void MLDisownRealList(MLINK *link*, double *a*, long *n*) disowns memory allocated by MLGetRealList() to store the array *a* of length *n*.

    See page 674.

- ## MLDisownString()

    void MLDisownString(MLINK *link*, char *s*) disowns memory allocated by MLGetString() to store the character string *s*.

    See page 675. ▪ See also: MLDisownUnicodeString.

- ## MLDisownSymbol()

    void MLDisownSymbol(MLINK *link*, char *s*) disowns memory allocated by MLGetSymbol() or MLGetFunction() to store the character string *s* corresponding to the name of a symbol.

    See pages 675 and 676.

- ## `MLDisownUnicodeString()`

    `void MLDisownUnicodeString(MLINK` *link*, `unsigned short *s`, `long` *n*`)` disowns memory allocated by `MLGetUnicodeString()` to store the string *s*.

    See page 679. ▪ See also: `MLDisownString`.

- ## `MLEndPacket()`

    `int MLEndPacket(MLINK` *link*`)` specifies that a packet expression is complete and is ready to be sent on the specified link.

    `MLEndPacket()` should be called to indicate the end of any top-level expression, regardless of whether its head is a standard packet. ▪ See pages 689 and 699.

- ## `MLError()`

    `long MLError(MLINK` *link*`)` returns a constant identifying the last error to occur on *link*, or 0 if none has occurred since the previous call to `MLClearError()`.

    You can get a textual description of errors by calling `MLErrorMessage()`. ▪ Constants corresponding to standard *MathLink* errors are defined in `mathlink.h`. ▪ See page 696.

- ## `MLErrorMessage()`

    `char *MLErrorMessage(MLINK` *link*`)` returns a character string describing the last error to occur on *link*.

    See page 696.

- ## `MLEvaluateString()`

    `int MLEvaluateString(MLINK` *link*, `char *`*string*`)` sends a string to *Mathematica* for evaluation, and discards any packets sent in response.

    The code for `MLEvaluateString()` is not included in the *MathLink* library, but is generated automatically by `mcc` or `mprep` in processing *MathLink* template files. ▪ `MLEvaluateString("Print[\"`*string*`\"]")` will cause *string* to be printed in a *Mathematica* session at the other end of the link. ▪ See pages 664 and 689.

- ## `MLFlush()`

    `int MLFlush(MLINK` *link*`)` flushes out any buffers containing data waiting to be sent on *link*.

    If you call `MLNextPacket()` or any of the `MLGet*()` functions, then `MLFlush()` will be called automatically. ▪ If you call `MLReady()`, then you need to call `MLFlush()` first in order to ensure that any necessary outgoing data has been sent. ▪ See page 700. ▪ See also: `MLReady`.

- ## `MLGetArgCount()`

    `int MLGetArgCount(MLINK` *link*, `long *`*n*`)` finds the number of arguments to a function on *link* and stores the result in *n*.

    See page 694.

- ## MLGetByteString()

  int MLGetByteString(MLINK *link*, unsigned char **s*, long **n*, long *spec*) gets a string of characters from the *MathLink* connection specified by *link*, storing the codes for the characters in *s* and the number of characters in *n*. The code *spec* is used for any character whose *Mathematica* character code is larger than 255.

  MLGetByteString() allocates memory for the array of character codes. You must call MLDisownByteString() to disown this memory. ▪ MLGetByteString() is convenient in situations where no special characters occur. ▪ The character codes used by MLGetByteString() are exactly the ones returned by ToCharacterCode in *Mathematica*. ▪ The array of character codes in MLGetByteString() is not terminated by a null character. ▪ Characters such as newlines are specified by their raw character codes, not by ASCII forms such as \n. ▪ See page 679. ▪ See also: MLGetString, MLGetUnicodeString.

- ## MLGetDouble()

  int MLGetDouble(MLINK *link*, double **x*) gets a floating-point number from the *MathLink* connection specified by *link* and stores it as C type double in *x*.

  MLGetDouble() is normally equivalent to MLGetReal(). ▪ See notes for MLGetReal(). ▪ See page 678. ▪ See also: MLGetFloat.

- ## MLGetFloat()

  int MLGetFloat(MLINK *link*, float **x*) gets a floating-point number from the *MathLink* connection specified by *link* and stores it as C type float in *x*.

  See notes for MLGetReal(). ▪ See page 678.

- ## MLGetFunction()

  int MLGetFunction(MLINK *link*, char **s*, long **n*) gets a function with a symbol as a head from the *MathLink* connection specified by *link*, storing the name of the symbol in *s* and the number of arguments of the function in *n*.

  MLGetFunction() allocates memory for the character string corresponding to the name of the head of the function. You must call MLDisownSymbol() to disown this memory. ▪ External programs should not modify the character string *s*. ▪ MLGetFunction(*link*, &*s*, &*n*) has the same effect as MLGetNext(*link*); MLGetArgCount(*link*, &*n*); MLGetSymbol(*link*, &*s*). ▪ See page 676. ▪ See also: MLGetNext.

- ## MLGetInteger()

  int MLGetInteger(MLINK *link*, int **i*) gets an integer from the *MathLink* connection specified by *link* and stores it in *i*.

  If the data on the link corresponds to a real number, MLGetInteger() will round it to an integer. ▪ If the data on the link corresponds to an integer too large to store in a C int on your computer system, then MLGetInteger() will fail, and return 0. ▪ You can get arbitrary-precision integers by first using IntegerDigits to generate lists of digits, then calling MLGetIntegerList(). ▪ See page 694. ▪ See also: MLGetShortInteger, MLGetLongInteger.

- ## MLGetIntegerArray()

  int MLGetIntegerArray(MLINK *link*, int **a*, long ***dims*, char ****heads*, long **d*) gets an array of integers from the *MathLink* connection specified by *link*, storing the array in *a*, its dimensions in *dims* and its depth in *d*.

  The array *a* is laid out in memory like a C array declared as int a[m][n].... ▪ *heads* gives a list of character strings corresponding to the names of symbols that appear as heads at each level in the array. ▪ MLGetIntegerArray() allocates memory which must be disowned by calling MLDisownIntegerArray(). ▪ External programs should not modify the arrays generated by MLGetIntegerArray(). ▪ See page 675. ▪ See also: MLGetIntegerList.

- ## MLGetIntegerList()

  int MLGetIntegerList(MLINK *link*, int **a*, long **n*) gets a list of integers from the *MathLink* connection specified by *link*, storing the integers in the array *a* and the length of the list in *n*.

  MLGetIntegerList() allocates memory for the array of integers. You must call MLDisownIntegerList() to disown this memory. ▪ External programs should not modify the array generated by MLGetIntegerList(). ▪ See notes for MLGetInteger(). ▪ See page 674. ▪ See also: MLGetIntegerArray, MLGetByteString.

- ## MLGetLongInteger()

  int MLGetLongInteger(MLINK *link*, long **i*) gets an integer from the *MathLink* connection specified by *link* and stores it as a C long in *i*.

  See notes for MLGetInteger(). ▪ See page 678.

- ## MLGetNext()

  int MLGetNext(MLINK *link*) goes to the next object on *link* and returns its type.

  The following values can be returned:

MLTKERR	error
MLTKINT	integer
MLTKFUNC	composite function
MLTKREAL	approximate real number
MLTKSTR	character string
MLTKSYM	symbol

  ▪ MLTKINT and MLTKREAL do not necessarily signify numbers that can be stored in C int and double variables. ▪ See page 694. ▪ See also: MLGetArgCount.

- ## MLGetReal()

  int MLGetReal(MLINK *link*, double **x*) gets a floating-point number from the *MathLink* connection specified by *link* and stores it in *x*.

  If the data on the link corresponds to an integer, MLGetReal() will coerce it to a double before storing it in *x*. ▪ If the data on the link corresponds to a number outside the range that can be stored in a C double on your computer system, then MLGetReal() will fail, and return 0. ▪ You can get arbitrary-precision real numbers by first using RealDigits to generate lists of digits, then calling MLGetIntegerList(). ▪ MLGetReal() is normally equivalent to MLGetDouble(). ▪ See page 694. ▪ See also: MLGetFloat, MLGetDouble, MLGetRealList.

- ## MLGetRealArray()

    int MLGetRealArray(MLINK *link*, double **a*, long ***dims*, char ****heads*, long **d*) gets an array of floating-point numbers from the *MathLink* connection specified by *link*, storing the array in *a*, its dimensions in *dims* and its depth in *d*.

    The array *a* is laid out in memory like a C array declared as double a[m][n]... . ▪ *heads* gives a list of character strings corresponding to the names of symbols that appear as heads at each level in the array. ▪ MLGetRealArray() allocates memory which must be disowned by calling MLDisownRealArray(). ▪ External programs should not modify the arrays generated by MLGetRealArray(). ▪ See page 675.

- ## MLGetRealList()

    int MLGetRealList(MLINK *link*, double **a*, long **n*) gets a list of floating-point numbers from the *MathLink* connection specified by *link*, storing the numbers in the array *a* and the length of the list in *n*.

    MLGetRealList() allocates memory for the array of numbers. You must call MLDisownRealList() to disown this memory. ▪ External programs should not modify the array generated by MLGetRealList(). ▪ See notes for MLGetReal(). ▪ See page 674.

- ## MLGetShortInteger()

    int MLGetShortInteger(MLINK *link*, short **i*) gets an integer from the *MathLink* connection specified by *link* and stores it as a C short in *i*.

    See notes for MLGetInteger(). ▪ See page 678.

- ## MLGetString()

    int MLGetString(MLINK *link*, char ***s*) gets a character string from the *MathLink* connection specified by *link*, storing the string in *s*.

    MLGetString() allocates memory for the character string. You must call MLDisownString() to disown this memory. ▪ External programs should not modify strings generated by MLGetString(). ▪ MLGetString() creates a string that is terminated by \0. ▪ MLGetString() stores single \ characters from *Mathematica* as pairs of characters \\. ▪ MLGetString() stores special characters from *Mathematica* in a private format. ▪ See pages 675 and 694. ▪ See also: MLGetByteString, MLGetUnicodeString.

- ## MLGetSymbol()

    int MLGetSymbol(MLINK *link*, char ***s*) gets a character string corresponding to the name of a symbol from the *MathLink* connection specified by *link*, storing the resulting string in *s*.

    MLGetSymbol() allocates memory for the character string. You must call MLDisownSymbol() to disown this memory. ▪ MLGetSymbol() creates a string that is terminated by \0. ▪ See pages 675 and 694.

- ## MLGetUnicodeString()

    int MLGetUnicodeString(MLINK *link*, unsigned short ***s*, long **n*) gets a character string from the *MathLink* connection specified by *link*, storing the string in *s* as a sequence of 16-bit Unicode characters.

    MLGetUnicodeString() allocates memory for the character string. You must call MLDisownUnicodeString() to disown this memory. ▪ External programs should not modify strings generated by MLGetUnicodeString(). ▪ MLGetUnicodeString() stores all characters directly in 16-bit Unicode form. ▪ 8-bit ASCII characters are stored with a null high-order byte. ▪ See page 679. ▪ See also: MLGetString, MLGetByteString.

- **MLInitialize()**

  MLENV MLInitialize(0) initializes functions in the *MathLink* library.

  An appropriate call to MLInitialize() is generated automatically when an external program is created from *MathLink* templates. ▪ Any external program that uses the *MathLink* library must call MLInitialize() before calling any other *MathLink* library functions. ▪ See page 698.

- **MLLoopbackOpen()**

  MLINK MLLoopbackOpen(MLENV *env*, long **errno*) opens a loopback *MathLink* connection.

  In an external program set up with *MathLink* templates, the environment stdenv should be used. ▪ You can use loopback links to effectively store *Mathematica* expressions in external programs. ▪ See page 692. ▪ See also: MLCreateMark.

- **MLMain()**

  int MLMain(int *argc*, char ***argv*) sets up communication between an external program started using Install and *Mathematica*.

  The code for MLMain() is generated automatically by mprep or mcc. ▪ MLMain() opens a *MathLink* connection using the parameters specified in *argv*, then goes into a loop waiting for CallPacket objects to arrive from *Mathematica*. ▪ MLMain() internally calls MLOpenArgv(). ▪ See page 664.

- **MLNewPacket()**

  int MLNewPacket(MLINK *link*) skips to the end of the current packet on *link*.

  MLNewPacket() works even if the head of the current top-level expression is not a standard packet type. ▪ MLNewPacket() does nothing if you are already at the end of a packet. ▪ See pages 697 and 699. ▪ See also: MLNextPacket.

- **MLNextPacket()**

  int MLNextPacket(MLINK *link*) goes to the next packet on *link* and returns a constant to indicate its head.

  See page 699. ▪ See also: MLNewPacket.

- **MLOpenArgv()**

  MLINK MLOpenArgv(MLENV *env*, char ***argv0*, char ***argv1*, long **errno*) opens a *MathLink* connection taking parameters from an argv array.

  MLInitialize() must be called before MLOpenArgv(). ▪ MLOpenArgv() scans for the following at successive locations starting at *argv0* and going up to just before *argv1*:

"-linkconnect"	connect to an existing link (LinkConnect)
"-linkcreate"	create a link (LinkCreate)
"-linklaunch"	launch a child process (LinkLaunch)
"-linkname", "*name*"	the name to use in opening the link
"-linkprotocol", "*protocol*"	the link protocol to use (tcp, pipes, etc.)

  ▪ MLOpenArgv() is not sensitive to the case of argument names. ▪ MLOpenArgv() ignores argument names that it does not recognize. ▪ MLOpenArgv() is called automatically by the MLMain() function created by mprep and mcc. ▪ With a main program main(int argc, char *argv[]) typical usage is MLOpenArgv(*env*, argv, argv+argc, *errno*). ▪ Avoiding an explicit argc argument allows MLOpenArgv() to work independent of the size of an int. ▪ On some computer systems, giving 0 for *argv0* and *argv1* will cause arguments to be requested interactively, typically through a dialog box. ▪ See page 698. ▪ See also: MLActivate, MLOpenString.

- ## MLOpenString()

  MLINK MLOpenString(MLENV *env*, char *string*, long *errno*) opens a *MathLink* connection taking parameters from a character string.

  MLInitialize() must be called before MLOpenString(). ▪ MLOpenString() takes a single string instead of the *argv* array used by MLOpenArgv(). ▪ Arguments in the string are separated by spaces. ▪ On some computer systems, giving NULL in place of the string pointer will cause arguments to be requested interactively, typically through a dialog box. ▪ See page 698. ▪ See also: MLActivate, MLOpenArgv.

- ## MLPutArgCount()

  int MLPutArgCount(MLINK *link*, long *n*) specifies the number of arguments of a composite function to be put on *link*.

- ## MLPutByteString()

  int MLPutByteString(MLINK *link*, unsigned char *s*, long *n*) puts a string of *n* characters starting from location *s* to the *MathLink* connection specified by *link*.

  All characters in the string must be specified using character codes as obtained from ToCharacterCode in *Mathematica*. ▪ Newlines must thus be specified in terms of their raw character codes, rather than using \n. ▪ MLPutByteString() handles only characters with codes less than 256. ▪ It can handle both ordinary ASCII as well as ISO Latin-1 characters. ▪ See page 679. ▪ See also: MLPutString, MLPutIntegerList.

- ## MLPutDouble()

  int MLPutDouble(MLINK *link*, double *x*) puts the floating-point number *x* of C type double to the *MathLink* connection specified by *link*.

  See notes for MLPutReal(). ▪ See page 678.

- ## MLPutFloat()

  int MLPutFloat(MLINK *link*, double *x*) puts the floating-point number *x* to the *MathLink* connection specified by *link* with a precision corresponding to the C type float.

  The argument *x* is typically declared as float in external programs, but must be declared as double in MLPutFloat() itself in order to work even in the absence of C prototypes. ▪ See notes for MLPutReal(). ▪ See page 678.

- ## MLPutFunction()

  int MLPutFunction(MLINK *link*, char *s*, long *n*) puts a function with head given by a symbol with name *s* and with *n* arguments to the *MathLink* connection specified by *link*.

  After the call to MLPutFunction() other *MathLink* functions must be called to send the arguments of the function. ▪ See page 667. ▪ See also: MLPutString.

- ## MLPutInteger()

  int MLPutInteger(MLINK *link*, int *i*) puts the integer *i* to the *MathLink* connection specified by *link*.

  You can send arbitrary-precision integers to *Mathematica* by giving lists of digits, then converting them to numbers using FromDigits. ▪ See pages 667 and 696. ▪ See also: MLGetInteger, MLPutShortInteger, MLPutLongInteger, MLPutIntegerList.

- `MLPutIntegerArray()`

    int `MLPutIntegerArray(MLINK` *link*, int `*a`, long `*dims`, char `**`*heads*, long *d*) puts an array of integers to the *MathLink* connection specified by *link* to form a depth *d* array with dimensions *dims*.

    The array *a* must be laid out in memory like a C array declared explicitly as int `a[m][n]`... . ▪ If *heads* is given as `NULL`, the array will be assumed to have head `List` at every level. ▪ The length of the array at level *i* is taken to be `dims[i]`. ▪ See page 667. ▪ See also: `MLPutIntegerList`.

- `MLPutIntegerList()`

    int `MLPutIntegerList(MLINK` *link*, int `*a`, long *n*) puts a list of *n* integers starting from location *a* to the *MathLink* connection specified by *link*.

    See page 667. ▪ See also: `MLPutIntegerArray`, `MLPutByteString`.

- `MLPutLongInteger()`

    int `MLPutLongInteger(MLINK` *link*, long *i*) puts the long integer *i* to the *MathLink* connection specified by *link*.

    See notes for `MLPutInteger()`. ▪ See page 678.

- `MLPutNext()`

    int `MLPutNext(MLINK` *link*, int *type*) prepares to put an object of the specified type on *link*.

    The type specifications are as given in the notes for `MLGetNext()`. ▪ See page 696. ▪ See also: `MLPutArgCount`.

- `MLPutReal()`

    int `MLPutReal(MLINK` *link*, double *x*) puts the floating-point number *x* to the *MathLink* connection specified by *link*.

    You can send arbitrary-precision real numbers to *Mathematica* by giving lists of digits, then converting them to numbers using `FromDigits`. ▪ `MLPutReal()` is normally equivalent to `MLPutDouble()`. ▪ See pages 667 and 696. ▪ See also: `MLPutRealList`, `MLPutFloat`, `MLPutDouble`.

- `MLPutRealArray()`

    int `MLPutRealArray(MLINK` *link*, double `*a`, long `*dims`, char `**`*heads*, long *d*) puts an array of floating-point numbers to the *MathLink* connection specified by *link* to form a depth *d* array with dimensions *dims*.

    The array *a* must be laid out in memory like a C array declared explicitly as double `a[m][n]`... . ▪ If *heads* is given as `NULL`, the array will be assumed to have head `List` at every level. ▪ The length of the array at level *i* is taken to be `dims[i]`. ▪ See page 667. ▪ See also: `MLPutRealList`.

- `MLPutRealList()`

    int `MLPutRealList(MLINK` *link*, double `*a`, long *n*) puts a list of *n* floating-point numbers starting from location *a* to the *MathLink* connection specified by *link*.

    See page 667. ▪ See also: `MLPutRealArray`.

- ## MLPutShortInteger()

    int MLPutShortInteger(MLINK *link*, int *i*) puts the integer *i* to the *MathLink* connection specified by *link*, assuming that *i* contains only the number of digits in the C type short.

    The argument *i* is typically declared as short in external programs, but must be declared as int in MLPutShortInteger() itself in order to work even in the absence of C prototypes. ▪ See notes for MLPutInteger(). ▪ See page 678.

- ## MLPutString()

    int MLPutString(MLINK *link*, char *s*) puts a character string to the *MathLink* connection specified by *link*.

    The character string must be terminated with a null byte, corresponding to \0 in C. ▪ A raw backslash in the string must be sent as two characters \\. ▪ Special characters can be sent only using the private format returned by MLGetString(). ▪ See pages 667 and 696. ▪ See also: MLPutByteString, MLPutUnicodeString, MLPutSymbol.

- ## MLPutSymbol()

    int MLPutSymbol(MLINK *link*, char *s*) puts a symbol whose name is given by the character string *s* to the *MathLink* connection specified by *link*.

    The character string must be terminated with \0. ▪ See pages 667 and 696. ▪ See also: MLPutString.

- ## MLPutUnicodeString()

    int MLPutUnicodeString(MLINK *link*, unsigned short *s*, long *n*) puts a string of *n* 16-bit Unicode characters to the *MathLink* connection specified by *link*.

    All characters are assumed to be 16 bit. ▪ 8-bit characters can be sent by having the higher-order byte be null. ▪ See page 679. ▪ See also: MLPutString, MLPutByteString.

- ## MLReady()

    int MLReady(MLINK *link*) tests whether there is data ready to be read from *link*.

    Analogous to the *Mathematica* function LinkReadyQ. ▪ MLReady() is often called in a loop as a way of polling a *MathLink* connection. ▪ MLReady() will always return immediately, and will not block. ▪ You need to call MLFlush() before starting to call MLReady(). ▪ See page 700.

- ## MLSeekMark()

    MLMARK MLSeekMark(MLINK *link*, MLMARK *mark*, long *n*) goes back to a position *n* expressions after the specified mark on a link.

    See page 693.

- ## MLTransferExpression()

    int MLTransferExpression(MLINK *dest*, MLINK *src*) transfers an expression from one *MathLink* connection to another.

    src and *dest* need not be distinct. ▪ *src* and *dest* can be either loopback or ordinary links. ▪ See page 692.

A.12 Listing of Named Characters

■ Introduction

This section gives a list of all characters that are assigned full names in *Mathematica* Version 5. The list is ordered alphabetically by full name.

The standard *Mathematica* fonts support all of the characters in the list.

There are a total of 727 characters in the list.

⦂aaa⦂ stands for ⎡ESC⎤*aaa*⎡ESC⎤.

Interpretation of Characters

The interpretations given here are those used in `StandardForm` and `InputForm`. Most of the interpretations also work in `TraditionalForm`.

You can override the interpretations by giving your own rules for `MakeExpression`.

Letters and letter-like forms	used in symbol names
Infix operators	e.g. $x \oplus y$
Prefix operators	e.g. $\neg x$
Postfix operators	e.g. $x!$
Matchfix operators	e.g. $\langle x \rangle$
Compound operators	e.g. $\int f \, d\!\!\!\!\rule[0.5ex]{1.2ex}{0.4pt}\, x$
Raw operators	operator characters that can be typed on an ordinary keyboard
Spacing characters	interpreted in the same way as an ordinary space
Structural elements	characters used to specify structure; usually ignored in interpretation
Uninterpretable elements	characters indicating missing information

Types of characters.

The precedences of operators are given on pages 1024–1029.

Infix operators for which no grouping is specified in the listing are interpreted so that for example $x \oplus y \oplus z$ becomes `CirclePlus[x, y, z]`.

Naming Conventions

Characters that correspond to built-in *Mathematica* functions typically have names corresponding to those functions. Other characters typically have names that are as generic as possible.

Characters with different names almost always look at least slightly different.

\[Capital...]	upper-case form of a letter
\[Left...] and \[Right...]	pieces of a matchfix operator (also arrows)
\[Raw...]	a printable ASCII character
\[...Indicator]	a visual representation of a keyboard character

Some special classes of characters.

style	Script, Gothic, etc.
variation	Curly, Gray, etc.
case	Capital, etc.
modifiers	Not, Double, Nested, etc.
direction	Left, Up, UpperRight, etc.
base	A, Epsilon, Plus, etc.
diacritical mark	Acute, Ring, etc.

Typical ordering of elements in character names.

Aliases

Mathematica supports both its own system of aliases, as well as aliases based on character names in TEX and SGML or HTML. Except where they conflict, character names corresponding to plain TEX, LATEX and AMSTEX are all supported. Note that TEX and SGML or HTML aliases are not given explicitly in the list of characters below.

⦂*xxx*⦂	ordinary *Mathematica* alias
⦂*xxx*⦂	TEX alias
⦂&*xxx*⦂	SGML or HTML alias

Types of aliases.

The following general conventions are used for all aliases:

- Characters that are alternatives to standard keyboard operators use these operators as their aliases (e.g. ⦂->⦂ for →, ⦂&&⦂ for ∧).

- Most single-letter aliases stand for Greek letters.

- Capital-letter characters have aliases beginning with capital letters.

- When there is ambiguity in the assignment of aliases, a space is inserted at the beginning of the alias for the less common character (e.g. ⦂->⦂ for \[Rule] and ⦂ ->⦂ for \[RightArrow]).

- ! is inserted at the beginning of the alias for a Not character.

- TEX aliases begin with a backslash \.

- SGML aliases begin with an ampersand &.

- User-defined aliases conventionally begin with a dot or comma.

Font Matching

The special fonts provided with *Mathematica* include all the characters given in this listing. Some of these characters also appear in certain ordinary text fonts.

When rendering text in a particular font, the *Mathematica* notebook front end will use all the characters available in that font. It will use the special *Mathematica* fonts only for other characters.

A choice is made between Times-like, Helvetica-like (sans serif) and Courier-like (monospaced) variants to achieve the best matching with the ordinary text font in use.

á   \[AAcute]

Alias: ⣀a'⣀. ▪ Letter. ▪ Included in ISO Latin-1. ▪ See page 998. ▪ See also: \[CapitalAAcute].

ā   \[ABar]

Alias: ⣀a-⣀. ▪ Letter. ▪ Included in ISO Latin-4. ▪ Used in transliterations of various non-Latin alphabets. ▪ See page 998. ▪ See also: \[CapitalABar].

ă   \[ACup]

Alias: ⣀au⣀. ▪ Letter. ▪ Included in ISO Latin-2. ▪ Used in transliterations of Cyrillic characters. ▪ See page 998. ▪ See also: \[CapitalACup].

ä   \[ADoubleDot]

Alias: ⣀a"⣀. ▪ Letter. ▪ Included in ISO Latin-1. ▪ See pages 190 and 998. ▪ See also: \[CapitalADoubleDot], \[EDoubleDot].

æ   \[AE]

Alias: ⣀ae⣀. ▪ Letter. ▪ Included in ISO Latin-1. ▪ See page 998. ▪ See also: \[CapitalAE].

à   \[AGrave]

Alias: ⣀a`⣀. ▪ Letter. ▪ Included in ISO Latin-1. ▪ See pages 190 and 998. ▪ See also: \[CapitalAGrave].

â   \[AHat]

Alias: ⣀a^⣀. ▪ Letter. ▪ Included in ISO Latin-1. ▪ See page 998. ▪ See also: \[CapitalAHat].

ℵ   \[Aleph]

Alias: ⣀al⣀. ▪ Hebrew letter. ▪ Sometimes called alef. ▪ Used in pure mathematics to denote transfinite cardinals. ▪ See pages 192 and 993. ▪ See also: \[Bet], \[Gimel], \[Dalet].

⣀   \[AliasIndicator]

Alias: ⣀esc⣀. ▪ Letter-like form. ▪ Representation of the indicator for special character aliases in *Mathematica*. ▪ \[AliasIndicator] is an inactive letter-like form, used in describing how to type aliases. ▪ An active character of the same appearance is typically obtained by typing ESCAPE. ▪ See page 1009. ▪ See also: \[EscapeKey], \[SpaceIndicator], \[ReturnIndicator].

\[AlignmentMarker]

Alias: ⣀am⣀. ▪ Letter-like form. ▪ Invisible by default on display. ▪ Used as a marker to indicate for example how entries in a GridBox column should be lined up. ▪ See pages 451 and 1008. ▪ See also: \[InvisibleComma], \[InvisibleSpace], \[Null], \[NoBreak].

α   \[Alpha]

Aliases: ⣀a⣀, ⣀alpha⣀. ▪ Greek letter. ▪ Not the same as \[Proportional]. ▪ See pages 175 and 990. ▪ See also: \[CapitalAlpha].

∧   \[And]

Aliases: ⣀&&⣀, ⣀and⣀. ▪ Infix operator with built-in evaluation rules. ▪ $x \wedge y$ is by default interpreted as And[x, y], equivalent to x && y. ▪ Not the same as \[Wedge]. ▪ Drawn slightly larger than \[Wedge]. ▪ See page 1001. ▪ See also: \[Or], \[Nand], \[Not].

∟   \[Angle]

Letter-like form. ▪ Used in geometry to indicate an angle, as in the symbol ∟ ABC. ▪ See pages 192 and 996. ▪ See also: \[MeasuredAngle], \[SphericalAngle], \[RightAngle].

Å   \[Angstrom]

Alias: :Ang:. ■ Letter-like form. ■ Unit corresponding to 10^{-10} meters. ■ Not the same as the letter \[CapitalARing]. ■ See pages 192 and 994. ■ See also: \[ARing], \[Micro], \[EmptySmallCircle], \[HBar].

å   \[ARing]

Alias: :ao:. ■ Letter. ■ Included in ISO Latin-1. ■ See pages 190 and 998. ■ See also: \[CapitalARing], \[EmptySmallCircle].

⋰   \[AscendingEllipsis]

Letter-like form. ■ Used to indicate omitted elements in a matrix. ■ See page 997. ■ See also: \[DescendingEllipsis], \[VerticalEllipsis], \[Ellipsis].

ã   \[ATilde]

Alias: :a~:. ■ Letter. ■ Included in ISO Latin-1. ■ See page 998. ■ See also: \[CapitalATilde].

\   \[Backslash]

Alias: :\:. ■ Infix operator. ■ $x \setminus y$ is by default interpreted as Backslash[x, y]. ■ Used in mathematics for set difference. ■ Also used to separate arguments of elliptic functions. ■ Sometimes used to indicate x divides y. ■ See pages 191 and 1002. ■ See also: \[RawBackslash], \[Colon], \[VerticalBar], \[Continuation].

∵   \[Because]

Infix operator. ■ $x \because y$ is by default interpreted as Because[x, y]. ■ $x \because y \because z$ groups as $(x \because y) \because z$. ■ See page 1001. ■ See also: \[Therefore], \[LeftTee], \[FilledRectangle], \[Proportion].

ℶ   \[Bet]

Alias: :be:. ■ Hebrew letter. ■ Sometimes called beth. ■ Used in pure mathematics in the theory of transfinite cardinals. ■ See page 993. ■ See also: \[Aleph].

β   \[Beta]

Aliases: :b:, :beta:. ■ Greek letter. ■ See pages 175 and 990. ■ See also: \[CapitalBeta], \[SZ].

˘   \[Breve]

Alias: :bv:. ■ Letter-like form. ■ Used in an overscript position as a diacritical mark. ■ See page 999. ■ See also: \[DownBreve], \[Cup], \[RoundSpaceIndicator], \[Hacek].

•   \[Bullet]

Alias: :bu:. ■ Letter-like form. ■ See pages 192 and 996. ■ See also: \[FilledSmallCircle], \[FilledCircle].

ć   \[CAcute]

Alias: :c':. ■ Letter. ■ Included in ISO Latin-2. ■ See page 998. ■ See also: \[CapitalCAcute].

⌢   \[Cap]

Infix operator. ■ $x \frown y$ is by default interpreted as Cap[x, y]. ■ Used in pure mathematics to mean cap product. ■ Sometimes used as an overscript to indicate arc between. ■ See page 1002. ■ See also: \[Cup], \[Intersection], \[CupCap], \[DownBreve].

Á   \[CapitalAAcute]

Alias: :A':. ■ Letter. ■ Included in ISO Latin-1. ■ See page 998. ■ See also: \[AAcute].

Ā   \[CapitalABar]

Alias: ⦂A-⦂. ▪ Letter. ▪ Included in ISO Latin-4. ▪ See page 998. ▪ See also: \[ABar].

Ă   \[CapitalACup]

Alias: ⦂Au⦂. ▪ Letter. ▪ Included in ISO Latin-2. ▪ Used in transliterations of Cyrillic characters. ▪ See page 998. ▪ See also: \[ACup].

Ä   \[CapitalADoubleDot]

Alias: ⦂A"⦂. ▪ Letter. ▪ Included in ISO Latin-1. ▪ See pages 190 and 998. ▪ See also: \[ADoubleDot].

Æ   \[CapitalAE]

Alias: ⦂AE⦂. ▪ Letter. ▪ Included in ISO Latin-1. ▪ See page 998. ▪ See also: \[AE].

À   \[CapitalAGrave]

Alias: ⦂A`⦂. ▪ Letter. ▪ Included in ISO Latin-1. ▪ See page 998. ▪ See also: \[AGrave].

Â   \[CapitalAHat]

Alias: ⦂A^⦂. ▪ Letter. ▪ Included in ISO Latin-1. ▪ See page 998. ▪ See also: \[AHat].

A   \[CapitalAlpha]

Aliases: ⦂A⦂, ⦂Alpha⦂. ▪ Greek letter. ▪ Not the same as English A. ▪ See page 990. ▪ See also: \[Alpha].

Å   \[CapitalARing]

Alias: ⦂Ao⦂. ▪ Letter. ▪ Included in ISO Latin-1. ▪ Not the same as \[Angstrom]. ▪ See pages 190 and 998. ▪ See also: \[ARing].

Ã   \[CapitalATilde]

Alias: ⦂A~⦂. ▪ Letter. ▪ Included in ISO Latin-1. ▪ See page 998. ▪ See also: \[ATilde].

B   \[CapitalBeta]

Aliases: ⦂B⦂, ⦂Beta⦂. ▪ Greek letter. ▪ Used in TraditionalForm for Beta. ▪ Not the same as English B. ▪ See page 990. ▪ See also: \[Beta].

Ć   \[CapitalCAcute]

Alias: ⦂C'⦂. ▪ Letter. ▪ Included in ISO Latin-2. ▪ See page 998. ▪ See also: \[CAcute].

Ç   \[CapitalCCedilla]

Alias: ⦂C,⦂. ▪ Letter. ▪ Included in ISO Latin-1. ▪ See page 998. ▪ See also: \[CCedilla].

Č   \[CapitalCHacek]

Alias: ⦂Cv⦂. ▪ Letter. ▪ Included in ISO Latin-2. ▪ See page 998. ▪ See also: \[CHacek].

X   \[CapitalChi]

Aliases: ⦂Ch⦂, ⦂Chi⦂, ⦂C⦂. ▪ Greek letter. ▪ Not the same as English X. ▪ See pages 175 and 990. ▪ See also: \[Chi], \[CapitalXi].

Δ   \[CapitalDelta]

Aliases: ⦂D⦂, ⦂Delta⦂. ▪ Greek letter. ▪ Not the same as \[EmptyUpTriangle]. ▪ Sometimes used in mathematics to denote Laplacian. ▪ See pages 175 and 990. ▪ See also: \[Delta], \[Del].

$\mathbb{D}$ \[CapitalDifferentialD]

Alias: :DD:. ∎ Compound operator. ∎ $\mathbb{D}$ can only be interpreted by default when it appears with $\int$ or other integral operators. ∎ Used in mathematics to indicate a functional differential. ∎ See page 994. ∎ See also: \[DifferentialD], \[DoubleStruckD].

F   \[CapitalDigamma]

Aliases: :Di:, :Digamma:. ∎ Special Greek letter. ∎ Analogous to English W. ∎ See page 990. ∎ See also: \[Digamma].

É   \[CapitalEAcute]

Alias: :E':. ∎ Letter. ∎ Included in ISO Latin-1. ∎ See page 998. ∎ See also: \[EAcute].

Ē   \[CapitalEBar]

Alias: :E-:. ∎ Letter. ∎ Included in ISO Latin-4. ∎ See page 998. ∎ See also: \[EBar].

Ĕ   \[CapitalECup]

Alias: :Eu:. ∎ Letter. ∎ Not included in ISO Latin. ∎ See page 998. ∎ See also: \[ECup].

Ë   \[CapitalEDoubleDot]

Alias: :E":. ∎ Letter. ∎ Included in ISO Latin-1. ∎ See page 998. ∎ See also: \[EDoubleDot].

È   \[CapitalEGrave]

Alias: :E`:. ∎ Letter. ∎ Included in ISO Latin-1. ∎ See page 998. ∎ See also: \[EGrave].

Ê   \[CapitalEHat]

Alias: :E^:. ∎ Letter. ∎ Included in ISO Latin-1. ∎ See page 998. ∎ See also: \[EHat].

E   \[CapitalEpsilon]

Aliases: :E:, :Epsilon:. ∎ Greek letter. ∎ Not the same as English E. ∎ See page 990. ∎ See also: \[Epsilon].

H   \[CapitalEta]

Aliases: :Et:, :Eta:, :H:. ∎ Greek letter. ∎ Not the same as English H. ∎ See page 990. ∎ See also: \[Eta].

Ð   \[CapitalEth]

Alias: :D-:. ∎ Letter. ∎ Included in ISO Latin-1. ∎ See page 998. ∎ See also: \[Eth].

Γ   \[CapitalGamma]

Aliases: :G:, :Gamma:. ∎ Greek letter. ∎ Used in TraditionalForm for Gamma. ∎ See pages 175 and 990. ∎ See also: \[Gamma], \[CapitalDigamma].

Í   \[CapitalIAcute]

Alias: :I':. ∎ Letter. ∎ Included in ISO Latin-1. ∎ See page 998. ∎ See also: \[IAcute].

Ĭ   \[CapitalICup]

Alias: :Iu:. ∎ Letter. ∎ Included in ISO Latin-2. ∎ See page 998. ∎ See also: \[ICup].

Ï   \[CapitalIDoubleDot]

Alias: :I":. ∎ Letter. ∎ Included in ISO Latin-1. ∎ See page 998. ∎ See also: \[IDoubleDot].

Ì   \[CapitalIGrave]

Alias: :I`:. ∎ Letter. ∎ Included in ISO Latin-1. ∎ See page 998. ∎ See also: \[IGrave].

Î   \[CapitalIHat]
Alias: ⦂I^⦂. ▪ Letter. ▪ Included in ISO Latin-1. ▪ See page 998. ▪ See also: \[IHat].

I   \[CapitalIota]
Aliases: ⦂I⦂, ⦂Iota⦂. ▪ Greek letter. ▪ Not the same as English I. ▪ See page 990. ▪ See also: \[Iota].

K   \[CapitalKappa]
Aliases: ⦂K⦂, ⦂Kappa⦂. ▪ Greek letter. ▪ Not the same as English K. ▪ See page 990. ▪ See also: \[Kappa].

Ϙ   \[CapitalKoppa]
Aliases: ⦂Ko⦂, ⦂Koppa⦂. ▪ Special Greek letter. ▪ Analogous to English Q. ▪ See page 990. ▪ See also: \[Koppa].

Λ   \[CapitalLambda]
Aliases: ⦂L⦂, ⦂Lambda⦂. ▪ Greek letter. ▪ Not the same as \[Wedge]. ▪ See pages 175 and 990. ▪ See also: \[Lambda].

Ł   \[CapitalLSlash]
Alias: ⦂L/⦂. ▪ Letter. ▪ Included in ISO Latin-2. ▪ See page 998. ▪ See also: \[LSlash].

M   \[CapitalMu]
Aliases: ⦂M⦂, ⦂Mu⦂. ▪ Greek letter. ▪ Not the same as English M. ▪ See page 990. ▪ See also: \[Mu].

Ñ   \[CapitalNTilde]
Alias: ⦂N~⦂. ▪ Letter. ▪ Included in ISO Latin-1. ▪ See page 998. ▪ See also: \[NTilde].

N   \[CapitalNu]
Aliases: ⦂N⦂, ⦂Nu⦂. ▪ Greek letter. ▪ Not the same as English N. ▪ See page 990. ▪ See also: \[Nu].

Ó   \[CapitalOAcute]
Alias: ⦂O'⦂. ▪ Letter. ▪ Included in ISO Latin-1. ▪ See page 998. ▪ See also: \[OAcute].

Ő   \[CapitalODoubleAcute]
Alias: ⦂O''⦂. ▪ Letter. ▪ Included in ISO Latin-2. ▪ See page 998. ▪ See also: \[ODoubleAcute].

Ö   \[CapitalODoubleDot]
Alias: ⦂O"⦂. ▪ Letter. ▪ Included in ISO Latin-1. ▪ See pages 190 and 998. ▪ See also: \[ODoubleDot].

Ò   \[CapitalOGrave]
Alias: ⦂O`⦂. ▪ Letter. ▪ Included in ISO Latin-1. ▪ See page 998. ▪ See also: \[OGrave].

Ô   \[CapitalOHat]
Alias: ⦂O^⦂. ▪ Letter. ▪ Included in ISO Latin-1. ▪ See page 998. ▪ See also: \[OHat].

Ω   \[CapitalOmega]
Aliases: ⦂O⦂, ⦂Omega⦂, ⦂W⦂. ▪ Greek letter. ▪ Used as the symbol for ohms. ▪ See pages 175 and 990. ▪ See also: \[Omega], \[Mho].

O   \[CapitalOmicron]
Aliases: ⦂Om⦂, ⦂Omicron⦂. ▪ Greek letter. ▪ Not the same as English O. ▪ See page 990. ▪ See also: \[Omicron].

Ø   \[CapitalOSlash]
Alias: ⦂O/⦂. ▪ Letter. ▪ Included in ISO Latin-1. ▪ Not the same as \[EmptySet] or \[Diameter]. ▪ See page 998. ▪ See also: \[OSlash].

Õ   \[CapitalOTilde]

Alias: :O~:. ▪ Letter. ▪ Included in ISO Latin-1. ▪ See page 998. ▪ See also: \[OTilde].

Φ   \[CapitalPhi]

Aliases: :Ph:, :Phi:, :F:. ▪ Greek letter. ▪ Used in TraditionalForm for LerchPhi. ▪ See pages 175 and 990. ▪ See also: \[Phi].

Π   \[CapitalPi]

Aliases: :P:, :Pi:. ▪ Greek letter. ▪ Used in TraditionalForm for EllipticPi. ▪ Not the same as \[Product]. ▪ See pages 175 and 990. ▪ See also: \[Pi].

Ψ   \[CapitalPsi]

Aliases: :Ps:, :Psi:, :Y:. ▪ Greek letter. ▪ See pages 175 and 990. ▪ See also: \[Psi].

P   \[CapitalRho]

Aliases: :R:, :Rho:. ▪ Greek letter. ▪ Not the same as English P. ▪ See page 990. ▪ See also: \[Rho].

ϡ   \[CapitalSampi]

Aliases: :Sa:, :Sampi:. ▪ Special Greek letter. ▪ See page 990. ▪ See also: \[Sampi].

Š   \[CapitalSHacek]

Alias: :Sv:. ▪ Letter. ▪ Included in ISO Latin-2. ▪ See page 998. ▪ See also: \[SHacek].

Σ   \[CapitalSigma]

Aliases: :S:, :Sigma:. ▪ Greek letter. ▪ Not the same as \[Sum]. ▪ See pages 175 and 990. ▪ See also: \[Sigma].

ϛ   \[CapitalStigma]

Aliases: :Sti:, :Stigma:. ▪ Special Greek letter. ▪ See page 990. ▪ See also: \[Stigma].

T   \[CapitalTau]

Aliases: :T:, :Tau:. ▪ Greek letter. ▪ Not the same as English T. ▪ See page 990. ▪ See also: \[Tau].

Θ   \[CapitalTheta]

Aliases: :Th:, :Theta:, :Q:. ▪ Greek letter. ▪ See pages 175 and 990. ▪ See also: \[Theta].

Þ   \[CapitalThorn]

Alias: :Thn:. ▪ Letter. ▪ Included in ISO Latin-1. ▪ See page 998. ▪ See also: \[Thorn].

Ú   \[CapitalUAcute]

Alias: :U':. ▪ Letter. ▪ Included in ISO Latin-1. ▪ See page 998. ▪ See also: \[UAcute].

Ű   \[CapitalUDoubleAcute]

Alias: :U'':. ▪ Letter. ▪ Included in ISO Latin-2. ▪ See page 998. ▪ See also: \[UDoubleAcute].

Ü   \[CapitalUDoubleDot]

Alias: :U":. ▪ Letter. ▪ Included in ISO Latin-1. ▪ See pages 190 and 998. ▪ See also: \[UDoubleDot].

Ù   \[CapitalUGrave]

Alias: :U`:. ▪ Letter. ▪ Included in ISO Latin-1. ▪ See page 998. ▪ See also: \[UGrave].

Û   \[CapitalUHat]

Alias: :U^:. ▪ Letter. ▪ Included in ISO Latin-1. ▪ See page 998. ▪ See also: \[UHat].

Υ　\[CapitalUpsilon]

Aliases: ⋮U⋮, ⋮Upsilon⋮. ▪ Greek letter. ▪ Not commonly used. ▪ Used in physics for $b\bar{b}$ particles, and in the quantum theory of measurement. ▪ See pages 175 and 990. ▪ See also: \[CurlyCapitalUpsilon], \[Upsilon].

Ξ　\[CapitalXi]

Aliases: ⋮X⋮, ⋮Xi⋮. ▪ Greek letter. ▪ Not commonly used. ▪ Used for grand canonical partition function, cascade hyperon and regular language complexity. ▪ See page 990. ▪ See also: \[Xi].

Ý　\[CapitalYAcute]

Alias: ⋮Y'⋮. ▪ Letter. ▪ Included in ISO Latin-1. ▪ See page 998. ▪ See also: \[YAcute].

Z　\[CapitalZeta]

Aliases: ⋮Z⋮, ⋮Zeta⋮. ▪ Greek letter. ▪ Used in TraditionalForm for JacobiZeta. ▪ Not the same as English Z. ▪ See page 990. ▪ See also: \[Zeta].

ç　\[CCedilla]

Alias: ⋮c,⋮. ▪ Letter. ▪ Included in ISO Latin-1. ▪ See pages 190 and 998. ▪ See also: \[CapitalCCedilla].

¸　\[Cedilla]

Alias: ⋮cd⋮. ▪ Letter-like form. ▪ Used in an underscript position as a diacritical mark. ▪ See page 999. ▪ See also: \[Hacek], \[Breve].

¢　\[Cent]

Alias: ⋮cent⋮. ▪ Letter-like form. ▪ Currency symbol, used as in 5¢. ▪ See page 994.

·　\[CenterDot]

Alias: ⋮.⋮. ▪ Infix operator. ▪ $x \cdot y$ is by default interpreted as CenterDot[x, y]. ▪ Used to indicate various forms of multiplication, particularly dot products of vectors. ▪ Sometimes used to indicate concatenation or composition. ▪ Used in the British mathematical tradition as a decimal point. ▪ See page 1002. ▪ See also: \[CenterEllipsis], \[RawDot], \[CircleDot].

⋯　\[CenterEllipsis]

Letter-like form. ▪ Used to indicate omitted elements in a row of a matrix. ▪ See page 997. ▪ See also: \[Ellipsis], \[VerticalEllipsis], \[CenterDot].

č　\[CHacek]

Alias: ⋮cv⋮. ▪ Letter. ▪ Included in ISO Latin-2. ▪ See pages 190 and 998. ▪ See also: \[CapitalCHacek], \[SHacek].

χ　\[Chi]

Aliases: ⋮ch⋮, ⋮chi⋮, ⋮c⋮. ▪ Greek letter. ▪ See pages 175 and 990. ▪ See also: \[CapitalChi], \[Xi].

⊙　\[CircleDot]

Alias: ⋮c.⋮. ▪ Infix operator. ▪ $x \odot y$ is by default interpreted as CircleDot[x, y]. ▪ Used in mathematics for various operations related to multiplication, such as direct or tensor products. ▪ Also sometimes used to indicate a vector pointing out of the page. ▪ See page 1002. ▪ See also: \[CircleTimes], \[CenterDot].

⊖　\[CircleMinus]

Alias: ⋮c-⋮. ▪ Infix operator. ▪ $x \ominus y$ is by default interpreted as CircleMinus[x, y]. ▪ See page 1002. ▪ See also: \[CirclePlus].

⊕   \[CirclePlus]

Alias: :c+:. ▪ Infix operator. ▪ $x \oplus y$ is by default interpreted as CirclePlus[x, y]. ▪ Used in mathematics for various operations related to addition, such as direct sum and addition modulo two. ▪ Also sometimes used to indicate a vector pointing into the page. ▪ See pages 191 and 1002. ▪ See also: \[CircleTimes], \[CircleMinus], \[Xor].

⊗   \[CircleTimes]

Alias: :c*:. ▪ Infix and prefix operator. ▪ $x \otimes y$ is by default interpreted as CircleTimes[x, y]. ▪ Used in mathematics for various operations related to multiplication, such as direct or tensor products. ▪ Also sometimes used to indicate a vector pointing into the page. ▪ See pages 191 and 1002. ▪ See also: \[CircleDot], \[Times], \[Cross], \[Wedge], \[CirclePlus].

∮   \[ClockwiseContourIntegral]

Alias: :ccint:. ▪ Compound operator (see page 1031). ▪ $\oint f \, dx$ is by default interpreted as ClockwiseContourIntegral[f, x]. ▪ See page 1000. ▪ See also: \[CounterClockwiseContourIntegral], \[ContourIntegral].

⌘   \[CloverLeaf]

Alias: :cl:. ▪ Letter-like form. ▪ Used on Macintosh and other computers to indicate command keys. ▪ See page 1009. ▪ See also: \[CommandKey].

♣   \[ClubSuit]

Letter-like form. ▪ See page 996. ▪ See also: \[DiamondSuit], \[HeartSuit], \[SpadeSuit].

:   \[Colon]

Alias: ::. ▪ Infix operator. ▪ $x : y$ is by default interpreted as Colon[x, y]. ▪ Used in mathematics to mean "such that". ▪ Occasionally used to indicate proportion. ▪ Used to separate hours and minutes in times. ▪ See page 1001. ▪ See also: \[SuchThat], \[VerticalSeparator], \[Exists], \[ForAll], \[RawColon], \[Proportion], \[Therefore].

[CMD]   \[CommandKey]

Alias: :cmd:. ▪ Letter-like form. ▪ Representation of the COMMAND or ALT key on a keyboard. ▪ See page 1009. ▪ See also: \[CloverLeaf], \[LeftModified], \[ControlKey], \[EscapeKey].

≡   \[Congruent]

Alias: :===:. ▪ Infix similarity operator. ▪ $x \equiv y$ is by default interpreted as Congruent[x, y]. ▪ Used in mathematics for many notions of equivalence and equality. ▪ See pages 191 and 1003. ▪ See also: \[NotCongruent], \[Equal], \[TildeFullEqual], \[CupCap], \[LeftRightArrow].

∴   \[Continuation]

Alias: :cont:. ▪ Structural element. ▪ Used at the end of a line of input to indicate that the expression on that line continues onto the next line. ▪ Equivalent in meaning to \ at the end of a line. ▪ Not the same as \[DescendingEllipsis]. ▪ See page 1009. ▪ See also: \[RawBackslash], \[Backslash], \[ReturnIndicator].

∮   \[ContourIntegral]

Alias: :cint:. ▪ Compound operator (see page 1031). ▪ $\oint f \, dx$ is by default interpreted as ContourIntegral[f, x]. ▪ See page 1000. ▪ See also: \[ClockwiseContourIntegral], \[DoubleContourIntegral].

[CTRL]   \[ControlKey]

Alias: :ctrl:. ▪ Letter-like form. ▪ Representation of the CONTROL key on a keyboard. ▪ See page 1009. ▪ See also: \[LeftModified], \[CommandKey], \[EscapeKey], \[ReturnKey].

∐   \[Coproduct]

Alias: ⦂coprod⦂. ■ Infix operator. ■ $x \amalg y$ is by default interpreted as Coproduct[x, y]. ■ ∐ x is by default interpreted as Coproduct[x]. ■ Coproduct is used as an abstract dual to the operation of multiplication, most often in infix form. ■ See page 1002. ■ See also: \[Product], \[Wedge], \[Vee], \[CircleTimes], \[SquareUnion].

©   \[Copyright]

Letter-like form. ■ See page 996. ■ See also: \[RegisteredTrademark].

∮   \[CounterClockwiseContourIntegral]

Alias: ⦂cccint⦂. ■ Compound operator (see page 1031). ■ $\oint f \, dx$ is by default interpreted as CounterClockwiseContourIntegral[f, x]. ■ See page 1000. ■ See also: \[ClockwiseContourIntegral], \[ContourIntegral].

×   \[Cross]

Alias: ⦂cross⦂. ■ Infix operator with built-in evaluation rules. ■ $x \times y$ is by default interpreted as Cross[x, y]. ■ Not the same as \[Times]. ■ \[Cross] represents vector cross product, while \[Times] represents ordinary multiplication. ■ \[Cross] is drawn smaller than \[Times]. ■ See page 1000. ■ See also: \[CircleTimes].

⌣   \[Cup]

Infix operator. ■ $x \smile y$ is by default interpreted as Cup[x, y]. ■ Used in pure mathematics to mean cup product. ■ See page 1002. ■ See also: \[Cap], \[Union], \[CupCap], \[RoundSpaceIndicator], \[Breve].

≍   \[CupCap]

Infix similarity operator. ■ $x \asymp y$ is by default interpreted as CupCap[x, y]. ■ Used in mathematics for various notions of equivalence, usually fairly weak. ■ $f \asymp g$ is often specifically used to indicate that f/g has bounded variation. ■ See page 1003. ■ See also: \[NotCupCap], \[Cap], \[Cup].

ϒ   \[CurlyCapitalUpsilon]

Aliases: ⦂cU⦂, ⦂cUpsilon⦂. ■ Greek letter. ■ Not commonly used. ■ Used in astronomy for mass to light ratio. ■ See page 990. ■ See also: \[CapitalUpsilon].

ε   \[CurlyEpsilon]

Aliases: ⦂ce⦂, ⦂cepsilon⦂. ■ Greek letter. ■ Not the same as \[Element]. ■ Used in physics for Fermi energy and dielectric constant. ■ See page 990. ■ See also: \[Epsilon], \[ScriptCapitalE].

ϰ   \[CurlyKappa]

Aliases: ⦂ck⦂, ⦂ckappa⦂. ■ Greek letter. ■ See page 990. ■ See also: \[Kappa].

φ   \[CurlyPhi]

Aliases: ⦂j⦂, ⦂cph⦂, ⦂cphi⦂. ■ Greek letter. ■ Commonly used as a variant of ϕ. ■ See pages 175 and 990. ■ See also: \[Phi].

ϖ   \[CurlyPi]

Aliases: ⦂cp⦂, ⦂cpi⦂. ■ Greek letter. ■ Not commonly used, except in astronomy. ■ See page 990. ■ See also: \[Pi], \[Omega].

ϱ   \[CurlyRho]

Aliases: ⦂cr⦂, ⦂crho⦂. ■ Greek letter. ■ See page 990. ■ See also: \[Rho].

ϑ   \[CurlyTheta]

Aliases: ⦂cq⦂, ⦂cth⦂, ⦂ctheta⦂. ■ Greek letter. ■ Used in TraditionalForm for EllipticTheta and RiemannSiegelTheta. ■ See page 990. ■ See also: \[CapitalTheta], \[Theta].

† **\[Dagger]**

Alias: :dg:. ▪ Letter-like form and overfix operator. ▪ $x^\dagger$ is by default interpreted as SuperDagger[x]. ▪ See pages 192 and 996. ▪ See also: \[DoubleDagger].

ℸ **\[Dalet]**

Alias: :da:. ▪ Hebrew letter. ▪ Sometimes called daleth. ▪ Used occasionally in pure mathematics in the theory of transfinite cardinals. ▪ See page 993. ▪ See also: \[Aleph].

– **\[Dash]**

Alias: :-:. ▪ Letter-like form. ▪ See page 996. ▪ See also: \[LongDash], \[HorizontalLine].

° **\[Degree]**

Alias: :deg:. ▪ Letter-like form with built-in value. ▪ Interpreted by default as the symbol Degree. ▪ 30° is interpreted as 30 Degree. ▪ The symbol ° is sometimes used in mathematics to indicate the interior of a set. ▪ Not the same as \[SmallCircle] or \[EmptySmallCircle]. ▪ See page 994. ▪ See also: \[Prime], \[DoublePrime].

∇ **\[Del]**

Alias: :del:. ▪ Prefix operator. ▪ ∇f is by default interpreted as Del[f]. ▪ Used in vector analysis to denote gradient operator and its generalizations. ▪ Used in numerical analysis to denote backward difference operator. ▪ Also called nabla. ▪ Not the same as \[EmptyDownTriangle]. ▪ See pages 994 and 1000. ▪ See also: \[CapitalDelta], \[PartialD], \[Square].

δ **\[Delta]**

Aliases: :d:, :delta:. ▪ Greek letter. ▪ See pages 175 and 990. ▪ See also: \[PartialD], \[Del], \[CapitalDelta].

⋱ **\[DescendingEllipsis]**

Letter-like form. ▪ Used to indicate omitted elements in a matrix. ▪ Not the same as \[Continuation]. ▪ See page 997. ▪ See also: \[AscendingEllipsis], \[VerticalEllipsis], \[Ellipsis].

⌀ **\[Diameter]**

Letter-like form. ▪ Used in geometry. ▪ Not the same as \[CapitalOSlash] or \[EmptySet]. ▪ See page 996.

◇ **\[Diamond]**

Alias: :dia:. ▪ Infix operator. ▪ $x \diamond y$ is by default interpreted as Diamond[x, y]. ▪ See page 1002. ▪ See also: \[EmptyDiamond], \[FilledDiamond], \[DiamondSuit].

◇ **\[DiamondSuit]**

Letter-like form. ▪ Sometimes used to indicate the end of a proof. ▪ Not the same as \[Diamond] or \[EmptyDiamond]. ▪ See page 996. ▪ See also: \[ClubSuit].

d **\[DifferentialD]**

Alias: :dd:. ▪ Compound operator with built-in evaluation rules. ▪ d can only be interpreted by default when it appears with $\int$ or other integral operators. ▪ $\int f \, dx$ is by default interpreted as Integrate[f, x]. ▪ \[DifferentialD] is also used in TraditionalForm to indicate total derivatives. ▪ See pages 185, 994 and 1000. ▪ See also: \[PartialD], \[CapitalDifferentialD], \[Delta].

ϝ **\[Digamma]**

Aliases: :di:, :digamma:. ▪ Special Greek letter. ▪ Analogous to English w. ▪ Sometimes used to denote PolyGamma[x]. ▪ See page 990. ▪ See also: \[CapitalDigamma], \[Koppa], \[Stigma], \[Sampi].

÷ **\[Divide]**

Alias: :div:. ▪ Infix operator with built-in evaluation rules. ▪ $x \div y$ is by default interpreted as Divide[x, y] or x / y. ▪ $x \div y \div z$ groups as $(x \div y) \div z$. ▪ See page 1000. ▪ See also: \[Times], \[Proportion], \[Backslash].

≐   \[DotEqual]

Alias: ⦂.=⦂. ▪ Infix similarity operator. ▪ $x \doteq y$ is by default interpreted as DotEqual[x, y]. ▪ Used to mean approximately equal, or in some cases, "image of", or "equal by definition". ▪ See page 1003. ▪ See also: \[TildeEqual], \[RightArrow].

ı   \[DotlessI]

Letter. ▪ Used when an i will have an overscript on top. ▪ May or may not match the ordinary i from the text font. ▪ See page 992. ▪ See also: \[DotlessJ], \[Iota].

ȷ   \[DotlessJ]

Letter. ▪ Used when a j will have an overscript on top. ▪ May or may not match the ordinary j from the text font. ▪ See page 992. ▪ See also: \[DotlessI].

⸬   \[DottedSquare]

Letter-like form. ▪ See page 995. ▪ See also: \[EmptySquare], \[Placeholder].

∯   \[DoubleContourIntegral]

Compound operator (see page 1031). ▪ $\oiint f\, ds$ is by default interpreted as ContourIntegral[f, s]. ▪ Used to indicate integrals over closed surfaces. ▪ See page 1000. ▪ See also: \[ContourIntegral], \[Integral].

‡   \[DoubleDagger]

Alias: ⦂ddg⦂. ▪ Letter-like form. ▪ See page 996. ▪ See also: \[Dagger].

γ   \[DoubledGamma]

Alias: ⦂gg⦂. ▪ Letter-like form. ▪ Not by default assigned any interpretation in StandardForm. ▪ Interpreted as EulerGamma in TraditionalForm. ▪ Not the same as \[Gamma]. ▪ See page 994. ▪ See also: \[DoubledPi], \[ExponentialE], \[DoubleStruckA].

⇓   \[DoubleDownArrow]

Infix arrow operator. ▪ $x \Downarrow y$ is by default interpreted as DoubleDownArrow[x, y]. ▪ Extensible character. ▪ See page 1006. ▪ See also: \[DownArrow], \[DoubleUpArrow].

π   \[DoubledPi]

Alias: ⦂pp⦂. ▪ Letter-like form. ▪ Not by default assigned any interpretation. ▪ Not the same as \[Pi]. ▪ See page 994. ▪ See also: \[DoubledGamma], \[ExponentialE], \[DoubleStruckA].

⇐   \[DoubleLeftArrow]

Alias: ⦂_<=⦂. ▪ Infix arrow operator. ▪ $x \Leftarrow y$ is by default interpreted as DoubleLeftArrow[x, y]. ▪ Extensible character. ▪ ⦂<=⦂ is the alias for \[LessEqual]. The alias for \[DoubleLeftArrow] has a space at the beginning. ▪ See page 1006. ▪ See also: \[DoubleLongLeftArrow], \[LeftArrow], \[DoubleRightArrow].

⇔   \[DoubleLeftRightArrow]

Alias: ⦂<=>⦂. ▪ Infix arrow operator. ▪ $x \Leftrightarrow y$ is by default interpreted as DoubleLeftRightArrow[x, y]. ▪ Used in mathematics to indicate logical equivalence. ▪ Extensible character. ▪ See page 1006. ▪ See also: \[DoubleLongLeftRightArrow], \[LeftRightArrow], \[RightArrowLeftArrow], \[LeftArrowRightArrow], \[Congruent], \[Implies].

⊣   \[DoubleLeftTee]

Infix operator. ▪ $x \dashv y$ is by default interpreted as DoubleLeftTee[x, y]. ▪ $x \dashv y \dashv z$ groups as $(x \dashv y) \dashv z$. ▪ Used in mathematics to indicate various strong forms of logical implication of x from y—often tautological implication. ▪ See pages 1001 and 1007. ▪ See also: \[LeftTee], \[DoubleRightTee].

⟸ \[DoubleLongLeftArrow]

Alias: ⦙<==⦙. ∎ Infix arrow operator. ∎ $x \Leftarrow y$ is by default interpreted as DoubleLongLeftArrow[x, y]. ∎ See page 1006. ∎ See also: \[DoubleLeftArrow], \[LongLeftArrow], \[DoubleLongRightArrow].

⟺ \[DoubleLongLeftRightArrow]

Alias: ⦙<==>⦙. ∎ Infix arrow operator. ∎ $x \Leftrightarrow y$ is by default interpreted as DoubleLongLeftRightArrow[x, y]. ∎ See page 1006. ∎ See also: \[DoubleLeftRightArrow], \[LongLeftRightArrow], \[RightArrowLeftArrow], \[LeftArrowRightArrow].

⟹ \[DoubleLongRightArrow]

Alias: ⦙==>⦙. ∎ Infix arrow operator. ∎ $x \Rightarrow y$ is by default interpreted as DoubleLongRightArrow[x, y]. ∎ See page 1006. ∎ See also: \[DoubleRightArrow], \[LongRightArrow], \[DoubleLongLeftArrow].

″ \[DoublePrime]

Alias: ⦙''⦙. ∎ Letter-like form. ∎ Used to indicate angles in seconds or distances in inches. ∎ See pages 996 and 999. ∎ See also: \[Prime], \[ReverseDoublePrime].

⇒ \[DoubleRightArrow]

Alias: ⦙_=>⦙. ∎ Infix arrow operator. ∎ $x \Rightarrow y$ is by default interpreted as DoubleRightArrow[x, y]. ∎ Used in mathematics to indicate various strong forms of convergence. ∎ Also used to indicate algebraic field extensions. ∎ Not the same as \[Implies]. ∎ Extensible character. ∎ See page 1006. ∎ See also: \[DoubleLongRightArrow], \[RightArrow], \[DoubleLeftArrow].

⊨ \[DoubleRightTee]

Infix operator. ∎ $x \vDash y$ is by default interpreted as DoubleRightTee[x, y]. ∎ $x \vDash y \vDash z$ groups as $x \vDash (y \vDash z)$. ∎ Used in mathematics to indicate various strong forms of logical implication—often tautological implication. ∎ In prefix form, used to indicate a tautology. ∎ See pages 1001 and 1007. ∎ See also: \[RightTee], \[DoubleLeftTee].

𝕒...𝕫 \[DoubleStruckA] ... \[DoubleStruckZ]

Aliases: ⦙dsa⦙ through ⦙dsz⦙. ∎ Letters. ∎ Treated as distinct characters rather than style modifications of ordinary letters. ∎ Contiguous character codes from the private Unicode character range are used, even though a few double-struck characters are included in ordinary Unicode. ∎ See page 993. ∎ See also: \[DoubleStruckCapitalA], \[GothicA], \[ScriptA], etc.

𝔸...ℤ \[DoubleStruckCapitalA] ... \[DoubleStruckCapitalZ]

Aliases: ⦙dsA⦙ through ⦙dsZ⦙. ∎ Letters. ∎ Treated as distinct characters rather than style modifications of ordinary letters. ∎ ℕ, ℤ, ℚ, ℝ, ℂ, ℍ are used respectively to denote the sets of natural numbers, integers, rationals, reals, complex numbers and quaternions. ∎ Contiguous character codes from the private Unicode character range are used, even though a few capital double-struck characters are included in ordinary Unicode. ∎ See page 993. ∎ See also: \[GothicCapitalA], \[ScriptCapitalA], etc.

⇑ \[DoubleUpArrow]

Infix arrow operator. ∎ $x \Uparrow y$ is by default interpreted as DoubleUpArrow[x, y]. ∎ Extensible character. ∎ See page 1006. ∎ See also: \[UpArrow], \[DoubleDownArrow].

⇕ \[DoubleUpDownArrow]

Infix arrow operator. ∎ $x \Updownarrow y$ is by default interpreted as DoubleUpDownArrow[x, y]. ∎ Extensible character. ∎ See page 1006. ∎ See also: \[UpDownArrow], \[UpArrowDownArrow], \[DownArrowUpArrow].

∥   \[DoubleVerticalBar]

Alias: ⦙_∥⦙. ▪ Infix operator. ▪ $x \parallel y$ is by default interpreted as DoubleVerticalBar[x, y]. ▪ Used in mathematics to indicate that x exactly divides y. ▪ Used in geometry to mean "parallel to". ▪ Not the same as \[LeftDoubleBracketingBar], \[RightDoubleBracketingBar]. ▪ ⦙∥⦙ is the alias for \[Or]. The alias for \[DoubleVerticalBar] has a space at the beginning. ▪ See page 1005. ▪ See also: \[VerticalBar], \[VerticalSeparator], \[NotDoubleVerticalBar].

↓   \[DownArrow]

Infix arrow operator. ▪ $x \downarrow y$ is by default interpreted as DownArrow[x, y]. ▪ Used to indicate monotonic decrease to a limit. ▪ Sometimes used for logical nor. ▪ Sometimes used in prefix form to indicate the closure of a set. ▪ Extensible character. ▪ See page 1006. ▪ See also: \[DownTeeArrow], \[DownArrowBar], \[DoubleDownArrow], \[LeftDownVector], \[UpArrow].

↓   \[DownArrowBar]

Infix arrow operator. ▪ $x \downarrow y$ is by default interpreted as DownArrowBar[x, y]. ▪ Sometimes used as an indicator of depth. ▪ Extensible character. ▪ See page 1006. ▪ See also: \[DownTeeArrow], \[DownArrow], \[LeftDownVectorBar], \[UpArrowBar].

⇕   \[DownArrowUpArrow]

Infix arrow operator. ▪ $x \Updownarrow y$ is by default interpreted as DownArrowUpArrow[x, y]. ▪ Extensible character. ▪ See page 1006. ▪ See also: \[UpDownArrow], \[DoubleUpDownArrow], \[UpArrowDownArrow], \[UpEquilibrium].

⌣   \[DownBreve]

Alias: ⦙dbv⦙. ▪ Letter-like form. ▪ Used in an overscript position as a diacritical mark. ▪ See page 999. ▪ See also: \[Breve], \[Cap].

¡   \[DownExclamation]

Alias: ⦙d!⦙. ▪ Letter-like form. ▪ Used in Spanish. ▪ See page 996. ▪ See also: \[RawExclamation], \[DownQuestion].

↽   \[DownLeftRightVector]

Infix arrow-like operator. ▪ $x \leftrightharpoons y$ is by default interpreted as DownLeftRightVector[x, y]. ▪ Extensible character. ▪ See page 1007. ▪ See also: \[LeftRightVector], \[Equilibrium], \[RightUpDownVector].

↤   \[DownLeftTeeVector]

Infix arrow-like operator. ▪ $x \leftharpoondown y$ is by default interpreted as DownLeftTeeVector[x, y]. ▪ Extensible character. ▪ See page 1007. ▪ See also: \[LeftTeeVector], \[LeftVectorBar].

↼   \[DownLeftVector]

Infix arrow-like operator. ▪ $x \leftharpoondown y$ is by default interpreted as DownLeftVector[x, y]. ▪ Extensible character. ▪ See page 1007. ▪ See also: \[LeftVector], \[LeftTeeVector], \[LeftArrow], \[LeftUpVector].

↜   \[DownLeftVectorBar]

Infix arrow-like operator. ▪ $x \leftharpoondown y$ is by default interpreted as DownLeftVectorBar[x, y]. ▪ Extensible character. ▪ See page 1007. ▪ See also: \[LeftVectorBar], \[LeftTeeVector].

¿   \[DownQuestion]

Alias: ⦙d?⦙. ▪ Letter-like form. ▪ Used in Spanish. ▪ See page 996. ▪ See also: \[RawQuestion], \[DownExclamation].

↦   \[DownRightTeeVector]

Infix arrow-like operator. ▪ $x \mapsto y$ is by default interpreted as DownRightTeeVector[x, y]. ▪ Extensible character. ▪ See page 1007. ▪ See also: \[RightTeeVector], \[RightVectorBar].

→ \[DownRightVector]

Infix arrow-like operator. ▪ $x \to y$ is by default interpreted as DownRightVector[x, y]. ▪ Extensible character. ▪ See page 1007. ▪ See also: \[RightVector], \[RightTeeVector], \[RightArrow], \[RightUpVector].

⇥ \[DownRightVectorBar]

Infix arrow-like operator. ▪ $x \to y$ is by default interpreted as DownRightVectorBar[x, y]. ▪ Extensible character. ▪ See page 1007. ▪ See also: \[RightVectorBar], \[RightTeeVector].

⊤ \[DownTee]

Alias: ⣿dT⣿. ▪ Infix operator. ▪ $x \top y$ is by default interpreted as DownTee[x, y]. ▪ See page 1007. ▪ See also: \[UpTee], \[RightTee], \[DownTeeArrow].

↧ \[DownTeeArrow]

Infix arrow operator. ▪ $x \downarrow y$ is by default interpreted as DownTeeArrow[x, y]. ▪ Extensible character. ▪ See page 1006. ▪ See also: \[DownArrowBar], \[RightDownTeeVector], \[DownTee], \[UpTeeArrow].

é \[EAcute]

Alias: ⣿e'⣿. ▪ Letter. ▪ Included in ISO Latin-1. ▪ See pages 190 and 998. ▪ See also: \[CapitalEAcute].

ē \[EBar]

Alias: ⣿e-⣿. ▪ Letter. ▪ Included in ISO Latin-4. ▪ Used in transliterations of various non-Latin alphabets. ▪ See page 998. ▪ See also: \[CapitalEBar].

ĕ \[ECup]

Alias: ⣿eu⣿. ▪ Letter. ▪ Not included in ISO Latin. ▪ Used in transliterations of Cyrillic characters. ▪ See page 998. ▪ See also: \[CapitalECup].

ë \[EDoubleDot]

Alias: ⣿e"⣿. ▪ Letter. ▪ Included in ISO Latin-1. ▪ See page 998. ▪ See also: \[CapitalEDoubleDot], \[IDoubleDot], \[ADoubleDot].

è \[EGrave]

Alias: ⣿e`⣿. ▪ Letter. ▪ Included in ISO Latin-1. ▪ See pages 190 and 998. ▪ See also: \[CapitalEGrave].

ê \[EHat]

Alias: ⣿e^⣿. ▪ Letter. ▪ Included in ISO Latin-1. ▪ See page 998. ▪ See also: \[CapitalEHat].

∈ \[Element]

Alias: ⣿el⣿. ▪ Infix operator with built-in evaluation rules. ▪ $x \in y$ is by default interpreted as Element[x, y]. ▪ Not the same as \[Epsilon]. ▪ See pages 191, 1001 and 1004. ▪ See also: \[NotElement], \[ReverseElement], \[Euro].

... \[Ellipsis]

Alias: ⣿...⣿. ▪ Letter-like form. ▪ Used to indicate omitted elements in a row of a matrix. ▪ \[Ellipsis] on its own will act as a symbol. ▪ See pages 996 and 997. ▪ See also: \[CenterEllipsis], \[VerticalEllipsis], \[AscendingEllipsis], \[HorizontalLine], \[LeftSkeleton], \[RawDot].

○ \[EmptyCircle]

Alias: ⣿eci⣿. ▪ Letter-like form. ▪ Not the same as the infix operator \[SmallCircle]. ▪ See page 995. ▪ See also: \[EmptySmallCircle], \[FilledCircle], \[Degree].

◇   \[EmptyDiamond]

Letter-like form. ▪ See page 995. ▪ See also: \[Diamond], \[FilledDiamond].

▽   \[EmptyDownTriangle]

Letter-like form. ▪ Not the same as \[Del]. ▪ See page 995. ▪ See also: \[EmptyUpTriangle], \[FilledDownTriangle], \[FilledUpTriangle], \[LeftTriangle], \[NotLeftTriangle], \[NotRightTriangle], \[RightTriangle].

▯   \[EmptyRectangle]

Letter-like form. ▪ See page 995. ▪ See also: \[FilledRectangle].

∅   \[EmptySet]

Alias: ⁝es⁝. ▪ Letter-like form. ▪ Not the same as \[CapitalOSlash] or \[Diameter]. ▪ See pages 192 and 994.

○   \[EmptySmallCircle]

Alias: ⁝esci⁝. ▪ Letter-like form. ▪ Not the same as the infix operator \[SmallCircle]. ▪ Used as an overscript to add ring diacritical marks. ▪ See page 995. ▪ See also: \[FilledSmallCircle], \[Degree], \[ARing], \[Angstrom].

□   \[EmptySmallSquare]

Alias: ⁝essq⁝. ▪ Letter-like form. ▪ Not the same as the operator \[Square]. ▪ Not the same as \[Placeholder]. ▪ See page 995. ▪ See also: \[EmptySquare], \[FilledSmallSquare].

□   \[EmptySquare]

Alias: ⁝esq⁝. ▪ Letter-like form. ▪ Not the same as the operator \[Square]. ▪ Not the same as \[Placeholder]. ▪ See page 995. ▪ See also: \[FilledSquare], \[GraySquare], \[DottedSquare], \[EmptyRectangle].

△   \[EmptyUpTriangle]

Letter-like form. ▪ Used in geometry to indicate a triangle, as in the symbol △ABC. ▪ Not the same as \[CapitalDelta]. ▪ See pages 995 and 996. ▪ See also: \[FilledUpTriangle], \[EmptyDownTriangle], \[RightTriangle], \[Angle].

ENT   \[EnterKey]

Alias: ⁝ent⁝. ▪ Letter-like form. ▪ Representation of the ENTER key on a keyboard. ▪ Used in describing how to type textual input. ▪ See page 1009. ▪ See also: \[ReturnKey], \[ReturnIndicator], \[ControlKey], \[CommandKey].

ϵ   \[Epsilon]

Aliases: ⁝e⁝, ⁝epsilon⁝. ▪ Greek letter. ▪ Not the same as \[Element]. ▪ See pages 175 and 990. ▪ See also: \[CurlyEpsilon], \[CapitalEpsilon], \[Eta], \[Euro].

==   \[Equal]

Alias: ⁝==⁝. ▪ Infix operator with built-in evaluation rules. ▪ $x == y$ is by default interpreted as Equal[x, y] or $x == y$. ▪ \[Equal] is drawn longer than \[RawEqual]. ▪ See page 1003. ▪ See also: \[LongEqual], \[NotEqual], \[Congruent], \[Rule].

≈   \[EqualTilde]

Alias: ⁝=~⁝. ▪ Infix similarity operator. ▪ $x ≈ y$ is by default interpreted as EqualTilde[x, y]. ▪ See page 1003. ▪ See also: \[NotEqualTilde].

⇌   \[Equilibrium]

Alias: ⁝equi⁝. ▪ Infix arrow-like operator. ▪ $x ⇌ y$ is by default interpreted as Equilibrium[x, y]. ▪ Used in chemistry to represent a reversible reaction. ▪ Extensible character. ▪ See pages 191 and 1007. ▪ See also: \[ReverseEquilibrium], \[RightArrowLeftArrow], \[LeftRightArrow], \[LeftRightVector], \[UpEquilibrium].

◠   \[ErrorIndicator]

Uninterpretable element. ▪ Generated to indicate the position of a syntax error in messages produced by functions like Get and ToExpression. ▪ Shown as ^^^ in OutputForm. ▪ \[ErrorIndicator] indicates the presence of a syntax error, and so by default generates an error if you try to interpret it. ▪ See also: \[LeftSkeleton].

ESC   \[EscapeKey]

Alias: ⁚␣esc⁚. ▪ Letter-like form. ▪ Representation of the escape key on a keyboard. ▪ Used in describing how to type aliases for special characters in *Mathematica*. ▪ ⁚esc⁚ is the alias for \[AliasIndicator]. The alias for \[EscapeKey] has a space at the beginning. ▪ See page 1009. ▪ See also: \[AliasIndicator], \[RawEscape], \[ReturnKey], \[ControlKey], \[CommandKey].

η   \[Eta]

Aliases: ⁚et⁚, ⁚eta⁚, ⁚h⁚. ▪ Greek letter. ▪ Used in TraditionalForm for DedekindEta. ▪ See pages 175 and 990. ▪ See also: \[CapitalEta], \[Epsilon].

ð   \[Eth]

Alias: ⁚d-⁚. ▪ Letter. ▪ Included in ISO Latin-1. ▪ Used in Icelandic and Old English. ▪ See page 998. ▪ See also: \[CapitalEth], \[Thorn], \[PartialD].

€   \[Euro]

Letter-like form. ▪ Sign for euro European currency, as in € 5. ▪ See page 994. ▪ See also: \[Epsilon], \[Element], \[Sterling].

∃   \[Exists]

Alias: ⁚ex⁚. ▪ Compound operator. ▪ $\exists_x y$ is by default interpreted as Exists[x, y]. ▪ See page 1001. ▪ See also: \[NotExists].

ℯ   \[ExponentialE]

Alias: ⁚ee⁚. ▪ Letter-like form with built-in value. ▪ ℯ is interpreted by default as the symbol E, representing the exponential constant. ▪ See pages 988 and 994. ▪ See also: \[DifferentialD], \[ImaginaryI].

●   \[FilledCircle]

Alias: ⁚fci⁚. ▪ Letter-like form. ▪ Used as a dingbat. ▪ See page 995. ▪ See also: \[Bullet], \[FilledSmallCircle], \[SmallCircle], \[EmptyCircle].

◆   \[FilledDiamond]

Letter-like form. ▪ See page 995. ▪ See also: \[Diamond], \[EmptyDiamond].

▼   \[FilledDownTriangle]

Letter-like form. ▪ See page 995. ▪ See also: \[EmptyDownTriangle], \[EmptyUpTriangle], \[FilledUpTriangle], \[LeftTriangle], \[NotLeftTriangle], \[NotRightTriangle], \[RightTriangle].

■   \[FilledRectangle]

Letter-like form. ▪ Used in mathematics to indicate the end of a proof. ▪ See page 995. ▪ See also: \[EmptyRectangle].

●   \[FilledSmallCircle]

Alias: ⁚fsci⁚. ▪ Letter-like form. ▪ Used as a dingbat. ▪ See page 995. ▪ See also: \[Bullet], \[FilledCircle], \[EmptySmallCircle].

■ \[FilledSmallSquare]

Alias: ⦂fssq⦂. ■ Letter-like form. ■ Used as a dingbat. ■ Not the same as \[SelectionPlaceholder]. ■ See page 995. ■ See also: \[FilledSquare], \[EmptySmallSquare], \[Square].

■ \[FilledSquare]

Alias: ⦂fsq⦂. ■ Letter-like form. ■ Used as a dingbat. ■ Not the same as \[SelectionPlaceholder]. ■ See page 995. ■ See also: \[FilledSmallSquare], \[EmptySquare], \[Square], \[GraySquare], \[FilledRectangle].

▲ \[FilledUpTriangle]

Letter-like form. ■ See page 995. ■ See also: \[EmptyDownTriangle], \[EmptyUpTriangle], \[FilledDownTriangle], \[LeftTriangle], \[NotLeftTriangle], \[NotRightTriangle], \[RightTriangle].

■ \[FilledVerySmallSquare]

Alias: ⦂fvssq⦂. ■ Letter-like form. ■ Used as a dingbat. ■ See page 995. ■ See also: \[FilledSmallSquare], \[Square].

ς \[FinalSigma]

Alias: ⦂fs⦂. ■ Greek letter. ■ Used in written Greek when σ occurs at the end of a word. ■ Not commonly used in technical notation. ■ Not the same as \[Stigma]. ■ See page 990. ■ See also: \[Sigma].

★ \[FivePointedStar]

Alias: ⦂*5⦂. ■ Letter-like form. ■ Not the same as the operator \[Star]. ■ See page 995. ■ See also: \[SixPointedStar], \[Star], \[RawStar].

♭ \[Flat]

Letter-like form. ■ Used to denote musical notes. ■ Sometimes used in mathematical notation. ■ See page 996. ■ See also: \[Sharp], \[Natural].

∀ \[ForAll]

Alias: ⦂fa⦂. ■ Compound operator. ■ $\forall_x \, y$ is by default interpreted as ForAll[x, y]. ■ See page 1001. ■ See also: \[Exists], \[Not].

☺ \[FreakedSmiley]

Alias: ⦂:-@⦂. ■ Letter-like form. ■ See page 995. ■ See also: \[HappySmiley], \[NeutralSmiley], \[SadSmiley], \[WarningSign].

γ \[Gamma]

Aliases: ⦂g⦂, ⦂gamma⦂. ■ Greek letter. ■ Used in TraditionalForm for EulerGamma and StieltjesGamma. ■ See pages 175 and 990. ■ See also: \[DoubledGamma], \[CapitalGamma], \[Digamma].

ℷ \[Gimel]

Alias: ⦂gi⦂. ■ Hebrew letter. ■ Used occasionally in pure mathematics in the theory of transfinite cardinals. ■ See page 993. ■ See also: \[Aleph].

𝔞...𝔷 \[GothicA] ... \[GothicZ]

Aliases: ⦂goa⦂ through ⦂goz⦂. ■ Letters. ■ Treated as distinct characters rather than style modifications of ordinary letters. ■ Used in pure mathematics. ■ Contiguous character codes from the private Unicode character range are used, even though a few gothic characters are included in ordinary Unicode. ■ See page 993. ■ See also: \[GothicCapitalA], \[ScriptA], \[DoubleStruckA], etc.

𝔄...ℨ   \[GothicCapitalA] ... \[GothicCapitalZ]

Aliases: ⦂goA⦂ through ⦂goZ⦂. ▪ Letters. ▪ Treated as distinct characters rather than style modifications of ordinary letters. ▪ I is used to denote imaginary part; R is used to denote real part. ▪ Used in pure mathematics and theory of computation. ▪ Contiguous character codes from the private Unicode character range are used, even though a few capital gothic characters are included in ordinary Unicode. ▪ See page 993. ▪ See also: \[GothicA], \[ScriptCapitalA], \[DoubleStruckCapitalA], etc.

⬤   \[GrayCircle]

Alias: ⦂gci⦂. ▪ Letter-like form. ▪ Used as a dingbat. ▪ Generated internally by *Mathematica*, rather than being an explicit font character. ▪ See page 995. ▪ See also: \[FilledCircle], \[GraySquare].

◼   \[GraySquare]

Alias: ⦂gsq⦂. ▪ Letter-like form. ▪ Used as a dingbat. ▪ Generated internally by *Mathematica*, rather than being an explicit font character. ▪ See page 995. ▪ See also: \[FilledSquare], \[EmptySquare].

≥   \[GreaterEqual]

Alias: ⦂>=⦂. ▪ Infix operator with built-in evaluation rules. ▪ $x \geq y$ is by default interpreted as GreaterEqual[x, y]. ▪ See page 1004. ▪ See also: \[GreaterSlantEqual], \[GreaterFullEqual], \[NotGreaterEqual].

≷   \[GreaterEqualLess]

Infix ordering operator. ▪ $x \gtreqless y$ is by default interpreted as GreaterEqualLess[x, y]. ▪ See page 1004. ▪ See also: \[LessEqualGreater].

≧   \[GreaterFullEqual]

Infix ordering operator. ▪ $x \geqq y$ is by default interpreted as GreaterFullEqual[x, y]. ▪ See page 1004. ▪ See also: \[GreaterEqual], \[GreaterSlantEqual], \[NotGreaterFullEqual].

≫   \[GreaterGreater]

Infix ordering operator. ▪ $x \gg y$ is by default interpreted as GreaterGreater[x, y]. ▪ Not the same as \[RightGuillemet]. ▪ See pages 191 and 1004. ▪ See also: \[NestedGreaterGreater], \[NotGreaterGreater], \[NotNestedGreaterGreater].

≷   \[GreaterLess]

Infix ordering operator. ▪ $x \gtrless y$ is by default interpreted as GreaterLess[x, y]. ▪ See page 1004. ▪ See also: \[GreaterEqualLess], \[NotGreaterLess].

⩾   \[GreaterSlantEqual]

Alias: ⦂>/⦂. ▪ Infix operator with built-in evaluation rules. ▪ $x \geqslant y$ is by default interpreted as GreaterEqual[x, y]. ▪ See page 1004. ▪ See also: \[GreaterEqual], \[GreaterFullEqual], \[NotGreaterSlantEqual].

≳   \[GreaterTilde]

Alias: ⦂>~⦂. ▪ Infix ordering operator. ▪ $x \gtrsim y$ is by default interpreted as GreaterTilde[x, y]. ▪ See pages 191 and 1004. ▪ See also: \[NotGreaterTilde].

˘   \[Hacek]

Alias: ⦂hc⦂. ▪ Letter-like form. ▪ Used primarily in an overscript position. ▪ Used as a diacritical mark in Eastern European languages. ▪ Sometimes used in mathematical notation, for example in Čech cohomology. ▪ See page 999. ▪ See also: \[Vee], \[Breve].

☺ \[HappySmiley]

> Aliases: ⁝:)⁝, ⁝:-)⁝. ■ Letter-like form. ■ See page 995. ■ See also: \[NeutralSmiley], \[SadSmiley], \[FreakedSmiley], \[Wolf].

ℏ \[HBar]

> Alias: ⁝hb⁝. ■ Letter-like form. ■ Used in physics to denote Planck's constant divided by 2π; sometimes called Dirac's constant. ■ See pages 192 and 994. ■ See also: \[Angstrom].

♡ \[HeartSuit]

> Letter-like form. ■ See page 996. ■ See also: \[ClubSuit].

– \[HorizontalLine]

> Alias: ⁝hline⁝. ■ Letter-like form. ■ Extensible character. ■ Thickness can be adjusted using the SpanThickness option in StyleBox. ■ See page 997. ■ See also: \[Dash], \[LongDash], \[VerticalSeparator].

≎ \[HumpDownHump]

> Infix similarity operator. ■ $x \asymp y$ is by default interpreted as HumpDownHump[x, y]. ■ Used to indicate geometrical equivalence. ■ See page 1003. ■ See also: \[HumpEqual], \[NotHumpDownHump].

≏ \[HumpEqual]

> Alias: ⁝h-⁝. ■ Infix similarity operator. ■ $x \doteq y$ is by default interpreted as HumpEqual[x, y]. ■ Sometimes used to mean "approximately equal" and sometimes "difference between". ■ See page 1003. ■ See also: \[HumpDownHump], \[TildeEqual], \[NotHumpEqual].

í \[IAcute]

> Alias: ⁝i'⁝. ■ Letter. ■ Included in ISO Latin-1. ■ See pages 190 and 998. ■ See also: \[CapitalIAcute].

ĭ \[ICup]

> Alias: ⁝iu⁝. ■ Letter. ■ Included in ISO Latin-2. ■ Used in transliterations of Cyrillic characters. ■ See page 998. ■ See also: \[CapitalICup].

ï \[IDoubleDot]

> Alias: ⁝i"⁝. ■ Letter. ■ Included in ISO Latin-1. ■ See page 998. ■ See also: \[CapitalIDoubleDot], \[EDoubleDot], \[ADoubleDot].

ì \[IGrave]

> Alias: ⁝i`⁝. ■ Letter. ■ Included in ISO Latin-1. ■ See page 998. ■ See also: \[CapitalIGrave].

î \[IHat]

> Alias: ⁝i^⁝. ■ Letter. ■ Included in ISO Latin-1. ■ See page 998. ■ See also: \[CapitalIHat].

i \[ImaginaryI]

> Alias: ⁝ii⁝. ■ Letter-like form with built-in value. ■ ⅈ is interpreted by default as the symbol I, representing $\sqrt{-1}$. ■ See pages 988 and 994. ■ See also: \[ImaginaryJ], \[ExponentialE].

j \[ImaginaryJ]

> Alias: ⁝jj⁝. ■ Letter-like form with built-in value. ■ ⅉ is interpreted by default as the symbol I, representing $\sqrt{-1}$. ■ Used in electrical engineering. ■ See pages 988 and 994. ■ See also: \[ImaginaryI], \[ExponentialE].

⇒   \[Implies]

Alias: ⌷=>⌷. ▪ Infix operator with built-in evaluation rules. ▪ $x \Rightarrow y$ is by default interpreted as Implies[x, y].
▪ $x \Rightarrow y \Rightarrow z$ groups as $x \Rightarrow (y \Rightarrow z)$. ▪ Not the same as \[DoubleRightArrow]. ▪ \[DoubleRightArrow] is
extensible; \[Implies] is not. ▪ See pages 1001 and 1006. ▪ See also: \[RoundImplies], \[SuchThat],
\[RightArrow], \[Rule].

\[IndentingNewLine]

Alias: ⌷nl⌷. ▪ Raw operator. ▪ Forces a line break in an expression, maintaining the correct indenting level based on
the environment of the line break. ▪ See pages 460 and 1008. ▪ See also: \[NewLine], \[NoBreak].

∞   \[Infinity]

Alias: ⌷inf⌷. ▪ Letter-like form with built-in value. ▪ ∞ is interpreted by default as the symbol Infinity. ▪ See
page 994.

∫   \[Integral]

Alias: ⌷int⌷. ▪ Compound operator with built-in evaluation rules. ▪ $\int f \, dx$ is by default interpreted as
Integrate[f, x]. ▪ $\int_a^b f \, dx$ is by default interpreted as Integral[f, {x, a, b}]. a and b must appear as a
subscript and superscript, respectively. ▪ $\int a \circ b \, dx$ is by default output as $\int (a \circ b) \, dx$ whenever ∘ is an
operator with a precedence lower than ∗. ▪ Note the use of d, entered as ⌷dd⌷ or \[DifferentialD], rather than
ordinary d. ▪ See page 1000. ▪ See also: \[ContourIntegral].

∩   \[Intersection]

Alias: ⌷inter⌷. ▪ Infix operator with built-in evaluation rules. ▪ $x \cap y$ is by default interpreted as
Intersection[x, y]. ▪ The character ∩ is sometimes called "cap"; but see also \[Cap]. ▪ ⌷int⌷ gives \[Integral]
not \[Intersection]. ▪ See page 1002. ▪ See also: \[Union], \[SquareIntersection], \[Cap], \[Wedge].

\[InvisibleApplication]

Alias: ⌷@⌷. ▪ Structural element with built-in meaning. ▪ \[InvisibleApplication] is by default not visible on
display, but is interpreted as function application. ▪ f ⌷@⌷ x is interpreted as f @ x or $f[x]$.
▪ \[InvisibleApplication] can be used as an invisible separator between functions or between functions and
their arguments. ▪ See page 1008. ▪ See also: \[InvisibleSpace], \[InvisibleComma], \[RawAt].

\[InvisibleComma]

Alias: ⌷,⌷. ▪ Structural element with built-in meaning. ▪ \[InvisibleComma] is by default not visible on display, but
is interpreted on input as an ordinary comma. ▪ \[InvisibleComma] can be used as an invisible separator between
indices, as in M_{ij}. ▪ See page 1008. ▪ See also: \[AlignmentMarker], \[Null], \[InvisibleSpace], \[RawComma].

\[InvisibleSpace]

Alias: ⌷is⌷. ▪ Spacing character. ▪ \[InvisibleSpace] is by default not visible on display, but is interpreted on
input as an ordinary space. ▪ \[InvisibleSpace] can be used as an invisible separator between variables that are
being multiplied together, as in xy. ▪ See pages 454 and 1008. ▪ See also: \[AlignmentMarker], \[Null],
\[VeryThinSpace], \[RawSpace].

ι   \[Iota]

Aliases: ⌷i⌷, ⌷iota⌷. ▪ Greek letter. ▪ Not commonly used. ▪ Used in set theory to indicate an explicitly
constructible set. ▪ See page 990. ▪ See also: \[CapitalIota], \[DotlessI].

κ   \[Kappa]

Aliases: ⌷k⌷, ⌷kappa⌷. ▪ Greek letter. ▪ See pages 175 and 990. ▪ See also: \[CurlyKappa], \[CapitalKappa].

\[KernelIcon]

Letter-like form. ■ Icon typically used for the *Mathematica* kernel. ■ This icon is a trademark of Wolfram Research. ■ See page 995. ■ See also: \[MathematicaIcon].

ϱ \[Koppa]

Aliases: ⦂ko⦂, ⦂koppa⦂. ■ Special Greek letter. ■ Analogous to English q. ■ Appeared between π and ρ in early Greek alphabet; used for Greek numeral 90. ■ See page 990. ■ See also: \[CapitalKoppa], \[Digamma], \[Stigma], \[Sampi].

λ \[Lambda]

Aliases: ⦂l⦂, ⦂lambda⦂. ■ Greek letter. ■ Used in TraditionalForm for ModularLambda. ■ See pages 175 and 990. ■ See also: \[CapitalLambda].

⟨ \[LeftAngleBracket]

Alias: ⦂<⦂. ■ Matchfix operator. ■ ⟨ x ⟩ is by default interpreted as AngleBracket[x]. ■ Used in the form ⟨x⟩ to indicate expected or average value. ■ Called bra in quantum mechanics. ■ Used in the form ⟨x, y⟩ to indicate various forms of inner product. ■ Used in the form ⟨x, y, … ⟩ to denote an ordered set of objects. ■ Not the same as \[RawLess]. ■ Extensible character; grows by default to limited size. ■ See pages 191 and 1002. ■ See also: \[RightAngleBracket], \[LeftFloor], \[LeftCeiling].

← \[LeftArrow]

Alias: ⦂<-⦂. ■ Infix arrow operator. ■ $x ← y$ is by default interpreted as LeftArrow[x, y]. ■ Sometimes used in computer science to indicate assignment: x gets value y. ■ Extensible character. ■ See page 1006. ■ See also: \[LongLeftArrow], \[ShortLeftArrow], \[DoubleLeftArrow], \[LeftTeeArrow], \[LeftArrowBar], \[LowerLeftArrow], \[LeftVector], \[LeftTriangle], \[RightArrow].

↤ \[LeftArrowBar]

Infix arrow operator. ■ $x ↤ y$ is by default interpreted as LeftArrowBar[x, y]. ■ Sometimes used to indicate a backtab. ■ Extensible character. ■ See page 1006. ■ See also: \[LeftTeeArrow], \[LeftVectorBar], \[DownArrowBar], \[RightArrowBar].

⇆ \[LeftArrowRightArrow]

Infix arrow operator. ■ $x ⇆ y$ is by default interpreted as LeftArrowRightArrow[x, y]. ■ Used in mathematics to indicate logical equivalence. ■ Sometimes used to indicate chemical equilibrium. ■ Extensible character. ■ See page 1006. ■ See also: \[RightArrowLeftArrow], \[LeftRightArrow], \[DoubleLeftRightArrow], \[Equilibrium], \[UpArrowDownArrow].

| \[LeftBracketingBar]

Alias: ⦂l|⦂. ■ Matchfix operator. ■ | x | is by default interpreted as BracketingBar[x]. ■ Used in mathematics to indicate absolute value (Abs), determinant (Det), and other notions of evaluating size or magnitude. ■ Not the same as \[VerticalBar]. ■ Drawn in monospaced fonts with a small left-pointing tee to indicate direction. ■ Extensible character. ■ See page 1002. ■ See also: \[LeftDoubleBracketingBar], \[LeftTee].

⌈ \[LeftCeiling]

Alias: ⦂lc⦂. ■ Matchfix operator with built-in evaluation rules. ■ ⌈ x ⌉ is by default interpreted as Ceiling[x]. ■ Extensible character. ■ See page 1002. ■ See also: \[RightCeiling], \[LeftFloor], \[LeftAngleBracket].

⟦ \[LeftDoubleBracket]

Alias: ⦂[[⦂. ■ Compound operator with built-in evaluation rules. ■ $m⟦i,j, … ⟧$ is by default interpreted as Part[m, i, j, …]. ■ Sometimes used in mathematics to indicate a class of algebraic objects with certain variables or extensions. ■ Extensible character; grows by default to limited size. ■ See page 1002. ■ See also: \[RawLeftBracket], \[LeftDoubleBracketingBar].

‖   \[LeftDoubleBracketingBar]

Alias: ⣉l||⣉. ▪ Matchfix operator. ▪ ‖ x ‖ is by default interpreted as DoubleBracketingBar[x]. ▪ Used in mathematics to indicate taking a norm. ▪ Sometimes used for determinant. ▪ Sometimes used to indicate a matrix. ▪ Not the same as \[DoubleVerticalBar]. ▪ Drawn in monospaced fonts with a small left-pointing tee to indicate direction. ▪ Extensible character. ▪ See page 1002. ▪ See also: \[LeftBracketingBar].

⟂   \[LeftDownTeeVector]

Infix arrow-like operator. ▪ x ⟂ y is by default interpreted as LeftDownTeeVector[x, y]. ▪ Extensible character. ▪ See page 1007. ▪ See also: \[RightDownTeeVector], \[LeftDownVectorBar], \[DownTeeArrow], \[LeftUpTeeVector].

↓   \[LeftDownVector]

Infix arrow-like operator. ▪ x ↓ y is by default interpreted as LeftDownVector[x, y]. ▪ Extensible character. ▪ See page 1007. ▪ See also: \[RightDownVector], \[LeftDownTeeVector], \[DownArrow], \[UpEquilibrium], \[LeftUpVector].

↓   \[LeftDownVectorBar]

Infix arrow-like operator. ▪ x ↓ y is by default interpreted as LeftDownVectorBar[x, y]. ▪ Extensible character. ▪ See page 1007. ▪ See also: \[RightDownVectorBar], \[LeftDownTeeVector], \[DownArrowBar], \[LeftUpVectorBar].

⌊   \[LeftFloor]

Alias: ⣉lf⣉. ▪ Matchfix operator with built-in evaluation rules. ▪ ⌊ x ⌋ is by default interpreted as Floor[x]. ▪ Extensible character. ▪ See page 1002. ▪ See also: \[RightFloor], \[LeftCeiling], \[LeftAngleBracket].

«   \[LeftGuillemet]

Alias: ⣉g<<⣉. ▪ Letter-like form. ▪ Used as opening quotation marks in languages such as Spanish. ▪ Not the same as \[LessLess]. ▪ Not the same as \[LeftSkeleton]. ▪ Guillemet is sometimes misspelled as guillemot. ▪ See page 996. ▪ See also: \[RightGuillemet].

⌐   \[LeftModified]

Alias: ⣉[⣉. ▪ Letter-like form. ▪ Used in documenting control and command characters. ▪ *key*\[LeftModified]*char*\[RightModified] is used to indicate that *char* should be typed while *key* is being pressed. ▪ Not the same as \[RawLeftBracket]. ▪ See page 1009. ▪ See also: \[ControlKey], \[CommandKey], \[RightModified].

↔   \[LeftRightArrow]

Alias: ⣉<->⣉. ▪ Infix arrow operator. ▪ x ↔ y is by default interpreted as LeftRightArrow[x, y]. ▪ Used in mathematics for various notions of equivalence and equality. ▪ Extensible character. ▪ See pages 191 and 1006. ▪ See also: \[LongLeftRightArrow], \[DoubleLeftRightArrow], \[LeftArrowRightArrow], \[LeftRightVector], \[Equilibrium], \[UpDownArrow].

↭   \[LeftRightVector]

Infix arrow-like operator. ▪ x ↭ y is by default interpreted as LeftRightVector[x, y]. ▪ Extensible character. ▪ See page 1007. ▪ See also: \[DownLeftRightVector], \[Equilibrium], \[ReverseEquilibrium], \[LeftRightArrow], \[RightArrowLeftArrow], \[RightUpDownVector].

≪   \[LeftSkeleton]

Uninterpretable element. ▪ ≪ n ≫ is used on output to indicate n omitted pieces in an expression obtained from Short or Shallow. ▪ \[LeftSkeleton] indicates the presence of missing information, and so by default generates an error if you try to interpret it. ▪ Not the same as \[LeftGuillemet]. ▪ See page 1009. ▪ See also: \[RightSkeleton], \[SkeletonIndicator], \[Ellipsis], \[ErrorIndicator].

⊣   \[LeftTee]

Alias: ⦂lT⦂. ▪ Infix operator. ▪ $x ⊣ y$ is by default interpreted as LeftTee[x, y]. ▪ $x ⊣ y ⊣ z$ groups as $(x ⊣ y) ⊣ z$. ▪ Used in mathematics to indicate the lack of logical implication or proof. ▪ See pages 1001 and 1007. ▪ See also: \[DoubleLeftTee], \[LeftTeeArrow], \[LeftTeeVector], \[RightTee], \[DownTee], \[LeftBracketingBar].

↤   \[LeftTeeArrow]

Infix arrow operator. ▪ $x ↤ y$ is by default interpreted as LeftTeeArrow[x, y]. ▪ Extensible character. ▪ See page 1006. ▪ See also: \[LeftTeeVector], \[LeftTee], \[RightTeeArrow], \[DownTeeArrow].

↤   \[LeftTeeVector]

Infix arrow-like operator. ▪ $x ↤ y$ is by default interpreted as LeftTeeVector[x, y]. ▪ Extensible character. ▪ See page 1007. ▪ See also: \[DownLeftTeeVector], \[LeftVectorBar], \[LeftVector], \[LeftTeeArrow].

◁   \[LeftTriangle]

Infix ordering operator. ▪ $x ◁ y$ is by default interpreted as LeftTriangle[x, y]. ▪ Used in pure mathematics to mean "normal subgroup of". ▪ See page 1005. ▪ See also: \[LeftTriangleEqual], \[LeftTriangleBar], \[LeftArrow], \[NotLeftTriangle], \[RightTriangle], \[EmptyUpTriangle], \[FilledUpTriangle].

◁| \[LeftTriangleBar]

Infix ordering operator. ▪ $x ◁| y$ is by default interpreted as LeftTriangleBar[x, y]. ▪ See page 1005. ▪ See also: \[LeftTriangle], \[LeftTriangleEqual], \[LeftArrowBar], \[NotLeftTriangleBar].

⊴   \[LeftTriangleEqual]

Infix ordering operator. ▪ $x ⊴ y$ is by default interpreted as LeftTriangleEqual[x, y]. ▪ See page 1005. ▪ See also: \[LeftTriangle], \[LeftTriangleBar], \[PrecedesEqual], \[NotLeftTriangleEqual], \[RightTriangleEqual].

↧   \[LeftUpDownVector]

Infix arrow-like operator. ▪ $x ↧ y$ is by default interpreted as LeftUpDownVector[x, y]. ▪ Extensible character. ▪ See page 1007. ▪ See also: \[RightUpDownVector], \[UpEquilibrium], \[UpArrowDownArrow], \[LeftRightVector].

↥   \[LeftUpTeeVector]

Infix arrow-like operator. ▪ $x ↥ y$ is by default interpreted as LeftUpTeeVector[x, y]. ▪ Extensible character. ▪ See page 1007. ▪ See also: \[RightUpTeeVector], \[LeftUpVectorBar], \[UpTeeArrow], \[LeftDownTeeVector].

↿   \[LeftUpVector]

Infix arrow-like operator. ▪ $x ↿ y$ is by default interpreted as LeftUpVector[x, y]. ▪ Extensible character. ▪ See page 1007. ▪ See also: \[RightUpVector], \[LeftUpTeeVector], \[UpArrow], \[UpEquilibrium], \[LeftDownVector].

↾   \[LeftUpVectorBar]

Infix arrow-like operator. ▪ $x ↾ y$ is by default interpreted as LeftUpVectorBar[x, y]. ▪ Extensible character. ▪ See page 1007. ▪ See also: \[RightUpVectorBar], \[LeftUpTeeVector], \[UpArrowBar], \[LeftDownVectorBar].

↼   \[LeftVector]

Infix arrow-like operator. ▪ $x ↼ y$ is by default interpreted as LeftVector[x, y]. ▪ Extensible character. ▪ See page 1007. ▪ See also: \[DownLeftVector], \[LeftTeeVector], \[LeftVectorBar], \[LeftArrow], \[RightVector], \[LeftUpVector].

↦   \[LeftVectorBar]

Infix arrow-like operator. ▪ $x ↦ y$ is by default interpreted as LeftVectorBar[x, y]. ▪ Extensible character. ▪ See page 1007. ▪ See also: \[DownLeftVectorBar], \[LeftTeeVector], \[LeftArrowBar].

≤   \[LessEqual]

Alias: ⦂<=⦂. ▪ Infix operator with built-in evaluation rules. ▪ $x \leq y$ is by default interpreted as LessEqual[x, y]. ▪ See page 1004. ▪ See also: \[LessSlantEqual], \[LessFullEqual], \[NotLessEqual].

⋚   \[LessEqualGreater]

Infix ordering operator. ▪ $x \lesseqgtr y$ is by default interpreted as LessEqualGreater[x, y]. ▪ See page 1004. ▪ See also: \[GreaterEqualLess].

≦   \[LessFullEqual]

Infix ordering operator. ▪ $x \leqq y$ is by default interpreted as LessFullEqual[x, y]. ▪ See page 1004. ▪ See also: \[LessEqual], \[LessSlantEqual], \[NotLessFullEqual].

≶   \[LessGreater]

Infix ordering operator. ▪ $x \lessgtr y$ is by default interpreted as LessGreater[x, y]. ▪ See page 1004. ▪ See also: \[LessEqualGreater], \[NotLessGreater].

≪   \[LessLess]

Infix ordering operator. ▪ $x \ll y$ is by default interpreted as LessLess[x, y]. ▪ Not the same as \[LeftGuillemet]. ▪ See page 1004. ▪ See also: \[NestedLessLess], \[NotLessLess], \[NotNestedLessLess].

≤   \[LessSlantEqual]

Alias: ⦂</⦂. ▪ Infix operator with built-in evaluation rules. ▪ $x \leqslant y$ is by default interpreted as LessEqual[x, y]. ▪ See page 1004. ▪ See also: \[LessEqual], \[LessFullEqual], \[NotLessSlantEqual].

≲   \[LessTilde]

Alias: ⦂<~⦂. ▪ Infix ordering operator. ▪ $x \lesssim y$ is by default interpreted as LessTilde[x, y]. ▪ See page 1004. ▪ See also: \[NotLessTilde].

♡   \[LightBulb]

Letter-like form. ▪ See page 995.

—   \[LongDash]

Alias: ⦂--⦂. ▪ Letter-like form. ▪ See page 996. ▪ See also: \[Dash], \[HorizontalLine].

=   \[LongEqual]

Infix operator with built-in evaluation rules. ▪ $x = y$ is by default interpreted as Equal[x, y] or $x == y$. ▪ \[LongEqual] is drawn longer than \[RawEqual]. ▪ Used as an alternative to \[Equal]. ▪ See page 1003. ▪ See also: \[Equal], \[NotEqual], \[Congruent].

⟵   \[LongLeftArrow]

Alias: ⦂<--⦂. ▪ Infix arrow operator. ▪ $x \longleftarrow y$ is by default interpreted as LongLeftArrow[x, y]. ▪ See page 1006. ▪ See also: \[LeftArrow], \[DoubleLongLeftArrow], \[LongRightArrow], \[LongLeftRightArrow].

⟷   \[LongLeftRightArrow]

Alias: ⦂<-->⦂. ▪ Infix arrow operator. ▪ $x \longleftrightarrow y$ is by default interpreted as LongLeftRightArrow[x, y]. ▪ See page 1006. ▪ See also: \[LeftRightArrow], \[DoubleLongLeftRightArrow], \[LeftArrowRightArrow], \[Equilibrium].

⟶   \[LongRightArrow]

Alias: ⦂-->⦂. ▪ Infix arrow operator. ▪ $x \longrightarrow y$ is by default interpreted as LongRightArrow[x, y]. ▪ Not the same as \[Rule]. ▪ See pages 191 and 1006. ▪ See also: \[RightArrow], \[DoubleLongRightArrow], \[LongLeftArrow], \[LongLeftRightArrow].

↙   **\[LowerLeftArrow]**

Infix arrow operator. ▪ $x ↙ y$ is by default interpreted as LowerLeftArrow[x, y]. ▪ Extensible character; grows by default to limited size. ▪ See page 1006. ▪ See also: \[LeftArrow], \[UpperRightArrow].

↘   **\[LowerRightArrow]**

Infix arrow operator. ▪ $x ↘ y$ is by default interpreted as LowerRightArrow[x, y]. ▪ Extensible character; grows by default to limited size. ▪ See page 1006. ▪ See also: \[RightArrow], \[UpperLeftArrow].

ł   **\[LSlash]**

Alias: ⦂l/⦂. ▪ Letter. ▪ Included in ISO Latin-2. ▪ See page 998. ▪ See also: \[CapitalLSlash].

✳   **\[MathematicaIcon]**

Alias: ⦂math⦂. ▪ Letter-like form. ▪ Icon typically used for *Mathematica*. ▪ Based on a stellated icosahedron. ▪ This icon is a trademark of Wolfram Research. ▪ See page 995. ▪ See also: \[KernelIcon].

∡   **\[MeasuredAngle]**

Letter-like form. ▪ Used in geometry to indicate an angle, as in the symbol ∡ ABC. ▪ See page 996. ▪ See also: \[Angle], \[SphericalAngle], \[RightAngle].

\[MediumSpace]

Alias: ⦂␣␣⦂. ▪ Spacing character. ▪ Width: 4/18 em. ▪ Interpreted by default just like an ordinary \[RawSpace]. ▪ Sometimes used in output as a separator between digits in numbers. ▪ See page 1008. ▪ See also: \[ThinSpace], \[ThickSpace], \[NegativeMediumSpace], \[NonBreakingSpace], \[SpaceIndicator].

℧   **\[Mho]**

Alias: ⦂mho⦂. ▪ Letter-like form. ▪ Used to denote the inverse ohm unit of conductance. ▪ "Mho" is "ohm" spelled backwards. ▪ Occasionally called "agemo" in pure mathematics. ▪ Used to denote characteristic subgroups, and in set theory to denote functions of sets with special properties. ▪ See page 994. ▪ See also: \[CapitalOmega].

μ   **\[Micro]**

Alias: ⦂mi⦂. ▪ Letter-like form. ▪ Used as a prefix in units to denote 10^{-6}. ▪ Not the same as \[Mu]. ▪ See pages 192 and 994. ▪ See also: \[Angstrom].

∓   **\[MinusPlus]**

Alias: ⦂-+⦂. ▪ Prefix or infix operator. ▪ $∓ x$ is by default interpreted as MinusPlus[x]. ▪ $x ∓ y$ is by default interpreted as MinusPlus[x, y]. ▪ See page 1000. ▪ See also: \[PlusMinus].

μ   **\[Mu]**

Aliases: ⦂m⦂, ⦂mu⦂. ▪ Greek letter. ▪ Used in TraditionalForm for MoebiusMu. ▪ Not the same as \[Micro]. ▪ See pages 175 and 990. ▪ See also: \[CapitalMu].

⊼   **\[Nand]**

Alias: ⦂nand⦂. ▪ Infix operator with built-in evaluation rules. ▪ $x ⊼ y$ is by default interpreted as Nand[x, y]. ▪ See page 1001. ▪ See also: \[And], \[Not], \[Nor], \[VerticalBar].

♮   **\[Natural]**

Letter-like form. ▪ Used to denote musical notes. ▪ Sometimes used in mathematical notation, often as an inverse of numbering operations represented by \[Sharp]. ▪ See pages 192 and 996. ▪ See also: \[Flat], \[Sharp].

\[NegativeMediumSpace]

Alias: ⁞-␣␣⁞. ▪ Negative spacing character. ▪ Used to bring characters on either side closer together. ▪ Width: −4/18 em. ▪ Interpreted by default just like an ordinary \[RawSpace]. ▪ See page 1008. ▪ See also: \[NegativeThinSpace], \[NegativeThickSpace], \[MediumSpace].

\[NegativeThickSpace]

Alias: ⁞-␣␣␣⁞. ▪ Negative spacing character. ▪ Used to bring characters on either side closer together. ▪ Width: −5/18 em. ▪ Interpreted by default just like an ordinary \[RawSpace]. ▪ See page 1008. ▪ See also: \[NegativeMediumSpace], \[ThickSpace].

\[NegativeThinSpace]

Alias: ⁞-␣␣⁞. ▪ Negative spacing character. ▪ Used to bring characters on either side closer together. ▪ Width: −3/18 em. ▪ Interpreted by default just like an ordinary \[RawSpace]. ▪ See page 1008. ▪ See also: \[NegativeVeryThinSpace], \[NegativeMediumSpace], \[ThinSpace].

\[NegativeVeryThinSpace]

Alias: ⁞-␣⁞. ▪ Negative spacing character. ▪ Used to bring characters on either side closer together. ▪ Width: −1/18 em. ▪ Interpreted by default just like an ordinary \[RawSpace]. ▪ See page 1008. ▪ See also: \[NegativeThinSpace], \[VeryThinSpace].

≫   ## \[NestedGreaterGreater]

Infix ordering operator. ▪ $x \gg y$ is by default interpreted as NestedGreaterGreater[x, y]. ▪ See page 1004. ▪ See also: \[GreaterGreater], \[NotGreaterGreater], \[NotNestedGreaterGreater].

≪   ## \[NestedLessLess]

Infix ordering operator. ▪ $x \ll y$ is by default interpreted as NestedLessLess[x, y]. ▪ Used to denote "much less than". ▪ Occasionally used in measure theory to denote "absolutely continuous with respect to". ▪ See page 1004. ▪ See also: \[LessLess], \[NotLessLess], \[NotNestedLessLess].

⊖   ## \[NeutralSmiley]

Alias: ⁞:-|⁞. ▪ Letter-like form. ▪ See page 995. ▪ See also: \[HappySmiley], \[SadSmiley], \[FreakedSmiley].

\[NewLine]

Raw operator. ▪ Inserted whenever a raw newline is entered on the keyboard. ▪ Forces a line break in an expression, fixing the indenting level at the time when the line break is inserted. ▪ \[NewLine] represents a newline on any computer system, independent of the underlying character code used on that computer system. ▪ See pages 460, 1008 and 1010. ▪ See also: \[IndentingNewLine], \[RawReturn].

\[NoBreak]

Alias: ⁞nb⁞. ▪ Letter-like form. ▪ Used to indicate that no line break can occur at this position in an expression. ▪ See pages 459, 460 and 1008. ▪ See also: \[NonBreakingSpace], \[NewLine], \[Continuation], \[AlignmentMarker], \[Null], \[InvisibleSpace].

\[NonBreakingSpace]

Alias: ⁞nbs⁞. ▪ Spacing character. ▪ Generates a space with the same width as \[RawSpace], but with no line break allowed to occur on either side of it. ▪ See pages 459 and 1008. ▪ See also: \[NoBreak], \[InvisibleSpace], \[NewLine].

V̄   ## \[Nor]

Alias: ⁞nor⁞. ▪ Infix operator with built-in evaluation rules. ▪ $x \; \bar{\vee} \; y$ is by default interpreted as Nor[x, y]. ▪ See page 1001. ▪ See also: \[Xor], \[Or], \[Not].

¬   \[Not]

Aliases: ⦂!⦂, ⦂not⦂. ▪ Prefix operator with built-in evaluation rules. ▪ ¬ x is by default interpreted as Not[x], equivalent to !x. ▪ See page 1001. ▪ See also: \[RightTee], \[And], \[Or].

≢   \[NotCongruent]

Alias: ⦂!===⦂. ▪ Infix similarity operator. ▪ x ≢ y is by default interpreted as NotCongruent[x, y]. ▪ See page 1003. ▪ See also: \[NotEqual], \[Congruent].

≭   \[NotCupCap]

Infix similarity operator. ▪ x ≭ y is by default interpreted as NotCupCap[x, y]. ▪ See page 1003. ▪ See also: \[CupCap].

∦   \[NotDoubleVerticalBar]

Alias: ⦂!||⦂. ▪ Infix operator. ▪ x ∦ y is by default interpreted as NotDoubleVerticalBar[x, y]. ▪ Used in geometry to mean "not parallel to". ▪ See page 1005. ▪ See also: \[DoubleVerticalBar], \[NotVerticalBar], \[UpTee].

∉   \[NotElement]

Alias: ⦂!el⦂. ▪ Infix set relation operator with built-in evaluation rules. ▪ x ∉ y is by default interpreted as NotElement[x, y]. ▪ See pages 191 and 1004. ▪ See also: \[Element], \[NotReverseElement].

≠   \[NotEqual]

Alias: ⦂!=⦂. ▪ Infix operator with built-in evaluation rules. ▪ x ≠ y is by default interpreted as Unequal[x, y]. ▪ See page 1003. ▪ See also: \[Equal], \[NotCongruent], \[GreaterLess].

≂̸   \[NotEqualTilde]

Alias: ⦂!=~⦂. ▪ Infix similarity operator. ▪ x ≂̸ y is by default interpreted as NotEqualTilde[x, y]. ▪ See page 1003. ▪ See also: \[EqualTilde].

∄   \[NotExists]

Alias: ⦂!ex⦂. ▪ Compound operator. ▪ ∄ₓ y is by default interpreted as NotExists[x, y]. ▪ See page 1001. ▪ See also: \[Exists], \[ForAll].

≯   \[NotGreater]

Alias: ⦂!>⦂. ▪ Infix ordering operator. ▪ x ≯ y is by default interpreted as NotGreater[x, y]. ▪ ≯ is equivalent to ≤ only for a totally ordered set. ▪ See page 1004. ▪ See also: \[RawGreater].

≱   \[NotGreaterEqual]

Alias: ⦂!>=⦂. ▪ Infix ordering operator. ▪ x ≱ y is by default interpreted as NotGreaterEqual[x, y]. ▪ See page 1004. ▪ See also: \[GreaterEqual], \[GreaterFullEqual], \[GreaterSlantEqual], \[NotGreaterFullEqual], \[NotGreaterSlantEqual].

≧̸   \[NotGreaterFullEqual]

Infix ordering operator. ▪ x ≧̸ y is by default interpreted as NotGreaterFullEqual[x, y]. ▪ See page 1004. ▪ See also: \[GreaterEqual], \[GreaterFullEqual], \[GreaterSlantEqual], \[NotGreaterEqual], \[NotGreaterSlantEqual].

≫̸   \[NotGreaterGreater]

Infix ordering operator. ▪ x ≫̸ y is by default interpreted as NotGreaterGreater[x, y]. ▪ See page 1004. ▪ See also: \[GreaterGreater], \[NestedGreaterGreater], \[NotNestedGreaterGreater].

≹   \[NotGreaterLess]

Infix ordering operator. ▪ x ≹ y is by default interpreted as NotGreaterLess[x, y]. ▪ See page 1004. ▪ See also: \[GreaterLess].

≱   \[NotGreaterSlantEqual]

Alias: ⦂!>/⦂. ▪ Infix ordering operator. ▪ *x* ≱ *y* is by default interpreted as NotGreaterSlantEqual[*x*, *y*]. ▪ See page 1004. ▪ See also: \[GreaterEqual], \[GreaterFullEqual], \[GreaterSlantEqual], \[NotGreaterEqual], \[NotGreaterFullEqual].

≵   \[NotGreaterTilde]

Alias: ⦂!>~⦂. ▪ Infix ordering operator. ▪ *x* ≵ *y* is by default interpreted as NotGreaterTilde[*x*, *y*]. ▪ See page 1004. ▪ See also: \[GreaterTilde].

≇   \[NotHumpDownHump]

Infix similarity operator. ▪ *x* ≇ *y* is by default interpreted as NotHumpDownHump[*x*, *y*]. ▪ See page 1003. ▪ See also: \[HumpDownHump].

≢   \[NotHumpEqual]

Alias: ⦂!h=⦂. ▪ Infix similarity operator. ▪ *x* ≢ *y* is by default interpreted as NotHumpEqual[*x*, *y*]. ▪ See page 1003. ▪ See also: \[HumpEqual].

⋪   \[NotLeftTriangle]

Infix ordering operator. ▪ *x* ⋪ *y* is by default interpreted as NotLeftTriangle[*x*, *y*]. ▪ See page 1005. ▪ See also: \[NotLeftTriangleBar], \[NotLeftTriangleEqual], \[NotRightTriangle], \[LeftTriangle].

⧏̸   \[NotLeftTriangleBar]

Infix ordering operator. ▪ *x* ⧏̸ *y* is by default interpreted as NotLeftTriangleBar[*x*, *y*]. ▪ See page 1005. ▪ See also: \[NotLeftTriangle], \[NotLeftTriangleEqual], \[NotRightTriangleBar], \[LeftTriangleBar].

⋬   \[NotLeftTriangleEqual]

Infix ordering operator. ▪ *x* ⋬ *y* is by default interpreted as NotLeftTriangleEqual[*x*, *y*]. ▪ See page 1005. ▪ See also: \[NotLeftTriangle], \[NotLeftTriangleBar], \[NotRightTriangleEqual], \[LeftTriangleEqual].

≮   \[NotLess]

Alias: ⦂!<⦂. ▪ Infix ordering operator. ▪ *x* ≮ *y* is by default interpreted as NotLess[*x*, *y*]. ▪ ≮ is equivalent to ≥ only for a totally ordered set. ▪ See page 1004. ▪ See also: \[RawLess].

≰   \[NotLessEqual]

Alias: ⦂!<=⦂. ▪ Infix ordering operator. ▪ *x* ≰ *y* is by default interpreted as NotLessEqual[*x*, *y*]. ▪ See page 1004. ▪ See also: \[LessEqual], \[LessFullEqual], \[LessSlantEqual], \[NotLessFullEqual], \[NotLessSlantEqual].

≦̸   \[NotLessFullEqual]

Infix ordering operator. ▪ *x* ≦̸ *y* is by default interpreted as NotLessFullEqual[*x*, *y*]. ▪ See page 1004. ▪ See also: \[LessEqual], \[LessFullEqual], \[LessSlantEqual], \[NotLessEqual], \[NotLessSlantEqual].

≸   \[NotLessGreater]

Infix ordering operator. ▪ *x* ≸ *y* is by default interpreted as NotLessGreater[*x*, *y*]. ▪ See page 1004. ▪ See also: \[LessGreater].

⪡̸   \[NotLessLess]

Infix ordering operator. ▪ *x* ⪡̸ *y* is by default interpreted as NotLessLess[*x*, *y*]. ▪ See page 1004. ▪ See also: \[LessLess], \[NestedLessLess], \[NotNestedLessLess].

⪕̸   \[NotLessSlantEqual]

Alias: ⦂!</⦂. ▪ Infix ordering operator. ▪ *x* ⪕̸ *y* is by default interpreted as NotLessSlantEqual[*x*, *y*]. ▪ See page 1004. ▪ See also: \[LessEqual], \[LessFullEqual], \[LessSlantEqual], \[NotLessEqual], \[NotLessFullEqual].

≴   \[NotLessTilde]

Alias: ⋮!<~⋮. ▪ Infix ordering operator. ▪ $x \nlesssim y$ is by default interpreted as NotLessTilde[x, y]. ▪ See page 1004. ▪ See also: \[LessTilde].

≫̸   \[NotNestedGreaterGreater]

Infix ordering operator. ▪ $x \not\!> y$ is by default interpreted as NotNestedGreaterGreater[x, y]. ▪ See page 1004. ▪ See also: \[GreaterGreater], \[NestedGreaterGreater], \[NotGreaterGreater].

≪̸   \[NotNestedLessLess]

Infix ordering operator. ▪ $x \not\!< y$ is by default interpreted as NotNestedLessLess[x, y]. ▪ See page 1004. ▪ See also: \[LessLess], \[NestedLessLess], \[NotLessLess].

⊀   \[NotPrecedes]

Infix ordering operator. ▪ $x \nprec y$ is by default interpreted as NotPrecedes[x, y]. ▪ See page 1005. ▪ See also: \[Precedes].

⋠̸   \[NotPrecedesEqual]

Infix ordering operator. ▪ $x \npreceq y$ is by default interpreted as NotPrecedesEqual[x, y]. ▪ See page 1005. ▪ See also: \[NotPrecedesSlantEqual], \[NotPrecedesTilde], \[PrecedesEqual].

⋠   \[NotPrecedesSlantEqual]

Infix ordering operator. ▪ $x \npreceq y$ is by default interpreted as NotPrecedesSlantEqual[x, y]. ▪ See page 1005. ▪ See also: \[NotPrecedesEqual], \[PrecedesSlantEqual].

⋨   \[NotPrecedesTilde]

Infix ordering operator. ▪ $x \precnsim y$ is by default interpreted as NotPrecedesTilde[x, y]. ▪ See page 1005. ▪ See also: \[NotPrecedesEqual], \[PrecedesTilde].

∌   \[NotReverseElement]

Alias: ⋮!mem⋮. ▪ Infix set relation operator. ▪ $x \not\ni y$ is by default interpreted as NotReverseElement[x, y]. ▪ See page 1004. ▪ See also: \[ReverseElement], \[NotElement].

⋫   \[NotRightTriangle]

Infix ordering operator. ▪ $x \ntriangleright y$ is by default interpreted as NotRightTriangle[x, y]. ▪ See page 1005. ▪ See also: \[NotRightTriangleBar], \[NotRightTriangleEqual], \[NotLeftTriangle], \[RightTriangle].

⊯   \[NotRightTriangleBar]

Infix ordering operator. ▪ $x \not\!\triangleright y$ is by default interpreted as NotRightTriangleBar[x, y]. ▪ See page 1005. ▪ See also: \[NotRightTriangle], \[NotRightTriangleEqual], \[NotLeftTriangleBar], \[RightTriangleBar].

⋭   \[NotRightTriangleEqual]

Infix ordering operator. ▪ $x \ntrianglerighteq y$ is by default interpreted as NotRightTriangleEqual[x, y]. ▪ See page 1005. ▪ See also: \[NotRightTriangle], \[NotRightTriangleBar], \[NotLeftTriangleEqual], \[RightTriangleEqual].

⊄   \[NotSquareSubset]

Infix set relation operator. ▪ $x \not\sqsubset y$ is by default interpreted as NotSquareSubset[x, y]. ▪ See page 1005. ▪ See also: \[NotSquareSubsetEqual], \[SquareSubset].

⋢   \[NotSquareSubsetEqual]

Infix set relation operator. ▪ $x \not\sqsubseteq y$ is by default interpreted as NotSquareSubsetEqual[x, y]. ▪ See page 1005. ▪ See also: \[NotSquareSubset], \[SquareSubsetEqual].

⊐̸   \[NotSquareSuperset]

Infix set relation operator. ▪ *x* ⊐̸ *y* is by default interpreted as NotSquareSuperset[*r*, *y*]. ▪ See page 1005. ▪ See also: \[NotSquareSupersetEqual], \[SquareSuperset].

⋣   \[NotSquareSupersetEqual]

Infix set relation operator. ▪ *x* ⋣ *y* is by default interpreted as NotSquareSupersetEqual[*x*, *y*]. ▪ See page 1005. ▪ See also: \[NotSquareSuperset], \[SquareSupersetEqual].

⊄   \[NotSubset]

Alias: ⣿!sub⣿. ▪ Infix set relation operator. ▪ *x* ⊄ *y* is by default interpreted as NotSubset[*x*, *y*]. ▪ See page 1004. ▪ See also: \[NotSubsetEqual], \[Subset].

⊈   \[NotSubsetEqual]

Alias: ⣿!sub=⣿. ▪ Infix set relation operator. ▪ *x* ⊈ *y* is by default interpreted as NotSubsetEqual[*x*, *y*]. ▪ See page 1004. ▪ See also: \[NotSubset], \[SubsetEqual].

⊁   \[NotSucceeds]

Infix ordering operator. ▪ *x* ⊁ *y* is by default interpreted as NotSucceeds[*x*, *y*]. ▪ See page 1005. ▪ See also: \[NotSucceedsEqual], \[Succeeds].

⋡   \[NotSucceedsEqual]

Infix ordering operator. ▪ *x* ⋡ *y* is by default interpreted as NotSucceedsEqual[*x*, *y*]. ▪ See page 1005. ▪ See also: \[NotSucceedsSlantEqual], \[NotSucceedsTilde], \[SucceedsSlantEqual].

⋡   \[NotSucceedsSlantEqual]

Infix ordering operator. ▪ *x* ⋡ *y* is by default interpreted as NotSucceedsSlantEqual[*x*, *y*]. ▪ See page 1005. ▪ See also: \[NotSucceedsEqual], \[SucceedsSlantEqual].

⋣   \[NotSucceedsTilde]

Infix ordering operator. ▪ *x* ⋣ *y* is by default interpreted as NotSucceedsTilde[*x*, *y*]. ▪ See page 1005. ▪ See also: \[NotSucceedsEqual], \[SucceedsTilde].

⊅   \[NotSuperset]

Alias: ⣿!sup⣿. ▪ Infix set relation operator. ▪ *x* ⊅ *y* is by default interpreted as NotSuperset[*x*, *y*]. ▪ See page 1004. ▪ See also: \[NotSupersetEqual], \[Superset].

⊉   \[NotSupersetEqual]

Alias: ⣿!sup=⣿. ▪ Infix set relation operator. ▪ *x* ⊉ *y* is by default interpreted as NotSupersetEqual[*x*, *y*]. ▪ See page 1004. ▪ See also: \[NotSuperset], \[SupersetEqual].

≁   \[NotTilde]

Alias: ⣿!~⣿. ▪ Infix similarity operator. ▪ *x* ≁ *y* is by default interpreted as NotTilde[*x*, *y*]. ▪ See page 1003. ▪ See also: \[Tilde].

≄   \[NotTildeEqual]

Alias: ⣿!~=⣿. ▪ Infix similarity operator. ▪ *x* ≄ *y* is by default interpreted as NotTildeEqual[*x*, *y*]. ▪ See page 1003. ▪ See also: \[NotTildeFullEqual], \[TildeEqual], \[TildeFullEqual].

≇   \[NotTildeFullEqual]

Alias: ⣿!~==⣿. ▪ Infix similarity operator. ▪ *x* ≇ *y* is by default interpreted as NotTildeFullEqual[*x*, *y*]. ▪ See page 1003. ▪ See also: \[NotTildeEqual], \[NotCongruent], \[TildeFullEqual].

⍯ \[NotTildeTilde]

Alias: :!~~:. ▪ Infix similarity operator. ▪ $x \not\approx y$ is by default interpreted as NotTildeTilde[x, y]. ▪ See page 1003. ▪ See also: \[TildeTilde].

∤ \[NotVerticalBar]

Alias: :!|:. ▪ Infix operator. ▪ $x \nmid y$ is by default interpreted as NotVerticalBar[x, y]. ▪ Used in mathematics to mean x does not divide y. ▪ See page 1005. ▪ See also: \[VerticalBar], \[NotDoubleVerticalBar].

ñ \[NTilde]

Alias: :n~:. ▪ Letter. ▪ Included in ISO Latin-1. ▪ See pages 190 and 998. ▪ See also: \[CapitalNTilde].

ν \[Nu]

Aliases: :n:, :nu:. ▪ Greek letter. ▪ See pages 175 and 990. ▪ See also: \[CapitalNu], \[Vee].

   \[Null]

Alias: :null:. ▪ Letter-like form. ▪ Can be used to place subscripts and superscripts without having a visible base. ▪ See page 1008. ▪ See also: \[InvisibleComma], \[InvisibleSpace], \[AlignmentMarker].

ó \[OAcute]

Alias: :o':. ▪ Letter. ▪ Included in ISO Latin-1. ▪ See page 998. ▪ See also: \[CapitalOAcute].

ő \[ODoubleAcute]

Alias: :o'':. ▪ Letter. ▪ Included in ISO Latin-2. ▪ Used in Hungarian, for example in the name Erdős. ▪ See page 998. ▪ See also: \[CapitalODoubleAcute], \[UDoubleAcute].

ö \[ODoubleDot]

Alias: :o":. ▪ Letter. ▪ Included in ISO Latin-1. ▪ See pages 190 and 998. ▪ See also: \[ODoubleAcute], \[CapitalODoubleDot].

ò \[OGrave]

Alias: :o`:. ▪ Letter. ▪ Included in ISO Latin-1. ▪ See pages 190 and 998. ▪ See also: \[CapitalOGrave].

ô \[OHat]

Alias: :o^:. ▪ Letter. ▪ Included in ISO Latin-1. ▪ See page 998. ▪ See also: \[CapitalOHat].

ω \[Omega]

Aliases: :o:, :omega:, :w:. ▪ Greek letter. ▪ See pages 175 and 990. ▪ See also: \[CapitalOmega], \[CurlyPi], \[Omicron].

ο \[Omicron]

Aliases: :om:, :omicron:. ▪ Greek letter. ▪ Not the same as English o. ▪ See page 990. ▪ See also: \[CapitalOmicron], \[Omega].

∨ \[Or]

Aliases: :||:, :or:. ▪ Infix operator with built-in evaluation rules. ▪ $x \lor y$ is by default interpreted as Or[x, y], equivalent to x || y. ▪ Not the same as \[Vee]. ▪ Drawn slightly larger than \[Vee]. ▪ See page 1001. ▪ See also: \[And], \[Xor], \[Nor], \[Not].

ø \[OSlash]

Alias: :o/:. ▪ Letter. ▪ Included in ISO Latin-1. ▪ Not the same as \[EmptySet]. ▪ See pages 190 and 998. ▪ See also: \[CapitalOSlash].

Õ   \[OTilde]

Alias: ⦂o~⦂. ▪ Letter. ▪ Included in ISO Latin-1. ▪ See page 998. ▪ See also: \[CapitalOTilde].

︷   \[OverBrace]

Alias: ⦂o{⦂. ▪ Letter-like form. ▪ Extensible character. ▪ See page 997. ▪ See also: \[OverBracket], \[OverParenthesis], \[UnderBrace].

︴   \[OverBracket]

Alias: ⦂o[⦂. ▪ Letter-like form. ▪ Extensible character. ▪ See page 997. ▪ See also: \[OverParenthesis], \[OverBrace], \[UnderBracket], \[HorizontalLine].

︵   \[OverParenthesis]

Alias: ⦂o(⦂. ▪ Letter-like form. ▪ Extensible character. ▪ See page 997. ▪ See also: \[OverBracket], \[OverBrace], \[UnderParenthesis].

¶   \[Paragraph]

Letter-like form. ▪ See page 996. ▪ See also: \[Section].

∂ \[PartialD]

Alias: ⦂pd⦂. ▪ Prefix operator with built-in evaluation rules. ▪ $\partial_x y$ is by default interpreted as D[y, x]. ▪ ∂ is used in mathematics to indicate boundary. ▪ ⦂d⦂ gives \[Delta], not \[PartialD]. ▪ You can use \[InvisibleComma] in the subscript to ∂ to give several variables without having them separated by visible commas. ▪ See pages 185, 994 and 1000. ▪ See also: \[Delta], \[Del], \[DifferentialD], \[Eth].

ϕ \[Phi]

Aliases: ⦂ph⦂, ⦂phi⦂, ⦂f⦂. ▪ Greek letter. ▪ Used in TraditionalForm for EulerPhi and GoldenRatio. ▪ See pages 175 and 990. ▪ See also: \[CurlyPhi], \[CapitalPhi].

π \[Pi]

Aliases: ⦂p⦂, ⦂pi⦂. ▪ Greek letter with built-in value. ▪ Interpreted by default as the symbol Pi. ▪ See pages 175 and 990. ▪ See also: \[DoubledPi], \[CapitalPi], \[CurlyPi].

□   \[Placeholder]

Alias: ⦂pl⦂. ▪ Letter-like form. ▪ Used to indicate where expressions can be inserted in a form obtained by pasting the contents of a button. ▪ Not the same as \[EmptySquare]. ▪ See pages 199, 587 and 1008. ▪ See also: \[SelectionPlaceholder], \[RawNumberSign].

±   \[PlusMinus]

Alias: ⦂+-⦂. ▪ Prefix or infix operator. ▪ $\pm\, x$ is by default interpreted as PlusMinus[x]. ▪ $x \pm y$ is by default interpreted as PlusMinus[x, y]. ▪ See pages 191 and 1000. ▪ See also: \[MinusPlus].

$\prec$ \[Precedes]

Infix ordering operator. ▪ $x \prec y$ is by default interpreted as Precedes[x, y]. ▪ Used in mathematics to indicate various notions of partial ordering. ▪ Often applied to functions and read "x is dominated by y". ▪ See page 1005. ▪ See also: \[PrecedesEqual], \[Succeeds], \[NotPrecedes].

$\preceq$ \[PrecedesEqual]

Infix ordering operator. ▪ $x \preceq y$ is by default interpreted as PrecedesEqual[x, y]. ▪ See page 1005. ▪ See also: \[PrecedesSlantEqual], \[PrecedesTilde], \[SucceedsEqual], \[NotPrecedesEqual].

≼   \[PrecedesSlantEqual]

Infix ordering operator. ▪ $x \preccurlyeq y$ is by default interpreted as PrecedesSlantEqual[x, y]. ▪ See page 1005. ▪ See also: \[PrecedesEqual], \[SucceedsSlantEqual], \[NotPrecedesSlantEqual].

≾   \[PrecedesTilde]

Infix ordering operator. ▪ $x \precsim y$ is by default interpreted as PrecedesTilde[x, y]. ▪ See page 1005. ▪ See also: \[PrecedesEqual], \[SucceedsTilde], \[NotPrecedesTilde].

′   \[Prime]

Alias: ⅰ′ⅰ. ▪ Letter-like form. ▪ Used to indicate angles in minutes or distances in feet. ▪ Used in an overscript position as an acute accent. ▪ See page 996. ▪ See also: \[DoublePrime], \[ReversePrime], \[RawQuote].

∏   \[Product]

Alias: ⅰprodⅰ. ▪ Compound operator with built-in evaluation rules. ▪ $\prod\limits^{imax} f$ is by default interpreted as Product[f, {i, $imax$}]. ▪ $\prod\limits_{i=imin}^{imax} f$ is by default interpreted as Product[f, {i, $imin$, $imax$}]. ▪ Not the same as the Greek letter \[CapitalPi]. ▪ See pages 994 and 1000. ▪ See also: \[Coproduct], \[Sum], \[Times].

∷   \[Proportion]

Infix relational operator. ▪ $x :: y$ is by default interpreted as Proportion[x, y]. ▪ Used historically to indicate equality; now used to indicate proportion. ▪ See page 1003. ▪ See also: \[Divide], \[Proportional], \[Colon], \[Therefore].

∝   \[Proportional]

Alias: ⅰpropⅰ. ▪ Infix relational operator. ▪ $x \propto y$ is by default interpreted as Proportional[x, y]. ▪ Not the same as \[Alpha]. ▪ See pages 191 and 1003. ▪ See also: \[Proportion].

ψ   \[Psi]

Aliases: ⅰpsⅰ, ⅰpsiⅰ, ⅰyⅰ. ▪ Greek letter. ▪ Used in TraditionalForm for PolyGamma. ▪ See pages 175 and 990. ▪ See also: \[CapitalPsi].

&   \[RawAmpersand]

Raw operator. ▪ Equivalent to the ordinary ASCII character with code 38. ▪ See page 1010. ▪ See also: \[And].

@   \[RawAt]

Raw operator. ▪ Equivalent to the ordinary ASCII character with code 64. ▪ See page 1010. ▪ See also: \[RawAmpersand], \[SmallCircle].

‘   \[RawBackquote]

Raw operator. ▪ Equivalent to the ordinary ASCII character with code 96. ▪ See page 1010. ▪ See also: \[RawQuote], \[Prime].

\   \[RawBackslash]

Raw operator. ▪ Equivalent to the ordinary ASCII character with code 92. ▪ Equivalent in strings to \\. ▪ See page 1010. ▪ See also: \[Backslash].

:   \[RawColon]

Raw operator. ▪ Equivalent to the ordinary ASCII character with code 58. ▪ See page 1010. ▪ See also: \[Colon].

,   \[RawComma]

Raw operator. ▪ Equivalent to the ordinary ASCII character with code 44. ▪ See page 1010. ▪ See also: \[InvisibleComma].

—   \[RawDash]

Raw operator. ▪ Equivalent to the ordinary ASCII character with code 45. ▪ As an overscript, used to indicate conjugation or negation. ▪ Also used to indicate an average value or an upper value. ▪ In geometry, used to denote a line segment. ▪ As an underscript, used to indicate a lower value. ▪ x^- is interpreted as SuperMinus$[x]$. ▪ x_- is interpreted as SubMinus$[x]$. ▪ Not the same as the letter-like form \[Dash]. ▪ See page 1010. ▪ See also: \[RawPlus], \[HorizontalLine].

\$ \[RawDollar]

Letter-like form. ▪ Equivalent to the ordinary ASCII character with code 36. ▪ See page 1010.

.   \[RawDot]

Raw operator. ▪ Equivalent to the ordinary ASCII character with code 46. ▪ As an overscript, used to indicate time derivative. ▪ $\dot{x}$ is interpreted as OverDot$[x]$. ▪ See page 1010. ▪ See also: \[CenterDot], \[Ellipsis].

"   \[RawDoubleQuote]

Raw operator. ▪ Equivalent to the ordinary ASCII character with code 34. ▪ Equivalent to \" in strings. ▪ See page 1010. ▪ See also: \[RawQuote], \[Prime].

=   \[RawEqual]

Raw operator. ▪ Equivalent to the ordinary ASCII character with code 61. ▪ See page 1010. ▪ See also: \[Equal], \[NotEqual].

\[RawEscape]

Raw element. ▪ Equivalent to the non-printable ASCII character with code 27. ▪ Used in entering aliases for special characters in *Mathematica*. ▪ See also: \[AliasIndicator], \[EscapeKey].

!   \[RawExclamation]

Raw operator. ▪ Equivalent to the ordinary ASCII character with code 33. ▪ See page 1010. ▪ See also: \[DownExclamation].

>   \[RawGreater]

Raw operator. ▪ Equivalent to the ordinary ASCII character with code 62. ▪ Not the same as \[RightAngleBracket]. ▪ See page 1010. ▪ See also: \[NotGreater].

{   \[RawLeftBrace]

Raw operator. ▪ Equivalent to the ordinary ASCII character with code 123. ▪ Extensible character. ▪ See page 1010. ▪ See also: \[RawRightBrace].

[\[RawLeftBracket]

Raw operator. ▪ Equivalent to the ordinary ASCII character with code 91. ▪ Extensible character. ▪ See page 1010. ▪ See also: \[LeftDoubleBracket], \[RawRightBracket], \[RightDoubleBracket].

(\[RawLeftParenthesis]

Raw operator. ▪ Equivalent to the ordinary ASCII character with code 40. ▪ Extensible character. ▪ See page 1010. ▪ See also: \[RawRightParenthesis].

<   \[RawLess]

Raw operator. ▪ Equivalent to the ordinary ASCII character with code 60. ▪ Not the same as \[RightAngleBracket]. ▪ See page 1010. ▪ See also: \[NotLess].

\#   **\[RawNumberSign]**

Raw operator. ▪ Equivalent to the ordinary ASCII character with code 35. ▪ Not the same as \[Sharp]. ▪ See page 1010. ▪ See also: \[Placeholder].

%   **\[RawPercent]**

Raw operator. ▪ Equivalent to the ordinary ASCII character with code 37. ▪ See page 1010.

+   **\[RawPlus]**

Raw operator. ▪ Equivalent to the ordinary ASCII character with code 43. ▪ See page 1010. ▪ See also: \[RawDash].

?   **\[RawQuestion]**

Raw operator. ▪ Equivalent to the ordinary ASCII character with code 63. ▪ See page 1010. ▪ See also: \[DownQuestion].

'   **\[RawQuote]**

Raw operator. ▪ Equivalent to the ordinary ASCII character with code 39. ▪ See page 1010. ▪ See also: \[Prime], \[RawDoubleQuote].

\[RawReturn]

Spacing character. ▪ Equivalent to the ordinary ASCII character with code 13. ▪ Can be entered as \r. ▪ Not always the same as \[NewLine]. ▪ See page 1010. ▪ See also: \[ReturnIndicator].

}   **\[RawRightBrace]**

Raw operator. ▪ Equivalent to the ordinary ASCII character with code 125. ▪ Extensible character. ▪ See page 1010. ▪ See also: \[RawLeftBrace].

]   **\[RawRightBracket]**

Raw operator. ▪ Equivalent to the ordinary ASCII character with code 93. ▪ Extensible character. ▪ Not the same as \[RightModified]. ▪ See page 1010. ▪ See also: \[LeftDoubleBracket], \[RawLeftBracket], \[RightDoubleBracket].

)   **\[RawRightParenthesis]**

Raw operator. ▪ Equivalent to the ordinary ASCII character with code 41. ▪ Extensible character. ▪ See page 1010. ▪ See also: \[RawLeftParenthesis].

;   **\[RawSemicolon]**

Raw operator. ▪ Equivalent to the ordinary ASCII character with code 59. ▪ See page 1010.

/   **\[RawSlash]**

Raw operator. ▪ Equivalent to the ordinary ASCII character with code 47. ▪ Extensible character; grows by default to limited size. ▪ See page 1010. ▪ See also: \[Divide].

\[RawSpace]

Spacing character. ▪ Equivalent to the ordinary ASCII character with code 32. ▪ See page 1010. ▪ See also: \[NonBreakingSpace], \[MediumSpace], \[SpaceIndicator], \[InvisibleSpace].

*   **\[RawStar]**

Raw operator. ▪ Equivalent to the ordinary ASCII character with code 42. ▪ In addition to one-dimensional uses, x^* is by default interpreted as SuperStar[x]. ▪ x^* is often used in mathematics to indicate a conjugate, dual, or completion of x. ▪ See page 1010. ▪ See also: \[Star], \[Times], \[SixPointedStar].

\[RawTab]

Spacing character. ▪ Equivalent to the ordinary ASCII character with code 9. ▪ Can be entered in strings as \t. ▪ See page 1010. ▪ See also: \[RightArrowBar].

~   **\[RawTilde]**

Raw operator. ▪ Equivalent to the ordinary ASCII character with code 126. ▪ In addition to one-dimensional uses, $\tilde{x}$ is by default interpreted as OverTilde[x]. ▪ See page 1010. ▪ See also: \[Tilde], \[NotTilde].

_   **\[RawUnderscore]**

Raw operator. ▪ Equivalent to the ordinary ASCII character with code 95. ▪ $\bar{x}$ is interpreted as OverBar[x]. ▪ $\underline{x}$ is interpreted as UnderBar[x]. ▪ See page 1010. ▪ See also: \[Dash].

| **\[RawVerticalBar]**

Raw operator. ▪ Equivalent to the ordinary ASCII character with code 124. ▪ Extensible character. ▪ See page 1010. ▪ See also: \[VerticalBar], \[LeftBracketingBar].

^   **\[RawWedge]**

Raw operator. ▪ Equivalent to the ordinary ASCII character with code 94. ▪ In addition to one-dimensional uses, $\hat{x}$ is by default interpreted as OverHat[x]. ▪ $\hat{x}$ is used for many purposes in mathematics, from indicating an operator form of x to indicating that x is an angle. ▪ See page 1010. ▪ See also: \[Wedge].

®   **\[RegisteredTrademark]**

Letter-like form. ▪ Used as a superscript to indicate a registered trademark such as *Mathematica*. ▪ Typically used only on the first occurrence of a trademark in a document. ▪ See page 996. ▪ See also: \[Trademark], \[Copyright].

↵   **\[ReturnIndicator]**

Alias: ⣿ret⣿. ▪ Letter-like form. ▪ Representation of the return or newline character on a keyboard. ▪ Used in showing how textual input is typed. ▪ See page 1009. ▪ See also: \[ReturnKey], \[EnterKey], \[Continuation], \[ControlKey], \[CommandKey], \[SpaceIndicator], \[NonBreakingSpace].

RET   **\[ReturnKey]**

Alias: ⣿ ret⣿. ▪ Letter-like form. ▪ Representation of the Return key on a keyboard. ▪ Used in describing how to type textual input. ▪ ⣿ret⣿ is the alias for \[ReturnIndicator]. The alias for \[ReturnKey] has a space at the beginning. ▪ See page 1009. ▪ See also: \[EnterKey], \[ReturnIndicator], \[ControlKey], \[CommandKey].

‶   **\[ReverseDoublePrime]**

Alias: ⣿``⣿. ▪ Letter-like form. ▪ See page 996. ▪ See also: \[DoublePrime], \[Prime], \[ReversePrime].

∋   **\[ReverseElement]**

Alias: ⣿mem⣿. ▪ Infix set relation operator. ▪ $x \ni y$ is by default interpreted as ReverseElement[x, y]. ▪ Not the same as \[SuchThat]. ▪ See page 1004. ▪ See also: \[Element], \[NotReverseElement].

⇋   **\[ReverseEquilibrium]**

Infix arrow-like operator. ▪ $x \leftrightharpoons y$ is by default interpreted as ReverseEquilibrium[x, y]. ▪ Extensible character. ▪ See page 1007. ▪ See also: \[Equilibrium], \[ReverseUpEquilibrium], \[LeftArrowRightArrow], \[LeftRightArrow].

‵   **\[ReversePrime]**

Alias: ⣿`⣿. ▪ Letter-like form. ▪ Used in an overscript position as a grave accent. ▪ See page 996. ▪ See also: \[DoublePrime], \[Prime], \[ReverseDoublePrime], \[RawBackquote].

⇃↾ **\[ReverseUpEquilibrium]**

Infix arrow-like operator. ▪ *x* ⇃↾ *y* is by default interpreted as ReverseUpEquilibrium[*x*, *y*]. ▪ Extensible character. ▪ See page 1007. ▪ See also: \[UpEquilibrium], \[DownArrowUpArrow], \[RightUpDownVector], \[Equilibrium].

ρ **\[Rho]**

Aliases: ⦂r⦂, ⦂rho⦂. ▪ Greek letter. ▪ See pages 175 and 990. ▪ See also: \[CurlyRho], \[CapitalRho].

∟ **\[RightAngle]**

Letter-like form. ▪ Used in geometry to indicate a right angle, as in the symbol ∟ ABC. ▪ See page 996. ▪ See also: \[Angle], \[MeasuredAngle], \[UpTee].

⟩ **\[RightAngleBracket]**

Alias: ⦂>⦂. ▪ Matchfix operator. ▪ ⟨ *x* ⟩ is by default interpreted as AngleBracket[*x*]. ▪ Used in the form ⟨*x*⟩ to indicate expected or average value. ▪ Called ket in quantum mechanics. ▪ Used in the form ⟨*x*, *y*⟩ to indicate various forms of inner product. ▪ Used in the form ⟨*x*, *y*, … ⟩ to denote an ordered set of objects. ▪ Not the same as \[RawGreater]. ▪ Extensible character; grows by default to limited size. ▪ See page 1002. ▪ See also: \[LeftAngleBracket].

→ **\[RightArrow]**

Alias: ⦂␣->⦂. ▪ Infix arrow operator. ▪ Used for many purposes in mathematics to indicate transformation, tending to a limit or implication. ▪ Used as an overscript to indicate a directed object. ▪ Not the same as \[Rule]. ▪ ⦂->⦂ is the alias for \[Rule]. The alias for \[RightArrow] has a space at the beginning. ▪ Extensible character. ▪ See page 1006. ▪ See also: \[LongRightArrow], \[ShortRightArrow], \[DoubleRightArrow], \[RightTeeArrow], \[RightArrowBar], \[UpperRightArrow], \[RightVector], \[RightTriangle], \[LeftArrow], \[HorizontalLine], \[Implies].

↦ **\[RightArrowBar]**

Infix arrow operator. ▪ *x* ↦ *y* is by default interpreted as RightArrowBar[*x*, *y*]. ▪ Used in mathematics to indicate an epimorphism. ▪ Sometimes used to indicate a tab. ▪ Extensible character. ▪ See page 1006. ▪ See also: \[RightTeeArrow], \[RightVectorBar], \[UpArrowBar], \[LeftArrowBar], \[RawTab].

⇄ **\[RightArrowLeftArrow]**

Infix arrow operator. ▪ *x* ⇄ *y* is by default interpreted as RightArrowLeftArrow[*x*, *y*]. ▪ Extensible character. ▪ See page 1006. ▪ See also: \[LeftArrowRightArrow], \[LeftRightArrow], \[DoubleLeftRightArrow], \[Equilibrium], \[UpArrowDownArrow].

| **\[RightBracketingBar]**

Alias: ⦂r|⦂. ▪ Matchfix operator. ▪ | *x* | is by default interpreted as BracketingBar[*x*]. ▪ Used in mathematics to indicate absolute value (Abs), determinant (Det), and other notions of evaluating size or magnitude. ▪ Not the same as \[VerticalBar]. ▪ Drawn in monospaced fonts with a small right-pointing tee to indicate direction. ▪ Extensible character. ▪ See page 1002. ▪ See also: \[RightDoubleBracketingBar], \[RightTee].

⌉ **\[RightCeiling]**

Alias: ⦂rc⦂. ▪ Matchfix operator with built-in evaluation rules. ▪ ⌈ *x* ⌉ is by default interpreted as Ceiling[*x*]. ▪ Extensible character. ▪ See page 1002. ▪ See also: \[LeftCeiling], \[RightFloor].

⟧ **\[RightDoubleBracket]**

Alias: ⦂]]⦂. ▪ *m*⟦*i*,*j*, … ⟧ is by default interpreted as Part[*m*, *i*, *j*, …]. ▪ Extensible character; grows by default to limited size. ▪ See page 1002. ▪ See also: \[RawRightBracket], \[RightDoubleBracketingBar].

∥ **\[RightDoubleBracketingBar]**

Alias: ⦂r||⦂. ∎ Matchfix operator. ∎ ∥ *x* ∥ is by default interpreted as DoubleBracketingBar[*x*]. ∎ Used in mathematics to indicate taking a norm. ∎ Sometimes used for determinant. ∎ Sometimes used to indicate a matrix. ∎ Not the same as \[DoubleVerticalBar]. ∎ Drawn in monospaced fonts with a small right-pointing tee to indicate direction. ∎ Extensible character. ∎ See page 1002. ∎ See also: \[RightBracketingBar].

⊺ **\[RightDownTeeVector]**

Infix arrow-like operator. ∎ *x* ⊺ *y* is by default interpreted as RightDownTeeVector[*x*, *y*]. ∎ Extensible character. ∎ See page 1007. ∎ See also: \[LeftDownTeeVector], \[RightDownVectorBar], \[DownTeeArrow], \[RightUpTeeVector].

↓ **\[RightDownVector]**

Infix arrow-like operator. ∎ *x* ↓ *y* is by default interpreted as RightDownVector[*x*, *y*]. ∎ Extensible character. ∎ See page 1007. ∎ See also: \[LeftDownVector], \[RightDownTeeVector], \[DownArrow], \[UpEquilibrium], \[RightUpVector].

↧ **\[RightDownVectorBar]**

Infix arrow-like operator. ∎ *x* ↧ *y* is by default interpreted as RightDownVectorBar[*x*, *y*]. ∎ Extensible character. ∎ See page 1007. ∎ See also: \[LeftDownVectorBar], \[RightDownTeeVector], \[DownArrowBar], \[RightUpVectorBar].

⌋ **\[RightFloor]**

Alias: ⦂rf⦂. ∎ Matchfix operator with built-in evaluation rules. ∎ ⌊ *x* ⌋ is by default interpreted as Floor[*x*]. ∎ Extensible character. ∎ See page 1002. ∎ See also: \[LeftFloor], \[RightCeiling].

» **\[RightGuillemet]**

Alias: ⦂g>>⦂. ∎ Letter-like form. ∎ Used as closing quotation marks in languages such as Spanish. ∎ Not the same as \[GreaterGreater]. ∎ Not the same as RightSkeleton. ∎ Guillemet is sometimes misspelled as guillemot. ∎ See page 996. ∎ See also: \[LeftGuillemet].

⌉ **\[RightModified]**

Alias: ⦂]⦂. ∎ Letter-like form. ∎ Used in documenting control and command characters. ∎ *key*\[LeftModified]*char*\[RightModified] is used to indicate that *char* should be typed while *key* is being pressed. ∎ Not the same as \[RawRightBracket]. ∎ See page 1009. ∎ See also: \[ControlKey], \[CommandKey], \[LeftModified].

≫ **\[RightSkeleton]**

Uninterpretable element. ∎ ≪ *n* ≫ is used on output to indicate *n* omitted pieces in an expression obtained from Short or Shallow. ∎ \[RightSkeleton] indicates the presence of missing information, and so by default generates an error if you try to interpret it. ∎ Not the same as \[RightGuillemet]. ∎ See page 1009. ∎ See also: \[LeftSkeleton], \[SkeletonIndicator], \[Ellipsis].

⊢ **\[RightTee]**

Alias: ⦂rT⦂. ∎ Infix operator. ∎ *x* ⊢ *y* is by default interpreted as RightTee[*x*, *y*]. ∎ *x* ⊢ *y* ⊢ *z* groups as *x* ⊢ (*y* ⊢ *z*). ∎ Used in mathematics to indicate logical implication or proof. ∎ See pages 191, 1001 and 1007. ∎ See also: \[DoubleRightTee], \[RightTeeArrow], \[RightTeeVector], \[LeftTee], \[DownTee], \[RightBracketingBar].

↦ **\[RightTeeArrow]**

Infix arrow operator. ∎ *x* ↦ *y* is by default interpreted as RightTeeArrow[*x*, *y*]. ∎ Used in mathematics to indicate a transformation, often the action of a mapping on a specific element in a space. ∎ Also used in logic to indicate deducibility. ∎ Extensible character. ∎ See page 1006. ∎ See also: \[RightTeeVector], \[RightTee], \[LeftTeeArrow], \[UpTeeArrow].

↦   \[RightTeeVector]

Infix arrow-like operator. ▪ $x \mapsto y$ is by default interpreted as RightTeeVector[x, y]. ▪ Extensible character. ▪ See page 1007. ▪ See also: \[DownRightTeeVector], \[RightVectorBar], \[RightVector], \[RightTeeArrow].

▷   \[RightTriangle]

Infix ordering operator. ▪ $x \triangleright y$ is by default interpreted as RightTriangle[x, y]. ▪ Used in pure mathematics to mean "contains as a normal subgroup". ▪ See pages 191 and 1005. ▪ See also: \[RightTriangleEqual], \[RightTriangleBar], \[RightArrow], \[NotRightTriangle], \[LeftTriangle], \[EmptyUpTriangle], \[FilledUpTriangle], \[RightAngle].

▷   \[RightTriangleBar]

Infix ordering operator. ▪ $x \triangleright y$ is by default interpreted as RightTriangleBar[x, y]. ▪ See page 1005. ▪ See also: \[RightTriangle], \[RightTriangleEqual], \[RightArrowBar], \[NotRightTriangleBar].

⊵   \[RightTriangleEqual]

Infix ordering operator. ▪ $x \trianglerighteq y$ is by default interpreted as RightTriangleEqual[x, y]. ▪ See page 1005. ▪ See also: \[RightTriangle], \[RightTriangleBar], \[SucceedsEqual], \[NotRightTriangleEqual], \[LeftTriangleEqual].

↾   \[RightUpDownVector]

Infix arrow-like operator. ▪ $x \upharpoonright y$ is by default interpreted as RightUpDownVector[x, y]. ▪ Extensible character. ▪ See page 1007. ▪ See also: \[LeftUpDownVector], \[UpEquilibrium], \[UpArrowDownArrow], \[LeftRightVector].

↿   \[RightUpTeeVector]

Infix arrow-like operator. ▪ $x \upharpoonright y$ is by default interpreted as RightUpTeeVector[x, y]. ▪ Extensible character. ▪ See page 1007. ▪ See also: \[LeftUpTeeVector], \[RightUpVectorBar], \[UpTeeArrow], \[RightDownTeeVector].

↾   \[RightUpVector]

Infix arrow-like operator. ▪ $x \upharpoonright y$ is by default interpreted as RightUpVector[x, y]. ▪ Used in pure mathematics to indicate the restriction of x to y. ▪ Extensible character. ▪ See page 1007. ▪ See also: \[LeftUpVector], \[RightUpTeeVector], \[UpArrow], \[UpEquilibrium], \[RightDownVector].

↾   \[RightUpVectorBar]

Infix arrow-like operator. ▪ $x \upharpoonright y$ is by default interpreted as RightUpVectorBar[x, y]. ▪ Extensible character. ▪ See page 1007. ▪ See also: \[LeftUpVectorBar], \[RightUpTeeVector], \[UpArrowBar], \[RightDownVectorBar].

→   \[RightVector]

Alias: ⁚vec⁚. ▪ Infix and overfix arrow-like operator. ▪ $x \rightharpoonup y$ is by default interpreted as RightVector[x, y]. ▪ Used in mathematics to indicate weak convergence. ▪ $\vec{x}$ is by default interpreted as OverVector[x]. ▪ Used in mathematics to indicate a vector quantity. ▪ Sometimes used in prefix form as a typographical symbol to stand for "see also". ▪ Extensible character. ▪ See page 1007. ▪ See also: \[DownRightVector], \[RightTeeVector], \[RightVectorBar], \[RightArrow], \[LeftVector], \[RightUpVector].

↼   \[RightVectorBar]

Infix arrow-like operator. ▪ $x \rightharpoonup y$ is by default interpreted as RightVectorBar[x, y]. ▪ Extensible character. ▪ See page 1007. ▪ See also: \[DownRightVectorBar], \[RightTeeVector], \[RightArrowBar].

⥽   \[RoundImplies]

Infix operator with built-in evaluation rules. ▪ $x \Rightarrow y$ is by default interpreted as Implies[x, y]. ▪ $x \Rightarrow y \Rightarrow z$ groups as $x \Rightarrow (y \Rightarrow z)$. ▪ Not the same as \[Superset]. ▪ See pages 1001 and 1006. ▪ See also: \[Implies], \[SuchThat], \[RightArrow], \[Rule].

⌣ **\[RoundSpaceIndicator]**

Spacing character. ▪ Interpreted by default as equivalent to \[RawSpace]. ▪ See page 1009. ▪ See also: \[SpaceIndicator], \[Cup], \[Breve].

→ **\[Rule]**

Alias: ⦂->⦂. ▪ Infix operator with built-in evaluation rules. ▪ $x \to y$ is by default interpreted as x -> y or Rule$[x, y]$. ▪ $x \to y \to z$ groups as $x \to (y \to z)$. ▪ \[Rule] is not the same as \[RightArrow]. ▪ See page 1006. ▪ See also: \[RuleDelayed].

⤇ **\[RuleDelayed]**

Alias: ⦂:>⦂. ▪ Infix operator with built-in evaluation rules. ▪ $x \Rightarrow y$ is by default interpreted as x :> y or RuleDelayed$[x, y]$. ▪ $x \Rightarrow y \Rightarrow z$ groups as $x \Rightarrow (y \Rightarrow z)$. ▪ See page 1006. ▪ See also: \[Rule], \[Colon], \[RightArrow].

☹ **\[SadSmiley]**

Alias: ⦂:-(⦂. ▪ Letter-like form. ▪ See page 995. ▪ See also: \[HappySmiley], \[NeutralSmiley], \[FreakedSmiley].

ϡ **\[Sampi]**

Aliases: ⦂sa⦂, ⦂sampi⦂. ▪ Special Greek letter. ▪ Appeared after ω in early Greek alphabet; used for Greek numeral 900. ▪ See page 990. ▪ See also: \[CapitalSampi], \[Digamma], \[Stigma], \[Koppa].

a...z **\[ScriptA]** ... **\[ScriptZ]**

Aliases: ⦂sca⦂ through ⦂scz⦂. ▪ Letters. ▪ Treated as distinct characters rather than style modifications of ordinary letters. ▪ \[ScriptL] *l* is a commonly used form. ▪ Contiguous character codes from the private Unicode character range are used, even though a few script characters are included in ordinary Unicode. ▪ See page 993. ▪ See also: \[ScriptCapitalA], \[GothicA], \[DoubleStruckA], etc.

𝒜...𝒵 **\[ScriptCapitalA]** ... **\[ScriptCapitalZ]**

Aliases: ⦂scA⦂ through ⦂scZ⦂. ▪ Letters. ▪ Treated as distinct characters rather than style modifications of ordinary letters. ▪ $\mathcal{E}$ is sometimes called Euler's E. ▪ \[ScriptCapitalE] is not the same as \[CurlyEpsilon]. ▪ $\mathcal{F}$ is sometimes used to denote Fourier transform. ▪ $\mathcal{L}$ is sometimes used to denote Laplace transform. ▪ $\mathcal{H}$ and $\mathcal{L}$ are used in physics to denote Hamiltonian and Lagrangian density. ▪ \[ScriptCapitalP] is not the same as \[WeierstrassP]. ▪ Contiguous character codes from the private Unicode character range are used, even though a few capital script characters are included in ordinary Unicode. ▪ See page 993. ▪ See also: \[GothicCapitalA], \[DoubleStruckCapitalA], etc.

§ **\[Section]**

Letter-like form. ▪ See page 996. ▪ See also: \[Paragraph].

■ **\[SelectionPlaceholder]**

Alias: ⦂spl⦂. ▪ Letter-like form. ▪ Used to indicate where the current selection should be inserted when the contents of a button are pasted by NotebookApply. ▪ Not the same as \[FilledSquare]. ▪ See pages 199, 587 and 1008. ▪ See also: \[Placeholder].

š **\[SHacek]**

Alias: ⦂sv⦂. ▪ Letter. ▪ Included in ISO Latin-2. ▪ See page 998. ▪ See also: \[CapitalSHacek], \[CHacek].

♯ **\[Sharp]**

Letter-like form. ▪ Used to denote musical notes. ▪ Sometimes used in mathematical notation, typically to indicate some form of numbering or indexing. ▪ Not the same as \[RawNumberSign]. ▪ See page 996. ▪ See also: \[Flat], \[Natural].

← \[ShortLeftArrow]

Infix arrow operator. ▪ Extensible character. ▪ See page 1006. ▪ See also: \[LeftArrow], \[LongLeftArrow].

→ \[ShortRightArrow]

Infix arrow operator. ▪ Not the same as \[Rule]. ▪ Extensible character. ▪ See page 1006. ▪ See also: \[RightArrow], \[LongRightArrow].

σ \[Sigma]

Aliases: :s:, :sigma:. ▪ Greek letter. ▪ Used in TraditionalForm for DivisorSigma and WeierstrassSigma. ▪ See pages 175 and 990. ▪ See also: \[CapitalSigma], \[FinalSigma].

✹ \[SixPointedStar]

Alias: :*6:. ▪ Letter-like form. ▪ Not the same as the operator \[Star]. ▪ See page 995. ▪ See also: \[FivePointedStar], \[Star], \[RawStar].

▪ \[SkeletonIndicator]

Uninterpretable element. ▪ ‹ *name* › is used on output to indicate an expression that has head *name*, but whose arguments will not explicitly be given. ▪ \[SkeletonIndicator] indicates the presence of missing information, and so by default generates an error if you try to interpret it. ▪ See page 1009. ▪ See also: \[LeftSkeleton], \[Ellipsis].

∘ \[SmallCircle]

Alias: :sc:. ▪ Infix operator. ▪ *x* ∘ *y* is by default interpreted as SmallCircle[*x*, *y*]. ▪ Used to indicate function composition. ▪ Not the same as the letter-like form \[EmptyCircle]. ▪ Not the same as \[Degree]. ▪ See pages 191 and 1002. ▪ See also: \[FilledCircle], \[CircleDot], \[CircleTimes].

␣ \[SpaceIndicator]

Alias: :space:. ▪ Spacing character. ▪ Interpreted by default as equivalent to \[RawSpace]. ▪ See page 1009. ▪ See also: \[RoundSpaceIndicator], \[ThinSpace], \[ReturnIndicator].

♠ \[SpadeSuit]

Letter-like form. ▪ See page 996. ▪ See also: \[ClubSuit].

∢ \[SphericalAngle]

Letter-like form. ▪ Used in geometry to indicate a spherical angle, as in the symbol ∢ ABC. ▪ See page 996. ▪ See also: \[Angle], \[MeasuredAngle].

√ \[Sqrt]

Alias: :sqrt:. ▪ Prefix operator with built-in evaluation rules. ▪ √ *x* is by default interpreted as Sqrt[*x*]. ▪ CTRL @ , CTRL 2 or \@ yields a complete SqrtBox object. ▪ \[Sqrt] is equivalent when evaluated, but will not draw a line on top of the quantity whose square root is being taken. ▪ See page 1000.

□ \[Square]

Alias: :sq:. ▪ Prefix operator. ▪ □ *x* is by default interpreted as Square[*x*]. ▪ Used in mathematical physics to denote the d'Alembertian operator. ▪ Sometimes used in number theory to indicate a quadratic residue. ▪ Not the same as \[EmptySquare]. ▪ See page 1002. ▪ See also: \[Del].

⊓ \[SquareIntersection]

Infix operator. ▪ *x* ⊓ *y* is by default interpreted as SquareIntersection[*x*, *y*]. ▪ See pages 191 and 1002. ▪ See also: \[SquareUnion], \[Intersection], \[Wedge].

⊏   \[SquareSubset]

Infix set relation operator. ■ $x \sqsubset y$ is by default interpreted as SquareSubset[x, y]. ■ Used in computer science to indicate that x is a substring occurring at the beginning of y. ■ See page 1005. ■ See also: \[NotSquareSubset], \[SquareSuperset].

⊑   \[SquareSubsetEqual]

Infix set relation operator. ■ $x \sqsubseteq y$ is by default interpreted as SquareSubsetEqual[x, y]. ■ See page 1005. ■ See also: \[NotSquareSubsetEqual].

⊐   \[SquareSuperset]

Infix set relation operator. ■ $x \sqsupset y$ is by default interpreted as SquareSuperset[x, y]. ■ Used in computer science to indicate that x is a substring occurring at the end of y. ■ See page 1005. ■ See also: \[NotSquareSuperset], \[SquareSubset].

⊒   \[SquareSupersetEqual]

Infix set relation operator. ■ $x \sqsupseteq y$ is by default interpreted as SquareSupersetEqual[x, y]. ■ See page 1005. ■ See also: \[NotSquareSupersetEqual].

⊔   \[SquareUnion]

Infix operator. ■ $x \sqcup y$ is by default interpreted as SquareUnion[x, y]. ■ Used in mathematics to denote various forms of generalized union, typically of disjoint subspaces. ■ See page 1002. ■ See also: \[SquareIntersection], \[Union], \[UnionPlus], \[Vee], \[Coproduct].

∗   \[Star]

Alias: :star:. ■ Infix operator. ■ $x * y$ is by default interpreted as Star[x, y]. ■ Used to denote convolution and generalized forms of multiplication. ■ Sometimes used in prefix form to indicate dual. ■ Not the same as \[SixPointedStar] or \[RawStar]. ■ \[RawStar] is the character entered for superscripts. ■ See page 1002. ■ See also: \[Times], \[Cross].

£   \[Sterling]

Letter-like form. ■ Currency symbol for British pound sterling, as in £ 5. ■ Used in mathematics to denote Lie derivative. ■ See pages 192 and 994. ■ See also: \[RawNumberSign], \[Euro].

ς   \[Stigma]

Aliases: :sti:, :stigma:. ■ Special Greek letter. ■ Appeared between ϵ and ζ in early Greek alphabet; used for Greek numeral 6. ■ Not the same as \[FinalSigma]. ■ See page 990. ■ See also: \[CapitalStigma], \[Digamma], \[Koppa], \[Sampi].

⊂   \[Subset]

Alias: :sub:. ■ Infix set relation operator. ■ $x \subset y$ is by default interpreted as Subset[x, y]. ■ Usually used in mathematics to indicate subset; sometimes proper subset. ■ See page 1004. ■ See also: \[SubsetEqual], \[SquareSubset], \[Element], \[Precedes], \[LeftTriangle], \[NotSubset].

⊆   \[SubsetEqual]

Alias: :sub=:. ■ Infix set relation operator. ■ $x \subseteq y$ is by default interpreted as SubsetEqual[x, y]. ■ See page 1004. ■ See also: \[NotSubsetEqual].

≻   \[Succeeds]

Infix ordering operator. ■ $x \succ y$ is by default interpreted as Succeeds[x, y]. ■ Used in mathematics to indicate various notions of partial ordering. ■ Often applied to functions and read "x dominates y". ■ See pages 191 and 1005. ■ See also: \[SucceedsEqual], \[Precedes], \[NotSucceeds].

$\succeq$ \[SucceedsEqual]

Infix ordering operator. ▪ $x \succeq y$ is by default interpreted as SucceedsEqual[x, y]. ▪ See page 1005. ▪ See also: \[SucceedsSlantEqual], \[SucceedsTilde], \[PrecedesEqual], \[NotSucceedsEqual].

$\succcurlyeq$ \[SucceedsSlantEqual]

Infix ordering operator. ▪ $x \succcurlyeq y$ is by default interpreted as SucceedsSlantEqual[x, y]. ▪ See page 1005. ▪ See also: \[SucceedsEqual], \[PrecedesSlantEqual], \[NotSucceedsSlantEqual].

$\succsim$ \[SucceedsTilde]

Infix ordering operator. ▪ $x \succsim y$ is by default interpreted as SucceedsTilde[x, y]. ▪ See page 1005. ▪ See also: \[SucceedsEqual], \[PrecedesTilde], \[NotSucceedsTilde].

$\ni$ \[SuchThat]   ▪

Alias: ⫶st⫶. ▪ Infix operator. ▪ $x \ni y$ is by default interpreted as SuchThat[x, y]. ▪ $x \ni y \ni z$ groups as $x \ni (y \ni z)$. ▪ Not the same as \[ReverseElement]. ▪ See page 1001. ▪ See also: \[Exists], \[ForAll], \[Colon], \[VerticalBar].

$\sum$ \[Sum]

Alias: ⫶sum⫶. ▪ Compound operator with built-in evaluation rules. ▪ $\sum_{i}^{imax} f$ is by default interpreted as Sum[f, {i, $imax$}]. ▪ $\sum_{i=imin}^{imax} f$ is by default interpreted as Sum[f, {i, $imin$, $imax$}]. ▪ Not the same as the Greek letter \[CapitalSigma]. ▪ See pages 994 and 1000. ▪ See also: \[Product], \[Integral].

$\supset$ \[Superset]

Alias: ⫶sup⫶. ▪ Infix set relation operator. ▪ $x \supset y$ is by default interpreted as Superset[x, y]. ▪ Usually used in mathematics to indicate superset; sometimes proper superset. ▪ Not the same as \[RoundImplies]. ▪ See pages 191 and 1004. ▪ See also: \[SupersetEqual], \[SquareSuperset], \[ReverseElement], \[Succeeds], \[RightTriangle], \[NotSuperset].

$\supseteq$ \[SupersetEqual]

Alias: ⫶sup=⫶. ▪ Infix set relation operator. ▪ $x \supseteq y$ is by default interpreted as SupersetEqual[x, y]. ▪ See page 1004. ▪ See also: \[NotSupersetEqual].

ß   \[SZ]

Aliases: ⫶sz⫶, ⫶ss⫶. ▪ Letter. ▪ Used in German. ▪ Sometimes called s sharp, ess-zed or ess-zet. ▪ Usually transliterated in English as ss. ▪ Upper-case form is SS. ▪ Included in ISO Latin-1. ▪ See pages 190 and 998. ▪ See also: \[Beta].

τ \[Tau]

Aliases: ⫶t⫶, ⫶tau⫶. ▪ Greek letter. ▪ See pages 175 and 990. ▪ See also: \[CapitalTau], \[Theta].

$\therefore$ \[Therefore]

Alias: ⫶tf⫶. ▪ Infix operator. ▪ $x \therefore y$ is by default interpreted as Therefore[x, y]. ▪ $x \therefore y \therefore z$ groups as $x \therefore (y \therefore z)$. ▪ See pages 191 and 1001. ▪ See also: \[Because], \[Implies], \[RightTee], \[FilledRectangle], \[Proportion].

θ \[Theta]

Aliases: ⫶th⫶, ⫶theta⫶, ⫶q⫶. ▪ Greek letter. ▪ See pages 175 and 990. ▪ See also: \[CurlyTheta], \[CapitalTheta], \[Tau].

\[ThickSpace]

Alias: ⦂⌴⌴⌴⦂. ▪ Spacing character. ▪ Width: 5/18 em. ▪ Interpreted by default just like an ordinary \[RawSpace].
▪ See page 1008. ▪ See also: \[MediumSpace], \[NegativeThickSpace], SpaceIndicator.

\[ThinSpace]

Alias: ⦂⌴⌴⦂. ▪ Spacing character. ▪ Width: 3/18 em. ▪ Interpreted by default just like an ordinary \[RawSpace].
▪ See page 1008. ▪ See also: \[VeryThinSpace], \[MediumSpace], \[NegativeThinSpace], \[SpaceIndicator].

þ   ### \[Thorn]

Alias: ⦂thn⦂. ▪ Letter. ▪ Included in ISO Latin-1. ▪ Used in Icelandic and Old English. ▪ See page 998. ▪ See also:
\[CapitalThorn], \[Eth].

~   ### \[Tilde]

Alias: ⦂~⦂. ▪ Infix similarity operator. ▪ $x \sim y$ is by default interpreted as Tilde[x, y]. ▪ Used in mathematics for
many notions of similarity or equivalence. ▪ Used in physical science to indicate approximate equality.
▪ Occasionally used in mathematics for notions of difference. ▪ Occasionally used in prefix form to indicate
complement or negation. ▪ Not the same as \[RawTilde]. ▪ See pages 191 and 1003. ▪ See also: \[NotTilde],
\[VerticalTilde], \[Not].

≃   ### \[TildeEqual]

Alias: ⦂~=⦂. ▪ Infix similarity operator. ▪ $x \simeq y$ is by default interpreted as TildeEqual[x, y]. ▪ Used to mean
approximately or asymptotically equal. ▪ Also used in mathematics to indicate homotopy. ▪ See pages 191 and 1003.
▪ See also: \[TildeTilde], \[TildeFullEqual], \[NotTildeEqual].

≅   ### \[TildeFullEqual]

Alias: ⦂~==⦂. ▪ Infix similarity operator. ▪ $x \cong y$ is by default interpreted as TildeFullEqual[x, y]. ▪ Used in
mathematics to indicate isomorphism, congruence and homotopic equivalence. ▪ See page 1003. ▪ See also:
\[TildeEqual], \[Congruent], \[NotTildeFullEqual].

≈   ### \[TildeTilde]

Alias: ⦂~~⦂. ▪ Infix similarity operator. ▪ $x \approx y$ is by default interpreted as TildeTilde[x, y]. ▪ Used for various
notions of approximate or asymptotic equality. ▪ Used in pure mathematics to indicate homeomorphism. ▪ See
pages 191 and 1003. ▪ See also: \[TildeEqual], \[NotTildeTilde].

×   ### \[Times]

Alias: ⦂*⦂. ▪ Infix operator with built-in evaluation rules. ▪ $x \times y$ is by default interpreted as Times[x, y], which is
equivalent to $x\,y$ or $x * y$. ▪ Not the same as \[Cross]. ▪ \[Times] represents ordinary multiplication, while
\[Cross] represents vector cross product. ▪ \[Times] is drawn larger than \[Cross]. ▪ See page 1000. ▪ See also:
\[Star], \[CircleTimes], \[Divide], \[Wedge].

™   ### \[Trademark]

Letter-like form. ▪ Used to indicate a trademark that may not be registered. ▪ Typically used only on the first
occurrence of a trademark in a document. ▪ See page 996. ▪ See also: \[RegisteredTrademark], \[Copyright].

ú   ### \[UAcute]

Alias: ⦂u'⦂. ▪ Letter. ▪ Included in ISO Latin-1. ▪ See page 998. ▪ See also: \[CapitalUAcute].

ű   ### \[UDoubleAcute]

Alias: ⦂u''⦂. ▪ Letter. ▪ Included in ISO Latin-2. ▪ Used in Hungarian. ▪ See page 998. ▪ See also:
\[CapitalUDoubleAcute].

ü   \[UDoubleDot]

Alias: ⠶u"⠶. ▪ Letter. ▪ Included in ISO Latin-1. ▪ See pages 190 and 998. ▪ See also: \[UDoubleAcute],
\[CapitalUDoubleDot].

ù   \[UGrave]

Alias: ⠶u`⠶. ▪ Letter. ▪ Included in ISO Latin-1. ▪ See pages 190 and 998. ▪ See also: \[CapitalUGrave].

û   \[UHat]

Alias: ⠶u^⠶. ▪ Letter. ▪ Included in ISO Latin-1. ▪ See page 998. ▪ See also: \[CapitalUHat].

⏝   \[UnderBrace]

Alias: ⠶u{⠶. ▪ Letter-like form. ▪ Extensible character. ▪ See page 997. ▪ See also: \[UnderBracket],
\[UnderParenthesis], \[OverBrace].

⎵   \[UnderBracket]

Alias: ⠶u[⠶. ▪ Letter-like form. ▪ Extensible character. ▪ See page 997. ▪ See also: \[UnderParenthesis],
\[UnderBrace], \[OverBracket], \[HorizontalLine].

⏝   \[UnderParenthesis]

Alias: ⠶u(⠶. ▪ Letter-like form. ▪ Extensible character. ▪ See page 997. ▪ See also: \[UnderBracket], \[UnderBrace],
\[OverParenthesis].

∪   \[Union]

Alias: ⠶un⠶. ▪ Infix operator with built-in evaluation rules. ▪ $x \cup y$ is by default interpreted as Union[x, y]. ▪ The
character ∪ is sometimes called "cup"; but see also \[Cup]. ▪ See page 1002. ▪ See also: \[Intersection],
\[SquareUnion], \[UnionPlus], \[Cup], \[Vee].

⊎   \[UnionPlus]

Infix operator. ▪ $x \uplus y$ is by default interpreted as UnionPlus[x, y]. ▪ Used to denote union of multisets, in which
multiplicities of elements are added. ▪ See page 1002. ▪ See also: \[Union], \[CirclePlus].

↑   \[UpArrow]

Infix arrow operator. ▪ $x \uparrow y$ is by default interpreted as UpArrow[x, y]. ▪ Sometimes used in mathematics to
denote generalization of powers. ▪ Used to indicate monotonic increase to a limit. ▪ Sometimes used in prefix form
to indicate the closure of a set. ▪ Extensible character. ▪ See pages 191 and 1006. ▪ See also: \[UpTeeArrow],
\[UpArrowBar], \[DoubleUpArrow], \[LeftUpVector], \[DownArrow], \[Wedge], \[RawWedge].

↑̄   \[UpArrowBar]

Infix arrow operator. ▪ $x \uparrow̄ y$ is by default interpreted as UpArrowBar[x, y]. ▪ Extensible character. ▪ See page 1006.
▪ See also: \[UpTeeArrow], \[LeftUpVectorBar].

⇅   \[UpArrowDownArrow]

Infix arrow operator. ▪ $x \upharpoonleft y$ is by default interpreted as UpArrowDownArrow[x, y]. ▪ Extensible character. ▪ See
page 1006. ▪ See also: \[DownArrowUpArrow], \[UpDownArrow], \[DoubleUpDownArrow], \[UpEquilibrium].

↕   \[UpDownArrow]

Infix arrow operator. ▪ $x \updownarrow y$ is by default interpreted as UpDownArrow[x, y]. ▪ Extensible character. ▪ See
page 1006. ▪ See also: \[UpArrowDownArrow], \[DoubleUpDownArrow], \[LeftUpDownVector], \[UpEquilibrium].

⥮   \[UpEquilibrium]

Infix arrow-like operator. ▪ $x \upequilibrium y$ is by default interpreted as UpEquilibrium[x, y]. ▪ Extensible character. ▪ See
page 1007. ▪ See also: \[ReverseUpEquilibrium], \[UpArrowDownArrow], \[LeftUpDownVector], \[Equilibrium].

↖ \[UpperLeftArrow]

Infix arrow operator. ▪ $x \nwarrow y$ is by default interpreted as UpperLeftArrow[x, y]. ▪ Extensible character; grows by default to limited size. ▪ See page 1006. ▪ See also: \[UpperRightArrow], \[LeftArrow].

↗ \[UpperRightArrow]

Infix arrow operator. ▪ $x \nearrow y$ is by default interpreted as UpperRightArrow[x, y]. ▪ Extensible character; grows by default to limited size. ▪ See page 1006. ▪ See also: \[UpperLeftArrow], \[RightArrow].

υ \[Upsilon]

Aliases: :u:, :upsilon:. ▪ Greek letter. ▪ See page 990. ▪ See also: \[CapitalUpsilon].

⊥ \[UpTee]

Alias: :uT:. ▪ Infix relational operator. ▪ $x \perp y$ is by default interpreted as UpTee[x, y]. ▪ Used in geometry to indicate perpendicular. ▪ Used in number theory to indicate relative primality. ▪ See page 1007. ▪ See also: \[RightAngle], \[NotDoubleVerticalBar], \[DownTee].

↑ \[UpTeeArrow]

Infix arrow operator. ▪ $x \uparrow y$ is by default interpreted as UpTeeArrow[x, y]. ▪ Extensible character. ▪ See page 1006. ▪ See also: \[UpArrowBar], \[LeftUpTeeVector], \[UpTee], \[DownTeeArrow].

∨ \[Vee]

Alias: :v:. ▪ Infix operator. ▪ $x \vee y$ is by default interpreted as Vee[x, y]. ▪ Used to indicate various notions of joining, and as a dual of \[Wedge]. ▪ Not the same as \[Or]. ▪ Drawn slightly smaller than \[Or]. ▪ Sometimes used in prefix form to indicate the total variation of a function. ▪ See pages 191 and 1002. ▪ See also: \[Wedge], \[Union], \[SquareUnion], \[Nu], \[Hacek].

∣ \[VerticalBar]

Alias: :_|:. ▪ Infix operator. ▪ $x \mid y$ is by default interpreted as VerticalBar[x, y]. ▪ Used in mathematics to indicate that x divides y. ▪ Also sometimes called Sheffer stroke, and used to indicate logical NAND. ▪ Not the same as \[VerticalSeparator], which is drawn longer. ▪ Not the same as \[LeftBracketingBar] and \[RightBracketingBar], which are drawn with a small tee to indicate their direction. ▪ :|: is the alias for \[VerticalSeparator]. The alias for \[VerticalBar] has a space at the beginning. ▪ See pages 191 and 1005. ▪ See also: \[RawVerticalBar], \[Nand], \[NotVerticalBar], \[DoubleVerticalBar], \[Backslash], \[HorizontalLine].

⋮ \[VerticalEllipsis]

Letter-like form. ▪ Used to indicate omitted elements in columns of a matrix. ▪ See page 997. ▪ See also: \[Ellipsis], \[AscendingEllipsis], \[VerticalBar].

∣ \[VerticalLine]

Alias: :vline:. ▪ Letter-like form. ▪ Extensible character. ▪ Not the same as \[VerticalSeparator] or \[VerticalBar], which are infix operators. ▪ Not the same as \[LeftBracketingBar] and \[RightBracketingBar], which are matchfix operators, drawn with a small tee to indicate their direction. ▪ See page 997. ▪ See also: \[RawVerticalBar], \[HorizontalLine], \[VerticalEllipsis], \[UpArrow].

| \[VerticalSeparator]

Alias: :|:. ▪ Infix operator. ▪ $x \mid y$ is by default interpreted as VerticalSeparator[x, y]. ▪ Used in mathematics for many purposes, including indicating restriction and standing for "such that". ▪ Also used to separate arguments of various mathematical functions. ▪ Extensible character; grows by default to limited size. ▪ Not the same as \[VerticalBar], which is drawn shorter. ▪ Not the same as \[LeftBracketingBar] and \[RightBracketingBar], which are drawn with a small tee to indicate their direction. ▪ Not the same as \[VerticalLine], which is a letter-like form, and is indefinitely extensible. ▪ See pages 191 and 1001. ▪ See also: \[RawVerticalBar], \[NotVerticalBar], \[DoubleVerticalBar], \[Colon], \[SuchThat], \[HorizontalLine].

≀ \[VerticalTilde]

Infix operator. ▪ $x \wr y$ is by default interpreted as VerticalTilde[x, y]. ▪ Used in mathematics to mean wreath product. ▪ See page 1002. ▪ See also: \[Tilde].

\[VeryThinSpace]

Alias: :_:. ▪ Spacing character. ▪ Width: 1/18 em. ▪ Interpreted by default just like an ordinary \[RawSpace]. ▪ See page 1008. ▪ See also: \[ThinSpace], \[NegativeVeryThinSpace], \[AlignmentMarker], \[Null], \[InvisibleComma].

⚠ \[WarningSign]

Letter-like form. ▪ Based on an international standard road sign. ▪ See page 995. ▪ See also: \[WatchIcon].

⌚ \[WatchIcon]

Letter-like form. ▪ Used to indicate a calculation that may take a long time. ▪ See page 995. ▪ See also: \[WarningSign].

∧ \[Wedge]

Alias: :^:. ▪ Infix operator. ▪ $x \wedge y$ is by default interpreted as Wedge[x, y]. ▪ Used to mean wedge or exterior product and other generalized antisymmetric products. ▪ Occasionally used for generalized notions of intersection. ▪ Not the same as \[And], \[CapitalLambda] or \[RawWedge]. ▪ See pages 191 and 1002. ▪ See also: \[Vee], \[UpArrow], \[Intersection], \[SquareIntersection], \[CircleTimes].

℘ \[WeierstrassP]

Alias: :wp:. ▪ Letter. ▪ Used to denote the function WeierstrassP. ▪ Not the same as \[ScriptCapitalP]. ▪ See page 992.

🐺 \[Wolf]

Aliases: :wf:, :wolf:. ▪ Letter-like form. ▪ Iconic representation of a wolf. ▪ See page 995.

ξ \[Xi]

Aliases: :x:, :xi:. ▪ Greek letter. ▪ See pages 175 and 990. ▪ See also: \[CapitalXi], \[Chi], \[Zeta].

⊻ \[Xor]

Alias: :xor:. ▪ Infix operator with built-in evaluation rules. ▪ $x \veebar y$ is by default interpreted as Xor[x, y]. ▪ See page 1001. ▪ See also: \[Nor], \[Or], \[CirclePlus].

ý   \[YAcute]

Alias: ꞉y꞉. ▪ Letter. ▪ Included in ISO Latin-1. ▪ See page 998. ▪ See also: \[CapitalYAcute].

¥   \[Yen]

Letter-like form. ▪ Currency symbol for Japanese yen, as in ¥5000. ▪ See page 994.

ζ   \[Zeta]

Aliases: ꞉z꞉, ꞉zeta꞉. ▪ Greek letter. ▪ Used in TraditionalForm for Zeta and WeierstrassZeta. ▪ See pages 175 and 990. ▪ See also: \[CapitalZeta], \[Xi].

A.13 Incompatible Changes since *Mathematica* Version 1

Every new version of *Mathematica* contains many new features. But careful design from the outset has allowed nearly total compatibility to be maintained between all versions. As a result, almost any program written, say, for *Mathematica* Version 1 in 1988 should be able to run without change in *Mathematica* Version 5—though it will often run considerably faster.

One inevitable problem, however, is that if a program uses names that begin with upper-case letters, then it is possible that since the version when the program was first written, built-in functions may have been added to *Mathematica* whose names conflict with those used in the program.

In addition, to maintain the overall coherence of *Mathematica* a few functions that existed in earlier versions have gradually been dropped—first becoming undocumented, and later generating warning messages if used. Furthermore, it has in a few rare cases been necessary to makes changes to particular functions that are not compatible with their earlier operation.

This section lists all major incompatible changes from *Mathematica* Version 1 onward.

■ A.13.1 Incompatible Changes between Version 1 and Version 2

- 260 new built-in objects have been added, some of whose names may conflict with names already being used.
- `Accumulate` has been superseded by `FoldList`; `Fold` has been added.
- `Condition` (`/;`) can now be used in individual patterns as well as in complete rules, and does not evaluate by default.
- The functionality of `Release` has been split between `Evaluate` and `ReleaseHold`.
- `Compose` has been superseded by `Composition`.
- `Debug` has been superseded by `Trace` and related functions.
- `Power` no longer automatically makes transformations such as `Sqrt[x^2]`→`x`.
- `Limit` now by default remains unevaluated if it encounters an unknown function.
- `Mod` now handles only numbers; `PolynomialMod` handles polynomials.
- `CellArray` has been superseded by `Raster` and `RasterArray`.
- `FontForm` takes a slightly different form of font specification.
- `Framed` has been superseded by `Frame` and related options.
- `ContourLevels` and `ContourSpacing` have been superseded by `Contours`.
- `Plot3Matrix` has been superseded by `ViewCenter` and `ViewVertical`.
- `FromASCII` and `ToASCII` have been superseded by `FromCharacterCode` and `ToCharacterCode` respectively.
- `Alias` has been superseded by `$PreRead`.
- `ResetMedium` has been subsumed in `SetOptions`, and `$$Media` has been superseded by `Streams`.
- `StartProcess` has been superseded by `Install` and by *MathLink*.
- Additional parts devoted to *Mathematica* as a programming language, and to examples of *Mathematica* packages, have been dropped from *The Mathematica Book*.

■ A.13.2 Incompatible Changes between Version 2 and Version 3

- 259 new built-in objects have been added, some of whose names may conflict with names already being used.
- `N[`*expr*`,` *n*`]` now always tries to give *n* digits of precision if possible, rather than simply starting with *n* digits of precision.

- All expressions containing only numeric functions and numerical constants are now converted to approximate numerical form whenever they contain any approximate numbers.
- Many expressions involving exact numbers that used to remain unevaluated are now evaluated. Example: `Floor[(7/3)^20]`.
- `Plus` and `Times` now apply built-in rules before user-defined ones, so it is no longer possible to make definitions such as 2+2=5.
- The operator precedence for . and ** has been changed so as to be below ^. This has the consequence that expressions previously written in `InputForm` as a . b ^ n must now be written as (a . b)^n. `V2Get[`*file*`]` will read a file using old operator precedences.
- `\^` is now an operator used to generate a superscript. Raw octal codes must be used instead of `\^A` for inputting control characters.
- In *Mathematica* notebooks, several built-in *Mathematica* functions are now output by default using special characters. Example: *x*->*y* is output as *x*→*y* in `StandardForm`.
- More sophisticated definite integrals now yield explicit `If` constructs unless the option setting `GenerateConditions->False` is used.
- `HeldPart[`*expr*`, ` *i*`, ` *j*`, ... ]` has been superseded by `Extract[`*expr*`, {`*i*`, ` *j*`, ... }, Hold]`.
- `Literal[`*pattern*`]` has been replaced by `HoldPattern[`*pattern*`]`. `Verbatim[`*pattern*`]` has been introduced. Functions like `DownValues` return their results wrapped in `HoldPattern` rather than `Literal`.
- `ReplaceHeldPart[`*expr*`, ` *new*`, ` *pos*`]` has been superseded by `ReplacePart[`*expr*`, Hold[`*new*`], ` *pos*`, 1]`.
- `ToHeldExpression[`*expr*`]` has been superseded by `ToExpression[`*expr*`, ` *form*`, Hold]`.
- `Trig` as an option to algebraic manipulation functions has been superseded by the explicit functions `TrigExpand`, `TrigFactor` and `TrigReduce`.
- `AlgebraicRules` has been superseded by `PolynomialReduce`.
- The option `LegendreType` has been superseded by an additional optional argument to `LegendreP` and `LegendreQ`.
- `WeierstrassP[`*u*`, {`g_2`, ` g_3`}]` now takes g_2 and g_3 in a list.
- `$Letters` and `$StringOrder` now have built-in values only, but these handle all possible *Mathematica* characters.
- `StringByteCount` is no longer supported.
- Arbitrary-precision approximate real numbers are now given by default as *digits`prec* in `InputForm`. This behavior is controlled by `$NumberMarks`.
- Large approximate real numbers are now given by default as *digits**^*exponent* in `InputForm`.
- `HomeDirectory[ ]` has been replaced by `$HomeDirectory`.
- `Dump` has been superseded by `DumpSave`.
- `$PipeSupported` and `$LinkSupported` are now obsolete, since all computer systems support pipes and links.
- `LinkOpen` has been superseded by `LinkCreate`, `LinkConnect` and `LinkLaunch`.
- `Subscripted` has been superseded by `RowBox`, `SubscriptBox`, etc.
- `Subscript` and `Superscript` now represent complete subscripted and superscripted quantities, not just subscripts and superscripts.
- `FontForm` and `DefaultFont` have been superseded by `StyleForm` and `TextStyle`.

In the notebook front end, changes that were made include:

- The file format for notebooks has been completely changed in order to support new notebook capabilities.
- Notebook files are now by default given `.nb` rather than `.ma` extensions; `.mb` files are now superfluous.
- The front end will automatically ask to convert any old notebook that you tell it to open.
- The kernel command `NotebookConvert` can be used to convert notebook files from Version 2 to Version 3 format.
- The default format type for input cells is now `StandardForm` rather than `InputForm`.
- The organization of style sheets, as well as the settings for some default styles, have been changed.
- Some command key equivalents for menu items have been rearranged.

■ A.13.3 Incompatible Changes between Version 3 and Version 4

- 61 new built-in objects have been added, some of whose names may conflict with names already being used.

- N[0] now yields a machine-precision zero rather than an exact zero.

- FullOptions has been superseded by AbsoluteOptions, which yields results in the same form as Options.

- Element[x, y] or $x \in y$ now has built-in evaluation rules.

- The symbols I and E are now output in StandardForm as $\mathfrak{i}$ (\[ImaginaryI]) and $\mathfrak{e}$ (\[ExponentialE]) respectively.

- A new second argument has been added to CompiledFunction to allow easier manipulation and composition of compiled functions.

■ A.13.4 Incompatible Changes between Version 4 and Version 5

- 44 completely new built-in objects have been added, some of whose names may conflict with names already being used.

- Precision and Accuracy now return exact measures of uncertainty in numbers, not just estimates of integer numbers of digits.

- Precision now returns the symbol MachinePrecision for machine numbers, rather than the numerical value $MachinePrecision.

- N[*expr*, MachinePrecision] is now used for numerical evaluation with machine numbers; N[*expr*, $MachinePrecision] generates arbitrary-precision numbers.

- ConstrainedMin and ConstrainedMax have been superseded by Minimize, Maximize, NMinimize and NMaximize.

- SingularValues has been superseded by SingularValueList and SingularValueDecomposition. SingularValueDecomposition uses a different and more complete definition.

- FindRoot[f, {x, {x_0, x_1}}] is now used to specify a starting vector value for x, rather than a pair of values. The same is true for FindMinimum.

- DSolveConstants has been superseded by the more general option GeneratedParameters.

- TensorRank has been replaced by ArrayDepth.

- $TopDirectory has been superseded by $InstallationDirectory and $BaseDirectory.

- The default setting for the *MathLink* LinkProtocol option when connecting different computer systems is now "TCPIP" rather than "TCP".

Index

This index includes not only specific words and phrases from the text but also concepts and topics related to them. This means that a particular term in the index may not appear in its literal form on any of the pages specified. Note that the terms are sorted in standard dictionary order, with most non-alphabetic characters ignored.

See the *Standard Add-on Packages* book for information on capabilities included in additional packages bundled with most versions of *Mathematica*.

You can also use the online Help Browser in the *Mathematica* notebook front end to search for topics that appear anywhere in documentation for *Mathematica* and for packages that you have installed.

Index